DICTIONARY
OF
AMERICAN
CHILDREN'S
FICTION,
1960–1984

DICTIONARY OF AMERICAN CHILDREN'S FICTION, 1960–1984

Recent Books of Recognized Merit

ALETHEA K. HELBIG

AND

AGNES REGAN PERKINS

Greenwood Press
New York · Westport, Connecticut · London

Library of Congress Cataloging-in-Publication Data

Helbig, Alethea.
  Dictionary of American children's fiction, 1960–1984.

  Includes index.
  1. Children's stories, American—Dictionaries.
  2. American fiction—20th century—Dictionaries.
  3. Bibliography—Best books—Children's stories.
  4. Authors, American—20th century—Biography—
Dictionaries. I. Perkins, Agnes. II. Title.
PS374.C454H45 1986   813'.54'099282   85–24778
ISBN 0–313–25233–5 (lib. bdg. : alk. paper)

Library of Congress Catalog Card Number: 85–24778
ISBN: 0–313–25233–5

First published in 1986

Greenwood Press, Inc.
88 Post Road West, Westport, Connecticut 06881

Printed in the United States of America

The paper used in this book complies with the
Permanent Paper Standard issued by the National
Information Standards Organization (Z39.48–1984).

10 9 8 7 6 5 4 3 2 1

CONTENTS

PREFACE

The *Dictionary of American Children's Fiction, 1960–1984: Recent Books of Recognized Merit* includes 1,550 entries on such elements as titles, authors, characters, and settings based on 489 books of fiction for children and young people. Like its companion book, *Dictionary of American Children's Fiction, 1859–1959: Books of Recognized Merit*, it is intended for the use of everyone who is concerned with children's literature in any way: librarians, teachers, literary scholars, researchers in American studies, parents, booksellers, publishers, editors—those to whom literature for children is of vital interest professionally or personally. A later reference will deal with award-winning books in Canada, the British Isles, Australia, and New Zealand. Periodic updates are planned.

Both professional inquiries and casual questions have long made us aware of the need for such reference. Originally, we planned to include all important American fiction in a single volume, but we soon realized that even if we considered only books which have won significant awards and been named on prestigious selection lists, the material would be far too extensive for one book. The year 1960 serves as a convenient separation line. It divides the material roughly in half. More important, fiction for children changed markedly about that date, often dealing with different and more controversial subject matter, much of it previously considered taboo for a young audience. Moreover, many writers began to introduce into children's literature styles and structures and other narrative techniques ordinarily associated with adult fiction.

Rather than depend upon our own subjective judgment about which books are best or most significant, we have included those books which have won or been finalists for major awards in children's literature, using the award lists in *Children's Books: Awards & Prizes* published by the Children's Book Council. We have not included translations or any strictly regional awards, nor those issued by organizations to their members only. We also excluded those given to books chosen by children, since the selection of books made available to the children who are polled is necessarily limited. In addition, we have included the fiction chosen annually by *Horn Book* magazine for its Fanfare list.

Some books, however, that clearly have become important as literature for children were overlooked at the time of their publication by editors and award committees. Others, though perhaps of less than award quality, have become popular or have come to be considered standard novels that should be part of any representative collection for young people. We have therefore added several other lists: the *Choice* magazine list of children's books for an academic library (1974 and 1978 editions); the list of Contemporary Classics published by *Horn Book* magazine; May Hill Arbuthnot's choices in *Children's Books Too Good to Miss* (1963, 1966, and 1979 editions); and lists published by the Children's Literature Association of the Top Ten American Books for Children and the Children's Literature Association Touchstones. We have also included two types that have become increasingly important among books for young people, westerns chosen by the Western Writers of America for their Spur Award and the Western Heritage Award winners, and mysteries which have been nominated and selected as winners of the Edgar Allan Poe Award. A compilation of awards and citation lists appears in the front matter.

These many inclusions have given us a broad spectrum of the literature recognized for merit by a wide variety of experts in children's literature for nearly twenty-five years. A number of the awards originated in this period and reflect contemporary critical attitudes toward books for young people. Of course, the selections on the various lists result from the application of somewhat different criteria, since the purposes of the awards vary. Though the selection committees all want to provide interesting, well-written books for children, some place more emphasis on social or spiritual values, like the Jane Addams, Christopher, and Child Study awards, others on entertainment, like the Edgar Allan Poe Award.

Because our study is of fiction and not of illustration, we have not included fiction in picture book form, since the texts of such books can seldom stand alone and their analysis requires a consideration also of the illustrations. Somewhat arbitrarily, we have set five thousand words as a minimum; most books need at least that number to develop a story that can work without pictures. Books of more than five thousand words, even if the illustrations are very prominent, are included.

Collections of short stories also require a different sort of analysis and plot summary from novels. Episodic books with the same characters in each chapter, like Beverly Cleary's Ramona books, are included. Books of unconnected stories are not, even if technically they are fiction.

A number of other books straddle the division between fiction and nonfiction. These are mostly novels based upon actual lives, realistic animal stories, fictionalized history, or retellings from oral tradition. Libraries we have consulted catalogue some of these with fiction, others with history, natural science, biography, or folktale. In most cases we have been able to follow the Library of Congress classification for these books.

In our author entries, we have focused on what in the author's life is most relevant to children's literature and to the particular books in *Dictionary of American Children's Fiction*. Although several other published sources give biographical information for authors, none considers all the authors whose books are in our study. Having the information in the same volume is not only of convenience for researchers, it is of particular value for those in areas where libraries are on limited budgets and do not own the other publications.

In presenting our entries we have tried to follow an arrangement that will be convenient for a variety of users. These entries are of several types:

A. Title entries. These consist of bibliographical information; the sub-genre of fiction to which the work belongs; the settings in time and place; a plot summary incorporating the plot problem, if any, significant episodes, and the denouement; a brief literary critical evaluation; sequels, if any; additional entries not mentioned in the summary, if any; and awards and citations in abbreviated form. A list of the complete names of the awards and citations appears in the front matter. Entries vary in length. Length in itself does not indicate the importance or quality of a book, since plots can be summarized more briefly and critical judgments stated more succinctly for some books than for others. Most readers will be acquainted with the terms we have used for sub-genres, but a few terms may need some explanation. By realistic fiction, we mean books in which events could have happened some time in the world as we know it, as opposed to an imaginary or fantastic world, not necessarily that the action is convincing or plausible. Historical fiction includes those books in which actual historical events or figures function in the plot, as in *The King's Fifth*, or in which the specific period is essential to the action and in which the story could not have occurred in any other time, as in *The Slave Dancer*. Books merely set in past times we have called period fiction.

B. Author entries, which consist of dates and places of birth and death, when available; education and vocational background; major contribution to children's literature; significant facts of the author's life which might have a bearing on the work; titles that have won awards; frequently titles of other publications, usually with brief information about them; and critical judgments where they can safely be made.

C. Character entries, which include physical and personality traits for important, memorable, or particularly unusual characters who are not covered sufficiently by the plot summary, and such aspects as how they function in the plot, how they relate to the major protagonist, and whether the characterization is credible and skillful. Characters are classified by the name by which they are most often referred to or by that by which the protagonist refers to them, e.g., Uncle Haskell Bishop; Crockett, Davy; Professor Cameron; Tucker Mouse. The name is also cross-referenced in the index under other most likely possibilities. If the plot summary gives all the significant information about characters, as with many protagonists, they are not discussed in a separate character entry. All major characters, however, are listed in the index.

D. Miscellaneous entries, which include particularly significant settings and elements that need explanation beyond mention in the title entry.

Every book has title and author entries. Entries are in alphabetical order for convenience. Asterisks indicate that the item has a separate entry elsewhere in the book. Accompanying entries do not duplicate one another. While a book's title entry gives the plot and a critical assessment, other entries provide additional information to give a more complete understanding of the book. Daggers indicate that the item appears in the companion volume covering American children's fiction from 1859 to 1959. The two books are intended to be used together to give a broader sense of the scope and development of children's literature in America.

Publishers' names have been abbreviated; a full list appears in the front matter. Similarly, the list of awards and their abbreviations appears in the front matter. The books classified by awards appear in the index.

The index also includes all the items for which there are entries and such items as cross references, major characters for whom there are no separate entries, specific place settings, settings by period, and such items as themes and subjects, books of first person narration, unusual narrative structures, significant tone, authors' pseudonyms, illustrators, and genres.

Throughout its history, children's literature has mirrored the society which produced it and has reflected its attitudes toward children. In looking back to the books of the earlier part of this century, one can easily see trends. After World War I, stories set in foreign lands dominated the award lists. In the 1930s, many of the books had a condescending, even coy, tone, or were transparently instructive, protecting children or preparing them for life in a hard world. In the 1940s, the tone was earnest, as befitted a country engaged in a serious world conflict. Books of the 1950s began to reflect social consciousness, with more black and other minority protagonists. Similarly, in the past twenty-five years books for children have reflected the preoccupations of the country. Through the 1960s and early 1970s, stories dealing with social problems predominated, with American cities edging out small town and rural areas as settings. Television produced a more sophisticated young audience and stimulated interest in more adult subjects. Recently, the trend seems to be toward psychological problems, with concentration on less sensational, more inner-directed character development.

Other changes are also noticeable in the narrative technique of books published. Television and modern movies have influenced the pace and structure of novels for children. Cinematic techniques of scene presentation and first-person narration are frequently used, sometimes quite skillfully. Omniscient author point of view and author intrusion are less common, while third person limited omniscience is often so strong that it has the same intimate effect as first-person narration. More authors who have had experience in writing for adults have entered the field of children's fiction, often with innovative techniques and greater competence than many of the earlier writers.

Not all the changes are improvements. While the plotting and style are overall more skillful than earlier in the century, the subjects often seem to have been chosen for their shock value, and characterization still is frequently shallow. Eccentric, even outlandish, characters have been the vogue. While fantasy is both more frequent and more varied, historical fiction, which was a particularly rich genre earlier, has suffered neglect, with very few examples winning awards except for a brief spate of books with American Revolutionary settings published for the bicentennial period. Over the past twenty-five years, realistic fiction set in the contemporary period has predominated.

An even more significant change has occurred in critical attitudes toward books for children. In this period, children's literature has been accepted into the main stream of academic consideration. College and university courses have proliferated, and graduate degrees with the emphasis on literature are now available. In the last decade such professional organizations as the Modern Language Association and its regional affiliates have instituted sections on literature for children. The Children's Literature Association, which is devoted to scholarship in children's literature, has grown into an influential organization and is now also turning its attention to the application of critical literary standards in the elementary and middle-school classroom.

As university teachers of literature for children and young adults for more than twenty years and as people trained in the study of literature as literature, we are dedicated to the idea that books for children must be judged by the same criteria as those for adults, keeping in mind, of course, that children are the intended audience. Our critical comments, therefore, judge each book as imaginative literature, not on other values, regardless of the particular emphasis of the award or list for which it was chosen.

As with the companion volume, we ourselves have read every book included in *Dictionary of American Children's Literature, 1960–1984: Recent Books of Recognized Merit* and have done all the research and writing in this volume. We have had some valuable assistance from a variety of sources. We wish to acknowledge the help of Eastern Michigan University and the Josephine Nevins Keal Fund with leaves and grants and to express our appreciation to the Eastern Michigan University Library and the Ann Arbor Public Library for the use of their extensive collections. Specifically, we thank Marcia Shafer of the Ann Arbor Public Library Youth Room and her staff for their encouragement and aid in research and Rita Bullard and her colleagues of the Interlibrary Loan Department of Eastern Michigan University Library for their invaluable help in obtaining obscure books.

ABBREVIATIONS

AWARDS AND CITATION LISTS

Addams	Jane Addams Peace Association Children's Book Award
Books Too Good	*Children's Books Too Good to Miss* (1963, 1966, and 1979 editions)
Boston Globe	*Boston Globe-Horn Book* Award
Child Study	Child Study Children's Book Committee at Bank Street College Award (formerly called Wel-Met)
ChLA Top 10	Children's Literature Association Top Ten American Books for Children
ChLA Touchstones	Children's Literature Association Touchstones
Choice	*Choice* magazine list of suggested children's books for an academic library (1974 and 1978 editions)
Christopher	Christopher Award
Contemporary Classics	Contemporary Classics list published by *Horn Book* magazine
Fanfare	*Horn Book* magazine Fanfare lists
IRA	International Reading Association Children's Book Award
Lewis Carroll	Lewis Carroll Shelf Award
Maxi	*Media and Methods* Maxi Award
National Book	National Book Award, Children's Book Category
Newbery Honor	John Newbery Medal Honor Book or Runner-Up
Newbery Winner	John Newbery Medal Winner
O'Dell	Scott O'Dell Award for Historical Fiction
Poe Nominee	Nominee for the Edgar Allan Poe Award Best Juvenile Mystery Category
Poe Winner	Winner of the Edgar Allan Poe Award Best Juvenile Mystery Category
Spur	Western Writers of America Spur Award
Stone	George G. Stone Center for Children's Books Recognition of Merit Award

Western Heritage — Western Heritage Award

PUBLISHERS

Abelard	Abelard-Schuman Limited
Abingdon	Abingdon Press
Addison	Addison-Wesley Pub. Co.
Ashford	Ashford Press
Atheneum	Atheneum Publishers
Atlantic	Atlantic Monthly Press
Atlantic/Little	Atlantic Monthly Press in association with Little, Brown & Co.
Avon	Avon Books
Ballantine	Ballantine Books, Inc.
Bantam	Bantam Books, Inc.
Bobbs	The Bobbs–Merrill Co.
Bradbury	Bradbury Press, Inc.
Carolrhoda	Carolrhoda Books, Inc.
Caxton	The Caxton Printers, Ltd.
Chilton	Chilton Book Co.
Clarion	Clarion Books
Communication Skill	Communication Skill Builders, Inc.
Cowles	Cowles Book Co., Inc.
Coward	Coward, McCann & Geoghegan Inc.
Criterion	Criterion Books
Crowell	Thomas Y. Crowell Co.
Crown	Crown Publishers, Inc.
Day	The John Day Co.
Delacorte	Delacorte Press
Dial	The Dial Press
Dodd	Dodd, Mead & Co.
Doubleday	Doubleday & Co.
Duell	Duell, Sloan & Pearce
Dutton	E. P. Dutton & Co.
Farrar	Farrar, Straus & Giroux
Feminist	Feminist Press
Follett	Follett Publishing Co.
Four Winds	Four Winds Press
Funk	Funk & Wagnalls
Gallancz	Victor Gallancz, Ltd.
Gallup	Gallup-McKinley Public Schools
Ginn	Ginn Custom Publishing
Golden	Golden Press
Golden Horseshoe	Golden Horseshoe Press

Greenwillow	Greenwillow Books
Greystone	Greystone Press
Grosset	Grosset & Dunlap, Inc.
Harcourt	Harcourt Brace Jovanovich, Inc.
Harper	Harper & Row Publishers, Inc.
Hastings	Hastings House, Publishers, Inc.
Hawthorn	Hawthorn Books, Inc.
Hodder	Hodder and Stoughton
Holiday	Holiday House, Inc.
Holt	Holt, Rinehart & Winston
Houghton	Houghton Mifflin Co.
Human Science Press	Human Science Press
Jordan	Jordan Valley Heritage House
Knopf	Alfred A. Knopf, Inc.
Lane	Lane Publishing Co.
Lippincott	J. B. Lippincott Company
Little	Little, Brown & Co.
Lothrop	Lothrop, Lee & Shepard Co. Inc.
Macrae	Macrae Smith Company
Macmillan	The Macmillan Publishing Co.
McCall	McCall Books
McGraw	McGraw-Hill Book Co.
McKay	David McKay Co., Inc.
Meredith	Meredith Corporation
Messner	Julian Messner, Inc.
Morrow	William Morrow & Co.
Nelson	Thomas Nelson Publishers
Northland	Northland Press
Norton	W. W. Norton & Co., Inc.
Obolensky	Obolensky Books
Oxford	Oxford University Press, Inc.
Pantheon	Pantheon Books, Inc.
Parents	Parents' Magazine Press
Parnassus	Parnassus Press
Penn	The Penn Publishing Company
Philomel	Philomel Books
Phillips	S. G. Phillips Inc.
Prentice	Prentice-Hall Inc.
Putnam	G. P. Putnam's Sons
Pyramid	Pyramid Publications
Raintree	Raintree Publishers
Rand	Rand McNally & Co.
Random	Random House, Inc.
Reynal & Hitchcock	Reynal and Hitchcock, Inc.

Rinehart	Holt, Rinehart & Winston
Scholastic	Scholastic Book Services
Scribner's	Charles Scribner's Son
Scott	Scott, Foresman & Co.
Seabury	Seabury Press, Inc.
Simon	Simon & Schuster
South and West	South and West
Stackpole	Stackpole Books
St. Martin's	St. Martin's Press, Inc.
Tower	Tower Press
Vanguard	Vanguard Press
Van Nostrand	C. Van Nostrand Co.
Viking	The Viking Press, Inc.
Walck	Henry Z. Walck, Inc.
Warne	Frederick Warne & Co., Inc.
Watts	Franklin Watts, Inc.
Wesleyan	Wesleyan University Press
Westminster	The Westminster Press
White	David White Company
Whitman	Albert Whitman & Co.
Whittlesey	Whittlesey House
Wilcox	Wilcox & Follett Co.
Winston	John C. Winston Co.
World	World Book Co.

DICTIONARY
OF
AMERICAN
CHILDREN'S
FICTION,
1960–1984

A

AARON THANE (*Freelon Starbird**), livery stable keeper who joins the army in Philadelphia in much the same involuntary way Freelon* has joined and who goes through the winter of 1776 cynical and complaining about everything. At Trenton he recovers and returns the splendid hunting piece which Jib* Grasshorn has abandoned in their first encounter with the Hessians. When the others voluntarily agree to spend six more weeks when their enlistment is up, Sgt.* Kite pulls Aaron forward by the ear to join them. He is killed shortly thereafter at the battle of Princeton.

ABADAN (*The First Two Lives of Lukas-Kasha**), Arabian Nights-like realm in which Lukas-Kasha finds himself and of which he becomes king and embroiled in a power struggle. His efforts to extricate himself result in his acquiring a more sober, less self-centered attitude.

ABBY KENNY (*The Secret of the Simple Code**), thirteen-year-old mountain girl who helps Paul solve the mystery of the cigar messages and develop a healthier attitude toward life. She has a beautiful singing voice and knows many traditional mountain songs. She hopes to find enough garnets or rubies in the abandoned mines to pay her way through music school. She plans to save her share of the reward money for her education.

ABEL'S ISLAND (Steig*, William, ill. author, Farrar, 1976), fantasy which tells with tongue-in-cheek seriousness a Robinson Crusoe story set in 1907 not far from a town called Mossville. Elegant, foppish Abelard Hassam di Chirico Flint of the Mossville Flints—Abel to his friends—is a cultivated Edwardian gentleman mouse. With his charming wife, Amanda, he is caught in a storm while picnicking and takes shelter in a cave. When the wind whips off Amanda's scarf of gauze, Abel impulsively rushes out to retrieve it, is caught by the tempest, and seizes hold of a nail protruding from a flat piece of board which is then washed down a gully, into a stream, over a waterfall, and eventually ends lodged in a birch tree on an island in the river. When the water recedes, Abel climbs down and assesses his situation. At first he expects immediate rescue; in a short while he realizes that it will be up to him to find his way home. Though he has lived a pampered life, he is resourceful. In the ensuing days he tries using the board with the nail for a raft, builds a boat with his jacket for a sail, constructs a catamaran to row, braids a grass rope which he tries to sling across the water for a guy line, rigs a catapult, attempts to make a bridge of stepping stones, even flings himself from the top of the birch with makeshift wings which he hopes will act as a glider—only to fail in all these efforts. In the meantime, he awakens long dormant instincts which help him find food and construct a shelter in a hollow log. He also manages to start a fire and makes clay bowls for cooking and also to carry messages down the stream. He also sends "mind messages" to Amanda. As summer turns to fall he amuses himself by sculpting figures of Amanda and his parents in clay and wood. He also runs across a pocket watch and a romantic novel about bears, which he reads by pacing back and forth along the lines. His island is not without danger: he narrowly escapes from an owl, which he later battles with a spear made from his penknife lashed to a stick. In preparation for winter he stores food in his log and weaves himself a cape of grass in two layers, stuffed with milkweed fluff. Through the bitter weather he exists in a somnolent state in his log home, but with spring he awakens to the beauties of nature. Spring also brings him a visitor, Gower Glackens, an elderly and forgetful frog. Gower sits for his statue in clay and points out that Abel seems to have found his vocation. The frog is well-meaning but unable to keep an idea in mind, and when the water subsides from the spring runoff so that he can swim back, he promises to send rescue, but, as Abel fears, he forgets. A long dry spell so reduces the water that Abel, now much tougher both physically and mentally from his year on the island, determines to swim across. He succeeds, though he is carried a long way down stream, and just as his problems seem solved, he is caught by a cat. With cleverness and determination, Abel escapes, makes his way home, finds Amanda out, and by the time she returns, he is bathed and dressed in silk shirt, purple cravat, and brown velvet jacket, and is reclining on the plush sofa, a stronger, braver, and better mouse because of his year-long adventure. The formal, pretentious style which mimics romantic novels of the turn of the century provides much of the humor, as also do Steig's illustrations and the irony of a Robinsonnade with a mouse protagonist. Abel is a plucky and appealing hero and his developing self-reliance is interesting in itself, not just as parody. Books Too Good; Fanfare; Lewis Carroll; Newbery Honor.

ABOUT THE B'NAI BAGELS (Konigsburg*, E. L., Atheneum, 1979), realistic novel about a suburban New York Jewish family and their involvement in Little League. When twelve-year-old Mark Setzer's mother, Bessie, volunteers to coach the B'nai B'rith team and names his older brother, Spencer, 21, coach, Mark's troubles begin. By sheer enthusiasm Mrs. Setzer wins over the team, who start calling her Mother Bagel, and they come from last place to the Point Baldwin finals. Mark, however, suffers because both Spencer and his mother lean over backward to give him no special favors and because his best friend, Herschel Miller, has changed his allegiance to Barry Jacobs, a boy whose well-to-do mother keeps a close watch on his every move under the guise of an open, "no-secrets-from-each-other" relationship. To get practice, Mark skips Hebrew school to play ball at a low-income housing project where the Rivera twins, Simon and Sylvester, live, and he finds that, without the pressure of parents and brother watching, he plays pretty well. Cookie Rivera, the twins' matter-of-fact little sister, takes a shine to him and teaches him how to tell her brothers apart. In the final game, when a substitution of an ineligible identical twin for the tiring pitcher brings a win but is noticed only by Mark, he is faced with a conflict between loyalty to his team and to truth. In the end his honesty seems to be rewarded by the return of Herschel as a close friend, as they both prepare for their Bar Mitzvahs. There are other, mostly amusing conflicts: Aunt Thelma frequently tries to show off her superior education to Bessie; Spencer, now in college, argues with his mother to show *his* superiority; Bessie appeals continually to God, who, Mark thinks, seems to live in the light fixture in the ceiling; Mark, on Spencer's advice, disguises his tuneless voice by singing his part for the Bar Mitzvah *fortissimo*. With a good deal of other humor based on dialect and customs, the book gives a picture of the ethnically mixed community that is sympathetic if stereotypical. Choice.

ACKERMAN, ERLO (*Bert Breen's Barn**), crotchety, authoritative, conservative, old partner in the Ackerman and Hook* Mill in Boonville, for whom Tom works for several years to get the money to buy Bert Breen's barn. Although he encourages Tom and occasionally gives him advice, he never indulges the boy, always expecting full measure in labor from him. In his younger days, he had chummed with Chick Hannaberry, Tom's shiftless grandfather.

ACROSS FIVE APRILS (Hunt*, Irene, Follett, 1964), historical novel set during the American Civil War near Newton in Jasper County in southern Illinois from April, 1861, to April, 1865. Although the family is sympathetic to the Union cause and two older brothers, John and Tom, a cousin, Eb Carron, and a good friend, schoolteacher Shadrach* Yale, join the Union army, nine-year-old Jethro* Creighton experiences hostility from neighbors because his brother Bill* is fighting for the Confederacy. Antagonistic local people pour coal oil in the well, burn the barn, and attack Jethro on his way home from town. After his brothers leave for the war and his father, Matt, has a heart attack, Jethro must take the responsibility of running the family farm and making the decisions with only the help of his sister, Jenny, 14, who later marries Shad. A major problem arises when Eb deserts from the army and returns home, and Jethro must decide whether or not to report him. He writes to Lincoln for advice and receives an answer giving details of amnesty for deserters. A final blow is the death of the president, for whom Jethro has developed a great admiration. A war book in which no battles appear, the novel emphasizes the hardships of those who remain at home during the conflict and gives a good sense of what it must have been like to live in border country and be suspected of having Rebel leanings. The reader is kept apprised of what happens during the conflict by word of mouth reports, letters from the boys who serve in different sectors, and newspaper accounts. Based upon the memories of Hunt's grandfather, who was a boy in southern Illinois during the war, incidents carry the conviction of reality. The style is mature in vocabulary and sentence structure, but the storytelling cadence makes for a pleasing narrative flow that carries the reader along, and characterization is strong. (Dave Burdow*; Ross Milton*) Books Too Good; ChLA Touchstones; Choice; Fanfare; Lewis Carroll; Newbery Honor.

ADAM BOOKOUT (Shotwell*, Louisa R., ill. W. T. Mars, Viking, 1967), realistic novel with detective story aspects in a family and neighborhood context covering about a month's time in the mid–1900s first in a small town in Oklahoma and then in a mixed-ethnic part of Brooklyn, N.Y. Since the death of his rancher parents in a plane crash, free-spirited, dreamy, grieving Adam Bookout, 11, has been living in Walnut Lick, Okla., with his two great-aunts, Vann, a teacher, and Meg, a motherly sort. Refusing to make friends in school and tired of Meg's joking attempts to cheer him and of Vann's imperious ways, Adam runs away to live with Cousins* Kate and Gideon Bookout, author of detective novels and professor of philosophy, respectively. They receive him with warmth and sympathy if surprise, and he soon feels at home in their comfortable apartment in Van Hooten Terrace. In public school he soon makes friends with Saul* Katz, a loquacious Jewish boy, Willie* Weggfall, a black youth from Alabama also new in school, and Magdalena, a very bright girl of Puerto Rican descent. A new plot problem then develops, which eventually leads to the solution of Adam's personal one. Willie's much loved mongrel, Honey, is stolen, and at Saul's suggestion, the children form a committee for getting her back, the Honey Recovery Task Force, or the H.R.T.F. They enlist the aid of authorities and collect and investigate clues. Adam's idea of consulting Cousin Kate about how her fictional detective, Aldrich Batt, would solve the mystery leads eventually to the dog's return. Kate suggests that they examine carefully for clues the picture Saul took of the group with the dog in front of Van Hooten Terrace the day Honey was stolen. Various difficulties intervene before Adam discovers that the thief is Hank Wilmot, the son of wealthy friends of the Bookouts, who has been shoplifting to punish his father for never listening to him, and who stole the dog just "for kicks." Adam has learned also that the Bookouts are planning a sabbatical in Europe. Although they offer him a permanent home and boarding school while they are away, Adam searches his soul, decides to confront his personal problems, and elects to return to Walnut Lick and the guardianship of kindly Aunt Meg. This story of a boy's attempts to come to grips with life's painful realities moves evenly with interesting if implausible complications to an abrupt and unconvincing conclusion. Conversation is natural, point of view consistent, and added details contribute color and texture. The adults are more credible than the children, who though individualized constitute a too-deliberate mix of ethnic groups, are stereotypes, or phony, like Hank Wilmot and breezy Beecy (B. C.) Carr, the young woman whom Adam meets on the bus and who wangles a ticket to Kennedy for him. Adam himself is a sympathetic protagonist. Choice.

ADAM EDDINGTON (*The Arm of the Starfish**; *A Ring of Endless Light**), almost seventeen in *The Arm of the Starfish*, he plans to go to Berkeley in the fall to major in marine biology. He gets a summer job with Dr. Calvin* O'Keefe on the island of Gaea off Portugal, working on experiments with the regeneration of the starfish. A bright, earnest, independent youth, he tends to be impetuous. His involvement with Carolyn Cutter (Kali* Cutter) leads to the death of Joshua Archer, the young embassy official, whom Adam has grown to admire and respect. Later, in *A Ring of Endless Light*, he is an experimental scientist at a marine biology station in New England where he comes into contact with Vicky Austin of *Meet the Austins**, who helps him with his experiments. He is somewhat disillusioned after the Kali Cutter affair, and Vicky restores his confidence in women.

ADAMS, SAMUEL (*Early Thunder**), American Revolutionary leader, an actual historical figure. Daniel West sees him as a shuffling, slack-faced man and thinks he is a fortuneteller, until Jeremy Packer tells him otherwise. Adams directs activities after the government of Massachusetts Colony is moved to Salem.

ADAM WAITE (*Dark Venture**), young surgeon of the slave ship *Orion*. Because he has a strong desire to be independent and is irritated by his contemptuous treatment by his godfather, in whose house he grew up, Adam accepts the chance to wipe out his debt by shipping as surgeon on his godfather's slave ship. A man of sensitivity and principle, he finds everything in the slave trade repugnant. When he buys twelve-year-old Demba to save him from a cruel master, he berates himself for his foolish impulse that has left him in debt and saddled with a dependent, but he is kind and patient with the boy.

AERIEL (*The Darkangel**), slave girl who in trying to avenge the kidnapping of her mistress, Eoduin, by a vampyre is herself captured and carried off to be a slave in his castle. Short and skinny, she has been scornfully teased by Eoduin as being clumsy, but she learns that her mistress has been secretly jealous of her endurance. At the vampyre's castle, she must spin and weave garments for the wraiths of his brides with no material but her emotions. At first she can spin only heavy, coarse thread from pity, but gradually she learns to make fine, light, golden thread from love. The Darkangel (the vampyre) rejects her at first as a bride because he finds her ugly, but during her quest in the desert she grows and develops physically and spiritually so he discovers she is beautiful when she returns.

AGGIE KILPIN (*Up a Road Slowly**), retarded, undernourished daughter of local ne'er-do-wells. Her schoolmates shun Aggie because she is dirty and pushy. She obsequiously follows them about, interjecting herself into their games. Aunt* Cordelia insists that Julie include Aggie in her activities and Julie repeatedly tries without success to convince her aunt that Aggie is an unsuitable playmate. In one of the book's most memorable scenes, Julie arranges for Aggie to be "queen," a game in which the children ostensibly honor Aggie but in reality effectively exclude her. Aggie dies of malnutrition and neglect.

AKAWA (*Saturday, the Twelfth of October**), daughter of Diwera, the Medicine Woman, and twin of the ugly Hiffaru*. Apparently a flighty girl without a serious thought, she is a disappointment to her mother, who had hoped she would become the tribe's next Wai Wai, or Medicine Woman. When Hiffaru kills Sonte*, Akawa acts out of character when she alone keeps her head. She surprises everyone by taking charge and bringing order out of the pandemonium that ensues because of the murder. Diwera changes her mind about her daughter.

ALAIN FAYAUD (*Janine**), childhood neighbor and friend of the Forel family, who has become estranged. Because of the difficulties of the war years and the strain of knowing that his father has been suspected of betraying the other miners to the Nazis, Alain is old for his years and serious. He has been a coal miner since he was twelve and during the occupation managed some minor sabotage to slow the flow of coal to Germany.

ALAN AND NAOMI (Levoy*, Myron, Harper, 1977), realistic novel set in Queens, New York City, in 1944, during World War II. The main interest in the life of Alan* Silverman, junior high age, is stickball, even though he is not very good, is frequently ridiculed by the neighborhood jock, Joe Condello, and might not even be chosen for a team if it were not for his friend, Shaun Kelly. Then his mother drops a bomb; she has agreed that he will go up to the Leibmans' apartment every day to talk to the crazy girl, Naomi* Kirshenbaum, 12, a French refugee who, with her mother, has come to stay with them. Mrs. Silverman explains that the girl has been upset by the terrible things she has experienced— seeing her father beaten to death by the Gestapo, hiding for days in the Paris sewers—and her psychoanalyst thinks she may improve if she has a friend her own age. Alan has already seen Naomi in the hall, where she was tearing maps to bits and cowered away from his stick when he came from playing ball. He grudges the time away from stick ball, he is afraid of being called a sissy, he rages, but he goes. He takes with him a Charlie McCarthy dummy he had some years before, and it proves a lucky inspiration. Naomi will not speak to him, but she gradually gets her doll, Yvette, to talk and even sing and dance with Charlie. Sometimes Alan says the wrong thing and scares Naomi back into her shell, but generally they become more at ease. Mrs. Leibman and Mrs. Kirshenbaum are pathetically grateful and push candy and fruit on Alan. Naomi's doctor is pleased and thinks now Alan must wean the girl away from using the doll as a crutch. With some setbacks Alan accomplishes this, discovering as he does so that he really likes Naomi. His teacher sends home books and assignments, and they study together. At first he insists that they be secret friends, so he will not have to acknowledge her greeting if they meet in front of the other neighborhood kids, but by the time Naomi's doctor thinks Alan should take her out on the street, he is so fond of the girl that he is willing. He takes his Piper Cub model, and they go on a long walk to the deserted field at Holmes Airport where he and Shaun sometimes fly their planes. They have a wonderful time, and Naomi tells him for the first time about her father's death, how he and she tried to tear up all his maps of the Paris sewers where the Resistance soldiers traveled and hid, tear them up and flush them down the toilet before the Gestapo came, and how she hid under the bed while they clubbed him to death. On the way home Shaun follows them and yells "Sissy" at Alan, and the next day they have a confrontation in which Alan realizes that Shaun has been hurt because he kept Naomi from him, and is not ready to forgive. Nevertheless, as Naomi starts school and seems to be doing well, Alan is happy. Then Joe Condello taunts them with yells of "Yid" and a remark that it's no wonder Hitler wants to wipe them out. Alan shouts at Naomi to run and dives into a hopeless fight with Joe. Before he is beaten too badly, Shaun joins the fight and helps him home, but when they look for Naomi she is nowhere to be found. The whole neighborhood and police search, and she is finally found cowering under the coal in the coal bin, totally irrational. Alan, with his father, visits her later in a mental institution where she sits unspeaking, tearing paper to bits. Despite the ending, which leaves little hope for Naomi, this is not a negative book. The relationship that develops between the youngsters is touching, often funny, and believable, and the effort at friendship seems to be worthwhile. Boston Globe Honor; Fanfare.

ALAN SILVERMAN (*Alan and Naomi**), bright young Jewish boy who is volunteered by his mother to be a friend of the deeply disturbed refugee girl staying with a family in the apartment building. Something of an outsider himself, Alan risks being ridiculed and tries to keep the friendship secret, but he is bright and clever and uses his wise-cracking Charlie McCarthy dummy to say things he couldn't say himself, thereby breaking through the girl's shell and coaxing her back to normality. He resents the way the adults have maneuvered him into the situation, and he is annoyed by their gratitude. He is himself haunted by a memory of a face in a news film of a girl being loaded into a truck to go to one of the Nazi death camps. Later, he becomes genuinely fond of Naomi* for her own sake.

ALCOCK, GUDRUN born in Stockholm, Sweden; editor and author of several books concerned with social problems published in the 1960s and 1970s. She worked as art director for Marshall Field & Co. and as women's editor for the Chicago *Sun*. Volunteer work in a children's home provided the background and incentive for her novels *Run, Westy, Run** (Lothrop, 1966), a story of a compulsive runaway, *Turn the Next Corner* (Lothrop, 1969), concerned with a boy whose father is in prison for embezzlement, and *Duffy* (Lothrop, 1972), about a girl who is ward of the court.

ALEXANDER, LLOYD (CHUDLEY) (1924–   ), born and grew up in Philadelphia, Pa.; educated at West Chester State Teachers College, Lafayette College, and the University of Paris (Sorbonne); author, free-lance writer, and translator. He achieved prominence for his novels of fantasy for children, chiefly the five frequently honored Chronicles of Prydain: *The Book of Three** (Holt, 1964), cited in Contemporary Classics; *The Black Cauldron** (Holt, 1965), a Newbery Honor book; *The Castle of Llyr** (Holt, 1966); *Taran Wanderer** (Holt, 1967); and *The High King** (Holt, 1968), winner of the John Newbery Medal and a National Book Award finalist. Among still other honors, all were Fanfare books and appear in the Children's Literature Association Touchstones and in *Choice*. Based loosely on the legends and mythology of the Welsh *Mabinogion* and set in a Wales-like land, they see the youth Taran, a foundling of no known parentage and an assistant pig keeper, resolve questions of identity and self-worth in an atmosphere of heroism and danger. Among other fantasies are the picaresque *The Cat Who Wished to Be a Man** (Dutton, 1973), *The First Two Lives of Lukas-Kasha** (Dutton, 1978), nominated for the National Book Award, and *The Marvelous Misadventures of Sebastian** (Dutton, 1970), which received the National Book Award. Alexander has also published picture books, among them, *Coll and His White Pig* (Holt, 1965) and *The Truthful Harp* (Holt, 1967), both introductions to the land of Prydain for younger readers, and *The Foundlings and Other Tales of Prydain* (Holt, 1973), six short fairy tales which take place before the time of the Chronicles. Recent companion novels, *Westmark** (Dutton, 1981), *The Kestrel** (Dutton, 1982), both Fanfare books, and *The Beggar Queen* (Dutton, 1984) form a trilogy that departs somewhat from his previous work, being realistic novels of adventure and conflict set in a fictitious medieval kingdom threatened by democratic revolutionaries. His style is exuberant, contemporary, and slyly witty, his plots are inventive and fast-moving if superficial, overly intricate, and too patly resolved, his hosts of characters are intriguing if shallow and static, and recurring themes include the triumph of good over evil, treachery foiled, and discovering one's hidden strengths. Before writing for children, Alexander wrote for adults, including the novel *And Let the Credit Go* (Crowell, 1955) and translations from the French of Sartre, Eluard, and Vialar. He was nominated for the Laura Ingalls Wilder Award in 1983.

ALEXANDER SCHMORELL (*Ceremony of Innocence**), Alex, an actual historical figure who appears as a character in the novel. Good friend of fellow medical student, Hans Scholl, and sweetheart of Hans's sister, Sophie*, Alex is a mischievous, easy going sort, whose motives to resist Nazism actively stem from observed Nazi oppression of the Jews. He is caught while trying to escape through the Alps to Switzerland and guillotined.

ALFRED BURT (*The Alfred Summer**), black retarded boy who becomes a friend of Lester* Klopper. Handicapped physically as well as mentally, Alfred limps and has one useless hand, and apparently has further problems that lead to his epileptic attack. His great pleasure is selling *Colliers* and *The Saturday Evening Post* and collecting match covers and foil on the beach. Sweet-tempered and friendly, Alfred does not see Lester as different and therefore forms a bridge which connects him to Myron* Kagan and the outside world.

THE ALFRED SUMMER (Slepian*, Jan, Macmillan, 1980), realistic novel of the friendship between a cerebral palsy victim and a black retarded boy, set in Brooklyn in 1937. Though fourteen, Lester* Klopper is tied to his mother by invisible strings, both depending upon her and hating her fierce defense of his condition, which makes walking and talking difficult. When he meets Alfred* Burt, about twelve, he is attracted to the younger boy's apparent lack of consciousness of his difficulties, but his mother is repelled by the idea of his knowing a retarded boy. At the beach, only Lester sees when Alfred slips on a rock and gets stuck. With great difficulty, he tells his father, who with the help of Myron* Kagan, about Lester's age, pulls Alfred out. So the three-way friendship starts, since Myron, though apparently normal, is just as handicapped as the other two by his dominating mother and sisters, who tease and criticize him continually. Myron is building a boat in the apartment-house basement so that he can get away from them all, and Lester and Alfred become part of the project, collecting scrapwood and watching Myron's crude building attempts. They are joined by Claire, a jaunty girl runner, who is hiding her cat in the basement. To see how seats are fitted into rowboats, the four take a picnic to Prospect Park (a real adventure for Lester, who has never been away from his mother), where Myron almost gets arrested for his thwarted attempt to steal oarlocks. To prove himself, Lester plans a second trip to the park with Alfred, so they can steal the oarlocks. They manage the theft, but on the return train home Alfred has an epileptic attack. Unable to summon help, Lester drags him from the train, and later, for the first time, is praised by his father. With Alfred in the hospital, Myron changes the boat's name from *The Getaway* to *The Alfred*, and they collect all the families to go to the beach for the big launching where Myron proudly sets off rowing—and sinks. With newfound confidence, Myron turns the ridicule into applause, and Lester realizes that it is one way of overcoming handicaps. In an unusual and somewhat jolting pattern, the first and last chapters are told in first person by Lester and all the rest in the omniscient author point of view. Characterization is the strong element in the book, in which Lester's struggles, Alfred's sweet acceptance, and Myron's clumsy resentment and rage all are portrayed without condescension. The parents, particularly Lester's with all their faults, and Alfred's, are pictured honestly and humanely, and their predicament and Lester's is not trivialized by an easy solution. Sequel is *Lester's Turn* (Macmillan, 1981). Boston Globe Honor.

ALICIA ALLISON TRELLING (*Up A Road Slowly**), the second wife of Julie's abstracted professor father. Her efforts at redecorating the family home Julie finds distasteful and disrespectful at first. She is also Julie's high school English teacher. She tries to get Julie to see that Brett* is using her and to realize the moral implications of giving him so much help with his studies.

ALLEY (*The Alley**), setting of the book and also of *The Tunnel of Hugsy Goode*, a real place about which faculty houses clustered just off the campus of Pratt Institute, where the author, Eleanor Estes*†, lived while her husband was a professor there.

THE ALLEY (Estes*†, Eleanor, ill. Edward Ardizzone, Harcourt, 1964), realistic novel of family and community life with detective story aspects. The action covers about two months and is set in Brooklyn, N.Y., in the mid–1900s. Twenty-seven faculty houses line the Alley* just off the campus of Grandby College. Thirty-three children of different ages play there, among them ladylike, sheltered Connie* Ives, 10, thoughtful, considerate Billy* Maloon, her best friend, and outgoing and imperious Katy* Starr, 11, who makes the rules and directs activities. On May 15, Alumni Day, the Iveses' house is ransacked. Mama is certain that one of the investigating policemen has stolen her diamond ring, which she kept affixed to the clip on Papa's pencil and stored in a dresser drawer. When the police fail to apprehend the culprits, the Alley children take a hand in the case. They collect clues, of which Billy takes charge: a Stanley screwdriver used to gain entry to the house, a bloodstained curtain, a cigarette butt, and a bone. They are positive that a bulletheaded man, who tried to make up with Connie's dog, Wags, and who smokes the same kind of cigarettes, is one of the thieves. The children hold a mock trial in the Alley, some of them pretending to be the burglars and two others pretending to be the policemen Mama believes had a part in the crime. Billy proves to be a persuasive and eloquent prosecutor and Katy a fair and effective judge. Near the end of the trial, Billy catches sight of the bulletheaded man talking to another Alley resident, artist Joe Below, called by the children Bully Vardeer, from the French term *boulevardier*, for his Parisian attitudes. Billy and Connie are sure he is next on the thieves' list and "case" his house for days to no avail. When Connie's school is evacuated for a bomb scare, Connie observes one of the policemen using a pencil that looks like her father's. During the summer, she forms the Alley Conservatory of Music and gives piano lessons to the little children of the Alley. On Recital Day, Billy observes thieves breaking into Bully's house and snaps pictures of them and the investigating policemen. Connie identifies her father's pencil, and the suspects, including the bulletheaded man and the two policemen, are arrested. Characterization is rich, and the activities, attitudes, and speech of the children accurate and very engaging. The plot ambles along unevenly. Its premise that children can succeed where adults fail seems dated and condescending to late twentieth century audiences. The style is warm, easy going, and affectionate, and language is simple. The book is chiefly memorable for its splendid detail of everyday life and quiet humor. (Nanny*, Hugsy* Goode). Choice.

THE ALLIGATOR CASE (DuBois*†, William Pène, ill. author, Harper, 1965), brief tongue-in-cheek mystery set in a small American town in the mid-twentieth century. The unnamed first-person narrator is a boy detective, perhaps twelve, who sees the first posters pasted on barns for Leed's Leading Circus where the top act is the Astrogater, an alligator fired by a cannon into a tiny water tank. The detective prepares a trap-trap (a pit shaped like a trapezoid) to catch the Astrogater, just in case he might escape. Acting as a porter, he sees three passengers arrive on the weekly train, two men named Mr. Bromwell and Mr. Fish, and a woman named Miss Journey. He fantasizes that Mr. Bromwell's long thin case that looks like a fishing pole case really contains a snake, and that Mr. Fish's case, which looks as if it contains a musical instrument, is really hiding a bazooka. Assuming a series of disguises—an old man, a bus boy, a dishwasher, a barefoot boy with cheeks of tan, a popcorn salesman—he proves these three to be the crooks who rob the hotel dining room and the circus cashier, tricks them into his trap-trap, and becomes the town hero. A light and ridiculous mystery, it gets considerable humor from mimicking the language of detective thrillers, though some of this may be lost on its intended audience of early readers. Choice.

ALL TOGETHER NOW (Bridgers*, Sue Ellen, Knopf, 1979), realistic novel set in North Carolina during one summer in the early 1950s. With her airforce pilot father, David, in the Korean War and her mother singing in a nightclub, Casey* Flanagan, 12, comes from South Carolina to spend the vacation with her grandparents in Greensboro, N.C. Lonely and a tomboy, she makes friends with retarded Dwayne* Pickens, a man her father's age but with the mind of a twelve-year-old, who plays a complicated solo game of baseball in the lot across the street, taking the parts of all the players in turn and announcing the plays like a radio sportscaster as he goes along. Because Dwayne scorns girls, Casey lets him think she is a boy. Casey's uncle, Taylor, 28, who works in his father's lumberyard but whose heart is in fast cars, takes them to the track where he races every weekend, and they get to know his girlfriend, Gwen*, a blond who works at the five-and-dime store. Casey's life also becomes involved with that of Hazard* Whitaker, a middle-aged sometime salesman and dancing waiter, who has been befriended by Casey's grandmother, warmhearted, practical Jane Flanagan, and her husband, Ben. For twenty-five years Hazard has admired Jane's best friend, Pansy, a spinster who works in a doctor's office, and after Casey repeats the women's conversation about him, Hazard surprises himself by asking Pansy to marry him, a proposal she calmly accepts. Their honeymoon is a disaster because the bumbling Hazard first forgets to reserve a berth, then gets drunk and forgets Pansy, who returns to her own home and starts proceedings for an annulment. Further complications occur when Taylor good-naturedly teaches both Casey and Dwayne to drive and Dwayne takes his brother Alva's Chrysler to the track and wheels it around, thinking he is in a race. Casey saves the day by announcing over the loud-speaker that Dwayne has won and should come to the stand for his trophy. Taylor alienates Gwen by giving Dwayne a trophy that was a gift from her. Alva seizes this opportunity, and a subsequent fight in which Dwayne protects Taylor, to have Dwayne committed to an institution, but the Flanagans and their friends attend a town meeting where they shame Alva, an alderman, into withdrawing his commitment order. Casey comes down with polio and while she is seriously ill, Dwayne overhears the doctor refer to her as a girl, but he is able to accept the truth and at book's end, Hazard has recovered Pansy, Taylor and Gwen are back together, Casey is returning to her home, and Dwayne is looking forward to another summer of palling around with her, a situation Casey knows is not likely to occur, since she is growing up while he is not. Although the plot has several interesting strands and the nostalgic setting rings true, the strength of the novel lies in its strong characterizations. Any of the handful of main characters could easily become stereotypes and the story sentimental, but sensitive handling prevents both of these possibilities. Boston Globe Honor; Christopher.

ALONE IN WOLF HOLLOW (Brookins*, Dana, Seabury, 1978), novel of mystery and suspense set near a Midwestern small town in recent times. Bart Cadle, 12, and his brother Arnie, 9, arrive in Jason after Cousin Jenny in St. Louis has tired of taking care of them since their mother's death and has sent them by bus to their Uncle Charlie Fleckson. When Uncle Charlie is not there to meet them, the station master sends them, along with the telegram which was supposed to precede their arrival, to the Blue Raven, a tavern on the edge of Wolf Hollow, the wooded area where their uncle lives. They get from the bartender the news that Charlie owes fifty dollars there, and from the waitress, Madge, a flashlight and directions to Charlie's isolated house. They arrive to find the house in a terrible mess and their uncle drunk. He tells them to find a bed but is furious in the morning when he finds them in the only clean room in the house, the room that had belonged to his recently deceased wife, Lou. Arnie, who has a lively imagination, is terrified of the dark Hollow, of the insane asylum on the hill, of the tree which sounds like a woman crying, of the sound of someone following them, of werewolves, and of other characters from horror movies. Bart is afraid that their uncle will reject them and they will be separated, since none of their other relatives want them both. As they go into Jason for supplies, they hear Madge arguing with a man, the sound of a slap, and they catch a glimpse of a khaki shirt, but Madge makes light of being hit and gives them a coke in the Blue Raven. Their uncle alternates between being drunk and acting fairly normal and friendly. With no commitment that they can stay, they start school and begin to enjoy exploring the Hollow, playing in an old boat on a mud-hole called Crazy Woman Pond, and spying on Old Lena, a youngish black woman who traps and lives in a shack, the only other resident of the Hollow. On their way to school one morning they come upon Madge's body, brutally stabbed. They find no one at the Blue Raven, so run on to Mr. Clenning's grocery store, where he calls the sheriff. Uncle Charlie, who has been consoled by Madge since Lou's death, goes into another drinking bout and when he comes out of it briefly, gives Bart seventy dollars and tells them to catch the bus for St. Louis. Then he leaves. They go into town but can't make themselves board the bus, and return to live alone in Wolf Hollow. As problems mount, Bart decides to wait through Christmas to face the inevitable, trying not to spoil Arnie's enthusiasm. On Christmas Eve, as they make some last-minute deliveries for Mr. Clenning to earn a little money, Bart realizes because of something Clenning has said to the sheriff that he must be the murderer. Bart tries to conceal his knowledge, but Clenning guesses, follows them back to the Hollow, tells them that he was once Madge's husband and has followed her to Jason and killed her in jealousy, that he knows Charlie is gone, and that he is going to shut them up for good. They escape, dash through the woods, and are saved by Old Lena and King, a mental patient who has been secretly living with her and who thinks he is king of a distant planet. In the middle of the night, Charlie returns, having joined Alcoholics Anonymous, and agrees to consider letting them stay. The two boys are well characterized, Bart prematurely responsible, hardworking and worried, Arnie a charmer, full of imagination and seemingly young for his age, but underneath tougher than he seems. The suspense is well sustained and events are plausible, even in the Gothic atmosphere. Poe Winner.

ALONZO WEBSTER (*Whose Town ?**), the black high-school student who is always looking for insults in any encounter with whites. David*† Williams, the protagonist, first meets Alonzo in school, where he is the hot-headed leader of a group of blacks who eat separately in the cafeteria and avoid acquaintance with white students. At football practice, Alonzo swings at a boy who is keeping the ball from him and is kicked off the team by the coach. Alonzo is the one who wants to go back to the gas station where Jimmy's car was smashed and to pressure the attendant to tell them who did it. At the station he starts from the car toward the frightened attendant, who grabs a gun and kills him. In *North Town*, the second in a four-book series starting with *South Town**†, he is called Alonzo Wells.

AMANDA (*The Headless Cupid**), Molly's daughter and the Stanleys' new stepsister. She is a spoiled child who is angry at her mother for bringing her to live in such a remote place, refuses to have anything to do with her stepfather, and takes her resentment out on the Stanley children by assuming a superior attitude toward them. At the beginning, she refuses to help with tasks or play with the children. Gradually she warms to them, and agreeing to instruct them in spiritualism is the first step in the process by which she becomes part of the family.

AMOSS, BERTHE (MARKS) (1925–   ), born in New Orleans and educated at Tulane University in Louisiana and at art schools in Hawaii, Germany, and Belgium. Originally an illustrator, she has done both words and pictures for a number of books for the very young, including *It's Not Your Birthday* (Harper, 1966) and *Tom in the Middle* (Harper, 1968), both based on incidents in the childhood of her six sons. *The Great Sea Monster: or, A Book By You* (Parents, 1975), is a dual-purpose book as the title suggests, being a story of a boy captured by an octopus while fishing plus suggestions for writing and illustrating the reader's own story. *The Chalk Cross** (Seabury, 1976) is for older children, a time fantasy that reflects her interest in art and her knowledge of New Orleans, both past and present.

AMY ENFIELD (*The Griffin Legacy**), protagonist of the novel, almost fourteen. She arrives at her Grandma* Enfield's house somewhat apprehensive about what she will find there, because it has been half a dozen years since she has seen her grandmother, because she knows imposing old Aunt* Matilda now lives there, too, and because the house stands all by itself outside of the village and seems forbidding. Amy does her best to fit in and please the two old women, and she is happy that Ben* and Betsy* Winters are friendly and soon make her feel at home in the village and the church. Most of her attention is focused on Lucy* Griffin's problems, toward which Aunt Matilda keeps pushing her. Amy resembles Lucy very strongly, and when she is dressed in old-fashioned paisley for the church heritage festival, the ghost of Seth* Howes mistakes her for Lucy and takes her to task for disloyalty. This is the first ghostly visitation. At the end Amy feels content with having helped Lucy and Seth and looks forward to returning to Grandma Enfield's and her Winters friends on summer vacation. Amy is well named, being an amiable, agreeable, respectful girl.

AMY TRELOAR (*The Dollhouse Murders**), twelve-year-old who rebels at her responsibility for her brain-damaged sister, Louann*, while her mother works and who goes to stay with her Aunt Clare in the old home that belonged to her father's grandparents. There she discovers strange happenings in the elaborate dollhouse in the attic, a replica of the house she is in, and she solves the mystery of a thirty-year-old murder with the help of the unquiet spirit that inhabits the dollhouse. Amy's frustration at her sister's behavior is tempered by real love for Louann and a realization that the girl is a family problem that she must share with her parents.

ANAMANDRA AMUDSAR (*A Gift of Mirrorvax**), charming, naive farm girl who rescues Michael* 2112439–851 and with whom he falls in love. Blond with dark eyes, she is graceful and intelligent, but so unsuspicious that she accepts him as a ''foreigner'' without attempting to pry into where he is from, little suspecting that he comes from another planet.

AND ONE WAS A WOODEN INDIAN (Baker*, Betty, Macmillan, 1970), humorous adventure story set just before the Civil War in the Gila River country of Arizona, which reflects historical events and contrasts current attitudes of whites and Indians. Two Apache youths, nearsighted Hatilshay, whose combination of wit, nearsightedness, and luck have earned him a reputation for medicine power, and earnest Turtlehead, staunch believer in omens, on a raid for Mexican horses, fall in with an American supply train bound for the gold field at the Gila bend. When the army doctor attached to the military escort treats Turtlehead's wounds, Turtlehead is terrified at the sight of a life-sized decorative wooden statue of an Indian upon which has been painted a blanket with the designs that Turtlehead's own blanket bears. This has been done as a joke at the suggestion of Chulito, white-educated Christian Papago, who travels with the train as translator, and whose tribe are traditional enemies of the Apaches. When his healing wounds stiffen, Turtlehead is convinced that the Yankees have captured his spirit and imprisoned it inside the statue. He persuades Hatilshay and his uncle, the shaman known as the old one, to steal and destroy the statue and thus save his life. The quest takes them cross country to the gold city and also involves the often arrogant Chulito and a miserable, white-dependent Yuma, Poor Lo. The Indians succeed, after a series of comic errors which both amuse and annoy the White-Eyes, cause the Indians themselves considerable consternation, and reveal basic differences in outlook between Papago and Apache, Yuma and Papago, Yuma and Apache, American and Indian, and converted and unconverted Indians. Turtlehead is relieved to be free from the White-Eyes' power, and Hatilshay has gained perspective on the shaman's role and his own identity. Characters are deftly drawn, but only Hatilshay, from whose point of view events are seen, changes in personality. This is a very sophisticated book, whose understated style is so cryptic at times as to render the action obscure. A reader who is alert for inferences, sensitive to subtleties of style and juxtapositions, and appreciative of the humor of irony and satire as well as of situation comedy, will probably discover that this is a very funny and very revealing novel. Western Heritage.

ANDREA HULL (*Homesick: My Own Story**), Jean Guttery's friend in the American community of Hankow in 1925. A year older than Jean and far more sophisticated, she is a source of all sorts of valuable information: where babies come from, how to bring out the ''hidden lights'' in your hair with a camomile rinse, what is the newest slang in America, and how important it is to be in love with a boy. One night on the voyage across the Pacific, Andrea, a ballet enthusiast, does an impassioned free-style dance for Jean expressing the forces drawing them back to China and away from it as the girls enjoy solitude on the upper deck.

ANDRECIA (*Enchantress from the Stars**), a society on a planet somewhere in space still in a feudal state, in which the people believe in witches, magic, and the like. Elana, Starwatcher*, and Evrek*, agents of the Anthropological Service of the Federation, have been sent to Andrecia to prevent the Imperialists, a more technologically advanced society, from establishing a colony there and destroying the Andrecians. The Andrecians think the Imperialists' earthmover is a Dragon* and make sacrifices to it.

ANDREW (*A Spell Is Cast**), Scottish caretaker at Tarnhelm, Mrs. Van Heusen's estate, and husband of Fergie*. He speaks with a brogue and loves to tell Scottish stories and sing Scottish songs. He sometimes sings them for his employer's guests. He helps make Cory feel at home at Tarnhelm, and she enjoys his company very much.

ANGELA WEXLER (*The Westing Game**), beautiful young woman whose mother dominates her until the Westing game gives her the opportunity to assert herself. She is responsible for the bombings, in one of which her face is scarred. She really wants to go to college to study medicine and eventually does. She becomes an orthopedic surgeon and marries the young doctor, Denton Deere, who also has a part in the Westing game.

ANGIE (*The Loner**), Boss's* former daughter-in-law, the widow of Boss's son, Ben, who was killed by a grizzly. She is a schoolteacher and is warm, friendly, and accepting. She helps David to believe in himself.

ANGUS TUCK (*Tuck Everlasting**), father of Jesse* and Miles*, who, with his wife, Mae*, has drunk from a spring in the woods near Treegap and has lived unchanged for the eighty-seven years since then. A big, gentle man with a sad face and baggy trousers, Tuck is the one to row Winnie* Foster out on the lake and explain to her why she must not drink from the spring nor tell anyone else about it.

THE ANIMAL FAMILY (Jarrell*, Randall, ill. Maurice Sendak, Random, 1965), deceptively simple fantasy set on an unnamed island in an unspecified time. A hunter, living alone on the island, becomes friends with a mermaid whose voice is liquid and who is quick to learn and adventurous to try the things of the land. Soon she comes to live with him and, although she never learns to cook well, preferring her food raw, she is so delighted with her discoveries and so clever at most things that the hunter doesn't expect her to be a housewife, and they are very happy. After a while the hunter begins to dream of his father, a disturbing dream in which his father is somehow double. One day he brings home a child for them, a bear cub. He is a charming pet, "like a little boy in a bearskin," but he soon grows into a monstrous furry clown. When he gets wet, "drying him was like drying a marsh," and when he gets into a bee tree, the hunter has to run to the beach with the mermaid in his arms and stay in the water until the bees leave. Later the hunter comes home with a lynx kitten, which grows into a beautiful, graceful creature, deft and noble. One day, after a storm, the lynx finds a stranded boat containing a woman, dead, and a little boy just able to walk and say a few words. The lynx gets the bear, and together they bring the child to the house. As the boy grows, the hunter and the mermaid almost forget where he came from, and it seems as if they are joking when they say the lynx brought him. The mermaid has come to understand that she cares for the others in a way the sea people can never care, but that even though it can make her cry, life on land is better for her than the careless life in the sea. They are a happy family, using as a motto the phrase that the mermaid initiated by mistake, "Let, and live let." Although little actually happens and the characters are never given names, the story is moving, warm, and gentle. The style is poetic, lyrical with skillful use of prose rhythm and figurative language, and the general tone is idyllic but not at all sentimental. Choice; Fanfare; Lewis Carroll; Newbery Honor.

ANNA (*The Little Fishes**), 11, beggar child who becomes a dependent and sister to Guido* and, with her little brother, Mario*, travels with him from Naples to Cassino during World War II. At first Anna is living with an aunt in a single room, until a bomb destroys the house and kills the aunt. The only information given about her own parents is that her father, whom she hates, is in prison. Anna predicts that Mario will die and, though she weeps at his death, she realistically knows that he was not strong enough to survive.

ANNA (*The Pushcart War**), old Anna, aged pushcart peddler who sells apples and pears outside hospitals and museums in New York City. She so strenuously urges her fellow peddlers to resist the intimidation of the truck drivers at their strategy meeting that she is made their field commander, or "general." Since she cannot aim the pea shooter straight enough to hit the tires, she sticks the pins in by hand, earning acclaim among her partisans for her great bravery. After her death, a statue of her is erected in Tompkins Square Park, upon which appears the brief inscription, "By Hand."

ANNA GUTHRIE (*A Wonderful, Terrible Time**), Mady's mother, a nurse. A black woman, whose husband was killed in a Civil Rights march in Mississippi about five years before the novel begins, Anna works hard to support herself and Mady. She is serious, impatient of whining and laziness, often tired and a little lonely.

ANN AURELIA AND DOROTHY (Carlson*†, Natalie Savage, ill. Dale Payson, Harper, 1968), realistic novel for intermediate ages set in an American town in the 1960s. Ann Aurelia, 10, a foster child and tomboy, meets Dorothy, a black girl her own age, when her swing chain breaks, catapulting her into Dorothy, who is passing through the playground. They tie the chain together with a handkerchief, swing together until it breaks and Dorothy is injured. Ann Aurelia hunts her up through the newspaper story of the accident, returns her broken glasses, and gets acquainted with her loving family, including her little sister, Louise. On Halloween she also meets Dorothy's older brother, Hughie, on leave from the Navy. Ann Aurelia's new foster mother, Mrs. Hicken, is a slovenly but good-hearted woman who bails them out when they pick out more goodies than they can pay for at the supermarket and who becomes involved in the PTA for the child's sake. Dorothy gets Ann Aurelia into the Safety Patrol, but playing around they get her flag stuck in a tree and are removed from the Patrol in disgrace. On a school nature walk, their teacher, strict Miss Wyckoff, tries to reach some mistletoe and falls into the river. Ann Aurelia reaches a branch to her, then runs for the principal while Dorothy keeps her busy reviewing the multiplication tables. In recognition they are both reinstated in the Patrol. When the children hear that their beloved fifth grade teacher, Miss Bennett, is leaving, Ann Aurelia assumes it is to be married, and they organize an elaborate surprise party, only to discover that Miss Bennett is going back to graduate school. Unexpectedly, Ann Aurelia's mother, who left her behind when she married a Mr. Lacy, returns, having left him. The girl is faced with a conflict in deciding whether to go with her mother or stay with Mrs. Hicken, who has been very good to her. Her decision to join her mother is influenced by the loving family relationships in Dorothy's family. Ann Aurelia's mother takes an apartment nearby and the girls take Louise to see Mrs. Hicken's new foster child, little Kathy. There is no real plot and the characters are one dimensional, but everyday incidents supply some mild humor. The integration theme and the idea that even a happy foster home is no substitute for one's own parents are over-obvious, even for the intended young audience. Choice.

ANNE CAMERON (*A Formal Feeling**), sixteen-year-old who returns from boarding school for Christmas, the first since her father has remarried. Anne is tall, musical, an excellent student, cool and self-possessed in manner. While she looks like her mother, she lacks her mother's beauty. Although she comes to realize that she has always resented her mother's insistence on perfection, she finds herself doing just as her mother did in little as well as major actions: she can't bear to see a dirty cup and saucer in the kitchen sink and quickly washes them; she covers the roses with dead leaves and plastic cones, though she has never cared much for the roses; she straightens the place mat with the tips of her fingers in a gesture she recognizes as her mother's. As the holiday progresses, memories begin to seep from her unconscious that deny the image she has of a perfect mother, memories of her mother's always choosing blue for Anne's clothes, memories of her mother's perfectionist piano teaching that was frustrating to Anne as a child, memories of how her mother's insistence forced Anne to go to the boarding school she had attended when Anne wanted to go to public school with her friends. When the deeply suppressed memory that her mother once deserted the family comes back, Anne is able to start to become her own person. The major problem that has paralyzed Anne emotionally and prevents her from analyzing the Conrad novel for her paper is her childhood fear that her behavior, her tantrum when she couldn't play the piece as her mother directed, caused her mother to leave home, and the projected illogical suspicion that her rejection of the blue sweater her mother knitted has somehow caused her mother's death. She is a precisely characterized protagonist for whom sympathy grows slowly and not easily but whose struggle to break from her self-protective shell is memorable.

ANNETT, CORA (SCOTT) (1931–   ), born in Boston; author of a number of books for young children including *How the Witch Got Alf** (Watts, 1975), *The Dog Who Thought He Was a Boy*, (Houghton, 1965), *Homerhenry*, (Addison, 1970), and *When the Porcupine Moved In*, (Watts, 1971). Educated at Boston University and the University of Massachusetts, where she received her Ph.D. in 1974, she has been a clinical psychologist and a psychotherapist.

ANN HIGHAM HALL (*A Gathering of Days**), Catherine's* stepmother, whom her father marries during the novel. She is a widow, with a son Cath's age, Daniel, and has been running her brother's store in Boston since her husband died before Daniel's birth. She is warmhearted, practical, caring but not effusive, principled but not rigid, and generous. She moves slowly to win Cath's confidence. To judge by Cath's observations, Ann at first fears she may not be adequate to her new responsibilities, but she sets out with will and restraint to teach Cath and Matty housewifely arts. When she sings "small funny songs" to Matty after the little girl has been stung by a bee, Cath notes with satisfaction and appreciation that Ann behaves just as their own mother would have done. Eventually at Daniel's suggestion, the children call Ann "Mammann," a term which happily solves the awkward problem for Cath of how to address her stepmother without compromising her feelings toward her own mother. Ann is a well-rounded character.

ANNIE JOHNSTON (*Mustang**), née Annie Bronn, a real historical figure, whose first name was Velma. A Nevada woman, she earns the epithet Wild Horse Annie for her work in championing the cause of saving the wild mustangs from extinction. In the novel, Annie tells the story of her life from early childhood to the time the bill protecting the mustangs is passed. Chronology is vague in the novel, but apparently Annie is in mid-life, when she finally achieves victory in her long campaign. Annie testifies that horses were part of God's Plan for her even before she was born. On her Bronn ancestors' journey west by covered wagon, her grandmother feeds Annie's father, then a small baby, on mustang milk. When Annie is five, polio leaves her crippled and racked with pain for several years, and a year in a hospital cast straightens her spine but leaves her facial features lopsided. Annie is plain, self-reliant, and hardworking, and her friendship with Charley Johnston, rugged, steadfast, part Delaware Indian youth six years her senior develops gradually into a low-keyed romance and marriage. Charley shares her love for the out-of-doors and animals and her strong moral sense. Theirs is a satisfying relationship, and they are liked and respected by their neighbors. When sometimes her horse campaign gets her down, Charley always encourages her. Annie matures believably in the novel.

ANSON PETRIE (*The Far-Off Land**), headstrong, selfish, impetuous elder brother of Ketty*. He says he came east to search for his family because he was homesick for them. Although it is never really clear why he takes Ketty west with him, he plans that she teach school when they arrive at French Lick. His inability to look ahead and consider the consequences of his actions, his recklessness, and his refusal to accept advice create difficulties for the travelers on several occasions. After his precipitous behavior results in broken legs for his son, Cal, he becomes steadier and more responsible and more loving toward his wife, Tish*.

ANTONIO (Potter*, Bronson, ill. Ann Grifalconi, Atheneum, 1968), very brief realistic story set on the coast of Portugal in the mid twentieth century. Antonio, 12, though the son of the fisherman Joachim, cannot work aboard his father's *Seabird* because he has one stiffened hand, the result of a childhood accident. Instead, he is the fishermen's ox-boy, the boy who tends the heavy beasts that drag the boats across the sand dunes. At this job he is extremely skilled, able to control the huge animals better even than Jacevi, the town's rich landowner, who was once ox-boy himself. The schoolmaster, Carceira, spends extra time with Antonio and hopes to make him a teacher, but the boy longs for the excitement of the sea. Seeing a storm approaching, Antonio and the teacher go with Jacevi in his truck to try to sight the boats. They spot the village fleet already having trouble, unable to get back to the cove. Antonio persuades Jacevi to bring the oxen to the open beach in his truck and, standing in front of a big fire they build, he signals his father to bring the boats in one by one, but, because his father is the leader, the *Seabird* is last. Since the weather has worsened, Antonio sees that his father must turn the *Seabird* broadside and let a wave carry him in. Antonio dives in, swims, and lets the strong rip tide carry him out to the boat, and tells his father his plan. The boat is saved, and all the village people, even the hard Joachim, celebrate. He agrees to let Carceira tutor Antonio for the teachers' exam. Though only about 7,000 words long, this is not a simple book for young children but rather a sparely written story for good readers. The atmosphere of a foreign setting and the excitement and danger are well evoked. Choice.

ANTON REIKER (*Summer of My German Soldier**), twenty-four-year-old German prisoner of war whom Patty Bergen befriends after he has escaped from the prisoner of war camp. He is the son of a university professor. Before being conscripted into Hitler's army, he was a medical student. He speaks excellent English, is well read, and is a thinker. He realizes that Patty has a fine mind and yearns for appreciation and affection. He reaches New York before he is shot by authorities while avoiding arrest. He is an unconvincing character.

ANYWHERE ELSE BUT HERE (Clements*, Bruce, Farrar, 1980), realistic novel set in Schenectady, N.Y., in the contemporary period. After her father's printing business fails, Molly Smelter, 13, wants nothing more than to leave Schenectady and set up a new life elsewhere. One reason is her aversion to Shelby Bissel (Uncle Shel), her father's know-it-all former partner, who has cheated him and who is to marry her Aunt Aurora. A mysterious man named Walter* Potrezeski comes to the auction and buys all the Polish things they have, mostly relics from her long-dead mother's relatives. She recognizes him as someone who has often stared at her, but not until she shows him her doll house, a perfect replica of her mother's house in Krakow, does she learn that as a Jewish child he had hidden in the attic of that home during World War II. Life is complicated by the visit of Aunt Aurora's friend, Fostra* Lee Post, a beautiful, affected divorcee, and her bratty son, Claude, 8. Mrs. Post is a devotee of a religion advocating hedonism, and she applies this principle to Claude, letting him do exactly what he feels like at any time. Molly wants her father to buy a printing business in Willimantic, Conn., and move there; Aunt Aurora wants him to get a job with General Electric and marry Mrs. Post; Mrs. Post appears to want to convert Molly but actually wants to get rid of Claude; Uncle Shel wants to buy back the printing business (which he could have saved with his money) and hire Molly's father to run it. Pressed into duty as a baby-sitter, Molly learns to manage Claude by appealing to his imagination, and a sort of affection develops between them. Mrs. Post seizes the opportunity to fly off to California, leaving her son behind. Afraid that her father will not have the drive to strike out on his own, Molly sells the doll house to Mr. Potrezeski for enough to make the down payment on the business in Willimantic. At the book's end they have moved to Willimantic, taking Claude with them. Molly gets some good advice about the business from Mr. Potrezeski and about Claude from a former teacher, Miss Simmons, but the adults in the story are mostly weak personalities, unable to direct their lives in a meaningful way. Molly, the first-person narrator, is a strong, decisive, and imaginative girl, a believable and attractive character, but the glut of ineffectual adults and the family's easy acceptance of Claude as a permanent responsibility make the book less than completely plausible. Fanfare.

THE APACHE GOLD MYSTERY (Thompson*, Eileen, ill. James Russell, Abelard, 1965), novel of suspense set on the Fort Apache Indian Reservation in Arizona in the mid twentieth century. Red-haired, competent Danny Collins,

12, has been staying since his father's death in Show Low with the Janders, an elderly couple for whom his carpenter father was building a cabin. Danny suspects that his father's jeep crash on the mountain road was really murder, not the result of drunken driving as the police report says, because his father was made very ill by alcohol and never drank. On a fishing-camping trip near the site of the accident, he slips away, leaving a note, and in the woods meets another runaway his age, Matthew Pinal, a Coyotero Apache, who is escaping being taken to boarding school by an uncle. They team up and with Matthew's woods lore have a pleasant, even comfortable, hike for several days, unaware that a major search effort is afoot for them. When a plane flies low, back and forth as if searching, then disappears, they realize that it has gone down. They head in what they hope is the right direction and, coming upon a mountain lion about to spring, scare it off and discover the wounded pilot, Tom O'Rourke, a mountain restaurant operator who is in the Civil Air Patrol. Matthew goes for help to Hawley Lake, the nearest settlement, while Danny stays with Tom and, to pass the time, tells him of his wandering life with his father, who was always trying to find treasure, and of his suspicions that his father was near a cache left by a prospector in the 1880s and that he was murdered for his maps which were not found at the wreck. Later, they manage to prove the acccident was a murder committed by Red Feather, an Indian from the Hawley Lake Store, and they find not the treasure but a few valuable coins. Matthew decides to go to school, after all, hoping to become a pilot like Tom. Danny is offered a home with Tom and his wife, Kit, and their two little girls, who want a big brother. The coins turn out to be worth enough to buy Tom a new plane and to help Matthew's family. The characters are one dimensional, but as recreational light reading the story is not demanding and provides a fast moving plot and enough suspense to keep a reader's interest. The ending is not entirely plausible, but the boys' trip and their rescue of Tom do not seem far fetched. Poe Nominee.

APRIL HALL (*The Egypt Game**), one of the originators of the Egypt game, who at first calls herself by a name she thinks more elegant, April Dawn. Her hobby is reading about ancient times. April comes reluctantly to live with her grandmother, Caroline, sure that she will stay with her only temporarily. She has never associated much with other children and is certain that she will not like her new school and neighborhood. At first she imitates her mother in her dress and behavior, piling her long blond hair up high on her head, wearing grotesquely long false eyelashes, and generally putting on a show of "cool." As the Egypt game proceeds, she gradually learns how to play with other children and grows to appreciate her gentle, understanding grandmother. When her mother invites her for Christmas, she has grown to like her new home and friends so much she declines the invitation.

ARABELLA MARLBOROUGH (*Ox Under Pressure**), beautiful, intelligent, but unstable girl with whom Ox* becomes involved. When she was younger, Arabella had been a victim of anorexia, because her parents had shown her no affection, and while she now seems to be no longer ill, she is subject to depression and fights the life her father leads by turning it into a fantasy. Although she is in love with Ox, she knows that she is too emotionally weak to run away and hide out until she is eighteen and can legally leave her parents. She decides to stay in the mental hospital where they have placed her until she is strong enough to make a move on her own. Whether this is a sensible decision or a cop-out is left to the reader to decide.

ARCHIE COSTELLO (*The Chocolate War**), assigner for the Vigils*, the vicious secret organization at Trinity High School. Diabolically clever, Archie thinks up the assignments that will pass as pranks but will torment the boys who receive them by wearing their nerves thin. Hated even by Obie, his continual sidekick and Vigil secretary, and by Carter, athletic Vigil president, Archie has only contempt for his seeming friends, his teachers, and his victims. Secretly he finds his post a growing strain and dreads the black box, from which he must draw a marble for each assignment, a box containing a black marble, one in six, which if drawn will mean that he will have to do the assignment himself.

ARE YOU IN THE HOUSE ALONE? (Peck*, Richard, Viking, 1976) sociological problem novel set recently in a middle-class New York suburb, which begins as a novel of suspense. The first nine chapters describe sixteen-year-old Gail Osburne's cooling romance with Steve Pastorini, bright, ambitious, reliable son of the local plumber, whom her parents regard as inappropriate for the daughter of an architect; her realization that her closest friend, Alison Bremer, is a social climber, determined to advance herself by marriage with unsteady, arrogant Phil Lawver, son of the most influential, respected family in town; her discovery that her father has lost his job and her worries about the effect this will have on him; and her increasing awareness that she is being followed and watched, wherever she goes about town, while she is baby-sitting Mrs. Montgomery's two small daughters, and when she and Steve meet clandestinely for sex at the cottage by the lake. Terror strikes when Gail finds a threatening, sadistic note stuck in her school locker, a terror that she is too immature to communicate to any adult and toward which Alison has a strangely ambivalent attitude. Ominous phone calls and another note follow. When Gail gathers her courage and takes her fears to school counselors, they stubbornly and myopically refuse to take her seriously. One Saturday night, as she baby-sits, the terror becomes embodied in the form of Phil Lawver, who rapes her, strikes her with a poker, and leaves her lying unconscious on the Montgomery livingroom floor. The novel now takes a turn, and in the last five chapters the author supplements the mystery mode with information about the medical, legal, and psychological aspects of rape. Although hospital workers and Gail's parents are sympathetic, the police are cold and accusing, and Gail feels even more isolated and alienated as she discovers that though victim she is put on the defensive while her assaulter goes unpunished. Obviously based on careful research, the book puts across its message frankly and explicitly but without pornography or sensationalism. Characters are types, who behave and change predictably. The effect of both plot and message is diminished by the author's choice of villains, and unconvincing, even given the setting, is the ending in which the psychotic Phil remains uncharged although authorities apparently have evidence that he has committed a second assault. The honest, unpretentious style builds credibility, and the otherwise careful plotting and close attention to atmosphere and small town setting results in a tension-filled if didactic thriller. Poe Winner.

ARE YOU THERE GOD? IT'S ME, MARGARET (Blume*, Judy, Bradbury, 1970), realistic episodic novel set in the late 1900s in New Jersey, in which Margaret Simon, almost twelve, tells about some of the things that happen to her from the Tuesday before Labor Day through the end of school, the first year that she, a somewhat shy only child, her mother, and father live in the town of Farbrook. Margaret speaks directly to the reader in relating her experiences during the year, while in brief, italicized inserts she communicates her innermost feelings about them to God. While Margaret hopes to get along well in school and make friends, her main anxieties involve whether or not she is developing normally physically and whether she should profess Judaism (her father's religion) or Christianity (her mother's persuasion). Her concern about making friends is soon and easily resolved even before school begins when Nancy* Wheeler, a classmate from down the street, invites her to join her secret club, the Pre-Teen Sensations. The clubmates meet every Monday for gossip, particularly about Laura Danker, who is extremely well endowed for sixth grade and is consequently the envy of the girls and ogled by the boys; to discuss boys; and to perform bust-enlarging exercises. After Nancy decrees that club members must wear bras, Margaret persuades her mother to buy her one. Her physical anxiety then revolves around her inability to fill it to her satisfaction. When her teacher assigns individual school projects, Margaret elects to do hers on religion, hoping thereby to solve her personal problems of whether to join the Y or the Jewish Community Center. She visits the temple with fun-loving, sprightly Grandma* Simon, attends church with friends Janie and Nancy, and almost goes to Confession at Laura's church. When her mother's parents, who cut off their daughter because she married a Jew, unexpectedly visit and pressure Margaret to adopt their religion, she reacts in anger, renounces all religions, and even refuses to communicate with God, with whom ironically she has been having daily conversations all along. Simultaneously, her greatest problem, not yet having started her periods, is aggravated when two of her clubmates report having theirs. End of school finds her without a religion. While she is preparing to leave for camp, her period comes, restoring her faith in herself and also in God. Although it is frequently very humorous, with irony, situation comedy, and lively, typical dialogue, the book deals with none of its superabundance of concerns effectively. Characters are shallow, and situations seem deliberately contrived for sensation and audience appeal. As in many such novels, Margaret is made to appear more sensible than the adults around her, and many of the children are offensive. Her story has been one of the most popular books of New Realism with pre- and teenaged readers. Choice.

ARILLA SUN DOWN (Hamilton*, Virginia, Greenwillow, 1976), realistic novel of an interracial family set in a contemporary southern Ohio town. Arilla Adams, 12, daughter of a light-skinned black mother, Lillian Perry Adams, and a mostly American Indian father, Sun Stone Adams, has a strong sibling conflict with her brother, Jack Sun Run, 16, who plays the Noble Redman to the great admiration of the local girls, particularly his favorite, Angelica Diavolad, daughter of Haitian parents. Jack, who calls Arilla "Moon" and thinks she has some power in the dark, sneaks her out at night to lead him and Angel to the out-of-bounds skating rink, teaches her to ride the appaloosa mare he has insisted she be given for her birthday, and generally tries to dominate her life. After Jack is thrown from his horse and injured in an ice storm, Arilla gets help in time to save him and sees him for the first time as vulnerable. When she takes Jack's place in traveling to Cliffville, their original home, to retrieve her "erratic" father, who periodically disappears, she gains self-esteem and heritage. The story is complicated by long flashbacks to Arilla's early childhood in Cliffville, when she was saved twice by an old Indian, James False-Face, who gave her a secret name, flashbacks told in a sort of pidgin English, possibly to express the Indian language or the confused memories of a young child: "Horse not stamping. Walking, not like Sun Run stamping, Me ride the walking, just like Sun. Me, a horse walking Sun. All the time. The tall tree-man talking sounds I don't know." As in her other books, Hamilton asks the reader to accept an element both grotesque and improbable, in this that Arilla's father returns to Cliffville not to drink or to see old friends but to go sledding on a dangerous hill in the dark and to howl like a wolf. Fanfare.

ARMINTA HAYES (*Come By Here**), Minty Lou's warmhearted and generous maternal grandmother. When she comes to visit, she picks up a poor girl and her baby on the ferry to Baltimore and brings them to her daughter's house, simply assuming that they will be welcome as they would be in her own home. With her rich voice, she sings spirituals to the hospital patients, and she tells Minty Lou about Harriet Tubman, whose original name was Minty and for whom she was named, since her slave mother had almost fled north with a group Harriet was leading. Although she has less than any of the other people Minty Lou lives with after her mother's death, Arminta Hayes is the only one with the genuine goodness which may help the embittered child.

THE ARM OF THE STARFISH (L'Engle*, Madeleine, Farrar, 1965), mystery-thriller with fantasy aspects set in the near future in Madrid, Lisbon, and Gaea, an island off Portugal, combining scientific advances with international intrigue. Adam* Eddington, 17, who plans to major in marine biology, feels fortunate to get a summer job helping renowned Dr. Calvin* O'Keefe, biologist, in his laboratory on Gaea with his experiments on the regeneration of the starfish. Adam soon finds himself caught between two opposing groups, both ostensibly working for good ends. On the one side are beautiful, sophisticated Carolyn Cutter, called Kali*, who warns Adam not to trust O'Keefe, her elegant, wealthy smooth-talking father, Typhon Cutter*, and the unctuous and overbearing Dr. Ball, a priest, while on the other are the noted Dr. O'Keefe, Canon* Tallis, a mild-mannered, confidence-inspiring English priest, and Joshua Archer, a pleasant, young embassy official, who advises Adam to consider carefully where right lies and to work actively for what he thinks is right and good. Adam is attracted to the articulate and persuasive Kali and would like to believe in her, but he mistrusts her father, particularly after he discovers that Cutter had a part in kidnapping O'Keefe's twelve-year-old daughter, Polyhymnia, yet he finds it hard at first to put his faith in the O'Keefe side either. After Adam gets to know the large, loving, gregarious O'Keefe family and learns with what affection and respect the doctor is regarded by the people of the village near his laboratory, he decides that Dr. O'Keefe must indeed be a good man and agrees to help him in a scheme to keep Cutter from getting information about O'Keefe's experiments. Dr. O'Keefe has been able to apply the information learned from his tests with starfish to humans, and he knows that if the Cutter forces acquire this information it would end up in the hands of those who might use it for morally questionable purposes. He asks Adam to be a courier to take this information to Canon Tallis, who will then see that it gets to Washington. Adam pretends to be in cahoots with Cutter, goes to Lisbon with the report and with another, a fake, which he gives to Cutter. In the attempt to get the valid information to Tallis, Joshua is shot and killed. Later Kali is attacked by a shark while swimming off Gaea and her arm severely lacerated. Dr. O'Keefe compassionately agrees to apply his new techniques in an effort to help her. Characters and events are stock for this genre, and only Adam grows as a result of his experiences. Events move fast, suspense is high, and message is obvious. The well-balanced plot, crisp style, and humanistic appeal of Dr. O'Keefe's work lift this book above the average. An undeveloped but potentially interesting character is Canon Tallis, while Dr. O'Keefe and his wife are Calvin O'Keefe and Meg* Murry from *A Wrinkle in Time**. Intelligent and perceptive as Adam is supposed to be, his dilemma about which side is in the right is not very convincing. Fanfare.

ARMSTRONG, WILLIAM HOWARD (1914–   ), born in Lexington, Va.; history teacher and author whose best-known works, *Sounder** (Harper, 1969) and *Sour Land* (Harper, 1971), reflect his interest in the life of southern blacks between the Civil War and 1900. Educated at Augusta Military Academy, Hampden-Sidney College in Virginia, and the University of Virginia, he has taught in Virginia and Connecticut. Other works for young people include the novels *The MacLeod Place* (Coward, 1972) and *The Mills of God* (Doubleday, 1973), biographies of Grandma Moses and of Lincoln, and other nonfiction books. For adults he has written a number of pedagogical works. His best-known book, *Sounder*, shows not only knowledge of the hardships of blacks in a white controlled society, but also their essential humanity and dignity. The 1972 movie made by Twentieth Century Fox changed the setting to the 1930s and elaborated the characterization of the fable-like novel.

ARNEATHA HAWKINS (*The Soul Brothers and Sister Lou**), Lou's lazy, selfish older sister. Momma indulges her because she is so pretty and makes excuses for her laziness. She has had a baby out of wedlock, Cora Lee, whom Momma and Lou care for. Momma is more strict with Lou because of Arneatha. Arneatha takes off when William* Hawkins insists that she repay the money she stole, money which was supposed to be used to buy musical instruments for the club. She represents shiftless black girls and is a foil for Lou.

ARORA, SHIRLEY L(EASE) (1930–   ), born in Youngstown, Ohio, but has spent most of her life in California, where she graduated from Stanford and the University of California at Los Angeles. A professor of Spanish at the University of Los Angeles, she has published many scholarly works on Spanish folklore. She met her husband, Harbans, while they were students at Stanford. After he completed his studies in research biology, they lived for four years in his native India, in a hill area like that in *"What Then, Raman?"** (Follett, 1960), for which she received the Jane Addams Award and the Charles W. Follett Award. Written to give young readers some idea of the problems confronting Indian youth, it is about an earnest, poor Indian boy whose ambition is to become a scholar and conveys a vivid sense of life among the poverty-stricken masses, but projects a decidedly didactic tone. *The Left-Handed Chank* (Follett, 1966), another novel set in India, follows the fortunes of an Indian boy who searches for a rare, luck-bringing shell.

ARREN (*The Farthest Shore**), young prince of Enlad, whose name means "sword" and whose true name is Lebannen, sent to Roke* to seek the aid of the Council of The Wise when word of a breakdown of order and loss of the powers of magic troubles his father's court. Impulsively, he swears fealty to Ged*, the Archmage, and accompanies him in the search through the western islands for the cause of the malaise affecting all Earthsea*. Brave, noble, courteous, Arren is in many ways the stock hero type, but he is made more human by the doubts and fears that afflict him during their travels and by his maturing realization that there may be no return from the journey they have undertaken. At last, having taken the initiative in their descent into the world of the dead and then both led and carried Ged back, he has attained the stature necessary to be crowned king of Havnor, thereby of all Earthsea.

ASA HALE SHIPMAN (*A Gathering of Days**), Cassie's* younger brother, who is Catherine's* age. He is a lively youth, assertive and decisive. Even before Cath and Cassie assist the phantom, Asa steals pies from the Shipman buttery to take to the fugitive and earns a whipping for his generosity. Cath thinks a good deal of him.

ASTORIA (*Hail Columbia**), wide-open port town in Oregon that Louisa's Aunt Columbia sets out to clean up in 1893. The book reflects actual conditions and events of the period.

ATTEAN (*The Sign of the Beaver**), grandson of Saknis*, chief of the local Penobscot band of Indians, who, at his grandfather's command, brings food to Matt* Hollowell in return for instruction in reading English. Although he doesn't want to learn to read and write, Attean is obedient to his grandfather and applies himself enough to gain some skill. He and Matt have revealing and somewhat humorous discussions about what goes on in *Robinson Crusoe*. Later in the story, Attean goes on a vision quest, acquires a gun of his own, and is accepted among the hunters of the band. To the very end, he remains somewhat cool and aloof toward Matt, though he appreciates Matt's saving his dog from the hunter's trap. Attean is being raised by Saknis because whites killed his parents, and, considering the circumstances, he is remarkably generous and helpful to Matt. Though roundly developed, Attean is not always convincing.

AUNT AMERICA (Bloch*, Marie Halun, ill. Joan Berg, Atheneum, 1963), realistic novel set in the mid-twentieth century during the Cold War in the Ukraine near Kiev. Lesya, 11, resents her father, Roman, who seems to her a failure and careless compared with his brother, Uncle Vlodko, because when she was four her father and mother were arrested for suspicion of subversive freedom fighter activity. Although they have endured and have been back for three years, she still feels that they deserted her and is closer to her aunt and uncle who took her in. A letter from America from her father's Aunt Lydia, explaining that she is coming to Kiev, sets the village into a fever of excitement, and even Uncle Vlodko, who has kept a discreet distance, comes to their house to read it. Lesya goes to Kiev with her parents and uncle and her cousin, Elena. They get permission to go to Aunt Lydia's room but walk to the park to talk so that their conversation cannot be overheard. Aunt Lydia gets permission to visit them in their village and to have them all ride back in a chauffered car, but the joy is spoiled for Lesya because she gives Elena a doll and Lesya only a book of Ukrainian folktales. When Elena carelessly leaves the doll outside, Lesya on impulse takes it and hides it, then suffers shame and remorse but is unable to admit her theft. Villagers ask Aunt Lydia to carry letters to their American relatives, and she readily agrees, not realizing the danger. Lesya sneaks out, returns the doll, catches the autobus to Kiev, reaches Aunt Lydia just before her train moves out, warns her, and confesses about the doll. Her grateful and understanding aunt gives her the letters to take home, saying that she will write to the relatives from the United States, and later sends fine gifts to the family, including a doll for Lesya, which she determines to keep for her younger sister. From her aunt's scorn of Vlodko's toadying to authority and praise of Roman's defense of freedom, Lesya learns to admire and love her father. Written from a cold war perspective, the book casts Aunt Lydia in the role of an all-wise Lady Bountiful and the other characters in stock roles, but Lesya is a more developed character and details of life in the Ukraine are of interest. Fanfare.

AUNT CORDELIA BISHOP (*Up a Road Slowly**), Julie's stern, proper, imperious aunt, who raises her. She loves Julie very much but never allows her affection to influence her principles of childrearing. More than anyone else, she helps Julie to grow from a self-willed and indulged child into a warm and compassionate young woman, able to use her abilities for worthy ends. Cordelia is a well-drawn, dynamic character.

AUNT DELIA (*Nilda**), very deaf elderly great-aunt, who constantly reads the newspaper and warns everyone she comes in contact with of rapists, purse snatchers, burglars, and other threats of the city. When the local grocery has been raided for taking bets on the numbers and the grocer, Jacinto, refuses to take her bet, she is furious, screams at him, and fetches two policemen to complain that after ten years he has changed his policy. Although ordinarily she speaks only Spanish, she manages enough English to call the policeman a son-of-a-bitch.

AUNT FAITH (*The Murder of Hound Dog Bates**), middle sister of the three spinster aunts who have raised Sassafras Bates from infancy. In the beginning of the book, when Sass is angry at her because he thinks she killed his dog, he describes her as a thin, black-haired, thin-lipped, ferocious woman. Later, after he learns how hard it has been for her and her sisters to raise him, he thinks better of her, and she appears to be mellower in disposition. As a character, she is less developed than the other two aunts.

AUNT HELEN ROBBINS (*Come By Here**), the religiously fanatical great aunt to whom Minty Lou is sent when her Grandma Payson* will no longer keep her. When the child of seven, who has been deafened by a blow from her white employer, regains her hearing, Aunt Helen claims credit because of her prayers. At the store-front Brothers of Christ and Sisters Church, she is a leading force, but she loves power, and when Uncle Elmer stops her from beating Minty Lou with a belt, she starts to punish her by locking her in her room without food for days at a time. Ostensibly to provide modest clothes, she sews high necklines made from old sheets onto Minty's dresses and black extensions to the skirts to make them reach the floor.

AUNT HOPE (*The Murder of Hound Dog Bates**), youngest of the three spinster sisters who have been raising Sassafras Bates since his mother died when he was born. Aunt Hope is about thirty, according to Sass, blond, and an excellent cook. Sass is angry at her when the book begins, because he thinks she killed his dog. He describes her to the reader as a hateful, terrible woman. In his attempts to find out who killed the dog, he interviews her in the manner of storybook detectives, hoping to trap her into an admission of guilt or some indiscreet statement that will indicate complicity in the crime. From their conversations, he quite unexpectedly learns some family history and begins to realize how much his aunts have given up in order to rear him properly. He feels better about them all as a result. Aunt Hope marries Kelly* O'Kelly at the end.

AUNT LILY (*To the Green Mountains**), Elizabeth* Rule's sister, Kath's aunt, who lives on a farm not far from South Angela and whom Kath loves to visit. Pretty, warm, and gentle, she usually obeys her husband without hesitation. But when he and Elizabeth have a falling out because he objects to Elizabeth giving the law books to Will Grant, Lily insists that she will continue seeing Elizabeth if she wishes, since Elizabeth is, after all, her own sister. Aunt Lily's religion provides her great comfort.

AUNT LUCY FARR (*The Genie of Sutton Place**), Timmy's aunt, a little, short woman whose clothes never seem quite appropriate and who "needs help in living," according to Timmy. A good-hearted sort, she is determined to do her very best to bring Timmy up correctly but, in spite of her good intentions, does everything a little bit wrong, because she does not understand him. She becomes better adjusted to the people around her as the story progresses and is quite likeable at the end.

AUNT MATILDA (*The Griffin Legacy**), eighty-five-year-old great-aunt of Amy* Enfield, half-sister of Grandma* Enfield, whom she raised, and direct descendant of Lucy* Griffin. Bony, arthritic, soft-spoken, half-blind, she likes to sit in the dim light of the living room by Lucy's portrait, is reputed by the villagers to have second sight because she seems to know everything that's going on, is keenly interested in everything, often speaks obscurely, and tends to take command of things. She says Amy has "Griffin bones" and, more than anyone else, gets Amy involved in the Griffin mystery. She tells Amy much about her ancestors. She wishes to have Amy solve the mystery because she herself failed.

AUNT RHODY HOLLINGSHEAD (*Half-Breed**), Hardy's Aunt Rhoda, sister of his father, Jesse, who, although she deplores Hardy's Indian upbringing and tries to change his ways, wins his admiration and loyalty by sticking up for him when others disparage him. Hardy often disagrees with her but always respects and obeys her. She arrives in Oregon with her cow, Sookie, and little money.

She is undaunted by Jesse's absence, and to support Hardy and herself, she makes and sells meat pies to sailors made of the venison Hardy hunts. In a both humorous and poignant episode, she sends the boy to church school, where he brings ridicule upon himself by his innocent assertion that Coyote made the world. Rhody readily sees that Jesse's invitation to Noah Tuttle to come for Christmas dinner is a scheme to get rid of her by marrying her off. Noah is looking for a wife so he can file a double claim (for 640 acres), and Rhody is unmarried, sturdy, and available. Though eccentric and not always convincing, Rhody is a well-rounded, memorable figure whom the reader, like Hardy, gradually gets to know and eventually to like.

AUNT VEELA (*The Murder of Hound Dog Bates**), eldest of the three spinster sisters who have raised Sassafras Bates from infancy. Sass says Aunt Veela is about fifty. At the beginning of the book, he is very angry at her because he thinks she has killed his dog, Hound Dog Bates, and his description of her at that time makes her seem formidable and vindictive indeed. She has red hair and a fiery nature, wears overalls, because she works the land, and smokes a corncob pipe. She is considered the head of the family, and her sisters defer to her because she is the oldest and does the hardest work of them all. After he learns how much Aunt Veela and her sisters have sacrificed to raise him, Sass thinks better of her. Like Sass, the reader comes to see that Veela is really a very sensible, hardworking, compassionate woman.

AVARIC (*The Darkangel**), country on the moon from which Aeriel* is captured by the vampyre to be a slave to his brides. It is one of the areas developed by the Ancients, as men from Earth are called, with an atmosphere created and bound to the surface and a race of people and animals developed who are able to live in its thin air.

AVI (AVI WORTIS), (1937–   ), librarian at Trenton State College, storyteller, teacher of children's literature, and author of children's books; born in New York and educated at the Universities of Wisconsin and Columbia. Since the publication of *Things That Sometimes Happen* (Doubleday, 1970), a book of short stories, and *Snail Tale* (Pantheon, 1972), a picture-story book about the adventures of a snail and an ant, his list has built rapidly into a dozen books that cover a wide variety of times, places, subjects, and treatments, including three mystery-detective novels, *No More Magic** (Pantheon, 1975), about the recovery of a bike stolen on Halloween, and *Shadrach's Crossing** (Pantheon, 1983), about how a youth brings some smugglers to justice, both nominees for the Edgar Allan Poe Award for best mystery of the year, and *Who Stole the Wizard of Oz?* (Knopf, 1981), involving thefts from a library, and two adolescent problem novels, *A Place Called Ugly* (Pantheon, 1981), about a youth's fight to save from demolition the house at the beach where his family has spent summers for many years, and *Sometimes I Think I Hear My Name* (Pantheon,

1982), concerning a boy's surprise visit to his divorced parents and his friendship with an emotionally disturbed girl. More highly regarded are his amusing, spirited, adventure-filled parodies on Victorian melodrama, *Emily Upham's Revenge** (Pantheon, 1978), also a nominee for the Poe Award, and *The History of Helpless Harry* (Pantheon, 1980), and two sensitive, revealing historical novels, *Night Journeys* (Pantheon, 1979) and the Christopher Award book, *Encounter at Easton** (Pantheon, 1980), set just before the American Revolution about two children who are runaway indentured servants. Avi is ranked among the most versatile and inventive of recent writers for the young. His best works are distinguished by fast-moving, imaginative plots, strong characterization, and considerable wit and irony.

AN AWFUL NAME TO LIVE UP TO (Hosford*, Jessie, ill. Charles Geer, Meredith, 1969), novel told in journal entries written from January, 1901, through September, 1902, in western Nebraska. Judy—Julia Ward Howe—Hoffman, 12, knows she will have to be a writer to live up to her famous name, and so she starts her diary for practice. Her family, she points out, is really two families. Eve, 20, Polly, 17, and George, 16, are Grants, children of her mother's first husband who drowned. She and Andy, 9, are Hoffmans, children of the German homesteader who married the young widow. To complicate matters, Mother is English, speaks very properly, and hates Nebraska; Papa twists his English into German word order and loves the open spaces. Mother has a new baby, which they name Elizabeth, but the baby soon dies, and Mother blames Nebraska where medical care is poor. Many of the journal entries are concerned with Eve's beaux—Ned Elliot, who teaches school, rides a sorrel horse, and is Judy's favorite, though she sees that he is not romantic; Everette Karlton, poetic and soulful but forty-five, older than Mother; Ben Ullery, who has a "bay-window" front, and Dexter Allen, the handsome new clerk in the drugstore. Eve is thought to be anemic, therefore pale and beautiful and not required to work hard. Judy saves her from running off with Dexter (who, she has discovered, happens to have a wife back east) by exchanging Eve's letters to Ned and Dex, and Eve happily marries Ned. Mother's sister, Aunt Edith, and her husband, Uncle Jim, come from Illinois for the wedding. Mother has always admired Aunt Edith and has tried to get Papa to move back to Illinois to work in Uncle Jim's store, but their long visit, with Aunt Edith bossy and Uncle Jim acting like a poor stick, convinces her at last that Nebraska is the place for the family. Aunt Edith announces that Julia will go east with them to attend high school and help in the store, but Papa forestalls that plan by finding a German family she can board with in Grand Island and go to school there. Before she leaves, Mother and Papa try to tell her the facts of life, explaining seriously that when she's older boys may try to kiss her, a funny scene since Judy has already been kissed (and rather liked it) by one hired man and has fought off an intended rape by another. The convention of the journal allows for some humor as Judy alternates between pretentious style and naive frankness, but it also works against the story, making dramatic events less exciting and cutting the narrative into ununified chunks. Mother and Papa are the most interesting characters, and their conflict about the beauty of life in Nebraska, "this desolation," as Mother calls it, is the main focus of the plot. Western Heritage.

B

BABBITT, NATALIE (MOORE) (1932–   ), born in Dayton, Ohio; fantasy writer who entered the children's book field as an illustrator but has become recognized as an author of increasingly skillful style. She is a graduate of Smith College, where she majored in art, and has taught writing and illustrating for children at Kirkland College, Clinton, N.Y., where her husband has been president. He was the author of the first book she illustrated, *The Forty-ninth Magician* (Pantheon, 1966). All her books have an element of humor, sometimes over-intellectual and contrived, but her most successful are very clever, like *The Devil's Storybook* (Farrar, 1974), a short story collection, and *The Eyes of the Amaryllis* (Farrar, 1977), for young adults. *Tuck Everlasting** (Farrar, 1975), a fantasy about the problems of eternal life, which is usually considered her best, is sometimes listed as a modern classic. Other award-winning books are *Goody Hall** (Farrar, 1971), a zany mystery, *Kneeknock Rise** (Farrar, 1970), a story in a folktale pattern, and *The Search for Delicious** (Farrar, 1969), a tale in a mock-heroic style. A more recent novel is *Herbert Rowbarge* (Farrar, 1982), a story of a self-made man, creator and owner of an amusement park, and his unloving relationships to friends and family. She was the United States nominee for the 1982 Hans Christian Andersen Medal.

BACON, MARTHA (SHERMAN) (1917–1981), teacher, poet, novelist for adults and children, and editor for *Atlantic Monthly* and other magazines. She was born in Berkeley, Calif., the daughter of Pulitzer Prize–winning poet Leonard Bacon, and attended the American Academy of Dramatic Arts. A member of the English faculty at Rhode Island College, she won critical acclaim for two books of poetry, two novels, and a book of essays before she began to write for children. She employed her knowledge of Africa, where she traveled extensively, as background for her first and still her most highly regarded novel for young readers, *Sophia Scrooby Preserved** (Little, 1968), a Fanfare book. This boisterous, romantic historical novel about the late eighteenth-century adventures of the daughter of an African chieftain who is bought and raised by a genteel American Tory family is told with sophisticated wit in the florid style of the period. Also energetic in pace and inventively concocted, the picaresque *In the*

*Company of Clowns** (Little, 1973), a Fanfare book, describes life among traveling players in eighteenth-century Italy from the point of view of a foundling who seeks adventure among them. Less convincing though polished and clever are her fantasies, *The Third Road* (Little, 1971) and *Moth Manor* (Little, 1978).

BAKER, BETTY (LOU) (1928–   ), born in Bloomsburg, Pa. Author of books for children, she is best known for her historical novels for adolescents about the southwestern United States and in particular about Indians. She has held various positions as dental assistant, owner of a gift shop, and lecturer and has been editor of *Roundup Magazine* and *Western Writers of America*. A resident of Arizona for many years, she has long held an active interest in the out-of-doors, Western history, and Indians. Of her more than twenty books for young people, *Killer-of-Death** (Harper, 1963), set during the last years the Apaches were free, and *And One Was a Wooden Indian** (Macmillan, 1970), tongue-in-cheek account of the comic misadventures of some Indians in the Gila River country, both received the Western Heritage Award. Selected by *Choice* was *Walk the World's Rim** (Harper, 1965), considered by many her best book, in which an Indian boy serves as guide for Cabeza de Vaca and other survivors of the ill-fated Spanish expedition on their trek to Mexico City. Paralleling this is *A Stranger and Afraid* (Macmillan, 1972), the story of a Plains Indian who becomes guide for the Coronado expedition. *The Dunderhead War** (Harper, 1967), which received the Spur Award of Western Writers of America, combines excitement and humor to take an odd couple, a methodical German immigrant and his restless nephew, into the Mexican War. Baker also wrote several books of non-fiction, including retellings of Indian myths, *The Night Spider Case* (Macmillan, 1984), a mystery-detective set in New York City in the 1890s, and for younger readers, *My Sister Says* (Macmillan, 1984), about two sisters in the 1850s who imagine the gifts their sailor father may bring them, *Little Runner of the Longhouse* (Harper, 1962), a controlled vocabulary story about an Iroquois boy, and short talking animal fantasies, *Dupper* (Morrow, 1976) and *Danby and George* (Greenwillow, 1981). Although her books carry the conviction of careful research and show a special sympathy and understanding for her Indian subjects, her plots tend to be weak and her characters flat and static.

BAKER†, CHARLOTTE (1910–   ), born in Nacogdoches, Tex.; author-artist whose interest in animal welfare is reflected in her books, many of which, both fiction and non-fiction, concern care of pets and kindness to animals. She attended Stephen F. Austin State College in Nacogdoches, received her B.A. degree from Mills College in California, and her M.A. at the University of California in Berkeley. She has taught art in Texas public schools, Ball State Teachers' College, and Texas College of Arts and Industries at Kingsville, Tex., and was at one time acting director of the Portland, Oreg., Art Museum. Among her books of fiction is *Necessary Nellie*† (Coward, 1945), a story of a dog in a Mexican-American family. More recently she wrote *Cockleburr Quarters**

(Prentice, 1972), a story of children and their pets set in a southern black neighborhood, which was named to the Lewis Carroll Shelf of books worthy to stand with *Alice's Adventures in Wonderland*. With her attorney husband, Roger Montgomery, she has been active in the Humane Society of Nacogdoches, where they have made their home, and in similar state, national, and international organizations.

BALL, ZACHARY (KELLY RAY MASTERS) (1897–   ), born in the Blackjack Hills near Princeton, Mo., and raised in Kansas along the Verdrigris River. He left school after the sixth grade to help support the family and worked at a variety of jobs before joining a repertory company and playing as actor and musician for twenty-five years in touring tent shows. At forty-five, he sold his first story to *True Detective* and has been a prolific free-lance writer since, producing short stories for magazines at first, then turning to books for young people, most of which reflect his varied background, including *Tent Show* (Holiday, 1964), and a number concerned with life on rivers, which draw from his childhood memories. *Bristle Face** (Holiday, 1962), a dog story set in Mississippi, was filmed by Disney Studios and shown on television.

BAPTIST RAMSAY (*The Far-Off Land**), strong-as-an-ox, cocksure, Indian-hating frontiersman, who sings back-country songs while poling the flatboat, the *Dragonfly*. He is much humbler and far soberer after his newborn son is tragically drowned during an Indian attack. Ketty* Petrie sings a Moravian funeral service for the child.

BARNEY YOUNG (*Child of the Owl**), gambling father of Casey* who steals Paw-Paw's* heirloom owl charm and loses his daughter's respect. Having been a straight-A high school student and then suffered ten years of frustration in being able to get only menial jobs, he is portrayed as a victim of anti-Chinese prejudice as much as of weakness of character.

BARNWELL, D. ROBINSON (1915–   ), born in Pageland, S.C. A graduate of Winthrop College at Rock Hill, S.C., she also studied writing at Elton College, in North Carolina, and has taught high school English and French in North Carolina. With her husband, George Shelby Barnwell, she has lived in Burlington, N.C. Besides *Head into the Wind** (McKay, 1965), a Depression era story set in the rural South which was named to the *Horn Book* Fanfare list, she received favorable notice for *Shadow on the Water* (McKay, 1967).

BASIDIUM-X (*The Wonderful Flight to the Mushroom Planet*†; *Stowaway to the Mushroom Planet*†; *Time and Mr. Bass**), small, previously unknown planet which is Mr. Tyco* Bass's homeland. It is thirty-five miles in diameter and fifty thousand miles from Earth. The atmosphere is pale green, and its surface is covered with light green, spongy moss, fern trees, and myriads of grayish white and pinkish mushrooms of various sizes and shapes. It is inhabited by the Mushroom* People. Earth, which comes between it and the sun, called the Hot One, serves as its Protector from the sun's heat.

THE BASSUMTYTE TREASURE (Curry*, Jane Louise, Atheneum, 1978), mystery novel set in Gloucestershire, England, in the last third of the twentieth century, which depends upon the tradition that Mary, Queen of Scots, had a lover and gave birth to a child while she was in custody. When Tommy Bassumtyte, 10, comes from New Hampshire to live with a distant cousin, also named Thomas, at the family home in the Cotswolds, he finds Boxleton House everything he could have hoped for, but there are also some problems. Thomas, who scaled Mt. Everest some years before, has been injured in a climbing accident and is still far from well. Moreover, he is worried about financial matters; inheritance taxes have left him insufficient funds to keep up the house and grounds, and though he has sold off the farm and keeps only Mr. Wickery, the gardener, and his wife, the housekeeper, instead of a large crew of servants, and even opens the house to tourists on certain days, he must seriously listen to the offer an Arabian prince is making for the property. The coming of Tommy, who looks just like the portrait of Small Thomas, a red-haired, lively-looking boy of the sixteenth century, awakens interest in the mysteries of the house which stem from Elizabethan times and concern the loyalty of the Catholic Bassumtytes to Mary, Queen of Scots. Tommy chooses for his room a small chamber with walls covered by needle-point panels depicting scenes from King Arthur, and, hunting for the priest's hole that Thomas tells him exists, finds a new passage into the secret room from his cupboard bed, a passage unknown even to Thomas. He also shows Thomas a medallion handed down to him by his grandfather and quotes a riddle his grandfather taught him that is supposedly the key to the family treasure. Gemma Harvey, the vicar's grown-up niece, who works in a museum, gets interested and makes two very important discoveries: that the first panel in Tommy's room was actually embroidered by Queen Mary and has her monogram stitched into the underside, and that the portrait of Grace, mother of Small Thomas, who never met her in-laws but was brought in a coffin to be buried at Boxleton, is actually a portrait of Queen Mary, overpainted to disguise the color of her hair. Thomas, Gemma, and Tommy discover that the coffin buried under the Boxleton chapel contains a heavy beam of wood but no body. After searching all the many chests at Boxleton to find the "box" that figures prominently in his riddle, Tommy finally realizes it is the central yew tree in the box-wood maze that was a feature of the Elizabethan garden, and there they find a box bound into a cleft in the tree so that the wood has actually grown around it. The box contains no great treasure but certain miniatures and relics that show that Small Thomas was not a Bassumtyte at all, but the son of Queen Mary brought as an infant by her loyal follower, Tall Thomas, who was later hanged for his part in a plot to free her. The portrait, however, is of enough value to rescue the house from its financial troubles and to provide for Tommy's schooling, and the search has brought Thomas and Gemma together romantically. The plot is tight-knit and plausible, except for the appearance to Tommy, three times, of the ghost of Lady Margaret, mother of Tall Thomas and supposedly grandmother of Small Thomas, a fantasy element that has little function and runs counter to the realistic tone of most of the book. The characters are attractive, though not particularly memorable, and the setting is interesting. Poe Nominee.

THE BAT POET (Jarrell*, Randall, ill. Maurice Sendak, Macmillan, 1964), unusual fantasy set in an American rural area in an unspecified time which also gives undidactic insight into poetic criticism. A little light brown bat sleeps with the other bats hanging from the porch roof in the summer, but in the fall when the others move to the barn, he doesn't go with them. Because he is alone, he is sometimes wakeful and sees things in the daytime, the squirrels, the chipmunks, the cat, and the birds. He begins to understand the mockingbird which sings in the moonlight of what has happened all day in the yard. He tries to make up songs like the mockingbird and finds his voice is not right, but he thinks, "If you get the words right you don't need a tune." When he makes up a poem about the daytime and tries to say it to the other bats, they are not interested. Finally, he gets up nerve to ask the mockingbird to listen to his poem about the owl. The bird, who would much rather have the bat for an audience, listens somewhat condescendingly and is surprised. "Technically it's quite accomplished," he says, and gives a brief analysis of the formal aspects. The bat is disappointed and says to himself, "The owl nearly kills me, and he says he likes the rhyme scheme!" Then he voices the poets' complaint, "The trouble isn't making poems, the trouble's finding somebody that will listen to them." He decides to suit his verse to his audience and offers to make up a poem about the chipmunk, charging a fee of six crickets because "they don't respect something if they get it for nothing." To show the chipmunk what he means, the bat says his owl poem, and the chipmunk is properly frightened by it. When the bat has composed a chipmunk poem, his chipmunk friend is pleased by it and suggests that he write one about the cardinal. The bat agrees but finds that he cannot summon poetry to order and has to give up, much as he admires the beautiful red bird. He does, however, make one about the mockingbird, which the chipmunk likes but rightly predicts that the mockingbird will not. Thinking he must find a more receptive audience, the bat composes a poem about a bat baby clinging to its mother and soaring through the night air. The chipmunk is impressed, but when the bat goes to the barn to say it to the other bats, he finds them asleep, so he snuggles in close to them to wait until they are awake. The lines of the poem begin to fade from his memory as he, too, falls asleep. The delicate story is a vehicle for presenting several of Jarrell's best known poems. It is also a gently ironic comment on attitudes toward poetry and on the plight of the poet in a world more interested in practical things. Choice.

BAUER, MARION DANE (1938–   ), born in Oglesby, Ill., teacher, writer of novels for children. She attended La Salle-Peru-Oglesby Junior College and the University of Missouri, and received her B.A. degree from the University of Oklahoma. She has taught high school English at Waukesha, Wis., and creative writing for adults at Hennepin County Technical School in Minnesota and for the University of Minnesota Continuing Education program. Her novel, *Foster Child* (Seabury, 1977), a story of a twelve-year-old sent to a foster home where a fanatically religious father presses his attentions on her, was named Golden Kite honor book by the Society of Children's Book Writers. Among her other novels are *Shelter from the Wind* (Seabury, 1976) and *Rain of Fire** (Clarion, 1983), which won the Jane Addams award. Like *Foster Child*, both have twelve-year-old protagonists, the first a girl who runs away when her father remarries, the other a boy who makes up a series of lies to cover the odd behavior of his brother who has returned disturbed from witnessing the horrors of Hiroshima, stories which lead the younger boy and his friends into nearly disastrous play. She has also written a novel for young adults, *Tangled Butterfly* (Houghton, 1980), about a disturbed seventeen-year-old girl. She and her family have made their home in Minnetonka, Minn.

THE BEARS' HOUSE (Sachs*, Marilyn, ill. Louis Glanzman, Doubleday, 1971), short realistic novel of family and school life set in New York City in the mid–1960s. Young-old, inarticulate Fran Ellen Smith, 9, has two homes and big problems. At PS 87 her classmates tease her because she sucks her thumb, tell her she stinks, and get her in trouble with the teacher. In her real home, she lives with her brother, four sisters, and emotionally ill mother. Her father has abandoned the family, perhaps gone home to Harlan, Ala., and her mother spends most of her time in bed, unable to cope with children or house since his disappearance. Twelve-year-old Fletcher* organizes his siblings to care for one another so they can stay together. The youngest sister, baby Flora, is Fran Ellen's greatest joy, and every day Fran Ellen races home at recess to look after her. Fran Ellen's other house stands at the back of her school classroom. In it live Goldilocks and the Three Bears, and there in her imagination Fran Ellen finds refuge from the pressures of home and school. Father Bear holds her, Mother Bear gives her a pretty dress, and they even have a birthday party for her. When her teacher, Miss* Thompson, catches Fran Ellen breaking school rules and going home at recess, she insists on talking to Fran Ellen's mother. She accompanies Fran Ellen home and discovers that Mrs. Smith is ill. When she asks to talk with the children's father, Fran Ellen and Fletcher equivocate and prevaricate, as Fletcher has long been doing with the social worker, and Fran Ellen buys some time by promising to be good and not suck her thumb any more. At schoolyear's end, six months after the novel begins, Fran Ellen wins the doll's house for her hard work in school. Then Miss Thompson helps her take it home and discovers the truth about the family. Fran Ellen realizes that social agencies will intervene but assures her Bears' House friends that she has persevered and done her best. Fran Ellen is a naive narrator whose childlike perceptions of things underscore the implied indictment of the impersonality of modern urban life in this "slice of real life" story for younger readers. Fran Ellen's fantasy and real worlds do not clearly mesh, but her escape from painful reality is original in conception and convincingly childlike. Her voice is believable most of the time, but the book lacks unity, and the chapter headings are the only clue to the novel's time span. The conclusion is predictable, and the story fails to achieve a proper climax. The author excels at creating the moment, and the scenes in which Fran Ellen takes care of Flora are especially good. Choice; National Book Finalist.

BEATRICE D'ESTE (*The Second Mrs. Giaconda**), historical figure, young wife of Ludovico*, powerful, wealthy, late-fifteenth-century Duke of Milan. Although she is very plain, her liveliness and wit make her popular with the court and people. She is also highly esteemed by the artist Leonardo da Vinci, whose patron is her husband, and by da Vinci's apprentice, young Salai*. Her advice to Salai, to see to it that da Vinci always keeps "something wild, something irresponsible in his work," leads the youth to accept the commission of Mr. Giaconda to paint his wife, Madonna Lisa, whose portrait becomes the da Vinci masterpiece known as the "Mona Lisa." Astute and warmhearted, Beatrice becomes loud and altogether too cheerful when she realizes that her husband has fallen in love with a court lady. Salai is put off by her new brashness and sudden concentration on acquiring more and more art objects, her way of compensating for her heartbreak. She dies giving birth to her third child. Beatrice is a well-drawn, pathetic figure.

BEATTY, JOHN (LOUIS) (1922–1975), born in Portland, Oreg.; educator, historian, author of books for adults and young people. He was a graduate of Reed College, where he met his future wife, Patricia Beatty*, of Stanford University, and of the University of Washington. For many years, he was a professor of history at the University of California at Riverside, where he specialized in English history of the sixteenth, seventeenth, and eighteenth centuries. He edited and wrote scholarly books for adults. With his wife he co-authored eleven books of historical fiction for young readers. One, a Fanfare book, *A Donkey for the King** (Macmillan, 1966), improvises upon the Biblical Nativity Story from the point of view of a mute Judean shepherd boy, vividly recreating the flavor and thinking of the time and the appearance of old Palestine. Three of their novels received citations from the New York *Times* as outstanding books for their years of publication, *At the Seven Stars* (Macmillan, 1963), *Campion Towers* (Macmillan, 1965), and *The Royal Dirk* (Macmillan, 1966), all meticulously researched historical novels of excitement and adventure set in the British Isles or London in the seventeenth and eighteenth centuries.

BEATTY, PATRICIA (ROBBINS) (1922–   ), born in Portland, Oreg.; educator, librarian, and author best known for her adventurous historical novels for young people. She graduated from Reed College and the University of Washington. She taught high school English and history in Idaho, was a technical and science librarian in Delaware and California, and contributed materials on English history to Science Research Associates. She wrote novels with her husband, John Beatty*, a professor of British history. This happy collaboration of historian and storyteller resulted in eleven historical novels for children and young people, many set in the British Isles, and including *A Donkey for the King** (Macmillan, 1966), a novel that takes place in ancient Palestine and was selected by the editors of *Horn Book* for their Fanfare list. Individually she has written more than twenty carefully researched novels about Indians, pioneer life, the Old West, and women's rights. Of these her *Hail Columbia** (Morrow, 1970) is the most highly regarded and is cited in *Choice*. This is a rousing, fast-moving, amusing account of one woman's campaign to clean up the far from wholesome port of Astoria, Oreg., in the 1890s. Among her recent novels are *Jonathan Down Under* (Morrow, 1982), set in the gold fields of Australia, *Melinda Takes a Hand* (Morrow, 1983), a tall tale for middle readers about two sisters in Colorado in the 1890s, and *Turn Homeward, Hannalee* (Morrow, 1984), which involves Georgia millworkers shipped North to work in Indiana against their will during the Civil War. Often intentionally outrageously exaggerated, her stories are fast-moving, full of peppery happenings, suspense, and the events and flavor of the times, and related in zesty, good-humored style, but her characters are flat and sometimes approach caricature, and her plots seem overly complex and contrived. She lives in southern California and has taught classes in writing fiction for children at the University of California at Los Angeles.

BEAUTY (McKinley*, Robin, Harper, 1978), fantasy retelling the story of "Beauty and the Beast." Told in first person by Beauty*, whose real name is Honour Huston, the story starts in a seaport much like those of sixteenth- or seventeenth-century Europe where her father is a wealthy merchant. Her eldest sister, Grace, is betrothed to Robert Tucker, a promising young sea captain, and the second daughter, Hope, is in love with Gervain Woodhouse, an ironworker in the shipyard. When bad news comes that her father's fleet, including Robert Tucker, has been lost, Gervain persuades them to go with him to a village in the north near his birthplace, where he can be blacksmith. Before they leave, a horse dealer, Tom Black, gives Beauty the large, magnificent horse she has helped raise, Greatheart, whose presence makes their move and start in the farm at the forest edge reasonably successful. After more than two years, word comes that one of Huston's ships has come at last to port, and when he travels to the city to handle the business, Beauty suggests that he bring some seeds of roses that she might plant around the house. To their surprise, he returns in a snow storm with a gorgeous rose in his hand. The next day he tells them of how he lost his way, came upon a marvelous castle where he was served by invisible hands, stayed overnight, and just as he was leaving, rode through a garden of beautiful roses. Remembering Beauty's request, he picked one and was confronted by a roaring beast, which agreed to spare his life only if he would give it one of his daughters. Beauty volunteers and, despite protests from father and sisters, sets out bravely on Greatheart and soon comes to the mysterious estate. There she, too, is given every fine thing to eat and wear and in the evening she finds the Beast, talks to him briefly, but is horrified when he asks her to marry him. As time goes by, they become quite companionable, but she can never bring herself to give an affirmative answer to the question he repeats each night. Finally in her longing for her family, the Beast lets her look into a glass-covered table where she sees Grace considering marriage to a local minister and then in another scene sees Robbie Tucker returning after long years of shipwreck. Frantic that Grace will not wait for Robbie, Beauty begs to be allowed to go home to warn her, and the Beast reluctantly agrees that she may go for a week. She warns Grace, who is still deeply in love with Robbie, and spends a happy week, but uneasily worries about the Beast. When she returns, she finds him dying. She tells him that she loves him and that she will marry him, the spell under which he has been living is broken, and he changes into the handsome young noble whose portrait she has seen in the hall. The old story has enough natural appeal to stand the expansion into a novel, and the realistic detail is well handled, particularly in the first part of the story. The end, however, seems rushed, as if invention had worn thin. Fanfare.

BEAUTY HUSTON (*Beauty**), protagonist of the fictional retelling of the old tale, "Beauty and the Beast." This Beauty, whose real name is Honour, is the awkward, intellectual younger sister of two lovely girls and has always thought her nickname ironic. When her father's business fails and they move to a remote country village, she is able to do much of the work in the house and fields and does not really miss the old life. Her love for horses and particularly her own large horse, Greatheart, is fortunate for the family who badly need his labor, and, when she goes to the Beast's castle, having Greatheart with her helps her to fill her time and to adjust to the strange life. She is frank and honest and comes in time to live up to both her given name and her nickname.

BECCA HANSEN (*Rain of Fire**), Rebecca, friend of Steve* Pulaski who invariably gets him into trouble. Daughter of the mill superintendent, she is uninhibited and full of ideas, easily able to manipulate slower Steve. In the past she has several times concocted pranks that landed him in difficulties while she escaped free. It is her idea that they swipe Donny's bike, repaint it, then leave it behind Ray* Celestino's house so the twins will think that he stole it. When she and Steve are tied up and left in the foxhole, she admits that she is sorry for some of the times she has landed him in trouble but is quick to blame him for lying when it comes out that Ray is not a bicycle thief, and she is the only one who escapes all injury in the explosion.

BECKETT FOOTE (*Early Thunder**), best friend of Daniel West, the same age and also fun-loving, occasionally mischievous, and Tory in political sentiment. In his company, Daniel roams Salem and learns the political news. Beckett and Daniel find messages in an old oak tree that appear to have been left by Liberty* Boys about conspiratorial activities against the Crown. Beckett's father chooses to leave Salem rather than sign a paper renouncing the family's Tory leanings. After the Footes leave for Halifax and the Wests' house burns down, the Wests move into the Foote house. Beckett's personality lacks definition. He is more of a functionary figure than a real person in his own right. Daniel's relationship with Beckett, and also with Peter Ray, whom Beckett and Daniel put to a "witch test" of loyalty, flesh out the picture of Daniel as a fairly normal boy who is growing up in politically explosive times.

BECKMAN, DELORES, Arizona resident, author of *My Own Private Sky** (Dutton, 1980), a novel of a friendship between a boy with problems and an older woman, which won the International Reading Association Award. She has also written *Who Loves Sam Grant?* (Dutton, 1983), about a high school girl who copes with an on-off relationship with the school's handsome quarterback.

BECKY MORGAN (*A String in the Harp**), cheerful, outgoing younger sister of Peter* and Jen*, aged ten. She introduces the family to Gwilym and Rhian, Welsh youths, who take the Morgans about the countryside and acquaint them with Welsh ways and beliefs. Becky insists that Jen try to mend the fractured relationship between their father and Peter and takes seriously what Peter says about the harp key's ability to conjure up scenes from the past. She is a convincing character, both catalyst and support.

BEFORE THE LARK (Brown*, Irene Bennett, Atheneum, 1982), realistic novel set in 1888 in eastern Kansas. Because she has a harelip, Jocey* (Jocelyn Belle) Royal, 12, hides her lower face in a scarf as she delivers laundry for her Grandma* Letty (Letitia) Stern in Kansas City, Mo., but still she is frequently tormented by The Chasers, youngsters who yell at her, call her "looney," and sometimes throw stones. When an offer comes from a lawyer seeking to buy a farm in the Neosho River country which her drifter father has abandoned, Jocey decides to go there, even though her grandmother has been ill. With all their belongings piled in the laundry cart drawn by their old horse, Napoleon, they set out despite Grandma Letty's objections, camping along the way. At the farm they find signs of her father, including a gun which they trade for food, but it is clear that he has been gone for a long time. Although Grandma Letty demands a great deal of care and attention, Jocey is happy in the isolated place and works hard to plant a small crop. When she dams the creek to water her potatoes and garden plants, their nearest neighbor, Edvard Pladson, a dour Norwegian, calls to demand that she tear out the dam, and, when he learns that she is Jim Royal's daughter, warns her to stay away from his family. Jocey is glad to be alone, but her grandmother, a sociable woman, is lonesome and welcomes an Indian peddler and a couple of sewing-machine salesmen. To scare them off, Jocey reveals her harelip, and later one of them returns to tell her of an operation for her affliction. When the Pladsons' sheep destroy much of her corn, Jocey rides to their house to complain and finds the mother and the children delighted to see her, familiar with her problem from her father's stories of her, and grateful to him for having taught them to read English, though their father strongly disapproves. They tell her that Jim Royal went to Mexico and that they heard he had been shot. The next morning Tosten Pladson, a boy about Jocey's age, brings her a cow on semi-permanent loan to pay for the damage by the sheep. Grandma Letty finally admits that she has been well for some time but has liked being pampered so much that she has continued to play sick. When the sewing-machine salesman returns with details about the operation available in Kansas City, Jocey takes the train alone and has the surgery, free because medical students observe it. As she is convalescing, her father shows up, weak but recovering from the gunshot, having returned to Kansas City and been alerted to her hospital by an old laundry neighbor. With an earnest tone, the story contains too much comment on the attitudes toward harelips and on Jocey's feelings, explanation that could better have been shown in action. This gives a modern, sociological feeling that detracts from the historical verisimilitude. Jocey's hard work on her farm and her love of the land seem genuine, however, and Grandma Letty is an exasperating but convincing malingerer. Spur.

BEHIND THE MAGIC LINE (Erwin*, Betty K., ill. Julia Iltis, Little, 1969), realistic novel concerning black family unity, set in Chicago and across the United States to the west coast, in the mid twentieth century. Bright, responsible Dozie Western, about ten, eldest of the six black children still at home in their crowded two-room apartment, watches the home birth of her baby sister, Erica, and becomes chief baby-sitter as soon as her mother, Marie*, goes back to work cleaning for white families. Occasionally her grown brother, Whitney, comes home, but neither he nor their two married sisters can help out the family, and their father, Josh*, has not been heard from for some months. Too busy to play with other children, Dozie is lonesome and is delighted when she makes friends with an old man, Samuel* Dan, who was once a stage magician and now has retired from the stage and "from the human race." Dozie helps him fix a shack in a vacant lot and believes he has real magic powers as he seems to "find" money to buy steak for the family. Prodded by old, bedridden Aunt Jean, who lives in the same decrepit apartment house as the Westerns, he even takes a job as a butler to earn enough to buy the children winter clothes. When he is brought back ill, Marie takes him in, and he gradually recovers. Then Whitney shows up, shot in a holdup where he was a bystander but nevertheless is chased by the police, and Samuel Dan saves him by pretending they are a couple of drunks staggering up the alley, taking him to his shack, and hiding him until he recovers. Josh comes home with some money he has saved, buys an old station wagon, and the family leaves in the middle of the night, Samuel Dan and Whitney with them, and heads for the west coast, camping along the way. When the car breaks down in Montana, a rancher lets them sleep in the barn and help around the place, but seeing how useful and hardworking they are, decides to force them to stay at gunpoint. Josh dares him to shoot and is prevented from attacking the man by young Jeremy, who dances in front of him, distracting the rancher until Whitney can get the gun. The family travels across the Rockies in a snowstorm and arrives in the coastal city where Josh has found a boarded-up house in poor repair that the family can afford to buy. Josh and Whitney get jobs as garbage men, and Samuel Dan agrees to stay as baby-sitter while Marie works and Dozie goes to school. The main emphasis is the strong love that holds the family together despite hard times and discrimination. Although more realistic than earlier books about blacks, the story still idealizes the family. The attitude that men should be forgiven for being irresponsible but women should willingly do the hard, day-to-day work with patience may seem dated since the women's liberation books of the 1970s. Choice.

BEHN†, HARRY (1898–1973), born in McCabe, Yavapai County, Ariz., and was living in Greenwich, Conn., at the time of his death; poet and novelist whose two callings complemented each other in his books for children. He was influenced by the Indians he knew in his childhood in Prescott, Ariz., to appreciate both nature and the telling of tales. After his education at Stanford University and Harvard University, he wrote scenarios for movies and taught creative writing at the University of Arizona, Tucson, from 1938 to 1947. He translated Rilke and Japanese haiku for publication and published three volumes of his own poems for adults and seven for children, among the best known being *The Little Hill* (Harcourt, 1949), *Windy Morning* (Harcourt, 1953), and *The Golden Hive* (Harcourt, 1966). Much of his philosophy of poetry, writing, and living is contained in *Chrysalis: Concerning Children and Poetry* (Harcourt, 1968). His novels, particularly *The Faraway Lurs** (World, 1963), a romance set in prehistoric Denmark, reflect his poetic vision in their view of the world and their lyrical style. He also wrote *The Two Uncles of Pablo†* (Harcourt, 1959), a lighter story set in Mexico.

BELL, CLARE (1952–   ), writer, test engineer for a computer company, and student of design. She was born in England but has become a naturalized citizen of the United States. She says she has been influenced by C. S. Lewis, Arthur C. Clarke, and Olaf Stapledon, and that her central theme is evolution. Her fantasy, *Ratha's Creature** (Atheneum, 1983), which was awarded the International Reading Association Award, reflects this interest, being concerned with large cats which develop intelligence and language and learn to control fire. She lives in Palo Alto, Calif.

BELLING THE TIGER (Stolz*†, Mary, ill. Beni Montresor, Harper, 1961), fantasy of short story length that improvises upon a familiar fable from Aesop. Portman*, tyrannical leader of the house mice, calls a meeting in a clothes closet to decide who shall bell Siri, the wicked house cat. The rigged vote falls upon Rambo and Asa, small twin cellar mice. They meekly accept the charge, scurry to the neighborhood hardware store, and steal a blue collar with a bell attached. On the way home, they spy a cat and flee to the docks, where they race up a rope onto a ship which then sets sail. Days later they find themselves in a land of exotic flora and fauna. They fall asleep under a trumpet plant and wake to find stretched out near them an immense black and gold creature that looks and smells like a cat but is two hundred times the size of Siri. Rambo urges immediate departure, but for the first time in his life Asa assumes the initiative and suggests they bell this "cat." Belling the creature's tail awakens the tiger*, who proves unexpectedly congenial. After introductions, the tiger says he has never before seen mice but knows elephants fear them. To prove the truth of his statement, he takes the mice to see an elephant, who, as predicted, retreats trumpeting wildly upon catching sight of them. On their return Portman demands to know why the mice have been absent without permission. The brothers find they are no longer afraid of Portman and insist on being elevated to pantry status. The other mice, admiring the manner in which the twins speak up to Portman, vote them in. Portman then says he has heard the father of the house reading a story in which the belling-the-cat scheme proved unfeasible and asserts that it is obvious that flying in the face of custom is impossible. The mice accordingly abandon the project of belling Siri, but Rambo and Asa know that impossible tasks can be done and that mice can even scare elephants. They have done both. As in the traditional fable, the animals are recognizable human types, and action and dialogue move directly to the implicit moral. More is made of the humor of irony and situation and satire on human behavior (e.g., government by steering committee), and other clever twists on the old tale lighten the tone and distinguish this as an authored story. Montresor's highly textured black and white sketches contribute to the entertainment in this short narrative in which the littlest triumph. Sequel is *The Great Rebellion*. Fanfare; Newbery Honor.

BEN (*The Sign of the Beaver**), heavyset, raggedy white man who steals Matt* Hollowell's rifle after Matt has fed him and given him a bed for the night. He has glittery, blue eyes and a sneaky way about him. He has apparently fallen afoul of the law and is on the run. A stock and minor character, he appears once only, but his action sets the stage for Matt to become friends with the Penobscot Indians, Attean* and Saknis*, and thus Ben is important to the story.

BENCHLEY, NATHANIEL (GODDARD) (1915–1981), born in Newton, Mass.; journalist, humorist, and writer of plays, articles, short stories, and novels for adults, children, and young people. He was educated at Phillips Exeter Academy and graduated from Harvard. A former reporter for the New York

Herald Tribune and assistant drama editor for *Newsweek*, he was well known as an author of articles and books for adults before he turned to writing for the young. His several controlled vocabulary books for the Harper I Can Read series of realistic and historical short stories exhibit greater skill with words and more careful attention to detail than such books usually do. These have remained consistently popular among younger readers, and *Sam the Minuteman* (Harper, 1969), one of the most requested, has sold over 75,000 copies. His historical novels for young people authentically recreate the problems and events of past times with vigor and occasional wit, but the plots are strained and move unevenly, and he seems more interested in conveying information than in telling a good story well. He received the Western Writers of America Spur Award for *Only Earth and Sky Last Forever** (Harper, 1972), about the Sioux attempts to stem the white westward tide. Other historical novels are *Gone and Back* (Harper, 1970), about the Oklahoma land rush, *Bright Candles* (Harper, 1974), about the Danish resistance to the Nazis, and *A Necessary End* (Harper, 1976), about a seventeen-year-old signalman in World War II, written with the conviction that came from his own personal experiences in the war. His most famous book, *The Off-Islanders* (McGraw, 1961), a novel for adults, was made into the movie *The Russians Are Coming, The Russians Are Coming*. He was the son of humorist Robert Benchley, whose biography he wrote for adults.

BEN MACDONALD (*Incident at Hawk's Hill**), six-year-old son of a Manitoba farmer who, in 1870, gets lost and spends two months in the company of a badger. Extremely small for his age, Ben has always been very shy and almost silent with humans but able to make friends with animals, watching them patiently for hours and imitating their motions and sounds. Although the neighbors and even his own father suspect that Ben is retarded, he is really intelligent, just overwhelmed by the relative size of other people and unable to make them understand his fascination with animals.

BENNETT (*The Runaway's Diary**), the middle-aged grocer in Harrisburg, owner of a chain of stores. Cat and other teenagers gather in his apartment behind one of the stores after school for conversation and, for some of them, marijuana. Unhappy at school, which she feels is impractical, and also at home, where her parents fight and her mother asks uncomfortable questions, Cat spends much time with Bennett, and from him she has gained many of her ideas about life and suggestions about the practical aspects of running away. A phony figure, he never appears directly in the story, but he is often in Cat's thoughts.

BENNETT, JAY (1912–   ), born in Brooklyn, N.Y.; mystery writer of novels for both adults and young people, as well as radio and television scripts. He attended New York University and lives in Brooklyn. His adult novel, *Catacombs* (Abelard, 1959), has been translated into eight languages and made into a movie. His mysteries for young people, including *The Long Black Coat**

(Delacorte, 1973) and *The Dangling Witness** (Delacorte, 1974), are well crafted with a strong sense of contemporary society.

BEN O'NEAL (*Teetoncey**; *Teetoncey and Ben O'Neal**, *The Odyssey of Ben O'Neal**), protagonist of this Cape Hatteras trilogy. Son of a surfman who was killed in a storm when Ben was a young child, the boy has been raised by his mother, who wanted a daughter and who even dressed him as a girl until he was five, hoping to make him gentle and to woo him away from the sea. Ben resents this treatment, particularly because it has made the fishermen and surfmen he admires suspicious of him, but at twelve he is still enough under her control so he must hide the boat he has found and named for his father, *Me and the John O'Neal*. In his attitude toward Teetoncey*, the girl he has saved from the wreck of the *Malta Empress*, he is a typical adolescent boy, often exasperated by her demands and her inexplicable behavior but taken in by her charms. In the first book, written in third person, he is a more complex and interesting character than in the other two, written in first person from his point of view.

BEN SILLS (*Words by Heart**), father of Lena, head of the only black family in the 1910 Texas community. An intelligent man, Ben had hoped to be a minister and has moved his family from the safety of an all-black community to West Texas in hope of giving Lena and his other children a better chance than he had in the South. When he is shot by a white-trash boy, he uses his last strength to help the boy, who has been thrown from his horse and badly injured. In his life he lives the part of the righteous man, patient but proud, and shows Lena the way she, too, must live.

BEN WINTERS (*The Griffin Legacy**), local youth, brother of Betsy* and friend of Amy* Enfield. He is funloving and adventurous and dares to enter the Griffin property without permission to try to find the silver. At first Grandma* Enfield and Aunt* Matilda don't want him and his sister around but change their minds when they realize the two are sincere in trying to help Amy help Lucy* Griffin. He also helps Amy to feel at home in the village and gives her historical information that is useful to her in her quest. He is able to see Lucy.

BERNADETTE SAVARD (*The Tamarack Tree**), fourteen-year-old orphan who comes to stay in Connecticut with the David Fry family, hoping to attend Miss Crandall's Seminary for Young Ladies. Her great desire for learning has been nurtured by David's minister brother in Ohio, who has fired her with ambition to attend newly started Oberlin College and then to start a school for girls herself. Although sidetracked for more than a year by her stay in Connecticut, she has learned a great deal about people, has become an abolitionist, and has come to realize that she must think for herself and not depend upon the judgments of others, no matter how kind they may be to her.

BERRIES GOODMAN (Neville*, Emily Cheney, Harper, 1965), realistic novel of family and community life revolving around prejudice against Jews. Events begin in New York City when Berries (Bertrand) Goodman, 16, gentile, has a quick and unexpected reunion in Times Square with his old chum, Sidney* Fine, Jew. Berries then flashes back to tell of the two years that begin when he is nine and the Goodman family, his brother, Hal, 17, sister Jennifer, 2, and their parents, leave their New York apartment and move to a big, old rented house in Olcott Corners, a suburb fifty miles out of the city. Berries becomes close friends with Sidney, whom the other youngsters shun because of his religion. New York reared Berries is confused and disturbed by their anti-Semitic attitudes and the remarks of the Goodmans' neighbors, the Grahams, and Hal's girlfriend, and even by the ready compliance of his mother, now a real estate agent, with the unwritten agreement among local realtors not to sell Olcott Corners property to Jews. After Sidney is injured ice skating, taking up Sandra* Graham's dare to leap the outlet to the pond, Sidney's over-protective, controlling mother refuses to allow the two boys to play together any more. The two meet secretly, however, for a time, until discovery puts a halt to their activities. Shortly thereafter, Berries's mother sells their house to old friends from the city, who are coincidentally named Goodman and ironically are Jewish, and the Goodmans quickly return to New York. The book ends with Berries following up on the reunion with a visit to Sidney's house. He finds Sidney still excelling in school, more independent and less easily intimidated by his mother, and apparently none the worse for his experience in Olcott. Lacking in drama, overforeshadowed, not always logical, filled with coincidence and typed or eccentric characters, the book is dated and a too obvious comment on prejudice against Jews. Not even Berries is convincing as a character, being a very apparent vehicle for relaying events. The author captures well the day-to-day attitudes and activities typical of children, however, the home life of the Goodmans seems authentic, and some humor adds interest. Addams; Choice; Fanfare.

BERT BREEN'S BARN (Edmonds*†, Walter D., Little, 1975), realistic period novel set at the turn of the century on a farm near the small town of Boonville (a real place) in upper New York State, covering about three years in the life of an impoverished farm youth who succeeds in his determination to provide a more comfortable life for his family. After her ne'er-do-well husband deserts her, thirteen-year-old Tom Dolan's mother, Polly* Ann, manages to feed him and his two younger sisters by doing housework and laundry in nearby Boonville. A quiet, proud, enterprising boy, Tom intends to "turn their lives around" by putting up a better barn. He plans to buy Bert Breen's, a sturdy and spacious if old structure, which stands on the Widow Breen's land several miles from the Dolan place. Tom quits school and gets a job for twenty-five cents a day at the Ackerman* and Hook* Feed and Flour Mill in Boonville. After scrimping and saving for many months, with the encouragement and advice of Polly Ann and many friends, he buys the barn for fifty dollars and the labor of demolishing the now ramshackle house. Although threatened by the three vicious Flanscher brothers, local hoodlums who are hunting for the treasure rumored to lie hidden there, Tom and Birdy* Morris, a kindly elderly neighbor, painstakingly tear down the barn and move the lumber, board by board, to the Dolan farm, where they equally painstakingly rebuild it. By barnraising time, Tom is sure he knows where the treasure is, and that night he and Polly Ann secretly return to the Breen place and on the old barnsite discover two trunks containing over $9,000 in bills and gold. After giving a share of his new-found wealth to Birdy, Tom pays the debt on the barn, buys the supplies he needs to finish it, and secures the equipment he needs to run a farm well, proud that he and his family are no longer "low-down Dolans" but can take their place among the respected members of the Boonville community. Although the treasure hunt contributes suspense, it strains credulity and weakens the theme that hard work and determination can result in success. It seems an unnecessary and melodramatic complication in an otherwise substantial picture of a period and a toughminded, perservering, plucky youth. Style is graceful with a homely plainness that seems to fit the time and place, the tone warm and conversational, and the storytelling finely paced. The descriptions of the barn building and raising are made very clear, and the evocation of farm and small town life is rich and vivid. (Billy-Bob* Baxter) Christopher; Fanfare; National Book Winner.

BERTHA ERICA CROW (*The Westing Game**), Samuel Westing's ex-wife, now a cleaning woman, who became estranged from Westing after the suicide of their daughter and who with Otis Amber runs a soup kitchen on skid row.

BESS TUTTLE (*The Unmaking of Rabbit**), best friend of Paul's grandmother, Emma*. Bess praises her grandson, Gordon*, so highly for his many accomplishments, among them, proficiency at tennis, that Paul feels quite inadequate and hesitates to associate with Gordon when he comes to visit his grandmother. Gordon turns out to be a regular fellow after all, and the two boys get on famously.

BETSY READ (*My Brother Sam Is Dead**), local girl on whom Sam* Meeker is somewhat sweet, to whom he writes, and who carries news about him to Timmy. When he comes home to visit, Betsy meets Sam in the hut belonging to Tom Warrups, an Indian, where Sam is staying. Caught up in the romance of war at first, she, too, changes her mind about it as it wears on and she observes what happens to the people of Redding.

BETSY WINTERS (*The Griffin Legacy**), local youth, sister of Ben* and friend of Amy* Enfield. She is very interested in local history, serving as a guide during the heritage fair, and is really more interested in finding out about the Griffins than in locating the silver. She helps Amy in her quest and also introduces

Amy to local youth and helps her to feel at home in the community. She is a pleasant, fun-loving girl.

BEYER, AUDREY WHITE (1916–   ), born in Portland, Maine; author of several works of historical fiction with diverse settings in time and place. She attended Westbrook Junior College, was graduated from the University of Maine, and did graduate work at both Northeastern University and the University of Maine in Portland. She has taught English at the preparatory school level and at Northeastern University. Besides *Dark Venture** (Knopf, 1968), concerned with the triangle slave trade, she has written novels about the War of 1812, Napoleon, and the burning in 1775 of Falmouth, Maine.

BIG MAMA LOGAN (*Roll of Thunder, Hear My Cry**), Caroline Logan, Papa Logan's mother, Cassie's grandmother, who lives with the Logan family. She is a sturdy, serious woman. She works in the cotton fields and helps with cooking, churning, washing, and other household tasks while Mama Logan teaches school. She even shoulders a rifle when the night riders threaten. She tells the children the story of how her husband worked to buy the Logan land and how much it meant to him. She tries to help them understand how important a part the land plays in insuring their independence. The children love and respect her very much. She is a well-drawn, admirable character, one of the memorable grandmothers in children's literature.

BILL CAMERON (*The Last Run**), nicknamed ''Broomtail,'' for his expertness in capturing mustangs when he was younger. Tough, knowledgeable, old cowboy and ex-mustanger, Lyle* Jeffries's mother's father, Bill has retired from life on the range and has taken a job in his son-in-law's (Frank* Jeffries) gas station, a position he does not enjoy and does poorly at. He is a demanding, but not insensitive, man, who scolds Lyle for being lazy and procrastinating. While they are in the mountains together, he helps Lyle see the importance of obedience and responsible behavior. He sometimes drinks too much, a factor which also contributes to Harry's* death. Bill's stories of the old days inspire Lyle to become a cowboy. After Bill and Lyle release the mustangs, Bill decides to hang up his mustanging spurs for good, pursue odd jobs, and give much of his time to teaching Lyle to ride and rope. Going after the mustang was the last run for him, too.

BILL CREIGHTON (*Across Five Aprils**), Jethro* Creighton's much loved older brother, 23, whose conscience forces him to enlist in the Confederate army, an action that brings trouble for the family. Bill is a strong, sober, gentle man, a thinker who is interested in learning and bothered by the rights and wrongs of things. He and his brother John, 24, a strong Northern sympathizer, have a terrible fist fight after Bill announces his decision to fight for the South, a physical struggle very hurtful psychically to them both. After Bill enlists, the family hears nothing further directly from him. He is last seen by John in a prisoner of war camp in the South, a meeting that John reports in a letter home to his folks. Bill and John exemplify on a personal scale what a civil war really is—strife between brothers.

BILL DELAMER (*Thunder on the Tennessee**), Colonel William Delamer, also known as Big Bill Delamer, Willie's* father and the brave, strong, respected commander of the Second Texas Regiment, decimated during furious fighting at Pittsburg Landing. Duty and honor are important to him. Having seen tough service in the Mexican War and against the Indians, he dislikes war and deplores the necessity to leave his beloved ranch on the Brazos and fight. He sees the Southern cause in the Civil War as a matter of fundamental principle, so that the South can continue to be self-determining. He is wounded the first day of the fighting at Pittsburg Landing and dies that night, a brave and wise commander whose loss is mourned.

A BILLION FOR BORIS (Rodgers*, Mary, Harper, 1974), comic novel of family life. A year after *Freaky Friday**, Annabel Andrews tells the story of another fantastical happening involving her, her boyfriend, Boris (Morris) Harris, who keeps house and cooks for his mother, a writer, and her little brother, Ape Face (Ben). The story is in the form of a long letter which Annabel writes to a university department of parapsychology and in which she seeks a "logical explanation" for what happens during three eventful weeks. After Ape Face, who is handy with tools, repairs Boris's broken TV set, Boris soon discovers that the set now plays programs scheduled for the next day. Idealistic Annabel immediately sees possibilities for using their foreknowledge to help people in need, but Boris more opportunistically senses possibilities for improving his family fortunes, particularly by betting on sports events. He wants to paint their dingy apartment and replace their worn-out, dilapidated furniture. He especially wishes to pay off his improvident mother's debts and hire a psychiatrist to help her conquer her irresponsible inclinations. Annabel and Boris agree to assist each other in accomplishing their special aims. Among other benevolent acts, Annabel helps a lost child and assists a reporter, Bartholomew Bacon, to some sensational "scoops" and incidentally to a love affair. On the strength of Boris's mild success at the race track, the two have his apartment repainted and select new furniture as a surprise for Mrs. Harris, who is away on a writing assignment. Predictably, Boris's good fortune hits a snag with some erroneous information on the Kentucky Derby, and then to their horror Annabel's parents give away the old TV set. Boris's mother unexpectedly returns, and without mincing words she informs her son that she likes her life the way it is and orders him to stop imposing his values on others. Furthermore, she says she now has a substantial contract with Paramount for a movie script and can meet their current obligations without help from him. Eccentric, one-sided characters and a full measure of mixups and hijinks makes for a hilarious romp that ends as expected but quite appropriately. Garrulous Annabel's contemporary chatter gets tedious at times, probably deliberately so, nor does it mask the author's winks at the audience or her voice, also probably deliberately so, because the intent is to spoof modern values and mores and have fun doing it. Choice; Christopher.

BILL JOHNSON (*Half-Breed**), actual historical figure, former seaman and veteran of *Old Ironsides*, whose wife, Nancy, is Cheyenne. In the novel, Jesse's cabin stands on Johnson land, and the Johnsons watch it while Jesse is off on his jaunts. The Johnsons are staunch friends of Aunt* Rhody and Hardy, giving them advice and material help. Bill likes to talk and tell stories, and he repeats the story of the battle between *Old Ironsides* and the *Guerrière*, in which he received the scar on his forehead, so often that Hardy soon knows it by heart. After Rhody burns Hardy's medicine bag, Bill gives the boy his own half-penny as a lucky piece, and Hardy subsequently carries the coin in his moccasin. Bill and Nancy return to the Cheyennes at story's end.

BILLY BEN COREY (*The Witches' Bridge**), ambitious handyman who seems at first friendly but is really sinister. From a family who have always lived at Pride's Point and worked for the Prides, Billy Ben seems to be a simple, hardworking young man, inclined to think up work for himself beyond what is required, but actually is scheming to find the briefcase which had disappeared when old Dan Pride was found dead. The Pride heirs have assumed that it was taken by the Bishop family, since, they believe, it contains the receipts for the purchase of the shipyards from the Bishops. Actually, Billy Ben knows it is full of cash, since old Dan never got to the Bishop house but was waylaid and killed by Billy Ben's father. When young Dan comes to Pride's Point, Billy Ben pretends friendship but taunts him by singing "Danny Boy" and eventually tries to murder him.

BILLY-BOB BAXTER (*Bert Breen's Barn**), wise and kindly old lawyer in Boonville, who gives Tom Dolan practical and legal advice without charge, helps him count the cache of money the boy and Polly* Ann have found on Breen's place, and lets them store it at his house until they can take it to the bank for deposit. He is a good friend to the Dolans.

BILLY MALOON (*The Alley**), Connie* Ives's best friend. He is a shy boy with large, hazel eyes, who likes to use long, hard words and often comes up with ideas for activities. On Recital Day, he is ill in bed with a cold but sneaks out anyway and catches the robbers in the act of burglarizing Bully Vardeer's house. The snapshots Billy takes of them help to catch and convict them.

BIMBY (Burchard*, Peter, ill. author, Coward, 1968), historical novel set on the plantation of Pierce Butler, a real person called in the story Massa* Pierce, on the Georgia coastal islands just before the American Civil War. A day he has long looked forward to with pleasure holds tragedy and a new direction in life for the young slave Bimby. On Sunday he happily accompanies Jesse*, aged former teamster boss of the plantation, to St. Simons Island to help with the white folks' picnic. Bimby looks forward to visiting with his mother, a servant in the Mansion, whom he has not seen for weeks. Bimby and Jesse row the old slave's boat to Butler Point where the Mansion slaves are holding a camp meeting. When Massa Pierce and his guests arrive by barge, Jesse and Bimby load a wagon with food and supplies for the picnic. Jesse informs Bimby that he has learned that Massa is planning to auction off his slaves to pay his gambling debts. When he sees that the wagons carrying the white folks have begun to race, Jesse whips up his horse and deliberately cuts off Massa's wagon, causing his own wagon to overturn and his own death. Grief-stricken, Bimby flees for comfort to his Ma, who in her tiny, dark cabin tells him, among other things, that his respected, blacksmith father died from a flogging after an unsuccessful attempt to reach freedom. She encourages Bimby to try to escape and gives him names of contacts left her by Massa Butler's former wife, Miss* Fanny, an ardent abolitionist. The end sees Bimby in Jesse's boat striking for freedom. Although the author builds tension surely and deftly and draws the principals clearly, a fuller treatment of both characters and plot would have kept the novel from sounding like a lecture on the evils of slavery. While it is possible that Bimby might not have heard about the impending auction, it is unlikely that a boy of an age to be trained for a trade and as intelligent as Bimby is supposed to be would be unaware of such sordid aspects of slavery as the selling apart of family members. Nor does it seem likely that Bimby has not learned from overheard conversations or from his peers about what happened to his father, if not from his own mother before. Miss Fanny was a real person also, and the proposed auction did, in fact, take place. Choice; Fanfare.

BIRDY MORRIS (*Bert Breen's Barn**), kindly, old farmer who lives near Polly* Ann Dolan and her family, who gives Tom Dolan the idea of buying Widow Breen's barn, and who helps the boy tear it down and rebuild it on the Dolan place. Since Birdy helped to build the barn originally, he is familiar with its construction. Without his skill, help, and encouragement, Tom probably would not have succeeded with his plans. Birdy treats Tom like a son, and Tom likes and respects him very much.

BISHOP, CURTIS (1912–1967), born in Bolivar, Tex.; writer mainly noted for sports novels, including many dealing with football, baseball, and basketball. He was a student at the University of Texas, a newspaperman, and was in the Foreign Broadcast Intelligence Service during World War II. He played championship tennis and semi-pro baseball, and coached little league and other junior sports in Austin, Tex., where he made his home. Under his own name and the pseudonyms of Curt Brandon and Curt Carroll, he published several hundred magazine stories and articles and many books for young people, including

*Little League Victory** (Lippincott, 1967). Five of his books were made into motion pictures.

THE BLACK CAULDRON (Alexander*, Lloyd, Holt, 1965), fantasy set in the mythical land of Prydain*, second in the series featuring Taran*, the Assistant Pig-Keeper of Caer Dallben. Summoned by Prince Gwydion, the leading warriors of Prydain assemble at Caer Dallben to prepare to attack Annuvin, the domain of the Death-Lord, Arawn, and seize the Black Crochan, the Black Cauldron that is the source of Arawn's ferocious and deathless army, the Cauldron-Born*. The task force includes King Smoit and King Morgant and their men. Doli* is to make himself invisible, enter Arawn's stronghold, and locate the Cauldron which the warriors will then capture. Taran, Ellidyr, son of Pen-Llarcau, and Adaon, son of Taliesin, are to serve as a rear guard. Eilonwy* and Gurgi* later also attach themselves to Taran's group. After Doli discovers that the Cauldron is not at Annuvin, there is a set-to with Arawn's forces, and Fflewddur* Fflam brings word that Gwydion wishes all to regroup at Caer Cadarn, Smoit's place. On the way, Taran's group, now swelled by Doli, finds shelter at the way-stop of Gwystyl of the Fair Folk. From him they learn that the three wise enchantresses, Orddu, Orwen, and Orgoch (the Fates), who live in the Marshes of Morvu, have the Cauldron. Taran persuades the others to travel there to get it. The route through the Forest of Idres is filled with hazards. Ellidyr, proud and spiteful, deserts the companions and rides ahead, eager for glory. Adaon is slain by Arawn's Huntsmen. As he lies dying, he gives Taran the magical brooch given him by his betrothed. After making their way through the treacherous marshes, the little party arrives at the hut of the three old enchantresses, who flaunt their powers before them. While seeking straw for bedding for the night, Gurgi finds the Cauldron hidden in a corner of a dilapidated shed. When the companions try to move it, they stick fast to it. Orddu releases them when Taran gives her Adaon's brooch. She then informs the companions that the Cauldron can be destroyed only if someone willingly casts himself into it, sacrificing his life that others may live. The companions depart for Caer Cadarn, intending to take the Cauldron to Gwydion. On the way, Ellidyr seizes the Cauldron, and, determined to take credit for its recovery, swears the others to secrecy on pain of death. Somewhat farther on, the companions fall in with King Morgant, who has seized the Cauldron from Ellidyr. A turncoat, Morgant now intends to overthrow Arawn and make himself Overlord of all Prydain. Ellidyr, who has sustained a fatal wound, casts himself into the Cauldron, thus making the supreme sacrifice and terminating its powers. Gwydion's forces arrive and defeat the evil Morgant. Although the Celtic sources seem superficially and overly exploited, characters are flat, their behavior predictable, and there are too many episodes, the book offers an abundance of action, suspense, and plenty of excitement, its essential seriousness lightened with generous amounts of humor, both physical and subtle. Style has polish and vibrates with energy, and the conclusion is filled with dramatic action and gripping conflict. (Drynwyn*; Golden* Peledryn) ChLA Touchstones; Choice; Fanfare; Newbery Honor.

BLACK HILLS (*Only Earth and Sky Last Forever**), mountainous area in the upper midwest sacred to the Indians and which was by treaty with the United States Government reserved for them forever. Whites entered the region in violation of the treaty to search for gold, and the result was a series of bitter, futile battles to evict them.

THE BLACK MUSTANGER (Wormser*, Richard, ill. Don Bolognese, Morrow, 1971), realistic novel set in northwest Texas about 1880 concerned with rounding up wild horses and with problems of discrimination, both racial and regional. Dan Riker, 13, and his father, Lafe, have come from Tennessee to build a herd by mavericking, branding wild cattle, hard work for a crew of men and only just possible for a man and a boy. They have some 290 wearing their Rx "Prescription" brand when a horse rolls on Dan's father, breaking his leg. Dan gets Lafe back to camp, where his mother can care for him, then rides out to get help from one of the big mavericking outfits. Although the Civil War ended before Dan was born, he finds the foreman, Pasan, reluctant to give help to a man from the South who fought in the Union army. A visitor to the camp volunteers to help, a part-Indian, part-black mustanger known as Mesteño* Will, a man who catches and sells wild horses. With the help of Dan and his mother, Will sets the leg and rides off, but Dan knows that alone he cannot continue mavericking, so he sets off to try to get a job as chore boy or herd boy, anything that will earn enough to keep the family until his father can work again. Trying Pasan first, he is refused a job, and when he tries to sell the foreman the right to rebrand the Prescrip steers, Pasan shows him that they can be branded over with the Railroad Connected, which he intends to file on. Legally, he will rebrand the Prescrip without paying when the Rikers are forced to leave Texas. Discouraged and upset, Dan rides off, joins up with two ne'er-do-wells he has met at the store, and with them comes upon Mesteño Will's camp. He lets the saddle bums leave without him and takes Will's offer to earn five dollars by helping him drive a herd of mustangs to an outfit heading east. There the foreman warns him that no white boy works for a colored man, but Dan, fascinated by the mustanger, heads home to ask his parents' permission to join Will. Pressed by necessity, they agree, and Dan becomes a partner in a unique way of catching wild mustangs by "becoming a horse," riding with a group until they accept a man as one of them, then challenging the stallion for leadership. Dan attracts the affection of a two-year-old he names Wattle for his reddish color. After living with the group for some time, they maneuver a challenge by Wattle to the old stallion and, with their help, Wattle wins, assuming leadership of the main part of the herd. When they have corralled and partly broken the herd, they have a sale attended by all those in the area, including Dan's parents and Pasan, who saves face by referring to Will as an Apache and who sells the Railroad Connected brand to

Lafe for a token twenty-five cents. Dan's future as a mustanger or a mavericker is left open. This is a well-written novel, with strong characterization, even of minor figures, and a tight and plausible plot. The racial conflict Dan and his southern-bred parents feel is believably presented, and the theme, that a man is what he is and not what a stereotype makes him seem, is clear but not over-obvious. Choice; Spur; Western Heritage.

THE BLACK PEARL (O'Dell*, Scott, ill. Milton Johnson, Houghton, 1967), realistic novel set among the pearl divers of LaPaz, in Baja California, Mexico, in an undetermined time, probably contemporary. At sixteen, Ramon Salazar becomes partner in the pearl dealership of his father, Blas, but his father disapproves of his real ambition, to dive for pearls. Partly Ramon dreams of diving for excitement, but partly to find a great pearl that will show up the braggart, Gaspar Ruiz, known as The Sevillano, the best diver in his father's fleet. While the fleet is out, Ramon persuades the Indian, Soto Luzon, to take him to his lagoon and teach him to dive, but the old man will not dive in the cave which he says belongs to Manta Diablo, a huge sea creature of such legendary fame that mothers scare their children into good behavior with stories about it. When Luzon injures his hand, Ramon goes alone to the cave and finds a black pearl of enormous size, 62.3 carats, which he takes home despite the Indian's warning that Manta Diablo will have it back. Unable to get the price he knows it is worth, Ramon's father summons Father Gallardo and gives the pearl to the church, to be displayed in the hand of the statue of the Virgin Mary. After a festival celebrating the gift, the fleet sets sail, confident that they are under special protection, but all the boats and men are lost except Gaspar Ruiz, who swims to safety. Reminded by Luzon that the pearl belongs to Manta Diablo, Ramon steals it from the church, takes it back to the cave, and throws it into the water, only to have Ruiz, who has followed him, dive in and retrieve it. Ruiz then makes Ramon his unwilling companion to sail to a distant market, where the name of Salazar will bring a better price, but their boat is followed by Manta Diablo. Ruiz spears it with a harpoon and, entangled in the harpoon rope, is dragged down by the dying manta. Ramon returns the pearl to the statue of the Virgin, now feeling that it is a true gift, not a bribe. As in other books by O'Dell, the narrator-hero is given to understatement, but the dramatic nature of the story makes a hero articulate about his own emotions less necessary in this than in others. The story gives a good sense of the culture of the Mexican people and of the difficulties and fascination of pearl diving. Choice; Fanfare; Newbery Honor.

BLANCO (*The Horse Talker**), realistic, sensitive, intelligent, middle-aged Mexican, captain of the mustangers, called Blanco because of his snow-white hair. Lan travels and works with his crew. Blanco is a firm, just commander, who has little liking for his work but sees it as a means to an end. He wishes to get enough money to build up his ranch in Mexico so that he, Marina*, and Miguel*, his daughter and son, can return there and live. He tries to help Lan see that the traditional Indian way of life is over. He takes the boy on his crew out of kindness but later becomes fond of him, though occasionally he becomes impatient, and even frustrated, with him, for example, when he learns that Lan has not been honest about his ability to "talk" to horses. Like Lan, Blanco is a respecter of animals, had lived as a captive of the Comanches, and belongs to more than one world.

BLIND EDDIE BELL (*The Soul Brothers and Sister Lou**), old, blind musician who plays guitar for the youth in Louretta Hawkins's club, teaches Lou how to chord on the piano, and instructs the young people in "soul music." A former recording artist with eminent jazz groups, Eddie has fallen on hard times, but he helps the quartet get started with the recording company that makes them famous. He also sets Fess's* lyrics to music.

BLOCH, MARIE HALUN (1910–   ), born in Komarno, Ukraine; writer whose best-known books reflect her native country, although she came to the United States when she was four and became a naturalized citizen in 1923. She lived in Cleveland, then Evanston, Ill., where she attended Northwestern University and later was graduated from the University of Chicago. She worked at one time as a junior economist for the Department of Labor in Washington, D.C. More recently she made her home in Denver, Colo., where she reviewed children's books in a regular column for the Denver *Post* and wrote several books about the Colorado mountains, including *Tony of the Ghost Towns* (Coward, 1956), *The House on Third High* (Coward, 1962), and *Mountains on the Move* (Coward, 1960). *Marya* (Coward, 1957), is about her own childhood as the daughter of immigrants and *The Dollhouse Story* (Walck, 1961) was originally written for her daughter. In 1960 she returned to the Ukraine for a visit; out of this experience have come several books, including *Ukrainian Folk Tales* (Coward, 1964), *Aunt America** (Atheneum, 1963), a story of the effect a visit from an American aunt has on a family in the Stalinist period following World War II, *The Two Worlds of Damyan* (Atheneum, 1966), and a historical novel set in tenth century Kiev, *Bern, Son of Mikula* (Atheneum, 1972).

BLOS, JOAN W(INSOR) (1928–   ), born in New York City; educator and author of books for children. She received the Newbery Award for her first published novel, *A Gathering of Days** (Scribner's, 1979), a young girl's journal of her life on a New England farm in the mid nineteenth century. This meticulously researched story is high in emotional appeal and conveys a clear and sympathetic picture of the times. She has also done picture books for the very young, among them, *Martin's Hats* (Morrow, 1984), in which a variety of headgear inspires a little boy to imagine himself having a series of exciting experiences. She has contributed numerous articles to periodicals like *School Library Journal* and *Merrill-Palmer Quarterly* and was United States editor for *Children's Literature in Education*. She was graduated from Vassar and studied psychology at Yale and City College of New York, from which she received her M.A. degree. She has been on the staff of the Bank Street College of Education in New York and has lectured in children's literature at the University of Michigan. Her professional life has revolved around teaching and writing. She regards herself as a teacher who once also wrote and now as a writer who also teaches. She lives in Ann Arbor, Mich., where she is often asked to speak for parents and professional groups on literature for the young. Her most recent book is *Brothers of the Heart* (Scribners, 1985), about the settlement of Southeastern Michigan.

BLOWFISH LIVE IN THE SEA (Fox*, Paula, Bradbury, 1970), realistic novel of family life set in the 1960s during the "hippie era" and the Viet Nam War in an urban area in the northeastern United States. Carrie, 12, lives in a big city apartment house with her mother, doctor father, and half-brother, Ben, 18. Ben is a long-haired, cynical school dropout, whose favorite expression is "blowfish live in the sea." Carrie loves Ben dearly, but he is often hard to understand and get along with. Her parents in particular find it hard to be patient with him, and there is a good deal of tension in the house. Carrie often feels like a punching bag, caught between her parents' and Ben's verbal thrusts and jabs, which if mostly good-natured can still be uncomfortable. When Ben's father, whom he has not seen since he was a child, invites him to spend the weekend with him in Boston, Ben asks Carrie to accompany him. After a wearying two-hundred-mile bus trip, the two discover that Ben's father is not at home in his skid row hotel room. The note he leaves says merely that he has been called away on business. As they are about to hop the bus for home, Ben has a hunch that they should go back to the hotel once more, and there they find Ben's father in his room, alone and half-drunk. Dan Felix has simply not had the courage to face his son. Although obviously low on funds, he puts on a bold front and insists on taking the two young people out to dinner at an expensive restaurant. The evening goes well, and they enjoy one another's company. Dan is a warm, ordinary man, footloose and free in spirit. He is a person with little sense of responsibility, who, he says, has never felt the need to be anything special. Ben soon adopts a protective, directive attitude toward his father. He decides to stay with Dan and help him fix up the ramshackle motel he has bought on the outskirts of Boston, his latest of many projects. Ben now has a purpose in life, and like the blowfish he has found a place of his own. This story of a youth's need to be needed offers humor and insights into contemporary family life. The simplistic conclusion undermines the very serious problems held up for consideration in the early part of the story. The plot is lean and some incidents seem improbable, and characters are one-sided and distorted for effect. Carrie reports events in a conversational tone, with natural, modern dialogue and some flashbacks. Choice; National Book Finalist.

BLUE, ROSE (1931–   ), born in New York City, surname originally Bluestone; author of realistic contemporary problem stories for middle readers. She is a graduate of Brooklyn College and has done graduate work at Bank

Street College of Education. As a teacher in New York public schools and in the Bedford-Stuyvesant Headstart program she saw the need for sympathetic treatment of younger children facing urban problems, and she has written about divorce, drug addiction, discrimination against minorities, and other topics which were formerly often limited to books for older children. *A Quiet Place* (Watts, 1969), her first book, is about a black child. Among her others are *A Month of Sundays* (Watts, 1972), *We Are Chicano* (Watts, 1973), and *Grandma Didn't Wave Back** (Watts, 1972), a brief novel concerning a child's difficulty in accepting her grandmother's senility, which appears on the *Choice* list. More recently she has written two non-fiction books, *Me and Einstein: Breaking Through the Reading Barrier* (Human Science Press, 1979) and *Bright Tomorrow* (Communication Skill, 1983), and has continued writing fiction, including *Cold Rain on the Water* (McGraw, 1979), for adolescents, and *My Mother the Witch* (McGraw, 1980).

THE BLUE SWORD (McKinley*, Robin, Greenwillow, 1982), fantasy set in an outlying section of a colonial country very like India in the Edwardian period. Harry* (Angharad) Crewe, presumably about eighteen, comes after the death of her father from the Homeland to Istan, a northern border town of Daria, where her very proper brother, Richard, is a junior military adjutant. She is given a home by Richard's superior, the stuffy District Commissioner, Sir Charles Greenough, and his wife, Lady Amelia, and is bored and restless with the round of teas and balls, for which she does not feel well suited. Rumors of strange powers used by the Damarians, the Hillpeople who are survivors of the old kingdom which has been subdued by Homeland, begin to reach her, but it is not until news of an impending uprising of the Northerners, half-human inhabitants of the country beyond the mountains, that she sees her first men from Damar. They are a group something like desert sheiks, riding magnificent horses and led by the magnetic king, Corlath*, who has come to Istan to seek help in holding the passes against their common enemies. Despite the efforts of Jack* Dedham, colonel in charge of Istan's garrison, Sir Charles refuses to believe in the imminent danger, and Corlath, insulted and furious, starts to leave, catching Harry's eye as he strides down the verandah steps. Later, he realizes that his *kelar*, his special extrasensory magical gift, has told him that he must have the girl on his side, and he returns secretly and steals her in the night. Harry is more bemused than frightened to find herself riding north with the Hillpeople and their king and to discover that when she sips the ritual drink, the Water of Sight, she has prophetic visions and can speak the Old Tongue of Damar. She is treated with respect, given a fine hill horse, and trained in sword play and riding by Mathin*, reticent but patient older member of Corlath's elite guard, the king's Riders. At the annual trials before the king's city, Harry takes first place, defeated only by Corlath himself, and is initiated as a king's Rider and given the sword Gonturim with a blue jewel in its hilt, the weapon that belonged to Lady Aerin, the legendary hero known as Firehair and Dragon-Killer, who seems to be guiding Harry in her visions and accomplishments. Corlath sees the threat from the north as coming mainly through the eastern mountains and sets off with his force, swollen by men and women from tribes which have not sworn allegiance to the king in generations, but still pitifully few against the horde of Northerners. When Harry tries to remind him of the narrow western pass, Ritger's Gap or the Madamer gate north of Istan, he angrily says the Outlanders, as they call the Homelanders, can take care of any Northerners who enter there. Harry's *kelar* tells her that this is folly, and reluctantly she sneaks off alone to warn the garrison at Istan. She is followed by her hunting cat, Narkon, and two young warriors, both of whom are devoted to her. At the fort she is at first denied entrance, but when she is able to talk to Jack Dedham, he astonishes her by agreeing with her and joining her group, along with some dozen of his older soldiers, although it is strictly against orders from headquarters and means court martial if they ever return. He also tells her, quite casually, since he thinks she already knows, that her *kelar* comes to her naturally since her great-great-grandmother was a Hillwoman, a fact that her family had kept a secret from her. In the north they are welcomed and recruit some more followers, but their force is extremely small against the less-than-human thousands from the North. At Ritger's Gap they are joined to Harry's surprise by her brother Richard, who has returned from a diplomatic mission, learned of her visit, and deserted to join her. In a brief sortie from the gate, they engage the advance forces, and Harry has a personal duel with Thurra, their demon leader, and manages to tear down his standard before her force must retreat to the gate. There they hope only to hold the enemy back a few days, at most, but as they rest and await attack, Harry, led by her *kelar*, climbs to a point overlooking the valley where the enemy approaches, raises her sword, and calls upon Aerin and Corlath for help. Blue lightning leaps from the blade, the thunder sounds, and the mountains collapse, burying the host of Northerners. Stunned and unbelieving, Harry is found by her friends, and they start the journey to join Corlath's army, though she is afraid of his anger and rejection because she deserted him. When they meet, however, his *kelar* has told him what happened, and he pledges his love to her. She reciprocates. The Homelanders who have followed her come to live with the Hillpeople, but eventually Harry opens diplomatic relations with Istan by naming her daughter after Lady Amelia. The ambitious story starts off well with an interesting situation, but what is evidently a desire to make feminist statements and to introduce elements as a foundation for further novels in a series about Damar makes the story lose some of its force toward the end. The defection of conventional Richard to join Harry's group is unconvincing, and the collapse of the mountains is reminiscent of the climax of Tolkien's *Lord of the Rings*. Fanfare.

BLUME, JUDY (SUSSMAN KITCHENS) (1938–   ), born in Elizabeth, N.J.; writer of over a dozen contemporary novels for children and young people controversial with adults and very popular with their young audiences because they are frank, breezy, and amusing. She began writing freelance after her children were in school, and her books are based on her memories of her own childhood experiences and on her observations of the behavior and attitudes of other children while growing up. *Are You There God? It's Me, Margaret.** (Bradbury, 1970), her third published book, catapulted her to fame and is of her novels still the most widely read. It describes an eleven-year-old girl's worries about menstruation, bosoms, and religion and has been recommended by *Choice*. Its male counterpart is *Then Again Maybe I Won't* (Bradbury, 1971), about a boy's concerns with wet dreams, erections, and shoplifting. *Deenie* (Bradbury, 1974) leans in a moralistic direction to relate how young Deenie develops empathy for others who have problems as she learns to deal with her own handicap of spinal curvature. In the *Choice* book, *It's Not the End of the World** (Bradbury, 1972), a twelve-year-old girl describes the effect on her family when her parents decide to get a divorce. Also didactic is *Forever* (Bradbury, 1975), a low-key, realistic depiction for teenaged readers of a high school love affair, often classified as an adult book. Widely enjoyed by younger readers is the humorous *Tales of a Fourth Grade Nothing* (Dutton, 1972), which episodically relates "Awful Incidents" in the life of nine-year-old Peter, whose greatest life burden is his little brother, Fudge, 2. Among her other novels are the largely autobiographical *Starring Sally J. Freedman as Herself* (Bradbury, 1977), *Super Fudge* (Dutton, 1980), and *Tiger Eyes* (Bradbury, 1981). Blume's novels often employ first person and are simplistic in character and situation. Her adult characters in particular are often satirized for sensation, her plots contrived and overburdened with themes, and her humor heavyhanded. She took her B.A. degree from New York University. Her children now in college, she spends part of the year at her suburban home in Los Alamos, N.Mex., and part in her New York City apartment. She is a frequent speaker at conferences of teachers and librarians and those interested in contemporary literature for children and young people.

A BOAT TO NOWHERE (Wartski*, Maureen Crane, ill. Dick Teicher, Westminster, 1980), realistic historical novel dealing with the refugees from Vietnam on the Gulf of Siam in the 1970s after the Communist takeover of South Vietnam. Mai and her little brother, Loc, have lived in the tiny isolated village of six families since they fled the city with their grandfather, Thay (teacher) Van Chi, when Loc was an infant. Hong, wife of Big Tam, cares for them, and Van Chi, an educated man who has travelled widely in his youth, works with the other adults and teaches the entire village from his knowledge of history, geography, and traditional lore, but he does not mention the war or the events of recent years. Into this little pocket of tranquility near the southern tip of the country stumbles a boy named Kien*, older than Mai, perhaps fourteen or fifteen, a city-bred orphan who has lived by his wits, impudent, disrespectful, very hungry. At first he jeers at the simple villagers, but he works hard and wins the trust of the adults, even Big Tam, who lets Kien sail his precious boat, the *Sea Breeze*, when he himself is injured. Only to Mai does Kien stay cynical, and she distrusts him, but he seems to be trying to mend bridges when he takes her and Loc sailing one day. They get into a storm and lose the precious fishing net, nearly get swept out to sea, and finally beach the boat some distance from the village. They return home to an even greater catastrophe: the agents of the new government have arrived, led by a doctrinaire woman, who informs them that their tax will be fifty percent of all they grow or catch, and who burns Thay Van Chi's precious books and arrests him to be taken to a "reeducation center." Only Kien seems to greet them eagerly, but he confuses Mai by claiming that the boat has been wrecked. That night he gets permission to guard the teacher and persuades him that they, with Mai and Loc, should flee. They get to the boat just as they are about to be recaptured and set out with little food or water and only the grandfather's navigational skills to head for Thailand. After surviving several terrible storms they arrive almost starving, only to be met by a police boat charged with preventing boat people from landing. A few kindly women bring them food, but even when Mai tries to give them Loc so that he will have a chance to survive, none of them are allowed to land. They set off again hoping to reach Malaysia, but they are beset by storms, illness, and pirates, who riddle their sail with bullets, destroy their mast, and throw Loc into shark-infested waters. Kien saves him, and with Grandfather very ill, they drift to an island inhabited by rough outcasts whose boat has been wrecked there. Kien realizes that their seeming kindness, giving food and medicine for Van Chi, is just to get the boat, which they plan to repair and sail off in, abandoning the family. Kien executes an escape first, and they sail off again with only a little food, into the beginning of the monsoon storms. Once a ship sights them but will not pick them up. Kien dives in and swims after it, and the sailors throw him a life raft, but when he realizes that the others will be abandoned, he lets go and returns to the *Sea Breeze*. In the terrible days that follow Grandfather dies and Mai becomes very ill. When an American ship finally picks them up, they are almost too far gone to care, but the reader is left with hope that they will be nursed to health and sponsored by the ship's officer to come to America. Although all the book is told in third person, the first part is from the point of view of Mai, a competent, bright, and ultimately courageous girl of undetermined age, perhaps twelve. From the time they set off for Thailand, the point of view switches to Kien, a much more complex character. His gradual integration into the family as he takes responsibility for and begins to love the others is the main psychological theme. The storm, hunger, and physical exhaustion are so well depicted that a reader feels the inevitability of their failure and death. The final rescue, therefore, is not particularly convincing and comes, ironically, almost as an anti-climax. Sequel is *A Long Way from Home* (Westminster, 1980). Child Study.

BOBBIE WALKER (*Time at the Top**), Vicky's* brother, Susan* Shaw's friend, a chubby, always hungry, twelve-year-old who wants to go to military school and become a soldier. He provides food and muscle for the treasure hunt. His full name is Robert Lincoln Walker.

BOND, NANCY (BARBARA) (1945–   ), born in Bethesda, Md.; librarian and author of books for children and young people. The daughter of a librarian and an elementary school teacher, she grew up in Concord, Mass., and received her B.A. degree from Mount Holyoke College. She lived for several years in the British Isles, where she attended the College of Librarianship in Aberystwyth, Wales, taking her diploma of librarianship in 1972. She was a member of the promotional staff of Oxford University Press in London from 1967–1968, then returned to the United States where she took a position as children's librarian and was two years director of a library in Massachusetts. Her first book, *A String in the Harp** (Atheneum, 1976), a fantasy improvising on Welsh folklore, was a Newbery honor book and a *Boston Globe-Horn Book* honor book, received the International Reading Association Award, and was a Fanfare book. *Country of Broken Stone* (Atheneum, 1980) is a realistic novel set at an archeological dig in northern England, while *The Best of Enemies* (Atheneum, 1978), *The Voyage Begun** (Atheneum, 1981), a *Boston Globe-Horn Book* honor book, and *A Place to Come Back To* (Atheneum, 1984), all take place in the United States, *Voyage* in the future after pollution and energy limitations have resulted in a much reduced standard of living for Americans. *A Place to Come Back To* is a sensitive, detailed novel of responsibility and friendship that returns to the characters and setting of *The Best of Enemies* to find the four friends of the first book now in high school. Although her books are sometimes ponderous with detail and occasionally didactic, they are credible in character and situations, project a keen sense of time and place, and deal especially convincingly with family relationships.

BOND OF THE FIRE (Fon Eisen*, Anthony, World, 1965), historical novel with animal story aspects set at the end of the last Glacial Age in Europe. Ash, sixteen-year-old hunter, acquires a dog, the first of his primitive, cave-dwelling tribe to have such a companion in work and leisure. Through the dog Ash has experiences that awaken him to new possibilities in life. Caught alone after dark on a hunt, Ash builds a fire for safety and is joined by a strange wolf-like creature hungry for company. The two seem instinctively to be bonded by the fire, and the youth names his new friend, Arkla, the "animal-who-talks." The dog, the author informs the reader, is the sole survivor of a nomadic tribe from the east. Although some members of Ash's tribe are suspicious of Arkla at first, the dog soon proves his worth. An accomplished hunter, Arkla helps Ash hunt aurochs and deer and escape from the dread wild boars, fights with him against wolves, and assists in diverting bison on their annual migration into traps in sufficient number to fill the tribe's winter storage cave with more meat than ever before. One tribesman covets the dog so much when he realizes his potential that he offers Ash his daughter, Oona, in marriage in exchange for the creature, but Ash declines. For Ash their greatest adventure together involves capturing the she-wolf Rascha. Eventually Rascha and Arkla have seven puppies that Ash plans to train to hunt like their father. For the tribe the most serious event that occurs involves a flood that results when the river rises with a tremendous surge from melting ice. The water destroys the storage cave and wipes out many cave homes. Game becomes extremely scarce, and, when even the most experienced hunters are unsuccessful and the tribe faces certain starvation, Arkla is instrumental in their survival. On a hunt, Ash and some companions discover the bodies of deer that wolves have driven over a cliff. The hunters seize the deer, then are attacked by several wolf packs combined. Even though Ash resourcefully manages to drive off the wolves by using fire against their leader, the hunters realize they will need help in getting the meat home. Ash sends Arkla with a message to his grandfather, Fire-maker, and a rescue party arrives just in time, to demonstrate still further how useful Arkla is. The hard winter over, Ash plans to travel and see what lies beyond the horizon, accompanied by Oona and his faithful, clever Arkla. The plot employs conventions common to animal stories and as a whole lacks urgency. Scenes stand out—the dog coming to the fire, the death and burial of Like-a-fawn, Ash's aged grandmother, the capture of the bison, and the stand against the wolves, among others. The author recreates with conviction the ancient way of life. Most characters are undeveloped, and Ash is a blameless, resourceful youth, who is quick to capitalize on his new acquisition. He is shown as being more intelligent than most of his tribespeople. An interesting, unexploited character is Fire-maker, the grandfather, a respected elder of the tribe, wise in the ways of people and the land, and a support to the young man. Lewis Carroll.

BONHAM, FRANK (1914–   ), born in Los Angeles, Calif.; author of adventure, mystery, and problem novels, the most successful of which have been concerned with minority characters in contemporary urban settings. He attended Glendale Junior College and has made his home in La Jolla, Calif. Ironically, he credits asthma with forcing him to leave college and to choose writing as a career rather than some more physically active pursuit. Since 1948 he has published widely for adults and young people—novels, television scripts, and magazine stories and articles—mostly realism set in the twentieth century, though *The Missing Persons League* (Dutton, 1976) is science fiction and *The Golden Bees of Tulami* (Dutton, 1974) is fantasy. His first novel for young people was *Burma Rifles* (Crowell, 1960), a story of the Niseis with Merrill's Marauders in World War II. Among his mysteries are *Honor Bound** (Crowell, 1963), concerned with the intrigue in the attempt to bring California into the Union as a slave state, *The Mystery of the Red Tide** (Dutton, 1966), concerned with getting marine biology specimens in the San Diego area, and *Mystery of the Fat Cat** (Dutton, 1968), about urban kids' efforts to save their dilapidated youth center, all nominees for the Edgar Allan Poe Award. Probably his best known novel is *Durango Street** (Dutton, 1965), about black youth gangs in Los Angeles. Among others with urban settings are *The Nitty Gritty* (Dutton, 1968) and *Viva Chicano* (Dutton, 1970). Two more recent novels are *Gimme an H, Gimme an E, Gimme an L, Gimme a P* (Scribner's, 1980), about a suicidal teenager, and *The Forever Formula* (Dutton, 1979), a futuristic fantasy.

THE BOOK OF THREE (Alexander*, Lloyd, Holt, 1964), fantasy set in the mythical realm of Prydain*, the first in a series featuring Taran*, a youth of unknown parentage who seeks to become a hero, and improvising upon stories from Welsh mythology. Taran lives at Caer Dallben, the farmstead belonging to Dallben, the enchanter who has raised him from infancy. His mentor is Coll, Dallben's farm manager, whom Taran serves as Assistant Pig-Keeper. Taran's particular responsibility is taking care of Hen Wen, the oracular pig of Prydain. The plot starts soon after Dallben tells Taran that evil forces are abroad in Prydain. Then Hen Wen burrows out of her pen and runs away. Impulsively, Taran follows her into the forests, where he soon encounters the terrifying band of warriors led by the dread Horned (antlered) King. He is rescued by Prince Gwydion, one of the Sons of Don and Taran's special hero. Gwydion has traveled to Caer Dallben to consult Hen Wen about combatting the Horned King. The pair soon encounter Gurgi*, a hairy, good-hearted creature who advises them of Hen Wen's route and accompanies them in seeking her. They are soon captured by the Cauldron-Born*, the terrible dead warriors revivified by Arawn the War Lord to fight his battles, and are taken to the Spiral Castle of the evil enchantress, Queen Achren. Separated from his friends, Taran is cast into the dungeon, from which he is rescued by spunky, golden-haired Princess Eilonwy*, now Achren's unwilling ward. On their way out through underground passages, they encounter a majestic figure lying on a stone slab surrounded by a circle of ancient, dead warriors. Eilonwy takes the sword, Drynwyn*, from the hand of the dead king, and she and Taran make it to freedom just before an earthquake demolishes the castle. Taran proceeds on with Eilonwy, Gurgi, and Fflewddur* Fflam, a king traveling as a bard. Believing Gwydion dead, Taran decides to give up his quest for Hen Wen and carry the news of the uprising to the capital, Caer Dathyl, instead. Gurgi breaks his leg, and the four soon run short of supplies. They are first helped by Medwyn, a kindly farmer, who is the special friend of animals, and later by grumpish, excitable King Eiddileg of the Fair Folk (dwarves), who gives them the dwarf Doli* as guide. When near Caer Dathyl they observe the Horned King's forces about to attack the city. Taran valiantly charges them on horseback. He draws Drynwyn, which leaps from his hand and sears him with its flame. At the critical moment, Gwydion appears and destroys the Horned King by shouting out his secret name. Gwydion bestows upon the companions rewards for valor, but all the sobered Taran really wants now is the peace and comfort of home. Hen Wen arrives home at Caer Dallben safely. It was she who provided Prince Gwydion with the Horned King's secret name, the means by which the evil king was destroyed. All the characters except Gwydion are touched with the comic, sometimes incongruously so, and Gurgi and Fflewddur Fflam in particular provide comic relief. Taran changes expectedly through his experiences, and Eilonwy's spunkiness makes her an attractive figure. The novel offers plenty of adventure and action and some suspense, but episodes are overly many and underdeveloped. Tone is more humorous than heroic, and the plot seems stretched out. (Golden* Peledryn) Books Too Good; ChLA Touchstones; Choice; Contemporary Classics; Fanfare.

BORINA, MAESTOSO (*White Stallion of Lipizza**), most famous dressage horse in the Spanish Court Riding School in Vienna, the world champion *courbetteur*, performer of a very difficult dressage movement involving a leap on the hind legs. In the novel, Borina is getting on in years when Hans Haupt becomes his rider. The horse has a fine ear for music and an excellent stage sense. He becomes the hit of the show when he contributes a *courbette* to the climax of the opera, *The Girl of the Golden West*, starring the beautiful and talented Madame Jeritza. Maestoso is his family name; Borina is his call name, the one Hans uses.

BOSS (*The Loner**), the woman who rescues David, names him, and gives him a home on her Montana ranch. She is rigid in her requirement that the sheep come first in their lives. Though she is good to David in the physical sense, she fails him spiritually and intellectually. She compares David unfavorably with her son, Ben, and demands a standard of performance with the sheep that David is not ready by training or inclination to give. An inarticulate woman, she longs to be able to express her feelings with greater ease and facility. Because she is unable to express herself, tension grows between her and the boy. Eventually, through her association with the boy, she becomes less of a loner, too.

BOSTON RITZ HOTEL (*The Trumpet of the Swan**), the place where Louis*, the mute swan, spends the night when employed as a one-hundred-dollar-a-week jazz musician on the swan boats in the Boston Public Garden. He dines elegantly on twelve watercress sandwiches, for which he graciously tips the waiter, and sleeps floating on water in the bathtub. Droll humor and carefully worked out details make this incongruous incident completely believable and one of the novel's most amusing moments.

BOWIE, JIM (*Their Shining Hour**), actual historical figure. In the novel, he is seen through Susanna* Dickenson's eyes as a kind, stalwart leader of the Texans' resistance against the Mexicans. He refuses to blow up the Alamo as Sam Houston has ordered him to do, instinctively recognizing the symbolic significance of making a stand at the old mission in the total war for independence. He is killed when the mission falls. Although a sick man, he fights to the finish.

A BOY OF OLD PRAGUE (Ish-Kishor*, Sulamith, ill. Ben Shahn, Pantheon, 1963), ironic period novel set in Prague in the mid–1500s about the hatred of the Christians for the Jews. A wiser Tomás looks back upon the events that lead to his becoming a clerk in a monastery. The eldest son in a family of half-starved, overworked serfs on the domain of proud, handsome, self-indulgent Lord Rainier near Prague, Tomás accepts without question the harshness of the feudal system and the stories of atrocities presumably committed by the Jews of the Prague ghetto. When Tomás removes a thorn from the paw of one of his master's favorite hunting dogs, he is rewarded with a position in the castle kitchen. When he is caught stealing a chicken to take to his starving mother, the lord first sentences the youth to be hanged, then changes his mind and orders him turned over to an old Jewish moneylender to whom the lord is indebted and to whom he has promised a bond servant. His head buzzing with stories of unspeakable atrocities attributed to the Jews, Tomás is so terror-stricken he is barely conscious when he arrives at the ghetto. To his immense surprise and relief, the Jews accept him as "the stranger within their gates," and ensuing weeks find him becoming quite fond of them. He has a room of his own for the first time in his life, and also for the first time he has enough to eat. He even sits at the same table and eats the same food as his master, the elderly Pesach ben Leib, his small grandson, Joseph, his granddaughter, Rachel, and their servingwoman, old Miriam. When pretty Rachel rejects the suit of Lord Rainier, the lord angrily takes revenge by inciting the Christians of Prague against the ghetto. Terrible carnage ensues as the crazed mobs turn the choked ghetto into a human bonfire. Things so fall out that Tomás rescues the lord's page, Lucien, from the flames, and in gratitude Lucien secures for Tomás the position in the monastery. A taut, understated style and unrelentingly even pace help to compensate for the one-dimensional characters, tailored events, and obvious message in this starkly dramatic and haunting account of how an intelligent if ignorant youth ironically finds loving kindness among those he has been taught to despise and fear. Choice; Fanfare.

BRADLEY, DUANE (1914–   ), born in Clarinda, Iowa; writer of a variety of books for young people, mostly non-fiction. She was educated in public schools, worked on newspapers in California, married George Sanborn, and has lived in Rhode Island, Washington, Delaware, and New Hampshire. Besides *Meeting with a Stranger** (Lippincott, 1964), a problem novel set in modern Ethiopia which won the Jane Addams Award, she wrote *Engineers Did It!* (Lippincott, 1958), which has been translated into Persian and Arabic, *The Newspaper: Its Place in Democracy* (Van Nostrand, 1965), which has been translated into French, and a number of books on science and sewing.

BRAD WILLETS (*The Cat and Mrs. Cary**), brave, forthright nephew of Mrs. Cary, who comes to stay with her for the summer to recuperate from a severe virus infection. He is well mannered and likes books, particularly on space. He learns to adjust to new situations and to look beyond surface appearances. He helps Mrs. Cary find the treasure and learn to appreciate her family.

BRADY (Fritz*†, Jean, ill. Lynd Ward, Coward, 1960), historical novel set in a farming area in southeastern Pennsylvania. Until the summer of 1836, happy-go-lucky, garrulous Brady Minton, about fourteen, has given little thought to the subject of slavery. He knows his Virginia-born mother favors it and that his father, Thaddeus, a minister and farmer, and his Uncle Earl, the sheriff, oppose it. Brady prefers prowling the woods, hunting, and fishing with his pal, Range Hadley, to thinking about social issues. He prattles on at dinner one day about how he and Range have discovered that Drover* Hull's secluded cabin is an Underground Railroad station. When his father severely reprimands him for his chatter and forbids him to discuss the matter further and his older brother, Matt, points out that the Underground Railroad is a matter of life and death, not a subject for idle chitchat, Brady realizes that his family thinks he is too irresponsible to be trusted with important secrets. Then a slave catcher and an abolitionist preacher visit the region, and feeling about slavery begins to run high. Mr. Minton preaches a sermon against it, and some church members sign a petition rejecting his leadership. Bill Williams, a shiftless but vocal demagogue, decides to run for sheriff against Uncle Earl, and signs vilifying the Mintons appear. Then Brady discovers a runaway black youth, Moss, in his father's Sermon House, the outbuilding Mr. Minton uses as a study, and Brady realizes that the Minton farm is also a station on the Railroad. He now realizes too that his father, Uncle Earl, and Parley* Potter, the itinerant clock repairman who occasionally visits their farm and with whom his father and Uncle Earl have long conversations, are agents by which slaves reach freedom. While visiting Matt at the college where Matt teaches, Brady encounters the slave catcher again, and, fearing that the man will discover Moss, Brady races home. When arsonists set the Minton barn afire, Mr. Minton is injured, and Brady realizes he must assume the responsibility for moving Moss to the next station. Brady has cast his lot with the abolitionists and has learned to curb his tongue. The author successfully combines Brady's problems in growing up with the social and political issues of the times. Although the story starts slowly and moves unevenly and some events occur altogether too felicitously, the novel is rich in details of family and rural life of the period and presents Brady's changing thoughts and feelings very convincingly. The story excels in showing how sentiment ran high in border country. (Tar* Adams) Choice.

BRAN DAVIES (*The Grey King**), white-haired youth of mysterious background raised as the son of Owen Davies, farmhand of Will* Stanton's Welsh uncle. Brave, intelligent, talented on the harp, he helps Will win the golden harp with which the Six Sleepers are awakened by correctly answering a riddle put to him by a lord inside the mountain. He and Will learn that he is the son of King Arthur, brought with his mother, Guinevere, forward in time for their protection by Merriman* Lyon. Bran's dog, Cafall, shot by Caradog Prichard, the agent of the villainous Grey King, was named by Owen after Arthur's dog. Bran also appears in *Silver on the Tree*, the last book in the series, where he cuts the mistletoe from the Midsummer Tree with the shining sword to defeat the Dark but chooses to live with those he has come to love in the twentieth century rather than return to Arthur's time.

BRANSCUM, ROBBIE (1937–   ), writer of regional novels for children and young people. She was born near Big Flats, Ark., the daughter of a farmer. She and her four brothers and sisters were raised by their grandparents on a small dirt farm in the Arkansas hills. Her only formal education was in a one-room country school, and the backwoods life she lived as she grew up has inspired her novels. Strong in their picture of mountain life, they employ humor, the colorful colloquialisms and rural imagery of the area, and a reminiscent tone, and successfully convey the vitality, courage, and inner resource of the people who live there. Her dozen and a half published novels include an autobiographical trilogy that has attracted critical attention, *Toby, Granny, and George* (Doubleday, 1976), *Toby Alone* (Doubleday, 1978), and *Toby and Johnny Joe* (Doubleday, 1979), about a mountain girl growing up with her grandmother and her romance with a young man who is killed in World World II. Winner of the Edgar Allan Poe Award is *The Murder of Hound Dog Bates** (Viking, 1982), a humorous mystery rich in regional flavor about how a boy's determined attempts to find out who killed his dog result in deeper understanding of his guardian aunts and changes in all their lives. *Cheater and Flitter Dick* (Viking, 1983) concerns Arkansas sharecroppers forced by disastrous circumstances to take into their home the family and servants of their landowner. More recent is *The Adventures of Johnny May* (Harper, 1984), also set in the Arkansas hills, which tells how an eleven-year-old girl copes with complications in her life at Christmas time. Branscum is often invited to speak on writing books for children, has made her home in California, and now lives in Eufaula, Okla.

BRETT KINGSMAN (*Up a Road Slowly**), Julie Trelling's temporary sweetheart and foil to Danny* Trevort. Country-reared Julie has had no opportunity to date, and, at sixteen, she falls madly in love with Brett, handsome, smooth-talking, new boy in school, for whose attention all the girls vie. Brett sweeps naive Julie off her feet, rushing her because he wishes her help in getting through his classes, particularly English composition, in which he is simply too lazy to apply himself. The realization that he has been using her is very damaging to Julie's ego. Brett is a phony figure, hard to accept as presented, and a too obvious foil to Danny Trevort.

BRIAN FAHERTY (*Shadrach's Crossing**), Shadrach Faherty's younger brother of eleven, who spies on him, tattles about what he sees and hears, and gets him into deep trouble with his parents, who have forbidden him to go out at night and generally to spy on the smugglers. Brian eventually joins Shad in the hazardous enterprise of bringing the smugglers to justice. Even as Brian provides moral support for Shad, he causes him trouble, since the younger boy is smaller and weaker and so is easily captured and lacks the strength to wade the shallows.

BRIDGER, MARY ANN, HELEN MEEK, DAVID MALIN (*Cayuse Courage**), half-Indian, half-white foster children of Marcus and Narcissa Whitman*, with whom Samuel becomes friends while he lives with the Whitmans. In particular, he develops a fondness for Mary Ann, the daughter of trapper Jim Bridger. She accepts Samuel without reservation and helps to nurse him back to health. A lively, outgoing girl, she teaches Samuel English in return for his teaching her Cayuse. His knowledge of English eventually makes it possible for him to become an interpreter. Samuel warns her during the uprising and thus she and the others escape the slaughter. Later the Indians bring her and the other two children into their camp, because the children are half-breeds, but finally the three are taken to the British.

BRIDGERS, SUE ELLEN (1942–   ), born in Greenville, N.C.; author whose novels reflect her interest in family relationships and in small southern towns and rural areas. She was graduated from Western Carolina University and has lived, with her husband and three children, in Sylva, N.C. Her novel, *All Together Now** (Knopf, 1979) won the Christopher award; it is the story of a summer friendship between a twelve-year-old girl and a retarded man, and of the lives that their friendship affects. She also received favorable critical comment for *Home before Dark* (Knopf, 1976), a novel in which a migrant family returns to the father's childhood home and which shows a nostalgic appreciation of the Carolina area where she has lived. More recently she has published *Notes for Another Life* (Knopf, 1981), about a brother and sister, both teenagers, who live with their grandmother because their father is in a mental hospital and their mother works in a distant city.

BRIDGET GUNTHER (*The Velvet Room**), Bonita McCurdy, the old woman who lives in the little stone cottage near the Las Palmeras mansion and whose special friends are birds and animals. While the children in the migrant village call her the *bruja*, witch, and avoid her, Bridget becomes Robin Williams's good friend and confidante. Hers is a strange story. Once she lived in the mansion as the daughter of the house, but she bravely and impulsively ran away to avoid causing a rift in the family, worked as a governess for a German immigrant family, married an artist, and returned in later life to take a position with her own cousin, Mr. McCurdy, as nursemaid to his daughter, Gwen*. Neither Gwen nor her mother nor anyone else in the area knows who Bridget really is, and Mr. McCurdy, who now runs the ranch, has out of respect for her wishes kept her identity secret. She is a stock figure of romance.

BRIDGE TO TERABITHIA (Paterson*, Katherine, ill. Donna Diamond, Crowell, 1977), realistic novel concerning friendship and death set in the country near Washington, D.C., probably in Maryland, in the late 1960s or early 1970s. Until the new family moves into the old Perkins place on the next farm, Jesse* Aarons, 10, has had no one with whom to share his interests, his fascination with drawing and love of music. Even his desire to be the best runner in the fifth grade, which he practices early mornings in the cow pasture, is known only to his skinny little sister, May Belle, 6. His laborer father is gone all day, his mother is overworked with the farm and baby Joyce Ann, and she gives in too easily to her loud, manipulative older daughters, Ellie and Brenda, leaving most of the work around the place to Jess. At first he isn't sure whether his new neighbor, Leslie* Burke, is girl or boy with her short hair, jeans, and sneakers, and at school he tries to avoid her because she doesn't fit in: she insists on racing with boys and, worse, beats them all; she writes about scuba diving as her favorite pastime; she admits publicly that they have no television at their house. When he saves her from the bullying seventh grader, Janice Avery, who is about to evict her violently from the favored back seat of the bus, he begins to learn more about her, how her parents, Judy and Bill, both writers for whom "money is not a problem," have moved to the country after "reassessing their values." Jess and Leslie become fast friends and build a hut in the woods, making up a magic world they call Terabithia, which they enter by swinging across a ditch on a rope tied to a tree branch. Leslie, who is articulate and has read widely, leads in all their play, developing a special formal language for Terabithia and telling Jess stories from books. At her home he sees for the first time people who live with books and music and the world of the mind. She admires his ability to draw, a skill discouraged at home because it wastes time and his father is afraid he'll be a sissy. At Christmas, after agonizing about what to give Leslie, he finds a free puppy, which she names Prince Terrien and they call PT. When Janice Avery steals May Belle's lunch treat, they get even by writing a love note, supposed to be from a boy Janice admires, but later, when Leslie finds Janice weeping in the girls' lavatory because her friends have found out that her father beats her, she comforts the older girl and makes a "half friend." After a spell of rainy days which have swollen the creek in the ditch so much that Jess fears to swing across it, his young, unconventional music teacher takes him to Washington, to the National Gallery and the Smithsonian. It is the best day he has ever had, but he returns to learn that Leslie has been killed when the rope broke as she was swinging to Terabithia. Leslie's parents move away, and, after May Belle, following him on a fallen branch that crosses the ditch, gets stuck and nearly falls, Jess builds a bridge to Terabithia and prepares to share his secret place with his little sister. The strength of the story lies in Jess's realistic and moving reaction to Leslie's death, his initial refusal to believe it, his anger at her for leaving him, his moment of pride that he will be singled out as her friend, his realization that he will now be the best runner in the fifth grade, his feeling of guilt, and his final, stormy, sobbing grief, which his inarticulate father helps him accept. There are also good characterizations of even the minor characters in the story and a strong sense of the conflicts in the poverty-stricken Aarons family. Less strong is the predictability of the plot and an elitist point of view which may make some readers uncomfortable. Contemporary Classics; Fanfare; Lewis Carroll; Newbery Winner.

BRIGHT MORNING (*Sing Down the Moon**), Navaho girl who is sold into slavery by Spaniards, escapes, and is driven with her people into relocation at Fort Sumner. In a culture where the wealth in the form of sheep is owned by the women, she is sought after despite not being considered a beauty. Her independence and spirit are best shown during the death march when, against the advice of her family, she carries a little girl belonging to a stranger who has two young children, shares her meagre food with the child, and grieves when the little girl dies. At the Bosque Redondo, where the Navahos are confined, she plans escape and waits for the opportunity, though she cannot persuade her husband, Tall* Boy, to join in her hopes until he must flee for his life. Even then it is Bright Morning who engineers the escape and who leads them to Hidden Canyon, where they can start life again with their infant son and with the remnants of her flock of sheep.

BRIGITTE (*The Happy Orpheline*†; *A Brother for the Orphelines*†; *A Pet for the Orphelines**), one of the twenty little girls who are orphans in a French village. In the first book she is accidentally separated from the others and has a strange adventure with a couple who think they are the rightful king and queen of France. Although she is a supporting character in the next two books, it is her choice of a cat which finally prevails in *A Pet for the Orphelines*.

BRISTLE FACE (Ball*, Zachary, Holiday, 1962), dog story set in Mississippi, about two hundred miles south of Memphis, around 1900. Having run away from a brutal uncle, Jase Landers, 14, comes upon a strange-looking dog with bristly hairs growing from his nose and unusual, glassy-looking eyes. Without much encouragement, the dog follows him to the little country store run by Lute* Swank, where Jase is given his first square meal in days, a place to sleep, and eventually a real home. Lute, though lazy and easygoing, has decided to run for sheriff against Red Toler, long-time incumbent, an unpleasant red-neck type. Lute's ambition is spurred by his boast to the good-looking Amazonian widow, Pansy Jarkey, who runs her farm single-handed and can outwork Lute easily. Bristle Face, as they call the dog, endears himself to the widow by tracing the route of the red sow through a hollow log into her oat patch. Against all expectations he also proves to be a fine fox hound, despite his puppyish ways. This frivolity is knocked out of him when he fights and kills a panther about to attack Jase. Red Toler, hoping to depict Lute as a harborer of a thief, declares that the dog must be a valuable animal lost by a Mr. Rinders some thirty miles south and holds a test to prove it. Old Emory Packer, who knows more about dogs than any man in the area, tests his response to a hunting horn and finds that he ignores it, but privately lets Lute and Jase know that the dog may be from a line of Irish dogs being bred as fox hounds. Lute risks his reputation by betting with a large group of men that Bristle Face will lead the pack and that the widow's little white Toots will come in second, then when he wins, giving all the money back to prove he wouldn't be dishonest as sheriff. Disaster comes to Bristle Face when he follows a fox that won't hole up, and since he can't be horned off the trail, he runs until the fox dies and the dog is so badly strained he is blinded. Emory chloroforms him, and Jase, grieving, decides to set out again for Memphis, but first travels south to tell Rinders about the dog. There he finds Lute, who has already bought him one of Rinders's bristle-faced young dogs and who takes Jase home to live with him and the widow, whom he is marrying, having been elected sheriff. The story has the easygoing pace of the southern setting, with a good deal of humor and a minimum of tension. Even the death of Bristle Face is less harrowing and less sentimental than the death of a loved pet in most stories. Scenes of fox chases are vivid, the strongest parts of the book. Choice.

BRITTAIN, BILL (WILLIAM BRITTAIN) (1930–   ), born in Rochester, N.Y.; teacher, mystery writer, author of fantasies for young people. He attended Colgate University, received his B.S. degree from New York State University at Brockport, and his M.S. degree from Hofstra University. He has taught English at LeRoy, N.Y., elementary school in Lawrence, N.Y., and remedial reading in Lawrence Junior High. Sometimes using the pseudonym of James Knox, he has contributed stories to *Ellery Queen's Mystery Magazine* and *Alfred Hitch-cock's Mystery Magazine*, some of them featuring a series detective, Mr. Strang, a high school science teacher. His *All the Money in the World* (Harper, 1979), a story of wish fulfillment that brings trouble, won the Charlie May Simon Award and *Devil's Donkey* (Harper, 1981), another story of fantasy and magic, was named an ALA notable book. *The Wish Giver: Three Tales of Coven Tree** (Harper, 1983), another fantasy of wish fulfillment, a variation on the three wishes motif of folktale, was cited on the *Horn Book* Fanfare list and was named a Newbery honor book.

THE BRONZE BOW (Speare*†, Elizabeth George, Houghton, 1961), historical novel set in Roman-occupied Palestine in the first century A.D. The story follows a year in the life of Jewish patriot, Daniel bar Jamin, 18, of Galilee, who, after his father is crucified by the Romans and his mother dies of grief, is sold into slavery to a blacksmith who is cruel to him. Daniel escapes to the hills, vowing vengeance against the Romans, and joins a band of outlaws headed by the unscrupulous Rosh, who is ostensibly preparing rebellion against the Romans. Forced by the death of his grandmother to return to his native village of Ketzah to care for his mentally ill younger sister, Leah*, Daniel organizes a group of youths, their symbol the bronze bow, to do undercover work for Rosh. Through Simon, the blacksmith whose shop Daniel operates, and Joel* and Thacia*, twin youths who are the children of a rabbi in Capernaum and whom he enlists to the cause, Daniel meets Jesus, more impressed by the unpretentious carpenter turned teacher each time he sees him. Disillusioned by Rosh's failure to move against the Romans and his refusal to help liberate Joel, who has been captured doing Rosh's work, Daniel breaks off with the rebel leader, realizing finally that

Rosh is more brigand than patriot. When Daniel angrily drives away a young Roman soldier with whom Leah has become friends and the girl reverts to her dark world of unspeakable fears, Daniel sees vividly the damage hatred can do. When Jesus cures Leah, Daniel decides that by following Jesus he can both find inner peace and better help his country, for only love is strong enough "to bend the bronze bow." This story of how an idealistic youth comes to terms with certain realities of life moves steadily toward a rather melodramatic ending. Characterization is effective, the fearful Leah and the huge black man, Samson, who is devoted to Daniel because Daniel helped save him from the Roman galleys and who gives his life in rescuing Joel from the galleys, are particularly memorable. The two leaders, patient, gentle, ascetic Jesus and cruel, domineering, self-seeking Rosh, are starkly contrasted. Daniel is always the central figure, not Jesus, though this is also a story of early Christianity. Especially outstanding is the sense of the times—the hatred patriotic Jews bore toward their Roman conquerors. The title is based upon II Samuel 22:35. Choice, Fanfare; Newbery Winner.

BROOKINS, DANA (MARTIN) (1931–   ), born in St. Louis, Mo. She was graduated from California State College in San Bernardino and has taught English at Chaffey Community College in Alta Loma, Calif., as well as English as a foreign language to Spanish speakers. Married and divorced with four children, she has made her home in Rialto, Calif. *Rico's Cat* (Seabury, 1976) is a short book about a boy who decides to hide and raise a cat and kittens despite his landlord's ban on pets. *Alone in Wolf Hollow** (Seabury, 1978), which won the Edgar Allan Poe Award for juvenile mystery novel, is set near St. Louis and is notable for good characterization of the two boys as well as skillfully crafted suspense. A more recent mystery is *Who Killed Sack Annie* (Houghton, 1982).

BROTHER LEON (*The Chocolate War**), corrupt and sadistic acting headmaster of Trinity High School, the Catholic boys' school that is controlled by the secret student organization, the Vigils*. In order to get credit for raising more money than ever before, Brother Leon has used unauthorized school funds to get for cash a special price on stale boxes of chocolates left over from Mother's Day and has doubled the number of boxes for the school's annual fund raising sale and also doubled the price per box. With a great deal at stake, he makes a deal with the Vigils, implying, at least, that for their support of the sale they will get his support of the vicious organization. Brother Leon is shown tormenting boys, humiliating them in front of the class, even watching Jerry Renault being beaten and possibly killed without interfering. A pale, soft-voiced man, he is shown as both insecure and evil.

BROTHER RUSH (*Sweet Whispers, Brother Rush**), younger brother of Vy* Pratt, who appears to her daughter, Tree, as a ghost and shows her episodes from the family past. A numbers runner and a stylish dresser, Rush is actually suffering from a painful rare disease, porphyria, complicated by his use of alcohol. On a drive to Cincinnati with Tree's father, Rush sees that an accident is imminent and, instead of warning the driver, he waits and actually dives out of the car to his death, a suicide to end his agonizing condition.

BROTHER SEBASTIAN (*The Empty Moat**), the elderly gardener at the monastery near Swaenenburgh Castle. He is a one-sided figure, apparently symbolic of dedication to the cause of country. Elizabeth is later given a start of one of the roses he developed, a rather obvious and sentimental symbol.

BROTHER SOLANO (*Walk the World's Rim**), kind monk of the Mercederian abbey in Mexico City, whose answer to every problem is to offer food. He represents the lure of easy living which could bind Chakoh to Mexico City and a life of relative uselessness and prevent him from fulfilling his responsibilities to his Avavare tribespeople.

BROTHER THOMAS (*A Solitary Blue**), kindly, understanding monk who teaches theology at Professor* Greene's University and who befriends the Professor and Jeff*. Brother Thomas has a good sense of humor and finds happiness in almost everything, although he can be sober enough when the occasion calls for seriousness. He enjoys good wine and fine food and often cooks meals for the lonely father and son. He affects the story in important ways; for example, he helps when Jeff comes down with a severe case of bronchial pneumonia, persuades the Professor to get Jeff to a counselor when the boy fails eighth grade after Melody* dumps him, pushes the Professor into submitting his manuscript to a publisher, gives Jeff some idea of the Professor's eminent reputation in the field, after Melody has consistently downtalked the Professor to Jeff, and generally helps both to see possibilities in life other than their own small, insulated for self-protection world. Though Brother Thomas appears mostly as the kind and caring friend, he, too, is shown as having his rougher moments and emerges as a round and believable character.

BROWN, IRENE BENNETT (1932–   ), born in Topeka, Kans.; journalist and novelist. When she was nine her family moved to Oregon's Willamette Valley, and she grew up near Harrisburg, Oreg., and attended Oregon high schools. In Salem, Oreg., she worked as a waitress, retail clerk, long-distance telephone operator, and wrote a weekly column on church activities for three Oregon newspapers. She has contributed articles to a variety of adult journals, has been Woman's Editor for *Capitol Press*, an Oregon farm weekly, and has had stories for children published in several magazines. Among her novels are *To Rainbow Valley* (McKay, 1969), a story of the dust bowl pioneers of the

1930s, and *Before the Lark** (Atheneum, 1982), about a girl of the 1880s in Kansas who suffers social ostracism because she has a harelip, a novel which won the Spur Award for the best juvenile novel. Her experience working for the telephone company is reflected in *Morning Glory Afternoon* (Atheneum, 1981), a murder and love story set in 1924 in Kansas, in which the Ku Klux Klan is defeated by a young switchboard operator.

BRY BISHOP (*Dreamland Lake**), Bryan Bishop, friend of Flip* Townsend and the one who tells the story in retrospect. Bry is a pensive, dreamy boy, who later realizes he should not have yielded so readily to Flip's suggestions about investigating the dead body and dealing with Elvan Helligrew. He has nightmares about the dead man, whom he calls Gold Tooth, and cannot forget the girl whose body he and his father find dead at the scene of a highway accident. He comes to see that what drew him and Flip together were a few temporary shared interests. Among other things, Bry learns to think for himself better. He has a positive relationship with his father, one of the book's assets.

BUDDY CLARK (*The Planet of Junior Brown**), streetwise, fourteen-year-old black who has developed a series of "planets," hide-outs in abandoned buildings for homeless boys in New York, where he supplies food and clothing and teaches them independence. Mathematically brilliant, he spends his days helping the janitor, a former teacher, construct a model solar system in a secret basement room of his school and escorting enormously fat Junior* Brown through the streets, and his nights visiting his "planets" and working at Doum Malach's newsstand. He calls himself a Tomorrow Billy, a keeper, and is pictured as tough but improbably good, an almost Christ-like figure, opposed to stealing and concerned for the poor and grotesque and willing to suffer cold, fatigue, and rejection almost beyond belief.

BULLA†, CLYDE ROBERT (1914–   ), born on a farm near King City, Mo.; author of many books, mostly for early readers. He attended King City High School, has lived in California, and has traveled extensively. He has published one novel for adults, *These Bright Young Dreams* (Penn, 1941), a book about opera for older children, and a large number of books for younger children to read to themselves, and wrote the music for a number of plays. Among his books for younger children are *John Billington, Friend of Squanto†* (Crowell, 1956), a story of the Pilgrims' trip to Plymouth, Mass., and their first months there, *The Sword in the Tree†* (Crowell, 1956), which has a medieval setting, *Viking Adventure** (Crowell, 1963), which tells of a Norse expedition to the New World, and *White Bird** (Crowell, 1966), a study of a lonely boy, which has more character development than most of his earlier books. More recently he has published *A Lion to Guard Us* (Crowell, 1981), a story of three children from London attempting to reach their father in the Jamestown colony, and *The Cardboard Crown* (Crowell, 1984), a novel of parent-child relationships in a rural setting. His books are noted for simple, direct language and uncomplicated though interesting plots.

BULL KALINSKI (*Smugglers' Road**), "El Toro," tough ex-marine sergeant who runs the Baja Zopilotes clinic in the Mexican village of La Ribera. A stern taskmaster, he rides Kern Dawson hard, grounds him indefinitely when he borrows the jeep without permission, and threatens to send him home to face Juvenile Hall, but worries about the boy when he is gone overlong and, in the final action, saves Kern's life. Although his night fishing, his prolonged trips in a jeep loaded with packages, and the mysterious payments listed in his notebook all lead Kern and Tony to suspect him of smuggling, they have innocent explanations: he goes "fishing" but comes back to spend the nights with Mama Rosa, his secret common-law wife; he loads the jeep with gifts for Mama Rosa's five kids, off at school at Santa Ynez, and he is paying installments on pipe to bring water to the village from a distant well.

THE BULLY OF BARKHAM STREET (Stolz*†, Mary, ill. Leonard Shortall, Harper, 1963), realistic novel of family and neighborhood life set in St. Louis in the mid twentieth century, in which the events of *A Dog on Barkham Street** are seen from the point of view of the neighborhood bully. Martin Hastings, 11, is on the outs at home, in the neighborhood, and at school. Big for his age, older than his classmates, overweight, he is failing in his subjects, has no friends, feels his parents never listen, is constantly in trouble with his older sister, Marietta*, and regularly smarts off to his teacher, Mr.* Foran, and other adults. Lacking in self-esteem, he takes his feelings of inadequacy out on smaller kids, like Edward Frost, who lives next door. Irresponsible and forgetful, he even loses his beloved puppy, Rufus, because he fails to live up to his promises to take care of the animal. Things start to change for Martin when Mr. Foran praises him for work well done, gives him a little extra attention at recess, and assigns him the part of bugler in the skit the sixth grade is putting on for parents' night. During the program things go wrong for Martin, but he gamely carries on, impressing even his mother with his sportsmanship and earning thunderous applause from the audience. He gradually comes to see that if his life is to improve some of the changes will have to come from within himself. He works harder at his studies, tries to see things from the point of view of other people, lets up on snacks, practices more on his bugle, and even gets a paper route to earn money for a saxophone. He slips occasionally, for example, when Edward's Uncle Josh arrives, whose dog, Argess, opens old wounds. When Mr.* Hastings remarks that it is hard to live down a bad reputation, Martin realizes that his parents are really very understanding. By school's end, Martin has too many positive projects on his mind to consider picking on Edward or smarting off. Humor, poignancy, and sympathetically treated children and adults contribute to an entertaining, thought-provoking character study for younger readers, which holds up well even though Martin changes too patly. (Otto* Sonberg; Mr.* and Mrs. Hastings) Choice.

BURCH, ROBERT (1925–   ), born in Inman, Ga.; author of modest, realistic stories set in the rural South. He was graduated from the University of Georgia in agriculture, was in the army in New Guinea and Australia during World War II, and has lived recently in Fayetteville, Ga. He started writing for children while taking classes at Hunter College, N.Y., under Dr. William Lipkind of the Will and Nicolas picture book team. He has written some books about animals for pre- and early readers, including *A Funny Place to Live* (Viking, 1962), *Joey's Cat* (Viking, 1969), and *The Hunting Trip* (Viking, 1971). For somewhat older children are *Tyler, Wilkin, and Skee* (Viking, 1963), a charming episodic story of three boys in depression era Georgia, *Skinny* (Viking, 1964), and *D.J.'s Worst Enemy* (Viking, 1966). His *Queenie Peavy** (Viking, 1966), a novel of a girl whose father is in jail, won numerous honors, and his *Ida Early Comes Over the Mountain** (Viking, 1980) was named a *Boston Globe-Horn Book* Award honor book. Its sequel is *Christmas with Ida Early* (Viking, 1983). All his stories have an understated, gentle realism without sentimentality.

BURCHARD, PETER (DUNCAN) (1921–   ), born in Washington, D.C.; free-lance illustrator and writer. He graduated from the Philadelphia Museum School of Art in 1947. During World War II, he did technical illustrations for the Navy, served as a radio operator aboard a troop transport in the North Atlantic, and drew for *Yank* magazine. He has illustrated over one hundred books for such writers as Virginia Haviland, Lonzo Anderson, Louisa R. Shotwell*, and Clyde Robert Bulla*, for whom he has done several. He started writing in 1956 and since then has completed over a dozen picture books, novelettes, and full-length novels for children of various ages, mostly set against a background of American history and often about the Civil War and slavery. Among these are *Jed: The Story of a Yankee Soldier and a Southern Boy** (Coward, 1960), *Bimby** (Coward, 1968), and *Rat Hell* (Coward, 1971), while *Stranded* (Coward, 1967) features a Scottish youth caught in the slums of Lower Manhattan in 1875 when his ship sails without him. *Jed* was elected to the Lewis Carroll Shelf and was a Fanfare book, *Bimby* is also a Fanfare book, and both are cited in *Choice*. Written in terse, unembroidered prose strong in pictorial quality, Burchard's novels place fictitious characters in actual situations to work out problems closely integrated with the times. More recently he has published *Sea Change* (Farrar, 1984), a three-part book for young adults beginning in the early 1900s which explores thoughtfully how three related girls of different generations cope with changes in their lives. Burchard was a Guggenheim Fellow in 1966 and lives and works in New York City. He has contributed many articles to nationally circulated magazines.

BURDOW, DAVE (*Across Five Aprils**), shiftless, despised neighbor of the Creightons, whose son was responsible for the death of Mary Creighton, Jethro's* older sister, and who helps Jethro when the boy is attacked on the way home from his buying trip to Newton. It is while he is on his way to thank Burdow that Matt Creighton is stricken.

BURLESON, ELIZABETH, author of novels set in ranch country of Texas. In *Middl'un** (Follett, 1968), which won the Spur Award for the best juvenile with a western setting, a girl of turn-of-the-century hill country near the Guadalupe River aids her father with the cattle and helps apprehend rustlers. She also wrote *Man of the Family* (Follett, 1965), a novel of a boy growing up on a sheep ranch, also in the early 1900s. She has made her home in Texas.

THE BURNING GLASS (Johnson*†, Annabel, and Edgar Johnson*†, Harper, 1966), historical novel, involving adventure and chase among trappers and Indians, which begins in 1833 and covers about a year's time and includes a few actual historical figures as minor characters. Jeb, 15, whose family has come west to trade at Santa Fe, longs for the wild, free life of a mountain man. At Independence, Mo., he overhears the doctor say that he will soon die of consumption. He runs away from home and persuades hard-bitten Armand Deschute*, a French fur trader, to include him with the pack train Deschute is leading westward for Grover Welsh. Welsh is a wealthy eastern banker and shipper, who wants to trade for beaver pelts at the rendezvous at the headquarters of the Siskadee, or Green, River. Also in the group are Ira Tate, a farmer looking for new land, Lobo*, the hard but kind French campmaster, and Etienne Pepin, French hunter. Apparently seeing in Jeb something of what he himself once was, Deschute teaches the boy skills of the trail and occasionally gives him fatherly advice, and over a year's time what had started as a business arrangement matures into friendship. Indians give the train problems, food is uncertain, and Welsh and Tate cause trouble by stubbornly disregarding Deschute's orders. At the rendezvous, competition is fierce, and pelts go high, as the American Fur Company, whose factor is Kenneth McKenzie, called the King of the Missouri, vies with the Sublette Company, which worldly, ambitious Jim Bridger supplies. Tate leaves the train for California, but Welsh, who has bartered for prime pelts, wishes to push further into the mountains. When the train meets Nat Wyeth, Welsh learns that two of his ships have gone down and that he is ruined financially. Later, Crow Indians steal his furs, and he leaves the story at Fort Union, McKenzie's post. Deschute now sets out to settle an old score with LaRoche*, a former partner who shot Deschute for trying to keep him from selling liquor to the Indians. The search for LaRoche takes Deschute, Etienne, and Jeb deep into Crow country, where they are captured and spend the winter. In the spring Jeb engineers their escape, and they make their way south to Bent's Fort where they encounter Lobo. Lobo tells them that LaRoche has headed east and that the rising popularity of silk has caused beaver prices to drop. Deschute decides to give up his search for LaRoche and return to Crow country. Now strong in body and clearer about his life's ambition, Jeb plans to continue with him, but it is unclear whether or not a chance encounter with his younger brother, Burr, will change his mind. Strong characterizations of the principals helps to compensate for the sometimes trite, only occasionally exciting plot. Most characters are types, and Jeb is an impassive, colorless protagonist. The book's strongest points arise out of its recreation of the times, done with a large palette—life on the trail and among the Indians, attitudes of trappers and Indians toward each other, and the possibilities and dangers of the fur trade. (Cuts-the-Turnip*) Spur.

BURNISH ME BRIGHT (Cunningham*, Julia, ill. Don Freeman, Pantheon, 1970), story of prejudice set in a French village, at an unspecified time. Monsieur Hilaire, aging mime, is startled when he finds the mute orphan boy who works for coarse, brutal Madame Fer watching and applauding his practice. Knowing that he does not have long to live, the old actor does not take in the boy, Auguste, but agrees to teach him secretly each evening, warning him that the people will be cruel to him because he is different. Auguste is an apt pupil, and Hilaire gives him the medal with which he was decorated at his last performance, then dies. Shortly after, Auguste surprises the mayor's brutish son, Gustave, and two other boys preparing to break into the actor's house and scares them off by acting as a ghost. When Gustave falls and hurts his ankle, Auguste helps him home and wins his friendship. News that Madame Cresson's daughter, Avril, is ill and refusing to eat prompts Auguste to climb in at her window and put on a show, juggling with imaginary props. The girl, recovering, becomes a devoted but secret fan of Auguste, coming to watch him practice in the evenings, eventually also bringing Gustave. The villagers are suspicious because all three children appear changed and happy. When a small dog acts strangely, they think it is mad, chase it, and are further suspicious when Auguste breaks through the crowd and leads the dog off. He is unable to tell them that he cures it by removing a burr caught at the back of its tongue. Shortly after, Gustave becomes ill and calls for Auguste. Avril fetches him, but the mob begins to stone him. He escapes and runs to Hilaire's house, which they then set on fire. Avril, believing him dead, comes three days later to find him exercising in the ruins, burned and ragged, but dancing with great grace and emotion. She takes the medal from its hiding place, presents it to him, and bids him farewell as he starts away from the village. Although this has some unlikely plot elements—Gustave's change from stupid bully to devoted friend, Avril's sudden recovery, Auguste's survival in the fire—it is more plausible than some of Cunningham's other realistic novels, perhaps because its unfamiliar setting gives it the quality of a fairy tale. The shortsighted, superstitious villagers are well drawn, as is the sensitive mute boy and the aristocratic old mime. As in a fairy tale the theme—that people destroy things of value that they don't understand—is obvious. Choice.

BURRUM (*Saturday, the Twelfth of October**), Zan's staunch friend and protector among the People. A warm and loving girl, she shares what she has with her "new found sister." She is a good daughter and a loyal cousin to Sonte*. When her beloved little brother, Lishum, dies, she conforms to tribal practice and sacrifices a finger to commemorate and mourn his loss.

BUTTERWORTH†, OLIVER (1915–   ), born in Hartford, Conn.; educator and author of comic science fantasies for children. He received his B.A. degree from Dartmouth College, did graduate work at Harvard, and took his M.A. from Middlebury College. He has been a teacher of Latin and English to boys, an elementary school teacher, and a teacher of English at Hartford College for Women. He began to write for children after teaching in elementary school for two years, his intention being to provide for the young imaginative and literate reading that would also be informative. His amusing stories involve outrageous incidents related in a dry and witty style and convey information without sounding instructive. His books take off on his own family's experiences. *The Enormous Egg†* (Little, 1956), elected to the Lewis Carroll Shelf and selected by *Choice*, rose out of an incident with backyard hens, while his children's experiments with homemade telephones and crystal radios led to *The Trouble with Jenny's Ear* (Little, 1960), also listed in *Choice*. His third book, *The Narrow Passage* (Little, 1973), again stars Nate Twitchell of *The Enormous Egg*. It resulted from a family visit to the famous cave of Lascaux in France.

BYARS, BETSY (CROMER) (1928–   ), born in Charlotte, N.C.; author of books for children. She grew up in Charlotte and graduated from Queens College, where she met her future husband, now a professor of engineering at West Virginia University. Although she has contributed many articles to *Saturday Evening Post*, *Look*, *TV Guide*, and other magazines, she is best known as a writer of realistic novels about contemporary family life for early adolescents, ideas for which come from the things that happen to her at home and with her family. Among her novels is one Newbery Award winner, *The Summer of the Swans** (Viking, 1970), about a girl and her retarded younger brother; a *Boston Globe-Horn Book* Honor book, *The Night Swimmers** (Delacorte, 1980), which pursues a theme of personal and family responsibility; and a Lewis Carroll Shelf book, *The Midnight Fox** (Viking, 1968), about a boy who develops a strong emotional attachment for a wild fox. Her style is lively and contemporary, her plots usually fast, but her characterization is shallow and often distorted for effect, her plots unfocused and occasionally quite thin, contrived and improbably concluded, and her attempts at humor sometimes heavyhanded. A very popular modern author, she has also written *The Pinballs** (Harper, 1977), a Child Study Award book about foster children; *The Cartoonist** (Viking, 1978), about a boy obsessed with drawing cartoon strips; and *The House of Wings** (Viking, 1972), a finalist for the National Book Award about how a boy and his grandfather come to terms. She has also written *The Two-Hundred-Pound Goldfish* (Harper,

1982), about a boy abandoned by his mother who escapes into horror movie fantasies, and *The Glory Girl* (Bradbury, 1983), about a family of traveling gospel singers. Several of Byars's books have been Fanfare selections and are listed in *Choice*. She lives in Morgantown, Pa., and, a dynamic and humorous speaker, she is much in demand for professional conferences.

BY THE GREAT HORN SPOON! (Fleischman*, Sid, ill. Eric von Schmidt, Little, 1963), historical novel told with vigor and gusto in hilarious tall tale style. Earnest Jack Flagg, 11, and his Aunt Arabella's impeccable, unflappable butler, Praiseworthy, outfitted with his trademarks of top hat and umbrella, leave Boston in 1849 for the California gold fields stowed away on the sidewheeler *Lady Wilma*. They are forced to shovel coal into the ship's furnaces to pay for their passage until Praiseworthy unmasks the thief who picked his pocket in Boston. In San Francisco, Praiseworthy's skill at barbering prospective bridegroom Quartz Jackson earns them their grubstake. When on the stage bound for the town of Hangman near Sacramento they are held up by highwaymen, Praiseworthy flattens one of them with a mighty punch, made more effective by the store of gold dust he carries in his glove and earning him the nickname of "Bullwhip." At the gold fields they are advised by Pitch-Pine Billy, a kindly prospector, who also teaches Jack to drink coffee and gives him the nickname of "Jamoka Jack." For weeks the two prospect unsuccessfully, while Praiseworthy brushes up on fine points of boxing that will enable him to defeat Mountain Ox, the local strong man. They meet an assortment of colorful Old West characters, who provide excitement and adventure, but a continuing problem involves Cut-Throat Higgins. This pickpocket and confidence man has stolen the treasure map belonging to veterinarian Dr. Buckabee, who has promised Jack and Praiseworthy a half share of his mine if they recover the map. When they save Cut-Throat from being hanged for horse stealing, he gives them the map, which they then discover is worthless. Ordered by the judge to dig a grave on a hill overlooking the camp in anticipation of Cut-Throat's execution for some infraction of the law, Praiseworthy and Jack strike a rich vein of gold. On the way back to San Francisco, they lose their newfound treasure when the boiler of the steamship explodes. The resourceful Praiseworthy, who has met their every difficulty with aplomb, ingenuity, and characteristic grace, proves up to the situation once more. He earns another grubstake by joining with Yankee trader Azariah Jones to auction off the cats from the now-abandoned *Lady Wilma* to the rat-bedeviled San Franciscans. The two comrades are delighted to discover that Aunt Arabella and Jack's two young sisters have followed them to San Francisco. Praiseworthy, now independently wealthy, proposes to Aunt Arabella, for whom he has held an enduring affection, and she accepts his suit. The pleasingly concocted plot unfolds with precision and considerable daring, and clever twists invest stock incidents of villainy and hair raising escapes familiar from the dime novels and Saturday movies with new interest. Although most other figures are caricatures or stock, Praiseworthy is given additional dimension and wins and holds the reader's sympathies and admiration, being the true central character of the story, compared to whom Jack is a colorless foil. Zesty language adds to the humor, excitement, and flavor of this Old West extravaganza, which if deliberately flamboyant succeeds in projecting a rich sense of time and place. Choice; Spur; Stone.

C

CADBURY'S COFFIN (Swarthout*, Glendon, and Kathryn Swarthout*, ill. Frank Mayo, Doubleday, 1982), realistic novel of suspense with detective story aspects set somewhere in New York State at the beginning of December, 1899, filled with melodrama in Victorian style, and related with the grandiloquence typical of the period. Events are seen mostly from the point of view of but not told by orphaned Joshua Overland, 14, innocent, obedient, highly moral choreboy of eighty-four-year-old, hard-fisted Lycurgus Cadbury, millionaire manufacturer of horse-drawn cutters. With the help of his lawyer, Brainerd Peckham, and his doctor, Silas Hopkins, both loyal if self-seeking, the stubborn, wily, irascible tycoon sets in motion a complex scheme whereby he hopes to test the love of his only remaining relatives, his greedy nieces, Hetta Mae Cadbury and Lillian Morgan. Apparently on his deathbed, felled by a stroke, he publicly begs not to be buried alive. Privately he instructs Dr. Hopkins to give him an injection, ostensibly to put him out of his misery, the act witnessed by his lawyer, who is in on the scheme, and by the virtuous but unknowing Josh, who is bound to strict secrecy about what has transpired. Pronounced dead by the doctor, the old man's body is accordingly placed in a coffin specially fitted out with air passages and bell for summoning help should he revive. The body is placed in the family tomb on the grounds of the Cadbury mansion, and Eli Stamp, half-senile Civil War veteran, who has served Cadbury as handyman for many years, and Josh are ordered to guard the coffin and report any suspicious sounds or activity, Eli during the day and Josh by night, for three days and nights. After that, if there has been no sign of life, Cadbury will be declared officially dead and his will read. While Eli and Josh carry out their master's orders, angry quarrels break out between the grasping nieces, each of whom had been told by Cadbury that she would inherit the bulk of his fortune; Lillian's malicious, evil-minded son, Montfort, who systematically sets out to drown Cadbury's numerous pet cats; and the servants, who also include pretty Verbena Huttle, 15, a scullery maid out to improve her lot in life, which at this point she thinks can best be done by hooking her wagon to Josh's star, since she is certain that Josh will be richly rewarded for his diligence and courage; and the loyal, workworn, warmhearted old housekeeper, Mrs. Minnie Pumpley, who tenderly mothers them both. The first night Josh hears sounds from the coffin and reports as directed to Dr. Hopkins, who, later, unbeknownst to Josh, helps Cadbury from the coffin (the injection was a drug without lasting effect) and takes the old man home. The second and third nights, as Josh continues to stand guard in considerable fear and trembling, the boy observes each niece attempt to make sure her uncle is truly dead by tampering with the coffin. When the will is finally read, all hopes are solidly dashed. The lawyer announces that Cadbury had indeed been alive when first placed in the coffin, had been assisted from the coffin, and then, while at the doctor's house, had died of a massive heart attack, ironically, before seeing the results of his grandiose scheme. Except for very modest bequests to relatives and retainers, his fortune is to be used to establish a foundation for homeless cats. The angry relatives systematically set about plundering the house, and the faithful servants are summarily turned out. Determined not to be returned to the orphanage, Josh decides to hop a freight west to seek his fortune. In pity and love for Verbena, he gives the girl, whom he regards as his sweetheart, his share of the Cadbury fortune, a twenty-dollar gold piece, with the understanding that she will wait for him. As soon as he has departed, however, realizing that youth is fleeting and reluctant to work in the cutter factory until he comes back, Verbena decides to try her luck in New York City, where she hopes to receive help from Montfort, who has not been unaware of her budding charms. After a slow start, in which the servants are introduced, Cadbury's character is established, and a tone of impending disaster created, the carefully calculated plot picks up speed. After that, the momentum never relaxes, and the story becomes elaborately intricate and readers are treated to a full measure of dastardly deeds, judiciously withheld information, deliberate overforeshadowing, and ironic twists on plot and character, all admirably supported by the deftly handled baroque style. The result is topnotch Gothic storytelling in which everybody becomes the victim of Cadbury's hoax, including Cadbury himself and the readers, too. Poe Nominee.

CAL JONES (*Hoops**), black ex-pro basketball player, known professionally as Spider, who pulls himself out of the gutter to coach a Harlem team in the city-wide Tournament of Champions. His own career having ended when he began shaving points for gamblers, he has since separated from his strong and loving wife, Aggie, and become a wino. He resists pressures from both the white O'Donnel, who is afraid his presence will taint the tournament and make sponsors leery, and from the black gamblers, who want him to throw the championship game by keeping Lonnie from playing. Although he is killed, he has demonstrated to the boys that they have to keep their games clean or they are lost forever, and in so doing has redeemed his life.

THE CALLENDER PAPERS (Voigt*, Cynthia, Atheneum, 1983), murder-mystery novel with detective story aspects set during the summer of 1894 in the Berkshire Mts. of New England. The story starts in Cambridge, Mass., where quiet, studious, over-serious Jean* Wainwright, almost thirteen, who tells the story, lives with capable, sensible Aunt Constance, who has raised her from infancy and who is headmistress of a respected girls' school. Mr.* Daniel Thiel, painter, trustee of the school, and widower of Irene Callender, Aunt Constance's girlhood friend, a dour, dark man, requests that Jean come to his large, comfortable, country home at Marlborough in the Berkshires to sort out his deceased wife's papers. Though she has misgivings about working for so cold and distant a man, Jean respects the judgment of Aunt Constance and accepts the assignment. Jean approaches the task of sorting out the dozen boxes filled with miscellaneous Callender papers with characteristic diligence, though she finds little to interest her at first. She thinks puzzling the presence of Mrs.* Bywall, the reticent, kindly housekeeper once imprisoned for stealing from the Callenders, and the behavior of Mr. Thiel himself, who seems to want to be friendly but who displays a stubborn sternness that puts her off. He lives almost as a recluse, having little to do with the villagers, and keeps strictly apart from his wife's younger brother, Enoch* Callender, and his family who live in a large house a little way down the hill. Jean gradually picks up information about the Callenders, from Mac* McWilliams, a youth her age who is the son of the local doctor, Mrs. Bywall, Mr. Thiel, and even from the pretentious but oddly poor Callenders, who invite her for modest Sunday lunches. She is especially attracted to handsome, congenial, charming Enoch, who had been raised by Irene after their mother's death and who shows Jean their special way of crossing the ravine over the falls where Irene suffered her fatal fall some dozen years earlier. Learning about Irene's death and the puzzling disappearance of Irene and Dan's child, who gossip says was carried off by a strange, hooded, witchlike nurse not long after Irene's death, arouses Jean's curiosity, and aided by Mac she scours the papers for the Callender will, which she is sure will shed light on matters. At the same time she is plagued by nightmares, suffers from food poisoning, and becomes increasingly uneasy about her safety. The will discovered, Jean finally puts together the pieces of the jigsaw, and at the critical moment she is rescued by Dan just as Enoch is about to engineer her fall into the ravine. Enoch, seeking the family fortune denied him by his father's will and left to Irene's child, was responsible for Irene's fall and also wishes to kill Jean since she is Dan and Irene's child, raised by Aunt Constance to keep her out of his greedy clutches. Though it is never quite clear why Constance and Daniel cook up such an elaborate scheme to introduce Jean to her mother's relatives, it is apparently to lure Enoch into revealing his true nature and motives. Still, the plot makes for a gripping, old-fashioned Gothic melodrama with its gloomy mansions, family mysteries, innocence beguiled, unfortunate love, longstanding animosities, a wastrel son, spooky night happenings, wronged faithful servant, and a strong sense of impending evil. Characters are sharply drawn and pacing carefully calculated for maximum effect. The reader early suspects Jean's true identity, and much of the story's interest lies in seeing how Jean will find out about herself and whether or not she will accept the distant man who is her father. Style is appropriately prim and slightly literary, and Jean changes believably as she learns about her relatives and adjusts to her new environment. Poe Winner.

CALL PURNELL (*Jacob Have I Loved**), McCall, Rass Island boy who progs for crab with Louise* Bradshaw and later culls oysters on her father's boat. At first a fat, nearsighted boy, he develops in the Navy in World War II into an attractive young man, but his sense of humor and his sensitivity to the emotions of other people stay at an elementary level. He is a great favorite of the Captain*, Hiram Wallace, to whom he becomes almost a son, and he marries Louise's twin sister, Caroline*.

CALVIN FITCH (*Smoke**), stepfather of Christopher Long. Cal has sold his Montana ranch when Chris's mother, Fran, his childhood sweetheart, was widowed, and has taken over her Oregon ranch. A well-intentioned but rigid man, he has easily won over Chris's little sister, Susie*, but finds Chris more difficult, resentful of Cal's place in the family group and of the chores that Cal insists he do on the ranch. When Cal learns that Chris has befriended a starving German shepherd, he cooperates with the boy to capture and treat the animal. It is Cal who insists that they advertise for the owner and, when the owner arrives and Chris runs away, will not allow his mother to call the police, insisting that Chris must be allowed to face the fear and pain that result from his choice.

CALVIN O'KEEFE (*A Wrinkle in Time**; *The Arm of the Starfish**), intelligent, decisive youth, a fine athlete and a good student, a "sport" in his own family but who fits in well with the intellectual Murrys. He is a sympathetic and understanding young fellow who has an unusual ability to communicate with people. He accompanies Meg* and Charles* Wallace Murry on the quest for their father in *A Wrinkle in Time*. He later marries Meg and becomes a world-renowned biologist, who conducts experiments on starfish in his laboratory on the island of Gaea off Portugal in *The Arm of the Starfish*.

CAMAZOTZ (*A Wrinkle in Time**), the controlled society somewhere in space where Meg* Murry's father is held captive by IT, a disembodied brain. On Camazotz, everyone must behave like everyone else, doing exactly the same thing at the same time in accordance with schedules and requirements set up by IT. The people have become automatons who live in fear.

CAMERON†, ELEANOR (BUTLER) (1912–   ), born in Winnipeg, Canada; librarian, critic, author of novels for children and young people. Her family moved from Canada to Ohio when she was three and three years later to Berkeley, Calif., where she grew up. She attended the University of California and the Art Center School in Los Angeles. Among other positions, she has been a research librarian. Her first published novel, *The Unheard Music* (Little, 1950), written for adults, gratified an early desire to become an author. Shortly thereafter the Mushroom Planet books launched her career as a children's writer, the area for which she is best known today. The first book in the popular series, *The Wonderful Flight to the Mushroom Planet†* (Little, 1954), was written in answer to her son's request for a story "about two boys his own age who would build a little space ship and fly away to discover a planet. . . . " The other Mr. Bass stories followed, entertaining, briskly told, if rather conventional science fiction for younger readers. The first of these and two of several sequels, *Stowaway to the Mushroom Planet†* (Little, 1956) and *Time and Mr. Bass** (Little, 1967), are cited in *Choice*. While these evidences of inventiveness and storytelling ability continue to be well liked, her later books for older readers and young people are more highly regarded by critics. *A Spell Is Cast** (Little, 1964), a Fanfare book and an Edgar Allan Poe Award nominee, is a lightweight, diverting mystery that straddles the line between her earlier merely entertaining pieces and her later portrayals of young girls attempting to find themselves. These later novels show greater sophistication in subject, treatment, and theme. Though quiet, they are strong in characterization, subtly humorous, and written with grace and verve. *A Room Made of Windows** (Little, 1971), a Fanfare book, a Jane Addams Award book, and a *Boston Globe-Horn Book* winner, and *Julia and the Hand of God** (Dutton, 1977), a Fanfare book, both set in San Francisco in the 1920s and featuring ebullient Julia Redfern, are loosely autobiographical and offer a convincing picture of a budding writer. Two of Cameron's more recent novels tell about Julia's earlier years for younger readers, *That Julia Redfern* (Dutton, 1982) and *Julia's Magic* (Dutton, 1984). *To the Green Mountains** (Dutton, 1975), a National Book Award finalist and a Fanfare book, grew out of her memories of her Ohio years but involves no actual experiences. *The Court of the Stone Children** (Dutton, 1973), winner of the National Book Award, is a time fantasy. *The Green and Burning Tree: On the Writing and Enjoyment of Children's Books* (Little, 1969) established her as a major critic of children's literature. Much in demand as a speaker on literature for the young, she lives in California.

CANALBOAT TO FREEDOM (Fall*, Thomas, ill. Joseph Cellino, Dial, 1966), historical novel set in the 1840s along the Delaware and Hudson Canal which ran from the Shawangunk Mountains in Pennsylvania to the Hudson River. It deals with the aiding of black slaves in their escape to freedom and, less directly, with questions of loyalty and of the similarity between slavery and indentured servantdom. Red-haired orphan Benja (Benjamin) Lawn, 12, arrives in New York from England and is illegally sold as an indentured boy for two years to work off the cost of his passage. His purchaser is Captain* Roach, mean, tight-fisted, hard-drinking canaler, owner of the *Bullfrog* that hauls lumber along what is locally called the "Delaware Ditch." Benja starts as a hoggee, driving the two horses and caring for them. The only deck hand is a black called Lundius*, a quiet, dignified man who saves Ben from a cruel flogging when the captain has had too much to drink, gently teaches the boy about nature, and becomes the friend and father he has never had. Two circumstances bring them closer. Ben jumps into the canal to unhitch the horses from the packet boat that have slipped in at Cuddlebackville, thereby saving them from drowning. His action is observed by a lady disembarking from the boat, Mrs. Robbins, who gives him a book though he cannot read and who turns out to be friend and wintertime employer of Lundius. Later, he observes that Lundius has sneaked two blacks aboard and hidden them in the woodpile for part of the journey downstream. Lundius is soon forced to take Ben into his confidence, explaining to him about his part in the Underground Railway, since a slave named Newt is to be taken aboard that night. They visit Mrs. Robbins's farm where Newt is hidden, warn her that a local slave hunter is bringing the constable, and her Indian hired man, George, takes Newt to the woods. The slave hunter suspects that Lundius is Newt, reads his papers, insists that he remove his shirt to prove he does not have five whip scars on his right shoulder as Newt does. Lundius reveals a back cross-hatched with deep whip scars. They get Newt aboard but learn that all boats are being searched for him. Lundius plans a diversion in which he will pretend to knock some lumber overboard and fall with it while Ben dashes out with Newt and takes him over the mountain to Mrs. Robbins's farm. The ruse works but Lundius is killed when a boat crashes into the *Bullfrog* while he is in the water. Ben deeply resents Newt, who runs instead of helping Lundius, and struggles with his conscience while Newt hides in a cave Lundius has shown Ben. Mrs. Robbins's daughter, Kate*, who shares Ben's love for Lundius, tries to help him come to terms with his grief. When Ben volunteers to take food to Newt, he is intercepted by drunken Captain Roach, who corners him with his bullwhip. He is saved by Newt, who has left the cave and pretends to be the ghost of Lundius and scares the superstitious captain. Learning that Lundius had his freedom papers, Newt begs Ben to whip him until his back resembles Lundius's, so he can pass for the dead man. When Ben cannot bring himself to do so, Newt takes a meat hook and scars his own back. After it heals the appearance is enough to thwart a second attempt by the slave catcher, and Ben, realizing Newt's bravery and his resemblance to Lundius, leaves the haven of the Robbins farm to go with him to work on the canal and to save until they can become owners of a canalboat. The action is lively and the device of telling the story through the naive perceptions of Ben, who knows nothing of American slavery, brings freshness to the frequent subject of escaping slaves. Lundius is a believable character, though exceptionally worthy, but the change of Newt from a cowering slave unable to sit down in the presence of whites even though urged to do so to a man of confidence and dignity like Lundius is too sudden to be plausible. Choice.

CANON TALLIS (*The Arm of the Starfish**), middle-aged, mild-mannered English clergyman. Though bald-headed, lacking eyebrows, and looking something like a very intelligent teddy bear, he inspires confidence. He has friends in high places and carries out super-secret international intelligence assignments. He is Dr. Calvin* O'Keefe's official contact with Washington. He is mysterious, knowledgeable, and influential, a man whose character and actions remain shadowy. He also appears in *The Young Unicorns*.

CAPTAIN HIRAM WALLACE (*Jacob Have I Loved**), elderly man who returns to Rass Island, having left as a youth after he acted cowardly during a storm. At first the subject of suspicion by the islanders, who are not sure he really is Wallace and think he might be a spy, he convinces them unwittingly that he is genuine when he calls old, befuddled Auntie Braxton by her first name, Trudy. It is the money he inherits from Trudy Braxton, whom he marries after she has had a stroke, that sends Caroline* Bradshaw to music school. A man of experience and intelligence, he is fascinating to Louise* Bradshaw, whose infatuation centers on his hands, so different from those of the rough island men. He does not seem to recognize the shock she feels when he gives the money for Caroline, but he later sees the blow that Call* Purnell's marriage to Caroline is, and he encourages Louise to leave the island and make something of herself.

CAPTAIN JOSIAH REDDY (*The Odyssey of Ben O'Neal**), captain of the bark *Christine Conyers*. Considered crazy by the other captains, he sticks to the old ways of sailing which are dying out in the 1890s, refusing to use a donkey engine to hoist sail and insisting on chanteys. He sits out on the jib boom and sings to the ocean and sprinkles sugar on the water to "rise" a breeze, but he also beats the other ships on the Barbados run. A rather small, trim man, he dresses in a business suit and takes his Siamese cat to sea.

CAPTAIN KRYLOV (*Ivanov Seven**), Prussian-trained Russian artillery officer, who flaunts his training and ridicules the other officers because their men do not perform as well as his do. He is a stickler for proper detail and deportment. He first encounters Stepan, that is, Ivanov Seven, with his head stuck in the mouth of a cannon, observing a bird who has built her nest in there. Captain Krylov gives Colonel Yermolov the idea of "reassigning" Stepan, that is, mustering him out of the army, as the best way of getting out of an embarrassing situation. Krylov affects the plot greatly.

CAPTAIN ROACH (*Canalboat to Freedom**), greedy, mean-tempered owner of the *Bullfrog*, the canalboat on which Benja serves as an indentured boy. Because delays lose him money, Roach usually drinks heavily when the boat is held up by weather or traffic jams at the locks and returns to the boat in a violent temper. Only Lundius*, the black deck hand, can manage him, usually verbally but with a strong crack to the chin if necessary. Since few people will work for the brutal man, he even puts up with Lundius telling him to stop "wiggling his whiskers." He knows that it is illegal to keep Ben working without wages and resents Lundius pointing this out to Ben, even when Ben's flattery makes him fond of the boy in his own way. Because he is highly superstitious, Newt is able to fool him by pretending to be the ghost of Lundius.

CARLETON, BARBEE OLIVER (1917–   ), born in Thomaston, Maine; educator and author of several mysteries and collections of stories for young people. She has been an assistant editor at Houghton Mifflin publishers and has taught in secondary schools in Maine and Massachusetts and on the elementary level in Brookwood Independent School. Her mystery, *The Witches' Bridge** (Holt, 1967), was named a nominee for the Edgar Allan Poe award.

CARLIE (*The Pinballs**), bossy, cynical, wise-cracking, prevaricating fosterling, along with Harvey* and Thomas J*, of Mr. and Mrs. Mason. Carlie is living with the Masons because her stepfather assaulted her. At first, she hates the place and writes letters begging her mother to fetch her. She likes novels about nurses and enjoys watching TV. She refers to herself as the "slave of the world" when Mrs. Mason asks her to help out about the house. Carlie changes predictably.

CARLOS (*The Pushcart War**), the pushcart peddler (Cartons Flattened and Removed) who proposes using pea shooters as weapons against the huge trucks that are threatening to run the pushcarts off the streets of New York City. Since Carlos speaks only Spanish, Maxie* Hammerman explains Carlos's proposal to the peddlers at their strategy meeting. Carlos gets the idea from the clever pea shooter that his youngest son has made, one that shoots not ordinary peas but peas with pins stuck in them.

CARLOS MARQUEZ (*The Girl from Puerto Rico**), Felicidad's older brother, principal breadwinner of the family in New York City. He wishes to move to New York from Puerto Rico because his sweetheart and her family have emigrated there. In New York, his job as a bus boy pays little, but it is more money than he could earn in Puerto Rico, and he is satisfied. He spends little time with his family, and he and Margarita often go out. Their behavior toward each other, typical of New York youth, shocks their parents, who believe that young people should always be chaperoned. When the Marquez family return to Puerto Rico, he remains in New York and marries Margarita. He adjusts better than the rest of his family to their new life, since he has Margarita to cushion the culture shock.

CARLSON, NATALIE SAVAGE (1906–   ), born in Winchester, Va.; author of several distinct types of books for children, each reflecting a different part of her experience. She grew up in a large family of girls with just one younger brother, worked on newspapers in California, married a naval officer and lived for three years in France, where he was stationed, and has more recently made her home partly in Newport, R.I., and partly in Florida. Her collections of French-Canadian stories are mostly tales she first heard from her mother's visiting relatives. Among them are *The Talking Cat and Other Stories of French Canada* (Harper, 1952) and *Alphonse, That Bearded One* (Harcourt, 1954). Her books set in France have been her most popular. *The Family Under the Bridge†* (Harper, 1958) was a Newbery honor book and her Orpheline stories (about twenty little orphan girls and their one orphan "brother") have become a series, among them *The Happy Orpheline†* (Harper, 1957), *A Brother for the Orphelines†* (Harper, 1959), *A Pet for the Orphelines** (Harper, 1962), and *A Grandmother for the Orphelines* (Harper, 1980). Her novels of social consciousness focus on questions of racial equality and integration and include *Ann Aurelia and Dorothy** (Harper, 1968), a story of a happy bi-racial friendship, *The Empty Schoolhouse** (Harper, 1965), which concerns a boycott of a Catholic school in the South when it first attempted integration, and *Marchers for the Dream** (Harper, 1969), about the 1968 Poor People's March on Washington, D.C. Though considered important at the time of their publication, they now seem naive and a trifle patronizing. Her two books based directly on autobiographical experience are *The Half-Sisters* (Harper, 1970) and *Lurvy and the Girls* (Harper, 1971). She has also published picture books, like *Spooky Night* (Lothrop, 1982), a story of a cat, a witch, and a scary night. In 1966 she was named the United States candidate for the international Hans Christian Andersen Award.

CARN BASSYD (*Time and Mr. Bass**), Tyco* Bass's home in Wales, built when he was a boy in 1593. "Carn" means "pile of stones," and "Bassyd" is the Welsh form of Tyco's name, which is really Tyco ap (son of) Bass. He has turned the place over to the Mycetian* League to use as a meeting place. It is a large hall made of rough, slate blocks, square and high, with two big chimneys. In the council room stands a large, oaken table, in whose supports the other twelve scrolls written by Elder Grandfather* are found.

CAROLINE BRADSHAW (*Jacob Have I Loved**), musical, favored twin sister of Louise*. Having been a delicate baby, Caroline has been the center of attention all her life and at adolescence is a pretty, sweet blond with a fine voice worth the family sacrifice to give her music lessons. By the end of the book she has graduated from Juilliard School of Music and is making her debut in an opera. Although she is self-centered and accepts more than her share without qualms, she is also charming and tactful, deserving of the devotion of the other islanders.

CAROSELLI, REMUS F(RANCIS) (1916–   ), born in Providence, R.I.; research chemist and mystery writer. He received his B.S. degree from the University of Rhode Island, was research manager at Owens-Corning Fiberglass Corporation and consulting chemist at the R. F. Caroselli Consulting Co. in Narrangansett, R.I., where he has made his home. He has contributed to a volume of articles on man-made fibers. *The Mystery Cottage in Left Field** (Putnam, 1979), his first novel for young people, is set in 1929 and is concerned with bootleggers and organized crime figures of the period, reflecting his special interest in the late 1920s and early 1930s. More recently he has published *Mystery at Long Marsh* (Holt, 1985), set in a summer resort town and concerned with a threat to the coastal marshland.

CARR, HARRIETT (HELEN) (1899–   ), born in Ann Arbor, Mich.; journalist and author of novels for children and young people. After growing up in North Dakota, she returned to Michigan to attend Michigan State Normal College in Ypsilanti and the University of Michigan. She was a reporter for and then editor of the Ypsilanti *Daily Press*, the first woman editor of a daily paper in Michigan, and feature writer for the Detroit *News*. Turning to educational journalism, she wrote for *Michigan Vocational Out-Look* in Lansing and became editor and director of field services for Scholastic Magazines in New York City. In 1963, she became a full-time free-lance writer of fiction. She has written non-fiction, girls' stories, mysteries, and well-researched, regional historical novels, among them, *Where the Turnpike Starts* (Macmillan, 1955), about a young woman's involvement with Governor Stevens T. Mason's plans to establish Michigan as a state, and *Wheels for Conquest* (Macmillan, 1955), about the development of Pennsylvania in the nineteenth century. *The Mystery of Ghost Valley** (Macmillan, 1962), a conventionally plotted and cast story set among the Pennsylvania Dutch which projects a strong regional flavor, was nominated for the Edgar Allan Poe Award. Other novels include *Against the Wind* (Macmillan, 1955), about homesteading in North Dakota, and *The Mystery of the Aztec Idol* (Macmillan, 1959). She has contributed many articles to newspapers and vocational, educational, and animal magazines.

THE CARTOONIST (Byars*, Betsy, ill. Richard Cuffari, Viking, 1978), realistic novel of family life set recently in Morgantown, W.Va., in which over several days a junior high youth comes to terms with his life. Alfie Mason lives with his overbearing, overdirective mother; capable, sensible, high school-aged sister, Alma; and garrulous grandfather, Pap. Alfie's mother wants him to become a star football player like her older son, indulged, ne'er-do-well Bubba, now married and living in another town. Pap wants Alfie's help in reviving Alfie's father's junkyard business. Even Tree Parker, his school chum, seems intent on managing his life, by constantly trying to involve Alfie in his various impractical schemes. Only Alma, herself in Bubba's shadow, understands Alfie's need to be himself and make his own decisions, a yearning he expresses by retreating to the attic and feverishly drawing cartoons. Every day Alfie rushes home from school and stubbornly isolates himself in his private domain at the top of the house where he fashions one cartoon strip after another in which he attempts to pare away the beauty and glory of life and show things the way he thinks they really are. When Bubba loses his job, Mom is delighted with the possibility of having her favorite son under her roof once more and makes plans to remodel the attic to accommodate him and his pregnant wife. Horrified at the prospect of losing the only place he can call his own, Alfie barricades himself in the attic and for one whole day refuses to come down or let anyone come up, in spite of numerous pleas, bribes, harangues, and threats. Fortunately for Alfie, however, Bubba and Maureen choose to live with Maureen's mother, a decision that leaves Alfie's mother hurt, deflated, and angry. Although Alma astutely points out to Alfie that he has not really won his battle, he nevertheless comes down from the attic with cartoons in hand, surer about himself than before but realizing that he must accept the naked truth of things: his life is as it is, and he must make the best of it. Itself a narrative cartoon, the story combines humor, irony, and pathos in examining the conflict between a boy and his mother. Most characters are caricatures, scenes are economically sketched, and dialogue carries the burden of the story. Fanfare.

CASEY FLANAGAN (*All Together Now**), girl who spends the summer with her grandparents and poses as a boy to become accepted as a friend by their neighbor, retarded Dwayne* Pickens. On the surface a confident tomboy, Casey is really vulnerable and lonely, missing her father, who is an airforce pilot in the Korean War, and feeling somewhat rejected by her mother, who has taken a second job as a nightclub singer and, the book hints, may be playing around in her husband's absence. Casey has inherited her mother's voice and, though shy about singing in public, can belt out a song like Judy Garland. Her presence serves as catalyst in a number of romances, and her friendship with Dwayne gives meaning to her summer.

CASEY YOUNG (*Child of the Owl**), streetwise twelve-year-old daughter of the gambler Barney*, who goes to live with her grandmother in Chinatown. Outspoken and realistic, Casey appalls her wealthy, conventional uncle's family but finds much in common with her grandmother, Paw-Paw*, and gradually comes to appreciate her roots, to learn about her mother, Jeanie, about whom Barney never talks, and to understand how frustration has led Barney into his obsession with gambling. Practical and strong-willed, Casey has been able to keep Barney from deep gambling debt, but apart they both show their vulnerability, Casey by breaking down and sobbing to Paw-Paw, Barney by getting into deep gambling debt and crime. As the narrator, Casey is convincingly a tough, wise-cracking kid and also an intelligent and lonely child.

CASSIE SHIPMAN (*A Gathering of Days**), dearest friend and confidant of Catherine* Hall. She helps Cath take food and a quilt to the fugitive slave. Cassie is a year older than Cath, and Cath values her friendship very much. Cassie is a prudent girl, serious minded, sweet of disposition, and less assertive than Cath. She and Cath have discussions about such matters as obedience, oppression, and affection. Although Cath does not make much of it as the book goes on, evidently Cassie is not strong physically and, when once she sickens, is soon gone. Cath grieves, but her New England farm upbringing demands that she not give in to her loss, and she sorrows quietly. The reader sees Cassie only through Cath's eyes, "each of us in the other's dear heart sees secret dreams reflected." Cath's stepbrother, Daniel, grows fond of Cassie, too, in the short time after he arrives in the Hall house and before Cassie dies, and Cath understands and does not resent his sorrow.

THE CASTLE OF LLYR (Alexander*, Lloyd, Holt, 1966), fantasy, third in the series set in the land of Prydain*. Taran* and Gurgi* escort unwilling Eilonwy* to her relatives of the House of Llyr on the island of Mona, King Rhuddlum and Queen Teleria, who are to teach her to be a lady. There Eilonwy is kidnapped by Magg, the chief steward, who secretly serves evil Queen Achren. King Rhuddlum puts his feckless son, Rhun*, in charge of the search party and prevails upon Taran to watch over the hapless youth. The search party breaks into small units, and Taran, Rhun, Fflewddur* Fflam, and Gurgi have harrowing adventures before rescuing Eilonwy with Gwydion's help. In a rude, thatched hut, they encounter Lyan, a cat as big as a horse, who attaches herself to Fflewddur, because she particularly enjoys his music. They also find a book with mostly empty pages. Kaw, the crow, reports that Magg has taken Eilonwy in the direction of the River Alaw, and the companions head that way. Rhun finds Eilonwy's golden bauble, the Golden* Peledryn, and soon after the companions tumble into an underground cavern inhabited by a monstrous giant, Glew*, who is forced to stay there because he is too large to pass through the entrance. The companions learn that Glew received the book from a wizard who said that it once belonged to the Royal House of Llyr. Glew wants to use the companions as guinea pigs for testing size-decreasing potions. Rhun blinds Glew with the bauble, enabling the companions to escape, and then discovers that the bauble brings out strange markings in the book. Gwydion helps the companions cross to the island where Achren holds Eilonwy prisoner. Taran scales the tower to Eilonwy's room and discovers that Achren's enchantments have erased the princess's memory and that Achren plans to take over Annuvin. Under pressure, Gwydion gives up the bauble and book to Achren, but once in Eilonwy's rightful hands, they precipitate an earthquake that destroys the island and Achren's power. Comic humor increases the excitement and suspense of the story which moves shallow characters through a series of underdeveloped incidents to an abrupt, puzzling, and hectic conclusion and makes generous though satisfying use of coincidence, features typical of Alexander's writing. Rhun, the bumbling prince, is a flat but likeable figure. (Cauldron-Born*; Drynwyn*) ChLA Touchstones; Choice; Fanfare.

THE CAT (*The Cat and Mrs. Cary*), egotistical, independent, manipulative, scroungy, patchwork tom, which had once belonged to Mrs. Crow, an elderly recluse. The Cat goes in and out of Three Corners, Mrs. Cary's house, at will through a tiny trapdoor. He speaks throughout the novel, but only to Mrs. Cary, often giving her advice. Only she can understand and converse with him. Most people find Mrs. Cary's assertion that The Cat speaks to her merely an old woman's comic eccentricity. The Cat persuades her to invite Brad* Willets to spend the summer, because he wishes a boy to chum with. He causes Brad to find the parakeet and is also the means by which the humans discover the treasure in the secret attic room.

THE CAT AND MRS. CARY (Gates*†, Doris, ill. Peggy Bacon, Viking, 1962), realistic mystery-detective novel with fantasy aspects set in the small town of Crow's Harbor somewhere on the seacoast of the United States in the mid–1900s. Meeting The Cat*, a self-assured, patchwork tom that speaks, brings unexpected adventures into the life of Mrs. Cary, a staid, independent widow of modest means, who has just moved into the old house known as Three Corners that was formerly owned by reclusive Mrs. Crow. Before long, under the subtle influence of The Cat, Mrs. Cary has invited her nephew, Brad* Willets, almost thirteen and just recovered from a virus, to recuperate for the summer at her house. She also meets Cricket* Mobray, whose grandfather, Grandy Mobray, is in Crow's Harbor on some mysterious mission. Cricket informs Mrs. Cary that Three Corners is thought to be haunted by a ghost. While Brad is exploring the coast one day, he happens upon a small cruiser outfitted with rifles and sidearms, and then shortly afterward in a deserted graveyard he finds a beautifully colored parakeet which he rescues from The Cat. These discoveries are followed by still more Gothic conventions, including the theft of the parakeet by a stealthy night intruder, the discovery of secret attic rooms with sliding panels and a treasure worth over $5,000 secreted in the bottoms of empty bird cages stored in the attic, and the apprehension by Mr. Mobray, who turns out to be an FBI agent, of a parakeet-smuggling ring. Mr. Mobray informs Mrs. Cary that the former owner of Three Corners had acted as a go-between for the smugglers for several years, that her attic served as their storeroom, and that the $5,000 were the fruits of their illegal trade. The money now hers, Mrs. Cary buys a housetrailer so that the entire Willets family can come to visit her. Now more comfortable around people, she realizes that The Cat has helped her to become more outgoing and more appreciative of her family and her friends, and she looks forward to spending more time with them. The Cat chooses to return to Kansas with Brad, but Mrs. Cary decides she cannot be without a cat and adopts three nondescript kittens, offspring of The Cat and just as ordinary in appearance as he. The formulaic plot starts slowly, moves unevenly, and offers few surprises. Dialogue is natural, the relationship between Mrs. Cary and Brad is convincing, and The Cat, if humanized to the extent that he speaks to Mrs. Cary and plans and executes schemes, exhibits otherwise typical feline characteristics. Most of the excitement takes place in the last third of the book, but the novel's warm tone and positive outlook exert a certain charm, and the diction shows skill with and appreciation for language. Fanfare.

CATHERINE HALL (*A Gathering of Days*), also called Cath, the fun-loving, dutiful, slightly vain child, who tells the story in her journal. She is a religious girl and sincerely wishes to do right in the eyes of God and those around her.

Since she rejoices in her father's praise and is proud of being able to handle household tasks to his satisfaction, with some help from Mrs. Shipman, their neighbor, she feels some reluctance and even resentment about her new stepmother, Ann* Higham Hall, taking over. Catherine is self-reliant and self-controlled, and, although she knows she will miss her home and family, she accepts her father's decision to send her to the Holts*. She realizes that she can be helpful to them and that the situation will provide opportunities for a full and useful life.

CAT IN THE MIRROR (Stolz*†, Mary, Harper, 1975), novel in which the frame story takes place recently in New York City in the world of reality and the remainder in a fantasy world set in Egypt 3,000 years ago. Plain, unsure of herself, Erin Gandy, about fourteen, adores her handsome, successful, wealthy father, Peter, whose interest in things Egyptian she shares. A loner, she is dissatisfied with herself and on the outs with the people around her, particularly her beautiful, socialite mother, Belle, and the students at her exclusive private school. The only people she gets on with are Flora*, the kindly housekeeper, and a new student at school, Seti* Gammel, the son of an Egyptian official at the United Nations. While at the Metropolitan Museum of Art with Flora, Erin overhears her schoolmates speak disparagingly about her. Frantic to get away from them, she strikes her head, plummeting herself backward in time to ancient Egypt, where as Irun, daughter of the rich and influential noble, Perub, she finds herself in circumstances very similar to those of twentieth-century Erin. Irun is in conflict with her mother, Bel, alienated from her peers, extremely close to her father, comforted by her old nurse, Fl'ret, and befriended only by a noble youth, Seti. She thinks that the girl inside her, Erin, is her "demon." On a visit to Perub's house, the King admires Ta-she, Irun's silvery-gray kitten. Fearing that he will appropriate the cat for himself, Irun screams her defiance of him, at the same time precipitating herself back to the twentieth century. Erin awakens in the hospital, where she is being treated for concussion. When she arrives home, her father gives her a kitten that looks just like the one Irun had, a kitten she names Ta-she. Reflecting on her experiences, Erin finds comfort in knowing that her Egyptian counterpart had the same sorts of problems and ponders the nature of time and human experience. The reader is left in doubt about whether or not Erin was actually transported back in time and space or whether she was hallucinating. Details of the ancient setting offset the modern one, and their texture adds sufficient depth to keep this from being just another problem story, but the theme that generational and peer conflicts have probably always existed seems overly obvious. More interesting is the exploration of the concept of time: is time circular, rather than linear, and have these people been living in the past, too, incarnated in that dimension also? The girls' conflicts with themselves and others are clear, presented melodramatically in keeping with the typical teen self-centered points of view and tendency to exaggerate, and characters, except for Flora, are one-dimensional. Although the conclusion is too abrupt and filled with incidents and questions to be satisfying, style is vigorous, pace is fast, and the almost Electra attachments to the fathers is compelling. Fanfare.

THE CAT WHO WISHED TO BE A MAN (Alexander*, Lloyd, Dutton, 1973), fantasy set in an imaginary medieval kingdom which improvises on folktale motifs. Lionel, a cat who belongs to Stephanus, the wizard of Dunstan Forest, wishes to become a man and visit the town of Brightford. With a good deal of reluctance and grumbling, Stephanus effects the transformation and sends Lionel on his way, warning him against the evils of humans, directing him to return to Dunstan, and providing him with a magic wishbone that will grant him one boon. Lionel soon has good reason to doubt his decision to become human, for he immediately runs afoul of the tyrant of Brightford, small-bodied, meager-minded, greedy Pursewig, who exacts exorbitant tolls from all who enter the city and has the inhabitants firmly under his avaricious thumb. Lionel bypasses the toll gate and the human impediment of lack of money by calling upon his cat powers and vaulting over the gate. Inside the town, he soon discovers that Pursewig, who has acquired most of the property in the town by devious means, is trying to take over the Crowned Swan Inn, owned by pretty, assertive Gillian, with whom Lionel falls in love. Events follow in rapid succession as Lionel employs both human and feline powers to prevent Pursewig from ruining Gillian's business and forcing her to sell to him. Aiding him is chubby, loquacious Dr. Tudbelly, who has an Armamentarium of marvelous cures and remedies. When they divert the hundreds of rats that Pursewig and his henchman, Swaggart, have planted in Gillian's cellar to Pursewig's own house, Pursewig has the pair arrested and imprisoned. But the townspeople courageously object to Pursewig's kangaroo court tactics, and then Lionel informs them that Stephanus, not Pursewig, is the real owner of the bridge by which Pursewig has been profiting illegally all these years. Lionel uses up his one boon with the bone to return to Gillian just in time to rescue her from the inn to which Pursewig has set fire. Pursewig is deposed, and Lionel heads home accompanied by his friends, in accordance with Stephanus's instructions. Although Lionel has encountered abundant baseness among humankind, he himself has consistently acted out of noble motives, and Stephanus fails in his attempt to transform Lionel back into feline form. Stephanus acknowledges that, while he himself gave Lionel human shape, Lionel himself has by his unselfish actions made himself into a true human being. The book is mostly plot. Action-filled, it moves rapidly, incidents pushing one another to happen, some outrageous, some redoings of conventional happenings. Also combined are a bit of romance, subtle and slapstick humor, extensive dialogue, an interesting assemblage of flat and stock characters, a worthwhile if obvious theme, and a vigorous style. Altogether they make for rousing entertainment, predictably but satisfyingly concluded. Boston Globe Honor.

CAUDILL†, REBECCA (1899–1985), born in Poor Fork, Harlan County, Ky.; author best known for her regional short stories and historical novels for children. One of eleven children whose parents were teachers, she grew up in Tennessee and graduated from Wesleyan College in Georgia and later took her M.A. degree from Vanderbilt. She taught English in a girls' school in Rio de Janiero, and then edited a Methodist church paper in Nashville. She married James Ayars, an editor, and lived in Urbana, Ill. After her marriage, she wrote short stories, novels, and verse for children and young people, publishing eventually about two dozen books, mostly drawing upon the history of the Appalachian area and her own memories of her childhood there for subjects and settings. One of her historical novels, *Tree of Freedom†* (Viking, 1949), was both a Newbery honor book and a Fanfare book, while another, *The Far-Off Land** (Viking, 1964), was also included in Fanfare. Both involve mid-teen girls in the movement westward into Tennessee and Kentucky in the 1780s. *A Certain Small Shepherd** (Holt, 1965) and *Did You Carry the Flag Today, Charley?** (Holt, 1966), both highly illustrated short books for younger readers, were Fanfare and *Choice* selections, and the latter book is included in *Children's Books Too Good to Miss*. Her historical novels show extensive research and integrate personal conflicts well with those of the period. Her stories for younger children, if sentimental and occasionally contrived, show awareness of and sensitivity for the needs and problems of children and capture convincingly the limitations and the flavor of the rural mountain setting. She also published the picture book *A Pocketful of Cricket* (Holt, 1965) and *Come Along!* (Holt, 1969), a book of haiku.

CAULDRON-BORN (*The Book of Three**; *The Black Cauldron**; *The Castle of Llyr**; *Taran Wanderer**; *The High King**), the mute, mindless, and deathless warriors who serve Arawn, Lord of Annuvin, the evil monarch who seeks to control all Prydain*. They are the stolen bodies of slain warriors, steeped in the Black Crochan, or Black Cauldron, to give them life again. They cannot be killed by ordinary means, and in the hands of Arawn, they are implacable weapons of murder and the slaves of evil. Taran* eventually defeats them with the dread and powerful sword, Drynwyn*.

CAVANNA, BETTY (1909–   ), born in Camden, N.J.; author of popular romances, mysteries, problem stories, and growing-up novels mostly for early adolescent girls, and of informational books for younger readers in the First Books and Around the World Today series for Watts Publishing Co. She also wrote under the names of Elizabeth Headley, Betsy Allen, and Elizabeth Cavanna Harrison. She graduated from Douglass College with a major in journalism, wrote for a year for the Bayonne *Times*, and subsequently held positions with Westminster Press in Philadelphia as advertising manager and art director. While she was working with Westminster, she became interested in writing stories herself and in 1943 began writing full time for young people. Her over fifty novels primarily feature stereotyped protagonists occupied with such teen interests as boys, dogs, horses, the arts, loneliness, and shyness, and such timely issues as divorce, alcoholism, and racial bias. She married George Russell Harrison, who was dean of the School of Science of Massachusetts Institute of Technology, and the couple traveled extensively. Her escapist novels in the Around the World mysteries for Morrow Publishers, while otherwise conventional, reflect her keen eye for the color and physical appearance of the places they visited. *The Ghost of Ballyhooly** (Morrow, 1971) and *Spice Island Mystery** (Morrow, 1969) were both nominated for the Edgar Allan Poe Award. Others in the series are *Mystery in Marrakech* (Morrow, 1968) and *Mystery on Safari* (Morrow, 1970).

THE CAY (Taylor*, Theodore, Doubleday, 1969), realistic novel set mostly on a Caribbean island in 1942, during World War II, a variation of a Robinsonnade dealing with an inter-racial friendship. Phillip Enright, 11, originally from Virginia, is living with his parents on Curacao, a Dutch island off the coast of Venezuela, where his father works with a petroleum company, when German submarines shell the island and the harbor. Phillip's mother, who has never liked Curacao or felt comfortable with its black population, insists that she and Phillip go back to Virginia. Aboard the *S.S. Hato* they reach Panama but are torpedoed two days later on April 6. Phillip, struck on the head by debris during the evacuation of the ship, is hauled aboard a raft by a huge old black man, a West Indian named Timothy*. The only other occupant is the cook's cat, Stew. At first Phillip has a terrible headache; then he loses his sight. After several days the raft is washed ashore on a deserted cay, a small island one mile long and half a mile wide, with a few palm trees. Timothy fears, correctly, that they are on one of the many bits of land in the Devil's Mouth, where banks of coral form a U fifty miles long and make navigation hazardous, therefore out of the paths of shipping. Timothy builds a hut, catches lobster, and builds a fire pile to light if they hear aircraft, but he needs Phillip's aid to spell "H E L P" on the sand with stones. At first Phillip is very much afraid, particularly when alone, and he acts like a spoiled baby, expecting Timothy to wait on him and screaming insults when the old man tells him to weave sleeping mats. A sharp slap on the face from Timothy brings him to his senses and a new phase in their relationship starts when he asks the old man to call him Phillip instead of "young bahss." The island has no water, but Timothy makes a catchment to trap rain. With the aid of a vine rope and a cane, Phillip begins to get around the island. Timothy says Stew Cat is bad luck, and when the cat disappears, Phillip is afraid the old man has killed it, but finds that Timothy has put it on the anchored raft, carved a replica and driven nails into it to kill the bad spirits, then retrieved the real cat unharmed. Phillip nurses Timothy through an attack of malaria. He learns to fish on the reef and gets up courage to climb a palm for coconuts. Together they ride out a hurricane lashed to palm trees, but soon after this Timothy dies. Phillip buries him, rebuilds the fire pile, and explores the debris by sense of touch. Early in August he hears an airplane and lights the fire pile but cannot attract its attention. Toward the end of the month, he hears another and dumps armloads of the oily sea grape on the fire to make black smoke, and the plane circles low but then leaves. A few hours later a small power boat alerted by the plane comes, and the sailors are astonished to find a naked, blind boy and a cat. He is taken to a destroyer, his parents notified (his mother having been rescued from the *Hato*), and later in New York, after several operations, his sight is restored. The end is unrealistically cheerful and detracts from the compelling portion set on the cay. Phillip's petulance and dislike of Timothy, at first, are somewhat overdone for a boy whose entire existence depends on the man, even for a white boy raised by a prejudiced mother, and the theme of man's oneness under the skin is rather too obvious. The details of the island, however, make this an interesting variant of the Robinson Crusoe story. Addams; Choice; Fanfare; Lewis Carroll.

CAYUSE COURAGE (Lampman*, Evelyn Sibley, Harcourt, 1970), historical novel set in the Place of the Rye Grass, the valley in Oregon Territory where Marcus Whitman* established his mission among the Cayuse Indians. Alert, sensitive Samuel Little-Pony, about ten and an aspiring warrior, witnesses events that lead up to the Indian attack on the Whitman mission in 1847. Most Cayuse, including Samuel's staunch, wise grandfather, Old* Beardy, a former chief, have ambivalent feelings about the Whitmans. They respect Boston Doctor, as they call him, and see advantages in his white medicines and technology, but they resent not being allowed to enter the Whitman house, not being given a share of the crops grown on their land, and, in particular, not being paid for the land on which Whitman built the mission. When Samuel injures his hand in a White-Eyes' (their term for whites) trap and gangrene sets in, and the medicine man, Cupup* Cupup cannot help, Old Beardy takes the boy to Whitman, who saves his life by amputating the hand. Narcissa Whitman, Marcus's wife, called Yellow* Hair Squaw by the Indians, nurses him back to health with the help of her foster daughters, Mary Ann Bridger* and Helen Meek, of whom Samuel becomes fond. Unable to fight or hunt and hence useless to his tribe, Samuel confidently expects to continue living with the Whitmans. But when they take in the seven orphaned Sager* children, they have no room for Samuel and send him back to the tribe. Angry, resentful, bitter, feeling rejected and abandoned, he turns for consolation to Joe Lewis*, white-hating, visiting Iroquois, who urges the Cayuse to band together and drive out the White-Eyes. When settlers bring with them an epidemic of measles that kills many Indians, the Cayuse believe they have been poisoned by the missionaries. After Amos, the son of Chief* Tilaukait, dies, the Cayuse attack the mission and kill almost all the White-Eyes there, including the Whitmans. The women and children who survive are eventually ransomed by the British of the Hudson's Bay Company, the leaders of the uprising are executed by avenging White-Eyes, and Samuel faces the inevitable and accepts a position as interpreter with the British trading company. This is a dramatic, emotion-gripping account of personal and tribal tragedy. The story combines good characterizations of the principals with a simple, fairly plausible plot which presents the historical events sympathetically if a bit too ambitiously from the point of view but not in the words of a boy on the periphery of events. The story neither sentimentalizes nor romanticizes the Indians, and its strength lies in the good sense it gives of their altered way of life and their perceptions of and attitudes toward the whites and those of the whites toward the Indians. Considerable irony and the ultimate tragedy grow out of the Indians' grasp of the tremendous disparity between the actions and the words of the White-Eyes. The many characters are sometimes hard to keep straight, but all of them except Samuel and all events except those immediately involving Samuel are historical. Old Beardy, the grandfather, is a particularly memorable character. Narcissa Whitman is sketched in bold strokes, epitomizing by her behavior and attitudes the characteristics of the whites that most antagonize the Indians. Some of the author's terminology is questionable, for example, the terms ''squaw'' and ''brave'' and referring to Joe Lewis as a ''renegade.'' Spur.

CEREMONY OF INNOCENCE (Forman*, James, Hawthorn, 1970), historical novel set in Munich, Germany, during World War II. Hans Scholl, 24, and his younger sister, Sophie*, both students at the University of Munich, are in Stadelheim prison awaiting trial for treason. They have been caught distributing leaflets urging resistance to Hitler's government. As he converses with the prisoner who shares his cell during the weekend of his imprisonment, responds to the questions of interrogators and his lawyer and to the suggestions of Franz Bittner, a childhood friend now an SS trooper, Hans reflects on significant events that lead to his being in prison. In linear narrative and in flashbacks, Hans recalls how Franz's father invites him to join the Hitler youth after he defends the ugly little boy against older bullies and how disappointed he is when his father opposes his joining. He remembers how proud he is when, finally a member of the corps, he carries the flag at a Party victory convention and how he doubts his leader's motives when the man refuses to call a doctor to care for Franz, who has suffered severe burns in an accident. He recalls an Octoberfest he attended with fellow medical students Alexander* (Alex) Schmorell and Christl Probst during which a Jewish youth is harrassed by Hitler youth and then shot to death. Service in France and Russia affirms his belief that death is an outrage and that the actions of Hitler's Party pose a threat to all humanity. He, Alex, and Christl write and distribute leaflets under the White Rose symbol for some time before Sophie discovers what they are doing and insists on joining them. She identifies with the unfortunate and the oppressed and has become increasingly religious. She staunchly supports their efforts to promote passive resistance. At the same time, Alex and Sophie become sweethearts, but Christl's resolve wavers when he realizes what harm his actions might bring to his young wife and babies. The little group adds members gradually, growing to about a dozen, and includes the eminent Professor Huber. Although Franz becomes an SS trooper, his philosophy the typical Party line, his concern for the welfare of the Scholls and especially for Sophie, of whom he is fond, seems genuine. Suspecting that they may be behind the seditious papers, he warns them on several occasions of the consequences if they are caught. At the end, all are captured and taken to trial. Unsuccessful in his attempts to persuade Hans to recant, Franz slips him a pistol, which Hans later gives to the priest as he is led away to execution. Hans rejects both suicide and escape as compromising his principles. All meet death on the guillotine. In an added note, the author states that all the main characters except Franz really lived, and that memorials to all were subsequently erected in Munich. The interrogation scenes are suspenseful but offer no horrors of torture or maltreatment, nor are Hans's Gestapo jailers shown as unfeeling, inhuman villains. Hans's political convictions grow and change believably, and his concern for his sister and friends and his fears for his own safety show that he has been no mere slave to ideology. Franz Bittner, however, whose motivations remain obscure, emerges for that reason as the most interesting character in the book. Scenes unfold like a series of snapshots in an album, recording details of action, emotion, and politics realistically and gradually. The novel's main concern is with examining what motivated these intelligent, life-loving young people to sacrifice their lives and bright futures for a cause so patently futile, when almost everyone else who shared their views simply played a waiting game. Lewis Carroll.

A CERTAIN SMALL SHEPHERD (Caudill*†, Rebecca, ill. William Pène du Bois*†, Holt, 1965), short realistic story set among the farmers of Hurricane Gap in the Appalachians in the mid twentieth century. Born on a freakish night in November, little Jamie is a beautiful child in all respects except that he cannot talk. Although he is teased by his playmates and their parents term him "no-count," Jamie's father recognizes that the boy has a good mind and enrolls him at age six in the local one-room school taught by Miss Creech. Soon Jamie excels in his studies but is frustrated by his inability to speak in oral language. He is proud to be given the part of a shepherd in the school Christmas play, and with cloak and crook he looks forward eagerly to the performance. To his dismay, a terrible snowstorm on Christmas Eve cancels the program. That night Jamie's father takes in a man and woman who come to his door seeking shelter. Although they elect to stay in the stable, he takes the couple to the little church nearby because it is warmer there. The next morning the family discovers that the woman has given birth to a child. Jamie, who knows well the story of the first Christmas, runs home quickly. He puts on his shepherd's cloak, grabs his crook, removes the orange from his Christmas stocking, and rushes back to the church. Clearly and strongly he speaks for the first time in his life, announcing that he has a "gift for the Child." This warm, sentimental account of a father's concern for his handicapped son and a small, loveable boy's unselfish gift engages the emotions from the outset. Language is rich and euphonious, and descriptions are sharp with imagery. Clear, framed, rather stiff watercolors contribute to the homey tone and rustic setting and add some details to this simple modern version of the ancient Nativity Story. Choice; Fanfare.

CHAFFIN, LILLIE D(ORTON) (1925–   ), born in Varney, Ky.; poet, educator, and librarian. She attended the University of Akron, was graduated from Pikeville College, and received her M.A. degree from Eastern Kentucky University. She has taught elementary grades and been a librarian, and has lived in Pikeville and Meta, Ky. Besides several hundred poems and stories, she has published three books of poetry for adults, including *A Stone for Sisyphus* (South and West, 1967), which won the International Poetry Prize. Among her books of poems for children are *Bear Weather* (Macmillan, 1969) and *In My Backyard* (Golden Horseshoe, 1970). In 1968 she was named poet of the year at Alice Lloyd College. Her novel for young people, *John Henry McCoy** (Macmillan, 1971), set in the eastern Kentucky country she knows well, won the Child Study Award. A more recent book set in the same locale is *Up Hatfield Holler* (Ashford, 1981).

THE CHALK CROSS (Amoss*, Berthe, Seabury, 1976), fantasy set in New Orleans which alternates between the present day and 1832. Stephanie Martin, 14, a talented but lonely girl, is sketching scenes in New Orleans from the 1830s for her class in the Bois, the famous art school properly called *l'Academe aux Bois, College des Beaux Arts la Nouvelle Orleans.* She feels a strange affinity with a particular cottage in St. Ann Street and finds herself drawn into the life of its early nineteenth-century occupants, Marie Laveau, the Voodoo Queen, and her daughters, Sidonie and Dede. This is just the first of a series of similar experiences in which Stephanie becomes Donie, a free black, the artistic daughter who is expected to inherit the Power by which her mother works voodoo, but who struggles to retain her identity and her religious belief. Through the summer of 1832, during which plague hits New Orleans, Stephanie-Donie attempts to undo Marie Laveau's gris-gris which makes a lovely young belle give up her love for an apothecary and submit, zombie-like, to marriage with an old marquis. Failing to prevent that, the girl tries to save the slave who is to be sold for trying to help her young mistress elope. Hoping to control the power, she agrees to be initiated into voodoo but eventually rejects it, even destroying the snake, Dumballah, which plays an important part in her mother's magic. Stephanie, returning periodically to the twentieth century, is increasingly disturbed by her double life but gets little help from the nuns at the Bois, who either try to explain it as the result of overwork or are too preoccupied with a financial crisis at the school to give it full attention. When Donie's mother sends her spirit forward in time, Stephanie accepts it as part of herself, and the drawings that picture the life of Donie and seem to Stephanie to have been done by the girl in the past are skillful enough to ensure her chance of staying on at the school. The time fantasy is not always convincing, but the scenes from New Orleans of 1832 are vivid and the Gothic elements of the house-like tombs and the voodoo ceremonies are excitingly spooky. Poe Honor.

THE CHAMPION OF MERRIMACK COUNTY (Drury*, Roger W., ill. Fritz Wegner, Little, 1976), lighthearted fantasy set in an American small town sometime in the mid twentieth century. To their astonishment, Janet Berryfield and her mother, Dorothea, find a mouse wearing a helmet riding a miniature bicycle around the rim of their newly installed old-fashioned bathtub. As they watch, fascinated, O* Crispin, expert bicyclist mouse who lives with his large family in the Berryfield cellar (the only cellar in the Bel-Air Park), tries an intricate maneuver he calls "Rolling Down to Rio" and slips on a sliver of soap on the floor of the tub. In the ensuing crash, not only is his tail injured and the front wheel of his bike ruined, but also a long scratch is gouged in the tub's enamel. Janet and her mother try to cope with all these problems before Mr. Berryfield comes home, since the tub is his pride and joy and he is so anti-mouse that he has invented a new trap to keep them from his workshop. Janet takes the damaged bike first to Harry's Bicycle Shop. Harry takes her on a bicycle-built-for-two to his Great-uncle Silvester Pye, clockmaker, where they find a wheel small enough but with cogs around the edge. Pye, riding in the bike basket, directs them down country lanes to Bangs the Blacksmith. Bangs decides it is a job for the fine tools of a dentist, and mounting his "sample horse," which wears a different shoe on each foot, leads them to his son-in-law, natty Dr. Norton, who fixes the wheel and, his curiosity aroused, jogs along behind the others to the Berryfield home. In the meantime Mrs. Berryfield has taken O Crispin to Dr. Potts, who misunderstands her and believes she is referring to her own rear end when she mentions a broken tail. He sends her to the hospital for an X-Ray where, after a series of misunderstandings, he finally splints O Crispin's tail, rigs a hook and miniature fishpole suspended from Crispin's helmet to hold the heavy tail up, and accompanies Mrs. Berryfield home. The assembled helpers are watching the mouse practice on the tub which makes an ideal racetrack when Arthur Berryfield comes home. He soon discovers the hiding men and the scratch, which Janet has disguised with toothpaste, but he refuses to believe the wild story. Crispin, in the meantime, has escaped to the basement and hidden in the box trap constructed by Mr. Berryfield. All the other mice are driven from the house by the eight pet-shop cats rented by Mr. Berryfield, but they can't get at Crispin in the trap. When Mr. Berryfield finally discovers the mouse, though he is reluctant to admit it, he is so delighted that his trap works that he brings food to the mouse and sneaks out at night to release him. This is just in time for Crispin to reach the race track where he wins and becomes Champion of Merrimack County. Returning triumphantly, he races around the tub edge while Mr. Berryfield soaks and snoozes, then hides, again in the trap, and again gets caught, so he is on hand when all the original helpers arrive with surprises, Bangs with a new foot to replace the missing one on the tub, Harry with a wire soap rack made from a bicycle basket, Mr. Pye with an ingenious spring to retract the plug so the mouse will not hit it, and the dentist with enamel to repair the original scratch. O Crispin puts on a great show for them all and plans new triumphs, perhaps to become Champion of the World. The story has a straight-faced tone that makes the ludicrous adventures seem somehow plausible. Christopher.

CHANCY AND THE GRAND RASCAL (Fleischman*, Sid, ill. Eric von Schmidt, Little, 1966), realistic adventure novel with period aspects told in tall-tale style and set along the Ohio River and then in Sun Dance, Kans., shortly after the

Civil War. When their doctor father is killed at Vicksburg and their mother dies of fever, Chancy Dundee and his brother and two sisters are parceled out to various families by a schoolteacher friend, Miss Russell, who keeps the two youngest, Mirandy and Jamie. Indiana, another sister, is apprenticed to a chair bottomer near Paducah, and Chancy ends up with the Starbucks on a farm in southern Ohio. Four years later, Chancy piles his few belongings in a wheelbarrow and bravely heads for the Ohio River, where he happens to encounter his Uncle Will, the younger brother whom his mother proudly called "a grand rascal." Tall, lean, very strong, an Indian fighter and adventurer, Uncle Will Buckthorn smokes thin black cigars and carries two carpetbags filled with clocks which he peddles as the two travel together. His keen knowledge of human nature, ready wit, and facile tongue enable them to make the best of every situation they meet as they go along. Uncle Will gets them a lift down the Ohio on Captain Harpe's logboat, where he plies the oars and Chancy works as a cook. At Paducah, they discover Indiana still working for the miserly chair bottomer, Micajah Jones, whom Will tricks into signing release papers in exchange for an empty strongbox that presumably contains Indiana's inheritance. Miss Russell has informed Indiana by letter that she has moved to Sun Dance, a cowtown near Abilene. When Uncle Will and Chancy arrive there, they find the place almost deserted because the people have heard that Indians are about to attack and have left in search of safety. Only a few hardy souls remain, including Miss Russell, Mirandy, and Jamie, who is too ill to be moved. When the Indians turn out to be the notorious Seven-Eyes Smith and his gang of outlaws in disguise, Uncle Will spreads the word that longhorns are bringing thirty dollars a head in Sun Dance. The rumor precipitates a cattle rush that pens the outlaws inside the town. Uncle Will then captures them easily and turns them in for the fifteen hundred dollars in reward money. The grateful residents elect Uncle Will mayor, and he decides to settle in Sun Dance, a jack-of-all-trades who will try being a family man for a change. The plot is elaborate but concocted with precision, and clever twists on stock incidents and characters, even pacing, and large doses of trickery, villainy, and near escapes result in a story that asks nothing of the audience but to enjoy. Choice; Fanfare.

THE CHANGELING (Snyder*, Zilpha Keatley, ill. Alton Raible, Atheneum, 1970), realistic novel of family life set in the late 1900s in the suburban community of Rosewood Hills somewhere in the United States. The story starts when Martha Abbott is a high school sophomore and drama major, then flashes back, not in Martha's words but from her point of view, to the time when she is seven, a shy, chubby, unpretty, underachiever in a family of extroverted doers and excellers. That year she becomes friends with Ivy* Carson, second youngest of the local ne'er-do-wells who live off and on in a rundown mansion nearby. Ivy is dark eyed and curly headed, a strange, unearthly looking child, with a powerful imagination and a strong desire to become a dancer. Not a typical Carson, Ivy thinks she may be a changeling, the child of water sprites or wood nymphs who was exchanged for the real Ivy at birth. In mostly summarized narrative, the author describes their ten-year friendship. Martha is the follower, while Ivy generates the ideas for their activities. Life is very exciting for Martha when Ivy is around, and, in spite of Martha's parents' disapproval, the two maintain their association, always resuming their relationship when the Carsons return to town. The girls meet in Bent Oaks Grove, where they live in a let's-pretend world, with rituals and ceremonies, imaginary monsters and strange animals, and people who inhabit a mythical kingdom in the trees whom they call the Tree People. In junior high, Ivy persuades Martha to join the new drama club. There Ivy comes into conflict with Kelly Peters, most popular girl, and the book reaches its climax when Ivy wins the part of lead dancer instead of Kelly. Then the school office is vandalized, and for revenge Kelly accuses Ivy and Martha of doing it. Her word is taken over theirs, and to avoid trouble the Carsons quickly move away. Then Martha's older brother, Tom, confesses that he and chums high on dope were responsible for the break-in. Two years pass, and Martha, now deeply involved in drama and grown more self-assured, learns from Josie, Ivy's little sister and her counterpart, that Ivy has inherited from her Aunt Evaline enough money to attend ballet school. The two changelings are making good lives for themselves, each in her own way. Martha's continuing friendship with Ivy is not wholly convincing, given the presentation of her parents as highly social-conscious and over-directive. Tension is low until late in the book, and the story comes down from the climax too quickly. Although the author hints at the dissatisfaction of Martha's brother and sister with their success-oriented upbringing, Tom's brush with the law seems contrived and brings the book close to a tract on how not to bring up children. Martha grows up convincingly, but Ivy is the book's most interesting character. The other people are stereotypes. (Mrs.* Smith) Choice; Christopher.

CHARLEEN MADLEE (*Summer of My German Soldier**), journalist who takes an interest in Patty Bergen and encourages her to pursue writing as a vocation. She takes Patty with her when she interviews the commander at the prison farm and presents her with a subscription to her newspaper while Patty is in reform school. She is a type figure but is important in giving Patty hope.

CHARLES HALL (*A Gathering of Days**), Catherine's* father, a farmer. He has strong convictions and holds firmly to certain principles, but he is not a rigid man. He loves to tell stories, enjoys jokes, and appreciates Cath's efforts to make a home. He knows his own mind and refuses to be drawn into a relationship with Aunt Lucy Shipman. While he is in Boston on a trading trip, he meets and marries Ann* Higham, a widow, who runs a store and has a son. Cath realizes that he is pleased to have a son at last, although she does feel a few pangs of jealousy. Charles is a well-realized, interesting, and sympathetic figure.

CHARLES WALLACE MURRY (*A Wrinkle in Time**), precocious, younger brother of Meg* Murry, a child prodigy, who is especially close to his older sister with whom he is able to communicate telepathically. His pride and reliance on intellect make him susceptible to IT, who captures him on Camazotz*.

CHARLEY KEMP (*The Mystery of Ghost Valley**), stagestruck youth from the Pennsylvania Dutch town of Kutztown, who, after graduation from high school, goes to New York City hoping to break into movies and TV. He is part of the movie company that has come to town to film the Arts Festival. Victim of the temptation for easy money, he joins Mr. Jennings and Mr. Taylor in counterfeiting antiques.

CHARLIE GODFREY (*The Summer of the Swans**), ten-year-old, mute, retarded, younger brother of Sara Godfrey, for whom she feels a deep affection and who gets lost while trying to make his way at night to look at some swans. A very realistically drawn figure, Charlie suffered brain damage at the age of three from high fevers accompanying two illnesses. He is a winning child and takes pleasure in and worries about small things. He sometimes endlessly repeats actions, like scuffling his feet in the same spot on the porch steps until he wears grooves in them and fingering a buttonhole until it becomes a large rent in the garment. Charlie is particularly fond of a wristwatch which once was taken from him as a prank by some boys. It was returned to him by Joe Melby, who Sara mistakenly thinks took it.

CHASE ME, CATCH NOBODY! (Haugaard*, Erik Christian, Houghton, 1980), historical novel set in Nazi Germany in 1937. Erik Hansen, 14, a Danish boy of a well-to-do, middle-class family, reluctantly joins a group from his school on a vacation trip to Germany. On the ferry a man in a grey raincoat gives him a package, with directions to deliver it to an address in Hamburg if the man is not able to take it back after customs inspection. Having seen the man obviously being arrested, Erik takes the first opportunity to open the package and finds it contains a stack of blank passports, a fact he communicates only to a boy with whom he has become friendly, Nikolai Karl Leon Linde, son of a Communist and politically far more knowledgeable than Erik. Nikolai, who is strongly anti-fascist, continually ridicules the Hitler youth and together with Erik earns the wrath of Mr. Nielson, the teacher known as The Lighthouse, who admires the Nazis. The other teacher, Stinker Larson, is more liberal and less tyrannical. In Hamburg, Erik leaves the group and delivers the passports, then discovers that Nikolai has told his secret. When the police approach the group at the zoo, Erik escapes. Later, seeing the dwarf to whom he delivered the passports taken into custody, Erik follows the offer of help of a young man who takes him to a low-type tavern, where he meets the fat, slovenly proprietress, Gretl, known as the Sow, and Freiherr von Klein, a young aristocrat high in the Nazi hierarchy. For reasons he does not understand, the Freiherr tells the Sow to give him a place to stay, but that night he discovers a half-Jewish niece of the Sow, Isolde, who calls herself Nobody, a girl who has been hiding for a year in an upper room. With the help of the Sow, Erik and Nobody start for the Danish border but are joined by Nikolai and followed by Freiherr. In a final effort they come to an inlet across from the Danish coast, steal a leaky scow with two paddles, and narrowly escape to Denmark. Because the story seems to be based on autobiography, there are some elements of the plot left unexplained. The characterizations of Erik and, even more, of exuberant but foolish Nikolai, are strong, and the picture of pre-war Germany is chilling. Fanfare.

CHAU LI (*The Man in the Box: A Story from Vietnam**), Vietnamese boy from a Montagnard village who saves the American soldier. Chau Li's own father has been tortured and killed by the Viet Cong in the bamboo box, in which a man can neither sit straight nor stretch out. The boy feels compelled to honor the memory of his father, the village chief, by helping the American prisoner now in the box, even if it is only to kill him with a grenade to prevent his further torture. Chau Li has been the chief provider for his mother, his old grandfather, and his two younger sisters, so he has become adept at getting food in the jungle and is a responsible boy for his age, which is not given but is clearly too young for him to be taken as a soldier by either side and so must be no more than fourteen.

CHEROKEE STRIP (*The Obstinate Land**), also known as the Cherokee Outlet, the Indian country in north-central Oklahoma which was opened for settlement on September 16, 1893, and became the scene of a tremendous land rush. The Rombergs, German-American farmers from Texas, hurriedly establish their claim on this marginally agricultural land. They soon come into conflict with a rancher who has a large herd of beef and wishes to add their homestead to his own.

CHESTER CRICKET (*The Cricket in Times Square**; *Tucker's Countryside**), the Connecticut country cricket whose fondness for liverwurst leads to his being trapped in a picnic basket and carried to New York City, where for a time he lives in a matchbox and then in a Chinese cricket cage belonging to Mario* Bellini. His marvelous musical talent brings financial success to the Bellini newsstand. Later returned to Connecticut, he summons Tucker* Mouse and Harry* Cat to help him keep his home meadow from being razed for apartments.

CHIEF TILAUKAIT (*Cayuse Courage**), leading chief of the Cayuse band to which Samuel belongs. He is a staunch, firm, usually fair and just man, and Samuel holds him in high regard. He arranges for Samuel to accompany the band on the hunt in Blackfeet territory during which Samuel's hand is injured. Clever and discerning, he long resists the urging of Joe Lewis* to attack the White-Eyes but loses his perspective after the death of his son, Amos. He is executed for his part in the uprising.

CHILD OF THE OWL (Yep*, Laurence, Harper, 1977), realistic novel set mostly in San Francisco's Chinatown during the early 1960s. Casey* Young, 12, whose Chinese name, Cheun Meih, means "Taste of Spring," must leave her gambling father, Barney*, in a hospital where he has landed after winning big and being robbed and beaten by thugs. Incompatible with the family of her deceased mother's brother, Uncle Phil, a wealthy Americanized lawyer, she is sent to her maternal grandmother, Ah Low, called Paw-Paw*, who lives in a tiny cluttered apartment in a Chinatown alley. Externally tough from years of batting around with Barney, Casey soon finds rapport with Paw-Paw, who is tough in a different way, tiny, round-faced but hardworking and independent. When Barney shows up and tells Casey he is deeply in debt from gambling and must run from his creditors, she begins to realize she is stuck for a long-term stay, breaks down and cries, and is comforted by Paw-Paw's long story of their supposed ancestors, owl people, and of the jade owl charm that is the only family heirloom. Gradually Casey begins to understand and like Chinatown and to meet people: Mr. Jeh, an elderly member of Paw-Paw's club which meets in Portsmouth Square, Mr. Jeh's grand-nephew Gilbert, the "Pachinko" or Chinese tough, who drives for a gangster and tries to act like James Dean, Sheridan, an alcoholic who was in high school with Barney and Casey's mother, and even Booger (Tallulah Bankhead Chew), a girl in her class at school. When Paw-Paw surprises a burglar and her leg is broken in the ensuing scuffle, Mr. Jeh, Casey, and Booger stake out the pool hall Gilbert frequents, suspecting him of being the thief who has taken the owl charm. Following him, they arrive in a third-rate apartment house in time to see him held at gunpoint, and Mr. Jeh, a devotee of Tai Chi, an exercise system, brains the gunman with a book. Only then Casey discovers that Barney is also there and realizes that he is the thief. Since neither Phil nor Paw-Paw's other son will contribute enough to pay the hospital expenses, Paw-Paw arranges to sell the charm to an art museum for enough to pay her debt and to extract Barney from his difficulties. Casey, disillusioned with Barney and finding that Gilbert has been leaving the five dollars every week she has thought was from Barney, refuses to have anything to do with her father, but in the end her resentment weakens and she calls to see how he is. Both the setting and the characters come alive in the first-person narration, particularly Casey, who is convincingly street-hard but bright and sensitive inside, and Paw-Paw, who displays an interesting mixture of American and Chinese cultures. The story about the owls, however, is intrusive, too long and complicated to seem folktale-like and not interesting enough to carry the symbolic weight assigned it. Addams; Boston Globe Winner; Fanfare.

CHILDRESS, ALICE (1920–   ), born in Charleston, S.C.; author, actress, lecturer. She attended Radcliff Institute for Independent Study, married Nathan Woodard, has one child, and has lived in New York City. She was director for New York's American Negro Theater, and two of her plays, *Wine in the Wilderness* and *Wedding Band*, were produced for television. Her best known book for young people is *A Hero Ain't Nothin' but a Sandwich** (Coward, 1973), a story of a thirteen-year-old heroin addict, which was a National Book Award finalist and was named to the Lewis Carroll Shelf. Both this novel and *Rainbow Jordan* (Coward, 1981), a story of a neglected black girl who comes to appreciate the fussy woman in charge of the Interim House where she has been placed, are written in first person with several different narrators, thereby reflecting events from divergent points of view. She also wrote *When the Rattlesnake Strikes* (Coward, 1975).

THE CHOCOLATE WAR (Cormier*, Robert, Pantheon, 1974), realistic novel set in the late 1960s or early 1970s in a modern urban Catholic boys' high school named Trinity. Though its existence is not officially recognized, an organization called the Vigils* really controls Trinity, and though the Vigils' president is Carter, the organization itself is actually controlled by clever, malignant Archie* Costello, the assigner. Assignments in Archie's hands are ingenious and usually psychological, more likely to wound the spirit than the body, a fact which helps the Brothers close their eyes. Assignments fall to seemingly random students selected by Archie and must be accepted if the student wants to stay alive at the school, which means staying out of trouble with the Vigils. Archie is controlled only by the black box containing five white and one black marble, out of which he must draw a marble after each assignment is made. If he should draw a black marble (as he never has), Archie would have to complete the assignment himself. The assignment of Roland Goubert, the Goober*, is to loosen all the screws on all the furniture in timid Brother Eugene's classroom, with a resulting chaos of collapsing chairs and desks that drives Brother Eugene to mental breakdown. The assignment for the skinny freshman, Jerry Renault, is to refuse for ten days to accept for sale any of the chocolates that the students are expected to sell "voluntarily," fifty boxes per student. The money-raising sale is of special significance because Brother* Leon, the acting headmaster, has doubled the number and the price of the chocolates and has spent unauthorized school money to finance the special cash price, and he is theatrically calling each name in assembly to ask for the number of boxes accepted for sale and the number sold. Privately Brother Leon has enlisted the help of the Vigils through Archie, who agrees, seeing this as a way of controlling Brother Leon. Jerry, the protagonist, is already upset, as Archie knows, by the recent death of his mother and his father's passive acceptance of the meaningless routine of his life. In his locker Jerry keeps a poster with the question, "Do I dare disturb the universe?" He has tried to find meaning in football, which he pursues with dogged determination, though he is too light to be good. He suffers through Brother Leon's sarcasm and anger for the ten days, and, when his assignment is completed, continues, in an unexpected stand for individualism, to refuse the chocolates. Other students, sick of the pressure to sell, begin to admire him, and Brother Leon, terrified that the sale will collapse, leans on Archie. Archie gets his side-kick, Obie, and the animalistic Emile Janza, whom he blackmails by letting Janza think he has a picture of him masturbating, to harrass Jerry in a variety of ways, including phone calls with only breathing on the line at all hours, and a vicious attack by a gang of little kids paid by Janza. The Vigils take over the sale, send out teams of sellers, and dispose of all the chocolates except the fifty boxes Jerry will not accept. Archie organizes a fight, Jerry against Janza, which turns out to be a raffle: for fifty cents, any student can call for a specific punch and assign it to either fighter. Tricked into coming, Jerry realizes too late that it will be a massacre. Only Goober makes any attempt to stop the fight until Brother Jacques ends it by shutting off the lights, while Brother Leon has been secretly watching all along. Before Jerry is taken away in the ambulance, he tries to tell Goober not to fight the system, not to try to disturb the universe. The picture of the school is of almost unrelieved corruptness and viciousness, and the theme is far more cynical than is usual in books for young people. Individual scenes are vivid and seem realistic, but the total effect is a disturbing view of life, with all the characters who might have been expected to support Jerry either ineffectual or evil. Sequel is *Beyond the Chocolate War* (Pantheon, 1985). Contemporary Classics; Lewis Carroll; Maxi.

CHRIS (*No More Magic**), impressionable, imaginative, persevering schoolboy who loses his bike on Halloween night, is certain it has been stolen, and sets out to recover it. He believes the bike is magic because it is a special green color. On Halloween, he dresses up as the Green Lantern.The idea that his best friend, Eddie, may have stolen his bike plunges him into a temporary depression. He feels sorry for parentless Muffin*, and, like her, is sure that when his green magic bike has been recovered, the magic will return to her parents' marriage and her family will all be together again, a naive assumption, but one in keeping with both their characters as presented and their ages.

CHRIS THEODORAKIS (*The Westing Game**), handicapped youth confined to a wheelchair for some sort of nerve disorder, one of the heirs in the Westing game.

CHRISTOPHER HERON (*The Perilous Gard**), younger brother of Sir Geoffrey, noble into whose custody Kate* Sutton is assigned. Blaming himself for the supposed death of Geoffrey's young daughter, Christopher has banished himself to live in an old leper's hut, returning to the castle and wearing decent clothes only when his brother is making a rare visit to the place. Idealistic and rather romantic, Christopher bargains with the "Fairy Folk" when he discovers they have the child and volunteers to trade places with her and become the *tiend* payer, the one to be ritually murdered as part of the religion of these survivors of the pre-Christian cult. In the interval between his imprisonment in their underground caverns and All-Hallows Eve, when the ceremony will take place, he is found by Kate, also a prisoner, and during her nightly visits reveals his secret desire, to buy and restore an old manor near his boyhood home. When

Kate interrupts the ceremony and her practical good sense breaks the spell, they both escape and at book's end are to marry.

CHUCK MASTERSON (*The Wonderful Flight to the Mushroom Planet†*; *Stowaway to the Mushroom Planet†*; *Time and Mr. Bass**), David* Topman's best friend. Chuck is short and square with brown skin and dark hair. While David is the planner and thinker, Chuck likes to do things. His grandfather, Cap'n Tom, gives the boys the materials to make the space ship with which they travel to Basidium-X*, the Mushroom Planet. Although likeable, Chuck is a flat character, almost indistinguishable from David.

CLAGGET, GEORGE (*Encounter at Easton**), constable in Easton, whose main concern in the Mawes case is doing his duty under the law, though he is not a cruel and inhumane man. He evidently is the link by which the tapman learns about Robert's* background and buys the rest of Robert's time. Clagget tells part of the story.

CLAPP, PATRICIA (1912–   ), born in Boston, Mass.; author of plays and books for adults and children. She studied journalism at Columbia University. Before she wrote her novels for young readers, she was well established as a writer of plays. More highly acclaimed than any of those, however, was her first novel, *Constance** (Lothrop, 1968), which was a finalist for the National Book Award the first year it was given for a children's book and was selected for the Lewis Carroll Shelf. A historical novel for older readers about the founding of Plymouth Colony, this rich, ambitious novel is well researched and full of the color of the times, if uneven in plot and heavy on history. Among her other novels for young people are *King of the Dollhouse* (Lothrop, 1974) and *Jane-Emily* (Lothrop, 1969), both fantasies, the first for younger girls and the other for adolescents, and, also for an older audience, *I'm Deborah Sampson* (Lothrop, 1977), which fictionalizes upon the real life experiences of the woman who disguised herself as a man in order to fight in the American Revolution, and *Witches' Children: A Story of Salem* (Lothrop, 1982), a historical novel about the witch trials of 1692.

CLAUDIA KINCAID (*From the Mixed-up Files of Mrs. Basil E. Frankweiler**), twelve-year-old suburban New York City schoolgirl, who, with her younger brother, Jamie*, runs away from home and hides out for a week in the New York Metropolitan* Museum of Art. Claudia feels unappreciated by her parents and not recognized for her individuality. A bright, resourceful, independent child, she plans the expedition and works out ways to evade detection. She also researches and discovers the origin of the Angel, a statue newly acquired by the museum. She feels better about herself at the end of the adventure.

CLEARWATER (*Gentle Ben**), old fisherman on the *Far North*, the salmon seiner owned by Mark Andersen's father, Karl. Having worked for Mark's grandfather, Clearwater has a paternalistic attitude toward Karl and toward Mark, whom he teaches to swim and encourages during the boy's first season aboard the boat. In a storm which wrecks the *Far North*, he is drowned. Karl is able to save only the black beret which Clearwater wore winter and summer.

CLEARY†, BEVERLY (BUNN) (1916–   ), born in McMinnville, Oreg.; prolific author, mostly of humorous, episodic stories for the eight-to-ten-year-old reader. She attended the University of California in Berkeley and received a degree in librarianship from the University of Washington in Seattle. After serving in the public library in Yakima, Wash., and as post librarian in an army hospital during World War II, she started writing books for children, her most popular being in two series, those of *Henry Huggins†* (Morrow, 1950) and its many successors and those about *Ellen Tebbits†* and her friends. These books are mildly humorous stories of a typical boy and a typical girl, written in simple language accessible to readers just beyond the primer stage. Henry has a dog of uncertain ancestry which is featured in *Henry and Ribsy†* (Morrow, 1954) and *Ribsy** (Morrow, 1964). The series takes on a new dimension, however, when it shifts to Henry's neighbors in *Beezus and Ramona†* (Morrow, 1955) and develops far more interest in such books as *Ramona the Pest** (Morrow, 1968), *Ramona and Her Father** (Morrow, 1977), *Ramona Quimby, Age 8** (Morrow, 1981), and *Ramona Forever* (Morrow, 1984). Ramona and, to some extent, her sister, Beezus, are individuals rather than types, and their stories incorporate subtler humor and more complex language, though still written for an audience of early readers. A somewhat more serious though still amusing tone dominates her Newbery Award–winning *Dear Mr. Henshaw** (Morrow, 1983), an epistolary novel of a boy's difficult adjustment to his parents' divorce, told in letters to an author of children's books. Cleary has also written light, down-to-earth fantasy in *The Mouse and the Motorcycle** (Morrow, 1965) and its sequels, *Runaway Ralph** (Morrow, 1970) and *Ralph S. Mouse* (Morrow, 1984), and a number of novels for young teenagers, among them *Fifteen* (Morrow, 1956) and *Sister of the Bride* (Morrow, 1963). She has received many honors besides the Newbery Medal, the most prestigious being in 1975 the Laura Ingalls Wilder Award for total contribution to children's literature and in 1983 the George G. Stone Recognition of Merit Award for her body of work.

CLEAVER, BILL (1920–1981), born in Seattle, Wash.; author of popular novels mostly of contemporary family life and problems set in the American South for pre- and early adolescents. Retired from the U.S. Air Force, he wrote many short stories for *McCall's* and *Woman's Day* and other leading popular magazines. With his wife, Vera Cleaver*, he published over a dozen novels in the new realistic mode that have been generally well received by audience and reviewers, if often criticized for melodrama and contrivance. The Cleavers won awards and citations for *Grover** (Lippincott, 1970), *The Whys and Wherefores of Littabelle Lee** (Atheneum, 1973), *Queen of Hearts** (Lippincott, 1978), *Where the Lilies Bloom** (Lippincott, 1969), *Dust of the Earth** (Lippincott, 1975), *Ellen Grae** (Lippincott, 1967), and *Trial Valley** (Lippincott, 1977). He and his wife traveled extensively and made their home in South Carolina and then in Winter Haven, Florida.

CLEAVER, VERA (1919–   ), born in Virgil, S. Dak.; half of a husband-wife team of authors, who have written novels for children and young people mostly about contemporary family life in the rural South. Her family moved from South Dakota to Florida when she was very young. She was employed for a number of years as an accounting officer for the U.S. Air Force and has lived in Japan and Europe, and now a full-time writer she has contributed many stories to such periodicals as *McCall's* and *Woman's Day*. Together with her husband, Bill Cleaver*, she has written a dozen and a half books of the new wave of fiction for the young that became popular in the late twentieth century and for which they have received numerous citations and awards. Four of the Cleavers' novels were finalists for the National Book Award, *Grover** (Lippincott, 1970), *The Whys and Wherefores of Littabelle Lee** (Atheneum, 1973), *Queen of Hearts** (Lippincott, 1978), and *Where the Lilies Bloom** (Lippincott, 1969), about a North Carolina mountain family's efforts to make ends meet by "wildcrafting" after their father dies, which many consider their finest book and which was a *Boston Globe-Horn Book* Honor book, was a Fanfare book, and is cited in *Choice* and *Children's Books Too Good to Miss*. *Dust of the Earth** (Lippincott, 1975) won the Western Writers Spur Award and was elected to the Lewis Carroll Shelf, while *Ellen Grae** (Lippincott, 1967) and *Trial Valley** (Lippincott, 1977), sequel to *Lilies*, were Fanfare books. The plots often develop against a background of rural hardship and are built around personal problems of adolescence or of family, timely social issues, and human frailties. The style is spare, lively, and humorous, even comic, but the characters are often eccentric, and plots sometimes melodramatic and contrived, with endings that diminish the impact of the problems. Very popular contemporary writers, their other titles include *Lady Ellen Grae* (Lippincott, 1968), *The Mimosa Tree* (Lippincott, 1970), *The Kissimmee Kid* (Lothrop, 1981), and *Hazel Rye* (Lippincott, 1983). Individually she has published *Sugar Blue* (Lothrop, 1984).

CLEMENTS, BRUCE (1931–   ), born in New York City; educator, minister, writer. He received his A.B. degree from Columbia University, his M.A. from the State University of New York at Albany, and his B.D. from Union Theological Seminary. He served as ordained minister of the United Church of Christ in Schenectady and has taught in college in New York and Connecticut. In 1975 he wrote, with his wife, *Coming Home to a Place You've Never Been Before* (Farrar), a documentary account of twenty-four hours in Perception House, a half-way house in Willimantic, Conn., for young people in trouble, a shelter in which he was deeply involved. He is also the author of *From Ice Set Free* (Farrar, 1972), a biography of his father-in-law, Otto Kiep, an international lawyer and diplomat who was hanged as a resister to the Nazi regime. Despite his religious vocation, none of his novels for young people is moralistic, his *I Tell a Lie Every So Often** (Farrar, 1974) even poking fun at an older brother who is self-righteously pious. Other novels which have received critical acclaim include *The Face of Abraham Candle** (Farrar, 1969), a story of a boy maturing in Colorado in the 1890s, *Prison Window, Jerusalem Blue** (Farrar, 1977), a gripping novel set in the Viking period, and *Anywhere Else but Here** (Farrar, 1980), a modern novel of a strong-willed girl who copes for her ineffectual father among a group of manipulative adults. His 1984 novel, *Coming About* (Farrar), a story of an unlikely friendship of two high school boys that contains one big lie, received enthusiastic reviews.

CLEM SINGLETON (*The Rock and the Willow**), Clement, brutal, red-neck father of Enie. Embittered by the hard life on a one-mule Alabama farm, he resents anyone with money or more land than he has, particularly his well-off neighbor, Tom Shane, and he treats Enie's aspirations to learning with contempt, as "uppity notions." His only tenderness seems reserved for Sue Ann, and when this toddler dies, he is even more rough and demanding toward his remaining children. His brutal whipping of the eldest, T.H., has already driven the boy off. Fate deals him two other blows—the rotting loft collapses under him and he breaks his leg, and his wife, Elnora*, sickens and dies. Not long afterwards, he starts keeping company with a middle-aged spinster, Miss* Elsie Mae Howells, with whom he has sung in the choir, and soon marries her, thereby acquiring more land, machinery, and a far better house. This comparative affluence makes him willing to sell a piece of land and their old house to Shane and to lend (or possibly give) enough money to Enie to start at teachers' college. He even shows up, characteristically too late, to see her off on the bus.

CLETUS ARMSTRONG (*The Leaving**), feckless father of Roxanne*, who lets his daughter do most of the farm work. Having come from a shiftless, coon-hunting family which drifted north from Arkansas, Cletus is a step above his father and brothers in responsibility and ambition, but he lacks the intelligence and drive to match Thora* Braun, the girl he has married. As a father, he has been mostly indifferent to his daughter, except for giving up his job in Waterloo when Thora returned to the farm, saying that a girl needs her daddy, and giving her a red-and-white pinto pony on her twelfth birthday. Both actions are inspired by romantic dreams that he and his daughter will be pals and co-workers, dreams that he does little to make into reality. Although he feels some guilt, he sells her horse for money to leave Thora, yet when a woman urges him to take off the night before Roxanne is to leave, he refuses because he feels he should be on hand to say goodbye to his daughter. Essentially a weakling, he is more a pitiful figure than a villain.

CLONE CATCHER (Slote*, Alfred, ill. Elizabeth Slote, Lippincott, 1982), futuristic science fantasy set in Australia in 2019. The narrator, Arthur Dunn, 25, is a clone catcher, a twenty-first-century detective made necessary by the practice of wealthy people cloning themselves and raising their clones as living spare-parts banks. When the parent becomes old or ill, the clones often attempt escape, since the continued life of the parent means the death of the clone. Dunn has been hired by Sir William Montagu of Montagu City, a small industro-scientific-recreational city near Perth, to find the clone of his wife, Lady Kate, who is ill and will need organ transplants. In defiance of cloning regulations, the clone has not been called simply Kate II and raised in the closed compound with the clones of Sir William and the high officials of his conglomerate, but has been given a name, Mary Montagu, and treated almost as one of the family, even allowed to become an actress as Lady Kate was in her youth. After her final performance in Perth, attended by ailing Lady Kate, Mary Montagu has disappeared. Dunn is picked up by Sir William's only son and heir, Norman, evidently a meek and ineffectual young man relegated to running one of Sir William's sheep ranches. He meets imperious Sir William, who was, like his wife, in the theater when he was young, and the evidently very ill Lady Kate, her protective nurse, Fitzsimmons, and the efficient administrator of the main house, attractive Alice Watson, 25. He also visits the clone compound, run by Archie III, where he meets Sir William's clone, Billy II, who is acting in a production of the compound playhouse, ostensibly a history of early Australia but evident to Arthur as an incitement to revolution. Billy II, a younger replica of small, peppery Sir William, attacks Arthur and is put in the "slammer," the disciplinary tower in the center of the compound. In a series of clever complications, Arthur proves that the attack was part of a plan of Billy II, Alice, Fitzsimmons, Norman, and Mary Montagu, who have been conspiring to hide the death of Lady Kate on her drive in to Perth to see Mary's last performance. Since then, Mary has been playing Lady Kate in order to effect the escape of Billy II, with whom she is in love, and to give liberty to the other clones. Alice, a highly intelligent young woman dedicated to wiping out cloning, persuades Arthur to give up clone catching, marry her, and live on one of Sir William's remote ranches, from which they can carry on her worldwide campaign. Sir William, resigned not to live forever, goes to stay with Norman, for whom he has new respect, after blessing the marriage of Mary and Billy II, to whom he turns over Montagu Enterprises, confident that as his clone Billy II will do as good a job as he has done. The plot has sufficiently intricate twists based on two sets of look-alike theatrical personalities to keep it interesting and culminates in an exciting chase and confrontation. Little effort is made at characterization beyond the needs of the plot and not much is made of the Australian locale. Poe Nominee.

CLOVER ALLEN (*Their Shining Hour**), talkative young woman, close friend of Susanna Dickenson. Clover's parents have emigrated from Tennessee just as the Texas war for independence from Mexico begins. Clover cheerfully makes the best of whatever happens. She fashions herself a patchwork skirt for a party, looking upon it as a panorama of history rather than a makeshift creation. The young soldier to whom she boldly proposes dies at the Alamo. Some of the story is told from her point of view.

CLYDE JONES (*Fast Sam, Cool Clyde, and Stuff**), thoughtful leader of the group of black kids from 116th Street, a boy about fifteen when the story starts and a new high school graduate at the end. After his father dies and he realizes how much Sam's* support helped him, he suggests the formation of The Good People, hoping that the club can help Gloria* and any others who need friendship. Clyde is the most questioning and mature of the kids in the gang, but he is capable of wild stunts like entering the dance contest with Sam, dressed as Claudette, as his partner.

CLYMER, ELEANOR (LOWENTON) (1906–   ), born in New York City; teacher and writer. She attended Barnard College, received her B.A. from the University of Wisconsin, and studied further at the Bank Street College of Education and New York University. She has held various positions, working in a doctor's office, for a publisher, and as a social worker, and she taught in nursery schools and worked with young children in camps and settlement houses. A prolific writer, during her lifetime she has published over fifty books, mostly of realistic fiction for young readers, under her own name and pseudonyms Janet Bell and Elizabeth Kinsey. Her books reflect her attempts to provide for young children interesting stories about their everyday lives. She has also written on Indians and about animals, among other subjects, and also for young people. Many of her books are set in an urban or inner city environment, including *Luke Was There** (Holt, 1973), which received the Child Study Award and is cited in *Choice, My Brother Stevie** (Holt, 1967), and *We Lived in the Almont** (Dutton, 1970), both also on the *Choice* list. Other titles include *The Spider, the Cave, and the Pottery Bowl* (Atheneum, 1971), about Indians, and *Santiago's Silvermine* (Atheneum, 1973), about Mexicans. Her style is simple and economical of words, dialogue unforced and revealing, but plots seem tailormade and lack conviction.

COATSWORTH†, ELIZABETH (JANE) (1893–   ), born in Buffalo, N.Y.; poet and novelist. After graduating from Vassar, she took her master's degree at Columbia University, studied further at Radcliffe, and traveled widely in Europe, Africa, and the Orient. She married Henry Beston, a writer and naturalist, and the couple made their home in Maine. She was known for her stories and poems for adults before she began writing for children. She published her first book for the young in 1927, launching a long and distinguished career in literature for children, during which she wrote over ninety books for young people, mostly fiction and ranging widely in subject, period, and setting. Her career as a writer for the young reached its height during the 1930s, when she received the Newbery

Award for *The Cat Who Went to Heaven*† (Macmillan, 1930), a short fantasy set in Japan. Also highly regarded were her historical novels and period pieces set in New England about little Sally and her family and friends, *Away Goes Sally*† (Macmillan, 1934), *Five Bushel Farm*† (Macmillan, 1939), and *The Fair American*† (Macmillan, 1940), all of which received citations of critical acclaim. Although plots are inept and characters types, her style has a poetic charm, descriptions are vivid, and the tone shows affection for New England, its people, and its history. Other books from this decade that won her critical acclaim are *The Golden Horseshoe*† (Macmillan, 1935), set in Colonial Virginia, and *Alice-All-By-Herself*† (Macmillan, 1937), about a little girl's adventures on the coast of Maine. Both of these and her later *Door to the North*† (Winston, 1950), a Fanfare selection about Viking exploration in Greenland in the fourteenth century, are less convincing than the Sally books. A still later novel, *The Princess and the Lion** (Pantheon, 1963), a short, contrived, rather condescending adventure novel set in Abyssinia, also appears on the *Horn Book* Fanfare list. Diverting and action-filled, it lacks the holding power and warmth of her earlier books. Considered a distinguished citizen of her state, she has received honorary degrees from the University of Maine and New England College.

COB (*The Trumpet of the Swan**), the garrulous, officious, old swan, fond father, who steals a trumpet for his son, Louis*, a trumpeter swan who has been born mute. Even though he is a very moral sort, the cob feels the theft is essential to enable his son to make the sounds necessary to win a mate and have a good life. The old Cob is a sympathetic, credible figure, if overdrawn for the sake of humor and theme.

COCKLEBURR QUARTERS (Baker*†, Charlotte, ill. Robert Owens, Prentice, 1972), realistic novel and animal story set in the poor black section of a southern town in the late 1960s. When Dolph Burch, 10, and his friends, Archie and Perry, find eight newborn puppies under the Kingdom of Heaven Church, Brother Biggers, the pastor, offers them a dollar to get the litter out. Dolph must first make friends with the starving mother dog, a half-blind stray, but when he realizes that Brother Biggers plans to abandon the pups in the dump, he enlists the help of his sister, Myrtis, 8, and makes plans to save them. He starts doing errands for old Mrs. Randall, a religious widow, and her group, the Little Leaveners, who save scraps and pay him for his work. He gives the money to his hardworking mother, Emeline, who needs it to help support her no-good brother, two grown daughters and their babies, and Albert, Dolph's older brother, as well as Dolph and Myrtis, but she gives back enough so he can buy some dog food. A letter from Dolph's oldest brother, James, fighting in Viet Nam, which tells that he is buying a lot to build them a house at one end of the section called Cockleburr Quarters, reminds Dolph of an old shack near the lot, and at night he transports the dog, whom they have named Tory, and the pups there. As the puppies grow, Dolph has a hard time getting enough food for them, so he and Myrtis give away three and one dies. Then a wandering tramp named Jake Brown shows up, starts to live in the shack, and cares for the dogs. A fire on Cockleblurr Hill drives Tory and the pups out of the shack, but makes Albert a hero when he jumps on a runaway bulldozer and swerves it to save an unconscious fireman in its path. At first the children despair of finding Tory, but Jake patiently lures the frightened dog back, the puppies having been killed. Jake settles into an empty house in the Quarters and starts caring for the dogs and cats, instructing the children how to worm them, treat them for fleas and mange, clean up their droppings, and have them neutered. All seems lost when the Quarters are sold to make way for apartments which will not permit pets or gardens. Emeline, who needs a garden, hunts vainly for a new place for the family, now reduced because she has thrown out her brother and daughter, Janetta. When daughter Clara marries her boy friend, a good young man who agrees to take in both her baby and Janetta's, Dolph is able to help persuade the owner of a small house right next to James's lot that the family, now only four, will not be too large for his place, and Dolph will be able to keep Tory on the lot next door. The setting and the family relationships are interesting and convincing, and Dolph is a believable little boy, but Jake appears like a *deus ex machina* and the book's message of how to treat animals kindly becomes didactic. Lewis Carroll.

COLLIER, CHRISTOPHER (1930–   ), educator, historian, and writer, one half of a brother team that has collaborated upon several American historical novels for young readers. He received his bachelor's, master's, and doctorate from Columbia. He has taught history to junior and senior high students in Connecticut and at Teachers College in New York. A professor of history at the University of Bridgeport, he has published scholarly books and articles in his discipline. With his brother, James Lincoln Collier*, he has published several novels with early American historical backgrounds. The first of these, *My Brother Sam Is Dead** (Four Winds, 1974), was a finalist for the National Book Award, a Newbery Honor book, a Fanfare book and is cited in *Choice*. About a Connecticut family's experience during the American Revolution as seen through the eyes of the second son, it is a tersely told, dramatic, and accurate recreation of the times, an exciting and moving blend of facts and story. Next came *The Bloody Country* (Four Winds, 1976), a story of war and conflict over territory claimed by both Pennsylvania and Connecticut in the mid–1700s, and *The Winter Hero* (Four Winds, 1978), set during Shays' Rebellion. Christopher does the research for the brothers' novels, and James does the writing. While the central characters in their stories are fictitious, every episode in the meticulously researched books actually happened as described. Other American historical novels on which the two have collaborated are *Jump Ship to Freedom* (Delacorte, 1981) and its companion, *War Comes to Willy Freeman* (Delacorte, 1983), with a background in slavery.

COLLIER, JAMES LINCOLN (1928–   ), born in New York City; musician and freelance writer. He grew up in Garden City, Long Island, graduated from Hamilton College, Conn., and served in the infantry during the Korean War. A specialist in social science reporting, he has contributed over six hundred articles and stories to magazines and written many books of fiction and non-fiction for adults, children, and young people on various subjects. He received the Child Study Award for *Rock Star** (Four Winds, 1970), a less conventional boy's story about a youth's try for the "big time" in the New York City music world. His other books include *A Visit to the Firehouse* (Grosset, 1966), *Why Does Everybody Think I'm Nutty?* (Grosset, 1971), *The Teddy Bear Habit* (Grosset, 1967), *Give Dad My Best* (Four Winds, 1976), and non-fiction books about music. With his brother, Christopher Collier*, a professor of history, he has written several notable novels based on American history. Their first, *My Brother Sam Is Dead** (Four Winds, 1974), an accurate, dramatic, and terse story about the experiences of a Connecticut family during the American Revolution, was a Newbery Honor book, *Choice* selection, and a finalist for the National Book Award. Other books they have collaborated upon with American historical settings include *The Bloody Country* (Four Winds, 1976), *The Winter Hero* (Four Winds, 1978), *Jump Ship to Freedom* (Delacorte, 1981), and its companion, *War Comes to Willy Freeman* (Delacorte, 1983).

COLMAN, HILA, born in New York City; author of novels. After attending Radcliffe College, she did promotion and publicity work for National War Relief in New York City during World War II and later was executive director of Labor Book Club in New York. Since 1949 she has been writing freelance, doing articles and stories for such magazines as *McCall's*, *Saturday Evening Post*, *Redbook*, and *Ingenue*, and primarily novels for older girls, some stories for younger children, career books, and, under the name Teresa Crayder, a set of books for reluctant readers. She received the Child Study Association of America Award for *The Girl from Puerto Rico** (Morrow, 1961). Other books are *Bride at Eighteen* (Morrow, 1966), *Thoroughly Modern Millie* (Bantam, 1966), a novelization of the movie, *Claudia, Where Are You?* (Morrow, 1969), *Rachel's Legacy* (Morrow, 1978), and its sequel, *Ellie's Inheritance* (Morrow, 1979), about Jewish immigrants from Russia, and *The Family Trap* (Morrow, 1982). She and her husband, Louis Colman, a medical writer with whom she published a cookbook, have lived in Bridgewater, Conn.

COLONEL ALOIS PODHAJSKY (*White Stallion of Lipizza**), Director of the Spanish Court Riding School in Vienna, Austria. He is a kind, dedicated, businesslike man, who gives Hans Haupt his chance to become a Riding Master. At the end of the story, Hans understands the meaning of the Colonel's statement, "Our Spanish Court Riding School is a tiny candle in the big world. Our duty, our privilege is to keep it burning. If we can send out one beam of splendor, of glory, of elegance into this torn and troubled world, that is worth a man's life."

COLONEL TURNER ASHBY (*The Spring Rider**), dashing Confederate officer who leads Jacob Downs on a daring foray behind Union lines. One of the dead who return each spring to refight a Civil War battle in the Virginia mountains, Ashby comes for love of fighting and the heroics involved. He is aware that he is drawing Jacob back into his own time and presumably into death, but he accepts Jacob's admiration as his due and feels no reluctance to have the boy follow him.

"COME AND GET IT" (*Their Shining Hour**), battle cry during the Texans' war for independence from Mexico. When the Mexicans demand the return of the Gonzales cannon, the Texas women fashion a flag. They use white material from a wedding dress for the ground and black taffeta lining from Susanna Dickenson's coat for the picture of a cannon. Beneath the cannon they put the words "Come and Get It," a cry of angry and bold defiance that becomes a slogan during the conflict.

COME BY HERE (Coolidge*, Olivia, ill. Milton Johnson, Houghton, 1970), sociological novel of an abused black child in Baltimore in the early 1900s. Minty Lou Payson, six when the book starts, is the pretty, bright daughter of Big Lou, the first black girl to escape from the poverty and ignorance of rural Cambridge and to have made something of herself in the city. A supervisor of kitchens at the hospital, she has the respect of her fellow workers, a nice apartment, a good husband—and the jealousy of her mother-in-law, a mean-spirited woman with children still at home only a little older than Minty Lou. Pert and a bit spoiled, Minty Lou thinks Grandma* Ellen Payson is fond of her until both her parents are killed in an accident at a dance hall. Because she wants the insurance money which should have gone to Minty Lou, Grandma Payson takes her in, but she resents her, lets her sons, particularly Gordie, the youngest, take advantage of the girl, and treats her as a slavey, even hiring her out at seven to a white woman who mistreats her and strikes her so hard with a ladle that she falls and is deafened. Grandma, unable to forgive Minty Lou for hurting Gordie when she fights back after he pulls a knife on her, sends her off to live with her father's Aunt* Helen Robbins, a fanatically pious woman. Underfed at Grandma's, Minty Lou is starved by Aunt Helen, who works her excessively and punishes her by locking her in her room for days at a time with no food. Seeing a white restaurant owner across the alley dumping leftovers, Minty Lou climbs down across a shed roof and raids the garbage pail. Shocked at seeing this painfully thin child dressed in deliberately ugly clothes made by Aunt Helen snatching garbage and devouring it ravenously, the man reports it to the truant officer, who makes rather perfunctory inquiries but scares Aunt Helen. The upshot is that Minty Lou is put on the ferry to Cambridge, sent to her other grandmother, warmhearted Arminta* Hayes, who has not even been told that her daughter is dead. No longer a cute, well-dressed child, but a gaunt urchin in a grotesque, floor-length garment, Minty Lou waits all day on the dock, stealing and eating raw crab, since no one knows to meet her. When a neighbor finally takes her to where the Hayes family lives, they are astonished and filled with consternation: they have no empty bed and little enough to eat without this extra mouth. Despite their poverty, they take her in and open their hearts to her, but by now she is so suspicious and hurt that there seems little chance that she will be happy. Not a pleasant story, this is probably one of the most honest pictures of the struggle of blacks in the first part of this century in any book for children, though the main emphasis is not on racial problems but on those of an unwanted and abused child in a poverty-stricken society. The characterizations are strong and convincing, particularly Minty Lou's rage and her progress into sullen despair. Boston Globe Honor; Fanfare.

COME TO THE EDGE (Cunningham*, Julia, Pantheon, 1977), fable-like novel set in an unspecified place presumably in the mid twentieth century. Red-haired Gravel Winter, 14, has spent four years at a foster farm for homeless boys, sustained by the trust that his alcoholic father will reclaim him and by his friendship with "Skin" (Wally) Kemp, a fat boy who loves Gravel's stories of life on the outside. When Skin disappears, Gravel doesn't believe the principal's explanation that he has been placed with foster parents. Gravel attacks the man, is placed in a bare room called the Cell, and there overhears his father saying that he doesn't want him. Stunned at first, Gravel breaks out, "crisscrosses three highways and five towns," and finally collapses at the door of Mr. Paynter, a sign painter, who takes him in with no questions. He lives with Paynter for some time, but the "greyness" that threatens to take him over physically and mentally when he thinks of his loss of Skin and his father's rejection finally drives him to move on. At another town he pulls an old, almost blind man, Mr. Gant, from the path of a speeding car and is rewarded by being offered a room in Gant's Victorian mansion. He chooses the attic and agrees to devote his mornings to "seeing" for Gant, despite the enmity of Gant's hulking servant, Williston. The next day a woman, Mrs. Prior, falls against him and after he helps her home, she offers him meals if he will help her in her arthritic condition, running errands and helping around the house. On his way home, he is struck by a handful of weeds, reacts angrily, then finds that they were thrown by a deaf woman, Ethel Ransome, who employs him to listen to her and shout occasional answers. He continues in this pattern, though resisting any emotional involvement with the three, until he finds that Williston has dug up Gant's hoarded money. When the servant first offers to split the loot in return for Gravel's aid in murdering Gant, the boy runs off, but, conscience-stricken, returns, only to find that Gant has killed Williston and plans to blackmail Gravel into taking his place. Gravel leaves, says goodbye to Mrs. Prior and Miss Ransome, and returns to Paynter, who has had faith that he will return. While Gravel's devastation after his father has rejected him is interesting, bordering on mental illness, events in the book happen so fortuitously that they are not believable. Characters are types used to illustrate influences upon Gravel. Because the theme (that everyone has worth and a place in the world) is over-prominent and the plot implausible, the story has some of the quality of fable, but this does not mix well with the realism of the style. Christopher; Lewis Carroll.

CONE, MOLLY (LAMKEN) (1918–   ), born in Tacoma, Wash.; author of more than forty books, both fiction and non-fiction, for young people, many of which reflect her Jewish heritage. She attended the University of Washington and worked as an advertising copywriter. She married, has three children, and has lived in the Seattle area. Under the joint pseudonym, Caroline More, she did some writing with Margaret Pitcairn Strachan. A strong element of humor enters into her fiction, including several books about Mishmash, a friendly dog, and her novel, *A Promise Is a Promise** (Houghton, 1964), about a Jewish girl whose concern over her religious and social status gets her into some amusing situations. Among her other titles are *The Amazing Memory of Harvey Bean* (Houghton, 1980), *Paul David Silverman Is a Father* (Houghton, 1983), and *The Big Squeeze* (Houghton, 1984).

CONNIE IVES (*The Alley**), protected, somewhat shy girl of ten, only child of a professor of English at Grandby College. She has long blond braids and a serious face. She loves to read and often reads aloud to Mama as Mama is going about her daily tasks. She takes piano lessons, although she does not like them, and after a year and a half of lessons considers herself qualified to give instruction to the little children of the Alley*, proving herself quite a competent teacher in the basics. She most enjoys swinging in her back yard and thinks of herself as "the famous swinger." In much of the story, she and Billy* Maloon swing together, and while they are swinging they think and plan. At the end of the book, Connie has grown more sure of herself.

CONRAD CATLETT (*Pistol**), cynical, overbearing, exploitive, older brother of Billy. He regularly belittles Billy, according to Billy, who tells the story, uses him for his own purposes, and generally avoids spending time with him. Conrad and their father argue almost incessantly, their bickering and haranguing often reducing their sensitive, timid mother to tears. They argue over the father's refusal to let Conrad participate in school activities like football, among other things, and Conrad despises his father for failing to succeed in his various rainbow-chasing schemes and for making life hard for their mother. After the move to Deal, Billy and Conrad, now almost men, hit it off better and actually become friends.

CONSTANCE: A STORY OF EARLY PLYMOUTH (Clapp*, Patricia, Lothrop, 1968), historical novel about the founding of Plymouth colony in which almost all the characters actually lived, including the protagonist. In her journal, Constance Hopkins tells of the colony's first five years, during which the settlement moves from near starvation to comfortable self-sufficiency and she from a rather giddy adolescent to a self-assured, useful, and contented young bride. Fifteen-year-old Constance, her father, Stephen, her stepmother, Elizabeth, and two younger brothers and a sister, arrive at Plymouth on the *Mayflower* with the other Pilgrims. Weary from the long, hard voyage, Constance is appalled by the bleak November coast and longs for the color and gaiety of London. She is conscientious, industrious, and high-spirited and gradually gets caught up in the satisfactions and challenges of the enterprise, assuming her share of the responsibility for making things go in the Hopkins house. She describes the terrible sickness that carries off half the colonists the first winter and through which she nurses her gravely ill father. Other historical events she describes include the coming of the friendly and helpful Indians, Samoset and Squanto, the courtship of Myles Standish and John Alden for the hand of Priscilla Mullins, the young woman who becomes her closest friend, and the Thanksgiving feast ordered by Governor Bradford at which the Indians are guests. Other actual events Constance talks about include Myles Standish's attack on the Indians, when the Pilgrims believe they are planning to cause trouble, the terrible drought of 1623, the arrival of several boatloads of settlers, among whom are John Oldham and John Lyford, troublemakers who scheme to undermine Governor Bradford's authority and set themselves up as rulers of the colony, and the development of trade in furs to pay off the settlers' debt to their London promoters. Although there are problems and sorrows, among them the deaths of the two youngest Hopkins children, such joys as parties, conversations before the fire, and visits of friends relieve the tedium and hardships of their existence. Pretty and lively, Constance attracts the attention of several young men in the village, with whom she is inclined to flirt until she realizes how her coquetry may affect her reputation. Two young men emerge as serious suitors, handsome, red-haired, rakish Stephen Deane and witty, yellow-haired, industrious Nicholas Snow. While both are away on a trading trip, she sorts out her feelings about them. She realizes that she loves Nicholas, and the end of the book sees them wed and settled in their new home. Except for Constance herself, characterization is shallow. The Indian girl, Minnetuxet, with whom Constance becomes friends and exchanges gifts and intimacies, is a non-historical figure whose potential for interest is not exploited. Constance's old-fashioned way of speaking builds credibility and helps establish setting, and the romantic element, though predictable, provides unity. This pleasant story of a young girl's growing up, learning to get on with her stepmother, and finding her place in life is most memorable for the detailed picture it gives of early Plymouth from the woman's point of view. Choice; Lewis Carroll; National Book Finalist.

THE CONTENDER (Lipsyte*, Robert, Harper, 1967), sports novel set in Harlem in the 1960s. Orphan Alfred Brooks, 17, lives with his widowed Aunt Pearl Conway and her three little girls, works as janitor and stock boy in the Epstein brothers' store, and has dropped out of school, seeing no point in continuing. His long-time friend, James Mosely, gets caught robbing the Epstein store with some tough, older boys because Alfred has inadvertently let it slip that the Epsteins leave cash in the register on Friday night but forgets to mention the new burglar alarm. Three of the others in the attempted robbery, Major, Hollis, and Sonny, beat Alfred up, and he is found dazed and wandering and is taken home by Henry* Johnson, a lame boy who works at Donatelli's gym. The next day Alfred goes to the run-down gym and tells Vito* Donatelli, the fight manager, that he wants to learn to be a champion. Donatelli explains to him that he must first become a contender, a person on his way up who knows he may never make it but is willing to put in the time and effort to try. When he comes back, Donatelli has left a ticket for him to see a fight with Henry, where he meets Spoon (Bill Weatherspoon), a teacher who did some fighting until Donatelli told him to stop before his brain or eyes were injured. Alfred soon is running every morning and working out every evening, a part of the group that includes a huge man called Jelly Belly and Dr. Corey, a dentist who helps around the gym. When Major and his friends threaten Alfred unless he will disconnect the burglar alarm at Epsteins', he stands up to them, and they back off. He even discovers that one of the Epsteins was a boxer, Lightning Lou Epp, in his youth. But he misses James, and when Major asks him to a party and says James will be there, he breaks training to go only to find that James, now on heroin, will have nothing to do with him. For several days Alfred doesn't go back to the gym, thinking he will quit, but when he does go back he works harder than ever and begins to improve. He wins his first two fights, but the knockout in the second worries him, and when the third ends in a draw though he could have won it, Donatelli tells him he's through, that he doesn't have the killer instinct, and that he will be put against much better fighters and really hurt if he continues. Alfred begs to have one more fight to see if he's able to keep going when hurt, and Donatelli reluctantly agrees. His opponent is much better than he is, but he fights gamely and feels that he has proven himself even though he loses. The only time he has seen James since the party is once when this old friend, desperate for a fix, begs money from him. When he gets back from his last fight, hurt but elated, Aunt Pearl tells him that James has broken into Epsteins,' right through the front window. Alfred goes to a cave in the park where they used to hide as little boys and finds James, badly cut and needing a fix, and with new confidence persuades James to come with him to the hospital, planning to get him into a narcotics clinic Spoon has told him about and to go back to school and get into neighborhood social work himself. Scenes in the gym and descriptions of the fights are vivid and interesting, and Alfred is a believable protagonist, going from aimlessness and fear to purpose and confidence. Although the ending is upbeat, the problems are not trivialized, and there is no assurance that James, or even Alfred, will succeed. Child Study; Choice.

COOLIDGE, OLIVIA (ENSOR) (1908–   ), born in London, England; writer known chiefly for her many biographies, her historical fiction set in the classical or early medieval period, and for her retelling of myths and hero tales from the oral tradition. She was educated at Wycombe Abbey School, Buckinghamshire, and at Somerville College, Oxford, where she received her B.A. and M.A. degrees. She has taught English and classics in Germany, London, Boston, and Connecticut, and was a member of the Board of Trustees of Mills College of Education in New York. She is married, has four stepchildren, and is a naturalized citizen of the United States. Among her best-known books are *Greek Myths* (Houghton, 1949), *Legends of the North* (Houghton, 1951), and *The Trojan War* (Houghton, 1952). She has written biographies for young people of Winston Churchill, Edith Wharton, Eugene O'Neill, George Bernard Shaw, Thomas Paine, Gandhi, Joseph Conrad, Lincoln, and a group of famous Romans. Her only book of fiction set in the twentieth century is *Come By Here** (Houghton, 1970), a story of a mistreated black girl in Baltimore.

COOPER, SUSAN (MARY) (1935–   ), born in Burnham, Buckinghamshire, England; journalist and author of books for adults and children. She grew up near London, spending time also with her grandmother in Wales. After taking her M.A. in English literature from Oxford, she worked as a reporter and feature writer for the London *Sunday Times*. In 1963 she married Nicholas Grant, an American college professor, and since then has lived near Boston. She received high critical acclaim for her series of five fantasies for middle-grade readers, called *The Dark Is Rising*, for which she drew on the major English and Welsh myths to produce an adventurous and suspenseful account of the endless battle between good and evil. The books move through various settings and times and feature several modern children as protagonists: *Over Sea, Under Stone** (Harcourt, 1966), a Fanfare and *Choice* book; *The Dark Is Rising** (Atheneum, 1973), a Newbery Honor book, a *Choice* book, a Fanfare book, a *Boston Globe-Horn Book* Winner, and recipient of the Jane Addams Award; *Greenwitch* (Atheneum, 1974); *The Grey King** (Atheneum, 1975), a Newbery Award winner and a Fanfare book; and *Silver on the Tree* (Atheneum, 1977). *Dawn of Fear** (Harcourt, 1970), a novel set near London at the height of the blitz in World War II, echoes her own childhood. It was a Fanfare book and is cited in *Choice*. More recently she has published *Seaward* (Atheneum, 1983), another fantasy which draws on Celtic myths. She has also written a novel, *Mandrake* (Hodder, 1964), a play, and books of non-fiction for adults.

CORBETT, SCOTT (1913–   ), born in Kansas City, Mo.; author and teacher. He attended Kansas City Junior College and received a degree in journalism from the University of Missouri at Columbia. During World War II, he was a war correspondent and editor of *Yank* magazine. After the war he became a free-lance writer of magazine articles and books for adults. He eventually settled in Providence, R.I., where he taught English in a preparatory school for eight years and began writing humorous, adventurous books for children. He has published some fifty books of fiction and several of non-fiction mostly for elementary and junior high boys, including the successful series of "trick books," among them, the perennially popular *The Lemonade Trick* (Little, 1960). He has also written a set of informational books which explain in simple language complicated mechanical and scientific processes, including *Home Computers: A Simple and Informative Guide* (Little, 1980). One of his mysteries, *Cutlass Island** (Little, 1962), received the Edgar Allan Poe Award, while *The Mystery Man** (Little, 1970), and *Here Lies the Body** (Little, 1974) were nominees. He has traveled widely, and *The Cave above Delphi* (Holt, 1965) resulted from a trip to Greece. It captures well the flavor and appearance of the area in central Greece sacred to the ancient god Apollo. His books are about ordinary boys that young readers can easily identify with. They employ an easygoing, engaging tone that invites participation and enjoyment. More recently he has published *The Discontented Ghost* (Dutton, 1978), a witty and lively retelling of Oscar Wilde's *The Canterville Ghost*.

CORBIN†, WILLIAM (WILLIAM CORBIN MCGRAW) (1916–   ), born in Des Moines, Iowa; newspaperman turned free-lance writer of novels for young people, many of them horse and dog stories. He was graduated from Drake University, did graduate work at Harvard, and wrote for the Athens (Ohio) *Messenger*, the Cleveland *Plain Dealer*, the Oklahoma City *Times*, and the San Diego *Union-Tribune*. Because he is married to Eloise Jarvis McGraw*†, with whom he has made his home in the Willamette Valley south of Portland, he uses his middle name professionally to avoid confusion. His newspaper background is employed in his novel *Deadline* (Coward, 1952) and to a lesser extent in *High Road Home†* (Coward, 1953), which concerns a cross-country search for a columnist by a refugee and an aspiring reporter. *Smoke** (Coward, 1967), a novel in which a reconciliation between a boy and his step-father results from their involvement with a starving German shepherd, is a good example of his dog stories.

CORCORAN, BARBARA (1911–   ), born in Hamilton, Mass.; teacher, journalist, and author of books for young people, also under the names Paige Dixon and Gail Hamilton. She received her B.A. from Wellesley and her M.A. from the University of Montana. She held positions as a researcher for Columbia Broadcasting in Hollywood and as a copywriter for a radio station in Missoula, Mont., and she taught English in Los Angeles, at the University of Colorado, and at Palomar College in California before becoming a full-time writer in 1969. She has written plays, contributed articles and stories to popular magazines, and published over two dozen novels of family life, adventure, and timely social concerns, set usually in Montana or the Pacific Northwest for junior high readers or up. *The Long Journey** (Atheneum, 1970), a contrived but interesting story of a Montana girl's long ride on horseback to get help for her blind grandfather is cited in *Choice*. Other titles include *Sasha, My Friend* (Atheneum, 1969), *A Trick of Light* (Atheneum, 1972), *The Winds of Time* (Atheneum, 1974), *You're*

Allegro Dead (Atheneum, 1981), *A Watery Grave* (Atheneum, 1982), and *The Woman in Your Life* (Atheneum, 1984).

CORDELIA SILL (*To the Green Mountains**), sharp-tongued, inquisitive, domineering wife of the local druggist in South Angela, a mousey little man. A self-righteous, judgmental, know-it-all, Cordelia gossips about Elizabeth* Rule and Will Grant. Her husband deserts her after she makes fun of a window display of which he is particularly fond. She is a flat character, very important to the plot.

CORLATH (*The Blue Sword**), young king of the Hillfolk, the remnants of the people of Damar who have been colonized by Homelanders. Like all other members of the royal family and some other Hillpeople, Corlath has *kelar*, the ability to prophesy, an extrasensory gift more often burden than pleasure. Like some Arabian sheik, he rides a magnificent horse and spends much of his time on the road with his select Riders, living in a tent spread with rugs and served by people of the royal household. Although he has been king for about ten years, he has not married and is not known for womanizing, so his decision to kidnap Harry* Crewe is a surprise to his followers.

CORMIER, ROBERT (1925–   ), born in Leominster, Mass., where he still makes his home; author of popular and highly controversial novels for young adults. A radio announcer and newspaperman, twice honored by the Associated Press with the Best News Story in New England Award, he had published short stories and magazine articles and written a column under the pseudonym of John Fitch IV before he published *The Chocolate War** (Pantheon, 1974), a novel set in a Catholic boys' school, whose ending, with the protagonist completely defeated by vicious and corrupt elements, caused much critical comment. *I Am the Cheese** (Pantheon, 1977), a story of a family given a new identity to escape the revenge of organized crime, and *After the First Death* (Pantheon, 1979), a novel of a school bus highjacked by terrorists, have similar themes. He has also published three adult novels, a book of short stories for young people, *Eight Plus One* (Pantheon, 1980), *The Bumblebee Flies Anyway* (Pantheon, 1983), a young adult novel concerned with ethics in an experimental medical facility, and *Beyond the Chocolate War* (Pantheon, 1985), which continues the story of the Vigils*.

COTTON MACKENZIE (*Of Love and Death and Other Journeys**), Andrew MacKenzie, teacher of English during the winter and painter during the summer, with whom Phoebe* and Peter* Smith and Meg Grant often live, who accompanies them in their travels about Italy, and who occasionally helps them out financially. Meg has been in love with him since she was a small child and often dreams of marrying him. She realizes that he regards her as a child and is aware that he has had a series of "popsies," as she calls his girl friends, but romantically she hopes that when she is a little older they will be married. When she proposes to him, he rejects her with kindness and understanding. At the end, she realizes that he, like her mother and Peter, is a free spirit and will never settle down.

THE COURT OF THE STONE CHILDREN (Cameron*†, Eleanor, Dutton, 1973), fantasy in which past and present intersect to solve the mystery of a murder in France during the time of Napoleon. Nina Harmsworth, about thirteen, new and slow to make friends in San Francisco, meets Gil* Patrick, a boy of about her own age, in the park near her apartment. He tells her about a privately owned French Museum nearby. Since Nina especially enjoys museums and aspires to become a curator, she soon visits the two-storied building, one end of which encloses a transplanted eighteenth-century French chateau, complete even to courtyard flagstones and statuary. In this part of the building, Nina's "Museum Feeling," a sense of the coming together of past and present, is particularly strong. Here Domi* (Dominique) de Lombre, a patrician young woman from the time of Napoleon, paintings of whom Nina has seen on the walls of the museum, appears to her. Domi seeks help in proving that her father did not murder his valet, the crime for which he was executed. She is concerned that Mrs. Staynes, a curator in the museum who is writing a biography of him, will be accurate in the way she presents him. Through Domi, Nina realizes the significance of the stone statues in the courtyard, in particular that of the child Odile*, whose father painted Dominique. Odile's journals, one of which is in French and is translated for Nina by Domi, and Odile's appearance to Nina in a dream are instrumental in solving the mystery. Nina discovers that at the time of the murder, Ms. de Lombre was in fact with Odile, to whom he was betrothed, and that he was actually executed for opposing Napoleon. As Nina applies herself to the unraveling of this mystery, the solution to which is vital to the emotional well-being of two women in the past and to the accurate portrayal of a biographical subject in the present, she learns much about the work of a curator, comes closer to understanding the basis of her own personality, and makes some friends, mostly adult, besides. This slow-starting, quiet story in which the essential plot problem is late in being revealed, grips with increasing intensity as the story unfolds, and once established, holds to the very end. Prediction dreams, discussions about the nature of time, objects that co-exist in two time dimensions, and careful attention to details of character, setting, and atmosphere combine for a richly conceived story related with style, dignity, and grace. Choice; National Book Winner.

COUSIN KATE (*Adam Bookout**), warm, motherly woman, cousin of Adam, whose children are grown or away at boarding school. Author of detective novels featuring hero Aldrich Batt, she is mostly instrumental in bringing about Adam's adjustment to life in Brooklyn and acceptance of the deaths of his parents. She loans the children books for school reports, opening new vistas especially for Magdalena. She is a round character.

CRAZY KATE (*It's Like This, Cat**), Kate Carmichael, Gramercy Park character and eccentric friend of Davey Mitchell. She gives Davey his pet tom, the stray tiger he calls Cat. Kate wears funny old clothes and sneakers, talks to herself, and befriends stray cats. Against the regulations of the apartment building, she has a half-dozen or more cats living with her at a time. She inherits a great deal of money from a brother with whom she has not spoken in twenty years, attracting the attention of the press. If it had not been for the help of the Mitchells, she might have lost her apartment and her independent way of life because of the money and the hullabaloo that comes with it.

THE CRICKET IN TIMES SQUARE (Selden*, George, ill. Garth Williams, Farrar, 1960), amusing talking animal fantasy set recently in a subway station in New York City's Times Square. Mario*, the lonely son of the Italian Bellinis who operate a rundown newsstand in the subway station, finds Chester*, a Connecticut country cricket who came to New York in a picnic basket, and keeps him as a good-luck pet. Chester's friends and protectors, Tucker* Mouse and Harry* Cat, inhabit a nearby drainpipe, unknown to the Bellinis. A summer of excitement follows, with Mario taking Chester to Chinatown to get a cage to keep him in and to learn about the care of crickets and where Mr. Sai Fong tells him the Chinese tale about how crickets came to be; with Chester accidentally eating a two-dollar bill while he is asleep and dreaming it is grass; and with parties among the animals in which they observe that Chester can play any tune he hears. While dancing to Chester's music, Tucker accidentally sets fire to the newsstand. In remorse, Chester plays an Italian song, "Come Back to Sorrento," which he had heard on the radio, for Mrs. Bellini, and his remarkable musical talent is discovered by the humans. Mr. Smedley, the music teacher who patronizes the stand and is opera-loving Mr. Bellini's friend, informs the New York *Times* about Chester's ability. Soon Chester's concerts of classical and popular music draw tremendous crowds and bring financial success to the newsstand. At the end of the summer, wearied by crowds and homesick, Chester sadly hops a train for Connecticut and home. Humorously told with much dialogue in contemporary speech and modified Italian dialect, this somewhat slow-starting story with its simple plot of two separate but interacting worlds picks up after the author has characterized his principals, which he does with obvious liking and amazing realism. The story has much emotional appeal, and scenes of Chinatown and bustling New York and the gentle satire on modern mores and commercialism add interest. The clear, representational black and white drawings contribute to character, clarify situations, and enhance the humor. Sequel is *Tucker's Countryside**. Choice; Fanfare; Lewis Carroll; Newbery Honor.

CRICKET MOBRAY (*The Cat and Mrs. Cary**), granddaughter of the FBI agent who has come to Crow's Harbor to search for parakeet smugglers. Throughout most of the book she and Brad* Willets are at odds because his pet, The Cat, and her Doberman, Doc, are enemies. Cricket is direct, candid, and honest, and never hesitates to speak her mind. She and Brad become reconciled through their common interest in finding the treasure.

CROCKETT, DAVY (*Their Shining Hour**), actual historical figure, a brash, loud backwoodsman who arrives at the Alamo from Tennessee with ten comrades. Always cheerful, he sings and plays his fiddle to keep the defenders' spirits up. Crockett goes down fighting when the Mexicans overrun the old mission during the Texans' fight for independence.

CROP-EAR (*Sophia Scrooby Preserved**), Silas, the mean and grasping slaver with a "gallows complexion," who buys Pansy and the other Scrooby slaves and through whom Pansy falls into the hands of Pedro Alvarez, the pirate. Silas lost his ears as a punishment for counterfeiting, and Pansy terms him "Crop-ear." He and his motley-garbed, dwarfish companion, Jonesy, called "Scarecrow" by Pansy, think Pansy is a witch. Although they bluster and threaten a lot, they never harm the slaves. They are the typical villains of melodrama.

CROSS-FIRE: A VIETNAM NOVEL (Graham*, Gail, ill. David Stone Martin, Pantheon, 1972), historical novel set during the war in Vietnam. Harry, a young American foot soldier who has been separated from his unit, falls in with four Vietnamese children. Mi, a girl of about twelve, her brother, Ton, 9, their little sister, Bong, and their baby brother are the only survivors of a village that has been destroyed by American bombs. Harry needs to regain his unit before he is caught by the enemy, and the children seek to join their father who works at the American air base in Saigon. After Mi shows Harry their devastated village, Harry understands their plight and feels responsible for them, but their relationship gets off to a shaky start. Harry distrusts the children, since the Viet Cong often employ children in their schemes, and the children have been taught to be suspicious of all Americans. The first night, while Harry sleeps, Ton steals his rifle, some food, and matches, and the children attempt to cross the river alone. Harry awakens and catches up with them just in time to save them from drowning, but the supplies and gun are lost, and Bong's leg is broken. After that, although they are unable to communicate in words, since neither knows the other's language, the soldier and the children become comrades in survival. While Ton remains hostile, Mi especially senses the American's good will and also realizes that they need his help if they are ever to reach their father. Their several days' journey through the jungle is lonely and difficult. The baby develops a sudden and mysterious fever and dies before they can reach medical help in Cai Nuoc. After burying the body in a shallow grave, they cross the river opposite Cai Nuoc, with Bong on a stretcher Harry fashions of sticks and vines. Then B–52s strafe the region, and Harry is killed trying to help Ton to safety. The children huddle in bushes that night. Dawn sees American planes drop paratroopers who shoot the children one by one as they come out of the business. Chapters alternate in relating events from Harry's and Mi's points of view, and most of the book is concerned with describing how they feel about each other and their situations and with Ton's persistent refusal to accept the American, who, ironically, dies for the boy. The scenes of the baby's death and burial are especially moving. Although Harry, Ton, and Mi have strong survival instincts, their efforts come to nothing in the end as the cold machinery of war envelops and obliterates with indiscriminate destruction everything in its path, whether friend or foe. Harry (called Haa-lee by the children) and Mi are acceptably drawn, but the implacable Ton remains a flat figure. The reportorial style is terse and factual, and the understated ending is all the more eloquent with horror for its lack of detail. In spite of the emotional impact of events, the reader is left with the feeling that message takes precedence over story. Fanfare.

CUMMINGS, BETTY SUE (1918–   ), born in Big Stone Gap, Va.; educator, author of novels with strong female protagonists who have survived hardships. She received her B.S. degree from Longwood College in Virginia and her M.A. from the University of Washington in Seattle. During 1942–1945 she served in the U.S. Coast Guard, where she became an ensign. She has taught junior high school in Virginia, high school in Thermopolis, Wyo., and has been an English teacher and counselor in schools of Brevard County, Fla. Her home has been in Titusville, Fla., the area of the setting of *Let a River Be!** (Atheneum, 1978), a story in which a retarded young man and an independent old woman work together to save the ecological balance of a river. *Hew Against the Grain** (Atheneum, 1977) is a Civil War novel set in Virginia.

CUNNINGHAM, JULIA W(OOLFOLK) (1916–   ), born in Spokane, Wash.; author of a number of books for young people which partake of the qualities of both fable and realism. She lived in New York and finished high school in Charlottesville, Va., afterwards attending art school there. She has worked for various publishers and in a bookstore in Santa Barbara, Calif., where she has made her home. Several of her novels are set in France, where she has also lived. Among those which have been critically commended are *Dorp Dead** (Pantheon, 1965), *Burnish Me Bright** (Pantheon, 1970), *The Treasure Is the Rose** (Pantheon, 1973), *Come to the Edge** (Pantheon, 1977), and *The Flight of the Sparrow** (Pantheon, 1980). Except for *The Treasure Is the Rose*, a story with a medieval setting, these all have orphans as protagonists and plots realistic in their grimness, including psychotic characters, but existing in the timelessness and abstraction of fable.

CUPUP CUPUP (*Cayuse Courage**), respected and feared medicine man of the Cayuse, who tries unsuccessfully to save Samuel's hand, who agrees to teach him to become a medicine man (after Samuel's vision quest on which the boy sees the medicine-man symbol of the wolf-snake), and who tells the boy to learn as much as he can about Boston Doctor's (Marcus Whitman*) medicines. After

Cupup Cupup dies of the measles, there is no one left who can teach Samuel the medicine, and he loses this vocational option, too.

CURRY, JANE LOUISE (1932–   ) born in East Liverpool, Ohio; painter and author of a large number of fantasies. She attended Pennsylvania State University and received her B.S. degree from Indiana State University, Indiana, Pa., in art education, her M.A. and Ph.D. degrees from Stanford University, and studied medieval poetry at the University of London. She served as art technician with the Mountain Playhouse, Jamestown, Pa., taught art for the Los Angeles public schools and English at Stanford University. Most of her writings contain elements of history or legend. Her fantasies known as the Abaloc stories—*Beneath the Hill* (Harcourt, 1967), *The Change Child* (Harcourt, 1969), *The Daybreakers* (Harcourt, 1970), *Over the Sea's Edge* (Harcourt, 1971), *The Watchers* (Harcourt, 1975), *The Birdstones* (Harcourt, 1977), *The Wolves of Aam* (Atheneum, 1981), and *The Shadow Dancers* (Atheneum, 1983)—postulate a link between medieval Wales, the mound builders of southeastern United States, and the Aztecs. *Poor Tom's Ghost** (Atheneum, 1977) is a time fantasy going back to sixteenth-century London, and *The Bassumtyte Treasure** (Atheneum, 1978) unravels a mystery concerning Mary, Queen of Scots.

CUTLASS ISLAND (Corbett*, Scott, ill. Leonard Shortall, Little, 1962), realistic detective novel set on an island off the New England coast about 1960, sequel to *Tree House Island*. Schoolboy sleuths, Harvey Harding and Skip Ellis, live in the seacoast town of Goose Harbor. The president of the local bank, crotchety, proper Ephraim Fairchild, whom the boys call Mr. Eph, summons them to his office, where he introduces them to an old friend of his, Bradshaw Kemberley. Mr. Kemberley owns Cutlass Island, once a pirate haunt. On the island are a fort and a mansion that serves as a museum for a valuable Civil War collection. Mr. Kemberley would like the boys to find out why the caretaker, John Hurd, has been behaving strangely lately. They are to pose as handymen, sent by Mr. Kemberley to assist Hurd around the place. Malcolm Sewell, also a Civil War buff and a friend of both Kemberley and Hurd, motors them over to the island. The boys immediately like easygoing, genial Mal, but are put off by Hurd who grudgingly accepts their assistance. He soon puts them to work, spading, raking the beach, and mowing and trimming lawns. Although the boys keep their eyes open, they cannot understand why Hurd seems so uneasy. Generally taciturn and demanding, Hurd warms enough to guide them proudly through the museum, but, when they ask to see the fort, he becomes aloof and uneasy again. He tells them he always keeps the fort locked, because Mr. Kemberley's Fourth of July fireworks are stored there. When Skip sprains his ankle, Hurd motors to the mainland for help. While he is gone, Harvey picks the lock on the door of the fort, and the boys soon discover a box marked "English bone china" buried under the floor. Hurd returns with Mal, Mr. Eph, and Gumbo, the "town squirt" of twelve, and the boys' activities come out. To their surprise and dismay, Mal pulls a gun and ties them up, then goes off in his boat to fetch accomplices. Hurd releases them, informing them that Mal and some others are mixed up in some sort of smuggling operation for which they are using Cutlass as a base. Mal has threatened to harm Hurd's nephew if Hurd informs on Mal. When Mal returns with his henchmen, presumably to pick up the box, the five attract the attention of the coast guard by shooting off the fireworks, then sink Mal's boat with the parrot cannon from the museum, and take refuge in the fort, until the coast guard cutter arrives. All characters are types, and events move with conventional twists and plenty of coincidence in rapid succession to an exciting, rambunctious climax. Tone is intimate and inviting, dialogue is extensive and convincing, and the good side comes up with an inventive defense. The contents of the box are never divulged. Information about Civil War weapons adds interest. Poe Winner.

CUTS-THE-TURNIP (*The Burning Glass**), Crow Indian boy with whom Jeb becomes friends. Jeb gives him a "burning glass," a lens with which fire can be made. It is one of the ways Jeb wins the boy's confidence and makes escape possible. This lens gives the story its title. Like most of the other characters in the novel, Cuts-the-Turnip is a stereotype.

CUTTER, TYPHON (*The Arm of the Starfish**), handsome, elegant father of beautiful Kali* Cutter, in whom Adam* Eddington has a romantic interest. Cutter is a large, bulky man, whose disproportionately thin limbs give him a sinister, spidery appearance. His manner of speaking is smooth and articulate, and he inspires confidence. He arranges to have Polyhymnia O'Keefe kidnapped while on the plane and in Adam's care, intending to use her as a hostage to get the information that her father, Dr. Calvin* O'Keefe, has learned from his experiments on the starfish, but abandons that plan when Adam takes the job as O'Keefe's laboratory assistant. Cutter then attempts to get the information through Adam, who is attracted to Cutter's daughter, Kali, and naively susceptible to her suggestions and insinuations. Already wealthy and influential, Cutter intends to peddle the information to the highest bidder because he is greedy for even more power and money. At the end, because of his intrigues, authorities give him a week to get out of Portugal. He is very close to being the stereotyped villain.

D

DABNEY PRATT (*Sweet Whispers, Brother Rush**), retarded seventeen-year-old brother of Tree, who dies of a rare disease, porphyria, complicated by his use of barbiturates. Dab seems to be very dependent upon his fourteen-year-old sister, yet he evidently finds it possible to meet street girls and bring them in to sleep with him and to buy drugs. In the fantasy episodes showing the past, he is abused by his mother, though treated well by Brother* Rush, his young uncle.

DAN AND THE MIRANDA (Gage*, Wilson, ill. Glen Rounds, World, 1962), realistic novel for younger children set in an unspecified modern time in a mid-American town. Because Miss Clancy, fifth grade teacher, wants the Oak Hill School to shine in the junior science fair, she has encouraged all the children to start early on their projects. Dan's friend, Hank, is making an electric motor, but Dan is more interested in watching living things and in playing baseball. His real ambition is to play first base for the Four-Eight club organized by Mr. Elsworth, the guidance teacher, and limited to boys who have attained that height. Dan decides to concentrate on spiders and discovers a great many varieties but is chiefly interested in a Miranda, which he watches with fascination. He learns a great deal but is reluctant to collect specimens and encase them in plastic, as Miss Clancy wants him to do. When the Miranda dies, he keeps its egg sac on the back porch, intending to get as specimens half the baby spiders before they molt and half just afterwards, but when the time comes he just opens the door and lets them float away. Although he still lacks one-quarter inch of four-eight, Mr. Elsworth makes an allowance for a new haircut and lets him join the club. The family interplay between Dan and his parents and his two sisters, Patricia, about thirteen, and Bitsy, younger than Dan, is amusing, and the theme, that science is in the watching and learning and not in collecting, takes a healthy dig at some teachers. Information dominates the story and may be a good deal more about spiders than most readers want in their fiction. Fanfare.

DAN COTWELL (*They Never Came Home**), sweetheart of Joan* Drayfus, superior student, skilled camper, who disappears while on a camping trip in the Mogollon Mts. with Larry* Drayfus. Late in the novel, the reader discovers that

Larry tried to push Dan to his death over a cliff. Dan suffered a head injury that produced amnesia. When first met, the two have been living as brothers, calling themselves Dave and Lance, in southern California for several months. They continue to do so until Dave's friendship with Peggy Richards leads to his identification.

DAN FORREST (*A Wonderful, Terrible Time**), college-educated black man, a taxi-driver, Sue Ellen's very loving father, and Mady's cherished "Uncle Dan." He likes to have fun and takes the girls riding in his cab and kite flying on the roof of their apartment house. He is a responsible, self-respecting, fair-minded person, who refuses to exploit the financial possibilities of Mr. Kusack's offer to reward him handsomely for saving his life. Mr. Kusack then offers to send the girls to camp. Dan arouses in Mady a longing for her own dead father.

DANGER BEATS THE DRUM (Madison*, Arnold, Holt, 1966), detective novel set in upper New York State in the mid–1900s and involving traffic in drugs. The tragic death of his policeman father, shot by a teenaged drug addict, has left Bob Carstens, 16, bitter, moody, and contentious. His mother has brought him and his sisters to a cottage at Shadow Lake for the summer in hopes the change in environment will improve his attitude. Bob soon meets Mark Shore, a confidence-inspiring, pleasant young writer; Alden Fawcett, unpopular bully, who soon baits him into an argument which reflects unfavorably on Bob; and Vern Brooks, well-liked, calm-mannered black youth, who involves Bob in efforts to build a Teen Center on the lakeshore. Unsettling events take place: the Carstenses' cottage is ransacked and several snapshots stolen; windows are broken in the Center, the plans stolen and later discovered in the piano in the Carstenses' basement; and strange postcards are found bearing obscure messages about flying now and paying later. Then Bob discovers Alden and two other boys in the woods, hyped up on barbiturates, and later he finds a can of kerosene in Tomahawk Cave. One night at the Teen Center practicing drums, he hears running footsteps, and soon a fire breaks out. Suspicion is directed at Bob, whose antagonistic attitude has aroused animosity toward him in the community. Mrs. Carstens summons Larry Rawlson, policeman colleague of her late husband, whom she plans to marry. Bob resents Larry but apprises him of what has happened. Larry suspects that the Count, the drug dealer who supplied the murderer of Mr. Carstens with his dope, may be operating in the area. Determined to prove his innocence, Bob consults Mark Shore, takes him to the cave to show him the kerosene can, and to his horror discovers that Mark Shore is the Count. At the critical moment, Vern and Larry show up and rescue Bob, who has come to realize the importance of self-control and positive thinking and to appreciate Larry's strengths. Addressing the topical social concern of drugs on a superficial level, the story moves with a full measure of conventional characters, cliched incidents, melodrama, and false leads, but its fast pacing, excitement, and suspense make for good entertainment anyway, and Bob's conflict with self, society, and mother's fiance contributes an additional dimension. Poe Nominee.

THE DANGLING WITNESS (Bennett*, Jay, Delacorte, 1974), novel of suspense set in Brooklyn in the 1970s. Matt Garth, working after his first year at the University as a summer theater usher, steps out the side door into the alley one rainy afternoon just in time to see a man shot. The murderer, later identified as Joe Rudd, a hit man for the mob, threatens Matt and disappears but returns throughout the story to assure him that he is being watched and beats him up slightly to drive home the point. Matt is questioned by Phil Gleason, the neighborhood cop, and by a detective named Andersen, but he tells them nothing. He is haunted by his personal tragedy, the memory of a football game in which he unintentionally killed an opponent. At the funeral, he sees Julie Leonard, the murder victim's young sister, and later meets her in the library and falls in love with her. Rudd warns him not to see her again and, when he does, tells Matt that he must see the big boss, Daniel Carson, apparently head of a respectable real estate firm. Carson says that he deplores violence, that Matt reminds him of his own elder son, now dead, and offers to send him through college if he plays their game. Caught between the contending forces, both of which watch his every move, Matt suffers. Carson lets him know that Julie was working for Andersen when she picked him up in the library, and, disillusioned, Matt breaks up with her. Finally, after his mother tells him that she is leaving his father because the man has no courage to face life, Matt calls Andersen and arranges to join his side but to pretend to be making a deal with Carson. On the way to Carson's home in his limousine, they are stopped by Rudd, who has a tommy gun. Full of hate because Matt has escaped his surveillance and knowing he is a marked man for having failed his assignment, he plans to kill Carson, then Matt. Carson shoots him first, then turns to Matt, who has begun to believe that Carson genuinely likes him and hates violence. Carson explains that he must kill Matt because the boy has seen him kill a man. At that moment Andersen appears, and in the exchange of fire Carson dies. Since he was the top man, Matt presumably is now safe, but the doubt left on that point is just one of the loose threads in the plot. These are not noticeable on first reading, however, since the suspense is built and maintained skillfully. Poe Winner.

DANNY TREVORT (*Up a Road Slowly**), the boy whom, at the end, Julie Trelling plans to marry when both have completed their education. Danny also attends Aunt* Cordelia Bishop's school, where he is a favorite pupil, since he is intelligent and conscientious. Julie varies in her opinion of him, because he sometimes joins her brother, Chris, and the other boys in teasing her, while, at other times, he comes to her defense. In high school, she rebounds to his arms after her unhappy affair with Brett* Kingsman. As a child, Danny is convincing, but, as a youth, he is too much the knight in shining armor, the anthithesis of Brett, to be credible.

DAN TURNER (*Wilderness Bride**), stalwart patriarch of his large, Mormon establishment of three wives and sundry offspring. He is a big, black-browed man of strong convictions, who is held in very high regard within the Mormon community. He is a carpenter whose skills are much in demand during the trip westward to Zion. He is determined to get to the Mormon destination and to remain steadfast in his faith, and he never deviates from the letter of the Mormon law as he sees it. He is a hard man, yet he can be generous and neighborly to a fault. Dan is a round character, the most interesting figure in the novel, one who arouses both respect and dislike, in particular, for the way he treats Corey and Ethan* Drake.

THE DARKANGEL (Pierce*, Meredith Ann, Atlantic/Little, 1982), fantasy set on the moon in the far distant future, after men, now known as the Ancients or the Unknown-Nameless Ones, have constructed domed cities, created an atmosphere, and bred a race of people and animals able to live in its thin air, then, because of wars in their homeland, left or retreated to the closed cities, leaving the moon creatures to survive without them. Aeriel*, slave girl to beautiful, graceful Eoduin, the daughter of the village leader, or syndic, is picking flowers with her young mistress in the mountains surrounding their country of Avaric*. As Eoduin goes ahead, Aeriel hears her scream and sees her carried off by a creature with a beautiful white body and many black wings whom she realizes is a vampyre, one of the icari, who drink the blood and the souls of their annual brides. Eoduin's mother blames Aeriel for not protecting her daughter; Dirna, the blind weaver slave, hints that Aeriel herself killed Eoduin from jealousy; and the syndic plans to sell her at the next slave auction, but no one is willing to face the vampyre except Aeriel, who steals a kitchen knife and sneaks away to climb back to the same spot on the mountain. When the vampyre returns, however, his presence and beauty overwhelm her, and she is unable to plunge the knife into him. He carries her back to his castle, not as a bride but as a slave to his wives, now mindless wraiths. Hunting for food in the neglected garden, she comes upon a gnome, a duarough named Talb*, who takes her to his underground caverns where food is plentiful. From him and from the wraiths, who gradually begin to remember things under her care, she learns that the Darkangel who carried her off is not yet a full vampyre but still retains some good, because he has not yet collected fourteen souls from his yearly brides to give as tribute to his "mother," the water witch. The thirteen which he has he wears in a necklace of lead vials. To pass the time until his next bridal flight, he gets Aeriel to tell him stories. When she gets to the last one she can remember, one Dirna told her about how she drowned her young charge, Prince Irrylath, at the request of the water witch, the Darkangel is strangely disturbed. The wraiths and the duarough urge Aeriel to kill him before he can become a full vampyre and join with his six vampyre brothers to control all the countries of the moon. With the duarough's magic help, Aeriel sets out in a boat on the underground river, gets to the edge of a desert, and is trudging across it when she is spotted and attacked by the Darkangel. She is saved by a huge white lyon, the Pendarlon, one of the creatures ordered by the last of the Ancients to guard the lands. He takes her to the Avarclon, a winged horse or equustel, who figures in an old rhyme about how to destroy a vampyre. They converse during the noon eclipse, but when the sun reappears he withers, and she realizes that he has been long dead and that she has been talking to his phantom. The rhyme, however, refers to his hoof, so she takes this with her and returns to the castle, only to learn that the Darkangel has not found a bride to his liking and has decided to make her his fourteenth. The duarough, whom she now knows is the Little Mage of Downwending, brews a bridal cup in the star horse's hoof, and when she persuades the Darkangel to drink it with her, he is poisoned and, in great pain, crumples before her. With the opportunity hers at last, Aeriel cannot kill him, and when she learns that he needs a heart, she removes his leaden one and cuts her own out to give him. Talb is able to melt the lead off the Darkangel's heart and plant it in Aeriel, so they both survive, the Darkangel now human again. Aeriel lets the wraiths drink their souls so that they can die in peace, and she and the Darkangel, who is really Prince Irrylath, set off to find his real mother. Although derivative in many ways from numerous other science fantasies, the created world is consistent and well maintained in the novel. Style is sometimes self-consciously inverted, and tricks like odd spellings—lyon for lion, for instance—call attention to themselves. Some elements appear to be introduced to provide a basis for sequels. Aeriel, however, is an appealing and plausible protagonist. IRA.

DARK HORSE OF WOODFIELD (Hightower*†, Florence, ill. Joshua Tolford, Houghton, 1962), realistic family novel with mystery and animal story qualities set in 1933 in the small town of Wolverton, Mass. The once influential and well-to-do Armisteads of Woodfield Farm have been hard hit by the Depression, and most of the beautiful, thoroughbred horses for which the estate was noted have been sold to pay expenses. Determined, imperious Gran and earnest Aunt Cinny, who pores over the family account books, manage to keep themselves and orphaned Maggie, 14, and Bugsy, 10, the last of the Armistead line, in food and other necessities and to pay small salaries to their faithful retainers, Miss Urquhart, their feather-headed, childish, elderly maid, and Michael, their garrulous old stableman. Ironically, it is the efforts of horse-crazy Maggie and butterfly-mad Bugsy to enter Maggie and her cherished Stardust in a local horse show to win money to buy back Aunt Cinny's beloved Amber that lead to a small fortune and also clear the reputation of the deceased family black sheep, Uncle Wally, a famous poet. Bugsy suggests raising butterflies to get entry money and sets up his hatching space in Grandfather Armistead's unused study. Then Martin Drew, newspaperman whose chance remark in praise of Uncle Wally's poems led to the deaths of Grandfather by a heart attack and Maggie and Bugsy's parents in an accident on the way to his funeral, arrives for the tenth anniversary of the deaths. He informs the family that a New York publisher is offering a vast sum for letters Uncle Wally had written to Grandfather. The family searches without success, and Martin even sifts to no avail through the voluminous collection of papers Miss Urquhart has snatched from wastebaskets for more than thirty years. With Martin's help, Maggie writes an essay about Uncle Wally's horse poems, in which she points out how skillfully he compares his relatives to their horses. The essay redeems him in Gran's esteem and ties for first prize in a community essay contest. With the money, Maggie enters the local horse show and wins. Then Bugsy spies a caterpillar on the pendulum of Grandfather's old clock, and, while rescuing the creature, he notices papers on the floor of the clock. These turn out to be the long-lost letters. The family fortunes take a turn for the better, and Martin and Cinny decide to marry. Eccentric characters, a well-paced, convoluted, consistently interesting if implausible plot, excitement, humor, and a literate style make for light, diverting entertainment. Choice; Fanfare.

THE DARK IS RISING (Cooper*, Susan, ill. Alan Cober, Atheneum, 1973), fantasy set recently in a village in Buckinghamshire, England, during the twelve days of Christmas, the second in The Dark Is Rising series, which also includes *Over Sea, Under Stone** and *The Grey King**. For his eleventh birthday, which falls on Midwinter Day, Will* Stanton, seventh son of a seventh son, receives from Farmer Dawson a circle of iron crossed by two lines, an emblem which he is instructed to keep with him at all times for his protection and subsequently wears on his belt. In evading a mysterious Black Rider, Will is transported on a white horse back in time to a great hall. There he meets a frail old lady and a tall, imposing man, Merriman* Lyon, who informs Will that he is an Old One, one of those immortals who are as old as the land, who represent the Light of Good, and whose responsibility is to defeat the evil ones whose power is of the Dark and who are attempting to bring all the world under their control. The lady and Merriman, too, are Old Ones, as are Farmer Dawson and two of his men. Will learns that he is the long-awaited Sign-Seeker and that when he has acquired the signs of wood, bronze, water, fire, and stone to put with the iron one and the knowledge of the ancient Book of Gramarye, the Old Ones will be able to overcome the forces of the Dark. Going back and forth in time and with help from the Old Ones, especially Merriman Lyon, all of whom also exist in the present as well as in the past, Will gradually finds the necessary signs, except for those of fire and water, and gains the knowledge of the ancient book by Twelfth Night. As the days pass, the weather worsens, until on Twelfth Night all England is in the throes of the most terrible snowfall and cold spell in recorded history. When on Twelfth Night Will acquires the sign of fire, a torrential thunderstorm occurs, melting the snow and causing a flood. The torrent unearths the burial ship of an ancient king, from whose body Will takes the last sign, that of water, thus breaking the power of the Dark. Characters are conventional good versus evil types, and not even Will is well developed and made sympathetic. The book's authority comes from its atmosphere of impending doom which is created early and well sustained. Skillful use of Celtic folklore strengthens the plot, which follows the quest pattern familiar from hero tale. Past and present are skillfully intermingled to support the theme of the continuing conflict between good and evil, but it is never clear why the Old Ones do not exert more control over circumstances. Addams; Boston Globe Winner; Choice; Contemporary Classics; Fanfare; Newbery Honor.

DARKNESS OVER THE LAND (Stiles*, Martha Bennett, Dial, 1966), historical novel set in Munich from 1939 to 1946, in which a few characters and the larger events are real. The complex plot carries a German family, the Elends, through World War II. The viewpoint is mostly that of impressionable, impetuous, young Mark, 9, who is puzzled by discrepancies between his teacher's vigorous support of German policies and his friends' energetic involvement in the *Jungvolk* and the lack of enthusiasm shown for the Nazis by his family: warm, discreet if outspoken Mutti, thoughtful Vati, a bookseller, Uncle* Franz, once a university professor of history and now a factory worker, and his beloved older brother, Gottfried*, a seminarian. Although intensely patriotic and fired up with the spirit of helping in a grand cause, Mark gradually finds himself engaging in acts of treason: taking food to his grandparents' elderly Jewish neighbors, keeping silent about and even hiding the questionable literature his father keeps at his shop, entertaining the seditious ideas of the historical Sophie* Scholl, who writes and distributes leaflets urging resistance, and even stealing a ration card from an air raid victim. As the war progresses and life becomes harder and more precarious, Mark observes the contradictions between what the Nazis report through the newspapers and what actually is happening. He loses dear ones and friends to army, prison, and air raids. Gottfried goes off to the army, and SS men take away Uncle Franz, whose manuscript on German history Mark hides in a secret drawer in an old French chest. Food and fuel grow scarce, the Allies press in on every side, and bombers are reducing Munich to rubble. Troubles continue even after war's end, when Poles rampage through the city, destroying property and helping themselves to whatever they wish, and the Americans seem obsessed with the idea of "collective guilt." The end of the novel brings out the secret of Mark's parentage, a plot complication that seems superfluous in view of the novel's overall intensity. Mark's Uncle Stefan, a Polish refugee, turns up and claims the boy. The reader then learns along with Mark the over-foreshadowed truth, that Mark is a Polish refugee rescued by Gottfried and subsequently raised by the Elends as their own son. Although Mark is much tempted to leave for America with Stefan, he realizes that his uncle is a hate-ridden man. Mark's love for the Elends, who have loved him so much and who need him now, and his desire to help dispel the "darkness over the land" motivate him to remain in Germany. There is a rich assortment of characters, and even minor figures are drawn with bold strokes: Grossvater, realist, philosopher, and abstract painter impressed by the government into fashioning signs for the cause; Gregor, the schoolmate who enjoys repeating snide jokes about Hitler and manages to maintain a degree of objectivity about things that Mark cannot and who ironically assumes his share of duties in the Hitler *Jungvolk*; Hanni (Esther), a coldly calculating "U-boat," a Jewish girl who travels under identification papers lifted from the body of a bombing victim; and Sophie Scholl, intense, hard-driving, doomed to execution. Mark himself grows up believably, and the way he handles the ironic discovery that he himself is a "U-boat" says much for the quality of his up-bringing and his character. Although the conclusion seems contrived, where a chance encounter with his little sister, Greta, who peddles books for food on the black market, sways Mark to his decision, the story is richly detailed, carries the conviction of careful research, and skillfully blends personal and historical problems. Without lapsing into morbidity or sentimentality, it proclaims the triumph of love and the human spirit, brings to life with drama and sympathy a troubled period, and gives a good sense of what it must have been like for those who found themselves having to support government policies opposed to their own political and ideological convictions. The title comes from Mark XV:33. (Father* Wlada) Fanfare.

DARK VENTURE (Beyer*, Audrey White, ill. Leo Dillon and Diane Dillon, Knopf, 1968), historical novel set in 1795 in Central West Africa, New England, and on the slave ship traveling between. The book, written in the third person, is divided into three parts, the first told from the point of view of Demba*, 12, a boy of the Fulani tribe who is captured by Mandingos and sold to Karfa, a wealthy black slaveholder. There he meets Nealee, a girl of his tribe, who has sold herself into slavery in exchange for food for her starving mother and sisters. When Demba's escape attempt is thwarted, he is badly beaten and made one of a slave coffle sent to the coast. Nealee, too, is part of this agonizing march, chained together, but when she becomes too weak to continue Demba gives up the knife he has acquired for another escape attempt in order to stay with her until she dies, promising to rejoin the coffle. The second part, set on the River Gambia and the return trip, with flashbacks to New England, is mostly from the point of view of Adam* Waite, 22, surgeon for the slave ship, *Orion*. When Ephraim Garrett, Adam's godfather, offers to cancel the large debt Adam owes him for his education if Adam will go as doctor on the ship, the young man seizes the chance, even though Garrett's daughter, Jenny, 16, objects. Adam is appalled at almost everything about the slave trade, including coldly calculating Captain Thomas Shaw, and he tries to protect Demba and Sam, 9, the only black children, who are not chained below decks. When some of the slaves make an attempt to break out and the knife they use is traced to the boys, Demba, to save Sam, admits he stole it from the galley and is flogged again. Adam aids him and tries to better the condition of the slaves during the passage, and when Demba gets a fever, which Shaw fears is smallpox, Adam threatens to charge the captain openly with murder when they return to New England if he should "lose" the boy overboard as he plans. Demba recovers from what turns out to be chicken pox just as they arrive in Barbados. Adam arranges that Sam be bought by a kindly owner, but Shaw takes Demba, still weak, to the auction of least desirable slaves. Impulsively, Adam bids on him and then must borrow money from Shaw to pay. Part III, set in Bristol, R.I., is told alternately from the point of view of Adam and Demba. Adam meets mixed reaction when he arrives with Demba: his landlady, Mrs. Steele, is at first disapproving but accepts the boy practically; Jenny is horrified but, when she hears the story, becomes Demba's advocate; Garrett, surprisingly, approves, thinking the slave will give status to a doctor. Adam is fined $200 for importing a slave, but Shaw and Garrett go free, though slaving is a criminal offense, and when the *Orion* is to leave once more Garrett asks Adam to go as surgeon again. Adam refuses and vainly begs his godfather to give up the trade. Later, when news comes that the *Orion* has been burned in a slave uprising and all hands killed, he feels some compassion for Garrett, real sorrow for the loss of Will Trask, the second mate whom he likes, and resolution to marry Jenny and educate Demba, then free him. Although predictable, the book has good character development and gives a strong but unsensational picture of the slave trade. Boston Globe Honor.

DARRY CURTIS (*The Outsiders**), Darrel, Ponyboy's overly serious and conscientious older brother. He is a fine athlete, who chose not to continue in college in order to go to work and keep the family together after their parents' death. He is so determined that Pony behave and not fall afoul of the law that he rides the boy quite hard, provoking him to rebellion. Darry's angry recriminations drive Pony away from home to the vacant lot the night the greasers are attacked by the Socs and Bob is killed. Later events help Pony to see that, if he expects Darry to understand his motivations, he must also try to understand Darry's. Sodapop* is a mediating influence between his two brothers.

DAVID BEN JOSEPH (*The Rider and His Horse**), son of a wealthy wine merchant of Tyre, student and protagonist. As first-person narrator, David expresses his confusion and conflicting emotions; his love for his father and his scorn for his father's sentimentality and worship of learning; his love and admiration for strong-minded Rachel* and his disapproval of her unwomanly assertiveness; his thrill at the high-minded resolve of Eleazar* ben Ya'ir, commander of the Massada, and his horror at Eleazar's decree that all in the fortress must kill their families and themselves. In his personal life, David has been confused by his study of the Torah and his reading of Greek, by his reverence for Jewish law and his realization of the excesses committed in its name, by his desire to follow the heroics of Eleazar and his understanding of the superiority of Rachel's practical virtue. In the end he has reached no certainties, only the position where he knows he must be the "memory" of this episode for his people and as such, perhaps, their conscience.

DAVID STANLEY (*The Headless Cupid**), patient, observant, understanding youth of eleven, who, since the death of his mother, has assumed much of the responsibility of caring for his younger brother and sisters. He looks forward to having a new sister when he hears that Amanda* is coming, even though she is a year older than he, but is perplexed and put off by her bossiness, refusal to help with household tasks, and sauciness toward her mother, his stepmother, Molly. Later he understands why she behaves as she does and makes allowances for her. He suspects that she deliberately makes the ordeals troublesome for the children in order to make herself feel superior and that she chooses tasks for the children to perform that will vex Molly. He resourcefully helps the children get through the ordeals. Later he and the others realize, to their surprise, that they have come to like Amanda.

DAVID TOPMAN (*The Wonderful Flight to the Mushroom Planet†; Stowaway to the Mushroom Planet†; Time and Mr. Bass**), youth of about ten, who lives with his parents in Pacific Grove, Calif. He and his best friend, Chuck* Masterson, build a space ship with which, with Mr. Tyco* Bass's help, they fly to Basidium-X*, the Mushroom Planet, and to Lepton. David's father calls his attention to the ad in the local paper for a space ship that starts the adventures out. David is freckled, tall, and quick, likes to plan things, and worries a lot. He is a courageous, persevering boy, who has doubts about the morality of taking scientists to Basidium. Although likeable, he is a flat character almost indistinguishable from Chuck. Sometimes he and Chuck influence the action. Most of the time Mr. Tyco Bass is the real hero, but David and Chuck are characters with whom young readers can more readily identify.

DAVID WIGGS (*Dawn of Fear**), mean, nasty boy, one of the Children of White Street toughs who wreck the camp belonging to Derek Brand, Peter* Hutchins, and Geoff* Young in retaliation for their having pelted him with stones until he released the small, black kitten he was torturing. He gets his older brother, Johnny, known in the area as a vicious troublemaker and black marketeer, to help his gang wreck the three boys' camp in the Ditch.

DAVID WILLIAMS (*South Town†; Whose Town?**), protagonist in four novels that trace the development of a black boy in the segregated South through his experience in high school and work in a northern city to his return as a doctor to the southern town where he started. Through his story the problems of blacks and the changes wrought by the early Civil Rights movement are illustrated. David is honest, hard working, and dedicated, but he gets into trouble with the law through no fault of his own. Others in the series are *North Town* (Crowell, 1965) and *Return to South Town* (Crowell, 1976).

DAWN OF FEAR (Cooper*, Susan, ill. Margery Gill, Harcourt, 1970), historical novel covering about two weeks' time in a suburban neighborhood about twenty miles from London during the height of the Nazi blitz in World War II. The story is told in third person mostly from the point of view of sensitive, earnest schoolboy, Derek Brand, who like his chums, Peter* Hutchins and Geoff* Young, is fascinated by the German bombers that daily raid southeastern England. They cheer the RAF interceptors and take an objective and technological interest in such aspects of the war as bomb craters and air raid shelters. Their main activity involves building a camp, or hideout, in the Ditch, a nearby excavation for an abandoned highway. One Sunday morning the boys proudly take Tom Hicks, a teenager from their street who is awaiting call-up into the Merchant Navy, to view their camp. They find that the gang of toughs from the next street, the Children of White Street, have wrecked it. Tom is certain that the White Streeters have been helped by Johnny Wiggs, a youth his own age whom he regards as a war slacker and general troublemaker. The four ambush the White Streeters on their home grounds, pelting them with mudballs. The ambush culminates in a particularly vicious fight-out between the two older boys. Tom flattens Johnny just before the sirens sound, but not before Derek sees violent adult hatred for the first time. The air raid continues through the night, and the next morning Derek discovers that Peter's house has sustained a direct hit and the entire familly killed. Derek's attitude toward the war changes. He has not only lost a dear playmate, but he also now understands what fear is. He has observed in his own neighborhood the violence that deep and longstanding hatred can produce. This finely crafted and powerfully written story of the potential for destruction of human emotion moves with steadily mounting intensity. Careful details of the boys' play, the neighborhood, and the ambush and pitched battle set the larger conflict in broad relief by providing a grim domestic parallel. (David* Wiggs) Choice; Fanfare.

A DAY NO PIGS WOULD DIE (Peck*, Robert Newton, Knopf, 1973), largely episodic novel of a boy growing up in a Vermont family that follows the austere Book of Shaker in the 1920s. Published originally for adult readers, the book is earthily explicit in some places, as in the opening episode in which Robert, 12, playing hookey, happens on a neighbor's cow as it struggles unsuccessfully to give birth. The boy ties one leg of his pants around the protruding head of the calf, the other around a tree, and drives the cow forward, then, when the animal continues to gasp, reaches into her throat and rips out a goiter, getting badly bitten in the process. In gratitude, the neighbor, Benjamin Franklin Tanner, gives him a newborn piglet, which Robert calls Pinky and which soon trails him about like a dog. Amusing episodes include Robert's misinterpretation of Ethan Allen as a baseball star, his bafflement when a family friend tries to teach him English by diagramming a sentence, and his delight when the Tanners take him to the Rutland fair and Pinky wins a blue ribbon for the Best Behaved Pig. Two chapters concern sins in the view of the adults not fully understood by the boy:

the Widow Bascom and her hired man, Ira Long, are reported to be scandalously laughing and giggling in a darkened house, and, more seriously, Mr. Hickman is found by Rob and his father at the graveyard on a rainy night, digging up the coffin of a child he fathered but did not acknowledge and now, contrite, wants to bury in his own family plot. In a grisly scene they help Ira Long "weasel" his dog, putting terrier and weasel in a barrel together to teach the dog to hate weasels, a plan that ends with the dog so badly injured it has to be destroyed. In a harrowing episode, Rob must help his father butcher Pinky, who has proven to be barren and must be eaten in the no-frills household. Having faced this loss, Robert is able to face the loss of his father, who, after a lifetime of butchering pigs, has known all winter that he is dying. Although on one level the book is a story of a boy losing his pet and growing up, it is a deeper study of the relationship and understanding between Robert and Haven Peck, a hardworking, illiterate man who feels deeply and loves the beauty of nature. In a sense, it is more the father's story than the boy's. Although in a few places it is overwritten for an easy laugh, at its best it is moving without being sentimental. Maxi.

DEAD MAN'S JOURNEY (*The Dunderhead War**), ninety-mile trail over rugged, exhausting desert south from Albuquerque into Mexico, followed by the Missouri Volunteers and Cy Petry's wagon train, with whom Quincy* Heffendorf and Uncle* Fritz travel with their wagon of trade goods. While on this demanding trail, the rag-tag army changes its estimate of Uncle Fritz, relying for survival more and more on his good sense, resource, strong sense of discipline, and careful attention to detail, and Quincy loses his romantic notions about travel and war.

DEAR MR. HENSHAW (Cleary*†, Beverly, ill. Paul O. Zelinsky, Morrow, 1983), epistolary novel set in Pacific Grove, Calif., in the early 1980s, composed of letters and diary entries in the form of letters, written to an author of children's books by Leigh Marcus Botts, a sixth grader through most of the book. The first few letters, written when Leigh is in second, third, fourth, and fifth grades, all express appreciation for *Ways to Amuse a Dog*, apparently the only book Leigh has read. The next is in reply to an answer to his fifth grade letter, which suggested that he read another book. He tells Mr. Henshaw that he read his *Moose on Toast* and makes a number of critical comments. The sixth grade letter is written for an assignment, asking ten questions. By the next, Leigh has received Mr. Henshaw's reply, which includes ten questions for Leigh to answer. At first Leigh is sure he won't take on that job, but a combination of the television set's breakdown and his mother's pressure finally pushes him to tackle it. We learn that his parents are recently divorced, that his father is a trucker, that his mother works for a catering service, that they used to live in a mobile home park, but that he and his mother have moved to a "garden cottage" in Pacific Grove, and that Leigh's dog, Bandit, now rides with his father. We also learn that in his new school Leigh has no young friends and has a problem: the good things from the catering service are being stolen from his lunch every day. His only friend, the custodian, Mr. Fridley, suggests that he needs a burglar alarm, and eventually with the help of the library and a hardware store man, Leigh rigs an alarm to ring when his old lunch box is opened. Unfortunately, he can't get it open at noon without alerting the whole cafeteria. To his surprise, this makes him the center of admiring attention and is responsible for winning his first friend, Barry, who wants to rig an alarm to go off when his little sisters get into his room. Leigh switches to a diary but still finds he can't get started writing without saying, "Dear Mr. Henshaw" or "Dear Pretend Mr. Henshaw." His diary entries reveal his hurt that his father never writes and seldom calls and tell of his delight when a trucker, contacted by CB, turns up on Christmas Eve with his father's gift, a down jacket. He eagerly awaits his father's phone calls, which never come when promised, and is angry and hurt because he learns that his father lost Bandit when he stopped to put on chains in a storm. Leigh starts up the real correspondence with Mr. Henshaw again when he is stuck for an ending to his story for the mimeographed *Young Writers' Yearbook*. At the author's suggestion, he junks his story and writes about a real trip he took with his father in the truck, hauling grapes to a winery. It wins honorable mention, and he gets to join a group having lunch with a woman author, who encourages him. About the end of March his father turns up with Bandit, having found the dog by persistent inquiries on his CB. He asks Leigh's mother if there is a chance of reconciliation, and she gently but firmly says no. He intends to leave Bandit with Leigh, but the boy, sensing his father's loneliness, sends the dog off with him, saying he can't keep Bandit happy in their little house. The style is simple and amusing, and the voice of the sixth-grader is well sustained. While there is no great depth, the emotions are honest and bitter-sweet as Leigh gradually gives up his dreams of riding in the big truck and comes to terms with his father's irresponsibility. Fanfare; Newbery Winner.

DEATHWATCH (White*, Robb, Doubleday, 1972), suspense novel set somewhere in the southwestern desert of the United States not far from a small town in the late 1900s. The story describes the four-day ordeal of desert-wise, sturdy, persevering Ben, a college student majoring in geology. Ben instinctively dislikes Madec, a wealthy and conceited businessman who boasts about how he bends people to his will. Since Ben needs money for tuition, he agrees to serve as guide for Madec on a hunt for bighorn sheep. After a couple of days in the desert, Madec accidentally shoots and kills an old prospector. Madec tries to persuade Ben with words and money not to inform the authorities, but Ben is a strongly moral sort and insists on taking the body to town. Madec then turns on him, takes him prisoner, and systematically sets out to kill him. After forcing Ben to disrobe, he drives him into the desert. Knowing that he can survive only about forty-eight hours without water, Ben calls upon all his physical and intellectual resources to outwit both Madec and the land. In the old prospector's camp, Ben discovers a rather complicated, highly effective slingshot, which eventually proves to be his salvation. He fashions sandals from the leaves of the sotol plant and during the night tramps painfully to a nearby butte, up whose side he scrambles. There he happens on a small, wind-formed tunnel that shelters a small pool where quail gather. The slingshot provides him with food and the pool with water. Realizing he must gain control of the jeep, the only means of leaving the area, Ben stealthily descends the butte, while Madec prepares to scale it, intending to flush Ben out. Ben then sets fire to Madec's camp, disables Madec with the slingshot, and finally takes the older man captive. But Ben's troubles are far from over. When he turns Madec over to authorities in the small town nearby, to Ben's amazement the police take Madec's word over his and charge Ben with murder and assault. Ticklish scenes ensue as Madec's high-powered lawyers almost succeed in pinning the crimes on the innocent youth, but irrefutable testimony by the perceptive, astute, young doctor at the local clinic corroborates Ben's story, and Ben is exonerated and Madec charged as deserved. The book starts fast, and Ben's struggle against humans, nature, and self moves dramatically, relentlessly, and somewhat fortuitously to its expected conclusion. Characters are clear types, and the most interesting part of the novel describes Ben's harrowing experiences in the desert. That Ben's hometown friends should be so ready to believe Madec instead of Ben seems incredible, anticlimactic, and fabricated to extend the tension. The title's significance is obscure. Poe Winner.

DEBORAH LEVIN (*Mom, the Wolf Man and Me**), Brett's mother. A professional photographer, she likes to wear jeans, take up causes, work until small hours, be independent, be honest with her daughter, and make up her own mind. She chose not to marry Brett's father and has never tried to hide from anyone, including Brett, her unwed motherhood. She prefers to live with the Wolf Man instead of marrying him, and her reasons for deciding to marry him are never clear. When she announces her change of heart about the Wolf Man, she shocks Brett, who has adjusted to and likes their current, self-sufficient, independent way of life.

DEGENS, T(UTI), author of books for adolescents; born and grew up in eastern Germany, from which she emigrated to the United States in 1956. She studied biology and psychology in Germany and has lived in Massachusetts. Three of her novels have contemporary settings: *The Game on Thatcher Island* (Viking, 1977), a gripping, horrifying story in which an apparently cordial invitation to friendship turns into a sadistic game of terror on an island off Cape Cod; *Friends* (Viking, 1981), a problem story of a broken family and a friendship; and *The Visit* (Viking, 1982), a psychological study in which a young girl in present day Germany unravels the mystery of the death of her aunt, once a member of the Hitler Youth. Degens's first book for young readers was *Transport 7–41–R** (Viking, 1974); it remains her best-known book, and for it she received the Jane Addams Award, the *Boston Globe Horn Book* Award, and the International

Reading Association Children's Book Award. It is a graphic first person narrative of the experiences of refugees on a transport train to Cologne in 1946. A fine storyteller firmly in control of her rather intricately constructed narratives, she pays careful attention to characterization and atmosphere.

DE JONG†, DOLA (1911–   ), born in Arnhem, Holland; writer and language specialist who reads and judges manuscripts for publishers in English, French, German, Dutch, Flemish, and South African. She was educated in the Netherlands and England and worked on a newspaper in Amsterdam. In 1940 she escaped from the Netherlands to North Africa, from there coming to the United States and becoming a citizen in 1946. Her novel, *The Level Land†* (Scribner's, 1943), though not strictly autobiographical, employs many incidents and scenes from her childhood and the immediate pre-war period in the Netherlands. *The House on Charlton Street** (Scribner's, 1962) is a very different sort of book, a mystery set in Greenwich Village, New York City. She also writes for adults in both English and Dutch, and in 1947 won the Literature Prize of the City of Amsterdam. In 1955 she was elected to the Dutch Academy of Arts and Letters.

DEJONG†, MEINDERT (1906–   ), born in Wierum, Netherlands; author whose unusual ability to express the point of view of animals and young children has won him a special place among writers for young people. When he was eight, he came with his family to the United States and settled in Grand Rapids, Mich., where he was graduated from Calvin College. During World War II, he served in the U.S. Air Force, where he was historian of the Chinese-American Wing, 14th Air Force, an experience employed in *The House of Sixty Fathers†* (Harper, 1956), about a Chinese boy adopted by American flyers. Among his other books two types predominate, those about animals, usually seen wholly or partly through the point of view of the animal characters, including *Hurry Home Candy†* (Harper, 1953), *Along Came a Dog†* (Harper, 1958), and *The Last Little Cat** (Harper, 1961), and those set in the Netherlands of his childhood, usually featuring young children, including *The Tower by the Sea†* (Harper, 1950), *Shadrach†* (Harper, 1953), *The Wheel on the School†* (Harper, 1954), *Far Out the Long Canal** (Harper, 1964), and *Journey from Peppermint Street** (Harper, 1968). He has won many honors including the Newbery Medal, the National Book Award, the Hans Christian Andersen International Medal, the Regina Medal from the Catholic Library Association, and the Aurianne Award for books which tend to develop humane attitudes toward animal life. His books have been translated into twenty languages and published in Europe, Australia, Japan, and South Africa.

DE LUCCA, NICK (*Gentlehands**), Nicholas De Lucca, Italian-American reporter, who, coincidentally, happens to be visiting at the Penningtons' estate, Beauregard, when Buddy Boyle develops his summer crush on Skye* Pennington. De Lucca dresses garishly, puffs away on a fake cigarette, wears a hearing aid he mostly tunes out, and skulks around the place, snooping and fitting in with no one, it seems. The first person Buddy meets at the Pennington estate, De Lucca ironically brings an end to Buddy's relationship with both Skye and Trenker*. De Lucca's cousin was an Italian war prisoner of Trenker's, and De Lucca tells the story of what happened to her to Buddy, Skye, and Skye's friends one day while Buddy is visiting. De Lucca plays the part of the spoiler in the story. He is a very unconvincing figure.

DEMBA (*Dark Venture**), African boy captured by alien tribesmen and sold as a slave, eventually being shipped on the New England vessel, the *Orion*. Although used to the idea of slavery, since his own tribe keeps slaves, Demba is appalled by the horrors of being a slave and is determined to escape. When he is thrice thwarted in attempts, his spirit is not broken. Gradually, he responds to the kindness of the young surgeon, Adam* Waite, and when Adam buys him in Barbados to save him from a cruel master, he realizes his good fortune and is grateful. Having been raised as a Moslem, he is able to speak and read some Arabic. Quick and intelligent, he learns English and adapts to the ways of New England cheerfully, but he does not give up his longing for his own country and his own people.

DESCHUTE, ARMAND (*The Burning Glass**), hard-bitten, stout-hearted French trader, whom Jeb nurses to health after he has been shot by his partner, LaRoche*, and whose pack train to the upper Missouri Jeb joins. Raised by the River Crows, he became so expert at trading their beavers with the whites that they dubbed him Cross-Finger, or Trader. He searches for LaRoche to kill him. The authors fail to exploit his personal problem, and it is only late in the book that the reader learns that Deschute is regarded as a peaceful man.

THE DEVIL IN VIENNA (Orgel*, Doris, Dial, 1978), historical novel set in Vienna, Austria, in early 1938 during the Anschluss, the time that Germany annexes Austria and sentiment turns strongly against the Jews. For six years, ever since they discover on their seventh birthdays that they share the same birthdate, Jewish Inge* Dornenwald and Lieselotte* Vessely, Catholic, whose father is a minor Nazi party official, have been best friends. In early February, on the weekend they turn thirteen, Inge begins writing in the book of blank pages Opa Oskar, her grandfather whom she calls O.* O., gave her for Chanukah. She tells the story of the last weeks her family live in Vienna and of her friendship with Lieselotte, which endures in spite of family disapproval and through which ironically the Dornenwalds eventually escape to freedom. Even though O. O. calls Inge's attention to the potentially fateful meeting between Austria's chancellor and Hitler on her birthday weekend, the girl's thoughts are mostly on Lieselotte, whose family has moved to Munich, on school, and on Mutti, her mother, who has broken her leg skiing. In March, Inge reports that O. O. plans to emigrate to the United States. He is certain that Hitler will annex Austria and that the

Jews are in danger. He urges Vati, Inge's father, to leave also. Although Inge is aware of increasing anti-Semitism, she is mainly interested in the approaching wedding of Mitzi*, their maid, at which she is to be a bridesmaid. When Tommi Löwberg, the son of close family friends, is injured in an anti-Nazi demonstration and then Vati and O. O. are impressed into a mercifully brief but very arduous work detail, Inge begins to awaken to reality. The Vesselys return to Vienna, and Inge and Lieselotte secretly resume their friendship. Then the Löwbergs and other friends leave the city, O. O. sets out for Genoa, and Vati's mother, Oma Sofie, departs for Switzerland. Vati loses his high position at his export-import house and Mutti her editorship, because they are Jewish. When troublesome Usch, Oma Sofie's aged housekeeper, threatens to denounce them, the situation becomes critical. Rescue comes through Lieselotte's uncle, Father Ludwig, who baptizes them and provides pre-dated baptismal certificates that enable them to secure entry to Yugoslavia, and March 31 finds the family gratefully on their way to Zagreb and safety. With a realism born of personal experience, the author brings to life a troubled and terrifying period. Chronology is difficult, however, because flashbacks and letters interrupt the narrative. Inge grows and changes believably through her experience, but she is too articulate and accomplished a writer for a thirteen-year-old who is presumably completing a school writing assignment. The novel convinces but not as the product of a schoolgirl's pen. Mitzi and O. O. are well drawn, and the family is close and loving. Child Study; Fanfare.

DEVOLA LUTHER (*Where the Lilies Bloom**; *Trial Valley**), Mary* Call's older sister, who the family thinks is "cloudy headed," or feeble minded, but who evidently is just flighty and lovestruck over Kiser* Pease. Devola spends a lot of time fixing her hair and making herself pretty. She begins to show better sense the summer after Roy Luther dies, and, when it is apparent that the children will have to move, marries Kiser. In *Trial Valley*, she and Kiser, now married, try to adopt Jack* Parsons.

THE DIAMOND IN THE WINDOW (Langton*, Jane, ill. Erik Blegvad, Harper, 1962), fantasy set in Concord, Mass., in the mid twentieth century. Orphans, red-haired Eleanor*, possibly nine or ten, and Edward* Hall, possibly seven or eight, live with their unmarried Aunt Lily, who gives music lessons to support the family, and her brother Uncle* Freddy, who is exceedingly eccentric and talks familiarly to the busts of Emerson and Thoreau. When the youngsters discover a small tower room containing toys and twin beds in their run-down Gothico-Byzantine house, Aunt Lily tells them the story of their other aunt and uncle, Ned and Nora, who disappeared from that room years before, along with the man she had planned to marry, Prince* Krishna, who had come from India to study with Uncle Freddy, then a great authority on the Transcendentalists. The disappearance of his young brother and sister has deranged Uncle Freddy's mind. The window of the tower room is of stained glass with a diamond-shaped piece in the center of the pattern and a clear panel below. Eleanor and Eddy discover a poem written in Prince Krishna's hand on the glass, entitled "Transcendental Treasure" and made up of a series of eight riddles in rhyme, each promising a different treasure. When they start sleeping in the room, the children begin a series of shared dreams, in each of which they discover the meaning of one of the verse riddles and obtain the treasure, usually of intangible value or an object of interest but little intrinsic worth. Most of the adventures are pleasant—in one they are mice in Thoreau's cabin, in another they find a doll that belonged to Louisa May Alcott—but some are distinctly frightening. In a world they enter through the mirror they see what they might become if their faults persist; in another they are tiny creatures trapped in a Chambered Nautilus; in the last they are caught in bubbles which become crystal spheres. In breaking out of hers to save Eddy, Eleanor also releases Ned and Nora, who promptly knock at the front door in real life, now grown up, and Prince Krishna, who renews his romance with Aunt Lily. The explanation for their disappearance is fuzzy: they have somehow been spirited away and imprisoned by Krishna's uncle, who used a sinister Jack-in-the-box as a surrogate. When the bust of Louisa Alcott falls on Uncle Freddy's head, he is miraculously restored to his own unusual but intelligent self. There are many clever bits in the story (the statue of Truth on the newel post whose light will no longer turn on, Eddy's solemn conviction that he will become president), and the fantasy scenes are imaginative, but most of the adventures are not truly convincing, and the denouement is weak. Sequels are *The Swing in the Summerhouse*, *The Astonishing Stereoscope*, and *The Fledgling**. Poe Nominee.

DICEY'S SONG (Voigt*, Cynthia, Atheneum, 1982), realistic family novel set in southern Maryland in the late 1900s. It is the sequel to *The Homecoming*, in which the four Tillerman children, fiercely independent Dicey, 13, intellectually advanced James, 10, musically gifted Maybeth, 8, and pugnacious Sammy, 7, have been abandoned by their mentally ill mother and spend their summer on a long, hard journey to find another home. *Dicey's Song* tells of the first four months, September to December, that they live with their mother's mother, Gram (Abigail) Tillerman, in her rambling, old farmhouse on Chesapeake Bay. The children cope with school and peers, while feisty Gram strives with Dicey's help to make ends meet, legally adopts them, and swallows her pride and applies for welfare, a decision she deplores but realizes is necessary to provide properly for the children. Dicey, her counterpart in personality, struggles with conflicting inclinations, too. Dicey yearns to leave decisions and problems to Gram and to have a life of her own now after months of taking care of her brothers and sister. She feels she has earned the right to be selfish, and sanding every day on the old sailboat in Gram's barn represents her need to be her own person. Gram admonishes her to reach out and keep on involving herself in the lives of her family, and Dicey reluctantly but conscientiously continues her efforts to make good lives for the younger ones. She and Gram ponder Sammy's uncharacteristic docility and then his sudden return to belligerence, recognize James's need for friends and his fear that succeeding in school will result in rejection from peers, and worry about Maybeth's inability to achieve in her studies. In some of the least convincing passages in an otherwise highly credible book, James bones up on theory and tutors Maybeth in reading at the urging of both Gram and Dicey. Dicey makes a few friends in school and even reaches out to teachers with whom she has been having difficulty. In the book's climax, she and Gram fly to Boston, where Momma dies in a mental hospital, arrange for her cremation, and bring her remains back with them for an intimate family burial. By the end, Dicey has learned that life brings problems, but like the melodies in the folksongs the Tillermans sing about Gram's old piano, life works itself out as it goes along. Successfully introduced are such secondary characters as Mr.* Lingerle, Maybeth's piano teacher; Mina*, the practical, expansive daughter of the local black minister; and Millie* Tydings, the owner of the local grocery. Rich characterizations, subtly depicted interpersonal and interfamily relationships, natural dialogue, humor, irony, and pathos make for a warm and touching story. Although the children are skillfully realized, the most memorable character is Gram. She takes the children in reluctantly but with good heart, although she knows that problems, heartache, and loss of independence will come with them and, as a result, gradually learns to reach out not only to the children but to the community as well. *Dicey's Song* lacks the urgency of its predecessor, but it seems true to this stage in the lives of the Tillermans and adds considerable texture to their story. The themes of courage, hope, confidence, love, and perseverance are well supported, and numerous references to music and song contribute unity. *A Solitary Blue** is a companion novel. (Jeff* Greene) Boston Globe Honor; Newbery Winner.

DICKORY DOCK (*The Tattooed Potato and Other Clues**), art student, called Haunted Dickory by Garson. She is haunted by the past (her parents have been murdered) and by the present (her inability to organize her personal life and harness her talent). Her association with Garson gives her greater self-confidence and leads to the discovery of who killed her parents. She is an interesting, sympathetic, if overdrawn, character.

DID YOU CARRY THE FLAG TODAY, CHARLEY? (Caudill*†, Rebecca, ill. Nancy Grossman, Holt, 1966), short realistic novel set in the mid–1900s in the Appalachian Mountains. Charley, almost five and the youngest of ten children, is so eager to attend Little School for the summer that the first day he is ready for the bus an hour before it arrives. He has heard how Miss Amburgey chooses the boy or girl who has been especially good to carry the flag and lead the line of march to the bus at the end of school each day. Of all the exciting activities school promises, Charley particularly looks forward to carrying the flag. Each of the book's four middle chapters describes the events of a day in which the irrepressible Charley's hopes go unrealized, his behavior inappropriate for reward.

He bangs his chair during the most exciting parts of Miss Sturgill's stories, and he accidentally drenches Miss Amburgey with water. For one whole day he stubbornly refuses to take off his hat, and he is so engrossed in fashioning a snake out of clay that he misses the bus home one afternoon. Just before school ends for the summer, Charley offers to assist Miss Sturgill in moving the library books to new shelves. His helpfulness prompts Miss Amburgey to choose him to carry the flag, and Charley's family celebrates his success with a big, just picked, juicy watermelon. Charley is a winning lad, a strongly drawn character, curious, a little mischievous, the slightly spoiled youngest. Although the author fails to motivate Charley's helpfulness, the plot moves pleasantly through several humorous episodes to its expected, satisfying if contrived conclusion. The teachers are positively drawn, shown as sympathetic, patient, and knowledgeable about the problems of the people among whom they work. This warm account of school life among the hill people gives younger readers some sense of the problems and limitations of life in Appalachia. Nancy Grossman's realistic full-page drawings reveal the hill setting, picture episodes, and capture the book's upbeat attitude toward life. Books Too Good; Choice; Fanfare.

DIES DREAR (*The House of Dies Drear**), wealthy abolitionist from Boston into whose large and mysterious house in southern Ohio the Small family move more than one hundred years after his death. Besides running a station on the Underground Railway with his elaborate system of secret passages and caves for hiding fugitive slaves and helping them on their way, he has devised a simple code of directions made from a triangle attached to any vertical surface to give fleeing slaves directions to the safety of the black church, and he has sent slaves back into slavery carrying money to help others escape. Because so much depended upon secrecy, he was called by the musical term "Selah" rather than by his name. Drear was murdered the same week two of his slaves, returning with money, were killed by bounty hunters. He willed his cavern with all the valuable antiques to the first son of slaves that was able to find it.

DIGGERS (*The Whisper of Glocken**), flittery creatures who live in the desert beyond the mountain tunnel. Their gray-brown coloring makes them almost invisible against the sand of the desert where they live. They have long fingernails with which they can dig easily and rapidly. When they dig, they make a loud humming sound. The Hulks*, who are builders, regard them as enemies and kill them.

DINKY HOCKER (*Dinky Hocker Shoots Smack**), Susan Hocker, grotesquely fat girl who favors outlandish garb and is unusually interested in the bizarre. Dinky, an ironic term, is her parents' affectionate name for her. Her mother runs her life and seems more interested in social unfortunates and outcasts than in Dinky's "fat problem." After Dinky embarrasses her mother by giving the impression that she is on dope, her mother takes an interest in Dinky's needs.

DINKY HOCKER SHOOTS SMACK (Kerr*, M. E., Harper, 1972), humorous, sociological problem novel of family life set in Brooklyn, N.Y., in the late 1900s. Loner Tucker* Woolf, 15, meets Dinky* Hocker, 14, when she answers his ad seeking a home for his calico cat, Ralph Nader*. Dinky, who loves to eat, is grotesquely fat, but her mother, a "do gooder" whose current interest is working with reformed drug addicts, seems unconcerned about Dinky's "fat problem." Living with the Hockers is Dinky's pretty cousin, Natalia* Line, an orphan who attends a school for the emotionally disturbed and for whom Tucker falls. When Tucker invites Natalia to the school Fifties Dance, she accepts on condition he find a date for Dinky. Dinky and P.* John Knight, fat, opinionated, ultra-conservative classmate of Tucker's, immediately hit it off, and P. John persuades Susan, as he calls Dinky, to try Weight Watchers with him. Dinky succeeds in shedding some pounds and appears happier. P. John's outspoken conservatism, however, offends Dinky's liberal parents, who forbid her to associate with him. Then P. John and his liberal father have a falling out, and P. John goes to live with an aunt in Maine. After Dinky tries several diets without support from her parents, she reverts to obsessive eating and becomes even larger than before. Tucker and Natalia's relationship also meets opposition from their parents, who believe they are far more serious about each other than they really are. In the spring, P. John returns, trimmed down and an ardent liberal. When Mrs. Hocker wins the Heights Samaritan award, Dinky reacts with anger, painting "Dinky Hocker Shoots Smack" all over the streets by the banquet hall where her mother is being honored. Tucker intervenes and helps the Hockers to see why Dinky is so angry with them. The Hockers resolve to spend more time with their daughter and begin by taking her on a trip to Europe. This story of insecure youths misunderstood by and at odds with their parents lacks credibility. Dialogue is vigorous and contemporary, but characters and situations are so distorted for sensation that they seem phony, and the conclusion is totally unconvincing. The story, which has been popular with middle graders and early adolescents, uses shots at parents and topical social concerns as the basis for the overtly absurd humor that appeals particularly to that age group. Maxi.

A DOG ON BARKHAM STREET (Stolz*†, M. S., ill. Leonard Shortall, Harper, 1960), realistic novel of family and neighborhood life set in the mid- twentieth century. The greatest wish of St. Louis schoolboy, Edward Frost, 10, is to have a dog of his own, a request his parents reject because they consider him irresponsible. Next to that, Edward longs to be free of the constant bullying of Martin Hastings, 11, who lives next door and takes every opportunity, it seems, to force Edward to cry uncle. Much of the book describes Edward's problems with Martin and the reflections on life of Edward and his closest friend, Rod* Graham. Life changes abruptly for Edward when his wandering Uncle Josh, his mother's brother and a self-acknowledged hobo, arrives with his dog, Argess, a frisky, young collie. Both capture the two boys' hearts, and good times follow with Uncle Josh's romantic stories about his ramblings and lively romps with

Argess. Uncle Josh's suggestion for ending Martin's bullying results in a grand brawl in which Argess comes to Edward's assistance, evoking screams of protest from Martin's mother. To Edward's surprise, Martin defends Argess. One morning, Edward awakens to a great blow. Without saying good-by, Uncle Josh has left during the night, taking Argess with him. Then on the way to school, Edward hears a rumor that Martin has organized the sixth grade boys to "get him." Edward and Rod, for whom problems have also accumulated, decide to leave their worries behind and play hookey. They wander to the freight yard, where they are accidentally locked inside an empty refrigerator car and carried off. Home again, Edward discovers that Uncle Josh has returned to leave Argess with the Frosts, because she refuses to accompany him this time. Edward's father, whom observation has convinced that Martin has a sense of fair play, visits Martin to discuss the two boys' difficulties. Afterward, he suggests to Edward that, if Edward stops calling Martin names, his troubles with Martin may be over. Edward now has the dog he longed for. He has also discovered that he does not want to be like Uncle Josh, irresponsible and self-absorbed, and looks forward to better times ahead with Argess and Martin. Plenty of humor of dialogue and situation, sharp insights into family relationships, sets of deliberately contrasting characters, and sympathetically portrayed adults and children compensate for the loose and tailormade plot and keep the book from lapsing into a lesson on responsibility. Intended for middle and later elementary readers, the story recalls the Henry Huggins books but lacks their warmth, subtle humor, and straightforward storytelling. *The Bully of Barkham Street** is a companion book. Choice; Fanfare.

DOLI (*The Book of Three**; *The Black Cauldron**; *The High King**), crimson-haired dwarf with round, red eyes, who can make himself invisible at will. He serves the forces of good in Prydain*, sometimes unwillingly, because becoming invisible hurts his ears. He is a comic figure.

THE DOLLHOUSE MURDERS (Wright*, Betty Ren, Holiday, 1983), mystery story set in the midwestern town of Claiborne in the modern period and concerned not just with solving a murder of some thirty years previously but also with the complicated family relationships caused by a brain-damaged child. While her mother is working, Amy* Treloar, 12, must take care of her retarded sister, Louann, 11. After an embarrassing trip to a shopping center with her new friend, Ellen Kramer, during which Louann wanders away, Amy blows up when her mother blames her for not watching her sister better. She runs off to her Aunt Clare, her father's older sister who has returned to Claiborne to clear out the house of their grandparents, with whom she and her brother lived for a few years after the death of their parents. Aunt Clare welcomes her, understands her conflicts about Louann, and persuades her father to let Amy stay with her for a few days "to keep her company." In the attic Amy finds and is delighted with a beautifully made dollhouse, a replica of the old house they are in, reproduced

in intricate detail, and she is surprised at her aunt's reluctance to talk of it and
her anger when she remembers that it was a gift from her grandparents for her
fifteenth birthday. Nevertheless, she asks Ellen to come home with her after
school and shows her the house, which Ellen, too, admires. They find four dolls
in a box nearby, scaled to fit the house, jointed and obviously designed to look
like the grandparents, Clare, and little Paul, who was thirteen years younger,
and they put them around the dining room table as if eating. When she goes
back to the attic a little later to close up the dollhouse, Amy is shocked to see
the grandmother doll standing in the parlor. Aunt Clare's obvious dislike of
talking about her grandparents and their deaths and the memory that her parents
never talked of them, either, makes Amy suspect a mystery, and she and Ellen,
checking old newspaper microfilms in the library, are excited to learn that they
were murdered and were found by Clare, then eighteen, and that Paul, then five,
was discovered sound asleep in a closet beside the fireplace, used for storing
wood. Aunt Clare is furious when she overhears Amy discussing it on the phone
with Ellen and even more outraged when she finds the dolls in the position of
the murder victims in the dollhouse and assumes that Amy has been playing the
tragedy for fun. They make peace, however, and Aunt Clare plans a joint birthday
party for Amy and Ellen, who are almost the same age. Plans for the party
dominate Amy's thoughts and almost blot out her worry about the dollhouse,
where she has seen a light when she went to the attic to get a blanket for Ellen.
She is angry and feels betrayed when she finds Louann at Aunt Clare's, ready
for the party, and learns that her mother decided to go with her father to Madison
to help a friend whose husband is ill. Although she is sick with dread that Louann
will ruin the party, one of her friends takes Louann under her wing, and Aunt
Clare firmly keeps the child from talking too loud and dominating the conversation.
The party turns out to be all Amy hoped for, in spite of an uncomfortable few
minutes when Ellen insists on showing the other girls the dollhouse. That night
Amy wakes to realize that Louann, who has been sleeping with her, is gone and
follows her to the attic, where she is crouching in front of the dollhouse, watching
the grandmother doll crying and knocking books from the shelf in the parlor.
The next day Amy, faced with her aunt's anger when she has found the dolls
again in the murder positions, tells her the story and is surprised to be backed
up by Louann, a circumstance that convinces Aunt Clare. She is also surprised
that her aunt seems crushed by the story and disturbed when her aunt admits
that she thinks her fiancé, of whom her grandparents disapproved, and who was
killed later that same night in an automobile accident, murdered them. She tells
Amy that she has been suffering from guilt for all these years and now is afraid
that an unquiet spirit in the house is getting revenge. That night in a thunderstorm
Amy forces herself to take Louann up to the dollhouse, hoping to decipher the
meaning of the phenomena, and they watch the murder reenacted by an invisible
character. They flee to Aunt Clare's room and are all in the kitchen, comforting
each other with hot chocolate, when Amy thinks of the books that the grandmother
doll seems to keep indicating. They find a letter in one of the books on the shelf,

a note grandmother evidently wrote after barricading herself in the parlor, saying that Paul is in the cupboard and the hired man has just killed her husband and is approaching down the stairs. Relieved from years of guilt, Aunt Clare decides to return to Chicago, and Amy goes home. Her mother has reached new understanding of the need for both girls to have some time away from each other, and Amy has learned something of the value of family, despite heavy demands. Although the solution depends upon a supernatural element, the story has a realistic picture of the problems of a child responsible for a retarded sibling. The suspense is well sustained. Poe Nominee.

DOMI DE LOMBRE (*The Court of the Stone Children**), Dominique de Lombre, noble young French woman, patrician in appearance, earnest in manner, who lived at the time of Napoleon. She speaks in a formal manner and in a husky voice with rich "r's." She enters the late twentieth century when she appears to Nina Harmsworth in the French Museum in San Francisco to seek help in proving that her father was not a murderer. Nina can see her only when Domi wishes her to. Domi had dreamed that a girl from the future would come to the assistance of her and her father.

DOMINIC (Steig*, William, ill. author, Farrar, 1972), lighthearted animal fantasy in picaresque pattern, set in an undefined time and place. Dominic, a dog of undetermined ancestry but highly developed senses of scent and adventure, sets off to seek his fortune. At a fork in the road he meets a witch-alligator, refuses her offer to tell his fortune, but listens when she predicts that the road to the right is safe and dull, the one to the left unpredictable. Predictably, he takes the left fork and encounters a fish who gives him a spear, invincible if used "rightly"—with such skill that no one can best him. This proves useful when he falls into a trap set by the Doomsday Gang, a group of thugs—foxes, ferrets, tomcats, dingoes, rats, etc.—and is able to fend them off, then dig his way out. Subsequently, he meets and aids a wealthy pig named Bartholomew Badger, a jackass named Elijah Hogg, a turtle named Lemuel Wallaby, a housewife goose named Matilda Fox, an artist mouse named Manfred Lyon, and other assorted characters. All have been harassed by the Doomsday Gang, and at the wedding of the boars, Barney and Pearl Swain, which Dominic has financed with the fortune left him by Bartholomew Badger, he leads the good animals to rout the hoodlums. In a rather extraneous final episode, Dominic wakes a Sleeping Beauty Dog in a magic castle, and they go off to adventure together. Although the fantasy is loose, with several *deus ex machina* rescues at critical times, the story is entertaining on several levels: the animals' names have obvious humor, there is frequent but unobtrusive use of word-play (Dominic flings himself down "dog-tired"), the pigs' favorite jewels are pearls, the bride is "as lovely as a wild boar can be." Dominic is a philosophical as well as active hero, given to wondering about the meaning of life, and, although never overbearing, he has a sense of his own worth, asking himself, "How did the world manage without me before I was born? Didn't they feel something was missing?'' The story rambles, but pleasantly. Choice; Christopher; Fanfare; National Book Finalist.

A DONKEY FOR THE KING (Beatty*, John, and Patricia Beatty*, ill. Anne Siberell, Macmillan, 1966), historical novel set in Palestine at the time of Jesus' birth which improvises upon the Nativity Story. Jesse is a twelve-year-old mute shepherd boy, whose only talents are his ability to handle animals and to play the shepherd's pipes. Orphaned by the death of his father and turned out by his uncle, Jesse trudges from his native Judean hills, bitter, friendless, and unwanted. North of Jerusalem he finds work as an animal handler in the rundown, traveling circus of hardfisted Nabal* and strikes up a casual friendship with an acrobat of his own age, Saul*. Nabal owns a white, bad-tempered old donkey, Belshazzar, which Jesse comes to love and which, alone of all creatures, returns his affection. When Nabal sells the donkey to a Galilean carpenter, Jesse runs away to get his donkey back. Discouraged after weary days of fruitless searching, he wanders into the Judean hills overlooking Bethlehem. One night, he observes three splendrous kings on camels bound for the village, led by the light of an extraordinarily bright star. Dazzled and curious, he follows the kings to a stable, where he discovers Belshazzar, the carpenter, his wife, and their new baby lying in a manger. Belshazzar shows a great interest in the child, and the old beast appears more alert and vigorous than when Jesse knew him. Jesse follows the carpenter and his family from Jerusalem to Ashkelon, traveling with a caravan and then a Roman party on their way to Egypt. When Jesse plays his pipes to cheer a little Roman girl who is ill, the child's nurse, Saphir*, an Israelite slave, remarks on Jesse's talent. Seeing that the boy travels by himself, the carpenter and his wife invite him to join them. At Ashkelon Jesse learns from the carpenter that the baby is the long-awaited Messiah and understands why Belshazzar is attracted to the child. Realizing how much the boy loves the old donkey, the carpenter gives him to Jesse, and at story's end Jesse returns to Israel, intending to give the world of humans another chance. He will earn a living playing on his pipes while Belshazzar dances. His faith in human nature has been restored by the kindness of the carpenter and the slave girl and the example of his own small donkey. Showcase views of Jerusalem, villages, and countryside and of the attitudes, customs, and thinking, the book's strongest aspect, bolster the appealing if occasionally implausible story of a youth afflicted both physically and psychologically. The intense tone and simple, almost ballad-like style actualize Jesse's frustrations and inner torment. Characters are acceptably portrayed, but Belshazzar's rejuvenation and attachment to the baby strike wrong notes, and some episodes approach sentimentality. That the carpenter should join a Roman party for safety en route to Egypt offers a plausible solution to the holy family's problem of escaping from Herod. Fanfare.

DONOVAN, JOHN (1928–   ), author, playwright, and executive director of Children's Book Council in New York City. He pioneered in the rise of the popular problem novel aimed at youth in their teens and dealing openly with such topics previously considered controversial or too sophisticated for young readers as homosexuality, alcoholism, loneliness, bitterness, and neglectful parents. His first book, *I'll Get There. It Better Be Worth the Trip.** (Harper, 1969), provoked wide critical attention and was a Fanfare book. It revolves around the traditionally forbidden subject of homosexuality and also concerns a broken home, irresponsible adults, alcoholism, and divorce, a multiplicity of topics for one book. *Wild in the World** (Harper, 1971), a stark and ironic story of loneliness and alienation, tells of the everyday life and death of a mountain man whose only friend is his dog. It was a National Book Award finalist and a *Choice* selection. Some of his other books are *Remove Protective Coating a Little at a Time* (Harper, 1973), *Good Old James* (Harper, 1975), and *Family* (Harper, 1976), about four apes who escape from a laboratory, form a family unit, and live in the mountains. Before writing novels, he published a picture book, *The Little Orange Book* (Morrow, 1961), and his play *Riverside Drive* was produced in New York City and translated into several languages. A native of Massachusetts, he graduated from the College of William and Mary and the University of Virginia Law School.

DOODLEHEAD YODER (*The Mystery of Ghost Valley**), eccentric old man who withdrew from society and has lived reclusively for many years in a ramshackle house in Ghost Valley not far from the Yoder farm. He is afraid he will be arrested because he thinks he killed his brother, Tommy* Yoder's grandfather, in an argument over the Hefs iron pieces. John* Yoder's family watches over the poor old fellow, who has suffered needlessly all these years.

DOOLEY (*The Genie of Sutton Place**), Abdullah, Timmy's genie, the character about whom the fantasy revolves. Years before the story begins, Al-Hazred, wizard of the caliphate of Haroun Al-Rashid, created the genie to be his servant. He fashioned Abdullah's flesh of the burning sand of the desert and the darkness of starless night, his blood of the salt sea, and his bones from the granite mountains. The wizard tore Dooley's deep and resonant voice from the "throat of the roaring simoom." Abdullah later angered the wizard by falling in love with a woman in the wizard's harem and, as punishment, was confined to the carpet in which Timmy finds him in the National Museum and from which Timmy liberates him.

DORANTES, ANDRÉS (*Walk the World's Rim**), historical survivor, with three other Spaniards and the slave Esteban*, of an ill-fated expedition to the New World. Dorantes owns Esteban, the black man who enables the group to reach Mexico City safely. A coward and weakling, often disagreeable and complaining on the journey, Dorantes calculates Esteban's value in terms of horses. He resents Esteban's strength and courage and vindictively reneges on his promises to reward Esteban when they reach Mexico City.

DORP DEAD (Cunningham*, Julia, ill. James Spanfeller, Pantheon, 1965), realistic novel set in an unidentified time and place, a "village," presumably in the modern period. At eleven, Gilly (Gillford) Ground is brilliant but withdrawn, carefully keeping uninvolved in the life of the orphanage where he has been for the year since his grandmother's death. Driven by hatred for the noise of the place and his need to be alone, he has found a ruined tower on the mountain, where he retreats in his free time. Here he meets the Hunter, an enigmatic character carrying an unloaded gun, whom he perceives as seeming "royal." When he plays hookey for a whole day, Mrs. Heister, manager of the orphanage, arranges for him to have a foster home with the strange ladder-maker, Mr. Kobalt. In this house everything proceeds on a strict time schedule, with exact duties and only essential speech. At first the good food, new clothes, and the order and quiet of the life suit Gilly, and he is contented. He even gradually lures some response to his friendship from Kobalt's cowed dog, Mash. Returning to the tower one day in his free hour, he meets the Hunter, who is shocked at his change and asks, "Are you bewitched, boy?" and gives Gilly his address in case he should need it. The encounter disturbs Gilly, but not as much as his discovery that Mash has been cruelly beaten or Kobalt's explanation that the dog "must learn to die." In protest, Gilly rearranges ladders out of their perfect order. This drives Kobalt berserk, into a rage in which he creates havoc in the workshop, forces Gilly to clean it up, and then makes him perch for hours on the top rung of the highest ladder. Later Gilly climbs from his window, inches along a ledge, and peers into Kobalt's room which is always kept locked. There he sees a cage, obviously intended for him, a sight that shocks him so severely that he falls and sprains his ankle. Mash has disappeared and so has any trust between Gilly and Kobalt. That night Gilly escapes from the padlocked house by inching a ladder up inside the chimney and letting himself down from the roof with Mash's rope. With difficulty he reaches his tower and waits until Kobalt appears, enraged, carrying a large, iron-headed hammer. Gilly fends him off briefly with stones, but when he tries to run he falls, and Kobalt moves in to kill him, only to be attacked savagely by Mash. Gilly pulls the dog off when Kobalt is unconscious but still alive. Before they make their way to the Hunter, Gilly passes Kobalt's door and scratches on it, "Dorp Dead." The story is presented as an account written by Gilly in the first person and "found after it was all over." Although the grim scenes are gripping, many inconsistencies keep the book from being convincing. In the modern period, an orphanage would hardly turn over an eleven-year-old so casually to a character known to be as anti-social as Kobalt, yet many elements seem to be modern: the indoor bathroom, the tee shirts Gilly wears, even the misspelled phrase that gives the book its title. The Hunter appears as a *deus ex machina*, without explanation or motivation. Choice; Lewis Carroll.

DORY (*A Formal Feeling**), Anne* Cameron's new stepmother, the secretary at the university history department where her father is a professor. The direct opposite of Anne's mother, Dory is small while her mother was tall, inclined to be disorganized and messy while her mother was a meticulous housekeeper, enthusiastic while her mother was emotionally controlled. Although she is evidently an excellent secretary, Dory is not an intellectual, cheerfully admitting about her new husband that "half the time I don't know what he's saying" and remarking that "this family always sounds like books." She serves not only as a foil to her predecessor but also reveals that Professor* Cameron was less than completely happy with his first wife and, by his choice, has put her perfectionism behind him.

DOUG HOO (*The Westing Game**), son of the owner of the Chinese restaurant in Sunset Towers, who is a runner and who trots hither and yon helping to gather information and keep tabs on the players in the Westing game.

DOWN THE RIVERS, WESTWARD HO! (Scott*, Eric, Meredith, 1967), historical novel based on an actual river voyage of some two hundred pioneers from Virginia a thousand miles to Big Salt Lick, Tenn., in 1779 and 1780. The actual diary of the leader, Col. John Donelson, is incuded at the end of the book, but the hero of the fictional story is Isam Massingale, 13, given the responsibility of getting the family through by his brother, Josiah, who has gone overland. With Isam on their homemade craft, the *Jonathan*, a ten-by-twenty-foot cross between a raft and a riverboat, is Josiah's pregnant wife, Nancy, and his grandparents. They survive a variety of hazards—rapids, short rations, high water which sweeps the boat away and partly wrecks it on rocks, illness, and attack by Chickamauga Indians under Chief Dragging Canoe. While Grandpappy is nearly dying of pneumonia, Nancy has her baby, and Grandmammy and Isam manage to nurse the invalids and steer the boat. When they reach the Ohio, they have to tear down the sides of the cabin to make possible poling against the flood current. Not all of the two hundred people on the flotilla of rafts, flatboats, and dugout canoes survive the terrible weather, Indian attacks, and smallpox, but Isam and his family, having reached the Cumberland river and poled the long trip upstream to Big Salt Lick, are all well again to greet Josiah, who is waiting for them. The story depends on the authenticity of the actual expedition to make it entirely credible. Isam is adequate but not a memorable character. The tough old grandparents are the best characters, believable and full of human strengths and failings. An Indian, Thanwa, whom Isam at first shuns but later befriends, seems to be in the story to diminish the strong anti-Indian attitude of the actual expedition. The events of the voyage are exciting enough to keep the story lively despite a style that often depends on stock phrases. Western Heritage.

DRAGON (*Enchantress from the Stars**), earthmoving machine which the Imperialists, who have invaded Andrecia*, use to clear land for establishing their colony. The Youngling Andrecians, whose society is still in a feudal state, think it is a Dragon and make sacrifices to it.

DRAGONSONG (McCaffrey*, Anne, Atheneum, 1976), science fantasy, third in a series set on the distant planet of Pern in the far future, and the first of the series published for children. Events occur during the time of the latter half of the second book, *Dragonquest*. Pern has been endangered by threads of spore life spun off from another planet which devour anything organic in their way, but the human settlers there have learned to control the threads by fire and by dragons which can travel by teleportation and can char the threads midair with their fiery breath. Most residents live in Holds formed from natural caves. At Half-Circle Sea Hold, a comparatively isolated and tradition-bound community, the old harper, Petiron, has died and in all the Hold there is no one capable of singing his deathsong except Menolly*, 14, second daughter of the Sea Holder, Yanus*. Although she has tended Petiron and learned all the traditional lore, Yanus is reluctant to let a girl perform the honor or teach the children, and when the new harper, Elgion, arrives, Yanus forbids Menolly to sing or play, and particularly to make up new songs. To Elgion, who wonders what person has taught the children so well and who has a mandate from the Masterharper Robiton to find the talented lad that composed songs Petiron has sent him, Yanus speaks evasively of a fosterling sent away. After she cuts her hand gutting fish and her mother, Mavi*, the skilled nurse of the Hold, lets it heal crippled so she will no longer be able to harp, Menolly runs away and stays in a cave some distance down the coast. There she assists a queen fire lizard, a small dragon-like creature believed in the Hold to be mythical, by getting her eggs from the warm sand up to the cave to escape an unusually high tide. When the eggs hatch, Menolly is there and "impresses" nine fire lizards by feeding them and talking to them when the first emerge from the shell, thereby binding them to herself emotionally for life. The effort of feeding them takes her some distance from the cave, and when she is caught out in a threadfall, she is unable to get back though she runs over the rough stone in a courageous effort. T'gran, rider of the dragon Branth, picks her up just in time and teleports her to Benden Weyr, a center for dragons and their riders, where her lacerated feet are treated. Unknown to Menolly, also present at Benden Weyr is Elgion, who has become a friend of Alemi, Menolly's brother, the only family member sympathetic to her, and who has also been caught out in threadfall as he hunts fire lizards, having heard from Alemi that there really are such creatures on the coast near Half-Circle. At Benden Weyr Menolly is treated better than she ever has been in her life; she is admired for her fire lizards, which have teleported to her side, and she witnesses the hatching of a clutch of dragon eggs and their impressing by chosen boys and girls. At the feast following the ceremony, Elgion finally realizes her identity, introduces her to Masterharper Robiton, and thereby assures her future as a harper and composer, the first woman in such a position, at least in recent memory. A long summary of the earlier events at Pern helps a reader starting with this novel. Menolly is an appealing heroine, and as an introduction to the genre, this is a satisfying novel. Those familiar with the conventions of science fiction will recognize a number of cliches, but the story moves well, with more characterization

in the Sea Hold figures and a stronger single focus than is found in the novels
of the series published for adults. Sequels. Fanfare.

DRAGONWINGS (Yep*, Laurence, Harper, 1975), historical novel of the Chinese
community in the San Francisco Bay area during the first decade of the twentieth
century. As the story starts in China in 1903, the narrator, Moon* Shadow Lee,
8, is taken to America to join his father, Windrider, whom he has never seen,
by Hand Clap, a teller of tall stories and one of the owners of the laundry where
Windrider works and lives. Chief owner and patriarchal figure is Uncle Bright
Star; third owner is White Deer, who also cooks. Other workers are Lefty, a
compulsive gambler who chopped off his right hand when he diced away his
savings for a return ticket to China, and dissolute Black Dog, Uncle's opium-
smoking son. When Black Dog robs and beats Moon Shadow, Windrider
challenges the secret brotherhood of The Sleepers who shelter him and kills a
man in defense, so the father and son leave the town of the Tang people,
Chinatown, to live among the demons, the white Americans. They become close
friends of their landlady, elderly Miss Whitlaw, and her niece, Robin, and when
the San Francisco earthquake of 1906 strikes, they together dig out survivors
and camp on the beach to escape the fire. This jolts Windrider into a decision:
he will follow the vision of flying given him by the Dragon King and will
construct an airplane that improves on the Wright Brothers' invention. In the
Berkeley hills, the father and son live in a barn and by scrimping and extremely
hard work they construct their plane, *Dragonwings*, which achieves a flight
actually recorded in history before it crashes. Windrider decides that the love
of family is a greater blessing than flight and saves until he is able to go to China
to bring back Moon Shadow's mother. A great many events are crowded into
this novel and a good deal of history of the Bay area. If it is sometimes a bit
heavy handed, it is full of interesting customs and attitudes of the Chinese
American people of the period. Boston Globe Honor; Fanfare; IRA; Lewis
Carroll; Newbery Honor.

DREAMLAND LAKE (Peck*, Richard, Holt, 1973), realistic novel of community
and home life with mystery-suspense and problem story aspects set in the late
1900s in the small town of Dunthorpe in what appears to be Indiana. The loosely
plotted story revolves around the efforts of two thirteen-year-old schoolboys,
Flip* Townsend and Bry* Bishop, to identify a dead man. Local history enthusiasts,
they are poking around the woodsy end of Dreamland Lake, once a popular
amusement park, when they discover the body. Bry has misgivings about their
probe, which uncovers nothing of value for authorities and which brings them
into a friendship of sorts with Elvan Helligrew, their sometime paper-route
substitute. Elvan is a grossly fat youth, generally disliked by his peers, who
persists in following Flip and Bry around. He is obsessed with the Nazi era and
collects Hitler memorabilia. The boys accept an invitation to Elvan's house,
where he shows them his Nazi artifacts, and then demand that he cease pestering

them. Summer finds them engrossed in various matters, and interspersed among the episodes that advance the fragmented plot are scenes that support the themes of personal responsibility and father-son relationships as well as friendship and death. Among others, the boys are invited to the home of wealthy old Mrs. Garrison, who tells them about her dead son and shows them his picture. Bry accompanies his trucker father on a run to Memphis, in which they discover a highway accident with two fatalities. The plot picks up again when in the fall Elvan lures the boys back to the park. He attempts to impress them with the unlikely story that he killed the man with his Nazi war knife. The boys ridicule him and chase him away. He flees over the bridge spanning one end of the lake, falls through its rotten webbing, and hangs himself to death. Bry tells the story in appropriately contemporary language, sufficient detail, and vivid dialogue. The action moves unevenly with some mild suspense to the grisly, ironic conclusion. The sense of small town life is strong. Characters are distinctively drawn, if an unlikely combination, and Bry changes believably because of his experiences. The plot is too insubstantial to support the several themes but still provides diverting, undemanding reading about recognizable characters and home and community situations intended to appeal to pre- and early-adolescent readers. Poe Nominee.

THE DREAM WATCHER (Wersba*, Barbara, Atheneum, 1969), realistic novel of a New Jersey high school boy and his friendship with an eccentric old woman set in the mid–1960s. Albert Scully, who tells the story in first person, is a failure in his own eyes and to all his acquaintances. His mother, a demanding, materialistic woman, wants him to be brilliant, popular, and accomplished, and he is none of these things. She has managed to disapprove of and break up the few friendships he has ever made and to put a barrier between him and his insurance salesman father, whom she considers a failure and an alcoholic. One day, reluctantly delivering his mother's protest about a rubbish fire, he meets Mrs. Orpha Woodfin, an old woman crippled by arthritis, who lives in a dilapidated house, the only old and different house in the modern development where the Scullys live. Mrs. Woodfin invites him in, gives him sherry, and discusses Shakespeare with him. She tells him about her life as an actress in Europe and is not contemptuous of his interests in gardening and in recipes. Their friendship grows to be a regular daily engagement for tea, which Albert conceals from his mother by saying he has joined extra-curricular clubs at school. Mrs. Woodfin's interest and admiration for his genuine intelligence gradually raise Albert's self-image. When he finds her gone one afternoon and learns from a neighbor that she has had a heart attack, he is shocked and nearly hysterical, but he finds the hospital and starts regular visits. He confesses the real story of his activities to his parents, and his mother is impressed because Mrs. Woodfin was a famous actress and the daughter of an earl. At the hospital she has been entertaining the other old women in the ward by giving dramatic readings and telling stories of her life. When she is due to return home, Albert buys and plants a rosebush in her yard and returns home late only to find that the hospital has called to say Mrs. Woodfin has suffered another heart attack and died. Albert's mother also cruelly tells him that the social worker said Mrs. Woodfin was born of a poor family in London, had been an English teacher but was fired for drinking, and was on welfare. At first Albert feels betrayed, but gradually he sees that the old lady has lived a rich life through her dreams of fame and wealth, of her poet husband, and of her brother Bertie's becoming a Buddhist monk. He also sees that she has given him a new perspective on life and the courage to finish high school and to be true to himself even if he does not fit the popular idea of success. The story has a tone of the 1960s, which dates it even more than its discussion of hippies and LSD. Although Albert is a great reader, the wealth of quotations from Shakespeare, Thoreau, Rilke, etc., seem out of place with his immature vocabulary and more an exhibition of the author's interests than good characterization. Both parents are stock figures: the Bad Mother, the Weak Father, and the outcome is predictable if not entirely convincing. Choice.

DREW THORNDIKE (*The People Therein**), Andrew, botany teacher from Boston who comes to Dewfall Gap and changes the life of Lanthy* Farr. Told by his doctor to seek a complete change of scene to cure his drinking problem, he is traveling as a naturalist in the Great Smoky Mountains when he comes upon the Farrs' cabin. Although his appearance—copper-red hair and beard, blue eyes, slight build—and his educated background mark him a "furriner," the mountain people accept him hospitably. The simple life seems to suit him, but he is called away by the illness of Carrie, his older sister who raised him after the death of their parents and to whom he feels obligation and love, although he also confesses to Lanthy that Carrie "smothers" him. A man torn between two very different lives, he at first resists his love for Lanthy, knowing she can never be transported to his Boston world, but in the end opts for life in the mountains where her love and steadiness will give him strength. His view of the mountain community is told through his journal entries and letters to Carrie.

DR. FINNEY (*Stormy, Misty's Foal**), veterinarian at Pocomoke City. The Beebes take Misty to his place because they fear she may have problems giving birth to her foal. Dr. Finney sleeps in the stall next to Misty during the night, and at dawn he is surprised and pleased to find that the colt has been born and is healthy. His son, David, watches over Misty tenderly during the hours she occupies the Finney stable, and knowing that David is there makes Paul* Beebe feel both better and jealous. David misses the excitement of moving Misty and her foal home again because he has the measles, but he gets to watch the action from his bedroom window.

DR. HENRY VICKERS (*The Voyage Begun**), Paul's officious, always busy, authoritarian father. He is sure that the changes in the environment have been caused by geologic and thermal variations. He is disappointed in Paul, the

Vickerses' only son, because Paul does not measure up to his expectations of a teenaged son. For example, Paul has no interest in sports and has made no friends among the boys of the community, who, unknown to Dr. Vickers, are mostly hoods. Dr. Vickers tolerates the complaining of his wife, Diane, about the lack of food and luxuries and her yearning for the days when people had plenty of the things that were identified with the good life. Diane has a better relationship with Paul than does Dr. Vickers. Paul understands her need for gaiety in her life and tries to give her some of the companionship that she fails to get from her husband. The Vickerses' counterparts in the community are the Caffertys (Mr.* Cafferty), Mickey's* parents. The Vickerses are also foils for Maggie* Rudd and Gabe Palazzola.

DR. MCLOUGHLIN (*Half-Breed**), an actual historical figure. In the novel, he is presented as an imposing man with booming voice, kind blue eyes, flowing cloak, and tall beaver hat. Hardy Hollingshead meets him when Hardy first arrives in Oregon City. The doctor takes the boy home, gives him a meal, and summons Joe Meek* to take him to his father, Jesse Hollingshead. The doctor proves helpful to Hardy on other occasions, too. His actions show Hardy that not all whites distrust and shun Indians.

DROVER HULL (*Brady**), an agent on the Underground Railroad. Regarded in the community as a hermit, he has a secluded farm at which Brady and Range see runaway slaves. The two boys realize it is a station on the Underground Railroad. Drover is an undeveloped character.

DRURY, ROGER W(OLCOTT) (1914–   ), born in Boston, Mass.; he was educated at St. Paul's School, where his father was headmaster, and at Harvard University. He was a reporter for the New York *Herald Tribune* and worked in the advertising department of Macmillan publishing company, and during World War II he engaged in alternative service as a conscientious objector. From 1946 to 1960 he was a dairy farmer, and since 1960 has been a free-lance writer. His *The Champion of Merrimack County** (Little, 1976) is a straight-faced, absurd fantasy of a mouse whose passion is bicycle racing and who is injured when his bike slips on a soap sliver in the practice track he has discoverd, the newly installed old-fashioned bathtub in the house where he lives. In addition, Drury has written *Drury and St. Paul's* (Little, 1964) and *The Finches Fabulous Furnace* (Little, 1971).

DRYNWYN (*The Book of Three**; *The Black Cauldron**; *The Castle of Llyr**; *Taran Wanderer**; *The High King**), Taran's* magical, very powerful sword in the Prydain* novels. Eilonwy* secures it for him from the dead king in Queen Achren's castle. Later it falls into the hands of the evil powers, and when recovered by Taran, it enables him to defeat Arawn and free Prydain from the dread king's threats.

DU BOIS†, WILLIAM PÈNE (1916–   ), born in Nutley, N.J.; artist who has been both author and illustrator for more than twenty books for children and who has illustrated many books written by others. The son of a painter and an art critic, at eight he went to France with his parents and was educated in a French boarding school and later in Morristown School, N.J. From 1941 to 1945 he served in the U.S. Army, most of the time as a correspondent for *Yank*. His books range from picture books through picture-stories, like *The Flying Locomotive†* (Viking, 1941) to longer works like *The 21 Balloons†* (Viking, 1947), a fantasy which won the Newbery Medal. One of his great enthusiasms is the circus, an interest reflected in *The Alligator Case** (Harper, 1965), a spoof of mystery novels concerned with the robbery of the receipts of a traveling circus. A number of his stories are about characters of unusual size, among them several about Otto, a Bunyanesque otterhound, and *Giant†* (Viking, 1954), a story about an enormous eight-year-old boy. All his books concern bizarre or eccentric characters and situations, told in straight-faced, mock-serious style. Action is fast paced, with little description, elaboration being left to the precise and detailed illustrations.

DUNCAN, LOIS (LOIS STEINMETZ ARQUETTE) (1934–   ), born in Philadelphia, Pa.; writer best known for her books of mystery, suspense, romance, and everyday life for teenagers. Since 1960, she has written a dozen and a half books as Lois Duncan and as Lois Kerry. She sold her first story to *Calling All Girls* when she was thirteen, and she was three times winner in contests for *Seventeen* magazine. Versatile as well as prolific, she has written for slicks and also for such national popular magazines as *McCall's*, *Reader's Digest*, and *American Girl*. She has published books for readers of all ages, but mostly for young adults. Two of her mystery-suspense novels, *Ransom** (Doubleday, 1966), and *They Never Came Home** (Doubleday, 1969), were nominated for the Edgar Allan Poe Award. Though unsubtle, these are well-plotted, suspenseful, and highly entertaining stories. *Debutante Hill* (Dodd, 1958) is a love story of teens who come from different social backgrounds, *Giving Away Suzanne* (Dodd, 1963) is a story of family life for younger girls, *Point of Violence* (Dodd, 1966) is a thriller for teens, and *Major Andre, Brave Enemy* (Putnam, 1969) is a biography. More recently she has published *The Third Eye* (Little, 1984), about a young girl who is called upon by police to use her psychic powers in a kidnapping case, and *Chapters: My Growth as a Writer* (Little, 1982), her own story.

THE DUNDERHEAD WAR (Baker*, Betty, Harper, 1967), historical novel set in the American Southwest in 1846–1847, during the war with Mexico. Quincy* Heffendorf, 17, who tells the story, has mixed feelings when his father, a storekeeper in Independence, Mo., suggests that he and Uncle* Fritz go on a trading trip to Santa Fe. Quincy has an "almighty itch" to see the places "beyond the prairies and over the mountains" that colorful trapper, Possible Gooch, yarns about, and he is too young to join the Missouri Volunteers against Mexico. But he realizes that Uncle Fritz, newly arrived from Germany, a strong advocate of law and order, and a severe and outspoken critic of the lawlessness and crude behavior of the Missourians, might be a handful to control. Before long, however, he has good cause to feel grateful for Uncle Fritz's insistence on routine, planning, and discipline, as other less carefully maintained wagons fall by the wayside. At Council Grove Creek, they join the wagon train led by prosperous, competent trader, Cy Petry, for whom Possible works, and both prove good friends in the ensuing months. The 200 wagons proceed to Bent's Fort, where they rendezvous with General Kearny's Grand Army of the West and the Missouri Volunteers, among whom are Quincy's hometown pals, Will* Dayton and Les* Young, and his archenemy, town bully Rufus* Purdy. The three eventually learn Rufus is in the pay of the Mexican governor of Santa Fe, Armijo. Quincy and Uncle Fritz's fortunes merge with those of the army from this point on. After Santa Fe falls, without a shot, the two continue southward over the dread Dead* Man's Journey through the desert into Mexico. After taking Chihuahua, they return home heroes, having survived plagues of mosquitos and flies, hailstorms, alkali dust, buffalo herds, mud flats, and numerous fords and flash floods, as well as enemy fire. Once considered an eccentric dandy, Uncle Fritz has resourcefully risen to all occasions, among other efforts nursing Will through the measles and bartering his cuckoo clocks for sheep to feed the army. His traveling companions have gained respect for the once-derided critic of laziness and ineptitude, and he for the Americans' bravery, devotion to freedom, and ability to pull together when necessary. Most characters are types and the enmity between Rufus and Quincy and Rufus's treachery interject an unnecessary complication into what is an already colorful, action-filled story that offers possibilities for character development not adequately exploited. Quincy tells his story in colloquial language and with a keen eye for the sights, smells, and sounds of city, trail, and conflict. The issues and thinking of the times are presented in easy-to-grasp fashion. The novel offers a lighthearted, usually exciting picture of a little-known war very important in the history of the United States. Spur.

DUNN, MARY LOIS (1930–   ), born in Uvalde, Tex.; school librarian and novelist. She received her B.A. degree from Stephen F. Austin College (now University) and her M.A. from Louisiana State University and has been a librarian in Houston schools. Her novel, *The Man in the Box: A Story from Vietnam** (McGraw, 1968), won the Sequoyah Children's Book Award of Oklahoma.

DURANGO STREET (Bonham*, Frank, Dutton, 1965), sociological problem novel set in a black area of a large city in the mid twentieth century. When Rufus Henry, 17, is released from the Pine Valley Honor Camp, where he has been serving his sentence for car theft and other offenses, he learns that his mother has moved and now lives near the Durango Housing Project, called the Flats. Although one of the conditions of his parole is that he stay unconnected to any gang, he knows that in this tough area survival on the street is dependent on being in a gang. When the Gassers, a gang from Cathedral Heights, attack him and threaten his sister, Janet, 12, Rufus hunts up huge, slow-thinking Baby (Walter) Gibson, a friend from Pine Valley, who is a member of the Moors, and proposes that he join them. In a ritual initiation led by the vicious head Moor, Bantu (Richard) Motley, 20, the Moors beat Rufus into the gang, only to be interrupted by the police, who round them all up and haul them in. Rufus's parole officer gets in touch with Alex Robbins of the Group Service Council, who is devoted to breaking up gangs. Only Bantu, who is carrying drugs, is held, and in his absence Rufus takes over leadership. At his direction, the Moors play along with Alex, mocking him by electing the least likely member, puny Leeroy Purvis, their fifteen-year-old errand boy, as president. Alex, however, knows Rufus's vulnerable spot, his secret belief, originated by his mother, that big Ernie Brown, pro-football halfback, is his real father, and he invites the Moors to a practice of the Marauders, the team which has just acquired Ernie. Since only Baby Gibson, to whom Rufus confided about his Ernie Brown scrapbook at Pine Valley, could have been the source of this information, Rufus is sore, but he hides his feelings. When Bantu returns, Rufus fights him for leadership, beats him, and Bantu is out of the Moors. Even Idell Southworth, Bantu's right-hand man, accepts Rufus's leadership. Wanting to go after the Gassers, Rufus approaches two other groups, the Bloods, blacks from the Escala Court Project, and the Aztecs, a Mexican gang, proposing they jointly provide alibis for each other, but he gets turned down by both. When the Gassers catch Janet and cut off one of her braids as a warning to Rufus, he formulates and carries out an ingenious plan that leaves the Gassers beaten and their car wrecked, and when the Moors are picked up for questioning, the Bloods surprisingly provide an alibi. Alex gets them off with the proposal that they and the Gassers together visit the Marauders' training field. At the tense meeting, Ernie throws some passes to Rufus, compliments him, and agrees to show them all some plays on the Big Lawn, the common park area, the next week. Rufus's mother avoids the subject of Big Ernie and will give him no details of her earlier assertion that they were once married. At the Big Lawn, Ernie and the Moors show up, and the Gassers' leader, Simon Jones, comes with Rufus's scrapbook, having stolen it from his house. Rufus tries to attack Simon, is caught and put in Ernie's car, humiliated, but Ernie cheerfully tells him it's a common sort of hero worship and makes light of the claim that Rufus is his son. Determined to destroy Simon Jones, Rufus pressures one of the Moors to get a gun, planning a series of "mystery snipings," but it is taken from its hiding place, presumably by Alex. Earlier, the Moors have been approached by two girls, Judy Williams and Nonie Emrey, who want to start a ladies' auxiliary, the Am-Moors. Now the girls start pestering about wanting a dance, since the graduation dance of the kids who have stayed in high school is coming up and the drop-outs feel left out. Rufus sees this as a way of getting Simon, since he is sure the Gassers will try to wreck the dance, and he knows they will be arrested and Simon, who is on parole, will be sent to prison. With Alex's help, they organize a dance, get caught up in the spirit, and are having a lovely party when smoke starts to come up the vents. With great presence of mind, Rufus avoids a panic and tips off the police who arrest the Gassers for attempted arson. The rest of the dance goes beautifully, and Rufus decides to go back to school and live right. An uneven book, many of its scenes have vivid power—Rufus, sparring verbally with the psychiatrist at Pine Valley, the fights and other street scenes—but the end is a letdown, unbelievable and insufficiently motivated. Rufus's obsession with his relationship to Big Ernie, an important element in the early part of the novel, is dropped lamely, and Rufus's strong feeling of responsibility for Janet and their younger brother, Curtis, also disappears from the story. Rufus is an interesting character, intelligent, tough but sensitive, and the other Moors are well differentiated and plausible, but the girls and Alex are stock figures. Choice; Stone.

DUST OF THE EARTH (Cleaver*, Vera, and Bill Cleaver*, Lippincott, 1975), realistic family story set probably in the 1920s or 1930s on a sheep ranch in the Badlands of South Dakota. Fourteen-year-old, hardworking, observant Fern* Drawn tells how her Mama, her Papa, Hobson*, 16, Madge*, 8, and Georgie, 3, throw their few possessions into their old car and move to Chokecherry to live on the farm they have inherited from Grandfather Bacon, Mama's father. Grandfather Bacon had disparagingly referred to them as the "dust of the earth," but Papa, in an analogy intended to boost their wounded self-esteem, reminds his family that without dust, there would be no atmosphere, and his words are a comfort and encouragement as they set out to meet the tests of survival in their unfamiliar circumstances. The next year holds many hardships and few but much appreciated joys. Making a success of the farm and sheep means a great deal to Papa, who takes a job in the local bank so they will have money for necessities. Fern does the work of a man herding the sheep by herself, until Hobson drops out of school to help her. Mama has another baby, and little Madge has to pitch in and do more than an eight-year-old's share to keep the house going. They suffer from the flu, lose sheep to a marauding wolf, and see a terrible windstorm wipe out their sheep wagon. Papa loses his job just before lambing season begins. As the family works to survive and make a go of the sheep, they gradually stop picking at and demeaning one another. They grow closer together, develop respect for one another, and share their feelings and hopes as they have never before been able to do. The Drawns make some friends in the community, among them, Dr. Iron Ross, the sympathetic physician who sees them through the flu; Nell Perrott, a sturdy young widow and a former gold prospector, who helps them with food; and Col. Webb Harbuck, the flamboyant neighbor who helps with the lambing and shearing. This story of a family that learns through adversity and need to love and talk to one another is told in slightly overblown schoolgirl style that helps to characterize Fern. Her sometimes astute, often naive and humorous reactions to things is convincing, although she appears to know a great deal about sheep for one who is new to the business. Lewis Carroll; Spur.

THE DWARF PINE TREE (Lifton*, Betty Jean, ill. Fuku Akino, Atheneum, 1963), folktale-like fantasy set in Japan at an unspecified time. A little pine tree, growing alone in a birch and oak forest, sees small pine trees being carried along the road to the capital and learns that they are being taken to the palace because a soothsayer has predicted that the ailing princess can be cured only by "a dwarf pine as pure of heart as it is of beauty." He longs to be one of them, but the arrogant oaks and birches tell him that the dwarf trees are hundreds of years old, trained by humans to stunted growth and beautiful shapes. One stormy night Sojobo, the wicked king of Goblin Tengu, the half-human, half-bird creatures, seeks shelter and only the little pine tree will offer it. The next day the goblin king, who really is kind and helpful sometimes, asks what reward the little tree wants and is surprised that he seeks only to be beautiful so he also may try to cure the princess. Sojobo points out that, although it is possible for his tengu to produce the results in months rather than hundreds of years, it will be very painful and, moreover, the little tree will live only six months after the process is complete. The tree still insists that is what he desires and submits without complaint to the painful cutting of his tap root and the wiring of his branches in unnatural positions. The other trees laugh scornfully and point out that no one will ever see him in the forest, and so it seems for several months. Then woodcutters come and cut all the big trees, leaving the pine only because he is so small. With just one month left, the tree is spotted by some of the emperor's men and taken to the palace where the emperor himself carries it to the princess. For the first time in months the princess sits up, starts to talk, and soon is running about happily in the gardens. When his time is up, King Sojobo and his tengu take the pine tree to the mountaintop where the good tree spirits live and where the princess can see him silhouetted against the full moon. The brief story has the tone of Japanese tales from the oral tradition, though the moral of the value of self-sacrifice is more obvious and didactic than most folktale themes. Choice; Fanfare.

DWAYNE PICKENS (*All Together Now**), retarded man in his thirties who becomes the devoted friend of twelve-year-old Casey* Flanagan, thinking she is a boy. Honest, good-natured, respectful, Dwayne is liked by almost everyone in town, where they are used to his baseball "games" in which he plays all the positions and announces at the same time. He spends all his money on a baseball mitt for Casey and follows her loyally all summer to the movies, the dime store, and the race track. His great dread is the institution to which his brother Alva once had him committed. When Alva's wife nags at him, Dwayne takes her Chrysler and drives to the track where his idol, Casey's Uncle Taylor, races, and he imagines himself in the race, too. Later, when Taylor is jumped by some out-of-town racers, Dwayne enters the fight and beats them off, then vomits because hitting people makes him sick. This fight incites Alva to have him committed again, but he is rescued by the interference of Casey's family. His discovery from the doctor's words that Casey is a girl shocks him, but he does not hold the deception against her and brings her flowers he has picked. Although he is described as having the mind of a twelve-year-old, he seems actually more severely retarded, barely able to read comic books, far less competent than Casey, who is twelve.

DYER, T(HOMAS) A(LLAN) (1947–   ), born in Newberg, Oreg.; educator whose experiences as head teacher on the Warm Springs Indian Reservation in Oregon from 1975 to 1977 led to his novel, *The Whipman Is Watching** (Houghton, 1979), which won the Child Study Award and is concerned with problems of modern Native American teenagers. He received his B.A. and M.A. degrees from Portland State University, his B.A. in education from Eastern Oregon State College, and his M.A. in linguistics from the University of Arizona. Since 1978 he has taught in the Klamath County Schools.

E

EAGER†, EDWARD (MCMAKEN) (1911–1964), born in Toledo, Ohio; playwright, lyricist, and author of children's books. He grew up in Toledo and attended school in Maryland and Massachusetts, where he also studied at Harvard University. Before writing for children, he worked primarily on plays and songs for the Broadway stage, radio, and television. Reading stories for his son, Fritz, led to his first book for children, *Red Head* (Houghton, 1951), a picture book in verse. His fascination with E. Nesbit resulted in his magic books, the stories for which he is best known and which are open imitations of the family fantasies of the renowned turn-of-the-century English author. The first of these, *Half Magic†* (Macmillan, 1954), became very popular. About what happens when some children find a magical coin that grants only half a wish, it was a Fanfare book and was widely praised by critics, though some complained that it is coy and cartoonish. Still the most highly regarded of his books, it now seems contrived and overextended compared to its more famous prototypes. Among six successors, *Knight's Castle†* (Harcourt, 1956), *Magic or Not?†* (Harcourt, 1959), and *Seven-Day Magic** (Harcourt, 1962), which describes how several children have exciting adventures in literary lands after they bring home a special red book from the library, employ similar narrative techniques and reveal much the same limitations. Like *Half Magic*, these books are listed in *Choice*. His several other titles include *The Time Garden* (Harcourt, 1958) and *The Well-Wishers* (Harcourt, 1960).

EARLY THUNDER (Fritz*†, Jean, ill. Lynd Ward, Coward, 1967), historical novel set in Salem, Massachusetts Colony, from the spring of 1774 to the spring of 1775, built around events that occurred just before the American Revolution and presenting both Tory and Whig points of view. Although he has some good friends among the Whigs, such as the Salem nightwatchman, Jeremy Packer, Daniel West, 14, follows his physician father in holding very strong Tory sympathies. He considers crude and unreasonable such acts of the Liberty* Boys, the radical wing of the Whigs, as dumping garbage on Tory doorsteps, breaking windows, and shouting slogans and obscenities in the streets. Like many people in Salem, however, he is uneasy about how the British will react to the Boston Tea Party. Daniel's political sentiments gradually change, as his personal circumstances and the political climate of Salem change. His widower father marries an elegant, imperious Boston lady, who is strongly pro-Tory. She convinces Dr. West that Daniel should go to school in England, a plan the boy heartily opposes. Then the British close the port of Boston and pass what become known as the Intolerable Acts, moves which offend both Daniel's moral sense and his belief in the rights of the governed. When the General Court moves its meetings to Salem, the new capital of the colony, Daniel and his close friend, Beckett* Foote, also Tory, catch glimpses of important leaders like Samuel Adams* and Robert Treat Paine and even overhear important political conversations. Daniel Leonard, a Tory leader who is a friend of Mrs. West, stays at the West house. After Daniel's parents insist that he leave for England when the ship sails in October, Daniel runs away in Beckett's small boat, the *Libera*, sailing to the Misery Islands, where he camps out for several weeks. He returns when Whigs set fire to the part of Salem in which the Wests live and burn down their house. On a warm Sunday morning in February, the British attempt to commandeer the colonial cannon and arms at Salem, and Daniel throws in his lot with the colonists to successfully oppose them, for him now the only morally right course of action. Characterization is strong, and even minor characters assume importance. Although the plot falters, the island experience, in particular, failing to convince, the author skillfully integrates Daniel's personal and political problems. Daniel changes realistically and believably, and the author conveys well the dilemma of the times in personal terms, without flag waving, blame, or sentimentality. Glimpses of actual historical figures and historical events and references to others provide texture, and the novel culminates with an especially well-drawn incident, the skirmish at Salem Bridge, a little-known historical happening that was really the first battle of the American Revolution. Choice; Fanfare.

EARNSHAW, THOMAS (*The Glorious Conspiracy**), brutal foreman in the Arkwright mill in Manchester where Benjamin Brown slaves as a child. Although it is treason for skilled workers to leave England, Earnshaw agrees to sail to the new United States and start the mill system for SUM, the Society for Useful Manufactures, of which Alexander Hamilton is the leader. Earnshaw, who has wanted to marry Ben's Aunt Bet, recruits the boy, although Ben hates him for the blows and kicks he deals the child workers and particularly for the beating that leads to the death of Noah Harkness. After SUM goes broke, Earnshaw turns up in New York, where he blackmails Ben, acts as a hired thug to intimidate voters at the polls, and accompanies the mysterious Marquis whose presence threatens Jean* Pierre Vinard. Earnshaw eventually is found dying in an alley, a victim of a gang of toughs.

EARTHSEA (*A Wizard of Earthsea**; *The Tombs of Atuan**; *The Farthest Shore**), fantasy group of islands characterized by wizardry, the largest being Havnor, the most important Roke*. The people on the archipelago are varied, each island having its own customs, but all exist in a pre-industrial culture roughly comparable to the late middle ages, a society of simple fishermen, farmers, and craftsmen, with trade carried on by sailing vessels, warfare by spear and arrow, and administration by king, local lord, and village chief. The few castles and large cities are on the central islands, while in the further reaches the people are isolated, almost unaware of the other peoples and of the myths and history they share. Magic is a serious study; every village has its witch or weathermonger, and the learned mages are honored men.

ECKERT, ALLAN W. (1931–   ), born in Buffalo, N.Y.; writer of novels, biography, nature books, plays, and television scripts. He attended Buffalo schools and served from 1948 to 1952 in the air force. He has been a reporter and editor for the Dayton (Ohio) *Journal-Herald*, has had articles and short stories published in most major American magazines, has written scripts for the Wild Kingdom television series, and has been nominated four times for the Pulitzer Prize. Many of his books for young people are based on history or biography, like *The Court-Martial of Daniel Boone* (Little, 1973), employing strong research but adding fictionalized elements, particularly dialogue. *Incident at Hawk's Hill** (Little, 1971), which was a Newbery honor book, is also based on a real happening, a Canadian child's adoption by a badger when he is lost.

EDGAR ALLAN (Neufeld*, John, Phillips, 1968), realistic novel dealing with racial prejudice in a conservative California town in the 1960s. The first-person narrator, Michael Fickett, 12, has always been close to his minister father, Robert, but otherwise something of a loner, finding social isolation the easiest way to cope with being a minister's son. His sister, M. N. (Mary Nell), 14, is much more social and involved in her peer group. S. A. (Sally Ann), almost six, is mostly interested in teaching Stephen Paul, almost four, and is delighted when her parents adopt a black baby, Edgar Allan, nearly three, as is Stephen. Michael is startled, but thinks E. A. the cutest kid he has ever seen. Only Mary Nell is upset, actually furious with her parents, and she refuses to have anything to do with her new brother. Through the summer Edgar Allan becomes a happy member of the family, but in the fall when the Ficketts enroll him in the nursery section of the church-run school of which the Rev. Fickett is principal, protests start, a cross is burned on their lawn, parents withdraw their children from the nursery school, and two prominent church officials suggest that either the minister send the child, still in the probationary year, back or he will be asked to seek another position. Michael is called "nigger lover" and threatened in school. Mary Nell insists that her life is being ruined and says that if they keep Edgar Allan she will leave. They are all astonished, however, to find that their father has taken the little boy back to the orphanage. The younger children, told a lie that Edgar Allan's parents have been found, are not upset at first. Their mother does not criticize her husband openly, but they all feel the tension of her disapproval. Mary Nell, strangely, is not pleased. Michael feels bitter toward his father. A newspaper reporter, writing an exposé of the town's prejudices, waylays the younger children on their way home from school and from his questions they realize what has happened. That night, afraid they, too, could be given away, they leave. Their father goes after them and gradually woos their confidence back, but Michael is less forgiving. Finally his father takes him for a walk, admits he was wrong to give in, and tells him that ironically the congregation has lost confidence and is now asking him to leave. Since Edgar Allan has been placed in another home, they decide not to try to get him back, but to make a new start in another community. There is some hope at the end that the father has learned from the experience and that the family will pull together again, but no certainty. This lack of a clear and easy answer is what gives the book its impact, since the situation itself is so predictable as to be a cliche. The first-person narration makes Michael seem considerably older than twelve. The only complex character, and the most interesting, is the idealistic but weak father. Choice.

THE EDGE OF NEXT YEAR (Stolz*†, Mary, Harper, 1974), sociological problem novel set in the late twentieth century in an unspecified rural area of the United States and covering about a year from fall through spring, in which a youth must cope with the death of his mother and his father's alcoholism. Life changes dramatically for responsible, intelligent Orin Woodward, 14, when his mother, Rose, is killed in an auto accident. While his younger brother, nature-loving Victor*, screams out his grief and then immerses himself in building vivariums, and his journalist father, Eliot, finds comfort in alcohol, for Orin the grieving process is more complex. In addition to missing his mother very much and feeling rage toward the man whose reckless driving took her away from her family, he chafes under the responsibilities of taking care of the house and of Victor, duties that require him to give up after-school activities and the social life that normally accompanies the first year of high school. As the weeks pass, Eliot's drinking becomes more intense and obvious. He suffers memory lapses, has fits of temper, hides bottles about the house and yard, eats less regularly, and devotes less time to his writing, all signs, according to Orin's research, of the progressive disease of alcoholism. Exacerbating their relationship further is Eliot's increasing unreliability, which makes it impossible for Orin to date pretty Jeanie Sager. When he discovers his father sleeping off his most recent drunk in the barn by his car, Orin carefully arranges in a circle in the center of the library, where his father writes, the many bottles he scrounges from their various hiding places and then retreats from the house on a spelunking expedition with Victor. On their return, the two boys are pleased to discover Eliot sober and cleaned up. Jolted by the sight of the bottles and the realization that he has probably lost his job, he has contacted the local chapter of Alcoholics Anonymous. Orin observes that he has become resigned to the loss of his mother and dares to hope that he can now begin a life of his own. Strong family relationships, realistic dialogue, except in the drunk scenes, and good characterizations of major figures combine with a vigorous style for engrossing reading. Small psychological and physical details of grieving make Orin's loss and his love-hate relationship with his father convincing. Eliot's alcoholism, however, appears to be a classic textbook case, and Orin is a typical non-alcoholic victim of the disease. The family's isolation violates logic, Eliot's "reformation" is simplistic, and the abrupt and open conclusion stimulates too many questions. The most believable part of the book revolves around Orin's attempts to deal with his bereavement, and flashbacks of life with mother grip and linger in the memory. Fanfare; National Book Finalist.

EDGE OF TWO WORLDS (Jones*, Weyman, ill. J. C. Kocsis, Dial, 1968), historical novel set in Texas in 1842, based upon actual events and involving real Indians. Calvin Harper (a fictitious figure), 15, son of a lawyer, is on his way east to study law when his wagon train is attacked by Comanches. The sole survivor of the raid, he tramps over the desolate prairie. Exhausted from fear, thirst, and hunger, he comes to a river, where he is taken captive by an old Indian, who lives in a cave in the riverbank. The old man wears a red and yellow turban, a blousy cotton shirt, and a silver medallion about his neck and, to Calvin's surprise, speaks fluent English. He gives Calvin food and water and, when the river floods its banks, takes the boy with him as he continues his own journey, interrupted by illness, toward Mexico. As they make their difficult way by foot and by raft, avoiding Comanches and hunting, fishing, and gathering their food, the boy learns that the old man is Sequoyah (George Gist), renowned leader of the Cherokees. Sequoyah plans to rejoin his son, Tessee, and their friend, the Worm. The three men have been searching for a band of Cherokees who once lived in Texas and who are thought to have fled into Mexico to escape the whites. Sequoyah tells Calvin about the Cherokee Trail of Tears and about the system of writing he has developed for his people and for which he was awarded the silver medallion. Calvin discovers that the old man has lived on the edge of two worlds, never really accepted by whites, though his father was white, or by the Indians, though he helped make possible a good life for them in Arkansas and developed for them his "talking leaf" through which they became literate. An astute man, Sequoyah soon realizes that Calvin is poised on the brink of manhood, also on the edge of two worlds, and places him in situations where he can develop confidence and maturity of judgment. After the two encounter Tessee and the Worm, the Indians give Calvin a horse and send him on his way to the nearest white settlement wiser, more capable, and more knowledgeable about Indians. The weak plot serves as a vehicle to acquaint the reader with facts about Sequoyah and to combat prejudice against Indians. Sequoyah is a plaster figure, and Calvin changes predictably. The few other whites in the book, some buffalo hunters, reflect the prevailing prejudices toward Indians. The style is descriptive and evokes the sights, smells, and desolation of the prairie. Choice; Lewis Carroll; Western Heritage.

EDIE CARES (*A Lemon and a Star†*; *Terrible, Horrible Edie**; *Edie on the Warpath**), Edith, youngest of the four original Cares children in the episodic family novels set in the early 1900s. Seen through the viewpoint of her siblings in the first book, Edie, then five and six, is a pest, spoiled by the servants, tattling to Father*, tolerated by the others mostly as a source of news she picks up in the kitchen and from Nurse's gossip with Gander, the parlor maid. In the last two books, both told from Edie's viewpoint, she is a sensitive, forthright child of ten and eleven, filled with rage at the unfairness of woman's lot and hers in particular and uninhibited and clever at getting revenge. The object of disparaging remarks from birth ("Everybody knew that Edie had killed Mother by having to be born," Ted* points out), Edie fights back with vitality and ingenuity.

EDIE ON THE WARPATH (Spykman*†, E. C., Harcourt, 1966), fourth in a series of amusing episodic novels about the Cares family of Summerton, Mass. (*A Lemon and a Star†*; *The Wild Angel*; *Terrible, Horrible Edie**), this one set in 1913. Edie*, now 11, smarting from the teasing, neglect, and derogatory remarks of her brothers, Ted* and Hubert*, and from being misunderstood by her father, declares war on men. Her first campaign is to join a suffragette march in nearby Canboro, acompanied by Fatty McHenry, whom she persuades to dress as a girl while she wears her French fisherboy's costume to show the ladies what she thinks is proper attire. As often happens, her scheme backfires: the ladies do not appreciate her "unwomanly" appearance; they are furious at Fatty's deception; Edie hits a policeman trying to keep her from the march; she and Fatty are arrested and Father*, who despises suffragettes, has to rescue them. Edie, setting out to be a Good Samaritan, as her plump and pious friend, Susan Stoningham, urges, gets the job of caring for her half sisters, Christine, 6, and Lou, 4, while their nurse is on vacation and their mother is in the hospital. Edie's idea of a good deed is to harden the little girls up and to give them new experiences with animals and mud, a reform they resist with considerable energy. Edie's most successful skirmish occurs when her eldest brother, Ted, plans a weekend dance and hunt party for his college friends and enlists her aid as "chaperone," their parents being away and her sister Jane* having flatly refused. Edie is flattered and delighted to be included, even willing to risk Father's certain wrath when he finds out, but Ted has second thoughts, finds someone more suitable, and bluntly tells Edie to "make herself scarce." Hurt and furious, Edie buys a bottle of rabbit scent, soaks a fabric ball with it, and she and Susan prepare a drag trail early in the morning of the hunt, one which leads the beagles and college students through the crowd emerging from church, into Aunt Charlotte's front door and Grandfather's cellar, through the dairy herd and the brook, ending in Father's car. A good half of the book concerns Edie's trip to Florida, where she and Susan go to stay with Madam*, her stepmother, a trip beset by difficulties and misunderstandings, but on the whole wonderful: Edie loses their tickets so they lock themselves in their stateroom to prevent their being put off Cousin Lyman's train; Edie mistakes a naturalist friend of Madam for a kidnapper; she and Susan explore the grounds of all the wealthy mansions at Palm Sands by moonlight and even take secret dips in the swimming pools; they are ejected from the grand hotel for racing through its elegant halls and so are not believed when they discover it is afire and try to give the alarm; they go alligator hunting with Tom Barlow, the naturalist, and find what is possibly a mastodon bone. Back in Summerton, at the Lawn House, a large and lavish replacement of the Red House, Edie finds one last way to assert her superiority to men: she lets the huge bull out of the pasture and leads it around the circular drive in the view of all her horrified family. Edie's arguments against the religious views of Susan, whose father is a minister, provide some of the more subtle humor in this volume. Her rebellion against the assumption of superiority of men ties the incidents together, and her rage when they hurt her feelings provides the motivation for her more outrageous actions, which are often touching as well as funny. Choice; Fanfare.

EDITH GRISWOLD (*The Refugee Summer**), orphan cousin of Oliver* Avery, who spends the summer of 1922 in a Greek resort village and gets to know Nikolas* Angeliki, son of a widowed seamstress. A straightforward, outspoken girl, Edith is more sensitive and compassionate than the idealistic Oliver. When he demands that each of them say in one word what they want to be when they are grown up and volunteers that he wants to be "leader," Edith decides that she will be "kind."

EDMONDS†, WALTER DUMAUX (1903–   ), born on a farm near Boonville, N.Y., not far from the Erie Canal; author best known for his novels for adults based on the history of upstate New York, including *Drums along the Mohawk* (Little, 1936) and *Rome Haul* (Little, 1929). He also wrote several books of fiction for children and youth on the history and life of the same area. He received the Newbery Award for his first novel for children, *The Matchlock Gun†* (Dodd, 1941), a brief account of an actual Indian attack on a Dutch settlement when New York was still a British Colony, which is also a Fanfare book and a Lewis Carroll Shelf book. His second book for young readers, *Tom Whipple†* (Dodd, 1942), also a Fanfare book, starts and ends in the Mohawk Valley to tell how a resourceful Yankee boy gains an audience with the Emperor of Russia. *Bert Breen's Barn** (Little, 1975), a longer and considerably more substantial period novel, won the National Book and the Christopher Awards and was selected for Fanfare. This unadorned, richly detailed, compelling story of how an impoverished farm boy succeeds in providing a more comfortable life for his family was modeled upon remembered people and scenes from the author's own upstate boyhood at the turn of the century. A graduate of Choate School and Harvard University, he also contributed many stories to such leading magazines as *Harper's*, *Atlantic Monthly*, and *Saturday Evening Post*.

EDWARD HALL (*The Diamond in the Window**; *The Fledgling**), brother of Eleanor* in a series of fantasies. A sturdy, adventurous boy, he likes to talk backwards language and has picked himself a new name, Robert Robinson, because it sounds so fine backwards. He also plans to become president of the United States in *The Diamond in the Window*, but in *The Swing in the Summerhouse*, the second in the series, his ambition has changed to owning the largest junkyard in the world. Like his sister, he is a red-haired orphan living with Uncle* Freddy. In *The Fledgling* he plays a secondary role as step-cousin to young Georgie* Dorian.

ED WILLIAMS (*South Town†*; *Whose Town?**), father of David* in the four-book series about a black family in the segregated South who move to the North. Although used to holding his tongue among white people, Ed has a strong sense of self worth and resents being expected to do the work of a skilled mechanic at laborers' wages. When he speaks up for his rights and is arrested for disturbing the peace, he is beaten in jail. His injuries later necessitate brain surgery, from which he eventually recovers though he is never as strong again. As a father, he is a strong support to his son, standing behind him in his various scrapes with the law in both *North Town* (Crowell, 1965) and *Whose Town?* and counselling non-violence but determination. His own self image is damaged when he is laid off and, unable to get a job, must watch his wife going out to clean for white families, and he begins to stay away from home and drink. In the last book of the series, *Return to South Town* (Crowell, 1976), he has died.

THE EGYPT GAME (Snyder*, Zilpha Keatley, ill. Alton Raible, Atheneum, 1967), realistic novel of family and community life set in a mixed-ethnic, rather run-down business-residential neighborhood in a city in California in the mid–1900s. The story starts in August, when her actress mother sends theatrical, imaginative, aloof April* Hall, 11, Caucasian, to live with her grandmother in her apartment house on Orchard Avenue. April becomes friends with generous, companionable Melanie* Ross, 11, and her little brother, Marshall*, 4, both black. One day the children crawl through the dilapidated fence that encloses the yard behind the old Professor's* curio shop, where out of broken statuary, old boards, and various other discards they fashion the props for the Egypt game, an outgrowth of their interest in things ancient and plenty of imagination. Later, little Elizabeth* Chung joins them, and they continue the game, their own secret affair, every day after school, until the murder of a neighborhood child temporarily halts their activities. Suspicion falls on the Professor, a reclusive, stony-faced man, who is generally disliked. By mid-October, the children resume their game, and on Halloween, two sixth grade classmates unexpectedly drop in, Toby* Alvillar and Ken* Kamata, who add imaginative twists to enliven the play. Near Christmas, the game assumes an ominous atmosphere of realism, when their oracle rightly predicts the location of Marshall's lost stuffed octopus, Security. Not long after that, someone grabs April one night, when she and Marshall return to the yard for her math book. The Professor fortunately observes the incident and summons help. Marshall identifies the assailant, who is apprehended, and the Professor is exonerated of suspicion. Out of gratitude, he fixes the fence and gives the children keys to the gate. April gets along better now with her peers, and people think much better of the Professor. The characters are a too obvious mix, and the murder mystery introduces a current adult concern, but on the whole the book works well. It moves along smoothly with just enough complications to a satisfactory if predictable and overly pat conclusion. The book excels in its description of children at play by themselves. Choice; Fanfare; Lewis Carroll; Newbery Honor; Stone.

EILONWY (*The Book of Three**; *The Black Cauldron**; *The Castle of Llyr**; *Taran Wanderer**; *The High King**), pretty, spunky, golden-haired princess of the House of Llyr in Prydain* with whom Taran* falls in love and for whom he seeks to prove himself. She is a major figure in the series, is often in the thick of things, and is an attractive and memorable if overdrawn character.

ELEANOR HALL (*The Diamond in the Window**; *The Fledgling**), red-haired, nearsighted orphan who, with her younger brother, Edward*, lives in a large old house in Concord, Mass., with her Uncle* Freddy. In *The Diamond in the Window*, *The Swing in the Summerhouse*, and *The Astonishing Stereoscope*, she and Edward are the protagonists who have a series of fantasy adventures, in the first induced by sleeping in the tower room in the beds of their long-lost aunt and uncle, in the second by swinging through the archways of a summerhouse, in the third through time and space when they enter stereoscope pictures. In *The Fledgling* she and Edward are secondary characters, as is their uncle, now married to his student, Alexandra Dorian. When Georgie*, Alexandra's daughter, believes she can fly, Eleanor tries unsuccessfully to distract her by providing suitable playmates.

ELEAZAR BEN YA'IR (*The Rider and His Horse**), actual historical commander of the fortress Massada, who inspired all his followers to kill their wives, their children, and then each other to deprive the capturing Romans of the profit of selling them as slaves. Eleazar is pictured as a zealot and a changeable man, sometimes warm and encouraging, sometimes bitter and sarcastic, sometimes angry and abusive. At times he seems to be of heroic stature, at other times self-serving and self-deceptive.

ELIPHALET MEEKER (*My Brother Sam Is Dead**), father of Timmy and Sam*. Openly a Tory and steadfastly loyal to the king in whose forces he had once fought, he really opposes all war, not so much on moral as on practical grounds. He is just as headstrong as Sam with whom he argues over whether or not Sam should quit Yale and enlist in the Continental Army, an exchange very hurtful to them both. He also argues with his wife, Susannah*, over whether or not she should answer Sam's letters. Ironically, he dies of cholera on a British prison ship to which somehow he is sent after he is captured by the cow-boys.

ELI TRAPP (*I, Adam**), itinerant peddler who takes Adam to the Sharkey-Crane farm. Mrs. Crane allows Adam to travel with Eli because Eli is so different from most traveling peddlers of the day. He had once wanted to become a preacher and has very strict morals, but his sense of humor got in the way of his calling. He jokes, makes up riddles, recites psalms and passages from the Bible, and sings as he drives through the countryside in his wagon, which he calls the Clapp Trap. He is well liked in the area. Adam relies on him for advice and help.

ELIZABETH (*Jennifer, Hecate, Macbeth, William McKinley, and Me, Elizabeth**), fifth-grader at William McKinley Elementary School, who tells of the year when she becomes friends with Jennifer*, the only black in school. New in town and lonely, Elizabeth is intrigued by Jennifer's claim that she is a witch and readily agrees to become her apprentice. Overprotected and pushed by her status-conscious mother, Elizabeth rebels against associating with Cynthia, the school paragon of young female virtue, whom her mother considers appropriate as a friend. Although Elizabeth sometimes chafes at Jennifer's bossiness and demands, she derives a certain satisfaction from fulfilling the requirements Jennifer places upon her as part of her witch's training, such as eating raw eggs and not using the phone. Elizabeth progresses to journeyman and is about to be made a master witch, when she finally asserts herself and refuses to allow Jennifer to add their pet toad to a flying ointment the two are preparing. Her refusal leads the two girls into a deeper understanding of the nature of friendship.

ELIZABETH CHUNG (*The Egypt Game**), gentle, quiet, self-effacing, little Chinese girl, whose idea it is to protect the Egypt game from being ruined by inviting Toby* Alvillar and Ken* Kamata to join. Her idea works.

ELIZABETH RULE (*To the Green Mountains**), strikingly beautiful mother of Kath, estranged from her husband, Jason, a farmer. Jason is a stubborn, foolish man who insists on remaining on his failing farm even though he cannot support his family. Elizabeth barely makes a living managing the local hotel, but Jason still takes money from her in his ill-conceived attempts to make the farm pay. Genteel, respected, Elizabeth is fond of Tiss*, Will Grant's wife, and with mistaken idealism she believes Tiss will encourage Grant to achieve his ambition of becoming a lawyer. Elizabeth is unsuccessfully courted by Dr. Franklin, the town physician.

ELLEN ANDERSEN (*Gentle Ben**), small but determined mother of Mark. She persuades her husband to buy Ben, the bear, because she knows that having Ben will force Mark into physical activity that may ward off tuberculosis, which killed Mark's brother. When a crowd of drunken men arrive determined to shoot Ben one night, she stands up to them and orders them off her property.

ELLEN GRAE (Cleaver*, Vera, and Bill Cleaver*, ill. Ellen Raskin*, Lippincott, 1967), realistic problem novel set recently near the small town of Thicket, Fla., in which a young girl ostensibly assumes and struggles with the moral responsibility of someone else's actions. Bright, imaginative Ellen* Grae Derryberry, 11, whose parents are divorced and who is known for telling weird and outlandish stories, lives with foster parents, the kind and pleasant McGruders. Her roommate is Rosemary, whom Ellen considers stuck-up and fussy, who likes to primp, and whose parents are also divorced. In this first person narrative, Ellen Grae tells of the dilemma she faces when she hears a terrible secret from Ira*, the gentle town character, who sells peanuts at a stand and never speaks to anyone. Ellen Grae tells the reader that Ira has confided to her a horrifying story—that his mother and her husband lie buried in a shallow grave in a marsh just outside of town, where they died from rattlesnake bites intended for Ira himself. When Ellen Grae and her best friend, Grover* Ezell, who lives a few streets over, and Ira and his goat, Missouri, are on a treasure hunting expedition in the swamp, Ira shows her what apparently is their grave. His secret torments her so much that she can neither sleep nor eat, no longer spins yarns as she did, and falls behind in her schoolwork. Since she thinks he is mentally incompetent, she feels a moral obligation to do something about the situation. Mrs. McGruder summons her parents, Jeff and Grace, to whom Ellen Grae finally divulges Ira's secret. Ellen Grae's father assures her that the moral responsibility for Ira's deed of burying his parents there in a secret, unmarked grave, without informing anyone, will be hers only if she accepts it. However, she is taken to the sheriff, Irby Fudge, a congenial man, who listens to her account but dismisses it as a fabrication, observing that it is well known in town that Ira's parents abandoned him and that Ellen Grae has an overactive imagination and a melodramatic bent. Rationalizing to herself that people who would try to kill a child in such a terrible way deserved what happened to them, Ellen Grae goes along with the adults' explanation that she has made the story up, neither admitting nor denying what they say. Her parents angrily leave for the city, and Ellen Grae is soon her cheery, lively, articulate, and exasperating self again. Characters are distorted for effect and tinged with the eccentric, and the plot if slight holds some moments of suspense and humor. As she tells it, Ellen Grae's dilemma is believable, but the end leaves the reader perplexed and wondering if perhaps Ellen Grae (or the authors) has "done a number" on her audience. Did she imagine Ira's story, for, if not, her so quickly accepting the adults' dismissal of the matter does not seem compatible with her character as presented. If one is to take the ending at face value, then the conclusion makes light of her concerns. At any rate, various moral implications raised by the novel leave the thinking reader ill at ease. A companion novel is *Grover**. Choice; Fanfare.

ELLEN GRAE DERRYBERRY (*Ellen Grae**; *Grover**), brash, imaginative schoolgirl, with whom Grover* goes fishing and who also likes to tell outlandish stories, so weird and grotesque that people refuse to believe much of what she says. She and their mutual friend, Farrell, paint Grover's boat red to be helpful to him after his mother dies, but he gets angry with them, and hot words are exchanged. The falling out is brief, however, for Grover realizes that he has been selfish, as they have said he is. Although moral problems bother Ellen Grae, she seems able to rationalize them away. She is a distinctive if eccentric character, overdrawn but memorable.

ELNORA SINGLETON (*The Rock and the Willow**), long-suffering mother of Enie and five other youngsters. She calmly faces the prospect of her youngest child's birth with only thirteen-year-old Enie to help her and stoically accepts the death of her toddler, Sue Ann, but grieves when her eldest, T. H., leaves home after a brutal whipping from his father. Hardworking and uncomplaining, she suffers the tyranny of her redneck husband, Clem*, and even tries to explain his attitudes to Enie, but when her daughter's suggestion that she would like to go to college is met by rage and contempt, Elnora faces up to her husband. Throughout, she encourages Enie to get an education, is delighted to hear of the approval Enie gets from her teachers, and even manages secretly to save enough from their meagre income for her daughter's graduation dress, but sickens and is too ill to attend the ceremony where Enie gives the valedictorian address. Her faith that "the Lord moves in mysterious ways . . . " proves ironically justified when her death and her husband's remarriage make it possible for Enie to go to college.

EMILIO RAMIREZ (*Nilda**), Spanish-born step-father of Nilda and her brothers. Since all the other members of his family were killed in the Spanish Civil War, he is a Communist and strongly anti-Franco and anti–Catholic church. When his wife, Lydia, employs a spiritualist to rid the apartment of evil spirits that may have made him ill, he rouses from his sick bed and throws the medium out. Although none of the children are his, he treats Nilda as his own child and encourages her to think for herself. His illness and death put the family on welfare.

EMILY UPHAM (*Emily Upham's Revenge**), spoiled, seven-year-old girl, who spouts the moral aphorisms of the day. At first, Seth* Marple waits upon her hand and foot, in hopes he will collect a reward for returning her to Boston. A passive character at novel's beginning, she ironically emerges as the dominant figure at story's end. She takes control of the story when she removes the money from banker Upham's black account box, where Seth has hidden it in retaliation for the banker's trying to pin the robbery on him. Emily is grateful to Seth for not exposing her father's part in the robbery and later bravely confronts her father with her knowledge of what he has done.

EMILY UPHAM'S REVENGE (Avi*, ill. Paul O. Zelinsky, Pantheon, 1978), comic melodrama set in Massachusetts in 1875. When the bankrupt father of prim, proper, pampered, seven-year-old Emily* Upham of Boston deserts his family, her distraught mother sends her to North Brookfield to live with her father's wealthy brother, George Upham, an unscrupulous banker. Deposited at the train station, lost and tearful, Emily meets town mischief, Seth* Marple, 11, who tells her his name is Deadwood Dick. On the dodge from town authorities, including Mr. Upham, sensing possibilities for financial gain, Seth offers to protect Emily from the batches of assorted evildoers he maintains afflict the town and help her get back to Boston. At his suggestion, they conspire to rob Mr. Upham's bank for train fare and, prepared to do so, are astounded to observe a robbery already in progress. Seth recognizes the robber as Emily's own father, but out of consideration for the little girl's feelings he keeps his knowledge to himself. An exciting and amusing assortment of misadventures and entanglements follows, involving blackmail, fraud, and treachery, as resourceful Seth strives to keep from being blamed for the robbery and at the same time maintain naive Emily's innocence concerning her father's part in this nefarious affair. Events reach a grand climax when all best-laid plans to entrap and inveigle go hilariously awry and only the suddenly assertive Emily knows the whereabouts of the $4,000 in loot, and she stubbornly refuses to tell. Seth emerges as noble hero, banker Upham gets his comeuppance, Emily's father acknowledges the error of his ways, and Emily secretly and righteously donates the money to charity, it having been abundantly proved once again that "money is the root of all evil." The inventively convoluted plot is rich with ironies and surprises. It quick-steps along for what on one level is an engaging spoof on the old dime novels, on another is just deliciously good entertainment. (Reverend* Farnlee) Poe Nominee.

EMMA (*The Unmaking of Rabbit**), Paul's grandmother, who has firm opinions about almost everything that touches on their lives and believes in expressing them. She cannot understand why Paul's schoolmates taunt him and is convinced that Mr. Barker, the local grocer, overcharges his customers. Paul senses that she is not always accurate in her estimations of people but comes to see that the disparaging remarks she has occasionally made about his mother have prepared him for his mother's ultimate rejection of him. Emma is basically a sensible, worthy woman, though touched with the eccentric, as are all the characters.

THE EMPTY MOAT (Shemin*, Margaretha, Coward, 1969), historical novel set in Holland in 1942 during the German occupation. For centuries Swaenenburgh Castle has been the family home of the Van Swaenenburghs. Major Schmidt, the German commander for whose detachment it is now headquarters, allows the present family to continue to live in the house, promising that no harm will befall the place if Elizabeth, 16, her father, Baron Nicolaas*, and Jacob*, their elderly servant, obey him and do not obstruct his men in any way. Since Elizabeth is very much attached to the family castle, she is eager to please him. When she discovers quite by accident that her father and Jacob have been hiding Jews in the dungeon, she sets out to enlist the help of her older sister, Eva*, now living in Amsterdam, to stop them. But Eva has become engaged to a German medical officer, and, when she brings her fiancé home, Nicolaas suffers a stroke from the shock. Now mistress of Swaenenburgh, Elizabeth forbids Jacob and Erik Timmermans, young local physician and active member of the Resistance, the use of the dungeon, provoking Jacob to accuse her of cowardice. Days pass as Nicolaas, though recovering, falls into apathy, which Jacob pointedly tells her is due to her un-Swaenenburgh behavior. Elizabeth plays chess regularly with the major, too frightened to refuse his invitations. She plays ostrich at school, too, but as the war wears on she comes to see that she can no longer remain detached from the larger events going on around her. When a British airman, David Greene, is shot down, Elizabeth reluctantly allows him to be placed in the dungeon briefly then relents when the local priest, Father* André, points out to her that many lives would be jeopardized by moving him away immediately. Although she helps nurse the airman, she lives in terror of discovery. After Erik and others take David away, Elizabeth and Erik learn from Father André that Brother* Sebastiaan, the elderly gardener at Father André's monastery, was captured while helping David and died of a heart attack in a German prison. Her conscience thus further pricked, Elizabeth agrees to help old friends, Roza Cohen and her father, now living in Amsterdam, to flee the city, because the Nazis have stepped up the reign of terror against Jews. In Amsterdam to escort them back to Swaenenburgh on the train, Elizabeth is appalled to see Jews brutalized as the soldiers herd them on the train for Westerbork. Eva appears just in time to pass her identity papers to Roza, redeeming herself in Elizabeth's eyes. Roza, her father, and Elizabeth arrive safely at the castle, where Elizabeth hides Roza briefly in the dungeon. These experiences in helping those in dire need have caused Elizabeth to look beyond herself and see the importance of cooperative effort against the common enemy. She is gratified to see swans in the moat once again at Swaenenburgh, from which German soldiers had driven them, and takes their arrival as a sign of better times to come. The plot is slight, built on coincidence, and predictable, and sometimes violates logic. The reader shares Elizabeth's fears and can sympathize with her determination, but the girl's change in attitude is quite expected and not esthetically satisfying. Some characters are sketched in well, if in need of development, but most are stock. The Germans are mostly represented as cruel, uncouth, and rather dull witted, but one of them helps Elizabeth out of kindness only to be sent in punishment to the Russian front. In context, he symbolizes resigned acceptance of duty. As a whole, the story is underdone and didactic. Child Study.

THE EMPTY SCHOOLHOUSE (Carlson*†, Natalie Savage, ill. John Kaufmann, Harper, 1965), sociological problem novel for younger children about the beginnings of school integration in the 1960s in Louisiana. Narrated in first person by Emma Royall, 14, a black motel maid, the story centers on her younger sister, bright, pretty Lullah, 10, who transfers into St. Joseph Catholic School when it first allows blacks to enter. Lullah's main reason is not to achieve integration, but to be in school with her good friend, Oralee Feury, a little white girl whose mother employs Rose, Emma's mother. Lullah is delighted by the school and the nuns until two troublemakers come to town, men whom Emma nicknames Mr. Gater and Mr. Buzzard when they check into the motel. Parents of school children, both white and black, begin to receive threatening phone calls, a rock is thrown through one family's window, children are withdrawn from the school, and a bomb threat sends the remaining children home. When Oralee transfers to the segregated public school, Lullah goes back to the "colored" school. The friendship doesn't survive the separation, despite Emma's effort of organizing a picnic to Resurrection Cemetery, and Lullah's insistence on seeking out old Uncle Vounie for a love potion to put in a box of birthday candy, which she plans for a peace offering. When she finds that Oralee is having a party without inviting her, she is crushed at first but decides to go back to St. Joseph's school. There she is the only pupil but is happy until Mr. Buzzard first points a threatening gun at her in a field and then shoots her at school, injuring her leg but not permanently. This incident turns the town's attitude around, and parents reenroll their children at St. Joseph's. While historically important as a record of attitudes in the early days of Southern school integration, the story is contrived and may now seem condescending in its portrayal of "good Negroes." Child Study.

ENCHANTRESS FROM THE STARS (Engdahl*, Sylvia Louise, Atheneum, 1970), science fantasy about heroism against great odds set sometime in the future on the planet Andrecia*. Elana, about twenty, brave, intelligent, and impetuous, has stowed away on the space ship of her father and her sweetheart, Evrek*, both agents of the Anthropological Service of the Federation, an old and highly advanced civilization to whom psychokinesis, ESP, and telepathy are commonplace. They have been sent to Andrecia, a society of Younglings still in a feudal state, on a mission to prevent invading Imperialists, particularly dangerous because they place technology higher than human values, from establishing a colony there. The Younglings think the Imperialists' machine for felling trees and moving earth is a dragon. Younglings Georyn* and Terwyn*, sons of a woodcutter, volunteer to slay the Dragon* in return for rich rewards from their king. Although she is not yet an agent, Elana's father decides that she can be of great use to the expedition, and she is accordingly initiated into the Service, taking the Oath of loyalty and secrecy. Her father plans to help the Andrecians by giving Georyn and Terwyn just enough power, which will appear to be magical, to accomplish their objective by frightening away the invaders who are superstitious people. Elana assumes the role of an enchantress who has come from a distant star to help them accomplish the seemingly impossible tasks imposed upon them by her father, known to them as the Starwatcher*. She teaches Georyn psychokinesis, convincing him that his ability comes from a particular Stone she gives him, and a romantic attachment develops between them. After Terwyn is slain in the attempt to defeat the Dragon, Elana decides to accompany Georyn in his turn but is captured by Andrecian villagers, who turn her over to the Imperialists as a sacrifice to the Dragon. Among the Imperialists is Jarel*, a doctor who has become increasingly disturbed about the callous way his people are treating the Andrecians, whom they regard as less than human, and about collecting captives to be sent back to his planet's Research Center for study. Elana soon perceives the potential he offers for escape. She breaks the oath to tell him just enough of what is transpiring to get him to free Georyn and give him back his Stone. She then eludes her captors and runs toward the Dragon, intending to kill herself to avoid being taken to the Imperialists' Research Center. Then Georyn uses his psychic powers to prevent a load of stone from crushing her, so frightening the Imperialists that they leave as soon as they can. Elana tells the story from three points of view: from her own, in a letter to her cousin in informal, conversational style; in third person, in the style and tone of a folktale featuring Georyn as the successful youngest of four brave brothers; and in third person in a formal, scientific style appropriate to one in Jarel's profession. Characterization is more skillful than in most books of this genre. Elana is a sympathetic figure, but Georyn is more memorable, the real hero. Although ideas sometimes inhibit action, Elana's voice gets tiresome, and plot and themes are fairly complex, the story is suspenseful and moves to a satisfactory if predictable conclusion. Bringing together people in three different levels of advancement provides an intriguing basis for a story, and the three modes of narration add interest and make the story more convincing. Sequel is *The Far Side of Evil*. Choice; Fanfare; Newbery Honor.

ENCOUNTER AT EASTON (Avi*, Pantheon, 1980), historical novel, sequel to *Night Journeys*, which takes place over a few days in Easton, Pennsylvania Colony, in April of 1768. The story is presented in the form of testimony given by several characters at a hearing into the death of a runaway indentured servant. Two indentured servants, Robert* Linnly, about eleven, and Elizabeth Mawes, about twelve, have run away from their cruel master, John Tolivar, of Trenton, New Jersey Colony, to seek freedom across the river in Easton. After Robert and Elizabeth ford the Lehigh River, just out of Easton, Elizabeth becomes too ill to travel further. Mad* Moll, a deranged recluse, comes upon the sleeping girl and with Robert's help takes her home to her cave in a bluff overlooking the river. Robert continues on into Easton, where he unwittingly takes a job as handyboy to Nathaniel Hill*, a bounty hunter working for Tolivar, who is unaware of Robert's identity. Hill suspects that "Peter York," as Robert calls himself, may be a runaway, and his suspicions are confirmed when the local ferryman reports that the boy and a young girl tried to cross at his ferry. From him, Hill also learns about Mad Moll and soon deduces that the old woman is sheltering the girl and that Robert knows where Elizabeth is. Although he has found papers mentioning Elizabeth in Hill's saddlebags, Robert would like to believe that Hill is his friend and innocently leads Hill to his prey. Hill then enlists the help of George Clagget*, local constable, in apprehending the girl. Moll holds off the men with a burning branch, attempting to protect the child she in her madness now regards as her own daughter. Hill shoots Moll dead when she attempts to flee with the ill girl, and, when found, Elizabeth is also dead. No charges are filed against Hill, since Moll was obstructing justice, and Hill collects the bounty. A local tapman buys the remainder of Robert's time, and the boy stays in Easton. Characters skillfully revealed by their own accounts of what they have said and done, a subtly realized setting with just enough detail of landscape, customs, and the ethic of the time to keep the reader informed and interested, a plot carefully calculated for suspense and irony, and an energetic, understated, slightly formal style that heightens the tension and underscores the tragic climax combine for a powerful exploration of both period and human nature. Christopher.

ENCYCLOPEDIA BROWN: BOY DETECTIVE (Sobol*, Donald J., ill. Leonard Shortall, Nelson, 1963), mystery for young readers set in an American town of Idaville in the mid twentieth century. The fifth-grade son of the police chief, Leroy Brown, 10, is called "Encyclopedia" because his mind is so full of facts, but his greatest achievement is in reasoning out the solutions to crimes. In his first instance of detection, he realizes that a store keeper has robbed his own partner because his story of having been held up by "Natty Nat" has a flaw: he identifies the robber by his coat belted in the back though he has also said that he was facing the wall when the thief left and he could not have seen the back of the coat. Encouraged by this success, Encyclopedia sets up his own detective agency, charging twenty-five cents per day plus expenses. Several of the cases involve other boys, usually Bugs Meany, leader of the Tigers' gang. Encyclopedia takes Sally Kimball, the assertive girl who beats up on Bugs, as a bodyguard and junior partner. Together they solve a bank robbery, the theft of a diamond necklace, and several lesser crimes. Each case gives the reader the clues, but he must turn to the end of the book for the solution. In most of them the miscreant convicts himself by some inconsistency in his statement. The language of the book, the crimes, and the solutions are all quite simple, and characterization is minimal. This is the first of several similar books about Encyclopedia. Choice.

ENGDAHL, SYLVIA LOUISE (1933–   ), was born and grew up in Los Angeles; computer specialist and freelance writer best known for her science fiction for young adults. After attending Pomona and Reed colleges and the University of Oregon, she received her B.A. from the University of California at Santa Barbara. She taught briefly in elementary school and then worked as a computer systems specialist in Massachusetts, Wisconsin, Washington, and California, developing programs for air defense computers. Since 1967 she has devoted her time to writing. Not as gimmicky as most science fiction, her novels of space travel and exploration are less concerned with technological innovation than with human values and particularly the ethical, practical, and psychological problems that might result from contact between two widely different civilizations, one technologically advanced, the other primitive. While her books are aimed primarily at teenagers, they are also enjoyed by more able or sophisticated younger readers and are appreciated by many adults. Essentially quiet books, somewhat too long for their stories, they dwell on psychological and emotional concerns rather than action. Her first novel, *Enchantress from the Stars** (Atheneum, 1970) was a Newbery Honor book, a Fanfare book, and a *Choice* book, and *This Star Shall Abide** (Atheneum, 1972) won the Christopher Award. *The Far Side of Evil* (Atheneum, 1971) and *Beyond the Tomorrow Mountains* (Atheneum, 1973) are their respective sequels. Her other books of fiction include *Journey Between Worlds* (Atheneum, 1970) and *Heritage of the Star* (Gallancz, 1973). She has edited collections of stories and has published books of non-fiction on discoveries about other solar systems, high energy physics, and genetics. She has made her home in Oregon with her mother, who is also a writer.

ENOCH CALLENDER (*The Callender Papers**), handsome, golden-haired son of the wealthy and respected Callender family of Marlborough, cut out of his father's will for irresponsibility. He has never really grown up. He was indulged by everyone, including his sister, Irene, who raised him, and whose marriage to Mr.* Thiel he resented. He longs for the more exciting life of the big city. He loses the use of his legs and refuses to speak after falling from the board over the ravine from which he hoped Jean* Wainwright would fall. He and his family eventually leave for Europe where they live on a generous allowance from the Callender estate administered by Mr. Thiel. Enoch is an elegant if stock villain.

ENRIGHT†, ELIZABETH (1909–1968), born in Oak Park, Ill., daughter of a political cartoonist and illustrator and niece of architect Frank Lloyd Wright; illustrator and author best known for her amusing, realistic, episodic family stories for later elementary readers. She studied at the Art Students League in New York City, in Paris, and at Parsons School of Design and worked as an illustrator for magazines before she began writing stories and books for children. Considered an outstanding writer for the young during the late 1930s and 1940s, she published twelve books of fiction for young readers, mostly realistic episodic novels and some short stories in picture book form that were praised for their storytelling, keen characterization, and vividly pictorial style. Less successful but still named to the Fanfare list by the editors of *Horn Book* is a late book, *Tatsinda** (Harcourt, 1963), a short thesis-oriented fantasy of the marchen type. Selected by *Choice*, it relates the tribulations and subsequent elevation to good fortune of the waif Tatsinda, who is brought as a baby into the land of Tatrajan by an eagle and raised by a huntsman. Her second book, *Thimble Summer†* (Farrar, 1938), a story of rural life in Wisconsin during the Great Depression, received the Newbery Award, and *Gone-Away Lake†* (Harcourt, 1957) and *The Sea Is All Around†* (Farrar, 1940), both realistic novels, were also Fanfare books. Although it won no major award at the time, *The Saturdays†* (Farrar, 1941), concerning the adventures of the Melendy children in New York City, has remained the most popular of her books and is cited in *Choice* and *Children's Books Too Good to Miss*. The story of the Melendys continues in *The Four-Story Mistake* (Farrar, 1942) and in *And Then There Were Five* (Farrar, 1944), all three books being published in a combined volume as *The Melendy Family* (Farrar, 1947). Other titles include *Spiderweb for Two* (Rinehart, 1951), another Melendy book, and *Return to Gone-Away* (Harcourt, 1961). She conducted writing seminars at Indiana University, the University of Connecticut, and the University of Utah, and was a lecturer in creative writing at Barnard College.

ERWIN, BETTY K., physician and author. She is a graduate of the University of Wisconsin medical college and has lived in Seattle, Wash. Her books include *Where's Aggie?* (Little, 1967) and *Who Is Victoria?* (Little, 1973), as well as *Behind the Magic Line** (Little, 1969), a story of a black family's move from Chicago to the West Coast.

ESCAPE FROM NOWHERE (Eyerly*, Jeannette, Lippincott, 1969), sociological problem novel set in Cedar City somewhere in the United States about the time of the Vietnam War. Plain, introverted, serious Carla Devon, about sixteen, disillusioned with her alcoholic mother and what she sees as her parents' materialism, describes how she becomes involved with a boy who introduces her to marijuana. At a party at the house of schoolmate Marcie Hamilton, Carla meets two boys. One of them is lanky, studious, serious-minded Tom Willard, to whom Carla is attracted and who seems interested in her. The author never develops this relationship, using it instead as a springboard for another less satisfactory one. At Marcie's party, Carla also meets Dexter Smith, big man in school. A few days later, Carla arrives home to discover her mother sleeping off a drunk, the phone off the hook. Her mother informs Carla that a boy had called her. Assuming that the call was from Tom, ashamed of her drunken mother, Carla lashes out in anger, slams out of the house, and runs wildly down the street, almost colliding with the car of Dexter Smith, who just happens to be driving by and who is cynical about almost everything in life. He takes her to a friend's apartment, where he introduces her to marijuana. Their friendship continues for some weeks, which see great changes in Carla's personality and behavior. She accompanies Dex when he buys and sells drugs and once even substitutes for him on a "drop." He claims he is conducting experiments on the effect of the various substances for a book he is writing. Carla avoids her parents, whom she now regards as overly concerned with money and who are having problems coping with her sister's elopement. Carla has little to do with her old friends but makes no new ones either, and her marks drop drastically. The climax occurs at the cabin of Dexter's father, where Dex passes out from an injection of some drug. Carla seeks help, and both are arrested. Carla receives probation, but Dexter's mind has been affected, and he is placed in a mental hospital, where he is last seen, almost a vegetable. The experience has taught Carla much about drugs, which she now regards as very harmful, and has brought her and her parants closer together. Ironically, Carla learns at the end that the fateful phone call was not from Tom but from her sister's boyfriend. The plot lacks conviction, and all characters are stock. The book is a tract, a "textbook case," concerned with teaching about Drugs and Alcohol rather than in telling a good story about some young people who have problems with family and drugs. It reflects the current attitude of many youth toward adult ways and values and the well-meaning, simplistic efforts of some adults to tackle a complex social problem. Christopher.

ESTEBAN (*Walk the World's Rim**), black man, historical survivor, with three other men, of a Spanish expedition to the New World. He was sold into slavery in Africa by his poverty-stricken parents and is now the slave of the explorer Andrés Dorantes*. Esteban is a man of complex character and motives, one to whom duty and honor are very important. He is physically large and strong, a courageous man who tries at first to dissuade Chakoh from accompanying the Spaniards to Mexico City. He repeatedly helps the travelers overcome difficult situations, even though he could have turned circumstances to his advantage and soon gained his freedom. While the group is with the Buffalo People, he pretends to have been bitten by a rattlesnake in order to enable the Spaniards to demonstrate their ability to heal and entertains the Indians by pantomiming a fight with a buffalo, and he fashions scarecrows to drive thieving birds out of the Pima cornfields. Wherever the little band wanders, he wins friends for them. When Dorantes reneges on his promise to reward Esteban for his faithful service, he becomes bitter but still maintains his principles, a circumstance that leads to his death. Although he could easily have escaped to the Buffalo People, Esteban obeys orders to lead Fray Marcos to Cíbola, where he is first captured and then shot to death. In a sense, he triumphs over those who have ill-used him, because his fate motivates young Chakoh to return to his people.

ESTÉBAN DE SANDOVAL (*The King's Fifth**), young cartographer who travels with Mendoza* in search of the Seven Cities of Gold of Cíbola and tells his story from prison in Vera Cruz. A restrained young man, he is aware neither of his own growing love for the Indian girl, Zia*, nor of hers for him. At first he is uninterested in the search for gold, his own fascination being with mapping the lands they pass through, and he is shocked at the violence toward the Indians that Mendoza, his leader, takes for granted, but after he finds a large nugget at Nexpan, the desire for gold begins to capture his imagination. As he tells the story, he is sadder and wiser.

ESTES†, ELEANOR (1906–   ), born in West Haven, Conn.; librarian and author best known for her first three books about the poor but happy Moffat family set in Cranbury, Conn., a community much like the town she herself grew up in: *The Moffats†* (Harcourt, 1941), *The Middle Moffat†* (Harcourt, 1942), and *Rufus M.†* (Harcourt, 1943). Episodic in structure, each is held together by a slight theme, but all are most appealing for their keen characterization, quiet humor, sincere warmth, and fidelity to the child's point of view. All are highly acclaimed critically. She has written over a dozen other books about children in family and neighborhood situations, including *Ginger Pye†* (Harcourt, 1951), a Newbery winner, *The Hundred Dresses†* (Harcourt, 1944), a Newbery Honor book, and *The Alley** (Harcourt, 1964), which is cited in *Choice* and tells of the efforts of several children to apprehend the thieves who ransack houses on their street just off a university campus. Much less convincing if entertaining is her Fanfare fantasy, *The Witch Family** (Harcourt, 1960), about the adventures of two little girls with their make-believe family of witches. After finishing high school, she served as children's librarian in the New Haven Public Library. She then attended Pratt Institute Library School and became children's librarian at the New York Public Library. She married Rice Estes, professor of library science and director of the Institute, and lived in a little faculty house on campus, one like the alley houses that serve as setting for some of her books. After publishing *The Moffats*, she turned to writing for children full time. Among her other books for children are *The Tunnel of Hugsy Goode* (Harcourt, 1972), *The Lost Umbrella of Kim Chu* (Atheneum, 1978), and *The Moffat Museum* (Harcourt, 1983), a less spontaneous continuation of the Moffat adventures, in which Jane opens a museum in the old barn behind the house on Ashbellows Place. Estes also wrote a novel for adults and magazine articles.

ETHAN DRAKE (*Wilderness Bride**), well-mannered, well-read, cultured English youth to whom Corey is betrothed. Ethan's dying mother, Sister* Elizabeth, is Mormon Dan Turner's third wife. Although his mother has converted to Mormonism, Ethan has not. He has a more objective view of Mormonism than Corey, because he lives within the community yet is not himself Mormon. He is a complex character, in conflict with self as well as surroundings.

EVA (*The Empty Moat**), Elizabeth's older sister, a beautiful young woman, described by the author as spoiled and willful. She adores her father, Nicolaas*, and younger sister but ironically never stays long at Castle Swaenenburgh, because she soon gets into frightful rows with her father. Also ironically, it is just before they sit down to the fine homecoming dinner of souffle and wine (for which Nicolaas stole the eggs and wine from the Germans) that Nicolaas discovers that her fiance is German. Their subsequent argument leads to his stroke. Later, Eva makes it possible for Roza Cohen to leave Amsterdam by exchanging clothes and identity papers with the Jewish girl.

EVARTS, HAL G. (1915–   ), born in Hutchinson, Kans.; free-lance novelist, screenwriter, reporter for trade journals and newspapers. He receieved his B.A. degree from Stanford University. From 1939 until the Nazi invasion, he worked for the New York *Herald-Tribune* in Paris, then served in the U.S. Army in Europe from 1943 to 1945. The son of a well-known writer of western novels, he has had more than one hundred stories published in magazines. One of his strong interests, camping, is reflected in his mystery novel for young people, *Treasure River** (Scribner's, 1964). Both this and *Smugglers' Road** (Scribner's, 1968), set in Baja California, were nominees for the Edgar Allan Poe Award.

EVELYN (*Mom, the Wolf Man and Me**), Brett Levin's very feminine friend, obvious foil for the more boyish, unconventional Brett. An unusually pretty child, Evelyn thinks women should always look attractive and should marry. Her mother is extremely conscious of her looks and often goes on dates, for the purpose, Evelyn reports, of looking over the available men in order to choose a good one for a husband and father. Jilted by the one she likes most, Evelyn's mother tries to commit suicide. Evelyn's mother is a foil for Brett's mother.

EVREK (*Enchantress from the Stars**), Federation Anthropological agent and Elana's fiance and partner, along with her father, on the expedition to Andrecia*. Competent, warmhearted, and understanding, he gives Elana moral support, advice, and actual help in accomplishing her part of the expedition's objectives. He acts as the evil force which ostensibly attempts to keep Georyn* and Terwyn* from completing the three tasks placed upon them by Starwatcher*, Elana's father, and which will presumably render them capable of achieving their objective of slaying the Imperialists' Dragon*.

EYERLY, JEANNETTE (HYDE) (1908–   ), born in Topeka, Kans.; journalist and author of adolescent novels. She grew up in Iowa, the daughter of a railroad executive, attended Drake University, and graduated from the University of Iowa. She has published over fifteen novels of romance, suspense, adventure, and personal problems for teenagers. She won the Christopher Award for *Escape from Nowhere** (Lippincott, 1969), which concerns a girl who becomes involved with drugs. Some of her other books are *The Girl Inside* (Lippincott, 1968), about a girl who attempts suicide after the death of her parents, *Bonnie Jo, Go Home* (Lippincott, 1972), about a midwestern teenager who gets an abortion in New York City, *He's My Baby Now* (Lippincott, 1977), about an unmarried father who seeks to keep his baby, *If I Loved You Wednesday* (Lippincott, 1980), about a boy who falls in love with his substitute English teacher, and *Goodbye to Budapest* (Lippincott, 1974) and *Leonardo Touch* (Lippincott, 1976), both thrillers. Her home has been in Des Moines, Iowa, where her husband, Frank Eyerly, has been managing editor of the Des Moines *Register and Tribune*. A contributor to national magazines like *McCall's* and *Ladies Home Companion*, she also wrote a column, "Family Diary," for Hall Syndicate.

F

THE FACE OF ABRAHAM CANDLE (Clements*, Bruce, Farrar, 1969), novel more of character than adventure set in and near Silverton, Colo., in 1893. Abraham Candle, a polite, serious boy about thirteen or fourteen, has roomed and boarded at the home of a widow, Pauline* Stent, since the death of his father. Mrs. Stent is sloppy, a poor cook, and unable to handle her three children, but she is very fond of Abraham, who competently manages Julie, 9, and Robie, 7, tells them stories of the Great McGregor, and genuinely loves two-year-old Jane, whom he cares for devotedly. He earns enough to pay his expenses unloading ore from trains of pack burros. Thornton Malone*, a dapper little man, who looks ''like a large baby with a beard,'' involves him in a scheme to collect Indian artifacts from the Mesa Verde, with Abraham doing the climbing and exploring, Mr. Green, a part-Navaho with an inclination to drink, leading them to the right caves, and Mr. Malone selling what they find. It is soon apparent that Green knows nothing about the caves and that Malone, who has told Abraham that he will be able to translate the wisdom of the ages from the ancient pottery designs, knows nothing practical. Abraham does find a good number of jars and bowls, working very hard, climbing ropes and shoveling dust and exploring caves. One day he falls and is hurt rather badly; Mr. Green comes to find him and helps him back to camp. The rapport between the two grows, as does their contempt for Malone. Abraham has some qualms about what they are doing, acting like vultures, he thinks, and his best find he leaves where it is, not telling Malone: a seated mummy, with a large jar of corn beside him. When they return to Silverton, they find that Malone, who has gone ahead, has sold the pots for very little and has married Mrs. Stent. Abraham thinks he will leave, but, because of Jane, he decides to stay a little while. The narrative is interspersed with strange philosophical stories that Abraham remembers from his father. The novel is more a story of relationships than of action, with subtle, unexpected characterization and an understated style that produces a tone of serious depth beneath the incidents. Abraham, a quiet, able boy, is concerned with his face, hoping it will lose its childish features and show more maturity. Ironically, he proves to be the most mature person in the story. Fanfare.

FALL, THOMAS (DONALD CLIFFORD SNOW) (1917–   ), born in the Ozark mountains of Arkansas and raised in Oklahoma. He graduated from the University of Oklahoma in business administration and worked for oil companies before becoming a writer. Of Cherokee Indian ancestry on one side, he has been particularly interested in native Americans, an interest reflected in several of his books including *Edge of Manhood* (Dial, 1964) and *The Ordeal of Running Standing* (McCall, 1970). He has also written several adult novels and magazine stories. He lives in the Shawangunk Range of New York near the site of the canal which is the setting of *Canalboat to Freedom*** (Dial, 1966), a novel that concerns escaping slaves and the canal's role in the Underground Railroad.

THE FARAWAY LURS (Behn*†, Harry, World, 1963), romantic novel set in the early Bronze Age, about 1000 B.C., in what is now Denmark. Heather Goodshade, 18, is daughter of the chief of a forest tribe, a gentle Stone Age people co-existing with the Sun People, the early Bronze Age tribes who worship the sun. When a wandering Sun tribe camps nearby, Heather is attracted to the sound of their lurs, trumpets that curl up over the players' heads and are used by the priests in their ceremonies. Though warned by her little slave girl, Buzz, 10, who was thrown into the swamp as a sacrifice by the Sun priests and rescued by Heather's father, she is curious and becomes acquainted with a young Sun warrior who is acting as a scout, Wolf Stone, youngest son of the chief, Great Elk, and they fall deeply in love. Wolf Stone reveals that the Sun tribe is looking for the sacred tree of the forest people, believing that a ship made with its wood for a keel will never sink. He proposes that the forest people guard a different tree, to throw his father off the track, but the tree, interpreted by Heather's mother, says they must sacrifice what they value most. When the spring, also a god, dries up, they are further convinced. In the meantime, Blue Wing, the forest warrior expecting to marry Heather, goes to the Sun camp intending to kill Wolf Stone, but in an exhibition of archery, a skill unknown to the Sun tribe, kills the priest, Troll Tamer. Great Elk, believed to be under a curse to die at the same time as the priest, also dies but actually from poison Buzz has provided. Wolf Stone, as new chief, gives orders to diminish the power of the priests and sends the bronze sun-disc his father had made for his mother to Heather, with word that he will come after the funerals and that they will not bother the sacred tree. Before he can come, Blue Wing shoots him. Buzz has been killed in a fire, set by lightning. Heather, seeing the coffin being made, notes that it is far too big for Buzz, and, realizing that she is to be the sacrifice demanded by the tree, goes willingly to her fate. The story was inspired by an early Bronze-age grave found in Egtved, Denmark, containing the well-preserved remains of a beautiful girl wearing rather crude bronze ornaments but in other ways more likely a girl of a Stone-age people. The story has a poetic quality, with modern language but a tone that makes the ancient setting convincing. Fanfare.

FARLEY, CAROL J. (MCDOLE) (1936–   ), born in Ludington, Mich.; teacher and writer of novels for children. She received a teacher's certificate from Western Michigan University in Kalamazoo and studied further at Michigan State University in East Lansing. She taught elementary school in Michigan and also has worked as a fruit picker, a secretary, and in a library. Married to a career army officer, she has lived in many different places. Her several novels for children and early teenagers, some set in Michigan, show diverse subjects and styles. Some are fast-moving mystery-detectives, *Mystery of the Fog Man* (Watts, 1966), *Mystery in the Ravine* (Watts, 1967), and *Mystery of the Fiery Message* (Avon, 1983); some are amusing family stories, *Sergeant Finney's Family* (Watts, 1969), about how the Finneys adjust to life in a Michigan town without Dad, who is in Vietnam, and *The Bunch on McKellahan Street* (Watts, 1971); some are hilarious tall tales, *Loosen Your Ears* (Atheneum, 1977) and *Settle Your Fidgets* (Atheneum, 1977). Some are sensitively written problem stories, like *The Garden Is Doing Fine** (Atheneum, 1975), which received the Child Study Award, a convincing story about how a young girl copes with the impending death of her father, and *Twilight Waves* (Atheneum, 1981), about how a boy seeks his father, whom he has never known, in a small town on the east shore of Lake Michigan.

THE FAR-OFF LAND (Caudill*†, Rebecca, ill. Brinton Turkle, Viking, 1964), historical novel which follows a small group of pioneers as they travel westward in 1780 through what is now the state of Tennessee. Orphaned Ketty* Petrie, 16, has lived among the Moravians in Salem, N.C., since she was eight. In late February, her older brother, Anson*, whom she has not seen since she was two, suddenly appears at the settlement and takes her back with him to Fort Patrick Henry on the frontier. His wife, Tish*, and their children and two other families are waiting for him to arrive so that they can leave for the new settlement of French Lick on the Cumberland River. The flatboat trip of several months down the Holston, Tennessee, and Ohio rivers to the mouth of the Red River is filled with dangers from treacherous shoals and hostile Indians, and lack of game brings the travelers close to starvation. Their hardships often cause Ketty to reflect upon her previous life of comparative safety and ease among the pious, hardworking Moravians. Although she is regarded with suspicion and some resentment at first, she soon earns respect by her courage, steadiness, and willingness to work. Her main responsibility is to look after the children, whom she occupies with games and lessons, but she also steers and poles the flatboat occasionally and fishes to augment their meager supply of food. A major problem for Ketty arises out of her positive attitude toward the Indians, a way of thinking instilled in her by the peace-loving Moravians. When the *Dragonfly* is stranded on a shoal at Poor Valley Creek, early in the novel, the little party is helped and later joined by surveyor George* Soelle. He and Ketty fall in love, and his efforts to help Ketty understand the attitudes of the frontierspeople toward the Indians add depth to the novel. Shubeal* Given is lost while hunting, Anson is wounded during an Indian attack, and Lettice Ramsay's baby boy accidentally drowns. Smallpox breaks out on a small flotilla to which they are temporarily attached, the legs of Anson's son, Cal, are broken in a buffalo stampede, and they rescue a minister, Preacher Luster, who is in serious condition from scalping. When the party reaches the Ohio, they laboriously bushwhack their way upstream to the Red River, where George and Ketty are married and the two depart for George's inland claim, leaving the rest to continue on their way to French Lick. A richly conceived pioneer story drawn with a broad palette in which incidents carry the conviction of careful research, the novel emphasizes the concerns and responsibilities of pioneer women on the move. Style is mature, and the themes of self-control, responsibility, and objectivity are weighty, but abundant action and extensive dialogue keep the narrative moving. The characters, even less important ones, seem real and change believably through their experiences on the journey and their relationships with one another. Although the romance between George and Ketty adds a gratuitous element, conversations between the two provide the author with the opportunity to inform readers about Moravian ways and beliefs and shed perspective on frontier attitudes. (Baptist* Ramsay; Farrer*) Fanfare.

FAR OUT THE LONG CANAL (DeJong*†, Meindert, ill. Nancy Grossman, Harper, 1964), realistic novel set in a northern village of the Netherlands, presumably in the early twentieth century. Moonta Riemersma, 9, is the only fourth grader who cannot skate in a village where skating is a passion and his parents are champions. The last time there was ice, four years before, he was sick all through the cold spell and didn't learn. When neighbor woman Less predicts cold, he is delighted but crushed when the schoolmaster bans the older children from the Children's Skate School Field, so that the babies can learn without competition while the canal ice hardens. He goes to the field anyway but, seeing the master approach, flees up a deep draught ditch, where the ice is thin and then is almost drowned when the young men, playing a game of running across the thinly iced ditches, sink the layer of ice under his feet. They rescue him, carry him home as a ''pickerel'' (one who fell in), but are reprimanded by the headmaster, who learns the whole story and promises to skate with Moonta when he learns. Moonta's father also promises to skate with him by moonlight to New Church's pipe after he and Moonta's grandfather come back from the Eleven-Towns Tour. Moonta, confined to bed to prevent pneumonia, fantasizes about New Church's pipe, imagining a great tower, and the next morning reluctantly takes a little red chair to the canal to help him learn to skate. He catches on rapidly but has some problems: a sweeper spanks him soundly when he takes Aunt Cora's advice and throws away the broom the sweeper has tripped him with, and he earns the anger of the headmaster, who is trying to avert a squabble between the villagers and a canal boat family, when he spits in the canal-boater's shoe instead of dropping his pennies into it, as expected. Discouraged and resentful, he skates off with his chair, determined to reach New

Church's pipe by himself, although it is snowing and the ice is beginning to melt. At one point, he meets a champion skater, who takes him flying over the thin ice by a hole and sets him on the right path to the pipe. When he reaches a strange-looking tunnel, which he later learns is New Church's pipe, he sees that the ice has melted beneath it and that his father and grandfather, approaching on the other side, will go into the water. Hearing his screams, his father stops, but his grandfather crashes in and is rescued by Moonta lying flat on the ice and stretching his chair toward the hole while his father pulls from stronger ice behind. Then, with Moonta on his father's shoulders and his grandfather soaked, they skim over the thin ice and meet Moonta's mother, skating out to meet them, and Moonta's Aunt Cora, who cannot skate, and the headmaster searching the holes for Moonta's body. The predominant element in the story is Moonta's obsession with ice and skating, which blinds him to caution and makes the attitudes of the adults incomprehensible to him. It is heightened by his desire to be a real part of the skating family. Characterization of Moonta is so strong and the concentrated picture of village life so vivid that the plot does not seem as simple as it is. Fanfare.

FARRER (*The Far-Off Land**), small nephew of Rachel Given and a passenger on the *Dragonfly*. His name is a colloquial corruption of the Biblical term "Pharaoh." Seeing his parents slain by Indians has left him shy and fearful, and the other children on the flatboat enjoy teasing him. Ketty* Petrie's warmth and firm insistence that the children respect his grief and fears endear her to him. Story's end sees him accompanying Ketty and George* Soelle to their new home.

THE FARTHEST SHORE (LeGuin*, Ursula, ill. Gail Garraty, Atheneum, 1972), third in the Earthsea* trilogy, a fantasy set in a great archipelago where magic is studied seriously and wizards are honored scholars and powerful men. Because news from the west tells of troubling failure of spells and loss of order and concern among the people, Arren*, young prince of Enlad, whose true name is Lebannen, has been sent to Roke*, to the school of wizards, to seek aid and advice from Ged*, the archmage, also known as Sparrowhawk. Since his news echoes rumors from other islands and the Council of the Masters of Roke cannot agree on a course of action, Ged sets out to investigate, taking Arren as his only companion. Traveling in his eighteen-foot sailboat, *Lookfar**, they have a series of six adventures: (1) In Hart, where sorcerers are now denying their power and much of the population is turning to chewing hazia, an addictive and debilitating drug, they find Hare, a failed wizard, who works for the pirate, Egre, and who seeks through hazia to find the door to the land of the dead, which he says has been opened to allow eternal life. A disgusting and horrifying figure, he is also treacherous, luring them into an ambush from which Arren tries to save Ged and is himself taken captive by Egre, now turned slave dealer, and is rescued only by the expenditure of much magic power by Ged. (2) At Lorbanery, an island of silk-makers, they find the craft neglected, the dye formulas forgotten, the silk production deteriorated by too much rain. They are joined by wild-looking, red-haired Sopli, a former dyer and wizard gone mad seeking the newly opened route to immortality and hoping to find it with them though he fears the sea. (3) Going south and west, they seek to land at Obehol, where they are attacked from the shore, Ged is wounded, and Sopli dives overboard and drowns. Arren loses faith in Ged and lets the boat drift until both are nearly dead. (4) He wakes to find they have been rescued by the strange, small-statured folk of Balatran, who live on rafts, following the whales and coming to land only once a year to cut timbers to repair their rafts. Here they enjoy a period of almost idyllic peace and recuperation, until midsummer night, when the rafts come together for the all-night Long Dance. Shortly before dawn, the chanters fail and forget their songs, and though Arren completes the night by singing, it is clear that the illness of spirit troubling the world has reached even to these remote folk. With dawn comes the dragon, Orm Embar, seeking Ged. (5) Again in *Lookfar*, they travel swiftly before a mage wind to the group of islands known as The Dragons' Run, where they find that even the dragons, oldest and wisest of creatures, have lost their speech and are destroying each other. (6) Coming at last to Selidor, northwesternmost island, they meet with the image of Cob, a mage of Havnor, turned evil through his fear of death, who, as they have suspected, has opened a door to the land of death. Having followed him in a grueling journey through the dry, dark land, Ged summons all his power to close the door and allow Cob to die and so weakens himself that Arren must lead and even carry him out again. In a brief denouement, they are carried back to Roke by the dragon, Kallessin the Eldest, where Ged pledges fealty to Arren, who will become king not only of Enlad but of Havnor and therefore of all Earthsea. Presumably by having again a true king, Earthsea will be restored to order. Ged, no longer capable of being archmage with his power gone, returns to his home island of Gont. Except for a brief interlude showing how during their absence trouble has come even to Roke, most of the story is seen through the perceptions of Arren, a lad grown but not yet a man, brave, trained to rule, and greatly attracted to Ged, yet not certain of himself or of his loyalty. Perhaps because his characterization is central but more on a stock pattern than those of Ged and Tenar*, the book does not stand as well alone as the earlier two. There is more philosophical dialogue, and the action, though it covers a vast area, is slower. As the culmination of the series, however, it satisfactorily continues the somber and momentous tone and concludes the life story of Ged. Choice; National Book Winner.

FAST SAM, COOL CLYDE, AND STUFF (Myers*, Walter Dean, Viking, 1975), realistic novel set in a black area of New York City about 1970. Stuff* (Francis Williams), twelve when the action starts, is telling the story when he is eighteen about the kids he knew during the first few years he lived on 116th Street. On the stoop of his building, where he meets Clyde* Jones, 15, an intelligent, self-possessed boy, Sam*, a hyperactive, fast-talking kid about the same age, and Gloria* Chisholm, 14, he brags that he can dunk a basketball and thereby gets his nickname, Stuff. With these three he has a number of adventures: they get arrested, briefly, when a friend named Binky gets the tip of his ear bitten off in a fight and they invade the hospital emergency room to get it sewed back on; Clyde, with Sam dressed as a girl, wins the dancing contest at the neighborhood center but gives the fifty-dollar prize to the runner-up, Carnation Charley, when Sam's real identity is discovered; they form a club with several others that they call The Good People, dedicated to helping each other with their problems; Clyde, Sam, and Stuff chase a purse snatcher and get arrested (again briefly) as the thieves; Stuff gets a hair-line fracture of his foot as he's showing off, trying to impress a girl with a karate kick; Kitty, Clyde's younger sister whom Stuff likes, runs away because her widowed mother has gone out with a man, and Stuff finds her on the roof; the boys worry about pre-marital sex, consult Gloria and two of her friends, and decide, tentatively, against it; they all go out for the basketball team at the center, all make the team, even Stuff, and win the big game. The most dramatic incident occurs when they get a frantic call from Carnation Charley's girlfriend, asking them to go to his house, pick up a package, and deliver it to an address where the three boys have been to a drug party earlier. They find Charley, obviously drugged and beaten up, help him to Clyde's apartment, then, worried that he might OD, call Sam's father, who helps them cope with him. Then they are all arrested, having been photographed by police who were staking out the building where they found Charley. It is a touchy situation, but they are all cleared with the support of their parents. Later they learn that Charley, who was supposedly reformed, has been killed while robbing a store. More interesting than the events are the family relationships explored. Clyde's father dies, and the boy decides to succeed in school and go to college in his father's memory. Gloria's father loses his job and leaves the family, and she grieves and isolates herself. Stuff's father gives him long lectures but buys him, unasked, a flute to supplement the saxophone that the boy plays. The book is strangely disconnected, with some of the episodes seeming to fit into the tough ghetto scene and some fitting in tone into a Norman Rockwell boyhood. The first person narration, in black street language, is made plausible by having the story told some years after the events by a more mature Stuff. Fanfare.

FATHER (*A Lemon and a Star*†; *Terrible, Horrible Edie**; *Edie on the Warpath**), John Cares, patriarch in a series of episodic novels set in Massachusetts in the early twentieth century. Explosive and dictatorial, he is respected but avoided as much as possible by his four children and only partially tamed by Madam*, his second wife. Although he works at "business" in Charlottesville, they live on a large estate-like farm adjoining the dairy farms of relatives—his sister Charlotte, his father, his brother Charlie. Occasionally he decides the children need discipline or hardening, and he sets up rules or organizes them with a sort of Teddy Roosevelt spirit, but much of the time, if they can manage it, he has little idea of what they are doing.

FATHER ANDRÉ (*The Empty Moat**), priest in charge of the local monastery. He is evidently a leader of the Underground Resistance in the area around Swaenenburgh Castle. His comments prick Elizabeth's conscience and motivate her to help the Underground in spite of her fears that such action might lead to the destruction of her beloved family castle.

FATHER FRANCISCO (*The King's Fifth**), lame Spanish priest who accompanies Mendoza* on his journey to find the fabled Seven Cities of Cíbola. Father Francisco's purpose is to convert Indians, and his great interest is in plants, which he collects as they travel. A naive but good man, he is never caught by the gold fever that conquers all the other men of the party.

FATHER WLADA (*Darkness over the Land**), Polish priest who was at Dachau with Mark Elend's Uncle* Franz. A walking skeleton, he turns up after the Liberation and lives for a while with the Elends. They are very uncomfortable with him around. He is a bitter, angry man who never misses a chance to remind them of the atrocities committed by the German government. His remarks about how the Germans set about deliberately annihilating the children of noble Polish families foreshadow the truth about Mark's background.

FAULKNER, NANCY (ANNE IRVIN FAULKNER) (1906–   ), born in Lynchburg, Va.; teacher, editor, and writer. She grew up in Lynchburg and graduated from Wellesley College and Cornell University with degrees in history. She has held a variety of positions, as teacher in high school and at Sweet Briar College, director of the drama bureau of the School of Continuing Education at the University of Virginia, editor of *Recreation Magazine*, editorial consultant to Walker and Co., and vice-president of Chandler Records, where she helped adapt and produce children's books for broadcast. She has written over two dozen novels for children and several for adults. Nominated for the Edgar Allan Poe Award was her mystery, *The Secret of the Simple Code** (Doubleday, 1965), an exciting but fairly conventional book of its form, which spins off from her interest in music. Among her historical novels is *A Stage for Rom* (Doubleday, 1962), set in colonial Williamsburg, *The Sacred Jewel* (Doubleday, 1961), *Traitor Queen* (Doubleday, 1963), and *The Great Reckoning* (Dutton, 1970). Her books reflect her extensive travels, her continuing interest in history, and her dedication to accuracy of incident and place. She has made her home in New York City and Charlottesville, Va.

FENTON, EDWARD (1917–   ), born in New York City; author and translator of about twenty books for young people. He attended Amherst College and served with the American Field Service and British 8th Army in North Africa during World War II. In addition to his books for young people, he has written two novels for adults and a book of poems, *Soldiers and Strangers* (Macmillan, 1945). His mystery, *The Phantom of Walkaway Hill** (Doubleday, 1961) won the Edgar Allan Poe Award. He has made his home in Athens, Greece, and three books that he translated by Alki Zei received the Batchelder Award, *Petros' War* (Dutton, 1972), *Wildcat Under Glass* (Holt, 1968), and *The Sound of Dragon's Feet* (Dutton, 1979). *The Refugee Summer** (Delacorte, 1982), set in a resort village near Athens, was a *Horn Book* Fanfare selection. It evokes the living style and attitudes of the 1920s expatriates as well as a critical period in Greek history.

FERGIE (*A Spell Is Cast**), Mrs. Van Heusen's Scottish housekeeper, wife of Andrew*, the caretaker. Warm and kind, Fergie soon makes Cory Winterslow feel at home at Tarnhelm. She realizes that Cory needs mothering and is tender and loving toward her. She can be firm, however, with the girl and advises her to let go of her pride and try harder to make friends among the neighborhood children. To cheer her employer, when Mrs. Van Heusen, also Scots-born, feels depressed or unhappy, Fergie shares tea and hot buttered scones with the old woman and reminisces about her childhood in Scotland. Fergie is an attractive, strongly drawn figure, who contributes insights into Cory's character.

FERN DRAWN (*Dust of the Earth**), fourteen-year-old elder daughter of the impoverished Drawns, who move to Chokccherry in the Badlands of South Dakota to work the farm left them by Mama's father. Fern is opinionated, given to making sententious remarks, and often dramatizes situations. She would like to have a better life than she has and hopes to marry a rich man, but she is embarrassed by Madge's naive efforts to promote a romance between her and the middle-aged Col. Webb Harbuck, who is well-off by comparison with the Drawns. She is very displeased when she discovers Mama is going to have another baby, because she feels there are already more than enough mouths in the family to feed. Much of the burden of running the farm falls on her, particularly taking care of the sheep, where she draws upon her experiences in helping an Indian friend, Ash Puck, with his sheep, and learns by trial and error. When Hobson* quits school and helps her with the flock, things are a good deal easier for her. The two get over most of their sibling bickering and grow close together as they share the work of the sheep. Fern tells the story with adolescent exaggeration and self-promotion.

FESS (*The Soul Brothers and Sister Lou**), Phil Sattertwaite, youth from Boston newly arrived in Southside, who tries to persuade Lou and her friends to be more militant against the whites. Angry and determined to fight for black rights, he tries to persuade Lou to join the Afro revolutionaries to which he belongs, and, when she refuses, tries to rape her. He writes the poem about Jethro which is set to music and Lou and the three boys sing at Jethro's funeral. When the quartet is offered a recording contract, Fess dubs them the Soul Brothers and Sister Lou. He is called Fess, short for Professor, because his grammar and diction are unusually good and he has an apt way with words. He is self-appointed leader of the group that meets in the clubhouse. He is a phony character, not at all convincing.

FFLEWDDUR FFLAM (*The Book of Three**; *The Black Cauldron**; *The Castle of Llyr**; *Taran Wanderer**; *The High King**), a king in Prydain*, he travels as a bard, often accompanying Taran* on his quests. A comic figure, he has a tendency to stretch the truth, and when he does his harp strings break, giving him away. Good at heart and in nature, he serves the forces of good against the powers of evil. He appears in many scenes, providing both heroism and comedy, and often affects the action.

FIGGS & PHANTOMS (Raskin*, Ellen, ill. author, Dutton, 1974), comic mystery-fantasy novel about an eccentric family of ex–circus performers, who have settled in the town of Pineapple. Sullen, disagreeable, lonely Mona Lisa Newton rejects her car-salesman father, Newt Newton, and her tap-dancing mother, Sister Figg Newton, much preferring the company of her mother's brother, Florence Italy Figg, called "Flo," midget bookseller and would-be pianist. Flo and Sister belong to the Fabulous Figgs, formerly itinerant performers, including Truman, the Human Pretzel, Romulus, the Walking Book of Knowledge, Remus, the Talking Adding Machine, and Kadota, Dog Trainer. The sensitive and tenderhearted Flo is concerned about the troubled Mona and worried about how she will take his impending death. When Flo dies (goes to Capri, as the Figgs call it), Mona is at first so distraught she refuses to leave her room. Then, determined to find him, she searches his books for clues to the location of Capri. She falls ill and has a wild and fantasy-filled dream about Flo, which reveals many curious subconscious wishes and problems. This frivolous romp with its assortment of zany characters and outrageous scenes, slapstick happenings, and literary allusions and quotations is perhaps best taken as a spoof on mystery stories. Whatever the author's intention, the book seems contrived, often arch, and unnecessarily ambiguous. Newbery Honor.

A FIGURE OF SPEECH (Mazer*, Norma Fox, Delacorte, 1973), realistic novel of middle-class family life set in a city somewhere in the United States in the late 1900s. Jenny Pennoyer, 13, the fourth of five children of a grocery store manager, is sure that she was an "accident." She has difficulty relating to most of the people in her often opinionated family and feels especially close only to her aging grandfather. Carl Pennoyer, 83, has lived with his son's family since Jenny was born and has practically raised her for her always busy mother and authoritarian and often impatient father. Carl has his own tiny apartment in the basement of the Pennoyers' small house. Jenny loves to go there to play cards, hear about the old days, and just be near the old man, whom she sees as very warm and loving and feels understands her as no one else does. But Carl does things sometimes that irritate Jenny's family. His little notes on the family bulletin board, comments during dinner, and physical awkwardness don't always go over well with his son and his wife. Sometimes Jenny's mother complains that Jenny spends too much time with Carl, and she worries that he may be struck while crossing the street. When Jenny's parents imply that Carl is getting on and can't take care of himself any longer, Jenny speaks up for him, and that irritates them, too. Then Jenny's older brother, Vince, his parents' pride, drops out of college and moves in with his bride, Valerie. The little house bulges with people, and tension causes emotions to run very high. After a small, accidental stove fire forces Carl to move upstairs, Valerie contrives to take over his living quarters, when the place has been redecorated. Mother complains about more work to do, and Carl has trouble fitting in with the family. When Jenny's parents go looking for a nursing home for him, Carl decides to take charge of his destiny by returning to the family farm, unoccupied for many years. Jenny insists on going with him, and they arrive to find the old house vandalized. Jenny struggles diligently to make the place habitable, but Carl soon realizes that the toil is in vain. During a storm one night, he leaves the house, and the next morning Jenny finds him dead of exposure under a favorite old apple tree. Ironically, his tragic death increases the alienation between Jenny and her family. Characters are one-sided types, and the overforeshadowed plot appears deliberately concocted to acquaint young readers with the topical issues of aging and ageism. National Book Finalist.

FILENE MIDGETT (*Teetoncey**; *Teetoncey and Ben O'Neal**; *The Odyssey of Ben O'Neal**), commanding officer or "Keeper" of the rescue station at Heron Head on the Outer Banks of North Carolina in this Cape Hatteras trilogy. A hard, square-faced, heavy-jawed man, he is determined to make his surf-rescue service the best on the Banks and drives his men hard, even in their housekeeping around the station. Since the death of Ben* O'Neal's father, also a keeper of the station, he has been something of a father figure to the boy but mostly has shown him little sympathy and no affection. He meets his match in Rachel*, Ben's mother and his cousin, who defies him to protect and hide the castaway girl, Teetoncey*, whom Ben finds washed up from a wreck. When Ben and Tee are in trouble in Norfolk, Ben calls Filene, and the surfman advises them to turn themselves in to the authorities and agrees to back them and to pay back the money Tee has taken from the British Consul.

THE FIRST TWO LIVES OF LUKAS-KASHA (Alexander*, Lloyd, Dutton, 1978), fantasy of magic and space and time travel. Lukas-Kasha of Zara-Petra, a roguish, sometime carpenter's apprentice apt for any exploit, responds to the challenge of Battisto, a traveling conjuror, and finds himself washed ashore in the distant realm of Abadan*, a place of exotic domed and pinnacled palaces and noisy bazaars, where turbaned and jeweled courtiers hail him as King Kasha.

Except for occasional twinges of homesickness and a good deal of puzzlement over what has happened to him, Lukas enjoys his new life of luxury and indolence, until a conversation with Nur-Jehan, an embittered, surly captive brigand girl from the mountain kingdom of Bishangar, opens his eyes to the realities of the political situation in this country and embroils him in palace power struggles. Nur-Jehan informs him that for years the Abadani have been trying to conquer her land for its wealth in precious gems and metals. Moved by moral rectitude and respect for the girl, Lukas unsuccessfully suggests to his Royal Council that they make peace with Bishangar. Since Lukas threatens his schemes for power, Shugdad, Lukas's officious, shifty vizier, tries to have Lukas assassinated. With Nur-Jehan and Kayim, a knavish, facile-tongued public versifier, Lukas escapes from the palace by a secret passage. The three make their way toward Bishangar, living off the land and by their wits, encountering an assortment of characters and learning that Shugdad has proclaimed himself king. After Nur-Jehan deserts them and rides off on some purpose of her own, the two men are helped by earnest, befuddled Locman*, one-time astrologer to Lukas, now mayor of a remote village. Hairbreadth escapes follow, including a blood and thunder scene when a water-vendor Lukas once befriended deliberately sets fire to his house as a diversionary tactic. The undauntable Lukas tumbles from one precarious situation to another, until eventually he and resourceful Kayim find themselves in a punishment company of soldiers that Shugdad rightfully considers of questionable loyalty, led, coincidentally, by Osman, the very man whom Shugdad had dispatched to murder Lukas and whose life Lukas had spared on that occasion. The group staunchly supports Lukas as rightful ruler, and soon they encounter a contingent of horsemen led by Nur-Jehan, who, it turns out, is rightful queen of Bishangar. They join forces, and, in a desperate ploy, Lukas acts as a decoy to entrap Shugdad, and Osman, to Lukas's dismay, beheads the Usurper, putting an end to the invasion. Lukas returns to the royal city of Shirazan, determined to do his best as king. With Kayim as his vizier, he proves a wise and capable ruler. One afternoon, he and Kayim go for an outing by the sea, and Lukas suddenly finds himself back in Zara-Petra. The main characters are distinctly drawn, if flat, and Lukas changes as a result of assuming responsibility in the fantasy world, but just what relationship these experiences have to his real-world life is never clear, as the two worlds are ineptly meshed. Tales and sententious sayings support the visual details of the old Middle Eastern setting and contribute credibility to the story. The elaborate plot moves at a hectic pace and is typically Alexandrine in its unexpected twists and turns and uncontrolled virtuosity, myriad complications, and puzzling conclusion. Style is energetic, and the author appears to have fun manipulating characters, language, and situations. National Book Finalist.

FITZGERALD, JOHN D(ENNIS) (1907–   ), born in Utah, author of the popular "Great Brain" books based loosely on his childhood with his brothers. He was at various times a foreign correspondent and a jazz drummer, and he wrote magazine stories until the market decreased. His memoir, *Papa Married a Mormon* (Prentice, 1955), established his popularity and was followed by two sequels. Using the same conversational style, he wrote *The Great Brain** (Dial, 1967) for children, the first of a number of episodic, humorous books featuring the con-artist abilities of his brother, Tom.

FITZHUGH, LOUISE (1928–1974), born in Memphis, Tenn.; artist, author-illustrator of children's books. She rocketed to prominence with *Harriet the Spy** (Harper, 1964), still her best-known book, an innovative, controversial novel which helped establish the new realism in children's literature. This is the humorous story of a girl whose ambition is to become a writer and who prowls about the neighborhood spying and recording in her journals her candid, frank observations and reactions to her parents and friends. Although the book seems overdrawn today, with episodes and dialogue deliberately contrived for sensation, it nevertheless remains popular with the young, and it and its sequel, *The Long Secret** (Harper, 1965), which contains a scene discussing the once taboo topic of menstruation, are listed in *Choice*. Her last novel, *Nobody's Family Is Going to Change* (Farrar, 1974), a realistic story of black middle-class family life starring two pre-teenagers, has not caught on. She also wrote and illustrated a picture book, *Bang, Bang, You're Dead* (Harper, 1969) and another novel, *Suzuki Brave* (Doubleday, 1961). Intending to get a degree in literature, she attended colleges in Florida and Bard College in New York but just short of graduation dropped out to pursue a career in art. She subsequently studied at the Art Students League and Cooper Union. Her realistic oil paintings have been exhibited at various galleries, and she illustrated her own books. She lived in Italy, France, Washington, D.C., and New York City.

5 THALLO STREET (*The Wonderful Flight to the Mushroom Planet†*; *Stowaway to the Mushroom Planet†*; *Time and Mr. Bass**), place where Mr. Tyco* Bass lives in Pacific Grove, Calif. His house is dome shaped like a mushroom, with a telescope jutting out from the dome. Within the dome is a perfectly outfitted laboratory, and Tyco has a workroom in the basement. The house becomes the headquarters for the Society of Young Astronomers and Students of Space Travel. The Mushroom Planet Books start and conclude on Thallo Street.

THE FLEDGLING (Langton*, Jane, Harper, 1980), fantasy set in contemporary times in Concord, Mass. Eleanor* and Edward* Hall, now fourteen and twelve (of *The Diamond in the Window**), live with their Uncle* Freddy Hall, his wife, Aunt Alex (Alexandra Dorian Hall), and her daughter, Georgie*, 8, in the house which also includes Uncle Freddy's school, The Concord College of Transcendental Knowledge. Georgie, intense and small for her age, is sure she can fly. After unsuccessful attempts down the stairs, she begins to get the hang of it and when she meets a large Canada goose, she is quite prepared to climb on his back and soar over Walden Pond. Nightly the Goose Prince, as she thinks of him, lands on the porch roof, taps at her window, and takes her for a ride which includes a stop at the site of Thoreau's cabin. Georgie learns to slip off his back and glide in solo flight. Nosy next-door neighbor, Madeline Prawn, who has caught glimpses of the flights, is sure Georgie is either a saint or a fairy, and she alerts her employer, Ralph Preek, president of the bank, who believes a dangerous goose is loose and buys a gun. Lurking at the pond, he tries to shoot the goose is flight, but Georgie dives between goose and shot and is injured in one arm. Terrified that the goose will be killed, Georgie allows the family to "protect" her, moving her bed, nailing up windows, and accompanying her everywhere, until the last night of hunting season, when she sneaks out of the house at midnight and pulls up enough of Miss Prawn's plastic flowers which spell "Welcome to Concord" until they spell only "Come." She has not realized, however, that daylight savings time is ending and Preek has an extra hour of hunting season. The Goose Prince arrives, gives Georgie a "gift," and Preek shoots and kills it. Unable to find the gift, Georgie goes to bed in shock for a week but eventually finds it, a small, hard-rubber ball, in the leaves of her play "house" under the bushes. To the others it seems a nearly worthless toy, but Georgie discovers that, when held in the dark closet under the stairs, it glows and expands into the whole world. Serious, intense, nature-loving, Georgie is an appealing character, and scenes of flying are convincing. Family relationships are also believably drawn, but Miss Prawn and Preek are caricatures, and the final revelation of the gift seems contrived. Newbery Honor.

FLEISCHMAN, SID (ALBERT SIDNEY) (1920–   ), born in Brooklyn, N.Y.; reporter, writer of screen plays and of fiction for adults and children. He grew up in San Diego with the ambition of becoming a magician. The summer he was sixteen, he put together his own traveling magic show and later published a book about magic. After serving in the Navy in World War II, he graduated from San Diego State College. He was a reporter for the San Diego *Daily Journal* until 1948, when he began writing full time. His first novel for children, the Fanfare selection *Mr. Mysterious and Co.** (Little, 1962), which involves a traveling magician and his family of performers making their way West in 1884, only hints of the boisterous tall tales to come for which this author is best known. *By the Great Horn Spoon!** (Little, 1963), set against the California gold rush, established him as the master of the modern American tall tale, zesty stories of adventure loosely concerned with American history but still conveying a good sense of the times. *By the Great Horn Spoon!* won the Western Writers of America Spur and the George G. Stone Awards, was a *Choice* book, and was made into the movie *Bullwhip Griffin*. *The Ghost in the Noonday Sun** (Little, 1965), a *Choice* book built around pirates on the high seas and a folkloric belief, departs from his usual form, but *Chancy and the Grand Rascal** (Little, 1966), a Fanfare book, *Humbug Mountain** (Little, 1978), also a Fanfare selection, and a Jane Addams Award winner, a *Boston Globe-Horn Book* winner, and a National Book Award finalist as well, and the short, zippy, outrageous fantasies about

Josh McBroom, among them *McBroom Tells the Truth** (Norton, 1966), a Lewis Carroll Shelf book, all have American pioneer settings. His other books include *Jim Bridger's Alarm Clock, and Other Tall Tales* (Dutton, 1978), *The Hey, Hey Man* (Little, 1979), *McBroom and the Great Race* (Little, 1980), *McBroom's Almanac* (Little, 1984), and a series of mysteries featuring the Bloodhound Gang. Several of his books are listed in *Choice*.

FLETCHER LARKIN (*Henry 3**), Henry 3's friend, outcast in Crestview because of his Grandfather* Larkin's efforts to have the area restored to agriculture. To preserve his ego, Fletch beats up every new boy in school, including Henry 3. When the X15* Club dumps Henry, Fletcher and Henry take up with each other. The two outcasts become friends. Fletch encourages Henry to think for himself and to be himself. It is at Fletcher's suggestion that the two make their less than convincing trip to Henry's father's corporate offices in the Empire State Building in an attempt to convince Mr. Matthews, president of American Lock and Locomotive, to implement Henry's plan for averting war and discontinue building bomb shelters. Since Fletcher wishes to remain in Crestview after his grandfather dies, Henry hides him for a while and finally succeeds in persuading his parents to adopt his friend.

FLETCHER SMITH (*The Bears' House**), Fran Ellen's older brother, 12, whom she describes as "pretty smart and not usually mean." It is his idea that the children take care of themselves until their mentally ill mother gets well. He organizes them for their independent existence, but the house is a mess and they live on beans, franks, cookies, and Kool Aid. He is a bright boy, on the junior high honor roll, and is a former student of Miss* Thompson's. When the social worker comes and Miss Thompson visits, he manages to make it seem that Mrs. Smith is in charge of things. He is an expert at dissembling and evasion, in what both he and Fran Ellen believe is a good cause.

FLIGHT OF THE SPARROW (Cunningham*, Julia, Pantheon, 1980), novel of a group of Paris street waifs, presumably at the contemporary time. The narrator, an orphan girl of nine, is helped to escape from a dreary orphanage by Mago*, 13, a philosophical street boy who also protects a tubercular girl, Friquette, and a retarded boy, Drollant. He names the new waif Little Cigarette, teaches her to make her way, gives her courage, and calls himself her brother. When they move into an abandoned building for the winter, Friquette drowns herself in the Seine. A slimy youth, Eel, returns evidently from prison with a plan to steal a valuable painting from a nearby artist, Michel Courier, and sell it to a shady gallery owner. This requires the aid of Cigarette, which she refuses until Drollant is hit by a car and taken to a hospital. To keep him from an unsympathetic institution and to finance private clinic care, Cigarette agrees to help steal the painting. The child, who is very moved by color, easily makes friends with Courier, who wants to paint her. The painting that she is to steal, a portrait of a lady in green by a famous artist, is of Courier's estranged wife. When he goes to visit his wife in the village of Chataigner, he shows Cigarette where he leaves his key. She takes the painting, Mago sells it to the dealer, and together they persuade the laundry lady to pose as Drollant's aunt to get him transferred to a private clinic. Although Mago divides the remaining money with Cigarette and tells her to get out of the city, Eel robs her before she goes and tells her he will use blackmail to get Mago to do his will. Cigarette decides to go to Chataigner to find Courier, confess, and get him to retrieve the painting to save Mago from this fate. She is aided and hindered by a series of people along the way, a kind truck driver, a "witch woman" who plans to enslave her, a small dog, Trotte, who joins her, and a lonely flower-shop woman who takes her in, teaches her to read, and plans to adopt her. Her guilt drives her on to Chataigner, where she finds Courier's wife, only to learn that the artist has returned to Paris. Without questions, Mme. Courier buys a railroad ticket for Cigarette to Paris, where she finds Eel in Mago's room, goes to Drollant's clinic and finds Mago, who is now wanted by the police. When he sends her away, so that she will not be caught with him, she finds Courier, who is hurt and angry with her, but he forgives her and offers to take her to live with him and his wife. Instead she insists she must turn herself in to save Mago, rushes off to tell him, finds Eel and Drollant also there, and Eel says he plans to turn Cigarette in himself to get in good with the police. When he tries to prevent her going, Mago attacks him, and Eel knifes and kills Mago. Cigarette takes Drollant to the laundry woman, leaves Trotte with him, and tries to throw herself into the Seine like Friquette, but Courier saves her. She recovers when she understands what Mago meant when he told her she must be his "chance" in life. In the end she returns to Mme. Bruneau's flower shop. Although the novel has some grim incidents and technically is classified as realistic fiction, the events are too coincidental and melodramatic to be realistic. The style is almost skillful enough to obscure the lack of logic in plot and characterization, which do not stand up to analysis. With the dear little waif as protagonist, the one-dimensional good Mago and evil Eel, the suicide of Friquette, and the kindhearted woman who adopts Cigarette at first sight, the novel is an up-dated collection of the conventions of the sentimental Victorian novel, now in disrepute. Boston Globe Honor.

FLIP TOWNSEND (*Dreamland Lake**), Philip Townsend, Bry* Bishop's friend. An assertive youth, he is a good organizer and thinks up most of the things he and Bry do together. He is much like his father, brusque, macho Naval Commander Townsend, who is seldom at home, but when he is, bosses everone around. Flip can be considerate, however. For example, he understands that Bry is upset about finding the tramp dead and gives him extra help with the paper route when he has to deliver in the dark.

FLORA (*Cat in the Mirror**), the Gandy's housekeeper, almost a foster mother to Erin. Practical, proper, a no-nonsense sort, she insists Erin wear dresses instead of pants and deport herself like a lady, but she never nags at the girl or makes her feel inferior. She and Erin are friends, sharing a love for beautiful things. Flora takes Erin to the New York Metropolitan Museum of Art for lunch by the pool and then for a tour of the Egyptian section, during which Erin hits her head in her efforts to get away from her unkind schoolmates and falls unconscious. Flora's Egyptian counterpart is Fl'ret. Like Flora, Fl'ret is conscientious and solicitous of her charge. She sees to it that Irun is well taken care of and gives her emotional support. Flora/Fl'ret is the most interesting character in the novel, next to the protagonist, and is the only other round figure. It is interesting that Flora seems to know about Erin's Egyptian experience. Readers are left in doubt about whether this is actual or simply another example of her supportive behavior.

FLORIAN (*Westmark**; *The Kestrel**), bold, idealistic, hard-nosed leader of the revolutionaries in Westmark*. He has gathered around him a small corps of insurgents who become known as "Florian's children." These insurgents wish to effect reforms in the government by overthrowing the monarch. Born a noble, Florian is the son of the Count of Montmollin, but he was moved by conscience and ideals to champion the cause of the peasants. In *The Kestrel*, peasants burn his family manor, La Jolie, during the Regian War. After his home has been destroyed, the Count, Florian's father, commits suicide. Florian's father is a tragic figure who has been betrayed by friends and whose suicide is one of the most poignant passages in the book.

FLUMBO (*I, Momolu**), father of Momolu and a leader in his Kewpessie tribe in Liberia. Stubborn and quick tempered, he causes the original trouble when he is furious to see his son dressed, for a friendly joke, in a soldier's clothes, since his tribe has suffered greatly in the past at the hands of the Liberian soldiers. While they are prisoners working in the army barracks, he beats his son with a broom when the boy uses the American greeting, "Good morning," that he has learned from the soldiers. Flumbo continually makes it impossible for the captain to free them by insisting that he still hates the soldiers, even in the face of good treatment.

FON EISEN, ANTHONY T. (1917–   ), born in Avon, Conn.; author of short stories and of novels for children. A products analyst for G. C. Heublein, Inc., a food and liquor manufacturer, he has made his home in West Hartford, Conn. His novel, *Bond of the Fire** (World, 1965) was elected to the Lewis Carroll Shelf. Conventional in plot and characters but powerful in its sense of place and time, it is the story of a Stone Age youth who is the first of his tribe to acquire a dog. Also about dogs are *Storm, Dog of Newfoundland* (Scribner's, 1948), a suspense story for older readers set at the turn of the century, and *The Magnificent Mongrel* (World, 1970), a lighter novel set in Nova Scotia about a boy's problems with his dog, while *The Prince of Omeya* (World, 1964) concerns love, treachery, and adventure among Bedouins in Africa. Critics have found his books consistently interesting in spite of stock characters and overwritten plots.

THE FORGOTTEN DOOR (Key*, Alexander, Westminster, 1965), science fantasy novel set in the Smoky Mountains of Tennessee or North Carolina. Little Jon, a boy from a peaceful, beauty-loving planet, has fallen through a long-blocked "door" into our world and, having hit his head, temporarily has lost his memory. He makes his way from the cave where he finds himself to a public road where by mind reading he picks the family of Thomas and Mary Bean, who run a small rock shop, to rescue him. Because of his advanced intellectual powers, he is able to learn English in a few days, but Gilby Pitts, who has encountered him earlier and whose aim he spoils when Gilby is poaching deer, starts rumors of a dangerous "wild boy" roaming the mountains. Concurrently, valuables have been stolen from a nearby summer home and suspicion falls on Little Jon, though he knows through mind reading that they were really taken by Tip and Lenny, sons of the no-good Angus Macklin, who tries to see Jon convicted of the theft. In court, Thomas Bean has to admit that Jon is not the son of a recently deceased friend who served in the marines with him, as he has been pretending, but asks the judge, Josie Cunningham (Miss Josie), to read a note detailing their experience with Jon and their supposition about his origin. Little Jon intervenes and first gives a demonstration of his mind reading to convince her, and she releases him in the care of the Beans, but news of the incident leaks out and soon reporters and thrill-seekers gather. More sinister is a Marine Intelligence Colonel, Eben Quinn, who wants to use Jon's powers, and other men, agents of some foreign power, who enlist the aid of Gilby Pitts. Suddenly through mental communication Jon becomes aware that his parents are seeking him. Realizing that the Beans will be in great danger if he suddenly disappears, he proposes to take them, including their children, Sally and Brooks, with him, and they make a break for the cave, accompanied by the dog, Rascal. In the ensuing chase, Little Jon is struck on the head by a rock, his memory returns, Rascal routs the enemy, and they all escape into the other world. Although the story is cleverly handled, the characters, except for Little Jon and the adult Beans, are types or non-entities, including the Bean children, who could have been developed to take a meaningful part. Beyond the use of the cave in the mountains, little is made of the Appalachian setting. Lewis Carroll.

A FORMAL FEELING (Oneal*, Zibby, Viking, 1982), realistic novel set in Ann Arbor, Mich., in the contemporary period exploring the ambivalent feelings of a teenaged girl for her deceased mother and her new stepmother. When Anne* Cameron, 16, returns from boarding school for the first time since her father's remarriage, she feels that there is a glass between her and the rest of the world. Her older brother, Spencer*, who has moved home from the dormitory for the Christmas holidays, her abstracted father, Professor* Cameron, who teaches classical history, her best friend, Laura* Dewitt, Eric, her boyfriend from the previous summer, her old classmates from University School—all are much as they used to be, but Anne looks at them as if from a distance. Her father's new wife, Dory*, whom she has long known as the secretary in the history department, is almost the direct opposite of her meticulous, perfectionist mother. Everything in the household, from the dirty dishes in the sink to the Christmas tree too big for the living room, points up the contrast. Anne, who is on the cross-country team at her school, retreats into long runs and tries to get back the Christmases of the past by singing again with Laura in the church choir. The ease she knew the summer before, when she was alone with her father and they read *The Divine Comedy* (his choice) aloud, is gone, though she is honest enough to admit that disorganized, non-intellectual Dory is trying to make her welcome. Anne struggles to write a paper on Conrad's *Heart of Darkness,* knowing that she must get an A to balance the D on her midterm, in which she, an excellent student, suffered a mental block in trying to analyze the Emily Dickinson poem which starts, "After great pain, a formal feeling comes—" and turned in an almost blank paper. Little overt action occurs in the novel. The sensitive story consists of Anne's struggle with her own perceptions and her gradual realization that she has been hiding from herself her mother's real character and influence on the family, her inflexible certainties, her rigid good taste, her domineering insistence on her own point of view. Moreover, when Anne goes alone for an early-morning skate on the ice pond in the park and sprains her ankle, the pain provides the final breakthrough of a memory she has suppressed for eight years, the memory that her mother left the family for several months, and that she and Spencer spent her eighth Christmas with her grandmother. With that period of her life now returned to her, she can begin to realize that her behavior was not the cause of her mother's desertion or her death and that she no longer needs to strive for perfection that will bring her mother's approval. With this realization, Anne can also appreciate her mother's fine points and feel some of the love for her she has never really allowed herself. A very skillfully crafted novel, the story is intellectually demanding but absorbing, with each phrase and image carefully placed to make the psychological study plausible and the end hopeful, if not certain. A slightly younger age for the suppressed memories might be more believable—five or six rather than eight—but Anne's gradual awakening to and admission of reality is convincing. Her protective shield against emotion—glass, ice, plastic, the images vary—prevents an easy identification with her, but a thoughtful reader not only understands but feels deeply the vulnerability under her coolness. All the major figures are strongly characterized and the picture of the university community is exact in tone and detail. Christopher.

FORMAN, JAMES (DOUGLAS) (1932–   ), born in Mineola, Long Island, N.Y., the son of a lawyer; attorney and author of novels, biographies, and books of history. A graduate of Princeton University and Columbia Law School, he has made his home on Long Island where he has combined writing with the practice of law. For teenaged readers he has written some two dozen novels, chiefly of colorful, well-researched historical fiction set in different times and places and involving such themes as the conflict between good and evil, courage, loyalty, and in particular anti-war and the survival of the human spirit in spite of tremendous adversity. *Ceremony of Innocence** (Hawthorn, 1970), about German resistance to the Nazis during World War II, was selected for the Lewis Carroll Shelf. *Horses of Anger* (Farrar, 1967) and *The Traitors* (Farrar, 1968) are also set in Nazi Germany, as is *The Survivor* (Farrar, 1976), which is about the holocaust. Among his best-known novels are those that take place in Greece during World War II and the Greek Civil War, *The Skies of Crete* (Farrar, 1963), *Ring the Judas Bell* (Farrar, 1965), and *The Shield of Achilles* (Farrar, 1966), while *The Cow-Neck Rebels* (Farrar, 1969) and *Song of Jubilee* (Farrar, 1971) have American historical settings. More recently he has published *Call Back Yesterday* (Scribner's, 1981), which postulates a dramatic ordeal during the takeover of the U.S. Embassy in Saudi Arabia. Although critics have found his characters stereotyped and wooden and his plots contrived, they have praised his ability to create exciting atmospheres and authentic backgrounds and to convey worthwhile themes provocatively.

FORSYTH, JOHN (*Sophia Scrooby Preserved**), jolly, flamboyant Englishman, bound for the New World to establish a plantation when he is captured by the pirate captain, Pedro Alvarez, and held for ransom. A gentleman of noble intentions and much flowery speech, he takes Pansy with him on his return to England and introduces her to London society. He takes her to Drury Lane, where she sees such notables as Boswell and Johnson and falls in with Master* Anthony, who brings her back to America and the Scroobys.

FOSTRA LEE POST (*Anywhere Else but Here**), childhood friend of Aunt Aurora who blithely abandons her distinctly unlikeable eight-year-old son, Claude, at the Smelter home. A follower of Dr. Spiros Avanti, who leads a cult devoted to Self Actualization, she believes she is traveling to freedom on the Good-Energy Path. One of the tenets of the group is that one must always do only what one wishes, a doctrine that has made Claude a confused and disagreeable brat and lets Mrs. Post justify her impositions on the Smelters.

FOX, PAULA (1923–   ), author best known for her contemporary novels for later elementary readers and young adolescents. She was born in New York City and attended schools in New York, Cuba, New Hampshire, and Montreal. She studied at Columbia University and has held various jobs as a reporter for newspapers, a machinist, and editor for a publishing company in England. She has taught emotionally disturbed children and English to Spanish-speaking children and worked as a reader for a film company. She began writing novels in 1963 and in 1971–1972 received a Guggenheim grant. In 1974 she won the Newbery Medal for *The Slave Dancer** (Bradbury, 1973), a taut, dramatic novel set against the African slave trade to the southern United States in 1840 and the most critically acclaimed of her books. It is cited in *Choice* and was a Fanfare book. *The King's Falcon** (Bradbury, 1969), a short fable-like story set in a legendary medieval kingdom, was also a Fanfare book. Most of her novels have been contemporary realistic problem stories, among them, *Maurice's Room** (Macmillan, 1966), *How Many Miles to Babylon?** (White, 1967), *The Stone-Faced Boy** (Bradbury, 1968), and *Portrait of Ivan** (Bradbury, 1969), all cited in *Choice*, and *Blowfish Live in the Sea** (Bradbury, 1970), a finalist for the National Book Award in the children's category and also a *Choice* selection. She has also written television plays and novels for adults, one of which, *Desperate Characters* (Harcourt, 1970), was made into a movie, several picture books, a book of short stories for children, *The Little Swineherd and Other Tales* (Dutton, 1978), which was a National Book Award finalist, and more recently *A Place Apart* (Farrar, 1980) and *One-Eyed Cat** (Bradbury, 1984), a Newbery honor book, also about adolescent adjustments and growing pains. Her books reveal recognition of children's emotional struggles, and lack of communication and understanding between people appear as recurring themes in her books, but her work has a disturbing, purposeless, static surrealism, characters are often distorted and made eccentric for effect, and many times the plots come to very little in the end. She is married to Martin Greenberg, a professor at C. W. Post College, and they have made their home in Brooklyn. In 1978 she received the Hans Christian Andersen Medal in honor of her total work for the young.

FRANK COTWELL (*They Never Came Home**), younger brother of Dan*, who grows in self-assurance during the time Dan is gone. He is suspicious of Mr. Brown, but when Joan* Drayfus insists on working for the mysterious stranger to repay the debt of her brother, Larry*, Frank decides to help her. In that way, he thinks he can protect her.

FRANK JEFFRIES (*The Last Run**), Lyle's* impatient, worried father. Frank fears he may lose the gas station he has operated for many years to the competition of the new self-serve station down the way in Silverfield. He often scolds Lyle for being late and slovenly about his tasks and chafes at having to give a job to Bill* Cameron, his elderly father-in-law, when he needs but cannot afford to pay a skilled mechanic, too. After the mustang episode, Frank sees a sobered son offer to work to help him in this time of need and also to save money for the horse he wants so much. He approves of his son's changed attitude and in return informs the boy that their postponed fishing trip is still on.

FREAKY FRIDAY (Rodgers*, Mary, Harper, 1972), comic fantasy, set in the late twentieth century in New York City. Thirteen-year-old Annabel Andrews chatters away in "now diction" to describe her "freaky Friday," which really starts on Thursday when she has still another fight with her mother over freedom. Annabel wants to eat, dress, behave, and keep her room any way she wants. When she shouts out that she wants to be responsible for herself, her mother replies curtly that she will be, soon enough. The next morning, to Annabel's surprise, she wakes up in her mother's body. Although she is delighted with her new appearance, since her mother is an attractive woman, her new responsibilities bring a day of errors and disasters that change her perspectives on life. In addition to having to run the house, she worries about where her mother is, how Mummy managed the body exchange, and whether or not she (Annabel) will ever regain her own form. She carries off breakfast well, getting her brother, Ape Face (Ben), 6, and Annabel off to school by yielding to their idiosyncratic demands. She has a disturbing conversation with Bill, her husband (father), that gives her new insights into family finances and pressures. Then the washer breaks down, and she has an argument with the cleaning woman, smug, opinionated Mrs. Schmauss, whom she fires. She forgets to meet Ben at the bus, learns she must entertain Bill's clients for dinner, attends a school conference in which she hears her behavior and underachievement thoroughly discussed by teachers, psychiatrist, and principal, and has a wild conversation with the police when she tries to get help from Missing Persons. There are some plusses: not having to wear braces on her teeth, playing games with goodlooking, fourteen-year-old Boris (Morris) Harris from upstairs, with whom she has been in love and whom she inveigles into baby-sitting and cooking dinner. When, in late afternoon, problems threaten to engulf her, she retreats to her room and screams for her mother, and all is soon set to rights. Annabel turns over a new leaf and records the day's events for the term paper she has been neglecting. This rollicking farce moves like a TV situation comedy. It improvises on the old theme of role exchange to poke fun at contemporary youth and aspects of family and school life. Situations are outlandish and characters eccentric or caricatures. The author is quite brazen about leaving unanswered the important question of how Annabel's mother brings about the body exchange. Sequel is *A Billion for Boris*. Choice; Christopher.

FREEDOM TRAIL (Williams*, Jeanne, Putnam, 1973), historical novel set in northeastern Kansas Territory in the 1850s. Although his good friend, Elijah Crane, is a strong abolitionist, Charles Hall, father of young Jared, wants no part of the political struggle going on between the anti-slave faction, led by New Englanders of the Emigrant Aid Society, and the pro-slave people, many of whom live in Missouri and come into Kansas to vote illegally. When a runaway slave, Nicodemus, and his son, Young Nick, appear at his farm, he sends Jared to take his mother and little sister, Betsy, to Lawrence and to bring back Elijah to take the slaves to an Underground Railway station. Jared returns with Elijah to find his father killed by a band called the Rattlers, led by smooth, gentlemanly Dave McMasters. Young Nick, who has hidden in the woods, tells of seeing his own father torn apart by McMasters's hounds. Jared becomes a courier, working with Mark Johnnycake, an Indian boy who lives at Cranes', aiding the anti-slavery group by helping slaves to freedom and keeping the Free State activities coordinated. One of the first underground stations beyond Lawrence is an old mill where Matthew, an old mountain man who has been an Indian slave, now lives with his goats and a few horses. He has been scalped and his tendons severed, and he has a reputation for being slightly crazy but is a strong link in the anti-slavery network. Matthew lets him try a beautiful horse named Whirlin' Willie that is gentle until something gets on his back, when he erupts like a volcano; eventually Jared tames him. Once, taking a slave to Matthew's, Jared finds the old man almost dead, with a broken leg and a high fever, a victim of the Rattlers. Jared nurses him and swears to kill McMasters. In the course of his work he also meets John Brown and his grim sons, but their form of anti-slavery does not appeal to him. Determined to draw McMasters out where he can kill him, Jared goes to McMasters's farm and persuades his foreman, Simba, to run away. He takes Simba to Matthew's mill, sends him on north with Young Nick, who is now a conductor on the railway, then waits for the Rattlers. To his surprise, McMasters shows up with Young Nick, having saved him from the other Rattlers though he was wounded when Simba got away. McMasters, disgusted with his own men, joins Matthew, Mark, and Jared as they are held siege in the mill which the Rattlers surround and try to burn. Jared, knowing worse is coming as war fever heats up, nevertheless feels free as he no longer is obsessed with killing McMasters. A great deal of history of the Lawrence region is told in an exciting way, and while the book leans toward the Free State side, it is clear that there are also good, honest men on the pro-slavery side and abuses caused by hot heads on both sides. McMasters's sudden switch at the end is a flaw in the plot, not sufficiently motivated to be believable. Spur.

FREELON STARBIRD (*Freelon Starbird**), first person narrator who, in his old age, tells of the miserable, hopeless winter of 1776, when he served in the Continental army and lost his leg. Bored with watchmaking, his father's trade, and hoping to impress Polly Lycott, with whom he fancies himself in love, he begins to talk about the revolutionary cause, but he enlists by accident when drunk and finds only one hour of the great war for independence enjoyable, the hour when they first set out from Philadelphia, a glorious start that soon turns sour as they become lost and have to retrace their steps. Without any real patriotic conviction, he endures great hardships and not until he is an old man does he question why and whether such inept soldiers as he was had any effect in the cause.

FREELON STARBIRD (Snow*, Richard, ill. Ben F. Stahl, Houghton, 1976), historical novel set in the Pennsylvania-New York-New Jersey area and subtitled "Being a Narrative of the Extraordinary Hardships Suffered by an Accidental Soldier in a Beaten Army During the Autumn and Winter of 1776." Freelon* Starbird, 20, apprentice to his watchmaker father, becomes involved in the revolutionary fervor in Philadelphia more to impress a girl he admires, Polly Lycott, than through any conviction, though he has been reading Tom Paine's *Common Sense*. On the day when they first hear the Declaration of Independence read, he and his friend, Jib* Grasshorn, get drunk with Freelon's Uncle Jonas and wake the next morning to realize that they have both enlisted in the army. For most of the hottest part of the summer they drill on the grounds of the foul-smelling tannery under the vitriolic direction of Sergeant* Kite, a British deserter who has joined the rebel cause, and are watched occasionally by Captain Samuel Totten, a veteran of the French-Indian wars, Lieut.* Godkin, an ex-schoolteacher, and Corporal Francis Curran, a foul-mouthed Irishman. In September they set out to join the 3rd Pennsylvania Battalion, a group they never manage to find. They are ferried across the Hudson by a rascal who steals the Captain's horse and finally reach the army at White Plains, though not the Pennsylvania contingent. There they experience their first encounter, in which they run in panic from the Hessian mercenary troops without even shooting their firelocks. They retreat to Fort Lee, from where they can watch the British take Fort Washington, across the river, against all odds and predictions. They retreat without fighting to Newark. Ill and nearly starved, Freelon walks out of Newark to a farmhouse and asks for bread and is given some by a Mrs. Collins, wife of a Tory who is fighting for the British. He rejoins his unit as it retreats from Newark past the house. The day after Christmas, in a dense fog, they attack the British forces in Trenton and, amazingly, win. Since their six-month enlistments are almost up, Washington asks them to stay another six weeks, and to Freelon's surprise most of the ragged, hungry, miserable soldiers, including himself, agree. Shortly afterward, at the battle of Princeton, his leg is shot and must be amputated. Later he returns to Newark, finds Mrs. Collins a widow, woos and marries her. All this is told by Freelon as an old man, trying to set the record straight and find a meaning in it all. The emphasis is not on the campaign or the cause, but on the cold and the rain, the hunger and pain of the ill-clothed, ill-supplied men who are marched with bleeding feet on futile missions in terrible weather. The tone, when it considers the bigger issues, is mostly ironic. Several historical characters appear, chiefly Washington, who is pictured as a figure of calm in disastrous conditions. Others include Thomas Paine and Henry Knox and, more briefly, Alexander Hamilton, Benjamin Franklin, and Thomas Jefferson. Freelon's unusual conclusion is that the rebellious Americans became a formidable army mainly because the British treated them as one, throwing men and money into the conflict and thereby unifying the straggling troops of opposition. If the troop movements and battles are rather difficult to follow, that is deliberate, since Freelon and his fellows usually know little of what is happening. The fever, dysentery, wormy bread, misfiring guns, and splitting shoes are clearly and vividly described. (Aaron* Thane) Fanfare.

FRITZ†, JEAN (GUTTERY) (1915–   ), born in Hankow, China; author noted in children's literature for her meticulously researched, skillfully crafted American historical novels for older children and her amusing, authentic biographies of early American figures for younger readers. Her parents were missionaries, and she lived in China until she was thirteen, attending a British school and *in absentia* developing a deep curiosity and affection for the America she regarded as her homeland. She graduated from Wheaton College in Massachusetts and continued her studies at Columbia. She married Michael Fritz, who has been affiliated with the Hudson Laboratory at Columbia, and the couple have made their home in Dobbs Ferry, N.Y. In 1952 she started a children's room in the Dobbs Ferry library. Working there sparked her interest in writing her own books for children. Since 1954 she has published over two dozen books for children and young adults, including picture books, animal stories, and books of non-fiction, as well as the historical novels and period pieces and lively, humorous biographies for which she is most highly acclaimed. For later elementary readers and early adolescents, she has written three finely crafted, substantial novels that feature boy protagonists who must make major decisions about their lives: *Brady** (Coward, 1960), a *Choice* book, involves the Underground Railway; *I, Adam** (Coward, 1963), a Fanfare selection, is set against the waning whaling industry, the lure of the goldfields, and the push westward; and *Early Thunder** (Coward, 1967), a Fanfare book also cited in *Choice*, tells of events in Salem, Mass., just before the American Revolution. For younger readers, *The Cabin Faced West†* (Coward, 1958) places a little Pennsylvania pioneer girl in a similar life-directing situation. More recently Fritz has turned her attention to biography, producing several popular, highly acclaimed authentic picture-book lives intended to give young readers realistic, humanistic views of eminent American figures, among them, *Why Don't You Get a Horse, Sam Adams?* (Coward, 1974) and *What's the Big Idea, Ben Franklin?* (Coward, 1976). She has written for Silver Burdett Co., been a research librarian, directed several writing workshops, and taught at Appalachian State University in South Carolina. She is often asked to speak at professional gatherings on children's literature, has contributed short stories to national magazines, and has written a non-fiction book for adults, *Cast for a Revolution: Some American Friends and Enemies, 1728–1814* (Houghton, 1972). Her autobiography is *Homesick: My Own Story** (Putnam, 1982), and she received for the Laura Ingalls Wilder Award in 1986.

FROM THE MIXED-UP FILES OF MRS. BASIL E. FRANKWEILER (Konigsburg*, E. L., ill. author, Atheneum, 1967), realistic novel set during the 1960s in New York City. Discontented, Claudia* Kincaid, 12, persuades her miserly brother, Jamie*, 9, to run away with her and hide out in the Metropolitan* Museum of Art to teach her parents "a lesson in Claudia appreciation." They cleverly evade the guards by standing on toilet seats during museum check, bathe in the restaurant fountain and raid it for coins, join troops of children to remain inconspicuous, sleep in an ornately carved, sixteenth-century English bed, wash their clothes in the laundromat, and eat at the automat. They become involved in attempting to learn whether or not a newly acquired statue, the Angel, is really the work of Michelangelo, to whom it is attributed, doing library research on the subject. This main story is framed by a letter from the contributor of the statue, wealthy, eccentric Mrs. Frankweiler, to her lawyer,

Saxonberg, who coincidentally is the children's grandfather. While the children's activities in the museum are exciting, convincing, and original, the frame story seems contrived and extraneous. Books Too Good; Choice; Contemporary Classics; Fanfare; Lewis Carroll; Newbery Winner.

G

GAGE, WILSON, pseudonym for Mary Q. Steele*.

GAITHER GRAYBEAL (*Trial Valley*), sturdy young farmer who lives down the road from the Luthers and becomes romantically interested in Mary* Call. Gaither often comes to visit her and help her with her work about the house. He is quiet, steady, and serious minded and exhibits a strong sense of responsibility toward family and friends. He understands that Mary Call's life revolves around her family and accepts the situation. When he rescues Jack* Parsons from drowning, Mary Call realizes that, unlike Thad* Yancy, Gaither is a giving person, one with whom she can be comfortable and compatible. He is an obvious foil for Thad.

GALAXY M81 (*Time and Mr. Bass*), the galaxy in Ursa Major to which Mr. Tyco* Bass travels by thought and to which he is sent on special assignment by the Ancient Ones after David* Topman and Chuck* Masterson return from their first trip to the Mushroom Planet, Basidium-X*.

GALE FRANKLIN (*The Secret of the Seven Crows*), daughter of the owner of Crauleia, where Shelley* Calhoun's father hopes to start a school. A competent girl, Gale cares for her crippled and widowed father, roams the woods with her pet crow, Dracula, and tries to solve the mystery left by her great-great-great-grandmother, who built the mansion. Gale is inclined to believe that her ancestor's ghost inhabits the old house and tries to help her, the last descendant, find the hidden treasure. She is especially kind to the youngest Calhoun, Bug, letting him hold Dracula and claim a special understanding with the talking bird.

GAMBO (*A Solitary Blue*), Eulalie Boudrault Melville, Jeff* Greene's great-grandmother and Melody's* grandmother. Gambo is the proud matriarch of an old Southern family, not pleased with Melody's flighty ways, and eager to acknowledge Jeff and inform him about his family. Gambo suffers a stroke the winter after the boy first visits Melody and the second summer wants little to do with him. Jeff stays out of her way because her illness has changed her personality a good deal and she is often hostile or detached. Gambo leaves most of her property to Jeff, since he is a boy and she believes property should go down in the male line. She callously forgets to provide for her faithful retainer, Miss Opal, also of advanced age. One of Gambo's proudest possessions is an elaborate jade ring, an heirloom of much sentimental but little monetary value. This she leaves to Melody, who gladly exchanges it for the large, far more economically valuable and flashy diamond one Gambo has left Jeff. Jeff gives the stone to Melody without hesitation, because he believes it wasn't really fair of Gambo to will her estate to him instead of Melody. But he gives the diamond to his mother with sorrow, because Melody's quick acceptance of the diamond shows once again her shallow sense of values. Gambo is a strongly drawn character.

THE GARDEN IS DOING FINE (Farley*, Carol, ill. Lynn Sweat, Atheneum, 1975), realistic problem novel set in the small town of Pointer, Mich., on Lake Michigan, for several days in December of 1945. The story is told from the point of view of, but not by, earnest, responsible Corrie Sheldon, 14, who at first refuses to believe her father is dying of cancer. Her mother, apparently reconciled to the inevitability of her husband's death, assures him that the garden he loves so much is doing well. But Corrie knows that it lies dead and forsaken under the winter cold. She refuses to believe that he will not return home from the hospital, and she also thinks that, when he does come home, he will see that Mother has been lying to him. Three days' events and her own thinking lead Corrie to realize that her father's true garden—his legacy of love and the values system he instilled in his children—lives on, and she is able to speak the words she once regarded as blatant and deceitful lies. There are views of Corrie in the hospital, at home with her mother, twin brothers, Alan and Arthur, and Lewie, the kindly old neighbor lady who baby-sits while her mother works at Mr. Peterson's awning shop or visits the hospital, and with her supportive and understanding schoolmate, Sandra. Much of the book is devoted to Corrie's often naive adolescent reflections about life and death and the nature of human existence and to recollections of life with father before he went to the hospital. She remembers how they took a walk in the woods, when he solicitously carried back to the lake a turtle that had strayed, how he took a day off from work to attend her sixth-grade play, how he lavished attention upon his garden, and how unselfishly he shared its produce. Corrie's recollections paint her father's portrait for the reader, gradually revealing him as a self-educated workingman, an idealistic, life-loving man with many friends, whose somewhat irresponsible and improvident ways often irritated her practical, worrying mother. Sometimes Corrie resents her father's illness and feels it is spoiling her life: she regrets having to give up a part in the school play in order to visit him in the evening; she must wear hand-me-downs; and she misses much school fun. And she feels guilty about feeling this way. But most of the time she pitches in freely, and their mutual worry about Joseph Sheldon brings her and her mother closer together. Because of their situation, Corrie sees facets of her mother's character and life that the usual adolescent her age would probably never observe or understand. Touches of humor keep the book from becoming gloomy or morbid. For example, Corrie and Sandra, convinced that Catholic prayers, with candles, must somehow be more effective than their Protestant ones without candles, intrepidly make their way into the neighborhood Catholic church to pray for Joseph's recovery. This story of how an intelligent, caring young girl gradually comes to see that the father she loves so much is going to die and finally accepts that agonizing fact, of family love and unity in the face of great adversity, and of a girl's growing relationship with her mother strongly affirms the beauty and value of life without sentimentality and sensation and is more convincing than most contemporary problem novels of its type. Child Study.

GATES†, DORIS (1901–   ), born in Mountain View, Calif.; librarian and author of novels of family and community life for children. She was educated at Fresno State College, Los Angeles Library School, and Western Reserve University and for ten years was head of the children's department of the Fresno County Library in California. She then taught library science and children's literature at San Jose State College, the University of California at Berkeley, and the University of San Francisco. She grew up on a prune ranch, where she had a little gray donkey like the one in her first novel, *Sarah's Idea†* (Viking, 1938), and the novel *The Elderberry Bush* (Viking, 1967) tells the story of her ranching childhood. Her most highly regarded novel grew out of her library work with migrant children in the San Joaquin Valley, *Blue Willow†* (Viking, 1940), which was, among other citations, a Newbery Honor book and a Fanfare book. Also selected by the editors of *Horn Book* for the Fanfare list was *The Cat and Mrs. Cary** (Viking, 1962), a formulaic mystery-fantasy about a talking cat who brings excitement into the life of a staid and independent widow. Other books show her varied interests: *North Fork* (Viking, 1945), a story for older boys set in the lumbering area of the Sierra Nevada which also involves Indians; *River Ranch* (Viking, 1949), about rustling on a western cattle ranch; *Little Vic* (Viking, 1951), about a race horse; and *Trouble for Jerry* (Viking, 1944), which is sequel to *Sarah's Idea*. More recently she has published a well-received series of retellings of stories from Greek mythology and the novels *A Morgan for Melinda* (Viking, 1980) and its sequel, *A Filly for Melinda* (Viking, 1984). She married William Hall, an attorney, and has made her home in southern California. She has also been associate editor for Ginn and Company, co-authoring several readers in their Enrichment Series, has contributed to professional journals, and has written a book about children's literature for adults.

A GATHERING OF DAYS (Blos*, Joan, Scribner's, 1979), realistic period novel of a girl's growing up and of family life, in which events of the times somewhat influence what happens in the story. Catherine* Hall, 13, is a schoolgirl, the daughter of Charles* Hall, a New Hampshire farmer of modest means. She keeps a journal from late 1830 to early 1832, in which she records her observations and experiences, revealing in them much about her thinking, her character, and the times. Cath is a dutiful, sturdy, industrious girl, who has been taking care of her father and younger sister, Matty, since their mother died a few years before. Cath describes her duties about the house, school life, visits to neighbors and church, and activities with her young friends. The Halls take Thanksgiving dinner with their good neighbors, the Shipmans, enjoy Fourth of July in town, participate in "breaking out" after a heavy snow, and make maple sugar in the spring. Three major, intersecting story strands unite the occasional entries: Cath's relationships with a fugitive slave, with her best friend, Cassie* Shipman, and with her new stepmother, Ann* Higham Hall. Although fully aware of the moral and legal implications of helping a runaway but feeling supported by the sentiments of her Uncle* Jack Hall and teacher Edward Holt*, Cath persuades Cassie to join her in secretly taking food and a quilt to a mysterious "phantom," who has requested help in a ragged, poorly written, pathetic note. Although Cath's thoughts return now and then to the phantom, her attention then focuses on her new stepmother. Ann Higham is a Boston widow with a son about Cath's age. Ann's arrival brings changes into Cath's life, and there are some tense moments, for example, when Ann learns that Cath has given the quilt to the runaway and insists that she make another to replace it, and Cath struggles against jealousy and resentment. Gradually, however, Ann's warmth, sincerity, and good sense win Cath's confidence and eventually even her affection. In late summer of 1831, Cassie takes a chill while picking berries, soon sickens, and within a week is dead. Cath mourns with a quiet but deep grief, determined to imitate Cassie's virtues and not "pine away with useless sorrow." In late September, she receives a packet from Canada containing a small gift and a note of appreciation. Thus she knows that her phantom was indeed a fugitive slave and is safe. At the end, Cath leaves for Boston to help care for the new baby of teacher Holt, who will in return oversee her continuing education. This episodic story succeeds completely neither as novel nor journal. Characterization is full and deft, but potential for suspense and unity is never realized. The slave is almost forgotten by the time his letter arrives near the end of the book and the reader learns along with Cath that he has achieved freedom. Episodes of everyday life are described with details that would probably not appear in a real journal, and language seems artificial now and then, with, for example, word inversions, the use of "z" for internal "s," and strike-outs. The book conveys a good sense, however, of what life must have been like on a small farm for a devoted family in mid nineteenth century New England. It seems accurate to the point of view of a young girl, and staunch, sincere Cath is a convincing and memorable figure. (Asa* Hale Shipman) Newbery Winner.

GED (*A Wizard of Earthsea**; *The Tombs of Atuan**; *The Farthest Shore**), known as a boy as Duny and later as Sparrowhawk, the protagonist of the first book of the Earthsea* trilogy and a major character in the other two. Unusually gifted in the abilities of a wizard, he is destined to become Archmage, but his pride leads him to summon a dangerous Shadow from the Unworld, which almost kills him. Humbled, he must relearn much of the lore and then seek first to escape, then to seek out and destroy the Shadow, which turns out to be one aspect of his own character. From a very bright, confident boy, Ged becomes a deeply hurt young man, then gradually a wise and courageous adult.

THE GENIE OF SUTTON PLACE (Selden*, George, Farrar, 1973), fast-moving comic fantasy with Arabian Nights motifs set in New York City in the late 1900s. After the death of his father, a student of Near Eastern studies, the narrator, Timothy Farr, 12, goes to live with his father's wealthy sister. Right away, Aunt* Lucy objects to Sam*, Tim's basset-springer, which exhibits an unfortunate fondness for her. Desperate to save Sam from some terrible fate, Tim consults his father's diary and discovers an old Arabian verse-spell. With the help of Mr. Dickinson, Arabic expert at the National Museum, he conjures out of a valuable old tapestry Dooley*, a six-foot, six-inch genie of imposing presence, kind heart, and considerable talent with magic. Dooley hires on as Aunt Lucy's chauffeur and eventually falls in love with her maid, Rose* Jackson, a music student. Dooley changes Sam into a man, just in time to save him from extermination at the Humane Society, and helps him establish a successful pet store. When it appears that Dooley's magic is waning, Tim again resorts to his father's diary. He discovers that the wizard who created Dooley in days of yore decreed that, if Dooley fell in love and heard the word "Allah," he would forthwith be compelled to return to the tapestry. Dooley forgoes associating with Rose, and all goes well, until at Tim's thirteenth birthday party, Felix, Sam's loquacious, mischievous parakeet, utters the fateful name. Sam reverts to canine form, and Dooley returns to the rug. Then Tim discovers that the paper on which he has written the verse-spell has been destroyed. He again calls upon Mr. Dickinson for help. The expert both solves Tim's problem and makes a major contribution to Arabic studies, when he discerns that the spell is woven into the decorative design edging Dooley's image on the tapestry. He also discovers that, if Dooley willingly gives his Ring of Immortality to a mortal maiden, he will retain his human shape. Dooley promptly declares his love for Rose and gives her the ring, thus insuring that he and Sam, the product of his magic, will remain human. At Dooley's suggestion, Tim writes down the story of that eventful summer. Just enough complications artfully spaced keep the plot flowing smoothly and the interest up. A little romance, some mild villainy in the form of Aunt Lucy's lawyer, the ambivalent Mr. Watkins, some hilarious slapstick, along with a polished style and a distinctive mix of characters makes for a lighthearted, unpretentious fantasy with an old, low-keyed message—love conquers all. (Madame* Sosostris) Fanfare.

GENTLE BEN (Morey*, Walter, ill. John Schoenherr, Dutton, 1965), realistic animal story set in coastal Alaska in the mid twentieth century. Without his father's knowledge, Mark Andersen, 13, has been for some time visiting Ben, the Alaskan brown bear which Fog Benson has kept in a shed since it was a cub. Now half-grown, Ben is too big for Fog to handle, and he plans to sell chances, with the winner having the right to turn Ben loose and shoot him for a trophy. Appalled, Mark finds courage to beg his father, Karl, to buy the animal and finds a surprising ally in his mother, Ellen*, who argues that Mark is susceptible to tuberculosis, which killed his older brother, and that caring for the bear would give him incentive to exercise in the open air. With some reluctance Karl agrees, stipulating that Mark take full care of the bear and help pay for him by acting as pickup, the third crew member on Karl's fishing boat during the salmon run. At first living and working on the *Far North*, a forty-nine-foot seiner, is strange to Mark, but the other crew member, old Clearwater*, is helpful. Mark has taught Ben to fish for salmon in the stream, but the bear will need a great deal of food, so, in towns where they put in, Mark contracts with stores to buy their stale bread and bakery goods, then, to his father's surprise, he is able to convince the superintendent of the cannery, scowling, unfriendly Mike* Kelly, to rent him space in the freezer to store it. All is going well until Fog Benson, drunk, brags that he can make Ben drink a bottle of beer. Unable to wake Ben immediately out of semi-hibernation, Fog prods him with a scythe, cuts his ear, and so enrages the bear that it cuffs Benson, clawing his face and disfiguring him for life. The townspeople of the village, Orca City, insist that the Andersens get rid of the dangerous animal, though Mark knows that Ben is extremely gentle unless harassed. Arnie Nichols, a scraggy boatman, volunteers to drop Ben off to freedom on an outer island on his trip to Ketchikan but actually plans to take him south for sale to a small zoo in Washington state. In rough seas the cage comes loose from where it is chained on deck, crashing into a steel winch and breaking up as it tips overboard. Ben swims to the nearest island. At the end of the fishing season Karl takes over the mail run for the regular man whose boat has been damaged. In a winter storm he strikes a rock and radios for help. Mark, in Kelly's office, hears the call, and they get a float plane to pick him up, but Clearwater is drowned and the *Far North* is lost. With his way of earning a living gone, Karl agrees to be watchman at the Windy Point fish trap, which has been plagued by losses when previous watchmen sold out to fish pirates. There he warns off Fog Benson, who wants to deal with him to sell out. When Fog and his men return with guns at night, they are scared off by a bear which turns out to be Ben. Arnie sells the name of the island where Ben landed to a sportsmen's guide, Mud Hole Jones, who then brings a wealthy older man, Peter King, by plane to hunt the great bear. Mark worries until he finds King with his leg pinned under a boulder from a rock slide and gets Ben to roll off the stone. King decides to give up hunting and turn to wild life photography and also to become a partner with Karl in the fish trap, insisting that Mud Hole will get his business only if he promises to allow Ben to live undisturbed. Despite the reliance on coincidence and a simplistic conversion of values for the resolution, the story has appeal mainly because of its presentation of Ben. The sensory descriptions of the huge bear are warm and convincing, and his actions are realistic and plausible, told objectively with no anthropomorphizing. The Alaskan setting with its salmon fishing culture is effective and interesting. Choice.

GENTLEHANDS (Kerr*, M. E., Harper, 1978), realistic novel with mystery story aspects set in the mid–1900s, when stories about the discovery of fugitive Nazi war criminals occasionally broke into the news. Buddy Boyle, 16, works at the local ice cream shop in the small town of Seaville, Long Island, N.Y. He reflects on his summer romance with beautiful, black-haired Skye* Pennington, 18, indulged only daughter of an oil millionaire, whose oceanside estate with beach house, servants, and flashy sports cars lies just outside of town. To impress Skye on their first date, Buddy suggests they visit his grandfather, cultured Frank Trenker*, whom he hardly knows and from whom his mother is estranged, at his comfortable home up the coast a short distance. On this and later dates, Skye and Trenker converse amiably about opera and art, about which Trenker is quite knowledgeable, while Buddy, previously scornful of such "culture," soaks up atmosphere and sees possibilities in life of which he has been ignorant. Buddy's hard-bitten, inarticulate father, a local police sergeant, and practical mother try to convince Buddy that Skye is out of his class, and indeed he does feel awkward among her friends, but it takes the summer before he apparently comes around to their way of thinking. In between, he openly defies his parents, disobeys them, lies, dissembles, and ignores his accepted responsibilities toward his little brother, Streaker. When his father grounds him, Buddy moves in with Trenker, with whom he now talks easily. Buddy finds the older man warm and understanding, a lover of birds and animals as well as the arts. Grandfather gives Buddy friendly advice, telling him that with confidence and persistence he can make his life anything he wishes to. Buddy's mother sensibly tries to maintain communication with her son, even to accepting an invitation to dinner with her father. Then Nick De* Lucca, an investigative reporter who is a house guest of the Penningtons, publishes a story identifying Trenker as a wanted Nazi war criminal. He says that Trenker is the notorious Gentlehands, the Nazi official who taunted Italian prisoners with the aria from *Tosca*, "O dolci mani." At first Buddy refuses to believe the story, but eventually he realizes the facts fit, and he phones authorities to give what evidence he can. It is now fall, and Skye prepares to enter Bryn Mawr, her summer romance a thing of the past, and a somewhat wiser Buddy plans to attend the annual fall policemen's outing, now reconciled with his family. The romance between Buddy and Skye lacks motivation on her part and seems phony, and the overforeshadowed plot is concocted of a too fortuitous set of circumstances and trendy scenes designed to appeal to an adolescent audience. There is some humor, and dialogue seems natural. Trenker is fake, but the parents are sympathetically if flatly presented and are ironically the most likeable and real-seeming characters in the book. Most other figures are simply eccentric or stock, a conveniently assembled conglomeration. Buddy's musings and actions seem appropriate for an impressionable youth struggling to sort out his values. Christopher.

GEOFF YOUNG (*Dawn of Fear**), Geoffrey Young, chum of Derek Brand and Peter* Hutchins. A fussy boy, youngest child and only son in his family, he collects birds' eggs, a hobby which the other two boys deplore. He has difficulty facing up to situations and is less daring and adventurous than the other two but joins in escapades once begun. The other two can always count on him for support.

GEORGE†, JEAN CRAIGHEAD (1919–   ), born in Washington, D.C.; naturalist, author of novels concerned with animals and natural science, mostly self-illustrated. She grew up in the Washington area, often out of doors with her twin brothers, both of whom became wildlife ecologists. She received her B.A. degree from Pennsylvania State College and studied further at Louisiana State University, Baton Rouge, and at the University of Michigan in Ann Arbor. In 1942 she became a reporter for the International News Service and from 1944 to 1946 wrote for the Washington *Post*. For many years she has been connected with *Pageant* magazine. In 1944 she married John L. George†, with whom she wrote her first book, *Vulpes the Red Fox†* (Dutton, 1948) and five others. They were later divorced, but she continued to write, publishing more than twenty novels for young people, frequently employing scientific study of nature, as in *Gull Number 737** (Crowell, 1964) and *Who Really Killed Cock Robin? An Ecological Mystery** (Dutton, 1971). Her most popular books are both stories of survival away from civilization, *My Side of the Mountain†* (Dutton, 1959), about a boy who lives alone in the Catskills, and *Julie of the Wolves** (Harper, 1972), about a girl on the north slope of Alaska, the winner of the Newbery Medal. Although her novels often suffer from weakness in plotting, her research is always meticulous and her natural science fascinating.

GEORGE SOELLE (*The Far-Off Land**), youthful head of a surveying party, who joins the Petrie flatboat, the *Dragonfly*, because he realizes they need another hand and because he is attracted to Ketty* Petrie. He is a steadying influence, and his knowledge of the countryside and the river are of considerable help to the travelers. Well-educated for the times, he is the mouthpiece through which the author communicates much of the information about the thinking and larger events of the period.

GEORGIE DORIAN (*The Fledgling**), eight-year-old stepdaughter of Uncle* Freddy Hall, who learns to fly from a Canada Goose and soars in nightly adventures over Walden Pond. A serious, intense child, she has long thought she could fly, if she could just get the hang of it, and she worries her family by trying off walls and stairs. She puts up with their well-meaning efforts to protect her, because she realizes the danger that her friendship has caused to the goose. Throughout, her attitude is more mature than that of most of the other characters.

GEORYN (*Enchantress from the Stars**), courageous, intelligent, perceptive young Andrecian, fourth and youngest son of a woodcutter, who sets out to slay the Imperialist Dragon* and who falls in love with Elana, a Federation agent. He is convinced that she is an enchantress who has come to Andrecia* from the stars, is inherently good, and has magical powers which she shares with him when she gives him a certain stone. Actually, Elana teaches him psychokinesis.

GERSON, CORINNE (SCHREIBSTEIN) (1927–   ), born in Allentown, Pa.; editor and free-lance writer. She received her B.A. degree from Moravian College and worked in a variety of publishing concerns before turning to free-lance work in both writing and editing. Her first novels for teenagers were full of serious timely concerns—*Like a Sister* (Funk, 1954), *The Closed Circle* (Funk, 1968), *Passing Through* (Dial, 1978), *Tread Softly* (Dial, 1979). More recently she has adopted a lighter treatment, as in *Son for a Day** (Atheneum, 1980), in which a clever boy lets himself be "adopted" for the day to ease the strain of single parents whom he picks up at the zoo, where they are trying to entertain their children, and its sequel, *Oh, Brother* (Atheneum, 1982). She has also published a novel for adults, *Choices* (Tower, 1980).

THE GHOST IN THE NOONDAY SUN (Fleischman*, Sid, ill. Warren Chappell, Little, 1965), adventure novel that takes place on the high seas and on a desert island during the days of sailing ships and pirates. Oliver Finch, 12, of Nantucket, who was born on the stroke of midnight, tells the rousing, action-filled, convoluted story. Captain Harry Scratch of the *Sweet Molly* (really *The Bloody Hand*, a pirate vessel), a brusque, evil-eyed man, shanghais Oliver, because he believes that those born at midnight can see ghosts where other people cannot. He is searching for the treasure Gentleman Jack, his former captain, buried on a remote desert island. Gentleman Jack was murdered, and his map has faded, but Captain Scratch is certain that the old pirate haunts the place where he buried his treasure, and he needs Oliver's help in locating the site. Weeks of excitement and tension follow as Oliver serves as grommet, or ship's boy, to as wicked a captain and as brazen and evil a crew of cutthroats as ever sailed the seas, among them, Hajji, a turbaned Red Sea sailor, Cannibal, a seaman from Fiji, whom the boy especially fears, and John Ringrose and Jack o'Lantern*, mates who prove friendly. A windstorm takes the lives of three men, leaving the crew, including Oliver, at thirteen hands, considered an unlucky number. Jack o'Lantern is condemned to walk the plank but is instead marooned on a desert island. He later turns up on Gentleman Jack's island, where he conspires with Ringrose, Oliver, and some others to claim the treasure. Events follow in rapid succession, with ghostly sightings, treachery, intrigue, and the arrival of Billy Bombay, another pirate, who, like Oliver, is thought to have the gift of sighting ghosts. Through reasoning, Oliver leads his friends to the treasure, three boxes overflowing with jewels and gold. They take the loot and set sail for home, leaving Captain Scratch on the island. No one benefits from the treasure, however. A bad storm disables the ship, and the crew members rescue the treasure, taking it with them in a longboat, which, ironically, capsizes under the weight. Ringrose, o'Lantern, and Oliver escape in the ship's skiff, are picked up by a passing vessel, and are returned to Nantucket. Oliver has had memorable adventures, and he is as brown as a nut from the sun. All characters are types, and events happen fast with a good measure of villainy and unexpected twists and turns laced with humor and melodramatic conflict. Some use of archaic and nautical terms adds credibility and interest. The novel echoes Stevenson's classic pirate thriller but lacks its texture and richly delineated characters. Choice.

THE GHOST OF BALLYHOOLY (Cavanna*, Betty, Morrow, 1971), detective novel set recently in Ireland. American Kristy Henderson, 16, whose father is a visiting professor of mathematics in Dublin, looks forward to spending the Christmas holidays at Ballyhooly, a seventeenth-century Irish castle. Her American grandparents have chosen this romantic old structure overlooking the Blackwater River in County Cork as the site for a pleasant reunion with Kristy's family and that of their daughter, Irene. Although Kristy and her brother, Sam, 11, find little to interest them in the village, the castle tower and grounds offer prospects for amusement and the company of their overachieving relatives assures lack of monotony. Then Sam discovers the body of Fergus O'Malley, dour caretaker and gardener, dead in the castle graveyard, and the tempo quickens. Pages about the Ballyhooly ghost torn from a book about castles in the castle library, mysterious lights at night in the presumably locked tower, gypsies camped nearby, and a man with a heavily loaded donkey strangely signaling to someone across the river are all incidents that puzzle the children. Although local tradition points to the resident ghost as the culprit, police discover that Fergus was poisoned. When a can of poison is found in Uncle Robert's room and he is arrested, Kristy and her boyfriend, Michael Curtis, 19, Dublin schoolboy who is interested in conservation and is vacationing with his aunt in a neighboring village, set about finding the murderer. Dead fish in the river, Fergus's old brown cap discovered on the bank nearby, and in his room the missing pages bearing a footnote about spurge, a plant with anesthetic qualities, and indications that a sack of spurge may have been stored in the graveyard are all clues connecting Fergus with local salmon poaching. When Kristy and Michael trap a prowler in the tower and then capture a poacher, police have what they need to unravel the mystery. In a grand climax, with everyone gathered together in the castle drawing room for the great revelation commonly found in this kind of story, the police superintendent explains that Fergus accidentally poisoned himself while attempting to use poison in poaching for fish. A straightforward, undistinguished style, a fast-moving plot with just enough complications carefully arranged to maintain interest, an appealing if unmemorable heroine, and other likeable if stock characters combine with a touch of romance, a little talk about ghosts, and a strong sense of the Irish countryside and attitudes to make for diverting if conventional detective fiction for adolescent girls. Poe Nominee.

GIAN-NAH-TAH (*Killer-of-Death**), the shaman's son with whom Killer-of-Death* has a bitter rivalry throughout most of the book. He has it in for Killer-of-Death after Killer-of-Death tricks him into following a non-existent deer trail on which Gian-nah-tah encounters a skunk. Gian-nah-tah tries to make Killer-of-Death look bad whenever he can and often casts hateful looks in his direction that set the boy on edge. As time passes, Killer-of-Death realizes that Gian-nah-tah is self-seeking, cruel, and treacherous. After the massacre, Gian-nah-tah changes very abruptly in his attitude toward Killer-of-Death. He is an unconvincing, stock character.

GIAN-PIERO (*In the Company of Clowns**), abandoned boy found by the priest of the village of Rocco, Italy, one evening in the confessional booth. The priest's housekeeper raises the boy, and the priest teaches him to read and write. When the novel begins, Gian-Piero has been working in the kitchen of the Convent of the Poor Clares, existing on scraps of food and handout clothing. Lies come easily to his lips, and he longs for the romance of faraway places. He reads books for the traveling players that he falls in with, selecting interesting quotations from the works of literary masters for them to use on stage. Eventually, he becomes uncomfortable in their zany world, where reality and unreality seem to merge and standards shift to suit the occasion. At the end, he is glad to go back to his little village. There, it is easier to tell the difference between truth and lies.

A GIFT OF MIRRORVAX (MacCloud*, Malcolm, Atheneum, 1981), science fiction set in a distant galaxy on two planets, Vax, and a planet in an identical orbit, Mirrorvax, exactly opposite so that most Vaxans have never suspected its existence. Michael* 2112439–851, a Vaxan advocacy trainee, is shocked when he is notified to report to be reauctioned, a shameful experience, but astonished when the strongest conglomerate, Transvax, bids an unprecedentedly high price for him. In Tandra, a distant province, he learns that he has been chosen to replace a recently killed astronaut on a secret mission to Mirrorvax, which Transvax hopes to colonize and control before the other conglomerates realize its existence. In his training he works with the other two astronauts, Judy, a sharp-tongued, highly intelligent scientist who resents him because of her attachment to the man he is replacing, and Jeremy, a thoughtful technician whose vocal chords have been partly removed for his criticism of Transvax. Although neither seems to share Michael's unquestioning loyalty to Transvax, they work together and travel to Mirrorvax, not without some suspicious near-tragedies to their ship, *The Arm of Transvax*. Landing in a mountainous, forested area, Judy first goes out to explore. When she does not return, Michael sets out to try to find her. He sees evidence that she has been captured and follows further than his good sense says he should, even removing his anti-bacterial filter and drinking the local water. As he leans over the canal, his weapon falls into the water and creates a tremendous explosion, knocking him backward and stunning him. He is approached by the first human he has seen, a girl named Anamandra* Amudsar, who assumes he is injured and suffering from shock and with her younger brothers helps him to her farm home. There with her mother, Katandra, Anamandra nurses him and brings two neighbors who have the Authority, a power from a God figure, to heal him of his high fever. From Transvax, he has a translating device which renders their talk intelligible to him, but he must learn slowly to speak their language. In the ensuing days, Anamandra teaches him, and, though he considers them members of an extremely primitive society, he becomes emotionally attached to her, a feeling considered beneath a true Vaxan. To his astonishment, he gets a message from Judy to return to *The Arm of Transvax* broadcast over his translator, but he persuades himself he needs more information about the local culture to give to Transvax. He is taken to the nearest town where he meets with the Revelator, Ecclesiarch Siwarth Cincura, an elderly man who explains to him that people on both planets originated on Colob, presumably Earth, but the Vaxans have forgotten Him, the God, and that he must prevent Transvax from taking over Mirrorvax and ruining it, as they have ruined Vax, and enslaving its people, as he has been enslaved. Confused and unable to accept this viewpoint, Michael runs off, returns to the Amudsar farm, sees Anamandra, and bids her a final farewell. He finds Judy and Jeremy determined not to cooperate with Transvax but to take over Mirrorvax themselves. He disarms them, forces them to seek aid from the natives, and sets out alone in *The Arm of Transvax*, planning to drive it into the sun rather than return to Vax, even though Judy has told him he was chosen for the project because he is the son of a member of the secretariat, a heredity he has never suspected, and that he would have a brilliant future if he returned. While the conception of the mirrored worlds is ingenious and Michael is better developed than protagonists of many science fiction novels, there are a number of elements that jar. Ultimately the resolution rests on accepting the religious idea that God, who is all powerful, nonetheless lets evil exist and cannot act to curb it except through the intervention of humans, an idea that is not sufficiently prepared for in the novel. There is also the question of who, in this non-belligerent culture of Mirrorvax, has been attacking Judy and Jeremy in the space ship and how, considering that they have killed a number of natives, they will fare unarmed on Mirrorvax. Christopher.

GILLY HOPKINS (*The Great Gilly Hopkins**), Galadriel, street-wise, tough, yet vulnerable eleven-year-old foster child, who defensively fends off affection and relies on her dream that her beautiful mother, whom she knows only from a photograph, will come to get her. Gilly fights, lies, steals, and terrorizes less confident children, but when her sympathies are aroused, as they are by little William* Ernest Teague, she can be surprisingly tender as well as clear headed, realizing that the boy must be given confidence, not over-mothered. Bright and independent, she tries to control her life, and when her efforts backfire, she faces the result with courage.

GIL PATRICK (*The Court of the Stone Children**), earnest, serious-minded, intellectual youth who tells Nina about the French Museum. He is working on a project about the concept of time, and he and Nina have discussions about it. Their shared interest in antiquities and in the meaning of past and present forms the basis of their friendship. He helps Nina see how the painting proves Ms. de Lombre innocent of murder.

GINESTRA (*In the Company of Clowns**), orphaned, stagestruck, Dominican novice, who runs away to join the traveling players to which Harlequin* belongs. She claims to be the illegitimate granddaughter of Count d'Ascanio-Lisci, but later she admits she made up the story to be different from the other girls in the convent. Her supposed connection is one of the reasons the Count decides to accede to Gian-Piero's* request to help the imprisoned Harlequin. Ginestra enjoys being a player, the world of make believe being more real to her than the world of reality. She is an attractive girl, bright and quick, and Gian-Piero likes her.

THE GIRL FROM PUERTO RICO (Colman*, Hila, Morrow, 1961), novel of family life set in Puerto Rico and in the Puerto Rican sector of New York City in the mid twentieth century, in which an immigrant family discovers that for them the good life lies in their home village in Puerto Rico. The story is told from the point of view of pretty, lively Felicidad Marquez, 16, who lives with her mother, father, older brother, Carlos*, 18, and younger brother, Willy, 12, on a small, productive banana farm near the little town of Barranquitas. The Marquez family is close and happy, secure in the affection and respect of relatives and neighbors. But Carlos dislikes the hard life of a farmer and yearns to emigrate to New York City, where many Puerto Ricans are going in hopes of more interesting lives and better money, and he often argues with his father about it. Felicidad has mixed feelings about moving. She longs to see the world, but she loves her village and enjoys being with steady, earnest Fernando, her sweetheart, who is quite satisfied with life as it is. After Father dies of a heart attack, the children persuade Mrs. Marquez to emigrate. In New York, they share three cramped, shabby rooms with old friends, the Esteves family. The apartment house is smelly, noisy, and rat infested. Poor as their living conditions are, they are typical for Puerto Rican immigrants. The streets are dark, dirty, and unsafe, particularly at night, when gangs of thugs roam the area. Carlos's job as a bus boy brings in too little money to support them, and Felicidad's attempts to get a well-paying job in a good restaurant fail because she is Puerto Rican. She finally takes an opening in a greasy spoon run by a countryman. Although the New York woman for whom she baby-sits, Mrs. Benton, tries to ease the culture shock for the girl and Felicidad does make friends among her co-workers, she is lonely and disappointed. Her English is poor, she feels shy and awkward, and the friendships with New Yorkers and the glamor and good times of which she dreamed do not materialize. Even Jim Duncan, handsome nephew of Mrs. Benton, does not ask her out, apparently fearing his family's disapproval, though he appears to enjoy her company. Like those of other immigrant Puerto Ricans, the Marquez family begins to splinter. Felicidad becomes more independent, makes decisions for herself, and even argues with her mother, behaving quite unlike a well-brought up Puerto Rican girl. Because her mother grows too fearful to venture outside the house, Felicidad enrolls Willy in school, and she keeps secret Willy's involvement in the Black Arrows, a street gang. After Willy is beaten and left for dead, the family decides to return to Puerto Rico. Felicidad is glad to be home and looks forward to a good life with Fernando among her familiar, friendly surroundings. The book appears to be a composite of experiences of immigrant Puerto Ricans in New York City. It remains interesting in spite of its obvious sociological intent because the central character wins sympathy. Most of the characters are types or functionaries, but Felicidad emerges as a real person, whose yearnings, fears, and joys the reader can understand and appreciate. The mother's deterioration illustrates how alien and intimidating big city life can be to her generation. The picture of life in Puerto Rico in the first half of the book establishes a firm contrast to that in New York and points up the different social and economic patterns that result in family conflict, estrangement from the church, and psychological trauma. Child Study.

GLENN KIRTLAND (*Ransom**), one of five high school youths kidnapped for ransom. Handsome, athletic, used to being the center of attention, Glenn uses people to his purposes without compunction. He has recently been involved in a hit-and-run accident in which he left the scene. Though the boy he injured is in serious condition in the hospital, Glenn feels no remorse and rationalizes his action easily to his younger brother. He is an accomplished liar and often takes credit for the positive acts of others. He is a flat character, the conceited, arrogant, rich youth.

GLEW (*The Castle of Llyr**; *The High King**), a character in the Prydain* novels. A feeble little fellow, he seeks a potion that will make him grow larger. He tries one out on a mountain cat, Llyan, who grows to the size of a horse, and then he himself grows to the size of a giant. Unfortunately, he is too large to escape from the cavern in which this happens and henceforth must make the place his home. Later he shrinks in size, then constantly mourns his lost days as a giant.

GLORIA CHISHOLM (*Fast Sam, Cool Clyde, and Stuff**), verbal, sharp-tongued fourteen-year-old, skilled at "signifying" and master of the put-down, whose misery when her father leaves home is the prime reason for the formation of The Good People. The departure of her father is especially painful because it takes place before the whole neighborhood on the street in front of the apartment house where he knocks his wife down and stalks off with Gloria futilely beating her fists on his shoulder.

GLORIA NORSTADT (*The Man Without a Face**), Charles Norstadt's obnoxious, older half-sister of seventeen. She is beautiful, intelligent, boy-crazy, and to Charles's way of thinking, thoroughly disagreeable. According to him, she has a nasty tongue and delights in degrading him before family and friends. When her boyfriend, whom Charles sarcastically calls Peerless Percy, kills Moxie, Charles's cherished pet tomcat, Charles goes berserk and attacks Percy with a baseball bat. Moxie's death helps to drive Charles quite literally into Justin's* arms and a homosexual experience. At first, Charles wants to go to St. Matthew's school mostly just to get away from Gloria. After Gloria marries Percy and Charles has been coached by Justin, Charles realizes that he really does want to attend St. Matthew's for positive academic reasons.

THE GLORIOUS CONSPIRACY (Williamson*, Joanne, Knopf, 1961), historical novel set in Manchester, England, and New York City in the late eighteenth century, culminating in the campaign which elected Jefferson president in 1800. At the age of seven, orphan Benjamin Brown, who can read and write, is apprenticed first to a cruel Liverpool cloth merchant, then to a fishmonger, but their beatings are kindness compared to the mill in Manchester where he at eleven and his Aunt Betty go to escape the workhouse when his cobbler grandfather dies. In Arkwright's mill, children as young as four years old are worked fourteen hours a day for only board and room—poor-quality, meager food and a squalid loft. For two years Ben slaves there under a brutal foreman named Thomas Earnshaw*, who is slightly less cruel to him because he has taken a fancy to Aunt Bet. Two other children, a red-haired girl named Nanny and a spirited boy, Noah Harkness, seem to be survivors and become Ben's friends, but Noah, whose father is arrested for being a union member, is badly beaten by Earnshaw and dies of "factory fever." The epidemic spreads, and Aunt Bet also dies, but only after extracting a promise that Earnshaw will be good to Ben. He fulfills this by more frequent blows and kicks but also by including Ben, now thirteen, in an illegal scheme of SUM, the American Society for Useful Manufactures, to lure skilled workers from English mills to start similar factories in the new United States. On the ship Ben meets an Irish girl his age, Eily Conneely, also sent to train children for factory work at Paterson. After being checked in by a young gentleman who is eager to make "women and children productive" (later identified as Alexander Hamilton), Ben escapes, heads for New York, and nearly starves on the road, though helped and hindered in various encounters along the way. At the edge of New York and of his strength, he is rescued by a young Frenchman, Monsieur Jean* Pierre Vinard, a musician, then fed and cleaned up. A friend of Vinard, William Mooney, finds him a job on the anti-Tory newspaper of Thomas Greenleaf. Jean Pierre, with whom he lives, teaches him manners, good English, and insists that he save money to repay SUM for his passage. At a political rally, Ben prevents a heckler from throwing a stone at Hamilton. When the man turns on him, he is assisted by two boys his age, who later are identified as Philip Hamilton and Troup Van Wyck, and through Troup

Ben meets (and falls in hopeless love with) Theodosia, intellectual daughter of Aaron Burr. Some friends of Jean Pierre pay a tutor to teach Ben Latin, and later an anonymous donor arranges that he attend Columbia College. Just as all is going well, he meets and is blackmailed by Earnshaw, now a hoodlum hired to intimidate voters at the polls. When yellow fever hits the city, Troup dies and so does Mr. Greenleaf. Jean Pierre becomes very ill, and Philip Hamilton helps Ben nurse him. The Alien and Sedition Laws threaten Ben and get Greenleaf's successor, David Frothingham, arrested, imprisoned, and heavily fined. This leads Ben to join the Bucktails, the Tammany group working for Jefferson's election. The brilliant Bucktail plan, the Glorious Conspiracy promoted by Aaron Burr, is to circumvent the requirement that a voter must have £100 worth of property by a little-known law stating that a piece of a freehold worth £100 is sufficient. Therefore, they buy into each other's property, until each has a vote. When Ben discovers that it is Burr who has been paying for his education, he agrees to spy for the Tammany society. At a Hamilton party, he finds a list revealing a plan for Hamilton to defeat Adams. As he is copying the list, he is interrupted by a maid, who turns out to be Eily Conneely. Eily tells him that SUM went broke, and she helps him get away with the list that makes a Democratic victory possible. In the meantime, Jean Pierre's past is catching up with him in the form of a French Marquis, who is using Earnshaw as his thug to settle an old grudge. When Jean Pierre disappears, Eily takes Ben to the filthy abandoned building where her family lives and Earnshaw occasionally comes and through her brother they find Jean Pierre badly beaten. He recovers, Ben asks Eily to marry him, and she refuses. The plot contains several unlikely coincidences, but the events are mostly convincing, and the actual historical figures are introduced in believable and natural ways. Best is the setting, the grim scenes in the mill and the filthy alleys of New York. Also strong is the evocation of Ben's emotions, his fear and helpless fury at injustices, his pride in his own worth, and his shame at realizing that he has all but forgotten Eily. Fanfare.

GO ASK ALICE (Anonymous, Prentice, 1971), realistic fiction set in the late 1960s in several California and Oregon locations. Supposedly based on a real diary of a young drug user, it is written in entries dated from just before Alice's fifteenth birthday to shortly after her sixteenth. When her professor father becomes Dean of Political Science at another university, the family moves to a new town, and the parents and younger siblings all settle in quickly, but Alice is lonely and feels awkward in her new school. During summer vacation she goes back to her original town to stay with her grandparents and is thrilled when Jill, a girl from a high-status crowd, asks her to a party. There she innocently drinks a coke laced with LSD, an experience she finds thrilling, and Bill, a boy she has met there, soon introduces her to speed and seduces her. Back at home she tells herself she is off drugs for good but is so worried at the possibility of pregnancy that she starts taking sleeping pills. She is depressed, but a new friend, Chris, gives her other drugs and introduces her to Richie, a college student, who soon has her selling drugs even to grade school youngsters. When she and Chris find Richie and Chris's boyfriend making love to each other, they are disillusioned and angry and decide to run off to San Francisco. There Chris gets a job in a boutique run by a very sophisticated woman who invites them to parties where she introduces them to heroin, and she and her boyfriend rape them repeatedly. The girls flee to Berkeley, where they start a small jewelry shop and get along fairly well until, as Christmas approaches, they get homesick, call their parents, and go home. At first all goes well in the forgiving atmosphere, but Chris turns back to drugs and takes Alice with her. Next time she is able to get high, Alice walks out and hitchhikes to Denver. From there she drifts in a drugged haze to Coos Bay, Oreg., then to Southern California, living by begging, mooching, and prostitution. Eventually she talks to an old priest who contacts her parents, and she goes home and is again welcomed by her family, including her grandparents. She starts a new diary and a new life, determined to break with her past, but she suffers flashback hallucinations and pressure from her former friends at school to start using drugs again. The death of her grandfather and, shortly after, her grandmother, depresses her, but she sticks to her resolutions, even though she incurs actual hostility from her former friends, particularly Jan and Marcie. At the university library, she meets Joel Reems, a straight young student who offers her decent friendship and hope. Just as she seems to be making good, she eats chocolate-covered peanuts laced with LSD, planted evidently by Jan, has a terrible trip, injures herself, and is arrested when Jan and Marcie both testify that she has tried to sell them drugs at school. When she gets out of the hospital she is sent to the Youth Center at the State Mental Hospital, where she suffers emotionally. Her father, trusting her innocence in her last LSD encounter, pressures Jan to retract her testimony, and Alice is released. The family goes to New York for a couple of weeks, and Alice has time to adjust a bit. Back at home, she seems to be accepted by a respectable group at school and is supported by Joel's confidence in her. An epilogue says she died three weeks later of a drug overdose. Although the book professes to be "based on" a real diary, it has clearly been written at least in part by an adult mimicking the language of an adolescent. The entries, particularly when Alice has disintegrated and is heavily under the influence of drugs, are too coherent to be convincing. The sudden change from the hopeful ending to the epilogue seems manipulated for shock effect, and the long case histories of some of Alice's acquaintances appear to be the result of research, not the girl's genuine diary. Unlike many novels dealing with drugs, however, the story has the honesty to describe their real attraction and to treat the parents as intelligent and supportive. Maxi.

THE GOLDEN GOBLET (McGraw*†, Eloise Jarvis, Coward, 1961), historical novel set in ancient Egypt. Before the death of his goldsmith father, Ranofer, about thirteen, had aspired to be a pupil of Zau, the greatest goldworker in Thebes, but his half-brother, brutal Gebu, a stonemason, who beats and starves him, has put him to work as a porter in the shop of Rekh. There, at least, he is able to watch beautiful things being made of gold, but he is troubled by being forced to carry wineskins from the Babylonian porter, Ibni, to Gebu, wineskins which he ralizes must contain the gold which has been missing from the shop. He enlists the help of the new apprentice, Heqet, to tell Rekh, but the maneuver backfires when Ibni is fired and Gebu, no longer needing a messenger, puts Ranofer to work as apprentice in his stone-cutting business. After finding a golden goblet of antique design in his half-brother's clothes chest, Ranofer suspects that Gebu and his sinister confederate, Wenamon the mason, are robbing tombs, and he and Heqet, joined by an old reedcutter known as the Ancient, start spying on the pair, but they cannot find proof until the day of the great festival of the rising of the Nile, when all Thebes has crossed the river for feasting. Ranofer follows Gebu and Wenamon to the City of the Dead, where they roll aside a stone and enter a passage leading to a tomb. Ranofer realizes that they have constructed this special passage when they built the tomb and that it must be the tomb of the queen's parents. Outraged at this desecration, he follows them and accidentally attracts their attention by breaking a vase. In a wild chase, he escapes and traps them by rolling the stone back over the entrance, and Heqet and the Ancient appear just in time to keep the stone in place while he goes for help. Since almost all Thebans are at the festival, Ranofer runs to the palace, climbs over the wall, and is chased by the guards but is able to tell his story to the queen's dwarf, who takes him before the queen herself. She rewards him with a donkey so that he will be able to earn his living cutting reeds like the Ancient and become a pupil of Zau. The picture of an unfamiliar culture is interesting, and Ranofer is an appealing character, terrified by Gebu and conscience stricken at being involved in the robberies, but intelligent and steadfast in his ambition to become a goldworker. The story is fast paced and plausible. Fanfare; Newbery Honor.

GOLDEN PELEDRYN (*The Book of Three**; *The Black Cauldron**; *The Castle of Llyr**; *Taran Wanderer**; *The High King**), Eilonwy's* golden bauble in the Prydain* books. A golden ball of great power, it shines for the bearer when he acts unselfishly. Its light brings out the magical markings in the book belonging to the House of Llyr that was found by Taran* in Glew's* hut.

THE GOLDEN TOUCH (Johnson*†, Annabel, and Edgar Johnson*†, Harper, 1963), mystery-adventure novel set in 1900 in the gold fields west of Denver, in which the gold rush plays an important part in the story. Andy Brett, 12, leaves Kansas, where he has been living with his Grandpa, to join the father he scarcely knows in the mining town of Black Hawk. He arrives to find that his father, Will, is a gambler and is being run out of town for cheating at cards. Since Will is a tall, grim, taciturn man, Andy is more attracted to his uncle, Will's younger brother, genial, pudgy, facile-tongued Hep, who, according to Will, knows everything there is to know about gold. The three travel on by train, until they come to the town of Victor in the Cripple Creek goldfields. Andy takes quite literally his former teacher's remark that he has a golden touch and looks forward to striking it rich. Will and Hep look for jobs unsuccessfully, and Hep makes plans to send Andy back east, while Andy restlessly prowls the streets against Will's orders. On his meanderings, Andy encounters a melancholy old miner, wealthy Misery Jones, who offers to share his home with the wandering trio, and also Remi and Josey, a French brother and sister, who own a mine, the Sidewinder, that they are unable to work by themselves. Will, Hep, and Misery agree to work the mine on shares. Soon Andy adds Adeline, a disillusioned, good-hearted, dancehall girl to their household as cook. The Sidewinder proves highly profitable, and all debts are soon paid off. Then Remi discovers that gold is mysteriously disappearing. It seems that one of their group is stealing from the others. Suspicion points toward Will, who has been trailed to Victor by Duke Dade, sheriff of Black Hawk, the town from which Will was expelled. Things so fall out that Andy discovers that Hep, who sets the blasting charges in the Sidewinder, has been "highgrading," that is, removing the best ore during the night. The book reaches its climax when Hep deliberately sets off a charge that traps Andy and Will in the mine. Andy finds a way out, and Hep is captured by Dade, who turns out to be Will's friend. All along the personable Hep has been committing illegal acts and putting the blame on the less likeable Will. Hep is sent to prison, Misery and Adeline turn Misery's big, old place into a boarding house, Remi and Josey return to France, and Will and Andy, who have come to like and admire each other, decide it is time to leave and seek a permanent home elsewhere. The plot grips immediately and moves with careful pacing through a series of well-conceived twists, turns, and red herrings that keep the reader, as well as Andy, guessing about who wears the black and white hats. The characters though flat are an interesting assemblage, and there is just enough detail about mining procedures and life in mining towns to ground the story in reality. On the whole, the novel works well and is better than average for its genre. Fanfare.

THE GOOBER (*The Chocolate War**), Roland Goubert, the nearest thing to a friend Jerry Renault has at Trinity High School. A runner by choice, Goober is pass receiver at football practice with Jerry. Disturbed by his own part in the Vigil* assignment that leads to Brother Eugene's nervous collapse, Goober quits football, deciding not to be manipulated by the school any further. He even stops selling chocolates but does not have courage to protest when the Vigil sales are ascribed to him so that his quota seems to have been fulfilled. When he sees Jerry being brutally beaten in the rigged fight organized by the Vigils, he protests but can't make himself heard. He alone stays with Jerry until the ambulance comes, and it is to him that badly injured Jerry tries to give the advice not to buck the system. As a foil to Jerry, he represents the well-intentioned person who opts out, refusing to aid or to fight the corrupt forces which Jerry stands up against, and though he survives, as Jerry may not, it is only the evil characters who are winners.

GOOD NELLIE (*I, Adam**), Captain Crane's whaling ship. The name also applies to a small replica of the whaler, one that Captain Crane carved in scrimshaw when he was a boy on his very first voyage and feeling homesick and disgusted with life. Adam takes the little *Nellie* with him to the Sharkey farm. It symbolizes for him courage and perseverance, and it is a reminder, too, of his father's faith in him.

GOODY HALL (Babbitt*, Natalie, ill. author, Farrar, 1971), light mystery novel set in the nineteenth century in a village some one hundred miles south of the imaginary town of Hackston Fen. Plagued with a heroic name and a mother who expects him to live up to it, Hercules Feltwright has left home, tried being a wandering actor, and at twenty-five applies to be tutor at Goody Hall, a pretentiously overdecorated house occupied by a widow and her son, Willet. The housekeeper, Mrs. Dora Tidings, the blacksmith's sister, is intensely curious about the strange doings at the hall, particularly the mysterious trips to the city Mrs. Goody takes twice a year, from which she returns with no packages or new clothes. Willet, immediately attracted to Hercules, confides that he believes his father is not dead and buried in the family tomb at the back of the garden, and this starts Hercules on a search for the truth. His inquiry takes him to the home of the gypsy gardener, Alfresco Rom, who is tight mouthed, but the gardener's daughter, Alfreida, who helps out at the hall, is more cooperative. She holds a seance, at which the spirit of Shakespeare chides Hercules for his frequent misquotations, but the contact denies that Midas Goody has yet "crossed over." To test this, Hercules dresses up as Mott Snave, a Robin Hood figure from Hackston Fen, sneaks into the tomb, and finds that the coffin contains not a body but a silver statue of Cerberus. As he returns to the house he sees, to his astonishment, another Mott Snave in the yard. Faced with the information about the coffin, Alfresco confesses that to escape Goody Hall, which he hated, Midas Goody traded places with a thief who was thrown from a horse and killed, and that Willet's mother gave the gardener a diamond to keep quiet. The mystery is unravelled when Mott Snave climbs through the window, returning from a five-year jail term for stealing, and reveals that he is the supposed Midas Goody, but he is really John Constant, a farmer of Hackston Fen. Willet, his parents, and Hercules leave to return to their old home. Mrs. Tidings and the hall are both fired. The story is self-consciously clever, with Hercules's misquotations ("To thine own self renew, and it must follow, as the knight the doe, thou cans't not then befall to any man") and with the contrived mystery, but it is good fun: Since none of it is meant to be taken seriously, the theme that wealth does not bring happiness is rather heavy handed at the ending. Poe Nominee.

GORDON (*The Unmaking of Rabbit**), grandson of Bess* Tuttle, who is the best friend of Emma*, Paul's grandmother. Gordon's parents push him into activities he really does not enjoy, such as tennis. Mrs. Tuttle praises him so highly to Paul and Emma for what she feels are his great accomplishments that Paul is reluctant to have anything to do with him when he comes to visit and only agrees to associate with him out of duty and respect to his grandmother. Gordon proves to be an "average guy," however, who likes quiet activities as Paul does, and the two become good friends. The prospect of continued friendship with Gordon makes it easier for Paul to stand up to the school bully.

GORO (*Of Nightingales That Weep**), stepfather and later husband of Takiko. A potter, Goro makes beautiful things with his hands but is himself ugly, short with a heavy chest and long arms like an ape. He is, however, kindly and sensitive, patient with Takiko when she finds him frightening and repulsive at first, and drawn to her music even when he blames her, with some reason, for the death of her mother and brother, whom he loved. He represents the genuine good in life, as opposed to the shallow, artificial, and lecherous men of the court.

GOTTFRIED ELEND (*Darkness over the Land**), Mark's older brother, who is preparing to become a priest. Although he has no sympathy for the Nazi cause, he serves in the German army against the Russians when he is drafted. Before the book begins, he is in Poland when the Germans invade that country and finds Mark at the seminary of his order there, homeless, orphaned, and in shock, and brings the boy back with him to Munich, where the Elends raise Mark as their own son but never tell him about his background. Throughout the book, the Elends are afraid that the authorities may discover that Mark is not German and take him away from them. At the end, Gottfried decides to abandon his ambition of becoming a priest and return to the university to study to become a historian. He intends to work for a better Germany in the post-war period.

GRAHAM, GAIL American author of books for children and young people about the Far East. She has lived and worked in Vietnam, and the story of how she was captured by and escaped from the Viet Cong during the Vietnam War was read into the Congressional Record. Her novel *Cross-Fire** (Pantheon, 1972), a Fanfare book, grew out of her experiences there. Earlier she wrote *The Little Brown Gazelle* (Dial, 1968), a picture-book story of the jungle, and compiled a collection of folktales, *The Beggar in the Blanket and Other Vietnamese Tales* (Dial, 1970), which includes an Oriental version of the Cinderella story. She has made her home in Australia with her husband and her family and has contributed frequently to magazines.

GRAHAM†, LORENZ (BELL) (1902–   ), born in New Orleans, La.; teacher and social worker, whose stories of the black experience have been widely commended. He attended the University of Washington, Seattle, and the University of California, Los Angeles, and received his B.A. degree from Virginia Union College, Richmond. He also did graduate work at Columbia University and New York University. From 1924 to 1929 he was a teacher in Monrovia College, Liberia, the setting for his novel, *I, Momolu** (Crowell, 1966). From this experience he also wrote *How God Fix Jonah* (Reynolds, 1946), a collection of Bible stories told as if by the African, which were more recently reprinted as picture books, *David He No Fear* (Crowell, 1971), *God Wash the World and Start Again* (Crowell, 1971), etc. Between 1930 and 1942 he worked for the Richmond Adult Schools and was Educational Director for the Civilian Conservation Corps in Virginia and Pennsylvania. Later he worked as a housing authority manager and a real estate salesman and building contractor. In the 1950s and 1960s he was a social worker in Queens and a probation officer in Los Angeles County. Of at least ten novels, his best known are *South Town†* (Follett, 1957), *North Town* (Crowell, 1965), *Whose Town?†* (Crowell, 1969), and *Return to South Town* (Crowell, 1976), a series about a black family which copes with prejudice in the segregated South and the bigoted North and whose son returns to a changed and hopeful but still imperfect South.

GRANDFATHER, ELDER (*Time and Mr. Bass**), ancestor of Mr. Tyco* Bass and founder of the Mycetian* League of spore people in the time of Uther Pendragon in fifth-century Britain. He trained Mycetians to serve as spies and messengers for the Britons because the spore people are small and quick. He was the Royal Bard to both Uther Pendragon and Arthur, and, because he possessed second sight, was also their advisor. His great opponent was Narrow Brain, personification of evil. Elder Grandfather wrote the Mycetian scrolls, which tell how Narrow Brain can be defeated. He and Tyco Bass, his descendant, are the only two Mycetians able to travel by thought transference. He appears several times to Tyco in visions.

GRANDFATHER DAVID RENTEMA (*Journey from Peppermint Street**), maternal grandfather who takes Siebren on his first trip away from his village in the Netherlands. As they walk through the countryside and the marsh in the dark, he seems to Siebren unpredictable and changeable, sometimes the stern church elder, sometimes willing to joke, sometimes oblivious to the boy or irritated by him, at other times kindly and understanding. The reader can realize that he is worried about his dying sister and unused to traveling with a young child, and that his every variation of tone is exaggerated by the sensitive and imaginative boy.

GRANDFATHER LARKIN (*Henry 3**), Fletcher's* grandfather. Mr. Larkin owns the big mansion, the biggest house in town, in which he and Fletcher live by themselves. He formerly owned the land on which the suburb of Crestview has been built. An eccentric, outspoken man of strong convictions and substantial means and the most unpopular man in Crestview, he has been waging a long-standing battle at law against the development company to which he sold the land and which he thought would use the property for a farm. Grandfather Larkin continues to hope that the houses will be razed and the land put into potatoes. When Fletcher takes Henry to meet his grandfather, the old man expresses the opinion that people put too much emphasis on security and style and are blind to the real values in life. After he dies during the hurricane trying to save his cherished old oak, Fletcher comes into his property. The boy finally decides to drop the suit and allow Crestview to remain as it is, to everyone's relief. Grandfather Larkin and Fletcher have a fine relationship.

GRANDMA BEEBE (*Misty of Chincoteague†*; *Stormy, Misty's Foal**), grandmother of Paul* and Maureen*. She is a home-loving lady, who protests, but never very strongly, interruptions to her normal routine of taking care of house and family. Although in *Stormy* she objects to being moved out of her kitchen so that Misty can stay there and she dislikes the idea of being airlifted to the mainland, she takes the inconveniences of the flood in good part when she realizes there is no acceptable alternative. She is a typical, loving grandmother.

GRANDMA DIDN'T WAVE BACK (Blue*, Rose, Ill. Ted Lewin, Watts, 1972), sociological problem novel for younger children set in a coastal city in contemporary times. Debbie, 10, enjoys having her grandmother, Mrs. Green, live in their city apartment, as she has since the death of Grandpa. Grandma cooks, cares for Debbie while her lawyer mother works, tells Debbie about her beautiful things that came from her girlhood in Europe, and welcomes Debbie's friends. Then Grandma begins to have days when she forgets, calls Debbie "Helen," her mother's name, seems to think she is a girl again. Sometimes, when Debbie waves from the corner as she returns from school, there is no answering wave from the terrace or Grandma's window, and she knows that this will be a confused day for Grandma. Debbie's aunts and uncles come and quarrel about who should take care of their mother and scare Debbie by suggesting that they should "put her away" in a nursing home. Debbie's friends begin to avoid the apartment, and nasty Jennifer calls Grandma crazy. One night a neighbor finds Grandma wandering in the street in her nightgown. Soon after, Debbie returns from school to find that Grandma has been taken to the Shore Nursing Home. She insists on going alone to visit, taking Grandma's clock and some of her favorite things with her. She finds Grandma contented, though weary, and when she leaves, Grandma waves to her from the window. The book is clearly didactic, written to illustrate the thesis that growing old is part of life and should not be feared. The Jewish grandmother has some individuality; the other characters are stock types. The style is deliberately simple, designed to be read by children Debbie's age or younger. Choice.

GRANDMA ELLEN PAYSON (*Come By Here**), Minty Lou's paternal grandmother who takes her in to get the insurance money when her son and his wife are killed, and who abuses the child. Even before the death of Minty Lou's parents, Grandma Payson has resented her daughter-in-law, Lou, who has a nicer apartment and keeps the little girl in pretty, clean, starched dresses. Grandma spoils her own youngest, Gordie, and lets him and his brothers bully Minty Lou. She neglects to send word to Lou's parents of their daughter's death, afraid that they may claim the money. Although they are very crowded and Minty Lou must sleep on the floor, Grandma Payson keeps the parlor closed and is enraged when she finds that the little girl has been sitting there to get away from the tormenting boys. Grandma's meanness and grasping, it is clear, come partly from the poverty she lives in and the hard life she has led.

GRANDMA ENFIELD (*The Griffin Legacy**), Louise Enfield, Amy* Enfield's grandmother, a plump, solid, warmhearted woman. She is motherly and loving, and Amy enjoys being with her. She takes loving care of imperious Aunt* Matilda, who had raised her. While she is in the cellar getting together jars of preserves to sell at the church heritage fair, she ironically shows Amy the tarnished cup and plate that turn out to be the lost communion silver, hidden there by Lucy* Griffin many years before, in a place so obvious that no one suspected.

GRANDMA LETTY STERN (*Before the Lark**), Letitia, grandmother of Jocey* Royal, a young girl who suffers psychologically from having a harelip in the days when such disfigurement was considered the will of God. Grandma Letty has been ill, and Jocey has had to take over her laundry in Kansas City of the 1880s, but as the story progresses she becomes well again yet continues to play the invalid and to demand care and service, because it is the first time in her hard life that she has been pampered. It is her knowledge of farm work, however, that makes it possible for Jocey to succeed, and it is her precious "burying money," with which she dreams of a fancy funeral, that pays the back taxes on the farm.

GRANDMA LEVIN (*Mom, the Wolf Man and Me**), Brett Levin's conventional grandmother, who quizzes Brett about what Deborah*, her daughter and Brett's mother, does and whom she sees. She thinks Deborah should adhere to accepted mores and is a rather fussy person.

GRANDMA LOUISE BRADSHAW (*Jacob Have I Loved**), Bible-reading, vindictive, old grandmother of the twins, Caroline* and (Sara) Louise*. Since she lives with her son and his family on tiny Rass Island and, fearing the water, will not even ride the ferry, she is virtually a prisoner in the strict, Methodist community. As her mind gradually deteriorates, she becomes obsessed with sex, first taunting her granddaughter, Louise, with the attraction the girl cannot hide to Captain* Hiram Wallace, a man older than the grandmother, then accusing him of wanting to share her own bed and of killing his wife with the help of Louise. As she becomes more senile, she denounces her long-suffering daughter-in-law as a whore and bombards her with appropriate biblical passages. A thoroughly disagreeable woman, she still has a tender moment when she admits that she had a childhood crush on the Captain and grieved when he left the island without returning her love.

GRANDMA SIMON (*Are You There God? It's Me, Margaret.**), Sylvia Simon, Margaret's Jewish grandmother, whose company Margaret thoroughly enjoys. Grandma Simon feels that Margaret's parents' decision to allow their daughter to choose her own religion is not wise. At the end of the book, in a communication to her teacher, Margaret expresses a concurring opinion: that parents should pass along to their children one faith about which the children can become knowledgeable. Grandma Simon changes hair color frequently, enjoys Florida and delicatessens, takes her granddaughter to such places as Lincoln Center, is relaxed about rules, and at the end visits the Simons with a prospective husband in tow. Although her character lacks depth and is tinged with the eccentric for effect, she is one of the most interesting people in the novel.

GRANDPA BEEBE (*Misty of Chincoteague†*; *Stormy, Misty's Foal**), one of the Chincoteague islanders, on whose horse farm Paul* and Maureen* Beebe are staying. He is their grandfather. In *Misty*, he agrees reluctantly to their plan to buy Phantom, not because he does not want them to have the horse, but because he feels that they will be disappointed when Phantom, which always eludes pursuit, is not caught in this year's pony drive either. He is generally very supportive of their plans, however, and on the night of the big storm, he moves Phantom and her foal inside his truck, so they will stay warm and dry. Paul is very grateful when he discovers what Grandpa has done and spends the night there with the horses. Grandpa Beebe is a practical, plainspoken man. He has a strong sense of community, and in *Stormy*, particularly, he works very hard along with his neighbors and the Coast Guard to get the island back in shape after the storm. He often teases Grandma* Beebe and good-heartedly tries to please her. Grandpa Beebe is a good family man, warm and caring, a typical grandfather.

GRANDPA LEVIN (*Mom, the Wolf Man and Me**), Brett Levin's imaginative, fun-loving grandfather, a psychoanalyst. He likes to play pretend games with Brett. They make believe he is a Mr. Jones who keeps an alligator in his bathtub. He and Brett both love "b, b, and c," bread, butter, and caviar. During the story, he has a very serious operation. After he recovers, he and Grandma*

Levin decide to move to Arizona. At book's end, Deborah*, Theo, and Brett are thinking of moving there, too.

GRAY DOWNS (*The Spring Rider**), pretty, dreamy sister of Jacob. Although she has been waiting for a man to appear and "carry her off" from her mountain farm home, she insists that the man who appears, Hannibal* Cutler, stay alive in her time and is not willing to join him as one of the dead who come back each spring to refight a Civil War battle. Her conversations with Lincoln, the Spring Rider, go from innocence to awareness as the story progresses.

GREAT-AUNT KATE (*The High Pasture**), seventy-year-old rancher, somewhat eccentric but respected and loved by her neighbors. She dresses in puttees, breeches, and moccasins, and she wears a lacy shawl to cover the hump on her back. She homesteaded her 640 acres herself, raising the cattle, breaking the horses, and dealing with thieves. She still runs the ranch with authority, though she has hired others to do the heavy work. The way she handles the loss of Mac, her loyal, old cattledog, helps Tim to deal with his mother's death. The character of Aunt Kate holds possibilities which the author never exploits. Static as she is, she is still the only interesting character in the book.

THE GREAT BRAIN (Fitzgerald*, John D., ill. Mercer Mayer, Dial, 1967), first of a series of humorous episodic books about the three Fitzgerald brothers, members of the Catholic minority in Mormon Utah in the 1890s. Narrated by the youngest, John D., 7, the book stars his brother Tom, 10, a junior con-man skilled in manipulating not only his peers but frequently the adults in their southwestern Utah town of Adenville. When their father, editor of the Adenville *Weekly Advocate*, installs the first indoor toilet in town, Tom charges kids one cent a look, employing John as a barker to drum up trade. This scam backfires because his mother makes him repay his earnings, but when two friends and their dog are lost in a nearby cave, Tom wins the town's applause by figuring out how to find them; he knows their dog is in heat and he uses John's dog to follow the trail. His ulterior motive is later disclosed when he sells the puppy which is his share of the litter to a rancher. Tom takes Basil Kokovinis, the new boy from Greece, under his wing, teaching him American games and how to beat up the bully, Sammy Leads, and is well paid for it by Basil's father. He figures out a way to get rid of the unpopular new male teacher who has paddled him unjustly. With the help of all the non-Mormon boys in the school, each of whom swipes an ounce or two from his father's liquor, he plants nearly empty whiskey bottles in the teacher's room and coat pocket, then alerts the school board with an anonymous letter. His father, however, points out the unjustness of this sort of attack, and Tom goes with him to the board meeting, confesses his part, and negotiates so the teacher is reinstated. He modifies his discipline, and Tom ends a hero to adults and children alike. His major accomplishment is inspired by his desire for an erector set, bought for Andy Anderson by his father after Andy's leg is amputated. Andy, despondent when he can't play games, overhears his father saying he is useless and enlists John's help to commit suicide. John tries unsuccessfully to help him drown and to hang himself; then Tom takes over, analyzes Andy's problems, and teaches him to play games, run, and do chores despite his peg leg, generously allowing him to do the Fitzgerald chores for practice. Andy's gratitude is so moving, even to Tom, that he refuses to accept the erector set and turns over a new leaf to use his great brain for less selfish ends. Other episodes include the time when the boys, including Sweyn, 12, all get measles, then mumps, and when the Jewish peddler, Abie Glassman, persuaded by their father to start a variety store, dies of malnutrition, too proud to ask for help. Much of the humor of the book comes from John's innocent admiration of his crafty brother's great brain, even when he is the victim. Though exaggerated, the incidents are all possible and have a genuine feel of the period. Sequels. Books Too Good.

THE GREAT GILLY HOPKINS (Paterson*, Katherine, Crowell, 1978), realistic problem novel set in contemporary eastern United States. Bright, tough Gilly* (Galadriel) Hopkins, 11, is determined to dominate in her new foster home, as she has in the others where her social worker, Miss Ellis, has placed her, but none of the others have been like this. In spite of her determination to keep emotionally aloof, Gilly soon finds herself becoming attached to the elephantine Maime* Trotter, the new foster mother, little William* Ernest Teague, a frightened foster son Maime defends vigorously, and Mr.* Randolph, a blind old black neighbor who eats with them, and even Miss Harris, her cool black teacher. She clings, however, to her dream that her beautiful mother, Courtney Rutherford Hopkins, will come from California to get her. When she finds some money in Mr. Randolph's house, she takes another $100 from Mrs. Trotter's purse but is apprehended at the bus depot by the police and taken back with love by Mrs. Trotter and William Ernest. In a last gesture of defiance, she writes to her mother, describing the foster home in the worst possible light, but forgets the letter as she is caught up in caring for the others when they have flu. With the house in disarray, she is astonished to have a woman come to the door announcing herself as Gilly's grandmother, Mrs. Rutherford Hopkins of Loudoun County, Va., who has never known of Gilly's existence but has been alerted by Courtney to go claim the child. Although Gilly resists, she must go with her grandmother, but her disillusion is complete when Courtney comes from California for a visit and proves to be not the beautiful queen of Gilly's dreams but a resentful, gone-to-seed ex-hippy. Gilly calls Maime Trotter, who gives her courage to face the truth and continue life with her grandmother. Gilly's streetwise, tough veneer combines with her vulnerable sensitivity to make a memorable characterization which escapes sentimentality. Although the theme of the importance of love, rather than blood ties, in making a family is obvious, it is not belabored, and while the group in the foster home seem selected to represent extreme types, they are made to seem real rather than grotesque. Fanfare; National Book Winner; Newbery Honor.

GREENE, BETTE (1934–   ), born in Memphis, Tenn.; writer who gained prominence in children's literature for her first novel for adolescents, *Summer of My German Soldier** (Dial, 1973), about an alienated southern Jewish girl who harbors an escaped German prisoner-of-war during World War II. Autobiographical in broad outline, a finalist for the National Book Award, it was praised as absorbing by some and criticized by others for its unconvincing soldier and excessive melodrama. The comparatively light *Philip Hall Likes Me. I Reckon Maybe.** (Dial, 1974) follows an eleven-year-old girl's attachment to her classmate, was a Newbery Honor book, and is cited in *Choice*. Each has a sequel: *Morning Is a Long Time Coming* (Dial, 1978) and *Get on out of here, Philip Hall* (Dial, 1981). More recently she has published *Them That Glitter and Them That Don't* (Knopf, 1983), about a small town Arkansas high school girl who aspires despite great obstacles to a career as a country-western singer. The daughter of a merchant, Greene grew up in a small town in the Arkansas Delta where she felt isolated by her Jewish religion. She attended the University of Alabama, Memphis State University, and Columbia University, married a physician, and has made her home in Massachusetts. She has been a reporter for the Memphis *Commercial Appeal* and public information officer for the American Red Cross in Memphis and for the Boston State Psychiatric Hospital. She has also published books for adults.

GREENE, CONSTANCE (CLARKE) (1924–   ), born in New York City; author of contemporary problem novels for adolescents. She was born into a newspaper family, her father an editor and her mother a writer. After attending Marymount Academy and Skidmore College, she worked for several years for Associated Press, realizing a long-held ambition to be a newspaperwoman. After two years with A.P., she married, to return to writing after her five children were almost grown. Her novels approach with wit, vitality, and unhackneyed prose the problems of modern family life from the standpoint of often eccentric and quirky young protagonists who associate with unconventional people. The plots are entertaining and fast moving but often seem contrived for sensation. *The Unmaking of Rabbit** (Viking, 1972), about a boy with a poor self-image, is cited in *Choice*. Her first book, *A Girl Called Al* (Viking, 1969), was a runner-up in the *Book World* Spring Book Festival of 1969 and was an American Library Association Notable Book. Al's activities continue in *I Know You, Al* (Viking, 1975), *Your Old Pal, Al* (Viking, 1979), and *Al(exandra) the Great* (Viking, 1982). *Beat the Turtle Drum* (Viking, 1976), which focuses on death, evolved from the remembered experience of her own thirteen-year-old sister's death when she was eleven. Other titles include *I and Sproggy* (Viking, 1978), *Double-Dare O'Toole* (Viking, 1981), and *Ask Anybody* (Viking, 1983). After living in

Connecticut for several years, she moved to Maine where her husband became owner of a radio station.

GREENFIELD, ELOISE (1929–   ), writer of biographies and books of the contemporary black experience for children. Of her several picture books, *She Come Bringing Me That Little Baby Girl* (Lippincott, 1974), received the Irma Simonton Black Award. Her book of poetry, *Honey, I Love* (Crowell, 1978), was an American Library Association Notable Book, and her episodic novel, *Sister** (Crowell, 1974), has been selected by *Choice*. She has also written biographies of such eminent blacks as Mary McLeod Bethune and Rosa Parks and received the Jane Addams Award for her book about Paul Robeson. She has published *Talk About a Family* (Lippincott, 1978), another novel of contemporary family life, *Daydreams* (Dial, 1981), another book of poems for children, and has contributed to Scholastic Book Services and to many magazines and journals. She was born in Parmalee, N.C., and attended Miner Teachers College. She married Robert Greenfield, a procurement specialist, and has made her home in Washington, D.C. She has been a clerk typist and patent assistant, a case control technician in the Work and Training Opportunity Center, and administrative assistant in the Department of Occupations and Professions. She co-directed a section on writing adult fiction and was director of children's literature for the District of Columbia Black Writer's Workshop and writer-in-residence with the District of Columbia Commission on the Arts.

GREG REDFERN (*A Room Made of Windows**; *Julia and the Hand of God**), older brother of Julia. He is deeply interested in learning about ancient Egypt and spends all his spare time reading books and completing self-appointed tasks on the subject. He bears a remarkable resemblance to a certain pharaoh. After he accuses Julia of selfishness, she begins to pay more attention to the needs and wishes of the people around her. His grandmother wants Greg to continue to live with her, but he chooses to move with his mother and Julia to the small apartment they share in *A Room Made of Windows*.

THE GREY KING (Cooper*, Susan, ill. Michael Heslop, Atheneum, 1975), fantasy novel set recently in Wales, fourth in The Dark Is Rising series. The story continues Will* Stanton's quest for the objects that will eventually enable the Old Ones to destroy the Dark. This time, he follows clues found in the inscription on the side of the Grail. Will is sent to recover from a bout with hepatitis at the farm of his uncle and aunt in the mountains of northern Wales. There he initiates the search for the golden harp with which he can awaken the Six Sleepers whose help the Old Ones need to win the final battle against the Dark. Will makes friends with Bran* Davies, a white-haired youth of mysterious background who is ostensibly the son of a farmhand, Owen Davies. Together the two boys travel an old pilgrim trail, Cadfan's Way, and enter the mountain where they win the harp by answering correctly riddles put to them by three blue-robed figures, one of whom is Merriman* Lyon. They are opposed by the Grey King, who, among other obstacles, causes a fire on the mountain, sends his foxes, the legendary *migwn*, to attack them and the sheep, and takes over bodily a mean-tempered, neighboring farmer, Caradog Prichard, inducing him to kill Bran's beloved, white dog with the silver eyes, Cafall, and to attempt to kill even Bran himself. Will is persistent, however, and with the help of the kindly, capable shepherd, John Rowlands*, finally awakens the Sleepers and learns from Owen that Bran is the Pendragon, true son of King Arthur. Dialogue is extensive and suits the story in vocabulary and tone. Characters are distinctly drawn and, though the plot is mechanical, incidents seem plausible and are adventurous. Suspense is particularly high at the end. Bran is the most interesting character, much overshadowing Will, the protagonist. As in the previous books in the series, Celtic folklore strengthens the plot, which is not in itself very compelling, contributes to setting, builds atmosphere, which is the book's strongest feature, and gives the story its sense of dealing with important, timeless, universal matters. Other books in the series are *Over Sea, Under Stone** and *The Dark Is Rising**. Fanfare; Newbery Winner.

THE GRIFFIN LEGACY (Klaveness*, Jan O'Donnell, Macmillan, 1983), fantasy novel of suspense involving detection and spirits of the past who come into the present seeking help in solving their problems. It is 1946, World War II is over, and while her parents search for a place to live in the Chicago area, Amy* Enfield, almost fourteen, is sent by train from their old home in Baltimore to stay with her Grandma* Enfield in her rambling, old farmhouse, Constitution Hill, just outside a village in the Massachusetts Berkshires. Although Amy barely knows her Enfield grandmother, she finds the old woman warm and welcoming, but she is uneasy about Aunt* Matilda, her grandmother's very old half-sister, a strange, forbidding woman, whose half-blind eyes appear to see everything and who seems extremely concerned that Amy learn about her Griffin connection. Given Aunt Matilda's childhood room, the one their ancestor of Revolutionary times, Lucy* Griffin, also lived in, Amy soon becomes involved in the ill-fated romance between Lucy and Seth* Howes, the rector of St. George's, the local church. A Tory sympathizer, Seth was slain by Lucy's strongly patriotic father and buried by the townspeople outside the churchyard as a traitor. Lucy's ghost appeals to Amy as the last of her line for help in restoring to their rightful place both Seth's body and the church Queen Anne communion silver, entrusted to Lucy for safekeeping by her lover. Amy is assisted in her task by Betsy* and Ben* Winters, a local brother and sister, with whom she becomes close friends during the year of her stay in the village. Such clues as a golden key found in the hollow bedpost of Amy's bed, a portrait of Lucy in the living room, Lucy's ghost who appears several times and chants, among other things, about an L* and an M, glimpses of figures from the past, Seth's ghost, inscriptions on gravestones, and information Amy gathers from Aunt Matilda, her grandmother, the Winters youths, and a family Bible eventually lead to the solution of the mystery about where the silver lies hidden and what Lucy and Seth really want. Things come to a climax on Halloween, when after a lively party at the church and then at the Enfield homestead, there is a violent thunderstorm, during which lightning strikes an elm tree near Seth's grave and Aunt Matilda suffers an attack, probably a mild stroke. While racing through the storm to fetch the doctor for Aunt Matilda, Amy realizes that the tree holds the answer, returns the next morning to investigate, and discovers a small box, whose lock the key fits and inside of which is a little book where Lucy has recorded her story. It contains the vital clue that sends Amy to the communion silver, a wine cup and plate now in the Enfield cellar. In a proper service both body and silver service are returned to the church and both Lucy and Seth are finally at peace. Strongly drawn elderly women, particularly Aunt Matilda, a clearly delineated rural setting, and a skillfully unraveled family history offset the conventional melodramatic Gothic plotting and otherwise stock characters, clumsily handled visitations, and occasionally florid style for a pleasing, well-sustained story of mystery and suspense. Poe Nominee.

THE GRIZZLY (Johnson*†, Annabel, and Edgar Johnson*†, ill. Gilbert Riswold, Harper, 1964), realistic novel set in the mid–1900s in which the characters' personal problems are worked out in an atmosphere of adventure in the wilds. A weekend camping trip in the wilderness of Montana brings positive change in the relationship between shy, overprotected David, almost twelve, and his father, Mark. David has not seen Mark since his parents separated when he was a small boy, and he often has nightmares about him. David is tense and apprehensive when Mark, an engineer on assignment in Africa, returns and invites David for an outing to the remote, untamed place he himself had loved when he was a youth. Since David is certain that his rugged and demanding father will put him through tests to determine his mettle, he is afraid that he will incur his father's contempt by failing to live up to the man's expectations. Though he fears his father, he still feels a certain admiration for this determined, energetic man of forceful personality and powerful physique who makes the fathers of his friends look like weaklings. But it happens that a female grizzly with cubs lives in the area Mark has chosen for their campsite. She makes off with supplies, chases David up a tree, wounds Mark's leg severely, and wrecks the starter system of their truck. Suddenly, David finds their roles reversed. He must care for his wounded father and see that the truck is repaired so that they can get safely back to civilization. The responsibility enables David to discover resources he did not know he had and see his father in a new light. Mark changes, too. The son of a demanding, hard-driving father, he has thought of David as feckless and cowardly, spoiled by an over-solicitous mother's attentions. Now he regrets jeopardizing the boy's life and respects him for his gritty attempts to help. The two manage to fish for food, tend the wound, and get the truck started again. At the end, David hopes that he, his father, and his mother can come together as a family unit again. The book offers many exciting moments, but events seem deliberately contrived to bring the two together, and the reconciliation is too pat to be believable. Some events seem implausible or gratuitous, and the plot is not well paced. David's quick change in attitude is very improbable. That he should so quickly accept this man for whom apparently he so long has harbored neurotic fears and should even want a permanent relationship with him strains belief. Choice.

GROVER (Cleaver*, Vera, and Bill Cleaver*, ill. Frederick Marvin, Lippincott, 1970), realistic problem novel set in Thicket, a small town near Tampa, Fla., not long ago, in which a young boy adjusts better to the death of his mother than does his father to the loss of his wife. When he discovers his father weeping in his mother's empty room, Grover* Ezell, 11, realizes that his mother, recently hospitalized for surgery, is not expected to live long. When she comes home, she and Grover have frequent talks. In one of them, she observes that Grover is like her side of the family, the Cornetts, who face disasters without "howling." After she commits suicide, Grover's father, who never has been close to his son, becomes even more cold and remote, lost in his grief and ashamed of his wife's act, and Grover becomes aware for the first time that adults have problems with which they have difficulty coping. Grover continues to play with his chums, Ellen* Grae and Farrell, helps his veterinarian uncle, Ab, as before, and has long chats with Rose*, the grizzled, sensible, old housekeeper who tries to keep his home life as normal as possible. He even talks with Reverend Vance, who urges him to be patient with his father. When Betty Repkin, town misanthrope, cruelly taunts him about his mother's suicide, Grover, enraged, enlists the help of Ellen Grae and Farrell to kill her favorite turkey in revenge. For a time, he is so surly and impatient that he even has a falling out with Ellen Grae and Farrell, who accuse him of being selfish for not sharing his worries and problems with his friends. When he and his father visit his mother's grave, he realizes that his father has let himself become overwhelmed by self-pity, and, recalling his mother's words about the durability of the Cornetts, Grover decides that the only thing to do is to accept the inevitable and go on living. The story lacks focus and moves to an abrupt and pat conclusion, its potential for suspense unrealized. The book's strengths lie in the dialogue, which is generous and convincing, and in its vivid scenes, even though they occasionally seem contrived and overdrawn for effect. Irony sets events in relief, and characterization in general is firm, although Grover's father and Betty Repkin seem made to order. Grover appears a bit too detached and accepting to be really convincing, but Rose is a likeable and genuine figure. *Ellen Grae** is a companion book. Choice; National Book Finalist.

GROVER EZELL (*Ellen Grae**; *Grover**), schoolboy who lives in Thicket, Fla., a few streets away from the McGruders' house, who is Ellen* Grae's best friend, and whose mother commits suicide. He is a year older than she, but in the same grade, since he lost a grade the year his mother died. Although he can spin tales as well as Ellen Grae can, he has a practical bent and is more of a realist than she. He owns a boat and likes to go fishing. Grover is a distinctive figure.

GUIDO (*The Little Fishes**), mature, realistic twelve-year-old, who protects Anna* and little Mario* and takes them from bomb-riddled Naples to Cassino during World War II. Originally from Messina in Sicily, Guido has come to Naples after the death of his mother in the village of St. Marco, her childhood home to which she returned when she became ill after the death of her soldier husband. The stories of her life which his dying mother has confided to Guido—of her hard "iron" father, of his selling her at fifteen into marriage with a thirty-five-year-old man so he would not have to give a dowry—have given the boy a premature understanding of the difficulties and ironies of life. He thinks of himself as two people, himself, who is scared, childish, and emotional, and Guido, who is a clever beggar, streetwise, watching the vicious and foolish impassively.

GULL NUMBER 737 (George*†, Jean Craighead, Crowell, 1964), realistic novel set on Block Island off the tip of Long Island, N.Y., in the late 1950s or early 1960s. After several seasons of assisting his professor father in his research project on sea gulls, Luke Rivers, 16, is bored and resents his father's refusal to let him go west on a work trip with his classmates from Columbus, Ohio, or to work on Captain Gregor's lobster boat. He is further outraged when his younger sister, Chinquapin, and Gregory's daughter, Ginny, get the lobster boat job he has been offered. At the gull laboratory he is helping band a newly hatched chick, Gull #737, and drops it just as a jet from a nearby naval base roars over. Luke names the chick, which is not seriously injured, "Spacecraft," returns him to the right nest in the gullery, and notes that the bird always crouches and tries to hide at the sound of a jet going over. The research project demands careful notes and records on all the birds banded, and involves considerable discomfort for Luke, who must wear a helmet and heavy raincoat when he goes to the gullery since the mature gulls defend their territory and nests by diving at human intruders and regurgitating foul-smelling food upon them. Luke does most of this part of the work since the gulls, who recognize individuals, especially hate Dr. Rivers, because he was clumsy in banding his first bird, Larus, who became the leader of the gullery and always leads a virulent attack on him, screaming his gull-hate cry, "Hahahahahahahahahahaha!" When Chinquapin swears in front of her father, he forbids her to go back to the lobster boat where she learned such language and decides to go to Boston to look for Audubon Society aid so his family will not have to live such a frugal life. With him he takes Luke and Abnormality, a Block Island beachcomber who keeps a pet pig, feeds the gulls on Tuesdays, and thinks he can cure people as long as he doesn't work. Abnormality is to fly to Chicago to a psychiatrist, but as they watch his plane take off they are horrified to see it crash. Very shortly Dr. Rivers, who was unable to get any grant from any of the groups to which he was referred, because gull studies are low priority, is in demand, since it is determined that the plane crashed because gulls and starlings were drawn into the jets. Luke, whose hope of independence by getting a National Science Foundation grant for an idea he had is dashed by the NSF's letter of refusal, is alternately elated and humiliated by his father's attitude toward him in Boston. The effort to scare the gulls off the runway by a record of their distress signal fails when it arouses only their curiosity after the first few days. Luke suggests to kindly Dr. Allard that they should get a recording of Larus screaming at Dr. Rivers. He also tells Dr. Allard of Spacecraft's fear of jets, and how he found a female gull in Boston who shared this fear. Dr. Allard encourages him to write up his findings and to capture and mate the two gulls, but Dr. Rivers treats it as a foolish, childish idea. Luke defies him, returns to Block Island with the Boston gull, and with the help of his sister captures Spacecraft. A group of scientists come by helicopter with Dr. Rivers and follow Luke's idea of getting a tape of Larus's screams, which ultimately proves successful at scaring the Boston airport gulls. Through Dr. Allard's recommendation, Luke gets money to continue his study of Spacecraft and his mate, Jetser. Although the conflict between Luke and his arrogant scientist father is the center of the plot, it never really comes alive in the story. The attitude toward Chinquapin's job is very dated, as are Luke's thoughts about girls' inferior abilities and even his sister's reasons for wanting a job, so she can have red shoes and pretty trinkets. The mother seems to be strictly a subordinate, functional home-maker with no ideas or interests of her own. The details of the gull studies and their findings, however, are fascinating. Fanfare.

GUNHILD (*Hakon of Rogen's Saga**; *A Slave's Tale**), slave woman who has nursed Hakon along with her own daughter, Helga, after his mother died at his birth. To Hakon she is a mother, and when she is captured by Rolf Blackbeard and given to Ulv Hunger as part of his booty, Hakon resolves to get her back if he is able. To Helga, she represents the slave spirit, and the girl is secretly glad when Gunhild, who has been set free by Thora, refuses to join their crew and eventually to return to Rogen in *A Slave's Tale*. Helga remembers too well her mother's slave mentality, which made her favor Hakon and treat her own child brutally, and she is relieved that she cannot ever see her mother again.

GURGI (*The Book of Three**; *The Black Cauldron**; *The Castle of Llyr**; *Taran Wanderer**; *The High King**), a comic figure, Taran's* faithful companion and loyal follower. He speaks in alliteration and rhyme and is very emotional. A hairy creature, ugly, but very kind hearted, he is Taran's closest companion in his travels and appears in all the Prydain* novels. He sometimes influences the action.

GWEN (*All Together Now**), blond girlfriend of Taylor Flanagan, Casey's* uncle who races cars. Although a secondary character, Gwen is memorable because she escapes the stereotype of a cheap racetrack girl and is shown as an insecure young woman, scared at the prospect of dinner with Taylor's family, uneasily coming to accept retarded Dwayne* Pickens, and finally admitting to Casey that she is genuinely in love with Taylor and willing to change to fit into his life. At the end she gives up her job in the dime store and enrolls in a secretarial course.

GWEN MCCURDY (*The Velvet Room**), outgoing, lively daughter of the owner of Las Palmeras ranch, who becomes Robin Williams's best friend. Although in the context of the times, their friendship seems unlikely, the relationship is very important in the novel. Robin's interest in literature and talent on the piano stimulate Gwen to try harder at her music and motivate Gwen's parents to encourage their friendship. Gwen even works a while in the pitting shed. She does so well and is so unaffected in attitude that the migrants accept her. She is a likeable, if not completely convincing character, the antithesis of the usual boss's daughter.

H

HAIL COLUMBIA (Beatty*, Patricia, ill. Liz Dauber, Morrow, 1970), lighthearted, historical novel set in Astoria*, Oreg., in 1893, focusing on several of the social concerns of the day and related in exuberant, tall-tale style. Louisa Baines, 13, tells what happens when her widowed Aunt Columbia Baines, an active suffragette, arrives with her two children, called the Pettigrews, to spend the year with Louisa's respectable, dignified family and changes their lives forever. Ladylike Louisa has mixed feelings about her uninhibited aunt. She admires Columbia's free spirit but fears her aunt's outspoken manner and radical views may embarrass the family. Captain Baines, a wealthy shipowner proud of his position in the community, is aghast when he discovers that his sister flouts custom by using her maiden name, and he refuses even to speak to her. Submissive, timid Mama attempts to avoid trouble by keeping Aunt Columbia in the house and away from the Baineses' friends. When Columbia demands to be introduced to Astoria society, Mama gives in and holds a tea party for her. Columbia's frank expression of her views results in Mama being ostracized by her friends. Ironically, Mama catches Columbia's spirit and spunkily fights back by inviting her sister-in-law to the local WCTU levee and eventually becomes one of Columbia's staunchest allies in her various crusades. By April, Columbia has become bored with a life of polite inactivity and looks for causes to champion. She sets about improving relations with the Finns of Union Town, starts a school to teach Chinese men to read and write English, also forestalling a scheme to deport them by writing to San Francisco for their birth records to establish their American citizenship, makes speeches in Liberty Hall and on the courthouse steps about temperance, women's rights, and capital punishment, and leads protest marches through Swill Town, that part of Astoria notorious for its saloons, cutthroats, and shanghaiing of sailors. Her efforts to clean up Swill Town bring her into direct and violent conflict with John McDermott, political boss and saloonkeeper. By October, Columbia has accumulated enough supporters and political clout to run for mayor but bows out in favor of the Captain, who has long been adamant against the corruption of Swill Town. He wins by a narrow margin in spite of McDermott's effort to buy votes with free whiskey. In a final attempt to retain control of Astoria, McDermott decides to shanghai the Captain, but Columbia foils that plot, too, and McDermott's arrest leads to a reconciliation between sister and brother. At the end of December, Aunt Columbia leaves for her home in Philadelphia to a twenty-one-gun salute and the cheers of her many staunch and grateful friends in Astoria. The good-natured tone draws the reader's attention away from noticing how contrived the plot is. It provides Columbia lots of opportunities to remedy the social problems of Astoria and thus inform the reader about the period. Although Louisa remains prim to the end, Mama becomes emancipated realistically, and the Captain reflects the attitude of many men of the period. Columbia is a refreshing and memorable heroine, flamboyant, determined, indomitable against the world, vulnerable and soft-hearted underneath, a woman of courage and principle. Indian Louie, the rock-swallowing Chinook Indian who becomes her faithful bodyguard, is an unusual minor character who is based on an actual historical figure. That leading citizens did receive invitations to a hanging, as happened in the story, is shocking but true, according to an author's note, and those who helped the Chinese, like Columbia, were indeed called White Chinamen. This exciting, fast-moving lightweight offers a splendidly entertaining picture of the times from the woman's point of view. An author's postscript discusses the historical background. Choice.

HAKON OF ROGEN'S SAGA (Haugaard*, Erik Christian, ill. Leo Dillon and Diane Dillon, Houghton, 1963), historical novel set on the small island of Rogen off the Norwegian coast toward the end of the Viking period, probably the late tenth century. Hakon, son of Rogen's chieftain, Olaf the Lame, has been raised mostly by the slave woman, Gunhild*, since his mother died at his birth. Helga, Gunhild's daughter, is his own age and, though a slave, more like a sister to him. When Hakon is about eleven, his father sails to Tronhjem and brings home a new bride, lovely Thora* Magnusdaughter, whom all the islanders soon love, but Magnus has not given her willingly and the next year sends his nephew, Rolf Blackbeard, to avenge the wrong. The people of Rogen retreat to a stronghold on Thor's mountain and by heroic efforts and good luck the men fight off Rolf's superior force for a while, but the invaders win the fierce fight, killing Olaf and greatly reducing the number of men from Rogen's nineteen families. Thora and Gunhild are taken prisoner; Helga is saved by being hidden by the slave, Rark*, in a cave on the Mountain of the Sun, at the opposite end of the island. Hakon's uncle, Sigurd, who has refused to bring the men from his village to help his brother, comes to claim Olaf's house and begins a cruel reign. He gives Helga to Eirik the Fox, who takes over Sigurd's old house, and Hakon is treated like a slave. When his uncle sends him to hunt on the Mountain of the Sun, he finds the cave and on his way home is shot at and almost killed by an arrow of Eirik the Fox. Later, for refusing to go live with Eirik, Hakon is brutally beaten by his uncle, and he knows he will be murdered if he recovers. Rark warns him and sends him off to the cave where he hides, exploring it to discover a narrow tunnel that leads to a safer chamber opening toward the sea. One night when he returns to his uncle's house to try to find Rark and Helga, he overhears plans to use Helga as a decoy to draw him into the open. He meets Harold the Bowbender and learns that in Harold and his sons he has three more defenders. The dog Trold follows him and is instrumental in scaring off Eirik when he finds the cave, since the dog's echoing howl convinces Eirik that the spirit of Fenris wolf inhabits the cave. On another night expedition to Eirik's hall, Hakon finds Rark beaten and bound, brings him back to the cave, and together with him and Harold makes a plan to retake the island with those men who are loyal to Hakon. In the ensuing fight he kills Eirik, and Rark, trying to rescue Helga, who is being dragged off to a boat by Sigurd, kills Sigurd and is wounded. Hakon, now chief of Rogen, swears to recover Gunhild and to see that Rark gets back to his home. A first-rate adventure, the story also convincingly evokes the period and the fierce but noble Vikings. Hakon is quietly courageous; he and the other characters are well drawn. The theme that each person deserves freedom and respect according to his true worth emerges without explicit statement. The first person narration is in language plausible and tonally correct for the people of the story. Fanfare.

HALF-BREED (Lampman*, Evelyn Sibley, ill. Ann Grifalconi, Doubleday, 1967), historical novel set in Oregon about 1850 that tells of one year in the life of a half-breed Crow Indian boy. When his mother remarries, proud, earnest Pale-eyes, 12, leaves his home and family to seek his white father, whom he has not seen for six years. Calling himself Hardy Hollingshead, he travels westward across the mountains to Willamette Falls in Oregon. There he marvels at such wonders as glass, lumber mills, parrots, chairs, and sailing ships but is horrified by the contempt the whites show for the Indians. With the help of Dr.* McLoughlin, leading citizen in Oregon City, and Joe Meek*, United States marshal in Linn City, both of whom have Indian wives, he finds his father's cabin in Little Stumptown (Portland). There a kindly ex-seaman, Bill* Johnson, whose wife also is Indian, informs him that Jesse is away in the gold fields, and Hardy resigns himself to a winter on his own. Then, unexpectedly, Miss Rhoda Hollingshead arrives from Vermont with her cow, Sookie, to keep house for her brother, the only kin she has left, and, to his chagrin, Hardy soon finds himself doing squaw's work for his tall, sturdy, strong-minded, old Aunt* Rhody, who sets about altering his speech, dress, behavior, and beliefs to conform to white standards, even insisting he wear underwear. Although Hardy sometimes longs for the life of the Crows, he employs patience and understanding and gives her the obedience due one's father's family according to Crow custom. When she burns his medicine bag, however, he firmly resolves to leave for home, but Bill persuades him to stay, appealing to the boy's well-developed sense of responsibility and propriety. In late fall, Jesse arrives, his gold dust improving their finances considerably. Jesse and Hardy get on well, but Jesse soon chafes under Rhody's demands, and, when he fails to marry her off to ambitious, sharp-dealing Noah Tuttle (in one of the book's most humorous episodes), he takes off for greener pastures. Hardy feels resentful and bitter and again resolves to go back to the

Crows, but once more his strong sense of duty binds him to his aunt. Rhody decides to file a claim for land and, with Joe's help, finds a likely spot on the Tuality Plains, where not only is the land good but also enough half-breeds live, including the Meeks, for Hardy to be accepted. When the agent refuses to enroll the claim of a woman, Joe fetches Jesse home to stake it and build a cabin for her and Hardy. Ironically, Jesse, succumbing to his characteristic wanderlust, then departs for Crow country, leaving Hardy, who has taken a liking to the soil and the Meeks, to work the land. Although unevenly paced and arriving at a dubious conclusion, the plot holds the interest well. There is some suspense and a good deal of humor to lighten the basic seriousness. Characterization is strong, and the epoch well created. Hardy serves as the author's window on the times, to contrast not only the Indian and white ways of life but, in particular, to showcase the whites' scorn for the Indians, especially the half-breeds, in their midst. Hardy's experiences illustrate the book's central irony. Though professing Christianity, the whites are hostile to the Indians, while the pagan Crows have accepted freely the whites who choose to live with them and attach no stigma to mixed bloods. Hardy and his family are fictitious, but most other characters really lived. (No-scalp-lock*) Spur.

HAL KENT (*Our Eddie**), thirteen-year-old son of an American businessman from Denver who tells part of the story of the Raphaels, a Jewish family, with whom he becomes acquainted while his father works in London. Hal admires the aggressive, fun-loving Eddie Raphael, who teaches him to play cricket and whose fourteenth birthday party he attends. When Hal encounters the family several years later, after they have emigrated to New York City, Eddie has died from an unsuccessful operation for what is apparently multiple sclerosis, the mother is an invalid from the same disease, and the father is on sabbatical from his duties as headmaster of a Hebrew day school.

HALL, LYNN (1937–   ), born in Lombard, Ill.; author of novels for young people, many of them about dogs. She attended schools in Iowa, worked as a secretary in Fort Worth, Tex., as a secretary and veterinary assistant in Des Moines, Iowa, and as an advertising agency copywriter until 1968, when she decided to devote full time to writing. She lives near Garnaville, Iowa, where she breeds and shows collies. *The Whispered Horse** (Follett, 1979), a haunting story set in nineteenth-century Scotland, was awarded the Edgar Allan Poe Award in 1979, and her sensitive novel of family relationships on an Iowa farm, *The Leaving** (Scribner's, 1980), won the prestigious *Boston Globe-Horn Book* Award. She has also used a rural setting in *Denison's Daughter* (Scribner's, 1983), about a girl coming to terms with her father and with farm life. In *Uphill All the Way* (Scribner's, 1984), a small-town Oklahoma girl who works as a farrier becomes involved with a boy of criminal tendencies.

HAMILTON, VIRGINIA (ESTHER) (1936–   ), born in Yellow Springs, Ohio; writer whose novels of black life in New York and the Midwest have won many honors. She attended Antioch College, Ohio State University, and the New School for Social Research, New York. She married writer-anthologist Arnold Adoff, lived in New York City, the setting for *The Planet of Junior Brown** (Macmillan, 1971), and returned to live on her family farm in Ohio. Her novels, *Zeely** (Macmillan, 1967), *The House of Dies Drear** (Macmillan, 1968), and *M.C. Higgins, the Great** (Macmillan, 1974), winner of both the Newbery Medal and the National Book Award, are all set in southern Ohio and draw upon the memories of her mother's family, the Perry clan. *Arilla Sun Down** (Greenwillow, 1976) explores the problems of a family of a black mother and an American Indian father. She has also written biographical books on Paul Robeson and W.E.B. Du Bois. Her fantasy, *Sweet Whispers, Brother Rush** (Philomel, 1982) was a Newbery honor book and won the *Boston Globe-Horn Book* Award. Although much admired and containing memorable scenes, her novels have been criticized for having prominent bizarre elements that are hard to accept in realistic stories yet seem intrusive as symbols.

HANNIBAL CUTLER (*The Spring Rider**), sergeant in the Second Maine Division of the Civil War dead who return each spring to refight a battle. Hannibal is really sixteen but has been accepted by swearing he is "over eighteen," having put a scrap of paper marked "18" inside his shoe. A straightforward farm boy, he differs from most of the soldiers who return because of a love of fighting. His love and pride is his bugle, by which he calls up the forces and by which, in the end, he sends them back to permanent rest. Though he insists to Gray* Downs that he is as real as she and that he can stay with her in the present time, he knows that it will work the other way, that he can take her with him into death. In his decision, therefore, to call back the troops, he is giving up not only his annual taste of life but also his first and only chance for love.

HANS (*Ox Under Pressure**), with his wife, Carmen, servants who come with the house rented on Long Island by the Olmsteads. They are Germans who have lived in Argentina, and there is some question about whether they are ex-Nazis. Hans is mostly memorable for his twisted English and Carmen for her abundant cooking, but both are more human than most of the characters and are genuinely fond of Ox* Olmstead.

THE HAPPY DAYS (Kim*, Yong-ik, ill. Artur Marokvia, Little, 1960), realistic novel set in Korea in the late 1950s. Sang Chun, 10, has fled during the war to Cheju Island, where his mother has been killed collecting edible seaweeds for sale from the slippery sea rocks. To fulfill her wish, Sang Chun leaves the home of the hatmaker, who has been kind to him, and returns to the village of Sonwaji, the mainland home of his grandparents. There also live his uncle and his cousin Koo, 11, and Small Cousin, 3. Doree the barber, a war veteran, starts an evening school in his shop which the boys attend eagerly, along with Mija, the lame girl who lives next door, Manchu-boy, who is always hungry, and other village children. For a permanent school site, they persuade Grandfather to let them remove the huge pile of stones at Road Guest, a pile left by travelers who drank at the spring and helped clear the nearby fields in payment. To keep the children from trampling the barley fields, Doree plants a hedge of trees. Sang Chun and Koo sell wood to buy a bell for the school. When Manchu-Boy does not want to go on the Buddha-birthday school picnic because his mother can give him no lunch, Koo and Sang Chun steal seed sweet potatoes from their family's store room, give him some, and take the rest for their teacher, who plants them on the new school site. When Uncle finds out, he insists that they dig the potatoes up, but Doree persuades him to let them grow, agreeing to give him the entire harvest. Still angry, Uncle apprentices Koo at the lacquer shop where they make inlaid pearl boxes. Ashamed, Sang Chun stays away from school. Mija sells her one possession, her flute, and gives the money to pay for the potatoes, but Sang Chun stays away until the whole school comes bringing him a rare "message," a coconut mailed to him from the illiterate hatmaker. Sang Chun tries to buy the flute back from the wine-shop man and failing, gives the nut to Mija, but her mother, angry that she has sold the gift of a dying soldier, will not let Mija return to school. Sang Chun starts selling candy, with the dubious help of Manchu-Boy. At first they have little success, but when Sang Chun starts trading for barley and other goods he becomes a crafty merchant, earning enough to buy Mija's flute back for her. The children practice running and even get fleet Koo to come to be on their relay team for the Harbor Field Day, but they are not allowed to participate because they have no "real" school. Humiliated, all the children except Sang Chun and Mija drop out of school. When the hatmaker comes repaying the money of Sang Chun's mother which he had borrowed, Sang Chun gives it to Doree, and they are able to actually start building. They use tile and some lumber from the old Study House. In the winter the boys are taking the heavy posts from the Study House and clever Koo thinks of a way to get them to the road; they tie the posts together into a raft and slide it down the frozen river. Riding on it when the ice breaks, Koo is drowned. This tragedy gives the final impetus to the village to finish the school. At the Sang Rang ceremony, marking the raising of the roof, Grandfather enlists the help of the villagers to complete the project, and the "happy days" that Sang Chun's mother looked forward to for him are coming at last. The intense interest in and devotion to the school is convincing, and the characters are believable in this rather quiet and modest book. Customs and mores of the Korean village come in naturally as part of the story rather than as didactic elements of research. Fanfare.

HARLEQUIN (*In the Company of Clowns**), traveling player whose troupe Gian-Piero* joins. He says his real name is Agostino Molino. A priest's garb over his motley, he accompanies Gian-Piero in his search for the players who have stolen the boy's donkey, Domenico. Harlequin actually seems to live the part of company clown, now imp, now benefactor, "first cousin to the devil." He says what he thinks people would like to hear and what will be of advantage to him at the moment. On the rack, he confesses to the murder of the pawnbroker. He is an intriguing and perplexing character who epitomizes the ironies and ambiguities of life. Gian-Piero is never sure that he can trust the man.

HARNDEN, RUTH (PEABODY), born in Boston, Mass.; author of realistic adventure and problem novels for middle readers. Her first book for children, *Golly and the Gulls* (Houghton, 1962), about a boy's efforts to save some gulls when the harbor of his New England coastal town freezes over, was praised as strong in drama and mood. Her next book, *The High Pasture** (Houghton, 1964), about a boy who is sent West to the ranch of his elderly aunt and tames a wild dog, received the Child Study Award. Her other novels for younger readers include *Summer's Turning* (Houghton, 1966), and *Runaway Raft* (Houghton, 1968), while *Wonder Why* (Houghton, 1971) contains poetry for a young audience. For adults she wrote the novels *Bright Star or Dark* (McGraw, 1945) and *I, a Stranger* (Whittlesey House, 1950) and short stories for national magazines. The daughter of a lawyer, she received her B.A. degree from Radcliffe and studied further at Trinity College in Dublin.

HAROLD HOFFER (*Wings**), small, fearful, quiet boy in Pip dePuyster's class at school. Since he has only three fingers, the children think he is strange and shun him. Pip manipulates him into cleaning the chicken coop for her. She hates taking her turn at mucking out the smelly chicken dirt and promises to be his friend if he will do the job for her. He does it willingly and well. Although Pip dislikes him, her conscience and Yamaji's* prompting motivate her to keep her promise to him. Yamaji points out to her that she is treating Harold with the same sort of contempt that the class shows for the chickens. Later, when Harold gets infantile paralysis and is hospitalized, Pip regularly writes encouraging letters to him. He is a round, pathetic figure.

HARRIET THE SPY (Fitzhugh*, Louise, ill. author, Harper, 1964), humorous, realistic novel of family and school life set in Manhattan, N.Y., about 1960, one of the first and most popular of the books of New Realism involving unlikeable children and unsympathetically presented adults. Daughter of a TV executive, bossy, intelligent Harriet Welsch, 11, spends little time with her socially active parents. She feels very close to her imperious, husky, middle-aged nurse, Ole Golly, who encourages her in her ambition to become a writer. Ole Golly advises Harriet to keep her eyes open and learn as much as she can about the world. To that end, every day after school, Harriet dons her spy outfit of ancient blue jeans and horn rims and spies on her neighbors: Mrs. Plumber, a healthy woman who prefers to stay in bed all day; the De Santis, the volatile Italians who run the neighborhood grocery; the Robinsons, a highly acquisitive couple; and Harrison Withers, who keeps twenty-six cats and builds bird cages. Harriet jots down her frank observations about them in a secret notebook. She also records her candid reactions about her friends and classmates, including Sport* Rocque, her best friend, who runs the house for his divorced father, an absent-minded writer, and Janie* Gibbs, who aspires to become a chemist and blow up the world. Two events alter Harriet's life; Ole Golly leaves to get married, and her classmates find her notebook and read what she has written about them. They react with anger and plan revenge, forming a club to punish her. They write nasty notes about her and leave them where she will find them, dump ink on her, steal her tomato sandwiches, and generally cut her out of their lives. Increasingly lonely and isolated, Harriet takes refuge in her notebook, finally spending most of her time writing. Her worried parents take her to a psychiatrist who advises them to get in touch with Ole Golly and to ask the school to help her by capitalizing on her writing talent. Accordingly, she receives a letter from Ole Golly in which her former nurse suggests that sometimes it is necessary to apologize and to tell lies. At school, Harriet is made editor of the class paper, and soon her gossipy bits become the hit of the school. She publishes a retraction and is pleased when Sport and Janie show signs of wanting to be friends again. Harriet's behavior, her classmates' actions, and Ole Golly's advice raise significant moral and social questions, which are not resolved in the novel. Characters are zany, their eccentricities distorted almost to comic book proportions, yet they are interesting. Dialogue is extensive and credible, and some poignant moments set the comedy in relief. Some incidents, such as that in which Harriet and her father practice being onions, are hilarious, if unlikely. Sequel is *The Long Secret**. ChLA Touchstones; Choice.

HARRIS, MARILYN (MARILYN HARRIS SPRINGER) (1931–   ), born in Oklahoma City, Okla., the daughter of an oil man; author of fiction for adults and of problem novels for adolescents. *The Runaway's Diary** (Four Winds, 1971), the first-person account of a sixteen-year-old girl who runs away from her Harrisburg, Pa., home and spends three months in Canada, was selected for the Lewis Carroll Shelf. Other novels include *The Peppersalt Land* (Four Winds, 1970), about the friendship between two girls of different races in a southern town, and *Hatter Fox* (Random, 1973), about a Navajo girl befriended by an Indian Bureau doctor. She has also published short stories in leading journals and collections of short stories. Previous to receiving her bachelor's and master's degrees from the University of Oklahoma, she studied at Cottey College. She and her husband, a member of the faculty of Central State College in Edmond, Okla., live with their children in Norman, Okla.

HARRIS, MARK JONATHAN (1941–   ), born in Scranton, Pa.; educator, producer, director, and writer of screen plays and of novels for adolescents. After graduating from Harvard University and serving with Associated Press in Chicago as a wire service reporter, he made documentary and educational films for eleven years. Recently he has divided his time between writing and teaching cinema at the University of Southern California at Los Angeles and at the California Institute of Arts. He received the Spur Award of Western Writers of America for *The Last Run** (Lothrop, 1981), about the efforts of a youth and his mustanger grandfather to capture a spirited wild stallion. Before that he published *With a Wave of the Wand* (Lothrop, 1980), which relates the attempts of a confused twelve-year-old girl to cope with her parents' divorce. His film honors include the Emmy Award for "The Golden Calf," an Academy Award for his short documentary film, "The Redwoods," made to help the Sierra Club establish the Redwoods National Park, and a special award from the Leipzig International Film Festival for "Huelga!," about grape workers' strikes to unionize. His films and his books reveal his concern for social issues. He has been a frequent contributor to magazines and newspapers, including *TV Guide*, the Washington *Post*, and *Newsday*. With his wife, a clinical psychologist, and their two children, he makes his home in Los Angeles.

HARRY (*The Last Run**), Paiute Indian, who has retired from work as a cowboy and mustanger and lives on the reservation near Silverfield, Nev. He knows a lot about horses and warns Bill* Cameron that the stallion the two men and Lyle* Jeffries seek will return for his herd of mares. Disappointed about the loss of the stallion and casual about the mares, Bill drinks too much whiskey, and, when Harry needs him later, Bill is unable to help his friend, and Harry is trampled to death when the mares stampede. Although he has lived and worked among whites most of his life, Harry has maintained his traditional Paiute beliefs about the Creator and animals and the respect of his Indian friends.

HARRY BERGEN (*Summer of My German Soldier**), Patty Bergen's father. A nervous, proud man, he takes offense very easily. He is very aware of being the head of the only Jewish family in town. He is afraid that his pretty, appearance-conscious wife, Pearl*, whose family is well off, will feel that she has married beneath her. He has a poor self-image and as a character is overdrawn for effect.

HARRY CAT (*The Cricket in Times Square**; *Tucker's Countryside**), huge tiger cat with gray-green eyes, black stripes, and a warm and loyal heart. He lives with Tucker* Mouse in a drainpipe in the subway station in Times Square in New York City. He and Tucker advise and protect Chester* Cricket. Harry is a good hunter, enjoys roaming, and appreciates the finer things in life. A cultured cat, he discovers Chester's musical talent. Later he helps to save Chester's Old Meadow by letting Ellen Hedley make a house cat out of him.

HARRY CREWE (*The Blue Sword**), really named Angharad, Homeland girl who comes, after her father's death, to join her brother at a colonial outpost in Daria and is kidnapped by the king of the still unsubdued Hillfolk. Although she had a wild temper as a child, she has learned to control it and to hide her restlessness, but her parents and her brother have kept from her the secret of her ancestry, that her great-great-grandmother was a royal Hillwoman. As a result, she does not understand that she possesses *kelar*, an extrasensory power of the king's family. Since she is tall and has been an excellent horsewoman, she has less trouble than other Homelander girls would in becoming an expert at sword play and other warlike skills. Because her *kelar* calls up a vision of the legendary female hero, Aerin, for a whole camp, the Hillfolk rally to her standard, calling her Harimad-sol, a name of honor. The seer, Luthe, tells her she must be a bridge between the two cultures, and though she is sometimes dismayed, she succeeds in saving the Hillpeople from the invading Northerners.

HARVEY (*The Pinballs**), despondent, withdrawn, thirteen-year-old youth whose legs were broken when his drunken father drove his car over them. He, Carlie*, and Thomas J* live in Mr. and Mrs. Mason's foster home. At first, Harvey does not tell the other children the real story of how his legs were broken because he is too ashamed of the way his father has been treating him. He takes refuge from reality by making endless lists on various subjects and is addicted to such "fast foods" as Kentucky Fried Chicken. His mother abandoned her family to live in a commune in Virginia. Like the other characters, he is too distorted to be convincing.

HAUGAARD, ERIK CHRISTIAN (1923–   ), born in Copenhagen, Denmark; Danish writer who has lived in the United States and whose distinguished historical novels are written in English and first published in this country. He emigrated to the United States, after his parents moved here, and attended Black Mountain College, N.C., then served in the Royal Canadian Air Force during World War II. From 1945 to 1947 he studied at the New School for Social Research in New York. His books for young people cover a wide variety of times and places, including *Hakon of Rogen's Saga** (Houghton, 1963) and *A Slave's Tale** (Houghton, 1965), both about the last part of the Viking period, *Orphans of the Wind** (Houghton, 1966), about the American Civil War, *The Rider and His Horse** (Houghton, 1968), about Roman dominated Palestine, *The Little Fishes** (Houghton, 1967), set in Italy during World War II, *Chase Me, Catch Nobody!** (Houghton, 1980), about Germany in the period just before the war, *A Messenger for Parliament* (Houghton, 1976) and *Cromwell's Boy* (Houghton, 1978), both about the English Civil War of the seventeenth century, and *The Samurai's Tale* (Houghton, 1984), a psychological novel set in sixteenth-century Japan. Despite their diversity of setting and period, all his novels concern an orphan or a child without the ordinary protection of a family who is thrown somehow upon the mercy of strangers. He is considered one of the most skillful current historical novelists and has won many honors, including the Jane Addams Award and the *Boston Globe-Horn Book* Award. He has also translated the fairy tales of Hans Christian Andersen.

HAWKS (*The Soul Brothers and Sister Lou**), the gang of local youths to which Louretta Hawkins's friends belong. Their rivals are the Avengers. At Fess's* instigation, the Avengers combine with the Hawks to take revenge for Jethro's death, but Lou dissuades them from launching an outright war against the police.

THE HAWKSTONE (Williams*, Jay, Walck, 1971), fantasy set in the country near Millbridge, Conn beginning in the 1960s. Because of changes in tax assessment, it appears that Colin Hyatt's family may have to sell their 300 acres on which they keep a few chickens and a pig but which is mostly going back to nature. Colin, about twelve or thirteen, who loves to roam over the land, follows a white deer and discovers a cave he has never before seen. Overcome by a strange feeling that he is someone else, wearing a yellow tarpaulin, he digs in the cave floor and finds, wrapped in cloth and leather, a greenish stone shaped like a hawk. A friend of his father, Mr. Perino, identifies it as at least pre–1750; he also invites Colin to join an archery club in which he is active. Colin finds that when he wears the stone, he is taken back in history and becomes one of the people who lived on his land—Quethepah, the Indian in ancient times who first brought his people to the area; Waghinacut, last of the Indians, who is buried on the land; James Todd, who leaves to fight in the Revolution and is killed at Ridgefield; John Linnett, a born trader, who swaps with James's aging sister, Abigail Vine, the property for his family to care for her in her old age; Orel Linnett, John's grandson, who saves the farm from fire in the time of the Civil War and first buried the hawkstone in the cave; Sarah Linnett Hyatt, Orel's daughter, who found the stone and under its direction proposed to Clive Hyatt, Colin's great-great-grandfather in 1905 and by marrying him saved the land. It is Sarah who has reburied the stone as Colin found it. In the meantime, Colin has learned much of the local history from old Miss Hillhouse, a human encyclopedia on the subject, and has tried archery, amazing his friend, Max Klein, and Mr. Perino by his incredible skill, acquired because the stone makes him momentarily Quethepah. Although his mean neighbor, old Jake Putnam, who has bought a piece of the Hyatt land and has warned Colin off it, objects, he is allowed to enter the club shoot though not a regular member. At first he is nervous and does poorly, but gradually he relaxes enough to be endowed with the Indian's skill and amazes the other members, being awarded an exceptionally fine hunting knife. This he swaps, prompted by John Linnett, to Jake Putnam for treasure rights to the land that used to be Hyatt's, the knife and one percent of any treasure found. He then goes out and digs up a box of coins buried by John Linnett, now worth far more than enough to pay the taxes on the land. The story uses the pattern established in Kipling's *Puck of Pook's Hill* in a slightly mechanical way, but it is still a pattern that works well and gives a strong feeling of place and continuity in history. Much of it is in dialogue, the historical characters coming out more convincingly than Colin and Max. Lewis Carroll.

HAZARD WHITAKER (*All Together Now**), a man in his fifties who finally marries spinster Pansy and almost loses her immediately. Having drifted from job to job, Hazard has found his true vocation as a dancing waiter, only to have the restaurant close because of the owner's illness. After twenty-five years of admiring Pansy, he asks her to marry him, then suffers misgivings about his ability to live up to her standards. His fear of failure increases his ineptitude and causes him to make a disaster of their honeymoon by forgetting to reserve a berth on the train, then finding old acquaintances in the Washington Hotel and getting drunk with them while Pansy waits in the hotel room. Faced with her rejection and the possibility of an annulment, he pitches a tent on her lawn and vows to stay there until she will talk to him again. Finally she accepts him with all his faults, knowing that at least he is loving and well meaning.

HAZELINE (*The Midnight Fox**), noisy, good-natured, kindhearted daughter of Uncle Fred and Aunt Millie and cousin of Tom. Although she is too caught up in her own personal problems with obesity and her boy friend to pay much attention to him, she does recognize that Tom is shy and feels out of place on her family's farm. She tries a couple of times to help him fit in and have some fun, but her attempts to place what happens to the foxes in its practical perspective does little to make him feel better. She has an on-and-off romance with Mikey Galter, whom she marries at the end of the book. As a character, she is tinged with the eccentric.

HEAD INTO THE WIND (Barnwell*, D. Robinson, ill. Avery Johnson, McKay, 1965), realistic novel set in rural North Carolina in 1934. It is a hard year for Toby Butler, 13, partly because of the Depression but mostly because his father has died and his best friend, Little Jim Miller, whose sharecropper father has lost a leg in a logging accident, moves to town. He chafes under his grandfather's orders and worries about his mother, Elizabeth, who is often ill. Unmarried Aunt Jenny, who shares their house, is often the only one who understands him. For a while his beautiful new teacher, Miss Bevins, occupies all his attention, but when he learns she is to be married at Christmas time, he is resentful and loses interest in her as Mrs. Marsh. A new girl, Holly Sue Camp, who moves into Little Jim's old house, gives him his first kisses, but the world of adult romance disgusts him. Jim's mother, widowed by Big Jim's death, comes back with her seven children to marry the hard-drinking old man Dawkins and be stepmother to his four scraggly youngsters. Worse to Toby, Jake Ransom, who has been his father's best friend and whose dead wife was a cousin of his mother, begins coming around courting. On the anniversary of his father's death, Aunt Jenny admits to Toby that she has always loved Jake Ransom, but that she is happy that Elizabeth will be his second wife, and Toby begins to understand how he, too, must accept the change. A quiet book, it gives a feeling for the fields where Toby picks cotton, the woods in which he hunts, the warm family and neighborhood ties, the pain of loss and change to a boy in his early teens. Although in many ways typical for his age, Toby is more than a stock character, and minor characters, particularly Aunt Jenny, are well drawn. Fanfare.

THE HEADLESS CUPID (Snyder*, Zilpha Keatley, ill. Alton Raible, Atheneum, 1971), realistic family novel set in a big old house in the California countryside in the mid–1900s. The Stanleys, patient, responsible David*, 11, chattery Janey, 6, and the twins, earnest Tesser (Esther) and silent Blair, 4, their father, a university professor of geology, and new stepmother, Molly, a painter, buy the Old Westerly House. Arriving soon thereafter is Amanda*, 12, Molly's daughter, a student of spiritual science, dressed in her ceremonial costume, with her familiar, a crow named Rolor, a snake, a horned toad, and several boxes of books on the occult. At first, Amanda is aloof and haughty toward the children, resentful toward Father, and angry at her mother for bringing her to what she regards as the utter boondocks, but before long she thaws enough to show the children her spiritualist's paraphernalia and take them on as students. She puts them through a series of nine ordeals, among others, refraining from using anything made of metal and from walking on wood, initiates them, and conducts a seance for them, all with unexpected and amusing results. Then old Mr. Golanski, the electrician, informs the family that the headless cupid on the stairway bannister was thought to be the work of a poltergeist. Almost immediately, strange and unsettling things occur. Rocks tumble down the stairway, apparently unthrown, Molly's philodendron is smashed by an unknown hand, and a portrait suddenly crashes to the floor. David suspects Amanda, but one evening, while the two are together, a box containing rocks and the cupid's head mysteriously rolls down the stairs. Frightened, Amanda soon confesses to the earlier acts and becomes more agreeable, but the box and head remain a mystery, until Blair confides to David that he found them hidden in a corner of his toybox and dropped them down the stairs. Both boys are so pleased with Amanda's change of heart that they decide to keep quiet about Blair's discovery and deed. Emphasis is on plot, but the children are distinct individuals. Amanda changes predictably but realistically, and David learns a little about people and life. The author reveals a sharp eye for details of family life and a keen ear for conversation. Some suspense, a little humor, and a pleasing sequence of events make for good entertainment in this mildly Gothic variation on the old theme of the taming of the shrew. Sequels. Choice; Christopher; Newbery Honor.

HELL-AND-DAMNATION HASTINGS (*The Long Journey**), the wayfaring stranger dressed in black who pursues Laurie James almost the entire route of her journey to Butte, because he wants the gold nuggets her grandfather gave her to use for money in an emergency. He is very tall, wears a long poncho and wide-brimmed hat, and rides a mule which seems much too small to carry him. He is rude, demanding, and disrespectful of Laurie's rights as a person. He calls himself a preacher and sings "This Is My Story" over and over again in a thin, high voice. He terrifies the girl, but she manages to elude him most of the time.

To Laurie's surprise, Uncle Arthur tells her that the man is considered odd but harmless. Laurie's experience with the stranger has been just the opposite, that he is exceedingly dangerous, but she does not pursue the matter with Uncle Arthur. Hell-and-Damnation is an overdrawn, under-convincing character, but he certainly serves his purpose of contributing suspense and thrills to the story of Laurie's trip.

HENRY†, MARGUERITE (BREITHAUPT) (1902–   ), born in Milwaukee, Wis.; writer of fiction and non-fiction for children, best known for her popular horse stories. She attended schools in Milwaukee, where her father had a printing business, and graduated from Milwaukee State Teachers' College. After her marriage, she went to live in Chicago, where she wrote articles for trade journals and various other publications, and then moved to a farm near Wayne, Ill., where she began writing for children. She first wrote picture geographies for early elementary readers and then storybooks and biographies and other non-fiction for the eight-to-twelve-year-olds, compiling an impressive total of more than three dozen books. One was a Newbery Medal winner, *King of the Wind*† (Rand, 1948), a historical novel which tells how the Arabian horse came to England, while another, *Mustang** (Rand, 1966), which tells about the efforts of a courageous, determined woman to save from extinction the wild mustangs that roam the American West, won the Western Heritage Award. Appearing in *Choice* are *Stormy, Misty's Foal** (Rand, 1963), which continues the story of the wild ponies from islands off Virginia begun in *Misty of Chincoteague*† (Rand, 1947), both still popular, and *White Stallion of Lipizza** (Rand, 1964), about the famous Austrian performing horses. Her novels combine action and drama with sound research and warm, quite readable if rather pedestrian writing. Her animals are not anthropomorphized or sentimentalized, yet they are invested with just enough personality to make them individual and memorable. The reader is kept aware that though the books are fiction the subjects and major events actually occurred. Other titles about horses include *Justin Morgan Had a Horse*† (Wilcox, 1945), *Brighty of the Grand Canyon*† (Rand, 1953), *San Domingo: The Medicine Hat Stallion* (Rand, 1972), *All About Horses* (Random, 1962), and *A Pictorial Life Story of Misty* (Rand, 1976), while *Benjamin West and His Cat Grimalkin*† (Bobbs, 1947) strikes off in another direction, being a biographical novel of the early years of the man who became known as the father of American painting. She also wrote for Bobbs-Merrill's Childhood of Famous Americans Series, contributed articles and stories to many magazines, and wrote several books for the Whitman Picture Geographies Series. Several of her books were made into movies.

HENRY JOHNSON (*The Contender**), polio victim who works at Donatelli's gym and becomes Alfred Brooks's trainer. A sweet-tempered boy, Henry goes out of his way to help Alfred and becomes a good friend, though he doesn't replace James in Alfred's affection. Henry is grateful to Alfred for getting him a chance to become a trainer.

HENRY LOVERING II (*Henry 3**), Henry 3's father, a sympathetically portrayed character. The father and son have a satisfying relationship, and Henry sincerely supports his father's aspirations to a vice-presidency in American Lock and Locomotive. Since he knows his father as a calm, controlled, sensible man, Henry is shocked when he is in his father's office and sees how nervous and fawning he is around Mr. Matthews, the company president. He feels contempt when he observes his father pretending to be something he is not in order to get ahead but fails to see the parallel between his own attempts to disguise his IQ in order to win friends and his father's efforts to win the approval of his superior. After the hurricane, during which Henry II deports himself with substantial approval from the community, Henry and his father have a thoughtful conversation about how circumstances affect behavior.

HENRY REED (*Henry Reed, Inc.*†; *Henry Reed's Journey**; *Henry Reed's Baby-Sitting Service**; *Henry Reed's Big Show**), teenaged son of a diplomat, who spends several summers with his aunt and uncle in Grover's Corner, N.J., and records his adventures first-person in the form of journal entries. An intelligent and inventive boy, Henry creates mild chaos with all his projects, though he never means to cause trouble and, being very literal minded, is usually surprised when people are annoyed or amused at the results of his ideas. According to his uncle, he resembles his mother in his ability to stir up unexpected action no matter what he undertakes, as well as in his interest in animals, insects, and other natural history. Much of the action occurs in the barn on land owned by his mother, which Henry rightfully feels is his property.

HENRY REED'S BABY-SITTING SERVICE (Robertson*†, Keith, ill. Robert McCloskey, Viking, 1966), third in a series of humorous, episodic novels about the inventive young man who first started his research firm in Grover's Corner, N.J. (*Henry Reed, Inc.*†; *Henry Reed's Journey**), all told as entries in his journal. Henry* Reed, now 15, has returned to spend another summer with his Uncle Al and Aunt Mabel. In response to a survey on services needed in the area, Henry and Midge* Glass start a baby-sitting service. They find that this is not all sitting and reading while a child naps. Danny Whittenberg, 4, slams a window shut on Henry's head. Belinda Osborne, 5, hides until they trick her with Henry hiding in a tree with a walkie-talkie while Midge pretends to find her by gazing into a crystal ball. The housetrailer where Herman Melick, 8, lives disappears while he and Henry are riding bikes. Henry takes Craig Adams, 5, camping in his new tent, and in the early morning hours they hear a woman screaming for help. Accompanied by the State Patrolman, they discover it is only a peacock owned by Mrs. Caribelli. Later, hired to sit with Mrs. Caribelli's animals and aging mother, Henry spends an exhausting day, only to be chided by the old lady for sitting around doing nothing. Twice they save the day for adults: when the Whittenbergs are both delayed the night the boss is coming to dinner, Henry and Midge pitch in and cook a fine barbeque picnic, only to learn later that they have made the hamburgers from the dog's horse meat; while Henry is sitting for the Sansome twins, whose house is for sale, a series of near disasters involves all the neighbors, and the prospective buyer who shows up is so impressed by the friendliness of the community that he buys the house. Chief antagonists in this book are the Sebastian twins, Ruth and Johnny, 17, who live where the Apples used to live. They drive a red MG and are scornful of the younger teenagers. Ruth steals one job from Henry. Johnny, who is rather stupid, manages to drain a full swimming pool into the basement, Ruth is fired, and Henry gets the job back. When Henry and Midge expand their service into a nursery school in the barn, Johnny terrifies the children by making the barn sound haunted, using a hidden microphone. Henry follows the wires to where Johnny is lounging in his hammock laughing, and Midge cuts the rope, dropping him with a thump. They get full revenge at the County Fair, where they are giving rides to children in a cart pulled by Uncle Al's lawn tractor. Henry comes upon the MG stalled and gives Johnny a pull, touring through the fair on the way, to Johnny's humiliation. The episodes are similar to those in the earlier books, exaggerated but not impossible, with much of the humor from the point of view, since Henry seldom sees the ludicrous side of the situation. Choice.

HENRY REED'S BIG SHOW (Robertson*†, Keith, ill. Robert McCloskey, Viking, 1970), fourth in a series of episodic, humorous novels (*Henry Reed, Inc.*†; *Henry Reed's Journey**; *Henry Reed's Baby-Sitting Service**), all told as entries in the journal of a bright, inventive teenager. Henry* Reed, presumably now sixteen, though his age is not mentioned, returns for a third summer at Grover's Corner, N.J. He has decided to become a producer and wants to put on a play. His first encounter with the theater is as a spectator at the Music Circus in Lambertville, a summer tent theater where his dog, Agony, who has escaped from the car, finds his way to the stage and drowns out the lead singer with his howls. His second is accidental, when a car pulling a trailer house of a traveling rock music group, the Willy Nillies, breaks down on the road running past Henry's barn. In exchange for letting them stay the night, Henry asks friends to listen to their practice and the affair balloons into an impromptu concert. Henry's friend and partner, Midge* Glass, has developed an interest in horses. On their first ride, on borrowed mounts, Henry falls off the horse while they are separated and gets a nosebleed. He washes his bloody clothes in a stream and hangs his head over the bank to stop the nosebleed as they dry. Later Midge tells him of helping the State Patrolman hunt for the ''murdered body'' which a birdwatching woman has reported having seen on the stream bank. When a friend gives Midge a horse, they fence in the pasture and fix a stall in Henry's barn, renamed the R & G Ranch. At first Midge is terribly disappointed at the awkward-looking animal, but Galileo soon shows himself an unusually clever horse, given to hiding and able to untie knots and get through latched doors, both of which skills cause considerable trouble. Henry attends an auction and by clever trading up comes home with all his money, a buggy with harness, and a supply of old clothes for costumes. They are hired to drive Galileo with the buggy in a Princeton protest march for a cleaner environment. Henry's plans to produce a play fall flat because, at a party Midge gives for the possible cast, one of the young people plays a tape Midge has made giving Henry frank opinions about each of the guests, and they all leave in a huff. Midge comes up with the idea of a rodeo instead. Since a lot of the young people in the area have horses and they are able to borrow a bucking Shetland pony and a burro which stubbornly resists being ridden, as well as some calves and sheep to be roped, they are not short of participants. Because the sheep owners are ten-year-old twins who own replicas of medieval helmets, they include a tournament in the event. Even though the jousters knock down the fences so that all the animals get away and have to be rounded up, the show is considered a big success. Although the Apples, the disagreeable couple who live next to the barn, have returned and occasionally call the police or protest in other ways, there is no real antagonist in this book. Perhaps because of this, the story lacks some of the liveliness of the earlier volumes of the series, but the episodes are entertaining in much the pattern of the earlier ones. Choice.

HENRY REED'S JOURNEY (Robertson*†, Keith, ill. Robert McCloskey, Viking, 1963), second in a series of humorous, episodic novels (*Henry Reed, Inc.*†), this one detailing a trip by automobile from San Francisco to Grover's Corner, N.J., in the mid-twentieth century. His diplomat father having been transferred from Italy to Manila, Henry* Reed returns to the United States for a second summer via San Francisco, where he meets Midge* Glass and her parents and travels with them to his uncle's home in New Jersey. As Mr. Glass, a research chemist, has apprehensively foreseen, Henry's presence acts as catalyst for chaos, though he never intends to cause trouble. In San Francisco, while Midge and Henry are waiting for her father outside a conference room, a female chemist asks them to watch her dog. Because they are reading, they are unaware that the dog is making trips into the conference room and stealing and hiding shoes, which the female conferees have slipped off during the lecture. That situation is scarcely straightened out when they meet a woman on a cable car giving her parakeet a ride and end up with the parakeet, Amos, as a gift. This is the first of their acquisitions which cause Mr. Glass distress as the station wagon gets more and more crowded. Another recurring theme is Henry's search for firecrackers to purchase. At each stop something unexpected occurs. They create a gold rush in Yosemite by pretending to find in a stream the nugget Midge has purchased in China Town. They lose and regain Amos and acquire a large bag of giant pine cones. At Disneyland Midge, stretching to see a man she thinks is a movie star, falls off the boat traveling through Adventureland Jungle. At Herman's Gulch, Ariz., they help out some Hopi Indians by replacing sick tribal members on the float in the seventy-fifth anniversary parade. As a result they are adopted into the tribe, acquire a "tan" made of a dye that won't wash off, and learn the Hopi "disappearing fire trick," which consists of burning their bonfire on a pan set on a hole filled with ice blocks; as the fire burns, the ice melts, and the fire sinks from sight. In Hansonville, Kans., Henry applies the same principle to lower a steel swimming pool into its hole in time for the big Fourth of July celebration and becomes the town hero. At the Grand Canyon, they trade a horned toad for an artist's unfinished landscape, and in Taos they put the picture, with some bright vegetables painted by Henry as surreal additions, in an exhibit, win honorable mention, and sell the painting for thirty dollars. Ironically the purchaser is Mrs. Glass. In Denver they lose Amos in a hotel and chase him as he flies across the large open central well and from floor to floor. In Kansas Mrs. Glass wins a large freezer in a Bingo game, and they rent a trailer to haul it. In Missouri, Henry finally buys a large supply of fireworks and stows them in the end of the trailer. When they arrive in Grover's Corner, one of the neighbors assembled to greet them drops a cigarette stub among the fireworks, and they all go up in one brilliant, exciting display. Although the episodes, all recorded first-person as part of Henry's journal, are like those of the first book, possible though unlikely and invariably lively, there is a good deal of travel information that slows this book compared with the first volume. Choice.

HENRY 3 (Krumgold*†, Joseph, ill. Alvin Smith, Atheneum, 1967), realistic "boy's growing up" novel, third and last in the author's series about modern American boys and their relationships with their fathers. Since thirteen-year-old Henry, who tells the story, is the third Henry Lovering, he calls himself Henry 3. Partly because the family has moved so much and partly because, Henry thinks, of his extremely high IQ, he has never formed any close friends. Now that the family has moved to Crestview on Long Island, a suburban community of rising young executives, Henry resolves to hide his considerable intellect in the interest of winning friends. At first, all proceeds according to family plan. Henry's father (Henry II*) wins his hoped-for vice-presidency in American Lock and Locomotive, and Henry's sisters, parents, and Henry himself receive floods of invitations to social functions. Henry is even offered a coveted membership in the X15*, the most exclusive boys' club in town. Ironically, his father's company's venture into producing bomb shelters and the installation of a prototype in the Lovering back yard result in the family being ostracized and Henry's friendship with Fletcher* Larkin, town outcast. Henry becomes convinced that the solution to the family problem lies in finding a solution to war. Fletcher persuades him to present his plan (having Russia and the United States take out insurance on each other) to the president of Mr. Lovering's company. Their scheme backfires, and Henry is shocked and repulsed by what he sees of high-level corporate pressures and politics. During a hurricane, Holy Hannah, Mr. Lovering redeems himself in his son's eyes by his decisive, capable leadership and the family in the community's by their refusal to take refuge in the controversial shelter. Circumstances cause the Loverings to appreciate the clearsightedness and lack of pretense of Fletcher, whose guardian-grandfather (Grandfather* Larkin) has been killed in the storm, decide they need him for ballast, and adopt him. Henry has become so involved with Fletch and community problems that he forgets about his personal IQ problem and begins to excel in school again. This thought-provoking story offers a graceful, conversational style and much ironic humor, and the Loverings are well drawn. But the novel seems more concerned with social comment than its predecessors, and the plot is unconvincing, contrived, and unfocused. Choice.

HENTOFF, NAT(HAN IRVING) (1925–   ), born in Boston, Mass.; jazz expert, columnist, novelist. He is a graduate of Northeastern University, attended Harvard University and, as a Fullbright Fellow, The Sorbonne in Paris. A radio writer, producer, and announcer, he became editor of *Down Beat* magazine, a founder of *Jazz Review*, a staff writer for *The New Yorker* magazine, and a columnist for the *Village Voice*. He has also taught at the New School for Social Research. Besides *Jazz Country** (Harper, 1965), set in the black jazz community in New York City, he has written several novels of the tough urban-drug culture for young people, two novels for adults, and many books of non-fiction.

HERB MAYHEW (*To the Green Mountains**), an albino youth of whom Kath has been fond since first grade when she championed him against the cruel taunts of the school children. More aware than she of the implications of his abnormality, he forces her to sort out her feelings for him. His mother resents being left a widow in poverty and occasionally vents her bitterness on him, while at other times she pities him for his disability.

HERE LIES THE BODY (Corbett*, Scott, ill. Geff Gerlach, Little, 1974), family mystery novel involving witchcraft set in the 1930s in a small town in New England about one hundred miles from Salem, Mass. A grown man, Howie tells what happened to him and his older brother, Mitch, the year Howie was eleven and Mitch was fifteen. Howie tells his story in a long flashback, but as though events are happening. Since times are hard, he and Mitch are delighted to get jobs mowing and trimming the grass around the gravesites in the town cemetery even though the burial ground is a gloomy, spooky place and Ezekiel Zenger, the caretaker, is a grim, taciturn, demanding man. An aspiring poet, Mitch makes up rhymes about the people buried there to lighten the atmosphere and make the time pass faster. Late one stormy afternoon, the boys overhear Zeke and Nathaniel, his brother, in a violent quarrel about something that Nathaniel presumably has done to the gravestone of a member of the Zenger family. The boys investigate and discover a strange geometrical symbol painted on the stone. They consult Mrs. Bradford, town historian, who identifies the mark as the sign of Satan used in the Black Mass. She warns the boys to stay away from the cemetery, since Midsummer's Eve, the time that witches traditionally gather, is very close. She also tells them that the Zenger family had been involved in prosecuting those suspected of being witches in Salem back in the late 1600s and that disasters have plagued the family since that time. The boys return to the cemetery where they observe another confrontation between the two brothers. They learn that Nathaniel is going to Nantucket, and Mrs. Bradford informs them that there have been rumors that witches' gatherings are held there. The next day it is reported that Nathaniel has died on Nantucket and later that the plane bearing his body home has been lost at sea. The boys go to Zeke's cottage to bring him the news about his brother and find him dead on the floor, the devil sign etched in frost on the window. They attend his funeral and the burying. As they leave the gravesite, they see the Satan sign on the dusty earth above the grave. The author sustains well the spooky, chilly, playfully eerie atmosphere. Events move rapidly, and there is always something happening to sustain the interest. The book abounds in conventions of the genre, but the ending is abrupt and lets the reader down, because too many questions remain unanswered. The Zengers are the stereotypical, one-dimensional eccentrics of the form, and the boys are likeable, inquisitive types. The book is mostly dialogue, and Mitch's verses add some humor. Poe Nominee.

HERJOLT (*Prison Window, Jerusalem Blue**), heir to the Viking lordship of Linkøbing. An unimaginative man, he is suspicious of his brother for good reason, since Kronhengst, a charismatic adventurer, plans to kill him. He is also suspicious of learning, of runes, of slaves who act like freemen, and of the loyalty of his own followers. Though stolidly conventional, he broods over the pointlessness of life, which has given him a retarded son and the responsibility for the people of Linkøbing but not their love.

HERKY KRAKOWER (*Sinbad and Me**; *Mystery of the Witch Who Wouldn't**), twelve-year-old genius friend of Steve* Forrester, whose computer-like brain and photographic memory help solve crimes. A victim of polio, Herky can't engage in all the physical activities of other boys and welcomes the excitement which Steve's problems bring into his life.

THE HERMIT (*The Whys and Wherefores of Littabelle Lee**), Winston Splitstone, former Yankee who lives not far from the Lees at Vulture Bluff in the Arkansas Ozarks and who marries Aunt Sorrow. It is from him that Littabelle gets the idea of going to court to force her city relatives to assume some responsibility for their aged parents for whom Littabelle has been caring.

A HERO AIN'T NOTHIN' BUT A SANDWICH (Childress*, Alice, Coward, 1973), sociological problem novel set in New York City in the contemporary period. Narrated alternately in the first person by the various characters, the story traces the drug problem of Benjie Johnson, 13, whose father has left the family years ago and who lives with his mother, Rose, her resident lover, Butler Craig, and Rose's mother, Mrs. Ransom (Elizabeth) Bell. All three are concerned for Benjie's welfare, as also are his best friend, Jimmy-Lee Powell, who is interested in education and has become estranged from Benjie, and two teachers, Bernard Cohen, a white teacher with high academic standards, and Nigeria Greene, a black nationalist with strong concern for the youngsters. Other chapters are narrated by the tired principal, holding on until retirement, by Jimmy-Lee's father, a street-corner speaker, and by Walter, the drug pusher. Despite the good will of several characters, they are ineffectual, Mrs. Bell retreating to hymn-singing religion, Rose to superstition, Butler to another apartment, Cohen to a defensive position in the all-black school, and Greene to a polemic anti-white rhetoric. Butler is the strongest character, a man of both firmness and compassion, who seems to have pulled Benjie back from heroin addiction and crime when he pulls him back from a rooftop fall. At book's end, however, Butler, now planning to marry Rose, is waiting for Benjie, who has been detoxified, to show up at the follow-up center. The boy is late, and the reader is left unsure whether he will come or has spent his clothes money on drugs. Benjie is a smart, swaggering, but vulnerable boy; other characters are familiar types. Each character speaks his own variation of language, with profanity sprinkled throughout. Although handled with some skill, the story has the predictability of a familiar case history and places the blame on society. It does not, however, offer a facile solution. Lewis Carroll.

HESTER FRY (*The Tamarack Tree**), wife of David, mother of Paul* and baby Rachel, with whom Bernadette* Savard goes to live in Connecticut, hoping to attend Miss Crandall's Seminary for Young Ladies. A genuinely good person, Hester has become an abolitionist despite her husband's disapproval and refuses to attend church after the black girls of the seminary are barred from attendance, walking instead a long distance to the Quaker meeting. Having had six children, four of them stillborn, she explains sex and childbirth to Bernadette gently but determinedly, knowing the girl has no mother to turn to for advice.

HEW AGAINST THE GRAIN (Cummings*, Betty Sue, Atheneum, 1977), historical novel of the American Civil War period set in Virginia. Even before her father, Bland Repass, Sr., frees all his slaves, Matilda, 12, has felt the injustice that her friend and companion, Docia Patrick, is in bondage while she is free. But almost immediately Docia's brother, Lucas, is killed by hoodlums fired up to fight, and the war is upon them. Jason Fisher, married to Matilda's favorite sister, Sarah, is set upon on his way to join the Union army and hanged by three poor whites led by Ray Beard. Sarah's twin, Bland, Jr., joins the Union army and is killed. Michael and Joe, twenty-two-year-old twins, join the Confederate army where Michael is killed and Joe loses a leg. Matilda's sister Marjorie loses her husband, but when her baby is born prematurely, Matilda saves it by her care. Her father's will and then his mind begin to fail; her brother

Bill, only a year older than Matilda, joins the Confederacy and loses most of his hand; her mother's spirit is wounded. Sarah, bitter because the family has Southern sympathies and has not brought Beard and his friends to justice, leaves and refuses to visit or correspond. Only Matilda and Grandpa Hume retain their spirit, and he warns her against "dwindling," giving up and allowing events to beat her. Temporarily, her father revives to direct them all in planting and nurturing corn to send to the Southern troops, but when it is harvested, Federal troops sweep down and confiscate it, raiding and burning the house. The family moves into the cabin where Sarah had taught school, and they add on rooms. As Matilda is shingling the roof, Daniel Durham, a boy she had met briefly before the war and who is now a Confederate soldier, comes courting and helps her shingle. They correspond and make plans, but Matilda is found alone and raped by Ray Beard, whom she then shoots and kills. Horrified that she has been violated and may be pregnant, she will have nothing to do with Daniel, who wants to marry her anyway. Grandpa Hume, now old and very weak, comes to urge her to fight, to "hew against the grain," and not to kill herself, as she has planned rather than have Beard's baby. When Sarah returns to thank her for killing Beard, she begins to recover, finds she is not pregnant, and in the end marries Daniel. Although the book has most of the standard romantic situations of Civil War fiction, it also has a realistic picture of the hardships and psychological trauma of the period. Matilda is an interesting, lively protagonist, and her relationship with outspoken Docia, who finally tells her that she, too, has been raped (by Matilda's Uncle George), is a different element, not the standard "dear faithful darky" friendship. Fanfare; National Book Finalist.

HIFFARU (*Saturday, the Twelfth of October**), ugly son of Diwera, Medicine Woman of the People, twin of Akawa*, a daughter. He is proud and often surly and aloof but so alert and intelligent that his mother wishes he had been born a girl so that she might train him to succeed her as Medicine Woman of the tribe. When Diwera orders him to destroy Zan's knife, lest it bring trouble to the People, he has become so attached to it and fascinated by its latent power that he cannot bring himself to give it up. He subsequently kills Sonte* with it, the first murder ever among the people, a tragic and ironic deed.

THE HIGH KING (Alexander*, Lloyd, Holt, 1968), fantasy novel, last in the series set in the land of Prydain*. Rhun* brings Eilonwy* home to Caer Dallben from Mona, and Dallben and Taran* welcome her. She is still very spunky but less stubborn and more considerate of others than before. After Gwydion is wounded by Arawn's Huntsmen, and the miraculous sword, Drynwyn*, is stolen, Dallben consults Hen Wen. When the pig's advice proves too cryptic and obscure to be helpful, Gwydion decides to ride to Annuvin to regain his sword, for with the sword, Arawn can subjugate all Prydain. Eilonwy, Fflewddur* Fflam on Llyan, and Rhun travel together, while Taran, Gurgi*, Coll, and Gwydion head for King Smoit's castle. There they discover that Magg has taken Smoit prisoner and has installed himself as king. Using eggs that produce smoke and mushrooms that cause fire provided them by Gwystyll of the Fair Folk (dwarves), Eilonwy's group rescues their friends, but Rhun is slain. Gwydion then realizes that they will be unable to penetrate Arawn's stronghold without help. Taran is dispatched to rally the Free Commots and Fflewddur to gather the people in the North, while Gwydion rides to Caer Dathyl to enlist the Sons of Don. Soon Smoit's vassals join the cause, too, and all the free men of Prydain gradually join forces to oppose the mighty Death-Lord, among them many characters met in the previous Prydain novels. Pryderi of Don proves treacherous, however, and joins with the Cauldron-Born* against Caer Dathyl, which falls. Math, the High King, is slain, and the golden stronghold burned. Now High King, Gwydion sets sail with an army for Annuvin, while Taran's forces travel overland to intercept the Cauldron-Born before they can rejoin Arawn. Coll is killed in the first encounter. Doli* and 100 men of the Fair Folk turn up, dispatched by King Eiddileg, and Doli leads Taran and his followers by a short cut under the mountains. Eilonwy and Gurgi are captured by Dorath, the brigand, and rescued by Medwyn's wolves, Kaw the crow having informed Medwyn of the dangers facing the good people of Prydain. Adventures continue in abundance in the same vein until Taran finds Drynwyn on Mt. Dragon, the highest point in the mountains. He wields it to defeat the Cauldron-Born, and Arawn's mortal warriors, the Huntsmen, surrender. Magg dies trying to assume Arawn's iron crown. Achren dies helping Taran kill Arawn. As the companions leave Annuvin, the dread palace crumbles into ruins. The heroes return to Caer Dallben to discover that Gwydion and the Sons of Don must fulfill ancient prophecy and depart for the Summer Country, the land of eternal peace and ever-life. Taran decides to remain in Prydain, to devote himself to many unfinished tasks and deeds of benevolence for the people. Dallben informs him that he was a waif rescued from a battlefield, and thus Taran finally finds out who he is in the literal sense, but he has matured enough so that it doesn't matter any more to him. Eilonwy, who proved herself a capable and resourceful leader, gives up willingly her magical powers and accepts Taran's proposal of marriage, and the two wed and rule worthily as High King and Queen of Prydain for many years. The reader is happy to see Taran and Eilonwy finally wed, and the book ties up other loose ends and fleshes out the background of several characters. It is very adventurous and sometimes very suspenseful, but as in the other books, luck and coincidence heavily influence what happens, and the comic characters and humorous effects make it hard to take the conflict seriously, as presumably it should be regarded. ChLA Touchstones; Choice; Fanfare; National Book Finalist; Newbery Winner.

THE HIGH PASTURE (Harnden*, Ruth, ill. Vee Guthrie, Houghton, 1964), realistic novel with animal story aspects set in the American West in the mid–1900s. Because his wife is seriously ill, Tim McCloud's father sends his thirteen-year-old son west to stay with Tim's elderly Great-Aunt* Kate on her cattle ranch in Colorado. Although Tim is soon accepted by the ranch hands, likes and respects Aunt Kate, and assumes responsibilities about the ranch, he often feels out of place, resentful at being sent away from home at such a critical time, and afraid of losing his mother. He catches sight of a handsome wolf-dog one day while he is inspecting an upper pasture. Aunt Kate tells him that the dog is Lobo, a German shepherd "ghost dog," which belonged to a mountaineer who was killed in an avalanche four years before. Since that time, Lobo has haunted the area where his master died. Tim sympathizes with the dog, and several times takes food to him in an effort to make friends. He is delighted when, after a few days, Lobo responds with a tentative tail wag. When Aunt Kate's venerable cattledog, Mac, dies, Tim sees even more clearly how quickly life can come to a stop and that change is inevitable in life. Tim attends a rodeo with Danny and Judy Hooston, children of a neighbor of Kate's. He is able to convey to Judy some of his fears about his mother's health. When Tim's father phones that Tim's mother has died, Tim is grief-stricken and seeks comfort in the hills with Lobo. Bucked off his fractious horse, he suffers a broken shoulder and numerous bruises. Lobo fetches the Hoostons who rescue Tim, and Tim's father accepts Kate's offer of a home on the ranch. Lobo attaches himself to Tim, and Kate and Tim's father allow the boy to keep the dog. The future looks brighter to Tim than it has in a long time. This story of a boy's grief and a dog's loyalty never really engages the emotions. The book lacks originality, is filled with conventional characters and events, and is burdened with passages of philosophy. The taming of Lobo occurs too quickly to be convincing. Characters are plaster figures who do and say appropriate things. Child Study.

HIGHTOWER†, FLORENCE (COLE) (1916–1981), born in Boston, Mass.; author of good-natured mysteries, some of them period pieces, in a family context, based loosely on the activities of her own family. She grew up in Concord, Mass., attended Concord Academy, where her mother taught, and later graduated from Vassar College. Her husband was James Hightower, professor of Chinese literature at Harvard, and the couple lived in China both before and after World War II but made their permanent home in Massachusetts. Of her six novels for young readers, *The Ghost of Follonsbee's Folly*† (Houghton, 1958), a mildly Gothic story about strange happenings after a large and lively family moves into and renovates a big, old, pre–Civil War house, and *Dark Horse of Woodfield** (Houghton, 1962), a lighthearted mystery about the restoration of the Armistead family fortunes, were both chosen for Fanfare by the editors of *Horn Book*, and the latter is also listed in *Choice*. Her settings are vivid, her style deft, literary, and witty, the pace vigorous, and interpersonal relationships well conceived, but her characters are often stock or tend to be eccentric and her plots mechanical, conventional, and overly intricate. She also wrote *Mrs. Wappinger's Secret* (Houghton, 1956), about an elderly lady and a ten-year-old boy who go treasure-seeking, *Fayerweather Forecast* (Houghton, 1967), about the strange disappearance of Aunt Lucy's fiance, *The Secret of the Crazy Quilt* (Houghton, 1972), which involves rum-running and a coded message in a quilt, and *Dreamwold Castle* (Houghton, 1978), about a girl who becomes innocently involved in illegal activities.

HILL, NATHANIEL (*Encounter at Easton**), cruel, ruthless, arrogant bounty hunter, self-styled gentleman, whom John Tolivar engages to apprehend his runaway indentured servant, Elizabeth Mawes. At the time, Tolivar thinks Robert* Linnly, another runaway, has already been captured. At the Lehigh River ferry, Hill happens upon Robert, who calls himself "Peter York," and, needing money, Robert accepts Hill's offer of a job as handyboy. Neither is aware of the other's identity. This ironic encounter leads to Elizabeth's death, which, terrible as it is, Hill with cold irony still regards as a successful conclusion to his quest. Hill tells part of the story.

HINTON, S(USAN) E(LOISE) (1950–   ), born in Tulsa, Okla.; author of problem novels for adolescents. She graduated from the University of Tulsa and has lived in California and Spain, as well as in Oklahoma. She gained prominence when at seventeen she published *The Outsiders** (Viking, 1967), a novel about conflict between street gangs with a highly contemporary flavor that became immensely popular, perhaps because of its youthful vigor and sympathetic voice. It received the *Media and Methods* Maxi Award and is listed in *Choice*. Subsequent novels include *That Was Then, This Is Now* (Viking, 1971), *Rumble Fish* (Delacorte, 1975), and *Tex* (Delacorte, 1979), which continue the theme of youth on their own attempting to survive in a hostile environment. Young readers like her books more than adults, who criticize their superficiality, contrivance, and overemphasis on violence. Witty and engaging, she receives numerous requests to speak at conferences on literature for the young. She is married to David Inhofe, and they have made their home in Oklahoma.

HIS ENEMY, HIS FRIEND (Tunis*†, John R., Morrow, 1967), historical novel in which sports significantly influence events, set in France during World War II, just before the Liberation; in 1948, during the War Trials; and in 1964, twenty years after the novel begins. In 1944, the Germans occupy the small Normandy fishing village of Nogent-Plage. In an ironic exception to the rule, the villagers regard the German commander as their friend. The hostile incidents that plague the authorities of other occupied villagers never happen in Nogent-Plage. The officer in charge, Sergeant Hans von Kleinschrodt, the son of a baron, is an unauthoritarian, easygoing young man, who chats with the townspeople over coffee and is interested enough in them to help them solve their personal problems. Before the war, Hans was a star soccer player, and he often joins in games with the local youth, teaching them to play correctly and skillfully. One of them, young Jean-Paul Varin, idolizes the German and tags him around town. Realizing Allied invasion is imminent, the German High Command assigns a higher ranking officer to the village, which is strategically located. When he is shot and killed, Hans is ordered to execute six hostages in reprisal, among them, a teenaged budding soccer star, a half-demented old man, and Jean-Paul's father. The dilemma too perplexing to deal with, Hans procrastinates and does nothing, and finally a new superior officer takes over and completes the assignment. Although this officer actually gives the order for execution, the villagers blame Hans for the deaths, and he soon becomes known as the Butcher of Nogent-Place. Four years later, after the Liberation, he is convicted of murdering innocent civilians and sentenced to ten years in prison. The story then leaps ahead twenty years. Now thirty-eight, Hans is recognized as the finest soccer goalie in Europe. In a hard-fought, highly tense, world-championship match, his team defeats the other major European team, that on which Jean-Paul is star forward. More ironies follow. As Hans' team's bus passes through Nogent-Plage on the way back to Germany, angry villagers take the German players prisoner and confine them in the same blockhouse in which the hostages were held years before. They set fire to the place, but Jean-Paul intercedes, pleading with them to heed his idealistic father's teachings, lay aside old hatreds, and forgive. Conscience-stricken, the mob decides to release the Germans, but as Jean-Paul leads the baron out of the burning building, a half-mad villager shoots the former sergeant dead. Jean-Paul weeps over the body of the man he loved as a friend but whom circumstances made his enemy. The sports scenes stand out; they are dramatically described and exciting. Other incidents in the baron's personal struggle against war and fate are sometimes powerful but usually too understated to be effective and too obviously support the theme that bygones must be allowed to be bygones, else where will the killing end. The concluding scenes are simply too ironic and coincidental to be convincing. The characters are faceless and seem deliberately assembled. Although one would like to sympathize with Hans, the author never really makes his presumed agonies palpable. Fanfare.

HIS OWN WHERE (Jordan*, June, Crowell, 1971), realistic novel set in New York City in the 1960s. His mother having left the family and his father having been hit by a car, Buddy Rivers, 16, spends most of his time at the hospital sitting futilely by the bedside with little hope. There he meets Angela Figueroa, 14, whose mother is a private nurse for the other patient in the room. Every evening Angela comes into the room to report that she has cared for and fed her three younger brothers and her baby sister, to get further orders from her mother, and to answer a long string of abusive questions her suspicious mother shouts at her. One evening when her mother, infuriated by her monosyllabic answers, slaps her, Buddy follows her out and walks her home. After that he walks home with her every night, then returns to his vigil in the hospital room. One night when, depressed by the whole situation, he does not go back to the hospital, Angela's mother calls her husband who has come home drunk after his late shift and pours out her suspicions of Angela. He goes to Angela's room and beats her, then throws her out. She stumbles to Buddy's house, and he takes her to the hospital, where he is suspected of being the cause of her injuries, which include a concussion. Frustrated by all these problems, Buddy organizes a revolt in his all-male school, demanding sex education including information about contraceptives. Mr. Jenkins, the principal, agrees and the boys start an impromptu celebration in the cafeteria with the four women who work there dancing while all the boys sing and beat time. Jenkins calls the police, who find no cause for arrests, but Buddy is suspended and cannot be reinstated until a parent comes with him, an obvious impossibility. Meanwhile, Angela is sent to a home for abused children, St. Margaret's in Middlebrook, N.Y. Buddy sets off to see her in the family car, but, terrified by the traffic, gives up and returns home. When she has earned enough good conduct points to merit a visitor, he does go and arranges that he will see her when she earns a weekend at home. Her mother does not welcome her, and Angela says she will go back to St. Margaret's but instead goes to Buddy's house, a strange place converted by him and his father to be completely functional, almost bare of furniture and belongings. They make love and spend one night; then, fearful that they will be traced there, they move to a cemetery which they have visited one Saturday, where they break into a tool shed and set up housekeeping of a sort, make love some more, and end by hoping that Angela is pregnant. Although published in the early 1970s, the story has all the cliches of the fiction of the late 1960s: unredeemingly hostile parents, school personnel so rigid that they are blind to genuine feelings, young people confident that the beauty of their true emotions will solve all their problems and potential problems. It is written in a third-person stream of consciousness black language that slips unconvincingly into literary vocabulary now and then and gets tedious long before the end of the fewer than 100 pages. Fanfare; National Book Finalist.

HOBAN, RUSSELL (1925–   ), born in Lansdale, Pa.; artist, writer, whose most widely popular works are picture books about Frances the Badger, illustrated by his wife, Lillian. He attended the Philadelphia Museum School of Industrial Design and worked in a film studio, as a television art director, and as commercial artist and copywriter for an advertising agency. During World War II, he served in the U.S. Army in the Italian campaign and was awarded the Bronze Star. Since 1953, he has concentrated on writing, producing three adult novels, many picture books, and books of poems for children, among them *The Pedaling Man, and Other Poems* (Norton, 1968) and *Egg Thoughts, and Other Frances Songs* (Harper, 1972). His *The Mouse and His Child** (Harper, 1967), a fantasy about a wind-up toy, is listed in *Children's Books Too Good to Miss* but is generally admired more by British than American critics.

HOBSON DRAWN (*Dust of the Earth**), sixteen-year-old older brother of Fern* Drawn, who does not want to move to Chokecherry because he has a crush on Maizie Green. Lazy and dreamy at first, he wants something better for himself than the marginal life of a sheep ranch. Later, he drops out of school, because he feels the teacher is ignorant, and proves an able and alert student to Fern's teaching about sheep. The two grow close and pretty much cease their bickering during the year they herd together. Because of his experiences on the farm, Hobson decides to go to Kansas City to attend a school of agriculture.

HODGES, CARL G. (1902–1964), born in Quincy, Ill., where he attended school; free-lance writer, author of mysteries for adults and novels for children. He was executive-secretary for the National Association of Petroleum Retailers, did public relations work for the Illinois Department of Public Welfare, was superintendent of the Illinois Information Service, and was columnist for the Peoria, Ill., *Star*. He was Midwest vice-president of the Mystery Writers of America and president of the Springfield Civil War Round Table, which he helped to organize. He made his home in Springfield, Ill. Of his seven published novels, four were for young readers. *Land Rush** (Duell, 1965), a substantial and exciting historical novel about the Oklahoma land rush of 1889, received the Western Heritage Award. He also wrote *Baxie Randall and the Blue Raiders* (Bobbs, 1962), *Dobie Sturgis and the Dog Soldiers* (Bobbs, 1963), and *Benjie Ream* (Bobbs, 1964). He was author of novelettes for Hearst Features and of articles for house and travel journals.

HOLLAND, ISABELLE (1920–   ), editor and freelance writer, best known in children's literature for her novels of contemporary family life. She was born in Basel, Switzerland, where her father, a U.S. foreign service officer, was consul. She lived also in Guatemala and England, where she attended private schools and studied at the University of Liverpool. When her family returned to the United States during World War II, she lived for the first time in her own country. After receiving her B.A. degree from Tulane University in New Orleans, she worked for various magazines and was publicity director for Crown, Lippincott, and Putnam publishing companies, and was for several years publishers' assistant at Harper's. Since 1969 she has devoted full time to her writing. Of her some dozen novels for young people, two have been Fanfare books: *The Man Without a Face** (Lippincott, 1972), a novel controversial with some because it involves homosexuality, and *Of Love and Death and Other Journeys** (Lippincott, 1975), a better-crafted and more convincing story of how a young girl attempts to cope with the death of her mother, that was also a National Book Award finalist. Her plots are often forced to carry too many themes and receive less emphasis than the characters, who struggle variously with self and the social environment. Other titles include *Heads You Win, Tails I Lose* (Lippincott, 1973), *Alan and the Animal Kingdom* (Lippincott, 1977), *Now Is Not Too Late* (Lothrop, 1980), *A Horse Named Peaceable* (Lothrop, 1982), *The Empty House* (Lippincott, 1983), *God, Mrs. Muskrat and Aunt Dot* (Westminster, 1983), and a book of non-fiction, *Abbie's God Book* (Westminster, 1982). She has also published several novels for adults.

HOLMAN, FELICE (1919–   ), born in New York City; poet, author of a variety of books for children. She grew up on Long Island and is a graduate of Syracuse University. During the 1940s, she worked as an advertising copywriter. Her first books for children were picture books. Others include two books of verse, *At the Top of My Voice* (Norton, 1970) and *I Hear You Smiling* (Scribner's, 1973). Her novel, *Slake's Limbo** (Scribner's, 1974), a story of a boy who lives in the New York subway, was named to the Lewis Carroll Shelf, and both it and *The Murderer** (Scribner's, 1978), an amusing and moving story of a Jewish boy growing up in a Polish-dominated Pennsylvania mining town, were *Horn Book* Fanfare list choices.

HOLT, EDWARD (*A Gathering of Days**), Catherine* Hall's teacher. An earnest young man, a strict disciplinarian, he is very interested in stretching the minds of his students. He causes a furor in the community, however, when he reads about current happenings from newspapers in school. He marries Cassie* Shipman's Aunt Lucy and moves with her to Boston.

HOMESICK: MY OWN STORY (Fritz*, Jean, ill. Margot Tomes, Putnam, 1982), autobiographical novel set in Hankow, China, and on the trip to Washington, Pa., in 1925 to 1927. Born in China, Jean Guttery, ten when the story starts, is very conscious of being an American and longs to go "home" to her grandmother in Pennsylvania. Her decision that she can't sing "God Save the King" in her English school precipitates a small crisis with her teacher; a schoolmate, Ian Forbes, threatens to beat her up, she skips school, and finally her father Arthur, a YMCA director, suggests that she sing "My Country 'Tis of Thee" softly. Life of the missionaries and other Americans in the turbulent period in China is well described. Her amah, Lin* Nai-Nai, is really not of the servant class but has been ostracized by her family because she left her husband when he took a second wife; Yang Sze-Fu, the cook, is a communist who becomes increasingly surly as the political unrest deepens; the family friends, the Hulls, are unconventionally free in talk and action and live like privileged rich but are getting a divorce. When anti-foreign feelings run high and the Gutterys are threatened by the dock coolies, the ricksha coolies, who know the family, rescue them. As they summer in Kuling in the mountains, Jean's mother, Myrtle, has a premature baby girl, whom they name Miriam and whom Jean adores, but the infant dies. Her anger turns on the minister who has described death as glorious. A plan that an orphan named Millie, brought to spend Christmas with the Hulls, will stay a few days with Jean makes her wildly expectant that she will find a "sister," but the reality is a disaster when the girl refuses to stay. As the civil war reaches Hankow, Jean and her mother leave the city with the other women and children on the Yangtse River boat for Shanghai, where they stay with the Hulls until Arthur can join them. The Hull children with their mother travel back to the United States with the Gutterys aboard the *President Taft*, and Jean learns some American slang from her more sophisticated friend, Andrea* Hull, who is a year older. The Gutterys travel across the United States by automobile, making sometimes as much as 300 miles a day. Jean's grandparents and their farm are everything she has hoped, but her first day of school leaves her with mixed feelings. Her outspokenness and her resistance to Palmer method penmanship start her off badly with the teacher, but Donald Burch walks her home and she realizes that what Andrea has been telling her about boys and being in love can apply to her, too. In her foreword the author says she has taken some liberty with time and minor details, but that the book, published as fiction, "does not feel like fiction to me." Except in a narrowly factual sense, it is *not* fiction; it moves like autobiography and even includes photographs of a number of the characters and places. The picture of a lively, intelligent child living among adults of two different cultures is vivid, often funny, and has the ring of truth. Her determinedly conventional mother and adventurous father, who enjoys having a narrow escape from disaster, are well depicted. A brief summary of the history of China in the twentieth century follows the story. Boston Globe Honor; Child Study; Fanfare.

HONOR BOUND (Bonham*, Frank, Crowell, 1963), mystery novel set in 1858 on the first westbound Overland Mail stagecoach to California. Young Cullen Cook, whose grandfather is to be the agent at the stagestop on their Arkansas farm, is frequently in trouble because he would rather draw than do farm work. When one passenger on the stage arrives too ill to go on, Cullen jumps at the chance to travel in his place to illustrate the stories of the trip by journalist J. Ross Boone. He is entrusted by the ailing passenger with some mysterious responsibilities: a pair of ferrets, a bottle of Atlantic water from President Buchanan to be delivered to California Senator Gwin, and an attractive girl, Jennifer Bradford, who is knitting a scarf for Gwin and whom he is to protect by shooting an assailant, if necessary. Cullen finds himself almost immediately at odds with slave-trader Colonel Fales and slave-catcher, brutal Mike Saddler, and he contrives to help in the escape of the slave Saddler expects to pick up. With Boone's help, he soon realizes that there is a bigger game afoot, a plot to have California secede and become a slave state, a conspiracy involving Fales, the scarf into which Jennifer knits a code, and the ferrets, which have a key word on a gold strip embedded under their skins. Jennie prevails upon Cullen to finance her trip beyond El Paso, and though he suspects her motives he feels honor bound to protect her and to deliver the ferrets. In San Francisco he discovers she is not a willing part of the treasonous conspiracy but also feels honor bound to knit and deliver the scarf for her guardian, a pro-slavery senator. With Boone's help, they manage to thwart the plot. As a mystery the novel provides exciting and unexpected turns of plot, but as historical fiction it is too implausible and lacks the characterization to make any of the people memorable. Poe Honor.

HOOK (*The Long Journey**), Laurie James's sturdy half-Hambletonian, half-quarter horse, of which she is very proud, and which she rides cross-country to Butte on the instructions of her grandfather to get help for him in his impending blindness. She named the horse for the fishhook marking on his forehead.

HOOK, GEORGE (*Bert Breen's Barn**), the younger partner in the Ackerman* and Hook Mill in Boonville. He sees to it that the mill is up-to-date, often having to persuade Mr. Ackerman to try new ways, and advises and encourages Tom Dolan. A bachelor, he shows an interest in Tom's mother, Polly* Ann, and they keep company. He spends Christmas with the family, but there is no clear indication at the end of the book that he and Polly Ann will marry.

HOOPS (Myers*, Walter Dean, Delacorte, 1981), sports novel set in Harlem in the contemporary period. Lonnie Jackson, black teenager, having finished high school, is at loose ends with a part-time job at the run-down Grant Hotel and no plans for the future. The one thing he knows is basketball. With his best friend, Paul, and others who hang around a local gym, he gets into a team to enter the city-wide Tournament of Champions but is disgusted that the coach will be a man he thinks of as a wino, Cal* Jones. Lonnie begins to be won over when Cal proves he can outplay the boy and is reluctantly impressed when Cal brings a pro-ball player, Sweet Man Johnson, to practice and seems to be a good friend. Eventually Cal reveals that he is Spider Jones, a pro star who was forced out of the league in a point-shaving scandal for gambling interests. Since then he has turned to drink, separated from his wife, Aggie, and lost his only child in a fire. He sees a chance of rehabilitation by coaching a team and perhaps helping some of the boys get scholarships and a chance at a future in basketball. The gamblers, however, will not let him alone. One particular hood named Jack Tyrone runs an after-hours place where Paul's sister, Mary-Ann, who is sweet on Lonnie, works. She tells Lonnie that Tyrone has an envelope with Paul's name on it, and together they steal it and discover it is welfare checks that Paul stole, needing money to keep up with some middle-class blacks he has become friendly with, and which Tyrone is obviously keeping for blackmail. Tyrone and his thug, Juno, try to get Cal to cheat again for them. He fights and ends up in jail. Mary-Ann steals bail money from Tyrone, is suspected, and is given a drug overdose so her death will look like an accident. Paul finds her in time, however, and she recovers. A white entrepreneur named O'Donnel also leans on Cal, first saying his presence may taint the tournament, then wanting him to make Lonnie quit so the white boy he is sponsoring will look better. At the final game, Cal keeps Lonnie from playing, pretending to go along with O'Donnel's and Tyrone's demands until they see one of Tyrone's underlings go out to place his bet. Then Cal sends Lonnie in and the team wins. Tyrone and Juno force their way into the locker room, a fight ensues, and Cal is killed. Lonnie realizes that Cal was right when he said it's not the money the underworld figures want as much as the control and that the only way to stay out of their clutches is never to take anything from them. In the end Lonnie has some possibilities for basketball scholarships, but mostly he knows he has to learn to control himself and to deal with the many figures trying to exploit him. The first-person narrative is in black street language, somewhat modified, therefore sounding a bit stilted. There is casual acceptance of stealing and sex, as well as some earthy descriptions that would not have appeared in books published for children ten years earlier, though no four-letter words or gross profanity. For the sports-conscious reader there are several basketball episodes, described in long and loving detail. Poe Honor.

HORACE MORRIS (*Unclaimed Treasures**), youth about Willa's age who lives next door and becomes a good friend of the Pinkertons, whom by the end of the story Willa accepts as her true love, and whom eventually she marries. He is calm and steady and likes to eat apples, his most distinguishing feature throughout the story. Willa gradually comes to see that he is perceptive and decisive. When, for example, Nicholas shows Matthew the picture he has drawn of Willa kissing the bedpost, Horace saves the day by diverting attention to the chicken pot pie Willa's mother is serving, and he alone realizes that Willa engineered the reconciliation between his father and mother.

THE HORSE TALKER (Williams , J. R., Prentice, 1960), historical novel set in Comanche country in Texas along the Rio Grande about 1860. Red-haired, blue-eyed Lan, 15, has lived with the Comanches since he was three and thinks of himself as Comanche. When he fails in his vision quest, surly Yellow* Wolf, who despises Lan because he is white and calls him Bloody Scalp for his hair, persuades Lan to help him steal the great white horse that belongs to the colonel at the American fort some distance from the Comanche camp. Lan has a remarkable ability to communicate with horses and sway them to his will. At the fort, Lan gets the horse for Yellow Wolf, who then treacherously abandons him to the white soldiers. When the soldiers are hostile to the boy because he has been raised Comanche, and the colonel decides to send him to a mission school, Blanco*, captain of a crew of wild mustang hunters, offers to take him. If Lan helps him capture the fabled stallion, the Ghost of the Plains, to replace the stolen horse, Blanco says he will allow Lan to return to the Comanches. An eventful two months follow during which Lan learns much about white ways; makes friends with Marina*, Blanco's high-spirited, resourceful daughter, and once-hostile Miguel*, Blanco's sturdy godson; is befriended by Javier*, the lame campmaster and ropemaker; and incurs the enmity of the disagreeable, blond American mustanger, the Inglés, who is Blanco's special friend because he rescued Marina from Comanches. At first angry and resentful, Lan soon realizes it will be to his advantage to learn Spanish and cooperate with the mustangers. The sooner they acquire the quota of horses they need for the fort, the sooner they can go after the Ghost, and the sooner he can return to the Comanches and settle the score with Yellow Wolf. He proves brave and resourceful in hunting for food and in rounding up horses. He gentles a big, black stallion for Blanco by talking to it, and when afterward he suffers an attack of conscience for his deed, Blanco understandingly releases the horse. Although Blanco feels indebted to the Inglés, he breaks off with him when the Inglés joins another American, Guero Connors, to steal Blanco's horses. After the mustangs are delivered to the fort, Blanco and his crew head after the Ghost. When both Lan and Blanco discover they have no stomach for capturing the monarch of the southern Plains, Lan proposes to return to the Comanches, explain what happened, and ask the chief to return the colonel's horse. After a happy reunion, to Lan's joy, the chief agrees. The two catch up with Blanco in time to see Ghost choose death to capture by leaping into a bog. In a showdown, the Inglés, Guero, and Yellow Wolf are shot. Lan has learned that an inheritance awaits him in Scotland, but feeling neither white nor Comanche, he elects to accompany Blanco to his ranch in Mexico. The leading positive characters have life and evoke credibility, and the plot, if occasionally cliche, proceeds at a good pace with a pleasing blend of personal and circumstantial problems to a plausible if overly dramatic conclusion. Although the author's voice can sometimes be heard when the characters are discussing current events or the ways of whites and Indians are compared, on the whole, the strongly depicted setting is well blended with the plot, and the reader gets a strong sense of what Comanche and white life is like at this time on the Plains. The proud Lan's dilemma about what to do with his life in this period of transition for the Comanches seems accurate. Native Americans are objectively presented. Spur.

HOSFORD, JESSIE (1892–   ), born in Nebraska. She attended Iliff School of Theology and received her B.A. and M.A. degrees from New Mexico Highlands University. She was active in community affairs in Los Vegas, N.Mex., and wrote juvenile novels, the best known being *An Awful Name to Live Up To** (Meredith, 1969), set in Nebraska in the first decade of the twentieth century, and its sequel, *You Bet Your Boots I Can* (Nelson, 1972).

THE HOUSE OF DIES DREAR (Hamilton*, Virginia, Macmillan, 1968), mystery novel set in the Miami valley of Ohio in the mid twentieth century. Thomas Small, 13, has come with his black parents and his young twin brothers, Billy and Buster, from North Carolina to live in a big house once owned by the abolitionist, Dies* Drear, near the town where his father will teach in college. On the evening they arrive, several mysterious occurrences are upsetting: their furniture has been arranged with strange formality by the caretaker, Mr. Pluto Skinner; a huge black horse appears followed by a boy about Thomas's age, M. C. Darrow, and ridden by a tiny girl called Pesty*; activated by a button on the front door, the front steps move, revealing a tunnel entrance which Thomas follows to a kitchen wall that slides up; exploring in the woods behind the house he falls onto a sort of platform which rises, revealing a fiery interior and a "devil" who chases him; the devil turns out to be Mr. Pluto, a blacksmith living in a cave, who has a strange, nervous conversation with Mr. Small. Ominous things continue to happen. Someone comes into their house in the night, leaving mysterious triangles. Their kitchen is trashed. Mr. Pluto seems sometimes old and friendly, sometimes cold and frightening. With his father, Thomas goes to Mr. Pluto's cave, finds a rope that makes a cave wall slide aside, and enters a much larger cave full of valuable antique furniture, books, carpets, tapestry, and glassware, which is kept polished by Pesty, who is there with Mr. Pluto. A second Mr. Pluto appears, who turns out to be Mayhew Skinner, Pluto's actor son. He has come back because he knows the neighboring Darrows, whose old father had a feud with Pluto, are trying to find the Dies Drear treasure, and he worries that the Smalls will somehow side with them. Mayhew works out a plan to scare off the Darrows, who are the ones trying to frighten the Smalls, afraid they will find the treasure first. Having let it be known that Mr. Pluto is going to the hospital for at least one night, a ruse to force the Darrows to make their move, they hide near the cave with Mayhew dressed as Dies Drear, Thomas and his father as runaway slaves, and Pesty on a horse fitted out with phosphorescent paint and wings perched on a rise above the cave. The Darrows are thoroughly terrified, then realize they have been fooled, but also that Mr. Pluto is still a match for them. Mr. Small convinces Pluto that all the antiques belong to a historical foundation, though the old man has a claim to them through the will of Dies Drear. Pluto, however, will inventory them before Small notifies the foundation, a job that will take the rest of his life. Despite some gripping scenes, the book is unconvincing, too full of gothic elements and unbelievable things, like the cave with movable walls and a treasure of antiques more than a hundred years old still perfectly preserved in a cave. The parts about the Underground Railroad are exaggerated in a way that diminishes the very real drama of the actual historical truth. Choice; Poe Winner.

THE HOUSE OF WINGS (Byars*, Betsy, ill. Daniel Schwartz, Viking, 1972), realistic novel of family life set recently in a farming area near a major highway in northern Ohio in which from one morning to the next a boy comes to appreciate his aged, eccentric grandfather. Spoiled, willful, saucy Sammy, 10, whose parents ''had allowed him to raise himself because he was the youngest of eight and they were worn out,'' runs away from his grandfather, whom he does not know and with whom he has been left while his parents look for work in Detroit. Hurt and angry at being left behind, he furiously rejects his grandfather's explanation for their departure, calling him a liar and despising him for his weakness of body and his dirty, rundown house with its mud-caked floors and the birds and geese that wander in and out at will. He races desperately down the overgrown country road, through the culvert under the highway, up the hill through the cornfield, and into the forest, his grandfather in protesting and dogged pursuit. Puzzled by the sudden realization that his grandfather has stopped following him, Sammy gingerly backtracks, sure the old man has some trick in mind. To his surprise, he finds his grandfather gazing in rapture at a beautiful sandhill crane, standing alone, wounded, and pathetic in the brush. His interest caught,

Sammy helps the old man capture the bird, carry it home, feed it, and tend its wounds. Sammy gets interested in the tragedy of the blinded bird and in the old man's remembered stories about creatures he has known and nursed. Sammy notes how tenderly his grandfather cares for the owl, parrot, and geese that now share his house. The next day, when he helps his grandfather move the crane to the creek so it can grub for insects, he discovers he has come to like his grandfather and wants the old man to get to know him as well as he does his birds. Less a story than a study in character, the book grabs with its exciting chase scene and proceeds well through passages describing setting and the boy's feelings. The plot is very thin, and motivations won't bear scrutiny. The quick change in attitude of as stubborn and headstrong a boy as Sammy is supposed to be violates logic. Individual scenes stand up, and the grandfather emerges as an interesting figure, more so than Sammy. Choice; National Book Finalist.

THE HOUSE ON CHARLTON STREET (De Jong*†, Dola, ill. Gilbert Riswold, Scribner's, 1962), mystery novel set in Greenwich Village, New York City, in the mid twentieth century. Even before the Bartlett family—musical John, 16, Phoebe, 14, David, 11, their father, Carl, and their artistic mother, Jessica— are settled in their newly purchased house at $33^1/_2$ Charlton St., they learn that the old house has a mysterious history. Their moving man, Mr. O'Connor, tells them of the strange old couple named MacLaughlin, who lived there and for whom his mother worked when he was a child. Jacob MacLaughlin and his wife were recluses, never spoke to each other, and kept an upstairs room ready with fresh sheets for a visitor who never arrived, a room with a fireplace about which the old man had a paranoid fear. David becomes particularly interested in the history of Greenwich Village and discovers that the house once belonged to a man accused of being a receiver of smuggled goods, a charge that could never be proved. Charley Williams, an old man who cares for their unpredictable furnace, adds to the mystery by mentioning letters from Civil War times which he once found when the coal bin was replaced. At the suggestion of their grandmother, a music teacher who visits frequently from Boston, they find boarded-up fireplaces in several rooms, including David's room, the same one kept ready by the MacLaughlins. When they uncover the fireplace, David discovers a drawer cleverly concealed in the woodwork just above the baseboard. When he puts his new watch in the secret drawer and later finds it gone, he is at first suspicious of his sister and of Williams, but Phoebe, in a door-slamming fit of annoyance, knocks loose the door lintel in her room below his and is pelted with gold nuggets and with the watch. They discover that the drawer is equipped with a spring, which dumps its contents into a storage space built over Phoebe's door, obviously the work of the early owner involved in smuggling. The nuggets are explained by Williams' letters which tell of MacLaughlin's brother, William, who struck it rich in California, returned to visit his brother Jacob, hid his gold in the secret drawer, and accused Jacob of theft when it disappeared. The room was kept ready for his expected return. The Greenwich Village setting is the most individual element in the novel, though the research involved in learning about it seems rather advanced for an eleven-year-old like David. A typical boy in other ways, he is the most developed character. Although the historical background is interesting, the plot is rather slow and the solution unlikely. Poe Honor.

HOW MANY MILES TO BABYLON? (Fox*, Paula, ill. Paul Giovanopoulos, White, 1967), realistic novel of urban life set mostly in a black neighborhood in Brooklyn, N.Y., about the time the book was written. Only child James Douglas, 10, shares a dingy, one-room apartment with his loving and imperious aunts, Althea, Grace, and Paul, who earn their living by cleaning houses. His father abandoned his family, and his mother has been in the hospital for three months. One Saturday in November, James finds a cheap ring with an imitation red stone, which he takes as a sign that his mother wishes him to meet her at a certain place. The following Monday morning, James runs away from school and goes to a ramshackle, deserted house, where he has a secret hidingplace, sure that he will find his mother there. Three street-wise toughs a little older than he, Stick, Blue, and Gino, capture him. They live by stealing dogs from affluent people, to whom they subsequently return the dogs for rewards. They take James by bicycle to an apartment house, where they force him to steal a poodle named Gladys, and, with James and Gladys, they bike to their hideout in a Coney Island funhouse. After a policeman locks the funhouse for the night, James helps them all to escape through an exit he has discovered, and, with two more stolen dogs, they return to the deserted house. That night while the boys are sleeping, James makes a break for freedom, releasing the dogs to create a diversion while he runs away. After returning Gladys, James goes home. His worried aunts, who have reported his absence to the police, greet him with great relief, and, to his joy, within the tiny apartment his mother is waiting for him. Characters are flat, and some are stock, and not even James changes as a result of his experiences. He is shown as an imaginative youth, who fantasizes about the stories his mother has told him about the African origins of the blacks. He thinks he may be a prince, and that is what the three boys call him, Prince. Scenes are well drawn, and James's longing for his mother is convincing. But the author neither prepares the reader for the mother's return, nor makes James's ingenuity in solving problems believable. The toughs seem more eccentric than dangerous, and their boldness and daring are rather admirable. The plot comes to little, and one is never really worried about James, but events do convey some sense of inner city life for blacks. Choice.

HOW THE WITCH GOT ALF (Annett*, Cora, ill. Steven Kellogg, Watts, 1975), picture story about a donkey named Alf, who believes himself misunderstood and ignored, and who sets out to remedy the situation. Alf envies the canary, who does nothing but sing all day, yet the Old Woman whistles and talks to it. He envies the cat, who does no work at all but can sit in the Old

Woman's lap and sleep at the foot of the Old Folks' bed. He envies the dog, who pretends to be guarding the farm and is always being praised and petted by the Old Man. When Alf tries to sing to wake the Old Folks in the morning, the Old Man pours a bucket of water over his head. When he tries to frolic and jump like the dog, the Old Man scolds him. When he tries to sit in the Old Woman's lap, the Old Man chases him back to the barn with the mop. Alf decides to run away, but he chooses somewhere close, so he can see what happens next, and clambers up onto the roof of the house. The Old Folks think at first the noise is a tornado or an earthquake, but when the Old Man sticks his head out the window and sees Alf's ears sticking up behind the chimney, he is sure it is a witch. The next morning, when the Old Man discovers Alf gone, they think the witch has taken him. At first Alf is quite happy, nibbling the leaves from an overhanging branch and watching the concern the Old Folks show. Eventually, when all the leaves are gone, he gets hungry and thirsty and very lonely. When there is a storm at night and Alf slips around, unable to keep his footing on the wet roof, the Old Folks think it is witches, and the Old Man goes out with a pot and a spoon and bangs on it with all his might and shouts to scare the witches away. Startled by this strange behavior, Alf forgets to hang onto the chimney and comes head over heels hurtling down from the roof. The Old Folks are sure that they have scared the witch into returning their donkey, and Alf is delighted and comforted by the fuss they make over him. This light but pleasant story manages to present Alf as an interesting character and gets some humor from the misunderstandings on the part of both the donkey and his people. Christopher.

HUBERT CARES (*A Lemon and a Star*†; *Terrible, Horrible Edie**; *Edie on the Warpath**), third child in the wealthy, motherless family of Summerton, Mass., in the early twentieth century. Neither concerned for his honor, like Ted*, nor worried about what is proper, like Jane*, Hubert concentrates on food and survival. Blond and, as a young child, solid, he reminds Jane of a sailor. Generally agreeable, he is a frequent companion in Jane's adventures and is less antagonistic to Edie* than is Ted, but he also has a mind of his own and can be stubborn and, on rare occasions, erupts with sudden spurts of bravery.

HUGSY GOODE (*The Alley**), friend of Connie* Ives. He also lives in the Alley*. He helps to collect clues and participates in the trial. He tends to be very emotional and to overdo things. The children often have to rein him in. He is the main character in the sequel, *The Tunnel of Hugsy Goode*.

HULKS (*The Whisper of Glocken**), enemies of the Minnipins. They have built a dam over the Watercress River, which has caused the Watercress to flow backwards and flood the Minnipin lands. The Hulks are huge, stocky, human-like creatures, three Minnipins tall. They wear billowy, white cloaks and hats like overturned bread baskets and carry powerful crossbows from which they shoot long, sharp arrows. Because of their arrows, the Minnipins sometimes call them Stickermen. The Hulks intend to take the captured Minnipins home with them and put them in a cage on public display. Their leader is a huge, red-haired brute called Red Carrot. It is hard to take the Hulks seriously as villains.

HUMBUG MOUNTAIN (Fleischman*, Sid, ill. Eric von Schmidt, Little, 1978), realistic adventure novel told in tall-tale style and set in Missouri in the Old Wild West. Wiley, 13, and Glorietta, 10, are used to wandering the West since their father, Colonel Rufus Flint, is an itinerant newspaperman. They anticipate further excitements when Pa, down on his luck, decides to move the family up the Missouri to join Ma's father, Grandpa Tuggles, in his new town of Sunrise at the foot of Humbug Mountain. To their amazement, neither the glorious, bustling town complete with opera house and hotel of Grandpa's advertisement brochures nor Grandpa himself materializes, only jackrabbits and prairie stretching to the horizon, two outlaws, Shagnasty John and the Fool Killer, the "terrors of the plains," and, some way inland, high and dry in a creek bed, Grandpa's riverboat, the *Phoenix*, where Ma sets up housekeeping. Pa's newspaper, *The Humbug Mountain Hoorah*, sparks a land boom and gold rush, which enable Ma to rent all the rooms on the *Phoenix*, and Sunrise begins to take shape. A bashful man in a dark blue coat with brass buttons, Mr. Slathers, formerly Grandpa's engineer, informs the Flints that Grandpa had left Sunrise, when, two years before, the Missouri capriciously shifted its course, leaving his fine riverfront lots worthless. He also informs them that Grandpa is now captain of a tin-clad riverboat, at that very time on its way downriver laden with gold dust from Montana. Shagnasty John and the Fool Killer plan to hijack the boat, but the hijackers are foiled when, at the most fortunate moment, the Missouri jumps back into its old bed, its new banks having been weakened by the extensive prospecting. The Flints are reunited with Grandpa Tuggles, and Wiley gets to meet his hero, Grandpa's companion, Quickshot Billy Bodeen, whose remarkable adventures have been recorded in the nickel novels to which Wiley is addicted. Wiley learns, to his surprise, that these popular adventure stories are written by his own father, during the Colonel's occasional, mysterious disappearances. Other happenings include a ghost on the *Phoenix*, the discovery of a petrified man, and a disaster-prone goose, Mr. Johnson. The book is all plot. Action follows action in rapid succession for a robust, hilarious, pleasingly preposterous extravaganza that features zany, intriguing characters and whose only purpose is to entertain. Addams; Boston Globe Winner; Contemporary Classics; Fanfare; National Book Finalist.

THE HUNDRED PENNY BOX (Mathis*, Sharon Bell, ill. Leo Dillon and Diane Dillon, Viking, 1975), more a brief picture than a story of the relationship between a young black boy, Michael John Jefferson, and his Great-great-aunt Dew. Mike and his parents have brought the aging woman, Dewbet Thomas, from her home in Atlanta to live with them, because she took in John, the father, as a child when his parents drowned and he loves her, but she refuses to speak to his wife, Ruth. In her wandering mind Mike is often John as a boy, and they play a game of counting the coins in her "hundred penny box," which contains one cent for every year of her life. She tells him rambling stories of what happened in the years represented by the pennies, of her husband, her own five sons, of his father as a child. When his mother proposes to burn the box, thinking that it is in the way and that Aunt Dew will "settle down" better if she doesn't cling to her old things, Mike becomes fiercely protective and plans to hide it in the basement. The love between the old woman and the boy and the way they share feelings, despite her inability to understand Mike's urgency about the box, are sensitively portrayed. The mother's frustration at having to care for a frail old woman who refuses to recognize her presence is believable, but her desire to get rid of all Aunt Dew's possessions seems rather overdrawn. The book escapes sentimentality but remains slight. Newbery Honor.

HUNT, IRENE (1907–   ), born in Pontiac, Ill.; teacher and author of books for young people. After growing up on a farm near Newton, Ill., she received her degrees from the Universities of Illinois and Minnesota and did further study in psychology at the University of Colorado. For many years she taught French and English in the Oak Park, Ill., public schools and for a brief period psychology at the University of South Dakota. She then returned to Illinois to teach and serve as director of language arts in the Cicero schools. Her first novel, *Across Five Aprils** (Follett, 1964), was published when she was fifty-seven. Very well received, it was the sole Newbery Honor book of the year and a Fanfare book, and was selected for the Lewis Carroll Bookshelf, *Choice*, and *Children's Books Too Good to Miss*. A substantial and very credible historical novel about the experiences of a fictitious southern Illinois family during the Civil War, it rose from family records, letters, and stories told by her grandfather, who was a boy of nine at the start of the conflict. Her second novel, *Up a Road Slowly** (Follett, 1966), a highly convincing girl's growing-up story, was also the result of personal experience and memory. It won the Newbery Medal, was a Fanfare selection, and is cited in *Choice*. In 1970 it was one of seven books presented by the American Booksellers Association to the Home Library of the White House. Critics have been less enthusiastic about her succeeding books: *A Trail of Apple Blossoms* (Follett, 1968), a fictionalization of the Johnny Appleseed legend, *No Promises in the Wind* (Follett, 1970), about the "wild boys of the road" during the Great Depression, *The Lottery Rose* (Follett, 1976), concerning child abuse in present day Florida, *William* (Follett, 1977), about three orphaned black children who are cared for by a white girl, and *Claws of a New Century* (Scribner's, 1980), about the women's rights movement at the beginning of the twentieth century. Since her retirement from teaching, she has made her home in Florida.

HUNT, LAWRENCE J. (1920–   ), born in Banks, Oreg.; professor of business administration and author. He attended Oregon State College, received his B.B.A. degree from the University of Oregon, his M.A. from New York

University, did graduate work at Ohio State University and received his D.B.A. degree from the University of Oregon. During World War II he served in the U.S. Army and during the 1950s and the early 1960s worked as a home furnishings buyer and factory sales representative. He has taught at the University of Oregon and the University of Montana and has published short stories and mystery novels, among them *Secret of the Haunted Crags** (Funk, 1965), set in the salmon fishing trade in Alaskan waters.

HUNTER, KRISTIN (EGGLESTON) (1931–   ), poet and novelist; born in Philadelphia, where she has made her home. She received her degree in education from the University of Pennsylvania and taught in public schools in Camden, N.J. Among her other positions have been columnist and feature writer for the Pittsburgh *Courier*, copywriter for an advertising bureau in Philadelphia, researcher for the School of Social Work at the University of Pennsylvania, and information officer for the city of Philadelphia. A free-lance writer since 1964, she has also taught creative writing at the University of Pennsylvania. In addition to writing poems, short stories, reviews, and articles that have appeared in such publications as *Nation*, *Seventeen*, and *Black World*, she has written for television and several novels for adults, among them, *The Lakestown Rebellion* (Scribner's, 1978), *The Landlord* (Scribner's, 1966), and *The Survivors* (Scribner's, 1975). *The Soul Brothers and Sister Lou** (Scribner's, 1968), tells how several inner city black youths triumph over their environment by forming a singing group which becomes famous. Her first novel for children, it was elected to the Lewis Carroll Shelf and selected by *Choice*. She continued to record the black urban experience for the young as she perceives it in its sequel, *Lou in the Limelight* (Scribner's, 1981), in which Lou and the Soul Brothers find that the world of show business does not offer instant success, and in a book of short stories, *Guests in the Promised Land* (Scribner's, 1976), which was a finalist for the National Book Award and received the Christopher Award. She has also written picture books for the young.

I

I, ADAM (Fritz*†, Jean, ill. Peter Burchard, Coward, 1963), historical novel set in Connecticut in 1850 as the whaling industry wanes, farming assumes new importance, and the gold fields lure New Englanders westward. Adam Crane, 15, of the small seaside town of Coveport, is delighted to have finished school and now considers himself a man. While his school chums, Mulie, Enoch, and Stump, are heading either for the sea or California, Adam looks forward to running the upcountry farm that his father, Captain Crane of the whaler *Good* Nellie*, has bought. After Captain Crane sails on what is to be his last voyage, Eli* Trapp, amiable itinerant peddler, takes Adam out to the farm, which the current owner, Old Man Sharkey, has agreed to help Adam work until the family joins him in the fall. Adam's arrival is inauspicious. Mr. Sharkey and his son, Tyler, about nine, are hostile, the house is almost bare of furniture, and the barn and grounds are unkempt. Mr. Sharkey goes back on his agreement to help Adam with planting and haying, pleading ill health. Adam manages, however, with the assistance of the friendly Newlands, his nearest neighbors, and Pen Jackson, the local schoolteacher. On a trip to town, Adam discovers that the townspeople feel Sharkey is in excellent health and that he appears to be involved in some mysterious business deal. Discouraged by Sharkey's persistent shenanigans, Adam is advised by the Newlands to hire help out of the money due Sharkey and to play along with the man until Captain Crane arrives in the fall and can deal with him. In August, while Adam is in town attending a Freak Show with the Newlands, Sharkey ransacks the house, steals the deed to the farm and Adam's money, and takes off for California. Then a farmer shows up, Noble Hanson, who claims Sharkey has sold the farm to him. Hanson proves a decent sort, and he and Adam trace Sharkey to New York City, where they find him in jail. Sharkey owns up readily to his crimes and turns over the deed and unspent money. By this time, Adam has begun having doubts about farming as a vocation, and Pen Jackson and young Sarah Newlands persuade him to give college second thoughts. Then Captain Crane returns home minus one leg from an accident at sea, and Adam feels trapped into continuing to work the farm. Pen encourages him to share his ambitions with his father. When he does, to Adam's surprise, Captain and Mrs. Crane are delighted with his decision to return to school, sell the farm to Hanson, and decide to remain in Coveport. Although the story moves along well with some suspense, good conflict, and some humor, the plot falls into place too easily, and, except for Adam, the characters are flat or stock. The book is chiefly memorable for the picture it gives of the period. Tyler, Old Man Sharkey's sullen, aloof son, who becomes the ward of the Cranes at the end, is a minor character who arouses interest and sympathy. (Mr.* Stone; Old* Bess) Fanfare.

I AM THE CHEESE (Cormier*, Robert, Pantheon, 1977), grim novel set largely in New England in the contemporary period. Written in three voices, the novel seems at first to be a first-person, present tense narration of a bicycle trip from Monument, Mass., to Rutterburg, Vt., undertaken by Adam Farmer, about fifteen. These passages alternate with transcriptions of taped interviews with the boy by an investigator, possibly a therapist, which fade into third person narration of Adam's memories of past events. Gradually it becomes apparent that Adam is really Paul Delmonte, whose father, a newspaperman, gave testimony in an important trial concerning government links with organized crime and was given a new identity to protect him from retribution. The interviews bring out Paul's discovery of the past, of his fear and distrust of Mr. Grey, the government agent who has arranged this new life and is their contact, and of the friendship and love he felt for Amy Hertz, a carefree, prank-loving girl he knew in school. In the first-person story, Adam frequently tries to call Amy, to tell her he is traveling to Vermont to visit his hospitalized father, but keeps getting the wrong number. Through the interviews, it is revealed that their identity has been discovered or disclosed and that his mother and probably his father were killed, and that he has been in custody, possibly in a private sanitarium, for at least three years. The bike trip is either in Adam's imagination or a pointless pedaling around the sanitarium grounds. The people who offer threats on his trip are fellow inmates. More shocking is the suggestion that the "therapist," Brint, is a representative of either the corrupt government or the crime syndicate, probing to see whether Paul knows more about his father's testimony than he has revealed. There is a suggestion that he will be drugged until the order comes for his "termination." The book is extremely clever in its construction and gripping in its tension. The theme, that it does not pay to stand up for what is right, is depressing and has caused some to question this sort of realism for young people. Fanfare.

IDA EARLY COMES OVER THE MOUNTAIN (Burch*, Robert, Viking, 1980), realistic novel set in Georgia in the 1930s. Since the death of their mother, Randall Sutton, 11, his father, his sister Ellen, 12, and the twins, Clay and Dewey, 5, have suffered under the good intentions of rigid Aunt Earnestine, who manages the household but would like to return to her home in Atlanta. When Ida Early, a tall, unkempt scarecrow of a woman, appears seeking a job, the Suttons are delighted, and Aunt Earnestine reluctantly turns the family over to her. Ida's unconventional ways and tall stories entrance the children, and the smoothness of the household and good meals please their father. Small incidents mar the felicity, like the visit from Uncle Ross, their bratty cousin, Kathy Alice, 8, and Aunt Myrtle, who is shocked by the way Ida handles things, but generally Ida's great humor and unexpected abilities (she is a dead shot with anything she throws, for instance, and can beat anyone at checkers) keep them all happy until she accompanies the twins on their first day to school. In the playground some of the older children see and taunt the strange-looking woman, and Randall and Ellen fail to defend her. After that Ida tries wearing a dress instead of her usual overalls and curling her wild hair, but she seems to have lost her spirit. She regains some of her enthusiasm when, to help Randall with a school program, she puts on an exhibition with a lasso, then ropes a rampaging bear and saves one of the schoolgirls from being mauled. Randall and Ellen, consumed by guilt, realize that Ida plans to leave soon, so they write a letter of apology and put it in her knapsack. When she disappears, the twins at first won't believe it, and Mr. Sutton fears he must send for Aunt Earnestine again, but the children persuade him they can get along. Their struggles are sure to be apparent at Thanksgiving, when both aunts are coming to visit, but shortly before that date Ida roars up on a motorcycle to rejoin the family. Although the low-key picture of family life is appealing and realistic, Ida Early is too bizarre to be entirely believable. The general good humor of the book makes this less of a disadvantage than it might be in many novels. Sequel is *Christmas with Ida Early*. Boston Globe Honor.

IDA FARRADAY (*The Skating Rink**), Tuck's complaining stepmother. Slatternly and querulous, she is nevertheless hard working and more appreciative of Tuck than any of the other family members. When she talks of his real mother, who was drowned when Tuck was three, he realizes that she is jealous of her predecessor, who was from a socially higher family. Ida's unhappiness with her lot concentrates on the decrepit wood-burning stove, symbol of all the hardship she puts up with as wife to unsuccessful Myron.

I, JUAN DE PAREJA (Treviño*, Elizabeth Borton (de), Farrar, 1965), biographical novel about the slave who was assistant to the famous court painter, Velázquez*, in the early seventeenth century. Born to a black slave woman in Seville, Juan is early made page to the mistress and taught by her to read and write. When he is perhaps twelve, she dies of plague, and he is sent, along with the household goods, in the care of a cruel gypsy, Don Carmelo, to her heir and nephew, Diego Rodríguez de Silva y Velázquez. The gypsy beats and starves him, and he escapes along the way, agreeing to work for a baker for forty days, then makes his way alone to seek his new master. When he is close to Madrid, Carmelo finds him again, beats him unconscious, and delivers him to Velázquez, a quiet, kindly man who teaches him to grind and mix his paints and do other work around the studio. The household besides Velázquez consists of his wife, their two little daughters, Paquita and Niña, and two apprentices, Alvaro, whom

Juan likes, and Cristobal, who steals and tries to trick Juan. After some time Velázquez receives a commission to paint the portrait of the king, Philip* IV, and they move to a studio in the palace. The king and Velázquez, both quiet men, become close, real friends over the years as the artist paints many pictures of the monarch, his family, his chief courtiers, even his dogs. The famous painter, Rubens, visits from the Netherlands, and Juan falls in love with a slave, a musician, in his party but can make no declaration. When Velázquez is sent by the king to Naples to paint his sister, soon to be married to the King of Hungary, Juan accompanies him. They return to find that little Niña has died in their absence, and Juan, very much part of the family, grieves. As Paquito grows up, Juan, who has played with her when she was a child and given her a kitten, Mooshi, becomes her confidante when she falls in love with her father's student, Juan Bautista. A young man comes from Seville, Bartolomé Esteban Murillo*, wishing to be accepted as a student. A deeply religious young man, he becomes concerned for Juan's soul, which he knows is troubled, and Juan confesses to him that he has secretly been painting, although it is a crime punishable by death for a slave to engage in the arts. In 1649 Juan accompanies his master to Italy again on a mission to collect art works for the palace. Velázquez injures his right hand, and Juan nurses him back to health, after promising in his prayers to confess openly about his painting if his master is healed. Asked to paint a portrait of the Pope, Velázquez encounters the enmity of Italian nobles who resent foreigners. He paints a portrait of Juan but gets no commissions until Juan takes the portrait and calls upon various nobles, displaying his master's skill. When they return to Spain, Juan chooses his time, places one of his own paintings of the king's favorite dogs among his master's works, and when Philip discovers it, falls upon his knees and begs forgiveness. Puzzled, the king turns to Velázquez, who studies the painting, then writes out papers of manumission for Juan. He also agrees that Juan may marry Lolis, his wife's slave, who is granted her freedom as a wedding gift. The end of the book records the death of Paquita in childbirth, of her mother, and eventually of her father. Juan and Lolis go to Seville to live and work with Murillo. Although the book is based on known facts in the life of a real man, these are few and much has been invented. Nevertheless, the tone of the book is more like biography than fiction, with events proceeding more in the manner of history than of structured plot. The personality of the actual Juan de Pareja can only be surmised. In the story, Lolis is resentful at being a slave, but Juan is not. His character, patient and loving toward his master, is the stereotypical "good black man" who is eventually rewarded, a picture of slavery more admired in the early 1960s when the book was published than in more recent years. Fanfare; Newbery Winner.

I'LL GET THERE. IT BETTER BE WORTH THE TRIP (Donovan*, John, Harper, 1969), realistic problem novel set in the late 1900s mostly in New York City in which a lonely, imaginative, sensitive youth comes to see that one's perceptions of one's self can affect the quality and direction of one's life. After the death of his grandmother, who has raised him, Davy Ross, 13, leaves the small New England town where he has grown up and goes to live with his divorced mother, Helen, whom he hardly knows, in her apartment in New York City. Over her objections, he brings with him his dachshund, Fred, his dearest possession and consolation in his bereavement. Classwork and sports at his exclusive Episcopalian school afford him some relief from his grief and loneliness. Saturday visits with his father, David, and his new wife, Stephanie, bring a welcome change from the tension of life with Helen, who writes for an advertising agency, drinks heavily, and often wallows in self-pity. At school, Davy finds he has much in common with Douglas Altshuler, a class leader. Altshuler's parents are divorced, too; he also lives with his mother, and his closest friend recently died of leukemia. Davy, however, is congenial, accommodating, and less sure of himself, while Altshuler is belligerent, self-confident, and contrives to control situations. While the two boys are alone in Davy's apartment one evening, their needs find expression in a homosexual encounter. For days afterward, "making out" with Altshuler preys on Davy's mind, and he becomes withdrawn and irritable with guilt and fear. The relationship between the two youths takes a critical turn when Helen discovers them on her living room floor, asleep after sampling her whiskey. She immediately assumes misconduct and summons Davy's father. While Davy and his father discuss things, the half-drunk Helen leaves the apartment to walk Fred. The dog breaks away from her, runs into the street, and is killed by a car. Heartbroken, Davy experiences again the various emotions of grieving, finally concluding that Altshuler is to blame for Fred's death. His anger toward Altshuler explodes in the school locker room, where the two slug out their resentment for each other. Later, Altshuler calls to apologize, and the two boys reunite for a Saturday outing, during which Altshuler helps Davy see that the past need not prejudice the future. Davy and Altshuler convince, and dialogue flows fluently and believably, but that Davy should fall in with someone like Altshuler seems too convenient, and the plot carries a burden of themes and occasionally violates logic. Most characters and incidents seem tailored for the purpose of examining a topical concern, but the many small details of everyday home and school life, Davy's love for Fred, and the use of first person and present tense make Davy's grief and guilt palpable and immediate. Fanfare.

IMA DEAN LUTHER (*Where the Lilies Bloom**; *Trial Valley**), Mary* Call Luther's younger sister, who has a willful nature and likes to play with paper dolls. She is a fun-loving child and increasingly complains about the work involved in wildcrafting. She likes Kiser* Pease's house and the pleasures of being with him and Devola* and thinks it would be pleasant to go to live with them.

I, MOMOLU (Graham*†, Lorenz, ill. John Biggers, Crowell, 1966), realistic novel set in Liberia in the mid twentieth century. Momolu, 14, is the son of Flumbo*, one of the important and respected men of the Kewpessie tribe in the town of Lojay, in the interior beyond the reach of roads. When a group of soldiers come, the villagers greet them courteously and quarter them in various houses, but when the guest at Momolu's house, in friendly fun, dresses the boy in his uniform, Flumbo, who hates soldiers, furiously rips the clothes from his son and starts a fight. In a village trial, it is decided that Flumbo and Momolu must take six bags of rice to Cape Roberts and there stand formal trial. They are accompanied by Flumbo's strong friend, Nisa-Way, and by old Tinsoo, interpreter. After a trip down river of several days, they are just arriving when Momolu, in enthusiasm for the new sights, dances in the canoe and overturns it, losing five of the six bags of rice. They visit at the home of Jalla-Malla, a Kewpessie tribesman now a city dweller, and Momolu makes a friend at the mission school, but when they are tried, they are thrown into a prison of unspeakable filth. Their friend, Jalla-Malla, however, buys rice and pulls strings and gets them released into the custody of an army captain, who puts them to work in the care of a Kewpessie soldier, Poobak. Momolu sees much good in the new life, but Flumbo stubbornly continues to insist that he hates soldiers, who in the past have caused much misery to his people. Unwilling to release them until Flumbo changes his mind, the captain takes them as bearers on a trip to Kewpessie country. Flumbo, afflicted with a lame leg and unused to long walking, breaks down and the captain treats the leg and has Flumbo carried in his own hammock. As they near Lojay, Momolu worries that his father will be shamed by being brought home a prisoner. Momolu helps his father see that the soldiers and the government are working for the people, and when Flumbo agrees and promises that when the road-building crews come to Lojay he will lead his men to help, the captain declares him free. There is a joyous homecoming, and Momolu plans to learn to read and understand new things. The thesis, that one must accept change, is obvious and heavily ridden, and the action is somewhat slow, but the picture of life and attitudes among the tribal people of Liberia is interesting. Momolu is an adequate character, bravely offering to work off their sentence to save his father from prison, but the interest centers upon Flumbo's change of heart. Choice.

INCIDENT AT HAWK'S HILL (Eckert*, Allan W., ill. John Schoenherr, Little, 1971), novel based upon an actual incident of a child living with an animal in Canada about twenty miles north of Winnipeg in 1870. William MacDonald and his wife, Esther, have been successful homesteaders west of the Red River and have four children, John, 16, Beth, 12, and Coral, 9, all healthy, normal children, but six-year-old Ben* is different, very small for his age and quiet, disinclined to talk to people but so skillful in imitating animals that he seems to talk with them. When a new neighbor, an unsavory character named George Burton, terrifies the child by his roughness and brutality toward animals, William is unreasonably impatient with the boy with whom he always has trouble communicating. A few days later Ben wanders off, following a bird, and, caught in a sudden storm, loses his way and takes refuge in a badger hole. The organized hunt by all the neighbors backfires when the first horseman Ben sees is Burton, from whom he hides. When the female badger, who has just lost her cubs, returns, she is more curious than hostile and brings Ben food as she would to her own young. For two months they live together, hunting at night and even killing Burton's vicious dog, Lobo. When Ben is finally found by John, he is at first like a wild thing, snarling and fighting off his brother, then clinging to him when they get to the farm, but suddenly he seems to recognize his mother. The reunion is interrupted by the sudden appearance of the badger, toward whom Ben now becomes fiercely protective. After a short time during which the badger becomes accustomed to the farm and Ben turns surprisingly voluble, Burton rides into the yard and shoots the badger. The book ends with the badger probably dying, but with Ben and his father finally reaching an understanding. Detailed and skillfully written descriptions of the life of the badger and of the way it adopts Ben make this unusual story believable. The adoption of the badger by the MacDonald family is somewhat less plausible, but the difficulties William has of understanding his strange son, despite his good intentions, and the tensions this causes in the family are convincingly handled. Newbery Honor; Stone.

INGE DORNENWALD (*The Devil in Vienna**), protagonist, a Jewish girl who writes as a school exercise the story of her family's experiences in Vienna just before World War II begins. An only child, she rebels against her parents' wishes that she have nothing to do with Lieselotte* Vessely because Lieselotte is the daughter of a minor Nazi official. Vati is angry when he discovers that Inge has resumed her friendship with the girl who shares her birthdate, after the Vesselys return to Vienna from Munich. Later he discusses their predicament with Inge, and she comes to see that the relationship is potentially dangerous to both families. Inge finally decides to put family love and loyalty above her personal feelings for Lieselotte. Inge grows up realistically. She is impressionable, rebellious, and changeable, typical adolescent behavior. She would like to be able to do the things that Lieselotte does, and she at first feels dislike for Tommi Löwberg, the son of family friends, then develops a crush on him.

IN THE COMPANY OF CLOWNS (Bacon*, Martha, ill. Richard Cuffari, Little, 1973), baroque, realistic novel set in central Italy sometime during the eighteenth century. Foundling Gian-Piero*, about ten, works in the scullery of the Convent of the Poor Clares in the village of Rocco, where the priest has taught him to read and write. Bored with routine chores and longing for some color in his life, he runs away with Domenico, the convent's donkey, which he is soon duped into selling to a traveling player. He falls in with the troupe's Harlequin*, a resourceful and mercurial personality, who has a long-standing grudge against the leader of the band, Schiavullo, a fat man who wears red satin pantaloons, the very one who cheated Gian-Piero. The two are later joined by Ginestra*, a Dominican novice, who has a beautiful singing voice and who claims she is the illegitimate granddaughter of a powerful nobleman, Count d'Ascanio-Lisci. After they catch up with the troupe, Ginestra is soon assimilated into the band, her lovely voice, ready wit, and nimble tongue bringing acclaim to the group as they make their way northward toward Venice. But the animosity between Harlequin and Schiavullo grows more bitter as Harlequin gradually assumes leadership of the troupe. As the intricate plot swirls across the landscape adding characters and complications, Gian-Piero feels increasingly uncomfortable in this world of zanies who speak in lines even when not performing, and he grows less confident of Harlequin's friendship. In Venice, Schiavullo contrives to have Harlequin arrested for the murder of a pawnbroker. When Harlequin is sentenced to the gallows, Gian-Piero writes to Ginestra's nobleman, asking him to help Harlequin. Intrigued by the ambiguities and contradictions of Gian-Piero's eloquent, if tangled, letter, the Count intervenes on Harlequin's behalf and adds him and Ginestra to his personal household. The end of the story sees Gian-Piero on his way back to Rocco and the convent, relieved to depart from the world of intrigue and violence, quite different from the life of which he had dreamed. This vigorously told, ironically humorous farce moves at a frenetic pace, with a motley cast, many coincidences, sophisticated and irreverent style, and Punch and Judy patter full of innuendo and double meanings. It offers some sense of period as it examines the nature of truth and reality. It is often hard to keep the details of the convoluted plot and the characters straight. The composer, Antonio Vivaldi, called the Red Priest because of his flaming red hair, appears as the friend of the nobleman. Fanfare.

IRA (*Ellen Grae**), a gentle, kindly man of thirty, evidently retarded, who makes a living by selling peanuts at a stand in the town of Thicket, Fla. He never speaks to anyone and is regarded as the town character. He likes Ellen* Grae and talks to her, however, and to her friend, Grover*. His story about the secret death and burial of his mother and her husband poses a tough moral dilemma for Ellen Grae. Ira lives in a tin shack by the river with his pet goat, Missouri, which he says is named after his dead mother.

ISABELLA (*The Marvelous Misadventures of Sebastian**), Princess of Hamelin-Loring, attractive young woman whom Sebastian assists in her flight from the evil clutches of the Regent of Hamelin-Loring, who is trying to force her to marry him. She travels disguised as an apprentice. Her purpose is to reach her Uncle Frederick in his neighboring kingdom and with his assistance gather an army to drive out the unscrupulous Regent. At first, she is stiff and pretentious and speaks in polysyllabics and the royal "we." Proud, pampered, not very sensible, she has been oblivious of how the Regent has been oppressing her people. Her adventures with Sebastian help her to understand what has been going on in her kingdom and how poor a view her people have of the monarchy. She resolves to change things when she accedes to power. At the end of the story, she has predictably become warmer, more approachable, and more aware of her responsibilities.

ISABELLA D'ESTE (*The Second Mrs. Giaconda**), Beatrice's* older sister and Ludovico's* first choice for a wife, an actual historical figure. Proud, willful, she enjoys acquiring beautiful and exotic things, among them dwarfs, whom she then breeds. She tries to entice da Vinci to join her court and paint her portrait. The painting of the "Mona Lisa," for Salai* the painting of Beatrice that da Vinci never accomplished, is in part an answer to Isabella's peremptory demands. Isabella's courtiers refer to her as "Isabellasays," their way of ridiculing her imperious ways.

ISH-KISHOR, SULAMITH (1896–1977), born in London, England; author of fiction and non-fiction for adults and children on religious themes and Jewish history and legends. Her childhood was spent in England, where she began to write at five and published some poems at ten. After emigrating with her family to the United States, she attended Wadleigh High School and Hunter College in New York City, specializing in history, English, and languages. A prolific and versatile writer, she wrote nine books of fiction and many books of Bible stories, Jewish customs, biography, legends, and holidays, and a history of Israel for young readers. Her reputation as a children's writer rests largely on two novels, *Our Eddie** (Pantheon, 1969), about Jewish immigrants to New York before World War II, and *A Boy of Old Prague** (Pantheon, 1963), about the hatred of the Christians for the Jews in the mid–1500s, both of which were Fanfare books and are cited in *Choice*, the first also being a Newbery honor book. Her other titles for the young include *The Master of Miracle: A New Novel of the Golem* (Harper, 1971), *The Carpet of Solomon: A Hebrew Legend* (Pantheon, 1966), and *Children's History of Israel from the Creation to the Present Time* (Jordan, 1930). Her articles on music, art, and theater appeared in national magazines.

ISLAND OF THE BLUE DOLPHINS (O'Dell*, Scott, Houghton, 1960), "Robinson Crusoe" novel of the lone survival of an Indian girl on what is now called San Nicolas Island, seventy-five miles southwest of Los Angeles, in the mid nineteenth century. Based on a real experience, this is the tale of Karana, 12, a member of the Ghalas-at tribe who are living on the small island shaped like a dolphin when a ship of Aleuts arrives hunting the fur of the sea otters that live in the kelp beds nearby. The Russian Captain Orlov makes an agreement with Karana's father, Chief Chowig, that he will give the islanders half the value of the furs in trade goods if they can camp on the island while they hunt. The suspicious islanders watch the Aleuts carefully but do not make friends. When the fur hunters are about to leave, the islanders demand their share, the Aleuts seem to be dealing in bad faith, a fight breaks out, and nearly two-thirds of the island men are killed, including Chowig. The new chief, Kimki, goes alone by canoe to the mainland to seek a new home for the tribe, and at his request a white man's ship comes to pick up the people. As Karana and her sister are leaving, their little brother, Ramo, 6, runs back for his spear and is left on the

island. Because bad weather threatens and the ship cannot return, Karana leaps
into the sea and swims back to the island to be with him. Within a short time,
however, Ramo is killed by wild dogs. Karana expects the ship to return for
her, at first daily, then next summer, but it is years before she sees another
human. Although it is against the rules of her people for women to make weapons,
she does make a spear and a bow and arrows. As her hope of prompt rescue
dwindles, she takes a canoe and heads for the mainland, several days' journey
away, but it springs leaks, and she barely makes it back to the island. Finding
the memory of the dead depressing, she burns the village and makes herself a
new home against the cliff with a stockade of whale ribs to keep out the wild
dogs. Some of these dogs she manages to kill. After wounding their leader, she
brings him back to her house, nurses and tames him, and names him Rontu.
This first animal friend is followed by others—a pair of birds which she takes
as fledglings, a wounded sea otter she names Mon-a-nee, a little fox, and years
later after Rontu's death, his son, Rontu-Aru. Always fearing the return of the
Aleuts, she hides a canoe and supplies in a sea cave, and when, finally, they
do arrive, she retreats there but runs into a girl, Tutok, who is with them. Though
they cannot converse, they see each other for several days and exchange gifts,
and the hunters depart without Tutok revealing Karana's existence. One other
time a ship of the white men comes but leaves again before Karana decides to
reveal herself. Two years later another ship comes, and she goes with it, taking
Rontu-Aru with her. There is considerable interest in how she makes her cormorant
skirt, how she finds the Black Cave containing a skeleton and images made by
earlier peoples, how she survives an earthquake. Because Karana is an Indian
in her native environment, the story is based less on how a character manages
physical survival than most Robinsonnades, however, but rather on her emotional
survival in isolation. She is competent and restrained, not giving away to joy
or despair, but she appreciates the beauty of her surroundings and the
companionship of the animals. The understated style and quiet tone seem
particularly well suited to Karana's character and make this an effective book.
ChLA Top Ten; Choice; Fanfare; Lewis Carroll; Newbery Winner.

THE ISLAND OF THE GRASS KING (Willard*, Nancy, ill. David McPhail,
Harcourt, 1979), fantasy subtitled *The Further Adventures of Anatole*, and set,
in the real world, at Anatole's grandmother's house, evidently some time after
the first volume, *Sailing to Cythera**, since Grandpa has died and Grandma has
developed asthma. Together she and Anatole search in the garden for fennel,
an old cure for asthma, but it seems to have died out. That night Anatole and
his cat, Plumpet, who has been told by Grandma to take care of Anatole, discover
a brilliantly shining winged horse in the garden and climb aboard to go find
fennel for Grandma, taking with them the silver coffeepot they have found that
day under the bathtub. The horse says Anatole will find the fennel by freeing
the King of the Grass, and for that he will need a key from Mother Weather-
sky's garden, and the story is of their many adventures in finding it. They are

dropped on the Island of Sycorax, meet the Keeper of the Roads, who gives them the road to the garden. On the way they dig up a girl made of glass, whom they name Susannah, and who joins them. They are captured by a Great Dane and his soldier dogs in the Kingdom of the Dogs, and, along with a green plush rabbit named Captain Lark, are condemned to be thrown into the sky from a giant swing. They come to rest in a field near the house of one of Mother Weather-sky's sisters, a maker of clouds, who sends them on to the house of her brothers, the winds, in a fish-shaped cloud. The North Wind, in exchange for Anatole's YMCA card, takes them on to the garden of Mother Weather-sky's garden, first giving them the *Red Calfskin Book of Magic*, which can be read only by the wild boar of the garden. Mother Weather-sky sends her club to beat them to her, turns Plumpet and Captain Lark to gold, and sets Anatole, Quicksilver the Coffeepot, and Susannah to work. Sent to weed the garden, Anatole meets the boar, who is charmed by his harmonica music. He helps Anatole get the key which will free the Grass King. Quicksilver saves Plumpet and Captain Lark by sprinkling them, which reverses the golden spell, and with Susannah they escape, join Anatole, and all ride off on the boar, pursued by Mother Weather-sky's club. They all get away except Susannah, who is hit by the club and turned into a real girl. They find the Grass King and his wife in an enchanted sleep and wake them with Susannah's whistle, which also changes Captain Lark back into a sailor and the boar into a gardener. Susannah realizes she is the child of the King and Queen of the Grass. The King gives Anatole a clump of fennel from his crown and sends him home to Grandma's garden. The story has a more cohesive plot-line than the earlier book, and it follows more the pattern of an extended quest tale than the dream-sequence of its predecessor. While there are entertaining and striking bits, it has less of the whimsical charm, and the unmotivated changes that occur are more confusing than trancelike. Sequel is *Uncle Terrible*. Lewis Carroll.

I TELL A LIE EVERY SO OFTEN (Clements*, Bruce, Farrar, 1974), humorous novel set in 1848 along the Missouri River from St. Louis to what is now Vermillion, S.Dak. Narrated by Henry Desant, 14, who "tells a lie every so often," the story relates the wild adventure that results from an innocent falsehood. At the instigation of his brother, Clayton, 17, Henry sneaks upstairs in a neighbor's house to see whether the undergarments of Caroline Burke, Clayton's girl, have ruffles sewn inside to produce a more curvacious figure, as her twin sister, Clytemnestra, has charged. Overcome by guilt, he does not pry into her wardrobe but tells Clayton that he has and that there are no falsifying ruffles. Then, to distract Clayton from further questions, he says he has learned from an Indian that a white girl with red hair is living with Indians up the river. This story inspires the zealous Clayton to start off to rescue their cousin Hannah, who disappeared nearly ten years before and is thought to have been kidnapped by Indians, a circumstance that inspired Henry's lie. Since the boys were to travel upriver to help out at a cousin's farm in Kanesville for the summer anyway, they leave early on the pretext of escorting Miss Eusebia Otis, fiftyish, who is travelling to Council Bluffs to meet and marry Thomas Johnson, a union arranged by her uncle, Titus Pewbrace. To insure her dowry chest, Aunt Eusie, a woman with considerable practical wisdom, bets ten dollars against four hundred fifty that the riverboat will sink, and when it does, even though Henry manages to save the chest, she collects from the reluctant captain. Fired by stories of a red-haired niece of an Indian, a Mr. Nowac, whom they have met on the boat, Clayton pushes on to Vermillion, where they see the girl. Henry, though he accepts the superiority of his older brother, of which Clayton constantly reminds him, worries over Clayton's idea that while Henry climbs under a teepee side to "rescue" their cousin, Clayton, a crack shot, will shoot all evil Indians from a distance with his high-powered rifle. When Henry approaches the girl, he cannot determine whether she understands him, but his fears of Clayton prove well founded. Unable to find any evil Indians to shoot, Clayton drills Henry, carefully avoiding vital organs. Religious Clayton is insufferably self-righteous and prone conveniently to forget his own part in any disaster, and though Aunt Eusie sees through him, Henry remains loyal. Much of the humor in the lively book comes from Henry's honesty and Clayton's self-deception. National Book Finalist.

IT'S LIKE THIS, CAT (Neville*, Emily, ill. Emil Weiss, Harper, 1963), realistic, boy's growing-up novel, one of the earliest in the wave of New Realism. It describes a year in the life of fourteen-year-old Davey Mitchell, as told by Davey himself. Davey lives in an apartment in the heart of New York City with his lawyer father, a "roarer," and his asthmatic mother. He gets on poorly with his father, and, whenever the two quarrel, as they often do, his mother has asthmatic attacks. From eccentric Crazy* Kate, Davey accquires Cat, a big, tiger-striped, egotistical tom, whose company comforts Davey when tension runs high. When Cat strays into the basement of a nearby apartment building and gets accidentally locked in a property cage, he is released by a nineteen-year-old burglar, Tom* Ransome, who is later picked up by the police. Grateful for Tom's help, Davey writes to him, offering his father's professional services, and a friendship develops between the two. Through Tom, Crazy Kate, and other friends of Davey's, his relations with his father gradually improve. When he realizes that Cat's nightly roaming will surely lead to an early death for his pet from fights, Davey makes the difficult decision to have Cat neutered. Davey's father helps Tom, an ex-student of New York University, down on his luck and estranged from his family, to a job and a more stable life, and the whole family helps Crazy Kate through the difficult time when she is hounded by reporters after her wealthy, estranged brother leaves her his money. Among Davey's other friends are Nick, the chum who introduces him to Mary, whom he shyly dates, and Ben, a Jewish boy who also likes animals. As the days pass, Davey spends less time with Cat and more with people. He comes to see that human relationships are the most important of ties and that responsibility is an essential quality in every friendship, whether with human or animal. The story confronts contemporary generational conflicts without sentimentality or blame and with honesty, if the episodic plot does often seem artificial and lacking in substance. The book's strong points are its unpretentiousness, its easygoing, humorous, sometimes witty, conversational style, and its warm insights into the feelings of young adolescents. Books Too Good; Choice; Newbery Winner.

IT'S NOT THE END OF THE WORLD (Blume*, Judy, Bradbury, 1972), realistic, contemporary, problem novel set in the late 1900s in suburban New Jersey from the end of February to mid-June, in which a girl comes to terms with her parents' divorce. Sincere, dependable, somewhat naive Karen Newman, 12, reports to the reader directly and writes in her daybook, where she rates days with letter grades, including plusses and minuses, her thoughts about and reactions to events that occur after she learns that her parents are getting a divorce. At first, she refuses to believe that there is anything wrong between her parents, although her older brother, Jeff, 14, seems quite aware that there has been trouble. During lunch with Aunt Ruth, her mother's sister, and Uncle Dan, Mother breaks the news of the separation to the children, but Karen refuses to accept facts. She tries to hide matters from her friends and worries about what will happen to her, Jeff, and little Amy, 6. She remains puzzled, bewildered, worried, and somewhat angry throughout most of the story. When Garfa (Grandfather) Newman of Las Vegas fails to reconcile her parents, he urges Karen to take up where he has left off, an injunction she takes quite seriously and ponders different possibilities for achieving. Most of the book concerns her tentative efforts to reunite the family. A new friend and child of divorce, Val* Lewis, who lives downstairs in Karen's father's apartment complex, shares insights and a book on the subject with her. Sometimes Karen has doubts about her parents' love for her and her mother's ability to provide for the children, in spite of reassurances from her parents, both of whom confuse her even more by praising the other, and from Jeff, who has some sense of the legalities involved. Jeff and Amy turn rebellious, and Jeff runs away after a tiff with Mother at a restaurant. This leads to a terrible argument between the parents and the destruction of Karen's Viking project, on which she had naively staked all for reconciling her parents, and her final realization that her parents will never get back together again. At book's end, she receives a letter from Garfa urging acceptance. She buys a book on divorce and looks forward to junior high. Implausibility affects this novel at ever turn. For example, it seems incredible that a girl of Karen's apparent intelligence and acumen should not be aware that for six or seven years her parents have been having problems. The plot is lean and moves with mostly underdeveloped scenes, one-dimensional and typed characters, some humor, a little excitement, simple, short sentences, and easy vocabulary to the over-foreshadowed, overly pat conclusion. The result is a concocted, superficial, simplistic look at divorce aimed at a later elementary and junior high audience. Choice.

IVANOV SEVEN (Janeway*, Elizabeth, ill. Eros Keith, Harper, 1967), realistic period novel set in Russia in the days of the Czars, which satirizes the military by improvising on the old folktale theme of the dolt who makes good when wiser men fail. Stepan Mgaloblishvili, an energetic country youth who has never been outside of his native village of Kahetia in the Caucasus Mountains, has an insatiable curiosity about the world. His elders consider him a bother because he has an endless supply of unanswerable questions. After a strangely dressed, smoothtalking fellow named Tushin conscripts him into the Czar's army, Stepan characteristically makes the best of things and looks forward to the adventure and fortune Tushin has promised him. At Gorodets, the enrolling officer considers Stepan's surname too difficult and changes it to Ivanov, the seventh one now in the Czar's Thirty-ninth Artillery Regiment. All that winter the recruits are drilled in a leisurely fashion. The commanding officer, Colonel Yermolov, feels no need to hurry the training process, until he learns that the Grand Duke intends to review the regiment. Hoping to bring his men up to the Prussian standards described to him by one of his officers, Captain* Krylov, who had trained there, Yermolov sets his training targets over a range that will destroy the fields of the villagers who live near by. When the villagers flock to their fields to protest, the Colonel orders Stepan to fire upon them. But Stepan makes up his own mind, this time answering his own questions, and refuses. He is arrested and imprisoned for mutiny. But Stepan's deed makes him a hero with soldiers and villagers alike, and the Colonel decides the best thing to do is to muster him out. He sends Stepan home with the gun of his choice, an old howitzer named Katya, a horse named Bear, and a purse filled with silver. With Tushin to escort him back over the thousand-mile journey, Stepan makes his way home, very practically hiring Katya out for peaceful purposes along the way. He arrives in Kahetia, satisfied that he has achieved the adventure and fortune promised him. Once home, he employs himself salting thunderclouds with Katya, breaking them up and distributing the moisture to insure fine harvests of grapes henceforth. The light, vigorous, conversational tone helps to relieve the obviousness of the strong, anti-war theme. Situations are often comic, and there is a lot of action. Characters are types, scenes are sketched quickly and deftly, and most things are seen from Stepan's point of view. Fanfare.

IVY CARSON (*The Changeling**), Martha Abbott's best friend who helps Martha discover talents she never knew she had. Ivy escapes from her alcoholic mother, shiftless father, and bullying older brothers always on the fringes of the law into worlds of her own imagining and into which she also draws Martha, also the odd one in her family. Ivy is encouraged by her Aunt Evaline, with whom she sometimes lives and who has artistic friends. When Ivy is junior high age and returns to Rosewood Hills after living in Chicago for a time, she has become cynical about life. When Kelly accuses the two girls of robbing the school office, Ivy reacts with bitterness and anger, because she realizes that people believe Kelly, who is lying, rather than Ivy simply because Ivy is a

Carson. She cynically rejects her childhood notion that she is a changeling, which was her way of coping with hurts when she was younger. Ivy is a round, complex character.

I WILL ADVENTURE (Vining*†, Elizabeth Janet Gray, ill. Corydon Bell, Viking, 1962), historical novel set in 1596 in the England of Shakespeare's theater. Andrew Talbot, 12, youngest of six sons in a ten-child family, longs to see a play but his slightly puritanical father considers plays at best a waste of money. His father's cousin, Sir John Talbot, visiting their home in Kent, suggests that he take Andrew for a page, and it is arranged that the boy will be sent to him in London in three weeks. On the trip, in the care of Wat Hobson, a carter, Andrew sees his first play, *Romeo and Juliet*, in an innyard and has a fight with Chris Wilson, apprentice to Burbage and boy actor of the troop, Lord Hunsdon's Men. He knocks Chris down so that the young actor hits his head on the corner of the stage. The next morning Andrew hunts up Burbage and volunteers to take Chris's place, since the boy cannot go on stage. The gentleman actor, William Shakespeare, who is talking with Burbage, takes an interest and has Andrew ride behind him to Rochester and rehearse, but Chris recovers enough so that Andrew has no chance to act. In London Andrew discovers that Sir John has forgotten about his suggestion and neglected to mention it to his wife. Andrew is assigned to sleep in a trundle bed in the room of Bingley, the steward, thereby winning that man's enmity, and when Sir John leaves for Westminster, Lady Talbot, preoccupied with preparing her daughter by a former marriage to appear in Court, has little time or sympathy for him. Knowing that he is not useful, badly treated by Bingley, and neglected by the family, Andrew is homesick and decides to travel home with Hobson. He is distressed when Hobson refuses to take him without the permission of his guardians, and when he tries to ask Lady Talbot, she assumes he is sulking for being scolded and thinks she is being kind to let him stay. Learning that Lord Hunsdon's company is in town, Andrew goes to the Swan Theater, meets Chris, who is now friendly, and finds out from him where Shakespeare lodges, thinking he will get the actor-playwright to take him as an apprentice. Shakespeare is friendly but explains why this is impossible. In despair, Andrew starts home alone and as night approaches is waylaid by a young thug, only to be saved by the arrival of Sir John, who has returned and learned of his departure and ridden out to find him. This sudden interest cheers Andrew, and the next day, when Sir John takes him to a play, he sees his older brother, Horace, now a knight just returned from service with Lord Essex in Cadiz. Horace and a friend join them at a tavern and, thinking to call Andrew's bluff when he says he knows Shakespeare, send the boy to invite the actor to join their table. They are all surprised when he accepts and suggests that school might be the place for Andrew. Sir John, who doesn't need a page, decides to send Andrew to school at St. Paul's and allows Horace to take him home for Christmas first. Though the research is obviously extensive and the character of

Andrew appealing, the events of the story are never really convincing and the historical characters seem brought in mechanically. Sixteenth-century England is pictured as cleaner and more innocently pleasant than it probably was in fact. Fanfare.

J

JACK DEDHAM (*The Blue Sword**), colonel in charge of the garrison at Istan, colonial outpost in Daria, a fantasy country very like India of the late nineteenth and early twentieth centuries. Though lean and muscular, he is an older soldier who has been some fifteen years on the frontier and has come to believe stories of the magic practiced by the Hillfolk, stories scoffed at by most of his fellow Homelanders. When the Hill king, Corlath*, comes to Istan seeking an alliance against the invading Northerners, Jack understands his hurt pride and impulsively pledges his personal allegiance in the ritual manner in the Old Damarian tongue. Later when Harry* Crewe, who has been kidnapped and trained as a warrior, returns to seek help in holding a mountain pass against the invaders, Jack gives up his future in the army by going with her against orders, knowing that if she does not succeed, all Istan will be destroyed.

JACK PARSONS (*Trial Valley**), five-year-old abandoned child, old in knowledge of human nature and the hardships of life, found and taken in by the Luther children. After his mother, whom he knows only as Babe, ran off, Jack was cared for by the Widder Man, who brought him to Trial Valley near the Luther home and left him for the Luthers to find, cooped up in a tiny cage, dirty, skinny, and hungry. Although Kiser* and Devola* Pease long to adopt him and lavish him with gifts, he prefers to live with Mary* Call Luther, who eventually does take him in.

JACKSON, JACQUELINE (DOUGAN) (1928–   ), born in Beloit, Wis.; author, illustrator, college teacher. She grew up on a dairy farm in southern Wisconsin and received her B.A. degree from Beloit College and her M.A. from the University of Michigan. She has taught children's literature at Kent State University in Ohio and Sangamon State University in Springfield, Ill. A cellist and a talented artist, she studied for ten years at the Wisconsin School of Music in Madison and has illustrated two of her own books and several written by others. Her novel set in a lumber camp in Vermont, *The Taste of Spruce Gum** (Little, 1966), won the Dorothy Canfield Fisher Children's Book Award in 1968.

JACK TAR (Larson*, Jean Russell, ill. Mercer Mayer, Macrae, 1970), lively farce set in British-controlled India in the days of sailing vessels when Victoria was queen. Jack Wookey, a young Northumbrian lad, ships aboard HMS *Begum of Bengal*, bound for India. At first he does well but disaster strikes when he unwittingly hands the Captain a tin of epsom salts for his tea, thinking it is sugar. He is clapped into irons and, when they reach Bombay, thrown off the ship in disgrace. He learns that the priceless string of black pearls, intended to be a gift to the Queen on her forthcoming visit, has been stolen, evidently by a fellow seaman, red-haired Mick Muxlow. Jack determines that he must redeem himself by finding the pearls, and he goes to Government House to offer his services. The British Resident, Lord Lummox, rebukes him for interfering and suggests he should drop out of sight permanently. Undefeated, Jack goes through the city seeking Muxlow and runs into a gypsy woman named Tootie living in a cave, who describes herself as a desperado, a dealer in stolen goods, to whom Muxlow has that very afternoon offered the stolen pearls. She has sent him to Delhi, where she secretly plans to buy the pearls, since they are too hot to buy in Bombay. Jack sets off confidently for Delhi, falling in on the way with a Chinese tumbling act, the three Wong brothers, whose fourth member has left to become a fish peddler. Jack agrees to try to make up their lack, but once on top of their human pyramid he catches sight of Muxlow in the crowd. Trying to get down, he upsets the pyramid and, chased by the furious Wongs, escapes into the kitchen of the Empire Hotel, where the chef puts him to work serving roast beef. To his consternation, the guests are Lord Lummox and his valet, Pippin-Fry. And so it goes, with Jack, Muxlow, the gypsy woman Tootie, and Lord Lummox continually running into each other in bizarre situations. For a while Jack and Muxlow share a room in a shabby hotel, one by day, the other by night, both working for their keep and both disguised. Discovering Muxlow's identity, Jack seizes the pearls and escapes in a cart, only to be taken to the summer home of Colonel Frobisher, where Lord Lummox is visiting. Jack hides in a costume closet, is taken in wig, bonnet, and dress for Miss Goodle, the new governess. He escapes this situation by changing to a Japanese kimono and finally makes his way back to Bombay, accompanied by Tootie. They hide in a mop and broom closet until the Queen arrives, but before they can emerge to present the pearls, Muxlow arrives in disguise. They engage in a wild chase through the parlor where the Queen waits, around the house, back through the parlor—Jack chased by Muxlow, chased by Tootie, chased by Pippin-Fry. Finally they upset the tea table, slip in the spilled cream, Muxlow is arrested, Jack is able to present the pearls, and he is reinstated in the Navy. Throughout, the book pokes fun at the conventions of Victorian British society, in the lighthearted manner of a Gilbert and Sullivan operetta. Although the action is slapstick, much of the humor has considerable sophistication. Lewis Carroll.

JACOB (*The Empty Moat**), feisty old servant of the Van Swaenenburghs, in whose tiny apartment they eat and converse during the German military occupation of Swaenenburgh Castle. It is through Jacob's apartment that access is gained to the dungeon, of which, quite strangely, the Germans remain totally unaware. Jacob finds the wounded British airman and, with Elizabeth's help and over her objections, moves the man to the dungeon. He accuses Elizabeth of being a coward and shaming her family by her behavior.

JACOB HAVE I LOVED (Paterson*, Katherine, Crowell, 1980), realistic novel set in the early 1940s on Rass Island in Chesapeake Bay, concerned with the difficulties of growing up the ugly-duckling twin in a small, restricted community with few options for independent development. Tall, dark, and tomboyish, (Sara) Louise* "Wheeze" Bradshaw at thirteen spends her summer of 1941 progging for crab with Call* (McCall) Purnell, a fat, nearsighted boy of fourteen. She bitterly resents her pretty, blond twin sister, Caroline*, a delicate, musically talented girl who preempts her parents' attention and endears herself to the other islanders. Louise and Call get to know an older man, Captain* Hiram Wallace, an islander who left under a cloud many years before and has returned to his long-empty family home, and they donate much of their free time to helping him repair the house and dock. When Louise discovers Auntie Braxton, a senile old woman, unconscious in her house surrounded by her numerous cats, the Captain, as they call Wallace, takes over, gets Auntie to the hospital, and enlists the youngsters to catch the half-wild cats and clean the house. Since they are unable to bring themselves to drown the cats, as they have planned, Caroline drugs them with paregoric and, using her winsome charm, gets the other islanders to adopt them. Shortly afterwards, a hurricane hits the island, destroying the Captain's house and washing away most of his end of the island. While he stays with her family, Louise develops a passionate attraction to him, a feeling which alarms her and which her pious, malicious old grandmother, Grandma* Louise Bradshaw, suspects. The Captain moves into Auntie Braxton's house and when the old woman, who was a girl with him, returns from the hospital, he takes Caroline's suggestion and marries her so that he will have a place to stay and Trudy Braxton will have someone to care for her. When Trudy dies, the Captain gives her legacy to send Caroline to boarding school in Baltimore to continue her musical education, which had to be given up when the storm wrecked the family crab house and caused other expenses. Seeing the shock this favoritism causes Louise, Grandma quotes to her, "Jacob have I loved, but Esau have I hated," and, looking the quotation up, Louise sees with despair that it is God speaking. When Call joins the Navy and World War II makes laborers scarce, Louise takes his place on her father's oyster boat, a thing no woman on the island has ever done, but at war's end when Call, slimmed down and much more attractive, returns, it is Caroline he marries. The last two chapters tell how Louise leaves the island, tries to become a doctor, but, unable to be accepted into medical school, becomes a nurse-midwife in an Appalachian valley, marries a widower with three small children, and, with a son of her own, at last comes to terms with her sibling rivalry when she delivers twins, one fragile and weak as her sister had been. Strong yet subtle characterizations make the book outstanding. Caroline is self-centered, but not mean; Louise, the first-person narrator, is a believable adolescent, aware of her own faults but unable to eliminate them. The claustrophobic Methodism of the island community is well evoked, and the gradual erosion of the island itself is symbolic. Although spanning a good many years, the story is told in an economical style and has unity; an argument could be made, however, for more complete development of the period after Louise has left the island, events which are more narrated than shown in scenes. Fanfare; Newbery Winner.

JAKE (Slote*, Alfred, Lippincott, 1971), baseball novel set in the town of Arborville, which closely resembles Ann Arbor, Mich., in the 1960s. Tough, independent Jake Wrather, 11, black, fatherless, and deserted by his mother, lives with his Uncle Lenny, 24, formerly a basketball star at the University, now a musician. Since Lenny practices or plays each night in Detroit, Jake is much on his own, and he lives for his kids' Recreation League baseball team, the Print-Alls, of which he is the real leader, although they have a token coach in Mrs. Fulton, mother of the catcher. At the game with the McLeod Builders, the plate umpire is making bad calls against the Print-Alls and the boys get upset. Their star pitcher is thrown out of the game, a critical penalty since they have only nine players and are not allowed to play with more than one short. Nonetheless, they keep their heads while the opposing coach, Mr. McLeod, blows up and pulls his team out, forfeiting the game. Their victory is short-lived, since the league president meets with them the next day and insists that they not only replay the game but that they have a man coach present at every game. This seems an impossible requirement for this interracial team, since the few fathers living with their families have already proved unable to take the job. When it looks as if their next game will be rained out, the boys persuade Lenny to put in a token appearance on his way to Detroit, long enough to agree to call the game. The rain slows down, however, and they have to play. Dressed in his fancy stage clothes, Lenny coaches them vigorously, insisting that they get twelve runs to nothing in the first two innings, a situation that automatically ends a game, so that he can get to Detroit on time. Amazingly, they do, but the rain stops the game before their opponents can play their half inning. That night two of the kids roust Jake out with a great idea: they've found an almost empty warehouse where Lenny's band could practice, making many of the trips to Detroit unnecessary and giving him time to coach. The team dives into cleaning the place up while Lenny and Jake have a conference with the principal, who is disturbed by Jake's tardiness and sleepiness in school and suggests that a foster home might be more appropriate for him. Lenny is surprised at the warehouse, but he has bad news: it belongs to McLeod, and as they are looking it over, the owner shows up with a policeman and accuses them of breaking in to steal. Lenny, who knows the cop, gets them out of the situation and is annoyed enough to agree to coach at the make-up game against the Builders. The Print-Alls are so angry that they keep making mistakes but Jake has a chance to even the score by coming in and crashing into the pitcher, Pat McLeod, at home base. At the last minute he swerves to avoid hurting Pat and breaks his own leg. In the hospital McLeod thanks him, agrees to let Lenny rent the building, and Jake ends with a coach and a father-figure. The games themselves take up a good deal of the book and are well told, plausible, and not condescending to the young reader. Jake is a gutsy little character, and the other boys are well differentiated, and though the ending is a little schmaltzy, the story is satisfying. Choice.

JAMIE KINCAID (*From the Mixed-up Files of Mrs. Basil E. Frankweiler**), nine-year-old suburban New York City schoolboy, who, with his older sister, Claudia*, runs away and hides out in the New York Metropolitan* Museum of Art. A miserly boy, who saves up his allowances and the money he wins by cheating at cards, he is enlisted by Claudia in her runaway scheme because of his money. Although he occasionally asserts himself and contributes ideas, he mostly follows Claudia's lead and acquiesces in her plans to evade detection and continue their absence from home.

JANE CARES (*A Lemon and a Star†*; *Terrible, Horrible Edie**; *Edie on the Warpath**), dreamy, worrying second child in the Cares family in a series of novels set in Summerton, Mass., in the early twentieth century. Plagued by her disparaging older brother, Ted*, and her own conscience, Jane nevertheless manages to assert herself and even to organize her younger brother, Hubert*, into various remarkable and unconventional activities. Sandy-haired and freckled, she resembles Ted. The first book (*A Lemon and a Star*), in which she is ten, is told mostly from her viewpoint, but in the last two she fades into a background figure, occasionally a supportive older sister to Edie* but not as important as either of the boys.

JANEWAY, ELIZABETH (HALL) (1913–), born in Brooklyn, N.Y.; critic, lecturer, spokeswoman for the women's movement, and writer for adults, who has also written novels for young people. She grew up in Brooklyn, attended Swarthmore, and graduated from Barnard College. While at Barnard, she won *Story* magazine's Intercollegiate Contest for a short story. Soon after graduation she married Eliot Janeway, noted economist and author, and they and their two sons have made their home in New York City. She has been a judge for the National Book Awards and the Pulitzer Prize in Letters and a member of the board of trustees of Barnard College. Her adult titles include *The Walsh Girls* (Doubleday, 1943), a highly praised first novel, *Daisy Kenyon* (Doubleday, 1945), and *The Third Choice* (Harper, 1958), all novels; and *Between Myth and Morning: Women Awakening* (Morrow, 1974), essays; and she has contributed to many literary and popular periodicals. For children she has written *The Vikings* (Random, 1951), an account of the explorations of Eric the Red and his son, Leif Ericson, in the Landmark Series; *Angry Kate* (Harper, 1963), two short, rhyming moral stories in picture book format for a very young audience; and

*Ivanov Seven** (Harper, 1967), a humorous, realistic, satiric, anti-war novel set in Russia in the days of the Czars, which was a Fanfare book.

JANIE GIBBS (*Harriet the Spy**; *The Long Secret**), Harriet Welsch's second best friend and sixth grade classmate. Janie likes chemistry and wants to discover a formula powerful enough to blow up the world. She can be very sharp tongued and often stands up to Harriet. In *Harriet the Spy*, she turns against Harriet when she hears what Harriet has written about her in her notebook. In *The Long Secret*, the two are friends again, and Janie visits Harriet at the seashore where she helps her a little in her attempts to discover who is writing the notes that are upsetting the community.

JANINE (McKown*, Robin, Messner, 1960), realistic novel set in Albia, a town in the "black country," the coal mining district of northeastern France in 1946, two years after the liberation of the area in World War II. Because her father helped organize a miners' strike for better food during the German occupation and was arrested, Janine Forel, 17, supports her family, which includes her mother, her brother Pierre, 13, and their Polish-born foster child, Annick, 8, with a job as a telephone operator for the miners' cooperative. Having learned of the return of their former neighbor, Jojo* (Georges) Fayaud, who was arrested by the Nazis before her father, Janine goes to see him even though she believes he betrayed the strike organizers. She hopes he will write an affidavit which will help her mother get a pension for widows and orphans of the Resistance heroes. She finds him willing, surprisingly friendly and unashamed, but far gone with silicosis from his mining and malnutrition during his imprisonment. Before he writes the letter, however, he dies, and soon his mother and son, Alain*, 20, move again next door to the Forels and resume friendly relations, though Janine finds it hard to be forgiving. In the meantime, Janine has two new friends: Felix Rostand, a university student she met through the cooperative, and Joan* Weston, an American penpal from York, Pa., who got her name through the Red Cross and who begins to send boxes of groceries and smart clothes. There are also two irritating family friends, Uncle Gustave, their father's joking brother, who seems to be courting Mother, a fact which annoys Janine since she cannot admit her father is dead, and Madame Trebigny, the stout gossip whose husband has been withdrawn and surly since the death of their little daughter shortly after the arrest of the strike organizers. The big surprise comes when Joan writes that she is coming to Europe with her parents and will visit in Albia. Soon the whole town knows, and the Forel family makes great preparations, possible mostly because another prisoner, Yves Gilbert, has returned blind and confused but able to give the necessary information for the pension. The Westons arrive, Joan, blond, friendly, frivolous, her mother a sociologist who speaks French fluently, her father a businessman somewhat bemused by the situation but enthusiastic about Madame Forel's cooking. Joan is attracted to Alain and fakes a sprained ankle so her parents will leave her while they go to England. As a distinguished visitor, she is invited to tour the mine, and Janine accompanies her, led by Alain and the engineer. When Janine is called back to work, Joan dives into housework and charms everyone, including Alain. At week's end, when her parents return for her, she announces that she and Alain are engaged. Madame Trebigny accuses her of stealing Janine's fiance, and, after a tempestuous session, Joan realizes that she has wanted Alain because she envies Janine. She returns to America and soon writes that she has met a marvelous Dartmouth man. In Albia, Uncle Gustave plans to marry Madame Fayaud, having been refused by his sister-in-law. Felix proposes to Janine by phone, and she is inclined to accept, but before she does, a mine accident occurs and as she waits with Madame Fayaud, she knows she loves Alain. He is trapped by the fire in the pit but is saved and proposes to Janine, who accepts. Monsieur Trebigny, injured and dying, confesses that it was he who betrayed Janine's father, for money which he hoped would save his daughter. Conditions in the immediate postwar period in the mining area are well depicted, but the characters are simplistic, particularly Joan, who is the stereotyped American teenager, and her father, the American businessman. The romances are predictable, as is the revelation of the betrayal. Child Study.

JAREL (*Enchantress from the Stars**), Imperialist doctor, who has doubts about the rightness of the Imperialist cause in colonizing Andrecia*. He deplores the way they regard the Andrecians as less than human, immobilize them with stunners, annihilate them with vaporizers, and capture some to take back as specimens for study in the Imperialist Research Center. He realizes that Elana is unique and frees Georyn* at her request. He puts his future in jeopardy by killing another Imperialist, who is trying to kill Georyn when Georyn psychokinetically keeps the Dragon's* load from crushing Elana.

JARRELL, RANDALL (1914–1965), born in Nashville, Tenn.; poet, critic, whose books for children make up a small but significant part of his large number of published works. He received his B.S. and M.A. degrees from Vanderbilt University and served in the U.S. Army Air Corps from 1942 to 1946. He taught at Kenyon College, Ohio, the University of Texas, Austin, Sarah Lawrence College, Bronxville, N.Y., and Women's College of the University of North Carolina at Greensboro, and was a visiting professor at Princeton University, the University of Illinois in Urbana, Indiana School of Letters in Bloomington, and the University of Cincinnati, Ohio. He also served as acting literature editor for *The Nation*, as poetry critic for *Partisan Review* and *Yale Review*, and as consultant in poetry for the Library of Congress. For adults he wrote one novel, one play, thirteen books of poems, four of critical essays, and edited a number of others, three of them works by Kipling. Among his many honors was the National Book Award for verse. Both *The Bat Poet** (Macmillan, 1964) and *The Animal Family** (Pantheon, 1965) are poetic fantasies of remarkable originality. *Fly by Night* (Farrar, 1976), a briefer story, was published long after his death. His translations of German folk tales appear along with those of Lore Segal in *The Juniper Tree and Other Tales from Grimm* (Farrar, 1973).

JASMIN (*The Mukhtar's Children**), twelve-year-old daughter of the leader of an Arab village in Israel and twin to his son, Khalil*. Although raised to be subservient to men, she has long carried on a conflict with her twin brother, managing by guile and cleverness to get the better of him while seeming to be his admiring servant. The building of an Israeli kibbutz near her village precipitates events that give her a chance to see women who consider themselves equal to men and to learn to read indirectly from Khalil's friend, Selim, who teaches his young sister, who in turn teaches Jasmin. An intelligent and spirited girl, she ends with hope of getting an education and controlling her own destiny.

JASON CALHOUN (*The Secret of the Seven Crows**), clever older brother of Shelley*. Jason is a gourmet cook, improbably producing delicacies of a French chef in the ill-equipped basement kitchen at Crauleia, an old mansion that has more recently been used as a convent. Jason deciphers the coded message that leads to finding the treasure.

JASPER (*A Wizard of Earthsea**), student at the school for wizards of Roke*, who goads Ged* into summoning up a spirit of the dead and with it a Shadow that attacks and nearly kills him. Jasper is from a noble family on Havnor and seems to look down on the goatherd from Gont but actually is jealous of Ged's greater power. After the incident of the summoning, Jasper leaves the school without winning his staff to become wizard to a lord on the island of O.

JAVIER (*The Horse Talker**), old, lame ropemaker, whom Blanco* orders to teach Lan Spanish. He was lamed when, a captive of the Comanches, his Comanche master cut the tendons at the back of his right knee so he could not run away. When Guero says he is going to lame the 100 mares he buys from Blanco, Lan compares what he wants to do to the horses to what happened to Javier. Blanco refuses to allow Guero to proceed with the maiming and thus incurs the man's hatred.

JAZZ COUNTRY (Hentoff*, Nat, Harper, 1965), realistic novel set in New York City in the 1960s. The narrator, Tom Curtis, 16, plays trumpet and is a true jazz lover but, being white and upper–middle class, finds it hard to break into the mostly black jazz community. He hangs around outside the club where Moses* Godfrey plays (Tom, being underage, is not allowed inside) and talks to Bill Hitchcock, bass player in Moses's band, who agrees to listen to Tom play. At Bill's apartment in Greenwich Village, Bill politely tells Tom that he is skilled but has no soul, while Bill's wife, Mary, is openly hostile. One night Moses spots him on the sidewalk and invites him to the home of Veronica, a fat white woman who is accepted by all the jazz musicians. There he meets

Veronica's daughter, Jessica, about his own age, and hears a long story about Charlie Wilkins, a blind guitar player who had been a great inspiration to Moses. Moses becomes much the same sort of figure to Tom. He lets Tom be present at a rehearsal in which he gets a white trumpet player, old Will Burke, to solo and produces a moving piece. Once with Jessica, Tom meets Frederick Godfrey, alienated son of Moses, a young man who doesn't want to get involved in civil rights activities. Later Tom is with Moses and Burke when they come upon a Puerto Rican being beaten up by two hoods, and Fred Godfrey saves him. Tom gets to know Danny Simmons, a young black trumpet player, who lives in a Lower East Side slum and practices in the basement, and there a policeman spots them, suspects it is a drug sale, throws them out, and later the same policeman finds Danny there and beats up his face. In the meantime a slick but superficial jazz band leader, George Dudley, offers Tom a job in a traveling group. Tom agonizes over whether to take the job or go off to Amherst to college and asks the opinion of everyone he knows. Veronica finally points out to him that Moses and Bill wouldn't have allowed him to hang around with them if they hadn't liked him and thought he had potential. That helps him decide not to sell out for the soulless jazz of Dudley, so he goes to Amherst. Moses's band plays there, with Danny a part of it, and in the end even Mary Hitchcock seems to have accepted Tom. The book has a lot to say about integration and about jazz, but unfortunately it says it through the characters' dialogue telling the reader, rather than showing him through action. Tom is more a vehicle for presenting ideas of racial problems and what makes music great than a compelling protagonist, and the other characters seem to be chosen to represent different types in a sociological study. Choice.

JEAN PIERRE VINARD (*The Glorious Conspiracy**), French musician who befriends young Benjamin Brown. A gentle, unpretentious man, Vinard lives simply but insists that Ben learn good manners and good English. He is a member of the Bucktails, a Tammany organization devoted to democratic principles and the election of Jefferson for president. A shadowy past haunts Vinard; a black coach carries a mysterious Marquis and the brutal ex–mill foreman, Thomas Earnshaw*. It is not until Vinard disappears and is found beaten close to death that Ben learns his story: in France he had been a court musician and was to marry a girl, but the son of a Marquis and his friends followed the couple and beat him up for insolence when he protested, and when he called the Marquis's son a coward, they in their drunken state determined to have a mock duel. To their surprise, Jean Pierre killed the nobleman, then escaped. It is the father of the slain man who has followed him to the United States to get revenge, with Earnshaw his hired tool.

JEAN WAINWRIGHT (*The Callender Papers**), girl of twelve, almost thirteen when the story begins, a studious, very serious child, much attached to the woman she knows as Aunt Constance who raised her from infancy. Jean expects some day to become headmistress of Aunt Constance's girls' school in her aunt's place. Jean is a proud, easily nettled child, often ungracious but intelligent and diligent, and it is apparently for these latter qualities that Mr.* Thiel requests her services in sorting out his deceased wife's papers. Jean seems slow at discovering that she is his child and heir to the Callender fortune and too quick to respond to the blandishments of Enoch* Callender. At the end she chooses to remain with Dan Thiel because she sees how lovingly he painted the portrait of her and her mother and realizes that beneath his forbidding exterior he has a loving and kind nature.

JED: THE STORY OF A YANKEE SOLDIER AND A SOUTHERN BOY
(Burchard*, Peter, ill. author, Coward, 1960), short, historical novel set in 1862 near Shiloh, Miss., just after the Civil War battle that took place there. Although Jed, 16, a former printer's devil from a small town in Wisconsin, is no longer a fresh and untried soldier and the "glitter" has gone out of soldiering for him, he has not become callous and cynical about the war as have most of his comrades. He still dislikes raiding farms and plantations for food and materials, even though he knows his side must forage to survive, and he particularly deplores burning the homes of defenseless women and children. While serving guard duty at dawn one day, he pulls a thorn from the paw of a stray dog that obviously belongs to someone nearby, and a little later he discovers the dog's owner, a little boy of about nine named Philip, who has a broken leg and whose father is a Confederate soldier. Over the boy's protests, Jed takes Philip to the camp surgeon, who sets the leg, and then Jed carries the boy home to his mother on her little farm in the hills behind the swamp near which the Yankee camp is pitched. Philip's mother shows Jed about her little place, exhibiting a friendliness he had not expected to find among the enemy. When he returns to the camp, he discovers that his relief picket, Davy, a disagreeable, opportunistic fellow, has organized a small party to raid the farm. Jed hurries after them, wrestles Davy's gun away from him, and shames the soldiers into leaving the farm and the little family unharmed. This essentially single-incident, very economically told story gives a limited sense of the pressures on some of the Northern soldiers, their homesickness, hunger, yearning to have done with the whole unpleasant business, and efforts to retain certain basic human values. Jed represents those who manage to maintain their decency, a quality that appears also in the tenderness with which he cares for his ill tentmate, Jim, and is reflected in the respect shown him by his officers. Except for Jed, the characters are one-dimensional, and Jed himself could use development. Dialogue occasionally seems inaccurate, but the narrative passages move well. Choice; Fanfare; Lewis Carroll.

JEFF GREENE (*Dicey's Song**; *A Solitary Blue**), Jefferson Greene, son of the Professor* and his estranged wife, Melody*, called Jeffie by his mother. Jeff is a careful, timid boy who, after his mother walks out, devotes himself to keeping the house going smoothly and everything in its place because he doesn't want to risk losing his father, too. Jeff is afraid of change, is never assertive, and practices being nobody because he believes it is simply safer that way. He shows some fire when he stands up to Melody the summer he is thirteen, after she has abandoned him in favor of her various projects and do-gooder friends, no longer finding him a novelty. He justly accuses her of lying and deceit. After he and the Professor move to the cabin, Jeff slowly begins to lose his timidity, to come out of himself, and to form attachments with other people, even though his relationships are always low-key. He never loses the feeling that he must protect and shield his father. The book is stronger because Jeff doesn't do a complete flip in personality. The reader is left to believe that Jeff will always be slow to give himself emotionally. A consistently interesting figure, he is in conflict with self, parents, and society throughout most of the book. In *Dicey's Song*, he is much less credible, one of the weakest characters in the book. He is a guitar-playing tenth grader who becomes interested in Dicey Tillerman through their mutual liking for music, teaches her some songs, and wants to hear Maybeth play the piano and sing. He invites Dicey to a dance, but she refuses, since, a little afraid of growing up, she feels she is not yet ready to date. Jeff is not really accepted by the other young people in the small, rural community, but, later, in *A Solitary Blue*, which follows *Dicey's Song* in time, we learn that he does make a few friends his age.

JEN MORGAN (*A String in the Harp**), Jennifer, sensitive, responsible, loyal, older sister of Peter* and Becky*, who is skeptical at first about the truth of Peter's story that the key he has found once belonged to Taliesin, the great Welsh bard, and that it calls up scenes from the past. She sets about repairing the strained relationship between Peter and their father and remains staunchly loyal to Peter when Dr. Owens, museum curator, inquires about the key. She is a well-drawn, older sister.

JENNIFER (*Jennifer, Hecate, Macbeth, William McKinley, and Me, Elizabeth**), fifth-grader at William McKinley Elementary School, who becomes friends with Elizabeth*, a white girl. The only black girl in their suburban community, the daughter of the gardener on the Samellson Estate, Jennifer leads a self-imposed, isolated life, asserting her individuality by claiming to be a witch. Intelligent, an avid reader, she goes to the library and checks out wagonloads of books on witches. Bossy, independent, and self-sufficient, she imposes stringent requirements upon Elizabeth and teaches her rituals and dances when she makes Elizabeth her apprentice. After Elizabeth rebels against adding their pet toad to a flying ointment, Jennifer controls her need to dominate and enters into a more natural relationship with Elizabeth, now more truly her friend.

JENNIFER, HECATE, MACBETH, WILLIAM MCKINLEY, AND ME, ELIZABETH (Konigsburg*, E. L., ill. author, Atheneum, 1967), realistic novel about the friendship of two suburban fifth-graders at William McKinley Elementary School, Jennifer*, who is black, and Elizabeth*, the white girl who tells the story. New in town and lonely, Elizabeth meets Jennifer on the way to school on Halloween, and an uneven, but close, relationship develops between the two. The dominant Jennifer, who maintains that in reality she is a witch, makes Elizabeth her apprentice, imposing upon her such requirements as eating raw eggs or raw onions every day for a week. Although they go their separate ways in school, they leave notes for each other in their "Jennifer tree" on the way to school, meet in the public library every Saturday morning to do research and check out books on witches, and perform dances while reciting magic spells in the park. Their friendship continues throughout the school year, with Elizabeth docilely obedient to Jennifer's commands and progressing to journeyman status. When Jennifer decides to add their pet toad, Hilary Ezra, to a flying ointment in imitation of the witches in *Macbeth*, Elizabeth rebels. Her refusal leads eventually to a deeper and more lasting relationship between the two girls as they learn that real friendship involves mutual give and take. Good characterizations, crisp, contemporary dialogue, and activities and attitudes typical of later elementary children combine to make this account of a growing friendship convincing. Choice; Fanfare; Newbery Honor.

JENNY PEARSON (*The Trouble with Jenny's Ear**), a somewhat shy little girl of six who develops supersensitive hearing because her brothers' electronic equipment is so loud. She discovers she is able to hear even what people are thinking. She courageously agrees to go on a national TV contest show to get money to buy the hill and brook on the land adjoining her family's before Mr. Watson, the owner, sells it to a developer. A moral child, she is bothered by the implications of what she has done and offers to give the one hundred thousand dollars back to the sponsors of the show.

JESSE (*Bimby**), proud, white-haired, old slave, whom Bimby regards almost like a father. Tall and authoritative, Jesse was once the boss of the teamsters on the Butler plantation and still has a cabin of his own. Although one-armed, he is still very strong and has built a boat with which he takes Bimby for rides. He is bitter about his situation and refers to himself wryly as "Massa* Butler's clown." After the accident, Bimby concludes that Jesse raced Massa Butler to prove he was still capable of doing such a feat. Jesse is the most interesting figure in the novel, a tantalizingly underdeveloped character.

JESSE AARONS (*Bridge to Terabithia**), sensitive ten-year-old whose passion for drawing is not appreciated by his uneducated family. Jesse's ability has been recognized only by his "hippy" music teacher, Miss Edmunds, with whom he has fallen in love. In his own family of four sisters, he does most of the farm work, milks the cow, and takes care of the garden, while his older sisters slide out from under any chores and wheedle money out of their mother, even though the family is barely scraping along. After the death of his friend, Leslie* Burke, who has opened a new imaginative world for him, Jess tries to share some of the good life he has glimpsed with his little sister, May Belle.

JESSE FRENCH (*Ransom**), one of several youths kidnapped for ransom. An "army brat," she is well read and fluent in several languages, but she has moved so often she has never had the opportunity to make friends. She is happy with books, music, and quiet conversation. She taps resources from her itinerant background and grows in self-esteem when she and Marianne* Paget try to cover for the boys who are "hotwiring" the kidnappers' car and when she gives Dexter first aid. She goes to pieces when first kidnapped and cries a lot, behavior that is not altogether convincing in view of her background and subsequent actions.

JESSE TUCK (*Tuck Everlasting**), boy who, though he has lived 104 years, is still a seventeen-year-old after drinking from a spring in the woods near Treegap eighty-seven years before the action of the book. The only one of the family to enjoy his perpetual life, he has a great idea: Winnie* Foster should wait until she is seventeen, then drink some of the spring water and join him in eternal adventures.

JESS JESSEN (*Torrie**), Steadfast-Under-Adversity Jessen, the cool, capable, young Virginian whom Thomas* Anders hires to drive his wagon and who is instrumental in getting the Anders family to California safely. Jess is sober and aloof at first, and he both awes and frightens Torrie. He is reluctant to associate with the family, and particularly with Torrie, to whom he is attracted, because he thinks he is not good enough to do so. He feels inferior because he has had no opportunity to get an education and cannot read and write. Thomas agrees to teach him in return for his help on the trip westward. Jess learns to think better of himself. His romance with Torrie grows gradually as they come to know each other better. At the end, she says she feels he has been well named. He is only partially credible as a character, too made to order to be really convincing.

JETHRO CREIGHTON (*Across Five Aprils**), southern Illinois farm boy during the Civil War. Nine years old when the conflict begins, he takes the major responsibility for running the farm during the war. A bright, steady child, he receives encouragement from his schoolteacher, Shadrach* Yale, and the editor of the local paper, Ross Milton*.

JIB GRASSHORN (*Freelon Starbird**), companion who drinks too much and enlists, then serves through the dismal winter of 1776 with Freelon* Starbird before returning to his ship chandler's trade. An enthusiast, he is continually falling in love with a woman or a cause, but after serving through most of the winter with a fever, he has lost much of his surplus weight and his bluster. Later he makes up tales of seeing Washington praying in the snow at Valley Forge which he tells "for the edification of the young."

JIRO (*The Master Puppeteer**), son of Hanji the puppet-maker, the spirited boy who becomes an apprentice in the theater. Because he is suffering near starvation in a famine year and because of the continual scorn of his mother, who seems to hate him because he survived when three older siblings died, Jiro is clumsy in helping his father, and he sneaks away to take up the invitation to join the Hanaza Theater as an apprentice partly because the theater has food. Well fed and away from his parents, he demonstrates his intelligence and ability and becomes devotedly attached to Kinshi*, head boy and son of the master puppeteer. In a culture where manners and tradition are paramount, Jiro is a little too independent, yet it is because he is spirited that he is asked to join the theater, and it is his spirit that eventually saves his mother and Kinshi.

J. J. FORD (*The Westing Game**), Josie-Jo Ford, black, woman judge, whose mother was a servant in the Westing house, with whom Samuel Westing played chess when he was a child, and for whose education Westing paid. She is clever, organized, self-assured, and one of the most interesting characters in the book.

JOAN DRAYFUS (*They Never Came Home**), elder sister of Larry* and sweetheart of Dan* Cotwell, both of whom disappear while on a mountain camping trip. A plain, steady girl, she takes over the house when Mrs. Drayfus suffers a nervous breakdown after Larry disappears. Under the circumstances, Joan is reluctant to add to her parents' burdens and thus undertakes, without their knowledge, to repay the debt mysterious Mr. Brown claims Larry owes him. She takes a job with Brown transporting jewelry from Mexico and innocently becomes involved with a ring of marijuana smugglers. She first suspects that Larry may not be dead when she discovers his favorite clothes are missing from his closet.

JOAN WESTON (*Janine**), American teenager about to start Wellesley, who becomes a penpal of the French girl and then goes to Europe to visit. Blond, stylish, and extroverted, Joan thinks Janine's experiences during the German occupation are "thrilling" and tries to emulate her hard work more as a game than with any real understanding. She is, however, goodhearted and generous. Her infatuation with Alain* Fayaud is genuine but proves to be temporary when she turns her attention to a college boy after her return.

JOCEY ROYAL (*Before the Lark**), twelve-year-old born with a harelip, who sets out from Kansas City with her sick grandmother to make a new life on a farm abandoned by her father. Although usually considered half-witted because of her disfigurement, she is intelligent and strong willed, and she succeeds through hard work to put in a crop and to make a living from market produce, at the same time caring for her gold-bricking grandmother. When she hears of an operation to correct a harelip, she travels alone back to Kansas City for surgery. Rejected by most people she sees, Jocey has become a reader and enjoys isolation, but she is pathetically grateful when a neighboring Norwegian family accepts her handicap without flinching and offers her real friendship.

JOEL BAR HEZRON (*The Bronze Bow**), son of a well-to-do rabbi in Capernaum of ancient Galilee and twin of Thacia*. Fired with patriotism and zeal for freedom from the domination of Rome, he is one of the youths whom Daniel enlists to help Rosh prepare resistance against the Romans. Rosh orders Joel to gather information about the activities of wealthy and influential people in Capernaum. Later the youths realize that Rosh wants the information so that he can rob the houses of these people. The youths come to see that Rosh is no self-sacrificing leader of a noble cause, but a common thief who has been using them for his own selfish ends. After Daniel and his friends free Joel from the Romans, Joel decides to go to Jerusalem to continue his rabbinic studies.

JOHN AUSTIN (*Meet the Austins**; *The Moon by Night**), scientifically minded high school youth, eldest of the four Austin children and the older of the two sons. Vicky, who tells the stories, admires John's good looks and keen mind and envies his warm and outgoing personality and his ability to take charge in tense situations and come up with just the right thing to say. In *Meet the Austins*, he is warm and sympathetic toward orphaned Maggy but able to maintain some detachment, unlike the other children who are closer in age to her. In *The Moon by Night*, he is often the teasing older brother.

JOHN CONLAN (*The Pigman**), high school sophomore who is almost compulsively zany and who, with his friend Lorraine* Jensen, gets to know a lonely man named Angelo Pignati*. John employs his considerable imagination and acting skill in pulling pranks and telling enormous lies. He skips school, drinks and smokes, apparently mostly as rebellion against his very proper parents and older brother. Because he is very good looking, he gets away with most of his jokes, but he is pictured as genuinely sorry when their misuse of Mr. Pignati's house and belongings indirectly causes the man's death.

JOHN HENRY MCCOY (Chaffin*, Lillie D., ill. Emanuel Schongut, Macmillan, 1971), realistic novel set in the Appalachian mountains of Eastern Kentucky. Tired of moving around as his luckless father loses one job after another, John Henry McCoy, 10, hopes that the family will stay in the shack up the hollow where he waits with his mother, his grandmother, and his two sisters for his father to fetch them to Columbus, where he has found a job. Sara, a little younger than John Henry, wants to go back to a city, but the boy hopes that little Clarabell can stay and go to Head Start as he did in the happiest time he can remember, and that he can stay in one school a whole year. When John Henry tells Granny about the fine house empty and going to ruin, owned by Mr. Thompson, who runs the crossroads store, she decides to break the family pattern and makes a deal with Thompson to live in the house and keep it from deteriorating further. After fighting Thompson's grandson, Si Brown, the school bully, John Henry makes friends with him and gets a job feeding Thompson's pigs. He also acquires some hens and a stray bluetick hound, which he calls Fido. When a letter comes from his father sending money for them to join him, John Henry loses it and stays out, finally falling asleep with the dog. His mother finds him, and also the letter, but Granny announces that she is not moving this time. The decision is at least put off when the letter with the money says Daddy has no apartment for them, and John Henry's mother decides to stay, at least for the present. Although the book deals with the problems of poor drifting families, it does not present the grimness of life in Appalachia without running water, electricity, or sufficient food in realistic detail. The characters are stock figures; John Henry has ambition and likes to read, and Granny is spunky, but the others have little life. The style is aimed at children of the middle grades. Child Study.

JOHNNY ANDERSON (*The Night Swimmers**), Retta's* nine-year-old younger brother, who resents her organizing the children's lives. He is beginning to assert himself and to look for friends outside the home, an action Retta regards with resentment, jealousy, and even anger. Johnny's friendship with Arthur leads to Retta's realizing that she has been trying too hard to control her brothers. Johnny was named after Johnny Cash, country-western singer his parents admired.

JOHNSON†, ANNABEL (JONES) (1921–   ), born in Kansas City, Mo.; with Edgar Johnson*†, one-half of the husband-wife team responsible for a dozen and a half novels of history and adventure set in the old American West. She attended the College of William and Mary and the Art Students League in New York City and worked in publishing houses, as a librarian, and as a secretary before becoming a full-time writer in 1957. The Johnsons have traveled extensively, absorbing atmosphere, information, and ideas for their novels, which develop such phases of the American past as the gold rush, medicine shows, the push westward, and the fur trade. By herself she published *As a Speckled Bird* (Crowell, 1956), her first book, a contemporary novel about life in an academy of fine arts. Four of the Johnsons' period and historical novels have been Fanfare books: *The Black Symbol†* (Harper, 1959), which takes place in a traveling medicine show; *Torrie** (Harper, 1960), historical novel and girls' growing up story about a covered wagon journey from St. Louis to California in 1846; *Wilderness Bride** (Harper, 1962), set from 1846–1847 as the Mormons trek westward in search of their Zion; and *The Golden Touch** (Harper, 1963), mystery-adventure novel set in the gold fields west of Denver in 1900. *The Burning Glass** (Harper, 1966), which received the Spur Award of Western Writers of America, involves history, adventure, and chase among trappers and Indians in the Rockies in 1833, while *The Grizzly** (Harper, 1964), a *Choice* selection, is a contemporary adventure and problem story in which a father and son come to terms while on a week-end camping trip in the Montana wilds. The Johnsons' work is distinguished by careful research, sympathetic protagonists, excitement, and judicious use of detail. Other titles include *A Peculiar Magic* (Houghton, 1965), companion to *The Golden Touch*, and *Count Me Gone* (Simon, 1968) and *The Last Knife* (Simon, 1971), both contemporary problem stories, and *The Danger Quotient* (Harper, 1984), a futuristic story, set among survivors of a nuclear holocaust, that represents a departure from their previous work. They have also written under the name A. E. Johnson.

JOHNSON†, EDGAR (RAYMOND) (1912–   ), with his wife, Annabel Johnson*†, one-half of the team of writers best known for their several novels of history and adventure set in the American West for older readers. He was born in Washoe, Mont., a coal mining town, at the time when stagecoaches were still in vogue there. After various jobs on the railroad, as a baseball player, and as a musician in a dance band, he studied art at the Billings Polytechnic Institute, the Kansas City, Mo., Art Institute, the New York State College of Ceramics, and the Art Students League in New York City. Before he became a full-time writer with the publication of the couple's first novel together, *The Big Rock Candy* (Crowell, 1957), about a young sculptor who comes from the Ozarks to New York City, he was a ceramicist, model maker, jeweler, and wood carver, and was head of the department of ceramics at the Kansas City, Mo., Art Institute. He has served the Smithsonian Institution in Washington as a restorer. With his wife he has published a dozen and a half novels, including the critically acclaimed *The Black Symbol†* (Harper, 1959), a period novel about a boy kidnapped by the operator of a traveling medicine show; *Torrie** (Harper, 1960), about a covered wagon journey from St. Louis to California in 1846 as seen from the viewpoint of a young woman who survived the harrowing experience; *Wilderness Bride** (Harper, 1962), about a young Mormon woman's experiences during the hard, harried trek westward in search of Zion in 1846–1847; and *The Golden Touch** (Harper, 1963), a mystery-adventure novel set in the gold fields west of Denver in 1900; *The Burning Glass** (Harper, 1966), a historical adventure novel set in the Rockies in 1833 among trappers and Indians and involving some real people; and *The Grizzly** (Harper, 1964), a present day adventure story about a father and son who work out their problems together on a camping trip in the Montana wilds, all books which have won awards or citations. The Johnsons also write under the name A. E. Johnson and are noted for their skill at blending research and story for consistently satisfying reading experiences.

JOHN TREEGATE (*John Treegate's Musket†*; *Peter Treegate's War**; *Sea Captain from Salem**; *Treegate's Raiders**), Peter's father, a Boston importer. At first he is staunchly loyal to the British king, because he believes the alternative to royal rule is anarchy under the Mob of Sam Adams. A man to whom duty to country is vital, he travels to England to try to persuade the government to relax its oppressive regulations against American trade. During his absence, he apprentices Peter to Tom Fielding. His action causes Peter to lose confidence in him and to feel abandoned and betrayed by his own father. Even after he and Peter find each other again at the end of the first book, John remains loyal to the British crown. Tension continues between father and son, until British action at Lexington and Concord impels John to cast his lot with the colonials. In *Peter Treegate's War*, he appears as a fighter. In it and in the later books he is also a high colonial official. He becomes the colonial man of business, borrowing money for the army and finding provisions wherever he can for the soldiers. He also becomes the head of the Continental Intelligence. He ages appreciably and realistically as the stories advance.

JOHN YODER (*The Mystery of Ghost Valley**), Tommy* Yoder's Pennsylvania Dutch cousin, about Tommy's age. John has a "round and honest face, blue eyes and red hair." He is naturally merry but cool toward Tommy because he thinks Tommy is after Doodlehead* Yoder's iron pieces. By using binoculars and standing on the Yoder barn roof, he can keep track of Doodlehead's movements and watch over the old man.

JOJO FAYAUD (*Janine**), really Georges, father of Alain* and former neighbor of the Forel family. A drinker, Jojo was talking too freely about the strike by the miners to get better rations from the Nazis and was arrested. When the organizers of the strike were arrested soon afterwards, the townspeople assumed that he had betrayed them and were slow to forgive, even though he had suffered greatly in a concentration camp. He dies of silicosis, a miners' disease brought on by the bad conditions and malnutrition of his imprisonment.

JONES, WEYMAN (B.) (1928–   ), born in Lima, Ohio, salesman, businessman, and writer for children and adults. He grew up in Tulsa, Okla., the descendant of settlers in that area, and early developed an interest in Cherokee Indians through stories told him by his mother, who was born in Oklahoma when it was still Indian territory. He graduated from Harvard, where his undergraduate honors thesis was on the mythology and folklore of the Cherokees, researched largely in his grandfather's library of Indian materials. After serving as a lieutenant in World War II, he held positions in sales, public relations, and management for International Business Machines Corporation and as director of public relations with Kennicott Copper Corporation, and has lived in Chevy Chase, Md. In addition to contributing fiction to magazines, he has written a book about computers and two historical novels for young readers. *Edge of Two Worlds** (Dial, 1968) was based on the account found in his grandfather's papers of an Indian named "The Worm" and published in a Cherokee newspaper. It tells how the venerable, stalwart, seventy-year-old Cherokee leader, Sequoyah, walked across Texas in search of a lost band of Cherokees. It received the Western Heritage Award, was selected for the Lewis Carroll Shelf, and is cited in *Choice*. Previously he published *The Talking Leaf* (Dial, 1965), also about the Cherokees and Sequoyah, who had developed for his people a very practical alphabet which could be mastered in only a few days' study.

JORDAN, JUNE (1936–   ), born in New York City; professor, novelist-poet of the black experience in America. She attended Barnard College and the University of Chicago and worked as an assistant producer for a filmmaker and as a research associate for Mobilization for Youth in New York City. She has taught English at City College of New York, Sarah Lawrence College, Yale University, and Connecticut College and in 1969 received a Rockefeller Foundation grant for creative writing. Besides a novel and verse for adults, she has written *Who Look at Me?* (Crowell, 1969), a book of verse for children, and two novels for teenagers, *His Own Where** (Crowell, 1971), a romance of two lonely black youngsters in New York City, and *New Life, New Room* (Crowell, 1973), in which three children move into and decorate their own room while their mother is in the hospital having a new baby sister.

JOSH WESTERN (*Behind the Magic Line**), absent father who returns to the Chicago home and takes his family to the west coast. A large, strong man who walks with a cat-like grace, he has left his family without support for months but returns to be loved and followed unquestioningly. His irresponsibility is credited to the frustrations that a black man faces in contemporary society.

JOSINE (*The Happy Orpheline*†; *A Brother for the Orphelines*†; *A Pet for the Orphelines**), youngest of the twenty little orphan girls in a village near Paris. Because she is too young to attend school classes with the others, she is often on hand to become involved in incidents, as when she finds the baby boy in the bread basket. Curly-haired and sweet-looking, she is notable for her stubbornness, and she is described as having a "strong character . . . with remarkable tenacity." She is a supporting character in the first book, but the chief protagonist in the second and third.

JOURNEY FROM PEPPERMINT STREET (DeJong*†, Meindert, ill. Emily Arnold McCully, Harper, 1968), realistic story set in the Netherlands in the early twentieth century, telling about the wonderful first trip a child takes away from his village. Siebren, about eight and a half, is bored and resentful that he must spend all his free time entertaining his brother Knillis, about one, who has been ill and who can say only one word, "Da." He also feels secretly guilty because one day he took Knillis to play on a pile of rusty rails from narrow-gauge track, and now the baby's scalp has a fiercely itching rusty scale infection. When the cap peddler gives Siebren a little tin of chocolates and he is amusing Knillis by shining the reflected light in his face, the baby grabs the shiny box with both hands, catching Siebren's thumb and cutting it on the box's sharp edges. Into the confusion that follows with Siebren sick and fainting and Knillis screaming comes Grandfather* David Rentema, announcing that he must leave the village of Wierom because his sister, Anna, is gravely ill. When Siebren asks to go along, to his surprise both his grandfather and his mother agree. This starts a night journey on foot that is both frightening and magical for the boy, who has never been farther away from home than the neighboring village. At Nes they are surrounded by the mean village dogs, and Grandpa strikes out with his cane, hitting by accident a little underfed black dog that runs off on three legs yipping. When the miller calls out to Siebren, terming him a "wayfaring stranger," the words seem magical to the boy, but Grandpa, who has been feuding with the man over a debt of seventeen cents, thinks it is a deliberate insult to him. Siebren's naive questions startle him into going back to make up the quarrel, while Siebren sits on a ditch bank and feeds his sandwiches to the little dog, which has returned. He keeps this news from Grandpa, but when they get to the next village, Lahsens, and stop while Grandpa visits with the storekeeper, Siebren keeps watch out the window, sees the little dog that he has named "Wayfarer," grabs some cookies from the table, rushes out, and shuts the dog with the cookies in a school building his father is constructing. Siebren writes a note explaining on the door in charcoal. Back in the store he is humiliated to discover his pants are unbuttoned and that he can't fasten them with his bandaged hand. Aal, the kind wife of the storekeeper, helps him, rebandages his hand, and slips him money to buy the large black ball that he covets. As they go on, they enter the marsh, in the center of which Grandpa's sister, Aunt Hinka, a tiny woman no bigger than Siebren, lives in an ancient monastery with her six-foot six-inch deaf-and-dumb husband, also named Siebren. In the dark, when Grandpa misses the road and is floundering in the dangerous muck, Siebren rolls him the ball, which holds him up until Aunt Hinka arrives in her little boat. Since the boat can hold only two, she leaves Siebren for a second trip but gets him singing so he is not too frightened. She puts him to sleep in a huge, bare room in the center of which is a cistern where her pet bullfrog, Vrosk, lives, while she goes on with Grandpa to see their ill sister. Siebren is terrified of being alone with a deaf-and-dumb giant he has never met, but a note left by this Uncle* Siebren reassures him in the morning, and when the uncle returns from work, it is just in time to help Siebren land an enormous pike that he has hooked. They get along famously, writing notes, and the next day Siebren finds Aunt Hinka to be the most understanding adult he has ever known, though she is sad because the sister has died. They plan to go fishing, but the monastery is struck by a tornado, which lifts the roof off and gently sets it down on top of Siebren and Hinka as they cower against the wall. Unable to get out, they try to dig and uncover an entrance to a tunnel that leads to the side of the cistern. In the tunnel is a room where Siebren finds a jar of "monastery balm," a salve for which the monks were once famous. Siebren thinks it is a miracle, sent to cure Knillis's head, and even sacrifices his precious ball to make a safe place to carry the balm when Uncle Siebren lifts him to his shoulders and tramps through the marsh to Wierom. There Siebren discovers his father has found his note and brought

Wayfarer home, and Knillis is so glad to see him that he says his second word, "Sieb." The recital of events does not give a good idea of the story, which depends for its effect almost entirely on the point of view of Siebren, told third person but consistently with the naive perception of a young child, to whom his Grandfather's sharp reprimand or the shame of an unbuttoned fly is equal in importance to a destructive tornado. Siebren's worry that he might be a "handball of Satan" and his confidence in miracles are convincing in the context, and his mercurial emotions, responding to the whims of adults, are touching reminders of the vulnerability of children. Choice; National Book Winner.

JOURNEY OUTSIDE (Steele*, Mary Q., ill. Rocco Negri, Viking, 1969), fantasy set in an imagined, pre-industrial country. Dilar is one of the raft people, a group who exist on rafts in an underground river, supposedly, his grandfather tells him, headed for "a Better Place," but actually, Dilar comes to believe, circling past the same rocks and passageways year after year. On impulse, Dilar swims to a ledge one night and lets the rafts drift away from him, then, scared by a horde of rat-like creatures which gather, he scrambles up and eventually out into open country, where he first sees sky, green growing things, and sunlight. Being unused to the sun, he is badly burned but rescued by a widow, Norna, and her daughter, Dorna, who take him in and nurse him back to health. Although they are generous and their summer life is easy in a plentiful land, they are improvident, and, in a culture which treats questions as impolite, they have no curiosity about Dilar's past nor about the other peoples outside their valley. Driven by a need to find out more, Dilar leaves them as winter approaches, makes his way over a mountain pass, is almost frozen and in danger of attack by tigers when he is taken in by Wingo, an enormous man who has great stores of food and spends his time feeding birds and small animals but is unwilling to admit that he makes them easy prey for predators. Delighted to have an audience, he tells endless stories but will not listen to Dilar nor let him go. As spring approaches, however, Dilar manages to leave and descends into another valley of mists, where the people are almost sleep-walkers, admitting neither pleasure nor pain, existing on a tasteless cactus plant and denying any curiosity or interest in anything. Leaving them, Dilar comes to a seashore and meets an old man, Vigan, who lives with goats and seems to know something of the raft people. He tricks Dilar into undertaking a dangerous climb to steal an eagle's egg but repays him by telling him something of the history of the raft people and the course of the circular underground river. Dilar determines to try to go back in an effort to bring the people, or at least his grandfather, to a "Better Place." Dilar is an interesting character, and the settings and events of the story are compelling. The nearly allegorical nature of the episodes keep it from being as believable as it might be. Choice; Lewis Carroll; Newbery Honor.

JOURNEY TO AMERICA (Levitin*, Sonia, ill. Charles Robinson, Atheneum, 1970), historical novel set in 1938 in Berlin, Germany, and then in Switzerland about a Jewish family's flight to freedom from Nazi persecution. Lisa Platt, 12, tells how her father, Arthur, a tailor, leaves in February for America, intending to send for her, her mother, Margo, her older sister, Ruth*, and her younger sister, Annie, 4, as soon as he has enough money to pay passage and gets the proper forms. Before he leaves, Papa tells Lisa to remain cheerful and to help her mother, and he gives her and Ruth each a ring with a precious stone to be used only in a grave emergency. In March, Hitler invades Austria, and Papa instructs Margo to take the girls to Switzerland as soon as she can "for a short vacation." The girls know they will never return to Berlin, and it is hard for them to leave their friends, home, and cherished possessions. Annie fusses until Lisa placates her by allowing her to take her bride doll along. They have some problems getting out of the country. The official at the passport office is reluctant to give Margo passports because they are Jews, and she must bribe another official to let their taxi through a parade in order to make the train. To Lisa's relief, a border authority confiscates Ruth's violin without finding the money she has hidden in the lining of the case. In Zurich, they live for a while in one cramped room. When Mama's money runs out, she refuses to let the girls sell their rings, stating that more difficult times may be in store for them, when they will really need that money. Ruth and Lisa stay for several weeks at a refugee camp for children, where they are poorly treated, and then all three girls board with Swiss families, who accept them as their own. Lisa comes to love the kind and generous Werfels and their daughter, Erica, and enjoys going to Erica's school. The Werfels help when Mama gets pneumonia and comfort them when it is learned that an aunt and uncle have been put to death back in Berlin. After celebrating Christmas with the Werfels, they take the money Papa sends and travel by train to Le Havre, where they embark for America. After a stormy voyage, they are reunited with Papa in New York. The book is mostly plot, a composite of plausible incidents and characters insufficiently developed. Lisa is a too matter-of-fact narrator and changes little. The book instructs later elementary and junior high readers on an intellectual plane about this aspect of World War II and never really engages the emotions. (Werner*) Choice.

JOY PORTER (*The Witches of Worm**), Jessica's beautiful mother of thirty. She has raised Jessica by herself since her husband walked out shortly after Jessica was born. Joy often works late to make ends meet, is openly husband-hunting, and dates frequently. She regards Jessica as an encumbrance, though she loves her dearly, and she avoids facing Jessica's behavior problems by making excuses for them. The effect is that Jessica feels inferior and bad about herself, while at the same time she realizes she can control her mother's actions. Joy is a round character, for whom the reader feels both sympathy and censure.

J. T. (Wagner*, Jane, ill. with photographs by Gordon Parks, Jr., Van Nostrand, 1969), brief story set in an urban slum area in the 1960s. When J. T., a black boy who looks perhaps ten in the illustrations, sees a transistor radio on the dashboard of a red convertible, he reaches in, grabs it, and runs before Boomer and Claymore, two bigger boys, can get it. The next day they lay for him, he escapes, and as he cuts through the rubble of a vacant lot he sees an injured, scraggly, one-eyed cat. At school he worries about the cat until, at noon, he takes his sandwich and some milk from the cafeteria and hunts for the cat, finding it in an oven in a partly wrecked building. He feeds the animal, wraps his hood around it, and constructs a house for it out of junk, forgetting completely that he was supposed to meet his grandmother, Mama Melcy, at the bus station and help her find their apartment. When he gets home his grandmother is there and quite proud of herself for having coped with the city transportation herself. J. T.'s mother, Rodeen, is upset at his thoughtlessness and at the radio, which she knows he must have stolen. When he asks her if he can have the cat for Christmas, she won't listen. J. T. begins charging cans of tuna fish at the store run by Abe Rosen and his wife, and he skips school. Boomer and Claymore catch him once in the lavatory, hold his face under the soap dispenser, and squirt liquid soap into his eyes. Every day he adds something to the home for the cat, which he names Bones. One afternoon when he goes to visit Bones, Boomer and Claymore are there, having found the cat and the radio he has left in the cat's house to keep it company. The bullies play keep away until the radio sails through Mr. Rosen's window and the terrified cat streaks into the street and is hit by a car. J. T. is heartbroken. His mother and his grandmother try to comfort him with no success. One evening Mr. Rosen appears at the door with a basket containing the radio, cans of tuna, a bag of kitty litter, and a scrawny kitten. At first J. T. will have nothing to do with it, but before he goes to sleep the cat is sharing his bed. The next morning, seeing the red convertible, J. T. puts the radio on the dashboard and asks Mr. Rosen for a job. Despite its realistic contemporary urban setting, this Christmas story has the sentimental elements of many of its forerunners. Without the photographs, taken while a television show was being filmed, the story would be slight, written in simple language and showing warmth but no subtlety. Choice.

JULIA AND THE HAND OF GOD (Cameron*, Eleanor, ill. Gail Owens, Dutton, 1977), realistic, episodic novel of family life set in the 1920s in northern California. Aspiring writer, Julia Redfern, her widowed mother, Celia, who works in a bookstore, and her older brother, Greg*, who has a consuming interest in ancient Egypt, have been living with Julia's grandmother since Mr. Redfern's death in World War I. For her eleventh birthday, Julia's beloved, indulgent Uncle Hugh takes the three to lunch at an elegant restaurant in San Francisco. During lunch, he tells once again at Julia's request the story of the San Francisco earthquake and then gives her a richly bound volume of blank pages for her to fill with "rags and tags of oddities that you might lose forever if you never put them down." Julia soon has several memorable experiences to record in her book. She and her family hear what they are certain are the footsteps of Uncle Hugh's dead collie, Jenny, dancing on the linoleum in his kitchen. To her surprise and chagrin, Julia learns that Uncle Hugh's stout, rigid wife, Aunt Alex, controls the purse strings. Julia and her chum, Maisie, ruin Maisie's mother's best saucepan in their ill-conceived, well-meant attempts to cremate a dead mouse. To earn money to pay for the saucepan, Julia weeds for Dr. Jacklin, a scholar, and the two become good friends, enjoying conversation and tea together. Julia later helps Dr. Jacklin rescue his French Impressionist paintings when a grass fire threatens the residential area. Julia's intemperate outburst accusing her grandmother of favoritism toward Greg results in the ruin of a chart on Egypt Greg has been painstakingly preparing. At the end, Julia's mother finds an apartment in Berkeley she can afford and moves her family to their new quarters over Grandmother's protests. In her new room, light and airy with its many windows, Julia reflects upon the rapidity with which life can change and about how much she has to record in the book Uncle Hugh gave her, which she decides to call *The Book of Strangenesses*. The novel's loosely connected episodes are held together by Julia's growing awareness of the complex interpersonal relationships between her adult relatives and of change as an essential part of life. Well-drawn scenes have life, characterization is rich and convincing, and style is graceful, literate, spiced with humor, which is often adult, and distinguished by faithful attention to detail. Julia is convincingly revealed as an imaginative, often impetuous, outspoken, and intellectually gifted child with a tendency to dramatize. Julia's story continues in *A Room Made of Windows**, a fuller and also richly detailed account of Julia and her friends and relatives. Fanfare.

JULIE OF THE WOLVES (George*†, Jean Craighead, ill. John Schoenherr, Harper, 1972), realistic adventure novel, a variation of the Robinsonnade, set in modern times on the north slope of Alaska. Miyax, whose English name is Julie Edwards, was born on the island of Nunivak, between the Aleutians and Nome, where after her mother's death she lived in a seal camp with her father, Kapugen (Charlie), until his Aunt Martha insists that the girl live with her in Mekoryuk to attend school. Before she leaves, Kapugen tells her she can go at thirteen to marry Daniel, son of his friend Naka, who lives in Barrow, a match arranged by the two fathers. Julie finds life with Martha, who insists on the old ways and isolates the girl from her school friends, difficult after Kapugen is reported dead at sea. She turns more and more to dreams of life in San Francisco with her pen pal, Amy Pollock, who repeatedly invites her to come. When Naka sends word that she should come to Barrow, she goes willingly, only to find that Daniel is retarded, Naka is alcoholic, and his wife, Nusan, wants Julie to help her sew parkas and mittens for the tourists, the gussaks. She tries to fit in, seeing as little as possible of Daniel, until one day he catches her alone and, having been taunted about having a wife he cannot mate, attempts to rape her. She quietly collects the essentials for travel and sets out to walk to Point Hope, where she plans to catch the boat for San Francisco. She greatly underestimates the time needed, and the book opens as she camps, nearly starving, near a wolf pack. Having been trained in some of the old Eskimo ways by Kapugen, she observes the wolves closely until she learns their ways. The group is made up of three grown males—Amaroq, the beautiful leader, Nails, his lieutenant, and Jello, a low-status hanger-on—one female, Silver, and her five pups, whom Julie, now Miyax, calls Kapu, Zing, Zit, Zat, and Sister. By watching carefully, she learns their signs for dominance and submission, and she mimics them until she is accepted. At first she is puzzled by how the pups, no longer nursing, are fed, since the adults seem to carry no food back to them, until she sees the pups put their noses into the corner of an adult's mouth, a signal which makes the older wolf regurgitate partly digested meat. She uses this technique and saves herself from starving. With the wolves doing the hunting, she gets caribou hide which she can soak and freeze into a sled and snowshoes, and other useful items. As winter approaches she sets off again for Point Hope and discovers that the wolves are traveling with her, even protecting her by driving away a grizzly. When Jello steals her pack for the food that she carries, she is panicky, knowing that without her boots, knife, and needles she will quickly die, but she finds that Amaroq has killed Jello, and she retrieves her essential implements. One day she finds a golden plover, for some reason not migrated, names it Tornait, and keeps it with her through the winter in her hut of snow blocks. As she approaches civilization, a plane, shooting wolves for sport, kills Amaroq and wounds Kapu, now a grown wolf. She nurses him, and he recovers and takes over leadership. From a hunter and his wife, the first humans Miyax has seen in months, Miyax learns that she is near the village of Kangik and that Kapugen is married to a gussak and is living there with modern appliances, even flying a plane for sport hunters. At first she goes off but concludes that the old ways are dead and returns to Kapugen. Plotting in the story is weak, with numerous coincidences and unresolved questions. Why Kapugen arranged a marriage without discovering that Daniel is retarded is unclear. Scenes in which Julie watches the wolves and learns their ways are fascinating, as are other bits of nature lore, and the general problem for the Eskimo caught between the old and new ways is well presented, but the ending, though valid intellectually, is underdeveloped and unconvincing. ChLA Top 10; Choice; Fanfare; National Book Finalist; Newbery Winner.

JULS (*Prison Window, Jerusalem Blue**), younger brother of Sydne*, a buoyant, imaginative boy. Naively unable to feel himself a slave, he rashly earns a brutal flogging. He accepts the devotion and companionship of retarded Thyri* before his sister does, and it is his plan to turn Thorolf's traitorous scheme back upon him by revealing his treachery rather than mocking Herjolt* in their harvest festival play.

JUNIOR BROWN (*The Planet of Junior Brown**), Virgil, an extremely heavy black boy, 14, who plays the piano and paints with great talent, and for whom Buddy* Clark and Mr. Pool construct and name a new planet in their model solar system in a secret basement room of their school. Junior's overprotective mother, who suffers from asthma, is clearly one of the factors in his gross weight problem. His mind snaps when he tries to help his music teacher, Miss Peelis, rid her apartment of an imaginary intruder, a filthy diseased relative whose presence, Junior fears, may force her to destroy her grand piano, which he loves. At Buddy's suggestion he is lowered by a winch rigged by Mr. Pool to a "planet," or hide-out, for homeless boys in a basement of a collapsed building, where he will, presumably, start to recover. Junior's confusion and suffering, both mental and physical, are described vividly but he is essentially a dependent character, whose future seems problematic in realistic terms.

JURGEN, HARRY (*Rock Star**), executive with Wolf Records who encourages Tim to come to New York City because he recognizes the boy has talent and the ability to make good but who also tries to give him a realistic idea of his chances for success in the big time. Jurgen is knowledgeable and tough minded, neither callous nor cruel, and seems sincerely interested in the psychological well-being of the young people with whom he comes into contact. He is perhaps too deliberate an antithesis of the stereotype of the "big-time recording exec."

JUSTER, NORTON (1929–   ), born in Brooklyn, N.Y.; architect and professor of design. He was graduated from the University of Pennsylvania, Philadelphia, in architecture and attended the University of Liverpool on a Fullbright grant. From 1954 to 1957 he served in the U.S. Naval Reserve Civil Engineer Corps in Morocco and Newfoundland. He has worked as an architect in New York and in Sherburne Falls, Mass., and has taught at Pratt Institute, New York City, and at Hampshire College, Amherst, Mass. In 1960 he received a Ford Foundation grant to work in urban aesthetics and a Guggenheim Fellowship in 1967. His best-known books for children are *The Phantom Tollbooth** (Random, 1961) and *Alberic the Wise and Other Journeys* (Pantheon, 1965).

JUSTIN (*Mrs. Frisby and the Rats of NIMH**), large, very handsome, courageous young rat, captain of the guard at the rats' rosebush headquarters on Farmer Fitzgibbon's farm. One of the twenty rats whose lives were changed by the special injections given them in the laboratory of NIMH*, Justin astutely discovers an escape route through an air shaft and bravely leads the rats to freedom. He later courageously releases Mrs. Frisby from the Fitzgibbon boy's bird cage. The reader never learns whether or not Justin escaped the exterminators' attempts to wipe out the rat colony.

JUSTIN MCLEOD (*The Man Without a Face**), older man who writes popular novels, who coaches Charles Norstadt for the St. Matthew's exams, who helps him see that he can control his life, and for whom Charles feels a sexual attraction which results in a homosexual relationship. A recluse, Justin was terribly scarred in a car accident some years before the story begins. A youth was killed in the accident, and Justin served a two-year prison term for driving under the influence of liquor. Some call Justin the Man Without a Face because of his terrible disfigurement, and rumors are rife about him in the community. Justin is a cardboard figure, never really fleshed enough to seem alive.

K

KALI CUTTER (*The Arm of the Starfish**), Carolyn Cutter, daughter of Typhon Cutter*. Beautiful young sophisticate, she helps her father in his efforts to gain the information Dr. Calvin* O'Keefe has learned from his experiments on the starfish. She encounters Adam* Eddington at Kennedy International Airport in New York City at the beginning of the story, where she warns him against trusting Dr. O'Keefe and his friend, Canon* Tallis, planting the seeds of suspicion in Adam's mind that influence his conduct throughout the novel and lead eventually to the shooting of Joshua Archer. When she later realizes that Adam has grown suspicious of her intentions, she pretends to have discovered that her father only wants Dr. O'Keefe's secrets in order to get more money. She demands Adam's passport as proof that he will help her get away from her father. Since Adam's passport has Joshua Archer's phone number in it, her action leads to Joshua's death.

KATE ELLIOTT MCPHEE (*The Whispered Horse**), competent, long-suffering older sister of Rowan*. A younger copy of their mother, Kate has been a thirty-year-old spinster when she marries Tam* McPhee. Although she suffers his physical abuse without complaint and does not doubt that he will kill her if he realizes that she knows he murdered their mother, she fiercely refuses to think of running off with Rowan and leaving their heritage of cottage and land to Tam.

KATE FARR (*The People Therein**), tall, competent sister of Lanthy*. Married after a long wait for the arrival of the traveling minister, she is shocked and unsympathetic when unmarried Lanthy tells her she is pregnant and at first refuses to believe it. Later, when she herself becomes pregnant, she confesses that she has feared that she would never have a child as punishment for her unkindness to her sister.

KATE ROBBINS (*Canalboat to Freedom**), daughter of the Quaker widow who befriends Lundius and Benja. A little older than twelve-year-old Benja, Kate is very competent and a good shot. She raises rabbits and mink, traps for fur, and cooks a good apple pie. When Benja decides to go off with Newt instead of staying on the Robbins farm, Kate is disappointed, but the story ends with a letter from Ben, badly misspelled but reminding Kate of their plan to go into partnership someday as owners of a canalboat.

KATE SUTTON (*The Perilous Gard**), strong-minded Elizabethan girl who becomes a prisoner of the "Fairy Folk," actually the survivors of a pre-Christian religion who carry on secretly in underground caverns in remote Derbyshire, where Kate has been banished by Queen Mary. Awkward and intellectual, Kate has been blamed for a letter written by her pretty, brainless sister, Alicia. Although her situation seems hopeless, she resists the drugged drink which makes other "mortals" who serve the "fairies" happy with their lot and eventually reasons out where Christopher* Heron is being kept, knowing that he is to be murdered to pay the *tiend*, the seven-year ritual killing of the king which is part of the religion. Her practical good sense and outspoken opinions keep his spirit alive as his ordeal approaches, and in the end her courage in challenging the "fairies" saves him.

KATHRYN SUSSO MUELLER (*Taking Terri Mueller**), now Mrs. Merle Newhouse, mother of Terri*, who was stolen from her custody eight years before by her ex-husband, Phil*. Now remarried and the mother of Leah, 4, she has never given up hope of finding Terri or stopped grieving for her loss. Each night she sleeps with Terri's picture under her pillow. Although intellectually her yearning for Terri and her hatred of Phil are believable, she never comes alive in the story, which does not tackle the problem of why the original marriage broke up.

KATHY BARDY (*When No One Was Looking**), talented tennis star who seems destined to win the New England championship for girls fourteen-and-under and to go on, eventually, to Wimbledon. Although she is ambitious and loves tennis, she is harassed by the driving pressure of her mother and her coach and to a lesser degree her father and by the expectations of the townspeople. After being coached all summer in algebra, she is given the make-up exam by the superintendent, who carefully puts the answer book in sight and then leaves the room. She cheats, then admits it, and is confused and shocked when he won't accept her admission. Part of her ambition to excel in tennis comes from her feeling of her family's inferiority to the Redmonds, wealthy family of her best friend, Julia.

KATY STARR (*The Alley**), friend of Connie* Ives. She is a little older than Connie and much more outgoing, self-assured, and assertive. Connie is somewhat afraid of her but admires her ideas and her organizational skills. Katy and Connie think along the same lines, however, and, when Billy* Maloon leaves for camp at the end of the book, it appears that Katy will take his place as Connie's best friend.

KAVIK, THE WOLF DOG (Morey*, Walt, ill. Peter Parnall, Dutton, 1968), animal story set in Alaska and Seattle in the mid twentieth century. When Charlie One Eye wins the North American Sled Dog Derby in Fairbanks, George C. Hunter of Hunter Enterprises insists on buying his lead dog, Kävik, meaning Wolverine, which Charlie has trained to be a fighter. The bush pilot flying him out crashes. Andy Evans, 15, checking his trap line, comes upon the crash site where the dog has suffered in his crate for three days. Unable to leave Kävik, Andy lashes him to a piece of the plane's wing and drags him as far as he can, until his father, Kurt, alarmed when Andy does not come home, meets him. With the support of his mother, Laura, Andy insists on calling the doctor, Vic Walker, who is reluctant to take the dog as a patient but becomes involved in trying to save him. They keep the news of Kävik's survival from Hunter temporarily until they learn whether he will recover. Under Andy's gentle care, he does recover and for the first time learns love of a human, but he also shows, when the village dogs in Copper City attack him, that he has lost his nerve. Kurt admits to his son that he, too, has lost his nerve since his boat sank five years before and now refuses to go seining, working as a watchman and handyman instead. When Hunter returns in the summer, Kävik is externally the same fine dog that led the championship team, and Hunter refuses to believe Kurt's story that the dog is now a coward. Shipped to Hunter's palatial home in Seattle, Kävik mourns and, on a walk with Hunter, shows his fear of a much smaller dog. Hunter plans to keep him just long enough to show him off at his club, then have him shot. Seeing the mountains that look like home, Kävik jumps through the closed window and, with the help of the sympathetic handy man, escapes. After a harrowing trip through the city, including a detour through a department store, Kävik becomes one of the strays that haunt the docks, living on the refuse in garbage cans. He is picked up by the dog catchers but rescued by an older couple, Martha and John Kent, who live on a boat and call the dog ''Mr. Mystery.'' The Kents take Kävik north with them, but when he gets ashore and starts determinedly north, they let him go. Kävik makes a grueling journey over mountain ranges and glaciers; he is taken for a wolf and injured by the men wintering at a mine; he fights a wolf for a female and, mating with her, goes far out of his way; when she is killed by a hunter firing from a plane, he leaves alone and finally gets to the edge of Copper City where Andy lives. This time Dr. Walker willingly treats him, and Kurt stands up to Hunter, who sees Kävik fight the village dogs and wants him again. Kurt agrees to take over management of Hunter's seiner in exchange for the right to buy the dog. Reminiscent of both *Lassie Come Home*† and *Call of the Wild*†, the story uses stock characters and situations. It is strongest in its description of the dog's struggles against nature and weakest in the contrived parallel between Kävik's loss of courage and Kurt's. Choice.

KEITH†, HAROLD (VERNE) (1903–   ), born in Lambert, Okla.; sports publicist and author noted for his books of historical fiction for young people. He grew up in Kansas, Missouri, and Texas, as well as in Oklahoma, attended Northwestern State Teachers College, and took his bachelor's and master's degrees from the University of Oklahoma. He has taught school, been an assistant grain buyer, and for almost forty years was director of sports publicity at the University of Oklahoma in Norman. In 1961 he received the Arch Ward Memorial Trophy as outstanding sports publicist and has been president of College Sports Information Directors of America. Previously he received the Helms Foundation Sports Publicist of the Year Award (1950). He has written a dozen books mostly for older youth and mostly novels, some of them about sports, the most critically acclaimed being historical fiction. One of these was a deservedly much honored book, receiving among others the Newbery Award, *Rifles for Watie†* (Crowell, 1957), a rich and substantial novel, well researched and convincingly written, set during the Civil War, which takes a young Kansas farm boy in the Union army behind the Southern lines to scout for the North. Two of his novels received the Western Heritage Award, *Susy's Scoundrel** (Crowell, 1974), about a little girl and the clever coyote she raises, vivid in its details of animal life, which also won the Spur Award of Western Writers of America, and *The Obstinate Land** (Crowell, 1977), about the land rush into the Cherokee Strip of northern Oklahoma in the 1890s, which excels in the picture it creates of the difficulties the settlers faced in that hard and inhospitable region, although story is thin and characterization minimal. He also wrote *Komantcia* (Crowell, 1965), which fictionalizes upon the true story of a Spanish youth taken captive by Comanches. His other titles include *Shotgun Shaw: A Baseball Story* (Crowell, 1949), *The Runt of Rogers School* (Lippincott, 1971), a football story, *Boys' Life of Will Rogers* (Crowell, 1937), and *Sports and Games* (Crowell, 1941). He has also written fiction and non-fiction for many periodicals. A runner as an undergraduate, he has pursued this interest in later life, winning trophies in competition for his distance running.

KELLY O'KELLY (*The Murder of Hound Dog Bates**), stranger in the Arkansas hills, who helps Sassafras Bates find out who killed his dog. Kelly was on the police force in Chicago for a while before he started knocking around. He offers to help Sassafras find Hound Dog's killer, under the mistaken impression that Hound Dog is a human being, Sass's chum, because Sass has neglected to tell Kelly that his murdered ''friend'' is really his dog. Kelly eventually discovers that Hound Dog has died from eating the poison that Clem Watts set out to kill weasels. Kelly falls in love with Sass's Aunt* Hope, and they get married at the end.

KELPIE (*Witch of the Glens**), girl of the gypsies who possesses second sight and is accused of being a witch but who gradually learns the meaning of loyalty and principle. Though betrayed repeatedly by the gypsies, Black Bogle and Mina

Faw, beaten by Mina, and used by her to see in the crystal, Kelpie stays with them in hope that Mina will teach her witchcraft and because she has known no other life. She is skilled at purse-snatching, knows all the wiles of a skillful beggar, and steals and lies as naturally as she breathes. In her stay at Glenfern, her better instincts are roused, and she returns to the gypsies only to save the Cameron family from their threatened curses. Intelligent, clever, a fine actress, she has lived by her wits. From what Bogle has said, she concludes that she was stolen as an infant because she has strange, "uncanny" eyes, with three rings of blue, a sure sign of unnatural powers, and it is for these eyes as much as for her possession of a few strands of his hair that Argyll condemns her to be burned as a witch.

KENDALL†, CAROL (SEEGER) (1917–   ), born in Bucyrus, Ohio; children's author, best known for her fantasies about the Minnipins. She graduated from Ohio University and married Paul Kendall, a writer and professor of English at Ohio University. She has traveled extensively, accompanying her husband on his trips abroad to collect material for his books, and speaks Chinese, German, French, and Russian. After publishing two novels for adults, she wrote a juvenile mystery, *The Other Side of the Tunnel* (Lane, 1956), and she has also published *The Big Splash* (Viking, 1960), a realistic story about what happens when six children decide to raise money for a hospital drive; *The Firelings* (Atheneum, 1982), a fantasy about little people who live in a land located on the slopes of a volcano; and a book of folktales, *Sweet and Sour: Tales from China* (Seabury, 1979). Most popular and critically acclaimed has been her fantasy, *The Gammage Cup†* (Harcourt, 1959), about Muggles and her friends and their conflicts with the Mushrooms. Less original than its predecessor is *The Whisper of Glocken** (Harcourt, 1965), a Fanfare book. It tells how Muggles and her friends, now called the Old Heroes, aid the New Heroes in returning safely from their journey across the mountains to investigate why the Watercress River is overflowing its banks and flooding the area.

KEN KAMATA (*The Egypt Game**), sixth grade boy, friend of April* Hall and Melanie* Ross, and chum and follower of Toby* Alvillar. He joins the Egypt game because Toby decides to. Unlike Toby, he adds little of imagination to activities. At first, he says, "Sheesh! " about almost everything the children do, but gradually he is caught up in their pretending and eventually really enjoys the game.

KERR, M. E. (MARIJANE MEAKER) (1927–   ), born in Auburn, N.Y.; free-lance writer; author of contemporary problem novels for early adolescents. After graduating from Stuart Hall in Staunton, Va., she studied at the University of Missouri and then received her degree from Columbia University in English literature. She has worked for E. P. Dutton Publishing Co., and since 1949, after selling her first story to *Ladies Home Journal*, she has been a full-time

writer, publishing about forty novels for adults and young people, some also
under the pseudonyms M. J. Meaker, Ann Aldrich, and Vin Packer. As M. E.
Kerr, another pseudonym and one which plays on her own last name, she has
written a dozen popular novels about youth attempting to come to terms with
themselves and problems of their environment, among them, a *Media and Methods*
Maxi Award book, *Dinky Hocker Shoots Smack** (Harper, 1972), about a bright,
overweight teenager and her do-gooder mother, a book very much liked by the
young but not so enthusiastically received by critics and other adults, and a
Christopher Award–winning book, *Gentlehands** (Harper, 1978), about a teenaged
boy whose grandfather turns out to be a Nazi war criminal. Her novels move
fast, are witty and humorous, and feature exaggerated, oddly assorted characters
in larger-than-life situations. She has also written an American Library Association
Notable book, *Is That You, Miss Blue?* (Harper, 1975), about a girl at boarding
school whose parents have just separated, and a Children's Spring Book Festival
honor book, *If I Love You, Am I Trapped Forever?* (Harper, 1973), in which a
boy must cope with losing his girl friend and the return of his estranged father,
I'll Love You When You're More Like Me (Harper, 1979), about a troubled
parent-children relationship, *Little Little* (Harper, 1981), a satirical novel about
some dwarfs, and *Me, Me, Me, Me, Me—Not a Novel* (Harper, 1983), her
autobiography.

THE KESTREL (Alexander*, Lloyd, Dutton, 1982), vigorously plotted,
energetically related, fulsomely cast novel of adventure and conflict, sequel to
Westmark*, in which Theo is again confronted by problems of right and wrong
posed by circumstances and Mickle* proves herself adept as general and queen.
King Augustine has died, and Mickle succeeds to the throne of Westmark* as
Queen Augusta. Aristocrats led by General Erzcour conspire with the neighboring
realm of Regia, ruled by King Constantine, a weakling who plays with toy
soldiers, and ambitious courtiers prompted by exiled Cabbarus to invade Westmark,
hoping to overthrow Mickle and kill Theo, now Prince Consort-to-be. The
aristocrats wish to forestall the democratic reforms demanded by Florian's*
rapidly growing faction of revolutionaries, and the Regians simply wish to add
Westmark to their empire. Theo, on a fact-gathering assignment for the crown
when war breaks out, joins Florian, who agrees to take his followers into battle
on the side of the monarchy in return for Theo's help in securing a constitution
that guarantees equal rights for all. While with the contingent led by Justin, for
whom ends justify means and whose lieutenant is Monkey, a lanky officer of
uncertain background and shifting ethics, Theo grapples with his misgivings
about killing and plundering. His doubts are rapidly dispelled after the Regians
brutally kill Stock, the poet, and other partisans, and, as Captain Kestrel, Theo
participates in raids as cruel and daring as those he previously deplored, more
than living up to his sobriquet. Early on, Mickle, accompanied by Las* Bombas
and Musket*, leaves the palace in Marianstat to search for Theo. Along the way,
she assumes control of her fleeing army, transforming the broken troops into a

formidable barrier against the better equipped Regians. Recognizing that defeat is inevitable and deploring the numerous casualties on both sides, Mickle decides to approach King Constantine with a treaty offering mutually beneficial terms of peace. More than a full measure of rapidly occurring coincidences, surprises, twists, turns, and ironies ensues as the book flashes from sector to sector. Mickle and Las Bombas have an ironic interview with General Erzcour himself. Justin is captured by the Regians and freed in a daring raid led by Theo, who unwittingly wounds Mickle. As a lark, King Constantine takes the field and is captured by two children, who also rescue the wounded Mickle, thus bringing the two sovereigns together and effecting peace between the warring nations. Back in the capital, Mickle cleverly forestalls dissension over the future of the government by suggesting that Theo join Florian and Justin in a triumvirate to advise her and to draw up a constitution. The plot offers humor, pathos, suspense, and plenty of action and excitement, all cleverly blended to maintain maximum interest. Style is witty, animated, and often satirical, but characterization is shallow, and many characters are stock. The themes of freedom, justice, and life's existential problems are obtrusive, and the pace is typically Alexandrine in its freneticism. The book adds considerably to the reader's knowledge of the land and politics of Westmark and is more convincing than its predecessor. *The Beggar Queen* concludes the series. Fanfare.

KETTY PETRIE (*The Far-Off Land**), sixteen-year-old woman, raised pacifist by Moravians in North Carolina, whose brother Anson* Petrie, claims her and takes her with him, his family, and some friends on their flatboat journey to French Lick on the Cumberland River. Advised by her Moravian teacher, Sister Oesterlein, "to be present" to the needs of those around her and to maintain a reverent heart, Ketty strives to control her fears and always to be useful. The travelers soon learn to appreciate her steadiness and willing hands. A major problem, indeed a dilemma, for Ketty arises out of the difference between the way she and her fellow travelers view the Indians. The Moravians have taught her that all people, even Indians, respond positively to kind and fair treatment, a way of thinking that conflicts directly with the frontierspeople's belief that Indians are bloodthirsty heathens to whom no moral obligation is due. Anson is very angry when he learns that Ketty has treated and fed a wounded Indian, though the group later learns that her action probably prevented an attack. George* Soelle, for whom she forms a romantic attachment, helps her to see that circumstances dictate how she must behave toward the Indians, regardless of her personal convictions about them, and that she has a prior responsibility for helping to preserve the safety of those with whom she is traveling.

KEY, ALEXANDER (HILL) (1904–1979), born in La Plata, Md.; painter, illustrator, novelist. Orphaned as a young child, he grew up on the Suwanee River in Florida and attended the Chicago Art Institute from 1921 to 1923. He later taught art at the Chicago Studio School of Art and during World War II served in the U.S. Naval Intelligence. In 1929 he started writing and produced magazine articles, short stories, and novels for adults and at least seventeen books for young people. For some time he lived in Chicago, then Florida, then moved to a home in the Smoky Mountains, the setting for his science-fantasy, *The Forgotten Door** (Westminster, 1965), which was named to the Lewis Carroll Shelf.

KHALIL (*The Mukhtar's Children**), twelve-year-old son of the leader of an Arab village in the newly formed state of Israel. As his friend Selim says, Khalil has "too much conceit and not enough," continually warring within himself between his honor and his doubts. Although he is convinced of the superiority of men, he is constantly being outdone by his twin sister, Jasmin*. Because he is insulted by an arrogant Israeli officer, he takes part in an ambush and in reparation must live and work in the nearby kibbutz until the young man he shot has recovered. There he learns many new ideas and on his return channels his restless energies to reforming his village and his people.

THE KIDNAPPING OF CHRISTINA LATTIMORE (Nixon*, Joan Lowery, Harcourt, 1979), mystery-detective novel set recently in Houston, Tex. Home late from a friend's house one Friday night, pampered, headstrong heiress Christina Lattimore, high school junior, is kidnapped in her driveway and held for ransom in the dark, cold basement of a rambling, old house somewhere in the city. Her rough, ski-masked captor forces her to sign a ransom note demanding $250,000 from her oil-rich grandmother. Christina is frightened but keeps her wits about her and soon identifies her kidnappers as none-too-bright Zack Tigus and his timid wife, Loretta, the couple who run a greasy spoon hamburger joint Christina has sometimes patronized while slumming for kicks. When the police free her a few days later, Zack and Loretta declare she is their accomplice and accuse her of engineering her own kidnapping. To Christina's astonishment, authorities believe their story. Although she maintains she was an unwilling victim and offers tenuous proof, her family also remain skeptical, since shortly before the abduction the girl had unsuccessfully sought money from them for a European trip her parents disapproved of. Her socially correct mother, weak, over-churched father, and imperious grandmother, Cristabel, fear publicity and hire a high-powered lawyer to get the charges dropped. When even her best friend doubts her story, Christina realizes that she must clear her reputation by proving her innocence herself. She is encouraged by kind, believing police detective Jason York and T. J. Kelly, cub reporter and college student. Christina then interviews principals and tracks down clues. Several people fall under suspicion, including her father's mousey, middle-aged secretary, Rosella Marsh, Della, the housekeeper, and even doughty Cristabel herself. Kelly, whom Christina envisioned as her hero-to-the-rescue, turns out to be an opportunist hoping to use her to gain an exclusive story and thus advance his career. Eventually, Christina learns that Della's son, who had met Zack while both were in prison, had masterminded the extortion attempt. Christina tells her story with unusual control, revealing herself as a spoiled, indulged child who changes quite expectedly through events to become more independent and mature in judgment. At the end, she decides to take a part-time job to earn money for the trip, an illogical and didactic tag to the story. Christina's account improvises on the notorious Patty Hearst kidnapping and is otherwise quite conventional in character and incident. The villains are unconvincing, but the plot is fast paced and carefully calculated hints and twists keep the reader engrossed. Poe Winner.

KIEN (*A Boat to Nowhere**), orphan boy who sails with a Vietnamese teacher and his two grandchildren to flee the Communist takeover of their village. As a young child Kien was abandoned by relatives in an overcrowded, filthy orphanage. He has become attached to an American airman named Jim, who has given him his watch and promised to return for him, but never has. Embittered, Kien has run away and lived by his wits, cynical, disrespectful, unprincipled. At the village he is treated well, but beneath his veneer of amiability he maintains his jeering contempt for the simple villagers, a side he displays only to Mai. His greatest fear, that of being taken over by the Communists, prompts him to trade his precious watch for a chance to guard the teacher and to engineer their escape. On the boat, the *Sea Breeze*, he assumes a man's role since the grandfather is elderly and, much of the time, ill, and the other two are children. His choice to be part of the loving family is measured when he leaps into the shark-infested waters to save Loc and later when he has a chance to be lifted aboard a passing ship but slides back into the water rather than leave the others on the *Sea Breeze*. Before he dies, Van Chi tells Kien that he is now officially head of the family and makes him promise to return some day to Vietnam.

KILLER-OF-DEATH (*Killer-of-Death**), Apache youth, protagonist, who tells the story. He grows and changes believably. He is a thoughtful boy, inclined to pranks, who worries whether he will ever have the courage to impress his girl, be a worthy warrior, and help his people. He discovers, however, as his father has assured him, that, when the time comes, he does have the strength to do what must be done. He has a good relationship with his father, and there is a pleasing tension between him and his adopted brother, Lazy* Legs, who gives him wise advice. At the end, approaching middle age and confined to a reservation, Killer-of-Death realizes that his efforts to resist the white tide have failed, but he looks forward to a better life for his people through education (though this idea seems really the author's) and is content that he himself has done the best that he can.

KILLER-OF-DEATH (Baker*, Betty, ill. John Kaufmann, Harper, 1963), historical novel set in the mid–1800s, just before and after the Gadsden Purchase, in the Arizona mountains not far from Tucson. Earnest, fun-loving Killer-of-Death*, Apache, begins his story by saying, "I was born too late." He then goes on to describe with honesty and increasing perceptiveness events of the years he grows to manhood, the last ones his tribe are free. When his story begins, his main concerns are keeping his Mexican foster brother, Lazy* Legs, from living up to his name, trying to prevent his family from spoiling his charming baby sister, Little One, and proving himself a worthy warrior so that he may win pretty Sky Maiden. But the treaty Juan José, the chief, makes with the Mexicans, allowing them to mine copper in Apache territory, changes things for his people. Killer-of-Death's father, a sub-chieftain, and his father's cousin, the noted warrior, Mangas Colorado, are certain that the Mexicans will not be content with the treaty land, and events soon prove them right. Adding a little tension to the story is Killer-of-Death's rivalry with Gian-nah-tah*, the shaman's surly son, which gradually grows into a bitter hatred. In spite of Gian-nah-tah's opposition, Killer-of-Death succeeds in his desert trial and wins acclaim as an apprentice warrior. On a raid Mangas leads against a ranch, Gian-nah-tah strikes Killer-of-Death with an axe, leaves him for dead, and returns to spread stories that Killer-of-Death was a coward. After a long ordeal through hostile country, described in limited detail, Killer-of-Death makes his way home, where to his surprise he finds almost everyone except his own family away attending a feast put on by the Americans and Mexicans. His family greet him joyfully, and then they, too, leave for the feast. A fight with Gian-nah-tah outside the festival camp ironically saves both their lives, for the whites treacherously massacre almost all the Indians who attend. Killer-of-Death then throws in his lot with Mangas, who spearheads resistance against the whites. On one occasion, Killer-of-Death saves Mangas's life (thus fulfilling a prediction that the boy would save the life of a chief) by taking him to a white doctor to remove a bullet. The Apaches soon become the object of an intense and massive bounty hunt, and Mangas joins Cochise, another Indian who has organized resistance against the whites. Killer-of-Death glosses over the raids and flights that span many years, and the last chapter finds him on a reservation where he takes the suggestion of a sympathetic missionary and sends his son to school. He has become convinced that this is the best way he can help his people. The first part of the book is especially convincing because of the clear way it shows what it must have been like to grow up in the midst of events too complex and fluid for a youth to comprehend. Apache customs and attitudes are described in sufficient detail to give a clear picture of what their life must have been like. Mangas Colorado is neither glorified nor romanticized. The rivalry between Killer-of-Death and Gian-nah-tah seems an unnecessary complication, and the shaman's son never seems real. There is good tension between Lazy Legs and Killer-of-Death, however, and the relationship between the boy and his father, a sensible man, rings true. This interesting blend of history and fiction, if unevenly plotted, offers excitement, adventure, and occasional humor through the overview it gives of a fast-passing way of life. Western Heritage.

KILL'S MOUND (*M. C. Higgins, the Great**), home of the strange Killburn clan, considered "witchy" by their neighbors on Sarah's Mountain because they all have six fingers and six toes, are seen to have healing power, and live a secluded life in a community where the children play on a huge net, which ropes the houses together and is suspended above the garden, thereby protecting their limited arable land.

KIM, YONG-IK, born in Korea; Korean author who writes in English and whose books are first published in the United States. He studied English in Japan, and from 1948 to 1957 he lived in the United States, receiving his B.A. degree from Florida Southern College and his M.A. from the University of Kentucky and taking further work at the University of Iowa. He returned to Korea to teach English at the University of Korea and to write. Among his books are *The Happy Days** (Little, 1960), a story of the struggle in a village to start a school after the Korean war, and *Love in Winter* (Doubleday, 1969).

KINGMAN, (MARY) LEE (1919–   ), free-lance writer, long associated with children's books as author and editor. Born in Reading, Mass., she attended Colby Junior College and graduated from Smith College with a major in English. After publishing some plays, she took a position as an editorial assistant with Houghton Mifflin Publishing Co., where she later became children's editor. A free-lance writer since 1946, she has written and edited over thirty books for adults and children. She has been associated with *Horn Book* since 1964 as council member or director and has edited for *Horn Book* several widely recognized critical works on Newbery and Caldecott books and on illustrators of children's books. Her books of fiction for children vary in length, concerns, and intended audience. They include picture books like *Peter's Long Walk* (Doubleday, 1953); mysteries like *Private Eyes: Adventures with the Saturday Gang** (Doubleday, 1964), which was nominated for the Edgar Allan Poe Award; realistic novels of contemporary family life like *The Year of the Raccoon** (Houghton, 1966), which is listed in *Choice*; stories of adventure and suspense set in the past like *Escape from the Evil Prophecy* (Houghton, 1973); and teenage problem novels like *Head over Wheels* (Houghton, 1978), about the physically handicapped, *Break a Leg, Betsy Maybe!* (Houghton, 1976), which combines theater, growing up, and first love, and *The Refiner's Fire* (Houghton, 1981), about a girl who goes to live in an artists' colony with the father she barely knows. Kingman and her husband, Robert Natti, a teacher, have lived in Massachusetts.

THE KING'S FALCON (Fox*, Paula, ill. Eros Keith, Bradbury, 1969), short, realistic novel set in a medieval kingdom. Troubled, ineffectual King Philip rules a tiny, impoverished realm tucked away in a remote valley near the sea. His cold and heartless queen enjoys belittling him, and the king spends much of his time dreaming of the days of medieval splendor that appear to have passed him by. He spends hours puzzling over riddles of fate, wondering why he was born a king and why a king needs no particular skill for his work, as do musicians or falconers. One day, while strolling by the tower on the cliff overlooking the sea, he and his old falconer spy a falcon's nest with two eyases in it. Later, they return and capture one of them, which they train to the lure. Jubilant over his success with the bird, unhappy with his life as ruler, and appreciative of his falconer's contentment, Philip leaves his kingdom. He travels to a distant realm where he takes a position as the king's falconer and lives contentedly for three years. One day, a minstrel arrives who entertains the court with a song about a far kingdom whose ruler a falcon has borne away in his talons. Philip realizes that what he has done has entered embroidered legend. He smiles at the thought that seldom can a king "exchange his crown for a song." This brief, fable-like story seems unnecessarily obscure, and it is hard to see the point of it. The smudgy black and white illustrations extend the story's brooding tone. Fanfare.

THE KING'S FIFTH (O'Dell*, Scott, ill. Samuel Bryant, Houghton, 1966), historical novel set in New Spain, mostly in what is now western Mexico, New Mexico, and Arizona, in the years 1539–1541. At fifteen, Estéban* de Sandoval is cartographer on the ship of Admiral Alarcón, part of an expedition traveling north up the western coast of Mexico to meet and resupply the army of the conquistador, Coronado. Approached by treasure-hungry Captain Blas de Mendoza*, who is planning to mutiny and seek the gold of the Seven Cities of Cíbola, Estéban is hesitant, but when Alarcón, aware of the unrest, sends Mendoza to find Coronado, Estéban volunteers to go with him, thinking not of gold but of the chance to map uncharted country. After a terrible time reaching shore, they make contact with Coronado, but Mendoza lies to him about Alarcón's whereabouts. Seeking the fabled cities of gold, they travel to Chichilticale, the "Red House," where they find a ruin inhabited by two aging Indians, who promise that the gold is in Háwikuh. There they find a defended city of many tiers and engage in a battle in which Estéban is injured, but even when the Indians leave and the soldiers sack the city, they find no gold. Mendoza gets permission to scout with his own small group consisting of two of his musicians, Roa and Zuñiga, his horse-keeper, Torres, a Nayarit Indian girl guide, Zia* Troyano, 13, a priest, Father* Francisco, and Estéban. They also acquire some horses and Tigre, a large, friendly dog that Mendoza starts to train in viciousness as an Indian killer. Following some vague directions from Indians, they travel to the "chasm," the Grand Canyon, where they find peaceful Indians of Nexpan, so unconcerned with gold that they don't bother to pick it up from their streams. While Father Francisco converts the Indians, with Zia as interpreter, Mendoza kills six of their sheep and uses their fleeces to collect gold in the streams. To stop the angered Indians from chasing them, Mendoza fires the dry grass, and Zuñiga, lugging two heavy fleeces, is enveloped by flames and lost. Winter catches them before they reach their next destination, Tawhi, the "Cloud City" perched above cliffs on a mountain top, and as they shelter in a cave, Torres steals the gold from Nexpan and the best horse, though Zia and Estéban manage to keep its foal, Blue Star. At Tawhi they find a ceremony much like that known from Peru where the chief, or cacique, Tlascingo, covered with oil and gold dust, walks into a small lake to greet the sun each morning. Over the years the gold dust washed from his body has covered the lake bottom thickly. Mendoza pretends friendship, but he and Roa dig a ditch which empties the lake, flooding the city and exposing the gold, which they scoop into leather bags and drop over the cliffs to Estéban. As they head back with their overloaded horses and mules, Mendoza, almost crazed by the gold, sends Roa off, ostensibly to get more mules from Háwikuh, but really to get him out of the way so that Mendoza will not have to divide the treasure. Mendoza, however, is killed by Tigre, trained too well in man killing. Estéban takes charge, decides to avoid Háwikuh, where there will be too many claimants for the gold, and to head for civilization at Culiacan. Zia, seeing the change gold has made in him, leaves with some Indians. Estéban gives her Blue Star, the colt she loves. Although Father Francisco urges him to bury the gold, Estéban presses on into "the Inferno," the desert, where Father Francisco dies. Brought to his senses, Estéban throws all the gold into bubbling craters of sulphur water. The structure of the novel is complex, being told in a series of first person present tense episodes set in the prison of San Juan de Ulúa in Vera Cruz, where Estéban is on trial for having defrauded the king of the fifth part due him of any treasure found. These episodes are interspersed among longer passages, told first person past tense, presumably written by Estéban in his prison cell, telling of the events of the journey. In San Juan all who come in contact with Estéban are greedy for the gold—his jailer, Don Felipe de Soto y Ríos, his defense counsel, Pablo Gamboa, Torres, who appears as a witness falsely accusing Estéban of killing Mendoza, the commander of the fortress, even the members of the Royal Audiencia—all except Zia, who is brought to testify and who is ready to wait for Estéban when he is sentenced to three years in the terrible prison. This difficult structure emphasizes the theme—that the desire for gold corrupts—but takes away some of the tension from the adventures. Estéban is articulate about his experiences but understated about his emotions, a characterization that distances a reader from the story. The picture of the conquistadors is one of the best in books for young people. Choice; Fanfare; Newbery Honor.

KINLEY ELLIOTT (*The Whispered Horse**), elderly father of Rowan* and Kate*, who live in Gowanbothy cottage, Scotland. Although past seventy and apparently unbalanced and confused mentally after the death of his much younger and much-loved wife, he nevertheless thinks up and carries out a plan to terrify his son-in-law, Tam* McPhee, that eventually causes Tam's death. Kinley believes he has an ancient power to get horses to do his will by whispering to them and in his youth belonged to a secret society of "horse whisperers" which originated in Druid times. Being a God-fearing and normally gentle man, he does not want to kill Tam himself but believes he can get the little horse, Bannet, to kill Tam and is able to convince Tam that this will happen on Lammas night.

KINSHI (*The Master Puppeteer**), head apprentice in the puppet theater and son of the puppeteer Yoshida. Kinshi is not only kind to Jiro* and long suffering under his father's abuse, he is idealistic about helping the starving of Osaka. When he tries to save Jiro's mother, who has joined the looters, his right hand is chopped off by the police.

KISER PEASE (*Where the Lilies Bloom**; *Trial Valley**), presumed owner of the house in which the Luther children live and whose land their father, Roy Luther, has been sharecropping. Because she thinks he is greedy, mean, and ignorant, and because her father willed it so, Mary* Call opposes his marrying her sister Devola*. But Kiser proves himself practical, generous, and sensible in the arrangements he makes for the children. He deeds the house and the twenty acres it stands on to Devola upon their marriage, and, thereafter, he helps out Mary Call and the children whenever they need it. He is a little afraid of Mary Call and cautions her against being too forceful, lest she frighten away suitors and never get married. He tries to push her into choosing between Thad* Yancy and Gaither* Graybeal. Kiser longs for a child and immediately is attracted to and wishes to adopt abandoned Jack* Parsons, whom he characteristically smothers with affection and gifts. He is a well-drawn character.

KLAVENESS, JAN O'DONNELL (1939–   ), born in York, Pa.; raised in Illinois and Michigan; author of novels for teenaged readers. After graduating from the University of Michigan, where she received a minor Hopwood Prize in the essay division, she traveled extensively in Europe and worked for a year teaching English in Florence, Italy. She then settled in Ann Arbor, Mich., where she married Charles O'Donnell, professor of English, and continued her interest in writing. The couple later moved to Hempstead, N.Y., where Professor O'Donnell served as chair of the English Department at Hofstra University. After Professor O'Donnell's death in 1979, she became associate director of financial aid at Hofstra, resigning in 1982 to write on a full-time basis. Previously, she also held positions as a secretary in a brokerage house, an assistant director of student affairs at the University of Michigan, and as a representative for a portrait studio. Her interest in colonial history and historic preservation resulted in *The Griffin Legacy** (Macmillan, 1983), a nominee for the Edgar Allan Poe Award. The old farmhouse in which this Gothic novel is set was modeled upon one she visited while vacationing in Lanesboro, Mass. Under the name Jan O'Donnell, she published *A Funny Girl Like Me* (Scholastic, 1980), also for young adults, in which a girl discovers that being funny isn't the best way to gain popularity. More recently, she has published *Ghost Island* (Macmillan, 1985), another novel of suspense. Klaveness lives in Hempstead, N.Y., with her husband, Charles

Klaveness, a copy editor for the *New York Times*, and her two children. Her other interests include theater, ballet, canoeing, fishing, gardening, and cooking.

KLEIN, NORMA (1938–   ), born in New York City; free-lance writer, noted in children's literature for her contemporary problem novels that deal openly with once taboo subjects. She attended private schools and took her bachelor's from Barnard in Russian and her master's from Columbia in Slavic languages. She first published short stories for adults for literary and popular magazines, receiving several O. Henry awards, and some of her stories have been selected for anthologies. She has published for adults a book of short stories and novels, and for children and young people a book of verse, *A Train for Jane* (Feminist, 1974) and over a dozen novels since the appearance of her first, *Mom, the Wolfman and Me** (Pantheon, 1972). About a girl's life with her never-married mother, this appears in *Choice* and is still regarded as the best of her books. Other novels involve divorce, mixed marriages, cross-racial adoption, desertion by parents, broken or disintegrating homes, awakening sexuality, and homosexuality. An avowed feminist, she portrays female protagonists that are strong, intelligent, interesting girls with minds of their own. She writes with wit and humor and is very skillful with dialogue, but the books have a strong sociological bent and tend to have short-lived popularity. Other titles include *Confessions of an Only Child* (Pantheon, 1974), *What's It All About* (Dial, 1975), *It's Not What You Expect* (Pantheon, 1973), *Hiding* (Scholastic, 1976), *A Honey of a Chimp* (Pantheon, 1980), and *Robbie and the Leap Year Blues* (Dial, 1981). She is married to a biochemist, and they and their children live in New York City.

KNEE-DEEP IN THUNDER (Moon*, Sheila, Ill. Peter Parnall, Atheneum, 1967), ambitious fantasy set in a world inhabited mainly by talking insects as large as dogs. With no real explanation, Maris, 13, slips with her dog, Scuro, from her home near an ocean into a strange world where the dog disappears, to be taught by "Them," and she starts on a mysterious journey with a talking beetle, the size of a large dog, whose name is Exi, short for Alexaminander. After a series of trials, they are joined by other creatures to form a company which "They" have called to rid the world of a threat of the Beasts, horrible talking creatures resembling wild hogs. Together with Carabus, a practical brown beetle, Mr. Green, a pompous green beetle, Red, a soldier ant, Isia, a woolly caterpillar, and Locus, a mouse (the only voiceless character), they travel near to the jungle where the Beasts live. Locus and Isia are captured; Maris, with the help of a spider named Arachne and a gopher named Botta, enters their stockade and rescues the two along with a boy named Jetsam, a bird, Parula, and a Toad, all of whom have been slaves of the hideous Beasts. Their further journey takes them across a desert to a mountain where they meet representatives of "Them" and come to realize that their mission is to lure the Beasts from their jungle to a place where they can come to an agreement with them for final peace. Scuro having rejoined them, now a talking dog, they work out a plan to entice the Beasts into following them and to lure them across a series of pits, into which some will fall, until their numbers are few enough so that the last will parley with Them. With the help of Brontasauras, a horned toad, and Arachne, who weaves covers for the pits which are both good camouflage and sticky, so the beasts cannot escape, they manage, but Red is killed in the final stage. They then carry his body to the "Mountain of Them," where each one goes through an individual trial and all come out somehow purified and deserving to meet Them, mysterious, godlike beings. A few of the journeyers are accepted to join Them, and the others part, going their separate ways. Maris finds herself back in this world with Scuro, now an ordinary dog again. The book has some good scenes and ingenious situations, but there are seldom reasons for occurrences. "They" are too vague to be compelling, and there is no explanation of why these powerful beings need the help of the oddly assorted company or of what the whole experience means, beyond giving Maris some much-needed confidence. The style is frequently marred by pretentious but meaningless statements: "The silence . . . was rolling outward in waves of soundless sound"; "The plunge did not actually end, it just ceased to exist"; " . . . she seemed very near and tree-tall, yet far off and diminishing." Fanfare.

KNEEKNOCK RISE (Babbitt*, Natalie, ill. author, Farrar, 1970), fantasy set in the imaginary village of Instep at the foot of Kneeknock Rise, where the fabled Megrimum lives, a mournful creature that wails on rainy nights and is reported to eat any who venture to climb the mountain. The delightful fear this causes makes Instep's annual fair a great success. To this fair comes a young boy, Egan, to stay with his Aunt Gertrude and Uncle Anson, a clockmaker, and his cousin, Ada, a bratty, red-haired girl about his age. Egan meets instant antagonism from Sweetheart, Ada's cat, but warm friendship from Anabelle, overfed dog of Uncle Ott, Anson's brother, who has recently disappeared. After enjoying the fair, Egan, goaded by Ada, climbs the Rise with Anabelle, romantically planning to slay the Megrimum. At the misty top, however, he finds only Uncle Ott, who is staying there because the humidity helps his asthma and who shows Egan that the Megrimum is really a hot spring in a cave, which steams and makes weird noises like a teakettle when the cold rain water hits it. Ott, taking Anabelle, goes off wandering, and Egan returns, full of the news of the real explanation, only to find that the villagers do not want to believe him. The book is brief and has a fairy-tale quality, with very little character development. The almost tongue-in-cheek tone helps to present the theme—people want to be fooled—which might otherwise seem too obvious. Newbery Honor.

KONIGSBURG, E(LAINE) L(OBL) (1930–   ), born in New York City; author best known for her realistic novels about contemporary family life, among them one Newbery Award winner and Lewis Carroll Shelf selection, *From the Mixed-up Files of Mrs. Basil E. Frankweiler** (Atheneum, 1967), and one Newbery

Honor book, *Jennifer, Hecate, Macbeth, William McKinley, and Me, Elizabeth** (Atheneum, 1967), and for *A Proud Taste for Scarlet and Miniver** (Atheneum, 1973), a fantasy-biography of Eleanor of Acquitaine, which was a finalist in the children's category of the National Book Award. Her style is lively and contemporary, her plots tight and fast moving, but her characterization is often shallow, and her attempts at cleverness sometimes result in contrived incidents and unconvincing dialogue. A popular modern author, she has written, among others, the novels *About the B'Nai Bagels** (Atheneum, 1979), a *Choice* book, *George* (Atheneum, 1976), and *Father's Arcane Daughter* (Atheneum, 1976), two books of short stories, *Altogether, One at a Time* (Atheneum, 1971), and *Throwing Shadows* (Atheneum, 1979), and a biographical novel, *The Second Mrs. Giaconda** (Atheneum, 1975), which was selected for Fanfare. She grew up in small towns in Pennsylvania, graduating from Carnegie Institute in Pittsburgh and studying chemistry further at the University of Pittsburgh. She married David Konigsburg, a psychologist, and moved to Jacksonville, Fla., where she taught in a private girls' school. She lived for a while in New York and New Jersey and took lessons at the Art Students League. She began writing when her children were in school, and ideas for her books have come from family experiences. She makes her home in Jacksonville, Fla.

KRUMGOLD†, JOSEPH (QUINCY) (1908–1980), born in Jersey City, N.J.; film writer, producer, and author noted in children's literature as the first writer to win the Newbery Award twice, for *. . . And Now Miguel*† (Crowell, 1953) and for *Onion John*† (Crowell, 1959). Both books also received several other honors. These two books and *Henry 3** (Atheneum, 1967), a *Choice* selection, form a trio about boys growing up in contemporary America and their relationships with their fathers and are unusually successful in employing the first person voice. The first book concerns a sheep ranching family in New Mexico that is very close to its Hispanic heritage, the second involves the residents of a small town in New Jersey, and the third, less focused, less spontaneous, and heavier with social comment than its predecessors, involves the family of a rising young executive on Long Island. Krumgold's father was a movie exhibitor who owned and operated movie houses, and Krumgold early decided on a career in film. After graduating from New York University, he wrote and produced scripts for Metro-Goldwyn-Mayer and other major studios in Hollywood and New York City and then formed his own company, writing and producing motion pictures and television films for Columbia Broadcasting, National Broadcasting, and National Educational Television. His films won awards at the Venice, Prague, and Edinburgh film festivals. He traveled extensively in the United States, Europe, and the Middle East and made his home in Hope, N.J., which provided the setting for *Onion John*. His best-known book, *. . . And Now Miguel*, began as a documentary film. It was prepared for distribution overseas by the U.S. Department of State and was originally titled *Miguel Chavez*. In addition to his numerous screenplays, he also wrote a novel for adults, *Thanks to Murder* (Vanguard, 1935). His first and last books for children were for younger readers, *Sweeney's Adventures* (Random, 1942), set in the Bronx Zoo, and *The Most Terrible Turk* (Crowell, 1969), a short adventure story set in modern Turkey.

L

LABAN FARR (*The People Therein**), mountaineer father of Lanthy*. A just and righteous man, Laban is also strongly family oriented and particularly close to Lanthy, his eldest daughter, who is lame from birth. Laban generously allows the young Bostonian, Drew* Thorndike, to live in the cabin on his property and helps him repair and strengthen the ancient structure, but he is angry when he finds Drew drunk and murderously enraged when he learns that Lanthy is with child by Drew. When, as he is about to shoot Drew, Lanthy purposely throws herself on a rake and pierces her hand, Laban is so overcome with remorse for not having waited for her when she called to him that part of his anger turns to self-accusation. Laban is both a hard man, expecting long hours of labor from his daughters, and a fond father, aging with worry and shame over Lanthy's pregnancy, yet delighted with her little girl, his first grandbaby.

LAKLAN, CARLI (1907–   ), born Virginia Carli Laughlin in Paoli, Okla.; freelance writer known mostly for sports books, both fiction and non-fiction. She grew up in Miles City, Mont., attended Stanford University, received her M.A. degree at the University of Washington, and did graduate work at both Columbia University and New York University. Among a variety of other jobs she was a summer fire lookout in the Bitterroot Mountains of Montana and Idaho, taught drama, and directed summer stock, but since 1951 she has been mostly a freelance writer. Among her works are a trio of nursing stories—*Nancy Kimball, Nurse's Aide* (Doubleday, 1962), *Nurse in Training* (Doubleday, 1965), and *Second Year Nurse* (Doubleday, 1967)—and sports books—*Competitive Swimming* (Hawthorn, 1965), *Surf with Me* (McGraw, 1967), *Ski Bum* (McGraw, 1972), and others. She has also published under the pseudonym, John Clarke. An athlete and researcher, she trained for the pre-Olympics in the 100-meter dash, learned to surf in order to write her book, and visited migrant worker camps before writing *Migrant Girl** (McGraw, 1970), which won the Child Study Award.

LAMPMAN, EVELYN SIBLEY (1907–1980), author of numerous novels for children and young people. She was born and grew up in Dallas, Oreg., a small town in the Willamette Valley, granddaughter of pioneers in that region. They told her stories when she was a little girl of what things were like there in those days upon which she later drew for her books. She graduated from Oregon State University and became a continuity writer for a Portland radio station and eventually education director of the Portland NBC station, responsible for in-school listening programs. Several of her radio scripts won national awards. Her first book for children was published in 1948, and after that she wrote about three dozen books, some under the name Lynn Bronson, including historical fiction, contemporary stories, fantasy, humor, and adventure, though she is best known for her books about racial minorities, especially Native Americans, for whose problems over the years, way of life, and point of view she shows a rare sympathy and understanding. Her *Half-Breed** (Doubleday, 1967), about a Crow Indian boy who meets prejudice when he goes to live with his white father in 1850, and *Cayuse Courage** (Harcourt, 1970), which tells from the Indian point of view the events that led up to the Indian attack on Marcus Whitman's mission in 1847, both received the Spur Award of Western Writers of America. She also published concerning Indians the novels *Squaw Man's Son* (Atheneum, 1978), about a Modoc Indian boy who is part white and who finds he fits in neither culture, *The Tilted Sombrero* (Doubleday, 1966), about the first Indian revolt against Spanish rule at the beginning of the Mexican War for Independence, *White Captives* (Atheneum, 1975), based on a report of a captive taken by Apaches who attacked a Mormon wagon train, and *The Potlach Family* (Atheneum, 1976), about a Chinook Indian family who try to regain their culture after their brother returns from Vietnam. She was married to a newspaperman, made her home in Portland, and also contributed to magazines. In a lighter vein, she earlier wrote *The Shy Stegosaurus of Cricket Creek* (Doubleday, 1955) and *The Shy Stegosaurus at Indian Springs* (Doubleday, 1962).

LAND RUSH (Hodges*, Carl G., ill. John Martinez, Duell, 1965), historical novel about the Oklahoma land rush of 1889. The action covers about a week's time and begins on April 17 in Arkansas City, Kans., where hundreds of "boomers" have gathered to wait for the United States Cavalry to escort them to the border of the Unassigned Lands, that part of Oklahoma previously Indian country that is to be opened for homesteading on a first come, first served basis at noon on April 22, 1889. Among the thousands of hopefuls are orphaned, fourteen-year-old, towheaded Ossie Bond and his uncle, Hiram Morris, merry, three-hundred-pound newspaper editor and publisher. The two have traveled by mule-drawn wagon from Jacksonville, Ill., hoping to start anew by staking a land claim and then establishing a newspaper business in Guthrie. To his dismay, Ossie discovers that fancy-dressing, smooth-talking Bert Gault from Wichita plans to start a newspaper in Guthrie, too. Uncle Hy, however, knows Gault has often been involved in shady deals and has doubts about the man's motives now. Along the way, Ossie and Hy share pleasant conversations with their friends, William Prettyman, a photographer who intends to make a pictorial record of the opening, and his youthful helper, Ruben "Windy" Mackay, about

Ossie's age, and enjoy the hilarious tall tales of comical Miny Moe, a boomer from the Ozarks of Missouri. Uncle Hy insists that Ossie help with tasks about the camp, learn some basics of journalism, and practice his spelling. As the lengthy wagon train moves toward the border, excitement mounts. A twister provides some anxious moments, and, when the travelers find the Arkansas River too flooded to ford, Ossie gets the idea of flooring the railroad trestle. He climbs the telegraph poles to release the wires so the telegrapher can send a message to order planks from Arkansas City. The worst problem occurs when Bert Gault steals the map an old "sooner" ("sooners" were those who settled in the territory too soon and were escorted out by the U.S. Army), Gimpy Coultas, gave to Uncle Hy for a claim on Goose Creek near Guthrie and beats them to the claim. Then Ossie remembers that Gault once referred to himself as a taxpayer. He persuades Uncle Hy's lawyer, Double-A Cummings, to wire to Wichita to verify Gault's landholding there. Since the law prohibits landholders from homesteading in the Unassigned Lands, Gault's claim to the Goose Creek land is nullified, and Uncle Hy files for it. Story's end finds Hy and Ossie preparing to publish their first paper in the new territory. Neither flat characters, contrived and predictable incidents, pedestrian style, nor heavy-handed foreshadowing diminish the excitement of this fast-moving story of a momentous period in United States history. Western Heritage.

LANGTON, JANE (GILLSON) (1922–   ), born in Boston, Mass.; writer best known for her fantasies in the E. Nesbit tradition which are set in Concord, Mass. She attended Wellesley College, Mass., and received both her B.S. and M.A. degrees from the University of Michigan and a second M.A. from Radcliffe College. She has worked in a television station and has lived in Lincoln, Mass., near Concord, the setting for *The Diamond in the Window** (Harper, 1962), *The Swing in the Summerhouse* (Harper, 1967), *The Amazing Stereoscope* (Harper, 1971), *The Fledgling** (Harper, 1980), which was named a Newbery honor book, and the opening of *The Fragile Flag* (Harper, 1984). The first three of these employ the pattern of an object which takes the protagonists, Eleanor* and Edward* Hall, on a series of adventures in other lands and places. The fourth and fifth feature their stepcousin, Georgie* Dorian, who flies on the back of a wild goose in *The Fledgling*, somewhat in the pattern of Selma Lageroff's *The Wonderful Adventures of Nils*, and who leads a children's march on Washington in *The Fragile Flag*. Her earlier book, *The Majesty of Grace** (Harper, 1961, reprinted in 1974 as *Her Majesty, Grace Jones*) is perhaps the most satisfying of all, being based on memories of her own childhood. She has also written novels for adults, among them a mystery story, *Emily Dickinson Is Dead: A Novel of Suspense* (St. Martin's, 1984).

LANTHY FARR (*The People Therein**), Ailanthus, mountain girl who falls in love with Drew* Thorndike, botanist from Boston. Born with misaligned hips so one leg is shorter than the other, Lanthy is still small at eighteen, but she is "stout spirited" and hard working, determined that she will do her share of the grueling field and house work. Although only her cousin, lumpish Cecil Higgins, has ever shown an interest in her, Drew falls in love and finds her beautiful, with her heavy blond hair, small face, and large, serious eyes. She is intelligent, so that her former school teacher, Mr. Colver, had tried to get Laban* to send her to town to high school; she has a sweet, clear voice and sings ballads and hymns, accompanying herself on her great-grandmother's dulcimer. Having been assured by the midwife that she can never have "chick nor child," she is surprised to learn that she is pregnant after making love with Drew. When she is to have his child while he is in Boston, she refuses to let Drew know, determined that she will not trap him into marriage.

LAROCHE (*The Burning Glass**), Deschute's archenemy. Jeb debates with himself about whether or not he should tell Deschute all he knows about LaRoche, when he and Lobo* find LaRoche's trail in the mountains. This adds both to plot and to character. LaRoche is called "Too-Many-Hands" by the Indians for his ability to juggle cards skillfully.

LARRY DRAYFUS (*They Never Came Home**), self-centered, callous, spoiled youth, who smuggles marijuana into New Mexico and peddles it to high school students in Las Cruces for the high, quick profits. Because his father thinks he is running wild and has decided to send him to military school, Larry plans a camping trip into the mountains where he intends to kill Dan* Cotwell and then disappear. When the plan goes awry, he takes Dan to southern California, where he concocts the story that they are brothers and continues to live fairly high on illegal earnings.

LARSON, JEAN RUSSELL (1930–   ), born in Marshalltown, Iowa; specialist in Arabic literature, whose books include two volumes of tales from Arabia. She studied at Winthrop College, Rock Hill, S.C., the University of Iowa, the University of Chicago, and the University of Northern Iowa. Despite having eight children, she has travelled widely. Her *Jack Tar** (Macrae, 1970), a rollicking spoof of Victorian manners and attitudes, is set in British India.

LAS BOMBAS, COUNT (*Westmark**; *The Kestrel**), bombastic mountebank of many names and disguises, who, in *Westmark*, provides Theo refuge in his company when the youth is fleeing for his life from the king's men, and, in *The Kestrel*, accompanies and advises Mickle* (Queen Augusta) as she searches for Theo and King Constantine and as she leads her army. Las Bombas also uses the names Dr. Absalom, General Sambalo, and Master Bloomsa, changing identities as he gets by on his wits. Although a rascal, he has a kind heart and cares about the unfortunate. He is both a comic and serious character.

THE LAST LITTLE CAT (DeJong*†, Meindert, ill. Jim McMullan, Harper, 1961), brief realistic book set in contemporary America about a nameless cat, the last born in a litter of seven. These kittens are born in an old chicken's nest, high in a barn converted to a dog kennel. The runt, a coal black kitten, barely survives, being pushed away from food and warmth by its huskier siblings. When the mother takes the others to the barn floor to teach them not to fear the dogs in cages stacked on each side, she leaves the last one behind. Trying to reach the others, this kitten falls into the cage of an old, blind dog and upsets his milk. By licking the milk from the lonely dog's face, the cat makes friends with it and cuddles down between its front paws for warmth. Because this cage is perched higher than the others, the man who cares for the dogs doesn't notice the little cat, and after he sets the dog's cage in the sun one day the kitten walks out to explore the world. When it returns, the cage is gone, and it has a night of terrible adventures: it meets a dog and scares it away by running toward it; it creeps into a bulldog's house and scares it out; it is chased up a tree by a big tomcat; it is found by seven children who want to adopt it but their mother refuses, and it at last falls asleep on the porch of the seventh and last house in the row. There the old man who turns out to be the kennelkeeper takes it in, gives it milk, and finally brings his own dog home, now that there is company for it in the house. The man's dog, of course, is the old, blind friend of the last little cat. The very simple story is told with no named characters, but the rejected kitten emerges as an individual. Without anthropomorphizing the animals, DeJong manages to show their point of view in this as in his other animal stories. Fanfare.

THE LAST RUN (Harris*, Mark Jonathan, Lothrop, 1981), realistic, contemporary, boy's problem novel with western story aspects set over a few weeks' time one summer recently in and near Silverfield, a small town in Nevada. Lyle* Jeffries, 14, is bored with school, on the outs with a couple of town bullies, overshadowed by his more personable younger brother, and dejected at the prospect of working all summer in the gas station belonging to his father, Frank* Jeffries. He dreams of being a cowboy and starring in rodeos, fantasies inspired by the stories of his ex-cowboy grandfather, hardbitten Bill* Cameron. When rancher Hansford hires Bill to capture the wily wild mustang that lures away his mares, Lyle sees possibilities for avoiding distasteful chores, having some excitement, and securing a horse of his own and persuades his family to allow him to accompany his grandfather. Bill enlists the help of Harry*, a Paiute Indian, an old friend of his and also an ex-cowboy. The two men and the boy set out on what proves to be an exhausting, often frustrating camping trip in the mountains to locate and trap the stallion and his herd. Lyle makes serious mistakes that prolong their work. He carelessly allows the stallion to get wind of him on one occasion, and another time, as they are about to drive the mustangs into a blind canyon, his rashness leads to the death of Bill's cherished horse, Mattie, and the escape of the mustangs. Later, after they have trapped the herd in a makeshift corral in Jawbone Canyon, the stud leaps the seven-foot gate to freedom.

A stampede ensues, and Harry is trampled to death. Bill and Lyle redouble their efforts, and after hours of dogged riding, they capture the weary horse, waterlogged from drinking too much after the long chase, and take him to the corral. When the horse proves intractable, Bill plans to shoot him, but Lyle cuts the mustang's tether, freeing the proud, indomitable creature. Both man and boy agree that the horse has earned his freedom. Sobered, more responsible, Lyle returns home, offers his services to his father in the station, and looks forward to earning the money to buy a horse, which Bill agrees to help him train for competition. Although the plot does not hold up under scrutiny and all ends as expected, there is plenty of action and conflict to hold the reader's attention. Lyle is less interesting than the men of the story: his father, whose surliness and scolding are traceable to his anxiety over the possible loss of his station and his son's irresponsibility; Bill, tough old mustanger whose failure to heed Harry's warning leads to his friend's death; and Harry, who has lived as a white but has never lost his basic Indian beliefs. The real hero of the story is the unsentimentalized mustang, whom the reader as well as Lyle cheers on to freedom. Information about horses and the modern West is subtly woven into the narrative. Spur.

LAURA DEWITT (*A Formal Feeling**), Anne* Cameron's best friend, a good-natured, more easy-going girl, not as good a student nor as self-controlled as Anne. She sings in the church choir with Anne and shares many childhood memories. Somewhat disheveled and not well organized, she serves as a foil for Anne, but she also illustrates the warmth of emotion that has been absent from Anne's life, particularly in her quarrels with her mother, who lets the house accumulate clutter while she writes her dissertation, and her sudden embrace of her mother when the puppy dies, an incident that shows their underlying closeness and for which Anne feels a sharp envious pang.

LAURA TRELLING (*Up a Road Slowly**), Julie Trelling's beloved, older sister, with whom on visits she loves to cuddle up in bed and chat far into the night. At first, Julie resents Laura's marriage but gradually learns that second best can be good, too. Later, she develops the same close, warm relationship with Laura's daughter, another Julie, having learned to make the most of situations. Laura provides a strong role model, as well as stability, in Julie's life. She is credibly presented.

LAUREL WOODFORD (*A Spell Is Cast**), beautiful and talented weaver who lives alone in a little house in the hills above Tarnhelm, Mrs. Van Heusen's oceanside, California estate. Cory first meets Laurel on the beach where Laurel helps her recover the unicorn necklace that Cory has lost. Cory goes often to Laurel's house to chat because she feels very comfortable with the young woman. At the end, Laurel marries Cory's Uncle* Dirk, from whom she has been estranged, and they adopt Cory. Laurel is an interesting, romantic figure, if stock.

LAWSON, JOHN, born in New York City. He is a graduate of Exeter and Harvard, served in the army in World War II, and has spent summers in Virginia in the area of *The Spring Rider** (Crowell, 1968), a haunting fantasy of Civil War soldiers who return annually to refight a battle, which won the *Boston Globe-Horn Book* Award. He is also the author of *You Better Come Home with Me* (Crowell, 1966), a story set in Appalachia of a boy and a scarecrow. He has been in the banking business.

LAZY LEGS (*Killer-of-Death**), Killer-of-Death's* Mexican foster brother, kidnapped by the Apaches from his Mexican family and adopted into the tribe. Apache now in appearance and behavior, Lazy Legs is a realist who questions traditional ways and tends to cut corners, an attitude which bothers Killer-of-Death at the beginning of his story. Lazy Legs cautions his brother against making an enemy of the shaman and his son, Gian-nah-tah*, and sees the danger of the Americans and Mexicans to the Apache way of life. He dies in the massacre at Juan José's camp. He is a well-drawn character, a good foil for the less astute, more naive Killer-of-Death.

L. C. LUCKABILL (*The Whys and Wherefores of Littabelle Lee**), red-haired, serious-minded, neighborly grandson of Merlie Bud Luckabill. It is L. C.'s idea that Littabelle take the examination to be substitute teacher when Merlie Bud is unable to work because of illness. L. C. helps her with her first day of teaching and occasionally to and from school. An accommodating boy, he is about Littabelle's age of sixteen.

LEAH (*The Bronze Boy**), Daniel's mentally ill younger sister, whose health improves dramatically after Daniel returns to the village. Although she never loses her shyness and fear of strangers, she cooks, gardens, and weaves, and is a much happier girl. Her friendship with the young Gallic soldier in service to Rome provides some of the novel's most poignant moments and heightens Daniel's personal conflict.

THE LEAVING (Hall*, Lynn, Scribner's, 1980), realistic novel set in the 1970s on an Iowa farm. Having finished high school and stayed through the summer and early fall to help get in the hay and the corn, Roxanne* Armstrong, 18, is ready to leave the Volga River Valley farm and go to Des Moines to get a job and try her wings. She has long done most of the farm chores while her shiftless father, Cletus* Armstrong, lounges in the house or drinks with friends in Wadena. Her last weekend is marked by conflict when he announces that he plans to sell her horse, a pinto pony he gave her six years before. Roxanne flares up but realizes that she cannot prevent the sale and mostly resents that her undemonstrative mother says nothing to defend her interests. Later, returning from a girls' basketball game at high school where she was a team member the year before, Roxanne accuses her mother of not caring what she does, of never having attended a game to watch her, of not loving her. Having enlisted the reader's sympathy for Roxanne, the author shifts to the point of view of the mother, Thora* Braun Armstrong, and then to Cletus, so that we see their backgrounds before their mismatched marriage and the pain they both feel, particularly Thora, at not being able to show affection for Roxanne. Thora is especially tongue-tied because she realizes that Cletus is selling the horse to get money to leave her, and she is afraid that if Roxanne finds out, the girl will feel obligated to stay. While Thora will be glad to see the last of Cletus and desperately wants Roxanne to stay on the farm, she wants more to give her daughter a chance to lead her own life in a way Thora never had opportunity. After driving a very apprehensive Roxanne to Des Moines and helping her rent a room, Thora returns to find Cletus gone, as she expected. Stoically, she starts to feed the stock but almost breaks down when she realizes that Roxanne, knowing her mother will take over the chores, spent her last day at home building a pen for the weanling calves besides the barn, so that she will not have to lug bales of hay across the barn yard. The story picks up in the early spring when Roxanne, having found a filing job, girls who want her to share an apartment, and even a boyfriend interested in marriage, realizes that she has conquered her fear of being on her own in the city and that what she really wants is to return and help her mother run the farm. Each of the three characters is well developed and believable. The Iowa farm is vividly portrayed but not idealized, shown as demanding hard work in frequently bad weather, but having a beauty of its own. Although the plot line is simple, the sensitive treatment of the theme that lack of communication in a family causes misery keeps the story interesting. Boston Globe Winner.

LEE, MILDRED (1908–   ), born in Blocton, Ala.; author of sensitive novels for teenagers, all set in the South. The daughter of a Baptist minister, she grew up in a number of small southern towns and attended Tift College in Forsyth, Ga., Troy Normal College in Alabama, Columbia University, New York University, and the University of New Hampshire. Her most successful novels are those set among the poor, including *The Rock and the Willow** (Lothrop, 1963), about an Alabama girl's struggle to get away from her brutish father and his dirt farm, and *The Skating Rink** (Seabury, 1969), in which a boy afflicted with a severe stutter finds freedom in roller skating. Departing from the recent past, she set *The People Therein** (Houghton, 1980) about the turn of the century in the Smoky Mountains. The most mature of her novels, this develops the characters even more skillfully than her other books and tells an unsensational but moving story of love between a mountain girl and an educated young man from Boston. Her novels are more noted for evocation of setting and character than for action or plot.

LEEROY (*Smoke**), elderly, transient hired man who plays an important role in helping Chris Long treat the starving German shepherd. In many ways a stock figure of the wise though uneducated rustic, he tells Chris of his own flight, in his youth, from his home when he thought he had killed a man and of how it has marred his life, but he does not dissuade Chris from running away.

LEGUIN, URSULA K(ROEBER) (1929–   ), born in Berkeley, Calif.; science fiction writer whose Earthsea* fantasies for young people are often listed as modern classics. She received her A.B. degree from Radcliffe College and her A.M. from Columbia University and taught French at Mercer University, Macon, Ga., and at the University of Idaho. Since she has been writing science fiction, she has won the Nebula Award twice and the Hugo Award, both prestigious in that field, three times, and has taught writing workshops at Pacific University in Forest Grove, Oreg., the University of Washington, Seattle, Portland State University, the University of Reading in England, and in Melbourne, Australia. Her realistic novel for teenagers, *Very Far Away from Anywhere Else** (Atheneum, 1976), is sensitive and was well received, but it is the Earthsea trilogy that has won her a distinguished place in children's literature, *A Wizard of Earthsea** (Parnassus, 1968), a *Boston Globe-Horn Book* Award winner, *The Tombs of Atuan** (Atheneum, 1971), a National Book finalist, and *The Farthest Shore** (Atheneum, 1972), which won the National Book Award.

L'ENGLE, MADELEINE (1918–   ), born in New York City; actress, teacher, and author highly regarded for her novels of contemporary family life for children and young people. The daughter of Charles Wadsworth Camp, a foreign correspondent, and Madeleine Camp, a pianist, she led a lonely life as a child, writing, drawing, and playing the piano. She attended schools in Europe and the United States, graduating from Smith College and studying further at Columbia University. She became an actress, taking the family name of L'Engle. After her marriage to actor Hugh Franklin, she left the theater permanently and turned to writing and teaching. The Franklins and their children have lived in New York City and Connecticut. Her writings, which include articles, plays, scenarios, and poems, as well as over twenty books largely of fiction and mostly for children, arise out of personal experience, memories, and observation and reflect her strong sense of family, her interest in the arts, and her practicing Christianity. Most highly regarded are her novels about the Austin family, including *Meet the Austins** (Vanguard, 1960), a Fanfare book also cited in *Children's Books Too Good to Miss* and *Choice*, and its sequel, *The Moon by Night** (Farrar, 1963), a Fanfare book; *The Arm of the Starfish** (Farrar, 1965), a Fanfare book, which introduced the O'Keefes; and the most highly praised of all, the space fantasy about the Murry family, *A Wrinkle in Time** (Farrar, 1962), published after it was rejected by several publishers because it was so unusual and which subsequently won the Newbery Medal and was chosen for Fanfare, the Lewis Carroll Shelf, *Children's Books Too Good to Miss*, ChLA Touchstones, and *Choice*. Other novels involving the same families include *A Wind in the Door* (Farrar, 1973), about the Murrys; the Newbery Honor book *A Ring of Endless Light** (Farrar, 1980), and *The Young Unicorns* (Farrar, 1968), both about the

Austins; and *Dragons in the Waters* (Farrar, 1976) and *A House Like a Lotus* (Farrar, 1984), both about the O'Keefes. She has also written several novels and autobiographical books for adults and was nominated for the Hans Christian Andersen Award for her total work for the young. Although she has a tendency to be overly energetic and intellectual, she is a writer of imagination, daring, and great technical skill, who can be counted upon to tell a good story well.

LEROY (*The Mysterious Red Tape Gang**), Mike* Cassidy's friend, member of the Red Tape Gang, a black youth of twelve. When Linda Jean Hartwell accuses the boys of discriminating against her on the basis of sex, Leroy announces that his father always says that discrimination is "the curse of the world." Mike agrees with Leroy that discrimination is bad but maintains that it is perfectly legal to discriminate against girls. Leroy has a good head and thinks quickly. He makes very sensible suggestions and often keeps Mike from blurting out things he shouldn't and giving the show away.

LESLIE BURKE (*Bridge to Terabithia**), imaginative, sturdy-minded ten-year-old whose friendship opens a new world to Jesse* Aarons and whose death seems to destroy it all. The daughter of liberal young intellectuals of the later 1960s, Leslie is an object of curiosity and ridicule to the rural community for her clothes and life-style, but she bears up without complaint after she becomes a friend of Jess.

LESTER KLOPPER (*The Alfred Summer**), highly intelligent sixteen-year-old handicapped by cerebral palsy. Fine-boned and tall, with fair straight hair and a sharp nose, he looks "aristocratic," but he walks and speaks with great difficulty. In addition to his other problems are those with his parents: he craves the approval his father is not able or willing to give him, and he is stifled by his mother's over-protectiveness. When he meets loving, accepting Mrs. Burt, mother of retarded Alfred*, Lester falls in love with her, realizing what a difference that kind of attitude would make in his life.

LES YOUNG (*The Dunderhead War**), naive, young friend of Quincy* Heffendorf, who hero-worships Rufus* Purdy. Les is irresponsible and undisciplined and pays for his lack of self-control and stupidity with considerable distress. When he learns that Rufus has been using him, he assaults Rufus. Because Rufus is an officer, Les is courtmartialed and dishonorably discharged. He is typical of the youth in the "dunderhead army."

LET A RIVER BE (Cummings*, Betty Sue, Atheneum, 1978), ecological novel set in contemporary times on the Indian River near Cape Kennedy in Florida. Ella Richards, 76, has become single minded in her fight to save the river from the destruction and pollution of developers, partly for the river's sake, partly in memory of her deceased husband, a pharmacist known as Doc, and partly because she supplements her social security by selling the fish and crabs she catches. Her main local antagonist is Ivan Maxwell, a narrow-minded businessman with dreams of wealth from river property. After Ella finds Ivan and other neighbors shooting what they describe as a "Swamp Beast," she is not too surprised to find an exhausted, shaggy young man collapsed on her dock. Bathed and fed, with his beard trimmed, he is quite handsome, but he is unable to tell her about his past except that his name is "Reetard" and to make occasional references to his fear of the cattle prod. With patience, Ella is able to teach him to fish and to care for himself and the motor boat, and together they lead a compatible if frugal life, Reetard's great strength supplementing Ella's and his mental ability growing with experience. He shares her concern for the river and even makes a simple speech at a hearing. His loving personality begins to draw back friends who had been avoiding Ella, having found her environmentalism strident and embarrassing, and, pressured, he finally admits that to himself he calls Ella "Mama." Out by himself one day he discovers that Ivan has been bulldozing an island at Headwaters Creek, polluting the water. When she checks out his story, Ella is almost murdered by Ivan and his son. With the Marine Patrol and a young newspaper woman, they catch Ivan red-handed, but while attempting to escape, Ivan purposely runs Reetard down with his boat and kills him. Reetard's death galvanizes public opinion to make Headwaters area into an aquatic preserve. Although the antagonism of the opposition seems somewhat overdone and there is an unembarrassed didactic message repeated frequently, the characterization of Ella and Reetard and the story of their growing love and interdependence keep the book interesting. Fanfare.

LEVITIN, SONIA (1934–   ), born in Berlin, Germany; teacher and author of books for children and young people. She came to the United States when she was four, with her father, mother, and two older sisters, and her first novel, *Journey to America** (Atheneum, 1970), a *Choice* book, recreates in fiction their experiences during the trip. She grew up in Los Angeles, attended the University of California at Berkeley, took her degree from the University of Pennsylvania, and studied further at San Francisco State College. She and her husband, Lloyd Levitin, a corporate planning director, and their two children have made their home in Moraga, Calif. She has been a teacher in elementary and junior high schools and at adult education centers. She has a strong interest in history and was founder and president of the Moraga Historical Society. She has published over a dozen books that vary in subject, length, literary form, theme, and intended audience. Some are picture books for the very young, others are stories of contemporary family or school life, fantasy, or historical fiction. She is at her best in fictionalizing actual events. *The No-Return Trail** (Harcourt, 1978), a novelization of the actual 1841 Bidwell-Bartleson expedition, which included Nancy Kelsey, the first woman to journey overland to California, won the Spur Award of Western Writers of America and was elected to the Lewis Carroll Shelf. She has also published *The Fisherman and the Bird* (Harcourt, 1982) and

A Sound to Remember (Harcourt, 1979), both picture books, and the novels *Roanoke: A Novel of the Lost Colony* (Atheneum, 1973), *Jason and the Money Tree* (Harcourt, 1974), and *The Mark of Conte* (Atheneum, 1976), the latter two fantasies, and a school story for teenagers, *The Year of Sweet Senior Insanity* (Atheneum, 1982). She also received the Jewish Council of America Award for *Journey to America* and has written for magazines and newspapers.

LEVOY, MYRON, born in New York City; chemical engineer and author. He received his M.Sc. from Purdue University and has worked on nuclear propulsion projects for rockets and spacecraft. His story of the friendship between a New York City boy and a disturbed French refugee girl, *Alan and Naomi** (Harper, 1977), was named an honor book for the *Boston Globe-Horn Book* Award and, translated into Dutch and German, received the Buxtehuder Bulle Award. He has also written novels, poetry, short stories, and plays for adults and other books for young people, among them *The Witch of Fourth Street and Other Stories* (Harper, 1972), eight stories about immigrants on New York's Lower East Side in the 1920s, and *A Shadow Like a Leopard* (Harper, 1981), about a friendship between a young New York street tough and a wheelchair-bound old man, a painter. Levoy makes his home in Rockaway, N.J.

LEWIS, JOE (*Cayuse Courage**), the Iroquois trader who hates the White-Eyes because they took his land and killed his people. He came west to urge armed resistance to the white advance and goes from tribe to tribe preaching rebellion. Among the Cayuse, he makes an ally of Nicholas Finley, the Cayuse ex-trapper who works for Marcus Whitman* and who eventually turns against the missionary. Lewis befriends Samuel for his own purposes.

LEWIS PHILLIPS (*Signpost to Terror**), the name, possibly false, by which Gail Schaeffer knows the young man who accompanies her on the hike to Spring Mountain Falls and who, she realizes almost too late, is one of the bank robbers. When she first sees him in the bank, Gail thinks that Lew is like a terrier and later revises her comparison to a chipmunk, quick, alert, afraid. He is personable and articulate, but his ideas seem to her cynical and somehow heartless, even before she grasps his evil intentions. He has been the brains of the robbery and has deliberately misled his accomplices so they will get lost and he can make off with the money.

LEXAU, JOAN M., born in St. Paul, Minn.; author of more than thirty books for children, among them a number of easy-to-read mysteries. She attended the College of St. Catherine and the College of St. Thomas in St. Paul and the New School for Social Research, New York. For some time she worked for publishing concerns, including four years in the children's book department at Harper & Row, before becoming a free-lance writer. Responsive to the market, she has written books about black children, stories of poverty and family love like *Striped*

Ice Cream* (Lippincott, 1968). *The Trouble with Terry** (Dial, 1962), based roughly on her own childhood, won the Child Study Award.

LIBBY FLETCHER (*The Taste of Spruce Gum**), Elizabeth, eleven-year-old girl who spends a winter in a Vermont logging camp with her mother and new stepfather, who is also her Uncle Charles. Having just lost her hair from typhoid, Libby is almost bald for the wedding and self-conscious, resentful, and somewhat scared of Uncle Charles. As the winter progresses, she shows her gumption in various ways, but just as she decides she might like Uncle Charles, he and Mama have a fight, and Libby lives miserably in the tiny shanty with parents carefully polite and distant to each other. An accident to Uncle Charles precipitates an understanding, but not until Libby has had to deal with preparing breakfast for the loggers, escaping from a drunken sawyer, stowing away in a load of lumber going to Rutland, and sneaking into her uncle's hospital room.

LIBERTY BOYS (*Early Thunder**), the radical arm of the Whigs in colonial Salem. They consist mostly, it appears, of misfits and mischiefs, including old Ding-Dong Allison, who lives in a shack not far from the Almshouse at the end of the Common, and sniveling Peter Ray, son of the Widow Ray, who has unsuccessfully set her cap for Dr. West.

LIESELOTTE VESSELY (*The Devil in Vienna**), Inge* Dornenwald's dear friend. She is assertive, fun-loving, inventive, and consistently loyal to Inge. The leader of the two girls, she has the idea of mingling their blood to swear Blood-Sisterly Love, or B.S.L. Although she enjoys the excitement and camaraderie of the *Jungmadel*, the Hitler youth group for girls, both in Munich and in Vienna, and participates in such activities as strewing flowers when Hitler visits the city, she is able to maintain some objectivity about Party activities. A decent, warmhearted child, she returns their dog to the Jewish Weintraubs and keeps quiet about the Jewish Dornenwalds' plans to leave Vienna, even though her father is a Nazi official. She helps Mitzi find a church to be married in, one that does not fly the Nazi flag, and agrees to substitute for Inge at Mitzi's wedding when the Dornenwalds leave Vienna. She, like Inge, is too articulate a writer to be convincing (she writes letters to Inge), nor is she entirely credible as a character, being just too good to be true.

LIEUTENANT GODKIN (*Freelon Starbird**), ex-schoolteacher who burns with patriotism and, at Hackensack, has the assembled ragged, feverish, hungry troops to listen to a long poem he has composed about his enlistment into the cause of liberty. On the surface a prissy man, he has already served at Boston and been wounded before he joins the Pennsylvanians, and in the battles they encounter, he fights even when the others are running. He is killed at the battle of Princeton.

LIFTON, BETTY JEAN (KIRSCHNER) (1926–   ), born in New York City; author whose books reflect her interest in the Far East, where she has lived for extended periods. She grew up in Cincinnati and was graduated from Barnard College and worked in television. With her husband, a professor of psychiatry who has been involved in psychological research, she lived in Tokyo from 1952 to 1954, in Hong Kong from 1954 to 1956, and returned to Japan in 1960, living for two years in Tokyo, Kyoto, and Hiroshima. *The Dwarf Pine Tree** (Atheneum, 1963) is a legend-like story with a typically Japanese philosophical theme.

LILLIAN FORREST (*A Wonderful, Terrible Time**), plump, practical, emotional black woman, mother of Sue Ellen. Lillian takes care of Mady while Mady's mother works. She treats Mady as if she were her own child, and Mady loves her "Aunt Lillian" very much.

LILY DEGLEY (*The Skating Rink**), young wife of Pete*, the roller rink owner. Small and almost child-like in appearance, she is a skillful skater and a hard worker, devoted to her husband and respectful of him as a teacher. She had been an orphan, bouncing from one unsympathetic foster home to another, when she started coming to Pete's rink and caught his eye. As partner to Tuck Farraday, she willingly shares the spotlight.

LIN NAI-NAI (*Homesick: My Own Story**), amah for Jean Guttery in Hankow, China. Of a background far above the servant class, she has been cast out by her family because she left her husband when he took a second wife. She agrees to teach Jean embroidery in exchange for lessons in English. When the siege of Wuchang by the communist army has been lifted, she insists on taking food to her starving family, only to have her father shut the door in her face. She runs back the long distance on her tiny bound feet.

LIPSYTE, ROBERT (1938–   ), born in New York City; reporter, columnist, writer of sports novels. He received his B.A. and M.S. degrees from Columbia University and was a New York *Times* reporter and columnist from 1957 to 1971, with a period in the U.S. Army in 1961. In 1966 he received the Mike Berger Award for distinguished reporting and the Dutton Sports Story Award in 1964, 1965, 1970, and 1971. His novel of prizefighting, *The Contender** (Harper, 1967), won the Child Study Award. Among his other books are *Nigger*, written with Dick Gregory (Dutton, 1964), *Assignment: Sports* (Harper, 1970), and *Something Going*, written with Steve Cady (Dutton, 1973).

LISA (*Lotte's Locket**), fat little friend of Lotte, who cannot understand why Lotte doesn't want to go to America with her handsome, rich, good-natured stepfather. With four brothers, Lisa is less used to being catered to than Lotte, and her delight in her friend's good fortune is more genuine than Lotte's for Lisa's first place win in the writing contest.

THE LITTLE FISHES (Haugaard*, Erik Christian, ill. Milton Johnson, Houghton, 1967), historical novel set in Italy in 1943, during World War II. In Naples, shelled frequently and full of refugees, Italian and German soldiers, and homeless natives, life is hard for all, but Guido*, 12, the first person narrator, fares better than some since he has a scavenged mattress and a portion of a cave in which a carpenter has a shop and old man called Sack of Bones lives and keeps his horse. The title comes from a remark of a German officer, talking to an arrogant Italian officer who has called the street children "scum." The German, throwing a couple of coins, says, "In the unclean waters live the little fishes. Some are eaten; most, I believe. But some will escape." A little boy, Mario*, 4, offers to eat dirt for a coin, tries, but chokes. When the officer gives him the coin and his sister, Anna*, 11, grabs it from him, Guido takes the child to the kind old priest, Father Pietro, who gives them most of his supper of bread, though the sour younger priest, Don Carlo, says he is a fool to do it. Guido goes to the harbor one day to work with Sack of Bones; the harbor is bombed, the old man and his horse killed. When Guido flees to Father Pietro, he finds the priest has died the night before. In the next bombing Anna's aunt is killed, and she and Mario move in with Guido, but soon the carpenter sells his right to the cave, and the children must leave. Guido decides to leave Naples, makes the others wash, and buys a second-hand dress for Anna so they will not be obviously beggars and picked up by the police. They head north for Cassino, simply a name Guido picks but a goal for Anna. On the way, they find evil and good people. A thief captures them to beg for him. They escape through a low roof of the shed where they sleep. A kindly miller lets them sleep in his mill, and arranges that they work for a nearby farmer for food. German soldiers come. Guido finds a Roman coin and gives it to one of them. They shoot an English parachutist, an act which arouses the resentment of the peasants, and in retaliation the officer insists that the children leave the mill and take back the coin. They meet a teacher who calls himself Jason, though his real name is Luigi. With him they get to the monastery at Cassino and spend a bitter winter in the place filled with hungry and sick refugees. Little Mario dies. To avoid sure starvation, they leave the monastery, wander in the mountains, and find shelter in a cave housing more than a hundred people, including a mother in childbirth. In an effort to get through to the Allies, who are shelling the area, Guido and Luigi crawl through a mine field. Luigi hits a mine and is killed. Guido crawls on and meets an American soldier. Since he is able to tell them where the German machine guns are, the Americans can take the mountain and get the refugees from the cave. The story ends with no certainty but with hope that Anna and Guido are among the little fishes who will survive. The war, as seen by its innocent victims, is shown in its horror and irrationality. Much of the power in the book comes from small incidents—Guido's realization that the young priest actually hates the beggar children; old Sack of Bones's explanation that the world must be run by the Devil, not God; Anna's fear of the lechery she recognizes in some men. The understated narration by Guido is convincing, giving the feel

of a foreign language and a prematurely aged observer. This is generally agreed
to be one of the best books dealing with World War II. Addams; Boston Globe
Winner; Choice; Fanfare.

LITTLE LEAGUE VICTORY (Bishop*, Curtis, Lippincott, 1967), sports novel
set in Austin, Tex., in the 1960s. Although small at eleven, Ed Bogart is a
natural athlete, fast and well coordinated. Nevertheless, he is unpopular because
he always insists on winning and picks fights continually, a situation not helped
by his solicitous mother, his child psychologist, Dr. Kreig, or his hard-driving
father, a former athletic star now usually absent on business. Ed's great desire
is to play on the regular Little League team as his only friend, big, good-natured
Luther "Luke" Cliff, and his archrival, Jim Cartwright, do, but his wealthy
family expect him to return to Camp Ticonderoga in the Catskills, where he has
spent the last three summers. Ed pressures his mother to let him go to the tryouts,
where he comes in first in the race and does moderately well in fielding and
batting but is not chosen by any team. Later that night, a call from Jim Tracy,
a friend of his father and manager of the Atlas Giants, tells him he has been
drafted by that team. First practice goes fairly well, but Ed is so tense that he
relies on his mother's tranquilizers to keep him from blowing up, and soon he
loses his quick reactions and bat control. His high-school-age sister, Susan, who
genuinely wants to help him, makes him confess to his father, who forces him
to go through a painful withdrawal. Ed's playing improves, but the team's record
does not. He blames their failures on the facts that he must play center field
instead of first base and that Luke, as catcher, is clumsy and easygoing. Ed
finally goads Luke into a fight, and when Luke stands up to him for the first
time, the big, slow boy gains confidence and Ed, unable to face the idea of his
teammates' jeers, turns in his uniform. That night Jim Tracy brings it back and,
in conference with Ed's father, reminds him that he, like his son, was unable
to play team sports until he learned to control his bad temper. Tracy had intervened
to persuade him to return to college at a crucial time. After his father tells him
the story, Ed goes back to the team. They lose all their practice games and, in
the first game of the regular season, with some important players ill, Ed pitches
a no hitter but the team loses anyway. Having learned real sportsmanship, Ed
refuses to blame Luke's catching. His proud father decides he can stay in Austin
instead of going to camp. Even Dr. Kreig is at the game and congratulates him.
For baseball fans, the details of the games are interesting, and Ed's frustrations
and conflicts are well portrayed. The solution, however, is simplistic, and the
discussions of Ed's problems by his mother and the psychologist in front of the
boy are hardly credible. Choice.

LITTLE MAN LOGAN (*Roll of Thunder, Hear My Cry**), Clayton Chester
Logan, precocious younger brother of Cassie. He is a staunch, earnest, proud,
rather finicky, little fellow. When, on the first day of school, the school bus
drenches him with dust, he shakes his fist in fury at the driver. He gets a whipping

at school when he refuses to use the cast-off schoolbook. Mama then glues paper over the offensive page in the front that provides the history of the book's usage. It is situations like this that prompt Mama to defy the Wallaces, an action which leads to her losing her position as a teacher in the local black school and provokes a financial crisis for the Logans. Little Man is a consistently interesting, credible, winning character.

L . . . M (*The Griffin Legacy**), part of Lucy* Griffin's chant that Amy hears but doesn't understand until the night the storm destroys the old family elm tree. Then she realizes the letters are referring to the tree and that Lucy was trying to tell her where the book is located. Finding the book leads to the discovery of the legacy, the silver communion service.

LOBO (*The Burning Glass**), an old French trapper, a mountain- and trail-wise man, who serves as campmaster for the Deschute* pack train. He is no respector of persons and often badgers his companions, but he is expert at his job and they respect him for it. He is kind to Jeb and teaches him much about how to behave on the trail and about the ways of the Indians and woodsmen.

LOCMAN (*The First Two Lives of Lukas-Kasha**), kindly, befuddled, earnest old astrologer at King Kasha's (Lukas's*) court, who, after Lukas's precipitous departure, also flees for his life. He refuses to prophesy falsely that Shugdad should be king. Although he has left hastily without his charts and instruments for calculating the future, he sets himself up as a soothsayer and does so well he is made mayor of a small village in Abadan*. He concludes that there is no way to predict the future and that there is nothing certain but uncertainty, a philosophy which is reflected in Lukas's own musings about why Battisto has sent him to Abadan, a question that is never answered in the novel. Locman is a sympathetic character, better developed than most in the book if distorted for effect.

THE LONER (Wier*, Ester, ill. Christine Price, McKay, 1963), realistic, problem novel set mostly on a Montana sheep ranch in the mid–1900s. A thin, underfed boy of about twelve, homeless, parentless, nameless, travels with migrant workers until, in Idaho, the young girl who has befriended him meets a tragic death. Determined to reach California on his own, the boy loses his way while hitchhiking. One cold night in early winter, exhausted with weariness, he sobs himself to sleep on the ground by some serviceberry bushes on a sheep ranch in Montana. The rancher, a tall, husky, commanding woman known as Boss*, finds him and takes him to the wagon in which she lives while she follows her flocks. Boss names him David, after the shepherd king on whose name the boy's finger falls in the family Bible. Because she regards this as a sign and because the boy reminds her of her own son, Ben, killed a few months back by a grizzly, she offers David a home in return for his help with the sheep. Gradually, David learns to tend the flocks, keeping off coyotes by night, hunting for strays, and digging sheep out from snowdrifts after winter hits. He often makes mistakes, for which Boss berates him, and once he even runs away after a scolding. At first, he is aloof and suspicious, but slowly, with the help of Angie*, Ben's understanding widow, and particularly of Tex*, the garrulous, kindly, young sheeptender, David comes to see his determination to go it alone as false pride and selfishness. On her part, Boss learns to appreciate the boy for his own good qualities of determination and perseverance. After David helps Angie rescue Tex from a bear trap Boss has set to catch the grizzly and later shoots a huge grizzly that has been stalking the flock, David knows that he has lived up to his new friends' and his own expectations and wants no longer to be a loner. Story's end finds him in sole charge of the flock and looking forward to going to school and to living with Angie and Tex on the ranch. Contrived episodes lead with some suspense to the dramatic if overforeshadowed conclusion. The parallels between David and the Biblical David and between David and "bum lambs" seem labored. Characters are flat, and David learns the ways of sheepherding and the skillful use of a gun too fast for belief. Even so, it is easy to sympathize with him, and the book's sense of place is strong. Books Too Good; Choice; Fanfare; Newbery Honor.

THE LONG BLACK COAT (Bennett*, Jay, Delacorte, 1973), mystery set in Brooklyn at the end of the Viet Nam war. Vincent Mathew Brant, Phil's older brother "Vinnie," has been killed in Viet Nam, but his shadow follows Phil, 17, and their grandfather, Len, with whom he lives and works in his repair garage. In the back of the garage is a room built by Vinnie and kept locked with only Phil knowing the combination, given him by Vinnie just before he left for the army. In the closet of the windowless room is a complete wardrobe, unworn, which Vinnie bought and sent home to be saved until his return from service, including a long black coat. In the coat is a letter which Vinnie has instructed Phil he must not read until eighteen months after Vinnie's death, should he fail to return. Two ugly characters, Ed Madigan, a heavy thug, and Joe Dawson, a smooth but cruel type, appear in Phil's life, both apparently acquaintances of Vinnie's from the army and both obviously looking for something they think Phil has or knows about. Edna Walsh, Vinnie's girlfriend, calls Phil to come to her apartment late at night, where he is beaten up. The next day she calls again, tells him she is scared and leaving town, but when he returns to her apartment, he finds her strangled. Phil realizes that Vinnie, whom he has always followed but whose character he has really known was bad, has somehow trapped him and Len, and he is not too astonished when, resting in Vinnie's room and wondering what to do, he is confronted by his brother, alive. Vinnie reveals that he has faked his death, that the "letter" in the black coat pocket has on it two stamps worth $125,000, stolen by him and the other two from a bank vault, and that he plans to take Phil to Mexico, having Len follow. Before they get away, he kills Madigan and is killed by Dawson, who in turn is shot by the airport police. An ironic twist is added when it is revealed that the two stamps were fakes, kept in the vault as decoys. Following the conventions of the mystery story, the novel depends more on action and clever plot than on characterization. Some inconsistencies appear (Len's last name is also Brant, though he is their mother's father, for instance), but in its genre it works well. Poe Winner.

THE LONG JOURNEY (Corcoran*, Barbara, ill. Charles Robinson, Atheneum, 1970), adventure novel set in Montana during the late 1900s. Laurie James, 13, has been raised by her grandfather, Peter Bent, since her parents died when she was three. She and her grandfather live in a ghost town, Hawkins Dry Diggings, where the old man owns the worked-out Saturday Mine. Laurie's grandfather and make-believe playmates have been her only companions, and her education has been by correspondence. Fiercely independent, Laurie's grandfather is scornful and suspicious of society's institutions. Fearing that he is going blind, he sends Laurie by horseback for help to his son, Arthur, in Butte. He orders the girl to stay out of towns, keep away from people, and live off the land on her journey. Laurie's trip on Hook*, her sturdy Hambletonian-quarter horse, takes many days and leads her cross-country on a route through Jasper and Missoula. Laurie's problems include getting food, finding suitable campsites, handling the people she meets, and controlling her emotions. As she travels, she gains a much broader perspective on the world and human nature. She is shot in the arm by an irate rancher, whose colt she is trying to rescue from a fence, gets caught in a forest fire, and returns a lost child to her parents. She herself is helped by warmhearted, motherly Miss* Emily Kimball, an ex-schoolteacher, when she is caught in a sudden rainstorm. At Miss Emily's house, Laurie first sees such ordinary conveniences of modern middle-class life as hot, running water, a dryer, and a phonograph. A continuing problem for her concerns a wild-eyed, wayfaring stranger dressed in black, who rides a mule and calls himself a preacher, Hell-and-Damnation* Hastings. He discovers that Laurie carries gold nuggets and tries to steal them from her. At Butte, she phones Uncle Arthur, who has a ranch outside of town. He and his kind wife welcome Laurie and offer her a permanent home with them. Arthur arranges for Grandfather to see a doctor and persuades him to have an operation for his cataracts. He also helps Grandfather reopen the mine, which Peter is certain contains a fortune in silver. Offered choices, Laurie decides to return to Saturday Mine with Peter. She likes life in the wilds, and the old man needs her. This story of an intelligent, courageous, quick-witted girl's eventful journey moves rapidly. Even though many events, and indeed the basic premise, are not very convincing, and characters and incidents appear gotten up for effect, careful attention to details of the journey sustains the interest. The wayfaring stranger is especially unconvincing but contributes a continuing element of danger. Laurie's reactions to the people she meets and to a world of bathtubs, parking meters, menus, and revolving doors are often humorous. She discovers that the world can be hard, but that it also offers beauty and goodness. Choice.

THE LONG SECRET (Fitzhugh*, Louise, ill. author, Harper, 1965), humorous, realistic novel of family life involving some of the same characters that appear in *Harriet the Spy**. Harriet Welsch and a school chum, Beth Ellen Hansen, whom Harriet calls Mouse because she is so shy, spend the summer with their families at the seashore at Water Mill, N.Y. Harriet is determined to find out who is writing the Biblical-sounding notes of warning and doom that are upsetting the community. Beth Ellen lives with her mother's mother, wealthy Mrs. Hansen, while her mother globetrots, and much of the book concerns her relationship with her mother, selfish, exotically beautiful, eccentric Zeeney Baines, who turns up along with her foppish, rich husband, Wallace, and sets out to make her daughter over in her own shallow, jet-set image. Harriet's suspicions about who is behind the notes are directed variously but focus mainly on the Jenkinses, a resident family who have moved to Water Mill from Mississippi and who include fat Mrs. Jenkins, a widow who hopes to become rich from the toe medicine she makes from watermelons; her son, Norman, and daughter, Jessie Mae, who hope to found a church; and the Preacher, a kindly black minister. A series of farcical incidents ensue, some of which include Bunny Maguire, pianist at the Shark's Tooth Inn, on whom Beth Ellen has a crush, and Agatha Plumber, on whom Harriet spied in *Harriet the Spy*. When Beth Ellen learns that her mother intends to take her back to Europe with her, she screws up her courage and shocks everyone by adamantly refusing to go. At the end, Harriet discovers that Beth Ellen has been sending the notes. The reason for her action is not clear, but it evidently stems from latent anger and hostility. The Welsches and old Mrs. Hansen are the only rational characters. The senior Welsches are much more sympathetically depicted than in *Harriet the Spy*, but Harriet remains as obnoxious as before. Many scenes are gratuitous, for example, that in which Harriet, Beth Ellen, and Janie* Gibbs, who comes to visit Harriet, discuss menstruation and the fracases in the inn between Agatha, Zeeney, and Bunny. Most characters are overdrawn, the humor is strained, and the plot is slight and not well meshed with the subplot. Choice.

LONZO (*The Taste of Spruce Gum**), cerebral palsy victim who works as chore boy at the lumber camp boarding house. Although he cannot talk intelligibly, he has a sharp intelligence, and although his arms and legs flail at random, he can drive a nail accurately, harness and drive the oxen, and do the kitchen chores efficiently. When Libby is escaping from the drunken sawyer, Vincent, Lonzo follows, ready to protect her.

"LOOKFAR" (*A Wizard of Earthsea**; *The Tombs of Atuan**; *The Farthest Shore**), eighteen-foot sailing boat in which Ged* sails vast stretches of the ocean of Earthsea*, pursuing the Shadow which he has, in his pride, loosed upon the world. It is also the boat in which Ged and Arren* travel to the south and west seeking to find what is destroying the power of magic and the sense of order in Earthsea, in *The Farthest Shore*. More briefly, it appears when Tenar* and Ged sail from Atuan back to Havnor (*The Tombs of Atuan*). Although like any ordinary sailboat it obeys the winds of the world, it also has unusual properties, being very seaworthy, especially suited to sailing before a mage-wind, and able to come from some distance when Ged "calls" it with his mind.

LORD, ATHENA V., born in Cohoes, N.Y.; author of biography and historical fiction. She was graduated from Vassar College, majoring in creative writing, and has lived with her husband and four children in Albany, N.Y. Her first published book was a biography for young people, *Pilot for Spaceship Earth: Buckminster Fuller, Architect, Inventor, and Poet* (Macmillan, 1978). Her novel of the early labor strike by the women in the Lowell, Mass., mills, *A Spirit to Ride the Whirlwind** (Macmillan, 1981), won the Child Study Award. More recently she has turned back to the scenes of her childhood in Cohoes, N.Y., in *Today's Special: Z.A.P. and Zoe* (Macmillan, 1984), a story set in 1939 of an eleven-year-old Greek-American who is responsible for his four-year-old sibling.

LORRAINE JENSEN (*The Pigman**), friend and side-kick of John* Conlan, who with him gets to know a lonely old man and helps cause his death. Told by her mother frequently that she is unattractive, Lorraine lacks self-confidence and goes along with John's wild pranks because it gives her a sense of belonging. She suffers more pangs of conscience than he as they fool the old man, and she blames both herself and John for the debacle that causes his final heart attack.

LOTTE'S LOCKET (Sorensen*†, Virginia, ill. Fermin Rocker, Harcourt, 1964), realistic novel set in Denmark in 1963. Lotte, 10, is upset and worried that her widowed mother, or Mor, Gerda, is to marry an American, Patrick* from Texas, and go to live with him in New York City. Since her pilot father died in a crash, they have lived with his mother at Lottegaard, her farm in Jutland, a place of long tradition named for an original Lotte of the eighteenth century, whose elderly husband willed that when he died she should remarry and that the farm should always be inherited by the eldest daughter named Lotte. The grandmother, Farmor, herself a Lotte, has had no daughters, so the farm and the heirloom locket will go to Lotte, who does not want to leave Denmark. The enthusiasm for Patrick and America of Farmor and of Lotte's best friend, Lisa*, irritates her, and even after the wedding, when she and her grandmother accompany Mor and Patrick to Copenhagen to see them off on a ship, Lotte tries to persuade her mother not to leave by "becoming a guidebook" and announcing all the wonders of Denmark as they pass them. When the king's guard band passes their restaurant, Lotte runs after it and gets lost. Eventually, she remembers Hr. Axel, a newspaperman who has admired Mor, and he helps her find her mother and writes her up with her picture in the paper. After they leave, Lotte, who is to stay with Farmor until school is out and she can join her mother and Patrick in New York, keeps trying to think of ways to bring her mother back. For the school writing contest about their heroes and heritage, she writes a poem which wins third place. Lisa, with an essay on Danish-American friendship, wins first place, a trip to Copenhagen. Hr. Axel's newspaper, however, takes the whole class, so that they all will see Lotte off. At the amusement park Lotte eats too much and is very sick. When she wakes, having missed the ship, her mother is flown to be with her. Seeing how generous Patrick is to send Mor all that way and how brave Mor, who hates planes, has been to come, Lotte is happy to go to America when Patrick comes to get them both. Too much information about Denmark too little disguised as fiction makes the pace very slow. Lotte's emotions are reported in detail but fail to ring true, and the patience of the adults dealing with her is unlikely. Fanfare.

LOUANN TRELOAR (*The Dollhouse Murders**), brain-damaged sister one year younger than Amy*, who is Amy's responsibility every day after school until their mother comes home from work and through much of Amy's weekend and summer vacation. Much larger than twelve-year-old Amy and indulged by her mother, Louann has not learned to control any of her impulses and talks constantly in a loud voice, embarrassing her sister and making Amy's friends unwilling to be with her. When Amy rebels and goes to stay with her aunt, Louann must spend her afternoons with a grandmother of a classmate in the school for exceptional children, and she learns skills and how to adjust to new people so that the time apart proves good for her as well as for Amy.

LOUIS (*The Trumpet of the Swan**), mute swan who accompanies his human friend, Sam* Beaver, to school where he learns to read and write but still is unable to woo his love, Serena, the beautiful swan. With a trumpet his father has stolen, he becomes a jazz musician. Resourceful and responsible and moved by filial concern, he leaves the Rockies he loves so much and flies east, where he gets jobs to earn money to repay his father's debt. He eventually marries Serena, who had previously ignored him.

LOUISE BRADSHAW (*Jacob Have I Loved**), Sara Louise, first-person narrator who is called "Wheeze" from the way her twin sister, Caroline*, first pronounced her name. A self-tormenting character, Louise is justifiably jealous of her favored twin but increases her own misery by assuming that she herself is unloved. The passionate attraction she feels for Captain* Hiram Wallace takes her by surprise, and because of her strict, Methodist upbringing, it seems to her sinful if not insane. Honest, hardworking, and sensitive, she grows into a woman who can cope with her own emotions and come to terms with her sibling rivalry.

LOWRY, LOIS (HAMMBERSBERG) (1937–   ), born in Honolulu, Hawaii; freelance writer and photographer. She attended Brown University and the University of Maine, where she received her B.A. degree and did graduate work. She has written several textbooks. Her own personal loss in the death of a sister motivated her to write *A Summer to Die** (Houghton, 1977), which won an International Reading Association Award. Among her other books are *Find a Stranger, Say Goodbye* (Houghton, 1978), *Autumn Street* (Houghton, 1980), *The One Hundredth Thing About Caroline* (Houghton, 1983), *Taking Care of Terrific* (Houghton, 1983), and a series about a lively child named Anastasia, *Anastasia Krupnik* (Houghton, 1979), *Anastasia Again!* (Houghton, 1981), *Anastasia at Your Service* (Houghton, 1982), and *Anastasia, Ask Your Analyst* (Houghton, 1984).

LUCY GRIFFIN (*The Griffin Legacy**), Amy* Enfield's ancestor of Revolutionary War times, who appears to Amy seeking the girl's help in restoring the so-called Griffin legacy, the communion silver given by British Queen Anne to St. George's church of which Seth* Howes, her lover, husband, and father of her child, was rector. The Tory Seth had entrusted the silver to Lucy for safekeeping and died thinking Lucy had betrayed him. She hid the silver, married Charles Griffin as her father ordered, and bore Seth's son, thought by everyone to be Charles's child. After Charles's death, his grown sons turned her out, and she returned to her home, laboring like a man to support herself and her son. She died still loyal to Seth, ordering that his name be placed on her gravestone. She appears several times to Amy and communicates to her by chanting. There is a portrait of her in the living room at Constitution Hill.

LUDELL (Wilkinson*, Brenda, Harper, 1975), realistic, girl's growing-up story set in the black community of the town of Waycross, Ga., in the mid–1900s. Spunky, fun-loving Ludell Wilson lives with her no-nonsense grandmother, whom she calls Mama*, a domestic. Her loosely plotted story starts with the everyday events of about a week when Ludell is in the fifth grade, then skips here and there until she is thirteen to show how Ludell's life appears to be following the pattern of the women in her neighborhood. Ludell enjoys chumming with her best friend, Ruthie Mae; chicken every Sunday; all the pie, cake, and cookies she wants on Christmas; a first romance with Willie Johnson, the boy next door; and knowing her strict, "ole timey" Mama loves her dearly. There are some things that bother her, too: the teasing of the sixth grade boys; having to wear sensible, brown scout shoes instead of the popular "tennises"; never having enough money for the goodies she craves; and the teachers in her segregated school who don't really care about their students. She doesn't think much of teenaged Mattie Johnson, fat, lazy, burdened with a baby, and stepping out with the middle-aged man across the street. She wonders what her mother, Dessa, whom she hasn't seen in years, looks like now and where her father is. She is outraged when Mis Johnson's white employer makes her work all day Christmas. She wishes Mama did not have to work so hard scrubbing other people's houses and that she were not so fussy and protective. Ludell recognizes the futility of protesting when the white lady she baby-sits and cleans for reneges on her agreed-upon price of a dollar an hour. When Ludell's eighth grade teacher acknowledges the girl's ability to write, new vistas open for Ludell, and she realizes that there might be more in life for her than Waycross and cleaning white folks' houses. Dialogue that is rhythmical and euphonious with black dialect carries the burden of Ludell's highly detailed story. Though slow starting and lacking in climax, the story gives a clear sense of some of the problems, joys, and hopes of a black community and blacks individually without being preachy, simplistic, or sensational. Ludell's sudden talent for writing strains credulity, but she is a round, dynamic, likeable character who grows up believably. Some characters are purely types, but Mama and Mis Johnson are particularly sympathetic, strongly delineated figures who command respect for their earnest attempts to achieve decent lives for their families. Sequels. National Book Finalist.

LUDOVICO (*The Second Mrs. Giaconda**), historical Duke of Milan, called Il Moro, the Moor, because of his dark complexion, patron of Leonardo da Vinci, husband of Beatrice* d'Este. He is a proud, rich, self-indulgent man, to whom appearances are important and who at first despises his plain young wife, his second choice for a bride. Later, won by her vivacious personality, intelligence, and wit, he falls deeply in love with her. He returns to form, however, when she is pregnant with their third child, and his affections stray to a pretty, young courtier. He is continually ordering Leonardo to begin on some new project of his fancy, thus keeping the artist from completing those that are really important to him.

LUKE EGAN (*Torrie**), a traveler in and later leader of the wagon train to which the family of Thomas* Anders is attached. Luke has a big buckskin horse of which he is very proud and which Jess* Jessen wins on a wager when Jess's bony mare defeats the buckskin in a race. Luke has carrot-colored hair and a booming voice and is brash and somewhat of a bully, but all the girls consider him a fine catch. He flirts with all of them, especially with plain Torrie, who for a time loses her head and becomes his willing servant, even milking his cows for him. Luke is a stock character.

LUKE MOREHOUSE (*Luke Was There**), young man, depicted as black in the illustrations, who is Julius's counselor at Children's House. He helps Julius with his homework, encouraging him in the pleasure of discovery. He gives Julius a magnifying glass which the boy cherishes, and he takes him to visit his apartment. Because Luke is a conscientious objector, he is assigned to hospital service and must leave Children's House for a tour of duty there. When Julius hears that Luke is leaving, he immediately assumes that Luke is abandoning him, as have his father and stepfather. He reacts with anger and has temper tantrums during which he throws and destroys things. Luke is potentially the most interesting character in the book but never rises above the stock.

LUKE WAS THERE (Clymer*, Eleanor, ill. Diane de Groat, Holt, 1973), short, realistic problem novel set in New York's inner city in the late twentieth century, in which a boy describes his search for security during one eventful spring. After his stepfather leaves home and his mother goes to the hospital for an operation, Julius and his younger brother, Danny, are taken to the Children's House, a neighborhood shelter for homeless children. Although he and Danny are treated kindly and Julius likes his new school and makes friends at the home, he worries about his mother and feels lonely and unsettled, until Luke* Morehouse, sympathetic, young black man, becomes his counselor. Luke plays baseball with Julius in the park, teaches him to box, and talks with him as to an equal. Julius likes his direct, friendly, accepting, but firm, manner and for the first time in months feels he has someone upon whom he can count. Ironically, on his birthday, Julius learns that Luke must go away. A conscientious objector, he has been assigned to duty in a hospital. Angry and discouraged at losing still another important adult in his life, Julius takes up with Max, an older, streetwise kid, who also lives in the House and who begs, shoplifts, and snatches purses. When Max puts the blame for a purse snatching on Julius, Julius flees. For several days he wanders the streets, begging and running errands, and even sometimes pilfering food. He stays one night with an old man he meets in a park, spends part of another in a junkie pad, falls in with a group of hippies, and even breaks into his old apartment to sleep. At Grand Central Station, he encounters little Ricardo, an abandoned child, whose need for love and the basic necessities of life are even greater than his own. Sincere concern for Ricardo moves him to take the boy to Children's House, even though he realizes that by returning he may be punished for a crime he did not commit. To his surprise and delight, he discovers that Luke has taken a leave from his hospital responsibilities to search for him. Luke believes his story about the theft, fixes matters up, and takes Julius to visit his mother in the hospital. Luke helps Julius to see that even adults must sometimes do things they do not like and that acceptance, trust, and hope are good qualities to cultivate. Before long, Julius and Danny are able to stay with their mother again. Julius tells the story of his search with honesty in detail and language suitable to an intelligent, well brought up boy of about ten. But his story is too dispassionate and summarized to be really moving. Luke is the ideal counselor, and Julius's involvement with Max is simply not convincing. Vocabulary is not difficult, and events seem designed to give elementary readers a picture of inner city life and show them how much neighborhood centers meet important needs, a book of social message without an emotionally satisfying climax and credible conclusion. Strongly executed drawings help with setting, clarify situations, and convey emotion. Child Study; Choice.

LUKE YOUNG (*The Secret of the Simple Code**), friend of Abby* Kenny, who helps Paul solve the mystery of the messages in the cigars. Since Luke has a summer job at the inn, he is able to keep an eye on the two strangers who pass messages to one another in the cigars. His unhappy home life makes him secretive and surly, and at first he resents Abby's growing friendship with Paul. After revenuers arrest his father for keeping a still and his stepmother runs off, he goes to live with Professor* Halstead. He knows a lot about nature and plans to use his share of the reward money for college.

LUNDIUS (*Canalboat to Freedom**), black deck hand on the *Bullfrog* who befriends Benja and is killed trying to save a runaway slave. Long before the story starts, when his wife and children were to be sold, Lundius tried to escape with them but was caught and whipped daily for several days with his family watching as an example to other slaves. Then they were all sold to different owners. Lundius, freed in his new owner's will, tried to find his family, only to learn that his wife has died and no trace can be found of his children. He has dedicated his life to helping other slaves escape. From Mrs. Robbins, for whom he works when the canal is frozen, he has learned to read and has made contacts with others in the Underground Railway.

LUTE SWANK (*Bristle Face**), store keeper and surrogate father to Jase Landers. Lazy, good-natured, and naturally clever, Lute has been earning a meager but adequate living in his country store where customers list their wants on a slate on the porch if he is not in and he delivers their orders at his convenience. This easygoing life changes when he boasts to the pretty widow, Pansy Jarkey, that he will be the next sheriff and then sets out to impress her by making good his boast. He is gentle, kindly, and understanding and makes a home for orphaned Jase and his dog.

LYDIA FARR (*The People Therein**), pretty, flirtatious youngest sister of Lanthy*. Although courted by Ben Cottrell, Lydia refuses to commit herself by "walking out" with him, because some other boy is always catching her eye. Though self-centered enough so that her first concern when the family learns of Lanthy's pregnancy is that her parents will restrict her own freedom, Lydia does have genuine family love for Lanthy.

LYLE JEFFRIES (*The Last Run**), lazy, self-centered youth, protagonist of the novel. The stories of his grandfather, Bill* Cameron, about mustangs and cowboy life have inspired Lyle to dream of becoming a champion rodeo rider. He hates working in his father's gas station, lies to his parents about what he is doing, procrastinates with his school work, and visits the local gambling casino even though he knows it is forbidden. He is not a sympathetic protagonist until near the end of his story when he has learned (if a bit too readily) to buckle down and think about others, as shown by his concern for Bill Cameron, his offer to work for his father, Frank*, and accompany him on the fishing trip, and his nonchalant handling of the teasing of the local bullies, who used to get under his skin very easily.

M

MACCLOUD, MALCOLM, born in the American West; science fiction novelist. He spent his summers on the North Rim of the Grand Canyon and is a hiking-camping-fishing enthusiast. He gave up the study of astronomy for science fiction, which he finds more satisfying, and has written two futuristic novels set on distant planets, *The Terra Beyond* (Atheneum, 1981), in which a highly mechanized society, descended from space travellers from Earth, has managed to suppress the search for truth, even in science, and *A Gift of Mirrorvax** (Atheneum, 1981), winner of the Christopher Award, in which an equally grim social system, also peopled by descendants of Earth space travellers, is planning to take over a planet in its solar system.

MACLACHLAN, PATRICIA, born in Cheyenne, Wyo.; teacher of English and creative writing and author of picture books and novels for later elementary and early adolescent readers. Her experiences as a teacher and member of the executive board of a family service agency have given her ideas for her books, which often place children in stressful family situations and concentrate on interpersonal relationships within family and small group settings. Among these is *Unclaimed Treasures** (Harper, 1984), a *Boston Globe-Horn Book* honor book, featuring a girl whose mother is about to have a baby and who becomes infatuated with the older man next door. Among her other novels is *Arthur, for the Very First Time* (Harper, 1980), about a boy who gains self-knowledge when he spends a summer with an unusual uncle and aunt, and *Cassie Binegar* (Harper, 1982), in which a young girl learns that changes are a normal part of life. *Through Grandpa's Eyes* (Harper, 1979) and *The Sick Day* (Pantheon, 1979) are among her picture books, while *Mama One, Mama Two* (Harper, 1982) is non-fiction about a foster child. Her books are vivid in style and briskly characterized. A graduate of the University of Connecticut, she lives in western Massachusetts with her husband, Robert, and three children.

THE MACLAREN OF SPEY (*John Treegate's Musket*†; *Peter Treegate's War**), Scots Highlander who discovers Peter Treegate washed up on the Carolina shore. He has been searching for salvage from shipwrecks, as is his custom, when he comes upon the half-dead boy. He adopts Peter into his clan, teaches him to fight, and takes him on raids against the Indians. The Maclaren is proud, stubborn, and sometimes cruel. He hates the British to the point of foolhardiness. He feels no loyalty to the colonial cause, however, and fights on the side of the Continentals only because he hates the British so much. His hatred goes back to the time when he lived in Scotland and was involved in the wars between the British and the clans. The Maclaren represents an older ideology, that of loyalty to family and clan rather than country, which is presented in the novels as outmoded. He is a foil for John* Treegate, Peter's father.

MACLEOD, CHARLOTTE (MATILDA HUGHES) (1922–   ), born in Bath, New Brunswick, Canada; artist and novelist. She attended public schools in Weymouth, Mass., and the Art Institute of Boston. For some years she was staff artist and copywriter for a grocery chain, then worked in an advertising agency. Among her novels for young people are *King Devil* (Atheneum, 1978) and *We Dare Not Go A-Hunting** (Atheneum, 1980), which was a nominee for the Edgar Allan Poe Award. *Cirak's Daughter* (Atheneum, 1982) is a mystery concerning an inheritance from a father that the protagonist did not know and whose life, she discovers, had many unexplained elements.

MAC MCWILLIAMS (*The Callender Papers**), Oliver McWilliams, about fourteen, local youth whom Jean* Wainwright meets while he is fishing the stream near Mr.* Thiel's house, who reluctantly seeks help from her with his Latin, who shares with her local gossip and knowledge about the Callenders, and who sustains her in her search for the truth about Irene Callender Thiel's death. He provides an occasional touch of comic relief.

MADAM (*A Lemon and a Star*†; *Terrible, Horrible Edie**; *Edie on the Warpath**), stepmother of Ted*, Jane*, Hubert*, and Edie*, whose real name is Elsie Cares, in a series of turn-of-the-century setting, humorous family novels. Sprung on the children in the last episode of *A Lemon and a Star* with no warning (except some rumors overheard from the servants which they can scarcely believe), she wins them over with great tact and firm control of Father*. Even Ted admits that she is good looking and fashionable when she puts on a big hat, and Edie loves the way she smells of violets. Later she has two daughters, the Fair Christine (so named by Hubert when she is a squally, red infant) and Lou. In the last book she is suffering from asthma, possibly brought on by nervous strain, and must spend winters in Florida.

MADAME FLATTOT (*The Happy Orphelines*†; *A Brother for the Orphelines*†; *A Pet for the Orphelines**), woman in charge of the twenty little orphan girls in a village near Paris. A maternal type, she has had no children of her own and treats the girls with affection and unconventional good sense. Her major concern is the decrepit state of their building.

MADAME MELANIE (*Sophia Scrooby Preserved**), wife of Pedro Alvarez, the pirate captain who buys Pansy from Crop-ear*, the slaver. A tall, red-haired black woman, she is a voodoo queen and quite frightening to the slaves. She runs the plantation in the alligator-infested swamp near New Orleans where Pansy and John Forsyth* are held captive. To prove that she has magical powers equal to those of Madame Melanie, Pansy sings an aria.

MADAME SOSOSTRIS (*The Genie of Sutton Place**), Muriel Glick, the flamboyant, generous, inept, highly emotional fortuneteller and antique dealer with whom Timmy Farr has been living and of whom he has grown very fond. He enjoys her relaxed way of life and would prefer to continue living with her but by terms of his father's will goes to live with his Aunt* Lucy. Timmy deliberately leaves his father's books in Madame Sosostris's shops so he will have an excuse to visit her. She is the chief comic figure in the story. Among other episodes in which she appears, Dooley* makes a seance she is attempting to conduct successful without her knowledge and to her delight and also helps her perform magic tricks for Timmy's birthday party.

MADGE DRAWN (*Dust of the Earth**), eight-year-old younger sister of Fern* Drawn. She sometimes whines and is willful. She has a keen awareness of what is going on in the family and first points out to Fern that Mama is going to have another baby. After Hobson drops out of school, she continues to attend and keeps the family informed about what is happening in the community. She pitches in to do tasks about the house when Mama has the baby.

MADISON, ARNOLD (1937–), born in Bayport, N.Y.; teacher and writer of fiction and non-fiction for adults and adolescents. He grew up on Long Island and received his B.S. degree from the State University of New York in Plattsburgh and taught in Bethpage, N.Y. He has directed and acted in community theater and summer stock, has directed several off-Broadway plays, and has been an instructor at the St. David's Writers Conference. His first novel for young people, *Danger Beats the Drum** (Holt, 1966), about traffic in drugs, was nominated for the Edgar Allan Poe Award of the Mystery Writers of America. His other mystery-adventure novels for youth include *The Secret of the Carved Whale Bone* (McKay, 1969), about buried treasure, and *Fast Break to Danger* (Pyramid, 1972), about basketball, while *Think Wild!* (Holt, 1968) is a novel of family life about a teenager who desperately wants a drivers' license. He has also written informational books on drugs, smoking, vandalism, vigilantism, treasure hunting, runaways, and surfing and has contributed serials, stories, and articles to juvenile and adult periodicals. He has made his home on Long Island.

MAD MOLL (*Encounter at Easton**), pathetic, deranged old recluse, called a witch by the local people, who shelters Elizabeth in her home in a cave overlooking the river near Easton. She was once a beautiful young woman whose fiance rejected her after she was raped by a soldier. She ran away from home and since then has been living alone in a cave. Her only friends have been the children of the area. She soon comes of think of Elizabeth as the daughter she never had and tries to protect her from the bounty hunter, Hill*, and the constable, Clagget*.

MAE TUCK (*Tuck Everlasting**), large, comfortable-looking woman, who has lived unchanged for eighty-seven years after drinking water from a spring in Foster's woods at the edge of Treegap. To save Winnie* Foster from being exploited by the man in the yellow suit, Mae clobbers him with a rifle held like a club and, when he dies, is arrested for murder. With Winnie's help, her family arrange her escape.

MAGGIE RUDD (*The Voyage Begun**), feisty, middle-aged woman who operates a game refuge and incurs Dr.* Vickers's dislike by complaining frequently about the hazards to local wildlife. She is Paul Vickers's first friend after his family moves to the cape. She lives by herself, a simple life, alone in her cottage with her effusive black Labrador, Hannah, and feels no need for the luxuries for which both Mrs. Vickers and Mrs. Cafferty yearn. She gets Paul involved with the local chorus at Christmas time, where he meets Dr. Heth, who agrees to help bring Walter home. Maggie's dear friend is Gabe Palazzola, whom she has not married because she realizes he cannot be tied down to one place. Maggie's adjustment to her circumstances contrasts sharply with the continuing dissatisfaction of Mrs. Vickers and Mrs. Cafferty.

MAGNUS THE FAIR (*A Slave's Tale**), young man who loves Helga but cannot win her from her devotion to Hakon. He tries to convince Helga that she will be better off marrying him, since he has the doubtful heritage of a Finnish grandmother, rather than highborn Hakon, but Helga is only hurt by his pointing out that, with her birth as a slave, she will never feel good enough to be Hakon's wife. Magnus is a thinker, able to verbalize his thoughts, and a more interesting character than Hakon is in *A Slave's Tale*. He is killed by the treacherous attack of Hugues's men and dies with Rigmor Ragnvalddaughter, who has loved him and has been bitterly jealous of Helga.

MAGO (*Flight of the Sparrow**), street boy who cares for an assortment of waifs in Paris, including nine-year-old Cigarette. A selfless youth, he shares his food and living space, gives the others courage, and puts himself in danger to protect them. When he steals a bunch of flowers, he takes them to a church as an offering to the Virgin Mary. He philosophically tells Cigarette she must be strong and live for his chance in life as well as her own. Since he is killed trying to protect Cigarette, he seems to be meant to be a sort of Christ-like figure.

MAHER, RAMONA (1934–   ), born in Phoenix, Ariz.; editor, author of plays, poems, and books for children and adults. After receiving her B.A. degree from Texas Christian University, she studied further at the Universities of New Mexico, Washington in Seattle, and Arizona State. She has been editor for the University of Washington Press, the Arizona Historical Foundation, and the Arizona Education Association, helped to found Baleen Press and *Inscape*, and was book review editor for *New Mexico Quarterly*. She has published poems, reviews, and stories in nationally distributed magazines, and many of her poems have been selected for anthologies. Her first novel for young readers, *Their Shining Hour** (Day, 1960), about the battle of the Alamo, received the Spur Award of Western Writers of America. She has also published several mysteries and a book of Eskimo myths. Her other titles, some under the pseudonym Agatha Meyer, include *Secret of the Sundial* (Dodd, 1966), *The Glory Horse* (Coward, 1975), *When Windwagon Smith Came to Westport* (Coward, 1977), and *Alice Yazzie's Year* (Coward, 1977).

MAIME TROTTER (*The Great Gilly Hopkins**), foster mother whose love is even larger than her enormous girth. Uneducated and a poor housekeeper, she seems at first to Gilly* to be a sloppy freak. Her sterling qualities are apparent, however, in her fierce defense of the timid, seemingly retarded, little foster son and her concern for her old, blind black neighbor and are confirmed when she welcomes Gilly back after the girl has stolen money. It is her solid good sense and love that finally give Gilly courage to face her disillusionment with her mother and to accept her new life with her grandmother.

THE MAJESTY OF GRACE (Langton*, Jane, ill. author, Harper, 1961) realistic novel set in the early 1930s in Cleveland, Ohio. Grace Jones, about ten, is convinced that she is a member of the British royal family being raised secretly in modest obscurity and therefore the Future Queen of England. She bases her conviction on two facts: her new neighbor has remarked that she looks like the Princess Elizabeth, and her mother has said that she was not born in the United States. Her older brother, Will, a clever boy who can spell and build radios, thinks she is crazy; her sister, Sophie, is too young to understand; her parents are preoccupied because the job which brought the family to Cleveland has disappeared when the department has been closed down. Family treasures begin disappearing to the pawn shop or being sold. When the Model A Ford, Petunia, is to be sold, Grace, who makes lists (her Six Faults, Seven Awful Things, etc.), institutes Plan A, which involves writing to King George for help and working a little sympathetic magic by doing seven chores. Since this fails and the nice old couple, the Dixons, come to pick up the car, she falls back on Plan B, Step 1 of which is to hide in the rumble seat. She cannot think of a Step 2 by the time the Dixons discover her, but they kindly take her with them to dinner at the home of their daughter, who welcomes her. Eventually, when she is ill and her mother convinces her that as plain Grace Jones she is not a non-entity, she gives up her royal pretentions, and it appears that they may have come round the corner toward prosperity when her father regains his job. This plot line is interspersed with episodes full of amusing incidents: they have a marvelous Fourth of July celebration; the children put on their own circus; Mom feeds a tramp who is a juggler and a sleight-of-hand artist and who rides away on a unicycle; Grace earns a quarter and buys gifts for the whole family from the dime store. The characters are well delineated and believable, particularly Grace herself. The tone is refreshingly genuine, humorous without being condescending, and the picture of the period is accurate in mood and detail. The book was renamed *Her Majesty, Grace Jones* when it was reprinted in paperback. Fanfare.

MALONE, THORNTON (*The Face of Abraham Candle**), talkative, baby-faced man who organizes the expedition to find Indian artifacts at the Mesa Verde but soon shows himself to be lazy, incompetent, and a little foolish. Even his one ability, selling, proves ineffective when he gets only about a tenth of what he expected for their collection of pots. His ideas about the Indian designs embodying the wisdom of ages, which he will translate, prove to be all talk, and Abraham becomes skeptical and even angry at Malone's claim to have known his father well. When Malone marries Abraham's landlady, Pauline* Stent, the household still lacks an adult more competent than young Abraham.

MAMA WILSON (*Ludell**), Mis Wilson, Ludell's grandmother, the elderly black woman who has raised Ludell from infancy. The girl calls her Mama. Ludell is the illegitimate child of Mama's daughter, Dessa. Mama refuses to let Dessa take Ludell to New York City where she works as a live-in domestic. Certain that she raised Dessa too loosely, Mama is quite strict with Ludell. A practical, hardworking, self-respecting woman, Mama is doing her best to bring Ludell up right and instill in her a good sense of values. She is unaware that Willie is romancing Ludell, a circumstance that raises questions about Ludell's ability to break the shackles of her environment and casts her story in relief.

THE MAN IN THE BOX: A STORY FROM VIETNAM (Dunn*, Mary Lois, McGraw, 1968), realistic novel set in a Montagnard village and the surrounding jungle in Vietnam during the 1960s war. Since the death of his father, who was village chief, Chau* Li has been the main support of his mother, his aged grandfather, and two young sisters, but when the Viet Cong put a prisoner, an American soldier who had been badly beaten, into the bamboo box in which his father died, the boy knows he must do something. He creeps close enough to the box, where the prisoner is cramped, unable to stretch out or sit upright, to see that he is bleeding, his feet have been broken, and, to the boy's astonishment, he has grey eyes. Although his mother knows she will never see her son again, she does not try to dissuade him from acting. To his surprise, Chau Li gets help from Ky, an older boy who lives in the jungle, coming to school occasionally, but who admittedly is provided for by the Cong. Ky works out a way to substitute a different box in the driving night rain that has forced the guards to take shelter and helps Chau Li to wheel the box containing the prisoner to a sampan in the swollen river. With great difficulty, Chau Li guides the craft downstream and brings it to shore below a secret cave shown him by his father, where the French had stored supplies. By using ropes like pulleys, with one end attached to the boat driven by the current, he manages to lift the cage to the cave, then cuts the sampan loose. Through the trip, the man has been unconscious and now develops a fever, and Chau Li fears he will die, though earlier he was determined to kill the man rather than let the Cong capture and torture him again. The boy kills a young gibbon and finds food and medicinal plants in the jungle, being careful to cover the traces from the sharp eyes of the Cong soldiers. When the man recovers consciousness, Chau Li tries to get him to drink broth and discovers that his mouth has been horribly burned by having a torch thrust into it. Gradually Chau Li nurses him and learns that his name is David Lee, which Chau Li interprets as "Dah Vid"; David hears his name as "Charlie." Dah Vid is able to use some morphine that is in the French medical kit, but the rest of the medicine is spoiled. To get food, Chau Li makes a long trip over the mountain to a village where he tries to trade wood for food. The only one who listens is a "crazy" woman with one lame foot, who takes him in and sends him off early in the morning with a pack full of food, though her son is a sergeant for the Viet Cong. Chau Li learns that the American soldiers are expected and a few days later falls into the hands of a patrol, but their black leader lets him go, after giving him chocolate and cigarettes. Dah Vid believes this is a group he knows but does not dare to try to get in touch with them. Chau Li whittles him crutches, and they make the long, painful journey to the village where the American soldiers are now in charge. The black captain, Louis, greets him and sends for a helicopter to take them both to DaNang, but the Vietnamese pilot, frightened, pushes the boy out when the Viet Cong shoot from the surrounding jungle. Although the men assure Chau Li that they will get him to DaNang the next day, the Cong attack the village in the night and many are killed, including Louis and the medic. Chau Li finds the hut of the old woman who was kind to him and who did not heed his warning to come into the village, utterly destroyed, but a black-clad Cong soldier tries to lead him into the safety of the woods. Chau Li throws a grenade in his path and kills him before he realizes it is Ky. Stunned, the boy stumbles off, unable to accept what he has done and unable to remember why he wants to get to DaNang. He gets into a sampan and starts the long journey down river, clutching the "amulet" he retrieved when he first stole the torture box, a pair of metal discs that he does not realize are Dah Vid's dog tags. In spite of the open ending, there is hope with their identification Chau Li may be reunited with Dah Vid, who planned to take him back to Texas with him. The grim realities of war are softened only by the idealized but believable relationship between Dah Vid and Chau Li. Although the Americans are pictured as the good side and the Viet Cong as the evil side, there is an attempt to show that the American presence brings disaster to the village and that some members of the Cong, like Ky and the sergeant who is the old woman's son, have some good qualities. The plot is simple but plausible, and Chau Li an appealing character. Choice.

MANOWAR (*Roosevelt Grady**), the orphan boy who becomes Roosevelt Grady's best friend. After his grandfather dies, Manowar falls in with the crew of slippery Digger Burton. A good storyteller, Manowar's spellbinding tales about his travels make him a great favorite with the migrant children. At first, Roosevelt is jealous of him, and he is sure the bigger boy's exciting stories are lies, in particular the one about geese weeding cotton fields in California. Manowar has treasures he has collected in his travels, a Navajo necklace, a tin Christmas star, a piece of petrified wood, a wooden horse his grandfather carved for him, and a book, *The Luck of Roaring Camp*, with which his grandfather taught him to read. Digger Burton, for whom he is camp handyboy, does not treat Manowar well. When Digger dumps out Manowar's treasures and breaks the horse, Manowar quits him and runs away to join the Gradys. Mr. Elliott then makes him handyboy at his camp where the Gradys now live.

THE MAN WITHOUT A FACE (Holland*, Isabelle, Lippincott, 1972), realistic novel set on the Atlantic seaboard not far from New York City in the late 1900s in which the protagonist faces problems connected with a broken home, sibling rivalry, school, and his developing sexuality. Charles Norstadt, 14, who tells his story, feels lonely and alienated from school and family. He looks upon St. Matthew's boarding school as a way of escaping increasingly intolerable everyday living circumstances and hopes one day to become an airplane pilot. In particular, he feels hemmed in by women. He thinks his four-times-divorced mother smothers him with questions and that his beautiful, bright, older half-sister, Gloria*, 17, continually puts him down. After he fails, through laziness, the entrance exams to St. Matthew's, his younger sister, Meg, 11, sympathetically suggests he ask Justin* McLeod to coach him for a retake. An older man whose face is horribly scarred, Justin is a writer who lives by himself and has little to do with neighbors. He agrees to help Charles provided Charles abides by his rules, which include a strict schedule for instruction and study. Reluctantly, Charles agrees, willing to accept the means in order to achieve the desired end of getting away, especially from Gloria. Charles's confidence in Justin's ability to help him grows when he discovers that Justin had once taught at St. Matthew's. After a shaky start, a deep friendship develops between the two. They go hiking, riding, and swimming, and the summer becomes what Charles calls his time of the "golden cocoon." Occasionally, he resents Justin's authoritarian ways, but mostly he appreciates his teacher's firmness, recognizes that the man cares about him, and comes to think of Justin almost as the father he never knew. At the same time, he is puzzled and disturbed by the intensity of his feelings for Justin. When, at summer's end, his mother decides to marry a family friend, Barry Rumbolt, and his cherished cat, Moxie, is cruelly slain, Charles has a homosexual experience with

Justin. A few months later, Charles is at St. Matthew's, Justin dies of a heart attack while on a visit to Scotland, and Charles is beginning to accept the loss of his dearest friend and to regard Barry as a friend and potential confidant as well as a stepfather. Although the plot is overburdened with topical matters, Charles's reporting of the summer's events conveys the exaggerated emotion and confusion typical of his age. Gloria is overdrawn, but that, too, seems appropriate to Charles's negative vantage point. Meg is a mite too sympathetic, perceptive, and articulate even for a highly intelligent eleven-year-old. The author arouses the reader's curiosity about Justin expertly, but the conclusion seems contrived and flat. Nor is it ever clear why Charles has never been told about what happened to his father. Fanfare.

MARCHERS FOR THE DREAM (Carlson*†, Natalie Savage, ill. Alvin Smith, Harper, 1969), realistic novel set mostly in Washington, D.C. during May and June, 1968, dealing with the protest march of the poor in the Civil Rights movement. When the Jackson family in a Massachusetts city must move from their run-down apartment house which is being torn down, they can find nowhere to go within their budget, no apartment or house open to rental by blacks. A widow, Mrs. Jackson supports her daughter, Bethany, 11, and Bethany's great-grandmother, Birdie Jackson. Her older daughter, Arva Williams, 22, is angry and bitter, one type of modern black, but the grandmother counsels patience and kindness. To the surprise of all of them, Birdie decides to join the Poor People's March on Washington, to go and live in the tent community by the Lincoln Memorial reflecting pool known as Resurrection City. To keep track of her great-grandmother, and because there is nowhere else for her to stay, Bethany accompanies the old lady. There they are assigned to a plywood tent and meet a variety of other protesters, including Shad Haphey, a former street-gang member turned marshal, and Ruby Nichols, 13, a veteran of Civil Rights protest arrests in the South. With Ruby, Bethany helps in the day care center, organizes a Kids' Freedom March, and joins a protest demonstration at the Longworth Building. They survive the terrible conditions when rain turns Resurrection into a mud hole and the dining tent caves in, they see the Reverend Abernathy and Mrs. Coretta King, and they join the big march on "Junteenth Day." When they return to their home city, they have a plan: they will have their own protest march to get a new place to live. Bethany's mother and Arva join, with Arva's two children, and as they march around city hall, sympathizers join them and a newspaper runs a story. At the end of the second day, a builder offers them a neat, small house, though he worries that they might have trouble from the neighbors. Sustained and encouraged by their experiences in Washington, they take the house and are confident they will stay. The Poor People's March is of interest historically, but the story is so artificial and the solution so contrived that it does not work as literature. Characters are types, the plot is predictable, and the tone is moralistic. Choice.

MARIANNE PAGET (*Ransom**), one of the youths who have been kidnapped, she dislikes her stepfather, Rod Donavan, intensely. Since her mother's remarriage, she has stubbornly refused to accept him and has remained steadfastly loyal to her real father, the reader learns via flashbacks, cutting Rod out of her life every chance she can. Ironically, if she had not been so stubborn and had accepted his offer of a ride home from school, she would not have been on the bus when it was hijacked. In scene switches during the story, the reader learns that her real father is a self-centered man, shiftless toward his family. He fails even to respond to Marianne's mother's pleas for help in arranging for Marianne's release, simply because he is too busy with his own life to be bothered. Rod, on the other hand, doggedly works to get the money to free her. At the end, Marianne realizes how Rod has put his own life in danger for her, changes her mind about him, and gladly prepares to ride home with him.

MARIETTA HASTINGS (*The Bully of Barkham Street**), Martin's older sister, with whom he has been on the outs, teasing and picking at her whenever he can, out of resentment for what he takes as his parents' partiality for her. When she complains to him about the restrictions girls must put up with, Martin begins to think about things from her point of view. She arranges for their mother to attend the assembly at which he plays the bugle.

MARIE WESTERN (*Behind the Magic Line**), mother of Dozie and ten other black children. A strong woman, she supports the family while her husband, Josh*, is absent, gets off welfare by cleaning for white families, cares for old, sick neighbors, sings to her children, and forgives Josh without question when he reappears. While the problems she copes with are realistic, she is a romanticized, warm mother figure.

MARINA (*The Horse Talker**), Blanco's high-spirited, vivacious, dark-haired daughter, about Lan's age. She travels with Blanco's mustang crew and does the work of a mustanger, helping with the drives, the roping, and the hunting. Although she enjoys making friends with the colonel's daughter at the fort, wearing a pretty dress, and being the center of attention at the dance, she has no desire to remain at the fort. She enjoys life with her father. It is learned late in the story that the Inglés did not rescue her from Comanches when she was a small child as he said he did. He killed her mother, and then he brought the child to her father, concocting the Comanche story to put Blanco in his debt and control him. Marina is the apple of Blanco's eye.

MARIO (*The Little Fishes**), little brother of Anna*, who is first seen offering to eat dirt if the officers will give him a coin. Though he is cared for by his sister and by Guido* in their travels through wartorn Italy, he is not a survivor and dies of starvation and fever in the monastery.

MARIO BELLINI (*The Cricket in Times Square**), boy who works weekends at his parents' newsstand in the subway station in New York's Times Square. An earnest youth, he persuades his mother to let him keep Chester* Cricket for luck, after he finds him under some grimy newspapers in the corner next to the stairway leading up to Forty-Second Street. He makes Chester a matchbox house and later buys him a Chinese cricket cage. His hopes for luck are realized when Chester brings financial success to the stand through his playing of both popular and classical music.

MARSHALL DAVIS (*The Noonday Friends**), Franny's beloved little brother, to whom she teaches numbers and letters when she sits with him after school. Occasionally naughty, Marshall is mostly a bright, happy little fellow, who loves the games and rhymes Franny makes up for him. The loving, optimistic side of Franny's nature is revealed through her relationship with Marshall. She likes to dance and sing and share her dreams with him. He introduces Mr.* Davis and Francisco and thus makes it possible for Francisco to get a job. Marshall's greatest wish is to stay up all night, and, in a charming episode, his parents give him his wish for his birthday. He lasts until five in the morning, by which time everyone else has given out.

MARSHALL ROSS (*The Egypt Game**), Melanie* Ross's little brother, April* Hall's friend, and one of the first children to play the Egypt game in the old Professor's* back yard. Marshall is a self-assured little fellow as long as he has his stuffed octopus, Security. Quiet and observant, he is the only one of the children who knows that someone sometimes watches them while they are playing, but he does not tell anybody about it.

MARTIN FLOWER (*Signpost to Terror**), eleven-year-old hostage seized in a bank robbery and abandoned with the telephone company jeep on a little-used fire trail in the Adirondacks. Fat and lazy, Martin is on his way home from a summer camp when he becomes the chance victim, and he is dressed in city clothes, including new shoes that soon blister his feet. Although he is terrified of being recaptured, he forces himself to follow Gail Schaeffer up the mountain after he sees Lewis* Phillips trailing her, and it is his yell at the critical time that startles the robber into falling from the fire tower. Gail's statement to Frank that Martin saved her life marks a turning point for him, giving him pride that eventually changes him into a more active, likable boy.

MARTY (*When No One Was Looking**), tough, driving tennis coach for Kathy* Bardy, who was herself a tennis champion, once beating Maureen Connolly at Wimbledon. An acid-tongued old maid, Marty is not loved by the staff of the country club or by most of her students, and she insults, pushes, and rails at Kathy in an effort to achieve through the girl the wealth and esteem that came to tennis after her day. She lets herself be suspected of Ruth's murder and suspended from the club until she is sure Kathy was not herself guilty.

THE MARVELOUS MISADVENTURES OF SEBASTIAN (Alexander*, Lloyd, Dutton, 1970), comic fantasy set in the imaginary eighteenth-century European realm of Hamelin-Loring. An impulsive, good-natured scamp, Sebastian is fired from his position as fourth fiddler to Baron Purn-Hessel and takes to the road to look for another position. His fiddle is smashed when he rescues a white cat with blue eyes that two townsmen propose to hang as a witch. The cat, Presto*, becomes his faithful traveling companion and occasionally influences the course of things. A little later, Sebastian helps out a skinny youth who turns out to be the Princess Isabella* in disguise. She is fleeing from the Regent, who is trying to force her to marry him. Sebastian, now showing a more sobered attitude and a greater sense of responsibility, sets out to help the Princess achieve safety. The action then swirls across the landscape through a series of outlandish and preposterous situations and hairbreadth escapes, as Sebastian and the Princess just manage to keep ahead of the Regent's cutthroats, among them a particularly murderous one disguised as a barber, or leech. The two fugitives briefly join Quicksilver's Gallimaufry-Theatricus troupe, where Sebastian acquires a fiddle that plays astonishingly moving music with little skill or effort on his part and Isabella dances with a bear, and go for a cross-country ride in a balloon which deposits them, to their immense consternation, in the capital city of Loringhold itself. Eventually Sebastian ends up in the dungeon of the Glorietta Palace, from which he is rescued through the efforts of Nicholas, a chubby, unassuming man of many devices, who turns out to be the popular, but obscure, revolutionary leader, Captain Freeling. Nicholas has quietly been organizing resistance to the increasingly corrupt and tyrannical government of the Regent. Sebastian blunders into the Grand Ballroom, where for safety he joins the Regent's orchestra. His music, played on the magical fiddle, so moves courtiers, guards, and musicians that they cannot stop dancing and mysteriously puts a convenient end to the Regent's life. Isabella's experiences have given her a new understanding of the responsibilities of a ruler, and she sets about righting wrongs in her realm and starts by making Nicholas her first minister. Sebastian's remarkable fiddle is accidentally smashed to smithereens, but he acquires a new one, and rejecting the Princess's offer of an easy life in the palace, he sets out to become a "noble among fiddlers." Like Isabella herself, he has learned that everyone must seek his or her own truth. The emphasis is on plot, which is highly convoluted, filled with incidents, action, and many surprising twists and turns. It makes little effort to command belief, the purpose being simply to afford fast-moving escapist entertainment. Characters and incidents are flat and underdeveloped, and the conclusion is abrupt and unclear. The style is witty, energetic, and distinctive. Choice; Fanfare; National Book Winner.

MARY CALL LUTHER (*Where the Lilies Bloom**; *Trial Valley**), serious, fiercely independent, resourceful second daughter in the Luther family. Before Roy Luther dies, he lays upon her the responsibility for his funeral and for keeping the family together. Mary Call is astute, observant, often judgmental, and too conscious of appearances. She is absolutely determined to preserve the family dignity and good name. She is unyielding in opposing Kiser* Pease's suit for Devola's* hand, even though she is quick to accept the help he gives the Luthers in his efforts to win Devola. It is Mary Call's idea that the children earn money by wildcrafting, and it's her warmth and strength that draw Jack* Parsons to their house. As she grows older, she begins to yearn for a life of her own and for something beyond her limited environment in Trial Valley, but her sense of responsiblity and love for them bind her to her family.

MARY ROSE GANZ (*Veronica Ganz**), Veronica's eleven-year-old, younger sister. A dreamy child, Mary Rose yearns for pretty things, but the Depression is on, and the family cannot afford them. Mary Rose is sure that her and Veronica's father, from whom their mother is divorced, is wealthy, will take them back with him to his ranch in the West, and will provide lavishly for them there. She is upset when she learns that their father will not visit and that the reason he is not coming is that he doesn't have the money. At first, Mrs. Petronski is very impatient with Mary Rose's despair, but she, too, has a dreamy side, and she really loves her children although she is often harsh with them. She supplements the Christmas money Mary Rose's father sends with enough to buy the girl some of the pretty bedroom furnishings she wants so badly. Veronica considers Mary Rose a fink but loves her anyway. The flatly characterized, feminine, and quieter Mary Rose is a foil for Veronica.

MASSA PIERCE BUTLER (*Bimby**), a real person, owner of the plantation among the Georgia coastal islands on which Bimby is a slave. In the story, Butler appears as a well-dressed, polite gentleman, a "good massa" to his slaves. He is shocked by Jesse's* death and moved by Bimby's grief but continues on with his picnic anyway, even though he shows annoyance at the callous behavior and insensitive attitudes of his guests. He enjoys the good life and has incurred huge debts "gamblin' and losin' up north," according to Jesse. Butler is an unsympathetic figure, in the novel the epitome of the Southern slaveholder, selfish, self-indulgent, and only somewhat bothered by the ramifications for the slaves of his decisions and actions. His ex-wife, Miss* Fanny, on the other hand, felt that slavery was evil, and this led to their divorce.

MASTER ANTHONY (*Sophia Scrooby Preserved**), Italian adventurer of many words and mercurial temperament, who, calling himself Signor Antonio, travels about the Connecticut countryside painting portraits and exhibiting his pet tiger. Squire Scrooby hires him to teach music and other school subjects to Prudence and Pansy. The Scroobys become very fond of him, since he is a faithful, kind, and happy person. He is an interesting, if flat, character.

THE MASTER PUPPETEER (Paterson*, Katherine, ill. Haru Wells, Crowell, 1976), historical novel set in the twelfth-century feudal Japanese city of Osaka. Jiro*, son of the puppet maker Hanji, starving in the famine year, does the unpardonable in accepting the invitation to eat when he and his father deliver a puppet to Yoshida, master puppeteer of the Hanaza Theater, and when the puppeteer praises his spirit and offers him a place in the theater, he does the unthinkable of going without his parents' permission. Afraid of the severe Yoshida, he goes to the blind old chanter, Okada, a more kindly figure, who accepts him. In the strict hierarchy of the theater, he is below the other apprentices, Kinshi*, Yoshida's son, mean Wada, fat, good-natured Minoru, and Teiji, who stutters, but with the help of Kinshi he is able to survive the initial trials and even learns the intricate manipulation of the feet, the first step in becoming a real puppeteer. As times become harder in the city, Jiro has several major worries: he learns that his father has lung disease and his mother, Isako, has taken him to the country; he realizes that the Robin Hood figure, the bandit Saburo*, has some connection with the theater and suspects that Yoshida may be Saburo, and he worries over the brutal way Yoshida treats Kinshi, who has become a friend and almost an idol to Jiro. When a roving band of rioters and looters called ronins come to the theater, he is shocked to recognize his mother among them and tries to devise a way to help her, though she has always seemed to despise him. Kinshi, who feels an obligation to help the ronins, offers to try to find Jiro's mother, and Jiro, in an effort to keep Kinshi off the dangerous streets, goes to Okada, telling him of the assistant magistrate's sword which he has found and which he thinks proves Yoshida's role as Saburo, but when he goes to get it, Okada himself confronts him and admits to being Saburo, with Yoshida and the others merely his puppets. Believing that Okada means to kill him, Jiro escapes and roams through the city on a wild night hunting for Kinshi, only to find his father not ill but a member of Saburo's band and his mother arrested with Kinshi, who has lost a hand in her defense. Jiro secures their release and takes them to the Hanaza, where, instead of the certain death he expects, he is accepted by Yoshida, who agrees to let his son work directly under Okada now that he cannot hope to manipulate puppets. The re-creation of the manners and mores of an unfamiliar culture, as well as the dramatic presentation of information about the puppet theaters, is skillfully woven into a story with strong characterization and a fast-paced plot. The complexities of loyalties are not oversimplified, and Jiro's ambivalent feelings toward his mother and the masters of the theater are convincing. Boston Globe Winner; Fanfare; National Book Winner.

MATHIN (*The Blue Sword**), older king's Rider who trains Harry* Crewe in the arts of riding the marvelous Hill horses and in swordsplay and other martial skills. He is close-mouthed but patient with her and at last unbends enough to tell her something of his own background, how he was a younger son of a horse breeder with a restlessness that led him to seek a place with the king's select guard. When Harry succeeds at the trials, he is extremely pleased. In the battle against the invading Northerners, he is terribly wounded but Harry's *kelar*, a magic power, heals him.

MATHIS, SHARON BELL (1937–   ), born in Atlantic City, N.J.; teacher, writer. She grew up in the Bedford Stuyvesant district of Brooklyn and is a graduate of Morgan State College in Baltimore, Md., and received her master's degree in library science from Catholic University in Washington, D.C. Among her honors are being writer in residence at Howard University, the Council for Interracial Books for Children Award in 1969, and the American Library Association Coretta Scott King Award in 1974 for a biography of Ray Charles. She has worked as an interviewer in Children's Hospital, D.C., and has taught in elementary and junior high school special education classes in Washington. She has also written a regular magazine column for *Ebony, Jr.* All her books consider some aspect of the black experience in America. *Sidewalk Story** (Viking, 1971) concerns an urban eviction; *The Hundred Penny Box** (Viking, 1975) is a brief story of the love between a little boy and a very old woman.

MATTHEW PULASKI (*Rain of Fire**), older brother of Steve*, who has spent a year in the occupation army in Japan where he saw the horrors of Hiroshima and who has returned disturbed and morose. Before the war, he was a fond companion to his brother, telling him fantastic stories and playing with him. In his efforts to explain the shame he feels for his country's part in the devastation of Japan, he is accused of being a coward and a traitor. Not only his neighbors in the mill town fail to understand him, but also his father, who is impatient that he doesn't get to work, and his mother, who is solicitous but baffled by his attitude. Finally, his injured little brother begins to share some of his horror of war, and that provides a hope that he may recover.

MATT HOLLOWELL (*The Sign of the Beaver**), Matthew Hollowell, youth of thirteen who survives in the wilderness of Maine through the help and generosity of local Penobscot Indians. Naive and imprudent at first, he learns from experience, observation, and Attean's* instruction in wilderness survival. A well-mannered boy, he always treats Saknis*, Attean's grandfather and also Matt's benefactor, with the respect and deference due the old man. When Matt realizes that he cannot save Attean's dog from the trap by himself, he bravely makes his way to the village to seek help from Attean's grandmother, who, Matt knows, hates whites. She charitably tends his wounded hand before allowing him and Marie, Attean's sister, to go back and rescue the dog. Attean often makes Matt feel uncomfortable, both by behavior and speech, and Matt realizes how dependent he is upon this Indian boy who has good reason to hate whites and whose questions about why whites do as they do he is hard put to answer. Matt matures in judgment and behavior predictably, but credibly, as the story progresses.

MATT MUSTAZZA (*Portrait of Ivan**), the painter whom Ivan's father commissions to paint Ivan's portrait. His interest in Ivan as a person, his joy in living, and his liking for his work broaden the boy's perspectives on life, help him look beyond his restrictive home environment, and spur his curiosity about the people in his family, his housekeeper, and his uncle.

MAUREEN BEEBE (*Misty of Chincoteague*†; *Stormy, Misty's Foal**), warmhearted and emotional girl, younger sister of Paul*. She is greatly moved by the beauty of the horses and works just as hard as Paul to accumulate enough money to buy the mare, Phantom, and her foal, Misty. When Paul wins the right to ride Phantom in the big race, she wills them to win, imagining herself flying along with them down the track. In *Stormy*, she works just as hard as Paul to make Misty comfortable and to get the stall ready for Misty and Stormy. She often regrets being a girl and complains to Grandma* Beebe. She feels girls are forced to miss excitement and fun just because they are girls. Grandma Beebe understands and consoles her.

MAURICE'S ROOM (Fox*, Paula, ill. Ingrid Fetz, Macmillan, 1966), very short realistic novel of family life set in a large city at an indefinite time but probably in the late 1900s. Maurice, 9, is a collector. His room is crammed with things that are important to him but that his parents call junk. They are baffled by his strong collecting impulse and have considered moving to the country to try to get him interested in something else. Maurice's uncle loans the family his dog, Patsy, hoping that Maurice will decide to acquire a dog instead of more "junk." When Patsy raids his treasures, Maurice becomes too ill to go to school and decides he must stand guard over his treasures. His parents misinterpret the situation, conclude he has developed a phobia for school and too great a liking for the dog, and get rid of Patsy. Then Maurice's mother insists he learn to play the trumpet, hoping music will divert him from collecting. On the way to his first trumpet lesson, Maurice and his friend, Jacob, pass a junkyard where Maurice spies some old headlights. Although he fails to acquire the headlights, he gets rid of the trumpet by leaving it in the junkman's office. Although angry about the trumpet, his parents next try to extend Maurice's interests by presenting him with a large and expensive toy sailboat. Maurice and Jacob wreck the boat on the lake in the park while they are salvaging some old bedsprings. The wreck prompts the long-threatened move to the country. Maurice packs his collection in a steamer trunk which topples off when the van rounds a bend. Even though Maurice is not upset about the loss, his father tells him he can start a new collection when they arrive at the farm. In the old barn, Maurice and Jacob see marvelous potential in discards for starting a new collection of valuables. Unless taken as satire on contemporary parenting, in particular, the book is preposterous. The plot violates logic, and the characters are thoroughly unconvincing. Maurice is entirely too eccentric, and the behavior of the parents is utterly ridiculous. Mr. Klenk, the genial, pipe-smoking apartment house janitor, who gives Maurice a huge, smelly teddy bear and who takes Maurice's compulsion to collect in stride, is a good figure, the only sensible person in the book. There is some humor, language is within the reach of eight-to-nine-year-olds, and the clear and vivid detail with which Maurice's room is described makes it easy to visualize the situation. Numerous black and white sketches help to tell the story. Choice.

MAVI (*Dragonsong**), mother of Menolly* and wife of Yanus*, Sea Holder at Half-Circle, and as such the organizer of the women's work in the Hold. Although more sympathetic to Menolly than Yanus is, Mavi is more interested in keeping her husband from being angry than in supporting her daughter, and she deliberately keeps Menolly busy at tasks that will prevent her from harping. When the girl cuts her hand badly, Mavi lets it heal with a scar that draws it together, thinking that it will be too crippled to allow Menolly to play again.

MAXIE HAMMERMAN (*The Pushcart War**), called the Pushcart King, because he is the leader of the some five hundred pushcart peddlers in New York City. Maxie repairs broken pushcarts and gives friendly advice to the peddlers. During the pea-shooting part of the conflict, he maintains a battle map on which he indicates with different colored stickpins the precise location of all flats achieved ("tires killed") by the peddlers. Later, he wins sixty thousand dollars gambling against The Three* on the night they had planned to kidnap him. With the sixty thousand dollars, he institutes a war chest to finance the fighting. Maxie's feat is considered one of the more brilliant achievements of the war.

MAZER, NORMA FOX (1931–   ), born in New York City; author mostly of realistic novels for adolescents. She grew up in Glen Falls, N.Y., in the Adirondack Mountains, attended Antioch College and Syracuse University, and has written plays for television and stories for such magazines as *Jack and Jill*, *Ingenue*, *Child Life*, and *Redbook*. Among her novels for young people are *A Figure of Speech** (Delacorte, 1973), National Book Award finalist about a girl and her grandfather, whose family puts him in a nursing home; *Saturday, the Twelfth of October** (Delacorte, 1975), chosen for the Lewis Carroll Shelf, about a girl who travels back in time to a pre-historic Stone Age society; *Taking Terri Mueller** (Avon, 1981), winner of the Edgar Allan Poe Award, about a girl whose father has kidnapped her from his divorced wife; and *The Solid Gold Kid* (Delacorte, 1977), about a youth who unwittingly assists with his own kidnapping, written with her husband, Harry Mazer, also a novelist for young people. For younger readers she has published *I, Trissy* (Delacorte, 1971), and her book of short stories, *Dear Bill, Remember Me?* (Delacorte, 1976), received the

Christopher Award. The Mazers live in the Pompey Hills of central New York State.

MCBROOM TELLS THE TRUTH (Fleischman*, Sid, ill. Kurt Werth, Norton, 1966), short fantasy in tall-tale style set in Iowa in the early part of the twentieth century in which Josh McBroom looks back upon a summer's difficulties with an overly productive farm and with the greedy farmer who tries to get it away from him. Finding their stony Connecticut farm unprofitable, Josh, his wife, Melissa, and their eleven red-headed children, Willjillhesterchesterpeterpollytimtommarylarryandlittleclarinda, pile into their old Franklin car and head west. In Iowa, they encounter tall, scrawny, sharpdealing Hector Jones, who sells them eighty acres for ten dollars, all the money McBroom has. The McBrooms soon discover that instead of eighty linear acres, Jones has sold them one acre of very deep bog. All is not lost, however, for extraordinarily hot weather sets in, evaporating the bog water and leaving McBroom with soil so rich it produces crops before McBroom has finished planting his field. Planting and harvesting three or four crops of vegetables in a single day keep the McBrooms very busy and soon put them on the road to wealth. The unexpected prosperity of the McBrooms arouses the envy of Heck Jones, who schemes to get the land back. After neighbors help the McBrooms eradicate the weeds Jones plants, Jones is attacked by a rapidly growing watermelon and then whisked away by a huge banana squash, leaving the McBrooms to enjoy the amazing productivity of their land. McBroom's manner of speaking is congenially conversational and tongue-in-cheek, and the inventive, outrageous incidents deliberately strain belief and produce a rollicking good yarn. One of a series about McBroom. Lewis Carroll.

MCCAFFREY, ANNE (1926–   ), born in Cambridge, Mass.; author of a series of fantasies about the dragons of Pern, a distant planet some time in the future. She is a graduate of Radcliffe College and studied meteorology at the University of Dublin, Ireland. She worked as a copywriter in New York City and as a professional stage director for several groups in Wilmington, Del. Her first dragon book, *Dragonflight* (Ballantine, 1968) won both the Hugo and the Nubula science fiction awards and was followed by *Dragonquest* (Ballantine, 1971). Both these books and some later in the series were published for adults, but *Dragonsong** (Atheneum, 1976), *Dragonsinger* (Atheneum, 1977), and *Dragondrums* (Atheneum, 1979), sharing the same setting and many of the same characters as the earlier books, were published for the juvenile market. The books for young people, though not as complex as the others in the series, are in some ways better novels, with stronger focus and in some ways better novels, with stronger focus and more fully developed characterization. She has lived in County Wicklow, Ireland, in a home known as "Dragonhold."

MCGRAW†, ELOISE JARVIS (1915–   ), born in Houston, Tex.; artist, novelist. She is a graduate of Principia College in Elsah, Ill., and studied at Museum Art School in Portland, Oreg. In 1942–1943, she taught painting at Oklahoma City University and has since taught at Lewis and Clark College in Portland and at Portland State University. With her husband, writer William Corbin* McGraw, she has owned and farmed a filbert orchard in the Willamette Valley, Oregon. Her novels for young people mostly have historical settings, including *Moccasin Trail*† (Coward, 1952), a story of the settlement of Oregon, and *The Golden Goblet** (Coward, 1961), set in ancient Egypt, both Newbery honor books. More recently she has turned to the contemporary period as in *A Really Weird Summer** (Atheneum, 1977), a psychological mystery which won the Edgar Allan Poe Award, and in *Hideaway* (Atheneum, 1983), a story of a twelve-year-old runaway. All her books are notable for well-developed characters and suspenseful action.

M. C. HIGGINS (*M. C. Higgins, the Great**), black boy of southern Ohio, who rides a forty-foot pole propped up by junk in his yard on Sarah's* Mountain, a pole given him as a prize by his father for swimming the Ohio River three miles away. M. C. is awakened to his first romantic feelings by Lurhetta Outlaw, a girl camping on the mountain, whom he first meets by jumping on her in the dark and cutting her back with his knife. Intelligent and responsible, he has ambivalent feelings toward his stubborn father, admiration for his strength but resentment at Jones's refusal to acknowledge the danger of the strip-mining spoil, which sits precariously above their house, threatening to crash down as it absorbs moisture from the rain, and at his suspicions of the neighboring "witchy," six-fingered Killburns, whose son Ben is M. C.'s friend. Finally putting aside his dreams of leaving, M. C. starts to build a wall behind the house to which Jones contributes the tombstone of his grandmother, Sarah, the runaway slave who first settled there.

M. C. HIGGINS, THE GREAT (Hamilton*, Virginia, Macmillan, 1974), realistic novel of a black family who live on Sarah's* Mountain in southern Ohio. Sitting on a forty-foot flagpole held up by a pile of junk in their yard, M. C.* (Mayo Cornelius) Higgins, 13, swings with precarious balance, surveys what is happening on the mountain, and keeps his eye on his younger brothers, Lennie Pool and Harper, and his little sister, Macie Pearl, swimming in a lake some distance away. M. C. is concerned that the spoil piled above the house after the top of the mountain has been strip-mined for coal will crash down and destroy their home. This fear is reinforced by the observations of a traveling folksong collector, James K. Lewis, whom M. C. expects will, after recording the beautiful voice of his mother, Banina, make records and move the family to fame in Nashville. M. C.'s father, stubborn Jones, refuses to acknowledge the danger. M. C. is also suspicious of newcomers, like Lurhetta Outlaw, a girl older than M. C., who is traveling alone and camping on the mountain, and of old-timers, like Ben Killburn, M. C.'s friend from a strange family who live on nearby Kill's* Mound and are considered "witchy" because of their near-white skin, reddish hair, and six-fingered hands. Lurhetta scorns M. C.'s fear of the Killburns and lures him to visit their strange community where the houses are netted together by a huge "spider web" on which the children play, suspended above their gardens. Awakened to action at last, M. C. resolves his problem of whether or not to leave the mountain by starting the construction of a protective wall above the house, made of earth, of the junk in the yard, and of the tombstone of Great-grandmother Sarah, for whom the mountain is named. Despite some vivid writing, particularly in the descriptions of the family singing and the natural features of the mountain, the book is unconvincing, with too many elements that are hard to believe realistically—the pole that defies physics, the wandering girl who is friendly despite being literally attacked by M. C., the Killburn settlement, even the value of M. C.'s solution to the problem of the spoil heap. Newbery Winner.

MCKINLEY, (JENNIFER CAROLYN) ROBIN (1952–   ), born in Warren, Ohio; author of fictionalized versions of stories from the oral tradition and heroic fantasy. Since her father was in the navy, McKinley lived in a number of different areas as a child. She was graduated from Gould Academy in Bethel, Maine, attended Dickinson College, Carlisle, Pa., and was graduated from Bowdoin College in Brunswick, Maine. She has worked in publishing and on a horse farm. Her first book, *Beauty** (Harper, 1978), is a retelling of the old story, "Beauty and the Beast." *The Door in the Hedge* (Greenwillow, 1981) is a collection of four stories, two borrowed from Grimm and two originals, "The Stolen Princess" and "The Hunting of the Hind." She has written that she loves "old fashioned British Empire adventure novels by writers like P. C. Wren and A.W.W. Mason and H. Rider Haggard and especially Rudyard Kipling." This influence shows in *The Blue Sword** (Greenwillow, 1982), a fantasy set in an imaginary country of Damar, which has colonial military outposts very much like the northern part of Kipling's India. Her Newbery Medal–winning *The Hero and the Crown* (Greenwillow, 1984), is described as a "prequel," a novel telling what happened many generations before the time of *The Blue Sword*. Both have strong female protagonists.

MCKOWN, ROBIN, born in Denver, Colo.; columnist, literary agent, author of books for teenagers, both fiction and non-fiction. She received her B.A. degree from the University of Colorado and did graduate work at Northwestern University School of Drama and at the University of Illinois. In New York she worked in sales promotion, wrote radio scripts and a column on books and authors for the Book of the Month Club and worked as a literary agent. During World War II she did volunteer work for a New York committee that helped widows and orphans of the French Resistance, and in this work she toured France for six weeks immediately after the end of the war. She returned later and lived for three years in the mining district of northeastern France, the setting for both *Patriot of the Underground* (Putnam, 1964) and *Janine** (Messner, 1960), winner of the Child Study Award.

MEEK, JOE (*Half-Breed**), an actual historical figure, trader and United States marshal in Oregon Territory. In the novel, he is a staunch friend of Hardy and Aunt* Rhody Hollingshead. He is married to an Indian woman, Virginia, with whom Aunt Rhody becomes friends, and his sons, Courtney and Hiram, also half-breeds, become Hardy's good friends. Self-sufficient and practical, they show Hardy how to prepare the soil and plant, and they convince him that a good future awaits him in this area where Rhody has a claim and where he can go to school. Because of them, Hardy elects to remain among the whites.

THE MEEKER MASSACRE (Overholser*, Wayne D., and Lewis Patten*, Cowles, 1969), historical fiction detailing the dispute between the Utes of the White River Indian Agency in northwestern Colorado and their stubborn Indian agent, Nathan C. Meeker, in the fall of 1879. Through the eyes of Dave Madden, 17, a boy who has come from Greeley to work at the agency, the reader sees the events that lead up to the tragic confrontation. Meeker is trying to turn the proud, roving, horse-loving Utes into farmers, knowing that only by showing they are productively using the land will they be able to hold it from the greedy whites, despite the treaty guaranteeing them the right. In an effort to prepare the land for crops and to discourage their horse-raising and betting, Meeker has plowed up their racetrack and has sent Shad Price, a man with a young wife and two young children, to plow up the large horse pasture. As Dave takes Shad his lunch, the first shots ring out from snipers, who hit the plow and force Shad and Dave to dive into the weeds. Although Dave bravely goes to unhitch the horses, no one dares to retrieve the plow, and the tension increases. Most of the white men deplore Meeker's stubbornness, as does Meeker's daughter, Josie, who runs the boarding house, and Tono, Dave's Ute friend. When Meeker tells Chief Johnson, his strongest supporter among the Utes, that they should shoot their beloved ponies, the furious Indian manhandles the agent and accuses him of sending lies to Washington. Tensions mount until Meeker sends a wire asking for troops to protect the agency personnel. Tono warns Dave that this will make violence erupt, but Meeker won't listen. The fiery younger Ute leader, Chief Jack, threatens to attack Major Thornburgh, who is leading a small force, if he crosses Mill Creek. Meeker tells Dave to get Tono and ride out with a warning and a proposal that Meeker and the top Ute, Chief Douglas, will meet Thornburgh on the road. Dave finds Tono helping to dismantle his family's lodge, a sure sign of trouble, showing that the women and children are being evacuated, but the young Indian agrees to go with Dave. They are shortly joined by a quarrelsome Ute, Badger, who can't read and won't believe Dave's story of what is in the letter he carries. Knowing that Badger will probably kill Dave, Tono holds him at rifle point until Dave can get away, despite knowing that he will be punished by his own people for siding with the whites. Dave finds that he has arrived too late, that the soldiers are already under siege, but he rides madly through the Indians and delivers his message to the second in command, since Thornburgh is already dead. For two weeks the handful of soldiers are penned up by the Indians, who try to burn them out and keep them from getting more food and water, until reinforcements come, first a single company of black soldiers from Middle Park and at last a force from Rawlins big enough to drive off the Utes. One chapter switches point of view to Tono, who rides back to the agency, hoping to warn the whites, only to see that the massacre has begun, and who foresees that this will be the excuse to strip the Utes of their land. In the end Dave returns to the agency with the soldiers and helps bury the dead. An authors' note tells that the women and children survived, having been taken captive and treated well. The events themselves are exciting enough to keep the book interesting, though it seems more fictionalized history than a novel. Dave is adequate for his part, but the main interest is on the conflict of cultures with stubborn but well-meaning Meeker clashing with the proud Utes. Spur.

MEETING WITH A STRANGER (Bradley*, Duane, ill. Harper Johnson, Lippincott, 1964), realistic novel set in Ethiopia in the mid twentieth century. Although he has been treated in a hospital run by foreigners, "ferangis," after an accident, Teffera, an Ethiopian boy, does not trust their motives or their manners. His uncle, Bekele, who lives in a city, has taken up many foreign ways, but his father, Paulos, points out that historically foreigners have brought trouble and sorrow to their country. Beset by twin difficulties of failing eyesight and a weakening flock of sheep, Paulos finally takes Bekele's advice to go to the hospital in Addis Ababa and leave his sheep in Teffera's care. A ferangi from America, Sam Jones, arrives in the village, saying he will help the people improve their sheep. Deeply suspicious, the villagers repeat rumors that ferangis in the next village have taken the wool from the sheep, leaving them cold and naked, and have even killed some of the flock. When his uncle, with his grandfather's approval, allows Jones to use Teffera's flock as a demonstration, the boy hides the best sheep behind a barrier of thorn bushes, hoping to save a few, at least, for his absent father. Jones, discovering the deception and understanding the motive, tells Teffera that they will use the hidden sheep as a control group in their experiment. He teaches the village boys to shear and spray the sheep to discourage insect infestation and to cull the flock so that stronger lambs will be produced. Instead of killing the culls, he pens them off to fatten for the festival food. Still suspicious, Teffera marks his best ram with dye, conceals the mark with mud, and puts him in with the culls as a test of Jones's honesty. His best friend, Retta, is even more suspicious and refuses to attend the evening sessions in Jones's hut where he teaches the boys to write their own names, but he is won over by a gift of paints from Jones, who recognizes his artistic talent. When Jones discovers the ram and refuses to have it killed, Teffera is deeply ashamed, but the American praises him for his skepticism, and they become fast friends. The theme that one must be open to new ideas without giving up the old values is rather heavy-handedly expressed, but despite its didactic tone, the book gives insight into the customs and thought patterns of the Ethiopian villagers and treats such ideas as the great respect for elders without condescension. The style is simple, aimed at the middle-range reader. Addams.

MEET THE AUSTINS (L'Engle*, Madeleine, Vanguard, 1960), episodic, realistic family novel set recently in the village of Thornhill, Conn., not far from New York City. Vicky Austin, 12, tells how her family's life is changed when Margaret Hamilton, 10, comes to live with them: her father, Dr. Austin; her mother, who was a singer before her marriage; John*, 15; Suzy*, 9; and little Rob*. Maggy, who was recently orphaned when her pilot father's plane crashed, has never known what it is like to live in a real family, since she has been mostly cared for by nurses and governesses. Spoiled and headstrong, she disrupts the entire household by demanding favors and special attention, disobeying family rules, and generally disregarding the rights of those around her. Among other misdeeds, she meanly grabs Rob's musical toy, Elephant's Child, and breaks it, and she induces Suzy to play in Dr. Austin's office, a place always off-limits to the children. Gradually, however, the firm and loving parents and the good-natured children help Maggy adjust to her father's death and to living in a family situation. The year holds other happenings for the Austins, too. Vicky breaks her arm in a fall from her bike. The family dresses up outlandishly as a practical joke on Uncle Douglas, a painter, when he brings a young woman, Sally Hough, to visit them. Instead of being his latest flame, as the family supposes, however, she turns out to be Maggy's cousin, sent by Maggy's wealthy grandfather, Mr. Ten Eyck, to determine whether or not the Austins are respectable people capable of rearing Maggy properly. The whole family visits Grandfather Eaton, a retired minister, at his island home by the ocean where Rob gets lost along the seashore and is found by the Austins' Great Dane, Mr. Rochester. At the end, it is decided that Maggy will continue to live with the Austins for a while. Legally, she will be the ward of her grandfather and the Austins' beautiful and beloved Aunt Elena, the concert pianist who is the widow of Maggy's father's co-pilot, Uncle Hal. Although the Austins solve their problems too easily and are a little too compatible to be convincing, they are individualized and likeable. The themes of death and grieving are handled sensitively if didactically, and the old subject of the taming of the shrew works well within the context of the story, even though Maggy does change too abruptly after the episode in Dr. Austin's office. Most events ring true to modern family life, except for the practical joke, which appears contrived and inappropriate. Vicky is an intelligent, loving girl, who reports happenings honestly and with a sharp eye for details of action and emotion in language pleasingly contemporary. Sequel is *The Moon by Night**. Books Too Good; Choice; Fanfare.

MEG MURRY (*A Wrinkle in Time**; *The Arm of the Starfish**), plain, warmhearted, sensitive girl, very close to her family, in particular, her younger brother, Charles* Wallace, with whom she can communicate telepathically. She is an average student, except for math, in which she excels, finds it hard to socialize with her schoolmates, and is very sensitive to remarks made about her family. She gains in self-assurance and appreciation of her capabilities as the books about the Murrys progress. Her ability to love saves the lives of her father and Charles Wallace in *A Wrinkle in Time*. She appears as the wife of Calvin* O'Keefe and the mother of a large family of happy, lively children in *The Arm of the Starfish*.

MELANIE ROSS (*The Egypt Game**), April* Hall's friend and one of the originators of the Egypt game. She lives downstairs in the same apartment house, and the two girls become acquainted when April's grandmother arranges for April to stay with the Rosses while she works. The Rosses are blacks, whose father is a university graduate student and whose mother is a teacher. Melanie shares her paper doll games with April, and the Egypt game is an outgrowth of those. Melanie knows April will have a hard time getting along with the children in school, unless she changes her dress and attitude. Melanie tries to help April adjust.

MELODY GREENE (*A Solitary Blue**), Jeff's* mother and the Professor's* estranged wife. Jeff gradually learns about her background as the story progresses. She was brought up by her grandmother, Gambo*, in the manner of a proud old Southern family of Charleston. She met the Professor when she took a class of his at the University, set her cap for him purely for the pleasure of the conquest, soon became pregnant and felt compelled to marry him, hated the role of wife and mother, and finally walked out when Jeff was seven. She is a fine case of arrested development, a woman of beauty and breeding who never grows up. She is strikingly attractive with dark hair and gray eyes and lively personality. Her vivacious charm is merely a veneer for the coolly calculating child-woman underneath. Once Jeff begins to see how she operates, how she uses the love other people feel for her to get what she wants, he begins to break the shackles that bind him to her and to become aware of what the Professor, whom she always deprecates to Jeff, is really like. Then he begins to realize just how much the Professor really loves him in comparison to Melody.

MEMBER OF THE GANG (Rinkoff*, Barbara, ill. Harold James, Crown, 1968), realistic problem novel set in a modern city in the mid twentieth century. Black Woodie (Woodrow) Jackson, 13, has conservative, hardworking parents, who caution him to stay out of trouble, but he enjoys hanging out with Sonny, a joking, easygoing friend, and Leroy, a semi-dropout from school, who is a natural leader. Together with two boys from another school, Taylor and Jess, they form a gang, the Scorpions. Jess is new to the neighborhood but is known to have been heckled by a Puerto Rican gang, the Tops, where he lived before. With some trepidation Woodie skips school and acts as "front man," distracting the store owner when they shoplift in Jake's variety story. Since only four knives were lifted, he goes without when they invade the Tops' territory to show them who's boss, and in the ensuing fight he is saved by Sonny from being stabbed. Sonny is knifed and the others all scatter, leaving only Woodie, who stays with the wounded boy until the police arrest him and get an ambulance for Sonny. At the police station he finds the others, who have already been picked up, and he refrains from telling about the Tops member who stabbed Sonny. His parents are grieved and angry, and they clamp down on him. His father walks him to school, his mother times his homecoming, and he is not allowed to go to the Settlement, the neighborhood recreation center he used to frequent nor to inquire about Sonny or any of the other gang members. At court the case is continued until a probation officer can report, with sentencing to be imposed later. At first Woodie resents the probation officer, a friendly young man named Frank Henry, but he is relieved when Henry tells him Sonny is getting along well and offers to take Woodie to see him. At the hospital, Henry leaves the boys together, and Woodie is shocked to have Sonny say that as soon as he's well they'll have another rumble with the Tops. Woodie admits to Henry that he doesn't think like Sonny and to himself determines to work hard and shun troublemakers like the other Scorpions, who will only end as nobodies. The novel is like a composite case history, completely predictable, with a simplistic conclusion. Woodie's fears and desire to belong are handled well, but the attempt at black dialect is inconsistent and unconvincing, and all the characters are typecast. Choice.

MENDOZA, CAPTAIN BLAS DE (*The King's Fifth**), leader of the expedition to the Seven Cities of Cíbola in search of the legendary gold. An elegant young man, he takes many changes of fancy clothes and three personal musicians on the trek into the wilderness, yet he is physically strong and has a determination that saves the party more than once. His ruthless desire for gold, however, makes him antagonize Indians and drive his companions to desperation.

MENOLLY (*Dragonsong**), musical daughter of the Sea Holder, Yanus*, who is forbidden by her father to play or sing when the new harper arrives, because he fears the Hold will be disgraced by having a female musician. A tall, athletic girl, Menolly is convinced that she is homely and awkward, a view reinforced by her mother and her pretty older sister, Stella. Menolly's natural sensitivity makes it possible for her to "impress" nine fire lizards, an unheard-of feat much admired at Benden Weyr, and she has also taught them to sing. She does not figure as a character in the earlier book, *Dragonquest*, although she is present as a minor element in events that occur in the latter part of that book. She is a prominent character in later books of the series, both those published for adults and those published for children.

MERRILL, JEAN (FAIRBANKS) (1923–   ), born in Rochester, N.Y.; editor and author of over two dozen books for children, two of which were Fanfare books and selected for the Lewis Carroll Shelf, *The Superlative Horse: A Tale of Ancient China** (Scott, 1961), a fictionalization of an ancient legend, and a lively, inventive fantasy about conflict between pushcarts and trucks in New York City, *The Pushcart War** (Scott, 1964), also a *Choice* selection. Also popular has been *The Toothpaste Millionaire* (Houghton, 1972), a novel about a boy who invents an inexpensive, very effective toothpaste, exploiting, like *The Pushcart War*, the theme of big versus little. Her fiction combines significant themes, wit, and a good sense of the absurd, and her meticulous attention to details of story and dialogue gives her books conviction and relieves their message and self-consciousness. She has also written plays and a book of verse, *Emily Emerson's Moon* (Little, 1960), has collaborated on an edition of haiku by Issa, *A Few Flies and I* (Pantheon, 1969), and has published romances, retellings, and picture books. Her books reflect the places she has lived in and her extensive travels. Other titles include *The Travels of Marco Polo* (Knopf, 1956), *Henry, the Hand Painted Mouse* (Coward, 1951), and *The Very Nice Things* (Harper, 1959), all picture books, *Shan's Lucky Knife* (Scott, 1960), a picture book retelling of a Burmese tale, and *High, Wide, and Handsome* (Scott, 1964), Burmese tall tales. When she was eight, her family moved from Rochester to the country, and she grew up on an apple and dairy farm near Lake Ontario in Webster, N.Y., where she attended a country school. She received her bachelor's degree from Allegheny College and her master's from Wellesley in English and was a Fullbright Scholar at the University of Madras in India. She was editor and writer for many years for Scholastic Magazines, Inc., and *Literary Cavalcade*, was associate editor and contributor to the Bank Street Readers series for Macmillan, and has published in various periodicals for children and young people. She has made her home in New York City and spends her summers in Vermont.

MERRIMAN LYON (*Over Sea, Under Stone**; *The Dark Is Rising**; *The Grey King**), Great-Uncle Merry, called Gummery by the Simon*, Jane, and Barney Drew, close friend of the Drew family, and friend and mentor of Will* Stanton. Ostensibly a renowned and distinguished Celtic scholar, he is in reality an Old One, one of those immortals as old as the land whose responsibility it is to defeat the Dark and save the world from its evil power. Mysterious in his ways, imposing in demeanor, striking in appearance with thick white hair and deep, dark eyes, he is able to go back and forth in time and represents the ageless, universal force for good. Barney Drew notes the similarity between Uncle Merry's name and that of Merlin. Merriman Lyon appears in every book in The Dark Is Rising series to affect the action and assist the good.

MESTENO WILL (*The Black Mustanger**), a part-black, part-Indian mustanger who sets Lafe Riker's broken leg. Although he has doctored only horses, Will offers to treat Lafe when the foreman of a big mavericking outfit hesitates because

Riker fought for the Union in the Civil War, already some fifteen years in the past. A loner, Will has success catching wild horses by "becoming a horse," rubbing himself with his sweaty horse blanket, eating only baked mescal so that the odor of bacon and other human food will not give him away, and riding with a wild band until they accept him as one of them. With some hesitation, he takes young Dan Riker as a partner but generously gives him full ownership of the two-year-old stallion, Wattle, that becomes the leader of the herd. Neither a full-blooded Apache nor a black, he has suffered rejection by both groups as well as by the white world, but he has dignity and compassion that sets him above the other men in frontier Texas.

METROPOLITAN MUSEUM OF ART, NEW YORK (*From the Mixed-up Files of Mrs. Basil E. Frankweiler**), the place where Claudia* and Jamie* Kincaid hide out when they run away from home. Described with detail which gives an authentic sense of place, the museum represents to Claudia an opportunity for self-expression and independence.

MEYER, EDITH PATTERSON (1895–   ), born in Chatham, Mass.; librarian, editor, biographer. She attended Pratt Institute School of Library Science, Western Reserve University Library School, and the University of Chicago. From 1916 to 1921 she worked at public libraries in Fond du Lac, Wis., and Cleveland, Ohio, and during the early 1920s did editorial work for the American Library Association in Chicago. In 1924 she joined Rand McNally and Co., publishers, where she worked in the children's book department until 1944, when she moved to Abingdon Press, New York. Her books are mostly non-fiction, including biographies of Alfred Nobel, Oliver Wendell Holmes, and Isabella d'Este, or biographical fiction like *Pirate Queen** (Little, 1961), a novel based on the life of a famous Irish woman chief in the time of Elizabeth I of England.

MICHAEL 2112439–851 (*A Gift of Mirrorvax**), young advocate trainee who becomes a replacement astronaut on the Transvax mission of discovery to Mirrorvax. Though extremely bright and capable of feats of memorization, Michael is shown to be insecure beneath his inflexible belief in the superiority of the Vaxan culture. He is shaken by the idea, which his fellow astronaut eventually tells him, that he may be the son of a member of the secretariat, since he cannot imagine such high-status people indulging in child breeding. His experience with Anamandra* Amudsar, the girl he meets on Mirrorvax, produces in him emotions he has considered shameful and which he doesn't really understand. Misinterpreting his fevered attempt to tell his name, she calls him Maicyl Tuwin. His final decision to destroy the space ship and thereby scuttle the Transvax plans to colonize Mirrorvax is prompted more by his love for Anamandra than philosophical acceptance of the non-violent Mirrorvax culture.

MICKEY CAFFERTY (*The Voyage Begun**), Michelle Cafferty, 11, daughter of the local grocer. A fiercely independent and often defiant middle child, she feels pushed around and used by her parents and by Shawn* and Maureen, her brother and sister. She often disobeys her parents and is slovenly about her work in the store. Her relationship with Walter Jepson is complex, as is her association with Paul Vickers. At first, she is openly antagonistic to the old man, as is he to her, but she gradually begins to feel responsible for what has happened to him and sets about rectifying matters. She resents assistance and only grudgingly accepts help from Paul and his friends. She gives Paul purpose in life, especially since he feels he has let his father down by not living up to Dr.* Vickers's expectations for a teenaged son. As the story goes on, Mickey develops a conscience and a sense of social responsibility. She is a round, dynamic character.

MICKLE (*Westmark**; *The Kestrel**), in *Westmark*, a pitiful waif, "drab as a street sparrow" with "a beaky nose in a narrow face," whose unusual talent for throwing her voice Count Las* Bombas employs in a spiritualist act. Her apparent ability to summon spirits brings her to the attention of the unscrupulous Cabbarus, whom the king has instructed to find a medium whereby he can contact his long-lost daughter whom the king supposes dead. Cabbarus intends to use Mickle to help him overthrow the king and gain the throne for himself, but, at the critical moment, Mickle is revealed as the lost princess, whom Cabbarus had tried to assassinate years before. In *The Kestrel*, she is the sturdy, resilient Augusta, Queen of Westmark*, field general of the army, and Theo's bride-to-be.

MIDDL'UN (Burleson*, Elizabeth, ill. George Roth, Follett, 1968), realistic novel set in 1899 in Kerr County, in Texas hill country near the Guadalupe River. Hannah Worth, 13, the "middl'un" between pretty Melissa, 16, and cute Martha, 6, has been her father's "boy" after the death of his sons, the first two children. On her pinto, High Stepper, she has helped her pa herd cattle and do the work of their large ranch. Despite her mother's efforts to make her ladylike, she fights with boys, particularly "Andy" (William) Andrews, and joins him in pranks like switching the teams around before the families drive their buggies and wagons home from the last-day-of-school program. More serious trouble looms when she joins her father for the big cattle roundup and finds that brands on some of his cattle have been changed, including a steer which Hannah has raised from a calf. Pa starts patrolling his land, but Ma keeps Hannah close to home, teaching her to cook and keep house. Escaping briefly, she rides to a nearby box canyon, leaves her horse while she hunts arrow heads, and comes upon rustlers branding a calf. She gets a good look at one of the horses and cuts a wide swatch from the underside of the mane as proof. Before she can tell Pa, he is stricken with acute appendicitis and almost dies, but when she sees the horse in town, ridden by no-good Wash Billings, she tells the marshal. He advises her to keep quiet so they can catch Billings's confederates. With Pa sick, Hannah tries to keep the cattle from spreading too far on the range and one day finds Hash and Buck, Billings's sons, laying for her. Hash tries to rope her, and to escape she rides up a dangerous series of natural steps or ledges where, trying to follow, Buck's horse falls and is killed, and Buck is injured. At the trial Hannah testifies against Wash, finally admitting that she has the piece of mane hidden under her mattress at home, by which the rustlers are identified. Seaton Andrews, sweet on Melissa, comes to help and proposes. At her sister's wedding, Hannah for the first time attracts admiring looks from Andy and decides being a girl may not be all bad. Hannah is a likable tomboy character and, despite the stock situation of rustlers, the picture of ranch life is authentic and interesting. Spur.

MIDGE GLASS (*Henry Reed, Inc.*†; *Henry Reed's Journey**; *Henry Reed's Baby-Sitting Service**; *Henry Reed's Big Show**), Margaret, slightly younger friend and partner of Henry* Reed in a series of humorous, episodic novels. Although most of the ideas for projects are Henry's, Midge is not a passive partner. She dives into any undertaking with great energy and spirit. Somewhat more excitable than Henry, she is frequently responsible for complications and occasionally for solutions. It is her family with whom Henry has his journey across the United States, and it is her interest in horses which gives the inspiration for their rodeo, which proves to be the "big show."

THE MIDNIGHT FOX (Byars*, Betsy, ill. Ann Grifalconi, Viking, 1968), realistic novel of family life set mainly on a farm in the late twentieth century. Tom looks back on the summer when he is ten and reluctantly goes to live with his Aunt Millie and Uncle Fred while his parents are on vacation in Europe. A quiet, retiring child, Tom is sure that farm life will require more courage and physical stamina than he can muster. To compensate for anticipated inadequacies, he fancies situations in which through both he contributes to running the farm. He feels even more unequal to life on the farm when kind and caring Aunt Millie gives him the room that once belonged to her active, outgoing son, Bubba. Just outside the room stands the tree that Bubba and his brother used to shinny down. Tom takes refuge from these threats by daydreaming about the things he did back home with his best friend, Petie* Burkis. One day, while in solitary contemplation in the grove on the hill by the creek, he sights a fox with fur as black as midnight cutting through the grass. Tom confides his discovery to his grown cousin, Hazeline*, who informs him that a neighbor has been having trouble with a fox and recently dynamited a den. After that, Tom spends his spare time watching for the fox. He trails her to the den she shares with her one small kit and concludes she must be the one whose den the farmer destroyed. After Tom has sighted the fox over a dozen times and has grown fond of it, to his dismay Aunt Millie announces she has lost a hen and a turkey, undoubtedly to a fox, and urges her husband to find and destroy the marauder. Although Tom tries to divert his uncle from the task, Fred soon finds the den and captures the kit. He takes it home and puts in into a rabbit hutch to serve as bait for catching the vixen. That night, during a driving rain, Tom steals through his bedroom window, shinnies down the tree outside, and releases the kit, whose mother soon claims it and races with it to safety in the woods. Tom apologizes to his aunt and uncle, certain that they will be angry for what he has done, but to his surprise they react with acceptance and understanding. Tom concludes that his uncle and aunt are extraordinarily fine people. Once home, he is happily reunited with Petie. He resumes his old life, and the episode soon becomes just another memory. This story of a boy's infatuation with a wild creature lacks focus and balance, characters except for Tom are flat or distorted, and the author never exploits the emotional potential of Tom's concern for the fox or the effect of the experience on Tom. Tom's fantasies and recollections characterize him and Petie and are often amusing, but they do little to advance the plot. The improbable conclusion makes light of both Tom's problems and those of Uncle Fred and Aunt Millie. Choice; Lewis Carroll.

MIGRANT GIRL (Laklan*, Carli, McGraw, 1970), realistic novel set in the eastern United States in the 1960s. With her parents, her grandmother, and her three younger brothers, Dacey Cotter, 16, follows the crops up the east coast, traveling and sleeping in their decrepit truck. The crew boss, Big Joe, resents such "ditch bankers" because he loses the rake-off he usually makes by overcharging for the rundown shacks most of his migrant workers rent. Big Joe, who drives a white Cadillac, also makes money by giving short weight on "day haul" picking, withholding social security payments even for those who have no cards, and lending money at high interest to his workers. Most of the "stoopers," dependent on him for jobs and transportation, meekly put up with the injustice. Only young Juan Aquilar is unafraid to protest. Having heard of Cesar Chavez, who organized grape workers in California, Juan talks up the idea of a union. Encouraged by his boldness, Dacey goes to Big Joe's cabin to protest her incorrect pay and finds him sexually threatening. In terribly hot weather, Dacey's youngest brother, Gaither, 6, jumps into the puddle around the communal water spigot and cuts his foot badly, but when Juan demands drainage, Big Joe says parents should make their children wear shoes. Juan further infuriates Big Joe by commandeering a truck to take the young wife, Maria, to a hospital to have her baby. That night Big Joe's thugs beat him up. Dacey and his friend, Miguel, get him to a cabin, wash and bandage him. In defiance, the camp stages a fiesta when Maria comes back from the hospital with her baby girl. The pattern of exploitation is interrupted by their stay at one good camp, Grovesville, where decent cabins are provided free, day care is available for the children, and school is taught at night for the older ones. Dacey's desire to be a teacher is rekindled, but Big Joe will not let the crew stay for the party the volunteer teachers have planned. As the season nears an end, most of the workers are trapped in the pattern of debt, but one girl, Valida, determined to change, has been practicing making change and is sure she can get a job in a store. An eager worker, she is picking potatoes so fast that, without realizing it, she catches up with the digger, and her arm is slashed by the machine's teeth. Juan takes her to a hospital but later disappears from camp for several days. A man making a ''survey'' shows up and asks Big Joe some hard questions. The next day a procession of cars with banners appears, a rally demanding better conditions for migrants, roused by a newspaper article engineered by Juan. For the first time, the workers have some real hope that the outside world may help them. Juan with Miguel sets off for California to work with Chavez. The field work with its backbreaking labor, the heat, the dust, the insecticides that irritate the skin and make breathing difficult, and the economic problems of the migrants are well portrayed. The characters, however, are one-dimensional types, and the action is predictable. Child Study.

MIGUEL (*The Horse Talker**), proud, capable godson of Blanco*, who excels in the use of the lariat. At first, he is hostile to Lan, but a hunting accident which almost takes their lives results in a friendship that grows over the months Lan spends with the mustangers, and the two become quite close.

MIKE CASSIDY (*The Mysterious Red Tape Gang**), Michael Francis Cassidy, 12, member of the Red Tape Gang, whose objective is to improve the neighborhood by doing things that red tape keeps city hall from getting done. As Mike tells the story, he appears to be the leader of the gang, but Leroy* often makes suggestions which lead to something. Mike attends Mass the Sunday after the children discover that Mr. Hartwell is involved in some sort of wrongdoing. The priest's statement that those who are aware of wrongdoing but do not do anything about it are just as guilty as the evildoers leads Mike to ask his father what options criminals have. The club then decides to try to keep Mr. Hartwell from going to prison. This leads to the capture of the car thieves.

MIKE KELLY (*Gentle Ben**), unsociable superintendent of the Northern Fisheries cannery. Although he will not listen to the proposition Mark's father presents to rent space in the cannery freezer for Ben's food, he makes a deal with Mark which allows the boy to work off the rent payments. His interest in Mark and Ben is demonstrated when he comes to Ben's shed the night some drunken men have tormented the bear and return to shoot him. Mike backs up Ellen* Anderson, Mark's mother, when she tells them to leave, takes away their gun, and spends the night with Mark in the shed, caring for Ben's wounds and guarding him. It is later revealed that Mike's own son, about Mark's age, was drowned three years earlier along with the boy's mother, an occurrence that has embittered Mike until his friendship with Mark mellows him.

MILDRED FLETCHER (*The Taste of Spruce Gum**), widow who marries her brother-in-law whom she hardly knows and lives in a rough logging camp with her daughter, Libby*, 11. A woman of both good looks and strong spirit, she copes with brawling loggers, life in a freezing shanty when her house burns, and a husband who has long been a bachelor and has difficulty communicating. She rises to the occasion by becoming the teacher when she finds there is none, the midwife when one of the shanty women has a baby, and, briefly, the boarding-house cook when the incumbent is killed. Her most daring feat, however, is taking the horse of her brother-in-law, Henry, and riding to Rutland at night when her husband has been injured and then commandeering the company account books to prove that Henry has been cheating in the partnership.

MILES TUCK (*Tuck Everlasting**), older brother of Jesse*, who drank from the spring near Treegap when he was twenty-two, some eighty-seven years before the action in the book, and like the rest of the family has remained unchanged. Eternal life has not been kind to Miles; he has lost his wife and children because he has been thought to have been dealing with the devil. Skilled at carpentry, Miles removes the window from the jail so that his mother, Mae*, can climb out and Winnie* Foster can take Mae's place.

MILLIE TYDINGS (*Dicey's Song**), owner of the local grocery and meat market, a contemporary of Gram Tillerman. She is slow witted but warm and outgoing. Dicey persuades her to hire her to help out around the place after school and on Saturdays. Through her, Dicey learns a little about Gram's past and about the way the community regards Gram. Millie sets an example for Gram about reaching out to others and not being so fiercely independent.

MILTON, ROSS (*Across Five Aprils**), editor of the county newspaper, called ''Red'' for his red hair by the townspeople of Newton, Ill. He stands up for Jethro* Creighton when local men taunt the boy about what his brother Bill* Creighton has done, encourages him to improve his speech, gives him a book on grammar, and helps the boy and his family in various ways after Matt Creighton is stricken. He stands for fairness, justice, and neighborliness.

MINA SMITHS (*Dicey's Song**), Wilhelmina Smiths, warm, expansive, outgoing daughter of the local black minister, who serves as a foil for Dicey Tillerman. Large, mature, both physically and emotionally for her age, she stands up for Dicey when the English teacher accuses Dicey, who can write better than most eighth graders and is new in town, of plagiarism. Mina reaches out to Dicey in a way that earns Dicey's confidence and respect, and the two girls become friends. Mina is an interesting, credible character, sharply realized.

MINERVA LANDRY (*Sinbad and Me**; *Mystery of the Witch Who Wouldn't**), motherless eleven-year-old daughter of the Hampton, Long Island, sheriff and friend of Steve* Forrester, who is involved with him in ferreting out the truth in various crimes. Blond and tomboyish, Minerva is often scornful of Steve's ideas and is inclined to report their activities in ways that leave out her mistakes and emphasizes Steve's, but they are generally good friends, and Sinbad, Steve's bulldog, worships her.

MINK (*To Spoil the Sun**), respected spiritual leader and medicine man of Rain* Dove's group of Cherokees, known as the Seven Clans. He is a kind, sensible, and considerate man, who asks Rain Dove to marry him because his first wife is ailing and because he has been impressed by the girl's courage, strength of character, and intelligence. He finds personal comfort and renewal in discussing tribal concerns with her. Even when Rain Dove leaves him for a younger husband, he continues to care for her, advise her, and show concern for the welfare of her family. When the "invisible fire" of smallpox strikes, he tells her to take her children and leave the village for a certain secluded cove and instructs her in how to care for herself and her children. Without his advice, Rain Dove would not have survived. Mink dies of the plague while Rain Dove and her children are at the cove.

MISS ELSIE MAE HOWELLS (*The Rock and the Willow**), silly, man-chasing spinster whom Enie Singleton's widowed father marries. Miss Elsie Mae, in her forties, has inherited a good deal of land and a house which she keeps for her brother, Sonny. With flirtatious ways and a strident laugh, Miss Elsie Mae has been a figure of fun, but she launches her campaign for Clem* Singleton vigorously through their common interest in church music and brings cakes and other treats for the family and gifts and affection for the two young children. When she realizes that Enie bitterly resents her encroachments on her mother's memory, Miss Elsie Mae drops her silly chattiness and talks as an understanding woman to the girl, explaining that she doesn't expect to take the place of their mother, who was a better woman than she is, but that she promises to love and do her best for Leeroy and Jenny and to make life easier for the others. Indirectly, it is through Miss Elsie Mae that Enie gets a chance for college.

MISS EMILY KIMBALL (*The Long Journey**), elderly, maternal ex-schoolteacher, in whose barn Laurie takes shelter during a driving rainstorm. Miss Emily finds the girl and takes her into the house, where she feeds her and gives her dry clothing and a comfortable bed. In her house, Laurie gets her first glimpse of what comfortable, modern, middle-class home life is like. All Laurie has known about the way people live has come from her life with her grandfather in their rustic mountain cabin and from books andd magazines she has read. Laurie resolves to acquire some "conveniences," like a phonograph, for her home with Grandfather.

MISS FANNY (*Bimby**), Fanny Kemble Butler, a real person, a popular and gifted English actress born in 1809. She never appears in the novel, but the slaves speak of her with affection and respect, even though she lived on their

Georgia island plantation only a few months. She taught Bimby's Ma to read, write, and sew. She was staunchly opposed to slavery, a way of thinking that eventually led to her divorce from Pierce Butler, the Massa* Pierce of the novel. Fanny's diary provided most of the background information for *Bimby*.

MISS MANDERBY (*Portrait of Ivan**), white-haired spinster whose task is to entertain Ivan by reading to him while Matt* Mustazza paints his portrait. She contributes ideas as Matt creates the imaginary sketch of the sledge carrying Ivan's mother and her relatives from Russia to Warsaw. She gives Ivan glimpses of the world of literature, of which he previously knew and cared very little. She is a likeable, literary, rather introverted, yet warm, woman, and at times Ivan feels she is taking the place of the grandmother he never knew. She is a credible, if flat, figure.

MISS OSBORNE-THE-MOP (*Miss Osborne-the-Mop**), an ordinary dust mop changed into a woman by Jody's power of transformation that is connected with the glasses she must wear for the summer. Because Jody is thinking of "The Sorcerer's Apprentice," which her fourth grade teacher, Miss Osborne, told them, the mop has a personality very like the teacher—elegant, imperious, and ready for no nonsense. Physically, she is still like a mop with arms, short legs, and Miss Osborne's face, but she is unable to eat or to smell. She considers herself to be in delicate health but can work steadily without stop and expects the children to do the same. Because she can know only what Jody has put into her or what she has learned in the broom closet and the supermarket, her knowledge of natural history is limited, but she confidently identifies everything they see, pointing out a lizard as "a good inner seal" which eats "active and inert ingredients" and a butterfly as a "Washday Product."

MISS OSBORNE-THE-MOP (Gage*, Wilson, ill. Paul Galdone, World, 1963), light fantasy set in the North Carolina mountains in an unspecified modern time. Jody (Joan) Ransome, 11, is unhappy that family circumstances make her spend the summer with her aunt and uncle and their annoying son, Dill (John Pickett) Tracy, 11, rather than at the beach as she had planned. She is doubly unhappy that she is overweight and has to wear glasses to correct an eye defect. She discovers, however, that she has the magic ability to work transformations. After accidentally changing Dill into a squirrel and carelessly changing the cat into a tiger, she agrees to make a useful creature by turning a mop into a woman, as Dill suggests, seeing a way to get out of the work of cleaning his room. Unfortunately, the mop as a woman resembles Jody's teacher, Miss Osborne, who is much more inclined to direct and criticize than to do the work herself, and more unfortunately, Jody cannot turn her back into a plain dust mop. To keep her away from Aunt Margaret, they persuade her to spend the night first in a cave, which she dislikes intensely, and then in a "mountain cabin," intending to take her to a shack Dill knows of. On the way, however, they meet reclusive old Mr. Poteet. Nearsighted, Mr. Poteet first shoots at them, then, not seeing the mop clearly, takes her for an ordinary woman and, gallantly welcoming her, asks her to stay in his cabin and look after his chickens while he visits relatives in town. The cabin is a disaster, run down, filthy, full of old bottles, newspapers, and rags, sitting in a junk-filled clearing. After a moment of dismay, the mop organizes the children to clean it up, and they start on an exhausting project to clear the cabin and the yard, scrub walls, floors, and windows. Day after day they pack a lunch and scramble up the mountain to labor, spending all their money on cleaning materials and on seed for the garden. When Mr. Poteet returns, wearing store-bought glasses, he is outraged and threatens them furiously. Jody grabs the mop and races up the mountain, but Miss* Osborne-the-Mop finds this undignified, breaks away, and, slipping on shale, cracks herself. She insists her heart is broken and that she will die and, when Jody wishes she were still just a mop, promptly becomes a plain mop with a cracked handle. By this accident, Jody discovers that she still has the power of transformation, which is connected to the glasses she wears, but before she has time to experiment further, the eye doctor finds she no longer needs them and unintentionally breaks them. Jody's mother arrives to find that the hard work has slimmed and browned her daughter and that her antagonism to Dill has changed to friendship. Although only Miss Osborne-the-Mop stands out as a character, the story is cleverly worked out and has pleasant humor. Choice.

MISS THOMPSON (*The Bears' House**), elderly teacher at PS 87, Fran Ellen Smith's teacher. Miss Thompson's father made the Bears' House for her when she was a child. For thirty years the children of her classroom have played with it. She awards the Bears' House to Fran Ellen when she retires from teaching at school year's end. She knows that Fran Ellen has had many problems and has worked the hardest of all the children. Miss Thompson is strict and kind but fails to understand why Fran Ellen behaves as she does because Fran Ellen is simply too fearful to communicate her problems. At the end of the story, the reader believes that Miss Thompson will find some way to help the Smiths.

MISS WORTHINGTON (*The Mystery Cottage in Left Field**), librarian who has befriended Jimmy Loughlin and on whom the twelve-year-old has a crush. Although she lets him run errands for her and walk her home, she does not let him into her apartment and seems to live there with the shades down and the radio blasting. When he finally does get in, she has been very slow answering his persistent knock and has opened the windows and turned the radio off. Suspecting that the missing Evo Montella is hiding there, Jimmy makes an excuse to get her out of the room and peeks up the chimney of the enormous fireplace, where he sees the feet of a man who is sitting in a sort of swing suspended there. Evo, it turns out, is innocent of wrong but is wanted by both the police and the gangsters since he is the only surviving witness of an incident in which four men were shot. Miss Worthington is his girl friend and has been hiding him in her apartment for a year.

MITZI (*The Devil in Vienna**), the Dornenwalds' maid and Inge's* good friend. When she comes to live with the Dornenwalds, she is a raw country girl who is easily taken in by Lieselotte* and Inge. But later she becomes wise to the girls' little tricks and develops a firm hand with them. She often expresses her views in homely sayings and proverbs. When she insists she will not be married in a church with a swastika flag flying over it, it seems that her wedding to Fredl will have to be called off. Then Lieselotte tells her about Lieselotte's Uncle Ludwig's church, which refuses to fly the flag. Mitzi and Inge often share confidences, and Mitzi helps the two girls continue their friendship in spite of strong family opposition. It is from a remark of Mitzi's about Hitler's visit to Vienna after the Anschluss that the book takes its title.

MLLE. LEGRAND (*A Pocket Full of Seeds**), cold, calculating teacher in the school which Nicole attends in France in World War II. Mlle. Legrand is an enigmatic figure, whose motives are obscure, and the writer might well have made more of her. She probably turned in to the authorities the Italian-born Fiori family, simply to score points. Not all bad, however, she does give Nicole help when the girl desperately needs it. Perhaps the teacher acts out of self-interest, to be sure that she is not branded a collaborationist after the war, but she probably saves Nicole's life.

MOERI, LOUISE (HEALY) (1924–   ), born in Klamath Falls, Oreg.; librarian, writer. She attended Stockton Junior College and received her B.A. degree from the University of California at Berkeley. From 1961 to 1978 she worked in the library at Manteca, Calif. Besides many magazine stories for children, she has written several novels, including *The Girl Who Lived on the Ferris Wheel* (Dutton, 1979), *Save Queen of Sheba** (Dutton, 1981), a story of a boy and his little sister who survive an Indian attack on their wagon train, and *Downwind* (Dutton, 1984), about the problems of a twelve-year-old boy who takes on mature responsibility for his family after an accident in a nuclear power plant in their California valley.

MOHR, NICHOLASA (GOLPE) (1935–   ), born in New York City; painter, printmaker, teacher. She studied at the New York Art Students League, the Brooklyn Museum Art School, and the Pratt Center for Contemporary Printmaking. She married a child psychologist and has taught in art schools in New York and New Jersey, where they have made their home. Her novel, *Nilda** (Harper, 1973), won the Jane Addams Award. Her collection of stories, *El Bronx Remembered* (Harper, 1975), is also about Hispanic experience in New York City. *Felita* (Dial, 1979) is for younger children, about a lively eight-year-old Puerto Rican girl growing up in a loving family.

MOMADAY, NATACHEE SCOTT, born in Fairview, Ky., of Cherokee, French, and English descent; teacher, artist, editor, and author of articles and short stories dealing with the culture and art of the American Indian and of books for children. The mother of the celebrated Kiowa novelist, N. Scott Momaday, she was educated at Haskell Junior College, Crescent College, the University of New Mexico, and the University of California at Los Angeles. She has lived in Arizona, where her husband became principal of a school at Jemez Pueblo, and beginning in 1936 she herself taught in reservation schools. Her oil, pastel, pen and ink, and charcoal paintings and drawings have been widely exhibited in the Southwest and have won major awards. A former newspaper reporter, she has published *American Indian Authors* (Houghton, 1971), an acclaimed anthology of writings by prominent Native American authors, and several books for young readers about Indian children that are strong in their picture of Indian life, including *Betty, A Navajo Girl* (Gallup, N.Mex.: Gallup-McKinley County Public Schools, 1976), about a Navajo girl who helps an elderly white neighbor, *Lucky Lobo* (Gallup, 1975), about a little boy who saves a dog, and *A Visit to Grandmother* (Gallup, 1975), all very short books for just readers. The highly regarded *Owl in the Cedar Tree** (Ginn, 1965; Flagstaff, Ariz.: Northland Press, 1975) is also about the Navajo and won the Western Heritage Award. In 1968 the New Mexico Press Women honored her as the outstanding woman writer in New Mexico.

MOM, THE WOLF MAN AND ME (Klein*, Norma, Pantheon, 1972), realistic novel of family life set in New York City in the late 1900s and covering a few weeks' time in the life of Brett Levin, 11, who tells the story. Brett enjoys the easy informality of her life with her never-married mother, Deborah* Levin, a photographer. The mother of her friend Andrew* insists on strict routine and proper behavior and speech, and the mother of her friend Evelyn* continually goes out on dates, Evelyn says, to look over possibilities for a new father for Evelyn. Brett concedes that it is often difficult to field people's awkward questions about why she doesn't have a father, and the curiosity of her mother's mother, Grandma* Levin, about Deborah's relationship with her boss, Wally, who often visits with his two sons, occasionally annoys Brett, too. Then Deborah becomes interested in Theodore, whom she meets when she and Brett participate in a Women's Strike for Peace March in Washington. Theodore is a teacher whom Brett calls the Wolf Man because he has a huge wolfhound. Brett likes Theodore a lot because he has kind eyes, a gentle manner, and mutual interests, but she still tries to talk each of them, in turn, out of marrying. Her arguments are based on observation, her understanding of what they are like, and her own self-interest in wanting things to stay the same. She'd be happy just to have Theodore continue to "sleep over" on weekends. After her mother decides to accept Theodore's proposal, Brett soon adjusts and even helps plan the wedding. One of the most popular books of New Realism, this is an amusing portrait of an unconventional family. Brett's comments about her friends, relatives, and herself are often naive, sometimes earthily frank, and often ironically humorous, probably more so for adult readers than for young. Dialogue is authentically modern, and characters are likeable, if eccentric. Although Brett is a sensible and well-adjusted child, she takes too easily to her mother's decision. It does not seem in character. The plot is meager, events often distorted, and Brett's comments about people and situations carry the book, though shock appeal may account for much of its popularity with the young. (Grandpa* Levin) Choice.

MONTGOMERY†, RUTHERFORD (GEORGE) (1894–   ), born in Straubville, N. Dak., prolific writer of fiction mainly about wildlife and adventure in the out-of-doors. He grew up in the country near Velva, N.Dak., and on a Montana ranch. After attending Colorado Agricultural College, Western State College in Gunnison, Colo., and the University of Nebraska, he taught in public schools in Wyoming and was a teacher and principal in elementary and high schools in Colorado. After that he managed a chamber of commerce, served as a judge, and was budget and efficiency commissioner for the state of Colorado in Denver. He moved to Los Gatos, Calif., where he became a free-lance writer and taught creative writing classes. He has published over ninety books, mostly of fiction for young readers, based on his own experiences in the outdoors through camping, ranching, and flying, including a Newbery honor book and Fanfare selection, *Kildee House†* (Doubleday, 1949), about an elderly man whose friendship with wild animals enables him to make human friends for the first time in his life, and *The Stubborn One** (Duell, 1965), which received the Spur Award of Western Writers of America. A book descriptive in ranch life if conventionally plotted, it tells how a plucky youth persists in maintaining the family ranch after his father dies. Montgomery writes fluently and compellingly, though his books are formulaic, and he manages to convey a good deal of information without sounding instructive. His service in the U.S. Air Corps in World War I and time spent with the Strategic Air Command afterward provided material for his books on aviation. Later titles include *Big Red, A Wild Stallion* (Caxton, 1971), in which a forest ranger and his son seek to protect a herd of wild ponies from poachers and another of his books that deal with human and animals together, and *Rufus* (Caxton, 1973), about a bobcat. For Western Writers of America he edited a collection of stories, *A Saddlebag of Tales* (1972), wrote a series of aviation novels for Grosset under the pseudonym Al Avery and several books under the name Everitt Proctor, wrote screen plays for Walt Disney Studios, and ghost wrote the Dick Tracy series for five years. He has published novels for adults and over five hundred stories in magazines.

MOON, SHEILA (ELIZABETH) (1910–   ), born in Denver, Colo.; psychotherapist and author. She earned her A.B. and M.A. degrees at the University of California at Los Angeles, her Ph.D. at the University of California, Berkeley, and also studied at the C. G. Jung Institute in Zurich, Switzerland. She has been a practicing psychotherapist in Los Angeles and San Francisco and taught psychology at Sonoma State College from 1965 to 1970. In 1956 she received a Bollinger Foundation grant for work in Navaho mythology, a study which formed the basis for *A Magic Dwells: A Poetic and Psychological Study of the Navaho Emergence Myth* (Wesleyan, 1970). Among her varied writings are *Knee-Deep in Thunder** (Atheneum, 1967), a fantasy of a world peopled by talking, dog-sized insects, and *Hunt Down the Prize* (Atheneum, 1971), another fantasy of an unknown world which two youngsters enter on a late walk on Halloween.

THE MOON BY NIGHT (L'Engle*, Madeleine, Farrar, 1963), realistic, episodic family novel continuing the story of the Austins (*Meet the Austins**) about three years later and taking them on a three-months' camping trip through the American Southwest, up the coast into Canada, and then back home to Thornhill, Conn., through Wyoming and Upper Michigan. Vicky, now almost fifteen, tells how her father has accepted a research position in New York City and the family decides to go on an extended vacation before they move to their new home. Aunt Elena and Uncle Douglas get married and move to California, taking Maggy with them. After the excitement of the wedding and the departure have cooled, the Austins leave on their western trip in high spirits, neophyte campers with new, untried equipment, who look forward to high adventure. The trip holds some events typical of camping trips and some that are a good deal more adventurous, that more than meet their expectations for thrills as they sight-see and encounter other travelers along the way. In a campground in Tennessee, they are molested by rowdy boys and meet the Greys, an ostentatiously rich family whose only son, Zachary, about seventeen, handsome, spoiled, and headstrong, becomes romantically interested in Vicky and pursues her throughout the rest of the trip. Vicky's feelings about Zach are ambivalent. She is attracted to him and is flattered by his attention but is put off by his cynicism and self-centeredness. In Texas, a flash flood threatens their camp in the middle of the night, and, after they escape the torrent, they help evacuate a group of girl scouts. The family is repelled by the commercialism of Las Vegas, take in such usual scenic attractions as Mesa Verde and the Grand Canyon, where Vicky is troubled by the way the Indians have been treated, and have a grand reunion with Uncle Douglas, Aunt Elena, and Maggy at their new home in Laguna Beach, Calif. In Canada, they experience anti-American sentiment and see the Queen of England when she passes through Edmonton while touring the Dominion. Rob* has climbed a tree the better to see her, and, when the branch on which he is perched breaks, he plummets down directly in front of her car. He nonchalantly picks himself up and bows most gallantly to her, invoking admiration for his composure in all concerned. In Yellowstone, the family makes friends with the three Ford brothers, one of whom, Andy, spends a lot of time with Vicky. His values and outlook on life correspond more closely with those of the Austins, and he contrasts sharply with Zach. Near Yellowstone, an earthquake causes a landslide in which Zach is injured. The family arrives home before school starts, and the children stay with Grandfather Eaton in his island home by the ocean while their parents look for a place to live in New York City and Dr. Austin gets ready for his new position. During the summer, Vicky, who has been bewildered by the many rapid changes in her life and wondering if there is a rational plan to things, has sorted herself out realistically. She has come to see that change is inevitable and has grown more self-confident. The story ambles along with descriptions of scenic attractions and Vicky's musings about herself, her family, the boys, and her place in life's scheme, as well as action scenes in the different places they stop. Vicky's feelings and reactions are fairly typical of an intelligent teenager at her stage in life, but Zach is the stock spoiled rich youth. As in the other novels about the Austins, philosophical discussions and an emphasis on ideas occasionally result in an intellectual, almost didactic atmosphere. Sequels include *The Young Unicorns* and *A Ring of Endless Light**. Fanfare.

MOON SHADOW LEE (*Dragonwings**), child of China, the Middle Kingdom, who joins his father in San Francisco in 1903, when he is eight. In the next seven years he comes to understand the attitudes and difficulties of the San Francisco Chinese, the Tang people, but also to know and understand a few of the demons, the white Americans. With considerable fortitude, he works for his relatives in their laundry, experiences the earthquake of 1906, and helps his father build an airplane to fulfill his dream or vision of flying. As narrator of the novel, Moon Shadow gives a strong idea of the fears of a child in a strange land where his countrymen have good reason to be afraid of the dominant people.

MORAG ELLIOTT (*The Whispered Horse**), strong-willed mother of Rowan* and Kate*, who is killed by her son-in-law, Tam* McPhee. A large, powerful woman who wears her red hair in a heavy braid, she is adored by her elderly husband. She confronts her daughter's husband when she learns that he has murdered his previous wife and sends him packing, but she is waylaid the next morning and is murdered by Tam, though it appears she has been victim of an accident.

MORDA (*Taran Wanderer**), evil wizard who captures Taran*, Gurgi*, Fflewddur* Fflam, and Doli*. He turns Gurgi into a mouse, Fflewddur into a hare, and Doli into a frog, and threatens Taran's life. Taran kills the wizard and ends his enchantments by snapping in two the splinter of bone which governs his life.

MORE MINDEN CURSES (Roberts*, Willo Davis, ill. Sherry Streeter, Atheneum, 1980), mystery novel set in the American town of Indian Lake in the last third of the twentieth century, sequel to *The Minden Curse*. Danny Minden, 11, living with his grandfather, Charlie Minden, and his Aunt Mattie while his photographer father is in Ireland on assignment, dreads starting seventh grade, since he has never been to regular school before and knows his father will be disappointed if he doesn't make friends among the boys. His only real friend is a newcomer and a girl, C.B. (Clarissa Beatrix) Hope, who was involved with him in earlier adventures which concerned bank robbers, his part-Irish wolfhound, Leroy, and the Minden "curse" to be present when trouble occurs. Immediately, he has problems in school. Miss Twitten, the teacher, takes a dislike to him; Leroy follows him and causes difficulties until even understanding Mr. Pepper, the principal, bans him; the boys think of nothing but baseball, a sport Danny has never played and doesn't understand. Moreover, though several of the boys are friendly and want to invite him into their secret club, the president, Frankie Sloan, is hostile and sets for his initiation assignment that Danny catch the vicious cat named Chester but called locally "Killer," owned by the old Caspitorian sisters. Danny and C.B. have already become acquainted with the two old ladies, Miss Rosie, frail but agile, and Miss Anna, deaf and confined to a wheel chair, and with some of their thirty-two or thirty-three cats which share their run-down mansion, all of which wear collars studded with fake jewels. Danny is present when the trash fire flares up explosively and burns Miss Rosie, and his quick use of the garden hose prevents the fire from spreading but seems to annoy the next-door neighbors, Mr. and Mrs. Holman, a banker and his wife. When Miss Rosie is hurt by a woodpile that collapses on her and is taken to the hospital, Danny is asked to come sleep in the house to help out Miss Anna. Gramps has fixed their furnace, and C.B. and Danny have started going through a great deal of stuff in the attic, hunting for a jewel box containing some trinkets which the old ladies hope might bring enough to pay for a new roof. Danny already knows that their nephew, Virgil, is trying to get them sent to a rest home and that someone has been exploring the upper floors, obviously hunting for the treasure their jeweler father is reputed to have hidden. Danny tries to make friends with Killer, but the cat disappears. In the meantime, the youngsters find the jewel box and see Mr. Holman pour gas on the trash burner and they alert the sheriff, who tricks Holman into admitting he has a key to the Caspitorian house. When Miss Rosie returns and they learn that the jewels were not worth a great deal, the old ladies decide to dip into their "reserve" and are very upset to find that Killer is missing. The time allowed for Danny to produce Killer for the club is running out, and he and C.B. search, more to comfort the old sisters than in hope of catching the cat. They find him on the Sloan farm, shut in a shed and hanging by his jeweled collar, but still alive. The collar, as they have suspected, contains the real diamonds of the Caspitorian fortune. Danny and C.B., leaving Killer with the veterinarian, go furiously to the club house and charge Frankie with cruelty to the cat. When the other boys say that Danny has fulfilled the initiation feat, he refuses to become a member, and the other club members desert Frankie. The bizarre element of hiding diamonds in a cat's collar is made to seem plausible, and the rest of the well-crafted plot contains only believable elements. Though the characterization is not subtle, it is a good-natured and enjoyable story. Poe Nominee.

MOREY, WALT(ER NELSON) (1907–   ), born in Hoquiam, Wash.; author of adventure and animal novels for young people. He grew up in Oregon, Washington, Montana, and Canada, attended Benkhe Walker Business College, and in his varied career has been a construction worker, mill worker, theater manager, burner foreman and superintendent for Kaiser Shipyards during World War II, deep-sea diver and fish trap inspector in Alaska, and filbert farmer in Oregon. Several of his books are set in Alaska, including *Gentle Ben** (Dutton, 1965), a story of a huge Alaskan bear, *Home Is the North* (Dutton, 1967) and *Kävik the Wolf Dog** (Dutton, 1968), both stories of Malamutes. *Kävik* won both the Dorothy Canfield Fisher and the William Allen White Awards. *Canyon Winter* (Dutton, 1972), a story of a boy marooned by a plane crash over the winter, differs from most of his other novels in its strong conservationist message.

MOSES GODFREY (*Jazz Country**), black jazz pianist and mentor for trumpet player, Tom Curtis. Although only a little past forty, Moses looks fifty, short, thickset, with a full beard and dark glasses. He often answers questions enigmatically or refuses to talk at all, but occasionally he speaks philosophically at length about jazz and how it has to be honest and to express the player's life experience. He is his own man and doesn't hesitate to put a rude critic in his place, but he is vulnerable to the contempt of his son, Frederick, whose mother he left when Frederick was an infant, and he is proud when his son endangers himself to save a Puerto Rican being mugged.

THE MOUSE AND HIS CHILD (Hoban*, Russell, ill. Lillian Hoban, Harper, 1967), fantasy featuring a wind-up toy made of two mice, a father who originally dances in a circle swinging his son up and down as he turns. The story starts in the toy shop, where they are displayed along with a seal, which balances a red and yellow ball on her nose, and an elephant, which paces back and forth in front of an elaborate doll house with turrets, porches, balconies, and a mansard roof. From there they are sold and become toys brought out only at Christmas, until one year a cat knocks a vase from a table and smashes them. A tramp retrieves them from the trash barrel and tinkers with them until they move again, but only in a straight line, the father pushing the son backward. He leaves them at the edge of a road near the dump, where they walk until their spring runs down on a bridge. There they are found by Manny Rat, the gangster boss of the dump, who impresses them along with an assortment of other wind-ups to work as foragers and beasts of burden. When Manny sends his assistant, Ralphie, to rob the bank of its treacle-brittle, they are taken along to carry home the loot, but Ralphie muffs the job, and they escape. They are joined by a bullfrog, who wears an old mitten and earlier has told their fortune, and they set out to seek the child's heart's desire, the elephant for a mother, the seal for a sister, and the dollhouse for a home. They have a series of adventures: they see a war of the shrews ended when weasels eat the shrews, followed by an owl eating the weasels; they are picked up by a crow and join his Experimental Theater Group;

when the audience riots and breaks up the troup, the parrot, Euterpe, takes them to the old Muskrat, who is clever and may be able to make them self-winding; the deep-thinking muskrat, who tries to solve all problems by logic, uses them as the motor power to cut down a tree, whose fall kills the muskrat, knocks out a beaver dam, and catapults the mouse and his child into mud at the bottom of the pond. There they talk to pedantic C. Serpentina, a snapping turtle and author of the play, *The Last Visible Dog*, which so enraged the theater audience, and they meet Miss Mudd, a dragonfly larva, who ties them to a fishing line that dangles from a branch and another end to a good-luck medal, which is swallowed by a fish, causing the mouse and his child to be thrown onto the bank. A hawk spots them, carries them off for food, and drops them on the dump when he finds them inedible. The frog, seeing them fall and smash, gets a bittern to carry him to collect the pieces, and, with the help of a kingfisher, who has adopted the seal, they are reassembled as separate beings with working parts. All this time Manny Rat has been pursuing them vengefully, and now they find him living in the dollhouse, which has been victim of a nursery fire and long since discarded, and using the elephant, no longer plush and aristocratic, as a beast of burden. The good characters work out an ingenious scheme to lift the dollhouse on a pulley and dump the rats, who are attending a party there, onto a passing freight train. Only Manny, with his teeth broken out, remains, and he fakes humility to get into their favor, helping them fix up the dollhouse for their use and making both the mouse and his child self-winding but all along plotting to blow up the house. Thwarted in this, he responds to the mouse child's love and becomes, along with the frog, the bittern, and the kingfisher, an honorary uncle. The house becomes an inn, named, like the play, The Last Visible Dog, a reference to the Bongo Dog Food label, which shows a dog carrying a can with a label showing a dog carrying a can, etc. The mouse father and the elephant marry, and the tramp, who, years before, peered into the toy-shop window, now looks into the doll house window and sees them celebrating Christmas. Throughout, the story is written in a skillful style, full of word play and references to academic ideas and literary works. Several of the episodes are satiric, the muskrat's reduction of all situations to formula and the pretentious nonsense of the play, for instance. Despite all this cleverness, the story is tedious, probably because the main characters are so passive, having to depend upon someone else to wind them until the very end. All the other characters are types, and their assemblage at the dump and Manny's conversion are not convincing. Books Too Good.

THE MOUSE AND THE MOTORCYCLE (Cleary*†, Beverly, ill. Louis Darling, Morrow, 1965), fantasy set in a California foothills inn in the mid twentieth century. When the Gridley family stops at the aging Mountain View Inn, Mrs. Gridley is reluctant to stay because she suspects there are mice, but her husband is too tired to drive further in holiday traffic, and their son, Keith, is happy because he can have a room to himself. Although they don't realize it, they have already been sized up by the regular resident, Ralph, a mouse whose home is behind the knothole beneath the sink in Keith's room. Ralph is fascinated with the model cars Keith has brought and particularly the little motorcycle, so much so that when the Gridleys go down to dinner he climbs to the bedside table and tries sitting on the cycle, pushing with his feet. A sudden ring of the phone so startles him that he forgets to turn and crashes into the metal waste basket, trapped. When Keith finds him, they strike up a conversation, and the boy explains how to start the motorcycle: you have to make a motorcycle noise. So begins a night of thrilling adventure. Keith allows Ralph to take the cycle out of the room and ride down the long expanse of empty hall, where he is spotted by the terrier in another room but not caught. When he returns, however, the door has blown shut, so he leans against the door jam until Matt, the elderly bellboy, unsurprised by a mouse on a motorcycle, opens the door for him. Keith agrees to bring food for the mouse family and to let Ralph ride the cycle at night but wants it parked under the bed in the daytime. This plan works until the maid starts a rare cleaning with the vacuum under the bed where Ralph is admiring the machine and almost sucks him into the hose. To get away, Ralph starts the motorcycle but is so worried that he rides right into the bed linen and gets dumped into the hamper, cycle and all. He is able to chew his way out but not to rescue the motorcycle. He is ashamed, and Keith, though sorry, forgives him and continues to bring food, upon which the mice are now dependent since the housekeeper has been alerted by the chewed sheets, and they must lie low for a while. Disaster seems imminent when Keith gets sick, so late at night that his parents can't buy any aspirin. Ralph starts on a mission of mercy to find an aspirin, which, after harrowing adventures, he does, under a bureau in a first floor room, and to get back to Keith's room on the second floor. With great ingenuity, he succeeds, and Keith, feeling better, gives him the motorcycle, which has been returned to him, before the family departs, agreeing to leave it under the television set in the lobby, a spot they both know is never dusted. Ralph's desire for adventure and his frustration at being thought too young, which parallel Keith's, are the main themes that give meaning to their friendship and to the book. The matter-of-fact treatment makes a believable fantasy, with clever little twists, like the mother mouse thinking Keith is Room Service and worrying about how to tip him. Choice.

MOUSSA (*The Mukhtar's Children**), Mukhtar of the village of Bab-il-Howa in Israel's Achula Valley near the borders of Lebanon and Syria. As leader of his people, he expects respect and obedience to his authority, and he also wants to stick to the old ways, refusing to admit that machines, modern medicine, or social reforms could be the will of Allah. He has a special ability to nurse sick animals and seeks peace for himself and his village. Because he is a clever judge of people and experienced in negotiation, he understands his children's strengths and weaknesses, and while he disapproves of women who are not subservient, he still sees his daughter Jasmin's* superiority and secretly admires her spirit.

MR. ANDERSON (*Rock Star**), Tim's father, an electrician who once was a professional musician but who left the business because he felt it was no good way of making a living. While he was on the road with bands, he saw many musicians fall to alcoholism and drugs. He became an electrician so that he and his family could have a proper home life. He is stern, strict, and hardworking and tries to maintain a beneficial relationship with his son by spending time with him and keeping lines of communication open. Tim loves his father, respects him, and tries to please him, but he does not feel he can discuss the issue of career objectives with him. However, he does feel that his father is doing what he thinks is best for his son.

MR. AND MRS. HASTINGS (*The Bully of Barkham Street**), Martin's parents, whom the reader views in a different light as Martin's attitude toward them changes. At first they seem too busy and unconcerned to care about him or feel any sympathy with his problems. Later they merely seem overworked and exasperated with his irresponsible and defiant behavior. When Mrs. Hastings, for example, yawns at the assembly, Martin interprets her action to boredom. Later he realizes she yawned simply because she was very tired from working so hard.

MR. BURBANK (*Pistol**), teacher from Chicago new in Billy's school in Great Plain. He innocently assigns to the class *Giants in the Earth*. Some of the students react with anger, because the people of Great Plain, a ranching town, despise the dry farmers the book describes. They call them ''honeyockers,'' a derisive term. Mr. Burbank is a convincing character who does not play a big part in the story but significantly influences Billy's thinking, extending the boy's horizons.

MR. CAFFERTY (*The Voyage Begun**), Frank Cafferty, father of Mickey* and Shawn*, sometime friends of Paul Vickers. Mr. Cafferty is a grocer in Warren on Cape Cod who has trouble making ends meet because food supplies are so limited. He spends a lot of time in his store, working on his books and ordering and shelving stock. Sharon, his wife, who runs a beauty shop, nags at him, blaming him for their limited circumstances. She yearns for luxuries which are beyond his means to give her. To get away from her harping, he often storms angrily out of the house and spends long evenings with his friends. The Caffertys are unable to control Shawn, who does pretty much as he pleases, are baffled by close-mouthed Mickey, indulge their obsequious, tattling younger daughter, Maureen, and take advantage of their reliable, older son, Patrick. Mr. and Mrs. Cafferty are foils for Dr.* and Mrs. Vickers and Maggie* Rudd and Gabe Palazzola.

MR. DANIEL THIEL (*The Callender Papers**), painter, trustee of the school of which Aunt Constance is headmistress, who turns out to be Jean* Wainwright's father. He is trustee also of the Callender fortune by the will of old Josiah,

Enoch's* father, who so decreed because of Enoch's irresponsible and wastrel ways. Mr. Thiel had been a Hider (draft dodger) during the Civil War, returned later to Marlborough where he was not particularly liked, and then married Irene Callender, for her money according to local speculation, but the two apparently loved each other. He employs Mrs.* Bywall out of a sense of decent responsibility. After story's end, he marries Aunt Constance, who had raised Jean for him. At first Jean thinks he is a pessimistic, discourteous, secretive, disagreeable man, but later she comes to see finer qualities in him and chooses to live with him.

MR. DAVIS (*The Noonday Friends**), Franny's improvident father, a struggling artist. He is a dreamy man who repeatedly loses jobs because he doesn't keep his mind on what he is doing. He has trouble facing facts and puts unpleasant thoughts out of his mind as much as possible. He is a pathetic, if type, character.

MR. FAHERTY (*Shadrach's Crossing**), father of Shad and Brian*, only mechanic on Lucker's Island. Since the money he makes repairing the smugglers' engines provides substantially for his family, he has an ambivalent attitude toward the smugglers. Though he threatens to beat Shad, something he has never before done, for disobeying him and leaving the house during the smugglers' landings, he cannot bring himself to do it. He is a pathetic, sympathetically presented figure, a man caught between what he feels is morally right and expediency. Shad understands his father's situation. The sympathy between boy and father is one of the book's strongest features.

MR. FORAN (*The Bully of Barkham Street**), Martin Hastings's sixth grade teacher who grows exasperated with the boy's slovenly schoolwork, inattention, and sarcasm. He continues to reach out to the boy, however, and relents on the remainder of the copying exercise that Martin considers so onerous when he sees that the boy is really trying to comply. He even apologizes to Martin for making the punishment excessive, and Martin respects him for his fairness and openness. Mr. Foran has much to do with changing Martin's life for the better.

MR. HARVEY (*A Promise Is a Promise**), cat-loving neighbor whose little house faces the alley and most of whose yard is vegetable and rose garden. Most of the neighbors treat him with scorn or avoid him. When Ruthy prevents her brother's dog from harming his half-blind cat, the old man presents her with a rose, to her embarrassment. Later, Ruthy warns him that Mrs. Boyd, a fussy neighbor, has lured the cats into her basement, intending to call the Humane Society. Mr. Harvey stalks into her yard and calmly breaks her basement window to retrieve his cats. When a doctor wants to take him to the hospital, he refuses to go until Ruthy volunteers to care for the cats until he gets back, and when his sister insists that he live with her and leave the cats behind, he will agree only after Ruthy says she will find homes for them.

MR. LAURITZEN (*Transport 7–41-R**), faithful, determined old man, a repatriate from the Russian zone, who is doggedly intent on burying his dead wife in Cologne as she wished and as he promised her he would do when the time came. On the transport train, his ill, aged, wheelchair-ridden wife dies, and "I" helps him get the body to its destination. The old man and the girl share food, their few comforts, and their many discomforts, and the old man becomes a stabilizing force in the girl's life. He helps her look more objectively at things and builds her faith in people. He is perceptive and calm and tells her stories about what his grocery store in pre-war Cologne was like.

MR. LINGERLE (*Dicey's Song**), Isaac Lingerle, Maybeth Tillerman's music teacher in school. He recognizes the little girl's great musical ability, encourages the family to develop her talent, and gives her piano lessons. A perceptive, kind, and sensitive man, he becomes almost like a father to the Tillerman children. He is nervous at first with the family, partly because he is so fat and partly becuse he is naturally shy and timid. He joins the Tillermans for meals occasionally, sometimes baby-sits with the younger children, and plays the piano while they sing. He is a bachelor, and the Tillermans satisfy his need to belong and to be needed. He is the only teacher who is sympathetically realized in the novel.

MR. MYSTERIOUS AND COMPANY (Fleischman*, Sid, ill. Eric von Schmidt, Little, 1962), realistic novel, which hints of the writer's later tall-tale approach, set in 1884 in the southwestern United States. Jane, 12, her younger brother, Paul, 9, their little sister, Anne, 6, and their parents are used to wandering the West in a brightly painted covered wagon. Pa is a traveling magician, who calls himself Mr. Mysterious, and the family form his company of performers. Jane is the sleeping princess who floats in the air, Paul provides the voice of the wise Sphinx, Mama plays the piano and oversees the props, and Pa juggles and performs feats of magic and sleight of hand to entertain their Old West, small-town audiences. Now the family heads for San Diego, where Pa intends to homestead a ranch so the children can go to a proper school. The children have mixed feelings about Pa closing the company. Although they all enjoy performing, the girls, in particular, see advantages to settling down. Jane looks forward to making friends, going to parties, and wearing the latest styles, and little Anne hopes to attend ballet school. For his part, most of the time Paul wishes they could continue their free and varied life of the road. Going through Texas, Arizona, and New Mexico, they have exciting adventures: Pa trades his cherished, chiming gold watch for a dog which has been mistreated and the children name Professor and teach to jump rope; Paul, as the Sphinx, helps a sheriff capture the notorious Badlands Kid and earns fifty dollars in reward with which the children plan to buy Pa a new watch; they deliver a horse to the sheriff's sweetheart on her birthday and rid her town of outlaws; and Ma scares off attacking Indians with Pa's magic lantern. The family arrives in San Diego on Christmas Day for a joyful reunion with Uncle Fred and Aunt Emma and a happy exchange of gifts, among which Pa gets his new watch and Ma a new sewing machine. But Uncle Fred has spread the word that a famous magician is staying at his house, and, when entertainment-starved friends and neighbors arrive by the dozens hoping to see a show, Pa agrees to put on what the family wistfully regards as their farewell performance. The morning after, Pa, now merely Mr. Andrew Perkins Hackett again, files a claim for the ranch next to Uncle Fred's. Then the owner of the town theater, Big Jim Norton, hears how well their performance was received and invites Mr. Mysterious and Company to put on a show once a month for his patrons. Pa and the family happily accept, delighted that they can have a settled home and the advantages that go with it and also continue their "magic for everyone" shows that they have enjoyed so much. The members of the lively family seem genuinely fond of one another, and the entertaining, well-sustained story moves fast through sometimes surprising twists to a very satisfying conclusion. Choice; Fanfare.

MR. RANDOLPH (*The Great Gilly Hopkins**), blind old black neighbor, who eats at Maime* Trotter's. A man of some education and considerable dignity, his courtly manner contrasts with the blunt, uneducated speech of Mrs. Trotter. He introduces Gilly* to poetry through his love of Wordsworth. When Gilly returns the money she has stolen from him, he accepts it quietly, and when he becomes very ill with flu, his main worry is that his lawyer son will discover his illness and make him move to the son's home in Virginia.

MRS. BYWALL (*The Callender Papers**), Mr.* Thiel's efficient, capable, reticent housekeeper, who befriends Jean*. She stole some silver spoons from the Callenders, for whom she was working as a maid, in order to pay for medical help for her consumptive younger brother. Enoch* Callender insisted that she be prosecuted, and she was sent to jail. She becomes more talkative as the days go by, consoles Jean after her nightmares, and makes her a cotton dress more appropriate for walking in the countryside. Jean likes her.

MRS. CLUTCHETT (*Time at the Top**), cook for the Shaws and housekeeper for Mr. Ormondroyd. A type figure, she is fussy, gossipy, and nosey. She eavesdrops when Susan* Shaw tells her father about her adventures at the top of the elevator and then passes on what she has heard to Mr. Ormondroyd, who subsequently records it in the novel. She is the device by which Ormondroyd creates credibility for the story.

MR. SCULLY (*One-Eyed Cat**), a small, stooped old man who always dresses in a green and black plaid wool shirt and black trousers. He lives in an old house that is cluttered with possessions accumulated over a lifetime. Ned does chores for the old man, like cutting wood and carrying out trash, for a few cents a week. It is at his place that Ned first sees the one-eyed cat. Mr. Scully says it is one of the feral cats that frequent the woods and his backyard. The cat sleeps on an old quilt on top of an abandoned icebox near the old shed. Ned and Mr. Scully become friends through their common concern for the creature, and, after Mr. Scully suffers a stroke, Ned visits him regularly at the nursing home. There Ned tells Mr. Scully that he wounded the cat. By this point in the story, Ned is convinced that he really did maim the cat.

MRS. FAHERTY (*Shadrach's Crossing**), mother of Shad and Brian*, a workworn, careworn woman, cowed into submission by circumstances on the island, her poverty, and the deepening Depression. She advises Shad to reconsider bringing the smugglers to justice, remarking that he is trying "to get to next year by crossing a bridge" (a comment which perhaps gives the book its title), when he'd do better, she thinks, by standing still. She also says that there are times when there is no shame in giving up, a comment that summarizes her own action and attitude. Shad understands her sincere concern for him but refuses to look at things her way, valuing independence more than expediency.

MRS. FORTUNE (*The Witches of Worm**), the elderly woman who owns the apartment house in which Jessica Porter and her mother live. She keeps cats, which Jessica regards as smelly, and shows Jessica how to care for the abandoned kitten. She often tells Jessica stories about strange and wondrous happenings and appears to regard Jessica's anti-social and erratic behavior as the result of an over-active imagination. When she announces to Jessica that Jessica must tell Brandon that she threw his trumpet out of the window, or she, Mrs. Fortune, will tell him, she forces Jessica to face up, which Jessica does, after a fashion. Mrs. Fortune is an only somewhat credible figure.

MRS. FRISBY AND THE RATS OF NIMH (O'Brien*, Robert C., ill. Zena Bernstein, Atheneum, 1971), popular, highly regarded talking-animal fantasy with a science fiction slant about a determined, courageous lady mouse and some ingenious, very intelligent rats. Mrs. Frisby, a widow, and her four small mouse children live in a cinderblock house in Farmer Fitzgibbon's garden patch. Every spring comes Moving Day, when Mrs. Frisby must move her family to summer quarters before Farmer Fitzgibbon plows the field and destroys their home. But this year, her son, Timothy, is ill, and Mrs. Frisby fears the move may be too much for him. She is advised by wise old owl to seek help from the rats who live under the rosebush at the corner of the Fitzgibbon yard. To her astonishment, she discovers beneath the bush a large apartment house complex with electric elevators, electric lights, running water, a library, a school system, and similar human accomplishments and conveniences, all constructed by the rats to fit their needs and all rat-scale in size. From their leader, Nicodemus*, she learns that the rats had been captured and subjected to experiments in the laboratory of NIMH* (which presumably stands for National Institute of Mental Health), where they were given injections to increase their size, their intelligence, and their longevity. Employing their newly gained powers of reasoning and inventiveness, they escaped from the laboratory and made their way cross-country to the Fitzgibbon farm where they established a home in keeping with their increased knowledge and advanced technical ability. One thousand per cent more intelligent than ordinary rats, they are now busily engaged in implementing the Plan, a scheme whereby they will set up a self-sufficient society in nearby Thorn Valley and no longer have to live by the traditional rat method of theft. They agree to help Mrs. Frisby when she offers to put sleeping powder in the food of Dragon, the mean, ferocious Fitzgibbon family cat. She dopes the food, according to plan, but is captured and imprisoned in a bird cage. There, while awaiting hoped-for rescue, she hears that plans are underway to exterminate the rats. This information proves very valuable and enables her to save the lives of the rats who move her house and save her family. Although the focus of the plot shifts and the problems and the history of the rats become more interesting than those of Mrs. Frisby, presumably the protagonist, this story of courage and cooperation is original and suspenseful, and the carefully detailed descriptions of the ways and concerns of the animals, especially the rats, create credibility. The book ends on a peak of emotion, and the reader never learns whether or not all the rats escaped the exterminators. (Justin*) Boston Globe Honor; ChLA Touchstones; Choice; Contemporary Classics; Fanfare; Lewis Carroll; National Book Finalist; Newbery Winner.

MRS. GIORDANO (*The Mystery Cottage in Left Field**), kindly Italian woman who lives in the well-kept small house at the edge of the playing field. Actually Mrs. Montella, she has been given a new name and home by the police, who supply her with groceries delivered at night to keep her from the dangerous gangster, Early Winters. Because her son was a driver of a bootleg truck which was involved in a highjack incident with four fatalities, both the police and the gangsters want him and are trying to get at him through his mother. She finds the isolation unnatural and makes friends with the boys who practice baseball on the field, supplying them with lemonade and cookies and flowers to take to their mothers.

MRS. MARY TOM CHISM (*Words by Heart**), white woman who owns the house where Ben Sills's family live and for whom Lena and her stepmother, Claudie, work. Mrs. Chism is fat and quarrelsome and unpredictably inclined to shift from anger to careless generosity but is also shrewd at getting her way. When she plans a big party, inviting all her married children and most of the town, only Jaybird Kelsey, the grocer, shows up. In fury, after he has left, she throws the fern he brought at the portrait of her long-dead husband, who was well liked in the community.

MRS. POST (*The Witches of Worm**), the fat wife of the apartment house caretaker. She often looks in on Jessica Porter when Jessica's mother, Joy* Porter, works late or goes out on dates, both frequent events. Jessica dislikes her, since Mrs. Post openly disapproves of Joy's actions and the way she brings up her daughter. She feels Mrs. Porter should spend more time with Jessica, pay more attention to what she does, and make her behave. Jessica's mother relies on Mrs. Post but openly resents her unsolicited advice on child rearing. Jessica is fully aware of her mother's attitude toward Mrs. Post and uses it to her advantage, playing one woman against the other.

MRS. SCALLOP (*One-Eyed Cat**), housekeeper for the Wallis family, whose voice is "as sharp and grinding as a woodcutter's saw," in Ned's opinion. She is often insulting to him, speaks of herself in the third person to him, and is so contradictory in her speech and behavior that he thinks she is quite silly. She seeks to compensate for feelings of insecurity by trying to dominate those around her, even Mrs.* Wallis, who speaks up to her quite often. Mrs. Scallop enjoys cooking and often praises herself. Reverend* Wallis gets her a position in a local nursing home, where she seems quite happily in control of things. Ned sees her there when he visits Mr.* Scully, and she is no less disrespectful to the boy then. She is a foil for Reverend Wallis.

MRS. SMITH (*The Changeling**), wife of the owner of the Onowora Stables near Rosewood Hills, where Martha Abbott and Ivy* Carson go to ride. They become fond of Dolly, the oldest horse there, and, when they learn that Mr. Smith intends to have her destroyed decide to rescue her. They are discovered in the act, but sympathetic Mrs. Smith persuades her husband to change his mind about getting rid of the horse so the girls can continue to play with her. A painter, she is the only supportive adult in the book, until the girls are in junior high and encounter the drama teacher.

MR. STONE (*I, Adam**), waspish, disagreeable, none-too-intelligent schoolmaster of Coveport. After he beats Adam Crane on the last day of school, Adam and his chums dump the man in a haystack for one of the book's few comic scenes. Adam leaves school in Coveport with relief, because life there with Mr. Stone has been so unrewarding. Later, with Pen Jackson teaching, Adam discovers a new joy in learning. The very positive educational experience with Pen, supported by the encouragement of pretty, young Sarah Newlands, a student of Pen's who also loves to learn, changes the course of Adam's life, and he decides to continue with formal schooling by going to college.

MRS. WALLIS (*One-Eyed Cat**), Ned Wallis's Mama, wife of the Reverend* James Wallis. She has suffered from arthritis for several years, so much so that she is largely confined to her room and can only leave it when carried downstairs by someone. Although removed from events by her illness, she knows what is going on in the house and does not let Mrs.* Scallop dominate her. She has an alert and perceptive mind and is, Ned observes, as much interested in what he is thinking as in what he does. Relieved of much of her pain by a new treatment at the end of the story, she is able to walk outside by herself and thus meets Ned at the Makepeace mansion where she confides that she saw him on the night he fired the rifle and that years before she had run out on her family because she felt intimidated by her husband's goodness. More than any other character, she helps Ned come to terms with what he has done. She also points out to him that he cannot be sure that he is the one who maimed the cat.

MUFFIN (*No More Magic**), imaginative, determined schoolgirl, very interested in magic, who helps Chris* solve the mystery of where his bike has gotten to. She has long, dark hair, which she wears in a single braid down her back, and a checkered coat with a Druidic pattern. She is new in town and lives with her aunt. A loner, by Halloween she still has not made friends among her schoolmates. She takes quite literally her father's remark that his marriage has failed because the magic is gone from it. She believes that by recovering Chris's green bike, which Chris thinks is magical, the magic will return to her parents' marriage and they will get back together again. Muffin makes herself a warlock costume for Halloween, and, when her aunt gives it away to Chris's brother because she thinks Muffin is too caught up in magic, Muffin dresses as a nurse. Muffin thinks her costume was stolen. At the end of the book, her father and mother have patched up their differences. Muffin attributes their reconciliation to the recovery of the bike.

THE MUKHTAR'S CHILDREN (Watson*, Sally, Holt, 1968), realistic problem novel set in Israel near the Lebanese border in 1949. Although Moussa*, the mukhtar or leader of the Arab village of Bab-il-Howa, has refused to let his people engage in the war against the Yahud, the Jews, he is not pleased when a kibbutz, Kfar Shalom, is built nearby, and he insists that his people live in peace but stick to the old ways with minimal communication with their new neighbors. Gradually, however, they are drawn together by curiosity and circumstances. Moussa's son Khalil*, 12, is fascinated by machinery; his twin sister, Jasmin*, the chief protagonist, chafes under the many restrictions for women and fervently desires to be educated; Ahmed, the eldest brother, loves the land and admires the way the kibbutz irrigates, fertilizes, and grows in the poor soil; Yusif, their young half-brother, a strutting copy of his firebrand grandfather, Kbeer Abou, wants to show the Yahud the superiority of all things Arabic. Though Moussa refuses to join a conspiracy to drive the young Jews out, he does allow Jawad, a young man of the village, to return from Lebanon, although this is against the law. Khalil is attracted to Jawad's fiery rhetoric and interested in the plan to visit the kibbutz and leave behind dynamite to blow it up, but he does not participate directly, and when the blast fails to go off and the Yahud return the dynamite, he escapes Moussa's anger. Later, however, after being insulted by the bitter Major Schoor, he joins three older boys in an ambush to shoot the officer but succeeds only in seriously wounding Moshe, the young Israeli who has befriended him. When Avram, the leader of the kibbutz, brings the case to Moussa, Khalil confesses, the others are exposed, and Moussa thunders that he will banish them. Avram tactfully persuades him, instead, to send Khalil to the kibbutz to live and do Moshe's work (and to act as hostage) and to let the other conspirators work there by day or be banished. Only Jawad chooses banishment. In the meantime, Jasmin has rebelled violently at Moussa's plan to betroth her as second wife to an old man, has been beaten, and has discussed her case with an Israeli girl. She is told that the new law will not let her marry until she is seventeen. But when Khalil goes to live in Kfar Shalom, her secret visits to this strange place, where women and men work together on equal terms and women shamelessly wear clothes exposing their legs, must stop. Selim, Khalil's quiet, thoughtful friend, who is attracted to Jasmin, starts to teach his little sister to read and lets her teach Jasmin, who in turn teaches the other village girls. Gradually all the young people—Katan, Selim, Yusif (who adores the Israeli Leo), Ahmed—are quietly visiting the kibbutz and making friends. When Khalil returns home, he gives up his long war for supremacy over Jasmin and encourages her to visit the kibbutz also and gets his mother to talk to the women of the village about sewing machines and health programs and labor-saving devices, but Moussa is still unaware of this mingling. The climax comes when a bomb set to kill Moussa goes off on a night when he has been called to the kibbutz himself to help with a sick cow, because he has great skill in healing. The collapsing wall pins Khalil on top of Jasmin, who is nearly killed and revives before being taken to the hospital long enough to extract a promise from her distraught father that he will let her be educated, choose her own husband, and even visit the kibbutz. The story contains fascinating details of the life in an Arab village of the period and clear insight into the frustrations of a bright girl in the repressive culture. The young Israelis are treated idealistically, and the story ends with a hopeful friendship that seems ironic in light of the more recent hostilities in the area. Fanfare.

THE MURDERER (Holman*, Felice, Scribner's, 1978), realistic novel set in Ashlymine, Pa., a coal-mining town on the Susquehanna River, in 1932 and 1933. Depression widens the longtime gulf between the Polish miners and the Jewish storekeepers, but Hershey (Hershel) Marks, 12, does not understand the antagonism, even though he is often on the receiving end of the Polish boys' physical retaliation. In particular, Hershey admires Lorsh Jabieski, the captain of the Patriots ball team and acknowledged leader of the Polish boys, and he dreams of becoming a runner, a track star who will merit Lorsh's approval. When the Jewish boys make an abortive effort to eat lunch under the trees at school, a preferred spot the Polish boys reserve for themselves, Hershey is the only one caught. Lorsh and the others try to make him admit he is a Christ killer. Troubled, Hershey tries to find out what this means but is unable to get answers from his father or the rabbi. In a series of episodes, Hershey copes with this problem and other occurrences of small town life: he makes the "hypnotized" girl in the furniture store window laugh but doesn't win the promised bedroom suite; he reads and worries about the rise to power of Hitler when he briefly takes over a paper route; tone-deaf, he suffers through piano lessons until he persuades the music teacher to take on his younger brother, Max, instead; he watches a rare total eclipse of the sun; he is beaten up by kids his father catches shoplifting in their hardware store; he worries about death when his sometime friend, Lenny Gorin, dares the others to cross the frozen river and is later found drowned; he and Nutty Cohen are caught and strung up to clothesline poles, arms outstretched as if crucified, by a group of Polish boys, including his idol, Lorsh. Because the mines are mostly closed and his father's business is threatened, the family go to Phillipsburg, N.J., to see his mother's half-sister, wealthy Aunt Milly, for a loan of $300 to save the store. Aunt Milly pretends not to hear and gives Hershey's mother her old furpiece. Furious and humiliated, Mrs. Marks throws it in the river, then frantically gets Hershey to try to retrieve it, since it might be saleable. The store is saved when Mrs. Marks's brother, Uncle Sam, offers the loan from his meagre savings. Ready for his bar mitzvah, Hershey finds the rabbi has given him the wrong text and he has less than a week to learn the new one, a problem complicated by his inability to cope with the chant. The nightmare is resolved when he develops flu and is in bed for his party, knowing that the following week, for his postponed bar mitzvah, the text will be the one he first learned and knows well. Although full of humor, the book treats realistically Hershey's problem of what causes the prejudice and antagonism that divides the town and, as he comes to see, the world. It also shows his gradual understanding that Jews throughout the world share a heritage and that his life isn't limited by the slag heaps of Ashlymine. Life in a Jewish family is gently satirized with more understanding and subtlety than in many books on the subject. Hershey is an appealing character, naive but bright, long suffering but not resigned to injustice. Throughout, the book is in present tense, a rather self-conscious style. Fanfare.

THE MURDER OF HOUND DOG BATES (Branscum*, Robbie, Viking, 1982), lighthearted mystery-detective novel set in the hills of rural Arkansas at an unspecified time but probably in the 1930s or 1940s. Orphaned Sassafras Bates, 13, has grown up on the poor dirt farm that belongs to his three formidable spinster aunts, Aunt* Hope, the cook, Aunt* Faith, the gardener, and Aunt* Veela, the one who tills the soil and acts as family leader because she does the hardest work. When Sassafras finds his dog and best friend, Hound Dog Bates, dead, he immediately assumes that the animal has been poisoned by his aunts, who have persistently complained about the dog's bad manners and thieving ways. Sass angrily buries the dog in the front yard in Aunt Faith's pansy bed that faces the front porch, erecting over the grave a cross bearing an inscription that indicates clearly that he suspects them of the crime. Certain that confronting them in this way will bring a speedy confession of guilt, he is quite taken aback when his aunts not only profess ignorance of how the dog died but react with expressions of unusual tenderness and sympathy for his loss. This leads the boy to suspect that perhaps his own life is in danger. He then interviews each of them individually, hoping thereby to trap them into expressions of guilt. Ironically, each conversation leads him into a deeper understanding of what his aunts are really like, why they have never married, and what they have sacrificed to bring him up. Then he encounters by the old swimming hole, bluff, hearty, capable Kelly* O'Kelly, a wandering man and former policeman, whose aid he enlists in ferreting out the murderer. Kelly's suggestion that Sass check up on people new to the area leads him to bad-natured Clem Watts, just returned to the hills and a sometime beau of the aunts. In rapid succession, the aunts primp and put on a sumptuous meal to impress Clem with what he has lost, Aunt Hope and Kelly fall in love, Kelly rescues Sass when a tornado strikes, and, on a trip to town, Kelly discovers that Clem bought poison to kill weasels that were raiding his chickens. Sass knows now what happened to Hound Dog and understands that his aunts were right about the animal and that Hound Dog deserved his fate, and he is happy to welcome Kelly as his new uncle. Characters are colorful and boldly sketched, plot, though not always convincingly motivated, holds the reader's attention well, and the enjoyment level is high. Reading pleasure comes mostly from Sass's naive, forceful, first person reflections, a full measure of ironic humor, the flavorful, unschooled, regional speech, and the strong emotional attraction of a boy's deep love for his dog. The book seems aimed at a somewhat older audience than its ninety pages and large print would indicate. Poe winner.

MURILLO, BARTOLOMÉ ESTEBAN (*I, Juan de Pareja**), actual seventeenth-century Spanish painter who comes to study under Velázquez*. Murillo, who became famous for religious paintings, is represented as a genuinely devout young man who accepts the black slave as a friend with true simplicity of spirit.

MUSHROOM PEOPLE (*The Wonderful Flight to the Mushroom Planet†*; *Stowaway to the Mushroom Planet†*; *Time and Mr. Bass**), the inhabitants of Basidium-X* and the humanoid race to which Mr. Tyco* Bass belongs. While primitive in many respects, they catch one another's thoughts instantly. They use the flesh of the bilba trees to make robes which they drape about themselves much like those of the ancient Greeks. They are smaller than people of Earth, are pale green in color when healthy, and have large, dome-like heads, small faces, and gentle, dark brown eyes. They are peaceful and kind by nature and live in igloo-shaped houses.

MUSKET (*Westmark**; *The Kestrel**), dwarf in the service of Count Las* Bombas and friend of Theo and Mickle*. In *Westmark*, Theo first meets Musket when the dwarf comes to Theo's employer's print shop and commissions Theo to print for a mysterious Dr. Absalom a pamphlet in which the doctor offers to cure for a fee any ailment that may afflict humankind. King's men break in and destroy the press when they discover that Theo is printing without a license. In the skirmish, Theo assaults one of them and then must flee for his life. Musket later introduces Theo to Dr. Absalom, then going under the name of Count Las Bombas, and hair-raising adventures ensue. In *The Kestrel*, Musket accompanies Mickle, then Queen Augusta of Westmark*, as, disguised, Mickle searches for Theo. Musket later enables Mickle and Las Bombas also to go in search of King Constantine. Musket is small but clever, loyal, and outspoken.

MUSTANG: WILD SPIRIT OF THE WEST (Henry*†, Marguerite, ill. Robert Lougheed, Rand, 1966), biographical novel with animal story aspects set mostly in the United States West in the mid twentieth century. Determined, courageous Annie* Johnston describes her long crusade to save the wild mustangs from extinction. Born Annie Bronn, she grows up on a ranch near Reno, Nev., where her special chore is grooming Pa's horses. Pa's "Pardner," she inherits his great love for the magnificent, spirited, sturdy, wild horses he captures, trains, and sells and also his intense dislike for anyone who mistreats animals. A year in a San Francisco hospital in a body cast when she is eleven strengthens her polio-crippled body and also her great love for the mustangs and her native hills. Not long after high school, she marries Charley Johnston, her father's hired man, and the young couple buy Pa's ranch, rename it the Double Lazy Heart, and turn it into a weekend dude ranch for children. Life seems complete, until one day, while on her way to her secretarial job in Reno, Annie sees a truck crammed with bruised, beaten, bloody, wild mustangs being hauled to a rendering plant, where they are to be slaughtered and made into pet food. This is a turning point in Annie's life. She identifies with the terror-stricken, confined creatures and launches a battle to save them from the canneries which are hunting them with increasing intensity in air roundups. Charley, Pa, friends, and her employer, Mr. Harris, encourage her efforts, which extend over many months. After the county passes an ordinance prohibiting hunting and herding by air, a local lawyer, Mr. Richards, points out to Annie that the victory is really a "puny" one. He advises her to carry her campaign further, to gather facts and to prepare statements that will result in a state law against the devastating raids. Annie takes his advice seriously, and her campaign gradually gains momentum. School children write hundreds of letters on behalf of the endangered ponies. Eventually, state and national legislators and the communication media rally to the cause of this quiet, plain, determined champion whom thousands now know as Wild Horse Annie. Powerful opposition comes from ranchers and pet food manufacturers and ironically even from the United States Bureau of Land Management. In spite of her worry over Charley, who suffers from a fatal lung disease, and her inexperience in government, Annie persists. Her reasoned, eloquent plea before a Senate subcommittee during the Eisenhower administration results in the passage in 1959 of a law to protect the remaining mustangs and triumph for Annie. Language is easy and sentence structure simple. Tone is earnest and sometimes preachy. Most of the characters really lived. They are presented as quite obvious types, and one can often hear the author's voice in Annie's recital of events. Descriptive details of place ground the story firmly in the reality of ranch life, incidents are easily visualized, and the story carries the conviction that comes from information gained from interviews as well as printed sources. The book is dated in style and approach; late twentieth century critical tastes require a more skillful blending of research and plot and more attention to plotting and characterization. Choice; Western Heritage.

MY BROTHER SAM IS DEAD (Collier*, James Lincoln, and Christopher Collier*, Four Winds, 1974), historical novel set mostly in the village of Redding, Conn., from April, 1775, to February, 1779, about one family's involvement in the American Revolution on the home front. Mischievous, occasionally irresponsible Timmy Meeker, about eleven when events begin and the younger son in the family, tells the story. His much-loved and admired older brother, rebellious, arrogant, headstrong Sam*, 16, a Yale student, enlists in the Continental army after Lexington. Following a terrible argument with his father, Eliphalet*, a Redding store- and tavernkeeper with Tory sympathies, Sam steals his father's gun, the old Brown Bess, and runs away to join General Arnold's forces. Months pass without much incident, except that on one occasion Continentals terrorize the Meeker household in search of weapons, and the family hears very little about Sam. Times get harder and nerves tenser, as the British move northward and westward, and people are uncertain where their neighbors' sympathies lie. Mr. Meeker disappears in late 1777, simply abducted by cow-boys (Rebel thieves who prey upon travelers ostensibly in the name of freedom) on the way back from a trading trip to Verplancks on the Hudson, and Tim and his mother are left to run the family business alone. The British take over the town and treat the people harshly, rooting out Rebel partisans to make examples of them. Later, the Rebels move into town and help themselves to food and supplies, dealing no less harshly with the people than did the British. When Sam's unit arrives, Mrs. Meeker (Susannah*) attempts to persuade him to remain at home, since he is needed and his term is up, but he refuses. General Putnam has given orders that anyone caught stealing will be executed. Sam, now serving with his forces, tries one night to prevent some soldiers from raiding the Meeker cattle and is himself accused of theft by the thieves. Even though Timmy and Mrs. Meeker stand up for him and assert his innocence, the authorities do not believe their testimony, and Sam is convicted and shot as an example by his own fellow soldiers. A far soberer Timmy observes the execution of the brother he had so dearly loved. In an epilogue, Tim, fifty years older and a prosperous merchant, looks back on those troubled, hurtful times and ponders whether indeed freedom was bought at too high a price and the same objectives might not have been accomplished by peaceful means. Related in terse, vigorous style, the story moves relentlessly with few extra details through a series of sharply conceived scenes to its stark and horrifyingly ironic conclusion. Convincing characters, roundly and dynamically drawn; credible family relationships; a believable plot that expertly blends history and story; and sound research authentically treated combine for an accurate and realistic picture of the war that avoids the sentimentality and melodrama of many American historical novels about crucial times. Although the reader never sees a full-blown battle, only skirmishes, and focus is on local happenings, larger issues and events are revealed through conversations in the tavern, reports, and letters, and early in the book the reader is apprised of the prevailing Tory and Patriot points of view through conversations. (Betsy* Read) Choice; Fanfare; National Book Finalist; Newbery Honor.

MY BROTHER STEVIE (Clymer*, Eleanor, Holt, 1967), realistic novel of family life for younger readers set mostly in New York City in the mid–1900s. Annie Jenner, 12, tells about her worries and struggles with Stevie, her eight-year-old brother, who is "full of the devil" and increasingly hard to control. Just before their mother ran away and left them to live with grandma in her small apartment in a housing project, their mother told Annie that she should be sure always to take care of Stevie. Annie loves Stevie very much, and she is determined to follow her mother's instructions, but sometimes she thinks that her mother is asking too much of her. She gets no help from grandma, who is self-pitying, rigid, and very impatient with Stevie. After Stevie starts running with older boys who break into subway candy machines and throw rocks at trains, Annie turns to Miss Stover, Stevie's new teacher, who is warm and accepting. Stevie becomes fond of her dog, Skipper, and for a while things are better with Stevie. But when Miss Stover takes a leave from her teaching position, Stevie returns to his old habits and haunts. In desperation, Annie takes Stevie and sneaks away by train to the little country town where Miss Stover lives. She finds the teacher caring for her ill foster mother and several younger foster brothers and sisters. Spending the weekend with Miss Stover and her happy, loving family opens new vistas for both Stevie and Annie. Stevie enjoys wholesome activities with these well-cared for, joyful children, and Annie gains confidence in herself and the courage to continue trying to help Stevie. After they come home, grandma is more patient with Stevie, who becomes more manageable, and she shows a greater interest in the things that interest her grandchildren. Annie's story of her dedicated and sometimes amusing efforts to keep faith with her mother and keep Stevie out of trouble is told with candor and feeling. But the plot is thin, and the conclusion flat and predictable. Characters and events seem gotten up to show just-fluent-readers some of the problems of growing up in the inner city. Vocabulary is easy and style uncomplicated, and the narrative moves right along. Choice.

MYCETIAN LEAGUE (*Time and Mr. Bass**), a kind of law court which keeps in touch with Mycetians, the five thousand or so spore, or Mushroom*, people, on Earth. The purpose of the League is to judge all cases of wrong done to or by Mycetians. The League meets every three months at Carn* Bassyd, Tyco* Bass's home in Wales. Mr. Bass is its president, and Towyn Niog is his chief assistant. The number of members is thirteen, a lucky number among the spore people.

MYERS, WALTER DEAN (1937–   ), born in Martinsburg, W.Va.; editor, novelist. Since the family had too many children and too little income, his parents let friends adopt him, and he grew up in New York City. He attended City College of New York, served in the U.S. Army 1954–1957, and has been senior trade editor in Bobbs-Merrill publishing company. In 1968 he won the Interracial Council Award for Children's Books for *Where Does the Day Go?* (Parents, 1969). His best-known novels have black characters in inner-city settings, including *Fast Sam, Cool Clyde, and Stuff**, (Viking, 1975), a story of growing up in Harlem, and *Hoops** (Delacorte, 1981), a basketball novel which was an Edgar Allan Poe Award nominee.

MY OWN PRIVATE SKY (Beckman*, Delores, Dutton, 1980), psychological problem novel set in Glenwood, Calif., in the last third of the twentieth century. Although Arthur Elliot, 11, is used to baby-sitters because his widowed mother works, he has never known anyone quite like Jennifer Kearns, sixtyish, his first sitter after they move to California from Minnesota, hoping the climate will ease his severe allergies. Mrs. Kearns, also a widow, has come from Arizona where she grew up on a ranch. She and her father, Pilgrim*, who is aging and often confused, and their dog, Tuffy Apple, live in the same apartment complex as the Elliots. Besides wearing moccasins, denim cut-offs, and Indian jewelry, Mrs. Kearns is unconventional in having a wood stove, a workshop full of petroglyphs, and no television. Arthur soon becomes very attached to her and resents the neighbor kids, Norrie (Norene) Willis, a know-it-all girl Arthur's age but a full head taller, and her little brother, Jack, who hang around Mrs. Kearns's apartment. Arthur's problems are multiple, chiefly being small and skinny, having buck teeth and allergies, and being deathly afraid of water, the result of having been held under water in a wading pool by a bigger kid when he was small and then threatened by the baby-sitter if he should ever tell. At the pool where he with great reluctance is taking swimming lessons, he is bullied by Greg Patterson, a boy with whom he's already had a run-in and who has nicknamed him "Roto-Rooter." When nearsighted Mrs. Kearns is hit by a car and has her leg amputated, Arthur and Norrie are brought together by their concern and by helping Mrs. Willis take care of Pilgrim. Mrs. Kearns's cousin, loud, positive Hattie Lilly, comes from Arizona to take over. Arthur goes with Hattie to visit Mrs. Kearns at the hospital where his mother works and is shocked at how she seems to have lost her nerve. He also overhears two nurses discussing a romance between the physical therapist, David Halverson, who wears braces on his teeth, and Arthur's mother. He and Norrie sneak into the hospital physical therapy room to see if Mrs. Kearns really is afraid to try to walk on her artificial leg; they are caught by Mr. Halverson, who very decently does not tell Arthur's mother and later helps Arthur fix Mrs. Kearns's shopping cart and frame a rubbing of a petroglyph he has made. Mrs. Kearns comes home from the hospital the same day Arthur's swimming class will get their certificates if they dive, a feat Arthur has not yet been able to make himself do. She insists she can get along on crutches without Hattie's help but falls. As he trembles on the diving board, Arthur sees her walking at the other end of the pool, using her artificial leg. Inspired by her courage, he dives successfully. The story is a little too pat, with the prospective stepfather being the only adult to wear braces on his teeth and Norrie as miserable about being too tall as Arthur is to be short, and the theme that misfits can give mutual support is too obvious. Nevertheless, the characterization of Arthur is good, with a sense of his inner sturdiness behind his numerous insecurities, and the relationship between him and his mother is nicely handled. IRA.

MYRON FARRADAY (*The Skating Rink**), failure-prone father of Tuck. Embittered by a long string of unsuccessful ventures, Myron often takes out his anger on Tuck and is particularly resentful when the boy, unable to speak without stuttering, refuses to answer him. Although he has never shown his son much affection, he waits up after the performance at the rink, afraid that Tuck will not come home again after his success.

MYRON KAGAN (*The Alfred Summer**), inarticulate "normal" boy who becomes a friend of retarded Alfred* Burt and cerebral palsy victim, Lester* Klopper, and who builds a rowboat in the apartment house basement. Though with no obvious handicaps, Myron is shy and psychologically hampered by living in a household of demanding women, his mother, his grandmother, and his twin younger sisters, all scornful of Myron's clumsiness.

THE MYSTERIOUS RED TAPE GANG (Nixon*, Joan Lowery, ill. Joan Sandin, Putnam, 1974), mystery novel involving some detection set in a residential neighborhood in Los Angeles in the late twentieth century and narrated by Mike*, one of the children who participate in the action. Mike, whose full name, he informs his audience, is Michael Francis Cassidy, 12, and his three chums, Leroy*, Jimmy, and Tommy, decide that their club should be devoted to doing good deeds. When Mike's dad complains that city hall is too tangled up in red tape to do anything about an overgrown hibiscus bush on the Hartwell property that has caused six auto accidents, the boys take the initiative, hack it back, and transplant it, their first good deed. Linda Jean Hartwell, whom the boys dislike mainly because she is a girl but also because she chews gum, is a snoop, and wears "smelly perfume" that she made herself, blackmails them into letting her join their club. Once accepted, however reluctantly, she proposes that the club continue to cut red tape, that is, act where adults do not, and call themselves the Red Tape Gang. The club's second beneficial deed, boarding up a dangerous, abandoned house, brings the children up against, first, a dope ring, and second, some shady goings-on that appear to revolve around Mr. Hartwell's auto repair shop. Overheard phone conversations, snooping, and midnight trysts lead them to the discovery that Mr. Hartwell is involved with auto thieves. The club's touchiest situation occurs when Leroy gets locked in Mr. Hartwell's shop, the place where the stolen cars and engines are received and dispersed. Because the club members feel Mr. Hartwell should have the chance to turn himself in to authorities, or at least assist in bringing the ring to justice, and because they respect Linda Jean's feelings, the children plant notes at strategic points to frighten Mr. Hartwell into action. In the showdown, while Tommy summons the police, Leroy lets the air out of the villains' tires, Linda Jean pretends the Hartwells' car is booby-trapped so the thieves won't use it to get away, and Mike turns on the Hartwells' lawn sprinklers, actions which so confuse the two villains that Mr. Hartwell gets their gun, takes them captive, and then turns them over to the police. The boys conclude that Linda Jean is not so bad after all, even if she is a girl, and cast about for other ways to improve their neighborhood. A fast, even pace, natural dialogue with late-twentieth-century idioms and allusions, good interpersonal relationships, some humor, irony, and satire on the ways of adults, and some sense of the importance of doing the right thing compensate for the stereotyped characters and events and keep this from being just another book in which enterprising, alert children succeed where adults fail. Poe Nominee.

MYSTERY AT CRANE'S LANDING (Thum*, Marcella, Dodd, 1964), mystery novel set in southern Missouri in the early 1960s. Paula Jordan, a high school senior from New England, accepts the invitation of Lucy Crane, her roommate in their St. Louis boarding school, to spend spring vacation with her at Crane's Landing near New Madrid, Mo., where the town is having a Civil War Centennial celebration. Pretty Lucy is rattlebrained but manipulative, and Paula rightly suspects that she has an ulterior motive: to have a visitor in the house to blunt the protest of her cousin and his wife, present managers of the estate, when she invites her new boy friend, a medical student from St. Louis, to come for the Centennial dance and be an overnight guest. Lucy has arranged that Paula's date will be her attractive neighbor, Dave Rallings, whom Paula meets under unfortunate circumstances while she is changing a tire for Lucy on an isolated road. Lucy's cousin Walter proves to have a charming surface over a hard, humorless interior; his recently married wife, Cora, is a meticulous woman, a former nurse, interested mainly in the antiques she has collected for the pre-war house. The girls visit Aunt Sissy, Lucy's invalid Great-aunt Melissa, to borrow a dress for Paula for the costume ball, and Lucy happens on an old unopened letter from Cousin Walter, whom Aunt Sissy has refused to see since he came recently from Brazil to take over Crane's Landing when her own illness forced her to leave, her resentment stemming from the fact that Walter's grandfather joined the Union army while his brother, her own father, fought for the Confederacy. Later Paula finds Lucy in an agitated state and that night overhears angry voices, then is awakened by the sound of Lucy trying to start her car. Looking out her window, she sees Lucy coming from the stables on the stallion, Diablo, which rears and throws her. Paula's suspicions rise when Cora will not let her see Lucy. She finds the gas tank empty in Lucy's car, she discovers Lucy's door locked, and when she does see Lucy briefly the next day in Walter's presence, her friend seems groggy, as if drugged, yet evidently trying to send her a message through a code phrase they developed at school. When she tells Dave, he is unimpressed. She tries to get to Aunt Sissy with her concerns but is sent packing by the old lady's nurse-companion, who calls Walter to report her attempt. She is further concerned when Flora, the black cook since Lucy's infancy, is fired and seems afraid to discuss Lucy's problem. Since the house is to be open for viewing as part of the celebration, Paula helps clean and realizes that Lucy's signals have meant that the picture of Cousin Walter from the old letter is hidden in the music box. After the open house, she finds it, realizes that it is a very different person from the man in possession of the house, tries to call Dave, is discovered by Walter, runs away, and is found by Walter and Cora with the aid of Lucy's dog, Poppy. Thoughtfully providing blankets, a lantern, and a little food and water, they lock Paula in an old ice house in an isolated woods, while they plan to make their getaway to Brazil with all the quickly convertible assets from Lucy's house and farm. Paula cleverly entwines a necklace Dave has given her into Poppy's collar as a signal, and after about twenty hours she is rescued by Dave and Lucy's boyfriend. They find Lucy still locked in and groggy, but alive, and they get the marshal to send out an alarm which captures Walter and Cora boarding a plane in St. Louis. Walter, it turns out, is actually Jim Tompkins, the business partner in Brazil of the real cousin Walter, who was killed in an accident while they were riding together. Their identifications became confused, and Cora met and married Tompkins thinking he was Walter Crane. The plot and suspense are well handled, but the social relationships seem dated even for the period of publication. It is doubtful whether, even in the South, girls in the 1960s wore skirts and stockings for casual walks in the woods, rather than slacks or jeans, nor did young people of high school and college age call each other ''Mr.'' and ''Miss,'' even at first acquaintance. Poe Winner.

THE MYSTERY COTTAGE IN LEFT FIELD (Caroselli*, Remus F., Putnam, 1979), novel of suspense set in 1929 in Providence, R.I. Jimmy Loughlin, 12, the first-person narrator, must take his five-year-old brother, Dennis, to baseball practice with him because their mother is giving birth at home to a baby sister, Agnes. To keep Dennis out of trouble, Jimmy makes him sit against the picket fence of a neat cottage out beyond the left field edge. Although none of the kids have ever seen anyone around the house, Dennis is soon talking animatedly to a woman who stands in the cottage yard and soon is eating a piece of pizza she has given him. Through Dennis, Jimmy becomes friends with the woman, Mrs.* Giordano, who talks with an Italian accent, tells them of her son, who played baseball when young, and provides lovely flowers from her garden for their mother. When she supplies lemonade for the ball players, Jimmy's friends, particularly Ding Coleman, also become interested, as do two bigger boys, the bully Roy* Oates and his sidekick, Eats Farrell. The attractive young librarian, Miss* Worthington also seems unusually curious about Jimmy's stories of Mrs. Giordano. Jimmy and Ding stake out the house one night and discover that past midnight a man brings Mrs. Giordano's groceries, then returns to a police car. Another evening, they spot two men, one with a bald head and broad shoulders, watching the house. They fear that the car is following them home, and the next day, when Jimmy sees the bald man at the library, he goes to Miss Worthington's home for advice. She is upset and advises silence, but on his way home Jimmy is waylaid by the bald man who tries to get information about a man in the librarian's apartment. Part of the mystery is cleared up when Jimmy and Ding, again staking out the cottage at night, stumble over Roy and Eats, who are watching the bald man and his companion threaten Mrs. Giordano and learn that he is the gangster, Early Winters. Mrs. Giordano is really Mrs. Montella, and her son, Evo, is the only survivor of a bootlegging shootout who can finger Winters as the mastermind. Winters hears the boys outside, captures Roy, and enlists his support to beat the whereabouts of Evo out of Jimmy, who, he thinks, must know since Miss Worthington is Evo's girl. To protect Mrs. Giordano, Jimmy stands up to Roy, even though the gangster gives Roy his gun, and this stand wins Roy over to the good side. Jimmy takes Mrs. Giordano to Miss Worthington's, where, as he has already figured out, Evo is hiding in the immense fireplace, resting out of sight in a sort of swing suspended in the chimney. There the gangsters confront them, Evo decides to come out of hiding and testify against Winters, and Roy and Jimmy together tackle the man who is holding a gun on them. Roy, reformed, goes to work for Jimmy's father in his garage, Evo testifies, and he, Miss Worthington, and Mrs. Giordano are given new identities by the police. Winters goes to prison. Although the first-person narration is consistent and quite effective, the characters are unconvincing types and the events are in the realm of melodramatic wish-fulfillment for twelve-year-olds. Roy's conversion is not believable, and Jimmy's interesting family situation, which starts the book, becomes a trite winning-of-father's-approval story by the end. Poe Nominee.

THE MYSTERY MAN (Corbett*, Scott, ill. Nathan Goldstein, Little, 1970), mystery-detective novel set in the late 1900s in a small resort inn near Bell Harbor, Mass. High school boy Tod Emmett is recovering from an appendectomy at the seaside inn of his favorite uncle, kindly Gary Emmett. With only one other guest in the rambling, leaky-roofed inn, Tod thinks there should be plenty of time for him to complete his summer reading assignment of several novels, including *Silas Marner*. Awakened by a midnight thunderstorm, Tod observes wealthy, eccentric M. M. Murkey, retired Mystery Man of radio serial fame, prowling the grounds, shovel in hand. The next day, he and Uncle Gary are dismayed to discover a packet intended for an expected guest rainsoaked from the storm. Relieved that the packet contains only a copy of *Silas Marner*, Tod replaces the damaged one with his own unused copy. After breakfast, M. M.

leaves for a trip to town, muttering something about a ''fool nephew'' and clues ''any schoolboy could figure out.'' Then arrive two A. G. Cartwrights, the one, large, crude, overbearing Bertie with his fat, disagreeable, perpetually eating son, Marvin, the other, short, snappy, bullying Phinny. Each of them claims to be M. M.'s nephew and each of them shows a great interest in the book. Soon Tod and Gary are embroiled in a family feud which is further complicated when Uncle M. M. suffers a stroke and dies. Recalling the admonition of his English teacher, Wild Bill Caxton, to reason through problems, Tod settles down to examine the rainsoaked *Silas Marner*. He discerns pin pricks that spotlight certain words and convey a message. Bertie takes command but is disappointed when the message leads only to the excavation of a small, black box with a promissory note for $25,000 he signed indebting him to Uncle M. M. Recalling M. M.'s words about a schoolboy, Tod turns his attention to the text of *Silas Marner*. The passage describing Dunstan's discovery of the treasure in the fireplace sends Tod and Uncle Gary to M. M.'s cottage, where they find $25,000 in a black metal box buried in the hearth, $2,000 of which they learn M. M. has designated for repairs for Uncle Gary's roof and the remainder to community organizations. The integration of *Silas Marner* into the plot provides a literary touch to this fast-paced, skillfully concocted, fairly uncomplicated, conventional mystery. Poe Nominee.

THE MYSTERY OF GHOST VALLEY (Carr*, Harriett H., Macmillan, 1962), mystery novel set against the background of a Pennsylvania Dutch Folk Arts Festival in the mid–1900s. Tommy* Yoder, 11, lives with his widowed mother in an old-fashioned, gray frame house in Detroit. For a sixth grade Americana exhibit, he takes some family heirlooms to school, a Conestoga toolbox, iron bells, and an andiron, all decorated with a distinctive fern pattern and bearing the signature ''Hefs.'' The pieces attract a great deal of attention when Professor Mertz, a museum curator, announces that they are the work of a very famous, skilled, early nineteenth century Pennsylvania Dutch craftsman and are very valuable. He thinks they are so valuable that, if Tommy and his mother could find the mate to their andiron and sold the pieces, they could realize enough money from them to finance Tommy's college education. After someone tries to steal the antiques, Tommy and his mother decide to go to Kutztown, Pa., for the annual Folk Arts Festival. There they hope to learn more about their ironworking ancestor and perhaps find the other andiron. Tommy immediately likes his Uncle Will and Aunt Anna, who live on a farm, but he is puzzled by the strange looks they give him when he talks about the ironwork and by his cousin John's* aloofness and secretiveness. His concern that something unusual is going on increases when Charley* Kemp, a friend of the family, takes him to Ghost Valley near by to a tiny isolated shop where two sinister-looking men ask questions about the Hefs signature and design. Charley attempts to put Tommy at ease by explaining that the men need information for a movie they are making about Tommy's ancestor. One night at the fair, a guard tells Tommy about old

Doodlehead* Yoder, local eccentric who lives in the valley in a ramshackle house supposedly haunted by the ghost of a Hessian soldier. On the way home from the fair that night, Tommy sees Charley's car turn in at Doodlehead's house. Suspicious, Tommy hurries to the place, arriving just in time to prevent a theft and maybe a murder. He discovers that the old man has several Hefs pieces, including the mate to his andiron. The police arrest Charley and his friends for counterfeiting antiques. The mystery grabs quickly and moves fast with a fair share of stock characters, mild villainy, acceptable coincidence, and good-natured contrivance. Tommy is a typical pre-teener, the friendship between the two cousins develops gradually and convincingly, and the rapport between Tommy and his mother provides a pleasing touch. The author sometimes works too hard to build suspense, and the end, where it is disclosed that Charley wants the pieces for their design and not their intrinsic value, is a twist that some readers may consider a letdown or implausibility. Details of the fair, about Pennsylvania Dutch foods and symbols, and about the unfortunate family quarrel, in which poor Doodlehead is a central figure, add texture. This is an exciting, better than average introduction to the pleasures and conventions of this genre for later elementary readers. Poe Nominee.

MYSTERY OF THE EAGLE'S CLAW (Wosmek*, Frances, Westminster, 1979), suspense novel set in Maine in the 1970s. After the death of both her adoptive parents, Quail Fleming, 14, a half-Vietnamese girl, goes to the old Kettle and Crane Inn run by her father's Aunt Louise, whom she has never met. On the bus she meets Elspeth, about sixteen, who claims to be a witch and says she controls a boyfriend named Marcus. At the inn, Quail finds Aunt Louise aproaching senility, sometimes so confused she doesn't at first seem to know who Quail is, later bright and even friendly, though clearly not accepting an adopted child as related to her. Quail finds Gus Kramer, the handy man, and Hui Kwang, the cook, and even the inn guest, Vera, who is an ecology nut, friendly, but Elspeth, who turns out to be a waitress, and Marcus, a sort of manager, are hostile. Marcus is extremely full of hate, so much that the gentle albino great Dane, Moonshine, rages like a mad dog in his presence. To keep Quail busy, Aunt Louise makes her a waitress, a job she gradually learns, despite Elspeth's sabotage, and she earns enough to buy a bike on which she explores the mountain roads with Nancy, 12, Hui's daughter. Several questions bother Quail: Why is the room next to her aunt's kept locked? What has happened to Aunt Louise's moonstone ring, her favorite? Who rolled the boulder from a path above, almost killing Nancy, who was wearing Quail's distinctive red jacket? Elspeth, suddenly turned friendly, confides that she has stolen the eagle claw that Marcus wears and involves Quail in a midnight ritual burning to drive out the evil in him and make him fall for Elspeth. With Nancy, Quail visits the mountain cabin of Omar, who grows herbs. He is not at home, but she sees a large check from the antique shop where she has spotted the moonstone ring. They return to find that someone has released Moonshine, and they alert Gus, who shoots the dog as he is mauling

Marcus. Quail is surprised by a summons from the invalid, who insists that she must help him save Aunt Louise by going to the locked room, to which he has a key, and triggering a tape recording device he has installed. She does so with trepidation, gets the recording of a conversation she cannot hear, but she is seen by Aunt Louise leaving the room and is made to feel like a betrayer. However, the recording proves to be of a "seance," conducted by Vera's nephew, Omar, during which he pretends that the spirit of Aunt Louise's son, Jeff, who was killed in Vietnam, directs her to sign the inn over to them for an animal sanctuary. The locked room turns out to have belonged to Jeff, the cousin of Bruce, Quail's adoptive father, and great friend in Vietnam of Marcus. The original hostility of Marcus toward Quail is explained by his having been a prisoner of war, her appearance having triggered horrible memories. Omar has been persuading Aunt Louise to give up her valuables at the request of Jeff's "spirit" and pocketing the money instead of buying land for Vera's pet project, the sanctuary. Elspeth is just a boy-crazy girl who has dabbled in magic with Omar. Marcus has Omar arrested and, best of all, reveals to Quail that she is the child of Jeff and his Vietnamese love, rescued and adopted by Bruce after Jeff's death, a revelation that makes Aunt Louise finally accept her fully. The plot is constructed more carefully than that of most mysteries for children, without reliance on coincidence. Although Vera is a caricature and some of the other characters are types, Aunt Louise is an interesting figure, and Quail's concern about her own identity and her distress at being unwanted at the inn give some depth to the story. Poe Nominee.

MYSTERY OF THE FAT CAT (Bonham*, Frank, ill. Alvin Smith, Dutton, 1968), mystery story set in a large city in the contemporary period. Only the boys' club keeps the youth of the run-down Dogtown neighborhood off the streets and out of trouble, but when Buddy Williams, a black high school student, is bitten by a rat in the club pool, the board of health closes the dilapidated building. The only hope for the club lies in the estate of an eccentric old woman who has left ample funds to the club, to come to it after the death of her five cats. Four have died but Buzzer, a cat with one white and one black ear, apparently lives on at the ripe old age of twenty-eight, guarded by the ex-chauffeur, burly Joel Shriker, a white woman lawyer, Mrs. Podesta, and a veterinarian, all of whom are paid handsomely for their care. At the instigation of the boys' club director, Mr. Hamilton, Buddy and his friends—Johnny Paslelita, a Mexican-American known as Little Pie, Cool, who has been in trouble with the law, and Rich, whom Buddy's sister Angie, 16, greatly admires—try to get a snapshot of Buzzer to compare with old newspaper pictures of the wealthy cat. Since the estate on which the cat is kept is highly protected, they use a telescopic lens, with Rich ingeniously planning to shoot a flash bulb attached to an arrow into the window-frame above where the cat naps. Unfortunately, the arrow breaks the window, Buzzer disappears, Buddy is caught, and the resulting picture reveals that the cat matches the newspaper picture, although the boys who have seen the present Buzzer are sure that his opposite ear is white. Buddy's retarded brother, Ralphie, 12, leads to the unraveling of the mystery when he is disturbed by the backward print on the bag of catfood shown in the snapshot, a clue that proves the picture was printed reversed and that a different cat has been substituted for the original. In addition to the cleverly handled plot, the book makes comments on the need for recreation in city slums and on race relations among the street kids. Most of the characterization is minimal, though Ralphie, whose damaged brain retains the entire lists of names and addresses of the boys' club patrons, is memorable, and Little Pie, who manages to disappear whenever he is needed, is drawn with some complexity. Choice; Poe Nominee.

MYSTERY OF THE HAUNTED POOL (Whitney*, Phyllis A., ill. H. Tom Hall, Westminster, 1960), mystery novel set in the Hudson River Highlands, N.Y., in the mid twentieth century. Because her father is ill and wants to recuperate in the Hudson River country of his youth, Susan Price, 12, has been sent to Highland Crossing, where her Aunt Edith Sperry has found a house which is big enough for the family of four boys and Susan. The only problem—and the reason Susan is sent ahead—is that the owner, Captain Daniel Teague, is not sure he wants to sell or even to rent, and Susan is to help impress him with the acceptability of the Price family. There are other complications: the Captain's grandson, Gene Foster, whose injuries after being hit by a car are the cause of their financial shortage, is strongly opposed to anyone else in their house, and a wealthy, strange-acting old maid, Altoona Heath, seems to be after something in the Teague house. In a barrel of books which Aunt Edith, an antique dealer, has persuaded Captain Teague to let her sell, Susan finds an old journal, a log of a sea captain ancestor of the Teagues. Despite Gene's opposition, Aunt Edith gets the Captain to rent, and she and Susan move into the big old Teague house while Captain Teague and Gene move into a cabin on the land. During the first night Susan hears a loud thump downstairs and finds a window open on the first floor. The next morning they find a deep scratch in the living-room floor. That day, peering into the pool in the yard, Susan thinks she sees a face in the murky bottom. The next night Susan sees lights moving around in the yard near the pool. The arrival of her brother, Adam, 14, relieves Susan of her secret fear of the ghost of Sarah Teague, mother of the original builder, who Altoona has told her haunts the house, but active, tactless Adam antagonizes Gene in their first meeting. And strangely neither Adam nor Susan can now see the face in the pool. At tea with Altoona, they catch a glimpse of a wooden figure in her library. On the edge of an old book, when the pages are fanned slightly, they find a fore-edge painting or diagram, which Adam figures out is a map of a secret compartment in the living room, but their investigation proves it empty. A fire at Altoona's mansion nearly burns the object of all the secret searching, the figurehead carved by Sarah Teague's husband for his sailing ship, kept in the secret compartment, removed by Gene at night and dumped into the pond because it is too hard for the crippled boy to drag, retrieved by Altoona, who hopes to sell it as an antique, and now returned slightly charred to the Captain. But the real find is the string of wooden beads which the figurehead wore, found by Susan so badly charred that the wood disintegrates, revealing a diamond and emerald necklace hidden within. With their fortunes restored, the Captain and Gene can move back into their house, but Altoona, deciding to travel, rents her house to the Price family. A good deal of attention is given to the work of the local volunteer fire department, of which the Captain is chief and Gene an honorary member. The plot proceeds without too much dependence upon coincidence, but despite the secret compartment, the disappearing face in the water, and the suggestion of ghosts, the story is never particularly suspenseful. Poe Winner.

MYSTERY OF THE HIDDEN HAND (Whitney*, Phyllis, ill. Tom Hall, Westminster, 1963), mystery novel set on the Greek Island of Rhodes in the mid twentieth century. Gale, 12, and Warren Tyler, 13, are visiting their mother's sister, Aunt Marjorie, whose Greek husband, Alexandros Castelis, owns and runs the new Hotel Hermes. Both Gale and her cousin, Tassoula (Anastasia), also twelve, suffer from having talented, beautiful older sisters, but their reactions are different. Gale simply longs for some talent that will distinguish her; Tassoula, who paints beautifully but is clumsy, insists that she will become a famous ballerina like her sister, Lexine. On Gale's first day in Rhodes, several mysterious things happen. She wanders into the garden of a handsome white house and meets the old man resident, who turns out to be Athanasios Castelis, Tassoula's grandfather. He welcomes her, asks her to call him grandfather Thanos, and introduces her to his grandson, Nicos (Nicolas), 15, and she senses great tension between them. Nicos intercepts her on the way home and sends a secret message to Tassoula that "all has been arranged." Gale and Warren meet a woman at the hotel who wears blue eye shadow and a bouffant "peanut butter colored" wig and who indicates Grandfather Thanos's house and says, "That is the house of my enemy." As they sightsee around Rhodes and visit at the Castelis house, these mysteries clear up. Grandfather, who was prevented from being an artist by his father, wants Nicos to develop his talent, but Nicos wants to take over the family pottery works. Tassoula has broken one tile of a table top Grandfather has designed for a gift to Lexine, and Nicos has arranged to have a new one made if she can paint the design on it. The woman with the wig is Geneva Lambrou, a former maid at the Castelis house fired by Grandfather years before for poking into a drawer in his desk and discovering a marble hand. Nicos asks Gale to get Warren to dig in a particular spot when they visit Camiros, one of the old cities of Rhodes, and to get him to give what he finds to a museum. Nicos has buried the hand, which is eventually revealed to belong to a statue Grandfather Thanos helped discover many years ago. He had later found the hand, but, enchanted by its beauty, had not made his find known. Nicos has stolen the hand from Grandfather's desk and buried it where Warren finds it, hoping this way to restore the treasure while protecting the family name. Before

Warren can give the hand to a museum, Geneva steals it from his hotel room. Gale privately tells the whole story to Grandfather Thanos. In a final scene at Lindos, where Lexine is posing for a photographic story, the boys, who have retrieved the hand from Geneva's family, confront the thief. Grandfather Thanos (who has already explained to the museum) is reconciled with Nicos; Tassoula realizes, with her grandfather's encouragement, that art is her talent, not dancing; and Gale understands that she has a talent for communication and honesty that is as valuable as those of her sister. The mystery and the psychological aspects of the story are forced, and the sudden reformation of Geneva at the end is implausible. Descriptions of Rhodes and its past are interesting but heavy for the flimsy plot. Poe Winner.

THE MYSTERY OF THE RED TIDE (Bonham*, Frank, ill. Brinton Turkle, Dutton, 1966), mystery novel for middle readers set on the coast near San Diego, Calif., in contemporary times. Because his mother is dead and his father unemployed, Tommy Kelly, 11, comes from Kentucky to stay in the San Diego area with his Aunt Louise and her husband, Mike Warren, a marine biologist who collects and sells specimens for research. With his cousin Jill, also 11, and Uncle Mike, Tommy visits Smugglers' Cove, a remote area on a point honeycombed with abandoned tunnels that were once naval installations. On the way they are stopped by two surfers, Rusty and Cotton, about seventeen, who rudely demand aid for their stalled car and later are apprehended by Mike with a rare and protected garibaldi among the fish they have speared. Tommy also has a brief run-in with a beach comber known as Smith the Barber, who calls Uncle Mike a poacher and threatens to report him to the game warden. Back at their truck, they are stopped by game wardens who find six of the bright red garibaldi in their bucket and issue a citation. The next day, while Uncle Mike confers with his lawyer, Jill and Tommy ride their bikes to the cove, accompanied by Jill's red-haired friend, Woody, a budding archeologist, who explores Indian graveyards hoping to prove that the early inhabitants of the region made pottery as well as tools. When they find that, for the second day in a row, one of their sandwiches and bottles of pop are missing, they decide to explore one of the tunnels, where they find one of their empty pop bottles and an Indian bowl containing berries. A visit to the museum the next day confirms that the bowl is an ancient Indian artifact. On the next trip to the cove, Jill keeps watch while the boys swim and sees a black-haired boy swipe their sandwich and run up the hill to a tunnel mouth. Following him, Tommy finds a makeshift bed, candles, and other junky living equipment. That night Uncle Mike goes to the cove alone and returns with a ten-year-old Mexican boy named Ramon, whose mother works nearby and has thought he returned to Mexico to live with an aunt, whereas he has been hiding out in the tunnels. The pot is explained when he admits he took it from the home of a professor for whom his mother works. Knowing that the little sea horses Tommy has found are not native to the area, Uncle Mike reasons out the solution to the mystery of the baby garibaldi in their buckets, alerts the game warden, and the next night they apprehend Smith the Barber receiving a milk pail of smuggled tropical fish dropped off from a boat to wash up on the cove beach. They discover that he planted the fish in their buckets to get them barred from tide-pool collecting and that once, in fright, he dumped the tropical fish into the water. Ramon is invited to stay with Tommy's uncle and, since they need more workers, Uncle Mike proposes asking Tommy's father and brother and sister to join them. Although to find that smuggling is the activity at Smugglers' Cove is a very obvious plot solution, the suspense is kept up by screams in the tunnels, flashlights that go out, suspicion that falls first on the surfers, then on Ramon, and the device of the ancient pot. Characterization is not strong, but the setting is well evoked and the information about the tide pool creatures is interesting. Poe Nominee.

MYSTERY OF THE SCOWLING BOY (Whitney*, Phyllis A., ill. John Gretzer, Westminster, 1973), mystery novel set in the Pocono Mountains of eastern Pennsylvania in the 1970s. Jan Sutton, 12, and her brother, Mike, 13, a talented guitar player, are spending the Christmas holidays with their grandparents because their parents, both concert musicians, have to be away for the holidays. Living in the strange Victorian house down the hill from Gramps's chalet-like home, Jan discovers, is the movie star she idolizes, Alanna Graham, in real life Mrs. Anna Nelson, and her son, Steven, about Jan's age. They are staying with Alanna's invalid grandfather, Burton Oliver, a former sculptor of strange, tormented figures which he keeps locked in a top-floor studio "so they won't get out." Jan, who is unhappy at being the only untalented member of her family, thinks she may be destined to be an actress and, dreaming that Alanna may help her, makes a great effort to get acquainted, both by calling at the house and by striking up conversations on the ski slopes. Cousin Daphne (Mrs. Price), the housekeeper and nurse for Mr. Oliver, is clearly hostile, as is Harry Mercer, Alanna's business manager, and Steven is sometimes friendly, sometimes rude and angry, but Alanna is welcoming. When the children's grandmother becomes ill and must be taken to the hospital, Gramps hesitates to leave them with the hired man, Joe Reed, a reclusive man who admittedly has been mentally disturbed, so he asks Alanna to take them in, which she does willingly. There the mysteries of the Nelson family deepen: Where is Steven's father? Why is the boy so hostile to his mother? What is the secret old Mr. Oliver wants to tell Jan? Who moves the statues in the studio? All these elements are neatly tied together when it becomes apparent that Mr. Oliver is not completely bedridden, as it has been assumed, that he has been hunting for a box of old newspaper clippings that detail some trouble with the police Alanna had in her youth, that Cousin Daphne and Harry Mercer are attempting to blackmail her with this information, that Steven has found the box and, disillusioned, is angry at his mother, and that Joe Reed is really Bruce Nelson, Steven's father, now recovered from alcohol and drug abuse. Jan, whose sympathetic understanding has brought all these elements together, comes to realize that she has a talent, too, and doesn't need to be an actress. Though the story depends partly on the Gothic atmosphere of the old house and the grotesque sculptures, it is all plausible, and the ski-country setting is well evoked. Poe Nominee.

THE MYSTERY OF THE VELVET BOX (Scherf*, Margaret, ill. Charles Geer, Watts, 1963), detective novel set in suburban New York City in the mid–1900s, in which the children solve the mystery. Eccentric Great-Gran has died, and the morning her legacy to the Adams family arrives, an eighteenth-century, carved English desk for Mother and a charming, little, red velvet box containing a rusty key and a red carnation for Harriet, 14, so does handsome Gerald, a cousin from Montana that no one has ever met before and whose company the family soon grows to enjoy. The Adamses and proper, crusty Great-Aunt Grace, who has inherited Gran's old mansion, are puzzled because Mother has not been left the valuable Bellini painting that Gran had said would be hers. That night, someone breaks into the Adamses' attic and tears apart the old desk, obviously searching for something, the first in a series of frightening and mysterious events that lead the family to believe that Gran had hidden the painting and that someone wishes to steal it. A large number of people become involved in searching for the painting and in sorting out the strange, unsettling things that go on, among them, Mr. Shively, a shady antiques dealer; Mr. Peel, the crotchety caretaker at Gran's mansion; Mr. Pittman, Gran's authoritative lawyer; and even Aunt Grace. Impressionable Harriet, whose box proves instrumental in solving the mystery, her active and inquisitive younger brother, Bertie, 10, Harriet's boyfriend, Walter Cameron, who is jealous of Gerald because Harriet finds him attractive and who has doubts about Gerald's authenticity as a relative, and Harriet's best friend, Cathy Cole, all pursue various clues and leads singly and together. Harriet and Cathy even travel to New York City where they visit Mr. Shively's office, Mr. Pittman's office, and the Metropolitan Museum of Art and interview employees of Mr. Pittman. Things fall together when Harriet realizes that Gran, who liked puzzles, had planted red carnations as clues to lead Harriet to the painting. She discovers that the picture has indeed come to the Adamses, hidden beneath the portrait of Gran's late husband. Walter's efforts reveal that Gerald is a bogus cousin. He is really John Craven, who read Gran's will while he was working for lawyer Pittman. He has been trying to find the painting and steal it and has been behind most of the mysterious goings-on. The many characters are stock for the genre, and the complicated plot with its embedded clues and false leads moves to its expected conclusion. Details of family life and interpersonal relationships and lots of realistic, often snappy dialogue combine to give a good picture of family life in the mid 1900s, the book's strongest aspect in addition to its high entertainment value. Poe Nominee.

MYSTERY OF THE WITCH WHO WOULDN'T (Platt*, Kin, Chilton, 1969), mystery set in Hampton on Long Island in the 1960s, narrated, like its predecessor, *Sinbad and Me**, by Steve* Forrester, 12, and also featuring his bull dog, Sinbad, his friend, Minerva* Landry, her father, Sheriff* Langwell Otis Landry, and Steve's genius friend, Herky* Krakower. When Minerva tells Steve that she has met a witch named Aurelia Hepburn in Mucker's Swamp, who can blow away clouds and who has warned her to keep her father from opening a string-tied package that will blow up, Steve decides to investigate this woman. He arrives at her cottage in the dark, hides when a car comes, and eavesdrops on a conversation between the witch and the local banker, Mr. Barker, who seems to want her to read someone's mind for him. She refuses, sends him on his way, then, with an elaborate ritual, calls up a weather demon, whom Steve does not wait to see, though he does get soaked in the storm localized in a very small area. After he learns that Barker has been badly injured when his garage door fell on him, he tells his suspicions of skulduggery to the sheriff, who is scornful, but later the sheriff asks him to come to the hospital and wait behind a screen while he questions Barker. A nurse with a soft voice, platinum blond hair, and a limp hands Steve a package "for Mr. Barker," but the sheriff takes it, rips off the string, and throws it out the window just as it explodes. Steve, hunting for the blond nurse, thinks he sees her climb into a hearse from the Happy Hills cemetery. The sheriff is hospitalized with many bandages over body and eyes, and Minerva comes to stay with Steve's family until her father recovers. The extremely complicated plot has many bizarre elements: the Landry's new housekeeper, Mrs. Wood, whom Steve suspects because her voice is like the nurse's, gives Minerva a bracelet that turns out to be poison; Steve calls on their former housekeeper, Mrs. Carleton, and finds her confused and groggy, wearing an identical bracelet; Barker, though supposedly suffering from broken bones, is released from the hospital and is seen walking around; young Dr. Downey, who is treating both patients, admits to Steve that he is highly interested in witchcraft; Minerva disappears; the witch disappears; Professor Van Noord, the Dutch scientist who designed the garage door for Barker and is thought to be working on a valuable invention involving high frequency sounds, disappears. In a culminating scene at about midnight on an island to which they have been directed telepathically by Ms. Hepburn, Steve and Herky find all the missing ones held captive, and, to attract police, they soak gunny sacks in pitch, fasten them to the wings of an old Dutch-type windmill, light them, and start the mill, creating a blazing circle that can be seen for miles. The denouement exposes a number of culprits, the chief being Dr. Downey, leader of a group of Satanists become extortionists and blackmailers, which include Mrs. Wood, also known as Mrs. Dow, the owner of the cemetery, Gamsun, also known as Magnus, and Mr. Carleton, also known as Mr. Dow, and involve Barker. Ms. Hepburn reads the plans for the invention from Van Noord's mind, Herky explains to him the adjustments needed to make it work, and the sheriff forgives the fifty-six dollars he was charging Steve for dumping a box containing his new golf shoes into the water, when the boy thought it might be a bomb. The fast-paced story requires suspension of disbelief in all sorts of psychic phenomena, including the witch's ability to call up a hurricane which forces the fleeing bad characters back to the island, as well as in secret passages, sinister rituals, complete disguises effected by wigs, and a number of unlikely occurrences. Loose ends are all tied up, if somewhat implausibly, and there is a pleasant amount of good-natured banter by Sheriff Landry about Sinbad and the prospect of marriage, in the future, between Steve and Minerva. Poe Nominee.

THE MYSTERY OF 22 EAST (Ware*, Leon, Westminster, 1965), mystery set on a freighter trip from California to Europe via the Panama Canal in the mid twentieth century. Tom Cameron, 15, is one of nine passengers aboard the German ship, *Hornbill*, on his way to join his father, an exchange professor in England. Fellow passengers include a quiet German couple, the Conrads, an annoyingly talkative American couple, the Jacksons, an attractive young lawyer, Evan Thorne, an independent, well-to-do older woman, Mrs. Cartwright, and a suspicious couple, thin, mustached Paul Bernini and his nearly silent wife. Almost at once Tom realizes that someone, or perhaps several people, are trying to search his cabin. He soon finds out why: a package containing microfilm is hidden behind the light fixture over his mirror. Frightened, he rehides it in the identical place in the only empty cabin. In the meantime, he has been preoccupied with the problems of a stowaway, a boy he has seen in Ensenada, whom he afterwards spots hiding in the smoke stack of the *Hornbill*. He has smuggled water and some food to the boy, whose name is Jose, and worries when the stowaway is discovered and locked in the laundry. When the Chinese laundryman must be put ashore with appendicitis, Tom slips a note to Jose telling him to start washing, and Mrs. Cartwright, falling in with the scheme, teaches the boy to iron so that he will be too valuable to the ship to be turned over to the police. Later Jose endears himself to gruff Captain Altman by capturing a monkey that escapes from a circus aboard a ship going through the Panama canal locks at the same time as the *Hornbill*. At La Libertad in El Salvador, Tom goes ashore with the captain, quite a feat in itself in the heavy swells, and is approached by a man who quizzes him about the passengers and describes a "friend" who might be aboard, obviously meaning Mr. Bernini. Later Tom learns from the steward that a man named Breck, who had occupied his cabin several trips before, had crushed his foot between the launch and the gangway in La Libertad and was killed when his plane to the hospital crashed. Tom suspects that Breck was the source of the microfilm, and when in Cristobal he sees Bernini talking to a fat man in Spanish—though he has previously pointedly denied knowing Spanish—and afterwards the fat man, Charles MaGill, joins the *Hornbill* as a passenger, he begins to feel closed in and genuinely worried. Thinking Tom has the microfilm, MaGill and Bernini threaten him but are interrupted by the captain. A big storm in which the *Hornbill* picks up survivors of a burning ship, some badly injured, makes a shifting about of cabins necessary, and Tom with relief agrees to bunk with Thorne, who then reveals that he is with the FBI. Alerting the captain, Thorne sets a trap with Tom as bait and catches MaGill and Bernini.

Though the villains are predictable from the first, the mystery is plausible, and Tom's worry and uncertainty keep some tension in the plot. Life aboard a tramp steamer and the visits to Latin American ports make an interesting background. Poe Winner.

N

NABAL (*A Donkey for the King**), hard, dissolute, cruel scoundrel, owner of the seedy traveling circus for which Jesse becomes animal handler and in which he finds Belshazzar, the donkey. Nabal works his performers hard and pays them so little that they must resort to pilfering to live. He says he will hire Jesse provided Jesse finds him a talented, limber acrobat. When Jesse brings him Saul*, Nabal allows Jesse to remain with the troupe as animal handler. Nabal is a Hebrew name that means fool.

NACAR, THE WHITE DEER (Treviño*, Elizabeth Borton [de], ill. Enrico Arno, Farrar, 1963), historical novel set in Mexico in 1630. When the Viceroy of Mexico receives a special shipment from the Orient, a white deer sent by the Governor of the Philippines for the King of Spain, he is particularly concerned because he is fond of animals and the beautiful creature is weak and sick from the trip. His young commander of the guard, Captain Diaz, suggests that they summon to Acapulco a young goatherd named Lalo, who seems to have a special affinity for animals, to care for the deer, which the Viceroy has named Nacar. Lalo, who is not deaf but has been mute since at about four he saw his mother and baby brother killed in a fire, is small, perhaps ten or twelve. Lalo and Nacar have immediate empathy, and the Viceroy lets them depart for Lalo's home pastures in the mountains, sending along a red velvet banner to put on the deer to show he is the king's property. They make their way, avoiding towns and bandits, visiting a hermit. Nacar is bitten by a snake, but Lalo is able to nurse him back to health, and he is shot, but not killed, by an Indian boy, Chapulin. Chapulin's grandmother nurses the deer this time, and Chapulin accompanies Lalo for a visit to his home on Sleeping Lady Mountain, where old Juan has been caring for his sheep. On Christmas Eve, Lalo takes Nacar and his dog, Noche, to the village for the fiesta and church service, where Nacar becomes part of the living nativity scene. On the way home, they are set upon by bandits who hope to hold Nacar for ransom. The deer escapes, but Lalo is beaten and survives only because Noche helps him home. Nacar finds his own way home. Captain Diaz visits and, not knowing of Lalo's difficulties but finding the deer thriving, goes off to report that all is well. In the spring, Nacar gets restless and escapes; a month later Lalo finds him with a doe and is able to lure him back with a special tune he has played on his flute to call him. In a year, Lalo delivers the deer back to the Viceroy, who decides to send Lalo all the way to Spain with Nacar. They cross the mountains to Vera Cruz in a caravan led by Captain Diaz. They sail on the *Guadalupe*, whose master is insulting and wants to take credit for the deer's good condition, but his officer, Don Alvaro, is more understanding. The king, who is delighted with Nacar, says the deer will be released in his forests and a special prize given to whoever kills him. This so shocks Lalo that he finds his long-lost voice to protest. The king considers this a miracle, changes his proclamation to have the deer protected, and gives Lalo the opportunity to stay in Spain, live near Nacar, and become one of his foresters. The story is simple and legend-like, written in a beautiful style that brings each episode vividly to life. Lalo's ability with animals and his love for Nacar are plausible, and even his final recovery of his voice is believable in the context. Fanfare.

NADER, RALPH (*Dinky Hocker Shoots Smack**), Tucker* Woolf's calico cat, called so because Tucker found her under a Chevrolet. Tucker shortens her name to Nader when he discovers she is a female. It is through her that Tucker becomes friends with Dinky* Hocker, Natalia* Line, and P.* John Knight. Dinky answers Tucker's ad for a home for Nader and then overfeeds her. When the Hockers decide to have her destroyed, Tucker takes her back.

NAMIOKA, LENSEY (CHAO), born in Peking, China; mathematician and author. She attended Radcliffe College and received both her B.A. and her M.A. degrees from the University of California in Berkeley. Besides teaching mathematics at Wells College, Aurora, N.Y., and Cornell University, Ithaca, N.Y., she has been a translator for the American Mathematical Society. Although she is Chinese by birth, she is married to a man of Japanese ancestry and her mother lived for many years in Japan, so it is not surprising that her series of novels with historical background, all of which follow the same pair of Samurai, are set in feudal Japan: *The Samurai and the Long-Nosed Devils* (McKay, 1976), *White Serpent Castle* (McKay, 1976), *Valley of the Broken Cherry Trees* (Delacorte, 1980), and *Village of the Vampire Cat** (Delacorte, 1981).

NANCY WHEELER (*Are You There God? It's Me, Margaret.**), Margaret Simon's best friend. She is bossy, often overreacts to situations and people, and does not always tell the truth, but Margaret enjoys her friendship anyway. Nancy is presented as a typical middle-class, suburban child, whose parents are joiners, church goers, and active in community and school-related activities. Nancy makes most of the rules for the Pre-Teen Sensations.

NANNY (*The Alley**), Connie* Ives's grandmother who lives with the Ives family. She is imperious, loving, possessive, and good with animals, but not so with Connie's friends who are a little afraid of her. She comes from the South and feels that Southern ways are best. She cooks a lot and writes dozens of letters.

NAOMI KIRSHENBAUM (*Alan and Naomi**), 12, French refugee who is mentally disturbed by the terrible things she has suffered during the Nazi occupation. Although she retreats into a frightened, cowering infant, compulsively tearing paper to bits, she is actually bright, clever, and loving when Alan* Silverman is able to lure her away from her fears.

NATALIA LINE (*Dinky Hocker Shoots Smack**), Dinky's* cousin, a pretty, soft-spoken girl whose clothes appear to Tucker* Woolf to be pleasingly old-fashioned. She has been attending a school for the emotionally disturbed and speaks in rhymes when she is nervous. Her mother was emotionally disturbed, too, and her father committed suicide. She is sensitive, supportive, and positive in her attitude. She and Tucker like each other but are very shy about expressing their feelings. Their first meaningful conversation occurs with the bubble game, in which they complete statements inside the conversation bubbles that Tucker sketches.

NATALIE FIELD (*Very Far Away from Anywhere Else**), almost eighteen, a well-organized, talented violinist and composer who is Owen* Griffiths's first real friend. Owen describes her as strong-minded, self-reliant, very decisive, but also young and green, because in her busy schedule she has never allowed time for fun and friendship.

NAYLOR, PHYLLIS REYNOLDS (1933–   ), born in Anderson, Ind.; educator, novelist. She attended Joliet Junior College and American University and taught elementary school in Hazelcrest, Ill. She also was assistant executive secretary for Montgomery County schools in Rockville, Md., and editorial assistant on the *NEA Journal* before deciding, in 1960, to devote her full time to writing. She is married to a speech pathologist and has two sons. Among her numerous books for young people are some non-fiction, including *Getting Along in Your Family* (Abingdon, 1976) and *How I Came to Be a Writer* (Atheneum, 1978). Her fiction, written mainly for a middle-level reader, includes a trio of books dealing with modern witchcraft, *The Witch's Sister* (Atheneum, 1975), *Witch Water* (Atheneum, 1977), and *The Witch Herself* (Atheneum, 1978). Her *The Solomon System** (Atheneum, 1983), a story of the relationship between two brothers whose parents are contemplating divorce, won the Child Study Award. *Night City* (Atheneum, 1984) is a story of menace and kidnapping set in Mississippi hill country.

NELS ANDERSON (*A Really Weird Summer**), eldest of the four Anderson children who are shipped off to the old inn at Reeves Ferry while their parents work out details of their impending divorce. Nels is burdened by his feeling of responsibility for the younger ones, a feeling increased by their unhappiness and insecurity in the new environment and by his mother's assumption that he will look after his siblings. Nels is the favorite of his impractical pilot father, who has taught him chess and has been teaching him to fly, and now Nels's worries are increased by hints that his father expects him to come live with him. A thoughtful, sensitive boy, Nels likes to play chess and read, and he retreats from his guilt, from the thoughts of the conflict between his parents, and from the conversation about it that Stevie keeps introducing. Awakened one night by an escaped peacock, Nels has dreamed that his father is killing his mother. The friend Nels finds living in an abandoned wing of the inn at first seems very real to him, then possibly a ghost from another time period, and at last, to his horror, a product of his own disturbed mind.

NEUFELD, JOHN (ARTHUR) (1938–   ), born in Chicago, Ill.; author of problem novels for teenagers. He was educated at Phillips Exeter Academy and at Yale University. *Lisa, Bright and Dark* (Phillips, 1969) is a story of a mentally disturbed girl. *Edgar Allan** (Phillips, 1968) is about a white family who attempt to adopt a black child. Among his other novels are *For All the Wrong Reasons* (Norton, 1973) and *Freddy's Book* (Random, 1973).

NEVILLE, EMILY CHENEY (1919–   ), born in Manchester, Conn.; author best known for her realistic novels of contemporary family life for adolescents. Born into a large, close-knit New England family, she played and attended school only with siblings and cousins until she was ten. After attending Oxford School in Hartford and graduating from Bryn Mawr with a degree in economics, she joined the New York *Mirror*, where she wrote a profile column, and later married Glenn Neville, a newspaperman with the Hearst Corporation. The couple made their home in the Adirondacks. After publishing several novels, she enrolled in law school and was admitted to the New York bar in 1977. She has also written readers for the Bank Street College of Education. Her novels are based on her own childhood memories and on her experiences in raising her own five children. Her first book, *It's Like This, Cat** (Harper, 1963), a humorous episodic boy's story set in New York City, won the Newbery Medal and is listed in *Children's Books Too Good to Miss* and *Choice*. Her second novel, *Berries Goodman** (Harper, 1965), about prejudice against Jews, won the Jane Addams Award, was a Fanfare book, and is listed in *Choice*. Her other novels are *The Seventeenth-Street Gang* (Harper, 1966), also set in New York City, *Traveler from a Small Kingdom* (Harper, 1968), a fictionalized account of her own childhood, *Fogarty* (Harper, 1969), about a law-school dropout, and *Garden of Broken Glass* (Delacorte, 1975), about alcoholism. Although flawed by weak plots and contrivance, her books tend to be less overtly didactic, sensational, and sociological than most books of the New Realism.

NEWMAN, ROBERT (HOWARD) (1909–   ), born in New York City; free-lance writer best known in children's literature for his mystery-detectives for later elementary and junior high readers, including *Night Spell** (Atheneum, 1977), a mildly Gothic novel of suspense set on the New England coast which was nominated for the Edgar Allan Poe Award, and especially his several breezy and exciting take-offs on Sherlock Holmes, among them, *The Case of the Baker Street Irregular* (Atheneum, 1978), *The Case of the Vanishing Corpse* (Atheneum, 1980), *The Case of the Somerville Secret* (Atheneum, 1981), and *The Case of the Threatened King* (Atheneum, 1982), in which young Andrew, his friends, and Inspector Wyatt of Scotland Yard foil plots and solve puzzles in old London of hansom cabs after the fashion of their more famous prototype. He has written fantasies set in England with a mystery theme, *Merlin's Mistake* (Atheneum, 1970) and *The Shattered Stone* (Atheneum, 1975), and retellings from myth and legend, *Grettir the Strong* (Crowell, 1968) and *The Twelve Labors of Hercules* (Crowell, 1972), also for the later elementary audience. He attended Brown University and, before he wrote for young people, worked in radio and was chief of the radio outpost division in New York of the Office of War Information. In addition to books for children, he has written verse, short stories and articles for magazines, novels for adults, scripts for radio and television, plays, and films. His wife, Dorothy Crayder, and daughter, Hila Feil, are also novelists.

NEY, JOHN (1923–   ), born in St. Paul, Minn.; author, scriptwriter. He grew up in New York and St. Louis, lived in the Blue Ridge section of Virginia, then in Italy, the West Indies, and Palm Beach, Fla. His "Ox" books are about the loneliness and neglect of a boy in an extremely wealthy Palm Beach family: *Ox: The Story of a Kid at the Top* (Little, 1970), *Ox Goes North* (Harper, 1973), and *Ox Under Pressure** (Lippincott, 1976), which was a National Book finalist.

NICHOLAS PINKERTON (*Unclaimed Treasures**), Willa's twin brother, whom she always introduces as her younger brother because he followed her by seven minutes, a statement he never bridles at simply, Willa says, because that's the way Nicky is. He likes to experiment with language and often comes up with well-turned phrases. He is a realist, occasionally a cynic, but on the whole rather easygoing and very perceptive. He warns Willa of trouble if she maintains her infatuation for Matthew. He and Willa get on very well and share confidences. He is a well-drawn and likeable figure. Usually quite mature in his behavior, he acts like a very pleased little boy when Matthew Morris takes an interest in his drawings. He grows up to become a successful painter.

NICODEMUS (*Mrs. Frisby and the Rats of NIMH**), wise and reliable leader of the rats of NIMH* who tells Mrs. Frisby the story of how the rats are captured in a city marketplace, how they are imprisoned in cages in the laboratory of NIMH, and how they are subjected to experiments. He describes their escape and journey through the countryside to the Fitzgibbon farm and their efforts to make a new life there. A long facial scar crosses his left eye, over which he wears a black patch. He was a friend of Mrs. Frisby's husband, Jonathan, and it is because of this association that the rats decide to help Mrs. Frisby with her moving problem.

NICOLAAS (*The Empty Moat**), Elizabeth's father, the Baron of Swaenenburgh Castle. He is a stern man, who ironically takes pleasure in violating the terms laid down by Major Schmidt by working in the Resistance and stealing eggs, wine, and the like from the Germans. He is very traditional and forbids Eva* to marry the German officer. When she refuses to obey him, he gets so upset he suffers a stroke. He never influences the action of the novel after that. His negative views of the Germans presumably represent those of most Dutch during the war.

NIGHT SPELL (Newman*, Robert, ill. Peter Burchard*, Atheneum, 1977), novel of suspense involving extra-sensory perception set in the late 1900s on the New England coast. Now that he accepts the loss of his parents, orphaned Tad Harper, 14, expects to continue living at his exclusive private school where he feels comfortable and secure until his education is complete. To his dismay, his schoolmaster insists he accept the invitation of elderly Martin Gorman, wealthy friend of the Harper family whom Tad barely knows, to spend the summer at the Gorman mansion on a small coastal island. Tad finds the house silent, brooding, and forbidding, and he feels intimidated at first by the deaf-mute couple who serve the old man. His host, who is confined to a wheelchair, is gruff, peremptory, and judgmental. Mr. Gorman harbors a strange resentment toward Tad's father, although for some reason he has been paying Tad's tuition. Tad soon senses a compelling but not fearful presence in his bedroom, and strange dreams arouse him from sleep. Left to his own devices, Tad explores the island and the village. He soon meets Karen Nelson, high-spirited daughter of the local lighthouse keeper, with whom he goes sailing and picnicking. From Karen, Tad learns about the Gorman mystery. Lisa Gorman, Martin's only child, disappeared suddenly about a year before the story began after the accidental drowning of her only child, Nonny. Tad has a dream which motivates the two young people to search the attic of the mansion. There they discover a painting of Nonny done by Tad's father. Although the picture was apparently hidden there by Nonny herself, Mr. Gorman thinks Tad's father stole it. A premonition of Karen's, which the two youths also feel has been inspired by Nonny, leads them to the State Hospital, where they discover Lisa is a patient, a victim of amnesia. Mr. Gorman acknowledges with appreciation Tad's help in locating the picture, clearing Mr. Harper's name, and locating his lost daughter. He invites Tad to make his home permanently at Gorman mansion. A sudden, violent hurricane strikes the area, affording Tad the opportunity to rescue Karen with Nonny's assistance, in what the youths are certain is Nonny's last intervention in the world of the living. The novel is low in characterization and high in action. It moves rapidly with expected, mildly Gothic conventions to its anticipated conclusion. Poe Nominee.

THE NIGHT SWIMMERS (Byars*, Betsy, Ill. Troy Howell, Delacorte, 1980), realistic family novel set somewhere in the southeastern United States, probably Tennessee, and covering a few days in the late 1900s. Retta*, Johnny*, 9, and Roy* are the children of widower Shorty* Anderson, a small-time, country-western singer whose great ambition is to become a big recording star. Although he loves his children, Shorty regards them as a hindrance in his otherwise quite satisfying life, and he habitually leaves them home alone at night while he performs. Since their mother's death two years ago, Retta has taken charge of the house and her brothers. She makes their meals, sees to their clothing, and organizes their leisure time. She is determined that they speak and behave properly and experience some of the luxuries that better-off people enjoy. One night, she takes them swimming without permission in the pool belonging to wealthy Colonel Roberts, whose family always retires early. Although uneasy about the morality of what they are doing, the children have fun and plan to return again with new swimming suits and inner tubes. The next day, Johnny makes friends with Arthur, a boy about his own age whom he meets in the park and who flies radio-controlled planes. Johnny enjoys a sense of achievement and social confidence he has never before known because for the first time he has made a friend all by himself. Retta resents the relationship and senses she is losing control of Johnny. Twice more the children swim in the Roberts pool. The following night, when Johnny sneaks out to meet Arthur, Retta follows him, leaving Roy alone in the house. When she observes the two boys making some sort of flying apparatus out of a plastic bag and candles, she angrily interrupts the activity. Arthur responds by telling her to stop trying to run Johnny's life. While this is going on, Roy awakens, and, finding the house empty, he assumes the other two have gone swimming without him. He rushes to the pool, dives in, and encounters, not his siblings, but Colonel Roberts himself. The colonel fishes the boy out and phones his father, and the story of the children's nocturnal activities comes out. Although Shorty characteristically shrugs things off, his girl friend, sensible, loving, responsible Brendelle, steps in. She convinces Shorty that they ought to get married and helps Retta see how she has been overprotective of her brothers. Although the conclusion is simplistic, events happen rapidly, scenes come alive, dialogue is extensive and natural, and humor abounds. The author describes the ways, feelings, and attitudes of the children with warmth and sympathy. Except for Arthur, a stock figure who functions as the author's voice, the children are dynamic characters, but the adults are types and somewhat eccentric. Retta's compulsive behavior is handled sensitively. Boston Globe Honor.

NIKOLAS ANGELIKI (*The Refugee Summer**), twelve-year-old son of a widowed Greek seamstress, a sensitive, intelligent boy, who has a taste of a different world when he becomes friends with an American boy, Oliver* Avery, and his cousin, Edith* Griswold, who are spending the summer in his resort village. Passionately interested in learning, he can think only of the word ''knowing'' when Oliver demands that they each say what they want to be when they are grown up. Because he has been asked to read aloud the journals of a dead soldier to the man's illiterate mother and wife, he understands the horror and misery of the war, which most of the wealthy Greek and foreign adults treat as a patriotic game. Through his friendship with Oliver and Edith, he experiences some of the high life of the resort society and has gained in understanding by summer's end.

NILDA (Mohr*, Nicolasa, ill. author, Harper, 1973), episodic, realistic novel set in New York City in the World War II period, July 1941-May 1945. The youngest in the family, Nilda Ramírez, 10, lives with her mother, Lydia, her stepfather, Emilio*, her great-aunt, deaf, eccentric Aunt* Delia, and her four brothers in the Puerto Rican barrio. Although she has her Spanish-born stepfather's name, Nilda knows that she is really the child of Leo, as are at least some of her brothers, and she is fond of Leo, but her mother, who disapproves of the woman Leo lives with, forbids her to visit him. Although Nilda's mother is both a devout Catholic and a believer in spiritualism, Emilio is an anti-religious Communist, conflicting influences that confuse Nilda. In separate episodes, Nilda goes to a Catholic summer camp, a dismal place she hates, and later to a girls' camp she loves; Emilio has a heart attack, and Nilda accompanies her mother to the welfare office; her eldest brother Jimmy's girlfriend, Sophie, turns up pregnant and is taken in; Nilda goes with Sophie to show the baby to Sophie's mother, who refuses to let them in; she attends the storefront Pentecostal church with her friend, Benji, where the drunk husband of one of the members breaks in, creates a disturbance, and urinates on the floor; she attends a street rally where they burn effigies of Hitler, Mussolini, and Hirohito, and Leo buys war-stamps for her; her mother engages a spiritualist to rid the apartment of bad spirits and thereby aid in Emilio's recovery; Nilda attends Emilio's funeral, a Catholic service despite his scorn for the church; she sees Benji's little brother, mistaken for a gang member, beaten and badly injured by the police. As the war ends, she visits her mother in the hospital and hears her final advice, to live for herself, not for her lover or her children as Lydia has done. Nilda's brothers show the diverse ways the barrio life may affect young men: Jimmy becomes a drug addict, is arrested for theft, serves time in federal prison, and seems to be returning to crime at the story's end; Victor, an intelligent, stable boy, joins the army; dark-skinned Paul, Nilda's favorite, kind and well liked, joins the navy;

Frankie, a handsome, rather spoiled youngster, is a gang member but not a real tough. Nilda, who expresses herself by drawing, grows up in the four years from a self-centered baby of the family to a "señorita," who accepts her mother's death and the break-up of the family with understanding. Although it is written somewhat clumsily and has no strong central action, the book gives a vivid picture of the world of drugs and holy water, the numbers racket and seances, prejudiced teachers, welfare inspectors, poverty, and family love. Addams.

NIMH (*Mrs. Frisby and the Rats of NIMH**), presumably the acronym for National Institute of Mental Health, in whose laboratory rats are the subjects of experiments conducted by Dr. Schultz and his assistants, Julie and George. For months, twenty rats in Group A are given special injections designed to make them bigger, smarter, and longer lived than ordinary rats. Some of these "civilized" rats escape, and for two years they journey through the countryside having various adventures, until they settle at Farmer Fitzgibbon's place where their colony thrives and grows to 115 in number. They are living there in a comparatively comfortable and luxurious human-like existence under the rosebush in the yard when discovered by Mrs. Frisby.

NIXON, JOAN LOWERY (1927–   ), teacher and author best known for her mystery and suspense novels for children and adolescents. Born in Los Angeles, she received her bachelor's degree from the University of Southern California in journalism and her teaching certificate from California State College. She married Hershell Nixon, a petroleum geologist, and made her home in Texas. She has been a teacher in elementary school in California and has taught creative writing in Midland, Texas, and at the University of Houston, has lectured on writing, and has participated as instructor in writers' workshops. Her first book, *Mystery of Hurricane Castle* (Criterion, 1964), grew out of her daughters' request for a mystery story with them in it. One of her books was nominated for an Edgar Allan Poe Award, *The Mysterious Red Tape Gang** (Putnam, 1974), a novel for later elementary children, while two have won the Poe Award, *The Kidnapping of Christina Lattimore** (Harcourt, 1979), a take-off on the Patty Hearst case, and *The Séance** (Harcourt, 1980), a murder-mystery set in an East Texas town, both for adolescent readers. These are fast-moving, well-paced stories, written with more attention to style and language than is usual with the genre. Recent titles include *The Valentine Mystery* (Whitman, 1979) and *The April Fool Mystery* (Whitman, 1980), both easy-to-read books, and *The Specter* (Delacorte, 1982) and *The Gift* (Macmillan, 1983), for young people. She has also contributed fiction and non-fiction to magazines for adults and children and has been a columnist for the Houston *Post*. She has traveled widely in the United States, and her books stem from her personal experiences in the places where she has lived or visited. Their backgrounds are authentic.

NOAH (*Orphans of the Wind**), carpenter, the Bible-quoting madman who blows up the ship. "I speak the words of the Lord," he says, and he becomes convinced that he has been divinely directed to destroy the arms-carrying ship as God destroyed Sodom and Gomorrah. When Jim, exploring the hold of the ship, meets old Noah wandering with a candle among the kegs of powder, the carpenter refers to the captain as Beelzebub and mentions the destruction of the Cities of the Plains, so Jim is apprehensively prepared when Noah fires the *Four Winds* and murders the captain, who has already been wounded by a marlinspike thrown by the topforeman. When the ship goes down, Noah is at the wheel.

NO MORE MAGIC (Avi*, Pantheon, 1975), realistic detective novel set in a small town in the United States at Halloween in the late 1900s. Impressionable, imaginative schoolboy, Chris*, tells the story of how he recovers the bike he lost on Halloween night. Chris is certain that his bike, which is a special, glowing green, has been stolen because it is magical. His father advises him to use reason and logic to locate it. He tells his son that, if he asks the right questions, he will arrive at the correct solution to his problem. Preliminary evidence indicates that the child costumed as a warlock stole the bike. Chris believes that the warlock was Muffin*, a new girl in town, and that she magicked his bike away. Muffin, however, informs Chris that her warlock costume was stolen before she had a chance to wear it. The two children then join forces to uncover the thief. At different times, evidence points to Eddie, Chris's best friend; Mr. Bullen, owner of the local junk yard; and even Muffin herself. Interviews with Police Chief Byers and Mr. Podler, town drunk, clues, and the process of elimination eventually lead the children to the bike. They find it at the bottom of the river under the bridge where Chris then remembers he carelessly left it early Halloween night. The children also learn that Muffin's aunt, who is also her guardian, determined that Muffin not be encouraged in her belief in magic, had given away the girl's warlock costume to Mike, Chris's older brother, who donned it to play a trick on Chris. In getting his bike back, Chris learns that asking the right questions is indeed essential if one hopes to arrive at the right answers. The story is amusing even though the narrative is spun out with stock characters, a good share of false leads, and obviously contrived incidents. Chris and Muffin are individualized and winning, and their strong belief in magic seems typical of imaginative children of mid-elementary-school age and adds a distinctive twist and some humor, much of it adult, to what would otherwise be a rather conventional mystery for middle readers. The use of short sentences and phrases produces an appropriately conversational tone. The slight subplot about Muffin's parents' marriage contributes human interest and a little suspense. Poe Nominee.

THE NOONDAY FRIENDS (Stolz*†, Mary, ill. Louis S. Glanzman, Harper, 1965), realistic novel of family and neighborhood life set in Greenwich Village in the mid twentieth century. Usually sunny, eleven-year-old Franny Davis loves school and her family, which also includes irresponsible Mr.* Davis, a would-be artist who works as a shoe salesman; patient Mrs. Davis, who works in a laundry to make ends meet; flip Jim, Franny's twin, who tosses off all problems; and clever, candid Marshall*, almost five. Some things bother Franny: having to wear outgrown clothes and use a free lunch pass, the fear that her father will lose this job as he has so many others, not having the money to give Marshall a proper birthday party, and, especially, never having time after school to spend with her lunchtime friend, Simone* Orgella, because she has to baby-sit Marshall. When Mr. Harney fires Mr. Davis for insulting a customer, and Franny and Simone have a spat, it seems that Franny's world is coming to an end. Everyone, even little Marshall, becomes tense and out of sorts. Relief comes in an unexpected way. Mr. Davis, who has painted a portrait of Mr. Harney in hopes Mr. Harney will give him shoes for the family in exchange for it, decides to use the picture instead to help Francisco, Simone's cousin from Puerto Rico, get his former job. Mr. Harney is so pleased with the picture that he not only hires Francisco but also displays it in his window, where it coincidentally is soon seen by Mr. Wheeler, who owns an art gallery. Mr. Wheeler gets Papa a job with an ad agency and displays his paintings in his gallery. Franny and Simone meet in the lunchroom, tension erased, and share their families' good fortunes. Events are seen mostly from Franny's point of view, but some chapters concern the other members of the family, for example, Jim and his friends collecting bottles ostensibly for charity but really for spending money; Mr. Davis helping Francisco get the job; and Simone and Lila Wimbledon playing together. There is some humor, and the characters seem real, their concerns authentic and easily appreciated, and family relationships are warm and accurate, but the plot is slight and contrived and the conclusion strains belief. Marshall's fifth birthday party is a particularly good episode. The Davises and Mrs. Mundy, the irascible baby-sitter, give him thoughtful, simple gifts, and everyone has a good time being together and sharing what for Marshall is a long-awaited, momentous, never-to-be forgotten occasion. Choice; Fanfare; Newbery Honor.

NORDSTROM, URSULA (LITCHFIELD) born in New York City; editor of the juvenile division of Harper and Row for many years. She attended Northfield School for Girls and Scudder Preparatory School and joined Harper's in 1930. In 1954 she served as president of the Children's Book Council. Her novel for middle-level readers, *The Secret Language** (Harper, 1960), is a story of a girls' boarding school.

THE NO-RETURN TRAIL (Levitin*, Sonia, Harcourt, 1978), historical novel, fictionalized account of the 1841 Bidwell-Bartleson expedition, which included Nancy Kelsey, 17, the first woman to journey overland from Missouri to California. Most of the characters really lived, and events are based on primary sources listed at the end of the book. Strong, resilient, assertive Nancy shares the enthusiasm of her young husband, Ben, for fabulous "Californ-y" of oranges, ocean, and easy living. In the spring, they pull up stakes, take their new baby,

Ann, and leave with Ben's brother, Sam, and his family, and two other brothers, Isaac and Andy, to join the Western Emigration Society at Sapling Grove, Mo. To their surprise and dismay, the expedition is small and the leaders uninformed about the route. Dissension soon arises, and headstrong, officious John Bartleson insists on the captaincy. He has a map of sorts and has brought with him armed men for protection. Sensible, ex-schoolteacher John Bidwell is elected secretary. The group then joins Father De Smet's missionaries who are guided by Thomas Fitzpatrick and bound for Oregon. Although chores are demanding, the journey is pleasant at first, and Nancy soon makes friends with chattery, good-hearted Jessica Williams, 16, who marries Isaac in a simple trail ceremony given a touch of elegance by the loan of Nancy's best bonnet. But Indians are a constant worry, river crossings are hazardous and taxing, and caring for little Ann poses special problems for the young mother. Nancy soon feels tired and harried all the time. Ben, too, loses his good nature and becomes curt and impatient. Since he is level headed and reliable, the group soon looks to him for leadership, and thus more responsibilities are added to his already heavy trail burdens. Wind and weather take their toll, aging even the young, and the expedition narrowly escapes death from a buffalo stampede and a tornado. At Fort Laramie, the travelers divide, and all the other Kelseys, except Andy, continue on with Father De Smet, leaving Nancy the only woman bound for California. When Bartleson deserts, Ben is elected leader. Troubles soon mount, as the group encounters barren desert, forbidding mountains, and bitter cold and snow, and many times all seems lost. Provisions run out, and the travelers abandon all but the most vital necessities. When Ben becomes ill and the men threaten to abandon him to the trail, Nancy grabs a rifle, which she has earlier persuaded Ben to teach her to use, and forces them to stay with the Kelseys until Ben recovers. Shortly thereafter, Andy, who has been scouting ahead, reports they have reached journey's end. During the long, terrible trip, Nancy has come to appreciate the value of life and has learned when to hold her tongue and when to be assertive, while Ben has gained greater respect for the mind and capabilities of his sturdy, enduring young wife. Characterization is superficial, and it is hard to keep the many characters straight. Few scenes are well enough developed to be memorable, but the sober tone and the sheer accumulation of authentic details add up to the picture of a long, very rigorous journey as seen from the woman's point of view. Lewis Carroll; Spur.

NORTH, STERLING (1906–1974), born in Edgerton, Wis.; editor, novelist, columnist. He was a graduate of the University of Chicago and became a reporter, then literary editor for Chicago and New York newspapers. For several years he wrote a syndicated column and in 1957 became the founding editor of North Star Books, a Houghton Mifflin history series for children. Altogether he wrote some thirty books, about half for young people, including biographies of Edison, Thoreau, and Mark Twain, and *The Wolfling* (Dutton, 1969), a biographical novel based on the boyhood of his father. His novel published for adults, *So*

Dear to My Heart (Doubleday, 1947), a story of an Indiana boy and his lamb set at the turn of the century, is often read by children, but it is his *Rascal** (Dutton, 1963), an autobiographical novel of his year with his pet raccoon, that is best remembered by both adults and youngsters.

NO-SCALP-LOCK (*Half-Breed**), Crow warrior, a white man whose white name is Abner Beacon. He once trapped beavers with Hardy Hollingshead's father. Both men married Crow women and settled down among the Crows when pelts became scarce. Beacon taught English to Hardy and his own son, Hardy's friend, White-arm. No-scalp-lock tells Hardy to search for his father at Willamette Falls. Because of him, Hardy has some idea of what to expect when he arrives among whites. Beacon advises the boy to treat his white family as he would his Crow, give them the respect due them, and not take offense easily, admonitions that the boy strictly adheres to and that help him win through the troubled times that follow.

O

O'BRIEN, ROBERT C. (ROBERT LESLIE CONLY) (1918–1973), editor and writer for magazines and newspapers and author of novels for adults and children most highly acclaimed for his two fantasics for young readers, *Mrs. Frisby and the Rats of NIMH** (Atheneum, 1971), a very convincing story about a group of rats with superior intelligence who develop advanced communication and technical skills, which won the Newbery Award and was a National Book Award finalist, a Fanfare book, a *Boston Globe-Horn Book* honor book, a Lewis Carroll Shelf book, and a *Choice* book; and *Z for Zachariah** (Atheneum, 1974), an absorbing novel of suspense and conflict about a girl's struggles to survive after a nuclear war devastates the United States, which won the Edgar Allan Poe and Jane Addams Awards and was a Fanfare book. O'Brien was born in Brooklyn, N.Y., of a large, established, literary family, and grew up on Long Island. His father was a teacher and later a reporter for the New York *Herald Tribune*. O'Brien studied at Williams College, Juilliard School of Music, Columbia, and the University of Rochester, from which he took his degree in English. He worked briefly in advertising, then entered the newspaper and magazine field. After a position as researcher and writer for *Newsweek* in New York, he and his wife, Sally McCaslin, also a researcher for *Newsweek*, moved to Washington, where for thirty years he lived and worked first as a reporter for the *Times-Herald* and *Pathfinder* and then as a member of the staff and senior editor of *National Geographic*, until his death of a heart attack. He came late to the writing of fiction, and his first novel for children, *The Silver Crown* (Atheneum, 1968), about a threatened society, was published when he was fifty. His only other novel was for adults, *Report from Group 17* (Atheneum, 1972).

THE OBSTINATE LAND (Keith*†, Harold, Crowell, 1977), historical novel dealing with the hardships of the pioneers of northern Oklahoma, set against the land rush into the Cherokee* Strip in the mid–1890s. When his German-born father dies, fourteen-year-old Fritz Romberg takes over the responsibilities of running their homestead and making a living for his mother and his younger brother and sister. Fritz finds a troublesome adversary in Sam Womble, the nearby rancher who covets the Romberg land, turns his cattle into Fritz's corn, hoards water, and reports Fritz to the marshal for cutting timber on government land when the family needs fuel. Among Fritz's friends are Jim Yoakum, a kindhearted cowboy who later turns outlaw, Ray Patterson, a nester neighbor who proves particularly supportive, and John J. Geist, a banker who recognizes that the boy is courageous, hardworking, and determined to make his father's claim succeed as a business. Problems with the weather and with outlaws also test the mettle of the enterprising and plucky youth, who grows to manhood having earned the respect of the settlers and the townspeople and who at the end plans to marry Mattie Cooper, the daughter of the Arkansas Sooners who have settled nearby and who is skilled at curing with folk remedies. Although characterization is shallow and the conclusion predictable, such details of everyday life as dry farming, planting, harvesting, food preparation, building sod houses, digging wells, caring for the sick, trips to town, foraging for wood and cowchips to burn for fuel, and attending social functions like box suppers and church give a very vivid sense of the times. Western Heritage.

O CRISPIN (*The Champion of Merrimack County**), single-minded and confident bicycling mouse, the epitome of the dedicated athlete who puts his sport first. When he finds the ideal racetrack in the Berryfield bathtub, he does not let the possibility of danger interfere with his practice. He is also a keen appraiser of character and can see at once that Janet has good sense, her mother a kind heart, and that Mr. Berryfield does not always understand his own motives.

O'DELL, SCOTT (1903–   ), born in Los Angeles, Calif.; writer of some of the strongest historical novels published in the United States in the last half century. He attended Occidental College in Los Angeles, the University of Wisconsin, Stanford University, and the University of Rome. During World War II, he served in the U.S. Air Force and in the 1940s he was book editor for a Los Angeles newspaper, but since 1934 he has devoted most of his time to writing. Undoubtedly his most popular book is *Island of the Blue Dolphins** (Houghton, 1960), a Newbery winner and one of the Children's Literature Association's choice of the Top Ten American Books. Its sequel, *Zia* (Houghton, 1976) lacks the strong appeal of the original survival story. *The Black Pearl** (Houghton, 1967), a story of pearl divers in Baja California, *Sing Down the Moon** (Houghton, 1970), about the disastrous relocation of the Navaho Indians in the late nineteenth century, and *The King's Fifth** (Houghton, 1966), a novel of the Spanish conquistadors seeking gold, were all Newbery honor books. A more recent trilogy concerns the Spanish conquest and destruction of the Mayan culture, *The Captive* (Houghton, 1979), *The Feathered Serpent* (Houghton, 1981), and *The Amethyst Ring* (Houghton, 1983). Typically, he employs a first-person narrator who is emotionally restrained, a device that works well in situations where understatement adds to the sense of endurance but which sometimes backfires in stories which demand a more highly developed characterization.

ODILE CHRYSOSTOME (*The Court of the Stone Children**), daughter of a French painter at the time of Napoleon, whose statue as a child stands with those of her brothers and sisters in the courtyard of the French Museum in San Francisco. Odile appears to Nina Harmsworth in a dream in which she leads Nina up a stairway. Nina later ascends the staircase she dreamed about and sees a painting which she discovers proves Ms. de Lombre did not murder his valet.

THE ODYSSEY OF BEN O'NEAL (Taylor*, Theodore, ill. Richard Cuffari, Doubleday, 1977), adventure novel set in 1899 in places from Norfolk, Va., to Barbados to London, much of it aboard ship. The third in Taylor's Cape Hatteras trilogy, this continues the story of the involvement of Ben* O'Neal, now thirteen, with Wendy Lynn Appleton, 13, known as Teetoncey*, the girl he rescued from the wreck of the *Malta Empress* near his home on the North Carolina Outer Banks. Thinking that Tee, with Ben's dog, Boo, is on her way back to London, Ben goes to Norfolk to get a berth as cabin boy on a ship to the Caribbean, hoping to find his brother, Reuben, who is mate of the *Elnora Langhans*. He providentially falls in with Michael Grant, an apple-seller on the train, who takes him to his boarding house run by Mrs. Crowe. At the ship chandler's, where he inquires for a job, he receives a note from Tee asking for help and directing him to a barge where she is hiding. First visiting Calderham, Ben finds the British Consul irate, furious that Tee has run away simply because he would not arrange for Boo to accompany her to London. Ben finds Tee and Boo and takes them to Mrs. Crowe's. The railroad men boarders work out a plan for Tee to reach New York and take a ship from there, and Ben leaves aboard the *Christine Conyers*, known as a backbreaker because of eccentric and demanding Captain* Josiah Reddy and the slave-driving German bosun, Gebbert. Ben is a steward's helper, working with a Bravaman, Eddie Cartaxo. Predictably for the reader, Tee turns up as a passenger for Barbados and charms all on shipboard, including tough Gebbert, to whom she speaks in German. When they pass the *Elnora Langhans* and see Reuben, Boo knocks Ben overboard, and Tee confesses all to the annoyed captain, enlisting his sympathies. His help is needed when Tee is arrested in Barbados, escapes, and must be rescued and spirited out with Ben and Boo aboard the *Harriet B. Ritter*, bound for Norfolk. There they find from Mrs. Crowe that news of their escapades has preceded them, but she gets their story to a newspaperman, and public sympathy turns against Calderham and gets them passage (Ben works his) aboard a steamer for London. Written, as is its predecessor, in first person from Ben's point of view, the book adds incidents but no depth to the story. The pace of the wildly improbable events is fast, but characterization is weak. We are told that Tee charms everyone she meets but see little reason why, and most of the new characters are caricatures or non-entities. Stone.

OFFICER LAFFERTY (*The Soul Brothers and Sister Lou**), the "Man," he harasses Louretta Hawkins and her friends in Southside. He represents the hostile, bigoted white establishment policeman, an obvious stereotype.

OF LOVE AND DEATH AND OTHER JOURNEYS (Holland*, Isabelle, Lippincott, 1975), realistic problem novel set in Italy during the late 1900s among a community of Bohemian expatriates and dealing with the death of a parent. Meg Grant, 15, very much loves her mother, Phoebe* Smith, an American who earns a living as a freelance tour guide showing "Goodie Packs" the sights of Italy. Meg feels close to her stepfather, Englishman Peter* Smith, scholar turned writer of borderline pornography, and has long been infatuated with their good friend, Scotsman Andrew MacKenzie, called Cotton*, a sometime university teacher of English and painter. The four humorously call themselves the Pride collectively and Flopsy, Mopsy, Cottontail, and Peter individually. Meg has never known her father, Alan Fraser Grant VI, who, Phoebe says, was an unfeeling cad, the callous, superior scion of a smug, aristocratic family. Meg describes the summer she turns sixteen, when her mother dies of cancer and she meets and goes to live with her real father. Just after Meg learns that Phoebe must have an operation, she also hears from Sylvia, her mother's friend who owns a large Italian country house, that Alan is to be Sylvia's guest. Meg has mixed emotions toward both him and her mother. She realizes her mother has deliberately withheld information about him from her, but she also feels that he has been mean to her mother. Invited to spend the week with him at Sylvia's, she is surprised to discover that he is a warm, kind man with a pleasing sense of humor, who freely admits that he should have been more supportive and loving to her mother. As Meg and Alan go on short sightseeing trips, they have long talks during which they get to know each other, and the reader and Meg gradually pick up information about Alan. Alan tells how he settled down after Phoebe left him, mended wild ways, and made a good life for himself as an Anglican clergyman. He and his second wife, Rachel, a physician, had a retarded son, Stephen, who died. After Phoebe's death, Meg reluctantly goes to live with her father in New York City. School is not satisfying to her, and she dreams of marrying Cotton and even plans to fly to join him until she learns he is traveling with a new girl friend and she realizes there is no room in his life for her. She drops out of school and takes a job in Rachel's clinic for children. Book's end finds her thrilling to a portrait of Phoebe Cotton has just completed, in which he has captured Phoebe's beauty and joy in living. Meg realizes that she, too, is loved for what she is and can make a good life for herself if she will. The simple plot is over-foreshadowed, proceeds according to expectations, and occasionally comes perilously close to sentimentality. Interest focuses on the characters, and remembered conversations take up much of the book. The author effectively describes Meg's emotions and reactions to people and situations. Setting is well realized, and some humor lightens the drama of a young girl coming to grips with some of the harsh realities of life. Fanfare; National Book Finalist.

OF NIGHTINGALES THAT WEEP (Paterson*, Katherine, ill. Haru Wells, Crowell, 1974), historical novel set in late twelfth century Japan during a struggle between two rival samurai clans, the Heike and the Genji. Daughter of the Heike

Lord Moriyuke, Takiko is eleven when he is killed and her mother remarried by the arrangement of her imperious aunt to a distant relative, Goro*, a potter. When Takiko first joins them she is horrified at Goro, who is deformed, short with long arms like an ape. Gradually she gets over her fear and loathing, finding solace in her expert playing of the koto and in learning to read and make pottery from Goro. Her contentment is shattered by the birth of a half-brother who claims Goro's delighted attention. A merchant who handles Goro's pottery arranges a place for her with the Princess Aoi, where she is treated coldly but makes a friend, Mieko, her maid. Her playing and her beauty attract the lecherous attention of her mistress's husband, Prince Kira, whom she fears, so that when a request comes for her to go to the court of the child emperor, Antoku, 5, she welcomes it and takes Mieko along. There she finds things actually run by the emperor's grandmother, Nii no Ama, Lady Kiyomori, a nun, who along with the child's mother, appreciates the pleasure Takiko gives him with her playing. The Heike suffer a disastrous defeat, and the court flees the capital city for the island of Kyiusu. There Takiko entertains the young emperor, enjoys a comparatively informal life, and dreams of Princess Aoi's Genji lover, Hideo, with whom Takiko has herself become infatuated. The Genji now in control of the capital set up a new emperor but cannot make him official because Lady Kiyomori has brought the imperial treasures, necessary for a coronation, with them. In the ensuing conflicts, Takiko from a ship witnesses a terrible defeat of the Heike forces. Later, trying to avoid a tryst with the defeated General Munemori, she meets Hideo again, realizes that he is spying, but carefully waits until he can get away before raising the alarm. Later she finds him posing as a Buddhist monk at a nearby temple and makes love with him. Her next possibility of a meeting with him is ruined by the appearance of Goro, who wants her to return to help her mother in childbirth. Takiko says it is her duty to stay with the emperor but knows she is hoping to see Hideo again. The Genji attack, the imperial party leaves by ship, the general miscalculates, and, seeing that they will face a terrible defeat, the Lady Kiyomori, with the young emperor and two of the imperial treasures in her arms, calmly jumps into the sea, followed by most of the ladies of the court, including Mieko. Takiko cannot give up her life and, when some of the ladies are saved, including the mother of the emperor, is shamed. She is rescued, however, by Hideo, who gets her peasant clothing and says he will meet her at Goro's farm. When she arrives there, she finds that her mother, brother, and the servants have died horribly of fever and that Goro, living in the ruin of the burned house, blames her. She nevertheless stays, stubbornly insisting on helping him with the rough labor. When the nephew of one of the servants tries to steal their crop and she thinks Goro is killing him, she interferes and receives a terrible burn across her face. Goro nurses her back to health, but when Hideo finally comes, he rejects her. Takiko goes to the nunnery where the mother of the emperor now resides, planning to join them, but is persuaded to go back to Goro, whom she loves, and to marry him. In the end she bears her first child, a girl, which he welcomes. The details of life in twelfth-century Japan are remarkably convincing, and the characters, despite their stylized behavior, are individualized and believable. The author provides a summary of the political situation and chief figures, but the intrigue is still somewhat confusing. A map would help. Fanfare.

OGION (*A Wizard of Earthsea**; *The Tombs of Atuan**), mage of Re Albi, known as Ogion the Silent, the wizard who gives Ged* his true name and becomes his first real teacher. When Ged, then the boy known as Duny, has overspent his power in calling up the fog to save his village from the Kargs, Ogion comes to heal him and wake him from his dumb stupor. A gentle man, he uses his great powers very little, knowing how dangerous they can be. It is to Ogion that Ged returns in falcon form when he is fleeing the Shadow, and it is to Ogion that he takes Tenar* after they escape from Atuan.

O'LANTERN, JACK (*The Ghost in the Noonday Sun**), pirate aboard *The Bloody Hand*, condemned to walk the plank. When the crew decides to maroon him on a tiny desert island instead, he convinces some of them to trick the captain by leaving a dummy behind in his place. He convinces them they should band together to get for themselves the treasure the captain seeks. He befriends Oliver Finch on several occasions.

OLD BEARDY (*Cayuse Courage**), Samuel's grandfather, whose real name is Chief Many-Spotted-Ponies. He has raised Samuel, who is his only grandson, and takes the boy to Marcus Whitman* when gangrene threatens the boy's life. Once a chief, now an old man, he is still respected and heeded, but during the rebellion, which, like Samuel, he opposes, the warriors threaten to whip him if he warns the White-Eyes. Old Beardy is a well-rounded figure, comic, vain, wise, enduring, accepting, and compassionate, a knowledgeable leader who feels the Indians must keep lines of communication open with the White-Eyes. When he dies of old age after the uprising, Samuel has no alternative but to leave the tribe and find another place to live.

OLD BEN (Stuart*, Jesse, ill. Richard Cuffari, McGraw, 1970), very simple animal story for early readers, set on an American farm in an unspecified time. On his way to the apple orchard, Shan, a fifth grader, finds a big, bull black snake. At first hesitant, he picks up the six-foot-long snake, strokes it, talks to it, wraps it around his shoulders, and takes it home, where he puts it into the corn crib to catch the mice there. His parents are reluctant to accept the snake, which Shan has named Old Ben, but soon come round to see him as interesting and valuable, because they normally lose a lot of corn to mice. Shan's cousin, Ward, is similarly cautious but soon so enthusiastic that he is very pleased when he finds a nest of black snake eggs. Although the cows are at first scared by Old Ben and the dog, Old Blackie, wants to kill him, the cows become used to him following Shan, and Shan's father trains Blackie to leave him alone. When

Old Ben disappears and his nightly milk is undrunk, Shan and his father fork through all the hay in the loft hunting for him. Shan's father is afraid that he may have gotten into the pigpen, where the hogs would stomp him to death and eat him. Shan is more hopeful, thinking Old Ben may have found a winter home and will return in the spring. Written in simple sentences and elementary vocabulary, the story is obviously meant for beginning readers, but even for that audience it is underdeveloped, wooden in style, and didactic. Its main recommendation is that it makes a snake seem an attractive pet. Lewis Carroll.

OLD BESS (*I, Adam**), fortuneteller of whom the youth of Coveport are a little afraid. For a lark, Adam consults her when he finishes school. She looks into her crystal ball and, with an obscure smile on her face, predicts that life will bring surprises for him. Her words stick in Adam's mind, and later, after the Sharkey incidents, he realizes that what she said has come true.

OLD GRANDFATHER (*Owl in the Cedar Tree**), Haske's great-grandfather, who sometimes lives in Haske's family's hogan. Mostly, Old Grandfather moves about among his relatives, his only possessions his clothing and an old tin cup. He is afraid that he might die in a hogan belonging to one of them. If that happened, the hogan would have to be burned, according to traditional beliefs. He never stays long at one place for that reason. Night Singer and Riding Woman welcome him whenever he comes, because they have been educated in public schools and do not hold with the old customs they believe unworthy. Old Grandfather stays staunchly to the old ways, however, and his advice puzzles the boy since it conflicts with what his mother and father wish for him. Old Grandfather is a good storyteller and often shares his memories and the old stories with the boy. Ill and tired, he goes off to the hills to die alone. Haske's mother says Old Grandfather has gone to join the Ancient Ones.

OLD HEROES (*The Gammage Cup*†; *The Whisper of Glocken**), the "outlaws" who save the Minnipins from the Mushrooms in the first book and who assist the New Heroes to triumph in the second. They are Walter the Earl, Curley Green, Muggles, Gummy, and Mingy.

OLD PEPPER (*Unclaimed Treasures**), great-grandfather of Porky Atwater, neighbor boy of Willa Pinkerton. He is an old, "dried apple" of a man who often speaks in run-on sentences, keeps an old parrot, Bella-Marie, who also speaks in run-on sentences, is pushed around the near-neighborhood by Porky in a wheelbarrow, sometimes wanders naked in his backyard, and hunts for birds. Although usually a comic figure, he can be shrewd and witty. He maintains that ordinary and extraordinary are the same thing, meaning that it is not the nature of the thing itself that determines its classification but the observer's point of view. In a wild, slapstick scene, he manages to get Horace and Willa to the hospital. He manipulates the steering wheel while Horace manages the pedals.

Once there, he gets them inside where the action is by stoutly asserting that he is *Dr*. Pepper, a stunt he pulls off with aplomb.

OLD RAMON (Schaefer*, Jack, ill. Harold West, Houghton, 1960), story of a man's life concentrated into a few days of a sheep drive to summer pasture in the mountains of the Southwest, probably Arizona, in a period that internal evidence indicates to be around the turn of the century. The old sheepherder and the son of his patron, a boy of unspecified age, perhaps ten or twelve, with two dogs and a burro, follow and tend the sheep and learn about each other. Ramon's old brown dog, Pedro, is a natural and experienced sheep dog; the younger black dog, Sancho, is foolish but eager to please and becomes the boy's friend immediately. Ramon gives Sancho to the boy and teaches them both from his deep knowledge about the handling of sheep. In the long dry stretch before they reach the hills, Ramon tells the boy about his terrible trek across the Mojave Desert with the boy's grandfather when they were young men, a drive in which they lost a large part of the flock and ended with Ramon crawling to the stream, carrying the other man on his back. The remainder of the sheep they sold to gold miners, and the grandfather invested in more sheep, becoming a wealthy stockman, while Ramon blew his away on liquor and women. When a sand storm hits, Ramon gets Pedro to drive the sheep into an arroyo where they are partly sheltered, and he goes back to help the boy to safety, then shelters him under his blanket and tells tall tales until the storm is over. That night he tells the boy about the time in lambing season when he got drunk and lost five lambs and was so ashamed that he left and worked for four years at other jobs—herding cattle and driving mule teams and building adobe houses—before he forced himself to go back. Then he found that his friend, the grandfather, had been killed in a fall from a horse, but the new patron, the boy's father, said that as long as the family has sheep there is a flock for Ramon. When they reach the summer pasture, Pedro rouses Ramon to come and shoot a wolf, and they find Sancho's body, where he has attacked the wolf and been killed. The boy resents Pedro as a coward until Ramon tells him of how the old dog saved his life by attacking a bear. Ramon lets the boy sob out his grief, then proposes that they drive the flock in such a way as to pass his cousin's house, where there is a young dog sired by Pedro that he will get for the boy. Partly because the rhythm of the language is like a translation from Spanish, the story has the quality of a legend yet at the same time is a strong and moving characterization of a wise and gentle old man. The natural features of the area are also beautifully evoked. Choice; Newbery Honor.

OLIVER AVERY (*The Refugee Summer**), American boy who naturally becomes leader of the group of youngsters summering in a Greek resort village who call themselves the Pallikars. A handsome, blond fourteen-year-old, he is somewhat bossy but good-natured and idealistic, accepting Nikolas* Angeliki, the son of a Greek seamstress, naturally as a friend and companion. When they buy bread for a boxcar full of starving refugees from Smyrna, he defies the police and pitches the loaves into the boxcar with his best baseball style.

OLIVER ENGLISH (*When No One Was Looking**), college boy who works at the tennis and swimming club with Kathy* Bardy and who becomes fond of her. He accepts the restrictions Kathy's family puts on their relationship and enjoys seeing her play but doesn't share in the burning drive to make her a champion that most of her friends and associates feel. Not a particularly convincing character, he represents a more moderate attitude toward sports success.

ONEAL, ZIBBY (ELIZABETH ONEAL) (1934–   ), born in Omaha, Nebr.; novelist, university English instructor. She attended Stanford University and was graduated from the University of Michigan, where she has been a lecturer in English. She is married to a plastic surgeon and has two children. Her novel for middle readers, *War Work* (Viking, 1971), which takes place on the American home front during World War II and which involves a mystery, received the Friends of American Writers Award. She has also published two books for younger children, *The Improbable Adventures of Marvelous O'Hara Soapstone* (Viking, 1972), illustrated by Paul Galdone, and *Turtle and Snail* (Lippincott, 1979), illustrated by Margot Tomes. Her reputation as a writer is based more strongly on two psychological novels for young adults, *The Language of Goldfish* (Viking, 1980), a sensitive story of a disturbed girl who attempts suicide and gradually works her way back to mental health, and *A Formal Feeling** (Viking, 1982), a meticulously crafted novel of a teenaged girl's resolving of her ambivalent feelings toward her deceased mother and her new stepmother. She is noted for her careful control of tone and precisely selected detail in a setting of restrained emotion.

ONE-EYED CAT (Fox*, Paula, Bradbury, 1984), realistic novel of family life set from September to April in 1935 in a semi-rural area in New York State overlooking the Hudson River. For his eleventh birthday, only child Ned Wallis receives a coveted Daisy air rifle from his Uncle* Hilary, the brother of his mother, Mrs.* Wallis, who has been invalided by arthritis. Ned's elation over the gift is soon dispelled by his father, the Reverend* James Wallis, a Congregational minister, who orders him to put the gun aside until he is fourteen. That night, Ned steals to the attic of their big, old family home, removes the gun from its box, and takes it outside, where he playfully sights and aims with it, then, attention caught by a shadowy shape by the old shed, involuntarily presses the trigger and fires at it. For weeks thereafter, Ned is haunted by the conviction that he has harmed a living being. He becomes convinced that his victim is a one-eyed cat "gray as a mole with matted fur," one of several feral cats that frequent the surrounding woods and the yard of old Mr.* Scully who lives down the road and for whom Ned does small chores, and by the fear that his deed is known. After firing the shot, Ned had glanced upward toward the attic where he thought he detected the outline of a person's head against the window. Was it his father who saw? or his mother? or sharp-tongued Mrs.* Scallop, the bullying housekeeper? Ned diligently sneaks scraps of food for the cat, lies to his parents about his abstracted manner and lowering grades, especially as cold weather intensifies and his fears for the cat increase. He refuses Uncle Hilary's invitation to spend Christmas vacation in the Carolinas, because of his obligation to the cat. Then Mr. Scully suffers a stroke and must enter a nursing home, his daughter sells the house, and Ned falls ill and is unable to continue caring for the creature. When recovered, he takes to tramping the hills and woods, sometimes stopping by the empty old Makepeace mansion whose grounds abut those of the Wallises, where on one occasion he sees what he thinks is the one-eyed cat. He visits the nursing home, where he confides his guilty secret to the old man and senses in the press of the dying fingers understanding and forgiveness. A new treatment gives Mrs. Wallis greater mobility, and one night in mid-April, when Ned goes on a night walk to the Makepeace verandah, she follows him there. The two watch the one-eyed cat and his family playing in the moonlight, Ned confesses, his mother informs him that hers was the face at the window, and conversation between the mother and son leads Ned to the relieved understanding that everyone makes mistakes and that it is all right to be less than perfect. Although the plot is thin and its resolution somewhat abrupt and puzzling and the book has a static air, characters are boldly sketched, and it is easy to sympathize with Ned whose fears and uncertainties seem appropriate for a youth of his religious and moral upbringing. Much of the book's appeal comes from the small details of Ned's reflections and observations of life with mother, father, and community, which seem seen at a distance, as though through a mirror, and create the impression of memoir rather than lived experience. Style is vivid with imagery: the family home is a "big, ailing old house," the parsonage appears as a "mean, small house," after treatments his mother "feels like silk," and his father sometimes speaks "in a cemetery voice." Some phrases, however, strike false notes. Ned was "pretty sure he'd never seen her [a neighbor woman] without an infant clinging to some part of her body" and a school chum Ned's age describes her friend as a "skinny little beetle," turns of expression which seem to voice the author's observations rather than those of the characters. Newbery Honor.

ONLY EARTH AND SKY LAST FOREVER (Benchley*, Nathaniel, Harper, 1972), historical novel set in the Sioux-Cheyenne territory of the Badlands and the Black* Hills from about 1874–1876, which involves actual events and people. Dark Elk, a fictitious Indian youth of about eighteen, tells the story of the Indians' desperate attempts to prevent further inroads into their traditional territory and to cope with broken treaties and continuing indignities inflicted upon them by encroaching whites. While some Indians, like Crazy Horse, strive to stem the white advance, others have capitulated, trusting in white promises and treaties, and are now suffering poverty and starvation. Dark Elk goes into the Black Hills, an area sacred to the Indians, where he hopes to receive a vision by which he may prove himself worthy of beautiful Lashuka. He is shocked and angered to find whites prospecting there in violation of the treaty guaranteeing the region to the Indians forever. He visits his Sioux family who are living in degradation and misery on the Pine Ridge agency with Chief Red Cloud. Dark Elk then joins the powerful, much respected, still free Crazy Horse, hoping to assist Crazy Horse's partisans in their efforts to hold out against the whites and live as Indians have traditionally lived. The remainder of the book describes how, under Crazy Horse's wise guidance, Dark Elk learns to fight and raid, develops self-control and patience, and receives a coveted invitation to join a warrior society. With Crazy Horse, he witnesses and participates in historical events. He observes the meeting of combined tribes and whites to discuss ownership of the sacred hills, is present when Crazy Horse's Oglalas join with Sitting Bull's Hunkpapas and other Sioux and Plains Indians for a sun dance. Shortly thereafter, he takes part in the victorious Battle of the Rosebud against General Crook. His story culminates with the Battle at Little Big Horn (Greasy Grass), where Custer falls, and where triumph proves bitter because Lashuka is killed. This is a sober, somber, starkly realistic picture of a dark period in American history, only here and there relieved by dry wit. The point of view is inconsistent, straying from that of an intelligent, observant Indian youth perplexed and overwhelmed by events he cannot understand and is powerless to control to that of the author who uses the youth as a mouthpiece to comment on events and convey information. Crazy Horse, an actual historical figure, is memorably portrayed, and other important Indians appear, among them the mystic Sitting Bull. The plot is strained, and events often seem fabricated for the purpose of making a statement. The title comes from a war cry. A bibliography of sources at the end indicates that the author used eyewitness accounts. Spur.

O. O. (*The Devil in Vienna**), Opa Oskar, Inge* Dornenwald's grandfather, her mother's father, who is very influential in her life. He shares with her his misgivings about Austria's future after the Anschluss and his hopes for emigrating and opens her eyes to some realities of the political situation in Vienna and of life for Jews under Hitler. After he moves in with the Dornenwalds, she becomes quite fond of him. A realist, he urges the family to leave Austria before it is too late for them to do so. He is both indulgent and firm with Inge and is one of the best-drawn characters in the novel. Inge is convinced that he would not disapprove of their professing to be Catholics in order to escape from Vienna.

ORA HIGGINS FARR (*The People Therein**), Ory, mother of Lanthy*. Mountain bred, Ory has lived her whole life within a few miles of her married home at Dewfall Gap, where she has borne seven children: three daughters, then three sons who were stillborn or died in infancy, and finally Little Labe. Given to melancholy, Ory spends her whole life protesting, weeping, or complaining, but at the same time she does the back-breaking work of the mountain wife, cares without question for her senile mother, and offers hospitality and food to any visitor, friend or stranger. Partly because Ora is terrified of doctors, Lanthy's lameness has never had medical help, though Ora also thinks her daughter's condition inevitable because she "marked" her by looking at a deformed calf while she was pregnant.

ORGEL, DORIS (DORIS ADELBERG) (1929–   ), editor and author and translator of children's books. She was born in Vienna, Austria, where she lived until she was nine. After Hitler came into power there, the family fled to Yugoslavia, to England, and then to the United States in the winter of 1940, and lived in St. Louis before settling in New York. Her most acclaimed novel, *The Devil in Vienna** (Dial, 1978), which received the Child Study Award and was a Fanfare book, fictionalizes upon her own family's experiences during the critical period before they left Austria. After attending Hunter and Radcliffe, she graduated from Barnard. She married Shelley Orgel, a psychiatrist and psychoanalyst, and has lived in Connecticut. Previous to writing full time, she worked for magazine and book publishers. She has published over a dozen other books which vary in form, subject, scope, and intended audience. Some are picture books, like *Sarah's Room* (Harper, 1963) and *The Uproar* (McGraw, 1970), some verse, like *Merry, Merry FIBruary* (Parents, 1977). Also acclaimed have been her translations of *Dwarf Long-Nose* (Random, 1960) and *The Tale of Gockel, Hinkel, and Gackeliah* (Random, 1962). Her other novels include *Next Door to Xanadu* (Harper, 1969), about friendship, *A Certain Magic* (Dial, 1976), about a girl's attachment to her aunt, and *The Mulberry Music* (Harper, 1971), involving the death of a grandmother.

ORMONDROYD, EDWARD (1925–   ), born in Wilkinsburg, Pa.; librarian and author noted for his time-slip fantasies for later elementary and junior high readers. He grew up in Swarthmore, Pa., and Ann Arbor, Mich. After service in World War II, including time on a destroyer escort in the Pacific, he attended the University of California at Berkeley, graduating with a degree in English. He later received his library science degree and has held positions in Berkeley and as a technical services librarian in Ithaca, N.Y. He wrote *David and the Phoenix* (Follett, 1957) while still in college. It was seven years before it was published, but then it won the Commonwealth Club of California Literature Award. *Time at the Top** (Parnassus, 1963), his best-known novel and a *Choice* book, tells the adventures of a girl whose elevator deposits her back in the Victorian era. His dozen published books include *Castaways on Long Ago* (Parnassus, 1969), *Imagination Greene* (Parnassus, 1973), also fantasies, *All in Good Time* (Parnassus, 1975), which is sequel to *Time at the Top*, several picture books, and *Jonathan Frederick Aloysius Brown* (Golden Gate, 1964), a book of verse.

ORPHANS OF THE WIND (Haugaard*, Erik Christian, Houghton, 1966), historical novel set on the voyage from Bristol, England, to Charleston, S.C., and through some southern states during the American Civil War. An orphan, Jim, 12, the narrator, is virtually sold to Captain Matthews of the *Four Winds* by his uncle, Robert Pond, who takes his hire in advance. On the ship he is befriended by the cook, Rolf*, who explains to him that at sea all sailors are "orphans of the wind." He incurs the enmity of Shanghai, a rough seaman, and Pimples and Fatty, two of the boys, but is friendly with Jack, 14, admires the topforeman, Keith, and fears mad old Noah*, the carpenter, who quotes the Bible continually. When they are far out at sea, the crew learns that they are not headed for Boston, as they have been told, but for Charleston with a cargo of ammunition for the Confederates. This information splits the crew, half for the aid to the Southern army, the other half, led by Keith, planning to mutiny and sail the ship to New York. This confrontation is averted by Noah, who, believing he is the tool of God who destroyed Sodom and Gomorrah, sets the ship afire and murders the captain. Though most of the crew escape in the long boat, Jim delays to rescue the ship's cat, Potiphar, and then must swim for the smaller boat, a damaged craft containing Jack, Keith, and Rolf. With great difficulty, they reach a beach surrounded by swamp, build a drift-wood raft, and pole their way along channels until they reach Edisto, an island plantation managed by charming, friendly Mr. Anthony, who thinks of the slaves he directs as children. When the owner, a despicable slaver, arrives, he brings news that the long boat has reached Charleston and that the men have joined the Confederate navy. The four depart, ostensibly to join the navy but actually to walk north in hope of finding and joining the Union army. They have some close scrapes with Confederate recruiters and finally link up with a Confederate army unit as civilian cooks and field kitchen workers in order to work their way north more safely. They reach Manassas Junction and shortly after find themselves in the Battle of Bull Run, where they become separated. Jack finds Jim and admits, with horror, that he shot a man. In desperation he runs away, starting toward the retreating northerners and inadvertently leads a charge. The Union army is routed, and Jack is killed. Jim walks off, is found by Keith and Rolf, and they reach a Union army unit, only to be considered spies. They convince a colonel that they are sincere; Keith and Rolf join the army but Jim is sent to Washington and allowed to sign on the *Luck of Gloucester*, bound for California. Although the events are exciting, the book is more than an adventure story. The conflicts of slavery and freedom are explored as they apply in the Civil War and also, in effect, in Jim's relationship to his uncle and the sailors' to their captain. Characterization is interesting, and the scenes on the *Four Winds* avoid most of the cliches of sea stories. Fanfare.

OTTO SONBERG (*The Bully of Barkham Street**), easygoing classmate of Martin Hastings, of all the children the only one to reach out to Martin. He is well adjusted and a good foil for Martin. Martin is grateful for his friendship but also realizes that Otto gets on well with everyone. Martin smarts off to Otto's mother and hence is unwelcome at Otto's house. In a humorous scene he burns up Otto's shoes trying to dry them in the oven after the two boys go sledding on the first snowy day.

OUR EDDIE (Ish-Kishor*, Sulamith, Pantheon, 1969), realistic novel of family life covering several years in London and New York City before World War II and revolving around the strained relationship between father and son. The story is told in the first and last chapters by Hal* Kent, 13, a family friend, and in between and mostly by Sybil*, a daughter about Hal's age. Except for their father, the Jewish Raphels appear to be a lively, happy, gregarious bunch, beautiful, black-haired Mama, pretty Lilie, breezy, "right guy," fourteen-year-old Eddie, capable Sybil, and impish Thad. Mr. Raphel, authoritarian, miserly, remote from his family, is headmaster of a Hebrew day school and an ardent Zionist. Even though the children are bright and do well in school, they have little hope of advanced educations because Mr. Raphel is more concerned about his religious causes than the well-being of his family. He even turns down a better paying position, because he prefers to continue teaching poor Jewish children whose parents cannot afford the salary which would properly support his family. Eddie, in particular, feels his father's harshness and one-sidedness. When the father suffers a nervous breakdown and is sent to the United States to recuperate with relatives there, Eddie, now fifteen, must leave school to help support the family. The mother suffers from a progressive disease which hinders her motor ability. Eddie first shows signs of the same disorder when he slips on stairs while carrying a pail of hot water. Some time later, the family emigrates to join the father in New York. Still very engrossed in his work, he hardly notices that his wife is almost an invalid from what appears to be multiple sclerosis, that the girls are running the household, and that Eddie has apparently fallen victim of the same disease. Unable to hold jobs which require physical exertion and encouraged by his physician, Eddie hopes to become a medical researcher, but his father angrily refuses support for the education to achieve the ambition. Insisting his son become a Hebrew teacher and involve himself in the Jewish movement in the United States and in Zionism, he even invests in land in Palestine for Eddie, a decision which leads to a complete break between father and son. Prodded by their aunt, the girls contact a neurosurgeon who operates on Eddie, but the youth dies. When Hal next sees the Raphels, the father appears shaken by events and less rigid toward his family. This study of an oppressive, obsessed, neurotic man and his unfortunate, adolescent son who is of an age to assert his independence lacks focus, and the multiple sclerosis interjects an unnecessary, overly poignant complication. The understated "snapshot of life" method of presenting events serves to point up their conflict even as it weakens it by making their problems seem melodramatic and deliberately fashioned for effect. Choice; Fanfare; Newbery Honor.

THE OUTSIDERS (Hinton*, S. E., Viking, 1967), sociological problem novel about life among street gangs set in the mid–1900s in a city somewhere in the southwestern United States, a groundbreaking book in the New Realism for adolescent readers. The story is a monologue, ostensibly a theme written by Ponyboy Curtis, 14, an intelligent, good student, for his English teacher, in which he describes the events that help him decide in what direction his life should go. Pony and his two older brothers, serious Darry*, 20, and happy-go-lucky Sodapop*, 16, have been living alone in the family house since the death of their parents in an auto accident a few months before the story begins. To earn money to keep Pony in school and stay together, Darry has foregone college, and Soda has dropped out of high school. They and their friends are greasers, youths on the fringes of the law whose trademark is their long hair. They live on the East Side of town and are held in contempt by the Socs (Socials), the middle-class and rich kids from the West Side who "have all the breaks in life," according to Pony, and who habitually beat up greasers. Feeling between the groups has run particularly high since Socs assaulted Johnny Cade, 16, leaving him weak and fearful. Much of the book presents Pony's reflections on the unfairness of life and on his relationships with his brothers. He idolizes handsome, cheerful Soda but resents Darry's strictness, until he sees that Darry's behavior is an expression of his deep love for Pony. The slight plot revolves around a murder. Johnny, Pony, and their friend, Dally (Dallas), meet two Soc girls, Cherry Valance and her friend Marcia, at a drive-in movie. Later that night, Cherry's Soc boy friend, Bob, and other Socs attack Johnny and Pony, and in the fracas Johnny kills Bob. With Dally's help, the two boys hop a freight to Jay Mountain where they hide in an abandoned church. They remain there for about a week, when Dally visits and Johnny decides to turn himself in. Before they leave the area, they are wounded rescuing children trapped in the church which has somehow caught fire, Johnny so severely he is not expected to live. The trio is celebrated as delinquents turned heroes. Then the Socs challenge the greasers to a "skin" rumble, that is, a fight without weapons, in which the Curtis side emerges triumphant. Pony and Dally go to the hospital to report their success to Johnny and find him dying. Dally rushes out of the hospital in a fury, robs a grocery store, and is shot to death by police. When Pony falls ill of exhaustion and shock, his brothers nurse him back to health. He becomes despondent, and his grades suffer. An argument with his brothers, during which he comes to see how much they are doing for him, and a letter from Johnny written before his death exhorting Pony to make something of his life prompt him to make the last few fateful weeks the subject of his theme. The formulaic plot is occasionally melodramatic, and some incidents seem very unlikely. They are so implausible as to be almost ludicrous upon reflection, but, interestingly, they hold up well during reading, probably because the author makes Pony's concerns and the warm relationship between the brothers seem very real. The author's occasional editorializing about the faults of society injects a startling didactic element into an otherwise quite emotionally engaging story. The author succeeds in making potentially unsympathetic characters believable and likeable. Vocabulary is fairly easy, some use of street language contributes authenticity to the setting and simple interest, and the street code comes through clearly. Choice; Maxi.

OVERHOLSER, WAYNE D. (1906–   ), born in Pomeroy, Wash.; author of many western novels who also wrote under the pseudonyms of John S. Daniels, Lee Leighton, Wayne Roberts, Dan J. Stevens, and Joseph Wayne. He attended Oregon Normal School, the University of Montana, the University of Southern California, and the University of Oregon. For nearly twenty years he was teacher and principal in Oregon public schools and from 1945 on was a freelance writer, having published more than four hundred short stories and at least forty novels. With Lewis Patten* he is joint author of *The Meeker Massacre** (Cowles, 1969), a fictionalized history of an incident in Colorado in the fall of 1879, which won the Spur Award for the best juvenile western. Two of his novels have won Spurs in the adult western division, four have been made into movies, and two short stories have been filmed for television. Among his other books are *Buckaroo's Code* (Macmillan, 1947), *Cast a Long Shadow* (Macmillan, 1955), and *Red Is the Valley* (Doubleday, 1967). Overholser stands out among writers of westerns for the research that often uses a historical background and always gives an accurate feel for the life of the pioneer and cowboy.

OVER SEA, UNDER STONE (Cooper*, Susan, ill. Margery Gill, Harcourt, 1966), mystery-adventure novel, the first in The Dark Is Rising series, set in Trewissick on the coast of Cornwall, England, recently. While exploring the attic of Grey House, the tall, narrow, rambling place their parents and Great-Uncle Merry (Merriman* Lyon) have rented for their summer holidays, Simon*, Jane, and Barney Drew find an old, crumbling, almost illegible, medieval manuscript containing a map. When Uncle Merry, a renowned and distinguished Celtic scholar, helps them decipher the handwriting and interpret the map, they discover that they have found clues to the location of the long-lost Grail which once belonged to King Arthur and his knights. This ancient source of power to combat evil was hidden nine hundred years earlier somewhere on the nearby Cornish coast by the monk who prepared the manuscript, entrusted "to this land, over sea and under stone." Clues lead the children to the headland overlooking the bay where several tall, slender stones are grouped in a particular fashion with relationship to sea, sun, and moon. The children find a large hole under one of the stones that evidently extends to the shoreline below and are convinced that the Grail is hidden somewhere in its depths. As they are attempting to unravel the secret of the manuscript, the forces of evil, which, Uncle Merry has explained to the children, periodically threaten the world, are gathering, among them, Norman Withers, seemingly the owner of a sleek pleasure yacht and, on the surface at least, friendly to the Drews; his elegant sister, Polly; and Bill, a surly urchin from the village in their employ. The opposition seems eventually even to embrace Mrs. Palk, their apparently innocuous, hymn-singing housekeeper, and the village vicar, Mr. Hastings. On the day of the village carnival, events rapidly reach their climax as the children urgently trace the shoreline at low tide. While Jane keeps watch, the boys enter the cave that extends under the stone on the headland. Deep in the earth beneath, Barney finds the Grail, an elaborately decorated gold chalice containing a small manuscript hidden on a shallow ledge. As the three hurry back to the village before they are trapped by the rapidly rising tide, they come face-to-face with the Witherses and Mr. Hastings. Just in time, they are rescued by Uncle Merry, but, although they save the Grail, the manuscript is lost in the sea. Although fairly predictable, this fast-moving, well-paced mystery holds the interest well, and the children are individualized and more convincing than in most books of this type. Other characters, except Uncle Merry, are stock, and the setting is clear and well integrated with the plot. Sequels include *The Dark is Rising** and *The Grey King**. Choice; Fanfare.

OWEN THOMAS GRIFFITHS (*Very Far Away from Anywhere Else**), 17, intelligent, humorous boy, something of a loner, who almost ruins his first real friendship with young composer Natalie* Field by trying to include sex in their relationship. Confused when she rejects him, he wrecks the car which has been an unwanted gift from his father and ends in the hospital. Though unable to communicate with his parents, Owen understands their problems and the worries they have about him, just as he understands, though cannot conform to, the society around him.

OWL IN THE CEDAR TREE (Momaday*, Natachee Scott, ill. Don Perceval, Ginn, 1965; Northland, 1975), short, realistic novel intended as a reading text set in the mid twentieth century and lasting a school year among the Navaho in Arizona. Earnest young Haske lives happily with his father, Night Singer, his mother, Riding Woman, and his little sister, Desbah, in their hogan on the side of a mountain. While he herds his mother's sheep, two things occupy the boy's mind: dreams of Night Wind, the sleek, black horse belonging to Store Sitter, the trader, and drawing pictures in the sand like those he sketches on paper in school. Although school has introduced Haske to new ways, he respects tradition, too, and, when he hears an owl hoot one morning, he worries that it may mean bad luck. The family holds a sing, a medicine ceremony to heal Old* Grandfather (really Haske's great-grandfather), who shares their hogan and who has been attacked by a bear. As he watches the sand painter at work, Haske thinks he would like to become one, too, and make healing magic flow through his fingers. He soon finds himself caught between Old Grandfather, who urges him to drop out of school and devote himself to the old ways in preparation for becoming a sand painter, and his father, who himself attended white school, as did Riding Woman, and who insists that Haske learn new ways. Haske's mother consoles her son with wise advice: "Keep the best of the old ways while learning the best of the new ways." Just before Christmas, Haske paints a picture of a battle

Old Grandfather has told him about, and then he gives the painting to his teacher, Miss Smith, as a present. Some time after school lets out, Miss Smith arrives with a check for one hundred dollars, first prize in an art show in which she had secretly entered Haske's picture. Interpreting the owl's hooting as a message of good fortune, Haske buys the black horse. Miss Smith urges him to continue to paint the stories Old Grandfather, who has died, told him. Haske realizes that this is the way in which he can keep the old ways, which Old Grandfather revered, and have the new ones, too. Style is stiff, and didacticism obvious. The author makes few demands upon the reader emotionally, and the linear plot proceeds artlessly to its expected success-story ending. Characters are types, intended to reflect differing points of view among the Navahos. The book appears intended both to bolster Indian pride and also to introduce neophyte readers to Navaho life and thought. Passages about religious beliefs, herding, recreation, preparation of food, trips to the store, the stories of Old Grandfather, descriptions of hogan and clothing, and a clear sense of Navaho respect for the earth combine for an illuminating picture of Navaho culture, which is neither sentimentalized nor glorified. Family relationships are strong, and Haske's parents seem to voice the writer's sentiments. Western Heritage.

OX OLMSTEAD (*Ox Under Pressure**), overgrown boy in an extremely wealthy family from Palm Beach, Fla. Somewhat cynical, Ox has suffered neglect from his alcoholic mother and his jet-setting father, and he suffers even more when his father occasionally decides to take him in hand. Ox is not at all stupid but has never worked at school or used his intellect. When he meets Arabella* Marlborough, his latent sympathy and love come to the surface as he attempts to defend the troubled girl.

OX UNDER PRESSURE (Ney*, John, Lippincott, 1976), third novel about Ox* Olmstead, this one set mainly in Locust Valley on the north shore of Long Island in the 1970s. Now seventeen, Ox reluctantly accompanies his father, Barry, and their friend, Sally* Bracken, from Palm Beach, Fla., to New York to rescue one of Sally's several ex-husbands, Bones (Davenport) Blossom, who, as head of The Friends of African Animals, has mislaid two or three million dollars of the organization's funds. Barry takes on FRAAN as a crusade, and Sally, mostly sober for a change, shows her organizational abilities: she rents Severn house from Winston* Lochmann, a man who has spent his fortune on representational art; she hires a tutor for Ox, Ted* Parkinson, a relative of an ex-husband, and she galvanizes the servants, Hans* and Carmen, into producing meals big enough for even Ox's appetite. Wandering into the estate next door, Ox meets a girl his own age, Arabella* Marlborough, who calls herself Arabella Anorexia, because she has been a victim of the illness. She and her parents live in one of the guest houses on the Waterlukker estate, where her father (whom she calls "Big Andy Candy") is an investment counselor for the owner, Lizzie Waterlukker Revere (whom Arabella refers to as "Tin Lizzie"). Arabella, who despises both of them, sneaks Ox into the Revere mansion where they secretly watch Mrs. Revere tormenting her servants to show her power, and later, when Arabella is dancing a "prayer dance" and referring to Mrs. Revere as "the Wicked Witch, the Supreme Torturer," Ox turns to find the old lady watching. To get attention off Arabella, Ox pretends to think Mrs. Revere is an apple peddler. She orders two gardeners to apprehend him, and, while he is holding them off, a third attacks him with a shovel. Finally annoyed, Ox swings him by the ankles and tosses him into a tree. Mrs. Revere sends Big Andy to put pressure on Barry, but Barry is annoyed enough to slug Andy and then threaten to prefer charges for attacks on Ox by the gardener and on himself by Andy. He supplies money so that Ox can support Arabella if she wants to run away. The two young people go to Manhattan, rent a hotel room, and have a wonderful afternoon trying it out, but Arabella decides she isn't strong enough to make it living alone. When she doesn't call the next morning, Ox and Sally go to the Revere estate, demand to know her whereabouts, and learn that she is in a mental institution in Connecticut. They actually are arrested this time. Sally gets out on bail, but Ox spends the night in jail with Jack Taffle, the gardener who hit him with the shovel, in the next cell. When he gets out he finds that Barry and Sally have gone to the hospital to find Arabella but have not been able to persuade her to leave. Ox takes a helicopter, lands in the sanitarium grounds, and talks at length to Arabella. She tries to make him see that she needs to stay a while to get strength to start out on her own and that even though she loves him, she doesn't want to go home with him. He leaves, not sure whether she is right or even whether she is sane. The missing money in FRAAN turns up, deposited and forgotten in a couple of banks, and Barry, Sally, and Ox go back to Palm Beach. Although secondary characters are caricatures, as are all the characters in the earlier books, Ox and Arabella are more rounded, and both Sally and Barry are shown with some subtlety. The humor, therefore, is somewhat more successful. Ox, more mature than in the earlier books, views the antics of the very wealthy with more irony. (Follows *Ox: The Story of a Kid at the Top*, Little, 1970, and *Ox Goes North*, Harper, 1973.) National Book Finalist.

P

PANZPRESSER, JULIUS (*The Tattooed Potato and Other Clues**), wealthy New York art patron at whose house Garson meets Detective Quinn. Quinn is impressed by Garson's assertion that he might help solve cases by painting the *nature* of suspects from witnesses' descriptions of their looks and behavior and asks for Garson's help. This leads eventually to the disclosure of Garson's true identity. Ironically, Panzpresser, who owns the only known painting done by the genius, Edgar Sonneborg (really Garson), commissions Garson to do a painting of his wife, the obese, jolly, good-natured Cookie. At the end, Dickory* Dock enlists Panzpresser's help in freeing pathetic Isaac, the deaf-mute, who is in jail for murdering the men who tried to kill Dickory. Panzpresser does so in exchange for a Sonneborg painting of his wife. He and his wife are eccentric, comic-strip characters.

PARLEY POTTER (*Brady**), the traveling clockman who Brady discovers is an agent on the Underground Railroad. He is a fat, amiable gentleman who likes games of mental arithmetic and is full of jokes. He makes Brady uncomfortable when he spouts out problems for the boy to solve. Brady views him in a different light when he learns about the man's political activities.

PATERSON, KATHERINE (WOMELDORF) (1932–   ), born in Tsing-Tsiang, China; missionary, teacher, author. The daughter of a clergyman, she spent her childhood in both China and the United States, attended King College, and received her M.A. degree from Presbyterian School of Christian Education. Later she studied at Naganuma School of Japanese Language in Kobe, Japan, and at Union Theological Seminary, New York, N.Y. She was a missionary in Japan from 1957 to 1962 and taught school in Lovettsville, Va., and Pennington, N.J. Except for various religious works, her first three books are set in ancient Japan: *Sign of the Chrysanthemum* (Crowell, 1973), *Of Nightingales That Weep** (Crowell, 1974), and *The Master Puppeteer** (Crowell, 1976), which was a National Book Award winner. She then turned to present-day settings for *Bridge to Terabithia** (Crowell, 1977), a Newbery Award winner, and *The Great Gilly Hopkins** (Crowell, 1978), a National Book finalist and a Newbery honor book.

For her second Newbery Medal winner, *Jacob Have I Loved** (Crowell, 1980), she uses an island in Chesapeake Bay during the World War II period. Despite her involvement in formal religious activities, her books are not preachy, *Jacob* even picturing the strong Methodist community of the island as claustrophobic and far from charitable. Her historical novels give a strong sense of the cultural patterns and ways of thinking of the period they concern, and the exciting action is subordinate to interesting character.

PATRICK (*Lotte's Locket**), rich Texan who marries Lotte's widowed mother, Gerda, and takes her from Denmark to New York City. Having flown over Denmark during the war and known Lotte's father, he has come back and fallen in love with Gerda. He has a stereotypically loud voice, and he drives a big American car, known locally as the "Dollar-grin." He shows remarkable patience with Lotte, who resents his intrusion into their lives.

PATTEN, LEWIS B(YFORD) (1915–1981), born in Denver, Colo.; author of many western novels. He attended Denver University, served in the United States Navy from 1933 to 1937, and worked as an auditor for the Colorado Department of Revenue. From 1943 to 1949 he operated a ranch in Colorado. Then he turned to writing novels with a western setting. He collaborated with Wayne D. Overholser* to write *The Meeker Massacre** (Cowles, 1969), about the last Indian uprising in Colorado. Altogether, he wrote more than one hundred novels. Western Writers of America awarded Spurs to three of his books and gave him the Golden Saddleman Award for his collected works. *Death of a Gunfighter* (Doubleday, 1968) was filmed in 1969.

PAUL BEEBE (*Misty of Chincoteague†*; *Stormy, Misty's Foal**), a practical and realistic youth of fourteen or fifteen, who, with his sister, Maureen*, buys and tames Phantom, a horse. He is the planner of the two children, and most of their ideas originate with him. The story of Misty is told more from his point of view than from Maureen's. Paul wins the right to ride Phantom in the big race in a wishbone pull, Grandma* Beebe's idea. Similarly, Paul is more involved in the action in *Stormy* than Maureen is.

PAUL FRY (*The Tamarack Tree**), fifteen-year-old son of David and Hester* Fry, with whom Bernadette* Savard goes to live in Connecticut. At first scornful of Bernadette, he is later curious about a girl who could want book learning and later is won over to admiration by her spirit and determination. He is one of the boys who harass the seminary for black girls, climbing down the tamarack tree at night and walking to town to throw rotten eggs, dump trash at the front door, and foul the well with manure, but when his friend Ingo suggests starting the building afire, he is shocked and refuses to be part of the "prank."

PAULINE STENT (*The Face of Abraham Candle**), ineffective mother and poor housekeeper, with whom Abraham Candle boards and rooms. Her relationship with Abraham is ambiguous. She tells him she would have been married to his father, had he not died, a statement Abraham doubts but politely refrains from questioning. At one point Abraham fears she is planning to marry him, at least when he is a year or two older, and Thornton Malone*, whom she does marry, seems to sense her greater affection for Abraham than for himself. She is slovenly, a poor cook, and unable to manage her three children, yet Abraham does feel a certain fondness for her and even more for her two-year-old daughter, Jane.

PAW-PAW (*Child of the Owl**), grandmother of Casey* Young with whom the girl goes to live in San Francisco's Chinatown. A tiny, ancient woman, whose real name is Ah Low, she is afraid to go outside Chinatown yet independently refuses to give up her piece-work sewing and live with one of her well-to-do sons. A curious mixture of cultures, she plays solitaire and slapjack and smokes, yet she fears to light the oven for heat and keeps a set of statues of the Eight Immortals on her bureau. Although she has a temper and is scornful of the pretentions of her wealthy son, she forgives him for not paying her hospital bills and even forgives Casey's father, Barney*, for stealing from her, because, she says, "you can't afford to stay mad at anyone."

PEACE OF GOD MANLY (*Peter Treegate's War**; *Sea Captain from Salem**; *Treegate's Raiders**), staunch, Bible-quoting, Salem fisherman, old enough to be Peter's father, who becomes Peter's comrade-in-arms during the early part of the Revolutionary War. Later, Peace of God becomes a captain in the Colonial navy, commanding several ships off Europe and in the West Indies. He behaves like a father to his sailors, and he especially tries to keep his gunner, Simmons, from destroying himself with rum. He fights and prays equally hard. Very fond of his daughter, Nancy, he writes long letters of practical and moral advice to her. He is a foil to both John* Treegate and the Maclaren* of Spey. Through him, the author shows the involvement of common people in the war for American self-determination and revolutionary activity on the sea.

PEARL BERGEN (*Summer of My German Soldier**), Patty Bergen's pretty, fashion-conscious, rather bossy mother. She is a shallow, proud woman who wishes Patty were prettier and cared more about clothes and looking nice. She often speaks disparagingly of her daughter and once cruelly sends Patty to the hairdresser for a cut and hairdo when the girl begs not to have to go. Pearl is so overdrawn as a character that it is hard to take her seriously.

PECK, RICHARD (1934–   ), born in Decatur, Ill.; author of popular, contemporary problem novels for adolescents that are better crafted and more convincing than most books aimed at this audience. He attended Exeter University in England and took his bachelor's from DePauw and his master's from Southern

Illinois University, studying still further at Washington University. He has been an instructor of English and English education in high school in Illinois and at Southern Illinois University and at Hunter College in New York, was textbook editor for Scott, Foresman Co., and has been assistant director of the Council for Basic Education in Washington, D.C. With the publication of his first novel, *Don't Look and It Won't Hurt* (Holt, 1972), he gave up teaching for full-time writing and since then has published over a dozen books, most of fiction but also of poetry, edited books of essays, written a column for the New York *Times*, and contributed poems to anthologies and periodicals and articles to professional and popular magazines. For youth he writes mysteries, thrillers, melodramas, and humor and books about the problems and concerns of growing up, stories with immediate appeal deliberately intended to lure young people to read. He often blends the bizarre with the realistic, the bitter with the sweet, and laces events with wit and satire. One of his novels won the Edgar Allan Poe Award, *Are You in the House Alone?** (Viking, 1976), a well-researched, gripping story of a rape, clinical in outlook, while *Dreamland Lake** (Holt, 1973), a grisly account of two boys' discovery of the body of a tramp in an abandoned amusement park and the subsequent death of a bumbling, obese youth who inflicts himself upon them, was nominated for the award. He has also published well-received anthologies of modern poetry, including *Sounds and Silences* (Delacorte, 1970) and *Mindscapes: Poems for the Real World* (Delacorte, 1971). Among his recent novels are *Secrets of the Shopping Mall* (Delacorte, 1979), a mystery-comedy about runaways who decide to make their home in a shopping center, *Close Enough to Touch* (Delacorte, 1981), in which a youth must cope with the sudden death of his girl friend, and *The Dreadful Future of Blossom Culp* (Delacorte, 1983), a time and space fantasy in which a girl travels both forward and backward in time.

PECK, ROBERT NEWTON III (1928–   ), born in Vermont; writer of a variety of different sorts of fiction. He attended Rollins College, Winter Park, Fla., and was a law student at Cornell University. From 1945 to 1947 he served in the U.S. Army infantry in Italy, Germany, and France and has been at different times lumberjack, paper-mill worker, hog killer, advertising executive, and writer of commercial songs and jingles. Among his books are some for older children, like *Millie's Boy* (Knopf, 1973), a mystery set in Vermont of 1889, and some light humorous stories like *Soup* (Knopf, 1974) and its numerous sequels, based loosely on his own boyhood. His most moving book, however, is his fictionalized autobiography, *A Day No Pigs Would Die** (Knopf, 1973), the story of the close relationship between a boy and his father who live in the austere Shaker tradition in the 1930s.

THE PEOPLE THEREIN (Lee*, Mildred, Houghton, 1980), realistic novel telling sensitively of the romance of a mountain girl in the Great Smoky Mountains of North Carolina with an educated man from New England at the turn of the century. Drew* (Andrew) Thorndike, past thirty, a naturalist from Boston, arrives at Dewfall Gap and asks permission to sleep in a tiny cabin on the land of Laban* Farr, mountaineer father of Lanthy* (Ailanthus), 18, Kate*, 17, Lydia*, 16, and Little Labe, 3. The Farr household also includes Ora*, Laban's melancholy wife, and her mother, shrunken, senile Granny Higgins. Although he is a "furriner," the Farrs are hospitable, and Drew stays on at the cabin (the miner's shack, they call it) to the particular pleasure of Lanthy, lame from birth, who shares his love of wild things and shyly listens to his stories of the outside world. They are brought closer through a series of events in the mountain community: Preacher Hollis makes one of his long-spaced visits and, besides conducting Sunday "sarvis" and praying over the graves of those buried since his last visit, marries Kate and Orin Cottrell, who have been "promised" and awaiting his arrival; Lanthy makes the long walk to the cave hut of a mute Cherokee, silent Mary, who makes the moccasins for her mismatched feet that can't be fit by store shoes, returning meets Drew, shelters with him under an overhanging rock in a terrible storm, and is astonished and thrilled when he kisses her; Drew helps Laban and Lanthy "pull fodder," a long hot day of field work, and he tells her he wants to stay in the mountains to be near her. Shortly after this, she goes to his cabin, and they make love. Lanthy, who has thought no man would care for her except her cousin, Cecil, whom she loathes, is transported by love, but the next morning, when Granny Higgins has taken a bad turn and Laban goes to seek Drew's slight medical knowledge, he finds Drew on the floor sleeping off a "master drunk." Hurt and afraid of Laban's anger, Lanthy goes to Drew and learns something of his past. Drew insists on returning with her to apologize; Laban gives him another chance and even recommends him as the new schoolmaster when the wild Possum Ridge boys run out the young schoolmarm. Granny Higgins recovers briefly but dies a few weeks later. Drew and Lanthy make love, once again, in the schoolhouse, and Drew wants to ask Laban for the right to marry her, but Lanthy puts him off, afraid there is some girl from his Boston life he will go back to, wanting him to take time to be sure. Shortly after his successful Christmas program at the school, Drew is called away to Boston by the pneumonia of his sister, Carrie, who raised him after the death of their parents in his infancy. Lanthy gets one love letter, delivered secretly by an Indian friend, but all other communications are impersonal letters to the family telling that Carrie's illness has become tuberculosis. Lanthy soon knows that she is with child but keeps it from the family as long as possible. She is terrified by Laban's murderous rage against Drew when he finds out but hopes it will moderate with time and deliberately does not write Drew of her condition. To her intense relief, the baby is born healthy, a girl, copper-haired like Drew, and Lanthy names her "Glory." Some months later Ellis Widcomb, the young preacher, proposes to marry and make an honest woman of her, but she bluntly refuses. When Glory is nearly eighteen months old, Drew returns, his sister having died. Trying to deflect Laban, who she knows is about to shoot Drew in cold blood, Lanthy throws herself on an upturned rake whose prongs drive through her hand. In the bandaging and getting her to town to the doctor after this "accident," Drew and Laban work together, and Laban's rage is gradually dissipated. While she recovers, Drew builds a room onto the shack, in time winning back enough of Laban's confidence so that on their wedding day he joins Uncle Pleasant Higgins and Miller Cottrell in asking Drew to take back the position of master at Peavine school. Besides the main plot, the book contains stories of other elements in the Southern Appalachian mountain life: the campmeeting, where Cecil and Melviny Stalmeir both come forward as sinners, thereby declaring their fornication, and are hastily married; Kate's wedding; Granny's funeral; the hog butchering; Kate's shock and cold disapproval when Lanthy confides to her the news of her pregnancy; the "birthing," superintended by the midwife "granny woman," Eliza Bunce; the waif with the strawberry mark on her face from "yon side Lonesome Mountain" taken in by openhearted Aunt Dorinda Farr; the coldness and contempt with which the neighbors greet Drew's return, having deduced his part in parenting Glory from her hair and intense blue eyes. The sensory element of the style is strong, with people, cabins, smells, weather, and work evoked in vivid detail. The characters, particularly Lanthy and Laban, are memorable, and the picture of mountain life of the period is compelling, treated with sympathy and dignity. Fanfare.

THE PERILOUS GARD (Pope*†, Elizabeth Marie, ill. Richard Cuffari, Houghton, 1974), romantic historical novel set in Derbyshire in 1558. When Alicia Sutton, pretty, empty-headed maid-in-waiting to the Princess Elizabeth, writes to Queen Mary complaining of the treatment of the princess, the queen blames her more intellectual and spirited sister, Kate* Sutton, instead and banishes Kate to house arrest at Elvenwood Hall in the northern forests in the care of its owner, stern but decent widower, Sir Geoffrey Heron. There she gradually learns that Sir Geoffrey's four-year-old daughter, Cecily, has disappeared in the vicinity of an old shrine in a cave known as the Holy Well while she was being cared for by his much younger brother, Christopher*. Assuming that she has fallen into the well, Christopher blames himself and has sentenced himself to live in a crude leper's hut except when his brother is in residence and has not tried to dispel the rumors told to Kate by the old housekeeper, Dorothy, that he killed the child to get the inheritance for himself. After Sir Geoffrey leaves to return to his property in the south, Kate learns more: the village and castle people are terrified of the Fairy Folk who inhabit the wood and caves nearby; some of the pilgrims, who throw valuables into the Holy Well and are given a drink, return ecstatic, as if drugged; the minstrel, Randal, believes he has had his wits stolen away by the fairies; the well is really a center where pre-Christian rites were performed. She is suspicious that the "Fairy Folk" are really survivors of the old religion, who have been protected, for a price, by the Wardens, the family of Geoffrey's deceased wife. Learning of this, Christopher offers himself in place of Cecily, who he realizes has been taken to pay the *tiend*, the seven-year ritual death necessary to rejuvenate the land. Because Kate has discovered this and also that the steward, wily Master John, is in league with the "fairies," she is taken prisoner by the Lady in Green, queen of the group, and becomes a slave in the underground kingdom, but she refuses the drugged drink which keeps the only other "mortals" happy in their servitude. Eventually, she discovers where Christopher is kept and creeps to talk with him at night, keeping both their spirits up, but she often despairs that the messages she has been able to send by Randal will ever come to Geoffrey. On All-Hallows Eve, when the *tiend* is to be paid, she escapes and comes to the standing stone and claims Christopher, after the pattern in the ballad of "Tam Lin." Geoffrey arrives shortly afterward, the Fairy Folk flood the caverns and disappear, and Christopher, having taken Cecily to an aunt in London, returns with Kate's father to say that Elizabeth has come to power so Kate is free, and Christopher has arranged to marry her. Although the plot involves such improbable elements as the intricate underground society of the Fairy Folk that it seems close to fantasy, its suspenseful writing and basis in such anthropological works as Frazer's *The Golden Bough* make it believable. The characterization, particularly of Kate and Christopher, is strong, and the theme, the triumph of common sense and use of the intellect, helps to balance the strongly romantic elements. Fanfare; Newbery Honor.

PESTY (*The House of Dies Drear**), small foundling who lives with the rough Darrow family but is not related to them. Also called Sarah, Sooky, and Little Miss Bee, she is independent but devoted to old Mr. Pluto, caretaker of the house. Only Pesty can manage his huge black horse, and only she knows the secret of his antique-filled cavern until the Smalls discover it. She moves around the cavern on a ladder set in a rail and polishes the crystal. Although her part is important in the story, she is not convincing in the realistic setting. She is more like an elfin character than a flesh and blood child.

PETE DEGLEY (*The Skating Rink**), entrepreneur of the roller rink, who spots Tuck Farraday and teaches him to skate. Wiry and tough, Pete is also compassionate and straightforward about Tuck's speech impediment. Although he is using his wife, Lily*, and Tuck to fulfill his own dream of a big show to attract crowds to the rink, he does so without exploiting them unfairly. He has deliberately chosen Tuck because he is a local boy and because he is young enough not to be a rival for Lily's affection, yet he is not unaware that Tuck will benefit by the confidence he will get from skating well.

PETER HAWTHORNE (*A Spell Is Cast**), lively, red-haired scamp who introduces Cory Winterslow to the hills, rocky paths, and caves of Tarnhelm, her grandmother's oceanside estate in California. Through him, Cory meets the members of the Explorers Club, a group of neighborhood children, with whom she gradually becomes friends. Peter is the club's current president. He shows Cory a beautifully carved wooden box he found in a cave. When Cory opens it, she finds clues which lead to a reconciliation between Uncle* Dirk and Laurel* Woodford, estranged lovers, and to a happier home life for herself.

PETER HUTCHINS (*Dawn of Fear**), playfellow of Derek Brand and Geoff* Young. A sharply drawn character, he is an unworried boy, often in trouble but never mean or malicious. More daring than the other two boys, he often comes up with ideas for adventures. He and his family are killed by a direct hit during a Nazi night-time air raid.

PETER MORGAN (*A String in the Harp**), discontented, unhappy, twelve-year-old American schoolboy, who finds the harp-tuning key which once belonged to the legendary Welsh bard, Taliesin. He is taken back in time by the key and given important views of the bard's life. Puzzled and curious about what is happening to him, he borrows a copy of *The Mabinogion* in order to learn more about Welsh beliefs. He is an interesting, convincing character.

PETER SMITH (*Of Love and Death and Other Journeys**), rotund, quiet Englishman, Phoebe* Smith's second husband and Meg Grant's stepfather. His ambition is to write the definitive book on canon law. To earn a living, he writes borderline pornography, a task at which he is not very good. Meg hopes to continue living with him after Phoebe dies, but Cotton* MacKenzie helps her see that Peter wishes to return to his scholastic interests and has no room in his life for her. Peter's finest attributes, according to Phoebe, are his ability to love freely and without possessiveness.

PETER TREEGATE'S WAR (Wibberley*†, Leonard, Farrar, 1960), historical novel, the second in the series about the Treegates, set variously in the American colonies during the War for Independence. The novel opens at Boston in June of 1775 with Peter's account of the Battle at Breed's Hill, later known as the Battle of Bunker Hill. Peter, now sixteen, fights alongside his father, John*, a respected merchant to whose house Peter has returned, and his foster father, the Maclaren* of Spey, the proud, undauntable, British-hating Scotsman from Carolina who has raised him. Although for personal and clan reasons, the Maclaren enjoys fighting the British, he has little sympathy with the cause of the Revolution, while John Treegate feels deeply committed to the colonial struggle for freedom. The battle over, John leaves for Philadelphia on a special mission for George Washington. The weeks pass with little activity, and the Maclaren grows restless and proposes taking prisoner a British soldier or two. The stunt goes awry, and he and Peter are captured and sentenced to hang. A superior officer, Sir John Pett, mysteriously countermands the order, after he notices the Maclaren's distinctive clan brooch, and assigns the two to a British prison barge in Boston harbor. Some weeks pass before they escape, along with Peace* of God Manly, a Bible-quoting ex-fisherman. The three soon find themselves on the *Betsy*, an American brig loaded with gunpowder bound for Lynn. In an exciting episode, the Americans unload the explosives under heavy British bombardment. The Maclaren soon returns to his Carolina wilderness home, but Peter continues to fight for the colonial cause. In 1776, he and Peace of God see action at Boston and at New York. Captain of his own company now, Peter has little confidence in General Washington, nor does a chance conversation with the colonial commander before Trenton change his opinion. Later, however, Washington's impassioned speech to the troops at Princeton deeply impresses him. The ragtag army crosses the frozen Delaware and soundly defeats the British at Trenton at Christmastime and later also at Princeton. Recovered from wounds, Peter heads for the Maclaren's place, convinced that his foster father needs him. In a heated argument, John asserts that Peter's loyalty is misplaced and disavows his son. Peter soon becomes embroiled in the conflict between the Maclaren and Farqueson clans, strife which leads eventually to the Maclaren's death. Although heir to the Maclaren's property, Peter chooses to make peace with John and return to duty with the colonial army. After Burgoyne surrenders, Peter encounters Sir John Pett in a British hospital. He learns that the officer spared their lives because Pett realized, when he saw the Maclaren's brooch, that he had found and reared the Maclaren's infant son after the Battle of Culloden thirty years earlier. The novel ends abruptly with Peter declaring to Pett that he intends to give himself wholly to the colonial fight for freedom. Peter's story of what happened during those fateful days often reads like a history-book recital of events, and his personal dilemma lacks impact because he is not good at expressing his emotions. Although unevenly paced, too full of underdeveloped incidents, and shallow in characterization, the book is an occasionally engrossing, often exciting overview for middle-grade readers of what it might have been like for an intelligent, courageous youth in the colonial army. Others in series include *John Treegate's Musket†*; *Sea Captain from Salem**; *Treegate's Raiders**. Choice.

PETER WEDEMEYER (*Veronica Ganz**), the classmate who defies Veronica Ganz and whom she desperately seeks to beat up. Once, he takes refuge from her in a fish market, where he foils her by dumping a basket of fish refuse over her. Another time, she traps him in the boys' bathroom at the park, but, while she stands waiting out in front for him to emerge, he escapes through the window. Since Peter is new and one of the brightest children in the class, Veronica is particularly set on bringing him in line. Eventually, they become friends.

A PET FOR THE ORPHELINES (Carlsons†, Natalie Savage, ill. Fermin Rocker, Harper, 1962), sequel to *The Happy Orpheline†* and *A Brother for the Orphelines†*, set in the same French village of Ste. Germaine near Paris. Since the castle to which the twenty girl orphans and the boy orphans, too, are to move is in need of lengthy repairs, Monsieur de Goupil, hoping to distract their attention from the delays, agrees that the orphelines can have a pet. This causes major dissension. Josine*, the stubborn youngest girl, insists she wants a swan, because she admires the swans in the park and had hoped they might keep the one that escaped and wandered to their orphanage. Brigitte* wants a kitten, Marie a dog, Louise a lamb, Charlotte a white rat. Genevieve, the girl who helps care for them, suggests a rabbit. Madame* Flattot, their "mother," buys a gold fish, a choice which proves to be a dud and eventually goes down the bathtub drain. When the girls learn that the Duchesse de Bailly, Monsieur de Goupil's sister, is in charge of a grand charity ball given for the orphans, they naturally assume they are invited and raid the charity box for cast-off finery for suitable gowns. Their disappointment is even greater when they learn that the orphan boys have been invited to sing at the gala event. The Duchesse tries to make amends by arranging that they shall visit the Parc de Bagatelle in a two-tiered London autobus. There Madame Flattot meets an old friend, Monsieur Croquet, who grows new varieties of vegetables, and Josine finds the egg of a black swan, which she breaks trying to sit on it in the bus. Because Madame Flattot makes such fine cabbage soup, Monsieur Croquet names a beautiful new cabbage variety for her, and at the ceremony he suggests that the pet problem can be solved by taking all the girls to the cat show at the Salle Wagram in Paris. There they see beautiful, pampered prize cats. On their way out they encounter the Duchesse, a woman of many good works, in charge of a Protective Society for Animals group giving away stray cats. The orphelines choose ten, to Madame Flattot's consternation, a cat for each pair of girls, and the Duchesse assures them that she will supply the money to feed them. Josine, stubborn to the end, names her cat "Swan." While the story has many amusing bits, it does not have quite the zest of the two earlier Orpheline books, nor do the pictures have the warmth of Garth Williams's illustrations. Choice.

PETIE BURKIS (*The Midnight Fox**), Tom's best friend at his home in the city. The reader meets Petie directly at the beginning and again at the end of the story and in between in Tom's daydreams. Petie is more active, self-confident, and assertive than Tom. He plans to be a newspaper reporter when he grows up and often speaks in headlines. He is an eccentric character, only credible as a distorted type.

PETRY, ANN (LANE) (1908–   ), born in Old Saybrook, Conn.; pharmacist, editor, author. She attended Connecticut School of Pharmacy, now part of the University of Connecticut, and later Columbia University. In addition to a career as a pharmacist, she has been a writer and reporter for the *Amsterdam News*, N.Y., women's editor for *People's Voice*, and visiting professor of English at the University of Hawaii, Honolulu. A black woman herself, she has written her best-known books for children about black women, including a biography of Harriet Tubman and *Tituba of Salem Village** (Crowell, 1964), story of a slave accused of witchcraft in the Salem trials. She has also written several novels for adults.

THE PHANTOM OF WALKAWAY HILL (Fenton*, Edward, ill. Jo Ann Stover, Doubleday, 1961), mystery novel set in the mountains near New York City in the mid twentieth century. The narrator, James Gregory Smith Jr., 12, spends a weekend with his Little cousins, Amanda, 12, and Obie, 13, whose family has just moved to an old house in the mountains where the author father, Uncle Oliver, thinks he will be able to write in peace. The household also includes Aunt Claire, Dee Dee, 6, Sieglinde, her overweight dachshund, and Mrs. MacMinnies, the housekeeper. When the youngsters explore the outbuildings, the odd-job man painting the house, Charlie Murofino, tells them about the past owner, an eccentric woman sculptor rumored to keep a lot of cash in her house, and her last hired man, shifty Barney Rudkin. The Littles have inherited her beautiful but wild collie, Maggie, who frequently starts frenzied barking for no apparent reason. A heavy late snowstorm isolates the remote house, and the family is further cut off when the phone stops working and the electricity goes off. The city-trained family has some difficulty coping. Obie, a practical boy with a mechanical bent, discovers that the phone wires have been cut and traces the electrical outage to a switch in the barn rather than a broken wire. With James, he explores and in the barn basement finds a man lying on a cot. Terrified, the boys race to the house but keep the presence secret until Charlie wades through the deep snow to bring groceries. When they take him to the spot, he discovers it is Barney Rudkin with a broken thigh and delirious with fever. Charlie splints his leg, directs the boys to bring blankets, water, and soup, and decides that they should not tell the Little parents. Barney's incoherent muttering has included the words, "She said the dog has it." Mrs. MacMinnies formally gives notice. Amanda, miffed at being excluded from the boys' secret, is haughty. Dee Dee is hurt because Sieglinde has deserted her for Maggie. Unable to settle down while they wait for the snowplow, James suggests that they explore the attic. There they find a terra cotta statue of Maggie and, when the head comes off, find a will hidden inside. This gives the house to whoever will care for it and Maggie, as clearly the Littles are prepared to do. When the snowplow comes through, followed by the doctor, Charlie also brings James's father and a "Wanted" poster that mystery-loving James has collected and on which he has recognized Barney Rudkin. Mrs. MacMinnies relents and decides to stay on. As a mystery, the novel is neither very suspenseful nor very believable, but it is not difficult and is a pleasant story for intermediate youngsters. Poe Winner.

THE PHANTOM TOLLBOOTH (Juster*, Norton, ill. Jules Feiffer, Random, 1961), humorous fantasy involving a journey to another world. Alone in his room and bored as usual, Milo discovers an enormous package containing a purple tollbooth, a map, and directions for using them. His curiosity aroused, he decides to visit the city on the map called Dictionopolis. He gets into his small electric car, pays the toll, and soon finds himself speeding along in the world on the map. As he goes, he encounters a series of comic characters who teach him truths about life. In the Land of Expectations, he meets the nervous, little Whether Man, who constantly repeats himself, while in the Doldrums he finds the Lethargarians, who always waste time. To get out of the Doldrums, he is advised to think by Tock, a giant watchdog that carries a clock in his side. In Dictionopolis, he visits the Great Market, the place that words come from, and meets the Spelling Bee, which can spell any word there is, and the Humbug, whose word can never be believed. Arrested for mixing up words, Milo is cast into a dungeon, where the witch Faintly Macabre tells him the story of how the royal princesses, Rhyme and Reason, were banished from the land. Pardoned, Milo attends a royal banquet at the palace of King Azaz the Unabridged. The guests behave so irrationally that Milo suggests that Rhyme and Reason be brought back to the realm and is promptly ordered to find them and bring them back. Milo now has a purpose in life, and he, Tock, and Humbug proceed toward the Castle in Air, where the princesses are confined. Alec Bing, a boy who grows downward instead of upward and represents varying points of view, shows Milo the non-existent City of Reality, which faded away because everyone was in too much of a hurry to care. In the Forest of Sights, Milo watches Chroma play a colorful sunset symphony. Farther on, Dr. Dischord gives him a prescription for noise, which Milo passes on to the awful Dynne. After helping to restore sound to the silent Valley of Sound, Milo feels quite satisfied with his efforts and soon finds that he has jumped to the island of Unfortunate Conclusions. After the three companions swim back to the mainland, they meet a man of many angles, the Dodecahedron, who leads them to Digitopolis, and the Mathemagician, who manages the local numbers mine. Still others Milo meets before journey's end are .58 of a boy, the offspring in an "average family" of 2.58 persons, the Everpresent Wordsnatcher, the "dirty bird," who steals words out of the speaker's mouth, and the Terrible Trivium, the faceless demon of petty and worthless tasks, who requires them to move a pile of sand grain by grain, empty a well drop by drop, and dig a hole through a cliff with a needle. After passing the Senses Taker and finding the princesses, the companions are attacked by assorted giants and demons, including Ignorance and Compromise, before they are rescued by the army of King Azaz. Milo is proclaimed a hero for succeeding in an impossible task, and a magnificent celebration is held in his honor. When he returns home through the purple tollbooth, he discovers that his journey has taken only one hour in "real" time. The tollbooth disappears, but Milo's restlessness is gone, and he understands that books, music, and inventions of the real world can bring excitement and satisfaction, too. The book is candidly a moral tale, its didacticism only slightly moderated by the humor, and every adventure conveys an obvious lesson. The characters personify abstractions, and the reader can identify only with Milo. Among the sources of humor are the oddball characters, slapstick situations, language, parody, and logic. The novel recalls the Alice books, but the writing falls far short of Carroll's finesse. Situations seem contrived, and there are too many of them. Characters are overdrawn, and humor becomes strained. The book moves fast, something is always happening, and dialogue is extensive and snappy. Stone.

PHILIP IV OF SPAIN (*I, Juan de Pareja**), king who is patron to the seventeenth-century painter, Velázquez*, and whose portrait he is known to have painted many times. Philip is a shy man, bored by his exceedingly formal court life but without the personal drive to change its pattern. He often escapes to sit quietly in the artist's studio studying the pictures while Velázquez continues to paint. They share a rare mutual affection and trust.

PHILIP HALL LIKES ME. I RECKON MAYBE. (Greene*, Bette, ill. Charles Lilly, Dial, 1974), humorous, realistic "girl's growing up" novel about the year in the life of bright, lively Beth Lambert, 11, in which she discovers the importance of being true to one's self. Beth, who tells the story, has a crush on Philip Hall, according to her, the smartest, most handsome boy in her class. The Lamberts, an industrious black family who raise turkeys and pigs, live next door to the dairy-farming Halls, also black, near the town of Pocahantas, Ark., in the Ozarks. Encouraged by her close and loving parents always to do her best, Beth feels inclined to hang back because she is afraid of alienating Philip by outshining him. During the year, she makes discoveries about herself, her feelings, and her motives, as, among other experiences, she manages to keep her head while he quakes in fear when the two stake out her father's turkey yard to try to discover why the birds keep disappearing at night, when she is acknowledged first in her class scholastically, and when she leads her club, the Pretty Pennies, in challenging his, the Tiger Hunters, to a relay race, and when she locates him when he disappears at the Old Rugged Cross church picnic. When she wins the Blue Ribbon for best calf at the 4-H Fair, she is afraid she has lost him for good, but Philip, too, has been maturing in attitude. He acknowledges there is no honor in being allowed to be first and that being first is only satisfying if one has earned the honor fairly and honestly through one's own efforts. Beth's mother excepted, most characters including Beth and Philip approach caricature, situations are often slapstick, and the humor is heavy handed. While Beth is a sympathetic character, it is hard to believe that a girl as intelligent and bright as she is supposed to be would allow Philip to sweet-talk her so obviously into currying his cows and putting up with his snubs, nor does it seem that, if Philip were as smart as people evidently think he is, he would behave as he does. The slightly colloquial dialogue is amusing and acceptable, but the plot, with its feminist message, seems contrived and obvious and deals much too trivially with a serious social problem. Sequel is *Get on out of here, Philip Hall.* Choice; Newbery Honor.

PHIL MUELLER (*Taking Terri Mueller**), father of Terri*, who, after a divorce, kidnapped her eight years before the story starts from her mother's custody and has kept the knowledge of her real background secret from her. A truly devoted father, he has given up a regular job and home for an itinerant lifestyle and work as a carpenter in order to keep from being traced and has raised Terri with love and care. Though attractive and good-natured, he is described by his ex-mother-in-law as "spoiled," and in the end he loses the woman he has planned to marry because he is unable to see the misery he has caused Terri's mother or to admit that what he did was wrong.

PHOEBE SMITH (*Of Love and Death and Other Journeys**), Meg Grant's mother, a proud, strong-willed woman, whose beauty, childlike charm, and love of life readily win her friends. She left Meg's father, Alan Grant, before Meg was born but never informed him of Meg's birth, nor has she told Meg the facts about their life together. When Phoebe realizes that she is dying of cancer, she sends for Alan so that he and Meg can get to know each other before she dies. Although Meg resents not being told the truth about her father, she remains intensely loyal to her mother.

PIERCE, MEREDITH ANN (1959–   ), author of a fantasy, *The Darkangel** (Atlantic/Little, 1982), written when she was a graduate student at the University of Florida. Inspired by reading of a case history in C. G. Jung's autobiography of a patient who imagined an existence on the moon where a cruel but handsome vampyre abducts women and children, the novel won the International Reading Association Award. Pierce makes her home in Gainesville, Fla.

THE PIGMAN (Zindel*, Paul, Harper, 1968), novel of New Realism set on Staten Island, N.Y., in the 1960s. John* Conlan and Lorraine* Jensen, both high school sophomores about fifteen, write alternate first-person chapters about their relationship with an "old" man, Angelo Pignati*, about fifty-eight. Supposedly, they are typing it on the machine in the school library. John, a wildly imaginative boy, has made up a game of calling at random a number from the phone book and seeing how long they can keep the answerer talking. When Lorraine picks a number at an address not far from their neighborhood, she pretends she is calling for a charity and the answerer, Mr. Pignati, pledges ten dollars. Unable to resist the temptation, John says they will come to pick up the check the next day. They find a pathetically lonely man living alone in a rather ramshackle house, pretending that his dead wife is away for a trip. He takes the young people to the zoo to see his friend, Bobo, a baboon, and when John finds the wife's charge card to Beekman's department store in Manhattan, the old man buys them strange foods, stockings for Lorraine's mother, and roller skates for all three of them. They begin to spend every afternoon after school at Mr. Pignati's house, even skipping school, drinking wine, eating and watching TV. Mr. Pignati shows them his collection of pigs—wooden, ceramic, glass, etc.—and urges them to be at home in his house. Since he genuinely likes them and they both have unfeeling parents, they care about him and finally confess that they are frauds. He breaks down in tears as he confesses that his wife is really dead. To cheer him up, John puts on his roller skates and starts a zany indoor chase, which Lorraine and Mr. Pignati, both on skates, soon join. Suddenly Mr. Pignati suffers a heart attack. At the hospital they say they are his children and try to give him his house keys, but he insists that they keep the keys and enjoy the place while he is away. At first they do nothing harmful, but John decides to have a party, which rapidly gets out of hand. While he is chasing a .friend who is stealing electrical equipment and Lorraine and a friend are dressed up in the late wife's clothes, Mr. Pignati in a taxi and the police arrive simultaneously. He is terribly hurt but the next day agrees to go to the zoo with them to see Bobo. When they find that Bobo has died, Mr. Pignati has another attack and dies. The tone is sensational, and the characters are all overdrawn. Lorraine's nurse mother is a man-and-sex hater; John's mother is a compulsive house cleaner; John's father, "The Bore," is a single-minded businessman, with no feeling for John's needs. The convention that John and Lorraine are writing alternate chapters makes it possible to characterize them through both first- and third-person point of view, and the attempt is made to draw them honestly, but they are both shown as more thoughtless and unpleasant than is realistic. The effort to be up-to-the-minute and to see through the eyes of teenagers makes the book seem dated already. Boston Globe Honor; Fanfare; Maxi.

PIGNATI, ANGELO (*The Pigman**), lonely old man who makes friends with two high school sophomores and, trying to share the kind of life they lead, has a heart attack and dies. Simple-minded in some ways, Pignati is described as always smiling. He loves to go to the zoo and has developed a special relationship with Bobo, a hideous baboon.

PILGRIM (*My Own Private Sky**), David Ward Wingfield, going on ninety, father of Jenny Kearns, Arthur's unconventional baby-sitter. Often confused about the present, Pilgrim remembers with clarity his youth when he was the last of the post riders, a job he got at fifteen, although sixteen was the lowest official age for the men who rode the broom-tail ponies with the mail. He can also tell stories about when he was a "rassler," a cowboy, and a frontier storekeeper, but the present is vague, and he often falls back on reintroducing his dog, "This here is Tuffy Apple. He's going on fourteen." Described by Arthur as "the biggest man I ever saw. Mostly bones," Pilgrim spends much of his time working on a needlepoint replica of a petroglyph, though his daughter lets him do what he can for himself, eating with a big napkin around his neck to catch the spills and making bologna sandwiches with mustard smeared on the table. He is a good example of a senile character treated with respect.

THE PINBALLS (Byars*, Betsy, Harper, 1977), realistic problem novel set in the late twentieth century in an urban area somewhere in the United States. Wise-cracking, teenaged Carlie*, whose stepfather assaulted her; dispirited, thirteen-year-old Harvey*, whose legs were broken when his drunken father drove his car over them; and shy, eight-year-old Thomas J, whose eighty-eight-year-old twin foster aunts have been hospitalized with broken hips, are all residents of the foster home of Mr. and Mrs. Mason. Carlie thinks of herself and the boys as pinballs, objects that spin around involuntarily and cannot determine what will happen to them. At first, Carlie's main aim in life is to get away from the home and back with her mother as soon as she can, even if it means running away. She rejects with barely a thought Mrs. Mason's sensible suggestion that she try to help Harvey develop a more cheerful attitude but becomes more interested in him when she learns how his legs came to be broken, intrigued by the sensationalism of his case. For his part, Harvey hopes that he will be able to live with his mother again, but, when he learns that she does not want him, he becomes even more despondent than he was, and Carlie sets about lifting his spirits. Then Harvey is hospitalized with infected legs, and Carlie and Thomas J visit him. They get him a puppy for his birthday and even smuggle it into his hospital room. The reader sees Carlie's cynicism diminish as she tackles Harvey's problems. As Thomas J helps her, he begins to come out of himself, too, and to gain more confidence in his ability to relate positively to people. Although the circumstantial problems of the three children remain unsolved at the end, Carlie sees that, unlike pinballs, people are able to influence their destinies and change the quality of their lives, in particular, by attempting to improve things for others. The extensive, often witty, contemporary dialogue carries the burden of the slight, rather obvious plot and reveals character. The child characters seem deliberately assembled and are overdrawn for effect, and the adults are flat and functionary. Conversation and behavior tend to provoke amusement rather than empathy. The conclusion is heavily foreshadowed, and the whole thing trivializes what is a serious, contemporary social problem. Child Study; Fanfare.

PIPPA PARKIN (*Poor Tom's Ghost**), ten-year-old step-sister of Roger* Nicholas. Pippa is an animal lover, described as "wonderfully decorative . . . with that cloud of red-gold hair" and her pet bushbaby, Sammy, on her shoulder. A practical, matter-of-fact child, she sees and hears the characters from the Elizabethan story but doesn't become personally engulfed in its problems as Tony* and Roger do and so is able to follow Roger in the middle of the night and literally to hold him from being drowned in the Thames and in the past.

PIRATE QUEEN (Meyer*, Edith Patterson, Little, 1961), biographical novel set in Ireland in the sixteenth century. At eighteen, Grania O'Malley is elected chieftain of her clan at the death of her father. Born at the O'Malley castle on the Island of Clare off the west coast of Mayo, Grania has often sailed with her father on his *Grey Wolf* and has even engaged in a sea battle against an English sloop, taking command when her father was wounded. Succession is not automatic, however, and has never gone to a woman. The brehons scarcely consider Grania's thirteen-year-old brother, Donal, who in the medieval custom has been fostered out since infancy and is more interested in music than in leadership, but Grania must maneuver politically to be elected over Eoin, a strong and ambitious follower of her father. She rejects the idea of marriage to Tomas, devoted captain of the guard, who thinks they might rule jointly. As O'Malley chieftain, Grania expands the activity on both land and sea, leading raids and amassing treasure, commissioning the building of *Grey Wolf II* and various new fortresses to strengthen O'Malley defenses and cleverly moving politically to either dominate or form alliances with her contentious neighboring clans. In one dangerous escapade she goes incognito with Don Felipe de Huelva, a Spaniard who had once visited as a potential suitor and now has been remet by chance, to a party in Galway, which is dominated by the English. Don Felipe encourages her to dance a wild Irish jig, and she admits her real identity, but as they are leaving, they are stopped and taken to the home of Mayor Lynch, who attempts to detain her to hand over to the English lord deputy. His guest, Sir Richard Burke, known as Iron Dick because he always wears armor under his dress clothes, is a man whose castle she has appropriated, but he is pleasant, requests that she dance for them, and it is then she is able to make a daring escape. In a storm she finds a man washed ashore from a wreck, has him taken to the abbey to be cared for, discovers he is Donnell O'Flaherty, tanist (heir apparent) to the chieftainship of Ballynahinch, a noble family with lands south of Clare. She marries him and divides her time between his lands and hers, has a daughter, Mary, whom she insists on keeping, and two sons, who are fostered out. After six years of marriage, Donnell is killed by MacMahons, and Grania gets revenge and the MacMahon castle at Doona. Some years later she marries Iron Dick, who has done a clever juggling act between the English, his rival Burkes, and the other clans. They have one son, whom she calls Toby. The years that follow are full of her piracy, her capture, imprisonment, and eventual release, her husband's death, her daughter's marriage, and the growing power of the English. At last, when Owen O'Flaherty has been killed and her two other sons and her brother Donal imprisoned by the soldiers of the English Governor Bingham, she petitions to meet with Queen Elizabeth, as one queen to another, and is granted an audience. Since London has plague, she meets Elizabeth at Windsor Castle, becomes a favorite partly because she refuses to be subservient, and eventually is granted release of her relatives. When Elizabeth suggests that she make Grania a countess, the Irish woman is astonished and scornful: why become a countess when she is already a queen? Throughout, Grania has a dream that the Irish can combine to drive out the English, a dream never realized among the feuding clans. The story follows history, particularly the reports of Grania's visit to Elizabeth, and probably for this reason large parts of it seem more to be recounting facts than to be developed into scenes and episodes. The life of this remarkable woman could fill a dozen novels, and the fictional treatment probably should have been limited to make a more interesting literary work. Fanfare.

PISTOL (Richard*, Adrienne, Little, 1969), historical novel set from June, 1930, to September, 1934. For Billy Catlett an almost perfect life begins the summer he is fourteen, when he signs on as wrangler for Sam Tolliver's outfit east of Great Plain, Mont., and becomes known as "Pistol", or "boy," to the cowboys. School months pass quickly and even the unsettling bickering between his authoritarian father and cynical, older brother, Conrad*, can be borne in anticipation of exciting summers on the range. There, muscle-tearing hard work and high excitement abound as Billy rounds up horses and punches cattle, rides the range on his sorrel, Sundance, goes to a Saturday night dance, helps with the branding and market drives, fights a prairie fire, takes his place at the bountiful kitchen table with the adult hands, thrills to their laconic, understated, deadpan humor, accepts his share of hazing and barbs, savors meals of thick steaks and wide bacon, and spends evenings and off hours with his first love, Allison Mitchell, daughter of the wealthy rancher down the way. Then the Depression hits, and Sam is ruined and no longer needs Billy. The Great Plain bank closes, businesses shut their doors, and Billy sees old friends drift away as their families move on in the search for jobs. He sees the cowboys he thought lords of the range drunk on the streets, despair in their eyes, among them even Tom* Driscoll, his idol, who tamed Sundance for him and taught Billy his ranch tasks. After the meat packing plant shuts down, Billy's father loses his job. The finance company repossesses the furniture, carting away almost everything in the house. Billy's father runs off, leaving a note that he will return when he finds work. Billy and Conrad pick up odd jobs, Conrad as a dishwasher and Billy in the local gas station, and their mother stretches the tiny horde of coins in the old sock to their limit. Billy finishes high school, and the father returns, then to move the family to a tarpaper shack in the anything-goes shantytown of Deal on the Missouri, where the government is building a dam and jobs are available. Conrad gets work on construction, his father works as a dispatcher, and Billy sells shoes in the mercantile. Billy adjusts well and is almost happy, until he observes his mother's despair and fright at living in such crude conditions. Father soon moves the family back to Great Plain, but Billy strikes out on his own and takes a job punching cows on a cattle train bound for Chicago. Natural dialogue, strongly realized characters, vivid descriptions of setting and events, and a point of view unerringly accurate produce a first person novel that is not only a rich picture of the end of one era and the beginning of another but also a highly moving and very convincing boy's growing-up story. (Richie* Greatbear; Seth* McCollum; Mr.* Burbank) Fanfare.

P. JOHN KNIGHT (*Dinky Hocker Shoots Smack**), fat, ultra-conservative, opinionated youth, in whom Dinky* becomes interested and who tries to help her reduce. He always calls her by her right name of Susan, treating her with the dignity he believes she deserves. Son of the liberal writer, Perry Knight, he rejects what he thinks his father stands for, because he believes his father foolishly wastes their living on spongers and ingrates. Because of P. John's politics and superior manner, the Woolfs and Hockers don't want their children to associate with him. He encourages Dinky to try Weight Watchers. After he and his father have an ideological falling out, he leaves to live with an aunt in Maine, where, ironically, he becomes a worker and converts to liberalism.

THE PLACE OF THE TOMBS (*The Tombs of Atuan**), isolated community of priestesses, novices, and eunuchs surrounded by desert in the Kargish lands of Earthsea*. Several cults are represented in the temples of the place, the newest being that of the Godking who at this time rules Atuan, the oldest being those who serve The Nameless Ones, powers of darkness that inhabit the passages and rooms beneath the Place. These underground areas include the Undertomb, a huge natural limestone cavern, the labyrinth, a series of winding passages which can be left only through the Undertomb, the Painted Room, a chamber in the labyrinth decorated with pictures of distorted, winged men, and the Treasure Room, at the heart of the labyrinth, where the half-ring of Erreth-Akbe has been hidden for centuries.

THE PLANET OF JUNIOR BROWN (Hamilton*, Virginia, Macmillan, 1971), realistic novel set mainly in a public school and on the streets of New York City in the 1960s. Junior* Brown, an enormously heavy black boy, and Buddy Clark, a highly intelligent, streetwise tough, both about fourteen, have been skipping their eighth grade classes for months to spend the time in a concealed basement room where the school janitor, Mr. Pool, a former teacher, has constructed a power-driven miniature solar system to teach them principles of math and science and good living. Junior, a talented pianist, is troubled by his overprotective mother, Junella Brown, who counters any independent moves on his part by having a severe asthma attack, by his father's continued absence, and by the erratic behavior of his mentally ill music teacher, Lynora Peelis. Buddy watches over Junior, just as, unknown to Junior or Mr. Pool, he protects homeless boys in his role as a "Tomorrow Billy" in a series of "planets," hide-outs in abandoned buildings where he provides food, clothing, and street know-how to the youngsters until they can become independent. When Mr. Pool's room is about to be discovered and Junior's tormented mind finally joins Miss Peelis's psychotic fantasies, Buddy moves both of them to his planet in the basement of a collapsed building where he has been keeping two strays, Franklin (Russell) Moore and Nightman Black and now has several new recruits, a group he renames The Planet of Junior Brown. Although there are some strong scenes of Junior's suffering and of Buddy's night-stalking in the city and early morning work at the newsstand of Doum Malach, the central idea of Buddy's network of planets is sentimentally conceived, and the solar system in the school's basement room is too obvious a symbol and unbelievable on a realistic level. Newbery Honor.

PLATT, KIN (1911–   ), born in New York City; cartoonist, painter, mystery novelist. During World War II he served in the air transport command of the U.S. Army Air Corps in the China-Burma-India theater and was awarded the Bronze Star. For the New York *Herald Tribune* he created the comic strip "Mr. and Mrs.," which was syndicated from 1947 to 1963, and "The Duke and the Duchess," which ran from 1950 to 1954. He was also a caricaturist for the Los Angeles *Times* and for the *Village Voice*. Since 1965 he has been a free-lance writer, mostly of mysteries for young people and adults. Among his books for children are *Sinbad and Me** (Chilton, 1966) and *The Mystery of the Witch Who Wouldn't** (Chilton, 1969), both fast-paced mysteries with extremely complicated plots involving ghosts, demons, secret passages, ciphers, occult happenings, hidden treasure, gangsters—all ingeniously if unconvincingly tied together in the denouement.

A POCKET FULL OF SEEDS (Sachs*, Marilyn, ill. Ben Stahl, Doubleday, 1973), historical novel about Jews in France just before and during World War II, drawn from real life. The story is told by thirteen-year-old Nicole Nieman and begins in February of 1944 in Mlle.* Legrand's girls' school in Aix-les-Bains, France, where Nicole has been living since the arrest of her parents and younger sister, Jacqueline, in a raid on Jews the previous November. In a series of snapshot scenes, Nicole flashes back to 1938 to describe the main events that lead to the arrest. The Niemans' is an average home, moderate in means, close in spirit. Papa sells sweaters, and Maman takes care of the girls. Nicole sometimes resents her little sister and is scolded for talking back to Maman and being too bossy and outspoken. She first notices that she is considered somehow different when Lucie Fiori, the girl who lives across the street and with whom Nicole would like to be friends, calls her a Dirty Jew. Maman speaks to Nicole's teacher, Mlle. Legrand, who orders Lucie to apologize, but the episode disturbs Nicole. Nicole says the war starts for her when in 1940 Papa enlists in the French army. Within a few months, France falls, and Papa is reported missing. Maman provides food and shelter to refugees who flock to their still unoccupied town. The horror stories of these displaced people frighten the girls. Happily, Papa returns, and life goes on fairly normally under the Vichy government, even though food and other supplies grow scarcer and more expensive. The Niemans become close friends with the Rostens, with whom they celebrate Passover in 1942. Deeply concerned about what the future may hold, Maman pleads with Papa to take the family and flee to Switzerland while they still can, but Papa is sure Hitler will soon be defeated. By November of 1943, their town is occupied, and the Rostens plan to flee. Nicole's dear friend, Francoise, invites her to spend the last night at her house. The next day, Nicole discovers to her shock and fright that, during the night while she was gone, her family was arrested and taken away, victims of the intensified German reign of terror against Jews and those Christians who have ties with the Underground. Now Nicole becomes an outcast; no one will dare to help her. Even the Catholic Durands who cared for her and Jacqueline when they were little are too frightened to take her in. One day, Mlle. Legrand finds her huddled by the school door and makes a place for her among her pupils. All that Nicole, now a young woman with the courage and wisdom to try to make the best of life, has to remind her of her previous life is a letter from her mother encouraging her not to give up and a tattered photo album of her family. Scenes are well drawn but seem carefully arranged to instruct later elementary and junior high readers about this phase of the Holocaust. Except for Nicole and

Mlle. Legrand, characters are indistinct and/or needed for plot or setting. The plot moves too quickly over the years, and what sticks in the reader's mind is the bones of the story. The climax carries well, but the conclusion leaves the reader somewhat in doubt about its connection with the first chapter, and the book calls for re-reading for coherence. The title comes from a sonnet of Edna St. Vincent Millay, "The broken dike . . . ," which appears as an epigraph to the novel. Choice.

POLLY ANN DOLAN (*Bert Breen's Barn**), hardworking, uncomplaining, patient mother of Tom Dolan. The prettiest of the five daughters of ne'er-do-well Chick Hannaberry, sometime farmer near Boonville, she often tells how her father would take his daughters back into the woods to pick blackberries. When their berry buckets were full, he would put the girls in his wagon and take them, berry stained and scratched, into the valley to peddle the berries to the rich people there. Polly's husband, Noh, proved as shiftless as her father, and almost as soon as her three children were born, she was working to put food in their mouths, just as she had had to do for the Hannaberrys. She does laundry and housework for wealthy people in the community, well aware that, although she is respected for her industry, she is still regarded as one of the shiftless Hannaberrys and "low-down Dolans." She encourages Tom to move the Breen barn to the Dolan place and helps him find the treasure.

POOR TOM'S GHOST (Curry*, Jane Louise, Atheneum, 1977), fantasy set in London and environs alternately in the 1970s and in the Elizabethan period. After years of a roving existence with his actor father, Roger* Nicholas, 13, wants nothing more than a real home and settled life for the family, now consisting also of his stepmother, Jo Parkin, and Jo's daughter, Pippa*, 10. When his father, Tony*, inherits a house in Isleworth, he has high hopes, but the house turns out to be dismayingly ugly, oddly proportioned with fake paneling and crumbling plaster facades. They find, however, as they start ripping off sagging paper and buckled wall board, a lovely old house beneath, with the arch above the fireplace dated 1603. At the same time, they seem to have awakened a set of characters and a story from the early seventeenth century, a "ghost" of actor Tom* Garland, who begins to merge with twentieth-century Tony, and his younger brother, unprincipled Jack, who begins to share Roger's personality. They find themselves acting out the early story in which Jack, jealous of Tom's pretty young bride, Katherine, has fooled his brother into thinking she has run away with a young nobleman, whereas she has simply left their Isleworth home, New House, for her parents' home to escape the plague. Tony as Tom, hunting for his "Kitten," begins to sleepwalk and actually falls ill, though not until after he has turned in the performance of his life in *Hamlet*. Roger, who is able to see both stories at once, realizes that he has to be Jack long enough to undo the harm the boy has done. There follows an exhausting search through plague-ridden early London in which Roger as Jack keeps narrowly missing Tom in his effort to reach the actor and tell him the truth, yet the spirit of Jack asserts itself to prevent him from leaving the notes he intends to drop off at likely places to set Tom right. In the present-day world, Tony is very ill from strain, while in the early story Jack contracts the plague. Roger escapes the body of the dying Jack, and in the twentieth-century story he is saved from drowning by Pippa, who matter-of-factly sees the ghosts, accepts the story, and tenaciously follows Roger at night and holds him from slipping into the Thames until he reawakens in his own body. Although all four of them know, to some degree, the dual story, they discover that the five-day period in which it occurred has not really elapsed, and they are able to relive it again without the spirits of Tom and Jack. Their efforts to find out the history of the house are aided by Alan Collet, an actor friend of Tony, and his wife, Jemima, an architectural historian, both characters not developed beyond their utilitarian roles. The four principals, however, are well developed and interesting characters, as are their seventeenth-century counterparts. The switches from one time period to the other are well handled, and the Elizabethan atmosphere is convincing. Poe Honor.

POPE†, ELIZABETH MARIE (1917–   ), born in Washington, D.C.; professor, Shakespeare specialist, novelist. She is a graduate of Bryn Mawr College, received her doctorate from Johns Hopkins University, and has been on the faculty of Mills College, Oakland, Calif., since 1944. In 1947–1948 she was a Folger Research Fellow at the Folger Shakespeare Library in Washington, D.C. In addition to a scholarly book on *Paradise Regained* and articles in *Shakespeare Survey* and *Shakespeare Quarterly*, she has written two novels, *The Sherwood Ring†* (Houghton, 1956), a fantasy, and *The Perilous Gard** (Houghton, 1974), a historical romance set in the Elizabethan period.

THE PORTLETTE PAPERS (*The Pushcart War**), the shorthand record of the conversation between The Three* in which they plan to capture Maxie* Hammerman, the Pushcart King. Miriam Portlette, a cleaning woman, who is studying shorthand in hopes of getting a better job, happens to overhear the conversation and records it as an assignment for class, not realizing its significance at the time. Her action enables Maxie to capture Big Moe's bulletproof Italian car, one of the most brilliant feats of the war, and to his winning the $60,000 with which he establishes the pushcart war chest. The Portlette Papers are among the most important artifacts of the war. Others include the Diary of Joey Kafflis, a truck driver, the Peanut Butter Speech, and the police record of Maxie Hammerman's interrogation.

PORTMAN (*Belling the Tiger**), fierce kitchen mouse, tyrant, who decides that the house cat, Siri, should be belled. Portman is silver, going on gray, uses high-sounding language, is pompous and self-important, and likes to make all the decisions himself, though he makes a show of democratic procedures. Events prove that he can be far from right in his judgments and conclusions. At the end, Rambo and Asa stand up to him, and the other mice applaud their courage.

PORTRAIT OF IVAN (Fox*, Paula, ill. Saul Lambert, Bradbury, 1969), realistic novel of family life set in an urban area in the eastern United States and for a brief time in Florida and covering a few weeks in the life of an introverted, over-protected, isolated child. Ivan, 11, has never known his mother, who drowned when he was a baby. His professionally successful, remote father often goes away on business trips and seldom talks with the boy. He has been raised by Giselle, the housekeeper, and feels very close to kind, indulgent Uncle Gilbert. When Ivan's father commissions a local artist, Matt* Mustazza, to paint Ivan's portrait, Ivan visits the painter's small, cluttered studio every Saturday for some weeks. There he has long conversations with Matt and with elderly Miss* Manderby, whose task is to entertain him by reading to him while the painter works. Conversations about literature and life raise questions in Ivan's mind about his family. He discovers that he knows very little about his parents, particularly his mother, whose people were Russian refugees, and he searches his mind for information and begins to ask questions about her. As he works on Ivan's portrait, Matt also sketches an imaginary picture of Ivan's ancestors escaping to freedom, to which he adds details as the portrait progresses. Matt also takes Ivan to the exhibit of a sculptor-friend and to Jacksonville, Fla., where he paints the picture of a mansion that is to be demolished. Ivan's experiences along the way with Matt and Miss Manderby and while in Florida, in particular with lively Geneva, 12, the neighbor girl who explores the river, and Amos, an intelligent youth whose hobby is horticulture, continue to broaden his perspectives on his family, human nature, and himself. At the end, he has enough confidence to exert his own will and to ask his father to show him a picture of his mother. Scenes come alive in this quiet, virtually plotless, foreshortened story. Characters, if a trifle eccentric, are well realized. The change in Ivan's outlook toward himself and those closest to him develops, like Matt's portrait, both subtly and authentically. Choice.

POTTER, BRONSON, engineer and writer. He is a Harvard graduate and has traveled in France, Portugal, Africa, and the Middle East, areas in which some of his books are set, including *Antonio** (Atheneum, 1968), the story of a Portuguese fisherman's son, and three books set in Iran: *Isfendiar and the Wild Donkeys* (Atheneum, 1967), *Isfendiar and the Bears of Mazandaran* (Atheneum, 1969), and *Chibia, the Dhow Boy* (Atheneum, 1971).

PRESTO (*The Marvelous Misadventures of Sebastian**), the white cat with blue eyes that Sebastian rescues and that becomes his faithful companion in his travels about Hamelin-Loring. Presto significantly influences the plot on several occasions. He discovers the magical fiddle that once belonged to a magician named Lelio and which will play only if the fiddler is worthy. In Sebastian's hands, the fiddle plays more beautifully than it has ever played before. Presto figures out how to make the traveling balloon descend and acts as a messenger for Nicholas to bring Sebastian the picklock with which Sebastian escapes from the Glorietta dungeon. Most significantly, at the end he saves his master's life. At a critical moment, Presto, who is immune to the power of the music of the magic fiddle, leaps onto Sebastian's shoulder. His action sends Sebastian hurtling headlong and knocking him unconscious. Sebastian drops the fiddle, and thus he is saved from its magical power and imminent death.

PRINCE KRISHNA (*The Diamond in the Window**), a transcendentalist scholar and magician from India, who is responsible for the fantasy adventures experienced by Eleanor* and Edward* Hall in a series of books. In *The Diamond in the Window* he has written the riddle verses on the window, which the children pursue and solve in their joint dreams, but he has somehow been caught in the last dream through the machinations of his wicked uncle. In *The Swing in the Summerhouse* he has built a summerhouse through the arches of which one swings to enter the various fantasies; in *The Astonishing Stereoscope* he has sent a set of cards that produce the adventures, and he himself appears as the photographer. He marries the children's Aunt Lily.

THE PRINCESS AND THE LION (Coatsworth*†, Elizabeth, ill. Evaline Ness, Pantheon, 1963), short, realistic novel of adventure set in Abyssinia about two hundred years ago at the court of the king and in the countryside near the palace. It is the custom in this ancient kingdom for the princes to be confined to a palace in the mountains until the king chooses one as his successor. Little Mariam's teenaged brother, Prince Michael, has been imprisoned there almost all his life. Since his village-born mother has no influence at court, there appears to be little chance that Michael will ever rise to the throne. Since she does not wish him to spend the rest of his life in confinement, too, his mother plans his escape. Then, to the astonishment of the entire court, the king proclaims Michael his heir. Disguised as a country boy, riding on the old donkey, Asafa, and accompanied by Menelik, one of the royal lions, Mariam makes a three-day journey across the barren countryside to reach her brother and give him the glad news before he tries to make the planned break for freedom and loses his opportunity for the throne. The greatest threat to Mariam's success comes when she is captured by an Arab slaver. When Menelik attacks the Arab, Mariam escapes. After determining that her brother is still at the palace, Mariam dresses herself in her royal garments and gains entry by imperiously declaring that she bears a message from the king. When Michael runs to meet her, the governor refuses to let her speak privately with him. Thinking quickly, Mariam announces her message that Michael is the king's choice loudly enough for all, including Michael, to hear, thus warning him to abandon the plan for escape. This mildly suspenseful story for younger readers unfolds against a clear sense of the intrigues and opulence of the Abyssinian court and the immense power of the king. The quickwitted, resourceful Mariam is the only fleshed character. Style is descriptive, vocabulary is mature but easily comprehended from context, and tone straightforward and rather formal. The boldly patterned illustrations, executed in shades of brown, gray, and black, illuminate incidents and contribute a brooding note. Choice; Fanfare.

PRISON WINDOW, JERUSALEM BLUE (Clements*, Bruce, Farrar, 1977), historical novel set in 831 A.D. in coastal settlements in England and Denmark. Jugglers and wandering players, Sydne*, a tall girl, and Juls*, her two-year-younger brother, spend their winters at Osso Wisoff, on the English coast. When Kronhengst, leader of the Vikings in the ship *Quick Serpent*, raids the settlement, they are captured and taken to Linkøbing, his Danish home, where his father has just died. Kronhengst plans to kill his older brother, Herjolt*, but dies, presumably from a heart attack, just before the ship lands. His ambition is taken over by his uncle, Thorolf, who brings the ship in and begins to plot against Herjolt. As slaves, the brother and sister have nothing of their own; even their prize possession, a small pane of glass stained Jerusalem blue, is taken from them, but their life is made bearable by an old slave, Augustine, originally also from England. Sydne is sustained partly by her strong religious faith, Juls by his naive inability to think of himself as a slave. To keep from losing their skills, they practice their juggling and acrobatics at night, going from the settlement to a clearing they call the amphitheater. Soon they discover that they are being followed and watched by Herjolt's ten-year-old retarded son, Thyri*, who is beautiful but "brain-struck" and rejected by his father. Thyri scares Sydne, but Juls has compassion for the child and tries to teach him, discovering that he can learn simple juggling and is a natural mimic. When he sends the boy with a rune-message to his father, Juls is flogged at the orders of Herjolt, who distrusts runes and slaves who act free. The pair are approached by Thorolf, who suggests that he will return them to England if they will help him by working out a play for the harvest festival which will mock Herjolt, giving Thorolf the opportunity to kill his nephew and seize power. Troubled by the idea of betraying the rightful lord and by their fear that Thorolf will also kill Thyri, they pretend to agree but instead rehearse a play that includes Thyri acting himself, revealing Thorolf's plot and showing Thyri's loyalty to his father. When their play is successful, Herjolt, still suspicious, sends for them, at first saying they should be killed or sold for mocking his uncle but, when Sydne asks only that he recognize his son, agreeing to take them back to England. Sydne and Juls give the stained glass, which has been returned to them, to Augustine, who says that now his prison has a window. A compelling story, the novel is skillful at recreating the period and lifestyle in a convincing way, and at characterization. Sydne's Christian faith and Juls's essentially non-religious humanity are both treated with respect. The theme that one creates one's own slavery or freedom is subtly presented. Point of view shifts from one character to another, a slightly demanding structure at first but effective in the long run. Fanfare.

PRIVATE EYES: ADVENTURES WITH THE SATURDAY GANG (Kingman*, Lee, ill. Burt Silverman, Doubleday, 1964), detective novel set in the mid–1900s on Clam Cove on Cape Mary near Boston. When Ted Tibbetts, 12, and his pal, Fizzy, hear mysterious voices on the bay during a sudden fog, they and the other three members of the Saturday Gang fear skullduggery is afoot in their peaceful cove. Then their plans for a summer of fun in their clubhouse on the old Benedict property are upset when the new owner, Mr. Russell, announces that he intends to build a marina on Clam Cove. Ted moors his sailboat there, and local fishermen use the cove as a base for their boats. A battle looms between the old-time residents and Mr. Russell's company. Ted discovers that an outside force appears to be stirring up trouble deliberately between the two groups by destroying nets and cutting lobster pounds. The trouble seems also to have some connection with the mysterious voices, two shady characters new in town, Pirate McGob and Windy Jackson, and a local painter, elderly, reclusive Mr. Brinker. While sleuthing, Ted visits Mr. Brinker, who shows him a painting done by an anonymous painter of the late nineteenth century, one of several which Ted later learns may have been done by a Mr. Pringle whose work has become the focus of local interest and much valued. Matters reach a climax when it is learned that Windy Jackson is fronting for a company which has bought up waterfront rights to the cove, and Mr. Brinker is assaulted and some of his paintings stolen. Ted goes to the Boston Museum of Fine Arts to identify the stolen paintings, and Jackson tries to kidnap him there. After Jackson is captured, it is discovered that he belongs to a gang that is smuggling stolen masters. They have been attempting to scuttle Mr. Russell's plans because the cove serves as their base. The residents and Mr. Russell come to terms on developing the area, and all returns to normal. Typical of its genre, the book starts quickly and moves rapidly through a series of stock complications and coincidences to a speedy unraveling of all plot knots. Characters are conventional detective-story types, although in an unconventional switch, Randy Russell, the developer's son, proves unexpectedly likeable for a rich newcomer. Particularly exciting scenes include the voices in the fog and the Coast Guard rescue of the boys during a hurricane, while the investigation of the history of the cove in preparation for the hearing of the town council adds a convincing, realistic touch. Poe Nominee.

PROFESSOR (*The Egypt Game**), Dr. Julian Huddleston, reclusive owner of a curio and antique shop, generally disliked by the people of the Orchard Avenue neighborhood. He was once an anthropologist, but, after his wife's death, he became isolated from society. After word gets out about how he saves April* Hall's life, business picks up at his store, and he feels better about life and people. He fixes the fence and gives the children keys to the yard, so they can continue their game without fear of being disturbed. He attributes the improvement in his life to the Egypt game.

PROFESSOR CAMERON (*A Formal Feeling**), Anne's* father, a university professor of classical history. He is an affectionate but abstracted man, not the perfectionist that Anne's mother was. His fond but impractical nature is shown in his choice of the largest Christmas tree on the lot, too big for the living room, to celebrate his first Christmas with Dory*, his construction of the bird feeder which will never stand quite straight as a welcome home for Anne's mother, and his choice of *The Divine Comedy* to read aloud through the summer with his teenaged daughter. His efforts to break through Anne's emotional shield are genuine but not forceful, since it is not in his nature to impose his personality on others. His choice of Dory as his second wife and his evident happiness with her shows that his relationship with Anne's mother was not as perfect as she wants to believe and helps her retrieve the memories that will eventually make her recover.

PROFESSOR GREENE (*A Solitary Blue**), Horace Greene, Jeff's* father and Melody's* estranged husband, friend of Brother* Thomas. The Professor teaches history at the University in Baltimore and is widely respected in his field, but Melody tries to lead Jeff to believe that his father isn't worth much, a way of thinking the boy accepts for a long time, until events prove otherwise. The Professor is quiet, introverted, and often abstracted, seemingly the typical ivory-towered intellectual. Like Jeff, the reader gradually learns that the Professor is really a very modest man who has been deeply hurt by the realization that Melody, whom he loves, cannot return love and excels at inserting knives and then twisting them to get her way. The Professor's abstraction and isolation from events is a form of self-protection. The Professor's favorite expression is, "It doesn't make any difference," another way he has of shielding himself from disappointment. Jeff gradually learns that his father loves him very much, with an enduring, accepting, generous love, quite different from that of his manipulative, demanding mother, who uses love to get what she wants and is incapable of truly giving affection.

PROFESSOR LYMAN CUMBERLY (*The Pushcart War**), professor at New York University who writes the foreword to the history of the war. He is the developer of the Large Object Theory, which he suggests as the rationale behind the truckers' action for initiating the war. More and more trucks have been appearing on the streets, and the trucks have been getting bigger and bigger. Professor Cumberly's hypothesis is that the truck drivers have figured out that in crowded traffic the only way to get where you want to is to be so big that you don't have to get out of the way for anybody.

PROFESSOR STUART HALSTEAD (*The Secret of the Simple Code**), scholar and geologist who stays at Paul Herriott's Uncle Reuben's house for the summer and takes his meals at the inn where Luke* Young works. He teaches Paul and Abby* Kenny much about rocks and helps Paul develop patience and perseverance.

It is through him that the children meet Bill Smith, insurance investigator. Professor Halstead figures out that the numbers and letters on the cigar messages refer to the places on the map where mines are located.

A PROMISE IS A PROMISE (Cone*, Molly, ill. John Gretzer, Houghton, 1964), realistic novel set in an American suburb in the 1960s. At twelve, Ruthy Morgen is jealous of the attention given her brother, Herbert, who is to have his Bar Mitzvah, particularly of the partiality shown by her grandmother, who lives with them. When Sandra Wright, Ruthy's best friend, points out that she can't invite Ruthy to her Sunday School's Halloween party because all guests have to be children thinking of joining the class, Ruthy lets her know that she is thinking of it, but at the party she is embarrassed and ill at ease. Without fully knowing her reasons, Ruthy insists on having a Bas Mitzvah, an idea to which her family agrees at first reluctantly, then with enthusiasm. Her ambivalence about being Jewish becomes complicated by Sandra's crush on Herbert and a neighborhood quarrel between their fussy next-door neighbor, Mrs. Boyd, and unconventional Mr.* Harvey, whose small house faces their alley. Mrs. Boyd objects to Mr. Harvey's two cats, and Ruthy becomes their defender, even though her father warns her sternly to stay out of neighbors' feuds, since Jews should not cause trouble. When Mr. Harvey goes to the hospital, Ruthy offers to care for his cats and spends most of her energies keeping them away from Mrs. Boyd's yard. Her father's annoyance at this is increased when their dog, Prince, is poisoned by fish Mrs. Boyd put out for the cats. Just before her Bas Mitzvah, Mr. Harvey returns from the hospital, but his sister insists that he go live with her and leave the cats behind. Ruthy assures him that she will find good homes for both of them and is astonished when Mrs. Boyd agrees to look after them during the ceremony. As her grandmother and father agree, it, like the Bas Mitzvah, is a beginning. The theme of the need to speak out for those who are different, of not just tolerance but advocacy, is explicit. Ruthy is a believable twelve-year-old, but the other characters are types. A good deal of information about Jews and the Jewish religion is included. Choice.

A PROUD TASTE FOR SCARLET AND MINIVER (Konigsburg*, E. L., ill. author, Atheneum, 1973), a fantasy-biography of Eleanor of Aquitaine, who is waiting in Heaven to see whether her second husband, Henry Plantagenet (Henry II) of England will be allowed "up" after serving a sentence in Hell for his sins. The story of Eleanor's turbulent life on earth is told in turn by the Abbot Suger, tutor to her first husband, Louis VII of France, by the Empress Matilda, mother of Henry, by William the Marshall, a "true and noble knight," who switched sides continually in conflicts among her husband and sons, and by Eleanor herself. They give a lively picture of the restless, luxury-loving, competent twelfth-century French and English queen, her brilliant court, and her quarreling husbands and sons: Henry III, Richard I (the Lion-Hearted), sensible Geoffrey of Brittainy, and "bad" King John. The style is irreverent and often facetious, but the history is well researched, and the characters are interesting and convincing. Choice; Fanfare.

PRYDAIN (*The Book of Three**; *The Black Cauldron**; *The Castle of Llyr**; *Taran Wanderer**; *The High King**), the Wales-like land of mythical monsters, enchanters, and heroes in which Lloyd Alexander's novels about Taran* the Assistant Pig Keeper take place. It is a medieval realm, in which travel is on foot or by horse, bards entertain, and fighting is by sword and spear. The novels detail the efforts of the forces of good led by Prince Gwydion to defeat the evil Arawn, the Death-Lord, and, on a more personal level, of Taran to establish his identity both literally and figuratively.

THE PUSHCART WAR (Merrill*, Jean, ill. Ronni Solbert, Scott, 1964), humorous fantasy novel set in New York City and intended to be futuristic. The author acting as historian employs a factual, journalistic style enlivened by a tongue-in-cheek tone and occasional verbal witticism to recount the events that lead up to the war, describe its progress, and give the details of the treaty of peace. The Daffodil Massacre of March 15, 1976, touches off the conflict. At 17th Street and Sixth Avenue, Mack, driver of a Mammoth Truck, deliberately runs down the pushcart belonging to Morris the Florist, flinging daffodils one hundred feet in every direction and sending Morris headfirst into a pickle barrel. Mack's action is part of a conspiracy to take over the streets of New York that has been organized by The Three*, the owners of the city's three largest trucking firms. The pushcart drivers retaliate with a pea shooter campaign financed by Wenda* Gambling, a movie star sympathetic to their cause. They "kill" truck tires by shooting peas with pins stuck in them so successfully they paralyze traffic. When the police Pea Squad catches Frank the Flower in the act of "killing" a truck, to protect his friends he confesses to flattening over eighteen thousand tires and immediately becomes a folk hero. School children take up the cause, using tacks instead of pins. Then the city council passes a Tacks Tax, and the war becomes a matter of international interest. England, a major exporter of tacks, protests the tax on tacks, and the president of the United States appeals to the mayor to repeal it. When the peddlers organize a peace march to dramatize their cause, the mayor revokes their licenses. At that very time, Buddy Wisser, editor of a local newspaper, publishes a newly discovered snapshot of the Daffodil Massacre. With public opinion now firmly on the side of the peddlers, the two factions come to the peace table. They adopt Frank the Flower's suggestion (the Flower Formula) for limiting the size and number of trucks that may operate at a given time and ensuring the freedom of the streets for pushcarts and other small vehicles. The elaborate plot of this fast-moving, warmly funny satire on war and contemporary city life in which the "little guy" appropriately triumphs works with precision. Scenes are deftly sketched, and the many characters are a consistently interesting mix, if well-known types or caricatures. References to and quotations from "primary sources" cleverly add to authenticity. (Anna*; Carlos*; Maxie* Hammerman; The Portlette* Papers; Professor* Lyman Cumberly; The Three*; Wenda* Gambling) Choice; Fanfare; Lewis Carroll.

Q

_____

QUEENIE PEAVY (Burch*, Robert, ill. Jerry Lazare, Viking, 1966), realistic novel set in Cotton Junction, Ga., in the 1930s. Because her father is in the penitentiary in Atlanta, Queenie Peavy, 13, is frequently the target of gibes and teasing, and she has a chip on her shoulder. Even for Depression times, the Peavy place, where Queenie lives with her mother, is run down, barely able to support Queenie's chickens, her pet rooster, Dominick, and their cow, Sweetheart, not nearly as good as the neat brick house of the Corrys, Queenie's black neighbors. The Corry children, Dover, 8, and Avis, 5, are good friends of Queenie, but at school she is inclined to fight, though her teachers say she is smart and some of her classmates admire her ability to chew tobacco and to throw stones with deadly accuracy. Her school troubles become more serious at an eighth-grade field trip when Queenie gets even with her chief tormentor, Cravey Mason, by rigging a log to slip into a stream, then daring him to walk up it. When he breaks his leg, Mr. Hanley, the principal, threatens to expel Queenie for one more misdeed and makes her promise to apologize to Cravey. Before she can find the occasion, Cravey announces publicly that his doctor's bill will be sent to Queenie's mother and privately he gets Persimmon Gibbs to break the windows in the tower of the Hilltop Baptist Church and blame Queenie. The sheriff questions her, and she worries that she might be sent to the reformatory, but outwardly she says, "I don't care!" It seems to her that her troubles are over when her father comes home on parole. At first she is hurt at his lack of interest in her, then she fantasizes that he is talking to the sheriff and the judge about her problems. She finds that this is not true; moreover, he is surly, ignoring or rejecting all her overtures. She decides to pretend that a big change has come over her, just to show everyone how pleasant and cooperative she can be before she is sent away. She nominates Cravey for an important committee, sings for the assembly, and knows all her lessons. The next day two important things happen: Queenie is cleared of the window-breaking charge, and her father is sent back to prison for carrying a gun and thereby breaking parole. In a sub-plot, Martha Mullins, who is called "Little Mother" because she talks like a grown-up, has already admitted to Queenie that she often goes without adequate food because there is little enough for her six siblings. When she faints in school,

Queenie helps take her to the doctor's office where she is diagnosed as being anemic because of malnutrition. The doctor is impressed by Queenie's practical ability when she helps with an emergency case. At the book's end, Queenie is started on a new path with a part-time job for the doctor and an invitation to the ninth-grade party from Martha's older brother, Dave, whom Queenie admires. The main emphasis in the book is on Queenie's recognizing her self-deception and admitting her father's limitations of character. There are warm and often amusing scenes of Queenie talking to her rooster and playing with the Corry children, and life in a small southern town of the period is well depicted. Queenie is a memorable character—tough, intelligent, honest, and vulnerable. The modest, unpretentious style helps make the story convincing. Addams; Child Study; Choice; Fanfare; Stone.

QUEEN OF HEARTS (Cleaver*, Vera, and Bill Cleaver*, Lippincott, 1978), realistic problem story set recently in the town of Timberlake in northern Florida, in which a young girl learns to accept the inevitable with grace and resource. After she suffers a stroke, the doctor says that Josie Lincoln, Wilma's willful and spirited seventy-nine-year-old Granny, can no longer live by herself. Granny refuses to move either to a home for the aged or to that of her son, Wilma's father. Accustomed to a free and independent life, Granny sends packing with insults and reprimands several housekeepers her son has engaged, leaving him baffled about what to do with her. He asks Wilma, 12, who is looking forward to a summer vacation of happy times with her company of make-believe friends and her little brother, Claybrook, 6, a pleasant and undemanding sort, to look after Granny until he can find someone else to live in permanently. Realizing that there is no feasible alternative, Wilma reluctantly agrees, but she regrets giving up her freedom to stay with an old woman who has never shown her any affection. Surprisingly, Granny accepts Wilma, who intrudes as little as she can upon Granny's life. Wilma enjoys Granny's stories of her youth in South Dakota, told with exaggeration and enthusiasm about a less inhibited era and colorful frontier figures, but she resents the old woman's cutting remarks, her quick changes of mind, and her obstinacy. For example, Granny accuses her and Claybrook of stealing some gold coins she has misplaced, an incident that withers completely the incipient friendship between Granny and the little boy. Wilma is given a slight respite from her duties when her father hires homebodies Walter and Azella Screechfield to live in, but Granny soon rebels against their overprotectiveness, and Wilma is back on the job. As the summer passes, Wilma comes more and more to appreciate her father's dilemma, even as she is learning to understand why Granny behaves as she does. She realizes that much of Granny's poor behavior arises from fear and her decreased physical ability and that Granny needs the self-respect that being busy and productive can bring. When Granny complains that no one bakes good bread any more, Wilma suggests that she bake bread and rolls which she, Wilma, will sell for her. Wilma is advised in her plan by Granny's next-door neighbor, aged Ben Frost, for whom

Wilma once felt only impatience and disdain, as she once did also for her grandmother. After school starts, Granny, whose baking business is flourishing, gets rid of still another housekeeper, and Wilma resigns herself to the inevitable, that she is the only person whom indomitable old Granny will accept. Events seem purposely contrived and characters deliberately fashioned to provide the opportunity to examine some of the problems of Aging. Wilma's ready and uncomplaining compliance do not seem in keeping with her character as presented, and her solution to Granny's problem is simply too pat and successful. The story moves rapidly, and there are occasional patches of humor. National Book Finalist.

QUINCY HEFFENDORF (*The Dunderhead War**), plucky, impetuous, not very sensible youth, who at first is ashamed of his Uncle* Fritz. He is annoyed at Uncle Fritz's outspoken criticism of the Americans and at his insistence on order and discipline while they are traveling. Before the two leave Independence, Quincy's father's store is robbed of gunpowder and guns by Armijo's men. Later Quincy discovers in Rufus's possession a gun that he favored because of its distinctive buffalo decorations and which was lost in the robbery, proof, in Quincy's opinion, that Rufus was involved in the robbery and is a traitor to the American cause. Events prove Quincy correct in his suspicions.

R

RACHEL (*The Rider and His Horse**), cousin of Eleazar* ben Ya'ir, commander of the Massada. The Romans have killed her own two children and her husband, refusing to let her bury him, a shocking omission under Jewish law. An assertive woman, Rachel defies Eleazar, declines to accord him the worshipful admiration he expects, refuses to marry the man Eleazar has selected for her, and tries to wrest her brother's children from the fate waiting for all the inhabitants of the Massada. Yet Rachel, who was a child with Eleazar, thinks of him more as a fool deceived by heroic stories than as an evil person, and she retains some love for him under her hatred of his actions.

RACHEL O'NEAL (*Teetoncey**; *Teetoncey and Ben O'Neal**), widow of the surfman, John O'Neal, and mother of Ben* in the first two books of the Cape Hatteras trilogy. A religious and strong-willed woman, she hates the sea that has killed her husband and one son and tries to keep Ben from it, even dressing him like a girl until he is five. Her desire for a daughter seems to be fulfilled when Ben rescues a girl from a wreck, a child of about twelve who suffers from amnesia. Rachel summons all her energy to nurse and protect the girl, whom they call Teetoncey*, meaning ''small,'' even conspiring to hide her from the British Consul and defying her cousin, equally strong-willed Filene* Midgett, the commander of the local surfman's station, who believes it is his duty to get the girl back to England. When the surfmen manage to raise the chests of silver from the wreck and it is apparent that the greed of the local people and the mainlanders will keep the money from going to Tee, the rightful owner, Rachel cuts the rope on the hoist, dropping the chests into deep water where they are irretrievable. As a result of her exposure that day, she dies of pneumonia.

RADYAR (*Wings**), motorcycle-riding astrologer, who is a friend of Pip dePuyster's mother and her Aunt Andrea. His real name is Hiram Joseph Smith, and he writes a widely read column on astrology. When Pip first sees him, he is dressed in leather helmet, goggles, riding breeches, and leather puttees, just like the movie star, Al Wilson, who is Pip's special aviator hero. Pip pretends she is in an airplane when Radyar takes her riding in his sidecar. He prepares her horoscope and is the only one astute enough to realize that what she most wants for Christmas is a helmet and goggles. Although he may be a fortune hunter, after Pip's mother's money, he takes his astrological studies very seriously, and to Pip he is always kind, warm, and understanding. He significantly influences the slim plot and helps to unify the book. He quite innocently is the reason she must go back to Kansas City early. Her father finds out that she and Radyar went swimming in their underwear. The kind of man who always thinks the worst, he concludes that Radyar is a shady character and forbids his children to associate with the man.

RAIN DOVE (*To Spoil the Sun**), traditionally reared, strong-minded, intelligent, family-loving Cherokee girl. At fourteen, she marries Mink*, the tribal medicine man, to insure safety for her family after her brother accidentally kills a fellow tribesman. At first, Rain Dove dislikes being Mink's second and much younger wife, but she soon finds the ailing Hawk Sister a congenial companion and worthy teacher and becomes fond of both her and Mink, and she enjoys being at the center of events involving the tribe. When she falls in love with young Trotting Wolf, she feels guilty, but Hawk Sister and Mink are understanding and continue to be her friends. In her account of these critical years for her people, Rain Dove is honest, observant, and articulate but never garrulous, melodramatic, apologetic, or self-promoting. Although she grows and changes believably and her story is emotionally moving, she is more a window to the times than a living, breathing human being.

RAIN OF FIRE (Bauer*, Marion Dane, Clarion, 1983), realistic novel set in Illinois about 1947, a year after the end of World War II, a story exploring the way small conflicts escalate into dangerous situations and strongly condemning the heroics of war. The coming of Ray* Celestino, 14, into the neighborhood disturbs the easygoing friendship of Steve* Pulaski, 12, and his friends, the twins, Kenny and Donny Riley. Under Ray's taunts Steve claims his brother, Matthew*, who has returned disturbed after three years in the Pacific war, the last in the occupation army in Japan, was given a medal for bravery. Actually, Matthew has been morose and preoccupied and has not told Steve anything about his years in the artillery. Ray knows Steve is lying and calls him "Blubber-butt," a name that amuses the twins and that chubby Steve fears will stick. His friend, Becca* (Rebecca) Hansen, whose father is superintendent of the mill and quarry where all the other fathers work, suggests that he get even and has a great idea—that they take Donny's bike and repaint it, then leave it behind Celestino's house so the twins will think Ray stole it—an idea inspired by another of Steve's lies, that Ray steals and resells bikes. Against his better judgment, Steve agrees, and they make a terrible mess of the bike with their after-dark paint job. The next day, pretending friendship, Ray lures both Steve and Becca to the foxhole the boys have dug in the woods, where the twins knock them in, tie them back to back, and leave them for hours, scared and miserable and bitten by ravenous mosquitoes, before they are found by Matthew. Trying to arbitrate, Matthew gets all five kids together, tells Donny that Steve will pay to have his bike professionally repainted and points out that they have all suffered through their quarrel. The twins seem ready to make peace, but Ray calls Matthew yellow for considering the Japanese human beings, and Matthew answers that what he saw in Japan made him ashamed and then walks away. Trying somehow to salvage his brother's reputation, Steve concocts a wild story of how Matthew always miscalculated the range on the big guns so that they wouldn't kill anyone, and Ray scornfully repeats that Matthew is a Jap-lover. Later Ray and the twins appear and show Steve a letter they have written to J. Edgar Hoover accusing Matthew of being a traitor, and they try to get Steve to sign it, too. That night, Matthew tries to explain to Steve the terrible sights of Hiroshima and tells him of a boy who reminded him of Steve, whom he watched die slowly of horrible burns. Although he still doesn't understand how Matthew can say he is ashamed, Steve sneaks out that night to try to retrieve the letter from the Celestino mailbox and turns to find Ray watching him. Ray not only takes the letter but also the Pulaski cat, Ginger, which has followed Steve, and which he says he will hold hostage, along with the letter, until Steve brings him some dynamite, so he can blow some more foxholes in the woods. Once more Steve takes his problem to Becca, who confidently suggests that they steal dynamite from the quarry. There they find the dynamite in padlocked containers, but Steve picks up a blasting cap from the office before they are chased away by Mr. Celestino, the watchman. When he and Becca take it to Ray, along with some flares from the highway stuffed with sand to look like dynamite, he unlocks the trunk of the car where he has kept Ginger, and they find her dead. Determined to get revenge, Steve, Becca, and the twins, who are now on their side again, lure Ray to the foxhole, attack and tie him up, and set off the blasting cap just a few feet from him. At the last minute, Steve has second thoughts, rushes up to try to kick it away, and wakes up in the hospital with Matthew sitting by his bed. Though the worst injured of the youngsters, Steve has at last begun to understand his brother's horror of the results of war, and Matthew, having a person to communicate with finally, seems to have a chance for psychological recovery. Though the anti-war message is explicit and far from subtle, the action is believable and gripping, as the boys and Becca move blindly from minor conflict into real danger. Steve's frustration at a brother who will neither act normal nor tell him what is wrong and at the jeering of the other boys is well depicted, and his conflict of loyalty and anger at Matthew is understandable. Dialogue is convincing. Addams.

RALPH SHANE (*The Rock and the Willow**), intelligent, compassionate son of the Singletons' well-to-do neighbor. Some seven or eight years older than Enie, he is set apart from the other Tired Creek youngsters not only by his money but by his education, his Catholic religion, and his limp, the result of infantile paralysis. Enie never tells but cannot forget about the time she came upon Ralph and the "white-trash" Bliss Atkins making love in a honeysuckle thicket. When Enie's father breaks his leg, Ralph comes and helps until the doctor arrives, and when the family is short-handed at bean-picking time, he arrives unasked and labors in the field all day. Just before Enie goes off to college, he gives her a ride in a truck in which he is carrying an undernourished calf he has bought from the Atkins family, hoping to nurse it to health, raise it, and give it back so the Atkins children will have milk. Although it is never clear whether he has any romantic interest in Enie, as her father and brothers suspect, he represents to her the better life available if she gets away from Tired Creek and gets an education.

RAMONA AND HER FATHER (Cleary*†, Beverly, ill. Alan Tiegreen, Morrow, 1977), humorous, episodic novel, one of a series, set in an Oregon town in the 1960s or early 1970s. Ramona Quimby, now a second grader, is worried because her father has lost his job, and the whole family seems upset and different. With all good intentions, she tries to help and keeps causing trouble. Hoping she might earn a million dollars by making television commercials, she practices being cute, an activity misunderstood by her family, and makes herself a crown like the one in the margarine ad, using burrs which stick in her hair and have to be cut out. When Beezus (Beatrice, her older sister) accuses their father of wasting money and making his lungs turn black by continuing to smoke, Ramona sees a way to help and starts a campaign by putting up anti-smoking signs around the house. He is not amused but has to admit the girls are right and agrees to try, a move that makes him cross and life more trying for the rest of the family, particularly Ramona, who spends the most time with him now that her mother works full time. Occasionally Ramona forgets her worries, as on the day she and her friend, Howie Kemp, make tin-can stilts and clank around the neighborhood, singing at the top of their lungs. But she inadvertently causes more trouble by volunteering to be a sheep in the Sunday School Christmas pageant, forgetting that her mother will not have time to make the costume. Mrs. Quimby agrees to try to make one out of an old terry-cloth bathrobe but can finish only the head and the tail, thinking Ramona can wear her faded pajamas for a body. Ramona sulks while Beezus, who is to be Mary, irritates her by acting holy. Humiliated, Ramona refuses to be in the program but changes her mind when one of the "three wise persons" paints her a black sheep's nose with mascara. Just before Christmas, Mr. Quimby gets a job as a checker in a supermarket. As in the earlier books, Ramona is an interesting character. The family tension and the relationship between her and her father are well-handled elements. Boston Globe Honor ; Fanfare; Newbery Honor.

RAMONA QUIMBY, AGE 8 (Cleary*†, Beverly, ill. Alan Tiegreen, Morrow, 1981), humorous, episodic novel, one of a series, set in an Oregon town in the 1960s or early 1970s. Now a third-grader, Ramona Quimby has reached an age where she demands accuracy and feels a great weight of responsibility. If she doesn't get along with bratty Willa Jean, Howie Kemp's little sister, Howie's grandmother will not take care of her after school, her mother will not be able to work full time, her father, now returned to school to become a teacher, will have to drop out, go back to checking at the supermarket, and come home tired and cross every night. She genuinely tries to do her part, but things keep interfering. At the new school, which she gets to on a bus, a boy she calls Yard Ape christens her "Superfoot." When she joins the third-grade fad of breaking the hard-boiled eggs in their lunches by knocking them on their heads, Ramona's turns out to be raw, a mistake by her harried mother, and the school secretary has to help her wash the mess out of her hair. Worst of all, she overhears her nice, casual teacher, Mrs. Whaley, refer to her as a show-off and a nuisance. When her mother serves tongue, because it is inexpensive, both Ramona and her older sister, Beezus (Beatrice) rebel, and their father decides that they can make dinner the next day. Forced into cooperation, they cook an eccentric but edible meal. Determined not to be a nuisance to Mrs. Whaley, Ramona doesn't mention that she feels strange and vomits right in the classroom. Troubles seem to pile up until the rainy Sunday with the whole family cross when her father suddenly announces that they are going out to dinner, hang the expense. At the Whopperburger, an old man salutes Ramona and keeps watching them, and when they finish they find he has paid for their dinner because they seem to be such a nice family. Ramona has grown in this book in a believable way into a genuinely interesting and appealing child. The humor is not as much in the situation as in her perceptions, always logical if unlike those of the adults around her. The style is not as overly simple as in the early books of the series. Fanfare.

RAMONA THE PEST (Cleary*†, Beverly, ill. Louis Darling, Morrow, 1968), humorous, episodic novel for early readers, one of a series set in an Oregon town in the 1960s. Ramona Quimby, 5, little sister of Beezus (Beatrice), starts kindergarten with a misunderstanding when the teacher, Miss Binney, tells her to sit in this seat for the present, and she confidently waits to be given a gift. Many of her best impulses turn into conflict, as when she admires Susan's curls and pulls one to see if it will go boing! boing!, for which misdeed she must sit on the bench while the other children play. Her practical, unimaginative friend, Howie Kemp, who likes to take things apart with tools, removes one wheel from her tricycle, and she discovers that, by leaning to one side, she can ride it as a two-wheeler. In her new boots she wades in the mud of a construction site and must be rescued by Henry Huggins, who is now a fifth-grade crossing guard. On Halloween, she has such a convincing witch mask that she feels lost inside it and makes herself a sign so that she will not be permanently mislaid. When Susan calls her a pest, Ramona can't resist boing!ing her hair again, and Miss Binney says she must stay home until she can leave Susan's hair alone. Sure that Miss Binney does not like her, Ramona decides she can't go back to school until the teacher has forgotten her and she can start fresh. In the neighborhood she becomes known as a kindergarten drop-out, and Henry, now a paperboy, scares her by wondering why the truant officer doesn't make her go to school.

To complicate matters, she has lost her first tooth and left it in Miss Binney's care, so she can't smile or her family will notice. When Howie brings a letter from Miss Binney with the tooth scotch-taped to the paper, asking when she is coming back, Ramona realizes that her teacher really does like her, and she is free to return. Told from Ramona's point of view, the incidents all have the logic of a five-year-old mind and reveal a character a good deal more well developed than those in earlier books in the series. This allows for humor that is more subtle and sophisticated, though the style remains simple. Choice.

RANSOM (Duncan*, Lois, Doubleday, 1966), novel of suspense set in the mountains of New Mexico in the 1960s. Five high school youths from an affluent suburb, three boys and two girls, Glenn* Kirtland, his younger brother, Bruce, and their friends, Dexter, Marianne* Paget, and Jesse* French, are kidnapped by Buck and Juan, who hijack the bus on which they are riding home from school. They take the youths to a remote mountain cabin, where Buck and his wife, Rita, hold them prisoner while Juan arranges for the ransom money. Through conversations, flashbacks, and their actions, the author reveals what the five young people are like. Extroverted, stubborn Marianne resents her stepfather, Rod, while introverted Jesse, who goes to pieces easily, understands people better than Marianne. Dexter is very self-conscious about his body, because he was crippled by polio, while timid Bruce has learned to live in the shadow of athletic, handsome, attention-grabbing Glenn, to whom the younger boy is doggedly loyal. After a couple of days at the cabin, the inevitable break for freedom occurs. Dexter suggests "hotwiring" the car while their captors are asleep, but Buck awakens, and Dexter is shot trying to escape. Buck tries to run down Bruce and Glenn with the car, but it skids on the icy road and plunges over a cliff, carrying Buck to his death in the ravine below. Marianne's stepfather, Rod Donavan, agrees to deliver the ransom money to Juan. Although he has been unable to secure the demanded amount, he meets Juan anyway, determined to put on a bold front. When Rod demands proof that Marianne is still alive, Juan takes him into the cabin. There the story of Buck's death comes out, and Rita angrily turns on Juan. During the altercation, the youths seize Juan's gun and take their captors captive. A taut, spare style and judiciously spaced flashbacks produce tension in an otherwise predictable formula story. The kidnappers are quite unvillainous and stereotypically named, and, although there are some tight moments, most of the story interest revolves around learning what the youths are like and whether or not they will change as a result of the experiences they are having. Quite predictably, Jesse proves steady, Bruce learns that he can be whatever he makes of himself and sees his older brother for what he really is, Dexter gains in self-appreciation because he influences the course of things substantially and because Jesse likes him for himself, Glenn remains a shallow, self-centered, attention seeker, and Marianne learns to trust and value her colorless, reliable, steady stepfather. Poe Nominee.

RARK (*Hakon of Rogen's Saga**; *A Slave's Tale**), slave born in Frankland, who befriends Hakon and Helga in *Hakon of Rogen's Saga* and whose return to his home is the main purpose of the journey Hakon undertakes after he comes to power in *A Slave's Tale*. Rark is a Christian and a man of education, captured by Norsemen some dozen years before the return journey. In his homeland he was Jacques de Bardinais, a man of property with a wife and children. He is instrumental in returning Hakon to his rightful position by killing the usurping uncle, Sigurd, and Hakon not only frees him but vows to take him home. In France, however, Rark discovers his wife has remarried and all his lands have gone to her new husband, Hugues. At the feast ostensibly to discuss the situation, Hugues has Rark treacherously killed, and his wife's mind snaps at the sight.

RASCAL (North*, Sterling, Dutton, 1963), autobiographical novel set in 1918, the year the author was eleven, in Brailsford Junction, Wis. Sterling is an independent child living with his absent-minded and frequently absent father, checked on occasionally by his adult sisters, Theo and Jessica, their brother Herschel being a soldier in France and their mother having died four years earlier. The book is arranged by months. In May, with his friend, Roger Sutherland, and his St. Bernard, Wowser, Sterling finds a baby raccoon and brings it home to join the large menagerie of pets which share the home with him and his tolerant father. In June, he introduces the raccoon, named Rascal, to the joys of riding in his bike basket, eating in the high chair, fishing at Indian Ford, and sleeping in his bed. When Theo comes for a visit and takes Sterling's room, Rascal, always attracted to shiny objects, takes her diamond ring from the washstand, then loses it to Poe, the pet crow, also a collector of bright trinkets. Sterling retrieves it from the tower of the Methodist church, where the crow nests, and wins a reprieve from Theo, who has wanted to banish the canoe he is making in the living room to the barn. In July, Sterling and Rascal spend a marvelous day at Lake Koshkonong with Sterling's father, who has been shocked that the boy has never heard a whippoorwill and takes a day to remedy that situation. In August, Rascal discovers sweet corn, and a delegation of neighbors call to complain. Sterling's diplomatic father persuades them that his son will provide a leash and a pen for his pet and then takes the boy and raccoon on an idyllic two-week camping trip to Lake Superior and Brule River in northern Wisconsin. In September, Sterling builds a huge pen for Rascal and takes him to the Irish Picnic and Horse Fair where the little raccoon helps him in the pie-eating contest and they cheer as their neighbor, Mike Conway, wins a race with his trotter, Donnybrook, against the terrible-tempered minister, Gabriel Thurman, and his Model T car. In October, Sterling takes Rascal to school, by invitation, but when the bully, Slammy Stillman, snaps Rascal with a rubber band and gets bitten, Sterling has to keep his pet confined for two weeks. In November, Spanish influenza strikes, and Sterling is taken to his long-suffering Aunt Lillian's farm to be nursed. News of the armistice comes to them there on Sterling's twelfth birthday. During the winter, Sterling builds a cage for the Christmas tree so

Rascal can't destroy the ornaments, goes ice skating with the new skates Jessica has given him with Rascal clinging to his hair like a living coon-skin cap, and makes a midnight trip with his father to the farm to help protect the tobacco when "case weather" hits. In the spring, Sterling finishes his canoe, and, when Jessica insists that they get a housekeeper, he realizes that Rascal will not fit into the household any longer. He takes Rascal in the canoe to an isolated area and leaves him with a female raccoon. In spite of the distant war, which is chronicled throughout, the story is almost an idyll, a nostalgic picture of a quieter and better period in a comfortable small town. Characterization is strong, including clever, bright little Rascal, Sterling's polite, remote father, his understanding Aunt Lillian, and many minor townsfolk. Sterling's parting with Rascal is voluntary and, while sad, not the traumatic wrench of loss of many animal stories. Fanfare; Lewis Carroll; Newbery Honor.

RASKIN, ELLEN (1925? 1928?–1984), born in Milwaukee, Wis.; commercial illustrator and designer, author and illustrator of books for children. She attended the University of Wisconsin and after college became a freelance illustrator in New York City, where within the space of ten years she had designed over one thousand book jackets and completed many illustrations for magazines and advertising. After the publication of her first book for children, the acclaimed picture book *Nothing Ever Happens on My Block* (Atheneum, 1966), she gave up illustrating freelance. After that she published a dozen and a half self-illustrated books, most of them picture books, that were well received, two books of verse, and several raucous, zany, self-conscious novels of mystery, humor, and occasional poignancy that show a strong sense of structure and an inclination for striking out in new directions. One novel won the Newbery Award, the Jane Addams Award, and Fanfare status and was a *Boston Globe-Horn Book* winner, *The Westing Game** (Dutton, 1978), in which an unlikely assortment of heirs seek to solve the puzzle of their relative's disappearance and win his fortune. *Figgs & Phantoms** (Dutton, 1974), about an eccentric family of ex–circus performers, was a Newbery Honor book, while *The Tattooed Potato and Other Clues** (Dutton, 1975), in which a girl answers an ad for an artist's assistant and finds herself embroiled in mysteries, was nominated for the Edgar Allan Poe Award. Her first novel was *The Mysterious Disappearance of Leon (I Mean Noel)* (Dutton, 1971), and her picture books include *Spectacles* (Atheneum, 1968), *Ghost in a Four-Room Apartment* (Atheneum, 1969), and *Twenty-Two, Twenty-Three* (Atheneum, 1976). She illustrated many books for such writers well known in children's literature as Claire Bishop†, Vera and Bill Cleaver*, and Rebecca Caudill* and published editions of Thomas's *A Child's Christmas in Wales*, Rossetti's *Goblin Market*, and the poems of Poe, and won awards and citations for her illustrations and picture books. She and her husband, Dennis Flanagan, editor of *Scientific American*, and their daughter made their home in New York City.

RATHA'S CREATURE (Bell*, Clare, Atheneum, 1983), fantasy whose characters are large, intelligent cats, in a world in which humans do not seem to exist. Ratha, a young female, has been trained as a herder by Thakur, against the practice of Meoran, the chief, who thinks females unfit for this high position, and against the wishes of her den-father, Yaran, who slavishly follows Meoran. Although she is young for the job, Thakur takes her to the meadow where the herdbeasts, both the three-pronged deer and the dappleback horses, must be protected from the raids of the Un-Named Ones. When she has a confrontation with one of the raiders, she is astonished to find that, contrary to all she has been told, the Un-Named One can talk and is very like her, a discovery that Thakur dismisses as illusion, though he seems uneasy when she tells him. It gradually becomes apparent to her that, under Meoran's rigid rule, the clan has too few herders and that he underestimates and misrepresents the raiders, who are becoming more and more successful. A lightning storm starts a forest fire and, in their desperate effort to drive the herdbeasts to the river, Thakur sees a dappleback stallion horribly killed, and Ratha is nearly drowned. When they return to their own territory, they must pass by burning remnants. Thakur is filled with fear, but Ratha is curious and, observing and playing with the burning embers, discovers that she can carry fire with her at the end of a branch, and she sees that, with her "creature" tamed, the clan will have a weapon against the Un-Named Ones. Meoran, however, sees her only as a threat to his leadership and drives her out of the clan. Only Fessran, a female trainer of herders, understands, and she must pretend to have chased Ratha away to protect her own position in the clan. Feeling rejected and betrayed by Thakur, who tried to persuade her to kill her creature, Ratha wanders far from familiar territory, and, unused to stalking and killing game, is nearly starving when the Un-Named One she previously met approaches her. Something about him reminds her of Thakur, and she learns from him how to hunt and begins to live with him, though she scornfully calls him Bonechewer. Eventually they mate and, while she is heavy with her cubs, they attend a meeting of the Un-Named Ones, some of whom are without intelligence, but some, like Bonechewer, are very like clan animals. He tries to persuade the others that their best plan is to keep raiding, being careful not to deplete the herds too much, but others are filled with hate for the clan and insist that they must wipe it out. Though she has only the lowest status among them, Ratha joins the Un-Named in their attack on the clan but afterwards cannot bring herself to live in a clan lair. She discovers that Bonechewer feels the same way and learns that he was born of a clan mother who had mated with an Un-Named One and had two cubs, one of whom was kept in the clan when he and his mother were driven out. When they return to Bonechewer's territory and Ratha has her cubs, she has great hopes for starting a new clan, training her cubs and gradually building a herd, but to her dismay she discovers that they are without intelligence. Bonechewer stops her from killing them, but she leaves him and wanders back toward the old clan grounds, where Thakur finds her and tells her that the clan remnants are again starting a herd and trying to survive. He takes her with him, sure that Meoran so needs her now that she will be accepted, but under Meoran's grilling she admits that she will not submit without question to his authority, and she leaves of her own free will, though Fessran and Thakur are grieved. She stays close to the territory, visited by Thakur and Fessran occasionally. When another storm starts a fire, Fessran persuades her to again pick up a burning branch and challenge Meoran. In the ensuing conflict, he is killed, mainly by Fessran. Having taught the clan how to use fire, Ratha leads them in defense against the attack of the Un-Named Ones in which Bonechewer is killed. Ratha, though grieved, realizes that Thakur is his brother and that she will find her true mate in him, now that her people are safe, though changed, with their power over her creature. The theme is a strong condemnation of being tied to conventional patterns. Although the idea of intelligent cats controlling fire and keeping herds for their own food is at first bizarre, the fantasy is exciting and mostly convincing. The Named Ones have human speech and human emotions but retain their animal characteristics. IRA.

RAY CELESTINO (*Rain of Fire**), fourteen-year-old who disrupts the friendship of Steve* Pulaski and the Riley twins when he comes from Chicago to live in the neighborhood of mill housing. Son of the mill watchman, a drunken, bigoted man who has been wounded in the war and can no longer handle the big machinery that was his vocation, Ray is tough and enjoys pushing the younger boys around. When Steve hides in the bushes near the Celestino home, however, he overhears a domestic fight and sees Mr. Celestino leaving for his job drunk, and the next day, when he sees the marks on Ray's back, realizes that the boy's father beats him. In the explosion of the blasting cap, Ray is injured but not as seriously as Steve.

A REALLY WEIRD SUMMER (McGraw*†, Eloise Jarvis, Atheneum, 1977), novel on the borderline between fantasy and realistic psychological fiction, set in Oregon in the 1970s. Because their parents are getting a divorce, the four Anderson children have been shunted off to an old inn at Reeves Ferry owned by their great-aunt and -uncle, Aunt Ruth and Uncle* Fred Webster, an elderly childless couple who run a mom-and-pop store at one end of the largely abandoned building. Dreamy, sensitive Nels*, 12, is especially disturbed because he feels responsible for the others and because he knows he may be expected to live with his father, leaving the others with their mother. Aunt Ruth is a fussy type, mostly concerned with her husband's poor health; Uncle Fred is kindly but distant, unable to remember the children's names. Weary of the emotional demands of Stevie*, 10, Rory, 8, and Jenny, 6, Nels escapes to the "General's room" in the unused end of the inn's second floor and there discovers a boy, Alan Reeves, and a bookcase which is really a door to a closet. With Alan he goes through a door in the back of the closet to a tower where he and Alan engage in exciting activities of the sort he most enjoys: they play chess, they learn and practice ciphers, they finish a mock-up of a British Spitfire that Alan and his father designed, and they design and build, with the help of Alan's father, whom Nels eventually meets, a mock-up of a space ship big enough for them to climb into. Nels has difficulty escaping to this sanctuary and at first spends only occasional mornings with Alan, devoting his afternoons to his siblings, but gradually he spends more and more of his days in the tower. Stevie suffers most from Nels's preoccupation, since the younger two are busy playing with fat Maureen, daughter of Alice Clary, the abrupt, ironic cook whom Stevie dislikes. Hurt, bored, and worried about his family's future, Stevie hangs around the store talking to Uncle Fred until Aunt Ruth shoos him out, rides his bike disconsolately to the school yard, the limit set by Aunt Ruth, and eventually is allowed to hang around the fringes of a crowd of older boys working there on their motorcycles, who tolerate him because he brings them cookies and runs errands for them. The crisis occurs on August 21, Stevie's birthday, which everyone else has forgotten, when he is discovered with a whole box of ice cream bars he has stolen from the store for the motorcycle boys. Nels, shocked by Stevie's misery and the realization that he has forgotten his brother's birthday, promises to come right back and makes a hurried trip to the tower to tell Alan that Stevie must be let in on the secret, but he inadvertently lets the bookcase door latch behind him, though Alan has warned him not to, and is trapped in the closet. With great effort he resists Alan's calls to join him in the tower, a possibility he now recognizes as a threat. When he doesn't come for lunch, Stevie feels betrayed, but when Nels does not show up for the birthday dinner Aunt Ruth belatedly has planned, Stevie tries once more to call him in the General's room where he has long suspected Nels goes, and, getting a faint answer from the bookcase, manages to release a half-dead Nels from the closet. Later, they search the back of the closet for the door to the tower, realize that it is solid plywood, and Nels begins to suspect that it has all been a fantasy created by his own mind as he crouched in the closet, hiding from his fears and the heavy responsibility of the younger children. He also realizes that practical Stevie is his link to the real world and his salvation from mental illness, and he decides definitely to stay with Jenny and his brothers rather than to live with his father. The psychology/ fantasy is handled skillfully, so the reader has a choice of a realistic explanation or, less believably, of a fantasy "time bubble" in which Alan, who resembles a boy in a 1940 photograph on the inn wall, comes from a period before the inn was remodeled and part of the east wing was sealed off. Characterization is skillful, with Nels and Stevie both believable, compelling personalities, and the minor characters are plausible and interesting. Although the problem for Nels is created by the impending divorce of his parents, the book's theme is that hiding from one's problems is more dangerous than facing them. Poe Winner.

THE REAL THIEF (Steig*, William, ill. author, Farrar, 1973), brief fantasy set in an imaginary kingdom ruled by a bear named King Basil. Gawain, an honorable and handsome goose, is the guard for the royal treasury to which only he and the king have keys. When the pile of rubies looks smaller than usual,

Gawain reports it, and he and the king count and find a sizeable number missing. This loss is followed by others—gold pieces, silver ornaments, and finally the world-famous Kalikak diamond. The Prime Minister, Adrian the cat, points out that there is only one entrance to the treasury and that only Gawain, besides the king, has a key. Gawain is arrested, brought to trial, and convicted on circumstantial evidence. Before he can be taken to the dungeon, he flies through the window and across Lake Superb. All his former friends have turned against him except Derek, a mouse who is the real thief. Derek has found a tunnel under the floor of the treasury and a chink between two stones in the floor. Out of curiosity he has entered and, dazzled by the beauty of the rubies, taken a few to decorate his shabby room. As his decor improves, his desire grows, and he soon has a wall decorated with gold ducats, silver ornaments around the room, and, finally, the wonderful diamond on his table. When Gawain is arrested, he is worried but certain that no one will really think such a trustworthy character could be guilty. He attends the trial, determined to confess if Gawain is convicted. After Gawain flies away, thereby seeming to confirm his guilt, Derek is miserable until he thinks up a scheme; he continues to steal to prove that Gawain could not have been the thief. After a while, he realizes that he could also prove it by putting the jewels and coins back. This turn of events makes Basil repent of his haste in accusing Gawain. He sends out emissaries to try to find the goose, but Gawain, hiding in a cave whose entrance he has cleverly concealed, thinks they want to take him to prison. Finally Derek, guessing where Gawain is, finds him, confesses, and urges him to return. Gawain is made the Royal Architect, forgives his friends, and never tells who is the real thief. The slight story is told cleverly in serious, straight-faced language bordering on the pretentious. Gawain dreams of a new palace: "It would be oviform—that is, it would have the ideal shape of the egg." Derek's gradual slide into his life of crime is a classic description of the psychology of the embezzler or other white-collar criminal. Choice.

THE REFUGEE SUMMER (Fenton*, Edward, Delacorte, 1982), realistic novel set in 1922 in the Greek village of Kifissia, a place where well-to-do Athenians and foreigners have summer villas or stay for the season in resort hotels. Nikolas*, 12, lives year-round at the Villa Pandora, where his mother, Kyria Angeliki, a seamstress, is caretaker. To their surprise, the owners have rented the villa to Americans, an author named Avery, with his wife, his son, Oliver*, 14, and his niece, Edith* Griswold, 12. Oliver, a born leader, quickly organizes Nikolas into his gang with Edith and adds the two Arnauld girls, Nadine and Stephanie, about twelve and ten, who move into the neighboring villa with their mother, Vivienne, a singer of sorts, and their wealthy Greek "uncle," Panos (Pandelis), obviously her current lover. The children form a secret society, the Pallikars, complete with a special language, Desperanto, dedicated to doing secret noble deeds to help Greece and to oppose Turks and grown-ups. Each child chooses a secret name: Oliver and Nikolas spell their own names backwards to become Revilo and Salokin; Edith is Electra; Nadine is Melisande, and Stephanie is

Mitsouko. The Greek boys from Egypt who have an adjacent villa and whose arrival the others await eagerly turn out to be very snobbish and not suitable to be Pallikars. About the time the Averys arrive, Nikolas is asked to read aloud the diaries of Manolis Kondylis, a Greek soldier who died in Asia Minor and whose journals have been returned to his illiterate wife and mother. A self-educated man, Manolis has written compulsively and vividly of the miseries of the war, a great contrast to the patriotic fervor of most of the wealthy Greeks and foreigners. At first Nikolas keeps this activity from the other Pallikars, but when they discover what he is doing, Oliver declares that he has planted the first *seed*, Desperanto for a worthy deed. Some of their other attempts are less successful. At a fancy lawn party they meet a real Roumanian princess, a dumpy, middle-aged woman obviously down on her luck, but when they later call on her and try to leave some money in her purse, she accuses them of trying to steal and of mocking her, and they retire humiliated. Then the Greeks experience their terrible defeat at Smyrna, and refugees begin to arrive by ship. The Pallikars go to Piraeus and try to distribute bread to the starving Smyrnans, only to be chased off and sent home by the police. Back in Kifissia, they run into three refugee children hunting for their aunt who presumably lives in the village but whose name is so common that, since they have no address, they don't know how to look for her. Oliver decides that they must be hidden in the empty coach house of the Arnauld's villa, while their friend Yannis, the waiter at the coffee house, tries to find the aunt. Their installation in the coach house coincides with the concert Mme. Arnauld is giving as a benefit for refugees, thereby attracting all the society of Kifissia. Unfortunately, the concert is interrupted by the wife of a lieutenant that Mme. Arnauld has been seeing on the side and ends in confusion and scandal. Uncle Panos departs, and Stephanie and Nadine set off with their mother to a new "uncle" in Beirut. The three refugee children disappear from the coach house. Mr. Avery, becoming bored with Greece, decides to go to Rome and to send the children back to Boston to school. Nikolas, whose life has been changed by the summer, loses track of all of them. The novel has some of the quality of the E. Nesbit "Bastable" stories mixed with a nostalgic, and somewhat ironic, evocation of the early 1920s among the wealthy expatriots. All this is against a background of violent war and devastation for Greece, which scarcely touches the adults but is sensed in varying degrees by the youngsters. Strangely, the book starts in first person, though all the characters are described in third, so that it is not until a switch back to first person in the last few paragraphs that one is sure Nikolas is telling about the summer more than fifty years later. Although there is little plot, the characterizations are strong and many of the scenes, both tragic and funny, are memorable. Fanfare.

RESERVED FOR MARK ANTHONY CROWDER (Smith*, Alison, Dutton, 1978), realistic novel of family and school life set in a semi-rural area somewhere in the United States. Sixth-grader Mark Anthony Crowder wants appreciation and a place of his own. At school, the kids tease him about being so tall, his glasses, and his good grades. He is so awkward and clumsy at sports that they avoid choosing him for teams, and his father, a university coach, is ashamed of him. At home, he yearns for some place to put his Indian artifacts and shells where his snoopy little sister, Georgette, cannot get them. Only affable Earl Jones wants to chum with him, but when Earl persuades him to show his Indian stuff to two classmates, they refuse to believe that they are genuine and that Mark Anthony really found them. Only Uncle* Edward (really Mark Anthony's great-uncle) sympathizes and encourages Mark Anthony to think beyond the immediate, forget about pleasing others, and develop his own assets. After Uncle Edward nurses him through a bad spell of pneumonia, Mark Anthony and Earl head off to Eberhart woods to build a tree house which Mark Anthony hopes will become his special place. But an electrical storm sets it afire, and old Mr. Eberhart complains that the boys have trespassed and berates Mark Anthony's father for not keeping better track of him. Upset also by Mark Anthony's low grades, his father gives him the choice of spending the summer at sports camp or gardening. Mark Anthony chooses to garden, and, with help from Uncle Edward, he produces a garden that exceeds all expectations. His grades improve dramatically, and the summer passes quickly, as the two raise more than enough for the family to use and find a ready market for the surplus at Mr. Roccio's vegetable stand. In the fall, Mark Anthony decides to use the bean poles to build a tipi as a kind of hideout for himself. His father ridicules the project as a waste of time and money, and Mark Anthony lights out for Eberhart woods. Mr. Eberhart takes him in and effects a reconciliation. Uncle Edward has become friends with a young archaeology student who has had Mark Anthony's artifacts appraised. They are specially exhibited when they are found to be a valuable record of Indian life in that area. Mark Anthony's father and schoolmates think better of him, and Mark Anthony decides to use some of the money he has made from his garden to learn karate so that he will have the confidence and ability to defend himself. Except for Uncle Edward, characters are shallow types. Events are contrived and predictable, and, even though things are seen from Mark Anthony's point of view, he has altogether too many problems. The author devotes one-half of the novel to establishing Mark Anthony's situation. The last quarter of the novel is told in Mark Anthony's own words, an account in diary form that works well. It tells about his gardening experiences and shows how gardening changes his life and makes him feel better about himself. The descriptive passages are rich with sensory language, but dialogue is stiff and inept. The book reads like a thinly disguised handbook for adolescents and their parents in how to help young people achieve self-esteem. IRA.

RETTA ANDERSON (*The Night Swimmers**), Loretta Anderson, eldest child of country-western singer, Shorty* Anderson, and sister of Johnny* and Roy*. An overly earnest child, Retta took over without complaint running the household after her mother died. She does not express her feelings easily. In fact, she has never had anyone to confide in, since her mother and father were both very much involved with show business, and her father's main concern now is his career. Retta likes Brendelle, her father's girl friend, and at the end of the book appears ready, though not very convincingly, to let Brendelle take over. Retta was named after Loretta Lynn, country-western singer her parents admired.

REVEREND FARNLEE (*Emily Upham's Revenge**), suitor of Seth* Marple's mother, and, at novel's end, her new husband. He recognizes Seth's innate good character, believes his story about Mr. Upham and the money (that Mr. Upham had conspired with Emily's* father to rob Mr. Upham's bank and collect the insurance money), and agrees to help Seth prove his innocence (when Mr. Upham tries to pin the crime on Seth). He blackmails Mr. Upham into withdrawing charges against Seth by threatening to expose the conspiracy. Contrary to presentation early in the novel, he proves an unexpected and valuable ally to Seth.

REVEREND JAMES WALLIS (*One-Eyed Cat**), Ned Wallis's father, a Congregational minister. He is highly regarded by his parishioners, whose ladies lavish food and attention upon him and his family. They appear to feel sorry for him because his wife, Mrs.* Wallis, has been invalided by arthritis. He is a kind and gentle man, solicitous of his wife, for whom he cares very tenderly, and of his son, for whose feelings he shows an unusual awareness. He is so considerate that he even finds another position for Mrs.* Scallop, the housekeeper, instead of firing her. Not perfect, he can become irritable about small things, for example, the condition of the road and the roof, and his quick and stern command that Ned not use the Daisy air rifle leads to the story's central problem. He insists to Uncle* Hilary and to Ned, "What is there to imagine with a gun. . . . [except] Something dead." He is a good, decent man, a foil character to Mrs. Scallop, who self-righteously wears her goodness on her sleeve.

RHODA COOPER (*Three of a Kind**), foster mother of Sally* Gray and grandmother of the withdrawn four-year-old, Benjie. A sensible, competent woman, Rhoda has been fun and interested in Sally until Benjie comes to live with them, but then her concern for him and her fear of criticism from her son, Nathan, and his stylish wife, Laurel, makes her lose her good judgment so she smothers the child with too much attention. After she realizes her mistake, she is able to loosen her hold on him slightly and even control her elation at his first words enough to treat them casually and avoid scaring him back into his shell.

RHUN (*The Castle of Llyr**; *The High King**), good-hearted, gentle, feckless son of King Rhuddlum and Queen Teleria of Mona in the Prydain* books. His parents hope that he and Eilonwy* will marry. He often influences the plot, usually quite by accident. For example, he just happens onto Eilonwy's Golden* Peledryn, which enables the Companions to escape from Glew*, the giant. At first, Taran* finds Rhun a great hindrance but later comes to appreciate the prince's greatness of spirit and unfailing optimism. Rhun dies in the final great struggle against Arawn.

RIBSY (Cleary*†, Beverly, ill. Louis Darling, Morrow, 1964), dog story in the episodic Henry Huggins series, this one concerned with the adventures of Henry's pet when he is lost in their Oregon city. Ribsy has been left in the new car at a shopping center, with his collar off so that he can scratch a flea bite, and, jumping around to bark at a passing Pomeranian, has hit the button that automatically opens the window. In hunting for Henry in the crowded center, he gets lost, smells another new car, and jumps in. This belongs to the Dingley family, whose four little girls and toddler brother are delighted to take him home and give him a bubble bath. Ribsy escapes, smelling of violets, and tries to find his way home. Being a friendly dog, he meets people as he goes, the first being Mrs. Frawley, a lonely old woman who overfeeds and underexercises him and shows him off, dressed in a straw hat and rhinestone-studded collar, to her club. After he gets away from this indignity, he hangs around a schoolyard and is adopted as mascot of the second grade, a position he enjoys until one of the youngsters brings a pet squirrel to Show and Tell. The resulting chase and commotion causes Ribsy to be evicted from the school, but he finds a crowd of older boys at a football game and joins eagerly, tackling the ball carrier at a crucial point, saving the day for the home team and getting his picture in the paper. On impulse, a boy named Joe Saylor claims him and takes him home. Henry, who has been despondent with Ribsy gone, sees the picture, calls up, and, to persuade Joe that it really is his dog, calls to Ribsy over the phone. Recognizing Henry's voice, Ribsy dashes out to hunt for him again, becomes lost, and makes friends with Larry Biggerstaff, a lonely boy who lives in an apartment house. Larry takes him inside to get him something to eat but is almost apprehended by the bad-tempered manager. Larry hides Ribsy by shoving him out onto the fire escape. Terrified of the slippery metal slats, Ribsy can go up but not down, and it is there that Henry finally spots him. Getting him down poses some problems, but at last they are reunited. Much of the book is from Ribsy's point of view, but he is not anthropomorphized nor pictured as overly clever, just a friendly, odd-looking mongrel. Choice.

RICH, LOUISE DICKINSON (1903–   ), born in Huntington, Mass.; teacher, writer. A graduate of Bridgewater State Teacher's College, she became an English teacher. For some time she lived in a camp in the Maine wilderness, the setting for a number of her books, including *We Took to the Woods* (Lippincott, 1942). Most of her writing for young people has been non-fiction, including a number of the Watts "First Book" series—*First Book of New England* (1957), *of World Explorers* (1960), *of Early Settlers* (1960), *of Vikings* (1962), *of China Clippers* (1963), *of Fur Trade* (1965), *of Lumbering* (1967). Among her books of fiction is *Three of a Kind** (Watts, 1970), set on an island off the Maine coast, concerning the close relationship between a girl and the autistic grandson in the family where she is a foster child.

RICHARD, ADRIENNE (1921–   ), born in Evanston, Ill.; author of novels for later elementary readers and young adults. Her early years were spent in Arizona and Illinois. After graduating from the University of Chicago, she studied further at the University of Iowa and Boston College. She has traveled extensively in India, Kuwait, and Egypt, has been on archaeological digs in Israel, and is deeply interested in traditional societies. She and her husband, James Richard, a management consultant, have made their home in Massachusetts. Two of her novels are of special note: *Pistol** (Little, 1969) and *Wings** (Little, 1974). *Pistol* began as a short story about a cattle drive through a blizzard based on an experience of her husband. A novel of ranch life and the Depression in eastern Montana, it was a Fanfare book. *Wings*, about a little girl's relationships with her mother's Bohemian friends in southern California after World War I, was a finalist for the National Book Award. Both books convincingly blend strong characters, credible incidents, and a vivid picture of the periods with a sympathetic understanding of children. *The Accomplice* (Little, 1973), her second novel for early adolescents, concerns a boy on a dig in Israel with his archaeologist father who becomes involved in an Arab terrorist plot, while *Into the Road* (Little, 1976) tells of two brothers who go motorcycling. She has also written articles, short stories, travel sketches, reviews for magazines and newspapers, and the script for an educational film, "Leonardo da Vinci."

RICHIE GREATBEAR (*Pistol**), a part-Cheyenne youth with whom Billy Catlett is friends. They become blood brothers and call each other "Cat" and "Bear." While both are in high school, Richie decides to live as a white and gets a job as circulation manager for the local newspaper. When the Depression hits, he is fired so that the owner's nephew can have his job. Richie then returns to the reservation. He is a strongly drawn, unsentimentalized figure, whose situation gives some sense of the treatment of and attitudes toward Indians without sounding instructive or judgmental.

RIDE A NORTHBOUND HORSE (Wormser*, Richard, ill. Charles Geer, Morrow, 1964), realistic novel set in Texas in the mid–1870s. Driving his ox team near Alexandria, La., Alabama-born Cav (Cavalier) Rand, 13, is alone, his parents and younger brothers having died of swamp fever on their way to Texas. A rider who shares his fire, Bruce Cavanaugh, suggests that Cav look him up in Alexandria. Cav does, and sells the oxen and wagon to Big Cav and his partner, Jeff Kane, for a good price. They start off to pick up their cattle in San Antone for a drive to Kansas but persuade Cav to invest some of his money in schooling in Alexandria. For a while Cav tries it but soon runs off and buys a good horse, Belle, at an auction where he has to outbid Shawnee the Peddler, a man he has given a ride on his way to town. Shawnee buys Belle's stiff-legged sister, a horse that looks exactly like her until they start to move. A few days into Texas, where he plans to catch up to Big Cav and Kane, Cav is jailed by a sheriff who has a description of Belle as a stolen horse and one of the bound-out boy who took her which fits Cav, all sworn to by a Homer C. Davis. After Cav has been in jail a week, Davis shows up and turns out to be Shawnee. Cav and Belle are turned over to him, and they travel on, but at the first opportunity Cav escapes, not with Belle, whose lead rope Shawnee ties to his wrist when he sleeps, but on a heavy-footed grey, better than the stiff-legged mare but nothing like Belle. In a few weeks he comes up to the Grolier brothers' herd, a half a day behind Cavanaugh & Kane, and helps turn a C & K stampede in the night. When he sees Big Cav, he gets a job driving his oxen and helping the cook, Pursely. Because he figures he really is a horse thief now, Cav does not tell of his trouble with Shawnee until they hit the Llano River and find it so low that they know they will have a dry drive, or *jornado*, of ninety miles. Big Cav, who needs all his men for the drive, sends Cav ahead with the ox cart loaded with barrels of water, to leave at strategic points so the men can drink and sponge out their ponies' noses. Before he starts, Cav tells Big Cav the story of his arrest and theft. Then he begins the grueling drive to the Colorado River where they arrive staggering, the oxen blind from the heat and lack of water. After the herd comes up to them, they are almost drowned in a cloud burst. Cav catches sight of a man riding Belle and follows him on foot. While he is watching the man's camp, he sees Shawnee come in riding the stiff-legged mare and trade her for Belle. He has already heard how the men in the Grolier outfit have been tricked by a peddler who rode a seemingly arthritic mare, offered to race the best pony they had, took bets, and won when the horse suddenly changed character in the morning. Cav carefully takes the stiff horse, gets the night wrangler to trade it back for Belle from the horse herd, hides Belle, and in the morning walks in to see the race. Big Cav, who is in on the secret switch, sees that Shawnee pays up when the cowboy, Yonder, easily beats him and then points out that the grey is Shawnee's and Belle is Cav's. The clever sting operation is plausible, but the book's strength is in its description of the dry drive—the dust, the rocky ground broken only by patches of cactus, the stumbling exhausted oxen, the hallucinations and weakness toward the end—and in the relationship between Big Cav and the boy. Spur Winner.

THE RIDER AND HIS HORSE (Haugaard*, Erik Christian, ill. Leo Dillon and Diane Dillon, Houghton, 1968), historical novel set in the first century, about 73 A.D., in what is now Israel, dealing with the last days of the Massada. In Caesarea, the narrator, David* ben Joseph, 14, son of a rich wine merchant from Tyre, with his father visits the scholar, Joseph ben Matthias, head of the Jewish defense of Galilee who surrendered Jotapata and went over to the Roman side. On their return trip, their caravan is attacked by bandits led by the "King of Samaria," who takes David hostage for ransom his father is to bring. On the second day of traveling, the bandits are attacked by Roman cavalry, and David is left for dead along with his Syrian guard. Because of his distaste for Joseph ben Matthias, he walks not back toward Caesarea but toward Jerusalem, hoping to see again the temple which he does not believe could be destroyed. On the way he meets four boys, refugees from Jerusalem. The eldest, crazed by his experiences, throws stones at David, then runs off into the desert. The others, Samuel, emotionless Saul, and little Daniel, return with David to the devastated city, where he tries to find friends of his father. In the stable of their deserted house, they find an insane old man who gives Saul a knife with directions to murder a woman living nearby who has food. David follows Saul, prevents a killing, but forces the old couple to share their meat and bread. The next day he learns of Simon* ben Judas, a Levite, who is feeding homeless children, and, using his learning from the Torah and his ability at languages to gain Simon's confidence, persuades him to take in Samuel and Daniel. With Saul, he walks around the city, but Saul becomes fascinated by a rabble-rousing street orator, and David returns alone. That night a crowd of rioters tries to break down the gate to Simon ben Judas's courtyard, are run down by Roman soldiers, and the next morning David sees the street speaker dead among them. David spends all winter and most of the spring with Simon ben Judas, helping him and studying with him. He learns that Simon has contacts with the defenders of the Massada, the great fortress built by Herod near the Dead Sea, and is not surprised when a woman, Rachel*, comes, her own husband and children having been killed, and begs Simon to intercede with Eleazar* ben Ya'ir, Jewish commander of the Massada, to let her take her brother's children, who are there with their father. Eleazar, her cousin, sends word that none will leave the Massada. Shortly after, Rachel disappears. That same day, David sees Saul's body on a cross where he has been executed as a thief. He sets out after Rachel. The journey across the desert is difficult, but he comes at last to the springs of Ein-Gedi, a beautiful oasis kept by the fanatically religious Essenes. There he gets help and goes on the next day to the Massada, where he finds Rachel and becomes scribe to Eleazar. Rachel cares for the children, more devotedly than ever when their father is killed in a foray. At first, the Massada seems invincible, with supplies to stand a seige of years, but the Romans build a great ramp, using Jewish slave labor, on which they can bring up their battering ram. Eleazar reveals his plan to destroy the fortress and to have each man kill his family, then himself, so the Romans will get no slaves or trophies of value. Because he needs someone to tell the story of the brave end, he arranges that David shall hide in a cave, along with Rachel, the two children, a senile old woman, and two other young orphans. The defense and end of the Massada is told with a curious mixture of admiration and irony, not as a heroic action yet more admirable than the capitulation of Joseph ben Matthias, who became Flavius Josephus. Individual scenes are vivid. The characters, particularly David, Rachel, Simon, and Eleazar, are complex and interesting, but, perhaps because the ironic tone predominates, not wholly sympathetic. Overall, the sense is one of the disillusionment and futility of war and heroics and even, to some degree, of learning. Fanfare.

A RING OF ENDLESS LIGHT (L'Engle*, Madeleine, Farrar, 1980), realistic family novel and girl's growing-up story, set recently on Seven Bay Island somewhere on the New England coast. This sequel to *The Young Unicorns* in the series about the Austin family brings together two characters from other books by L'Engle, Zachary Gray (*The Moon by Night**) and Adam* Eddington (*The Arm of the Starfish**). The Austins are spending the summer in their grandfather's house near the ocean. To Vicky, almost sixteen, death seems everywhere: their dear friend, Commander Rodney, dies of a heart attack while rescuing the foolish, rich youth, Zachary Gray, from the water, Zachary's mother has been killed in an auto accident, the baby dolphin at the nearby marine Biology Station dies at birth, Dr. Nutteley of the Station has lost his wife and child in an auto accident, and, in particular, her grandfather has been slowly dying of leukemia and is not expected to live much longer. At the same time, Vicky recognizes that she is surrounded by affirmations of life: nesting swallows over the door of the house, the love and support of her family, and the attentions of three young men. Earnest, responsible Leo Rodney is looking for romance, seeking her warmth to assuage the grief of his father's death and her encouragement to continue his education at Columbia. Zachary sees her as an anchor against his wild and reckless ways and takes her flying and to fancy restaurants. Rebounding from an unfortunate romance with Kali* Cutter, Adam enlists her help in conducting his dolphin project at the Station. There are also the three dolphins, Basil, Norberta, and Njord, part of Adam's project, with which Vicky appears to have a special ability to communicate non-verbally. As the summer days pass, Vicky must balance her own need for love, security, and intellectual expression in poetic form against the needs of the boys and those of her family and particularly her grandfather. At the end, while Vicky is at the hospital awaiting word of her grandfather's condition, a little girl dies in her arms, and for a short time Vicky is unable to cope with the seemingly constant and senseless loss of life about her. After Adam takes her back to the beach and the three dolphins, she comes to realize that death as well as life is part of the "endless ring of light" (Henry Vaughn). The three boys are obvious foils, and Vicky writes poetry too easily to be convincing as a poet, but her adolescent problems are sympathetically and believably handled. L'Engle tries to do too much within the scope of the novel, which is underdone, moralistic, and didactic. Events often appear contrived, and there are problems with continuity. L'Engle's characteristically sure, deft style tempers the instructive tone. Newbery Honor.

RINKOFF, BARBARA (JEAN RICH)(1923–1975), born in New York City; social worker, writer. A graduate of New York University, she became a medical social worker and wrote some twenty-five books for children, both fiction and non-fiction. *Member of the Gang** (Crown, 1968) is based on cases she knew as a social worker in Harlem.

ROB AUSTIN (*Meet the Austins**; *The Moon by Night**), youngest child and younger son of the warm, close, happy Austin family. A clever, persevering boy, he does his best to join in family activities and often pops up with precocious, perceptive comments. His companion and guard is the Austins' Great Dane, Mr. Rochester. Rob has the calamitous adventures typical of the active, curious five- or six-year-old.

ROBBIE AND RUTHIE ROBBER (*The Runaway's Diary**), the middle-aged couple, hippies, who offer Cat Toven a ride in their Volkswagen bus that is painted brightly with various flower designs. A former professor of philosophy at Temple University turned skeptic, Robbie has gone on the road, he says, to take away from people only those things they do not want, such as unhappiness. Skinny, graying, he is an incongruous and repulsive figure. Extremely garrulous, he is far less astute than his wife, Ruthie, who realizes right away that Cat is a runaway. Robbie and Ruthie have in the back of their bus a sick youth, the nature of whose illness Cat never learns, but the reader suspects that the couple may be dealing in drugs and that the boy may have overdosed. Cat wonders from time to time how the boy is. Robbie is a stereotype; both are sham figures.

ROBERT LINNLY (*Encounter at Easton**), pale, dull appearing, poorly clothed boy of about eleven, indentured servant fleeing with Elizabeth Mawes from their cruel master, John Tolivar. Since they need money, Robert innocently accepts Nathaniel Hill's* offer of a job running errands, not realizing that he is hiring out to the man whom Tolivar has engaged to hunt for Elizabeth. Although he could have run off and left her and thus saved himself, Robert remains loyal to Elizabeth. He has a trusting nature and wants to believe that Hill is kind and good, and his mistaken estimation of the man leads to Hill finding Elizabeth. Robert's conscientious application to duty, however, attracts the attention of the local tapman, who buys the remainder of his time from Tolivar, and Robert remains in Easton. Robert tells most of the story.

ROBERTS, WILLO DAVIS (1928–   ), born in Grand Rapids, Mich.; paramedical worker, novelist. She attended Pontiac schools and worked in hospitals and doctors' offices. Her novels cover a wide range of types—Gothic, historical fiction, nurse stories, mysteries—and she has also written non-fiction, more for adults than for children. Her first book for young people, *The View from the Cherry Tree* (Atheneum, 1975), is a mystery of a child who sees a murder but cannot convince adults. *Don't Hurt Laurie* (Atheneum, 1977), a story of a young girl physically abused by her mother, won the Young Hoosier Award and other honors, including one from Australia. In a lighter vein, two books about a family propensity to precipitate exciting events, *The Minden Curse* (Atheneum, 1978) and *More Minden Curses** (Atheneum, 1980), are mysteries more humorous than spine-tingling.

ROBERTSON†, KEITH (CARLTON) (1914–   ), born in Dows, Iowa; freelance writer since 1947. He lived in Wisconsin, Minnesota, Oklahoma, Missouri, and Kansas as a boy, attended the U.S. Naval Academy at Annapolis, Md., and served in the navy from 1930 to 1945. For two years he worked for a publisher but started writing full time and has published more than twenty-five books for young people. A number of them star the youthful Carson St. Detectives, as in *Three Stuffed Owls†* (Viking, 1954). His most popular books have been his four episodic, humorous novels of Henry Reed: *Henry Reed, Inc.†* (Viking, 1958), *Henry Reed's Journey** (Viking, 1963), *Henry Reed's Baby-Sitting Service** (Viking, 1966), and *Henry Reed's Big Show** (Viking, 1970).

THE ROCK AND THE WILLOW (Lee*, Mildred, Lothrop, 1963), realistic novel set in Covington County, on Tired Creek in southern Alabama, in the 1930s. Depression and bad luck have embittered Clem* Singleton and made him a tyrant on his little, one-mule farm. Enie (Earline), 13, shares his red hair but feels no love for him since he has never shown any affection for her or his three sons, sullen T.H., 16, Henry Jim, about 14, or skinny little Leeroy, 5 or 6. Only Sue Ann, with her red curls and her baby ways, escapes his bullying. Her mother, Elnora*, is long-suffering but unable to avert his wrath that culminates in a beating to T.H. which makes the boy leave home. Enie, who longs for a world of books and learning, secretly envies T.H., especially when she spends the summer doing housework and caring for her new sister, Jenny, whom she almost has to deliver before the midwife arrives. Enie's teacher, Miss Cecily Pritchard, is impressed with her writing and encourages her. When Papa is nearly crushed by Sue Ann's sudden illness and death, Enie realizes that her hatred for him has changed to pity, but she is afraid to make any move to offer comfort. The summer before Enie's senior year, a stranger named C. D. Cullpepper—Seedy—shows up and talks Papa into letting him work for his keep. Seedy is a drifter, young and attractive, and even Papa has to admit that he is a good worker. Enie is attracted to him, happier when he admires her than she has ever been, but also confused and worried by his attentions. When they escape together to her secret place on the flat rock under the old willow by the stream and he wants to make love, she remembers coming upon the wealthy neighbor, Ralph* Shane, having intercourse with poor-white Bliss Atkins and the later scandal when Bliss became pregnant. She suddenly realizes that even if Seedy should marry her, she would be trapped in Tired Creek, and she breaks away. Hurt and angry, Seedy leaves and moves out of their lives. After months of painful memories, Enie recovers and is pleased to learn that she will be valedictorian of her class. Papa, however, squelches her desire to go to college, though Mamma encourages her to keep trying. Her slim hopes are shattered by a series of family disasters: Papa falls from the loft and breaks a leg, and at graduation time Mamma, who has been poorly for months, becomes seriously ill. The day after Enie gives her speech as valedictorian, her mother dies. Enie takes over the housework and tries to be mother to the younger children. To save Leeroy, who is delicate, she also works in the fields. Ralph Shane comes to join them, and with his help they get the beans picked on time, though Papa bitterly resents help from the Shanes and is suspicious that his motives might involve Enie. It is Papa who starts courting, however, with much encouragement from Miss* Elsie Mae Howells, who takes to dropping in, bringing food and presents for the children and suggesting that she could give piano lessons to Leeroy, who shows musical talent. Enie resents her interference, even the attractive skirt and blouse she makes Enie for Christmas. When Papa decides to marry Miss Elsie Mae, Enie tries to talk Henry Jim into staying and running their farm with her, but he is excited about the bigger Howells acreage and not interested in her proposal. Miss Elsie Mae, though silly and strident on the surface, turns out to be understanding and sensible underneath, and she makes Papa see he can sell a piece of his land to Tom Shane, who has long coveted it, so that Enie can go to college. The day after her father remarries, Enie leaves on the bus for the nearest teachers' college. The book covers about five years of Enie's adolescence, and although this makes a tight dramatic structure impossible, it allows time to show her growth and change. Each of the characters is individualized and believable, and the depression-era southern setting is strongly evoked. Enie's emotions are well depicted, and her struggles are realistic. This is a moving novel which escapes sentimentality and sensationalism. Child Study; Choice; Fanfare.

ROCK STAR (Collier*, James Lincoln, Four Winds, 1970), contemporary problem novel set first in the small city of Hammerton somewhere in the midwestern United States and then in Manhattan. Tim Anderson, about sixteen, lead guitarist of the Silver Sunshine rock group, wants to become a professional musician. This ambition brings him into sharp conflict with his father, Mr.* Anderson, who insists he go to college, and, since Tim is failing math, forbids him to continue playing. When Wolf Records, a New York outfit, announces a national contest, Tim is certain that Silver Sunshine can win. His good friend, Charlie, urges him to ignore his father's orders and stay with the group, while Susan, Charlie's sister and Tim's sometime date, makes the more positive suggestion that he tell his father outright how he feels about music. Respectful and affectionate of his father, Tim can bring himself to do neither, but on the sly, following, he realizes, the letter but not the spirit of his father's command, he trains Sammy O'Neil to sub for him. When Sammy falls ill on the big night, Tim fills in, and the group takes first place. Tim's father then angrily asserts he will do everything he can to keep Tim from continuing in music. Tim concludes that the only way he can have the future he wants is to travel to New York and seek help from Harry Jurgen*, the executive from Wolf who complimented him on his playing. While hitchhiking, he falls in with a hippie group, among whom is a folksinger, Helen McCord, also on her way to Jurgen, and an unpleasant man called Crazy who forces Tim to shoplift and sells his guitar and clothes. Tim flees the group, arrives in New York almost penniless, and eventually gets an interview with

Jurgen, who, he discovers, played hard to get in order to test Tim's persistence and courage. Jurgen gives him the position of rhythm guitar with the Sound System, with whom Tim has some ticklish moments. In New York's East Village, he again runs afoul of Crazy, and Helen McCord, who is performing there, summons police who call Mr. Anderson. Harry Jurgen mediates between the two, advising Tim's father to be less rigid, and father and son return home friends. Tim is still determined to become a musician, but harrowing experiences have taught him that he has much yet to learn about music, and he decides to enter a conservatory when he graduates from high school. Tim tells his story honestly and perceptively, and he and his father both change believably. Other characters are types, but the story is well plotted to sustain the interest, if contrived to illustrate the value of education and possible dangers of running away to the big city. The conflict between father and son is handled tastefully, unsensationally, and sympathetically toward both. Child Study.

ROCKWOOD, JOYCE (1947–   ), born in Ames, Iowa; author of novels for children and young adults primarily about American Indians. She has spent most of her life in Georgia. After receiving her B.A. from the University of Georgia, where she studied anthropology, she did further work at the University of Wisconsin. She is married to Charles Hudson, a professor of anthropology, and they have made their home in Danielsville, Ga. She relies on her extensive knowledge of anthropology and history to create the illusion of reality among the Indians before their lives were changed by the coming of the whites. Her first novel for young readers, *Long Man's Song* (Holt, 1975), about a long ago Cherokee youth who proves himself as a medicine man, won critical acclaim. Her second, *To Spoil the Sun** (Holt, 1976), about how initial contact between the whites and the Cherokees in the Southeast resulted in a decimating smallpox plague as related by a Cherokee woman who lived through it, received the award of the International Reading Association. *Groundhog's Horse* (Holt, 1978) tells for younger readers the adventures of a small Cherokee boy, but *Enoch's Place* (Holt, 1978) strikes off in another direction, being the story of a youth whose family belongs to a hippie community in the Blue Ridge Mountains. Rockwood has also written for journals and magazines.

RODGERS, MARY (1931–   ), born in New York City; composer, lyric writer, and author best known in children's literature for her comic fantasies for later elementary and young adolescent readers, *Freaky Friday** (Harper, 1972), about what happens when Annabel Andrews wakes up in her mother's body, and *A Billion for Boris** (Harper, 1974), its sequel. Both books won the Christopher Award and are listed in *Choice*. Characters are zany and idiosyncratic, and events rush by at a riotous pace, raucously combining realism and fantasy for pleasingly preposterous if ephemeral entertainment. The daughter of composer Richard Rodgers, she attended Wellesley, has been script writer for and assistant producer of New York Philharmonic's Young People's Concerts and script writer for the Hunter College Little Orchestra Society, and with her mother, Dorothy Rodgers, has written a monthly column, "Of Two Minds," for *McCall's* and a book, *A Word to the Wives* (Knopf, 1970). She has composed musical scores for several Broadway shows and written children's musicals, among them, *Young Mark Twain*, *Davy Jones' Locker*, and *Pinnochio. Summer Switch* (Harper, 1982), sequel to her first two novels, tells how a boy quite literally finds himself in his father's shoes, while *The Rotten Book* (Harper, 1969) is a picture book for much younger readers. She and her husband, Henry Guettel, a film executive, and their five children live in New York City.

ROD GRAHAM (*A Dog on Barkham Street**), classmate and closest friend of Edward Frost. He also yearns for a dog, but his parents, like Edward's, consider him too irresponsible to have one. He and Edward often have conversations in which they discuss the injustices of life. The two boys have good times playing with Argess and listening to Uncle Josh's stories. Both boys idolize Uncle Josh, who to them epitomizes the good life, which is a life without responsibilities. Although Rod considers being an uncle a great distinction, he resents having to give up his room when his sister and her two children, one a new baby, move in with his family. Disgruntled with his situation, Rod joins Edward in playing hookey from school.

ROGER NICHOLAS (*Poor Tom's Ghost*), thirteen-year-old protagonist, a tense, apprehensive boy, who has learned to cover his protective love for his actor father and his desire for a settled life with a studied nonchalance. He is a cello player, a sensitive boy, old for his years, and he genuinely loves his new stepmother, Jo, and her daughter, Pippa*, a fact which adds to his confusion when he becomes involved with the "ghost" of the Elizabethan Jack Garland, who wants to destroy the marriage of Jack's actor brother, Tom*, whose personality has been merging with that of Roger's father, Tony*.

ROKE (*A Wizard of Earthsea**; *The Tombs of Atuan**; *The Farthest Shore**), Isle of the Wise of Earthsea*, where the great school of Wizardry or art of magic is taught and to which boys who show promise in sorcery are sent to become novices in the long training of wizards. The nine mages of the school are held in reverence throughout the islands. On Roke are the town of Thwil; the school itself, known as the Great House of Roke; the Isolate Tower, some thirty miles away, where the Master Namer teaches; the Immanent Grove, where the council meets, and Roke Knoll, the hill that stood first above the sea at creation and on which Ged* summons the spirit of Elfarren. Although not one of the largest islands of the archipelago, Roke, protected by strong spells of magic and the repository of ancient lore, is the most important.

ROLF (*Orphans of the Wind**), cook of the *Four Winds*. Rolf is kind to Jim and also is philosophically against slavery. He tells the boy of a voyage of his youth aboard a slaver, of the terrible conditions that killed more than half the cargo, and of the eyes of a young black girl when they took her dead baby from her, an expression that has haunted him since. After the ship blows up, it is the efforts of Rolf and Keith, the topforeman, which get their little boat to shore and get the party eventually to the Union army.

ROLL OF THUNDER, HEAR MY CRY (Taylor*, Mildred D., Dial, 1976), realistic novel about problems encountered by a rural black family in Mississippi during the Depression year of 1933–1934. Cassie, 9, second eldest child in the close-knit Logan family, the only black landowners in a community of sharecroppers, overhears conversations and has experiences that awaken her to the realities of life for blacks in the deep South. She describes how the year brings many indignities, some serious and troubling, some fairly small and ephemeral but still puzzling and hurtful. She and her brothers, Stacey*, 12, Christopher-John, 7, and Little* Man, 6, must walk to school while white children ride the bus, whose driver takes a perverse pleasure in drenching them with dust or mud. They must use schoolbooks the whites no longer regard as suitable and endure derogatory remarks and snubs. The children are secure in the love of Mama, a schoolteacher, Papa, who works on the railroad to pay the taxes and the mortgage, and Big* Mama, their grandmother, whose husband arduously acquired the land on which they all live. Times are hard, and feeling against blacks rises. After night riders throw kerosene over and set fire to the men in the Berry family, burning them badly, Papa brings strong, wise old Mr. Morrison to protect the family while he is away. The Wallaces, whites who own the community store at which the Logans' sharecropping neighbors trade, gouge customers and encourage black youth in improper behavior in their gaming hall. After Mama, with the help of fair-minded Mr. Jamison, a white lawyer, organizes her neighbors in boycotting the store, she loses her teaching position. Night riders attack Papa while he and Stacey are returning from Vicksburg with supplies, and Papa suffers a broken leg. Then matters get even more tense when Harlan Granger, the white plantation owner who covets their land, persuades the bank to call in their mortgage. Uncle Hammer, who works in Chicago, sells his big, silver Packard to pay off the debt. The novel concludes with a near-lynching, after attention-seeking T. J. Avery takes up with some white youths who use him to rob a store and then abandon him to a charge of murder. Papa thinks fast and sets fire to the cotton, diverting the mob from their purpose, and for the space of one night blacks and whites work side by side to save the crops. Fine characterizations and rich details of family and community life keep the story from becoming a book about Prejudice. Cassie is a spunky, resilient girl, whose attitude is sometimes perplexed or angry but never self-pitying or hateful. The stories the adults tell about family and black history, if a trifle didactic, add texture and build credibility. Although many events are stock, this novel of spiritual and physical survival has several memorable scenes, among them the badly burned Mr. Berry on his deathbed, Little Man rejecting the cast-off schoolbook, and Cassie getting sweet revenge on snooty Lillian Simms. There is some humor, and the story never becomes sentimental or melodramatic. Sequel is *Let the Circle Be Unbroken*. Books Too Good; Boston Globe Honor; Contemporary Classics; Fanfare; National Book Finalist; Newbery Winner.

ROMEY LUTHER (*Where the Lilies Bloom**; *Trial Valley**), Mary* Call Luther's younger brother. He is a great help and comfort to her in her struggles to hold the family together. He helps her bury Roy Luther, in one of the book's most vivid and memorable scenes, and does much of the wildcrafting. As time passes he, like the other two children, tires of the hard work, yearns for more leisure and some fun, and complains and talks back to Mary Call.

A ROOM MADE OF WINDOWS (Cameron*, Eleanor, ill. Trina Schart Hyman, Little, 1971), realistic novel of family life, sequel to *Julia and the Hand of God**, set in Berkeley, Calif., in the 1920s, in which the main reading interest lies in revelation of character. The room of Julia Redfern, 12, at the head of the stairs of her family's small apartment, is tiny, just big enough for her desk, chair, and campbed, and so open and light that her brother, Greg*, 14, says it is "positively made of windows." In this haven, Julia, an aspiring writer, fashions her short stories, dreams her dreams, and records her observations about the people around her of whose individual lives, hopes, and needs she grows gradually and often acutely aware. Daddy Chandler, an old man of eighty-four, who encourages her to write, works diligently on a history of San Francisco he will probably never finish. Her closest friend, Addie Kellerman, remains cheerful and fun-loving in spite of a domineering grandmother and drunken father, trying to make the best of a home situation that has become intolerable for her brother, Kenny, who takes refuge in deceit and lies. Reclusive Mrs. Moore, a former concert pianist, introduces Julia to the world of classical music and takes her to a concert featuring her son, a famous pianist. Julia's brother has a consuming passion for Egyptology, and her widowed mother, Celia, struggles to support her family by working in a bookstore. No single plot question unifies the scenes in which the author describes Julia's day-to-day interactions with those around her, but some suspense arises from her opposition to her mother's plans to remarry, an antipathy that diminishes as Julia gradually comes to see her mother as a person in her own right. The end finds Julia writing good-by to her room in her journal. With her family, she looks forward to a new life with her stepfather, Uncle Phil, in his house in the hills overlooking Berkeley. Julia's candor and naivete are probably more amusing for adults than for children, and her journal entries are too detailed to be convincing as such, but she is an intelligent, perceptive, highly literate child with a gift for words. Julia's interactions with those around her are described in richly conceived scenes, remarkably accurate in details of conversation, action, emotion, and setting. The author uses language with much grace and makes Julia and her friends believably real. Addams; Boston Globe Winner; Choice; Fanfare.

ROOSEVELT GRADY (Shotwell*, Louisa R., ill. Peter Burchard*, World, 1963), realistic novel of family life set in the southeastern United States about 1960 and concerning migrant workers whom the illustrations depict as black. Roosevelt Grady yearns for a permanent address. In his nine years, he has attended thirteen schools as his family has moved around following the crops. Roosevelt, his cheerful, hardworking father, Henry, and his practical, patient mother, Addie, and his younger brother and two sisters, dainty, dimpled Sister, 7, lame Matthew, 5, and Princess Anne, the baby, are very close and happy, in spite of their poverty and crowded living conditions. They are part of the crew of Cap Jackson, a preacher, who, unlike many crew leaders, treats his people fairly and is concerned about their welfare. Mama and Roosevelt share a Secret. They hope that some day they will find just the right house for their family and that Papa will get a permanent job so they can live in it. This particular summer, they stay for a while at Quinby's Quarters, where the entire attic is theirs to live in, there is a real front porch for the workers to sit on and relax at night, and Roosevelt encounters Manowar*, a big, strong orphan his age who is handyboy for slippery Digger Burton, who smooth-talks workers into his crew. At first, Roosevelt does not like Manowar, whose friendly personality and exciting stories make a hit with the children and rouse Roosevelt to jealousy, but, later, he and Manowar become fast friends. At Willowbrook, the children go to a special school just for migrants, and Roosevelt and Manowar play ball after school. Roosevelt shares his Secret with Manowar, who recalls seeing a pleasant place called Elliott's Camp not far away. There the migrants live in buses that have been remodeled into houses. Roosevelt is excited, because this camp seems exactly like what he and Mama have been wishing for. In an unexpected stroke of good fortune, Cap decides to take the crew there to pick pears. Then Mr. Grady gets a job at a nearby fertilizer factory, and the family, which now includes Manowar who has run away from Digger, decide to settle there. Roosevelt attributes their good fortune to the Providence Papa believes directs life. Characters are types, incidents are stock, and the conclusion is too pat to be convincing. The book seems intended to teach middle grade readers about the hard lives of migrant workers, particularly the children, but Roosevelt himself is a winning and memorable figure. Choice; Fanfare; Lewis Carroll.

ROSE (*Grover**), kindly, capable old woman who keeps the Ezell house after Grover's* mother dies. She is steady, reliable, and very patient, and her commonsense attention to the details of everyday living provides stability for the boy during a turbulent period in his life. She is illiterate, and Grover offers to teach her to read.

ROSE JACKSON (*The Genie of Sutton Place**), the young woman who is Aunt* Lucy's live-in maid, housekeeper, and cook. She works for Aunt Lucy to pay for vocal lessons. She tries to keep Sam*, the dog, from upsetting Aunt Lucy, generally befriends Timmy, and tries to keep him apprised of what Aunt Lucy and Lawyer Watkins have in mind. She discovers that Dooley* has an exceptional singing voice, and they often vocalize together. At the end, she and Dooley plan to wed.

ROWAN ELLIOTT (*The Whispered Horse**), red-haired Scottish ten-year-old, protagonist whose mother is killed by her sister's husband. Rowan has a deep love for her home, for her flock of sheep and their fine white ram, Hughie, and particularly for Bannet, the shaggy, grey pony her father trades for but which Rowan thinks of as her own. Although she hates her brother-in-law, Tam* McPhee, with good reason, she tries to keep her father from getting Bannet to kill him, partly because she realizes that Kinley* will not live happily as a murderer and partly because she fears that Bannet will be destroyed if he's considered a killer horse.

ROWLANDS, JOHN (*The Grey King**), steady, capable, kindly Welsh shepherd, friend of Bran* Davies, who helps Will* Stanton achieve his objective of awakening the Six Sleepers. When the Dark rises, he chooses to give up his wife, Blodwen, whom he dearly loves, so that Bran can assist the Light.

ROXANNE ARMSTRONG (*The Leaving**), Iowa farm girl who tries her wings in the city and returns to the land. Sturdy, heavy in hips and ankles, Roxanne resembles her mother, Thora*, in appearance and in her love for the farm, for the animals, and for the land. She has been a regular guard on the girls' basketball team, but not a star; she has been an adequate student, but not brilliant; in Des Moines she gets a low-grade filing job but learns to do it competently. Realistically, she resents the way her father, Cletus*, has turned the farm chores over to her and what she perceives as her mother's indifference. She fears the big city, she desires love, and she feels triumph at having performed well at her job and found a boy friend, but her clear-sighted, practical nature tells her that she will be happier doing the grueling farm work than being a suburban housewife.

ROY ANDERSON (*The Night Swimmers**), the younger of Retta's* two brothers, the one whose actions put an end to the night swimming and to the children's very independent way of life. He is an engaging, imaginative little fellow, who still likes to be cuddled and protected but who is beginning to strike out on his own. He was named after Roy Acuff, country-western singer his parents admired.

ROY OATES (*The Mystery Cottage in Left Field**), bully who is fascinated with gangster stories. Charming when he wants to be, Roy hangs around the garage owned by Jimmy Loughlin's father and helps with mechanics and wins the approval that Mr. Loughlin denies his own son. Roy also charms Mrs.* Giordano, then turns on her, treating her with contempt and stealing money from her. When he is actually recruited by the gangster, Early Winters, he is not wholeheartedly in support and wavers when Jimmy threatens to tell his father, who will obviously not let Roy work in the garage again. Given the opportunity and Jimmy's lead, Roy turns against Winters and courageously tackles a gangster who is holding a gun on them.

RUFUS PURDY (*The Dunderhead War**), loud-mouthed bully who asserts that he will never be so foolish as to serve his country in the Missouri Volunteers during the Mexican War, then suddenly enlists, arousing suspicions about his motives. Quincy* Heffendorf surprises him robbing the Heffendorf store on the night of the send-off party Independence holds for the Volunteers. Rufus gets away, and no one believes Quincy's story. Later Rufus's treachery is proved, and he eventually becomes an Indian bounty hunter for the Mexicans. The subplot concerning his relationship with Quincy and the Mexicans seems melodramatic, extraneous, and contrived to hold the interest of young readers.

RUNAWAY RALPH (Cleary*†, Beverly, ill. Louis Darling, Morrow, 1970), fantasy set in the Sierra Nevada foothills in the mid twentieth century, sequel to *The Mouse and the Motorcycle**. Having discovered speed and freedom with the miniature motorcycle left him by a boy visitor to the run-down hotel which has been his home, Ralph, a mouse of a large family, is more impatient than ever with exhortations of his pompous Uncle Lester, the worries of his over-cautious mother, and the demands of his many mouse siblings and cousins. After one particularly frustrating night, he decides to run away to the summer camp whose bugle he has heard morning and evening and which he envisions as a delightful source of peanut-butter-and-jelly sandwiches. Just as he arrives at the entrance, however, he meets Sam, the watchdog of Happy Acres Camp. Though basically friendly, Sam feels duty-bound to prevent anyone who doesn't belong from entering. Ralph dives down a gopher hole, is trapped between Sam, trying to dig him out on one side, and an unwelcoming gopher on the other. When Sam leaves for dinner, Ralph gets away, only to be caught by Catso, the wicked tomcat, who plays with him for the instruction of a family of kittens. Thinking himself a sure goner, Ralph is astonished when one of the campers, an unhappy boy named Garf (Garfield), scoops him up in a butterfly net. Established in a cage in the window of the craft shop, Ralph is fed and has an exercise wheel and a good view of camp life, but he is worried about his motorcycle and about Catso, who is able to enter the craft shop through a hole in the screen door. Also, he doesn't dare talk to Garf because he has heard the boy singing a horrid song about banging mice on the head. Soon a hamster named Chum is installed in an adjoining cage. Garf insists on feeding his "personal mouse" himself, and Ralph is just beginning to trust him enough to try to talk to him when Catso takes a watch left by one of the girls on the window ledge and dumps it in the bamboo clump which also hides Ralph's motorcycle. Suspicion of watch theft falls on Garf, and he stays away from the craft shop and stops feeding Ralph. Chum occasionally flicks an alfalfa pellet over to him, but Ralph is getting so desperate that when Garf finally comes, he speaks up and tries to make a deal with him. Garf won't believe him then, but when Catso comes and bats the cage off the shelf so it opens and Ralph gets away, Garf is upset to have lost his mouse and is more ready to listen to him when Ralph approaches him again. They make a deal: if Ralph can return the watch so that Garf will be cleared of suspicion, the boy will give back the motorcycle, which he has found, and carry Ralph back to the Mountain View Inn in his pocket. With some help from Sam, Ralph manages to hide the watch in the girl's sleeping bag, so it looks as if she lost it there, and in the end is happily reunited with his motorcycle. Ralph is a mouse with a spirited personality and his adventures are humorous in a light but satisfying story. Choice.

THE RUNAWAY'S DIARY (Harris*, Marilyn, Four Winds, 1971), realistic problem novel set in Pennsylvania, New York, and in Canada in June, July, and August of 1970. After her parents separate, unhappy, resourceful, intelligent Cat (Catherine Anne) Toven, almost sixteen, of Harrisburg, Pa., runs away from home with forty-two dollars and seventy-five cents, some peanut butter, a small tent, a worn copy of Thoreau, and her diary. As she travels, she records her day-to-day impressions of the people she meets and the places she visits and her reflections on life. She says she and Mike, a black, German shepherd-like pup she finds along the way and adopts, are looking for a green place with a stream where they can be alone and at peace. She tells about the kind, elderly, church-going couple who accept at face value her story about needing to hitchhike to visit her sick grandmother and give her five dollars to help her on her way, and about Robbie* and Ruthie Robber, the middle-aged hippies who transport her to Watertown in their flower-painted Volkswagen bus, then by truck to Alexandra Bay, and from there by boat to Ontario. She tells how in Montreal she stays for a while with Theresa*, the old French-Canadian woman who sells flowers and vegetables in the market. She tells of sleeping on a Dairy Queen bench, behind billboards, in the front seat of the Volkswagen while the Robbers make love in the back, and in Theresa's homey trailer that she comes to love almost as much as she does Theresa. She describes how she carefully conserves her meager resources of food and money, reads her Thoreau, ponders Emily Dickinson, scrounges for bones for Mike, and reflects on her life with her dissatisfied mother and about Bennett*, a grocer with whom she has had many philosophical discussions and from whom she has gotten ideas about how to run away successfully. East of Quebec City, she buys two grocery bags of food in the store of an old French-Canadian, Mr. Gebel, and then hikes into the mountains, where she sets up a small camp by a stream and lives peacefully for several days. She augments her small supply of food by painting for Mr. Gebel. After a terrible rainstorm, she becomes seriously ill with a cold and is nursed back to health by a mysterious man, who, she later learns, has escaped from a mental hospital. After working briefly for Mr. Gebel, who is injured when his store is robbed, Cat plans to return home. She has decided that life can be beautiful, if one makes it that way. Her diary stops at that point, and, in an afterword, the author reports that Cat died after being struck by a car along a Canadian highway between Montreal and Toronto and was buried in Harrisburg. Cat's account is detailed and interesting, but her voice gets monotonous, she changes predictably, she spends far too much time writing for belief, and many events and characters seem phony and dated. The book attempts to capitalize on topical concerns of the time. Particularly hard to accept is the sequence about the mysterious man and Cat's illness. Cat's factual style at the beginning, however, and the brief introduction and conclusion, in which in newspaper reporting style the author tells how she acquired the diary and about Cat's ironic death, tone down the melodrama and sensationalism. Lewis Carroll.

RUN, WESTY, RUN (Alcock*, Gudrun, ill. W. T. Mars, Lothrop, 1966), realistic story of an eleven-year-old Chicago boy set in the 1960s. Westy (Robert Weston) has run away so many times that the truant officer is scheduled to call, and he has been locked in his room so that he cannot escape again. The windowless room in the apartment behind his mother's beauty parlor causes a claustrophobic need to escape. When his mother lets him out so that he can work for Mr. Post, the grocer next door, Westy takes the twenty dollars Mr. Post has given him to get change and runs again, planning to take a train he has seen in a poster, the Mountain Express, and travel west to a place where he can live in the woods. He first gets his red hair cut short, goes to a "farm in the city" for children in a park, and misses the train. He sleeps in some bushes in the park near the beach and the next morning encounters an old man who takes him fishing and introduces him to Jane Fredericks, "Lady Jane," who feeds the birds and plans to share their breakfast of fish. Before they can eat, a freak wave, a *seiche*, comes, drowns Frank, and almost drowns Westy, who has run back to warn him. Lady Jane pretends he is her grandson, takes him to her hotel where she gets him a hot bath, dry clothes, and breakfast, but when the house detective arrives, Westy escapes down the fire escape and is arrested. He is taken to Ogden Detention Home, where he at first refuses to talk but finally breaks down and tells all his frustrations to his caseworker, Jonathan Healy—his horror of his room, which he shares with two younger brothers, his frustrations at having to work so he can't take part in school sports, at having to give all his earnings to his father, at having to be quiet all day so his father, who works at night, can sleep. His mother visits him briefly, but his father refuses to come. In court the kindly judge elicits an explanation from Westy's father of why he keeps driving himself and his family to save money, because he had to go on relief when the meatpacking plants left Chicago. The judge points out to him that Westy has some needs, too, and Westy is put on probation and ordered to repay the unsympathetic Mr. Post. Being clever with his hands, Westy first builds and tries to sell bird houses, with little success, so he swallows his pride and returns to Mr. Post's store to work. At home he finds that his father has traded bedrooms with the children so Westy can have a window. Written to illustrate a thesis, the book has some of the interest of a case history, but as a novel the characterization is wooden, the situations, except for the *seiche*, predictable, and the solution simplistic. Choice.

RUTH PLATT (*Journey to America**), Lisa's older sister. Ruth is growing up in turbulent and dangerous times. Her attempts to be independent and help out sometimes threaten the family's safety. She hides some money in the lining of her violin case, even though she knows that, if the Nazi border guards discover it, they will not let her family out of the country. What she does worries Lisa a great deal. Fortunately, in one of the book's tensest scenes, the guard confiscates Ruth's violin but never examines the case. Ruth speaks up to Frau Strom, the director of the refugee camp, who steals the money the relief agency sends for food and supplies and uses it to buy clothes for herself. Ruth also tries to pawn the ring her father gave her, but the broker refuses to take it because he thinks it is too valuable for a child to pawn without parental permission. Ruth is a round character, more believable than Lisa, who seems often to be merely the author's eyes and mouthpiece and never really emerges as a person in her own right.

S

SABURO (*The Master Puppeteer**), bandit in twelfth-century Osaka who, like Robin Hood, steals from the rich merchants and gives to the starving poor. He is cheered by the populace for his caring and cleverness in defying authority, as well as for his generosity. After it becomes apparent to Jiro* that Saburo has some connection with the Hanaza puppet theater, he suspects that Saburo's true identity is the bad-tempered puppeteer, Yoshida, but he discovers in a terrifying confrontation that it is really the kindly seeming, old, blind chanter, Okada, who describes the others of his band, Yoshida included, as puppets and himself as the Master Puppeteer.

SACHS, MARILYN (STICKLE) (1927–   ), born in New York City; author of popular novels about contemporary urban children in family and neighborhood situations. She grew up in the Bronx and wrote for school papers and magazines. She graduated from Hunter College and took her degree in library science at Columbia University. Before writing books, she was a children's librarian for the Brooklyn Public Library. She married Morris Sachs, a sculptor, and in 1961 they and their two children moved to San Francisco where she was for four years a part-time children's librarian in the San Francisco Public Library. Since the publication of her first book, *Amy Moves In* (Doubleday, 1964), she has written a dozen books for later elementary readers, mostly amusing, lively stories of everyday life and problems with a contemporary tone which show her growing maturity as a writer. She draws her ideas for her books from memories of her own city childhood in a family of modest means. Several books feature Veronica Ganz, neighborhood bully introduced in *Amy and Laura* (Doubleday, 1966) and more fully revealed in *Veronica Ganz** (Doubleday, 1968), a novel listed both in *Children's Books Too Good to Miss* and *Choice*. Two other novels continue Veronica's story, *Peter and Veronica* (Doubleday, 1969) and *The Truth about Mary Rose* (Doubleday, 1973), which sees Veronica a mother and stars her daughter. *The Bears' House** (Doubleday, 1971), about a family whose mother is mentally ill, was a finalist for the National Book Award and a *Choice* selection. Also in *Choice* is *A Pocket Full of Seeds** (Doubleday, 1973), which departs from her usual form, being a historical novel about the experiences of a Jewish family in France during World War II. Her recent novels include *A December Tale* (Doubleday, 1976), about an abused foster child, *Hello. . . . Wrong Number* (Dutton, 1981), in which a wrong number leads to a relationship between teenagers, *Call Me Ruth* (Doubleday, 1982), a historical novel about Russian immigrants and labor unions at the turn of the century, and *Fourteen* (Dutton, 1983), about a fourteen-year-old girl's problems with her artistic family and the new boy next door.

SAGER CHILDREN (*Cayuse Courage**), the seven Sager orphans to whom Marcus Whitman* and his wife give a home. Because of them, Samuel is forced to leave the Whitman house and return to the tribe. Samuel and Francis Sager become friends, however, and Francis often visits the Cayuse camp and even picks up enough Cayuse to understand what the Indians are saying without much difficulty. Joe Lewis* takes an especial dislike to the boy and shoots him in the head during the uprising. The other children are slain, too. The Sagers were actual historical figures.

SAILING TO CYTHERA (Willard*, Nancy, ill. David McPhail, Harcourt, 1974), fantasy in three episodes, all of which start in the real world of a very young American boy, the first two in his own yard, the third (the title story), on a visit to his grandparents. In the first, Anatole goes off with his cat, Plumpet, to the christening party of Plumpet's Aunt Pitterpat, who is entering her ninth life. They travel on the Gospel Train full of animal passengers, find Aunt Pitterpat on the merry-go-round, and eat with her, but when they reboard the train, the last on which they can ever return to the mainland, they learn from the goat conductor that the engineer, a fox, has drunk too much blackberry juice and has not come back. Anatole drives the train home. In the second, Anatole finds a soldier sitting on the garbage pail, a blond young man who has been robbed of his name, address, and destination. On a war medal in his pocket, he finds his name, Erik Hanson. In Anatole's book, *So You Want to Be a Magician*, they find a spell for The Quickest Way of Going to Anywhere, try it using the destination, "Erik's Home," and travel running through the clouds and across the sea to the Norwegian village of Sellebak, but Erik can remember only leaving and returning and none of the thirty years in between. Anatole sets out to the house of the Sun to get the thirty years back and gets for Erik not the years but the memories. The third is the most complex in the real world. Anatole's grandmother loses things, cares for her aging and confused husband, and tells Anatole stories about the pastoral scene in the wallpaper. When Jon, the man who helps with Grandpa (who is twenty years older than Grandma and has forgotten how to walk), sings Anatole to sleep one night, the boy slips into the wallpaper scene and finds himself on a trip to the island of Cythera. Since he cannot remember his name, he says he is Frere Jacques. He and Therese, one of the wallpaper shepherdesses, pass the bridge at Avignon, where there is dancing and a fair, and take ship for Cythera, though warned that a monster called the Blimlim raises storms near the island and wrecks boats. Many of the things Grandma has lost turn up on Cythera. Anatole gets to the garden of the golden bough and finds the Blimlim, who offers him tea. The golden bough is like a tree of heaven, surrounded by flowers of precious stones. The Blimlim confesses that he is lonely and would like to find a quiet, dark place on the mainland. Anatole offers him the dark space under his bed, which has always frightened him, and flies home sitting on the Blimlim's head. Grandpa, later, remarks, "I saw Anatole this morning in the wallpaper," and Grandma says, "Of all the nonsense I ever heard," and kisses his ear. All three episodes move in a dream-like pattern with bits of the actual world, quotations, and literary references moving in and out of the story. Anatole is a trusting little boy, wide-eyed and unafraid. The tone is reminiscent of *Alice in Wonderland* but gentler, a mixture of the fanciful and the misperceptions of early childhood. The stories are charming to read but too amorphous to be easily memorable. Lewis Carroll.

SAKNIS (*The Sign of the Beaver**), grandfather of Attean*, Matt* Hollowell's benefactor. He is a strong, dignified man, generous and shrewd, the respected leader of the local band of Penobscot Indians. Foresighted, he believes that it is important for Attean to learn English so that he will be able to deal with the whites on their terms. He is a strongly drawn, interesting, and credible figure.

SALAI, ANDREA (*The Second Mrs. Giaconda**), historical figure, whose real name was Gian Giacomo de'Caprotti, servant of the artist Leonardo da Vinci. He serves da Vinci during the years that Ludovico*, Duke of Milan, is da Vinci's patron. At the beginning of the story, Salai is a handsome, blonde, curly-headed, roguish, ten-year-old pickpocket, son of a bootmaker. Uninhibited and irrepressible, Salai becomes a favorite with his master, interjecting levity and laughter into the life of the serious, self-absorbed genius. Lazy, deceitful, self-seeking, Salai is nevertheless strongly loyal to da Vinci and is particularly attached to plain, witty, vivacious Beatrice*, Ludovico's young wife. She advises the youth that he can best serve his master by helping da Vinci keep "something wild, something irresponsible in his work," and Salai always heeds her words. Although Salai never completely loses his mischievous manner, he does become more responsible as time passes. He is thoroughly dedicated to his master, but he still appropriates for his own purposes da Vinci's scribblings and rough sketches. He picks up extra money by selling them and also audiences with da Vinci, much of which he contributes to support his father and sister. His relationship with Beatrice leads to da Vinci's painting the "Mona Lisa." Salai is a round, dynamic, consistently interesting character.

SALLY BRACKEN (*Ox Under Pressure**), alcoholic friend of Ox* Olmstead's parents, who organizes the expedition of Ox and his father, Barry, to the New York area to rescue one of her ex-husbands about to be accused of embezzling.

At first Sally is shown as far gone in liquor and the Palm Beach lifestyle, even coming close to propositioning seventeen-year-old Ox, but when they get to New York she stops drinking heavily, shows herself efficient and perceptive, and is an active support to Ox, even joining him when he invades the Revere mansion to find out what has happened to Arabella* and being arrested with him. She lives with Ox and Barry on Long Island, but it is not clear whether she is having an affair with Barry. She is more intelligent than Barry and, ultimately, more humane, but back in Palm Beach she is certain to revert to her old habits.

SALLY GRAY (*Three of a Kind**), 11, red-haired orphan, ward of the state, who is foster child of Rhoda* and Ben Cooper. An independent child, Sally has learned to adjust to new situations and to be honest with herself, but she has not allowed herself to love until she becomes involved with Benjie, 4, the Coopers' withdrawn grandson. Since she has always considered herself unattractive (except for her hair) and unwanted, she identifies with Benjie and with the homely, tailless kitten, Ree-ject, as "three-of-a-kind," no bargains, who will have to stick together to make out all right.

SAM (*Fast Sam, Cool Clyde, and Stuff**), quick-talking, fast-running, constantly moving black kid in the 116th St. group who, along with Clyde*, allows Stuff*, the younger narrator, to join their urban adventures. Apparently supremely confident, Sam actually is crazy about Gloria* and suffers from her rebuffs and follows Clyde's lead in most serious situations.

SAM (*The Genie of Sutton Place**), basset-springer dog which, at story's beginning, is Timmy Farr's pet. Dooley* changes Sam into a man to save his life after Aunt Lucy's lawyer, Mr. Watkins, takes him to the dog pound. Sam the man's doglike looks and manner provide some of the story's comedy. Timmy must stay on his toes to cover for Sam, since Aunt Lucy is unaware that Dooley has changed Sam the dog into Sam the man. Although she dislikes Sam the dog, she is ironically much attracted to Sam the man and, to the consternation of all in the know, often visits him at his pet store. When Dooley chooses to become mortal, Sam is assured of continuing as a man, since part of the magic is that Dooley's works remain permanent.

SAM BEAVER (*The Trumpet of the Swan**), nature-loving, eleven-year-old schoolboy who, while on a camping trip with his father in southwestern Canada, observes the hatching of a brood of rare trumpeter swans, one of whom, Louis*, is mute. Sam takes Louis to school with him, where the swan learns to read and write, and later, after Louis has learned to play his trumpet, helps him get jobs so that he can pay for the instrument which his father, the old Cob*, has stolen. Sam keeps a diary in which he records his experiences with Louis and asks interesting, philosophical questions about nature. Because of Louis's friendship with the keeper of the Philadelphia Zoo, Sam decides that he will make zoo work his vocation. He is a convincing and interesting character.

SAM MEEKER (*My Brother Sam Is Dead**), Timmy's older brother and the Sam of the book's title. He enlists in the Continental Army in opposition to the wishes of his father, Eliphalet*, and, at the end of the story, is executed by the Rebel forces as a thief. Quick-tongued, impulsive, he idealistically expresses the Colonial views. As the war wears on, he sees hard service with Washington, among others, but, when his mother (Susannah*) urges him to come home since his enlistment is up and she needs him to help run the tavern, he refuses. Timmy ruefully observes that Sam chooses to continue in the army for the wrong reasons. His motive for re-enlisting is the desire for glory rather than conviction for the cause or sense of duty.

SAMUEL DAN (*Behind the Magic Line**), black hobo who makes friends with Dozie Western and joins the family trek west. A former stage magician, he easily convinces Dozie that the gifts he produces for her family are obtained by magic and that there is power in the magic line he draws around his shack with his obeah bag to keep evil out. Because he feels sorry for the child, he helps out the family, even taking a job as butler for an aging actress, fooling her by acting the old family retainer.

SANDOZ†, MARI (SUSETTE) (MARI MACUMBER)(1901–1966), teacher, editor, lecturer, regional novelist, historian and biographer, noted in children's literature for her books of fiction and non-fiction about Indians for children and young people. She was born in Sheridan County, Nebr., the eldest of the six children of a hard-bitten Swiss immigrant for whose biography for adults, *Old Jules* (Atlantic, 1935), her first book, she received the *Atlantic Monthly* fiction prize of $5,000. She grew up in the Sand Hills cattle country of northwest Nebraska, early working as a hand about the ranch. Beginning when she was nine, she attended rural school for four and a half years. She took the examination for a teacher's certificate and taught country school for five years, while attending the University of Nebraska. The college refused her a degree because she had never been to high school but later awarded her an honorary doctor of letters. She was a proofreader and researcher for the Nebraska State Historical Society, associate editor of *The School Executive* in Lincoln, proofreader for the Lincoln *Star* and *Nebraska State Journal*, and associate editor of *Nebraska History* magazine. She was staff leader for writers' conferences and director of courses in writing, and lectured, taught, and wrote for over thirty years until her death, receiving many awards and honors for her work. She published over a dozen and a half critically acclaimed books of fiction and non-fiction and a collection of short stories, and was a frequent contributor to magazines. For young people she wrote novels about Indian youths seeking to identify their roles in their societies that are rapidly changing because of the inroads of the whites. *The*

Horsecatcher† (Westminster, 1951), set among the Cheyenne, was a Newbery honor book and a Fanfare book. *The Story Catcher** (Westminster, 1963), winner of the Spur Award of Western Writers of America, tells of a Sioux youth who has a special talent for scouting and also catching in words the scenes important in the life of the tribe and who becomes tribal storyteller and historian. She also wrote for young readers *Winter Thunder* (Westminster, 1954), a short novel recently reissued along with some of her short stories in an edition for young adults, *The Battle of the Little Bighorn* (Lippincott, 1966), and *These Were the Sioux* (Hastings, 1961), a book of non-fiction. She was noted for her crisp style, her careful attention to detail, and her authentic portrayals of the Old West.

SANDRA GRAHAM (*Berries Goodman**), 11, daughter of the people who live next door to the Goodmans. The Grahams are rigid, judgmental, and very prejudiced against Jews. Sandra is bossy, pushy, loud-mouthed, and as self-righteous and over-assured as are her parents. She parrots their anti-Jewish remarks. As a character she is the author's overly obvious way of showing how prejudice is perpetuated. Sandra changes abruptly after the accident, when her mother tries to cover up for what Sandra did to Sidney* Fine, and becomes more friendly and less domineering.

SANDY MCSOUTHERS (*The Westing Game**), Alexander McSouthers, doorman at Sunset Towers, really Sam Westing in disguise. Westing's other identities are Barney Northrup and Julian Eastman.

SAPHIR (*A Donkey for the King**), kind and discerning Israelite slave of Marcus Tullius, the Roman governor of Egypt at the time of Jesus' birth. She notes Jesse's ability on the shepherd's pipes and asks him to play for her charge, little Tullia, 7, the governor's ill daughter. Saphir's remark to Jesse on the road to Ashkelon, that he could earn money by playing his pipes, encourages him to try once more to make a good life for himself.

SARAH'S MOUNTAIN (*M. C. Higgins, the Great**), mountain in southern Ohio, three miles from the Ohio River, whose top has been cut off by strip mining for coal, leaving a spoil pile that threatens the home of the Higgins family below. It has been named for M.C.'s* great-grandmother, a slave who escaped carrying her child and settled there.

SATURDAY, THE TWELFTH OF OCTOBER (Mazer*, Norma Fox, Delacorte, 1975), time fantasy novel, framed by a realistic story set in the late 1900s and focusing on the only daughter of a middle-class family living in an apartment complex in an unspecified American city. Intelligent, imaginative, sensitive Zan (Alexandra) Ford, 14, is generally dissatisfied with her life. She is bothered by her inability to communicate with her family, tense because of their crowded living conditions, upset at having been mugged, and worried about herself because she has not yet menstruated. On Saturday, October 12, she discovers her brother, Ivan, reading her diary to two of his friends. Furious, she runs to a nearby park where she flings herself down by an ancient boulder. A terrible storm comes up, envelopes her, and deposits her in another time dimension. On a meadow covered with exotic vegetation, she is found by Burrum*, a girl her own age, and Burrum's boy cousin, Sonte*, who call her Meezzan (from Me, Zan) and take her home to the People, the tribe of pre-historic, Stone Age cave dwellers to which they belong. At first, Zan is terrified of these strange beings with their curious eyes and prying fingers and resists their proffers of friendship and food, retreating into a kind of stupor until she is shocked by Diwera, the Wai Wai, or Medicine Woman, into realizing that her survival depends upon adjusting to her surroundings. She never loses her desire to return to her own dimension, but she gradually adapts to the People's ways and even learns their language. For almost one year, she shares the existence of these peaceful, family-oriented tribespeople, living in the cave with Burrum's large, extended family, who treat her like a daughter and for whom she develops affection and respect. Burrum, who also awaits her first period, becomes her special friend and protector. Diwera thinks Zan has special powers and fears that she will bring trouble to the tribe. She blames the girl for various calamities, chief of which is the death of Lishum, Burrum's little brother, and tries to drown her. Finally, Diwera's son, Hiffaru*, steals Zan's jackknife, which the People think is magic, and fatally wounds Sonte, the first murder ever among the People. In the ensuing pandemonium, Zan flees to the meadow and shortly wakes to find herself back in the city park on the ground by the boulder. She returns home to discover that it is still October 12. No one believes her story about the People, and, when she becomes tense and despondent about it, she is sent to a psychiatrist. Eventually, she simply refrains from discussing her experiences further. She has her first period and is pleased when her mother hugs her and congratulates her about it. She is now more at peace with herself and her surroundings. Zan's otherworld journey is never satisfactorily explained or integrated with her real life story. The ways, customs, and beliefs of the People, such as the birthing and burial practices and the Sussuru, the coming of age ceremony held for Burrum after she first menstruates, their stories, their recreation, their food gathering, and everyday life in the cave, are described in clear, vivid detail. The picture the author draws of the People steals the interest from Zan and her plight in the fantasy, and, compared to the story of the People, Zan's real-life story lacks originality and reads like just another account of an adolescent with growing-up pains. Both plots are unevenly sustained, and characterization is weak, but the author handles language with skill. (Akawa*) Lewis Carroll.

SAUL (*A Donkey for the King**), limber, energetic, young gymnast with Nabal's* circus, whose ambition is to perform in Rome. He strikes up a casual friendship with Jesse, the mute shepherd boy, and for a time is Jesse's only means of communication. An opportunist with few scruples, Saul has no compunctions about stealing, and Jesse soon follows his example, resorting to light thievery thereafter, in spite of his fear of crucifixion if caught.

SAUL KATZ (*Adam Bookout**), breezy Jewish boy, friend of Adam. Self-confident and outgoing, he is the first schoolmate with whom Adam makes friends. A blonde, curly-headed fellow with glasses, he is infatuated with dinosaurs and suggests that they use dinosaurs' names as passwords. He suggests and leads the H. R. T. F., the Honey Recovery Task Force, to get back Willie's dog.

SAVE QUEEN OF SHEBA (Moeri*, Louise, Dutton, 1981), historical novel set in the mid nineteenth century in what is now Nebraska. King David, 12, wakes after a Sioux attack on their wagon train to find himself half scalped, seven wagons scattered and burning, and bodies lying in awkward positions nearby. He realizes that several wagons, his father's among them, must have gotten away, and though dizzy and in pain, he carefully checks each body, finding only the wagon master showing any sign of life, and that quickly fades. Then he discovers his little sister, Queen of Sheba, alive and unhurt, under a feather mattress where she was hidden by the woman with whom she had been riding. King David gathers up the pitifully few stores not taken or spoiled by the Indians—a little corn meal, a few apples, matches, a quilt, a couple of canteens containing a little water, and then discovers that under the body of the wagon master is his rifle, with a few bullets and caps. He also finds a pair of shoes, those belonging to Margaret Ann Beecham, whom Queen of Sheba has disliked, and he forces his sister to wear them. With these meager supplies, the two children start out, though King David is so weak and sick that they can go only a short distance. Queen of Sheba, spoiled and willful, is a burden he can hardly cope with. They camp near the creek and find one of the wagon horses, Maggie, caught by her harness among the willows. Realizing that his head wound is getting infected, King David slashes off the flap of scalp and bathes the wound in the stream, but he is so weak and feverish that he can't move on for a full day. Following Queen of Sheba, who keeps wandering off, he sees a rabbit and shoots it, so they start off with at least one meal inside them. For about seven days they struggle on with great difficulty. During a terrific rainstorm, they shelter in a cave, and King David has trouble finding the trail again. With that on his mind, he fails to notice that Queen of Sheba is not following him. He retraces his trail, can't find her, and is almost relieved to turn and go on without her. Then he remembers that she is always attracted to water, turns back again, and finds a draw with a couple of small pools of water. As it gets dark, he walks down the draw a bit and stumbles on Queen of Sheba's shoes. The next morning he finds her at the same moment an Indian woman finds her, and as she clearly threatens to kill the child rather than give her up, King David points the rifle at the Indian's child. The Indian woman does not flinch at his bluff, but when he lowers the rifle, she releases Queen of Sheba, grabs her own child, and scrambles off. Later, almost starving as they plod on, King David shoots a rabbit and scares Maggie, who bolts, knocking off Queen of Sheba, then whinnies at approaching horses. It is some men from the wagon train, including Pa, returning to search for survivors. Exciting and well conceived, the book covers a single episode with essentially two characters. Further development might have made it a more fully satisfying story. Queen of Sheba's fussing and lack of cooperation makes her an unattractive character, but that and King David's ambivalence about her keep the story from being the usual children-survive-in-the-wilderness tale. There is no particular thematic purpose in their unusual names. Fanfare.

SCHAEFER, JACK WARNER (1907–   ), born in Cleveland, Ohio; editor, writer of western novels and stories. He is a graduate of Oberlin College and studied further at Columbia University. In the 1930s and 1940s he worked for the United Press and in an editorial capacity for newspapers in New Haven, Baltimore, and Norfolk. From 1949 on he has been a free-lance writer, living in the Southwest and using that area as setting for most of his fiction. Among his works for adults his novel, *Shane* (Houghton, 1949), was widely popular and became a movie and television series. For young people his sensitive story of the relationship between an elderly sheepherder and a young boy, *Old Ramon** (Houghton, 1960), was a Newbery honor book.

SCHERF, MARGARET (LOUISE) (1908–1979), born in Fairmont, W.Va.; author of mysteries for adults and children. She grew up in New Jersey, Wyoming, and Montana, attended Antioch College, worked as a secretary, copywriter, and reader for publishers in New York City, and later made her home in Kalispell, Mont. She traveled to Europe, where she taught English to French children, the Far East, and India, married Perry Beebe, and served a term in the Montana House of Representatives. After 1940 she was a full-time writer, publishing over two dozen books, mainly for adults. *The Mystery of the Velvet Box** (Watts, 1963), a detective novel set in New York City in which the children solve the mystery, was nominated for the Edgar Allan Poe Award. Her other juvenile titles are *The Mystery of the Shaky Staircase* (Watts, 1965) and *The Mystery of the Empty Trunk* (Watts, 1966).

SCOTT, ERIC, author of *Down the Rivers, Westward Ho!** (Meredith, 1967), historical novel based on the expedition of Col. John Donelson, who in 1779 and 1780 led two hundred pioneers on a river voyage from Virginia to Tennessee. It was the winner of the Western Heritage Award.

SEA CAPTAIN FROM SALEM (Wibberley*†, Leonard, Farrar, 1961), historical novel set in 1777–1778, third in the Treegate series about the American Revolution. The story features no member of the Treegate family, instead focusing on the valiant achievements of their good friend, Peace* of God Manly, in naval maneuvers off Great Britain. His work there is instrumental in bringing about the alliance between the French and the Americans that determines American victory in the conflict. The novel begins with a meeting between Peace of God and Benjamin Franklin in Paris, during which Franklin persuades the intrepid American sailor, now captain of the brig *Hornet*, to harry British ships in the channel between Britain and France. Franklin aims to strengthen the cause of the Americans at the court of the French king by demonstrating American sea might and by stirring up hostilities between the British and French. The former Salem fisherman soon proves a capable and inventive commander. After stocking the *Hornet* with arms and food, he slips out of Le Havre in a fog. He cleverly and daringly maneuvers two British frigates into firing upon each other, an episode that arouses considerable furor in the British House of Lords. In still another example of masterly seamanship, he lightens his load and thus evades the British frigate *Cerberus*, whose commander thinks he has the American bottled up in a Dutch port. Within three weeks' time, Peace of God has sunk or hauled away as war prizes into French ports so many tons of British shipping that insurance rates on British ships skyrocket. Then a British spy, who has learned that Peace of God has a special affection for common fishermen, approaches Lloyds of London with a scheme for capturing the American and they agree to finance his plan. In the channel between England and Ireland, Peace of God attempts to intercept four ships from West Indies bound for England. He sights a fishing boat that is apparently in distress but is actually a British gunboat in disguise. The *Hornet* is sunk, but Peace of God and two crewmen are rescued by Irish fishermen, led by Michael Reagan, a bold, British-hating rogue, who agrees to take them over to France. On the way, they capture a British schooner and arrive just in time to convince the French Count of Vercennes that the Americans are brave, tenacious, and thoroughly dedicated to the cause of freedom. The result is the alliance between France and the colonies that eventually results in independence for the Americans, just what Franklin had hoped to accomplish. Historical figures, among them also the Earl of Sandwich and Lord North, are credible and interesting, if flat, and the reader learns the American, British, and French points of view from conversation and exegesis. But plot and history are not well knit, although the author attempts to avoid sounding instructive by drawing lively and graphic action scenes that are made realistic by such details as the use of period nautical language. Peace of God dominates the book, but he is overdrawn, and his success is credible only if one can accept the premise that a Salem fisherman can within a few short months become extremely skilled at handling and commanding a good-sized gunboat. The master gunner, Simmons, who drinks too much and who, we later learn, has while under the influence given the spy the tip he needs to bring Peace of God low, and Michael Reagan are interesting minor figures. Others in the series include *John Treegate's Musket†*, *Peter Treegate's War**, and *Treegate's Raiders**. Choice.

THE SEANCE (Nixon*, Joan Lowery, Harcourt, 1980), contemporary novel of mystery and suspense. Plain, orphaned Lauren, 17, lives with her practical, outspoken, respected Aunt Melvamay in a small East Texas town near a swamp called the Big Thicket. Lauren dislikes pretty, boy-crazy Sara Martin, also seventeen, a ward of the court who has recently come to live with them. Lauren worries about the late-night jaunts Sara takes behind Aunt Mel's back and is reluctant to have anything to do with a séance that Sara insists she take part in. During the séance, Sara mysteriously disappears, and the next day her dead body is found in Big Thicket, murdered by drowning. Shortly thereafter, the body of Roberta Campion, the Cajun girl who conducted the séance, is discovered under similar conditions, and Lauren soon begins to fear for her own life. Suspicion falls upon the men Sara had been seen with or was thought to be interested in, including Lauren's middle-aged, next-door neighbor, Fant Lester, deputy Jep Jackson, and even the sheriff himself, Ashe Norvell. Red herrings and other such conventions of the genre as withheld information, a re-enactment of the séance, a visit to the swamp, night prowlers, and threatening phone calls keep the pot boiling and lead suspensefully and relentlessly to the tense climax, in which Ila Hughes, embittered, superstitious grandmother of Carley Hughes, town star athlete and top student, is apprehended as she attempts to kill Lauren. Ila readily and righteously admits she killed Sara, with whom she had discovered Carley was planning to elope, because she was afraid the girl would ruin Carley's future, and that she also killed Roberta, because she thought Roberta was Sara's confederate. Better than average for the genre, the story combines a well-paced plot, well-drawn if stock characters, some sense of small-town life, and literate writing. Poe Winner.

THE SEARCH FOR DELICIOUS (Babbitt*, Natalie, ill. author, Farrar, 1969), fantasy set in an imaginary small kingdom in a period roughly comparable to the Middle Ages. In the beginning of things, Ardis, a mermaid, is keeper of a house of stone built by dwarfs over the spring at the bottom of the lake, but her special whistle, which opens and closes the door, has been taken by a man, and her doll has been locked in the house. Now, generations later, when most people no longer believe in mermaids or dwarfs, the Prime Minister, working on his dictionary, is stuck for a definition for "delicious," since the King disapproves of his original "Delicious is fried fish," proposing instead "apples." The Queen wants "Christmas pudding," and the General, "a mug of beer." The Prime Minister's Special Assistant, Gaylen (Vaungaylen), 12, an orphan adopted by the Prime Minister, is sent out to the four towns of the kingdom to poll the populace. He meets a variety of characters including Medley, the mayor's daughter in the first town, who insists that Gaylen hear the story of the woldweller, whom she says she has seen. He later meets the woldweller himself, an ancient who descends from his tree to talk, Canto, a minstrel who sings a song of Ardis weeping and gives him a strange key for good luck, and Mrs. Copse, a kindly old woman whose crow talks of Ardis. Everywhere Gaylen goes people fight over what is most delicious, and everywhere the Queen's brother, Hemlock, has been ahead of him, stirring up trouble. Gaylen gets help from the dwarfs when his horse, Marrow, loses a shoe, and he meets the personified winds. When he despairs of completing his poll, he retreats to the mountains where he discovers Hemlock damming up the outlet to Ardis's lake, planning to gain control of the kingdom by shutting off the water supply. Gaylen gives Ardis the key so that she can regain her doll, in exchange for which she promises to weaken Hemlock's dam. At the critical moment, as the King and the Prime Minister arrive to confront the angry populace, the dam breaks, and they all agree that "delicious is a drink of cool water when you're very, very thirsty." Perhaps because the central idea of the quest for "delicious" is a bit too cute, it is hard to take the adventure seriously, and the moral statement of how wars start over trivialities is far from subtle. However, it is a pleasant story attractively illustrated. Choice; Fanfare.

SEBESTYEN, OUIDA (1923–   ), born in Vernon, Tex., in a family with roots in the South. She attended the University of Colorado but stopped to work in an airplane plant during World War II. More recently she has lived in Boulder, Colo. *Words by Heart** (Atlantic/Little, 1979), about a black family in Texas, won the International Reading Association Award and has been filmed for television. She is also the author of *Far from Home* (Atlantic/Little, 1980), a story of a boy's gradual discovery of the secrets in his past and of his real father, and *IOU's* (Atlantic/Little, 1982), a novel of a boy's coming of age and his strong relationship with his independent mother.

THE SECOND MRS. GIACONDA (Konigsburg*, E. L., Atheneum, 1975), biographical novel about Leonardo da Vinci set in Italy in the 1490s as told from the viewpoint but not in the words of his apprentice, young Andrea Salai*. Chosen by the master because of his golden-haired good looks, free spirit, and daring, the ten-year-old pickpocket, son of a Milanese bootmaker, adds balance and levity to the life of the serious, self-conscious, dedicated genius. Salai serves da Vinci while the master has as his patron Ludovico*, the powerful, wealthy, hedonistic Duke of Milan, called Il Moro. Among da Vinci's many projects during this period are a huge horse and "The Lord's Supper." Ludovico's vivacious, witty, sixteen-year-old bride, Beatrice*, becomes a favorite of both master and apprentice, but she steadfastly refuses to allow da Vinci to paint her portrait. Once despised for her plainness, Beatrice wins the hearts of courtiers and her philandering husband with the help of da Vinci and Salai. After the birth of his longed-for heir, Ludovico sends Beatrice as ambassador to Venice, and she soon manages to perfection the three roles of wife, mother, and diplomat. After she dies at twenty-two, while giving birth to her third child, all Milan mourns their lighthearted, life-loving, capable young duchess. When the French invade soon after, Ludovico flees into Germany, leaving da Vinci to return to his native Florence. On the way there, the master and Salai visit Mantua, where Beatrice's imperious, haughty, and acquisitive older sister, Isabella*, attempts unsuccessfully to add da Vinci to her retinue and persuade him to paint her portrait. In Florence, without his master's knowledge, Salai accepts a commission for da Vinci to paint the second wife of an obscure Florentine merchant, Mr.

Giaconda, who one day appears at the master's studio. Salai, whose mischief the years have not eliminated, although he has grown more responsible, shrewdly observes that this plain young woman with her intriguing, inscrutable smile, Madonna Lisa, is excellent portrait material. Like Beatrice, she is "beautiful in a deep and hidden way." Hers will be the portrait of Beatrice that da Vinci wanted to do but never achieved. The painting of Madonna Lisa Giaconda becomes da Vinci's masterpiece, the "Mona Lisa." Although the story of the "Mona Lisa" seems tacked on instead of the focal point of the action, this account of da Vinci's work, associates, and period is very compelling. In spare, understated, slightly formal language and excellent characterizations, Konigsburg has created a memorable view of an abstracted genius at work amid the proud, willful, often shallow nobles of Milan and Florence. Fanfare.

THE SECRET LANGUAGE (Nordstrom*, Ursula, ill. Mary Chalmers, Harper, 1960), school novel for younger girls set at the Coburn Home School in the northeastern United States in the mid twentieth century. Arriving as a new girl, Victoria North, 8, has a severe case of homesickness exacerbated by her snippy roommate, Ann Speare, and their martinet housemother, Miss Mossman. It begins to diminish when she makes friends with rebellious Martha Sherman, 9, who hates the school and has a secret language she shares with Victoria, words like *ick-en-spick* for anything silly or sentimental and *leebossa* for anything especially great or fine. When Ann leaves, Martha and Victoria become roommates, go to the Halloween party as ice cream cones, and turn a gift of tiny dolls into Ralmadil School inside a bureau drawer, a school where children are treated as they wish they were. After Christmas Miss Mossman is replaced by Miss Caroline Denton, who asks the girls to call her "Mother Carrie," an idea they think is ick-en-spick. She does various things to win them over, including allowing them to have the first double-decker beds and to build a hut in the woods, putting a quarter under Victoria's pillow when she loses a tooth, and giving them a locked box in which to bury their treasures. She is even understanding and doesn't punish them when the ice cream of their forbidden late night feast melts on the rug after they fall asleep trying to wait for midnight. A longed-for visit from Victoria's mother turns out disappointing because she fails to understand things and doesn't like Martha. By the end of the school year, both girls are calling their housemother Mother Carrie, and Martha, who has insisted she will not come back, is reluctantly admitting that if her parents force her to return, it will not be too bad. Martha, supposedly a free spirit, exhibits her rebellion mostly by singing a derogatory song and whispering after lights out, and Victoria is embarrassingly good for a child in modern fiction. Although the problems of a homesick child could be genuinely touching, the treatment, with trivial difficulties and tame situations, is so geared to the little girl reader that only a limited audience could find the story interesting. So little mention is made of the boys that one easily forgets that the school is co-educational. Choice; Fanfare.

SECRET OF THE HAUNTED CRAGS (Hunt*, Lawrence J., Funk, 1965), mystery novel set in southern Alaska in the early 1960s. Young King Stewart, returning to his home on Crystal Bay from his junior year in college, is full of plans to get a corporation job when he graduates and get his parents away from the hard work and poor living of the salmon-boat men, who are dependent on the prices set by the local absentee-owned cannery. On the last leg of his trip by mailboat, he meets a tenderfoot college boy, Roger Harrington, who is hoping for a job and adventure in an Alaskan summer. The boat runs into a storm and just before it pulls into a temporary harbor near the dangerous Haunted Crags, they hear a faint distress signal saying, "I'm going aground. . . . " When he reaches Crystal Bay and finds his father, Red, missing on the *Barbara Lee VI*, King realizes that the distress signal was from Red, and he recruits old Salty Gustafson, who lives aboard the *Sea Queen* with his granddaughter, Anne, to take him and Roger on a night search. With difficulty, they maneuver the *Sea Queen* in behind the Seven Ghosts, pillars of rock in the sea off the Haunted Crags, and send Blackie, Red's Labrador retriever, into shore with a message in a syrup bottle attached to his collar. Blackie brings back an answer telling them to send a helicopter the next day, but King, fearing his father cannot last the night, takes supplies and Blackie in the skiff in to shore, where Red waits with a broken leg near the grounded *Barbara Lee*. After his father is flown to the hospital, the Coast Guard pulls the *Barbara Lee* off. Several problems have developed in the Crystal Bay fishing community: the fish-buying barge usually anchored south of the Haunted Crags is missing (Red was hunting this when he went aground); the new cannery operator, Bear Hodge, has upped prices in the company store; he is also giving the fishermen short weight for their fish and has somehow rigged the cannery's books to show such poor profits that it must soon be closed. In a fog, Hodge's boat, the *Brown Bear*, runs down the *Sea Queen* without stopping, and only King's quick action saves Salty and Anne. When King wins the salmon derby he donates the five-hundred-dollar prize to start a fund for these two, but the incident has roused his suspicions, and he gets Roger, who now works at the cannery, to watch for unusual activity. They soon determine that Hodge is hijacking canned salmon and fixing the books to disguise the truth. To get proof, they follow the *Brown Bear* in behind the Seven Ghosts; King takes the skiff to explore and returns to find a storm coming up and the *Barbara Lee* gone. He follows the sea lions and discovers a cave whose entrance is underwater at all but low tide, and inside is the company barge with Roger, Blackie, and Tom Hanley, the barge tender, prisoners aboard. They tell him of the hijacking of the barge early in the summer and the sinking of the *Barbara Lee* while he was exploring. Since the skiff is their only hope of escape, King takes off to hide, is discovered, and there follows a suspenseful chase through the watery caverns in which King discovers a large amount of money stolen from the cannery years ago and is able to turn tables on the villains, leaving them on the barge until the Coast Guard can arrest them, and takes Roger, Tom, and Blackie to safety. His actions insure the continuation of the cannery as a cooperative with Red as manager. Salty and Anne return with a new boat and take King into a partnership, with the promise of a blossoming romance. Although the skullduggery and the Gothic elements of secret watery caves are not very convincing, the plot is adequately action filled for a suspense novel. Characters are functional rather than well developed, but the setting and the salmon-fishing information are interesting. Poe Nominee.

SECRET OF THE MISSING FOOTPRINT (Whitney*, Phyllis A., ill. Alex Stein, Westminster, 1970), mystery novel set in New Jersey in the mid twentieth century. Because her parents are solving their marital problems by going to Europe and Africa for several months and leaving her behind, Marcie Sawyer, 12, is angry—angry at them and at her young uncle, Evan Farris, and his new wife, Gwen, who don't particularly want her but are taking her in, and at the world of adults in general. At their rural New Jersey home she meets a neighbor, Timothy Rainbow, 12, who is even angrier than she is with much the same reason: his mother has gone to Hollywood, and his father, who travels in his business, has turned him over to his artist uncle, Robert Rainbow, whose charming son, Alex, 14, resents the interest Robert takes in Timothy's artistic ability. Timothy has already become known in the neighborhood as difficult. Evan, a junior-high science teacher, has found a common interest with the boy in geology but has felt betrayed when Timothy evidently stole some geodes. In a partly water-filled abandoned quarry near the two homes, Evan has found a valuable specimen, a rock that shows rain drops from extremely ancient times, but it has disappeared from his collection. Timothy, who begins to trust Marcie because of their mutual grudge against the world, gives it to Marcie to return to her uncle and tells her that Hector Dowd, a strange, half-crazy old man who lives near, took it because he thinks the spirits of Indians are disturbed by the taking of artifacts. Timothy also tells her that he didn't steal the geodes but makes her promise not to tell Evan about either incident, since he wants to nurse his anger and get revenge, not make a conciliatory gesture. He also shows her a cave he has found leading to the steep, dangerous side of the quarry and the specimens he found, one containing a clear footprint of an early dinosaur, which he keeps hidden in the cave. At first Marcie is reluctant to go along with his great plan to get revenge on all the adults by having her disappear from the county fair and hide, at least overnight, in the cave, but when Aunt Gwen accuses and scolds her unjustly, she is angry enough to follow his plan. In the middle of the night, when she sees them hunting for her in the quarry, her better nature and good sense surface, and she decides to give herself up, but first Alex appears, admits that he has been spying on them, and is now going to be a hero by "finding" her and blaming Timothy for her disappearance. He also gloats over how he took Timothy's fossil footprint and is going to tell the newspapers that he found it himself. Before he can carry out his plan, Marcie sends Timothy's dog, Fenris, for him. Timothy comes and fights Alex, giving Marcie time to turn herself in and explain. In the end both Marcie and Timothy are reformed, and Alex is getting much needed attention from his father. The psychology of the youngsters, while sound, is treated heavy-handedly. The mystery elements are contrived, though the setting of the old quarry is interesting. Hector and a couple of minor characters—a girl at the next farm and a warmhearted housekeeper—are invented and manipulated for plot purposes and never seem real. Poe Nominee.

THE SECRET OF THE SEVEN CROWS (St. John*, Wylly Folk, ill. Judith Gwyn Brown, Viking, 1973), mystery novel set on the Gulf Coast of Mississippi in the mid twentieth century, some years after World War II. Since their father hopes to start a boarding school in the old mansion, Crauleia, Shelley* Calhoun, 12, her cousin, Pam Jones, 12, and her brothers, Jason, 14, and Bug, 9, are exploring the empty house when they meet Gale* Franklin, about 12, daughter of the owner, and her pet crow, Dracula. Gale explains that her crippled father cannot sell the place until she finds the "secret of the seven crows" left by her great-great-great-grandmother and relates a rhyme giving clues and ending, "Seven crows a secret/ That's never been told." Because she greatly desires her father's approval, which she thinks goes all to Jason, Shelley eagerly enters the search so that Gale and her crippled father can get the money they so badly need to fix their hurricane-damaged house and Mr. Calhoun can start his school. The other three are soon caught up in the excitement, but before they make any discoveries, they find a note, apparently left by Cap'n Boney Willis, a shrimp-boat captain, warning, "Don't stay here. This place is dangerous." A series of disturbing incidents follows: doors open mysteriously, lights go out, candles are found burning in the Crauleia chapel, newly washed dishes are scattered and dribbled with catsup and broken egg, strange noises bump around the third floor and the basement. Jason theorizes that a poltergeist is responsible and arranges an exorcism ceremony. Gale, however, finds Taz and Raymond Willis, sons of Cap'n Boney, and Michael and Patricia Lummus, children of Roscoe, Cap'n Boney's black deckhand, running from the house, and it is apparent that they are the poltergeists. Shortly afterward, Cap'n Boney is killed in an automobile accident, and they capture a strange man who has been hanging around Crauleia and is discovered to have a hoard of drugs hidden in the attic, as part of a drug-smuggling operation which has Boney's boat, the *St. Boneface*, and his shrimping operation as a cover. In the meantime, Pam finds a note in the hollow bedknob in the "priest's house," so named when Crauleia was once a convent, a small cabin where Gale's ancestor had let an old man live in the 1870s. The note speaks of "blood money" and quotes Shakespeare's *Julius Caesar*. While polishing a carved molding in the chapel, Shelley comes upon a secret compartment containing an 1873 silver dollar, and Pam discovers a box in the attic with six crows on the cover, both fulfilling clues to the secret. Behind the picture of the crows is a coded message which clever Jason deciphers, "Under crows claw is what you seek." Baffled at first, Shelley discovers the roots of a large tree forming a crow's claw, and when Jason digs they find a box full of gold coins and a note explaining that they were left to Gale's ancestor by the old man who claimed to be John Wilkes Booth, assassin of Lincoln. The coins, now greatly appreciated in value, will help Gale's father fix their house and make possible the sale of Crauleia for Mr. Calhoun's school. A lively story, this has highly unlikely events, with stock elements of mysteries—drug dealers, possible ghosts, hidden treasure, codes, secret panels—all employed to add suspense or to explain strange occurrences. The children are individualized arbitrarily—Jason is clever, a gourmet cook, a reader; Pam is practical; Bug is fascinated by the pet crow—without being fully realized as characters. The setting has a touch of the Gothic, a decaying mansion set in deep woods hung with Spanish moss. Poe Nominee.

THE SECRET OF THE SIMPLE CODE (Faulkner*, Nancy, ill. Mimi Korach, Doubleday, 1965), mystery-detective novel set among the mines and farms of the Appalachians of North Carolina in the mid–1900s. An auto accident has put an end to the promising football career of Paul Herriott, about fifteen, leaving him with a crippled leg and an embittered and self-pitying attitude. Paul looks forward to a boring summer on the farm of his uncle and aunt, where he has been sent to recover his strength. But two strangers move into the local inn, and Paul discovers in the cigar one of them leaves in the ashtray on the terrace of the inn a message in what seems to be a simple code of letters and numbers. The tempo of life picks up as Paul seeks help in solving the mystery from lively and optimistic Abby* Kenny, 13, who hopes to attend music school; surly, dispirited Luke* Young, about the same age, who does odd jobs about the inn; and accommodating Professor* Stuart Halstead, a visiting geologist. The plot thickens with several mysterious cigar messages, the realization that the strangers are potentially dangerous men, and the arrival of still another stranger, Bill Smith, who informs the quartet that a magnificent ruby ring worth $60,000 belonging to a famous New York actress has been stolen and that he has traced the thieves to this inn. After the professor figures out that the messages refer to the location of mines in the area and the three young people encounter the two men in the hills, they suspect that the men may be planning to hide the stolen jewel in one of the mines. When Abby's goats mischievously run away and hide inside an abandoned mine, Paul discovers the gem concealed there in common feldspar. The thieves are apprehended, and the youths share the $6,000 reward. Paul changes believably, if predictably, as he gradually becomes involved in the interests of his new friends and in unraveling the mystery. Novel's end finds him able to relate with compassion and understanding to Luke's situation and feelings when the boy's parents abandon him. Characters are individualized if one-dimensional. The stretched-out plot lacks tension and makes generous use of coincidence. The many details about rocks and minerals slow up the story's action but add interest and depth not usually present in this kind of story. Poe Nominee.

SECRET OF THE TIGER'S EYE (Whitney*, Phyllis A., ill. Richard Horwitz, Westminster, 1961), mystery novel set in Cape Town, South Africa, in the mid–1900s. Aspiring writer Benny (Benita) Dustin, 13, who narrates the story, is delighted that she and her brother Lanny, 8, are accompanying their journalist father to South Africa and that they will be staying with Aunt Persis Ware, the elderly woman with whom her father lived when he was a boy in Cape Town, but she does not welcome as a traveling companion the son of her father's editor, Joel Monroe. She has taken a strong dislike to Joel, who has a logical, practical mind, and who seems to delight in scorning her imaginative fantasies. They all love genteel Aunt Persis and her strange, many-roomed house on a hill overlooking Cape Town and are fascinated by the wild garden which contains a cave. They are also curious about a legend that it is haunted by the ghost of a one-eyed tiger that Aunt Persis's husband, now deceased, once shot in India. The house has been recently the target of prowlers, and the mystery involves a circular staircase, a face at the window, ghost tigers in the garden, a tiger's skin with a loose eye, a sinister sailor with a tattooed thumb (The Man with the Blue Thumb), who calls himself Tom* Kettle, and the tragic death of Malcolm, Aunt Persis's son, who was killed in an accident after quarrelling with his father and robbing the house some years before. Benny discovers his explanatory note to his mother, secreted behind the eye of the tiger skin, telling that he was a reluctant participant and that he had stolen worthless jewels after hiding the real ones in the cave. In their cooperation when Aunt Persis is injured, Benny and Joel learn to appreciate each other's qualities and to be friends, fortunately, since they will soon be stepsiblings. A secondary plot concerns Benita's friendship with talented young Charis van Clief, a Cape Colored (mixed blood) granddaughter of Aunt Persis's gardener, who suffers discrimination because of the South African policy of apartheid. As a story of friendship despite differences—Joel and Benny, Benny and Charis—the novel is contrived and predictable, though the exotic elements keep the action fast moving and descriptions of local scenic attractions give a strong sense of physical setting. Poe Nominee.

SELDEN, GEORGE (GEORGE SELDEN THOMPSON)(1929–   ), born in Hartford, Conn.; free-lance writer best known for his amusing talking animal fantasies for children. He was educated at Loomis School, received his degree from Yale University, where he majored in English and classical literature, was a member of the Elizabethan Club, and contributed to the literary magazine, and spent a year in Rome on a Fulbright Scholarship. He gained renown among critics and a permanent position in the hearts of young readers for his third book, *The Cricket in Times Square* (Farrar, 1960), about the adventures of a Connecticut cricket and his friends, cultured Harry Cat and acquisitive Tucker Mouse, in the New York subway station, which was a Newbery honor, a Fanfare, and a *Choice* book and was elected to the Lewis Carroll Shelf. *Tucker's Countryside* (Farrar, 1969), sequel to *Cricket*, won the Christopher Award and is also cited in *Choice*. *The Genie of Sutton Place* (Farrar, 1973) is a departure, a more sophisticated novel about a genie conjured out of a tapestry, which was a Fanfare selection. *Harry Cat's Pet Puppy* (Farrar, 1974), *Chester Cricket's Pigeon Ride* (Farrar, 1981), a picture book, and *Chester Cricket's New Home* (Farrar, 1983), continue the adventures of the animal friends. The characters in the Cricket series are vivid and memorable, the style simple, clear, and unaffected, the humor gentle and affectionate, and the tone pleasant, warm, and relaxed. In addition to his dozen books for older and younger readers, he has written television plays and biographies. He has lived in Greenwich Village, and his interests in music, archaeology, and conservation are reflected in his writings.

SERGEANT KITE (*Freelon Starbird**), tough, canny ex–British soldier who has deserted, become a blacksmith, and, for undisclosed reasons, chosen to fight for the colonies in the American revolution. A short, long-armed man with a ferocious tongue, he drills the Philadelphia recruits into a semblance of soldiers and in battles and the dismal camps is the strongest force in keeping up discipline and spirits. He fights through the entire war and returns to Philadelphia to his smithy.

SETH HOWES (*The Griffin Legacy**), Tory sympathizing priest of St. George's church, driven out by his American patriot parishioners for his loyalist leanings and killed before he reached the British lines by Philo Coburn, Lucy* Griffin's father. As Seth is crossing the meadow to join Lucy and take her away with him to England, Philo shoots him, then gives Lucy in marriage to Charles Griffin, an elderly neighbor. Seth had entrusted to Lucy the silver communion service given to the church by British Queen Anne and died believing that Lucy had violated his trust and betrayed him. His ghost appears to Amy* Enfield in the church during the heritage festival. Seth mistakes Amy for Lucy to whom Amy bears a striking resemblance. Seth is a stern, curt, impatient man.

SETH MARPLE (*Emily Upham's Revenge**), glib-tongued, opportunistic schoolboy, seemingly without scruples at the beginning of the novel but who suffers pangs of conscience at Emily* Upham's unreserved faith in him. He is the catalyst for events that humble banker Upham, bring his mother and Reverend* Farnlee together, and restore Emily's happy home. He calls himself "Deadwood Dick" from the dime novels to which he is addicted.

SETH MCCOLLUM (*Pistol**), elderly cowboy who works for Sam Tolliver. In Billy's eyes, he is a romantic figure, epitomizing all of what Billy has heard about the old-time cowboys. Seth dies in a fall on the last great drive before Sam Tolliver loses his place in the Depression. Billy is with Seth when he dies. Billy thinks Seth's death foreshadows the terrible events that followed.

SETI GAMMEL (*Cat in the Mirror**), Egyptian youth who attends Erin Gandy's exclusive private school and is her only friend there. He insists she be given a part in the class movie about Egypt, noting that with her dark hair, short stature, and long, graceful neck, she is the most Egyptian in appearance of any of the American students. He walks her home from school and stays for tea, and Erin feels fairly comfortable with him. As the twentieth-century Seti gives Erin emotional support, so also does the Egyptian one attempt to think along with Irun when she discusses Erin, the girl within her she calls her "demon." At the end, the twentieth-century Seti addresses Erin as Irun, an action which raises the possibility that he really shared her experiences in Egypt. On the other hand, Irun may simply be the Egyptian way of pronouncing her name.

SEVEN-DAY MAGIC (Eager*†, Edward, ill. N. M. Bodecker, Harcourt, 1962), episodic family fantasy set in the mid–1900s. Two families of children in a town in Connecticut near the ocean have become fast friends. Athletic John and calm, sensible Susan, orphans in fifth grade, live with their Grannie. Resourceful Barnaby, the leader of the five, mild, warmhearted Abbie, and fierce-tempered Fredericka have a father who sings on TV in New York City and a mother who sells real estate. They all enjoy magic books, particularly those of E. Nesbit. One Saturday, while the children are on their weekly visit to the local library, Susan checks out a small, shabby, red book, which circulates for seven days only and which launches them into a series of bookish, but exciting, adventures. When Fredericka wishes upon the book for an adventure with wizards and witches, a red dragon with green eyes swoops down and carries her off to an Oz-ish land, where a rotund, ineffectual wizard and a respectable witch rescue her. While on a time travel, the children encounter the little girl who picked up the magic charm at the end of *Half Magic†* and teach her how to use it. She wishes herself and her baby brother fifty years into the future into the present of the other five children. The brother, grown in body but still a baby inside, causes quite a commotion when he tries to drive a passenger train. Grannie's wish takes them back to the Dakota prairie and the little one-room school in which she once taught and to a Laura Ingalls Wilder Little House adventure. Caught in a blinding snowstorm, they are rescued by Grannie's future husband. Abbie's wish transports them to the New York studio where her father is performing. Her efforts to get his talent recognized by the "right" people result in getting him fired and then in a part for him in a play by a famous playwright. On the Saturday the book is due, John and Barnaby argue over who should next use the book, and it is torn. With his half, Barnaby quickly wishes himself into enchanted, literary lands from which he is rescued when the others put the pieces of the book together again. John's wish, the last one, causes them to sprout wings with which they fly the book back to the library, still containing plenty of magic for others to enjoy. The children have learned to be more charitable toward one another and more aware of the needs and concerns of those around them. The characters are barely individualized, but the dialogue is lively, extensive, and credible, and the humorous, inventive adventures, though occasionally arch and overly extended, cleverly combine contemporary and literary settings. Wit, satire, and irony keep the incidents from seeming too young for the intended audience of later elementary children. Choice.

SHADOW OF A BULL (Wojciechowska*, Maia, ill. Alvin Smith, Atheneum, 1964), realistic problem novel set in the town of Arcangel in Andalusia, Spain, in the mid twentieth century. Son of the great bullfighter, Juan Olivar, Manolo has known from the time he was very young that he is expected by the people of his town to follow the footsteps of his famous father, even repeating the feat of killing his first bull, with no practice, at the age of twelve as a fortuneteller had foretold of Juan. Manolo feels special responsibility because the townspeople, particularly six *aficionados*, have supported him and his mother since his father was killed in the bull ring when Manolo was only three. When Manolo is nine, the six men begin to take him to bullfights and point out to him the fine points of the sport. Manolo, afraid to tell them that the whole idea terrifies him, practices secretly at night with the cape and muleta which belonged to his grandfather, also a bullfighter but not as great as Manolo's father for whom the town has a museum and two statues. Each year also the Count de la Casa, a wealthy man who raises bulls, comes to look over Manolo. When the boy is ten, the Count announces that they will not wait until he is twelve, like his father, but will let him fight a specially raised bull the next year at the *tienta*, the time of testing of bulls in the spring. Manolo's best friend, Jaime Garcia, has a brother, Juan, 14, who passionately wants to be a torero. Manolo goes to see him and is intercepted by Juan's bitter father, a former torero badly wounded many times in the ring and deeply resentful of the ease with which the Olivar men get their chances to fight good bulls. Manolo persuades Juan to take him to "cape" a bull, to practice secretly with the bulls in the pasture at night, a forbidden activity for which they could easily be shot. Manolo sees as Juan makes passes with his cape that the older boy has true grace and, though Manolo distracts the bull at a decisive moment so that Juan can get away, that he himself has none of the desire Juan feels for the sport. The next day, when the matador is horribly gored, Manolo helps the doctor as he treats the wound and discovers that medicine is what really interests him. He persuades his six men to write the Count for permission to bring Juan with him to the *tienta*. There he finds a great many people gathered in the elegant house, including Alfonso Castillo, the greatest author of the bull ring and biographer of his father. Castillo talks to him privately and urges him not to let people push him into what he does not want for himself. In the ring, Manolo performs creditably through the first part of the event, then announces that he will not be a torero, but that Juan will, and he calls on Juan to perform with the bull. Manolo goes to sit with the doctor. The story, though essentially a simple one, has a good deal of power in its depiction of Manolo's emotional struggles and the conflicts he feels. The style evokes a feel of the foreign culture. The doctor's part, however, is contrived and makes the otherwise dramatic ending too pat. Choice; Fanfare; Newbery Winner.

SHADRACH'S CROSSING (Avi*, Pantheon, 1983), realistic novel of suspense covering about a week's time in 1932 on a tiny, impoverished, sparsely populated, offshore Atlantic island, in which a determined and courageous youth brings criminals to justice and restores his community's self-respect. Liquor smugglers terrorize and bribe the people on Lucker's Island into helping them unload and transport their illegal cargo to the mainland United States. When Kinlow, their chief, humiliates Shad's father and mother publicly for not keeping him in the house as agreed on a delivery night, Shad Faherty, almost thirteen, decides to bring Kinlow and his confederates to justice. Against his parents' bitter and fearful opposition and the threat by his father, Mr.* Faherty, of physical punishment, Shad impulsively and rebelliously lays his plans for turning in the smugglers. Complicating matters for him is a new arrival on the island, Mr. Nevill, who owns a large pleasure boat. Shad is certain Nevill is in cahoots with the smugglers and takes at face value the promised assistance of Mr. Sheraton, the government official who comes now and then to read the island rainfall meter. After trying unsuccessfully to enlist the help of his good friend, Davey, Shad rejects and then accepts the help of his younger brother, Brian*, 11, and scouts the island, even daring to enter Kinlow's house while the man is out. There he discovers the place where the contraband is kept. All the while unbeknownst to him, the islanders are aware of what he is doing. When it appears that something important is going to happen on a particular Monday night, Shad leaves a note in the government rainfall instrument box for Mr. Sheraton, confident that the official will inform the appropriate authorities, and on the day itself refuses Mr. Nevill's offer of a fun excursion to the mainland, because he thinks Nevill just wants to keep him from identifying him as a smuggler. That night he and Brian creep out, observe the smugglers landing and unloading their latest cargo, and suddenly realize they are surrounded by Kinlow's men and allied islanders. Brian is captured, but a sympathetic islander helps Shad get away. Then Shad helps Brian escape while the men are loading the contraband onto the ferry, and both attempt to trudge the shallows to the mainland to summon authorities. Their strength rapidly ebbing, they are found by Mr. Nevill, who informs them that he is Coast Guard Officer Costello. High excitement and action follow as they discover that Sheraton is the brains behind the smuggling operation, Mr. Costello (Nevill) leads an attack upon the smugglers, Kinlow gets away and takes Shad hostage, Shad by sheer audacity and luck gets Kinlow's pistol, forces Kinlow to apologize publicly to his parents for treating them so shamefully, and then delivers him into Mr. Costello's custody. Though the plot is typical of the genre and offers the usual full measure of red herrings and twists, much of the interest comes from the reader's perception of the irony of the situation. The smugglers' activities sustain the islanders' precarious economy and make it possible for them to continue living there in spite of the increasingly hard times.

Shad's idealism—he maintains it is a free country and the islanders ought to stand up for their rights and do what they wish—brings him into conflict with his parents and neighbors who maintain a more pragmatic view. Tension runs high from the very beginning, made so by short, pithy sentences, curt dialogue, superb pacing, and plenty of action. (Mrs.* Faherty) Poe Nominee.

SHADRACH YALE (*Across Five Aprils**), Jethro* Creighton's school teacher and good friend, who encourages the boy to continue his education, shows him how to follow the course of the Civil War on the map, and instills in the boy a strong respect for Lincoln. While serving with the Army of the Potomac, Shad is wounded. Jenny, Jethro's sister, goes east to nurse him, and the two are married there. At story's end, Shad plans to return to college, and he and Jenny intend to take Jethro to live with them so that the boy may continue his education.

SHAWN CAFFERTY (*The Voyage Begun**), 15, openly defiant son of the local grocer, Mr.* Cafferty. He is contemptuous of his parents, bullies his brother and sisters, and runs with the Salvages, a street gang which loots houses and terrorizes the people of the town. He and Gabe Palazzola become friends while making seaworthy the abandoned sailboat Shawn has found to replace the one of Walter Jepson's the Salvages burned. Shawn is a foil for Paul.

SHELLEY CALHOUN (*The Secret of the Seven Crows**), protagonist, a middle child who believes that her father always favors her clever older brother, Jason*, and that her mother loves her younger brother, Bug, best. Shelley tries hard to win her father's approval, continually downgrading her own accomplishments, until her new friend, Gale* Franklin, points out that her father treats the boys specially to compensate for loving her the most. She comes to see that her parents love each of them differently but equally.

SHEMIN, MARGARETHA (HOENEVELD) (1928–   ), librarian and writer; born in Alkmaar, Netherlands, the daughter of a physician who was active in the Underground Resistance during World War II. She came to the United States after receiving a law degree from the University of Leiden but has never been a practicing attorney. She married a physician and has made her home in Pleasantville, N.Y. She took a master's in library science from Columbia University with honors and has been a children's librarian in White Plains, N.Y. She speaks and reads German, French, and Dutch. All her books have been set in Holland and have as one aim correcting traditional stereotypes about the country and its people. *The Little Riders* (Coward, 1963), her first book, is a short novel for younger readers about a little girl's attempts to save the leaden figures from the church carillon from being melted down for ammunition during the Occupation, while *Mrs. Herring* (Lothrup, 1967) is a story of family life and seafaring for more mature readers. She received the Child Study Award for *The Empty Moat** (Coward, 1969), an absorbing but flawed novel about a sixteen-year-old Dutch girl's growing awareness of the need to work with the Resistance against the Nazis during the Occupation. Both it and *The Little Riders* are based on Shemin's own experiences during the war.

SHERIFF LANGWELL OTIS LANDRY (*Sinbad and Me**; *Mystery of the Witch Who Wouldn't**), of Hampton, Long Island, father of Minerva* and family friend of Steve* Forrester. Sheriff Landry is frequently annoyed by Steve's propensity for jumping to conclusions instead of acting only upon facts, but he has to admit that Steve's hunches lead to solutions in some cases. The Sheriff has a standing joke about Steve being his future son-in-law.

SHORTY ANDERSON (*The Night Swimmers**), father of Retta*, Johnny*, and Roy*, the three children who swim without permission at night in the pool of wealthy Colonel Roberts. Shorty is the caricature of a country-western singer. He favors gaudy, eye-catching outfits and is constantly composing that one great hit that will make him a great recording star. He neglects his children; even his wife's death marked just a brief interruption in his career. He is pleased at the end to leave the responsibility of the house and children to Brendelle and accepts her proposal of marriage with characteristic casualness, relieved to be able now to devote his full time and attention to his music and advancing his career, which the reader expects will always be small-time.

SHOTWELL, LOUISA R(OSSITER) (1902–   ), born in Chicago, Ill.; educator and author of fiction and non-fiction for adults and children. Her family lived in Des Moines and Philadelphia before settling in the Finger Lakes village of Skaneateles, N.Y., where she grew up. After graduating from Wellesley, she taught English in her home town, then took her master's from Stanford and taught in college, eventually becoming a dean of women. She has taught promotional and interpretative writing for the National Council of Churches Division of Home Missions, and she traveled extensively throughout the United States, researching migrant farm laborers. Out of these experiences came several books of non-fiction for adults and for children the highly acclaimed *Roosevelt Grady** (World, 1963), a simply written, earnest novel featuring the son of black migrants in the southeastern United States who longs for and finally attains a permanent home, that was both a Fanfare and *Choice* book and was elected to the Lewis Carroll Shelf. Her best-known book, it has been published also in German and Danish. A trip to Thailand, India, and Indonesia resulted in *Beyond the Sugar Cane Field* (World, 1964), a non-fiction book about UNICEF in Asia for young readers. She also wrote for children the novels *Adam Bookout** (Viking, 1967), a story set in Brooklyn, about a boy who runs away to the city after his parents die in a plane crash, which is cited in *Choice*, and *Magdalena* (Viking, 1971), about the daughter of Puerto Rican immigrants in Brooklyn. She has made her home in Brooklyn and Skaneateles, N.Y.

SHUBEAL GIVEN (*The Far-Off Land**), frontiersman with the flatboat, the *Dragonfly*, who disappears while hunting and is given up for dead by the Petrie party, which continues on without him. He rejoins them some days later, after a harrowing journey overland through rugged country. While he is gone, his wife, Rachel, becomes discouraged, because she fears that without his help she and her children will not be able to survive in the wilderness. His return is received with joy and relief.

SIDEWALK STORY (Mathis*, Sharon Bell, ill. Leo Carty, Viking, 1971), realistic story for younger readers set in the black area of a large American city in the late 1960s or early 1970s. When Lilly Etta Allen, 9, finds that the mother of her friend, Tanya Brown, and Tanya with her six younger siblings, are being evicted, she decides to do something, even though her mother, a welfare recipient, says there is nothing they can do to help without endangering the payments that support Lilly Etta and her younger twin brothers. Despite her mother's orders to stay away from the Brown apartment, Lilly Etta takes her brother, Greg, and at first is rejected by Tanya, who is too ashamed to face her. However, she enlists Tanya's aid and calls first the police, who will not interfere, then the newspaper, where the reporter talks her out of her pretense of being Mrs. Brown and listens to her story but points out that evictions are too common to be news. Before she leaves, Tanya gives for safe keeping her grandmother's gold earrings to Lilly Etta, who is wearing straws to keep her recently pierced ears from healing over. That night Lilly Etta takes sheets and baby blankets to cover the Browns' furniture and clothes piled on the sidewalk and protect them from the rain, and when the wind blows the sheets off, she climbs onto the pile to hold them down and goes to sleep there. She is awakened by lights and noise, to find that the reporter has brought camera men and is getting pictures. When the paper runs her story and pictures, Mrs. Brown is offered free storage, a new job, child care for the younger children, and a new apartment. Lilly Etta is sent a large number of earrings. Although the solution is simplistic and unbelievable even in a book for younger readers, the problems are real and treated realistically. Lilly Etta's mother threatens punishment in a convincing way and is equally believable in her concern but lack of action to help her neighbor. Choice.

SIDNEY FINE (*Berries Goodman**), bright, timid boy, who is always careful not to get dirty or hurt, lest he offend or frighten his over-protective, over-directive mother, the stereotype of a Jewish mother as he is the stereotype of a Jewish boy. He is the only Jewish child in the Olcott Corners school. When he is hurt ice-skating, his mother characteristically over-reacts and refuses to allow him to have anything more to do with either the Goodmans or the Grahams. Sidney and his mother are intended to show how prejudice isolates and harms innocent people.

THE SIGN OF THE BEAVER (Speare*†, Elizabeth George, Houghton, 1983), substantial historical novel set for six months in 1768 in the wilds of Maine in which a white youth acquires some understanding and appreciation of the way of life and problems of the Penobscot Indians through associating with them. In early July, after they have completed their cabin and planted corn and pumpkins and his father goes back to Quincy, Mass., to fetch the rest of the family, young Matthew Hollowell, 13, is left alone in the wilderness to care for the place. At first, Matt* looks forward to proving himself during the six weeks his father expects to be gone, though he feels some loneliness and the pressure of unfamiliar responsibilities. Disasters strike: a renegade white man, named Ben*, to whom Matt extends hospitality, steals his rifle; a bear ransacks the cabin, destroying his small store of meal and molasses; and he is severely stung while raiding a bee tree. He is rescued from the bees and nursed back to health in his cabin by an elderly Indian, Saknis*, and his grandson, Attean*, about Matt's age. The three "make a treaty," at Saknis's suggestion, that Matt teach Attean to read and write English in return for Attean bringing Matt food. Using *Robinson Crusoe* as a text, Matt finds Attean a reluctant, but apt, pupil. The Indian boy's remarks move Matt to think about life from new perspectives and examine common white assumptions about Indians. Attean teaches Matt to snare animals, fish in the Indian way, and make a bow, and the two tramp through the forest, where Attean shows Matt the beaver symbol that indicates that his band has hunting rights in the area. The relationship between the two boys remains strained and uneasy, although they spend much time together. Matt realizes that Attean continues to feel contempt for him and understands how dependent he is upon the Indians' generosity for survival. The boys' greatest adventure, killing a she-bear, leads to Matt being invited to visit the village and participate in the feast to celebrate the deed. Attean loses some of his aloofness when Matt rescues the Indian boy's dog from a white hunter's trap. In late fall, the Indians prepare to move to the far north where they can continue undisturbed their traditional way of life. They invite Matt to go with them, but he refuses, certain that his father will eventually return. Before they leave, the boys exchange gifts. Attean gives Matt his dog, which he loves very much, and Matt gives Attean his father's watch, the family's most cherished possession. Because of the Indians' generosity and help, Matt lives comfortably until his family arrives about Christmas time. Told in the third person from Matt's point of view, the story moves in a familiar way with just enough complications carefully spaced to hold the attention of the intended later elementary audience. Although the plot lacks originality and won't bear scrutiny, style is literate, tone is straightforward, and history and story blend well. The book is strongest in characterizaton and setting. Although Matt is a sympathetic protagonist, he changes predictably, and Attean never completely convinces, but the Indian grandfather commands respect and belief. Such aspects of Indian life as making traps, hooks, and bows, dances, games, and village customs and practices are described in just enough detail to be clear, and Indian attitudes about such matters as ownership of land, sex roles, and the vision quest are presented without judgment. Fanfare; Newbery Honor; O'Dell.

SIGNPOST TO TERROR (Sprague*, Gretchen, Dodd, 1967), mystery thriller set in the Adirondack Mountains of New York in the early 1960s. Gail Schaeffer, 15, is sorely at odds with her noisy, sloppy, unrestrained sister, Karen, 12, and their feuding and bickering threatens to ruin a family camping trip. After Karen taunts her for her fear of heights that keeps her from climbing a forest-service observation tower, Gail decides to shun family outings and gets permission to hike the next day with a girl she has met in the campground. When an emergency takes the girl and her family away, Gail gets a campground worker, a student from Cornell named Frank, to give her a lift in a garbage truck to the trail's start and, without her family's knowledge, sets off alone. A little way up the trail she startles a deer, then hears a loud crash and, going to investigate, sees that on a little-used fire road a VW camper has hit the deer and wrecked. As she watches, two men and a woman get out a shovel, a tarp, and three airline bags. More startling, the older man starts to shoot the still-living deer with a revolver and is stopped by the younger, a boy about nineteen she has seen in the bank a few days before. Before she flees to avoid seeing the animal killed, her eyes meet his, and shortly afterward he catches up with her on the trail, saying he is Lewis* Phillips and that he was just hitchhiking with the others. He seems nervous but not threatening, and when she hears of a bank robbery on her portable radio, he confesses that he is the boy taken as a hostage and that he is trying to escape. This changes her plan, which was to hike to the falls and turn back, and she decides that, to avoid his captors, she must go with him all the seventeen miles to the spot where the trail crosses the highway. As they descend the steep and dangerous trail along the falls and he tries to lure her to the edge, she sees that he has a pistol in his back pocket, and she realizes that he is one of the robbers. She throws herself down the slope, manages to elude him, and while he searches, she gets back up the trail, knowing all the while that he can go faster than she can. At one point she meets the other man and the woman, but they take her for an ordinary hiker. In the meantime, the real hostage, a fat boy named Martin* Flower, 11, has waked up from the sedative they gave him, climbed out of the telephone company jeep they used for the robbery before switching to the camper, and started up the trail, thinking he will find a ranger. Gail and Martin meet, both nearly exhausted, get to the ranger's empty cabin, and break in only to find the telephone dead. Martin, unable to go on, hides under the bed, and Gail goes on to the fire tower, where she is sure she'll find the ranger. She conquers her fear of heights to climb the tower, but it is padlocked. Lew catches up at this point, climbs the tower, grapples with her, and is almost pushing her off when he is startled by a call from Martin, whose conscience has driven him to follow Gail. Lew slips and crashes from the tower but is not immediately killed. Gail gets his gun, then tries to shield him from the driving rain. There Frank, who has heard about the robbery and worried about her, finds them and gets help. The mistaken identities and the pattern of recurring hopes and disappointments are built skillfully into a tense plot in a setting which makes the action more plausible than in many novels of this genre. Poe Winner.

SILENCE OVER DUNKERQUE (Tunis*†, John R. Morrow, 1962), historical novel which follows the fortunes of a British soldier during the evacuation of Dunkerque in May and June of 1940. The story begins and ends in Dover with the family of Sergeant Edward Williams, recently dispatched to France with the British Expeditionary Forces, and twice returns to describe the sergeant's sons' involvement in the evacuation, but the bulk of the story belongs to the soldier himself. By luck and resource, the sergeant manages a bold escape when captured by German soldiers, then takes captive German officers who are carrying master plans for the invasion of France and Belgium, and, after Belgium falls, maneuvers his weary men to the coast and on board the destroyer *Wakeful* for return to Britain. Along the way, he adopts an abandoned Airedale, which he names Candy after his family Airedale. The scene then switches back to Dover where his sons, Richard and Ronald, fifteen-year-old twins, stow aboard an evacuating boat, the *Shropshire Lass*. As they help with the evacuation, they experience some of the harsh realities of war. Ironically, they observe the *Wakeful* fall prey to a mine, unaware, of course, that their father is aboard the ill-fated ship. Back with Sgt. Williams again—he and his driver, Fingers Brown (so named because he has lost fingers on one hand) luckily survive the explosion, and, clinging to a bulkhead, are carried ashore south of Calais. Here they are found and helped by Gisèle, a determined and resourceful fourteen-year-old French Girl Scout, staunch for the cause of freedom. Over the protests of her Anglo-hating mother, knife-tongued, shrewish Madame Bonnet, Gisèle hides the two men in the family barn, secures fake papers for them, and eventually smuggles them up the coast road to Calais. En route, they encounter German soldiers, but the bedraggled and battered Candy turns up at the critical moment, and the joyful reunion between man and Airedale convinces the Germans that these people are indeed legitimate French refugees. While the twins vainly search the Dover docks for their father, in Calais the two men and Candy are befriended by Gisèle's grandfather, a veterinarian with whom they live until more false papers are secured. Then, in a series of tense scenes, they are ferried by night in the fishing boat *Marie-Louise* into the channel under the very noses of the Germans by Gisèle's uncle, a bold and resourceful fisherman, and cast afloat in a small boat. They row desperately for the Dover side, and, in an extraneous and melodramatic episode, they capture a shot-down German airman, with whom they and Candy triumphantly return home where the sergeant is welcomed by his joyful family. After a ponderous beginning overly concerned with the facts of the situation, the book perks up with the shipwreck. Gisèle, the "French woman" of tender years and intense determination, and Candy, the winsome dog of felicitous presence, stand out. Otherwise, characters are stock or functionary, and there is a superabundance of fortunate coincidences and ticklish encounters too conveniently resolved. The conclusion to be drawn is that the book presents history let down through a plot contrived to interest young readers. Choice.

SILKY (*The Whisper of Glocken**), maternal Minnipin, one of the New Heroes, who joins the expedition to the land of the Hulks*. She insists on caring for Wafer, the green-eyed little Digger, and, because she does, the Diggers* are friendly to the New Heroes and help them against the Hulks.

SILMAN, ROBERTA (KARPEL) (1934–   ), born in Brooklyn, N.Y.; free-lance writer. A graduate of Cornell with an M.F.A. degree from Sarah Lawrence College, she worked as secretary and science writer for *Saturday Review* from 1957 to 1961, before turning to full-time writing. *Blood Relations*, a book of short stories, received honorable mention in both the Hemingway Prize and the Janet Kafka Prize contests, and she was awarded a Guggenheim fellowship in 1979. Her book for younger readers, *Somebody Else's Child** (Warne, 1976), a story of an adopted boy, won the Child Study Award.

SIMON, JANE, AND BARNEY DREW (*Over Sea, Under Stone**), children of a doctor and a painter, who vacation with their Great-Uncle Merry, Merriman* Lyon, in the Grey House, the large, rambling establishment of a sea captain on the coast of Cornwall. When Barney tosses his apple core under an attic baseboard, they discover an old manuscript with a map showing where the Grail of Arthur is hidden and setting off the events of The Dark Is Rising fantasy series. Simon, the eldest, is usually the leader of the three, Jane, the middle child, is the practical and warmhearted one, and Barney, the youngest, is the adventurous and impulsive one.

SIMON BEN JUDAS (*The Rider and His Horse**), learned and wealthy man, benefactor of the poor and homeless in Jerusalem. To David* ben Joseph, he protests that he is neither a scholar nor a holy man, yet he sees more clearly the self-deception of both Joseph ben Matthias and of Eleazar* ben Ya'ir, and he does good works, helping the poor and giving a home to orphans while others comfort themselves by quoting the Torah. He differs from other men of learning and action in the book in his sense of irony and his sense of humor.

SIMONE ORGELLA (*The Noonday Friends**), Franny's noonday, that is, school lunchroom, friend. Puerto Ricans, Simone's family is large, and their apartment is cramped. A pretty, dark-eyed child, she yearns to live in Puerto Rico, which she has heard from friends and relatives has a much better climate than New York City. She loves beautiful things. On weekends, she and Franny Davis spend hours filling scrapbooks with cutouts of things they think are beautiful. They have a tiff over Franny picking a scab, which Simone considers a very ugly thing to do, and Franny thinks Simone is being unreasonable and petty. Later, the two patch up their differences and make friends again.

SINBAD AND ME (Platt*, Kin, Chilton, 1966), mystery set in Hampton on the eastern end of Long Island in the 1960s. The first-person narrator, Steve* Forrester, 12, is alone with his English bulldog, Sinbad, because he has to take a summer make-up course after flunking science, and his parents must make a hurried trip to Maine. As their stay lengthens because of a series of accidents to his father, Steve's adventures at home become more complicated. In trying to help his old friend, Mrs. Teska, who runs a small grocery store, he encounters two gangsters who seem to be threatening her and then trash her store. They deliver poisoned hamburger to his home, but Sinbad is too smart to eat it. Because Steve has seen an IOU signed by Mrs. Teska's son, Frankie, he knows she needs money and decides to try to find the treasure left by Captain Billy Murdock, who died in 1800. Together with Minerva* Landry, 11, daughter of the chief of police and sheriff, he discovers a cave in a cliff below the vacant house known as Captain Billy's Castle. On the roof of the cave is painted a series of Xs and Os, evidently a cipher; on Captain Billy's tombstone is a riddle, and on other Murdock stones another one. The last Murdock, Big Nick, is not buried but is assumed to have gone down with his floating gambling casino, which burned and sank in 1920. Steve discovers that Mrs. Teska was once married to Big Nick, that she fears the curse of her "kum," a sort of old-world godfather, which she thinks will cause Steve's death, and that his science teacher, Mr. Snowdown, is also interested in the cave and treasure, as is a young newspaper reporter named Defoe. The complications are numerous: Steve finds a silver dollar Mrs. Teska has given him is worth a great deal; his genius friend, crippled Herky* Krakower, teaches him how to decode ciphers; Captain Billy's ghost visits him at night; he sees Defoe and a girl from a real-estate office make an illicit visit to Captain Billy's house; the gangsters reappear and force him to go to the house at night; he finds a secret tunnel and traps them in it; he discovers a hidden fortune in the panels of a fake door; Sheriff* Landry finds him with the money; they rescue Mrs. Teska about to throw herself off the widow's walk to appease the curse of the "kum"; Big Nick, having returned from Naples, reappears; Steve finds the last clues to the treasure written in invisible ink on a square of paper concealed in the head of Mrs. Teska's cane; the gangsters are arrested, and one turns out to be Frankie Teska; Steve helps find out the true murderer of Mayor Bagler in an old case which appeared to be a suicide but which Mrs. Teska has thought was a killing done by Big Nick. Steve's great interest in and knowledge of old styles of houses help him unravel several of the many mysteries. Sinbad and his uncanny presentiments help with others. An old-coin dealer named Mr. Newbury provides other important information. The story is extremely complex with far too many elements to be in any way believable, but it is so ingeniously worked out and fast paced that mystery fans may overlook the implausibility. Sequel is *Mystery of the Witch Who Wouldn't**. Poe Winner.

SING DOWN THE MOON (O'Dell*, Scott, Houghton, 1970), historical novel about the Navaho Indians set in 1863–1865. The action is divided into two nearly equal parts. In the first, Bright* Morning, 15, and her friend, Running Bird, who are herding their families' sheep, are kidnapped and sold into slavery by Spaniards. As servants in a southwestern town they meet Rosita, a slave from a poor tribe, who likes her present position, and Nehana, a bitter Nez Perce, who helps them run away. Their escape seems doomed until Tall* Boy, the Navaho intended as husband to Bright Morning, finds them and is wounded while protecting them, losing the use of one arm. The second half of the book concerns the evacuation of the Navaho people from their own land, their death-march to Fort Sumner, and their miserable confinement at Bosque Redondo, where many die and most of the others lose their spirit. Bright Morning marries Tall Boy and, when she finds she is pregnant, decides that the baby must not be born in captivity, yet she cannot persuade Tall Boy out of his apathy. When he injures an Apache trying to steal the wood he has collected, he is imprisoned in the fort but escapes through a garbage hole. This provides the needed impetus for an escape from the camp, and he and Bright Morning leave, eventually returning to their old home, the Canyon de Chelly, where, in a small side canyon, they find a cave to live in and discover some of her sheep still alive. The structure of the book is unfortunate. The most exciting portion is the first half, and the second half, which contains the most important and serious material, seems foreshortened as if it has been condensed. As a result, the historical situation, which should have great impact, is not as moving as it might be. Bright Morning, the narrator, is typical of O'Dell's protagonists, convincing but so emotionally inarticulate that her devastating adventures seem somewhat flat. Choice: Fanfare; Newbery Honor.

THE SINGING FLUTE (Worcester*, Gurdon S., ill. Irene Burns, Obolensky, 1963), brief story set at an unspecified time, probably the mid–1900s, at Cape Ann, Mass., among the stone quarriers of Finnish descent. Hilli, 11, whose mother died at her birth, lives alone with her unsmiling father, Waino, in an isolated stone house. Because of a crippling illness, Hilli walks with a limp, but she knows every path on the mountain and has even seen, though never spoken to, her Uncle Lauri, her father's estranged brother, whose beautiful flute music attracts and fascinates her. An old woman tells her of the feud, started beause the hard-driving Waino thinks Lauri, five years younger, is frivolous and resents being responsible for his brother's lameness, caused by an accident, and because of Lauri's being often right in decisions and suggestions. The quarrel came to a head when Waino's homesick Finnish wife found comfort in Lauri's music, and Waino divided his father's land and forbade Lauri to come onto his half. When Hilli learns that village men are trying to shoot a large black dog, gone wild since its stonemason master died, she takes meat, finds the dog, stands beside it so the men won't shoot, then takes it silently to her uncle. Later she witnesses a scene between the brothers, when her father warns Lauri that he will shoot the dog if it comes on his land and then, seizing Lauri's flute, throws it into a water-filled quarry pit. The next spring Hilli spots the flute on a ledge under water, reaches for it, slips in, and is rescued by the dog. Her father, wrapping her in his coat, carries her to Lauri's house, where they are reconciled. The story, though realistic, has a fanciful quality, with detail of the woods and quarry pits but the abstractness of legend in its characterization. Its symbolism and evocation of beauty are somewhat self-conscious. Fanfare.

SISTER (Greenfield*, Eloise, ill. Monica Barnett, Crowell, 1974), short, episodic, realistic novel of family life set among urban blacks in the late 1900s. Doretha Freeman, 13, lives with her widowed mother, Thelma, who works in a laundry, and her older sister, Alberta, 16, a school dropout. The elation Doretha feels at attending a concert of Lonnie and the Celebrations is tempered by the growing friction between Mrs. Freeman and Alberta. Since everyone says that Doretha is "just like" Alberta, Doretha is afraid that she will turn out to be shiftless and antagonistic like her sister. After the concert, Doretha gets out her Notebook, the memory book her father gave her when she was nine, and reflects on the special days in her life. Each chapter in the novel takes up one of those days. When Doretha is ten, her father, Clemont, dies of a heart attack during a birthday party his family and friends hold for him. Shortly after that, Alberta's best friend moves away, and Mama explains to Doretha that Alberta feels insecure because she is afraid that Mama and Doretha might leave her, too. When Doretha is eleven, she visits her Grandpa in North Carolina. He tells her about her great-great-grandfather, proud, hardworking Grandpa Jack, who was born in slavery and who avenged an insult to his son by shooting the whites responsible. When her new teacher, Mrs. Garner, tries to put her down, Doretha responds by walking "slow, slow, and loose," as if she doesn't care. Then Mr. Anderson, who knows he's going to die soon, gives her his flute and offers to teach her to play it, Mama is jilted by the man she hopes to marry, and Aunt Mae teaches Doretha how to walk properly past the boys. At thirteen, Doretha joins the Black Freedom School, and Alberta walks out of public school after a fight with another girl. When Doretha reflects on her special days, she concludes they've been mostly bad. She decides she will remember the good ones, however, like the concert, and determines to beat the tough times as Grandpa urged. She realizes she doesn't have to cave in to adversity as Alberta has. Lacking suspense and climax, the book is a series of short, self-contained vignettes, both instructive and encouraging in purpose. They inform readers about black life, offer hope to blacks, and urge taking pride in being black. Their style is simple, poetic, and sharp with imagery, and events are understated. Black dialect contributes to realism. Choice.

SISTER ELIZABETH TURNER (*Wilderness Bride**), Ethan* Drake's mother and Corey's mother-in-law-to-be. An invalid, Sister Elizabeth is a pretty, gentle, home-loving, confused woman. Corey, who has never known a mother's love, feels very close to her. Elizabeth's wagon is beautifully and comfortably furnished, with tapestries, rich carpeting, figurines, scented candles, a bit of England transported to the American frontier. She sometimes thinks that her husband, Dr. Drake, is still alive. Ethan loves her very much and secretly uses sleeping powders and potions to ease her discomfort on the trip westward to the Mormon Zion, even though he knows such remedies are forbidden by Mormon law.

SISTER TRUDE TURNER (*Wilderness Bride**), Mormon Dan* Turner's first wife, the one of his three wives who manages the household. She shares his determination to get to Zion. She seems hard and callous to Corey at first, but Corey later discovers that Trude is not as rigid and unfeeling as she seems. A perceptive woman, she pretty much knows what is going on in the Turner family. She married Dan because she loved him but has some regrets about having to share him with his other wives. This feeling motivates her to help Corey escape from the wagon train before Dan forces Corey to marry Shad Turner. The reader shares Corey's feelings about Sister Trude.

THE SKATING RINK (Lee*, Mildred, Seabury, 1969), realistic novel set in the 1960s in south Georgia, tracing the development, after he learns to roller skate, of a shy, poor-white boy handicapped by a speech impediment. Life changes for Tuck (Tucker Holland) Farraday, 15, the day he stops to watch construction begin on the new building near the poor, run-down chicken farm where he lives with his father, Myron*, his stepmother, Ida*, his older twin brothers, Tom and Cletus, and his young half-sister, Karen. Tuck has always been a loner because of his agonizing stutter, a problem which started when, as a three-year-old, he saw his mother drown. Because of the teasing, particularly of Elva Grimes, Tuck hates school, plans to quit as soon as he is old enough, and walks the long distance every day to avoid the school bus. In his family he speaks as little as possible and is treated like a dummy by all but Ida, whose defense he resents even as he recognizes her good motives. At the construction site he is surprised when a short, wiry man introduces himself as Pete* Degley and explains that he is building a skating rink which he expects will draw roller skaters from all the small towns nearby. Every day after that, Tuck hurries home so he can talk a few minutes with Pete without being so late for chores that he will anger his embittered father. Tuck's sense of isolation is increased when Elva Grimes waylays him, seductively sits with him in the woods, then slaps him when he tries to kiss her, calls him a dummy and screams that she was only trying to win a bet that she could make him talk. He is astonished when Pete, having sized him up as a natural athlete, suggests that he secretly learn to skate. At first he has difficulty but suddenly catches on. Several nights later, Tuck finds Pete with a girl, a small girl about half Pete's age whom he introduces as Lily*, his wife. Pete begins to train them as a team to give an opening night performance. As the time approaches for "Elysium on Wheels" to open, Tuck discovers that Karen has spied on him. Partly with threats, partly with the bribe of a shared secret, he gets her to swear not to tell, but he is nervous about her knowledge and at the speculation about the rink both at home and at school. His life is complicated by illness among the chickens which he doctors more skillfully than his father. The night of the performance his whole family and most of the town are at the rink. The show goes as well as Pete has hoped, and to Tuck's surprise Pete gives him one hundred dollars and a chance to give lessons Saturday mornings. Tuck finds Myron waiting up for him and gives him the money to get an electric stove to replace the decrepit wood-burning stove which Ida hates. With his new confidence, Tuck's speech has improved, and he decides to stay in school. The book is unpretentious and completely convincing, with the details of skating, of Tuck's speech impediment and consequent isolation, and of the family relationships all skillfully drawn. Even minor characters are individualized and portrayed with understanding, particularly Tuck's failure-prone father and his complaining stepmother. It treats a usually sleazy segment of society with compassion that gives their lives dignity. Fanfare.

SKURZYNSKI, GLORIA (JEAN FLISTER) (1930–   ), born in Duquesne, Pa.; author of several brief, illustrated books based on folktale and some more substantial novels and books of non-fiction. She attended Mt. Mary College in Pittsburgh, married an aerospace engineer, and has five daughters, one of whom is a doctor, a profession which has influenced three of her mother's books: *Bionic Parts for People: The Real Story of Artificial Organs and Replacement Parts* (Four Winds, 1978), *What Happened in Hamelin** (Four Winds, 1979), in which a mold on grain that produces a psychedelic condition is presented as an explanation for the children's dancing, and *Manwolf* (Houghton, 1981), about a boy affected with an obscure disease that causes its victims to become like werewolves in appearance. She has also written *Lost in the Devil's Desert* (Lothrop, 1982), about a girl lost in the Utah desert.

SKYE PENNINGTON (*Gentlehands**), beautiful, dark-haired young woman of eighteen, who is Buddy Boyle's summertime romantic interest, a relationship far more serious on his part than on hers. Indulged by oil-rich parents, she drives an expensive sports car, always dresses in costumes combined carefully of clothes all of one color, and has lots of young, trendy guests at the family seaside estate, Beauregard. For reasons undisclosed, she accepts a date with Buddy one day when she visits the ice cream parlor in which he works. Although she has plenty of friends of both sexes in her own set, she continues to date Buddy throughout the summer, evidently for novelty, or perhaps because she really likes him. However, she never invites him to any social function away from her estate. She is an improbable character.

SLAKE'S LIMBO (Holman*, Felice, Scribner's, 1974), realistic novel set in New York City, mostly in the subways, in the early 1970s. Aremis Slake, 13, an orphan, is underfed and undersized, nearsighted and afraid of almost everything in his life. In his neighborhood, where he has lived with an aunt, Slake often escapes from the gangs of kids who bully him by running down into the subway and jumping aboard a train. He even keeps a token in his pocket for such emergencies. One day he does this but emerges at a station which is not a transfer point, walks through Central Park, climbs a tree, is chased off by an attendant who calls the police, and dives under the turnstile back into the subway. Scared by a gang of boys and the shouts of the man in the booth, he leaps off the platform and runs into the dark tunnel. Feeling for an alcove where workmen can stand as the train passes, Slake discovers a jagged opening in the wall, a crack leading into a concrete-walled room that resulted from a blasting error when the Commodore Hotel was being built. The crack, caused by fifty years of wear and vibration on the concrete, is big enough for Slake to slip through, and he makes the room near Grand Central Station his home for 121 days. Slake discovers that he can wash in the restrooms, find newspapers left by commuters in the train cars, and smooth and resell these for enough to buy a little food. At first he watches at the quick food stand for a cup of coffee which someone does not finish and drinks it himself; later the man in charge offers him a meal in exchange for sweeping the floor during the rush hour, and the kindly waitress, noticing that he always puts half his sandwich in his pocket, begins to wrap something for him to take with him each day. He soon gets some regular customers for his papers, a cleaning lady who gives him some old clothes her son has outgrown and a turban-wearing man who at first frightens him. He rummages in the trash cans for an assortment of "treasures" with which he furnishes and finally decorates his room. He even begins to feed a rat which frequents the area. The narrative about Slake is interrupted by passages entitled "On Another Track," about motorman Willis Joe Whinny, who has always longed to be a sheepraiser in Australia and has come to look at his passengers angrily as sheep he is herding. The two stories are joined when a large piece of concrete near Slake's room falls on the train and the city decides to repair the aged and cracking concrete. Slake hides in his room until he hears the workmen approaching. Then he takes a felt pen, writes STOP on a large piece of cardboard, and runs with it down the tunnel into the path of an oncoming train driven by Whinny. The motorman jams on his brake, rushes out, and picks up the collapsed body of Slake, and thereby is jolted out of his fantasy to see his passengers as people like himself. Slake is taken to the hospital and there receives a card written to "The Boy in the Subway" from Whinny and saying, "Thinking of you." Given new clothes and some glasses, Slake is scheduled to be sent to a "juvenile facility," but instead he slips out of the hospital and sets out to find a new place to make his home, possibly on the roof of a building, in an untended pigeon coop or an abandoned water tank. A curious book, it holds the reader at a distance just as Slake holds the world at a distance. Because he is so self-absorbed and remote from other people, one can feel sympathy for Slake but not much empathy. Yet the story of what happens to him is absorbing and plausible. The end, since Slake is heading up, seems intended to be hopeful, though an objective analysis would not suggest that Slake's chances are very good. Lewis Carroll.

THE SLAVE DANCER (Fox*, Paula, ill. Eros Keith, Bradbury, 1973), historical novel set in New Orleans and on an American sailing ship engaged in the African slave trade in 1840. Thirteen-year-old Jessie Bollier lives with his mother, a seamstress, and his younger sister, Betty, in New Orleans. He tells how he often earns a few coins by playing his fife for the sailors who come to the great market near the levee. One night, while running an errand for his mother on a back street, he is kidnapped by gruff sailors who take him to an ocean-going vessel moored in the bay. He learns that *The Moonlight* makes regular and illegal voyages to Africa for slaves to be sold to Southern plantation owners. Captain Cawthorne has had Jessie kidnapped because he wishes him to play his fife to exercise the slaves so that their muscles will remain strong during the long voyage. En route to Africa, Jessie becomes "everybody's boy," running errands for Captain and crew, a band of vicious cutthroats who blink at the horrors of the traffic in slaves and put up with the Captain's sadistic behavior in anticipation of high profits at the end of the voyage. The trip over to Africa is fairly uneventful, though rations are short and both Captain and crew frighten him, and Jessie seldom thinks of his mother and Betty, he becomes so caught up in the microcosm of life aboard ship. He comes to admire the crew's skill at managing the ship and their fearlessness in executing often demanding and hazardous tasks. When the Captain has crewman Purvis flogged for stealing an egg and crewman Stout, who is really guilty, allows Purvis to take the punishment for his deed, Jessie realizes the true nature of the men among whom he has fallen. The return voyage affords daily horrors. The stench- and disease-filled hold is jammed with moaning blacks of all ages. There are frequent floggings, and dead bodies are callously tossed overboard. Worst of all for Jessie are the morning "dances" for which he must provide the music. These are hours he dreads, when the slaves must move their emaciated bodies painfully and dispiritedly in time to his thin, agonized tunes. Jessie's narrative reaches its climax when, off Cuba, as the Captain is negotiating for the sale of his ill-gotten, brutalized cargo, the men sight an American coastal patrol ship. Without hesitation and in great haste, the crew dump overboard slaves, irons, and all other evidence of their illegal activity. A sudden storm strikes, and ship and men are soon lost. Only Jessie and one black youth, Ras, survive, borne to the coast of Mississippi on a broken spar. There a runaway slave, Daniel, provides for them until they are well enough to travel. Daniel arranges for Ras to be smuggled to free territory in the North and gives Jessie directions to New Orleans. A much soberer Jessie is soon reunited with his family, studies to become an apothecary, and eventually moves to Rhode Island. Throughout his life, however, the sound of music evokes memories for him of the joyless, grotesque dancing of bone-thin slaves being exercised. Jessie proves an observant and honest witness to historical horrors, but as a character in his own right he never quite convinces. He fails to articulate the terror, shock, and revulsion one would expect of a youth in his circumstances. Captain and crew are stock villains. Style is graphic with extensive, selective detail, but the book's strength lies less in narrative than in historical perspectives. Choice; Contemporary Classics; Fanfare; Newbery Winner.

A SLAVE'S TALE (Haugaard*, Erik Christian, ill. Leo Dillon and Diane Dillon, Houghton, 1965), historical novel, sequel to *Hakon of Rogen Saga**, set toward the end of the Viking period with the main action in what is now France. Because Rogen's has been so devastated by conflict and bad crops, Hakon is not able to keep his vow to retrieve his foster mother, Gunhild*, and his stepmother, Thora*, from Tronhjem, or to return Rark*, the former slave, to his home for about two years after he comes to power. He and the former slave girl, Helga, who narrates the story, are fifteen when he sails aboard the *Munin* with about twenty-five men, four women, and Helga, who has stowed away below the deck. Before they reach Tronhjem, Helga emerges and is forgiven by Hakon, but at Tronhjem they find Magnus Thorsen dead and his hall in disrepair, held by his half-mad, half-invalid grandson, Hjalte Gudbrandson. Neither Thora nor Gunhild wish to return to Rogen. Kark, the insolent, cruel slave of Earl Hakon, greets them with contempt, but the Earl, who is cousin to Hakon's mother, receives them courteously if not warmly. As they leave Tronhjem, they almost meet the ships of King Olaf Trygveson, a Christian come from the Orkney Islands to attack the Earl, who follows the old gods. As they sail, Helga, who loves Hakon, is aware that Magnus* the Fair, who has a way with words, would like to marry her. His attentions win Helga the enmity of Rigmor Ragnvalddaughter, who wants Magnus herself. In Frankland their first stop is at the island of Saint Michel, where the rather frightened priests sell them bread and tell them that Rark's uncle has become the high priest of Saint Malo, a large and thriving island community joined to the mainland at low tide by a land bridge. At Saint Malo they camp on a nearby island while Rark stays with the priest and learns that his wife and children are alive but that his wife has been remarried to a Frank named Hugues, who has powerful relatives. Leaving a few to guard the *Munin*, most of the Vikings set off for the church of Saint Meen, near Rark's hall. As they camp, the sentry captures a slave who pretends to be loyal to Rark and urges them to attack at once. Helga knows he has been sent to trick them, and when he tries to escape in the night, Helga shoots him with her bow and arrow. At Saint Meen, the high priest, Father Christopher, is new, the previous priests having all been killed by raiding Norsemen. Only a young priest named Michel, whose parents came from Norway, is genuinely friendly and tries to warn them. Through Father Christopher, they receive an invitation to a feast given by Hugues. Though suspicious, five, including Rark, Hakon, and Helga, decide to go, with the priests guaranteeing their safety. Rark is treacherously slain in front of his wife. As the others leave, Hakon throws a dagger at Hugues, and they race their horses back to their camp. There they find all their companions slain. Father Michel gets them fresh horses, and all four ride all night to Saint Malo. There Rark's old uncle, the head priest, visits the *Munin* at night to bring them supplies and to urge them to leave before hoodlums encouraged by Hugues attack them. An epilogue tells that Helga marries Hakon, that Olaf Trygveson has turned all Norway Christian. The tale is a grim, almost bitter comment on the treachery and slaughter performed in the name of religion or with the blessing and connivance of priests of both the Norse and Christian beliefs. It is also a study of slavery, the condition of the spirit which remains even after the body is free. Helga finally achieves real freedom, but the trip has been a costly and bitter experience that has aged both her and Hakon. Helga and several of the minor characters are well developed. Hakon is not as interesting a character as he is in the earlier book but the story is absorbing and gives a good picture of the period. Fanfare.

SLEPIAN, JAN (1921–   ), born in New York City; speech pathologist and author. She took psychology at Brooklyn College and at the University of Washington and received her M.A. degree in speech pathology from New York University. She has collaborated on a series of language arts concepts books and has written more than a dozen books for children, her best known being *The Alfred Summer** (Macmillan, 1980), a story of a boy with cerebral palsy, which won the *Boston Globe-Horn Book* Award, and its sequel, *Lester's Turn* (Macmillan, 1981). *The Night of the Bozos* (Dutton, 1983) has a carnival setting, a story in which two isolated young people are drawn into the world of freaks and clowns.

SLIPPER-ON-THE-WATER (*The Gammage Cup*†; *The Whisper of Glocken**), the Minnipin village from which the Old* Heroes are outlawed. It received its name, according to Minnipin legend, when the Minnipins first entered their valley, the Land-Between-the-Mountains. Their leader, Gammage, lost his left slipper in the water, and it floated three days and three nights in the same spot. The Minnipins decided to found a village there and name it for the observed phenomenon. Over the years, the village grew to some size.

SLOTE, ALFRED (1926–   ), born in Brooklyn, N.Y.; television producer and author of sports novels. He received his B.A. and M.A. degrees from the University of Michigan, served in the U.S. Navy in 1944–1946, and studied at the University of Grenoble in 1950 on a Fullbright scholarship. For three years he was an instructor in English at Williams College, Williamston, Mass., then returned to Ann Arbor to join the University of Michigan Television Center, where he was a producer, writer, and director until his retirement. In addition to three adult novels, one book of non-fiction, and many scripts and educational television programs, he has written a number of popular sports novels for children, including *Jake** (Lippincott, 1971), a story as much about a little black boy's search for a father figure as it is about his baseball team. Most of Slote's books are baseball stories, based on his experience in playing baseball and coaching Little League, but he has also written about kids' hockey. Although sports are central in his novels, and descriptions of games are accurate and vivid, the emphasis is usually on the personal relationships and family problems of the characters. In a departure from most of his earlier books, he switched to futuristic fantasy in *Clone Catcher** (Lippincott, 1982), which was a nominee for the Edgar Allan Poe Award. Other titles include *My Father, the Coach* (Lippincott, 1972), *Hang Tough, Paul Mather* (Lippincott, 1973), *Tony and Me* (Lippincott, 1974), and *Matt Gargan's Boy* (Lippincott, 1975).

SMITH, ALISON (1932–   ), author of realistic novels of contemporary family life for young readers of later elementary and junior high age. She has written *Reserved for Mark Anthony Crowder** (Dutton, 1978), which involves a sixth-grade boy who grows in self-esteem by tending the family garden one summer and received the International Reading Association's Children's Book Award, and the more humorous *Help! There's a Cat Washing in Here!* (Dutton, 1981), in which a twelve-year-old boy takes over the household while his mother works on her art portfolio. Critics have praised her realistic grasp of family life today and her smooth, contemporary style, though they have found her story lines slight and fabricated.

SMITH, DORIS BUCHANAN (1934–   ), born in Washington, D.C.; author of books for children on relevant social topics. She has lived in Georgia since she was nine, attended South Georgia College, and has been a free-lance writer since 1971. In addition to their own four children and one permanent foster child, she and her husband have been foster parents to more than twenty children. Her novel, *Tough Chauncey** (Morrow, 1974), reflects this experience, being about a boy abused by his grandfather, who finally seeks help as a foster child. Her best-known book, *A Taste of Blackberries** (Crowell, 1973), deals with a child's grief and guilt at the death of a friend. More recent books include *Salted Lemons* (Four Winds, 1980), set in Atlanta during World War II, about a friendship between a Yankee girl and a Japanese-American girl, both outsiders, *Last Was Lloyd* (Viking, 1981), in which a coddled, overweight boy in Georgia takes his first steps toward independence, and its companion novel, *The First Hard Times* (Viking, 1983), about Lloyd's friend, Ancil, who is disturbed by having a new stepfather and moving to Georgia. *Moonshadow of Cherry Mountain* (Four Winds, 1982) is about an Appalachian mountain boy who must cope with his resentment against people moving into the area and his newly adopted sister.

SMOKE (Corbin*, William, Coward, 1967), realistic novel set in the 1960s in western Oregon. Ostensibly a dog story, it is really a story of the relationship between Christopher Long, 14, and his stepfather, Calvin* Fitch. Unreconciled to the marriage of his widowed mother, Frances, Chris is surly and resentful to Cal, who is polite in return but rigid, insisting on certain ranch chores and rules of behavior that rob Chris of his time to read and dream. When some animal, possibly a wolf, kills a couple of chickens, Cal intends to shoot it, but Chris, reading in his tree house in the woods, discovers that it is a starving German shepherd. With advice from the veterinarian and help from the seasonal hired man, Leeroy*, Chris starts to feed the dog secretly and to give it medicine. Chris's little sister, Susie*, 11, let into the secret, names the dog Smoke and blithely lies to cover Chris's actions. When Chris discovers that Smoke, suffering from advanced malnutrition, can't retain the food, he blurts out the whole story to Cal, who calls the vet and organizes Leeroy to help Chris and Doc capture the dog so that it can be treated. As Smoke recovers, Cal insists that they advertise for the owner. Cal drives one false claimant away, but when Mr. Stone arrives and obviously knows and loves the dog, even Chris has to admit that Smoke belongs to him. Suffering severely, he lashes out when his mother suggests that Cal will let him get a puppy, pointing out that one dog is not the same as another and accusing her, in Cal's presence, of thinking one man as good as another. That night, telling only Susie, Chris runs away with Smoke, heading east over the coastal mountains, unsure of his destination or his own intentions but unable to face Cal after that insult. He braves and subdues his irrational fear of the dark (caused by being lost overnight when he was a toddler) and is descending the east side of the divide when a fisherman's boxer attacks Smoke. Chris leaps into the fight but is badly cut on the back by a misplaced jab from the fishpole. The fisherman's uncle, a paramedic, sews his wounds up without anesthetic, and during the pain Chris come to terms with his own conflicts, hikes to the nearest phone to call and apologize to Cal, and learns that Cal has bought Smoke from Mr. Stone. The conflict between Chris and Cal is well developed, and both Susie and Fran are characterized interestingly, but the resolution, from the time Chris runs away to the end, is full of overt macho statements about facing fear and pain, mostly put into Cal's mouth but also contributed by the author, which change the tone of the book and over-simplify it. There is no logical reason presented why the fisherman doesn't simply drive Chris to a hospital or doctor, except to provide the opportunity for him to suffer and withstand pain. Choice.

SMUGGLERS' ROAD (Evarts*, Hal G., Scribner's, 1968), mystery novel set in Baja California in the 1960s. In trouble for fighting, poor school work, and a prank that looks like car theft, Kern Dawson, 17, is offered an alternative to Juvenile Hall by his counselor and Spanish teacher, Bob Barth: a summer working at the Mexican village of La Ribera for the Baja Zopilotes, the Baja Buzzards, who operate a small clinic four hundred miles south of the border, flying in volunteer doctors at irregular intervals to bring medical aid to the isolated community. Kern is put under the stern direction of the only permanent employee, ex-marine sergeant Bull* "El Toro" Kalinski, and prospects for the summer look grim, but he is well fed by warmhearted Mama Rosa and meets Tony Vela, who grew up in East Los Angeles and now helps on his grandfather's fishing boat. Tony thinks that smuggling is still being practiced on the old Smugglers' Road, and there are suspicious circumstances: a trucker, traveling alone, which is uncommon, goes off the road and must be rescued with great effort by Kern and Bull; an American, Hugo Hendryx, operates nearby La Serenidad, a resort with no patrons; Bull regularly takes his boat out for night fishing, though the catch is notoriously poor after dark. Tony persuades Kern to "borrow" the jeep to explore the area of the trucker's accident, where Kern finds a clay jug with a handle in the shape of a monkey, which later proves to be pre-Columbian and very valuable. Things heat up when the jug disappears. Tony and Kern, investigating a nearby island, are shot at and spend a harrowing night in a cave barely above water level, and later Kern and Ramon, a young boy whose club foot has been repaired by the Baja Zopilotes, see a cruiser off a deserted beach and are chased back to the jeep by rifle shots. While Bull Kalinski is away, a ranchero, Luis, summons Kern to aid his brother, who has been gored by a bull. Kern operates by following instructions in a medical book and earns the respect of the villagers and Kalinski. Luis, in gratitude, brings him an even older bowl, also from the site of the accident. In an exciting denouement, Kern visits Hendryx, who has offered him a job decorating, comes upon the smugglers, is nearly caught aboard Hendryx's cruiser, swims under rifle fire, and is rescued by Bull. The smuggling proves to be of pre-Columbian art treasures, crudely disguised as tourist junk (presumably the painting job Kern was to have) with Hendryx as chief culprit. Frankly an adventure mystery, the novel has an involved, fast-paced plot and an interesting setting but little characterization and some rather careless writing. Poe Nominee.

SNOW, RICHARD F(OLGER) (1947–   ), born in New York City; editor, author. He grew up in Westchester County and is a 1970 graduate of Columbia University. He is managing editor of *American Heritage* magazine, where an assignment about the battles of the American Revolution awakened his interest and led to his novel, *Freelon Starbird** (Houghton, 1976), a story of the war seen through the misery, fear, and confusion of a common soldier, who endures great hardship and tries to find meaning in his experience. The author has also written a book-length poem about Coney Island and two novels for adults.

SNYDER, ZILPHA KEATLEY (1927–   ), born in Lemoore, Calif.; teacher and author of popular realistic novels of family life for children and young people. The daughter of a rancher and oil driller, she grew up in rural Ventura county in southern California. She graduated from Whittier College and studied further at the University of California at Berkeley. She taught school in several states and became master teacher and demonstrator for education classes at the University of California at Berkeley. She and her husband, a professor of music, have lived near Santa Rosa, Calif. Since 1964 every year has seen the publication of another book, among them, *Today Is Saturday* (Atheneum, 1969), a book of verse, and several books of fantasy, including a trilogy about the futuristic land of Green-sky, *Below the Root* (Atheneum, 1975), *And All Between* (Atheneum, 1976), and *Until the Celebration* (Atheneum, 1977). Far more popular with young readers and critically acclaimed have been her realistic novels, several of which have won awards and citations: *The Velvet Room** (Atheneum, 1965), which was chosen for Fanfare and cited in *Choice*; *The Changeling** (Atheneum, 1970), which received the Christopher Award and is cited in *Choice*; *The Headless Cupid** (Atheneum, 1971), which received the Christopher Award, was a Newbery honor book, and is cited in *Choice*; *The Witches of Worm** (Atheneum, 1972), a Newbery honor book and a finalist for the National Book Award; and most popular with children and most highly regarded by critics, *The Egypt Game** (Atheneum, 1967), which was a Newbery honor book, elected to the Lewis Carroll Shelf, chosen for Fanfare, given the George G. Stone Award, and listed in *Choice*. Snyder draws her ideas chiefly from her own childhood, teaching, and family life, and recurring themes involve friendship, coming to terms with one's self and life, and the power of the imagination. Although her conclusions often seem unsatisfying and characters are sometimes types or overdrawn, she builds suspense well, uses literate and vigorous language, and creates interesting, imaginative, intelligent protagonists. Recent titles include *The Famous Stanley Kidnapping Case* (Atheneum, 1979) and *Blair's Nightmare* (Atheneum, 1984), which continue the story of the family first met in *The Headless Cupid*, *A Fabulous Creature* (Atheneum, 1981), and *The Birds of Summer* (Atheneum, 1983).

SOBOL, DONALD J. (1924–   ), born in New York City; journalist and free-lance writer. He attended Oberlin College and the New School for Social Research and served in the U.S. Army Combat Engineers in the Pacific theater in World War II. For some years he worked on the editorial staff of New York newspapers, in merchandising, and for both pulp and slick magazines but became a full-time free-lance writer. Among his many books for children are a number in the Watts "First Book" series—*First Book of Medieval Man* (1959), *of Barbarian Invaders* (1962), *of Stocks and Bonds* (1963)—and a biography of the Wright brothers. His *Encyclopedia Brown: Boy Detective** (Nelson, 1963) has at least a dozen sequels and shows his skill with the cleverly plotted story.

SODAPOP CURTIS (*The Outsiders**), Ponyboy's older brother of sixteen, very handsome and well liked. He has dropped out of school, partly because his wages are needed to keep the three brothers together and partly because he is no longer interested in school. He tries to keep peace and promote understanding between Darry* and Pony. Pony idolizes him.

A SOLITARY BLUE (Voigt*, Cynthia, Atheneum, 1983), richly detailed, very convincing realistic novel of family life with problem story aspects set mainly in the early 1970s, first, in Baltimore and Charleston, S.C., and, later, along the Chesapeake Bay not far from the home of the Tillermans of *Dicey's Song**, a companion book. Events are seen from the point of view of Jeff* Greene, who, when he is seven, returns home from second grade to discover that his mother, Melody*, has walked out on him and his father, because, as she explains in a note, she wishes "to try to make things better" for the world's starving children and ecology. For years, Jeff devotes himself compulsively to being very good and taking meticulous care of his abstracted, intellectual father, the Professor*, who teaches history at the University. With the help of a series of live-in college boys as housekeepers and Brother* Thomas, a kindly, understanding monk, the two manage to get along. Five years later, the summer Jeff is twelve, at her invitation, he visits his mother in Charleston, revels in the glow of her vibrant beauty, her enchanting smile, and her love, and makes the acquaintance of Gambo*, her grandmother with whom Melody lives, the dignified matriarch of a proud, old Southern line, from whom he gains some sense of family. Enraptured by his mother's considerable charm, he returns to Baltimore envisioning himself her knight protector, his ardor for her dimmed only by his unanswered letters. His return visit the next summer soon turns sour, and she neglects him throughout for boy friend and do-gooder projects. He confronts her with lying to him to get her way, struggles to keep her from using his love to "break him in pieces," returns to Baltimore feeling betrayed, used, and cast off, goes into a decline, plays truant from school, and, failing exams, is eventually discovered by the Professor and Brother Thomas at the amusement park that has become his haven and solace. Jolted out of the self-absorption caused by his own hurt from Melody, the Professor for the first time shares with Jeff some of his own experiences with Melody and his feelings about her, sees the need for both of them to leave behind unwholesome associations, sells the Baltimore house, and buys a cabin the two of them have found near the marshy seashore along a creek that empties into Chesapeake Bay. As they fix up the cabin to suit their simple needs, father and son grow to a new appreciation of each other. Jeff resumes playing the old Martin guitar his father gave him for Christmas after his first trip to Charleston, makes the honor roll in school, explores the region in his boat, takes up crabbing, and achieves a place among the local youth, respected and included though never popular, among them, Phil Milson, a steady, cheerful farm youth, Andy Barrows, a science nut, who provide ballast, Mina* Smiths, a warm and outgoing black girl, and the several Tillerman children. With the help of Brother Thomas and these school and neighborhood friends, he and the Professor, who has also published a well-received book, learn to be less withdrawn for emotional self-protection and begin to risk forming attachments. In short, they learn to love. When Melody sues for divorce and Jeff's custody and comes to claim him, Jeff has developed sufficient wisdom and self-confidence to see through the veneer of her charm, deduce her motives (which are self-seeking and, he learns later on, financial, for he stands to inherit Gambo's property), and reject her firmly though compassionately. Like the blue heron he has seen in the tidal marshes, Jeff remains essentially a loner, but also like the heron he is self-sufficient, projects an air of calm dignity, and enjoys the fellowship of his kind, though only on occasion. Both father and son will never lose the emotional scars Melody inflicted on them, but Jeff and the Professor can look forward to a satisfying life together. Though she appears in relatively few scenes,

Melody dominates this quiet, thought-provoking, unsensationalistic, substantial story of the relationships between father and son, mother and son, and husband and wife, a story less of plot than of character that explores such themes as giving love, emotional and psychological survival, and learning to know and appreciate one's self. Jeff gradually and convincingly grows in awareness of what his parents are really like. He gradually learns to see and cope with his mother's selfishness and deceit and to appreciate his introverted father, who, in turn, learns to give and receive love. Even minor characters are invested with life, though the Tillermans strike a false note, not because of the way they are portrayed, which is thoroughly consistent with *Dicey's Song*, but because they simply do not seem to fit. The symbolism of the heron, that develops and alters as does Jeff himself, the frequent allusions to music, and consistency of point of view, supported by restrained, effective detail of well-realized emotion, unify what would otherwise be merely a series of loosely connected vignettes covering a ten-year span of time. Boston Globe Honor; Fanfare; Newbery Honor.

THE SOLOMON SYSTEM (Naylor*, Phyllis Reynolds, Atheneum, 1983), realistic novel about the family disruption caused by an impending divorce, set in Kensington, Md., in recent times. Both Ted Solomon, 13, and his brother, Nory (Norman), 16, are well aware that their parents have not been getting along well for two or three years, but the two boys are very close and always work together, in what the neighbors jokingly call the Solomon System. Ted, the first-person narrator, is an emotional, vocal boy, while Nory is self-contained, apparently not letting the parental difficulties bother him. When their maternal grandmother, Grandma Rose, whom both parents like, visits, the tension is reduced, but shortly before both boys go to camp their mother tells them that she is going to ask their father to move out. Even though Camp Susquehannocks in the Poconos, which the boys have attended for years, is always fun, Ted worries about his parents and is annoyed that his grandmother's letter gives him no information. Some things about camp are changed, too. Though the boys are in the same bunkhouse, as they have wished to be in previous years, Nory does not fall in with Ted's plan to learn survival skills, an idea he has so that they can make their own way if their parents split up, but seems more interested in the girls than Ted thinks he should be. On visiting day, their grandmother comes instead of their parents. Ted gets a crush on one of the counselors, Marilyn Davis, and is dismayed when Nory seems to be making time with her. During the fifth week at camp they get a letter from their father, saying that he and their mother have mutually agreed to split up, but that neither one wants to be the one to move out, and that they will let the boys help decide when they come home. Nory's reserve is shattered, and in fury at having the decision thrown to them, he takes the beautiful dugout canoe that the head boys' counselor, Mel Kramer, has been making for several seasons, and he and Ted go out on the lake where he talks and cries, letting out all the misery and anger he has been bottling up. When it begins to get dark, Mel comes out in the rowboat to find them, furious at their breaking all the camp rules but understanding of their misery. The brief closeness with Nory doesn't last, however, and as they leave camp Ted's only consolation is that Marilyn has really liked his parting gift to her, his preserved tapeworm. The one thing the boys agree upon is that they will not make the decision for their parents. They think they are prepared for whatever arrangements their parents make, but the announcement, made on a weekend when their grandmother is again visiting, is a real shock. The parents have decided that their father will move out, and Ted will live with him for a year while Nory stays with their mother, then the boys will switch. Ted is stunned, but Nory seems indifferent and asks for the car to take Ted swimming. Instead, however, he gets out on the Beltway and drives like a madman, heading for Frederick, where Mel has a farm. Ted, terrified, pretends that a police car is following them and when Nory stops, leaps out and accuses him of wanting to kill them both in his anger at their parents. When they find Mel gone for the weekend, they quarrel again and Nory leaves but later returns and they go back together. At home, with their grandmother's encouragement, they confront their parents and say that they are a team and won't be broken up. The parents revise their plan so that the father will rent an apartment, live in it six months, and then trade places with their mother, so the boys can go on living together in their accustomed house. Nory gets jobs as newspaper carriers on a double route for himself and Ted so they can earn money as a team for camp next year. Though predictable, the story does an excellent job of portraying the uncertainty and pain of the children of a breaking marriage. At sixteen, Nory seems a bit old to be so enthusiastic about camp life, as described by Ted, but both boys are believable in their anguish over their family problems. The wise old Jewish grandmother is a stock figure. Child Study.

SOMEBODY ELSE'S CHILD (Silman*, Roberta, ill. Chris Conover, Warne, 1976), realistic story for younger children set in an American suburb in the 1970s. The narrator, Peter, a fourth grader, is very fond of the school bus driver, an older man known as Puddin' Paint, who calls Peter "Smiley." When the bus gets stuck near Peter's house, the last on the route, the driver comes in to call and in the conversation with Peter's mother says he has no children and wouldn't want to adopt and raise "somebody else's child." Peter, who knows he is adopted, is crushed, and his mother's kind explanations don't console him until the driver loses his two dogs, Black and Brown, and Peter helps look for them in bitter snowy weather. They are able to find the dogs, which are in deep woods caught in side-by-side traps, mostly because Peter is able to hear a whimpering inaudible to the driver. They make a stretcher from blankets they have handy, trudge a long distance to the car, and take the dogs to a veterinarian fortuitously living in a nearby village. Peter collapses from the strain but sleeps off the effects and realizes that his parents and his sister, Kate, care as much for him as Puddin' Paint cares for his dogs. The first person narration is fairly successful for a character as young as Peter, but the story is obviously contrived to teach about adoption. Child Study.

SON FOR A DAY (Gerson*, Corinne, ill. Velma Ilseley, Atheneum, 1980), humorous, realistic novel set in the Bronx in the last third of the twentieth century. While his mother is in Hollywood seeking a career in films, Danny Turner, 11, lives with his Aunt Dorothy, who works most evenings and weekends, leaving him to his own devices. At the Bronx Zoo, Danny observes that many of the visitors are single men with a child, "zoodaddies" he learns, that is, divorced men having their day out with their sons and usually feeling ill at ease. He figures out his MO, a system for engaging a boy, usually a couple of years younger than he is, in conversation about the young gorillas and providing a third party to ease the strain between father and child, so that he is invited to lunch, often to dinner and to share further treats. At his first try, with Donald Sutherland from Scarsdale and his father who drives a Cadillac, Danny learns that it is a mistake to tell the truth about his own father, who abandoned his mother before he was born. After that he always says that his father died when he was little. In the next months, Danny picks up a variety of boys and zoodaddies, who treat him to interesting experiences and good meals, some of them "regulars," who make dates for further weekends, among these Jeff Murdoch and his father, a teacher who drives an old Ford; Brad Hall and his father, Tony, a non-stop joker, who works in public relations and drives a red sports car; Bobby Remler and his doctor father, who owns a Mercedes. Once, by accident, he acquires a whole family by picking up Carlos Rivera and his father, who is not divorced but lives near Danny and is merely getting relief from a large family in a small apartment. In Carlos he finds a week-day friend and in the Rivera household a place where he can get a home-cooked meal and introduce his Aunt Dorothy. His big mistake occurs when he takes on Mike Andersen and his mother, Gretchen, his only zoomommy. Gretchen proves to be a TV commentator to whom Danny confesses, while Mike is visiting his father in California, his whole con scheme. Gretchen uses the story on her "Real People" program, keeping Danny's name secret but giving enough information so that other reporters zero in on him. Exposed, Danny fears he might go to jail but actually is the feature of Gretchen's next program, where she has assembled all his zoodaddies and, to his astonishment, his mother. The TV exposure gets her several job offers, of which she chooses one in Chicago, where Danny discovers in the Museum of Science and Industry the possibility of a new MO to provide him interest, friendship, and high life, involving museumdaddies. The story is essentially light-weight and amusing, though some comment on the problems of children and parents in divorces is implied. The first-person narration is mostly convincing, since Danny is a very bright, self-confident eleven-year-old. Christopher.

SONTE (*Saturday, the Twelfth of October**), cousin of Burrum*, who hopes to marry her until she is betrothed to Hiffaru*, to whom afterward he remains hostile. Sonte stands up for his mother, N'ati, when she is displeased with Farwe,

Burrum's mother, who is defended by Hiffaru. The two have a Quarrel, in which they insult each other verbally until their mothers are satisfied, the tribe's traditional way of handling disputes. Later, pride impels Sonte to insist that Hiffaru give him Zan's knife when he requests it. Hiffaru then stabs him to death, the most terrible thing that has ever happened among the People, who have never before known murder.

SOPHIA SCROOBY PRESERVED (Bacon*, Martha, ill. David Omar White, Little, 1968), romantic, historical novel which begins somewhere in Africa in 1768 and ends in Connecticut in 1782. Daughter of a minor African chieftain, Nono (Nameless) is the only survivor of a Zulu attack on her village. She lives with impala, roaming the forests and countryside, until hunger drives her to Mozambique, where she falls in with a band of slaves belonging to a Portuguese trader. With them she is shipped northward to the Gold Coast and loaded on a slave ship bound for the New World. Although prisoners die by the scores in the filthy, cold, and overcrowded hold, tough little Nono survives the rigors of the Middle Passage. She shares her stale and moldy bread with an equally emaciated young sailor, who, in gratitude, gives her a bit of sail for a garment and calls her Pansy from her big, dark eyes. On her arrival in New Haven, Connecticut Colony, the bewildered seven-year-old is purchased by a gentle Tory family, the Scroobys, as a companion for their willful and frivolous daughter, Prudence. Noting her wit and willingness to learn, Squire Scrooby names her Sophia. Pansy teaches herself to read and write and shows a talent for music, and the Scroobys' schoolteacher, Master* Anthony, finds Pansy a more apt student than Prudence. Pansy soon reads daily to Squire Scrooby, who is blind, and is to be trained as his amanuensis. The Revolutionary War brings financial ruin to the Tory Scroobys, and they are forced to sell their slaves and move to Canada. Pansy becomes the property of slavers, Crop-ear* and Scarecrow, who sell her to a pirate captain, Pedro Alvarez, who is holding a British gentleman, John Forsyth*, for ransom. Forsyth and Pansy escape from Alvarez and his wife, the voodoo queen, Madame* Melanie, and Forsyth takes the girl to London with him. There her cultured ways, quick wit, and rich singing voice win her the adulation of polite society. She discovers Master Anthony performing at Drury Lane and returns with him to Connecticut, where she is joyfully reunited with the Scroobys, who, now that the war is over, have settled on a farm. This well-sustained, entertaining story of the lively, melodramatic, often preposterous adventures of a slave girl's rise to culture, fame, and comfortable circumstances is related in a mannered style that parodies the writing of the period. Characters, some serious, some comic, are distinctly drawn, but Pansy-Sophia rises above them all as a charming and memorable heroine. Brave, kind, and enduringly optimistic, Pansy employs the necessary cunning and resource to overcome her many adversities and to make the most of any good fortune that comes her way. The reader sees what a refined, modest home of the period is like and gains limited views of polite London society, of the miseries of the Middle Passage, and of conditions in New Haven jail, which is debtors' prison, madhouse, and quarters for slaves and sundry unfortunates. Fanfare.

SOPHIE SCHOLL (*Ceremony of Innocence**; *Darkness over the Land**), a real historical figure, a German university student in her teens who was guillotined as a traitor by the Nazis in Munich during World War II. She helped to write and distribute leaflets signed with a White Rose which urged resistance to Nazi policies and sabotage as a way of ending the war sooner. In *Ceremony of Innocence*, she appears as warmhearted and life-loving but fiercely determined to act upon the dictates of her conscience, even though it might cost her own life and those of her brother, Hans, and sweetheart, Alex* Schmorell. At first she promotes passive resistance in Munich and other German cities but decides to resist Nazism more actively when she discovers that authorities are practicing euthanasia on the mentally retarded children among whom she works. She acts increasingly out of religious motives as opposed to Hans's intellectual and humanitarian ones. Her Catholicism gives her strength to meet her fate. In *Darkness over the Land*, Sophie visits the Elend bookshop, where she leaves some leaflets and discusses her views about things with Mark. Mark also becomes acquainted with and tries to help another member of her group, Professor Huber, a real person, too. Sophie is presented as intense and thoroughly dedicated to her cause.

SORENSEN†, VIRGINIA (1912–   ), born in Provo, Utah; novelist for both adults and children. She grew up in Utah's Sanpete Valley, received her A.B. degree from Brigham Young University, and did graduate work at Stanford University. She was awarded two Guggenheim fellowships for work in Mexico and in Denmark, which is the setting for *Lotte's Locket** (Harcourt, 1964), a story which has more description of locale than plot. Among her other books for young people are *Plain Girl†* (Harcourt, 1955), a story of a young Quaker, which received the Child Study Award, and *Miracles on Maple Hill†* (Harcourt, 1956), a story celebrating the wonders of nature in Pennsylvania mountains, which won the Newbery Medal. She and her writer husband have lived in Tangiers, Morocco.

THE SOUL BROTHERS AND SISTER LOU (Hunter*, Kristin, Scribner's, 1968), realistic novel of family and community life set among blacks in Southside, a city in the eastern United States, in the late 1900s and covering a few months in the life of Louretta Hawkins, 14, her family, and friends. Louretta, her seven brothers and sisters, and her mother occupy a too-small house on Carlisle Street. Louretta longs for a place to go "between school and suppertime," where she can talk and have fun with her friends. When the Cheerful Baptist Church moves out of its store-front building, Louretta persuades her older brother, William*, 21, to rent it for the printing business he wishes to start and let her and her friends use the rest of the place as a clubhouse. With the help of Miss Hodges, her English teacher, Mr. Lucitanno, the music teacher, and Blind* Eddie Bell, an old, black jazz musician, Lou and four boys practice singing soul songs, some of which Fess*, a new boy with militant ideas, helps write. During a dance, the police, led by zealous and hostile Officer* Lafferty, raid the store, and one of the singing group, Jethro, is shot. For a while, Lou becomes very bitter and even attends one of Fess's revolutionary meetings. When Jethro dies, Fess plans a ''war'' of retaliation against the police, but Lou urges her friends to express their love for Jethro more positively through their music. The teachers persuade city hall not to close the clubhouse. At the funeral, Frank, Ulysses, David, who are the Soul Brothers, and Lou attract attention for their fine singing, are offered a recording contract, and soon become wealthy. Lou finds that, while life is easier for her and her family, there are still problems to face. Once begun, the story moves fast. Touches of black idiom contribute authenticity. Most characters are clear types, and the book seems written to thesis, its events contrived for purpose. The author broaches too many black problems for one book to handle, and the conclusion is too pat to be credible. Sequel is *Lou in the Limelight*. (Arneatha* Hawkins; The Hawks*) Choice; Lewis Carroll.

SOUNDER (Armstrong*, William H., ill. James Barkley, Harper, 1969), fable-like novel set in the deep rural South in the last third of the nineteenth century. None of the characters is named—simply the man, the boy, his mother, the younger children—except the dog Sounder, half Georgia redbone hound and half bulldog, named for his clear, mellow hunting call. With hunting bad, field work over for the year, and the family hungry, the man steals a ham and some sausages. Before they have even finished eating the meat, a coarse, red-neck sheriff and two deputies come to the isolated cabin, handcuff the man, and brutally throw him into a wagon. When Sounder tries to follow, the sheriff blasts him with a shotgun. Terribly wounded, the dog drags himself under the cabin. The next day, while the mother walks to town to return the remainder of the meat, the boy crawls under the cabin but cannot find the dog. For Christmas, the mother makes a cake and sends the boy to town to give it to his father, since women are not allowed in the jail. The jailer breaks the cake to crumbs and treats the boy with contempt. After a little constrained talk, the father tells the boy not to come again. Two months later Sounder, three-legged, blind in one eye, horribly scarred, returns. The mother learns through the people for whom she washes that the father has been sent to hard labor. The boy starts doing field work in summers but in the fall goes around the state to road camps and prison farms and stone quarries, hunting for his father. Sometimes he finds a convict who has worked with him, or who suggests where he might have been sent, but he never finds his father. Once as he is looking through the wire fence around a road camp, a guard smashes his finger with a piece of metal. The boy stops in the yard of a one-room school to wash his bleeding hand, and the teacher, a gentle man, takes him home to treat the injuries. He reads to the boy from the essays of Montaigne, a book the boy has found in a trash can and carried, though he can barely read. The teacher offers to have the boy live with him, do chores, and get some education. The boy goes home, more than a day's walk, gets his mother's permission, and starts living with the teacher in the winters when the field work is done. One summer day, more than six years after his arrest, the man returns, half-paralyzed, dragging one foot, having been injured in a dynamite blast in the prison quarry and let out because he can no longer work. Sounder, who has never made more than a whine since he has come back, greets the man with a full-throated bark. In the fall, while the boy is back on a last visit before winter, the man and the dog go hunting, but Sounder returns alone. The boy follows the dog back to the wood to find his father dead. Before he goes back to school, the boy digs a grave for Sounder, knowing that he will not live through the winter. Though beautifully written and moving, the book has a remote feel. Only the boy's character is developed, with his fear and loneliness, his impotent fury at the cruel sheriff and brutal guards, his great desire for learning. The mother is long-suffering and patient. The man and dog are more symbols of endurance than characters. Choice; Fanfare; Lewis Carroll; Newbery Winner.

SPEARE†, ELIZABETH GEORGE (1908–   ), born in Melrose, Mass.; author most noted for her two Newbery Award–winning historical novels: *The Witch of Blackbird Pond†* (Houghton, 1958), set among the Puritans of Connecticut Colony in the late 1600s, and *The Bronze Bow** (Houghton, 1961), set in Palestine in the first century after Christ, which was also a Fanfare book and selected for *Choice*. *Witch* grew out of her interest in the history of Wethersfield, Conn., where she once lived, while *Bow* resulted from her wish to give the teenagers in her Sunday School class some sense of what it must have been like to live in Palestine under the Roman occupation. It tells of a young Jewish blacksmith's ill-conceived efforts to free his people from the domination of the Romans. Before that, she published the absorbing but less well crafted *Calico Captive†* (Houghton, 1957), a Fanfare book about a real New England settler woman who was captured by Indians during the French and Indian War. More recently she has published *The Sign of the Beaver** (Houghton, 1983), a Newbery honor book for younger readers in which a boy left alone on the family farm in the wilds of Maine in the late 1700s survives with the help of friendly Indians. For this book, in 1984 she was the first recipient of the prestigious new prize for historical fiction, the Scott O'Dell Award. Although their plots lack conviction, Speare's novels present serious, well-researched, and vivid pictures of their times and blend skillfully the protagonists' personal problems and those of their periods. Speare has also written a book of non-fiction for children, *Life in Colonial America* (Random, 1963), a novel for adults, *The Prospering* (Houghton, 1967), about the Stockbridge experiment in western Massachusetts, and has published articles and stories for women's magazines and plays. She has lived all her life in New England, attending Smith College and receiving her bachelor's and master's degrees from Boston University. Before marrying Alden Speare, an industrial engineer, and settling in Wethersfield, Conn., the locale of *The Witch* *of Blackbird Pond*, she taught English in Massachusetts high schools for several years. She now lives in Easton, Conn.

A SPELL IS CAST (Cameron*†, Eleanor, ill. Beth Krush and Joe Krush, Little, 1964), realistic mystery novel set in southern California in the late twentieth century. Imaginative, lonely young Cory Winterslow flies from New York to Monterey, Calif., for a several weeks' visit with her grandmother, Mrs. Van Heusen, and her Uncle* Dirk, while her foster mother, Stephanie, an actress, is on tour. Shifted from school to school and cared for by a succession of "lady helps," Cory looks forward to the comfort and security of the Van Heusen oceanside estate, Tarnhelm, to the pleasure of the company of her relatives, and to making friends her own age among the neighbor children. Shortly after she arrives, she is dismayed and perplexed to learn that Stephanie has never legally adopted her. Other puzzles intrigue her, too: why Uncle Dirk is so moody and often withdrawn, why a tower and a certain room in the house are off limits to everyone, and what connection the beautiful Laurel* Woodford has with the Van Heusens. When Cory dares both to enter the secret room and to make friends with lively young Peter* Hawthorne, president of the Explorers, a club made up of children who live in the neighborhood, she is on the way to unraveling all these mysteries. In the process, she repairs the fractured romance between Uncle Dirk and Laurel, who decide to adopt her and give her the permanent home and loving parents for which she has been longing. Stephanie protests briefly and theatrically, and Cory looks forward to being a real Van Heusen. Voices and music in the dark, a sleepwalking scene, fragments of love poems, affectionately carved, unfinished masks, and a locked, wooden box are valuable clues, and a dangerously rising tide and the recurring motif of the unicorn are among other Gothic conventions that appear in this gracefully written and carefully plotted romantic mystery for middle grade readers. Andrew* and Fergie*, the Scottish couple who keep Mrs. Van Heusen's house and garden, are especially good characters, and Cory comes out of herself believably. Choice; Fanfare; Poe Nominee.

SPENCER CAMERON (*A Formal Feeling**), older brother of Anne*, a college student who lives at the dormitory but has moved back for the Christmas vacation. Although he resembles his abstracted father in appearance and in his slow eating, his intense concentration on one thing at a time, and his disinclination to force the communication that might help Anne, he is generally sympathetic and fond of her. He picks her up at the airport, moves home early for the holidays to help break the awkward situation for her, takes her out to lunch, and, after she has been coolly disagreeable to her stepmother, advises her, "This is a brave new world, my friend. You might try joining it." He is aware that she has somehow forgotten the memory that is very clear to him of how his mother left the family when he was about twelve and he was sent with eight-year-old Anne to stay with his grandmother. He plays the recorder and shares the family musical and intellectual approach to life, but he is a realist about family relationships, in contrast to Anne, who has denied the painful past.

SPICE ISLAND MYSTERY (Cavanna*, Betty, Morrow, 1969), realistic mystery novel involving some detection set on the Caribbean island of Grenada in the late 1900s, in which two young people are instrumental in capturing a ring of marijuana smugglers. Bright, articulate, ambitious Marcy Baptiste, 17, has just returned to her native island after living for four years with an American family in Massachusetts as resident sitter and household helper while attending high school. Since there are few jobs for an educated girl on the island, Marcy eagerly accepts a position as girl-Friday with a construction company that builds expensive summer homes for Americans. She soon makes friends with the company architect, serious-minded, intelligent, young Richard Strang from Trinidad, who is also American-educated. A number of troubling questions vex Marcy. Coffee Parkinson, her old beau, and some other island youths are spending money more freely than the island's depressed economy and their curiously spotty work records would justify, and a classy schooner, the *Black Pirate*, strangely frequents the dangerous, off-shore waters. After she and Richard are captured and tied up by unknown assailants while they are trying to assist a troubled skiff during a storm, the two set out to get to the bottom of things. Their investigations lead them to a pagan devil-exorcising ceremony, to a cave containing a suspiciously empty cask, and to the discovery that marijuana is being grown locally. Their attention finally focuses on a nutmeg factory, which they enter stealthily by night. There they observe marijuana enclosed in spice bales for shipment to the United States. Richard is captured, and Marcy's screams attract help, to their great surprise, from Coffee. They discover that, while several island youths have indeed been involved in the illegal trade, Coffee's extra money has come from selling old Spanish gold he discovered while snorkeling. A good measure of red herrings, false leads, and unexpected twists extend the mystery which remains consistently interesting from beginning to end. From September to December, carefully calculated complications unfold against the more serious matter of Marcy's gradual re-involvement in island society, her growing romantic interest in Richard, her realization that she has outgrown Coffee, and her eventual decision to go to college. Richard is a plaster figure, the stock black man suspicious of white society and intentions, while Coffee is the typical misjudged local boy, who has not gone wrong as everyone believes. Marcy is well drawn, a self-reliant, curious, strong-minded young woman, just impetuous enough to become involved in such adventures. A little dialect and descriptions of the island economy and ways result in an unusually strong sense of setting for a mystery. Poe Nominee.

A SPIRIT TO RIDE THE WHIRLWIND (Lord*, Athena V., Macmillan, 1981), historical novel of the textile mill workers in Lowell, Mass., set in 1836. Binnie (Arbinia) Howe, 11, decides that the only way out of her life of slaving in her widowed mother's boarding house and taking care of her younger brother, Aleck, 5, is to earn a lot of money. To her surprise, the Irish boy, Packy (Patrick) McCabe, whom she helps out in a fight, has the same ambition, and they become friends, though her sort of people usually have nothing to do with the "Paddies" from the Acre. She admits to him that she wants a nice house, with a piano in the living room, just for her family with no boarders. When her mother collapses from overwork and flu, Binnie struggles to provide meals to the boarding women, all of whom work in the mills, to take care of Aleck, and to direct Mary Kate, the dim-witted Irish girl who helps out. She gets unexpected help from some of the boarders, particularly horse-faced Florilla Nappet, and from Iyam Andre Malenfant, the Frenchy who has been doing odd jobs and surprisingly knows how to cook. When Mrs. Howe, recovered, agrees to let Aleck go to stay with Cousin Cornelia at New Bedford, Binnie is both jealous and relieved of many of her duties, and she seizes the opportunity to ask her mother to let her start work at the mill. Reluctantly, her mother agrees, particularly because they need money for tuition at Harvard, where Binnie's older brother, Adam, is studying theology. At first Binnie is thrilled to be a "doffer" in the spinning room, to run up and replace full bobbins with empties though she soon tires of the noise, long hours, and almost unbearable heat. She especially dislikes Franklin Quimay, the sanctimonious manager. She does, however, enjoy belonging to the working women of the house, a mixed lot, notably tall, intelligent Maria Teasdale, who lends her books, flirtatious Dorcas Boomer, even complaining Phoebe Little. Florilla and Frenchy, an oddly assorted couple, leave together for Buffalo, where he will be a carpenter and she can have a small farm. Trouble starts when the boarding house keepers, who are paid by the corporation out of money withheld from the workers' wages, ask for higher board allowances to meet rising costs. Mrs. Howe is as shocked as the workers when the corporation withholds more money from the wages. Binnie has already become aware of abuses that occur, despite the corporation's paternalistic care for the women's morals and welfare: husbands can claim all a wife's wages and collect them directly; windows are nailed shut to keep the threads from drying out, even if the workers faint from the heat; women must work a full year and give two-weeks notice before leaving or be blacklisted but can be fired at the overseer's will; women are not paid for the part of the month they've worked if they leave or are fired before the end; when a storm closes the plant, the workers are docked for the time lost. Binnie and Packy fight when he tells her some of his radical uncle's ideas, but they make up, and she tries not to be jealous when he gets to be an apprentice in a machine shop. The "Premium System," which gives the overseers a bonus for greater production and results in a speedup, and the extra withholding of board wages so enrage the women that they start a walk-out. Binnie, allowed by her mother to choose, joins the strike and becomes a messenger. As it drags on, many women go back to their farm homes. Maria Teasdale is a leader and gives speeches written by Binnie but leaves when her father orders her home. Phoebe Little joins the strike but is revealed to have given her two-weeks notice at the first sign of trouble, so she won't be blacklisted. Mrs. Howe is torn between solidarity with the women and her need for a charter for her boarding house. Dorcas turns out to be one of the strongest strikers and cleverest in strategy. The strike ends limply with the corporation giving up the extra withholding, but the workers win no real gains. Binnie, however, has learned from the experience and decides to work through the winter, then go back to school. When she tells her mother that she wants to keep her wages for her own education instead of sending them to Adam, she is surprised to find that her mother approves. Binnie is a spirited girl, intelligent and feisty, a hard worker who refuses the condescending phony concern of the corporation. Other characters are well developed and interesting. Conditions of work in the "model" mills of Lowell are presented as intrinsic and interesting elements in the story. The theme that underdogs must stand up for themselves is clear but not overstated. Child Study.

SPORT ROCQUE (*Harriet the Spy**), Simon Rocque, Harriet Welsch's best friend and sixth grade classmate. He runs the house and manages the money for his absent-minded, divorced father, a writer. Sport is a serious-minded, young-old boy who wants to become either a ball player or a CPA when he grows up. Sport generally lets Harriet have her way when they play together and supports her in votes at school. He turns against her when he hears what she has said about him in her notebook but later makes up with her. He is the most likeable of the book's assortment of unlikeable characters.

SPRAGUE, GRETCHEN (BURNHAM) (1926–   ), born in Lincoln, Nebr.; attorney and mystery novel writer. She attended the University of Nebraska and Columbia School of Law and has been both an instructor of English and a practicing attorney. With her husband, a Rhodes Scholar, she has lived in England as well as in Arkansas and Brooklyn, N.Y. Her tense novel of a teenage girl and a young bank robber who meet on an isolated mountain trail, *Signpost to Terror** (Dodd, 1967), was a winner of the Edgar Allan Poe Award. Among her other titles are *A Question of Harmony* (Dodd, 1965) and *White in the Moon* (Dodd, 1968).

THE SPRING RIDER (Lawson*, John Crowell, 1968), fantasy set in the mountains of Virginia in the 1960s. Jacob Downs, 12, and his sister, Gray*, 17, live in a valley where one of the battles of the Civil War was fought. Local tradition has it that in April a rider wearing black with a stovepipe hat can be seen and recognized as Lincoln, but before his horse gets close, he disappears. When Jacob finds a young soldier in a Union uniform sleeping in the log barn, he realizes that it is one of the Civil War dead come back to refight the war for a few days every spring. He watches the soldier as he climbs the hill and plays assembly on his bugle. Then they get to talking, the soldier introduces himself as Sergeant Hannibal* Cutler of the Second Maine Division, and he helps Jacob feed the lambs. Jacob's sympathies, however, are with the South, particularly with dashing Colonel* Turner Ashby, who was in the local battle. The same day Gray, who waits for someone to come down the road to carry her off, meets the Spring Rider, and they talk of their dreams, hers to meet that special someone and his to get the fighters to stop. That night, Jacob sneaks out and meets the Confederate army coming, led by Stonewall Jackson. At first he is considered a spy, but he convinces General Jackson that there is a better way to the Big Sinks, a logging road over the mountain, and finds himself leading the army up the old road, an army that seems to move in its sleep. As they reach the top, Ashby arrives, a very wide-awake, headstrong gallant riding a white horse. Jackson sends him ahead to scout and sends Jacob with him in a wild ride down the mountain. With sheer audacity, Ashby overrides the sentries guarding a bridge, and when they reach the main camp of the Second Maine Regiment, wearing a poncho which covers his uniform, rides boldly in as if coming off sentry duty and asks for coffee. Their masquerade is discovered when Hannibal recognizes Jacob, and as they make a mad ride to escape, Ashby seizes and carries off their regimental standard. Jacob gets separated, falls off, and is almost captured before Ashby rides up, catches him up onto his horse, and speeds off to a cave he knows of. There they can make a fire and get food and dry clothes from a stock of provisions. Hannibal, wanting to retrieve the standard, recrosses the mountain and meets Gray, who doesn't understand at first that he is not from her time. They have a sweet, innocently romantic morning and meet Lincoln, who knows that as Hannibal calls the dead up to this battle, only he can send them back for good. When Hannibal returns to his outfit, they want to take him prisoner, and he escapes, realizing that Lincoln has asked for him and that is why he is being hunted. In the meantime, Jacob, left by Ashby in the cave, has begun to explore and gets stuck near an upper entrance. Ashby comes back for him but riding and shouting fails to hear Jacob's cries for help. Both Ashby and Hannibal realize that they can draw their new friends back with them, to live for only a few days of fighting each year, but they cannot reverse the process to remain in the modern world. Hannibal rescues Jacob and, understanding that Lincoln's solution is the best one, blows his bugle to call all the soldiers back from the world for good. The fantasy succeeds by building a haunting atmosphere which makes the mingling of times and of the dead and living plausible. Hannibal's self-sacrifice in giving up his annual taste of life is made deeply moving by his matter-of-fact, understated attitude of a Maine farm boy. The heroics of Ashby are nicely contrasted to Hannibal's quiet courage, and the whole story is pervaded by a sadness that points up the theme of how precious life is. Boston Globe Winner; Choice; Fanfare.

SPYKMAN†, E(LIZABETH) C(HOATE) (1896–1965), born in Southboro, Mass.; author of four humorous and authentic-sounding, episodic family novels set in the first decade of the twentieth century. She had a childhood much like that of Jane* Cares in her stories, living on an estate-like farm surrounded by those of her relatives, with an autocratic father and numerous servants. She traveled widely and wrote articles published in the *Atlantic Monthly*, but her contribution to children's literature consists of four books with memorable characters about a life now departed, seen not with nostalgia but through the matter-of-fact perception of a child: *A Lemon and a Star** (Harcourt, 1955), *The Wild Angel* (Harcourt, 1957), *Terrible, Horrible Edie** (Harcourt, 1960), and *Edie on the Warpath** (Harcourt, 1966).

STACEY LOGAN (*Roll of Thunder, Hear My Cry**), 12, elder brother of Cassie. He concocts the plan to get revenge on the school bus driver by miring the bus in mud. He sometimes does not use his head, for example, when he lets T. J. Avery talk him out of his new coat, but he becomes more sensible as the year goes on. When T. J. is captured by the lynch mob, Stacey and Cassie report what is happening to Papa Logan, and Papa's quick action saves T. J.'s life. Stacey thinks of himself as the man of the house when Papa is away. He is a convincing, well-drawn character.

STANLEY PETRONSKI (*Veronica Ganz**), Veronica's simpering, little half-brother, who hiccoughs when he is nervous, and he often gets nervous. Veronica loves him, feels very close to him, and takes care of him after school while her mother works at her stepfather's store. Veronica's relationship with Stanley reveals a tender side to her character that no one outside the family is aware of.

STARWATCHER (*Enchantress from the Stars**), Federation Anthropological agent, Elana's father and chief of the expedition to Andrecia*. It is his idea to have Elana initiated into the Service before she has completed her training so that she can help their expedition accomplish its objective of keeping the Imperialists from establishing a colony on Andrecia. To Georyn* and Terwyn*, Andrecians, he is known as Starwatcher, who appears to be an all-knowing, omnipotent being from another time and place. He imposes tasks on them which they think will render them capable of defeating the Dragon*.

STEELE, MARY Q(UINTARD GOVAN) (1922–   ), pseudonym: Wilson Gage; born in Chattanooga, Tenn.; writer of books for children, primarily on natural history. She attended the University of Chattanooga and married William O. Steele*, a writer. Among her books of fiction for children are some that clearly have their primary interest in science, as in *Dan and the Miranda** (published under Wilson Gage, World, 1962), a story about spiders. She has also written fantasies, among them the light but clever *Miss Osborne-the-Mop** (published under Wilson Gage, World, 1963) and the more complex and serious *Journey Outside** (published under Mary Q. Steele, Viking, 1969), a Newbery honor book.

STEIG, WILLIAM (1907–   ), born in New York City; humorous artist and writer. He attended College of the City of New York and the National Academy of Design and since 1930 has been a freelance artist, with work appearing frequently in *The New Yorker* magazine and at least thirteen books of his collected drawings published. His books for children have been a rather late development in his career, starting with picture books like *Sylvester and the Magic Pebble* (Simon, 1969), which won the Caldecott Medal. Since then he has written other picture books and some longer stories, all self-illustrated, like *Dominic** (Farrar, 1972), a picaresque dog fantasy, and *The Real Thief** (Farrar, 1973), a light fantasy mystery story. *Abel's Island** (Farrar, 1976) is the most skillfully written, a Robinsonnade starring an Edwardian mouse in a pseudo-pretentious style that parodies books of the period, a Newbery honor book. Another Newbery honor book, more a picture book than a novel, is *Doctor De Soto* (Farrar, 1982), again with a mouse protagonist, this one a clever dentist. Among his other recent titles are *Gorky Rises* (Farrar, 1980), about a frog who mixes a magic concoction that enables him to fly, and *CDC?* (Farrar, 1984), a picture book riddling on the sounds of letters.

STEVE FORRESTER (*Sinbad and Me**; *Mystery of the Witch Who Wouldn't**), competent twelve-year-old crime solver whose intuition and naive blunders lead to the capture of a number of criminals. Although directed frequently by Sheriff* Landry to act only upon facts, Steve often has hunches that lead to solutions in bizarre mysteries.

STEVE PULASKI (*Rain of Fire**), pudgy twelve-year-old whose lies about his brother, newly returned from the army, get him into a conflict with his friends that nearly ends tragically. Baffled and hurt that Matthew* is so changed and doesn't want to tell him about his three years in the war, Steve invents a medal and other exploits to brag about to the other boys, but his biggest lie comes from his own fantasy that Matthew has always mis-aimed the big guns so that no one would be killed, a lie that leads to the other boys writing a letter to J. Edgar Hoover accusing Matthew of being a traitor. In his efforts to undo the harm he has caused, Steve gets into continually bigger trouble, until finally, badly injured in the hospital, he begins to understand why Matthew has such horror of war.

STEVIE ANDERSON (*A Really Weird Summer**), practical, physically active younger brother of Nels*. Shut out by his younger siblings, Rory and Jenny, who are happy playing young-child games, and abandoned by Nels, who has retreated into a fantasy world, Stevie is miserable, bored to distraction, and apprehensive about his parents' divorce, which has sent the children to the old inn at Reeves Ferry for the summer. At first he tries to recapture Nels's attention and to get him to ride bikes and collect beetles with him, but when Nels rejects him verbally, he tries to make friends with a group of older boys who repair their motorcycles in the school yard, even though he uneasily realizes that they are using him and making fun of him. On Stevie's birthday, his faith in Nels's promise to return prompts him to a final search which saves his brother from suffocation in a closet.

STILES, MARTHA BENNETT, born in Manila, Philippine Islands; writer. After studying at the College of William and Mary, she took her bachelor's from the University of Michigan, where she received Hopwood awards for her writing. She married Martin Stiles, a professor of chemistry, and has made her home in Ann Arbor and in Kentucky. She received the certificate of Central State University of Missouri for outstanding contribution to children's literature, and her absorbing and well-crafted historical novel of World War II in Germany, *Darkness over the Land** (Dial, 1966), which grew out of travel to Germany after World War II, was selected as a Fanfare book by the editors of *Horn Book*. Her other novels with historical settings include *One among the Indians* (Dial, 1962), about colonial Virginia, and *The Star in the Forest: A Mystery of the Dark Ages* (Four Winds, 1979). She also published a picture book, *Dougal Looks for Birds* (Four Winds, 1972), a short novel, *Tana and the Useless Monkey* (Nelson, 1979), and *James the Vine-Puller* (Carolrhoda, 1975), a retelling of a Brazilian folktale. She is the granddaughter of John Bennett, who was the author of the well-known novel set during the time of Shakespeare, *Master Skylark*, and other stories.

ST. JOHN, WYLLY FOLK (1908–   ), born in Ehrhardt, S.C.; journalist, novelist, short story writer. She was graduated from the University of Georgia in journalism and has been a staff writer for many years on the *Atlanta Journal and Constitution Magazine*. Under the pseudonyms of Eleanor Fox, Eve Larson, Katherine Pierce, Mary Keith Vincent, and Michael Williams, as well as her own name, she has published more than a thousand short stories and articles, as well as a number of novels for adults. For children her books have been mostly mysteries set in the South, like *Uncle Robert's Secret** (Viking, 1972) and *The Secret of the Seven Crows** (Viking, 1973), both nominees for the Edgar Allan Poe Award. In 1968 she was named Georgia Author of the Year.

STOLZ†, MARY SLATTERY (1920–   ), born in Boston, Mass.; for over a quarter of a century a prolific author of popular novels of romance and growing up for older girls and of children in family and neighborhood situations for younger readers. Her more than forty published books include picture books, easy-to-reads, as well as novels of fantasy and realistic fiction. She attended Birch Walthen School, Columbia University, and Katherine Gibbs School, sold books at Macy's, and worked as a secretary at Columbia Teachers' College. She married Thomas Jaleski, a doctor and amateur painter, and has lived in New York and in Connecticut. She began writing her first novel, *To Tell Your Love*† (Harper, 1950), a Fanfare book, while she was recovering from a long illness. A much honored writer, she has since published two Newbery honor books,

Belling the Tiger* (Harper, 1961), a fantasy that takes off on the familiar Aesopic fable, and *The Noonday Friends** (Harper, 1965), about a Greenwich Village family, both of which are also Fanfare books; four other Fanfare books, *A Dog on Barkham Street** (Harper, 1960), about a boy who longs to have a dog and to be free from the neighborhood bully, *The Edge of Next Year** (Harper, 1974), in which a boy must cope with the death of his mother and his father's alcoholism and which was also a finalist for the National Book Award, *Cat in the Mirror** (Harper, 1975), a fantasy set in ancient Egypt, and *Because of Madeline*† (Harper, 1957); and a Child Study Award book, *In a Mirror*† (Harper, 1953). *A Dog on Barkham Street*, *The Bully of Barkham Street** (Harper, 1963), which sees the events of *A Dog on Barkham Street* from the viewpoint of the bully, and *A Wonderful, Terrible Time** (Harper, 1967), about two city girls at summer camp, are also cited in *Choice*. Slipshod in plotting and hastily assembled, her novels are perceptive and understanding accounts of human emotions and desires. *Emmet's Pig* (Harper, 1959), an I Can Read Book, and *Frédou* (Harper, 1962) are among her popular books for younger readers. Her recent novels include *Go and Catch a Flying Fish* (Harper, 1979) and *What Time of Night Is It?* (Harper, 1981), in which children must face disintegrating family circumstances. She has also been a frequent contributor to such popular magazines as *Seventeen* and *Ladies' Home Journal* and has written books and short stories for adults as well as children. Some of her books have been translated into foreign languages and issued in Braille. She received the Recognition of Merit Award from the George G. Stone Center for Children's Books in honor of her body of writing for the young.

THE STONE-FACED BOY (Fox*, Paula, ill. Donald A. Mackay, Bradbury, 1968), realistic novel of family life set in a country area somewhere in the eastern United States in the late twentieth century. Shy, fearful Gus, 10, third of the five children in the extroverted family of Dr. Oliver, an optometrist, has learned to mask his feelings so well that his family and friends refer to him as "stone face." At the same time, Gus feels locked in by his face, which will no longer register the emotions that at times he would like it to. His inability to express his feelings increases when imperious Great-Aunt Harriet, who drives a Stutz Bearcat, unexpectedly comes to visit. Since Mother assigns her to Gus's room, Gus must sleep in the blue room in the attic, a place he particularly dislikes. During the night, his little sister, Serena, asks his help in recovering a hurt dog, Tippie, that she has befriended and that has run away. Even though Gus fears the dog, he sets out to locate the creature for her. His search leads him through the snowy night and past a scary well in the family orchard. Fingering the geode stone that his aunt has given him and knowing it is safe in his pocket gives him some comfort. On a ridge opposite the house, he comes upon the dog caught in a trap. The old man to whom the trap belongs and whom Gus also at first finds intimidating proves friendly and releases the dog. The man takes Gus to his little house to warm up. After tea with the old man and his spry, wispy wife, Gus leaves for home with Tippie leashed with a rope the old man has furnished him. At breakfast, Gus quite confidently and effectively silences his teasing younger brother, Simon, and Great-Aunt Hattie compliments him on the plucky way he has rescued the dog. When brother Zack suggests they break open the geode, Gus refuses, determined to break it open in his own good time, if ever. The simple plot moves smoothly and quickly to a predictable conclusion, but the reader's questions about Great-Aunt Harriet are never answered. She departs as abruptly and enigmatically as she arrives. While her empathy for Gus helps to build his self-esteem and give him confidence, it is mainly Gus's own perseverance during the fearful night that enables him to succeed and subsequently to assert himself against his more aggressive brothers. Characters are flat and overdrawn, and events occur much too fortuitously to be convincing. Style is informal and conversational, and dialogue is extensive and believable, but the book promises more than it delivers. Choice.

STORMY, MISTY'S FOAL (Henry*†, Marguerite, ill. Wesley Dennis, Rand, 1963), realistic animal novel which involves actual events and which continues the story of Misty, the pony Paul* Beebe found on Assateague Island off Virginia when she was a foal. Paul and Maureen*, his younger sister, who live with their grandmother and grandfather on neighboring Chincoteague Island, anxiously await the birth of Misty's foal. In early March, a terrible storm with seventy-five-mile-an-hour gales brings bitterly cold weather and torrents of rain. The sea rises to flood levels, threatening to destroy everything on Assateague and Chincoteague islands. After Paul and Grandpa* Beebe help the Coast Guard evacuate the islanders to the mainland, Grandpa, Paul, and Maureen move Misty from her stable to Grandma's* kitchen. They make her comfortable there along with Wait-a-Minute, the cat, and prepare to leave the island. The Beebes have an exciting, if uneventful, ride by helicopter to Wallops Station, Va., where they join other cold and weary refugees, many of whom ask how Misty is faring. Even though the blow continues, the next day Paul and Grandpa join the men in mopping up operations. When they return to Chincoteague, they find houses smashed, streets littered with debris, many ponies dead, and soldiers on patrol to prevent looting. Misty is safe, and Wait-a-Minute has four kittens. The fourth day of the storm, Grandpa and Paul move Misty to the veterinarian's place at Pocomoke City, because the foal is now overdue. At Dr.* Finney's, Paul buys a goat and kid, just in case Misty's foal will need supplemental feeding. That night, Grandpa smuggles Grandma and Maureen back to Chincoteague, because he wants Grandma's company and because he knows that both she and Maureen feel left out of the excitement. He hides them in the back of his truck along with the goats, behind some bales of hay, but it is Paul's quick thinking that gets them past the check-point safely. The next day, Paul, Maureen, and Grandma scrub the house and Misty's stall, while Grandpa helps airlift carcasses of dead ponies off Chincoteague, a task that moves the horse-loving old man to tears. Early Sunday morning, Misty's foal is born. She is a tiny sorrel filly, which the children eventually name Stormy, choosing from names submitted by schoolchildren from all over the United States. The plight of the Chincoteaguers and the birth of Misty's foal attract nationwide attention. When it appears that the Chincoteaguers will be unable to hold their annual Pony Penning Day, because there are not enough ponies left on Assateague for a round-up, the public responds with help. The movie company that filmed Misty's life story contributes the proceeds from special showings to a Misty Disaster Fund to buy back ponies for Assateague. Contributions from schoolchildren pour in. Paul, Maureen, and Grandpa take Misty and Stormy on a personal appearance tour to promote the movie, and their first appearances in Richmond are to loudly cheering audiences. The story ends at this point, but an epilogue adds that by June the Disaster Fund has grown large enough to restore the herds on Assateague, enabling the islanders to hold their annual festival. The story is based on actual happenings and involves real people. The Beebe family is more fully revealed than in *Misty of Chincoteague†*, and the descriptions of the storm and its aftermath are very vivid, but tension is lacking, and there is never any doubt that the Beebes and Misty will win through all right. Maureen's misgivings about being a girl, because girls are so often left out of things, elicit sympathy. The narrative ends abruptly, if satisfyingly. The reader actually sees very little of Misty and Stormy, even though the well-being of the little pony provides the core of the novel. The story is aimed at a middle-grade audience and is filled with details of family and animal life that would appeal to that age group. The illustrations add details to character, story, setting, and atmosphere. Choice.

THE STORY CATCHER (Sandoz*†, Mari, Westminster, 1963), historical novel set for about two years in the mid–1800s among a band of Oglala Sioux who maintain their traditional way of life in spite of growing white influence. Events are seen from the point of view of, but are not related by, Lance, a youth who has been named after the sacred lance which his father, the respected warrior, Good Axe, carries into battle for his people. Lance longs to become known as a brave fighter like his father, to earn a name of his own, and to win the shy and pretty maiden, Blue Dawn. He has acquired a reputation for impulsiveness and disobedience, however, and even though he gradually gains renown for brave deeds, he still is not invited to join a warrior society. He brings home a Ree boy, capturing him singlehandedly in enemy territory, who is adopted as a son by Lance's family and who, late in the novel, shows his regard for the Sioux by freely choosing to remain with them instead of returning to his own tribe. Lance captures an eagle by himself and shoots three buffaloes on his first big hunt. Wounded while scouting Crows near the Black Hills, he survives on his own the long, hard winter on the Plains, making a tortuous way home, the arrowhead still festering in his knee. He fights valiantly at the battle of Crow Butte, and, after Crows raid the Sioux camp and carry off the little Ree, he invades the enemy camp itself to rescue his adopted brother. He brings safely home from the camp of the drunken Loafers (Indians who live off white handouts and have become addicted to whiskey) two Sioux women who have gone there to visit relatives and are endangered by a brawl. Always Lance carries the details of his deeds and those of his people in his mind's eye, recording them later on bark or hide. While Lance grapples with personal problems, the band struggles to maintain their traditional way of living, raiding for horses or captives among the rival Crows, Pawnees, and Rees, against whom they must also always be on guard, joining with other Sioux for the annual Sun Dance, and searching for buffalo, now grown scarce because of white wagons and hunters crossing the Plains. Late in the book, Lance acquits himself with honor as a scout, making possible victory against the hated Pawnees in a grudge battle. He is rewarded with three horses, has earned the right to court Blue Dawn, and is praised before the village as a "watcher." His people give him the honorable name of Story Catcher. They recognize that he not only has a special talent for scouting but also a remarkable ability for catching in pictures the important things that have happened to the tribe so that others will always be able to learn about them. Characters are types, wooden, and too numerous to keep straight, and only Lance and the little Ree have personality. Lance's personal problems quite obviously serve to provide the author with a vehicle for conveying information about the Sioux. The plot moves slowly, at times tediously, is enlivened at others by rapid-action scenes, and ends abruptly in a quite adequately foreshadowed conclusion. Style is compact, almost dense, and requires close attention. The strength of the book comes from its extremely convincing, well-researched re-creation of Sioux life, which emerges in clear, picturesque, panoramic views before the reader's eyes. Spur.

A STRING IN THE HARP (Bond*, Nancy, Atheneum, 1976), family fantasy set in the seaside village of Borth, Wales, recently. After his wife's death, American David Morgan accepts a position teaching at the University of Wales, bringing his three children with him and then totally submerging himself in his work. Jen*, 15, and Becky*, 10, adjust fairly readily to their new surroundings, but Peter*, 12, suffers from homesickness, misses his friends, dislikes his new school, and feels resentful toward his father for bringing them to what he regards as a cold, dismal, wet dump and then leaving them to create new lives for themselves all by themselves. He finds on the beach a strangely constructed and decorated Y-shaped object, which, he later learns, is the key the great sixth-century Welsh bard, Taliesin, used to tune his harp. The key pulls Peter back in time, enabling him to view important scenes in the poet's life from his youth to the time, when, now an old man, he is set adrift on the sea in a corracle by enemies who wish him dead. Becky and Jen observe that Peter becomes increasingly abstracted and removed from the life of their family. Worried, they set about trying to rebuild family spirit and to heal the breach between their father and brother. Then they, too, become aware of the power of the key and the magic of the ancient hills in which they are living as with their new friends, Gwilym, the son of the lady who helps keep their house, and Rhian, the daughter of the sheep-raising Evanses, they tramp the highlands and shores and learn something about the lore of the country and the thinking of the people. This substantial book offers sound characterizations, genuine dialogue, convincing family relationships, and a well-depicted setting which functions as an integral part of the plot. The two stories, each of which deals with the interrelatedness of time and human existence, one arising out of a modern problem, the other utilizing folklore, are skillfully interwoven, and suspense arises out of whether or not Peter will be able to return the key to its ancient owner before Dr. John Owen, curator of antiquities at the National Museum at Cardiff, finds out about it. Boston Globe Honor; Fanfare; IRA; Newbery Honor.

STRIPED ICE CREAM (Lexau*, Joan M., ill. John Wilson, Lippincott, 1968), realistic novel for younger readers set in a black section of an American city in the mid–1900s, probably in the early 1960s. Becky (Rebecca Jane) is looking forward to her eighth birthday and is hoping for striped ice cream, like last year, but Mama, supporting five children by domestic work, says times are hard this year and they all need shoes. Cecily, 14, shy Florence, 13, Abe, 11, Maude, 10, and even Becky earn money when they can and give it all to Mama for the shoes and living expenses. Some unexpected joy comes into their lives when one of the women Mama works for gives her a "Goodwill" bag of castoffs, and they all find treasures: a steam iron and umbrella for Mama, clothes for most of the children, a fairy-tale book to share, and a first reader and corduroy bathrobe (too large and with a hole) for Becky. The older girls buy some fabric and, with advice from the sales lady in the dime store, start to make a dress by hand for Cecily. They insist that Becky play outside while they work so she won't bother them, and, bored and lonely, she begins to resent their secrecy and to be sorry for herself because she is the youngest. Mama tells her that chicken and spaghetti, Becky's favorite meal, is too expensive for her birthday dinner but agrees to beans and franks, her second choice. The three older children chip in to send Becky with Maude to the swimming pool for the afternoon, a treat almost ruined when they learn that bathing caps are required for girls. The attendant lends them caps, however. After supper, which does include a surprise of striped ice cream, the girls give Becky her main present, a dress they have secretly made of striped fabric to match the ice cream, the first dress not a hand-me-down in Becky's life. Although there is a mild conflict between bossy Maude and Becky, the family gets along with incredible accord, all doing their chores willingly, contributing uncomplainingly to the family finances, generously sharing what little they have. Mama never scolds. They keep the house scrupulously clean. They are self-respecting but grateful for favors from the better off. There is no suggestion of crime, temptation, or rebellion. The earnest tone is reminiscent of the nineteenth-century stories of the Deserving Poor written by the Generous Rich. Even the younger children for whom this is intended must recognize it as unreal. Choice.

STUART, (HILTON) JESSE (1907–   ), born near Riverton, Ky.; teacher, very prolific writer. He is a graduate of Lincoln Memorial University and studied further at Vanderbilt University and Peabody College. After varied work as a laborer and newspaper editor, he taught school in Kentucky and Ohio, was a visiting professor of English and education at The American University, Cairo, Egypt, and during the summer at the University of Nevada, Reno. For the State Department Bureau of Educational and Cultural Affairs, he became an American Specialist abroad and lectured for the U.S. Information Service in Iran, Egypt, Greece, West Pakistan, East Pakistan, the Philippines, Formosa, and Korea. He has been Writer in Residence at Eastern Kentucky University and has received numerous honors, including a Guggenheim fellowship and a $5,000 prize from the American Academy of Poets for distinguished poetic achievement. For children he wrote warmhearted stories, among them *Old Ben** (McGraw, 1970), about a friendship between a farm boy and a large black snake.

THE STUBBORN ONE (Montgomery*†, Rutherford, Duell, 1965), realistic novel of life on a small, struggling ranch in the mountains of Colorado not far from Grand Junction in the mid-twentieth century. After his father dies, orphaned, eighteen-year-old Brett Sherman stubbornly sets out to maintain their Box Bar Ranch on the big Blue River. His bank-appointed guardian, Uncle Wilbur Barns, paunchy, authoritarian storekeeper in Bank City, insists he sell the stock and lease the spread to a recreation outfit. Faithful to his father's hopes for their ranch, Brett protests so strongly that they compromise and give Brett a year to prove himself capable of running the place. The horses will be sold immediately, and if Brett can get the cattle through the winter, Uncle Wilbur says he can keep the ranch. With the help of Rusty, his trusty wolf-dog, Brett kills a cougar and a bear that have been raiding his stock, and then, in deliberate defiance of Uncle Wilbur, turns the young mares and colts into the hills to run with Old Baldy, the wild stallion, from which he knows he can eventually retrieve them. Brett captures a wild stallion colt, with which he intends to protect the remainder of his herd. Helped by his cousin, Donna Barns, who openly opposes her father, and her accommodating boy friend, Budge Carson, and Hank and Edna Grady and their daughter, Mavis, a family prospecting for gold on Sherman land, Brett cuts five stacks of hay, enough to get the cattle through the cold winter. He feels assured of success when disaster strikes. Rusty almost dies of rabies after being bitten by a coyote, and a forest fire caused by lightning from an intense late-summer storm sweeps through the area, destroying the stacked hay. Mavis then saves the day. Now Brett's almost constant companion, she has discovered a deep pool whose water comes from the river that she thinks may hold gold. Budge dives and brings up gravel which proves bountiful in gold dust, and the partners look forward to sharing $100,000 in gold. Luck, pluck, and friendship predictably win through in this always interesting story that melds together conventional characters and situations, plenty of action, and some fine descriptions of ranch life and animal behavior. Spur.

STUFF (*Fast Sam, Cool Clyde, and Stuff***), Francis Williams, narrator and youngest kid in the black 116th St. group, tolerantly accepted by the fourteen- and fifteen-year-old others, so that he is in on their escapades and is a founding member of their club, The Good People. Stuff gets the best grades, plays the saxophone, and cries easily in any sad, frightening, or dramatic situation.

THE SUMMER I WAS LOST (Viereck*, Phillip, ill. Ellen Viereck, Day, 1965), realistic adventure novel set mainly in the Pemigewasset Wilderness Area of New Hampshire in the mid–1900s. At fourteen, Paul Griffin, the first-person narrator, feels like a failure. He is no good at team sports, he has let friends get him into trouble, he has let a school counselor bully and pressure him, he has made a fool of himself trying to show off for a girl, and he has just been fired from his job on McNary's farm, even though he worked so hard he passed out. His parents' idea that he go to camp sounds attractive when he learns that Jack Perker, his sixth-grade teacher, whom he remembers with enthusiasm, works at the New Hampshire Camp Sunlight. When he arrives, he is met by Jim Whit, a college boy acting as camp naturalist, and a truck full of boys, and he soon feels at home among them. After his two weeks are up, he decides to spend his own savings for another week so that he can go climbing in the White Mountains with the other boys his age. Led by Hank Tracy, the only counselor that Paul doesn't admire, the boys climb Mt. Lafayette and walk along the ridge to Mt. Lincoln, while Jim Whit drives the truck to the south end of the ridge and climbs to meet them. Because Hank stops to talk and then walk with some girls, the boys get ahead of him and are waiting at the top when a sudden storm comes up. Panicking, Hank yells at them to run and then heads down without waiting for them. Paul rushes down in the blinding rain and lightning, pushes through trees and underbrush, and when he finally stops, realizes that he has run down the wrong side of the mountain into the Pemigewasset Wilderness and that he can't get up the steep slope again through the tangle of fallen trees and heavy vegetation. Fortunately, he has his father's machete, some matches, a package of brownies from his mother, and some newspaper articles sent by his father and fastened together with a paper clip. During the next four days he gets along quite well. He makes a fish line from the strings on the brownie package and a hook from the paper clip. Although raccoons get most of the brownies, Paul has plenty of trout to eat. His only real difficulty comes when his hook snags and he has to go into the icy stream to get it. He hits his head on an overhanging rock, almost knocking himself out. By the time Whit and Perker find him, he has made his way a good distance down the stream toward civilization. The details of his survival in the wilderness are interesting and believable, though weighted by good fortune. The lengthy description of life before camp is tedious and of life at camp is slow, and Paul seems younger than fourteen to be so enthusiastic about most of it. The theme of finding oneself by self-reliance and keeping one's head is over-stressed, and the style is stiff and marked by some carelessness: Paul's last name isn't given until half way through the book and then, inexplicably, is the same as one of his friends introduced earlier. Lewis Carroll.

SUMMER OF MY GERMAN SOLDIER (Greene*, Bette, Dial, 1973), realistic problem novel, in which the times influence events, set in the small town of Jenkinsville, Ark., during World War II. Plain, garrulous, lonely Patty Bergen lives with her proud, self-conscious, socially aware father, Harry*, her attractive, appearance-conscious mother, Pearl*, and her pretty little sister, Sharon. The only Jewish family in town, the Bergens run the local department store. During the day, the girls are cared for by Ruth, the kind, comfortable, portly black housekeeper, who treats them as though they were her own children. Patty yearns for her parents' love. She feels she has let her mother down because she is not as pretty as Sharon, and she sometimes makes up stories, hoping to impress her father with her wit. Both her parents consider her willful and stubborn, and her father sometimes beats her. The story begins with Patty describing the biggest event of the summer, the arrival of a contingent of German war prisoners who are parceled out as laborers to local farmers. When several of the men are brought to the Bergen store to buy personal items, Patty meets discerning, intelligent Anton* Reiker, 24. When Anton escapes a few days later, he makes his way to the Bergen neighborhood, and Patty hides him in the unused servants' quarters above the garage. She smuggles in food and a shirt for him. When Ruth becomes suspicious, Patty lets the housekeeper in on her secret but tells no one else, nor does Ruth give the situation away. When, in a little while, discovery seems imminent, Anton departs, giving Patty a family ring as a sign of his esteem for her. After Anton is shot by authorities in New York City, FBI agents discover Patty's part in his escape. Although her father hires a lawyer to defend her, her parents reject her emotionally. A woman reporter, Charleen* Madlee, takes an interest in her, and she and Patty's maternal grandmother console the girl and encourage her to look ahead. Patriotic fervor runs high, however, and Patty is sentenced to a short term in reform school. Only Ruth, who has been fired from her job with the Bergens, visits her there. She gives Patty affection and encourages her to get an education. Patty hopes eventually to rise above her bitter family situation and make a good life for herself. Most of the characters are types or overdrawn and distorted. The most winning and convincing figure is Ruth. Patty herself is an unlikeable heroine, who still arouses sympathy. The plot seems contrived and often implausible, and the family's Jewishness seems labored. Sequel is *Morning Is a Long Time Coming*. National Book Finalist.

THE SUMMER OF THE SWANS (Byars*, Betsy, ill. Ted CoConis, Viking, 1970), realistic novel of family life set recently in a West Virginia mining town and revolving mainly around a teenaged girl's close relationship with her retarded younger brother. Half-orphaned Sara Godfrey, 14, lives with her brusque, conscientious Aunt Willie, her attractive, older sister Wanda, 19, and her mute, brain-damaged brother, Charlie*, 10. Generally dissatisfied with herself, Sara finds life during the summer full of ups and downs, though she feels secure in the affections of her aunt and sister and enjoys and loves them both. She genuinely loves Charlie and feels no resentment at having to look after and make allowances for him. When swans alight on the lake near their home, she takes Charlie on an outing to see them. Later that night, the pajama-clad boy slips out of the house intending to return to the swans but gets lost in the darkness. The next day, a hunt is organized to find him. Among the searchers is Joe Melby, a youth against whom Sara has long held a grudge, because she is certain he once stole as a prank the wristwatch of which Charlie is particularly fond. While hunting for Charlie, Sara learns from a school friend the truth about the watch and feels obligated to apologize to Joe. He accompanies her in her search for Charlie, and they soon discover the little boy, frightened but safe, in a wooded ravine not far away. Joe invites Sara to a party that night, and Sara is more satisfied with her life. This lightweight story of the importance of acceptance and not jumping to conclusions lacks focus and moves to an improbable conclusion. Sara's adolescent growing pains ring true, but that her problems should be so easily solved by an invitation from Joe is simply not convincing. Although most of the principals are well drawn, Joe Melby is a plaster figure and particularly unbelievable. The best character is Charlie, memorably and sensitively portrayed, his actions and attitudes typical of mentally retarded children. Choice; Fanfare; Newbery Winner.

A SUMMER TO DIE (Lowry*, Lois, ill. Jenni Oliver, Houghton, 1977), realistic novel concerned with the death of a sibling set in rural New England in the 1970s. The narrator, Meg (Margaret) Chalmers, 13, both admires and is jealous of her beautiful, blond, good-natured sister, Molly, 15. In segments each of which is told at a different time, like journal entries, Meg tells of the year her family lives in a house in the country so that her professor father can finish his book on irony. Though at first dismayed to give up her cheerleader position in her old high school, Molly is soon happy in the consolidated school they now attend, having acquired a new cheerleading post and a boy friend. Meg is slower to find substitutes for her art class and her photography club but makes a friend in their landlord, Will Banks, 70, who lives in a small house at the end of the road and who encourages Meg's photography by letting her use his fine German camera in exchange for lessons in use of the dark room her father has rigged up. Molly suffers a mid-winter session of severe nose-bleeds, which keeps her away from school, but it is not until she wakes up with blood soaking her pillow that she is taken to the hospital. Meg continues to think she will recover shortly and is annoyed by her demands and listlessness when she comes home. Molly finds new interest in the young couple who move into another old house owned by Banks, Ben Brady and Maria Abbott, and in the child they are soon to have. She also collects and classifies flowers, an interest encouraged by Will. A protest about the "hippies" by the local librarian seems to be scotched when Meg learns that Ben and Maria are married and from well-to-do families. Molly has to return to the hospital, and Meg blames herself, because she tells her parents when she sees red swollen spots all over Molly's legs. Molly wants Ben and Maria to wait to have the baby until she is back, but it is apparent that she will not be back soon, and Meg learns for the first time that Molly has leukemia. When the baby, a boy, is born at home as Ben and Maria planned, Meg photographs the whole thing as they have asked her to. They name him "Happy," and Meg goes to the hospital for the first time to tell Molly. A threat to Will from a nephew who wants to have him declared incompetent so he can get the land for development disappears when Ben greets him, recognizing him as a junior member of his father's law firm. Molly dies, and the last episode is written after Meg and her parents have moved back to town. A photography exhibit includes a lovely picture of Meg at the burial, taken by Will and titled "Fringed Gentian." Meg goes back to see Will, and he takes her to see the gentians, flowers that bloom late and almost secretly. The characterization of Meg is convincing and sensitively handled. Her ambivalent feelings toward her more popular sister, her own conflicts and tensions of adolescence, and her love and grief are realistic, not sensationalized or falsified. It is rather questionable, however, that she would take so long to know the nature of her sister's illness, and the structure of the book, skipping forward each chapter in time period of narration, as if it were a journal, forces the reader to adjust continually and works against the illusion of reality. Fanfare; IRA.

THE SUPERLATIVE HORSE: A TALE OF ANCIENT CHINA (Merrill*, Jean, ill. Ronni Solbert, Scott, 1961), short story set in ancient China, suggested by a Taoist tale in the *Book of Lieh Tzu* of about 350 B.C. Duke Mu, the most powerful of the rulers in The Five Provinces, is said to have twenty thousand blooded horses in his Imperial Stables. His chief groom is Po Lo, well known for his judgment in horses. But Po Lo is nearing seventy, and Wang Ho, the Duke's Chief Minister, who is jealous of Po Lo, suggests to the Duke that it is time Po Lo retired. Po Lo agrees with him. He suggests to the Duke that he be succeeded by young Han Kan, the son of a fuel hawker. When Wang Ho ridicules Po Lo's nomination, the Duke gives Han Kan a trial assignment. The youth and Wang Ho, who makes arrangements for them, travel for many days the length and breadth of The Five Provinces. Everywhere they stop, the boy carefully scrutinizes the steeds but never buys. Wang Ho is sure that the Duke will soon realize Po Lo has been mistaken and that the boy is either a fool or a faker. His opinion of the youth is reinforced when Han Kan passes over a magnificent white stallion in favor of a nondescript black horse he sees grazing in a field, one its owner has not even seen fit to groom for sale. On their return, the Duke considers Wang Ho's report and then wisely notes that the proof of a good horse is in achievement, not looks. He arranges for the black to race the gray stallion considered the finest horse in the Duke's stables. Although the gray bursts his heart in the attempt to win, the black easily outdistances him. Wang Ho is demoted to the position of Chief Postmaster, Han Kan becomes Chief Groom and eventually also Chief Minister, and Po Lo retires with reputation intact. The horse becomes the most renowned of all the Duke's many great steeds, a truly superlative horse. This story of the triumph of the despised falls somewhere between the modern short story and the traditional Eastern folk-fable in style. The emphasis is on plot; diction is appropriately formal; characters are types. Stylized black and yellow, chalky pictures support the ancient, Far Eastern setting and create mood. Fanfare; Lewis Carroll.

SUSANNAH MEEKER (*My Brother Sam Is Dead**), mother of Timmy and Sam*. After her husband (Eliphalet*) disappears, she takes over the family tavern and figures more prominently in the story. After Sam is arrested and convicted, she philosophically and bitterly observes that it makes little difference to men in war who have seen so much killing whether or not one more man dies, even though he may be, like Sam, innocent of wrongdoing. A woman of principle, deeply hurt by events over which she has no control, she refuses henceforth to serve Continental soldiers in her tavern.

SUSAN SHAW (*Time at the Top**), main character in the novel. She wants to go on the stage and wear long dresses that swish about her ankles. When she first finds herself at the world atop the seventh floor of her apartment house, she thinks she is in some sort of theatrical setting. She comes up with the schemes by which the children get rid of the unwanted suitor, Mr. Sweeney, restore the Walker family fortunes, and bring about a marriage between Mrs. Walker and Susan's father. She is somewhat old-fashioned in her tastes and so fits in well with the Victorians.

SUSIE LONG (*Smoke**), eleven-year-old sister of Christopher. An imaginative, open child, Susie is also a fine actress, a talent she uses to protect her brother from criticism and to cover up his attention to the starving dog he has found in the woods. She is charming, bright, and willing to lie whenever the occasion calls for it. She also is very loyal to her older brother, though at the same time fond of the stepfather whom he resents.

SUSY'S SCOUNDREL (Keith*†, Harold, Crowell, 1974), realistic animal novel set in the late 1900s in the wilderness of western Oklahoma, a vast expanse of buttes, canyons, cactus, mesquite, and small wildlife. Peter Zook*, Amish farmer, purchases from a bounty hunter two coyote pups as pets for his daughter, Susy, 8. Unlike his ranching neighbors, Zook thinks coyotes are beneficial in keeping down the rabbit and rodent populations. Susy raises the pups on a bottle and becomes very fond of her two intelligent pets, the distinctively colored Reddy, who also becomes known as Susy's Scoundrel for his playfulness, and mischievous Skeezix, Reddy's brother. When their mother reclaims her pups, the scene and point of view shift to the Wilderness, where she has her lair, and most of the rest of the book follows the pups' adventures in the wild, with the mother and father, Smoky and Buff, who train them to be wise in the ways of the Wilderness, occasionally returning to look at things from the humans' perspectives. Skeezix is the bolder of the two coyotes, an inventive rascal who even entices Ranger Clack's watchdog into playing with him on the ranger's lawn, goes for swims in the Ranger's pool, and brashly puts his feet on the window sill to watch Mrs. Clack do her housework. Although Reddy is less daring and more observant, he, too, enjoys adventures. He joins the wild Old One, also known as Old Social Security, in raiding a watermelon patch and learns from him and other older coyotes how to evade the traps, snares, and poison the coyote hunters set. He is a particularly canny runner and comes perilously close to *hubris* in his reliance on this talent. Eventually, he comes to be regarded as one of the cleverest coyotes ever to live in the region, a fine runner and a good strategist, with an excellent memory, who can capitalize on his foes' weak points. On one occasion, to lose the hounds which are trailing him, he lopes in front of Zook's tractor while the farmer is plowing, apparently aware that the plow will obliterate his scent and divert the hounds. Life continues without serious difficulties for the little family until ranchers become incensed over the killing of lambs, the work, unknown to them, of a maverick coyote, and hire Jack Dietz of Predator Control. For Dietz, who has a team of strong, vicious, and well-trained dogs, killing coyotes is a personal vendetta. One by one, he slays the coyotes, until only Reddy remains in that particular community. A showdown run finds Reddy streaking across the countryside to safety in Susy's barn. When Dietz discovers that a yellow female is the real sheepkiller, Reddy's reputation is cleared. In an afterword, the author notes that the humans are fictitious, but the coyotes and hounds are drawn from real life. The ways and manner of life of the coyotes are described in vivid, sympathetic, observer detail, but the animals are never sentimentalized. The human characters are types, but this does not detract from the appeal of this exciting and suspenseful novel, and the shifts in point of view are skillfully achieved. Spur; Western Heritage.

SUZY AUSTIN (*Meet the Austins**; *The Moon by Night**), younger daughter and third child in the warm, close, happy Austin family. Pretty, bright, and quick, Suzy hopes to become a doctor like her father. In *Meet the Austins*, she is spoiled Maggy's co-conspirator at first, but eventually she becomes once again her responsible, good-natured self. Vicky, who tells the stories, envies her younger sister her good looks, winning personality, and agreeable self-confidence.

SWARTHOUT, GLENDON (FRED) (1918–   ), born in Pinckney, Mich. A professor of English and writer of novels for adults and children, he graduated from the University of Michigan and received his Ph.D. from Michigan State University. In World War II he served as a sergeant in the U.S. Infantry. He has taught at the University of Michigan, University of Maryland, Michigan State University, and Arizona State University. His stories have appeared in such nationally circulated magazines as *Cosmopolitan*, *Collier's*, *Esquire*, and

Saturday Evening Post, and he has written some two dozen novels, mostly for adults and including several for children with his wife, Kathryn Swarthout*, some of which fictionalize upon their own experiences in growing up in Michigan. Their novel *Cadbury's Coffin** (Doubleday, 1982), a witty and amusing mystery, was nominated for the Edgar Allan Poe Award. Among other awards for fiction and plays, he has received the O. Henry Prize for Short Stories and the Golden Spur Award from Western Writers of America for his adult novel *The Shootist* (Doubleday, 1975). His adult novel *The Melodeon* (Doubleday, 1977), a humorous, suspenseful account of a Christmas on a Michigan farm in the 1930s, has much appeal also for young readers, as does *Bless the Beasts and Children* (Doubleday, 1970). Several of his books, including *Bless the Beasts and Children* and *Where the Boys Are* (Random, 1960), also for adults, were made into movies.

SWARTHOUT, KATHRYN (BLAIR VAUGHN) (1919–   ), born in Columbus, Mont.; writer of novels for children with her husband, Glendon Swarthout*, a professor of English. She grew up in Michigan, did her undergraduate work at the University of Michigan, received her master's degree from Michigan State University, and taught elementary school for several years. She began writing for children in mid-life, and all her novels have been in collaboration with her husband. They include *The Ghost and the Magic Saber* (Random, 1963) and *The Button Boat* (Doubleday, 1969), both of which reflect experiences from her Michigan childhood, *Whichaway* (Random, 1966), based on Arizona history, *TV Thompson* (Doubleday, 1972), a fantasy, and *Whales to See The* (Doubleday, 1975), about a group of children with learning disabilities. *Cadbury's Coffin** (Doubleday, 1982), was nominated for the Edgar Allan Poe Award. She has also written a column "Lifesavors," for *Woman's Day*. She and her husband live in Arizona.

SWEET WHISPERS, BROTHER RUSH (Hamilton*, Virginia, Philomel, 1982), fantasy set in Dayton, Ohio, in the last third of the twentieth century. Tree (Teresa) Pratt, 14, is almost completely in charge of her retarded brother, Dabney*, 17, while her mother, Vy* (Viola or M'Vy) works at live-in jobs as a practical nurse. Tree knows little about the family background until she starts being visited by the ghost of her mother's youngest sibling, Brother* Rush, an elegantly dressed numbers runner. Through a sort of mirror he takes her back for episodes from her early childhood in which she briefly sees the father she never knew, takes fast rides in Brother Rush's car, and sees her mother abusing Dab when he is a young child, beating him and tying him to the bed post. She also observes Rush's suffering from a strange malady that makes sunlight very painful, causes lesions and sores on his hands, and afflicts him with intense internal pain. In one episode, she sees the automobile accident in which Rush is killed and realizes that it was really suicide to escape his suffering. When Dab beomes ill and suffers severe pain, Tree does not know what to do and cannot reach her mother at the place where she supposedly works. Later her mother returns and summons her man-friend, Silversmith (Sylvester Wiley D. Smith), with whom she has bought a car and started a catering business. They take Dab to a hospital, where M'Vy produces a folder of medical history of her four brothers, all of whom suffered and died of a rare disease, porphyria. It is clear that Dab is also porphyric, his condition complicated by the use of barbiturates, just as Rush's was by alcohol. When Dab dies, Tree is inconsolable, blaming M'Vy for the treatment of Dab she has seen in the episodes shown by Brother Rush. At the funeral she meets Silversmith's son, Don, about eighteen, who treats her well and takes her to a movie. The feeling she has had that Brother Rush is her boyfriend fades. M'Vy has arranged for an old street woman, Cernithia Pricherd, to move into Dab's room and care for Tree, who has thought about running away but decides against it. The story has a number of inconsistencies: Dab, who is so retarded that he is very dependent upon Tree, has no trouble finding girls to share his bed frequently; M'Vy, who has some nurse's training and knows all about porphyria, has never had her children tested or recognized that Dab is porphyric; Brother Rush returns to show Tree her past to no particular purpose. Whether M'Vy's abuse of Dab contributed to his retardation is not clear. The language is also inconsistent, an unconvincing mixture of black English and literary usage, often consecutively in the same person's thoughts. Boston Globe Winner; Fanfare; Newbery Honor.

SYBIL RAPHEL (*Our Eddie**), thirteen-year-old, younger sister of Eddie, the bright, capable, plain, second daughter in the Jewish Raphel family, who tells most of the story. She gives Eddie moral support for his efforts in helping the family financially and tries to assist him in getting the education he longs for by arranging a conversation in which he can discuss his ambitions with their father, all to no avail.

SYDNE (*Prison Window, Jerusalem Blue**), sister to Juls*, who with their parents form a traveling players and jugglers troupe. A devout and sensitive girl, she is sustained when captured and enslaved by Vikings by her Christian faith and her sense of responsibility for Juls, who is two years younger. Unusually tall and aware of her ability as a tumbler, she does not take on the look of a slave. When one of the Vikings, Brand, makes advances toward her, she is justifiably fearful, and she is far more cautious than her brother in accepting retarded Thyri* and the plan to expose Thorolf, but her tenderness is shown when she nurses the sick slave, Augustine, and comforts Thyri in what appears to be an epileptic attack.

T

TAKING TERRI MUELLER (Mazer*, Norma Fox, Avon, 1981), realistic novel set in Michigan and California in the last third of the twentieth century. Having lived and moved frequently for as long as she can remember with her carpenter father, Phil*, and her dog, Barkley, Terri* Mueller, 13, has become an independent, competent girl. In Ann Arbor, Mich., Terri makes a best friend of Shaundra, a classmate from a divorced but happily normal family, and Phil becomes seriously interested in a young divorcee, Nancy Briet, who is attending graduate school and has a son, Leif, about four. Phil has told Terri that her own mother was killed in an automobile accident when she was four, but he will not discuss her further. Even before the annual brief visit from her Aunt Vivian, Phil's older sister, Terri has begun to wonder whether there isn't "something wrong." When she finds among her aunt's things pictures of Vivian, supposedly a single woman, with a man and two boys and later overhears Vivian urge Phil to tell Terri the truth, she tries to press her father for more information, but he clams up. With Shaundra, Terri breaks into her father's locked box and is stunned to find a certificate of divorce for her parents dated a year after her mother was supposedly dead. Confronting her father with this information in front of Nancy, she forces him to admit that he has lied, that, having been denied custody and finding that Terri's mother was planning to marry a man and move with him to Italy, he kidnapped his own daughter and has moved frequently and covered his tracks to keep from being traced. Terri first tries to call her mother in Oakland, Calif., but can find no listing under her maiden name, Kathryn Susso, or under Mueller, or even under the name of the man she was to marry. She then pressures her father to give her Vivian's address, which has always been a secret, and Vivian answers her letter, telling of her own ethical struggle in keeping her brother's secret and giving Terri's mother's address. With trepidation, Terri calls her mother, now Mrs. Merle Newhouse with a four-year-old daughter, Leah, makes her promise not to take any action against Phil, and sets in motion the plans to go visit her, with offers of financial help from both Shaundra and Nancy. Her arrival is something of a shock, since her Susso grandparents, Merle, Leah, and a large crowd of neighbors and well-wishers are present, but after a few days Terri begins to enjoy the family life, to overcome Leah's jealousy, and to consider staying permanently. A letter from Nancy, saying she is breaking off her relationship with Phil because he will not admit that taking his daughter was wrong, causes Terri to reconsider. Knowing he is really alone now, she returns to her father, planning to spend part of the year with her mother. A sub-plot of her interest in a boy at school and her giving him up to Shaundra is believable but relatively unimportant. The effort to make both Phil and Kathryn attractive, likable people backfires by robbing them of individuality and making them plastic figures. Portions of the story are told from each of their points of view, not too convincingly, but the major portion is through the point of view of Terri, who is a credible and interesting character, mature for her age and torn by conflicting loyalties. Poe Winner.

TALB (*The Darkangel**), a duarough or gnome who lives in the caverns below the vampyre's castle and helps Aeriel* in many ways. A garrulous, sociable creature, he has some comic aspects but in reality is the Little Mage of Downwending, an ancient creature with considerable ability as a sorcerer. Like a troll, he is paralyzed by direct sunlight, although he is not turned permanently to stone.

TALL BOY (*Sing Down the Moon**), handsome, macho young leader of the Navaho warriors, who loses the use of one arm when he is wounded helping his intended wife, Bright* Morning, escape from slavery among the Spaniards. He teaches himself to use his one good arm, even to throw a spear skillfully. When the soldiers, the Long Knives, come to drive the Navahoes from their land to Fort Sumner, however, his resistance is futile, and his spirit is broken. Like many of the other Navaho men, he becomes apathetic and dreams of the past, unwilling to face the future with their land and way of life gone. Even when he escapes from the fort prison, he has no will to flee the Bosque Redondo, and only Bright Morning's determination to bear their child in their own land keeps him from staying and being recaptured.

THE TAMARACK TREE (Underwood*, Betty, ill. Bea Holmes, Houghton, 1971), historical novel set in Canterbury, Conn., in 1833, concerned with an early attempt to run a school for black girls. Orphan Bernadette* Savard, 14, comes from Ohio, where she has been befriended by the Rev. Robb Fry and has lived as almost a daughter in his large family. She is to live with his brother, David, David's wife, Hester*, and their son, Paul*, 15, and attend Miss Prudence Crandall's seminary for young ladies in preparation for entering the new college of Oberlin. Before she even sees the school, however, she helps the midwife with the birth of Hester's daughter, Rachel, the first child after four stillborn, an experience that shocks and frightens her, though she is devoted to the baby. Only some weeks later, when she sees a group of black girls attending church and hears the minister give a bigotted sermon about the children of Ham, does she learn that the seminary has turned to educating free black girls and has aroused the ire of the town. News gets back to the Fry farm that local merchants won't sell to Miss Crandall and that a law is being passed against educating black girls from outside Connecticut. One day, when Bernadette is taking a basket of garden stuff to the school, she comes upon Ingo Lewis and other boys stoning one of the black students, Miriam Hosking. Bernadette shames a carter into driving off the boys and takes Miriam to the Fry's farm, where Hester nurses her. This event crystalizes family attitudes: Bernadette, who has been curious but afraid of the black girls, admires and likes Miriam and becomes a partisan; Paul, who is humiliated by having to help Miriam return to school, climbs down the tamarack tree at night and joins Ingo and his friends in throwing rotten eggs at the school and fouling its well; David considers the teacher a trouble-maker and hopes she will be driven out of town; mild, docile Hester refuses to attend the church where the seminary girls are not welcome and takes Bernadette instead to the Quaker meeting, to her husband's annoyance. Bernadette meets Miriam each week, becomes a good friend, and learns some of the slave history in her friend's family; she attends the trial where Miss Crandall is accused of trying to burn down her own school, though Paul knows Ingo was to blame; she finally asks to be taken as a pupil, only to be refused, since mixing races would be even more controversial. When Ingo comes to the farm and tries to corner and terrorize Bernadette, Paul fights him, then confesses his previous harassment of the school to his father. His scorn and resentment of Bernadette turns to admiration, and one day, as he is trying to teach her to swim (fully clothed), Ingo and his friends come to the stream, and Bernadette and Paul, hiding, overhear plans to wreck the school that night. Paul promises to go and warn them but falls asleep, and when Bernadette realizes he hasn't gone, she sneaks out and goes to town in the dark, arriving just before the mob which breaks windows and furniture. Paul, having waked, shows up and sees Bernadette home, but Miss Crandall's new husband, not as brave as she has been, insists on sending the girls home and closing the school. Bernadette realizes that she will get no education in Connecticut, and, though fond of the Frys, decides to return to Ohio and somehow enter Oberlin College. Though the novel does not reveal how much is historical fact, it does give a strong picture of the anti-black prejudice even in the North and also of the feeling against educating girls and of the subservient positions wives must endure. Bernadette, Paul, Hester, and David are convincing characters, the historical figures less so. Addams.

TAM MCPHEE (*The Whispered Horse**), Tammas, drunken, weasely husband of Kate*, Rowan's* older sister. Although Kate has married him not for his love but to get another worker for Gowanbothy cottage, he does little of the farm work and spends what money they have in the tavern. He abuses his wife, beats Rowan, and is surly to Kinley*, his elderly father-in-law. Rowan rightly fears that he may kill her and Kate if he realizes that they know he murdered their mother, but Kinley plays upon his superstitions so that he causes his own death.

TAR ADAMS (*Brady**), black freedman, the barber in Manna, the town nearest the Minton farm. Although he always does his barbering on crutches and is thought to be a cripple, Brady sees him walking unaided at Drover* Hull's place. Brady learns later that Tar uses crutches in order to avoid being taken by slave hunters as a runaway for bounty. He is an undeveloped character who illustrates how precarious life was for even freed slaves during this period before the Civil War.

TARAN (*The Book of Three**; *The Black Cauldron**; *The Castle of Llyr**; *Taran Wanderer**; *The High King**), youth who solves questions of identity and self-worth in an atmosphere of heroism and valor. A waif found on a battlefield and raised by Dallben, wizard of Prydain*, Taran seeks to prove himself noble and worthy of the hand of Princess Eilonwy* and becomes involved in assisting Prince Gwydion and the Sons of Don in saving Prydain from the evil Arawn, the terrible Death-Lord who wishes to conquer the land.

TARAN WANDERER (Alexander*, Lloyd, Holt, 1967), fantasy novel set in the mythical land of Prydain*, fourth in the series about the Assistant Pig-Keeper of Caer Dallben. Dissatisfied with his humble life on Dallben's farm, Taran* longs to accomplish heroic deeds. With his faithful friend, Gurgi*, he sets out on a quest to learn who his parents were. He hopes that they were noble, because he wishes to declare his love for beautiful, golden-haired Princess Eilonwy*. His quest leads him to the Marshes of Morva where dwell the three venerable enchantresses, Orddu, Orwen, and Orgoch, who advise him to consult the Mirror of Llunet in the Llawgadarn Mountains. Event follows event in rapid succession as Taran and Gurgi, and soon also Fflewddur* Fflam mounted on Llyan, traverse much of Prydain in search of the mirror that can give the youth the answers he seeks. After they are set upon by brigands who steal Taran's horse, are befriended by Aeddan, a humble farmer, and recover Taran's horse, they push on to the stronghold of King Smoit. He informs them that the mountains they seek lie among the lands of the Free Commots, hamlets and small villages a far ride away. Many harrowing adventures befall the trio before they arrive. There Taran works some weeks successively for four people each of whom has a trade he likens to life, Llonio, the lucky farmer, Hevydd, the smith, Dwyvach, the weaver woman, and Annlaw, the potter. Annlaw tells Taran where he can find the mirror, and he and Gurgi go there. As Taran gazes into the mirror, really a pool of water a finger's length in depth, Dorath, a brigand who has been following Taran in hopes Taran will lead him to treasure, destroys the pool, but not before Taran has seen himself for what he is, a youth with a mixture of talents, characteristics, and inclinations. Taran's journey has led him to the realization that true nobility is not to be found in a family tree but in what one does with one's life. Taran returns to Caer Dallben a wiser and soberer youth, resolved henceforth to make the most of his abilities and opportunities. Emphasis lies in action rather than suspense. Dialogue is extensive, the diction formal and elevated in tone. Luck and coincidence play a large part in the plot. Taran is the only dynamic figure, and he changes as expected. Though his journey gets tedious, because there are simply too many episodes and characters inadequately developed, the book is the most skillfully constructed and convincing of the several Prydain novels. (Cauldron-Born*; Drynwyn*; Golden* Peledryn; Morda*) ChLA Touchstones; Choice; Fanfare.

A TASTE OF BLACKBERRIES (Smith*, Doris Buchanan, ill. Charles Robinson, Crowell, 1973), a brief realistic novel set in an unidentified American town in modern times, dealing with the death of a child. The unnamed first-person narrator, a boy possibly nine to eleven, is often annoyed with his friend Jamie, a show-off who never knows when to stop, but the two are nevertheless very close, going blackberrying together, swiping apples from a cranky neighbor, signaling with flashlights in Morse code from one house to another. Jamie has an unusual fondness for his four-year-old sister, Martha. When their fussy neighbor, Mrs. Houser, hires all the children to scrape Japanese beetles off her grapevines, Jamie pokes a stick in a bee hole, and all the other children run, ignoring the act Jamie seems to be putting on when he falls on the ground and screams. To their astonishment and horror, they learn that he is dead, having been allergic to bee stings. The narrator suffers shock and guilt that he didn't even try to help Jamie. His parents are understanding and try to help him when he can't eat or talk about the death. He helps take care of Martha and attends the funeral, but he does not feel right until he remembers that the blackberries are ripe and picks them, as he and Jamie had planned, then gives the basket of berries to Jamie's mother. The book is written to thesis, to tell about death, and the purpose outweighs the story. Most of the scenes seem contrived to illustrate a point. While the subject of guilt feelings in a survivor is tastefully handled, the narrator's voice does not always ring true. Speaking of Heather, the girl who has been their best friend, he says, "She tossed that golden hair of hers . . . ," an observation too adult for a boy who usually thinks in simple sentences. "First I went and told my mother. Then I went and told Jamie." Child Study; Choice.

THE TASTE OF SPRUCE GUM (Jackson*, Jacqueline, ill. Lillian Obligado, Little, 1966), realistic novel set in a lumber camp near Rutland, Vt., in 1903. Libby* (Elizabeth) Fletcher, 11, has come with her widowed mother, Mildred*, from Illinois to her father's family in Vermont, a new life, complicated by the facts that her hair, lost through typhoid fever, has only begun to grow back and that she is to have a new father. Mildred has been wooed by mail by her husband's older brother, Charles, whom she met only once, years before at her wedding. To the surprise of both Libby and her mother, Charles does not live with his mother and eldest brother, Henry, his partner in the lumber business, but at the lumber camp on Shrewsbury Mountain where he handles the tree-felling and sawmilling while Henry handles the sales in town. Libby is horrified to find that Charles and his family expect her to live in town and share a room with her spoiled cousin, Hattie (Harriet), and relieved when Mama insists that Libby live with her and Uncle Charles. She is scared at overhearing Grandma Fletcher and Aunt Charlotte discuss the wild, rough, drunken men of the camp. On the long buggy ride up the mountain, she tries the spruce gum her uncle gathers for them and doggedly chews it until she begins to find it enjoyable. At the camp there are many new and disturbing experiences: the white hog, Hiram, knocks her over hunting for chocolates, and Uncle Charles laughs; the new house is made of rough lumber that oozes resin; Libby's mattress is straw-filled; Jewel Vincent, the boarding-house keeper, has been beaten by her drunken husband; the men's dormitory, the "pasture," is infested with bedbugs. There are two mysteries in camp: why does the cow give plenty of milk one day and almost none the next, and who is bringing in the liquor that sometimes turns the camp into drunken, brawling chaos. Libby no sooner learns that there are other children in the camp, the Moranvilles, "ignorant foreigners" no one has thought to mention, than a crisis involving the family develops. Albert, the boy about Libby's age, brings word to the boarding house that his mother is in labor. Since Mrs. Vincent is terrified, Mama delivers the baby while Libby bullies Albert into building up the fire and entertains the younger children with the doll Uncle Charles has given her and she has disdained. Another thing Uncle Charles has not mentioned is that there is a school but no teacher. Mama hitches up the buggy, drives to the nearest phone, and arranges to take the certification examination so she can teach. When Albert defies her, she thrashes him with a ruler, but he fights back and is finally cowed when Libby bites his finger. On Thanksgiving the family from town comes up for dinner, but Libby is in disgrace because of the mischief Hattie has led her into. Hattie does discover the milk thief: Hiram, the pig, actually suckles from the cow! After Christmas in town Libby begins to warm up to Uncle Charles, who has made for her little nesting barrels with a tiny mouse inside, but her affection turns to hate when she overhears him fighting with Mama, who tries to convince him that Uncle Henry is cheating him. That night the house catches fire; they are saved, but the house is ruined, and they move into a shanty in bitterly cold weather, almost as cold as the relationship between Mildred and Charles. As spring comes, Mrs. Vincent, badly beaten by her husband, finally decides to file for divorce. Charles drives her and one of the sawyers to town, and that night Uncle Henry appears, saying their buggy was hit by the train, the two passengers killed, and Charles injured. Although Henry tries to pretend that Charles's injury is slight so that Mama will stay and run the boardinghouse, she takes his horse in the night, leaving a note for Libby. Instead of staying to work and protect Libby, Uncle Henry leaves on a sawdust truck. Libby organizes Lonzo*, the cerebral palsied choreboy, to bring crippled Mrs. Moranville on the stone boat to run the kitchen for the workers, now many of them drunk. As she starts to leave for town, Libby sees Mr. Vincent drunk, thinks he has spotted her, and runs down the stream with him following. Terrified, she hides in a cave by Albert's trout pond, only to have him stop there, too, fumble behind a stone, and pull out a bottle. She waits, trembling, while he drinks and eventually staggers off, and then she explores and discovers a large cache of liquor. With the help of Lonzo, who has followed, she sinks it all into the pool, where it will be available for evidence but not to increase the camp uproar. Then she catches a ride hiding on a lumber truck, gets to Rutland, and learns from Hattie that Charles is in the hospital. There she is told she may wait for her mother, who has gone out to eat, but she cannot see her stepfather. When the nurse is not looking, she sneaks into his room where he is in traction and has a concussion, tells him the whole story, and makes her peace with him. She also discovers that her mother has made up with him and has taken the company books, which prove that Uncle Henry has been cheating Charles. Besides having lively and completely plausible action, with vivid detail of setting, the book has strong characterization of both major and minor characters. Libby's fears, resentments, worries, and misunderstandings are believable and often humorous. The style is unpretentious but skillful. Choice.

TATSINDA (Enright*, Elizabeth, ill. Irene Haas, Harcourt, 1963), fantasy modeled upon the marchen of folktale. Far away at the top of the world, nestled among the mist-encircled peaks of a towering mountain, lies the small, magical kingdom of Tatrajan. The silver-haired, blue-eyed Tatrajanni are a kindly, peace-loving people, who respect tradition and encourage conformity. Among them lives little golden-haired, brown-eyed Tatsinda, a waif brought into Tatrajan by an eagle when she was a baby and rescued by a huntsman. The hunter and his wife raised Tatsinda as their own. Although she has become the most skilled weaver in the land and her fine rugs inspire admiration, the Tatrajanni look down upon her because her hair and eyes are different in color from theirs. When she is ten, her mother consults the kind witch, Tanda-nan, and Tanda-nan assures her that her foster countrypeople will some day appreciate Tatsinda for herself alone. Years pass, and trouble comes to the Tatrajanni from the world outside their mountain. On the other side of the mountain live huge, destructive giants called Gadblangs, who loathe the light of the sun and spend all their time collecting a mineral called greb. A visiting owl, Skoodoon, who hates the Tatrajanni, leads one of the giants, greedy Johrgong, through the mist and over the peaks to Tatrajan, where greb is as common as gravel. Johrgong arrives on the day the Tatrajanni have gathered to celebrate Prince Tackatan's eighteenth birthday. In his haste to grab all the greb he can get his hands on, Johrgong creates general havoc among the little Tatrajanni. He seizes Tatsinda, because she looks prettier than the others, intending to take her home as a doll for his niece. Tackatan vows to rescue her. Tanda-nan gives him a vanishing powder, which goes awry and causes the owl, not the giant, to disappear. Tackatan locates Tatsinda, who suggests that the giant can be conquered by subjecting him to the light of day. She weaves a net of special silk that Tanda-nan supplies, and the Tatrajanni cooperate to shove aside the boulder at the entrance to his sleeping place. They wake him up and cast the net about him. He soon fades away in the noonday sun, eventually going out in a puff of black smoke. The prince proposes to Tatsinda, who has loved him all along. They marry and live happily ever after among their people in peace and usefulness. The witch's prediction about Tatsinda has come true. A distinctive, descriptive style, humor, and inventive, if strained, elaborations on folktale plot and characters combine for a pleasing, though didactic, story about prejudice, perseverance, patience, and being true to one's self. Numerous full-color paintings and black and white drawings illuminate situations, develop setting, add humor, and contribute much to the attractive appearance of the book. Choice; Fanfare.

THE TATTOOED POTATO AND OTHER CLUES (Raskin*, Ellen, Dutton, 1975), detective novel, set in the late 1900s in Greenwich Village, N.Y. Dickory* Dock, 17, an art student, answers the ad of painter Garson for a neat, observant, quiet assistant and soon finds herself embroiled in several mysteries, including that of the identity of the painter himself. Through astute observation and clever deduction, Garson helps cigar-smoking, nursery rhyme–reciting Chief of Detectives Joseph P. Quinn capture, among others, a hairdresser whose secret formula causes baldness, a counterfeiter whose five-dollar bills feature his own likeness, and a jewel thief. As the cases proceed, Dickory is increasingly intrigued and sometimes put off by her employer's many-faceted personality and mercurial temperament. Now a shoddy pop artist who plays up to his patrons, then knowledgeable, talented master, now acerbic taskmaster, then a kind father figure, he puzzles and impresses her with his attitude toward her and his clients and especially by his compassion and love for his huge, brain-damaged, deaf-mute servant, Isaac Bickerstaffe. Garson enjoys games, and, when he is detecting, he calls himself Inspector Noserag and Dickory Sergeant Kod (both reversals). He enjoys playing Sherlock to her Watson, complete with costume. Blackmail, extortion, suspicious neighborhood figures, tattoos, disappearing characters, murder, and an attack on Dickory's life—the author plays with these and other conventions of the form, revealing all in a grand climax which brings together the several story strands. Dickory and the reader learn what both now suspect. Garson is Edgar Sonneborg, a missing genius. Isaac is his former colleague for whose unfortunate accident Garson holds himself responsible. The convoluted, intricate, fast-paced plot is set up with a frame story which encloses the other mysteries. Characters and events in all of them are tied to the jigsaw of the main plot. There are twists and turns at every hand, and small details assume great importance. The theme of deceptiveness of appearances is reinforced at every level. Style is exuberant, dialogue is extensive and lively, and the book projects a good sense of fun. The characters are many and obvious mystery types that have been distorted and made eccentric for effect, though Raskin improvises upon the form with perhaps a little too much virtuosity, since the texture sometimes gets in the way of the story. (Julius Panzpresser*) Poe Nominee.

TAYLOR, MILDRED D., born in Jackson, Miss.; teacher and author of books for children, most noted for her Newbery Award–winnng novel, *Roll of Thunder, Hear My Cry** (Dial, 1976), about the efforts of the Logans, a close, sturdy, warm black family in the Depression South to survive on their farm and keep their self-respect against whites who seek to destroy them. Taylor grew up in Toledo, Ohio, receiving her degree from the university there, and did graduate work at the University of Colorado in journalism. While there, she was a member of the Black Student Alliance and helped organize a Black Studies program. A volunteer for the Peace Corps, she taught English and history in Ethiopia. After returning to the United States, she became a recruiter for the Corps. Her books have the flavor of actual story retold and evolved from the stories her father told her about the history of the blacks and his own people, many of which had been handed down in the family for many years. She has written other books about the Logans: *Song of the Trees* (Dial, 1975), a short story that introduces the family and involves their fight to save the magnificent stand of trees on their property, and *Let the Circle Be Unbroken* (Dial, 1981), which continues the account of the hardships and problems of this stalwart and determined family, picking up the story at the end of *Roll of Thunder*. *Roll of Thunder*, her first novel, was also a Fanfare book, a National Book Award finalist, and a *Boston Globe-Horn Book* honor book, and is cited in *Children's Books Too Good to Miss* and *Contemporary Classics*.

TAYLOR, THEODORE (1921? 1924?–   ), born in Statesville, N.C.; journalist, film producer, and writer. He attended Fork Union Military Academy in Virginia and worked on newspapers in Virginia, Washington, D.C., and New York. Later he attended the U.S. Merchant Marine Academy and served in the merchant marine from 1945 to 1946 and in the U.S. Navy from 1950 to 1955. Among various other occupations he has been a Hollywood press agent and has produced and directed documentary films. His best-known book for young people is *The Cay** (Doubleday, 1969), a story of a blind boy and an old black man stranded on an island in the Caribbean, an area where he has lived. His Cape Hatteras trilogy—*Teetoncey** (Doubleday, 1974), *Teetoncey and Ben O'Neal** (Doubleday, 1975), and *The Odyssey of Ben O'Neal** (Doubleday, 1977)—was winner of the George G. Stone Recognition of Merit Award. It traces the relationship of an English girl, only survivor of a wreck on the Outer Banks of North Carolina in the 1890s and the local boy who finds her.

TED CARES (*A Lemon and a Star†*; *Terrible, Horrible Edie†*, *Edie on the Warpath**), Theodore, imperious eldest son in the wealthy turn-of-the-century family of Summerton, Mass. To his three younger siblings, Ted is a power to be placated and avoided most of the time, though Jane* and Hubert* rebel occasionally and he is the main object of Edie's* war against men. When his stepmother arrives, only Ted holds out against her, and she wins him over by defending him firmly when Father blows up and by even arranging that Ted, then 13, learn to drive the Ford. In *The Wild Angel*, second book of the series and the only one with some episodes from Ted's point of view, he is revealed as having heroic if misguided impulses.

TED PARKINSON (*Ox Under Pressure**), relative of one of Sally* Bracken's ex-husbands, who is ineffectual tutor to Ox* Olmstead during their stay on Long Island. Ted, recently emerged from graduate school, is easily side-tracked by any liberal cause, but he is also a snob so impressed by the old-family wealth of the Waterlukkers that his liberalism is shown up as shallow. He makes almost no impression on the anti-intellectualism of Ox.

TEETONCEY (*Teetoncey**; *Teetoncey and Ben O'Neal**; *The Odyssey of Ben O'Neal**), girl Ben* O'Neal rescues from the wreck of the *Malta Empress* and continues to help out of troubles in this Cape Hatteras trilogy. Actually a wealthy English girl named Wendy Lynn Appleton, 12, Tee is given the name which means "small" because she is little and fragile and her mind is so stunned by her experience that she has amnesia. After she regains her memory at the end of the first book, she shows herself a formidable woman, independent, wily, and able to charm everyone she meets with her beautiful manners, command of several languages, and delicate blond beauty. Although Ben refuses the marriage at thirteen which she suggests, he is caught in her machinations and continually comes to her assistance, finally marrying her eleven years later and returning to North Carolina.

TEETONCEY (Taylor*, Theodore, ill. Richard Cuffari, Doubleday, 1974), realistic novel set in 1898 on the Outer Banks of North Carolina, first of Taylor's Cape Hatteras trilogy. At twelve, Ben* O'Neal is fascinated by the sea, which nearly ten years before killed his father, a Heron Head surfman directing a rescue boat in a storm, and an older brother, who was swept off a fishing boat, and which has taken his other brother, Reuben, to the Caribbean. His mother, Rachel*, who so wanted a daughter that she kept Ben in skirts and long hair until he was five, fears and hates the sea and wants to keep him from it. When Ben is watching Filene* Midgett, the Keeper, commanding officer of the rescue boat, directing the surfmen in a storm, he discovers the only survivor of the wrecked *Malta Empress*, a half-drowned girl about his own age. He carries her to his home, where his mother nurses her back to physical health, but she does not talk, and the Bankers think she has lost her mind. Ben and his mother, however, see signs of intelligence, and Ben takes her all over the island, vacillating between exasperation and growing fascination for the little, golden-haired girl they call Teetoncey, meaning "small." In annoyance one day he takes out the boat he has found, kept secret and named for his father, *Me and the John O'Neal*, and he capsizes in a sudden storm. Saved by one of the Banker fishermen, he is scorned for his foolishness, and his angry mother tells him that his father, also, was a fool to go out in the high sea which killed him. Shocked by this slight to his hero, Ben asks Filene if this is true and is answered with a question, "Do you think he could turn his back on the people pleading to be saved?" At the instigation of Rachel, during the next big storm Ben takes Teetoncey back to Heron Shoal where the ship grounded and her parents drowned, and the shock restores her memory and her speech. Besides the setting, which is stark and dramatic, the book has an interesting characterization of Ben, who suffers the scorn of the surfmen, particularly Filene, for what has been his mother's attitude, but who longs to be a seaman like his father and brothers. Although one of a trilogy (*Teetoncey and Ben O'Neal** and *The Odyssey of Ben O'Neal**), this book is the best and can stand alone, having unity of structure and a coherent theme of the necessity of doing what one thinks is right despite opposition or ridicule. Stone.

TEETONCEY AND BEN O'NEAL (Taylor*, Theodore, ill. Richard Cuffari, Doubleday, 1975), realistic novel set on the Outer Banks of North Carolina in 1898–1899, second in Taylor's Cape Hatteras trilogy. Teetoncey*, the only survivor of the wrecked *Malta Empress*, having regained her memory, Ben* O'Neal learns that she is really Wendy Lynn Appleton, of a wealthy family in London, traveling with her parents from Barbados to New York when the ship grounded off Heron Head and was smashed to pieces. Although she is vague about the ship's cargo when Filene* Midgett, Keeper of the Heron station, questions her for his official report, she confides to Ben that the ship carried two chests of bullion worth $100,000 from the sale of their Barbados estate. Since she hopes to try to recover it, she does not want to leave the island with the British consul, Mr. Calderham, who has been notified by Filene to come and pick her up. To their surprise, Ben's mother, Rachel*, God-fearing and law-abiding and unaware of the silver, is so fond of the girl that she suggests hiding her from the Consul, leaving the details to Ben. He takes her first to the isolated home of Mis' Credy, an eccentric former schoolteacher who paints birds, and then hides her in a rat-infested old millhouse, at the same time arranging that Jabez Tillett, an older surfman, will give the Consul a rough boat ride when he fetches him from the steamer at Skyco, so he won't be tempted to return. Thwarted and angry, the Consul leaves without Tee, and Ben enlists his friends, clever Kilbie Oden and Frank Scarborough, to help find the sunken treasure. At the lowest tide in January, the four young people take Ben's boat, *Me and the John O'Neal*, out to the bar where the ship grounded and find the boiler stack, but the Widow O'Neal spots them, and when they are almost to shore the boat capsizes and she forbids them to go out again. The next big storm, however, washes sand away and uncovers the remains of the *Malta Empress*. After the official surfmen's investigation finds nothing to salvage, the three boys go out again and, digging in the sand which fills the *Empress*, discover another body. Filene, who has spotted them, pressures the story of the silver from Frank, and soon the whole island knows. The surfmen organize a salvage mission, using an old barge with a block and tackle, and when Filene suggests that Tee may have a claim if she is present, Rachel O'Neal promises to go with her, and Ben begs a place as part of the family. British Consul Calderham, a U.S. Treasury man, a state taxman, a county taxman, and any number of volunteers swarm around, each planning to get the treasure, or a share of it, for himself. When the chests are located and lifted, Rachel produces a butcher knife and cuts the rope, dropping them in deep water where they will be unsalvageable. At first stunned, the island people soon rally to her support, realizing that she saved them from squabbling and making fools of themselves over money. The Widow O'Neal's bad cold, however, changes to pneumonia, and she dies. Tee agrees to go to England, and Ben plans to go to sea. Partly because this book switches to first person, the tone and characterization of Ben are quite different from the first of the series. This is a more standard improbable adventure story, the most interesting part being the battle of wits between Filene and Rachel. Stone.

TENAR (*The Tombs of Atuan**), child who becomes Arha, the One Priestess of the Tombs of the Nameless Ones. Chosen as an infant, she is taken at five from her village home and at six undergoes a ceremony which strips her of her name and identity, making her only one incarnation in a long line of priestesses who serve the spirits of darkness in the underground labyrinth. Tenar is a very intelligent girl, and her gradual awakening to the realization that not all the priestesses are pure believers as she is and then to the horror of the cult she serves is believable and moving.

TERRIBLE, HORRIBLE EDIE (Spykman*†, E. C., Harcourt, 1960), third of four episodic, amusing, family stories about the Cares family of Summerton, Mass. (*A Lemon and a Star†*; *The Wild Angel*; *Edie on the Warpath**), this one set in 1912. Now ten, Edie is the central figure in this book, which concerns a summer at Aunt Louise's house on the beach at Mount Harbor. Even the trip to the beach is exciting as Edie* rides in the Ford driven by Hubert* and carrying her goat, Ted's* monkey, Father's* beagle, and Madam's* bird, as well as Edie's dog, Widgy: they catch fire, they are arrested for speeding and released only after Father, coming along on the same road in his Packard, is also arrested; they get lost in fog and almost drive into the water. Edie's first major conflict is with Miss G'nan Black, a muscular young woman hired by Aunt Charlotte to look after the Fair Christine, 5, and Lou, 3, Edie's half-sisters. When she locks Edie in the boathouse for fighting, Edie escapes and takes the two little girls for a wild sail in the dory, which loses its rudder and is kept from being washed out to sea only by Edie's expert sailing and Christine's obedient help. After Miss Black leaves, a Mr. Silas Applegate Parker comes to keep track of the older Cares children while their parents are in Europe, and a nurse named Hood takes over for the younger ones. As all the older ones find interesting things to do away from the house, Edie, in the middle and feeling left out, sails to Millard's Cove to camp out, without telling anyone. Tormented by mosquitoes, she is rescued by Mr. Fawkes, the owner of the island, and commandeered to ride in his annual sheep roundup, where two of the young men, as old as Theodore—almost eighteen—make much of her, and, though she is almost swamped coming home, she has a wonderful time. A hurricane nearly destroys the house, washes all the furniture across the bay, and strands a sloop at their front doorstep. The next morning, finding herself alone and soldiers guarding every approach to the house, Edie assumes that a war has started, and when a man with a gun enters the house, she retreats to the roof, sure he is The Enemy. Later she finds that the jewels belonging to fat Mrs. Johnson next door have been stolen, that Mrs. Johnson has called the militia, and that all the rest of the Cares household have been arrested on suspicion but released. At dinner at Mrs. Johnson's, Edie recognizes James, the new butler, as The Enemy, and knows he must be the burglar. She hunts all over for the jewels and finally finds them, by accident, in the sloop which has remained on the front lawn, locked and guarded by Ted, mainly to keep her from exploring it. When their parents return from Europe, Lou will not recognize her mother, and Edie convinces her by laying a trail of violet toilet water, which the child follows to Madam, the source of the lovely smell she remembers. Although the jewel episode is a stock incident in children's fiction and less convincing than the rest of the family adventures, Edie makes an interesting and lively protagonist with her fury at her older siblings and her independent spirit. The summer area of the wealthy makes an interesting setting. Choice.

TERRI MUELLER (*Taking Terri Mueller**), 13, tall, dark-haired girl who discovers that the mother she has been told was dead is actually alive and that she was stolen eight years before by her father, who had lost her custody after a divorce. Mature for her age and intelligent, Terri is devoted to her father but understandably curious about her background, which he never mentions and, when she discovers clues to the real story, is torn by conflicting emotions.

TERWYN (*Enchantress from the Stars**), courageous, bold young Andrecian, older brother of Georyn*. He, too, thinks Elana is an enchantress come to Andrecia* from a distant star. He is less thoughtful and more impetuous than Georyn. He is killed when he tries to slay the Dragon*. Along with Georyn, he undergoes the ordeals presumably designed to make them capable of overcoming the Dragon.

TESSERACT (*A Wrinkle in Time**), a fifth-dimension method of traveling through space and time by taking a "wrinkle in time," thereby to cover vast distances with little perceptible lapse in earth time. The three witches* take the Murry children and Calvin* O'Keefe tessering to various planets and, finally, to Camazotz*, where Dr. Murry is held captive by IT.

TEX (*The Loner**), sheeptender on Boss's* ranch. He is outgoing, kind, and very talkative. His easy ways and accepting attitude soon win David's confidence and liking. Tex, too, is an orphan, but, unlike David, he was raised in an orphanage. By his own testimony, he had also once been aloof and afraid to trust but came to recognize that what he thought was self-sufficiency was pride and selfishness. At the end, the reader believes that he and Angie* will get married.

THACIA (*The Bronze Bow**), Malthacia, twin of Joel* and Daniel's friend. A pretty, warmhearted, courageous girl, she understands that the Jews must be realistic about Roman domination. She is instrumental in helping Leah* lose some of her fear of the outside world and is a steadying influence on Daniel.

THAD YANCY (*Trial Valley**), social worker from a well-off Virginia family, who takes an interest in the Luther children. He is romantically attracted to Mary* Call, and marrying him would mean escape from the hills and a more varied and economically secure life for her. A little aloof and superior, he never really understands how strong the ties are that bind her to the hills and her family. He is a foil for Gaither* Graybeal. He serves as the means by which Mary Call defines her values.

THEIR SHINING HOUR (Maher*, Ramona, Day, 1960), historical novel that fictionalizes the events surrounding the battle of the Alamo, the mission that fell to the Mexicans on March 6, 1836, after a bitter, two-week struggle. Most of the characters are true, including high-spirited, intelligent Susanna Dickenson, who was in the Alamo at the time and from whose perspective events are mostly seen. Susanna, about eighteen, her husband, Almaron, and their baby daughter, Angelina, are living in Gonzales in southeastern Texas, at that time still part of Mexico. In September of 1835, Susanna welcomes Clover* Allen and her family, who have emigrated from Tennessee, intending to settle at Goliad not far away. Susanna looks forward to a pleasant visit with her old girl friend. Soon word arrives, however, that the Mexicans intend to reclaim the cannon given the people of Gonzales in 1831 for defense against the Indians. The men of Gonzales mobilize and rout the Mexicans. Almaron's contingent takes San Antonio and remains there to defend it, staunchly determined to resist Santa Anna, the dread dictator of Mexico, who wishes to take away freedoms guaranteed by the Constitution. Because she feels her place is with her husband, at the end of November Susanna takes Angelina and joins Almaron in San Antonio, arriving to find the soldiers busily fortifying the Alamo. Susanna becomes acquainted with such leaders of the resistance as Buck Travis*, Davy Crockett*, and Jim Bowie*, whom she particularly admires. On February 23, the mission bells signal the approach of the Mexican army, and the Texans take refuge within the mission walls. After Bowie is hurt in a fall, Travis takes command. He sends out several pleas for reinforcements, with little response from the Texans. Susanna takes care of Bowie, who grows steadily weaker, and she also copies for Travis a letter containing a final plea for help and rallying Texans to the cause of freedom. After a bloody siege during which the Mexican forces swell to five thousand, the garrison of about one hundred eighty defenders falls. Since Santa Anna has sounded the *deguello*, the "no quarter" bugle call, all the defenders are put to the sword, including Almaron, who has been chief of artillery. Santa Anna is impressed by Susanna's courage and offers to adopt Angelina. Although Susanna is afraid of the cold, hard-eyed dictator, she flatly refuses the suggestion and is sent back to Gonzales with her child. On the way, she learns that the Texans declared independence on March 3, and she realizes how vital was the resistance at the Alamo in the Texans' struggle for liberty. The book is often exciting and stays close to the known facts. Susanna's helping a young enemy Mexican soldier and Clover's ill-fated romance are fictional events that seem gratuitous to the story and condescending to readers, and more might have been made of the relationship between Susanna and Almaron. Susanna's behavior during the collapse of the mission seems too stoic to be convincing. Almaron is a shadowy figure, but the girl, Bowie, Travis, and Crockett are round, and Santa Anna makes a memorable cameo appearance. The book is aimed at later elementary girls. An author's note giving background information concludes the book. ("Come and Get It."*) Spur.

THERESA (*The Runaway's Diary**) aging French-Canadian woman who sells flowers and vegetables in the Montreal market. She shares her trailer home, food, and few creature comforts with Cat Toven while Cat looks for a ride east to Quebec City. Theresa feeds the girl strawberries and ice cream, gives her a small, silver crucifix, which Cat proudly wears, and helps her find the ride she seeks. Theresa is not well and has some sort of red growth on her neck which Cat feels has something to do with her poor health. Cat becomes very fond of Theresa, and the old woman is one of the more believable characters in the book.

THEY NEVER CAME HOME (Duncan*, Lois, Doubleday, 1969), novel of suspense set in New Mexico and California in the 1960s. In late April, two youths, Dan* Cotwell, 19, and Larry* Drayfus, 17, fail to return home to Las Cruces, N. Mex., from a camping trip in the Mogollon Mts. After searching diligently, authorities assume they are dead. The noisy and easygoing Cotwell family copes well with the loss of their eldest son, but high-strung Mrs. Drayfus suffers a nervous breakdown. Larry's sister, Joan*, 18, also Dan's sweetheart, decides not to attend college in the fall since she is needed at home. Voluntarily and secretly, she assumes payment of over two thousand dollars mysterious John Brown claims Larry owes him. To pay off the debt, she takes Larry's job with Brown. The job involves driving occasionally to Juarez, Mexico, to pick up packages of jewelry. She is told that the designs are to be copied by Indian artisans for sale in the United States. For several weeks, she and Frank* Cotwell, Dan's younger brother, make occasional and increasingly uneasy trips to Juarez. On the way back from one of them, they have a flat tire. While fixing it, they discover packets of marijuana hidden in the hubcaps. They report to the police, who arrest Mr. Brown. Not unexpectedly, it comes out that Larry had not only been smuggling marijuana but also peddling it to area high school students. Intermingled with the accounts of these activities are scenes concerning two young men who share an apartment at a southern California seaside resort, Dave Carter and his younger brother, Lance. Dave suffers from amnesia which Lance tells him is the aftermath of a severe fever. All Dave knows about himself and his family he has learned from Lance, who says they are New Yorkers. He says that they came west some weeks ago after their parents were killed in an auto accident. Dave becomes fond of a college girl who works nearby as a waitress. A chance encounter one evening in her restaurant with a girl whom Dave does not recognize but who addresses him as Dan (actually a school friend from Las Cruces), jolts his memory, and bits and pieces of life as Dan Cotwell begin to emerge. Lance (Larry) tells Dan who they really are, but he attributes his own background to Dan. He says that Dan had gotten into trouble smuggling marijuana and had enlisted his aid in disappearing. Once the two were in the mountains, Lance says Dan fell and hurt his head, thus inducing loss of memory. The girl who had seen Dan in California phones Joan, saying she believes she has seen Dan. The two girls trace Dan to where he is living with Lance-Larry. When Dan sees Joan, his memory returns. Realizing the game is up, Lance-Larry attacks Dan and in the scuffle accidentally falls to his death from the balcony of the apartment house. Although events are stock, and all goes as expected, the author grabs the reader early and sustains interest well. The lean style and extensive use of credible dialogue create a brisk pace and heighten tension. Flashbacks skillfully and judiciously fill in information important for the plot and help in understanding the characters. The two-strand plot structure works well, and the main figures are quite firmly drawn for this genre. Joan is especially so, and, although Frank's determination to accompany her on her trips to Juarez seems improbable, the experience helps him to develop into a steady, sensible youth with a more positive self-image. This problem-adventure story deals with a subject that has received considerable attention in the late twentieth century, but the handling of it here already seems obvious and trite. Poe Nominee.

THIS STAR SHALL ABIDE (Engdahl*, Sylvia Louise, ill. Richard Cuffari, Atheneum, 1972), science fantasy set in a future on an arid, sterile planet somewhere in space inhabited by humans. The much-feared Scholars of the class-oriented society live behind the high walls of the City. They rule the villagers, farmers who lack even the wheel and are dependent upon the superior technology of the Scholars for their existence. The Scholars have aircars, machines that fertilize the soil, electricity, and various other advances, the use of which is denied to the villagers who consider them magical and the exclusive right of the Scholars. The Scholars' injunctions are carried out by a specially trained class of Technicians and are supported by religious teachings and prophecies dating back to a remote, mythical founding. The people worship the Mother Star, at whose future coming they are told that all will be revealed to them. Those who dare to question openly are tried as heretics by the villagers and delivered to the Scholars for punishment. From childhood, Noren, highly intelligent son of a farmer, has been skeptical of the teachings and ways of the Scholars.

Despondent after Talyra, the girl he loves, breaks their engagement, he travels to a nearby village where he blurts out his conviction that power and knowledge should be shared by all. He is tried for heresy and denounced as a blasphemer. He escapes, has some adventures, is captured, and taken inside the City, where he meets Stefred, High Priest and Scholar. Through a series of dreams he is caused to enter the mind of the First Scholar of old and share the experiences that led to the Founding. He discovers that much of what the people have been taught is indeed true, but much has been distorted by their imagination, fear, and ignorance. The First Scholar was one of a few survivors of the destruction of the Six Worlds. Highly trained technicians, they arrived on this planet in starships and set up a benevolent dictatorship to insure the survival of the human race. Noren learns that the Scholars have been aware of his feelings of dissatisfaction and suspicion, have marked him as one who might make a good Scholar, and have been testing the strength of his character and convictions. The story has clever twists and many suspenseful moments, but long passages examining Noren's feelings and motives inhibit the action. Characters are stock for this genre, and story is subordinated to philosophy in exploring, among other conventions of the form, the question of whether or not any group has the right under any circumstances to control the lives and direct the thinking of others without their informed consent. Sequel is *Beyond the Tomorrow Mountains*. Christopher.

THOMAS ANDERS (*Torrie**), slight, bookish father of Torrie. He is earnest, sober, and courageous and a dedicated family man. He believes that experience is the best teacher, until events prove to him that he also needs to discuss problems with his children. He is a schoolteacher and is well read and often quotes from literary works. Torrie's attitude toward him changes, and she comes to appreciate what a fine father, husband, neighbor, and leader he is as their journey westward wears on. She learns that he has decided to move west to give the family opportunities to develop cohesiveness and purpose. Also, the doctor has advised him that a warmer climate would be beneficial to Torrie's health.

THOMAS J (*The Pinballs**), along with Carlie* and Harvey* he is one of the residents of Mr. and Mrs. Mason's foster home. Inarticulate, undemonstrative, overly earnest, shy child of eight, he was raised by Thomas and Jefferson Benson, twin ladies in their eighties, each of whom he calls Aunt Benson and after whom he was named. Thomas J has never learned how to converse because the twins never talked much and then usually only in phrases. Because they showed little affection to each other or to him, he longs both to receive it and to show it to others but doesn't know how. Mr. Mason helps him understand why he is inhibited and not to feel guilty about it. Thomas J helps Carlie lift Harvey's spirits and gradually begins to relate more positively to those around him, as the reader anticipates he will.

THOMPSON, EILEEN (PANOWSKI) (1920–   ), born in Nebraska; mystery novelist. A graduate of Miami University of Oxford, Ohio, she won first prize in the American Association of University Women short story project in 1962 and attended the Famous Writers' School in Westport, Conn. She has lived at Los Alamos, N. Mex., where her husband is a chemist at the science laboratory, and she has worked there as a radio chemistry technician. Her books for young people have been mysteries, among them *The Apache Gold Mystery** (Abelard, 1965), an Edgar Allan Poe nominee.

THORA BRAUN ARMSTRONG (*The Leaving**), hardworking farm woman, mother of Roxanne*. A strong, thick-set woman, she has married Cletus* Armstrong at the end of World War II mainly because her three brothers have been killed and her parents need a man to help work the farm. When Cletus proves useless on the farm and decides to take a job in a Waterloo factory, she follows him and lives twenty-two unhappy years in a trailer park, lonely and cut off from the land she loves. Her pregnancy after twelve years of marriage brings her a daughter she loves deeply, but, being undemonstrative by nature and upbringing, she finds it difficult to express affection. Because Roxanne has never suggested that she come to watch her play in a basketball game, Thora has driven the stock truck and stood in the back, watching secretly, but when Roxanne accuses her of indifference, she is unable to tell her the truth for fear her daughter will give up her plan to get a job in Des Moines and will stay to help on the farm. Knowing that her husband is planning to abandon her and that, with Roxanne gone, she will be alone to cope with the farm, she nonetheless keeps her own counsel and urges Roxanne to do what she wants in her life with no compromises.

THORA MAGNUSDAUGHTER (*Hakon of Rogen's Saga**; *A Slave's Tale**), lovely stepmother to Hakon. After being unable to secure her father's permission to marry her, Hakon's father steals her from Tronhjem, thereby incurring the wrath of Magnus, who sends his nephew, Rolf, to destroy Rogen and get her back. After Hakon, who has loved the gentle Thora deeply, comes to power on Rogen, he sails to Tronhjem to bring her back, but he learns that she has married Ulv Erickson, called Ulv Hunger for his cruel ways, but has managed to dominate him, and she sends back to Hakon part of the treasure Ulv stole from Rogen.

THE THREE (*The Pushcart War**), the owners of the three biggest trucking firms in New York City: Moe Mammoth, of Mammoth Trucking, better known as Big Moe; Walter Sweet, of Tiger Trucking, known as The Tiger; and Louie Livergreen of LEMA (Lower Eastside Moving Association). The Three form a conspiracy to take over the streets of New York City. The first step is to drive the pushcart peddlers from the streets. They hope to do this by waging psychological warfare against the peddlers. The Three instruct their truck drivers to push the peddlers around and cause a lot of small, seemingly unintentional accidents.

They also publish articles in their house organs intended to turn public opinion against the peddlers. They are a devious crew.

THREE OF A KIND (Rich*, Louise Dickinson, ill. William M. Hutchinson, Watts, 1970), realistic novel set on Star Island, seven miles off the coast of Maine in the mid twentieth century. Sally* Gray, 11, an orphan "State Kid," who has bounced from one foster home to another, has found a place where she seems to fit at last with Rhoda* and Ben Cooper, whose three sons have grown up and left. Seven other wards of the state besides Sally have been taken in by the Island families to join the three youngsters so that the one-room school taught by Miss Mills can keep going. Sally is completely happy until the Coopers' oldest son, Nathan, who has been transferred to Boston from a West Coast job, comes to visit with his New York wife, Laurel, and his daughters, Tracy, 8, and Nan, 7, but without his four-year-old son, Benjie, whom the grandparents have never seen. Reluctantly, Nathan and his wife admit that they have put Benjie into a school because he is withdrawn, evidently autistic, though the word is not used in the book. Rhoda and Ben are shocked and, after some time and consultation, insist that Benjie come to stay with them. Nathan brings him, a beautiful, well-cared-for child, who is utterly unresponsive, who walks if someone leads him but does not move of his own volition or talk or show any interest in his surroundings. Rhoda turns all her attention to him, with no perceptible results, and Sally feels shut out and, she admits to herself, resentful. After two months there is still no change, but sometimes Sally thinks she almost catches Benjie looking at her and once is sure he has been noticing the birds at the feeder she has made. One day, when Rhoda is forced to leave Sally in charge because the girl has sprained her ankle and can't run a necessary errand, Sally experiments, seeming to ignore Benjie while she whistles and tosses his cap in the air, and she is sure he notices. Rhoda will not believe her, but Ben, when she tells him, accepts her observation and convinces Rhoda that she must stop "smothering" Benjie with constant attention and give Sally opportunity to help care for him. Three times he makes sudden, dramatic advances. When Sally and her friend, Linda, are taking him for a walk, he starts keeping time with their singing and, when they stop, stamps his feet in time to get them to start again. When Sally takes him to visit the old lobster man, Perley Stevens, Benjie of his own accord leaves his chair to follow a kitten. Later, when he seems to have disappeared and all the island people are searching for him, Sally and Rhoda come upon him confidently walking home with the kitten, Ree-ject, and he explains in his first words, "Ree-ject ran away but I caught her." After his second advance, his family visit, and he withdraws into his old shell, coming out only when he sees Ree-ject and, laughing spontaneously, runs out to bring her inside. At the book's end, Sally must face the possibility that, as Benjie improves, he may eventually be reclaimed by his own family. In the meantime, he has brought out in her a real commitment and love that she has always withheld before. Although the story, like many based on psychological problems, suffers from over-simplification, it makes an honest attempt to depict the difficulties faced by the family of such a child. The islanders are portrayed, somewhat unrealistically, as salt-of-the-earth, and life on the island as idyllic. Choice.

THUM, MARCELLA, born in St. Louis, Mo.; librarian, author. A graduate of Washington University of St. Louis, she studied library work at the University of California. After working as an advertising copywriter in St. Louis, she joined the U.S. Army Information Service as a civilian writer in Okinawa and in Germany. When she received her library degree, she became a civilian librarian with the U.S. Air Force in Korea and Hawaii. Later she worked for five years as a school librarian in Afton, Mo., then became a reference librarian at Meremac Community College in Kirkland, Mo. Her books for young people include some history and non-fiction, a novel set in Hawaii, *Anne of the Sandwich Islands* (Dodd, 1967), and *Mystery at Crane's Landing** (Dodd, 1964), a novel of suspense that won the Edgar Allan Poe award.

THUNDER ON THE TENNESSEE (Wisler*, G. Clifton, Dutton, 1983), historical novel in which most of the action takes place on April 6–7, 1862, at the Civil War battle of Pittsburg Landing on the Tennessee River. The book opens on a dark, wet April night, as sixteen-year-old Willie* Delamer, Confederate infantryman, awaits the morrow's engagement with Grant. After this quick establishment of setting and mood, the story turns back and traces the events that bring Willie here and follow him through the encounter. Willie joins up with his father, Colonel Bill* Delamer of the Second Texas Regiment, leaving behind his sweetheart, pretty, spunky Ellie Cobb from down the way, and the spread on the Brazos that holds tight both his and his father's hearts. Willie is motivated by gallant spirit and the strong call of duty and honor, not to preserve slavery as an institution, which means little to him, but to defend the broader issue of self-determination. The soldiers' training completed, Houston residents give the regiment a grand send-off party, and by April 1 the men have trudged their miserable way to Corinth in upper Mississippi. Settling in amidst pounding rains that turn the landscape into a quagmire, they expect to strike Grant's Federals before they are reinforced by Buell's men. Willie's comrade-in-arms is Travis* Cobb, Ellie's brother, and his sergeant is war-wise Tom* Stoner, grizzled veteran of the Mexican War. Rumors are rife, complaints rampant, expectations unreal, and altercations many between the various Southern detachments. Willie serves briefly as a mounted courier, then returns to his father's unit, and soon makes corporal. The enemy is joined on Sunday, April 6, and much of the story describes in reporting style the deployment of troops, presenting both sides as valiant and worthy heroes. The Confederates push the Yanks back, at great cost to both sides, but by Monday morning Buell's men have arrived, and the bitter retreat begins. General Albert Sidney Johnston, seen in a cameo appearance before the battle as wistful, pensive, and rather pathetic, is killed, Bill Delamer falls to two minié balls, Tom Stone dies from bullets to the stomach, leaving Willie in charge of their now severely decimated company, and then Willie himself is taken from action with severe shoulder wounds. Piled into a wagon, he is carried to Corinth and nursed to health, learns there that the South stood firm at Shiloh Church, makes plans with Travis for getting his father's body home to the Brazos, and looks ahead to resuming his duty for the South, in accordance with his father's remark, "Delamers always stand in the first line of battle." Willie has come to "know the smell of death and see the darkness that can possess the hearts of men," but feels his duty lies in the conflict, now one of fewer than four hundred men left of the once-proud, high-spirited Second Texas. Scenes are well drawn, carefully placed to bring out the irony, the gala party, slugging through the muck, "liberating" a herd of goats, Willie easing the passage into death of a little Yankee drummer boy, bantering with captured Yank soldiers, raiding Yank camps for essentials like boots and shirts. The author gives a starkly realistic picture of the war in understated style based on sound research from the standpoint of an intelligent, tough, young foot-soldier, who knew something of war from his father, a veteran of the Mexican conflict, who discovers that the reality of it falls far short of even the tiny touch of glamor that story may imply, but for whom duty remains duty. Dialogue often seems forced, and foreshadowing is heavyhanded, but the relationship between the father and son is warm and convincing, and other main characters are sketched in vividly if economically. The emphasis is on what the engagement shows about war and what and how Willie learns from it. Spur.

THYRI (*Prison Window, Jerusalem Blue**), retarded ten-year-old son of the Viking lord, Herjolt*. A beautiful child, he is rejected by his father, who never uses his name and avoids speaking to him directly but sometimes at night goes to the shack where the child lives alone and gazes at him. Most of the time Thyri sits on the beach, wearing his cap with runes on its band to drive out the devils from his mind, banging two stones together with an expression of great sadness on his face. Though "brain-struck," Thyri is in some ways far more clever than his father suspects, being able to follow the slaves, Sydne* and Juls*, at night to watch them practice their juggling and acrobatics. A natural mimic, he willingly becomes part of their play and is able to learn, though slowly, when they treat him with patience. He becomes very attached to them, since they are the first to treat him kindly. At the book's end, there is a suggestion that he may go with them to England to become part of their players' troupe.

TIGER (*Belling the Tiger**), congenial black and gold creature who allows Rambo and Asa to bell his tail. Associating with him gives the two little mice courage to stand up to Portman*, the tyrant of the house mice.

TIME AND MR. BASS (Cameron*†, Eleanor, ill. Fred Meise, Little, 1967), science fantasy, last of its series, that mingles such futuristic elements as space travel and travel by thought with aspects of the Arthurian legend. It is set in

California, Wales, and Basidium-X* one year after *The Wonderful Flight to the Mushroom Planet†*. Mr. Tyco* Bass is at home on 5* Thallo Street in Pacific Grove, Calif., when he receives an urgent phone call for help from Towyn Niog of the Mycetian* League in Carn* Bassyd in Wales. Tyco, David* Topman, and Chuck* Masterson rocket to Wales, landing in the mountains on a meadow near the Roman Steps not far from the Artro River in Arthurian country. Towyn distressfully reports that Penmaen Parry, Welsh antiquarian, has stolen the great rope of magical stones, called the necklace of Ta, and a scroll belonging to the League. The stones have the power to distort behavior and cause evil when in the wrong hands. Tyco and the boys pursue Penmaen across southern England, recovering the stones gradually from those to whom Penmaen has given or sold them by appealing to the most characteristic quality in each person. At Stonehenge, Mr. Bass fills the boys in on some of the history of the Mycetians and on some of his own background as well. He is sure that the evil Narrow Brain, murderer of his ancestor, Elder Grandfather*, bard to Arthur, still exists. Near the British Museum, Davis spies Penmaen and chases him to his apartment where Mr. Bass persuades Penmaen to give up the scroll. The last half of the book takes Mr. Bass and the boys to Basidium for clues to the meaning of the scroll. Upset because Mr. Bass plans to stay on Basidium until he gets the key to the writing on the scroll and hence will miss the surprise party the boys have planned for his three hundred eighty-fifth birthday, David wanders off by himself. While exploring in the ancient Basidium ruin, Lost City, David discovers a room on whose wall is the key to the scroll. After they return to Carn Bassyd, Mr. Bass translates the scroll, which was written by Elder Grandfather, and learns that to break the power of Narrow Brain and save the Mycetians from execution he must find the bones of Elder Grandfather and rebury them in the Mycetian burial grounds above the Roman Steps. Although Narrow Brain sends shrieking winds and freezing clouds against them, they and the Mycetians recover the body and reinter it in its proper location, and Narrow Brain disappears with a long cry of despair and defeat that echoes through the mountains. Narrow Brain is too shadowy and remote to be a convincing villain, and the story offers more adventure than suspense. It moves at a fast pace through a series of fairly well motivated events to a predictable conclusion. Language is not difficult but more demanding than that of *Flight*, dialogue is ample, and details about the League, Elder Grandfather, and Arthur, as well as the background of Mr. Bass himself, add depth and interest. Though strained like its predecessors, the novel contributes appropriately to the series. (Galaxy* M81; Mushroom* People) Choice.

TIME AT THE TOP (Ormondroyd*, Edward, ill. Peggie Bach, Parnassus, 1963), fantasy novel of time travel and family life, told by the author in the "I" person from details a minor character has passed on to him. The action begins in the world of reality of 1960 in a city somewhere in the United States. On her way home from a taxing day at school, teenaged, stage-struck, Susan* Shaw meets a frowsy, windblown old woman, who mysteriously grants her three trips back in time to another dimension. When Susan takes the elevator to the seventh floor of the apartment house where she lives with her widower father, the elevator transports her back in time to 1881 and deposits her in a large, comfortable, old Victorian country house that stands where the apartment house was later built. Susan becomes friends with the occupants, pretty, romantic Vicky* Walker, about Susan's age, her younger brother, Bobbie*, 12, and their beautiful, widowed mother. The children are certain that Mr. Sweeney, a persistent suitor, is courting their mother for her money. Susan dresses up as a maid and calls upon her resources as an actress to convince him that Mrs. Walker has lost her money, and he promptly withdraws his suit. Ironically, the children then learn that bad investments have indeed left them almost penniless. Susan returns to her own time, accompanied to her dismay by Toby, the Walker cat, for a recent newspaper article describing the discovery of a buried treasure of valuable, old United States coins. The children figure out its nineteenth-century location and dig it up, at the same time changing history and restoring the Walker family fortunes. Susan returns one last time to the twentieth century, where detectives have been called in to locate her. She persuades her father to return with her to the Walker house, and he and Mrs. Walker eventually get married. In addition to such tangible evidence of Susan's experience as Toby, Ormondroyd finds at the local historical society a picture of the old house which shows the now enlarged Shaw family gathered on the verandah. This verifies Susan's story, the details of which Ormondroyd says he learned from Mrs.* Clutchett, the Shaws' cook. A graceful, literate style, a warm and affectionate tone, distinctively drawn, if static, characters, and a carefully worked out, fast-moving, if predictably concluded, plot with some low-keyed suspense and gentle humor produce a fantasy that works well and entertains with a certain old-fashioned charm. Sequel is *All in Good Time*. Choice.

TIMOTHY (*The Cay**), the huge black man from Charlotte Amalie in the Virgin Islands who pulls Phillip onto the raft after their ship is torpedoed. Illiterate, superstitious, and unsure how old he is—more than seventy, he finally says— he is nevertheless clever in ways of survival and wise enough to force Phillip to become independent despite his blindness, since Timothy knows he may not survive long enough to be rescued with the boy. He suffers from malaria and dies after being severely battered by a hurricane during which he shields Phillip from the worst of the storm with his body.

TISH PETRIE (*The Far-Off Land**), wilderness-wise, very capable young wife of Anson* Petrie, mother of his three young children and the steady one in their marriage. She at first resents having Ketty* Petrie along but later draws the girl into their little group, adhering to the law of the wilderness that requires that travelers care for one another for their mutual survival. She takes charge of domestic duties on the flatboat while the men pole and hunt. Anson displays no affection for her and repeatedly disregards her advice, even though it is obviously sound. She remains steadfastly loyal to him even when his irresponsibility results in broken legs for their son. She is skilled in medicine and capably nurses the boy back to health. She relieves pressure on the brain of Preacher Luster, after he has been scalped, by boring holes in his skull for one of the books most memorable scenes. She becomes less surly, more relaxed with the other members of the flatboat party as she gets to know them better, and seems happier, as Anson's attitude toward her changes and she grows to trust Ketty.

TISS GRANT (*To the Green Mountains**), wife of Will Grant, reliable, young, black waiter in the hotel Elizabeth* Rule manages. Tiss is high-spirited and fun-loving and is Elizabeth's closest friend. She helps around the hotel and sews for Elizabeth, who appreciates her talent with pattern, cloth, and needle. Tiss is certain that nothing can come of Grant's studying for the bar and bitterly resents Elizabeth's encouraging him by giving him a set of law books. She misses her husband's companionship, because he studies very hard, and she goes out with another man. As a character, she is a foil for Elizabeth.

TITUBA OF SALEM VILLAGE (Petry*, Ann, Crowell, 1964), biographical and historical novel dealing with the events leading up to the witch trials of the 1690s in Salem Village, Mass. The book opens in Bridgeport, Barbados, in 1688, when the slaves, Tituba and her husband, John, are sold by their mistress to pay a gambling debt. Their new master, the mean-spirited Reverend Samuel Parris, takes them aboard the *Blessing* bound for Boston along with his ailing wife, his daughter, Betsey, 5, and his orphaned niece, Abigail Williams, 8. Their trip is mostly one of suffering, with only two events of importance: the rechristening and remarriage of the slaves by Parris, who gives them the surname, Indian, and the discovery by Tituba of a red-haired stowaway boy, Pim, whom she feeds until he is revealed to the captain by sly Abigail. During a miserable year in Boston, Tituba meets two people of later significance to her, a young woman named Judah White, thought to be a witch, who gives her herbs and recipes to ease her mistress's pain, and Samuel Conklin, a weaver who rents her from Parris and teaches her to spin and weave skillfully. After much dickering, Parris accepts the church position in Salem Village and moves the family there but immediately starts quarreling with his parishioners about whether they will supply his firewood, whether he will get a deed to the house, how much of his pay will be in cash, etc. He rents John to the "ordinary" or tavern, and with the mistress mostly bedridden, Betsey sickly, and Abigail lazy and resentful, almost all the work of the house, garden, and farm animals falls to Tituba. During the long, cold winters, Tituba entertains the girls with stories of Barbados, and Betsey sometimes falls into a hypnotic trance. Some time later, Tituba finds that Abigail, with other girls, usually Anne Putnam and the Putnams' bound girl, Mercy Lewis, are deliberately inducing these spells in Betsey. Mercy produces a pack of tarot cards loaned to her by Pim, who has been sold as bound boy to the ordinary, and, against her better judgment, Tituba tells some fortunes as she used to in Barbados. Other events feed the superstitions of the villagers, including Tituba's cat and her success at gardening, spinning, and nursing. When Pim decides to run away and to take Mercy with him, she agrees but changes her mind when he burns her golden hair he has chopped off so that she can pass as a boy. To fool her suspicious master, she pretends, at Pim's suggestion, that she was approached by the devil who cut her hair, overturned the furniture, scattered cornmeal, etc. Soon a number of other girls, mostly bound-out girls and orphans who crave attention, are feigning seizures, until the hysteria sweeps the village. A wife makes a "witch cake," which, with ritual, is supposed to draw the witch. When Tituba, a tramp woman, Goody Good, and old Gammer Osburne, a non-churchgoer, come in at the same time, they are marked for witches. As suspicions rise and the girls warm to their audience, the three are arrested and tried as witches, with the unpopular Parris participating to escape suspicion of being himself aligned with the devil. Good is hanged, Osburne dies, and Tituba stays in jail for more than a year, while some fifty others are arrested and nineteen of them hanged. When the governor pardons all the prisoners, those who can pay their jail fees are freed. Parris will not pay Tituba's fees because she will not admit her guilt, but the weaver, Conklin, pays her fees and later buys John so they can live and work together in Boston. The psychological reasons for the "fits" indulged in by the adolescent girls and the gradual net of suspicion that closes in around Tituba are well shown. At times, though, the book seems as long and cold as the Massachusetts winters, and the tension in the plot depends upon the reader's foreknowledge of the Salem witch hunts. After the trial, no attempt is made to create scene, and the events of Tituba's imprisonment and eventual release are summed up in brief narrative. Choice; Fanfare.

TOBY ALVILLAR (*The Egypt Game**), sixth grade boy, classmate of April* Hall and Melanie* Ross. He and Ken* Kamata, also in sixth grade, trail the children on Halloween and drop in on them while they are playing the Egypt game. The children are horrified, sure that the two boys will tell on them. But Toby is an intelligent, imaginative youth, whose interest is caught by their inventiveness and the game's exotic aspects, and he becomes a creative participant. Among other things, he suggests that they adopt Egyptian names, and he fabricates answers for the oracle. Because Toby joins the game, Ken does, too.

TO CATCH A KILLER (Woods*, George A., Harper, 1972), novel of suspense set in a small town called Keenton in the Adirondacks in the 1960s or early 1970s. After an argument with his widowed mother, Andrew Morgan, 12, slams out of the house determined to let her worry a bit before he comes back for dinner. To get warm and to pass the time, he sneaks into the basement window of an empty house owned by summer people. He discovers that someone has been in the house: a mattress is unrolled on a bed, a dirty dish and glass are on the kitchen counter. Scared, he has returned to the basement to leave when he hears footsteps above and voices which he recognizes as those of Jack Savage and Bill Hardy, two local policemen on a routine check of the house. In terror he hides beside the furnace and witnesses the murder of both men as they start down the stairs and are shot by someone hiding in the shower stall. He then is almost choked to death, bound, shoved through the window, gagged, and marched about nine miles through woods and swamps, barefoot up an icy stream, and up a mountain to a lean-to in the woods. There his captor builds a fire, gives him a blanket while his clothes dry, and, after he sleeps, shares food with him. Although Andrew doesn't know it, this is Craig Corso, a young army deserter, who has wanted only peace but who has been persecuted since childhood because he will not fight back. After being badly beaten by three red-necks in the South, Craig has left the army, acquired a gun, and become a slightly brain-damaged wanderer, entering the empty house on impulse after hiking to town from his lean-to in the mountains. He has shot the police in sudden fear and rage but is unable to kill Andrew, though he realizes that the boy's knowledge is a great threat. In the meantime, the local police chief, hunting his men who have failed to check in, discovers the grisly scene and is able to gasp out only a few words on the radio before he dies of a heart attack. The dispatcher, Sgt. Gladston, contacts ambulance, doctor, and state police, who find the chief's body but not the dead officers until they are joined by Dan Tawney of the state Bureau of Criminal Investigation. Gladston, contacting Tawney after his shift, suggests a suspect: Andrew Morgan, reported missing by his mother. A scrap of jacket fabric caught on a nail by the window and fingerprints confirm Andrew's presence in the house, but the unexplained set of prints convinces Tawney that someone else is involved. When a forest ranger's report of smoke is relayed to him, Tawney hikes into the hills to where Craig has been trying to bring himself to kill Andrew. Finally, he has tied the boy to a tree and rushed off to hop a freight train he hears, only to discover that it is a passenger train. When Tawney surprises him, Craig has released the boy and is leading him to the fire to get warm. Tawney manages to shoot Craig and is himself wounded but is rescued by a couple of state police. Both Tawney and Andrew are taken to the hospital, where they recover and become friends. The book shifts rapidly in point of view and back and forth in time. Despite some carelessness in language (endless quarrels, endless wrangles, endless forests) and detail (1972 mothers wearing "housedresses"), the suspense is convincing, and the small town police detail of some interest. The explanation that a pacifist like Craig is always a victim is facile, however. Poe Nominee.

THE TOMBS OF ATUAN (LeGuin*, Ursula, ill. Gail Garraty, Atheneum, 1971), second book (but complete in itself) of the Earthsea* fantasy trilogy, set in the Kargad land of Atuan, east of the main islands of the Earthsea archipelago (follows *A Wizard of Earthsea**; sequel is *The Farthest Shore**). Chosen because her time of birth corresponds to that of the death of the former priestess of the Tombs, Tenar* is taken at five to the isolated Place* of the Tombs surrounded by desert, and at six, in a lengthy ceremony intended to take away her identity, she becomes Tenar no more, but Arha, the Eaten One, dedicated solely to the service of the spirits known as the Nameless Ones which inhabit the labyrinth beneath the ancient temples. Trained mainly by Thar, the ascetic priestess, she learns as she grows older the rituals she must perform and also the way through the Undertomb, where no light is allowed, and the labyrinth, which she alone is permitted to enter. The only affection she is shown comes from the eunuch warden, Manan; otherwise, though she shares the work of the Place with the other girls, she is set apart from the others who believe, as she believes herself, that she is simply the present incarnation of the continually reborn priestess. Her convictions are not shaken by the comments of cheerfully unbelieving Penthe, a novice priestess of the Godking now ruling Kargad, but she is deeply troubled when she must order the death by thirst and starvation of prisoners sent to the Godking to be executed. One day she sees a forbidden light in the Undertomb and traps the man who carries it in the labyrinth, where she knows he cannot escape and will die slowly, a death she can watch from peepholes to the labyrinth located in the temples above. At first she exults in the fitting punishment for a desecrater of the holy place, but gradually she finds excuses to prolong his life and eventually begins to visit him and talk with him, learning that he is Sparrowhawk, Ged*, a great mage from the islands of the west, come to find and steal the half of the ring of Erreth-Akbe, most important of the treasures stored in the labyrinth, which, united with the half in Ged's possession, will bring peace to the archipelago. When she discovers that Kossil, head priestess of the Godking, has been spying on her visits, she realizes that Kossil is an unbeliever interested only in power. Arha is called her true name, Tenar, by Ged, and, having regained her identity, she sides with him and together they make a desperate escape, in which Manan is killed and the Place of the Tombs wrecked by an earthquake. Together they cross the mountains to the coast and sail to Havnor, bringing the potential for peace to Earthsea. Although the theme and the use of the ancient lore are not as compelling as in *A Wizard of Earthsea**, the story is intense and concentrated. Tenar's change is subtly foreshadowed and convincing. The scenes of moving through the absolute darkness of the underground passages are particularly evocative. Choice; Fanfare; National Book Finalist; Newbery Honor.

TOM DRISCOLL (*Pistol**), lean, weatherbitten cowboy to whom Billy Catlett is assigned when he joins Sam Tolliver's outfit. Tom breaks the little sorrel, Sundance, to which Billy becomes attached, with patience and understanding, so that he will not become mean, and, in the same way, he teaches Billy his tasks about the ranch, helping the lad into a satisfying life on the range. Billy admires Tom very much and is shocked later to see what the Depression does to his hero. Tom loses his tiny spread and lapses into drunkenness for a while. He pulls out of it though, marries Sam Tolliver's hired girl, and settles down on a rented ranch.

TOM GARLAND (*Poor Tom's Ghost**), Elizabethan actor, whose story becomes involved with that of a modern family. When Jack, Tom's irresponsible fourteen-year-old brother, is jealous of Tom's bride, Katherine, and tricks his brother into thinking she has gone off with a nobleman, Tom is crushed and his tormented spirit, presumably, has continued to seek Katherine over the centuries. In order to save his father, whose personality is merging with Tom's, Roger* Nicholas deliberately merges with Jack to force him to tell Tom the truth. Although he cannot change Jack's selfish vindictiveness, he does influence events enough to lay Tom's ghost and release Tony* Nicholas from his influence, actually turning time back, so that the events in the modern world have never happened. Research by various characters turns up a few facts about this actual historical character, his marriage and death record, the death of his son, the marriage of his daughter.

TOM KETTLE (*Secret of the Tiger's Eye**), seafaring man with a thumb tattooed blue, who makes friends with Joel and Lanny and whom Benny rightly suspects of ulterior motives. In the denouement, it is revealed that Tom was the ringleader in a robbery that the disreputable friends of Malcolm Ware perpetrated and in which Malcolm was killed. Because he has betrayed some of his confederates in crime, they have branded him by having his thumb tattooed. He is a type figure, not particularly convincing, though adequate to his role in the plot.

TOMMY YODER (*The Mystery of Ghost Valley**), eager, impetuous schoolboy. His remarks about looking for iron work at the Pennsylvania Dutch Folk Arts Festival arouse concern among his Pennsylvania Dutch relatives. He later learns that their anxiety is not that he might find the iron pieces that old Doodlehead* Yoder has but that he might distress the old man who has been deranged for many years. Tommy wishes his cousin, John*, would let him help with the 4-H booth at the Festival but his offers are spurned or ignored. John gradually thaws toward Tommy, however, and at the end is very pleased when the sign Tommy has made to advertise Pennsylvania Dutch Distelburgers attracts hordes of buyers.

TOM RANSOME (*It's Like This, Cat**), nineteen-year-old youth, expelled from New York University for a prank, out of work, estranged from his family, and picked up by police for burglary. He becomes friends with Davey Mitchell after he helps Davey rescue Cat who has been locked in a basement property cage. Davey's father, a lawyer, helps Tom to a better job with a florist who lives nearby. Tom decides to marry his sweetheart, Hilda, join the army for the training he will receive, and perhaps continue college at night.

TOM STONER (*Thunder on the Tennessee**), war-wise, grizzled veteran of the Mexican War who breaks Willie* Delamer into battle. Tom's great fear is being wounded in the stomach, a terrible way to die, and, when he receives such a wound, he grabs a saber and lashes out at Yank soldiers, deliberately provoking a volley of shots that end his life. He is always good to Willie, and Willie respects him. He represents the highest type of enlisted man.

TONY NICHOLAS (*Poor Tom's Ghost**), actor father of Roger* and stepfather of Pippa* Parkin. Footloose and mercurial in temperament, Tony becomes interested in the house left him by an aunt when he discovers the early seventeenth century house within it. In some mysterious way, he seems to be taken over by the personality of Elizabethan actor, Tom* Garland, original resident of the house, who is distraught at what he believes is his betrayal by his bride with a young nobleman. Under Tom's influence, Tony turns in a superlative performance in *Hamlet* but cannot handle the transition between the two time periods and must be taken to the hospital.

TORRIE (Johnson*, Annabel, and Edgar Johnson*, Harper, 1960), historical novel about a covered wagon journey from St. Louis to California in 1846. Fourteen-year-old Torrie (Victoria) Anders is out of sorts with herself and the world. She regrets her plainness and dreams of fancy dresses, handsome swains, and elegant balls. She feels ashamed of her sturdy, practical mother, Liza, and her slight, bookish father, Thomas*, a teacher, and her rowdy brother, Cal (Caleb), 10. Her father's decision to emigrate to California crowns her restlessness, and she decides to run away. Stymied, she reluctantly settles in for the journey. The family travels by covered wagon to Independence, Mo., where cautious Thomas adds supplies, takes on a driver, aloof, sullen, young Jess* Jessen, and joins the wagon train of ineffectual Colonel Carroll. Carroll is unable to maintain discipline, and the train splits after Pawnees attack. The Anders family joins the party of better organized, swaggering Luke* Egan, on whom Torrie develops a crush. When Luke becomes too forward, Jess fights him on Torrie's behalf, and Torrie belatedly realizes the consequences of her childish, rash, flirtatious behavior. Separated from Egan's train, the little party reaches Fort Bridger, where Thomas hears about a new, southerly, shorter route through the Wasatch Range, but after scouting, he wisely decides to use the more accessible if longer northerly one. They are joined by several other families, who elect Thomas leader of the train. He proves very capable and prudent, in particular, on their passage through the mountains, made extremely difficult by the increased elevation, rough terrain, oncoming winter, threat of Indians, and lack of food, water, and forage for the animals. After Cal breaks a leg and Liza falls ill, Torrie calls upon resources of which she was unaware. Jess goes ahead to Sutter's Mill for relief and returns in time to assist the travel-weary party to win through to their destination in California. The Anders family celebrate Christmas on their new farm on the American River, and a much soberer Torrie looks foward to marrying Jess, whose steady ways she has come to appreciate. The plot is troubled by too many incidents insufficiently motivated and underdeveloped and moves pretty much as expected in this girl's growing-up story. Torrie develops a much sounder set of values and learns not to judge by appearances. Torrie, her father, and Jess are dynamic characters, the others are individualized, if flat, and the details of the family's migration are convincingly described, well integrated with the plot, and reflect extensive research. There are a number of references to the ill-fated Donner expedition. Fanfare.

TO SPOIL THE SUN (Rockwood*, Joyce, Holt, 1976), historical novel set in the first half of the sixteenth century in Cherokee Indian territory. The plot finds its source in the exploration of the Spaniards along the coast of Florida, Georgia, and South Carolina, during which they captured some Indians to train as interpreters and attempted to establish a colony. When De Soto came through the southern Appalachians some years later, he found abandoned towns and only a few people left in what had once been a populous region. Making use of her studies in history, anthropology, and archaeology, Rockwood improvises upon discoveries among the southern Cherokees to present an unromantic and starkly realistic picture of how life changed among these Indians after first contact. Rain* Dove, a Cherokee woman, tells the story. In her childhood, a series of four omens indicates that misfortunes will befall her tribe. Shortly thereafter, traders and travelers bring tales from the south about huge townhouses that float on the water, have cloths that catch the wind, and are inhabited by spirits who wear metal garments. Rain Dove grows up under this threat of trouble, marries Mink*, a respected elder and medicine man of her tribe, then the young warrior, Trotting Wolf, and becomes a mother. Trouble strikes when her brother accidentally slays a tribesman, when the war party with Trotting Wolf and her two brothers fails to return, and particularly when the "invisible fire" of a smallpox epidemic sweeps through the Cherokee villages, killing one of Rain Dove's two children and decimating the tribe. In spite of flat, mostly functionary characters and pedestrian style, this is an absorbing, low-keyed account of two generations of personal and tribal history. It reveals much about the beliefs and ways of the hill Indians, their hunting, gathering, planting economy; their intricate system of family relationships; their continual strife with the neighboring tribes; the position of the elders; the roles of the sexes; their politics; the system of justice; the training of children. A wealth of information is woven into the story line and into the speeches and actions of the characters. The Spaniards never appear, but their influence pervades the novel. From the skillfully created sense of impending doom and from the reader's conviction that Rockwood knows her history and anthropology come the novel's force. IRA.

TO THE GREEN MOUNTAINS (Cameron*†, Eleanor, Dutton, 1975), realistic novel of family and small town life set in the rural community of South Angela not far from Columbus, Ohio, during World War I. Kathryn Rule, called Kath, about thirteen, hates living in a small, dingy room in the hotel her mother, Elizabeth*, manages. She longs for her grandmother's home in the Green Mountains of Vermont, a place she has not seen since she was four but about which she often dreams. She has two close friends her own age, Herb* Mayhew, an albino toward whom she feels protective, and Chattie, a managing sort of girl, but her special friends are Will Grant, the steady black waiter who aspires to become a lawyer, and his vivacious, fun-loving wife, Tiss*. When Elizabeth generously and well-meaningly provides Grant with a set of law books, hoping to start him on the path to a law degree, she unwittingly sets in motion a succession of events that drastically affect both the lives of the Grants and those of her daughter and herself. Cordelia* Sill, sharp-tongued wife of the local druggist, spreads rumors suggesting an improper relationship exists between Elizabeth and Grant. Tiss resents the time that Grant spends on his books, misses the fun they used to have together, and steps out with another man. Gossip intensifies when Elizabeth decides to seek a divorce from her ne'er-do-well husband. The carefully plotted narrative moves relentlessly to a logical, if melodramatic, conclusion when Tiss dies, struck by a train while attempting to join her lover. Elizabeth deplores the innocent action which has resulted in the rift between Grant and Tiss, realizes she has misjudged Tiss, and decides to leave South Angela for Vermont. The novel, which involves elements of a girl's growing-up story, perceptively and sympathetically examines the lives of several women and their relationships with the men in their lives. With verbal artistry, the author paints a richly detailed, if a trifle too studied, tapestry of life in a small, rural community. Although Kath significantly influences the action when she impertinently, if realistically, forces her mother to acknowledge the failure of her marriage and again when she urges her mother to return to Vermont, she functions mostly as the vehicle by which the author makes the reader aware of the cross-currents of emotions that swirl among the grownups in the town. (Aunt* Lily) Fanfare; National Book Finalist.

TOUGH CHAUNCEY (Smith*, Doris Buchanan, ill. Michael Eagle, Morrow, 1974), realistic novel of an abused child set in contemporary times in a town called Rambleton in South Georgia. Although Chauncey Childs, 13, is a pale, skinny little kid who looks younger, he has made himself tough and has intimidated all his seventh grade peers except black Jack Levitt. Always in trouble, Chauncey is actually hurt and vulnerable, torn between his love for his often-married mother and his knowledge that he can't count on her for security. Grandpa Sellers, with whom he lives most of the time, thinks he can beat good conduct into the boy with his strap and cow him by locking him in a closet. Chauncey's hate for his grandfather crystallizes in an incident when Grandpa, with obvious pleasure, shoots kittens. After begging his mother to take him permanently, Chauncey overhears her agreeing to sign him over legally to her parents, and he hops a freight and is badly injured trying to leap off. For a brief period he basks in the concern of neighbors and his mother's love, but his grandparents come to fetch him to their home. Stubbornly, he refuses to talk until he hears his grandfather shooting a new batch of kittens. Desperately, he flounders out on his crutches, grabs the remaining kitten, and dares Grandpa to shoot them both. His main concern thereafter is to hide the kitten, Little Orange, from Grandpa, although proper, precise Grandma, who usually bows to her husband's wishes in everything, says he may keep it "for a week or so." Deciding to run away, Chauncey enlists the aid of his old enemy, Jack Levitt, who admits that he has run away from foster homes until his grown sister took him in and who takes Chauncey to a deserted garage where he hides out with Little Orange for two days. When Jack tells him that the police are looking for him and that Grandpa has been on the radio asking him to come back, Chauncey takes the situation in his own hands, gets Jack to call a taxi, and goes to the Foster Care Office to tell his story and to try to find a new home. While Chauncey's character is explored in depth and is convincing, the story has the predictability of a case history, and the solution is facile. Boston Globe Honor.

TRANSPORT 7–41–R (Degens*, T., Viking, 1974), historical novel set in Germany just after World War II, beginning on April 25, 1946, and covering about a week's time. It deals with the repatriation of German refugees from the Russian-occupied zone to Cologne in the British zone as seen by "I," a girl of thirteen. "I" travels by herself on Transport 7–41–R, an old train whose dingy boxcars are crammed with refugees of different ages and backgrounds. Because they want to get rid of her, "I's" parents have arranged for her to attend a boarding school in Cologne. Resentful and cynical, "I" has decided to sever ties completely, to be totally self-sufficient, and to have nothing to do with her fellow travelers. In spite of her resolve, she gets caught up in the plight of her neighbors in the boxcar, old Mr.* Lauritzen and his seriously ill wife, who is confined to a wheelchair. When the old woman dies en route, "I" helps the old man get his wife's body to Cologne, so that he can fulfill his promise to bury her in Central Cemetery beside the body of their daughter. The two must keep what they are doing secret, so that the authorities won't take the body away from them. At first, "I" finds helping Mr. Lauritzen a game, an exercise in wit and deceit, a pleasurable challenge. Gradually, however, she becomes genuinely concerned about the old man and helps him because he is kind to her, loved his wife, feels strongly the obligation to keep his promise to the old woman, and simply needs "I's" help. The two make a perilous way through checkpoints and past border guards. Several times, "I" considers running out on the old man, but conscience prevents her from abandoning him and his precious burden. Once, a Russian soldier helps them, evidently reminded of his own old grandmother back home, and he even kisses and hugs "I," much to her embarrassment. The two conspirators join souplines, endure delousing procedures, share cold, wet, and drafty barracks, and worry that the decomposing body will attract attention. At the cemetery, they barter pillow, wedding rings, the wheelchair, and even the girl's boots for a dignified, if simple, coffin and funeral. Surprisingly, "I" then decides to stay on with the old man because he still needs her help. She who had shunned responsibility and close human relationships now realizes that caring for one another is all that really matters in life. "I" not only describes the difficulties that confront her and Mr. Lauritzen, she also tells in vivid detail the hardships and frustrations of the repatriates and relives in her mind some of her everyday experiences during the war. The story tells of a grotesque and exciting adventure, of a courageous old man and a quick-witted, persevering youth, and of a time when the German people were beginning to believe that a good life may indeed be in store for them after a dark period of destruction and terror. Mr. Lauritzen is strongly drawn, and "I's" experiences change her believably. The book is mostly narrative, dramatized with dialogue here and there but never melodramatic or sensationalized. Addams; Boston Globe Winner; IRA.

TRAVIS, BUCK (*Their Shining Hour**), actual historical figure; red-haired, hot-tempered commander of the Alamo at the beginning of the Texans' war for independence from Mexico. In one of the novel's most dramatic scenes, Travis outlines the odds to his men, draws a line with his sword in the dirt, and declares that those who will be with him to the death should step over the line. All do except one, and all of these die in the battle of the Alamo.

TRAVIS COBB (*Thunder on the Tennessee**), Willie* Delamer's best friend and his comrade-in-arms at the battle of Pittsburg Landing. Travis is about Willie's age, fun-loving, active, quick with a quip or yarn, reliable, serious underneath, and brave. He was Willie's chum back home on the Brazos in Texas and is the brother of Willie's sweetheart. He keeps an eye on Willie and helps him out on several occasions, for example, getting him into a dry tent the night Willie's father dies and arranging for the body to be sent home. Travis is also moved by duty and honor, like Willie, and the reader expects that, like Willie, Travis will fight to the end.

THE TREASURE IS THE ROSE (Cunningham*, Julia, ill. Judy Graese, Pantheon, 1973), brief, legend-like novel set in 1100 in an unspecified medieval kingdom. The Lady Ariane, whose husband has been killed five years before, lives in a chateau gone to ruin with her faithful servant, Moag. Impoverished, she maintains her dignity and her beautiful rose garden but does not believe in the village stories of hidden family jewels, though she puzzles over her husband's dying words, "The treasure is the Rose." Three young hoodlums, led by Yarrow, a young man of striking beauty, arrive and hold the two women hostage, insisting that they tell where the treasure is hidden. As each guards her, Ariane learns of his true background—of the prison birth and abused childhood of Toadflax, of the rich but neglected life of Ragwort, of the respectable but useless boyhood of the dangerous Yarrow. Moag, escaping briefly, alerts the arrogant neighbor, the Baron de Rincon, who suggests that he may buy the land of Ariane and is obviously thinking lecherously of her, but she refuses his offer. When she has at last not told Yarrow of the hidden wealth, he ties her to a tree where she will freeze, then suddenly realizing that the dying husband's message refers to the damask rose on his shield, he digs the only damask rose plant and strikes a casket full of jewels just as the Baron, this time summoned by Toadflax, who cannot bear to see her killed, arrives with his men. The Lady Ariane forbids him to set foot on her land and will not allow him to arrest the three ruffians but offers Yarrow a diamond necklace to help them in their travels. Overcome by her goodness and simple dignity, they beg to stay with her. After the villainous conduct of the three, the redemptive power of her trust would be hard to accept in a more realistic novel, but the legend-like quality of the style makes it acceptable. National Book Finalist.

TREASURE RIVER (Evarts*, Hal, Scribner's, 1964), mystery adventure novel set on the Thunder River in the Pacific Northwest, in an area that resembles the Salmon River country of Idaho. To earn money for college, where he hopes to study forestry, Dave Sherman agrees to guide two unlikely writers, Tommy How, a pre-med student, and Jay Kelso, a mineralogist, on an exploration trip to old mines along the river. The trip, on rubber raft fitted with an outboard motor, starts off badly when Dave forgets the life preserver vests, they receive threats from a regular tourist guide, Frank Fox, and Kelso gains the enmity of Hank the Hermit, whom they ask about the possible location of the Eagle Circus mine. When Kelso defects and joins Fox, Tommy shows Dave the true reason for their expedition, a diary kept by his Chinese grandfather who worked over the tailings of the Eagle Circus mine and describes a solid ledge of what Tommy has discovered from his samples to be pure jade, very valuable. Discouraged, they return to their starting point, but when Tommy tries to save the dog of Dave's great-uncle, Ben Bright, which has been mauled by a bear, the old man joins them. After a series of disasters which include losing their motor overboard and fighting a forest fire, the boys hike far upstream to a mining ghost town, Thunder City, where they surprise Kelso with the diary he has stolen. In trying to hide it, Kelso is in a mine cave-in, and Dave rides down the wild creek on an air mattress to call on the forest service phone for help. A helicopter picks up the injured man, but when the forest service supervisor arrives, Dave learns that Fox has filed trumped-up charges against him. In the few minutes they have left, Dave and Tommy figure out that because of his pronunciation, the grandfather has written Eagle for Regal, and that Tommy has mistranslated his Clown as Circus, so the Regal Crown mine, where they are, is the one indicated in the old diary. Following the diary's directions, they discover the ridge of jade hidden behind a waterfall. The story is action packed and exciting, so full of physical adventure that a reader is inclined to overlook implausibilities. One gets a good sense of the rugged mountainous setting, with its icy, rapids-filled rivers and narrow canyons. Poe Nominee.

TREEGATE'S RAIDERS (Wibberley*†, Leonard, Farrar, 1962), fourth in the series of historical novels about the involvement of John* and Peter Treegate and their friend, Peace* of God Manly, in the American Revolution. In the fall of 1780, Peter, now twenty-one and convinced that victory over the British lies in the South, travels to New York City. He forcefully requests Washington to send to the South a commander capable of inventive leadership and of uniting regulars and partisans in the common cause of independence. He then returns to the Carolina Wilderness, where, with stubborn bravery, some difficulty, and a few swashbuckling fights, he assembles a small fighting force of Highlanders, some from his foster-father's clan and some from hostile families, among them a number of Farquesons, who become known collectively as Treegate's Raiders. Under Peter's skillful and bold leadership, the Raiders harry British regulars and Tory partisans across countryside and through mountains, inflicting heavy losses in such vital engagements as King's Mountain. Throughout, Peter has difficulty keeping the individualistic clansmen united in fighting for a cause greater than family or clan. His pride and intense self-assurance also bring him into conflict both with self and with Donald Oge, a Farqueson. Moreover, his arrogance alienates his men to such a degree that they fail to shield him at Cowpens, with the result that he is captured by the British and sentenced to hang. Donald Oge, who earlier had killed his own brother to save Peter's life and whom Peter has continued nevertheless to scorn, comes to Peter's aid once again and is also captured. His unselfish act humbles Peter and demonstrates also quite effectively the importance of loyalty to comrade in achieving the common good. The two are rescued at the critical moment by Mr. Paddock, a timid bookseller, who, emboldened by Peter's example, has rallied a small force of Southerners. Simultaneously, Peace of God, now commanding a sloop in the West Indies, carries a message from French Admiral de Grasse to Washington informing the American general that the French are making for Chesapeake Bay. Washington mobilizes there, and Peter joins in the battle that culminates in Cornwallis's defeat at Yorktown, the surrender of the British, and independence for the Americans. Peace of God returns to Salem and his daughter, Nancy. The book concludes with an incongruously and absurdly romantic scene. Peter arrives in Salem, quite literally sweeps Nancy off her feet, and a marriage between the two seems imminent. An assortment of historical figures including Washington, the American generals Greene and Morgan, and the British leaders Ferguson, Tarleton, and Cornwallis parade through the pages, some of them in cameo appearances, others in more detailed scenes, during which the reader learns something of what they are like as people. The novel excels in showing the intense hatred that existed between Rebel and Tory Americans in the South, the passing of clan loyalties, and the importance of effective military strategy to the American triumph. The author sketches action scenes with dexterity, but the book blends research and story poorly, and one often feels that one is reading history ''let down'' with dramatized action. It is hard to accept what has happened to Peter through the four books as typical of a well-born youth of the period. He has too obviously been the author's instrument for acquainting young readers with the issues and progress of the Revolution. Previous books in the series are *John Treegate's Musket*†; *Peter Treegate's War**; *Sea Captain from Salem**. Choice.

TRENKER, FRANK (*Gentlehands**), Buddy Boyle's grandfather, his mother's father. Trenker's daughter dislikes him because she thinks he is a snob and because he abandoned her mother before she was born. Her mother brought her to the United States just before World War II, when she was a baby, and she has had little contact with her father. Trenker arrived in Seaville some time before the story begins. He is regarded in the community as a polite, learned, cultured gentleman, and people are shocked when he is identified as a Nazi war criminal. He gives Buddy new perspectives on life and opens horizons for the boy. While Buddy lives with him, Trenker tells Buddy a little about his past. These details fit in with what De* Lucca says about him and help Buddy to see that De Lucca is right about his grandfather. Trenker flees at the end of the story and apparently eludes authorities. He is the best-drawn character in the novel, though stereotyped and made to order to capitalize on current interest.

TREVIÑO, ELIZABETH BORTON (DE) (1904–   ), born in Bakersfield, Calif.; violinist, novelist. She was graduated from Stanford University with a B.A. degree in Latin American history and studied further at the Boston Conservatory of Music. After working as a reporter on the *Jamaica Plain Journal* in Boston and for Ginn & Co. in production and advertising, she became an interviewer on performing arts for the Boston *Herald American* and, while on assignment in Mexico for that publication, met the man who became her husband. They have lived in Cuernavaca, Mexico, where she has continued to play in musical ensembles and to write both fiction and non-fiction for adults and young people. Her first five books for children, published under her maiden name, were in the Pollyanna series originated by Eleanor Parker. *Nacar, the White Deer** (Farrar, 1963) had its origin in a historical document telling of an albino deer brought to Mexico from the Philippines by sailing vessel and shipped to Spain as a gift to the king. Similarly, *I, Juan de Pareja** (Farrar, 1965) is based on an actual person, the black slave who became assistant to his master, the painter, Velázquez*, set, like *Nacar* in the seventeenth century. *Turi's Poppa** (Farrar, 1968) has a twentieth-century setting, a story of a half-gypsy boy's journey through southern Europe with his father, shortly after World War II.

TRIAL VALLEY (Cleaver*, Vera, and Bill Cleaver*, Lippincott, 1977), realistic family novel set recently on a small farm in Trial Valley in the Great Smoky Mountains, sequel to *Where the Lilies Bloom**. Mary* Call Luther, now sixteen, maintains her practical, serious, and independent attitude as she and her younger brother and sister continue to make their living by wildcrafting, Now that they are a little older, Ima* Dean, 7, and Romey*, 12, often complain that Mary Call works them too hard, occasionally refuse to work, and frequently talk back to her. Mary Call is beginning to find caring for them and coping with their rebellious ways burdensome and frustrating and longs for a life of her own. Although she gets on well with Kiser* Pease and Devola*, she will accept only advice and occasional help in labor from them. She deplores the effect their easier way of life has had upon Romey and Ima Dean, who tend to be less steady than she would like them to be. Two young men become romantically interested in Mary Call, Thad* Yancy, social worker from a well-off family, and Gaither* Graybeal, a youth from a farm down the road. To complicate her life further, an abandoned, five-year-old boy, who says his name is Jack* Parsons and whom childless Kiser and Devola yearn to adopt, attaches himself to her. Since she already has quite enough to handle, she insists that he go live with Kiser and Devola. Although they treat him with love and indulge him with gifts, he runs away from them. As a result of the search for the child, Mary Call and the two young men sort out their feelings. It is predictable, but satisfying, that Thad goes back to Virginia and that Jack is added to Mary Call's little family. Mary Call tells her story of this eventful summer in the formal style and regional diction of the hill people. She is sometimes pensive and often humorous as she continues to grow and develop in her appreciation of life and the people around her. The book lacks the spontaneity of its predecessor but seems true to this stage in the lives of the Luthers. Fanfare.

THE TROUBLE WITH JENNY'S EAR (Butterworth*†, Oliver, Little, 1960), amusing science fantasy with family story qualities set in the mid–1900s in the small town of Pearson's Corners, Mass., in which a young girl's talent for mental telepathy saves the community recreational area from becoming a housing development. The Pearson family receives with dismay the news that houses are to be built on and around the hill and brook on the Watson property that adjoins theirs. Uncle* Harold gives Joe, 12, and Stanley, 10, many boxes of used electronic equipment with which they construct an astonishing complex of wires and amplifiers that produces a noise of great intensity. Soon the ears of Jenny, their sister, become so supersensitive to sound that she can hear even what people are thinking. Joe gets the idea of exploiting Jenny's special, new talent to earn money to buy the hill and brook and preserve them for recreation. He and Stanley arrange for Jenny to appear on a New York TV show where she wins $100,000, only to discover to their dismay that there will not be enough money left after taxes to buy the property. Jenny's success on TV attracts the attention of the Federal Government which commands her services on an FBI case in Boston, but, ironically, the defendant complains that by reading his mind Jenny has violated his constitutional right to privacy. When the Defense Department declares Jenny's ability of the utmost importance to national security, the family hopes the government will provide the money to buy the place, now considered vital to maintaining Jenny's peace of mind, but that expectation also soon comes to nothing. On the day the property is to be sold, Teddy Watson's family discover that Teddy is missing, and the whole town turns out to look for him. Jenny finds him, and, in gratitude, Mr. Watson deeds the hill and brook to the entire community. Jenny discovers that her marvelous talent has departed as suddenly and mysteriously as it arrived. Subsidiary adventures to which Jenny's unusual ability contributes include helping the boys tune in on what the school principal is thinking and facilitating a budding romance between lively, fun-loving Uncle Harold and pretty Miss Romaine, Jenny's first grade teacher. Touching lightly on such concerns as privacy and ecology, the mildly suspenseful plot proceeds smoothly from the well-delineated world of reality into the equally convincing, inventive fantasy. Positive and believable family relationships, likeable, if flat, characters, authentic dialogue, lots of action, originality of concept, and humor of situation and concept more than compensate for the undistinguished style to produce highly entertaining reading for later elementary and junior high youths. Choice.

THE TROUBLE WITH TERRY (Lexau*, Joan, ill. Irene Murray, Dial, 1962), realistic novel set in an unnamed town on the northern Mississippi River in the mid twentieth century. Terry (Teresa) Seth, 10, fails fifth-grade mathematics, can't seem to do anything right, and thinks her mother is always scolding her. In their fatherless family, Terry's brother, Tommy, 12, is a great comfort to their mother. He gets good grades, is hardworking and well organized, but is no sissy. Terry is a tomboy yet likely to burst into tears of frustration and self-pity. Tommy and his friends, Mike, Greg, and Danny, let her tag along, and she takes special responsibility for Soupy O'Halloran, Danny and Mike's five-year-old brother, since his mother has deserted the family. When the older boys try to cross the river on the concrete arches under the bridge, Terry follows cautiously, then discovers that Soupy, on roller skates, is coming after her. She knocks him to safety but almost falls in herself and is rescued by the boys. Tommy, a model paper boy, gets her a substitute route for a week, and she manages, with some complications from Soupy, but when Tommy's good record is spoiled by the complaints of Mrs. Pinehurst, in a neighboring apartment, they find that someone has been taking her paper. Terry puts flour in the paper and traps the thief, another neighbor. Terry's tenuous position with the boys' gang is threatened when Greg has an all-boy party and his father plans a tree house they will build for their boys' club, excluding girls. Terry hunts up Cindy, an old friend whom she seldom sees since Kim has moved into the neighborhood, and the three girls take over the tree house while the boys are absent then trick the boys into joining their girls' club. This humiliation makes the boys willing to negotiate a compromise: the girls will form a ladies auxiliary. When her mother works extra hours for two weeks, Terry takes over the cooking, with some mishaps, but finds it worthwhile when her mother's earnings go toward her heart's desire, a bicycle. Thrilled, she spends all her time cycling with Cindy or Kim or alone and only realizes that she has neglected Soupy and forgotten his birthday when he runs away. She finds him down by the river, persuades him not to go swimming or to throw his father's valuable camera in, and is surprised when he confesses that he knows his mother "runned away." Remorseful, she teaches him to write his name and takes him to the library to get a card. In an attempt to make her a lady, her mother has made (by hand) a dress with a jumper that Terry really likes, and she promises to keep it clean a whole day. Although she has to get it washed and ironed by Cindy's mother, she does return home clean and realizes that her mother loves her as she is. Even though Terry's struggles to fit into a pattern for which she seems unsuited is a timeless problem for some children her age, the worry about her tomboy fun, the double standard that places Tommy's virtues higher, the compromise of the second-class auxiliary all seem to date the book to a period even earlier than 1962 when it was published. The sibling rivalry and the neighborhood conflicts are well handled but not particularly engrossing. Terry's concern about Soupy is a more interesting sub-plot. Child Study.

THE TRUMPET OF THE SWAN (White*†, E. B., ill. Edward Frascino, Harper, 1970), talking animal fantasy which begins in the Canadian Rockies, moves to the Red Rock, hot-spring lakes of Montana, and then to other locations, including the Boston Public Garden, the Boston* Ritz Hotel, and the Philadelphia Zoo. Sam* Beaver, 11, observes the hatching of a brood of rare trumpeter swans, one of whom, Louis*, turns out to be mute, a great handicap to a swan who needs his voice to attract his mate. The old Cob*, Louis's father, sees this as a tribulation, vows to help his son, and flies off to Billings, Mont., where he literally breaks into a music store and steals a trumpet. Disturbed by his father's guilt, Louis sets out to make money to repay the store by becoming a jazz musician, and, with the help of Sam Beaver and others, he goes east, plays in various night spots, and becomes famous for his ability. His virtuosity also wins him the love of Serena, a beautiful female swan. Less original in style and incident than White's earlier *Stuart Little*† and *Charlotte's Web*†, *The Trumpet of the Swan* is still emotionally moving and clever in its handling of tone and humor. Choice; National Book Finalist.

TUCKER MOUSE (*The Cricket in Times Square**; *Tucker's Countryside**), excitable, warmhearted, talkative, home-loving mouse who lives with his good friend, Harry* Cat, in the drainpipe in the Times Square subway station in New York City. A scrounger, he has a store hole packed with "collectibles" like cloth, buttons, jewelry, small change, and food. He cannot bear to see anything go to waste. He significantly affects the plots in both books. In the first, he accidentally sets fire to the Bellinis' newsstand, and, in the second, he gets the idea of "planting evidence" to save Chester* Cricket's Old Meadow.

TUCKER'S COUNTRYSIDE (Seldon*, George, ill. Garth Williams, Farrar, 1969), amusing, talking animal fantasy, sequel to *The Cricket in Times Square**, set the next summer in a New York City subway and then in a meadow in the small town of Hedley, Conn., in which animals and humans in their separate but interacting worlds come to grips with the environmental concern of diminishing open space. In the spring, Chester* Cricket sends John Robin from Hedley with a message for his friends, Tucker* Mouse and Harry* Cat, who still live in the drainpipe in the subway station. Chester wants them to help him prevent developers from building an apartment complex in the Old Meadow where he lives. The two hop the Late Local Express for Hedley and are joyfully reunited with their old friend. Tucker moves in with Chester in his house in a hollow stump. Harry Cat soon attracts the attention of Ellen Hadley, 12, the eldest child in the family that lives at the edge of the meadow, who thinks he is a stray cat, takes him home with her, and indulges him as the household pet. The animals have good times exploring, visiting their animal friends, and chatting, until a summer flood, which temporarily forces many of the creatures from their homes, results in a town council decision to enclose the brook in a conduit. When the steam shovel begins excavating, Ellen and several neighbor children form a picket line in protest. While visiting Henry Chipmunk, Tucker discovers in an abandoned cellar near Henry's home an old family Bible, which once belonged to Joseph Henry, whose house presumably this once was. Tucker gets the idea of planting evidence to convince people that the old house was the homestead of the man who founded Hedley. On Hedley Day in August, the "evidence" is discovered, there is a celebration, and the council declares that Old Meadow is of such historical significance that it should be set aside as a permanent memorial. Detailed descriptions of the life and behavior of the animals build credibility, and gentle satire on the ways of people adds depth. The story is high in emotional appeal, if slow moving, and the anthropomorphized animals are very likeable and more convincing than the humans, who are clear types. The realistic illustrations add greatly to the humor and the believability of the story. Sequels. Choice; Christopher.

TUCKER WOOLF (*Dinky Hocker Shoots Smack**), friend of Dinky*. A dabbler, by his own admission he never finishes any task. He likes libraries and hopes to become a librarian. He has never, according to Tucker himself, had any real relationship and has always relied on his parents to do his thinking for him. He is a sensitive youth, alert to the feelings of others. He cares enough for his cat, Ralph Nader*, to remonstrate with Dinky about overfeeding her, and he willingly assumes household tasks when his mother begins law school. He has a crush on Natalia* Line. Although both Woolfs and Hockers discourage this relationship, because they think the two are getting overly serious, he continues to see Natalia and try to understand her. He is the most normal of the novel's curious assemblage of youths.

TUCK EVERLASTING (Babbitt*, Natalie, Farrar, 1975), fantasy set in the village of Treegap, somewhere in the United States in 1880, dealing with the problems of eternal life. Winnie* Foster, 10, child of a well-ordered, proud, rigid family, decides rebelliously to walk in the woods that her family owns, possibly even to run away. When she sees a boy about seventeen removing a pile of rocks to reveal and drink from a spring, she strikes up a conversation and is told that he is Jesse* Tuck, 104. When his mother, Mae*, and his older brother, Miles*, appear, they view Winnie with consternation, bundle her onto their horse, and rush her away, apologizing all the time. They are seen by only a sinister man in a yellow suit, who had called at the Foster home the previous evening. The Tucks take Winnie to their cabin where she meets Angus* (Pa) Tuck, who explains their problem. Eighty-seven years earlier, as they were travelling west, they stopped in the woods, drank from a spring (all except the family cat), and have grown no older since (except the cat, which eventually died). Tuck takes her out on the pond in his rowboat and tries to convince her that the spring must remain a secret, that its revelation would cause terrible conflicts and overpopulation. Winnie spends the night, alternately repelled and fascinated by the Tucks' disorderly life and considering them in turn crazy, criminal, and the most loving people she has met. Jesse thrills her by proposing that she wait until she is seventeen, them drink from the spring and go off with him. She sees some of the pain of their condition when Miles tells her how his wife left him, taking his two children, when she became convinced he was dealing in witchcraft. In the morning the man in the yellow suit shows up, having overheard them, then traded his knowledge of Winnie's whereabouts for a deed to the woods. The constable arrives just in time to see Mae crack the yellow-suited man's skull with the rifle butt. Mae is jailed, but when the man dies, Winnie sneaks out at night to help with the escape. After the Tucks remove the jail window and haul Mae out, Winnie takes her place on the jail cot so the alarm will not be raised until the Tucks have a chance to get away. Later, out of pity for a toad harassed by a dog, she pours over it a little water from the spring, which Jesse has given her in a bottle to keep until she is seventeen. In an epilogue Mae and Tuck return to Treegap in 1950 and find Winnie's gravestone. The fantasy is convincing and the characters well developed, with Winnie far more than merely an adequate child character and the Tucks individualized and memorable. Christopher; Fanfare; Lewis Carroll.

TUNES FOR A SMALL HARMONICA (Wersba*, Barbara, Harper, 1976), realistic novel set in New York City in the 1970s. The first person narrator, J. F. (Jaqueline Frances) McAllister, 16, looks and dresses like a boy, to the dismay of her wealthy, fashion-conscious mother. At Miss Howlett's School for Girls, she has one friend, Marylou Brown, a responsible, scholarly girl whose parents are playwrights and who does most of the housework and care of her six-year-old brother, Nelson. To Dr. Waingloss, her psychiatrist, J. F. reveals nothing, and only to Marylou does she confess her sudden, irrational love for their poetry teacher, Harold Murth, a pallid man of about thirty. The attraction becomes an obsession, and she trails Murth to his apartment, records his daily habits, and, when she meets him at a play-reading of the work of Marylou's mother, she walks home with him and sees the stark bareness of his apartment. From Esther Tilley, a teacher who is typing Murth's thesis on Christopher Smart, she learns that he has almost no money but needs to get to England to finish his thesis. After pumping Miss Tilley, who has a crush on her, or on the teenaged boy she resembles, J. F. starts sending Murth gifts. Although her parents are wealthy, she decides she must raise a thousand dollars for Murth by playing her harmonica on the street, imagining romantically that she will present him with the check, and they will go off together. Although he maintains a cool reserve, she comes close to him when she discovers him with a bad case of flu and is genuinely helpful in nursing him. With only about eight hundred dollars earned, J. F.'s street musician career halts abruptly with her discovery on a snowy night, when she is ostensibly baby-sitting Nelson, begging with him outside a concert attended by her parents, Nelson's parents, and Miss Howlett. She borrows the rest of the money from Marylou, dresses for seduction, and goes to Murth's apartment on Christmas Eve, only to learn that he is married, independently wealthy though with Spartan tastes, and actually just a shy, rather dull young man. She is offered a part in a movie playing a girl who looks like a boy, but, realizing that the director is exploiting her individual look, she turns it down. Disillusioned even by her psychiatrist, who is in bad need of therapy, she heads for the East River, contemplating suicide but instead plays her harmonica and finds peace in just being what she is. The book has the hip, with-it language which dates a novel fast, and the characters, except for posssibly J. F., are stereotypes, the father preoccupied with business, the frivolous mother, the faithful friend, etc. Although the narrative voice of the teenaged protagonist is sustained rather well, the outcome of the Murth infatuation is predictable and the wise-cracking tone belittles the seriousness of the situation it is developing. National Book Finalist.

TUNIS†, JOHN R(OBERTS) (1889–1975), born in Boston, Mass.; sportswriter, sportscaster, and author noted for his authentic, fast-action sports stories for older boys and teenagers. He was born in Boston and graduated from Harvard University where he played tennis and ran distance track. After service in France in World War I, he became a sportswriter for the New York *Evening Post* and Universal Service and a sportscaster for NBC, covering major sports events at home and abroad for many years. He was himself a title-winning tennis player, and in 1932 he had the distinction of announcing the first broadcast by short wave from Europe of a Davis Cup match. He was forty-nine when he published his first novel for young people, the Fanfare selection *Iron Duke†* (Harcourt, 1938), about a Harvard athlete in football and track. Twenty other novels for young readers followed over the next thirty years, including the sequel *The Duke Decides* (Harcourt, 1939), *Keystone Kids†* (Harcourt, 1943), a baseball story which received the Child Study Award and is cited in *Choice*, *Highpockets* (Morrow, 1948), which received the junior book award of the Boys' Clubs of America, *All-American* (Harcourt, 1942), and *Grand National* (Morrow, 1973), about horse racing and his last book. Two late books take their readers into World War II, *Silence over Dunkerque** (Morrow, 1962), also a *Choice* Selection, a non-sports novel which follows a British soldier during the evacuation of the British Expeditionary Forces after the fall of France, and *His Enemy, His Friend** (Morrow, 1967), also a Fanfare book, which involves a German soldier in France during the occupation who is a star soccer player. Tunis's first-hand experience as an athlete combined with his expert knowledge of the sports world gained as an announcer gave his books their authenticity, and his plots, though formulaic and didactic with social values and lessons in sportsmanship, are exciting and peopled by very human protagonists to whom it is easy to relate. He also wrote a novel for adults, *American Girl* (Brewer, 1930), loosely based on the life of Helen Wills Moody, ten books of non-fiction, and hundreds of articles for national magazines like *Collier's*, *Esquire*, and *New Yorker*.

TURI'S POPPA (Treviño*, Elizabeth Borton (de), Farrar, 1968), novel set in southern Europe, sometime not long after World War II. Turi, 8, who has spent the summer with his gypsy grandfather, Zoltan, because his mother is ill, returns to Budapest to find her dead and his non-gypsy father, Istuan Hubay, depressed and in debt because of her illness. Turi's efforts to help, mostly by stealing cleverly as he has done with the gypsies, grieve his father and backfire when he is arrested and fined. Hope comes in a letter from the Violin-Making Institute of Cremona, Italy, where Istuan was trained, asking him to become their director. Having sold a violin to discharge debts, they start off on foot. On their long journey they have a variety of trials, particularly at the borders where they do not have the necessary papers, but they are helped, mostly by simple peasants who share what little they have. To get out of Hungary, they pretend they are part of a gypsy band who, alerted by Turi's quick thinking, claim them and let them travel with the caravan for some distance. As they journey, Turi's gypsy training helps them through a variety of difficulties, and gradually his father adopts some of his clever strategems, even claiming to be named Gabelich, a name that gives them the advantage of being relatives of half the families in the mountains. In northern Italy, where they pick peaches, a jealous worker causes Istuan to injure his ankle, but the kindly owner sends them on his truck with his fruit to market, and that driver finds them a ride with a load of fish to Cremona. There the trustees of the Institute question Istuan's identity, since he has no papers, and some are hostile since they are reluctant to have a non-Italian director, though so many Italian violin makers were killed in the war that they have been forced to seek a foreigner trained at the Institute. At Turi's suggestion, they allow Istuan to make a violin to prove his skill, and when a famous violinist comes to play on the Stradivarius violin made at the Institute and kept there, he also tries Istuan's new instrument and declares it a worthy descendant. The story is loosely based on a real incident, but the characters themselves are fictional. Turi is a resourceful child, with a special affinity for animals and a great desire to be useful to his father. His baffled dismay when his efforts fail is the best characterization; other characters are more stock types, and the story ends moralistically with Turi giving up his gypsy ethic for respectability. Boston Globe Honor.

TURTLE WEXLER (*The Westing Game**), Tabitha Ruth Wexler, plain, bratty, adolescent daughter of a podiatrist and his pretentious, social-climbing wife who live in Sunset Towers. Turtle is an angry child, hostile because her mother's pride is Angela*, Turtle's beautiful, older sister. Turtle's partner in the Westing game, Flora Baumbach, a dressmaker whom Turtle calls Baba, serves Turtle well as a surrogate mother. The Westing game provides for Turtle the opportunity to demonstrate leadership and develop the financial acumen that result in her eventually becoming a lawyer and chairman of the board of Westing Products. She is really the winner in the Westing game. She is the best developed, most memorable character in the book.

TYCO BASS (*The Wonderful Flight to the Mushroom Planet*†; *Stowaway to the Mushroom Planet*†; *Time and Mr. Bass**), born at 11:00 P.M. on June 28, 1580, he has always had second sight. A rare Mycetian, he has a life expectancy of four or five hundred years on earth and received from the Ancient Ones the gift of travel by thought. A wispy-haired, dome-headed, perky little man, he arrived on earth as a spore. A scientist and inventor, he wills his house and observatory to David* Topman and Chuck* Masterson as headquarters for their Society of Young Astronomers and Students of Space Travel.

U

THE UNCLAIMED TREASURES (*Unclaimed Treasures**), the three great-aunts who live next door to Willa Pinkerton's family. When Mab dies, Willa meets Matthew for whom she develops an immediate infatuation. Vigorous and sharp in spite of their age, Aunt Crystal, once an eminent violinist, and Aunt Lulu run the house since Winnie, Matthew's wife, left. They often go for bird walks and picnics and generally lead full, rich lives, though their actions and speech are tinged with the eccentric. They have a musical ensemble, in which Winnie also performed. When she returns, they immediately include her in their group. Though caricatures, they are handled with sympathy and provide some comic interest in the story.

UNCLAIMED TREASURES (MacLachlian*, Patricia, Harper, 1984), amusing realistic novel of family and neighborhood life set one summer not long ago and seen from the viewpoint of fierce, independent, romantic Willa Pinkerton, almost twelve, who longs for extraordinary happenings and watches constantly for her true love. She, her father, Ted, a writing professor, her very pregnant mother, and her twin, Nicholas*, an aspiring painter, have just moved next door to the Morrises, Matthew, a painter, whose wife, Winnie, has "gone to seek her fortune," their son, Horace*, about Willa's age and a perpetual eater of apples, and their three musical, cat-loving, eccentric maiden aunts, called the Unclaimed* Treasures. When Great-aunt Mab dies, Willa meets Matthew, in her opinion an extraordinary figure and the true love for whom she has been seeking. Her intense but controlled passion, kept secret from all but perceptive Nicholas, works itself out in a series of understated scenes in which dialogue carries the details of the story and principals are subtly revealed, and there is abundant humor of situation, language, understatement, and character, much of it overt and some even slapstick. Sitting for Matthew to finish the portrait of his wife proves less joyous than Willa anticipates as she comes to see that she is merely the means by which he can express on canvas his enduring love for absent Winnie. Other events also claim her attention. She learns that her mother had once wanted to be a dancer, an ambition she gave up when Willa and Nicholas were born, and grapples with mixed emotions about the baby-to-be. She practices kissing on her bedpost, happens upon a love story about two characters named Ted and Wanda written by one of her father's students and reads it while she is supposed to be vacuuming the study, accompanies her mother on a visit to the obstetrician, has discussions about ordinary and extraordinary with Matthew, Nicholas, Horace, and aged Old* Pepper, who lives nearly, speaks in run-on sentences, and is pushed about in a wheelbarrow by his great-grandson, and observes the Unclaimed Treasures go on picnics and birdwalks. Her mother's remark, that there are "some things you can't do just for yourself, Willa. You have to consider others," gives her food for thought. Events take a turn, and Willa resorts to extraordinary measures after two strangers enter her life. One is a young woman named Wanda, who turns up at the door. Willa soon connects her with the story, realizes that she is a student infatuated with Ted, and gets rid of her by telling her that Ted has a "grand array" of children. Then Winnie turns up, and after pondering Winnie's obscure remark about everyone being an unclaimed treasure, Willa makes more connections and then cleverly manipulates Winnie into returning to Matthew by affixing to the finished portrait her own love note signed with a W. This accomplished, she realizes that calm, steady, ordinary Horace is her true love after all. Near summer's end, the book reaches a climax of emotion and action when an unexplained fire breaks out in the Morrises' house, Nicholas breaks his leg rescuing the painting and is taken to the hospital in the same ambulance that takes their mother to obstetrics. Old Pepper drives Horace and Willa on a wild ride to the hospital after them, Willa's mother gives birth to a little girl, and Willa happily welcomes an ordinary little unclaimed treasure named Jane, having learned that everyday life holds plenty of excitement and that everyone is important in his or her own way. An italicized frame story with unnamed characters occasionally reverted to piques the curiosity and helps to unify the fragmented story. At the end the reader learns that they are Willa and Nicholas a dozen years later, Nicholas now a painter, Willa now married to Horace and pregnant with her first child, and young Jane now the age of Willa in the story and much like her elder sister in early adolescent temperament and inclination. It seems the story may repeat itself. The plot is weak, but the characters are consistently interesting, if a too fortuitous mix of ordinary and extraordinary, and it is easy to like intelligent, life-loving Willa, an early adolescent who yields to her common sense. Unerringly accurate point of view and dialogue add much to the interest and credibility, and even if much of the humor is best appreciated by adults, the themes are labored, continuity is questionable, and the elderly are caricatured, the total effect is pleasing, a girl's growing-up story related with flair in which parents and children like each other and are treated with sympathy and respect. Boston Globe Honor.

UNCLE DIRK VAN HEUSEN (*A Spell Is Cast**), Cory Winterslow's uncle, brother of her foster mother, Stephanie Van Heusen, the actress. A gifted wood carver, he has made several wooden masks and some fine chess pieces, among them, unicorn knights. He plays chess with Cory and takes her on outings, and they enjoy each other's company. While outsiders consider him moody and irritable, he is always pleasant and agreeable with her. He and Laurel* Woodford became engaged during their last year in college, but she broke their engagement because she felt he lacked initiative and was too content to live on his mother's money. He then turned to architecture and became respected in his field. He approaches the stock unhappy lover of Gothic romance.

UNCLE EDWARD (*Reserved for Mark Anthony Crowder**), Mark Anthony's great-uncle and the only memorable character in the novel. He is a big, elderly, white-haired man with a mustache and a deep, resonant voice. He loves words and uses them with accuracy and flair. He is an ex-radio show actor and once was a barker at Atlantic City. After his wife died, he came to live with the Crowders. Like Mark Anthony, he is an outsider, and he is very careful not to intrude on family conferences and violate family privacy. He encourages Mark Anthony, gives him the understanding he seeks and needs, and does more than anyone else to raise the boy's self-esteem. He does not always handle the boy well but has the grace and sense to apologize. He works alongside Mark Anthony in the garden and treats him as an equal. Uncle Edward is a fully rounded character.

UNCLE FRANZ ELEND (*Darkness over the Land**), Mark's uncle. Once a university professor of history, he resigned his post in protest over the Nazi policy of excluding Jews from holding positions on university faculties. In the novel, he represents those who try to stand up for what they believe is right but are not supported in their stand by their colleagues. Then a factory worker, he helps a French prisoner of war to escape and is arrested and sent to Dachau. He returns to the Elends some months later, his mind gone and extremely fearful. He often reads from the Bible, particularly passages having to do with personal responsibility.

UNCLE FREDDY (*The Diamond in the Window**; *The Fledgling**), uncle to Eleanor* and Edward* Hall and step-father to Georgie* Dorian. He is enamoured of the great minds of Concord, Mass., where he lives, and he quotes Emerson and Thoreau at the slightest provocation. In *The Diamond in the Window* he is slightly lunatic, talking to the busts of his heroes as if they were alive, but by the book's end he is cured and in subsequent books he runs the Concord College of Transcendental Knowledge. He marries his brilliant student, Alexandria Dorian, and is the kind and interested step-father to her little daughter, Georgie, protagonist of *The Fledgling*.

UNCLE FRED WEBSTER (*A Really Weird Summer**), great-uncle to the Anderson children and owner of the inn at Reeves Ferry where they are sent by their parents' impending divorce. Elderly and in poor health, he is kindly but remote, tolerating Stevie's* questions but not always answering them and never bothering to remember the children's names. At the formal noontime dinner, he asks them in turn one ritual question a day: to Stevie, what is nine times nine? to Nels*, what is the capital of South Carolina? to Rory, how do you spell *receive*? and to Jenny, what is your doll's name? Evidently a stroke victim, he moves slowly and is fussed over by Aunt Ruth, with whom he manages a small store at one end of the largely abandoned inn.

UNCLE FRITZ VANDERBECK (*The Dunderhead War**), Quincy* Heffendorf's dead mother's younger brother. A tall, well-built man, he embarks on the trail west wearing a black frock coat and stiff black hat with stovepipe crown. He is a clockmaker by trade and has come to America to make a new life with the only kin he has left. A recent immigrant, he arouses antagonism in Independence by his open criticism of the lawlessness and roughness of the people of Independence and the lack of discipline of the American soldiers, whom he calls a "dunderhead army." In spite of great hardships on the journey west, he never complains about the trail's inconveniences and difficulties, just about what he feels is American ineptness and naivete. He teaches Qunicy to harness the mules in a certain fashion every morning, crying out, "Eins, Zwei, Drei!," during the process and earning for himself these words as a nickname. Uncle Fritz is a colorful figure who contributes much to the novel's lighthearted tone.

UNCLE HAROLD (*The Trouble with Jenny's Ear**), generous, good-natured uncle of the Pearson children, an electrician. If he had not given Joe and Stanley their electronic equipment, Jenny's* ears would not have become so sensitive to sound that she can hear what people are thinking. He meets Miss Romaine, Jenny's first grade teacher, at the sliding party the Pearsons hold on the endangered hill. At the end, he marries Miss Romaine, moves his business to Pearson's Corners, and hires Joe and Stanley to help him run his new enterprise.

UNCLE HASKELL BISHOP (*Up a Road Slowly**), Aunt* Cordelia's affected, pompous, lazy, self-deluded, alcoholic, older brother, who loves playing the role of the accomplished writer. Aunt Cordelia has always resented his position as their mother's favorite, and the brother and sister show little affection for each other. Keenly aware of how things are between Julie and Brett* Kingsman, at Cordelia's request, he intervenes at the critical moment when Brett takes Julie on a late night stroll and probably prevents a seduction. Haskell is genuinely fond of Julie and encourages her to write. Without her knowledge, he sends off what becomes her first published story. He is a roundly drawn, gradually and convincingly revealed character, pathetic, attractive, and sometimes repulsive.

UNCLE HILARY (*One-Eyed Cat**), Ned's uncle, Mrs.* Wallis's brother. A writer, he travels a great deal. He visits the family on Ned's eleventh birthday, bringing with him as a gift for Ned the Daisy air rifle which contributes to the story's central problem. He is a warm, outgoing man, affable and affectionate, and Ned and the family enjoy his company. Ned wants very much to accept his invitation to spend Christmas in the Carolinas but refuses because he feels he must take care of the cat he is sure he has unwittingly maimed. Uncle Hilary's engaging letters to the family only increase Ned's feelings of guilt. Although Uncle Hilary makes only one appearance in the novel, he greatly influences the action.

UNCLE JACK HALL (*A Gathering of Days**), fun-loving, footloose, bachelor uncle of Catherine* Hall. Cath overhears discussions between him and her father about how to handle the problem of fugitive apprentices and slaves, and she favors Uncle Jack's point of view that runaways flee because their situations have become intolerable and that they should be helped. Uncle Jack drops in and out of the story, and Catherine learns about current affairs in the larger world whenever he visits.

UNCLE ROBERT'S SECRET (St. John*, Wylly Folk, ill. Frank Aloise, Viking, 1972), mystery story set in a small town in Georgia, presumably in the 1960s. The narrator, Debbi Howard, 11 $^1/_2$, knows that her older brother, Bob, 13, has a secret in which he must involve her and their younger brother, Sonny, 9. Disappointed that he can't baby-sit the new daughter of his older sister, who has moved away shortly after the birth, he has brought home a little boy, Tim, whom he has seen badly beaten and tied up in a shack in the woods. Since the Howard children are temporarily being cared for by their very deaf great-aunts, they are able to keep Tim secretly in their basement playroom. Seeing Tim's father, Clay, trying unsuccessfully to get into the house of their reclusive and nearly blind next-door neighbor, old Mr. Peregrine, Debbi and Bob follow him to the shack in the woods and overhear him and his wife, Adele, planning to persuade Mr. Peregrine to alter his will in their favor. Neither of them is much concerned that Tim is missing. That night, Debbi sees a light moving in Mr. Peregrine's yard and, fearing it might be Clay, she sneaks out and climbs the tree that overlooks his high wall. When Sonny, following her, edges out behind her, the branch they are on breaks, and they crash into the family graveyard in Mr. Peregrine's back yard. Though startled, Mr. Peregrine, who has been evidently hunting for something with a flashlight, treats them kindly, takes them through his home to get back to their yard, lends them a book, and invites them to come again. In the meantime Bob, who has followed them to Mr. Peregrine's yard, has found a human skull at the surface of the grave marked only "M.C.," where the earth has washed away and their cat has been digging. When Clay and Adele return and move in on Mr. Peregrine, the children try to scare them with the skull covered with phosphorescent paint. They overhear enough to realize that Clay is Mr. Peregrine's grandson, son of his only daughter, Rose, and Merton Claymore, a good-for-nothing she ran off with, disgracing her family. The Howards are so astonished when Adele, trying to soften up the old man, produces an imposter posing as Tim, that they let their presence be known. Debbi recognizes the child as one recently missing from the school for the deaf and dumb. The wild scuffle that follows stops suddenly when Sonny threatens to throw the dynamite he found near a construction site. Realizing that it is old and therefore highly volatile, the adults freeze while Bob calls the police. Later, after Mr. Peregrine has been introduced to Tim, his real great-grandson, and Clay and Adele have been arrested for kidnapping and child abuse, the children arrange that their old baby-sitter, Mrs. McHenry, will come to keep house for Mr. Peregrine and Tim. Debbi discovers while reading the old man's letters he has saved from Rose that Merton Claymore, who never married her, had tried to extort money from her father. He had suffered a heart attack, died, and was secretly buried by Mr. Peregrine in a shallow grave. Bob quietly reburies the skull. As a mystery, the story has action and tension but depends too much on conversations overheard and the unlikely gimmick of the skull. Setting is immaterial and characterization, even of the first-person narrator, is thin. Poe Nominee.

UNCLE SIEBREN (*Journey from Peppermint Street**), huge deaf-and-dumb man married to Siebren's Great-aunt Hinka and living with her in an ancient monastery in a marsh. Though Siebren is terrified of the idea of him, he proves to be good-natured with a surprising sense of humor. Perhaps because he must be quiet, he thinks deeply and has sensitive answers to some of the boy's questions.

UNDERWOOD, (MARY) BETTY (ANDERSON) (1921–   ), born in Rockford, Ill.; writer, editor, worker with disenfranchised teenagers. She grew up in the Allegheny Mountains of Pennsylvania and later lived in Portland, Oreg. She attended Pennsylvania State University and worked for Houghton-Mifflin as a reader and assistant editor, for George Washington University as a staff writer for medical publications, for the Lane County Council on Alcoholism in Eugene, Oreg., and for the American Civil Liberties Union in Portland as assistant
to the executive director. Her novel, *The Tamarack Tree** (Houghton, 1971), about an early nineteenth century attempt at education for black girls, won the Jane Addams Award. *The Forge and the Forest* (Houghton, 1975) is about the conflict of a French orphan girl with her guardian, an iron-willed pastor.

THE UNMAKING OF RABBIT (Greene*, Constance C., Viking, 1972), problem story whose events take place one week in the late 1900s in a small town not far from New York City. Timid, small-for-his-age Paul, almost twelve, lives with his opinionated, kind grandmother, Emma*. His schoolmates tease him about not having a father and call him "Rabbit" because he is shy and stutters. His only friends are the Barkers, the couple that own the neighborhood grocery. While Paul yearns to be "one of the gang," his greatest wish is to go to live with his vivacious, pretty, divorced mother in New York. Within just a few days' time, Paul's mother marries an artist; Gordon*, grandson of Paul's grandmother's best friend, Bess* Tuttle, comes to visit; and Freddie, the leader of the school gang, makes overtures of friendship. To Paul's surprise, he and Gordon prove compatible and have a good time together at dinner with the Barkers. Paul "chickens out" on Freddie's requirement that he break into a house in order to prove himself worthy of membership in the gang, and his visit to his mother and his stepfather falls so flat that he loses enthusiasm for another New York trip. When the teacher declares his essay about his experiences with Freddie the best in the class and Paul shares it at her request with his schoolmates, he gains courage to stand up to the bully and demand to be called by his right name. An invitation from Gordon further boosts his self-esteem, and life with grandmother looks good. Although too many problems occupy the brief time span and events seem tailor made for the theme, characters are sharply realized, if distorted and made eccentric, and appear true to Paul's pre-adolescent point of view. Dialogue is extensive and accurate and contributes to the novel's fast pace. Choice.

UP A ROAD SLOWLY (Hunt*, Irene, Follett, 1966), realistic novel of a girl's growing up, which takes Julie Trelling from her seventh to her seventeenth years, set in a rural area somewhere in the United States in what may be the late 1920s or early 1930s. Julie tells the story of how, after her mother's death, she and her older brother, Chris, go to live with their mother's older sister, Aunt* Cordelia Bishop. Aunt Cordelia, a prim and proper rural schoolteacher who has never married, lives in a big, comfortable, old house in the country not far from a small town. The road to maturity for Julie is slow and lonely, but one she travels with the support and love of many friends and relatives and, in particular, her aunt, whom she grows to love and respect more as the years pass by. Julie learns to cope with the loss of her mother and separation from her father; her aunt's strictness; jealousy when her beloved older sister, Laura*, marries; schoolgirl snobbishness; the death of a schoolmate; and the sense of being an unwanted burden to her aunt. She adjusts to a new mother, the death of her Uncle* Haskell, and the loss of her first love. She comes to realize that her imperious, sober aunt was herself once young and beautiful and must inevitably face decisions about her own future. At the end, Julie has developed into a gracious young woman, confident that she is ready for college and whatever challenges life may bring to her and to her future husband, childhood sweetheart, Danny* Trevort. Vocabulary is mature but easily apprehended from context. In spite of Hunt's tendency to tell rather than to show, this richly detailed, finely crafted novel moves with control and the conviction of lived experience and is one of the best books of its type. With the exception of Julie's temporary heart throb, Brett* Kingsman, and Aunt Cordelia's old flame, aristocratic Jonathan Eltwing, and his pathetic, mentally ill wife, who never quite convince, characterization is rich and memorable. Dignified, egotistical, alcoholic Uncle Haskell and dirty, underprivileged, retarded Aggie* Kilpin, Julie's shunned schoolmate who dies, stand out. Julie grows up realistically to understand that the everyday experiences of life, no matter how unsettling or demanding, can be handled with equanimity and are finally what make life worthwhile. (Alicia* Trelling) Choice; Fanfare; Newbery Winner.

V

VAL LEWIS (*It's Not the End of the World**), Karen Newman's new friend, whose mother and father are divorced. She acquaints Karen with some of the realities of divorce based on her own experience and on information gained from a book which Karen later also buys a copy of. Karen stays with her one night, and the two do "girl things" together and enjoy one another's company. Val helps Karen to see that life can be good even though parents divorce.

VAN STOCKUM†, HILDA (1908–   ), born in Rotterdam, Netherlands; painter and translator, author, and illustrator of books for children. Because her father was a naval officer, the family traveled extensively in Europe and the Far East while she was growing up. She attended art schools in the Netherlands, France, and Ireland, where she met the family about whom she later wrote in the novels about the close and loving O'Sullivans, the peasant family who live in a peat burning cottage on the shores of Bantry Bay, and their friends and neighbors: *The Cottage at Bantry Bay*† (Viking, 1938), a Fanfare book which is also listed in *Children's Books Too Good to Miss*; *Francie on the Run*† (Viking, 1939); and *Pegeen*† (Viking, 1941), both Fanfare books. She married an American who was studying at Trinity College in Dublin, came to the United States, and lived in New York, Washington, and Montreal, all places to which his work took the family. She also studied art at the Corcoran School of Art in Washington and Thomas More Institute in Montreal. She specialized in portraits and still life, and her work has been exhibited in numerous shows and galleries. She speaks Dutch, German, and French and has translated books for children by such writers as Siny R. van Iterson and Achim Bröger, and has illustrated editions of *Little Women*, *Hans Brinker*, and many books by other writers. She has published two dozen books for older and younger readers, mostly self-illustrated, among them, the acclaimed *The Winged Watchman** (Farrar, 1962), about a Dutch family's problems during the German occupation of World War II, which was both a Fanfare book and a *Choice* book. Her first novel was a Newbery Honor book, *A Day on Skates*† (Harper, 1934), an amusing story about the adventures of some Dutch children while skating on a canal on the first day of winter. Her novels have been praised for their warm humor, liveliness, and understanding of the ways and needs of children. They carry the conviction of personal experience gained with her own six children and the young people she has met in her travels and the places where she has lived. Her family provided the models for *The Mitchells* (Viking, 1945), a novel about five lively children in Washington, whose father is away in World War II. She has also published several picture books.

VELAZQUEZ, DIEGO RODRIGUEZ DE SILVA (*I, Juan de Pareja**), actual seventeenth century painter at the court of Philip* IV of Spain, master of Juan, a black slave who becomes a painter in his own right. Velázquez is pictured as kindly, reserved, and abstemious, and preoccupied with painting truth rather than superficial beauty. When he frees Juan to save him from prosecution, he rightly apologizes for not realizing that he should have done it long before.

THE VELVET ROOM (Snyder*, Zilpha Keatley, ill. Alton Raible, Atheneum, 1965), realistic novel of family life set in rural California during the Great Depression of the 1930s. When her father's old Model-T breaks down in front of the gateway to the Las Palmeras estate, dreamy, intelligent Robin Williams, 12, has no idea how the old mansion will change her life. For several years, she, her father, mother, and four brothers and sisters have been moving from one migrant workers' village to another. They have been following the crops since illness cost Father his job and the family their home. Mr. Williams gets a job on the Las Palmeras apricot ranch, and Robin makes friends with old Bridget* Gunther, the former nursemaid of Gwen* McCurdy, the owner's daughter. Sensing that Robin needs something of her very own to give her hope and relief from her unsettled and humdrum existence, Bridget lends her the key to the tunnel which leads to the Spanish section of the boarded-up mansion in which the owners used to live. Robin investigates and finds the library, which she calls the Velvet Room, from its rich furnishings. The Velvet Room becomes Robin's special haven. There she finds the diary of Bonita McCurdy, the cousin of the present owner, who mysteriously disappeared when she was in her teens, was given up for dead, and is now believed to haunt the old house as a ghost. Robin also makes friends with bouncy, assertive Gwen, just her age, with whom she shares books and music. During the summer, when the work in the pitting shed gets her down or when Gwen goes away on trips, Robin retreats in imagination and reality to her Velvet Room and the puzzle about Bonita. Winter brings a dilemma for Robin. Father accepts a job in Uncle Joe's grocery in Fresno, and along with the new position comes the prospect of a permanent home for the family. Knowing that Robin loves the place, the McCurdys invite her to stay on with them. Realizing that Robin is tempted to accept their offer, Bridget reveals that she herself is Bonita. Bridget's story of her turbulent youth helps Robin see that she is valuing places over people and that she rightly belongs with her own family. The Williamses prepare to leave for Fresno and a settled life when Robin prevents robbers, led by Fred Bailey, the overseer's ne'er-do-well son, from looting and burning the mansion. Mr. McCurdy thinks it is high time he realizes his long-held dream of developing the mansion into a museum and hires Robin's father as caretaker. Robin has both her family and her Velvet Room. This mildly Gothic story remains consistently interesting, but the conclusion seems too fortuitous, and some scenes, such as that in which Robin frustrates the thieves, seem made to order to thrill a young audience. Some characters strain belief, too, but the book does convey some idea of what unsettled and difficult lives migrants lead. Choice; Fanfare.

VERONICA GANZ (Sachs*, Marilyn, ill. Louis Glanzman, Doubleday, 1968), realistic novel, with family and school story aspects, set in New York City in the early 1930s. Veronica Ganz, 13, lives with her mother, an impatient woman who yells at and smacks her children, her mild-mannered, not very successful stepfather, Ralph Petronski, who runs a drycleaning business, her dreamy younger sister, Mary* Rose, and her simpering, little half brother, Stanley*, who hiccoughs when he is nervous. Veronica is a social misfit who handles problems the way her mother does. The biggest child in her class, she is a chronic underachiever and is often sent to the pincipal's office for misbehaving. She has cowed by fists or reputation all her classmates except one, Peter* Wedemeyer. New in the area, he taunts her with scurrilous verses, enraging her to the point of desperation. Small, wiry, quick-witted, he has managed to evade every trap she has set for him since school began. Not even the anticipation of a longed-for visit from the father she has not seen since she was a small child can divert her from the prospect of forcing Peter to tow the line. After-school practice for the French Christmas program provides her with what she hopes will be an opportunity to get even with Peter. But, unknown to her, Peter has ironically organized the class into a Vigilante committee. When she attacks him, he and two companions beat her up. Fortunately for her, she is rescued by a man bystander, who berates the boys for treating a girl this way, large as she is. The shoe is now on the other foot, however, and Veronica dreads meeting Peter at school, sure he will pursue his advantage. She discovers to her relief that he is thoroughly ashamed of the way he has acted. She discovers, too, that all along he has admired her size and persistence, and she also realizes that she has appreciated his pluck and wit. The two establish a friendly, teasing relationship. Events move fast, people and incidents are readily recognizable, if exaggerated or stock, and language is fairly simple, easily apprehended by the middle grade readers. This is an often humorous, rather predictable, awkwardly plotted novel of social realism for younger readers that remains consistently interesting. Sequel is *Peter and Veronica*. Books Too Good; Choice.

VERY FAR AWAY FROM ANYWHERE ELSE (LeGuin*, Ursula, Atheneum, 1976), realistic novel set in California in the contemporary period. By his own description, Owen* Thomas Griffiths, 17, is a "bright little jerk," accustomed to being the youngest in his class and something of an outsider. On his seventeenth birthday, his father gives him a new car, a gift Owen finds more burden than pleasure. Almost by accident he gets to know Natalie* Field, nearly eighteen, a strong-minded violinist and composer, with whom he forms his first real friendship. Only Natalie, herself ambitious and determined, though somewhat young socially, can understand his desire to study biology and psychology at MIT instead of going to the local state college as his mother wishes. Spurred by the suspicions of Natalie's grim fundamentalist father and by the pressures of advertising, peer groups, and the pervasive culture, Owen feels that sex is an essential part of such a relationship, and when Natalie refuses he is so hurt and confused that he wrecks the car. Owen recovers physically but not emotionally, until he attends a concert where three of Natalie's compositions are played and she insists on talking the matter out with him. With new courage, he shows his parents the scholarship offer from MIT, and they agree to use the insurance money from the car for other first-year expenses. Although there is comparatively little action in this brief book, the characterization of two young people struggling to be different from their peers is deep and sensitive, and Owen's parents, who fail to understand him, are pictured sympathetically. Owen's first-person narration is handled convincingly to present an insecure but intelligent boy. The title refers not only to the location of an imaginary island country, Thorn, which Owen has invented, but also to Owen's own nature in relation to the society around him. Fanfare.

VETCH (*A Wizard of Earthsea**), friend of Ged* in the school for wizards on Roke*, a boy from a simple village in the East Reach. Heavy-set and dark-skinned, Vetch is a good man but not destined to be a great wizard. After Ged has been injured and is shaken in spirit, Vetch gives him the great gift of complete trust by telling him his true name, Estarriol. At the end of Ged's search for the Shadow, Vetch joins him and travels into the unknown eastern seas.

VICKY WALKER (*Time at the Top**), Victoria Albertine Walker, Susan* Shaw's friend in the fantasy world of the 1800s. Vicky is a genuine romantic, reads a lot, and believes in fairy tales. She is the first to realize that the old woman has granted Susan three trips to the Victorian era.

VICTOR WOODWARD (*The Edge of Next Year**), younger brother of Orin Woodward. He is ten years old when his mother is killed in an auto accident. Hospitalized himself for a while with injuries from the crash, he copes with his grief by immersing himself in his hobby of building vivariums for the wild creatures he collects. He persuades Orin to move their bedroom to the attic of the house, where he constructs several vivariums for his snake, Fergus, salamanders, and various other creatures. Eventually the attic is a little jungle of philodendron, ferns, ivy, potted yew, lemon tree, and crated creatures, most of them nocturnal types, as well as singing crickets destined to serve as their food. Steady, pragmatic Vic helps Orin see that life can go on.

VIERECK, PHILLIP R. (1925–   ), born in New Bedford, Mass.; teacher, novelist. He is a graduate of Dartmouth College and studied further at Plymouth Teachers College. During World War II he served in the U.S. Naval Air Corps. In his teaching career he has worked for the Bureau of Indian Affairs in Alaska, the setting for *Let Me Tell You About My Dad* (Day, 1973), about a young boy who spends a summer with his father in Alaska. Among other titles is *Sue's Secondhand Horse* (Day, 1973), recounting the complications for the family of a thirteen-year-old girl who realizes her dream when she gets a mare for Christmas. He has also been associated with Vermont schools as teacher, principal, and district supervisor and has co-authored social studies texts. For his survival novel, *The Summer I Was Lost** (Day, 1965), he hiked into the Pemigewasset Wilderness of New Hampshire with only a string and a paper clip to see whether his story idea was possible and discovered that he lived quite well on trout, as his character does.

THE VIGILS (*The Chocolate War**), vicious secret society in the Catholic boys' high school. The Vigils not only perpetrate pranks and terrorize non-members, but they also manipulate the Brothers who run the school and drive one of them to a mental breakdown.

VIKING ADVENTURE (Bulla*†, Clyde Robert, ill. Douglas Gorsline, Crowell, 1963), historical adventure for younger readers set in Norway and the North Atlantic in the days of Vikings. Sigurd, only son of Olaf the Strong, has been trained by his father in the skills of fighting. His father has even brought Sigurd's cousin, Rolf, more than two years older, to live at the family farm to be a combatant against Sigurd, a position he relishes, though he never becomes a friend. When Sigurd is twelve, raiders come to the coast, and a refugee from one of the devastated settlements arrives, Bard, a scholar and storyteller, who was a friend of Olaf's father. Bard, after being there some time, offers to teach Sigurd to read and write, but the boy has no desire to learn. The next year his father's great friend and companion, Gorm, comes, seeking Olaf's company on a voyage to Vineland, a dream of their youth. Since Olaf has a wound which never healed, he refuses, and Gorm finds Sigurd too young. The next day, however, the boy gets permission to follow Gorm to Torvik, where he proves his strength by lifting the test-stone and is taken into the hundred-man crew, although the financer of the expedition, Halfred, is angry at the decision. They sail to Iceland and from there on, but a storm blows them out of the way so they miss Greenland and come to the shores of Vineland, though Halfred proposes turning back because he has had a warning dream. Gorm as captain overrules him and they go ashore, but Halfred shoots an Indian for his necklace of shells, which the Viking thinks is pearls, and they must escape to their ship. Though Halfred still wants to turn back, Gorm sails down the coast, finds a good spot to winter, and is on shore with Halfred and Sigurd when he is pushed off a cliff by Halfred, though the treacherous man says it was a savage who attacked them.

On the way back, Halfred realizes that Sigurd knows the truth and makes an attempt on his life. When they reach the Faroe Islands, Halfred does not put ashore, though a storm is coming, fearing that Sigurd will escape and spread word of his treachery. With the help of Aron, a friendly young sailor, Sigurd gets off the ship in a tub and is washed ashore in a storm. The simple islanders nurse and feed him but do not believe his story of reaching Vineland. In the storm the ship is wrecked and all the other voyagers are killed. In the spring Sigurd finds a ship to take him home, where he learns his father has died. Since he is the lone survivor of the voyage, he asks Bard, who is still in the household, to teach him to write so that he may record the story for the future. For an audience of early readers, the book provides an action-filled adventure, but there is no attempt at subtle characterization or any but the simplest style. Choice.

VILLAGE OF THE VAMPIRE CAT (Namioka*, Lensey, Delacorte, 1981), mystery story set in a village in sixteenth century Japan. Zenta, a ronin, an unemployed samurai, and his younger companion, Matsuzo, return to the village where, ten years before, Zenta had studied with Ikken, a tea-ceremony master, learning grace, self-control, and calmness of spirit from the old man and skill with his sword from Ikken's son, Shunken. They find the village greatly changed, poverty-stricken, with the villagers apparently living in fear. At the tavern they have a run-in with a group of medicine peddlers who are extorting money from the villagers in exchange for medicine to protect their daughters from the phantom cat that has already killed four girls. As they proceed to the isolated house of Ikken, Zenta is attacked by a large, black creature that inflicts a bad scratch on his neck and utters a mewing sound. At the entrance to Ikken's yard they meet his lovely niece, Asa, and her mother, Toshi, widow of Ikken's brother. Asa's large dog, Kongomaru, at first attacks Matsuzo but soon becomes friendly, and Matsuzo is much attracted to the girl. The house of Ikken shocks them, however—unkempt, devoid of the lovely things Zenta remembers, and quite without food—and the old man himself seems broken and frightened. Fortunately, the two have brought food with them, and, after eating, Zenta is invited to the tea ceremony which calms both him and his old master. The two ronin set out to unravel the mystery and learn a number of important facts: Asa was betrothed to Shunken, who was killed three years ago in battle; Hirobei, a cousin of Toshi, is handling her affairs and hopes to marry her, though he is of the merchant class, lower than her samurai first husband; the girls who have been killed were first subject to fainting spells, and their throats have been slashed as if by claws; Ikken will have nothing to do with Toshi's offers of help, since her money comes from her merchant father, but he loves Asa and would like to marry her to one of the two samurai; the Cat is said to be after the fortune to be left Asa by her merchant grandfather. Ryutaro, chief of the outlaw medicine peddler's band, tries to get Zenta to join forces with him to destroy the Cat, but Zenta is cautious. On New Year's evening, Matsuzo goes to an abandoned house where Asa has been lured and there encounters the Cat, whom he wounds with

Kongomaru's help. Zenta, meanwhile, is defending Toshi's home from an attack by the peddler band, despite the fact that his right hand has been wounded by Kongomaru, who inexplicably has attacked him. When Zenta realizes that it is the tea-ceremony incense that maddens the dog, he thinks Ikken may be the Cat, but this seems impossible. At last all the clues point to the Cat as Shunken, not killed but disfigured in a battle and turned mad by the reaction of girls to his hideous face. Ikken, who is shamed by his son's behavior, commits hara-kiri, and Zenta and Shunken duel, both with left hands. Zenta defeats Shunken, who also commits hara-kiri to finish himself off. Although the ceremonies, the details of village life, and the values expressed all appear to be faithful to the samurai period in Japan, there is no feel in the thoughts, language, or actions of the characters of a time past. The pace is fast, but as if twentieth-century actors were cast in a fancy-dress play. This is the fourth book with Zenta and Matsuzo as chief characters. Poe Honor.

VINING†, ELIZABETH JANET GRAY (1902–   ), born in Philadelphia, Pa.; educator, novelist, librarian. She is a graduate of Bryn Mawr College and studied library science at Drexel Institute of Technology. At one time she taught high school in a New Jersey resort town, a setting used for her novel *Sandy*† (Viking, 1945). She was married and lived in North Carolina, but after only a few years of married life her husband was killed in an automobile accident. During World War II, she joined the American Friends Service Committee in Philadelphia, writing reports, appeals, and articles, and was recommended by the Friends Service to become tutor to the Crown Prince of Japan, a position she held for four years and which is the subject of her autobiographical book, *Windows for the Crown Prince* (Lippincott, 1952). Her Japanese experience is also used in her novel, *The Cheerful Heart*† (Viking, 1959). She has also written biographies for young people of Walter Scott, William Penn, and John Greenleaf Whittier, but her most successful books are historical fiction, like *Meggy MacIntosh*† (Doubleday, 1930), set mostly in North Carolina during the American Revolution, *Adam of the Road*† (Viking, 1942) set in England in the medieval period, and *I Will Adventure** (Viking, 1962), a story of a boy in Renaissance England who becomes a friend of William Shakespeare. Her long writing career has continued with an autobiographical work, *Being Seventy: The Measure of the Year* (Viking, 1978).

VITO DONATELLI (*The Contenders**), fight manager who runs the gym where Alfred Brooks trains. An honest man and therefore unusual in the fight business, Donatelli is known for telling his fighters when to stop before they are hurt too badly, if he knows they can't make it big, even though he loses the time and investment he has put into them. His influence is one of the big factors in changing Alfred from an aimless failure to a young man with purpose and confidence.

VOIGT, CYNTHIA (1942–   ), born in Boston, Mass.; teacher and author of novels for children and young adults. She was raised in Connecticut and graduated from Dana Hall School and Smith College in Massachusetts. After traveling in Europe, she worked in advertising and odd jobs for a while before getting her teaching certificate from St. Michael's College. She has taught English in high school in Glen Burnie, Md., and at the Key School in Annapolis, where she has also been department chairman. She and her husband, who teaches Latin and Greek, and their two children live in Annapolis and spend their summers on an island in the Chesapeake Bay. She received the Newbery Medal for *Dicey's Song** (Atheneum, 1982), which was also a *Boston Globe-Horn Book* honor book. This is a generously detailed, strongly characterized account of how the Tillerman children, introduced in *Homecoming* (Atheneum, 1981), find a home with their Grandmother Tillerman on Chesapeake Bay. She has also written *Tell Me If the Lovers are Losers* (Atheneum, 1982), a young adult novel set at a college for gifted women, *The Callender Papers** (Atheneum, 1983), a novel of suspense that won the Edgar Allan Poe Award, and *A Solitary Blue** (Atheneum, 1983). This story concerns a youth introduced in *Dicey's Song* whose mother deserts her family and then re-enters his life. It was chosen for the Fanfare list and was a *Boston Globe-Horn Book* honor book.

THE VOYAGE BEGUN (Bond*, Nancy, Atheneum, 1981), fantasy novel of family and community life set one school year on Cape Cod sometime in the twenty-first century. Energy limitations and pollution have resulted in widespread food shortages, ghost towns, vandalism, thievery, unemployment, and a much reduced standard of living in the United States. Paul Vickers, 16, bookish and introverted, at odds philosophically with his parents, but respectful to them, has made no friends among the town youth since his family moved to the cape where his father, Dr.* Vickers, directs the Environic Research Station. The local people resent the government employees at the coastal laboratory because they enjoy a higher standard of living than the residents of the once affluent, now severely depressed, resort area. Paul's first local friends are middle-aged, ecology-conscious Maggie Rudd*, self-appointed game warden, who helps Paul rescue a Canada goose caught in a snare, and then her friend, ex-fisherman turned itinerant painter, Gabe Palazzola. An equally important character is Mickey* Cafferty, 11, daughter of the local grocer, Mr.* Frank Cafferty, and also at odds with her family. After quarreling with aged, but spirited, Walter Jepson over a salvaged raft, tough-minded, persistent Mickey forms a grudging friendship with the old man. Walter lives in a shack in an abandoned shipyard where he is secretly building a sailboat. When Mickey unwittingly leads the Salvages, a notorious local street gang to which Shawn*, Mickey's bullying brother, belongs, the Salvages ransack Walter's place and burn down the yard, destroying his boat. Walter is taken to a nursing home, where he grows despondent. Paul meets Mickey when he encounters her trying to fix up Walter's shack so that Walter can come home. Paul gradually becomes involved in her project and enlists the help of Maggie and Gabe. After Paul is beaten up by the Salvages, Paul blackmails Shawn into finding another boat for Walter. The five "borrow" the Research Station cruiser to tow the boat to the shipyard. Dr. Vickers is embarrassed and angered by the scheme, which takes place during a government inspection of the research facility, and transfers to Washington. While Paul feels no closer in spirit to his parents at book's end, he has made friends on his own and is satisfied with knowing that Walter has a new lease on life, that Mickey respects him, and that Shawn has developed new, more constructive interests. Skillful characterization, a carefully crafted setting well integrated with plot and characters, adroitly caught interpersonal and family relationships, and carefully calculated ironies alleviate the didacticism and compensate for the sometimes plodding, too-coincidental plot. Boston Globe Honor.

VY PRATT (*Sweet Whispers, Brother Rush**), Viola or M'Vy, mother of Tree and Dabney*, who is more frequently absent than present in their lives, though she returns often enough to bring them money for groceries. When the ghost of Brother* Rush, her youngest brother, shows episodes of the past, Vy is revealed to have been an abusive mother to her son. Although a practical nurse with some formal nurse's training, she has neglected to observe the signs of the rare disease from which all four of her brothers died, even though Dab has a far-advanced case. Vy admits she has been wrong and seems belatedly to be attempting to make better decisions for Tree.

W

WAGNER, JANE, born in Tennessee; composer, designer, lyricist, and playwright for television. Her first book for children, *J.T.** (Van Nostrand, 1969), a story of the friendship between a black inner-city boy and a stray cat, was filmed for television. The book is illustrated with photographs taken in the filming.

WALK THE WORLD'S RIM (Baker*, Betty, Harper, 1965), historical novel involving real people, set in what is now Texas, New Mexico, Arizona, and Mexico in the mid–1530s. The story fictionalizes the varying fortunes of the four survivors of the ill-fated Spanish expedition to the New World led by Pámfilo de Narváez: Álvar Núñez Cabeza de Vaca, whose memoirs form the basis of the novel, Alonso del Castillo Maldonado, Andrés Dorantes*, and his black slave, Esteban*. After spending the winter with the poor but friendly Avavare Indians west of the Mississippi in what is now Texas, the four Men-From-the-Sun, as the Indians call them, begin their long trek to Mexico City. They take with them as interpreter and guide, simple, courageous Chakoh, the fourteen-year-old son of the Avavare headman. Chakoh elects to accompany them, lured by the marvels of Mexico City and hoping to learn how he might help his people economically. The three Spaniards and Esteban assume the role of medicine men, gaining some fame as healers among the tribespeople as they travel. The little band would never have reached its destination without Esteban, whose gift for languages, friendliness, wit, and resource several times save them from tight situations, and the Spaniards promise that Esteban will be rewarded for his great helpfulness. The travelers encounter the comparatively well-off Buffalo People of the southern Plains and stay for a while with the friendly Pima. Aunt Maria, the Pima woman whose hut they share, teaches Chakoh to grow corn and weave sandals. From the Pima, the travelers hear about Cíbola, a city of vast wealth which lies to the north. They hurry to Mexico City with the information, certain that the Viceroy will reward them richly. In Mexico City, Chakoh lives in the Mercederian abbey, where the brothers treat him with great kindness and teach him about Christianity, and he soon adopts Spanish ways. Thrilled by the splendors of the city, he enjoys his easy life and almost forgets about the Avavare. A year passes with no word from Esteban, which strikes Chakoh as strange, but he hears that the three Spaniards have failed to receive the rewards they anticipated. A chance encounter with Cortés in the Plaza in front of the Palace leads to Chakoh's discovery that Esteban is in charge of the Viceroy's stables and that he is Dorantes's slave, a fact he had not previously picked up. The knowledge leaves the youth confused about his relationship with Esteban, since in Avavare culture, slaves are regarded as cowards and weaklings. Furthermore, Esteban's remark that Chakoh appears to value easy living too highly pricks his conscience. The expedition northward under Fray Marcos to Cíbola leads to a reconciliation between the two, to Esteban's death from an arrow at Cíbola after great heroism, to Chakoh's realization that loyalty and honor have little to do with whether or not a person is physically free, and to his understanding that among the Spaniards he has, like Esteban, little but utilitarian value. The end of the story sees him returning to his people, resolving to improve the Indians' lives by his newly acquired knowledge and skills. Serious in tone, the plot moves inexorably, if unevenly, fortuitously, and somewhat illogically, to its expected conclusion. Focus wavers between Chakoh and Esteban, though the latter, while too stoic and inarticulate about his plight, engages the emotions with greater intensity than the protagonist. Most of the characters are types, the setting is indistinctly realized, and the story is too understated and inadequately developed to support the many themes it must examine from several perspectives, freedom, honor, courage, duty, and greed. Simply put, although the book holds the attention, the author has tried to do too much in 168 pages. The title comes from a rueful statement of Esteban's, that he appears destined always to "walk the world's rim like a blind horse chained to a waterwheel. Around and around with never an ending." (Brother* Solano) Choice.

WALTER POTREZESKI (*Anywhere Else but Here**), a man who has a deep interest in Molly Smelter because as a Jewish child in Poland he and his parents had been sheltered by Molly's grandfather during World War II. Hidden in the attic, Walter has watched the daughter of the family at her play in the yard and has become deeply attached to her, although she is unaware of his presence until the Russians are approaching Krakow and she, at eleven, and her mother decide to leave and walk west to meet the American army. Ironically, when the Russians arrive they arrest Walter's parents, even though they are Communists, and put the boy in a labor battalion for a year, after which he escapes to West Germany and eventually comes to Canada, then to the United States. By the time he tries to trace the girl he had watched, she has married, given birth to Molly, and died. He buys the dollhouse, an exact replica of the house in Krakow, from Molly to give her the down payment on a printing business for her father and suggests that he will help her with college expenses when she is older.

WARE, LEON (VERNON) (1909–   ), born in Plainview, Minn.; freelance writer of novels, movies, television scripts, and magazine articles. He grew up in Winnetka, Ill., graduated from Northwestern University, and served in the

U.S. Navy during World War II. After several years in business, he became a full-time writer. Sailing is his hobby, an interest reflected in such books as *The Threatening Fog* (Westminster, 1962). He has traveled widely, often by freighter; *The Mystery of 22 East** (Westminster, 1965), a winner of the Edgar Allan Poe Award, is about a freighter trip through the Panama Canal.

WARTSKI, MAUREEN (ANN CRANE) (1940–   ), born in Asiya, Japan; teacher, writer. She attended the University of Redlands in California and Sophia University in Tokyo. In 1957–1958 she was a reporter for *English Mainichi*, Kobe, Japan, and in 1962 became a United States citizen. She has taught history in public schools in Sharon, Mass. For five years she and her husband lived in Bangkok, Thailand, and during this period she visited Vietnam, seeing first hand the countryside and seas that form the setting for her story of refugees, *A Boat to Nowhere** (Westminster, 1980), which won the Child Study Award. Its sequel is *A Long Way from Home* (Westminster, 1980).

WATSON, SALLY (LOU) (1924–   ), born in Seattle, Wash.; novelist. She graduated from Reed College in Portland, Oreg., after studying at Colorado State College of Education for two years. From 1944 to 1946 she served in the U.S. Navy and later worked as a Great Books representative in Los Angeles and with a reading institute. Her fiction is mostly of two kinds, historical romances set in the Scottish highlands, like *Witch of the Glens** (Viking, 1962), and novels of the Near East like *The Mukhtar's Children** (Holt, 1968).

WE DARE NOT GO A-HUNTING (MacLeod*, Charlotte, Atheneum, 1980), mystery novel set on the island of Netaquid, near Nantucket off the Massachusetts coast in 1932. Island society is divided between the Ledgers, the wealthy who come in their yachts and summer in their wealthy palatial cottages on Netaquid Ledge, and the Islanders, the year-round residents who fish and get most of their cash by selling sea food, garden truck, and services to the Ledgers. Until Molly Bassett, newly graduated from high school, is drafted into baby-sitting Sammy Truell, $4^1/_2$, because emergencies take both his parents away, she hasn't realized that none of the Ledgers have been hiring Islanders this summer. When Upton Sotherby, wealthy Ledger, protests to Sammy's father, Jack Truell, Molly discovers that Sotherby has organized a boycott because the summer before his daughter, then six and a half, was kidnapped for a week, and though she was returned after he paid the ridiculously small ransom of two thousand dollars, he blames and distrusts the Islanders. Molly, an outspoken girl, points out that everyone on the island spent a week hunting for Annette Sotherby and got not even a thank you for their efforts, but she privately wonders whether some hard-up Islander was responsible. Annette is back this summer with her own baby-sitter, pretty, flighty Barbara Ackerley, and her own psychologist, Dr. Putnam, who is trying to cure her of a hallucination that she was with fairies during her week's absence. Molly is thrown into their company frequently, because Sammy and Annette are the only young children on the ledge, and she is attracted to the personable young doctor and can see that the feeling is mutual. She also makes a hit with the Truell servants, an elderly Italian couple, because she learned Italian from a hired hand and can converse in their own language. To fill in at the Bassett family vegetable-and-fish stand, her mother invites Tom Nevers, the son of an island girl who moved to Maine, to come for the summer. Among the other characters is Mrs. Hairweather, housekeeper at the isolated cottage of Mr. Frisben, an anti-social invalid; Mrs. Hairweather often rows to the stand for groceries, but Mr. Frisben is seldom seen. When, after a week, Jack Truell returns, Sammy gets the ride with Dr. Putnam and Annette in the Sotherby speedboat which conscientious Molly has steadfastly refused him, since she has promised not to let him out of her sight. To the horror of both her and the boy's father, a black boat with a powerful outboard motor swoops in and two figures in black oilskins knock Dr. Putnam into the water, lift the children into the black boat, and zoom off. Trying to follow in the red speedboat, which runs out of gas, Molly is first infuriated at the stupidity that would take children out with a nearly empty tank and no reserve gas; later this gives her second thoughts about Dr. Putnam. With Tom, she explores at night the empty boatyard and discovers that the owner, Peleg Gray, is doing a little liquor smuggling. They also call at the lighthouse, where their visit startles the keeper's wife out of mental confusion caused by her son's drowning, five years earlier. By sensible deduction Molly at last figures out that the children must be at Mr. Frisben's house at Little Netaquid, and the mystery unravels in an exciting raid in which many bizarre elements are revealed: Mr. Frisben is non-existent, just a dummy's head propped on a wheel chair in blankets; the fairies are midgets; Mrs. Hairweather is a former circus strong-woman, drawn with her midget friends into the crime by Dr. Putnam, actually a stage illusionist; Barbara is his assistant. While the solution is far-fetched, the story of the life on the island and Molly's forthright, no-nonsense character are far better developed and more interesting than is usual in this genre. Poe Nominee.

WE LIVED IN THE ALMONT (Clymer*, Eleanor, ill. David K. Stone, Dutton, 1970), realistic novel of family life set in New York City in the mid–1900s. Young Linda Martin, a chronic complainer, assembles her recollections about the several months when she is twelve and her family lives in the Almont, a large, once-elegant apartment house in a mixed neighborhood, and life changes for the better for the Martins. The family's small apartment, if shabby, is better than any they have had before in the buildings of which Linda's father has been resident Super. For the first time, too, Linda makes some close friends, among them, lively and generous Sharon Ross, who lives just around the corner in a big, luxury apartment house by the park. Linda becomes particularly fond of Sharon and spends a great deal of time with her before Sharon's parents decide to get a divorce and she is sent to a private school. Linda also becomes acquainted with several occupants of the Almont, including eccentric Miss Clark, who is called the Plant Lady, because her apartment is filled with house plants, and who keeps two cats. Ashamed of her home, which, before meeting Sharon, Linda had thought quite nice and to impress her friend, Linda gossips about the tenants. She also longs for a guitar like the one Sharon's sister has. One day, in the basement storeroom, she finds a guitar belonging to Miss Clark, which she "borrows" and hides in her closet. When the residents of the Almont learn that the building is to be sold, they protest their eviction in court but lose the case. While packing to move, Mrs. Martin discovers the guitar in Linda's closet. When Linda claims that Miss Clark loaned it to her, Mrs. Martin checks on her story. To Linda's surprise and relief, Miss Clark, probably because Linda has been kind to one of her cats, announces that she gave the guitar to her. Mr. Martin finds another job, and the family leaves the Almont. When Linda later returns to see what her old neighborhood looks like, she finds it quite changed, a supermarket standing where the Almont used to be. Characters are types, the plot lacks focus, and motivations are fuzzy. Not one of the plot problems is developed much or exploited for suspense, nor does the author work up the tenants for human interest. The story moves fast and presents a kind of overview for younger readers of life in a big city apartment house from the standpoint of a girl who grows a little less selfish and more aware of the implications of her actions. Choice.

WELLS, ROSEMARY (1943–   ), born in New York City; illustrator, novelist. She attended Boston Museum school and started her career as a book designer. Her first book of her own was made of her illustrations for a Gilbert and Sullivan song, *A Song to Sing, O!* (Macmillan, 1968). Since then, she has alternated doing picture books and young adult novels, among them *The Fog Comes on Little Pig Feet* (Dial, 1972) and *When No One Was Looking** (Dial, 1980), a mystery story of the junior tennis circuit, which was an Edgar Allan Poe nominee.

WENDA GAMBLING (*The Pushcart War**), movie star who gets to the heart of the problem of the constant traffic snarl in New York City when she sagely remarks on a TV panel show that there are simply too many trucks in the city and that they are too big. She finances the pea shooter campaign. After the war, she stars in a film about the conflict.

WERNER (*Journey to America**), sixteen-year-old youth at the refugee camp, who encourages Lisa to read and use her mind. He tries to help her see that the world offers interesting and valuable things to learn and do even though one's personal circumstances are filled with despair. He is the leader of the refugee children, who are usually hungry because the director, Frau Strom, uses their food money to buy clothes for herself. He leads the children in a raid of the pantry of Pop Wagner, their cook, the doddering, kindly, old man who likes to talk about the days when he was a cook at a luxury hotel. They steal potatoes which they roast in a glorious picnic in the woods, stuffing themselves for a delightfully satisfying change. Werner's father was shot by Nazis, and he doesn't know where his mother is. When Lisa compares his situation with her own, she concludes she is better off than he is.

WERSBA, BARBARA (1932–   ), born in Chicago, Ill.; actress, novelist. She grew up in San Mateo, Calif., was graduated from Bard College, and studied acting at the Neighborhood Playhouse and the Paul Mann Actors' Workshop in New York. For fifteen years she was a professional stage and television actress, then started writing books for young people. Her first five were for younger children, but she is best known for her novels for teenagers, including *The Dream Watcher** (Atheneum, 1969), a story of a friendship between a lonely boy and an aging actress, and *Tunes for a Small Harmonica** (Harper, 1976), about a girl's infatuation with her English teacher, which was a National Book finalist.

THE WESTING GAME (Raskin*, Ellen, Dutton, 1978), detective novel set in a town in Wisconsin on the shore of Lake Michigan in the late 1900s. Sixteen people from the swank Sunset Towers apartment house are invited to the reading of the will of reclusive, self-made millionaire, Samuel Westing, manufacturer of paper products. His unusual will specifies that the heirs be paired and that each pair be given ten thousand dollars and an envelope containing clues that are to be used to win something, just what is unclear, but the stakes are presumably high. In a rapid accumulation of swiftly shifting scenes, like a camera zooming in and abruptly receding in a TV thriller or soap opera, the most eccentric characters attempt to make sense of the clues (which prove to be the words to "America"), reveal themselves, and develop new interests and self-awarenesses as they do. There unfolds a bizarre chain of events, bombings, thefts, blizzards, and other mysterious comings and goings, and hardly anyone or anything is as he, she, or it appears. The podiatrist turns out to be a bookie; his wife, a self-styled decorator, goes into the restaurant business; the restaurateur is an inventor; a bratty child scores on the stock market; a black, woman judge sleuths into all their backgrounds; the cleaning woman turns out to be Westing's wife; the doorman is revealed as Westing himself, not dead as has been supposed but parading under several identities; and the heirs' prize, for the fun and games they have provided Westing, is the deed to Sunset Towers. The imaginative, convoluted plot moves with many inventive twists for a jig-saw puzzle of events, word clues, and character clues that lead the reader on with some humor, some excitement, and plenty of ambiguity and irony. The result is an overly complicated and sometimes precious, but certainly never dull, take-off on the traditional detective story. (Turtle* Wexler; Angela* Wexler; J.* J. Ford; Chris* Theodorakis; Doug* Hoo; Sandy* McSouthers; Bertha* Crow) Addams; Boston Globe Winner; Fanfare; Newbery Winner.

WESTMARK (*Westmark**; *The Kestrel**), the medieval kingdom that, in *Westmark*, the villainous prime minister, Cabbarus, rules for ailing King Augustine, who has become increasingly despondent since the loss of his daughter years before the story begins. Westmark has fallen upon hard times because Cabbarus is a despot who ruthlessly jails everyone who speaks against him and his tyrannical policies or attempts to initiate reforms. In *The Kestrel*, Westmark has been invaded by the Regians. Dr. Torrens, prime minister under Queen Augusta, maintains order during the conflict, ironically suppressing freedom of speech in much the same way that his predecessor did.

WESTMARK (Alexander*, Lloyd, Dutton, 1981), flamboyant, realistic adventure novel, first of a trilogy, set in the fictitious, medieval kingdom of Westmark*. Theo, printer's devil, under a criminal charge for assaulting a king's man, takes up with Count Las* Bombas, a roguish mountebank of many identities, in whose entourage is Musket*, a dwarf, and Mickle*, a pinched and starving street urchin who is a remarkable ventriloquist. Theo becomes fond of Mickle, whose pathetically thin body and pitiful weeping in her sleep stir his protective instincts. Las Bombas develops an interest-catching, spiritualist act around the girl, in which as an oracular priestess she speaks through a disembodied head, a stunt that attracts large and enthusiastic crowds. Ashamed of taking money under such false pretenses and fearful that his presence may endanger the troupe, the highly ethical Theo departs and falls in with revolutionaries led by Florian*, a man of good family, considerable leadership ability, and noble principles. Florian and his "children," as his motley group of followers are known, wish to overthrow the corrupt regime of Westmark and set up a democracy. The nation is now in the clutches of Cabbarus, ambitious, unscrupulous prime minister, who has suspended civil rights. After a succession of exciting adventures that carry Theo about the country and put him in one morally ambivalent situation after another, Theo arrives at the palace, in the custody of Cabbarus, along with Las Bombas and Mickle. The king and queen, still grieving over the loss years before of their only child, Princess Augusta, wish Mickle to contact the spirit of their lost child. In the process, it is discovered that Mickle herself is the missing princess, whom Cabbarus thought he had assassinated. Enheartened King Augustine replaces Cabbarus with loyal Dr. Torrens, who has consistently opposed Cabbarus's efforts to manipulate affairs. Mickle adjusts to her new life, and Theo accepts a commission from Torrens to serve as representative of the crown to determine the will of the people regarding their government. Theo has discovered that things are seldom as they seem and that choosing the right course is often difficult. Two story strands co-exist, one, detailing Theo's adventures, the other, describing the troubled situation at the palace. The two come together in a grand climax with the discovery of Mickle's true identity. Style is witty, now tongue-in-cheek, now satirical, the plot is convoluted, filled with underdeveloped scenes, and offers plenty of action and surprise after surprise, and characters are interesting, if shallow. This is a fast-moving, entertaining, often amusing story, typical of Alexander in its vigor, ironies, wry commentary, this time on the nature and responsibilities of government, and its overplotting. Sequels to complete the trilogy are *The Kestrel** and *The Beggar Queen.* Fanfare.

WHAT HAPPENED IN HAMELIN (Skurzynski*, Gloria, Four Winds, 1979), novel based on historical records of events in Hamelin, Germany, in June, 1284, which may have given rise to the Pied Piper legend immortalized in the poem by Robert Browning. Abused and underfed, the orphan Albert, 14, is known as Geist, or "Ghost" because his usual paleness is intensified by the flour of the baker's shop where he is a servant. In the midst of a plague of rats, an opportunistic piper shows up and becomes known as Gast, or "Stranger." With cleverness and charisma, he persuades the baker, Herman Meinersing, and the other village elders to put their problem in his hands, and he entices all the village children, including the baker's daughter, Hilda, to do as he says. He picks Geist as his special helper and insists the boy be freed of his regular duties to serve him. First he provides very salty meat for the rats to gorge on, directs that all water butts be sealed, then positions all the children along the river bank to club to death the thirst-crazed rats as they try to reach the water. Geist is appalled at the delight the children find in the slaughter. Although he and, to some degree, Hilda, are Gast's favorites, he feels some misgivings at following the piper's directions to make special sweet buns for all the children using a flour made of partly-rotted rye on which, the reader is told in an afterword, grows a fungus ergot, 46from which LSD is derived. Geist has been warned not to eat a bun and to keep Hilda from eating one, but she has one before he knows it and is afflicted along with the other children with manic energy which becomes, after several days, a terrible itching somewhat relieved by dancing. Gast, who has confided to Geist that he is a gypsy—"of the tribe of Rom"—persuades Father Johann that all the adults should attend a special mass while he plays for the dancing children. Geist, now with great misgivings, obeys Gast because he sees it as the only way to escape from his servitude to the baker, but when Gast leads the children up toward the mountain pass and Hilda suddenly loses her sight, he protests. Gast tells him he is taking the children to the eastern provinces where he can sell them to replace workers killed by the plague and that together they will be rich. Appalled, Geist tries to stop him, and Gast strikes him across the throat with his flute, injuring his windpipe so he can't speak, then creates a landslide to block the pass and prevent pursuit. Geist flees to the nunnery where he had lived as a young child and eventually regains enough speech to tell the story and to send word to Father Johann, who brings Hilda. The realistic explanation of the legendary elements of the story, including the report that only two children fail to get shut in the mountain, one dumb and one blind, is very clever but to some degree dominates the development of character. Christopher.

"WHAT THEN, RAMAN?" (Arora*, Shirley L., ill. Hans Guggenheim, Follett, 1960), problem novel set in the hills of southern India in the mid-twentieth century. Twelve-year-old Raman is the first person in his village to learn to read.

The star pupil in his school, he dreams of one day becoming a scholar and owning many books. His family makes a meager living by peddling firewood and vegetables to the Merkins (Americans) who live during the hot season in the bungalows that perch on the crest of the hills. When, after the monsoons begin, the Merkins return to the cities, it becomes very hard for the family to find customers for their produce. Raman's father leaves the hills to go to the Plains to seek work, and Raman must leave school to help make a living for his family. His father is proud that his son can read and promises him a share of whatever Raman earns to buy the books he so covets. Raman gets a job gathering flowers for a Merkin lady who wishes to paint pictures of them for a book she is preparing on native plants. Her question, "And then what?," when he confides his hopes to her, leads him to see that learning carries with it a responsibility to help others. Raman teaches his sister, Vasanti, and a friend of hers to read, and then he agrees to teach the boys who had taunted him and called him a bookworm. Another ethical problem confronts Raman when he gathers some especially rare flowers for the Merkin lady and earns nine rupees, more than enough to buy an elegantly decorated copy of the *Ramayana* that he has yearned for. He fully intends to keep the money secret from his mother and to buy the book with it, but his conscience bothers him so much that he finally spends it on a much-needed blanket instead. This predictable story of how a boy sorts out the priorities in his life narrowly escapes treatise, and the matter of the *Ramayana* adds an unnecessary complication to the already bland and instructive plot. Characters are types and style plodding. The best part of the book lies in the author's sympathetic, detailed re-creation for young readers of the living conditions of the poverty-stricken, illiterate masses, and, in particular, of their never-ending, discouraging, relentless quest for food. Addams; Choice.

WHEN NO ONE WAS LOOKING (Wells*, Rosemary, Dial, 1980), sports and mystery novel set in the late 1970s in Plymouth, Mass. At fourteen, Kathy* Bardy is well on her way to becoming a major tennis champion, although, unlike most of the young contenders, she has not been playing since early childhood but only since her talent was discovered when she was twelve. Nor does she come from a wealthy country-club family. She plays at the Plymouth Bath and Tennis Club because her coach, Marty*, is the tennis pro there, but Kathy works to pay her expenses—life guards, cleans the pool, sweeps the courts—as does her twelve-year-old sister, Jody, a reader, good at school but bored with Kathy's tennis. Family finances are further strained by transportation to meets, entry fees, etc., so that Kathy's grandmother must be moved to a less expensive nursing home. Kathy likes tennis and is willing to put in the long hours of practice necessary, but she feels guilty at using so much of the family resources (a guilt Jody jealously feeds) and pressured by the driving ambition of her parents, Marty, and even the superintendent of schools, who encourages her to cheat on an algebra exam. Only at the home of her wealthy friend, Julia Redmond, does Kathy feel at ease, and Julia willingly shares her glory and devotedly waits while

Kathy practices and works. Kathy can beat most of her opponents until Ruth Gumm, a large girl who plays a distinctly inferior game, manages to get her angry by delaying tactics and becomes her nemesis. In a critical tournament, Kathy is to play Ruth, but her opponent does not show up and Kathy wins by default, then learns that Ruth has drowned in the club pool that morning. This win gets Kathy an invitation to a meet in Florida, where she goes with Julia, stays with Julia's very wealthy aunt, and plays so well that it seems likely she may be New England champion in the coming tournament. She returns home to learn that Ruth Gumm's death was not accidental but that she died because the pool was overchlorinated, and that Marty, Oliver* English, a boy who works at the club and who likes Kathy, and even her family have been questioned. Kathy herself seems to have an alibi for the night before Ruth's death until she admits that she skipped her algebra lesson and went to the baseball game at Fenway Park. She is shocked at the way everyone tries to cover up for her. Through a complicated set of circumstances, she realizes that it was Julia who, in an effort to help Kathy's career, caused Ruth's death. In the end she seems determined to give up Julia, and probably also tennis. The pressure, hard work, driving adults, and tension for a young sports figure are well developed, though the adults are a particularly unlovable crew, and Kathy's own ambition and burning desire to win are convincing. The mystery of Ruth's death is also a cleverly handled plot, but the two don't fit together comfortably, and the novel seems to shift gears half-way through. Fanfare; Poe Nominee.

WHERE THE LILIES BLOOM (Cleaver*, Vera, and Bill Cleaver*, ill. Jim Spanfeller, Lippincott, 1969), realistic novel of family and community life set in the Great Smoky Mountains not long ago, in which a young girl comes to see that accepting help will not compromise her family's dignity or reputation for being able to care for themselves. Resourceful, independent, serious-minded Mary* Call Luther, 14, tells of the year in which she is forced to resort to desperate and sometimes funny measures in her struggles to hold together her poverty-stricken family, demanding Ima* Dean, 5, staunch Romey*, 10, and pretty Devola*, 18, and carry out the wishes of their sharecropper father, Roy Luther, after he dies of "worms in the chest." Naively believing that it is a legal document guaranteeing that they will not be put off the farm on which they have been living, Mary Call, Romey, and Devola induce Kiser* Pease, the next-door farmer on whose land they live, to sign a paper deeding them their house and twenty acres, while he lies ill of pneumonia. For cash, Mary Call organizes them in wildcrafting, the gathering of saleable plants, roots, buds, barks, and the like for Mr. Connell, who owns the general store five miles down the road. Kiser Pease wishes to marry Devola, but Roy Luther had specifically instructed Mary Call to oppose Kiser's suit because they believe Devola is "cloudy headed," that is, simple minded, and that Kiser is a grasping, superstitious, mean miser who would not be a fit husband for her. Because he is genuinely in love with Devola, he takes an honest interest in the family, something they do not really understand but take advantage of anyway. On different occasions, Kiser loans them a radio, a cow, and a car and gives them food. Even though they manage to lay in a fair store of food by fall and to buy clothes for school, winter brings hardships, among others, snow destroying part of their roof. When Kiser's sister, Goldie, who really owns the property, insists they be evicted, Mary Call plans to move to a cave. But Kiser comes to their rescue by buying the land and house from his sister, and he even puts them in Devola's name. He and Devola, who all along has been attracted to him and his nice house with its yellow kitchen and who has lost a good deal of her flightiness, get married, and spring sees the children independent and still on their own in the family home. Although Devola and Kiser change too abruptly, even seen from Mary Call's adolescent point of view, the characters are well drawn, and the rigors of hill life are depicted in clear and interesting detail. Mary Call is a strong and winning figure, her old-fashioned, semi-educated, mountain speech with its striking regionalisms adding depth to her character and helping to create a splendid sense of place. Scenes stand out, among them, that in which Mary Call and Romey at night secretly put Roy Luther's body in their wagon, drag it up the mountain, and bury it in the shallow grave he had dug for himself. The title comes from an old hymn. Sequel is *Trial Valley**. Books Too Good; Boston Globe Honor; Choice; Contemporary Classics; Fanfare; National Book Finalist.

THE WHIPMAN IS WATCHING (Dyer*, T. A., Houghton, 1979), novel of modern Indian life set on a reservation in the Northwest, presumably Oregon. Angie Wolfe, 13, is torn between her love for her Katla, her maternal grandmother with whom she has lived since the death of her alcoholic mother, and her scorn for the Indian customs and language which she and her best friend, Lois Tewit, show to get along in the off-reservation junior high they attend. Other attitudes toward traditional Native American ways are shown by Carysa, 7, Angie's younger sister, who brattily tries to get out of all the work, by Marta, 16, Angie's cousin, who accepts and appreciates the old ways, and by Cultus, Marta's brother, a rebellious high-school boy, all of whom live with Katla, and by Uncle Dan, Katla's son, a grade-school dropout who has a job with the tribe. These problems come to a head when Cultus purposely causes trouble on the bus, so that he will be suspended and not have to go to school. When Katla confronts the bus driver and is unable to persuade him to relent, she rides the bus herself to talk to the principal, Mr. McGilvra, although she speaks English with difficulty. To Angie's humiliation, she must accompany her grandmother, then have the old woman with her in her classes all day. As they line up for the return bus, Katla scolds Lois, who turns and knocks her down, causing her to break her arm. Despite her injury, Katla leads in her position as ringer in the Longhouse worship service, a mixture of Christian prayer and Indian custom, in which Angie dances the pattern of seven sevens—seven groups of seven songs. Katla also is a leader in the Powwow, to which dancers and drummers come from distant reservations and the Native American culture draws them together. His suspension ended, Cultus returns to school and, half in jest, attacks Lois, fights the bus driver who intervenes, then runs off, steals and wrecks a pickup truck, and ends in Group Home. In court the female Judge Edwards listens to Katla's impassioned statement of what troubles Indian youth, puts Cultus on probation in the charge of Jobie Sohappy, the police officer who is also Whipman for the Powwow, and asks Katla to come to the school board meeting to repeat her statement. At book's end, Cultus is planning to stay out of trouble because Jobie has promised to help him become a traditional Indian hunter. Although the story is told in third person through Angie's point of view, her character is not as well developed or interesting as that of Cultus. Katla is the strongest character, but all seem to have been chosen to represent types, and this gives the story a feeling of predictability. Except for the judge, the non-Indian characters seem excessively insensitive. Child Study.

THE WHISPERED HORSE (Hall*, Lynn, Follett, 1979), realistic but mysterious novel set in 1877 in the southern uplands of Scotland. Rowan* Elliott, 10, from her curtained-off bed alcove in Gowanbothy cottage, overhears a great deal more than her family knows. The night after Morag*, her mother, receives a letter, she hears the most shocking thing of all, her mother's confrontation outside her window with Tam* McPhee, husband of Rowan's older sister, Kate*, 30. Morag accuses Tam, who is returning drunk from the village, with the news that she has from her cousin, that he killed his first wife and wasted the money he inherited from her before coming to Midleith valley and marrying spinster Kate. Morag orders him to be gone and threatens that, if he returns, she will kill him with her own hands. When, the next morning, Tam "finds" Morag dead in the stream, having apparently fallen and struck her head, Rowan is afraid to face her own suspicions, afraid also to confide in Kate, who is a strong, competent woman like their mother, for fear Tam will kill them if he realizes they know. She also suspects that their old father, Kinley*, past seventy, whose mind seems to have broken with the death of his much-loved wife, also knows the truth about Tam. She is still shocked when Kinley tells her he needs a horse to kill Tam for him, a horse which will respond to his whispered instructions as he learned when he was a member of The Society of the Horseman's Word. When, after numerous trips to market, he trades his gold picture frame for a sturdy, grey pony named Bannet, Rowan falls in love with the horse and tells herself that her father's mind is wandering, that he cannot really commit murder by proxy. She worries, though, when Tam has a series of accidents involving Bannet, enough so she confesses her knowledge about Tam to Kate and gets her permission to ride off to find another horse whisperer, Auld Galbraith, blacksmith of Ballyforth, who assures her that Kinley has no real powers and tattoos crescent moons inside Bannet's ears to protect the horse. Kinley laughs off the charm and openly warns Tam that the horse will kill him Lammas night, August 1, or, if Tam shoots the horse, its spirit will destroy him that night. As the date approaches, Rowan and Kate, though they both hate Tam, combine forces to try to ward off a violent incident. Kate is to watch Kinley while Rowan hides Bannet in a neighbor's shed and then watches Tam getting drunk at the Lammas celebration in the village. Mistaking the rising moon for sunrise and thinking the fateful night over, Tam staggers for home, but at the point in the stream where he killed Morag he looks up, sees in the mist the white ram, thinks it Bannet, and panics, crashing into the stream and striking his head on the rocks. As Kate and Rowan wait, full of relief and peace, for the coroner, their father worries over his failure to be the cause of Tam's death and hits upon the explanation that satisfies him: Morag's ghost must have killed Tam, who had killed her. The power of the superstitions and folk beliefs is deftly handled, so that while all the events have a logical or psychological explanation, there remains a suggestion of mystery. All the Elliotts are well-rounded, interesting people, and the sense of their love for their home is conveyed strongly. A rather brief but satisfying novel. Poe Nominee.

THE WHISPER OF GLOCKEN (Kendall*†, Carol, ill. Imero Gobbato, Harcourt, 1965), fantasy-adventure involving the Minnipins, sequel to *The Gammage Cup*†. The action begins in the neighboring village of Water Gap when the Watercress River mysteriously floods. Scumble, keeper of the sluice gate, Glocken, the bell-ringer, and villagers Crustabread, Silky*, and Gam Lutic paddle for safety to Slipper-on-the-Water*. There the five renowned heroes of the Mushroom War (Old Heroes*) disregard their protests and outfit them with the magic swords, Muggles's *Maxims*, food, and advice for the expedition over the mountains to seek the cause of the flooding. The subsequent adventures provide them ample opportunity to demonstrate hidden resources for valor, and, through cleverness, courage, and considerable luck, the five adventurers become New Heroes among the Minnipins in spite of themselves. They are helped by hordes of desert-colored, flittery creatures called Diggers*, after kindhearted, maternal Silky rescues an injured Digger baby, Wafer, who becomes an invaluable ally. Silky and acerbic Gam Lutie have a falling out because Silky has used their small supply of Mushroom salve on Wafer's injured leg. Later, Gam Lutie takes charge when the others fall ill, slays strange egg-like beings that attack them, and, with Wafer's help, discovers that the eggs are the source of the salve. The Minnipins are captured by Hulks*, ugly, aggressive, human-like beings, who imprison them in a tower in their mountain stronghold. Then the Minnipins discover that the dam the Hulks are building has caused the flood. After several unsuccessful attempts, the Minnipins escape to a cave where Wafer unearths the bells of the legendary, lost carillon with the miniature bell known as the Whisper of Glocken. When Glocken strikes the Whisper, the dam cracks, and the mountain collapses, sealing the five in the cave, from which they are rescued by the Old Heroes and the Diggers. New and Old Heroes return home in triumph, bearing the golden carillon with its mighty Whisper with them. The story is fast paced and amusing, with humor, action, and suspense, but it lacks the originality of conception of its predecessor, characterization is shallow, events seem artificially constructed, and the theme of courage seems labored. The Hulks are stock villains, the Diggers are too comic, and it is hard to visualize the itinerary and the problem with the dam. The novel is less effective than its predecessor. Fanfare.

WHITE†, E(LWYN) B(ROOKS) (1899–1985), born in Mount Vernon, N.Y.; journalist, humorist, author for adults and children. Although he is best known for his essays for adults, he became noted in children's literature for the three fantasies for which he received the Laura Ingalls Wilder Award in 1970: *Stuart Little†* (Harper, 1945), about the second son of Mr. and Mrs. Frederick C. Little, who looks "very much like a mouse in every way," listed in *Choice*; *Charlotte's Web†* (Harper, 1952), about the spider who spins words in her web to save the life of a runt pig; and *The Trumpet of the Swan** (Harper, 1970), about Louis, the trumpeter swan, who was born without a voice and who learns to play the trumpet, listed in *Choice* and a National Book Award finalist. Among the most popular stories ever written for children, these are landmark books, particularly *Charlotte's Web*, whose numerous honors include the George G. Stone Award, election to the Lewis Carroll Shelf, and selection for the Children's Literature Association Touchstones and Top Ten, Children's Classics, and *Children's Books Too Good to Miss*. Deceptively easy in style and language, these books have strong characterization and deep themes, and they appeal to readers of all ages. White was educated at Cornell University, served in the United States Army in World War I, and worked as a reporter for the Seattle *Times* and as a production assistant in an advertising agency in New York. He was associated with the *New Yorker* magazine for many years as a writer and editor, doing the "Talk of the Town" column, and also wrote "One Man's Meat" for *Harper's* magazine. He made his home in North Brooklin, Maine.

WHITE, ROBB (1909–   ), born in the Philippine Islands, son of a missionary; freelance writer of screenplays, television scripts, and books of suspense and adventure for later elementary and teenaged boys. After irregular schooling in his early years, he attended Episcopal High School in Alexandria, Va., and graduated from the U.S. Naval Academy at Annapolis. He served in the Navy in the Pacific during World War II, later holding a commission in the Naval Reserve. His life has been filled with travel and adventure. He has lived in the Virgin Islands on a deserted island he purchased from the British government, was a member of a Harvard anthropological expedition to the Near East, has been a pilot, and has served on submarines, carriers, battleships, and sailing ships. Over his forty-year writing career, he has written a great many short stories and articles for such widely circulated magazines as *Reader's Digest*, *Saturday Evening Post*, and *Atlantic*, many screenplays for Hollywood and television scripts for "Perry Mason" and other programs, and more than two dozen popular novels of adventure. Many of them have been sea and war stories, like *The Survivor* (Doubleday, 1964), *Silent Ship, Silent Sea* (Doubleday, 1967), and *Up Periscope* (Doubleday, 1956), all of which take place during World War II. His novel of terror and chase set in the desert of the southwestern United States, *Deathwatch** (Doubleday, 1972), won the Edgar Allan Poe Award. If regarded as implausible and melodramatic, his novels have been praised for their fast action, high tension, and knowledge of subject matter. Recent publications include *Fire Storm* (Doubleday, 1979), about a ranger and a youth trapped in a forest fire in a national forest in the Sierra Nevada, and *The Long Way Down* (Doubleday, 1977), about a girl who wishes to become a trapeze performer. He has made his home in Malibu, Calif., and Lake Havasu City, Ariz.

WHITE BIRD (Bulla*†, Clyde Robert, ill. Leonard Weisgard, Crowell, 1966), novel for early readers set in Half-Moon, Tenn., in the late eighteenth century. Luke Vail, who has come to the valley in 1785 with an expedition led by his father, finds a baby in a cradle washed down a stream by high water. With the help of the only neighbors who have stayed in the rocky area, he raises the youngster, whom he calls John Thomas after the two initials on the cradle, but when the neighbors decide to move on to better land, he makes the boy hide. Left with Luke, John Thomas learns to work and how to read, but he longs for a friend. Luke refuses to take him to town or to let him have a dog, but the boy finds an injured white crow and cares for it lovingly. When a trio of brothers pass through, Luke lets the youngest take the bird, and John Thomas runs away to try to get it back. He finds the world, unlike Luke's descriptions, friendly and inclined to be helpful. The storekeeper gives him food, a girl takes him to a dance, and a boy finally tells him that the White Bird was shot by his brother. John Thomas returns to the store and is persuaded by the storekeeper to go back to the valley. The boy tells Luke that he intends to leave again but, realizing the man's loneliness, suggests that next time they can go together. Although written in simple, almost primer sentences, the book catches the loneliness and need of both Luke and John Thomas and sustains the interest of the boy's search. Stone.

WHITE STALLION OF LIPIZZA (Henry*†, Marguerite, ill. Wesley Dennis, Rand, 1964), realistic animal novel set in Vienna, Austria. The action occurs probably in the early part of the twentieth century and covers several years in the life of Hans Haupt, the son of a baker who is about twelve when the story begins. Hans so greatly admires the Lipizzaners, the splendid, white stallions who perform dressage movements at the Spanish Court Riding School at the Imperial Palace of Hofburg, that he thinks about them most of the time. After Fraulein Morgen, a librarian, gives him a ticket to a performance, he decides his life's ambition is to become a Riding Master with the school. Night after night, Hans studies everything Fraulein can find for him on the Lipizzaners and on the training of horses, particularly for dressage. He visits his "Oncle" Otto at Piber in the Alps where the famous horses are foaled. Back in Vienna, he tours the stables where the stablemaster introduces him to Borina*, one of the greatest of the dressage champions. After his sympathetic and encouraging father dies and his sister's husband takes over the bakery, Hans applies for entry to the riding school but is told to come back when he is sixteen. Then an unexpected assignment comes to him, walking Borina to and from the Opera House while the horse plays a part in the grand climax of *The Girl of the Golden West.* Hans handles the temperamental mount so well that Colonel* Podhajsky, the Director of the Riding School, gives him a job. After proving himself obedient and responsible in tasks about the stables, Hans embarks upon a five-year training period. Borina is his "horse professor"; his human teacher is the famed Riding Master, Bereiter Wittek. Both prove exceedingly exacting in their requirements of the boy. Months and months of hard work follow as Hans strives to develop the "perfect seat" that will complement the balance of the horse. Hans learns to merge his identity with that of Borina and dreams of some day producing more *courbette* leaps, a particularly difficult movement, than any horse has ever accomplished. He and Borina progress to ever more demanding steps. In his first public appearance, Hans performs creditably, and later, by sheer will power, he takes Borina into two splendid leaps and earns for himself a permanent place on the program. He and Borina execute five leaps in succession in a special show for the visiting Prince of Wales, from which Hans derives so electrifying a sense of satisfaction that he finally really understands the attraction of the dressage. Although drawn from real life, this story of how a youth realizes a cherished ambition lacks focus and narrative tension. Moments are well realized, and the action proceeds without sentimentality and melodrama. The plot is awkward, and the characters are mostly types, and not even Hans changes much through his experiences. Style is descriptive but not burdened with excess detail, and mundane. The book is chiefly memorable for its clear picture of how the youths are trained for dressage and of the excitement and appeal of the performances. The author's understanding and appreciation for horses comes through very strongly, and the story has the conviction of real incident. Black and white illustrations follow the progress of the story and show the horses in various attitudes and actions. Choice.

WHITMAN, MARCUS (*Cayuse Courage**), historical American missionary to Oregon Territory. In the novel, he is known as Boston Doctor to the Cayuse ("Bostons" are Americans), who are in awe of him but are puzzled and put off by his apparently hypocritical attitude toward them. For example, they cannot understand why he still cannot speak their language after eight years in their country. He appears detached from events, a busy man not much concerned about the needs and wishes of the Indians but very ready to make use of them if it suits his purposes. He is killed in the uprising.

WHITNEY, PHYLLIS A(YAME) (1903–   ), born in Yokohama, Japan; writer of junior novels and mystery stories. She attended high school in Chicago and later lived in China and the Philippines. In the 1940s she was children's book editor for the Chicago *Sun* and for the Philadelphia *Inquirer* and has taught writing for children at Northwestern University and at New York University. Altogether she has written more than twenty novels for adults, two books about writing for children, and more than thirty books for young people, most of them mystery stories like *Mystery of the Haunted Pool** (Westminster, 1960), *Secret of the Missing Footprint** (Westminster, 1970), and *Mystery of the Scowling Boy** (Westminster, 1973). Often the action occurs in exotic places, as in *Secret of the Tiger's Eye** (Westminster, 1961), set in South Africa, and *Mystery of the Hidden Hand** (Westminster, 1963), set on the Greek Island of Rhodes. Two of these have won the Edgar Allan Poe Award and the others have been nominees. Typically they are from the point of view of a young adolescent girl who feels unloved or inferior because of a lack of talent and who, with a boy her age or slightly older, unravels a series of mysterious events, often involving crime but not murder, and in doing so comes to self-understanding.

WHO REALLY KILLED COCK ROBIN? (George*†, Jean Craighead, Dutton, 1971), "ecological mystery" set in a small town in the northeastern United States in the 1960s. Tony Isidoro, 11, has been keeping up the research notes on the birds of Saddleboro for the graduate thesis his older brother had started before being drafted. He becomes involved in the question of what has killed Cock Robin, the bird whose mate is nesting in Mayor Joe Dambrowski's stetson hat and which the mayor is using as a symbol of the clean environment he claims to have brought to the town. Also concerned is assertive Mary Alice Lamberty, 11, who wants to prove that the bird was not killed by wastes from the Missatonic Mill owned by her father. Tony enlists the aid of Rob Cunningham, a graduate student friend of his brother, who is specializing in histochemistry. The mayor's propaganda campaign is reported by David Lowenthal, editor of the local paper, the *Patent Reader*. The mayor has planned "Cock Robin Day" to celebrate the hatching of the five eggs in the hat nest. Instead, they have a funeral for the bird. Two eggs hatch and a new male robin joins the mother, so the Cock Robin Day picnic proceeds with fulsome rhetoric from the mayor. Tony continues to investigate as the mother robin disappears, one fledgling dies, and the other three eggs fail to hatch. He discovers a series of ominous facts: the frogs have disappeared from the swamp; large numbers of ants and bees appear; water in the Missatonic tests high in some undefined chemical; the mayor and others in town use weed killers and fungicides on their lawns; a tree nursery upstream uses a product containing mercury on its logs; some noxious chemicals are in smoke from a yellow fabric burning in the dump. Mary Alice raises the remaining hatchling, named Saddle, but the bird is unable to make normal robin sounds, indicating some problem in its development. With the combined efforts of Tony and Rob, aided by others, it is finally determined that the cloth burning was from a secret NASA project for which the mill was making a fabric that contained PCB, that DDT in weed killers and insecticides are used in orchards upwind, that the mercury is killing the river but not Cock Robin directly. Mary Alice's father starts investigating the use of natural dyes, which Tony's mother knows from her gardener father, instead of the synthetics his mill has been employing. The final piece of the puzzle is found in a newspaper story about migrating sparrows which died by eating seeds treated with mercury so that millions of parasites leaving their bodies attacked the robins of the next wave of migration. Tony remembers seeing insects leaving the dead body of Cock Robin, so in the end a combination of forces is shown to be the murderer, including, as in an old rhyme, the sparrow. The elements of the investigations are, in themselves, interesting, but as with many mystery stories, the characters are merely figures to be used by the plot. The didactic purpose of the story is obvious, but there is some fun in the complexities of the detection. Choice.

WHOSE TOWN? (Graham*, Lorenz, Crowell, 1969), third in a series of realistic novels about David* Williams, this one set in North Town some two years after the last book. David, now eighteen, a high-school senior, goes to a meeting led by the Rev. Prempey Moshombo, a black activist, where he meets Head, back in town, and gets his first taste of the move for Black Power. Ed*, his father, is laid off from the plant where he works, and times are hard, but David works at a hardware store run by Sam Silverman, a decent and fair man, and his mother gets day work in white homes. After a party at the home of Maybelle Reed, a schoolmate, David and his girl, Jeanette Lenoir, get a ride with Jimmy Hicks and Alonzo* (Lonnie) Webster (called Wells in *North Town*) to a drive-in, where David, who has gone to get the food, is bumped by some white toughs and caused to spill his order. He fights to protect himself, then flees with the others, but they are pursued and arrested. Police Sergeant Reed, Maybelle's father, gets them all released. When they return to Jimmy Hicks's car, parked at a gas station where they were arrested, they find all the windows and lights smashed, though the attendant says he did not hear anything. Jimmy's mother blames David and demands that he pay for it. While David is waiting for the case to come up, Jimmy and Lonnie try to talk him into going back to the gas station to persuade the attendant to talk. David is reluctant, but he does drive them by. Lonnie turns the wheel into the station and climbs out, only to be met by sudden gunfire and killed. At school David finds formerly friendly students avoid him or are hostile, with the exception of sensible Becky Goldberg. The principal threatens that he may not allow David to graduate. Even the coach, who tries to be fair, seems to be telling him not to fight back. At the hardware store an older black employee, John Bowman, talks him into going to a meeting of militant blacks led by Moshombo. The different ideas and values confuse David. At the coroner's inquest, the verdict is justifiable homicide. The charge of battery against David is dismissed, but the possibility of being charged with a felony at the gas station is kept hanging over him. The tensions in the town increase as there is more unemployment, and tensions at home increase as Ed starts drinking, resenting his wife going out to work while he is idle. The town erupts when a black child is drowned after being thrown into a swimming pool by white youths in horseplay.

David finds himself in the middle of the riot, both horrified and exhilarated. Afraid to be out on the streets, he calls his parents from the Community Center and eventually gets home, but his girlfriend, Jeanette Lenoir, and her parents, trying to get to his house to sit with his parents, are arrested. That night and the next few days the family relive their terrible experience with night riders in the South. When he returns to work, David finds that Sam Silverman's store has been burnt out. With John Bowman and Sam, David helps board it up, and Sam gives words of hope that the trouble is over. Characters and incidents are types, used to illustrate the unrest of the period. The discussions showing the various points of view slow the book, despite melodramatic action. Even David's parents, who have some individuality in the earlier books, are stock figures in this one. Series includes *South Town*†; *North Town* (Crowell, 1965); and *Return to South Town* (Crowell, 1976). Choice.

THE WHYS AND WHEREFORES OF LITTABELLE LEE (Cleaver*, Vera, and Bill Cleaver⁺, Atheneum, 1973), realistic novel of family and neighborhood life set in the 1920s or 1930s in the Ozarks of Arkansas, in which a young girl learns to use her wits, common sense, and intelligence, and to let society's rules work for her. Littabelle Lee, who lives on a small farm with her grandparents, Paw Paw Lee and Maw Maw Lee and her Aunt Sorrow, an herb doctor, tells of the year that she is sixteen and disasters strike her family. In late summer, the house burns down during a storm, and all their winter store of food with it. They set up housekeeping in the barn, intending to build a log cabin as soon as they can, but the work stops abruptly when the neighbor who is helping them is called away because of an illness in his family. Then Aunt Sorrow, who began behaving queerly after a fall from a horse, runs away to live with The Hermit*, an old beau, who operates a whiskey still. Littabelle is left to provide for her grandparents and herself. Now she regrets not having paid more attention to the "whys and wherefores," as her aunt terms them, of making a living. Although there is a need for an herb doctor to take Sorrow's place and Littabelle does creditably well at birthing a baby and performing an emergency tracheotomy at the school when a boy chokes on a piece of chalk, she feels doctoring is not for her and lands a job as a substitute teacher for seven dollars a week. When Paw Paw falls ill with the grippe, the storekeeper presses them for unpaid debts, and the cows run off, Littabelle knows that their situation is desperate and decides to bring suit for parent-neglect against her uncle and aunts who live in the city, Hutchens, Ora, and Estie. Judge Marriage, a shrewd and practical man who maintains that the "pettifoggers" in Little Rock don't always understand the hill folk and make proper provisions for them, decides in her favor. He requires the city relations to pay twenty dollars each on the first of each month to support their aged parents. As a result of her experiences, Littabelle has acquired a more serious attitude and a new sense of direction for her life. She decides she likes teaching so much that she would like to train to be properly licensed. Although characters are eccentric and approach caricature and some scenes are overdrawn,

Littabelle is a memorable character and changes believably. The story moves rapidly with humor, extensive dialogue, and enough detail to give some sense of the way of life, problems, and attitudes of the hill people. (L.* C. Luckabill) National Book Finalist.

WIBBERLEY†, LEONARD (1915–1983), born in Dublin, Ireland; reporter, editor, and author of books of fiction and non-fiction for adults and young people, best known in children's literature for his ambitious series of historical adventure novels that span the American Revolutionary period and involve the Treegate father and son and their associates. One of these was a Fanfare book, *John Treegate's Musket†* (Farrar, 1959). It and three successors have all been *Choice* books, *Peter Treegate's War** (Farrar, 1960), *Sea Captain from Salem** (Farrar, 1961), and *Treegate's Raiders** (Farrar, 1962). After Peter is reconciled with his father, John, from whom he was estranged in the first book, Peter, John, and the Maclaren of Spey, who has raised Peter, see service in various sectors of the Revolution, until in the last book Peter, now in charge of his own detachment of soldiers, participates in the events that lead to the British surrender. *Sea Captain* is mainly the story of Peter's stalwart friend, Peace of God Manly, whose naval achievements off Great Britain are instrumental in bringing about the alliance between the French and the Americans. Wibberley was educated in schools in Ireland and in England. After serving as apprentice to a London publisher, working for London newspapers as a copy boy, reporter, and editor, and becoming editor of the *Chronicle* in Trinidad, where he also worked briefly for an oil company, he came to the United States in 1943 as a foreign correspondent. He later served as editor of the *Independent Journal* in San Rafael, Calif., and then took a position as columnist with the Los Angeles *Times*. He has made his home in California. After 1947, under his own name and also under the pseudonyms Patrick O'Connor, Leonard Holton, and Christopher Webb, he published for young people over forty books of fiction, chiefly romantic historical novels in the vein of *Treasure Island*, his favorite book from childhood, as well as two books of verse and several books of non-fiction, including *The Epics of Everest* (Farrar, 1954) and the highly regarded four-part biography, *Man of Liberty: A Life of Thomas Jefferson* (Farrar, 1963–1966). Regarded as a fine storyteller, he also published the novels *Attar of Ice Valley* (Farrar, 1968), about a Stone Age youth who seeks new hunting grounds for his tribe, *Leopard's Prey* (Farrar, 1971) and *The Last Battle* (Farrar, 1976), both in the Treegate series, *Flint's Island* (Farrar, 1972), his sequel to *Treasure Island*, and *The Crime of Martin Coverly* (Farrar, 1980), about pirates in the 1700s. He also wrote over forty novels, plays, and books of non-fiction and personal experience for adults, and several of his novels have been made into motion pictures.

WIER, ESTER (ALBERTI) (1910–   ), born in Seattle, Wash.; poet and author of realistic novels for later elementary readers. She attended Southeastern Teachers College and the University of California at Los Angeles. She married a naval officer, now retired and a professor of mathematics, in Hankow, China, and they have lived in many places in the United States and abroad. Before writing novels for children, she published books for adults about army and navy social customs. Her first and still her best-known novel for children, *The Loner** (McKay, 1963), set on a Montana sheepranch and about a boy's search for a place to live, was a Newbery honor book, was selected by the editors of *Horn Book* for Fanfare, and is cited in *Children's Books Too Good to Miss* and *Choice*. It was produced for television by Walt Disney Productions. There followed a dozen and a half books of fiction for boys with nature settings, some about animals and mainly about children who are seeking to find themselves and their place in life. Critics have found that her later books show a growing maturity and surer narrative technique and that she reveals a sincere appreciation of youth's problems. Other titles include *The Winners* (McKay, 1967), set in the Florida Everglades, *The Space Hut* (Stackpole, 1967), about a boy whose tree house is endangered, *The Wind Chasers* (McKay, 1967), set in the Arizona Strip, *Action at Paradise Marsh* (Stackpole, 1968), about urban spread, *The King of the Mountain* (Walck, 1975), about trophy hunting for bighorn sheep, *The Hunting Trail* (Walck, 1974), which traces the early years of a coyote's life, and *The Straggler* (McKay, 1970), about a year in a gannet's life. She has contributed extensively poems, stories, and articles to national periodicals, has been a reporter for the Chicago *Tribune*, and conducted a radio program for women. Her manuscripts are in the Kerlan Collection at the University of Minnesota.

WILDERNESS BRIDE (Johnson*†, Annabel, and Edgar Johnson*†, Harper, 1962), historical novel set in 1846–1847 among Mormons at their settlement in Iowa and then on the covered wagon trek westward toward the Mormon Zion, the place where the Mormons feel they are destined to settle. When Brigham Young orders him into the war against Mexico, Judd Tremain betroths his tomboy daughter, Corey (Corrine), 15, to cultured, well-mannered Ethan* Drake, English stepson of Dan* Turner, devoted follower of Prophet Joseph Smith. Although she protests at first, Corey has been taught to be obedient, quells her rebellious impulses, and tries hard to do her share among the large and sometimes quarrelsome Turner family of three wives and many offspring. Corey's special responsibility is caring for gentle, patrician, confused Sister* Elizabeth, Ethan's mother, Dan's third wife, whom he converted on his recent mission trip to England. The Turners regard Ethan as lazy and feckless, and on the trail Dan insists that the youth work at tasks for which he lacks strength and know-how. Even though he fails, Corey comes to respect him for the loving way he treats his ailing mother, his perseverence, and independence of spirit. At winter quarters on the Missouri, Ethan secretly defies Mormon doctrine to heal with potions Lucy, daughter of Sister* Trude, Dan's first wife and manager of the household, and others who are ill. Corey learns that his ambition is to become a doctor like his father was. Gradually, affection develops between these two young people, who differ from their peers on the train in upbringing and outlook on life and who share doubts about

Mormon doctrine. Ethan's medical activities come out, and Dan gives him a choice: clear out or officially become a Mormon. Ethan chooses to stay, bound by his mother's need for him. His baptism in frigid March waters results in a congestive ailment from which Corey nurses him back to health. When, later, Ethan operates on an infection Corey has on her hand, Dan tells Ethan to leave or stand trial for treason. Ethan gets out this time, but Corey continues to care for Elizabeth, who she now knows has only a few days left to live. Then Dan betroths Corey to bullying Shad, another stepson of his, to be Shad's second wife, a prospect for which Corey feels great distaste. When Elizabeth dies, having glimpsed Zion from the summit of the pass through the mountains as she wished, Corey leaves the Turners. She rides back through the train until she finds Ethan and looks forward to a useful life with her young doctor husband. Some finely-drawn characters and a richly conceived background compensate for the trite plot. The novel is most memorable for the picture it gives of its times. Details of the Mormons' preparations for their journey, the persecutions and difficulties they encounter, the authority of the elders, the position of and attitudes toward women, and especially the strong sense of family relationships convey a substantial picture of this aspect of our country's history. Brigham Young makes a cameo appearance. Fanfare.

WILD IN THE WORLD (Donovan*, John, Harper, 1971), realistic novel in which an animal plays a major role set in the mountains of New Hampshire at an unspecified time but probably in the mid–1900s. Ironically, the large dog that gives lonely John Gridley new purpose in life is thought by John's neighbors to have killed him. The Gridley brothers, Amos, Abraham, and John, are the sole dwellers of Rattlesnake Mountain. The last of a hardfisted family of seven brothers and four sisters, they live in the old farmhouse where all of them were born. In the spring, Abraham dies of an infection, and a few days later a cow kicks Amos's chest in, leaving John, the youngest and still quite active, to keep the homestead going. One day, while John is shucking corn for canning, a large brown and white wolf-like dog appears. Man and dog gradually become friends. John shares his food with Son, and they swim together in the Gridley brook, romp on the grass, and take naps together on John's couch. With the help of Gridley whiskey and Son's highly attentive ear, the normally inarticulate John chats freely to the dog, reminiscing about his family and confiding to Son his dream of bringing back to the farm the bodies of his brothers and sisters who are buried in the town graveyard down the mountain. The reader learns about the farm and the Gridleys and about John's attitudes toward the country- and townspeople (the Gridleys are "mountain") through John's one-sided conversations with Son. When John goes down the mountain to borrow the grasping Woodis brothers' team for haying, Son refuses to leave the mountain. Standoffish and laconic as usual, John does not tell the Woodises that Amos and Abraham have died, nor does he tell them about Son. When Son is bitten by a rattler, John nurses the dog tenderly, leaving Son's side only when he must care for the other farm animals. After Son recovers, John catches a cold swimming in the brook. Although he becomes progressively weaker, he tries to continue working. Being fiercely independent and suspicious by nature of all but the mountain people, he never seeks help from his neighbors. Ironically, at the same time, he seems to develop new interests. But his illness worsens, and he dies in the early fall, sitting outside his kitchen under the big maple tree. When the Woodis boys come to collect the rent for their team, they think Son has killed John and shoot at the dog, who runs off into the woods. Even though an autopsy shows John died of pneumonia, word spreads that Son was responsible and that a pack of wolves roams the region. People avoid the farm, but Son comes occasionally to nose through the abandoned house and sleep in his lost friend's bed. An understated style, strong characterization of both humans and dog, some flashbacks, judicious use of detail, and numerous ironies give drama and power to this simple, stark story of pride and alienation and of two dedicated loners who cannot find companionship among their own kind but find comfort and contentment with each other. Choice; National Book Finalist.

WILKINSON, BRENDA (1946–   ), born in Moultrie, Ga.; poet, writer of short stories and novels for children. She attended Hunter College in New York City and has made her home in the Bronx. She has given poetry readings in elementary, junior, and senior high schools and has been a member of the Sonia Sanchez Writers' Workshop at the Countee Cullen Library in Harlem. Her first novel, *Ludell** (Harper, 1975), was a finalist for the National Book Award. It reflects her own experiences as a black child growing up in a small town in Georgia in the 1950s. Her other novels continue Ludell's story, *Ludell and Willie* (Harper, 1976), and *Ludell's New York Time* (Harper, 1980). Her novels have been praised for their warm, sympathetic, and authentic portrayal of the black experience.

WILLARD, NANCY (1936–   ), born in Ann Arbor, Mich.; poet, author. She received her B.A. and Ph.D. degrees from the University of Michigan and attended Stanford University on a Woodrow Wilson Fellowship. She was honored with a Hopwood Award, the Devins Memorial Award, and the O. Henry Award for short story. She has published several books of poems, essays, and stories for adults, and one novel. Her book of verse for children, *A Visit to William Blake's Inn* (Harcourt, 1981), won the Newbery Award, the only book of poetry so honored. Among her other writings for children are several picture books and three fantasies, *Sailing to Cythera** (Harcourt, 1974), *The Island of the Grass King** (Harcourt, 1979), and *Uncle Terrible* (Harcourt, 1982), all featuring a young boy named Anatole, who goes on a series of dream-like adventures, and all notable for the clever allusions to literature and philosophy.

WILL DAYTON (*The Dunderhead War**), Quincy* Heffendorf's best friend. Bright, quick, and astute, he has been to school in the East. One of the Missouri Volunteers, he keeps an eye on Rufus* Purdy and once discovers him slipping off, probably to carry information to the Mexican governor, Armijo. When Will falls ill of measles, Uncle* Fritz nurses him back to health. Functionally, he provides a link between Quincy's wagon train and the Missouri Volunteers of the Grand Army of the West.

WILLIAM ERNEST TEAGUE (*The Great Gilly Hopkins**), timid young foster brother of Gilly* Hopkins, who gains a little confidence when Gilly teaches him to stand up for himself. At first he is almost unable to speak, throws his hands up in front of his face as if he is used to being struck, and is considered probably retarded. Gilly sees that he is really bright, and after initially terrorizing him, helps him with his reading and wins his devotion. It is because of his pleas that she returns to Maime* Trotter's after she has stolen the money.

WILLIAM HAWKINS (*The Soul Brothers and Sister Lou**), Louretta's kind, earnest, hardworking, older brother. He hopes to earn enough money through his printing business to send his younger brothers to college, an opportunity for advancement he himself has not had. He also encourages Lou to set her educational sights high. After their sister, Arneatha*, steals the money the club earned at the dance and uses it to buy a gaudy red suit, he insists she pay back the money by getting a job. He also tells Momma she must stop spoiling Arneatha. He and Lou are very close, and he has a steadying influence on her. Like most of the characters in the book, he is a type figure.

WILLIAMS†, JAY (1924–1978), born in Buffalo, N.Y.; actor and entertainer, prolific writer for both adults and children. He attended the University of Pennsylvania in Philadelphia and Columbia University and served in the U.S. Army during World War II. For some years before the war he was a night club entertainer and film and stage actor. For adults he wrote some fourteen novels and several books of non-fiction. For children he wrote thirteen books of non-fiction, one of verse, and thirty-three books of fiction, besides the thirteen Danny Dunn science fiction books written in collaboration with Raymond Abrashkin†, of which *Danny Dunn and the Homework Machine†* (McGraw, 1958) is typical. Among his other books for young people are *The Sword and the Scythe†* (Oxford, 1946), historical fiction set in southern Germany in the sixteenth century, and *The Hawkstone** (Walck, 1971), a time fantasy set in Connecticut.

WILLIAMS, JEANNE, born in Elkhart, Kans.; writer of both fiction and non-fiction for children and adults. She grew up in the Midwest and attended the University of Oklahoma. Under her own name and the pseudonyms Jeanne Crecy, Megan Rhys, and J. R. Williams, she has written a number of novels, including *Oh Susanna* (Putnam, 1963), a story of homesteading in Kansas, *New Medicine*

(Putnam, 1971) and *Trail of Tears* (Putnam, 1972), both stories of Indian life, and *Freedom Trail** (Putnam, 1973), a story of the struggle between Free Staters and pro-slavery forces in northeastern Kansas just before the Civil War, which won a Spur Award from Western Writers of America. *The Horse Talker** (Prentice, 1960), set among the Comanches, also won the Spur.

WILLIAMSON, JOANNE SMALL (1926–   ), born in Arlington, Mass.; pianist, author of historical novels. She attended Barnard College and the Diller Quaile School of Music. She was engaged in newspaper work and writing and editing for periodicals until 1956, when she turned her attention to writing historical novels for young people, including *The Glorious Conspiracy** (Knopf, 1961), which deals with the democratic process in the first years of the United States after the Revolution.

WILLIE DELAMER (*Thunder on the Tennessee**), William Delamer, sixteen-year-old Texas youth who fights in the battle of Pittsburg Landing where he comes to "know the face of battle, to feel the sharp-edged sword of war." His father is Colonel Bill* Delamer, a veteran of the Mexican War and many Indian skirmishes. Like his father, Willie loves their Texas ranch but enlists in the Confederate Army because Delamers are always in the front lines. Some time before the book begins, Willie ran away from home to avoid being sent away to school and lived for some months with the Comanches, earning among them a fine reputation as a fighter and horseman. His skill with horses wins him a job as a courier, but he elects to return to the infantry. Willie is a tough youth, but he often thinks of his sweetheart and is never too busy to give someone a helping hand. He has something of the Indians' fatalism and stoicism, and, a religious boy, he occasionally prays as a Comanche. He is motivated by honor and duty. His father's death is a bitter loss. At the end, Travis* Cobb brings him his father's sword, a weapon he is proud to possess.

WILLIE WEGGFALL (*Adam Bookout**), tall black youth, friend of Adam. He is sent to Brooklyn from Alabama to live with his grandmother, Gran Dee, the kind and capable Mrs. Dee, who keeps house for the Bookouts. He has been involved in civil rights marches, and, fearing for his safety, his parents think a change of environment advisable. His dog, Honey, is stolen, and getting her back leads to Adam's decision to return to Oklahoma.

WILL STANTON (*The Dark Is Rising**; *The Grey King**), bright, serious-minded, persevering boy, son of a Buckinghamshire jeweler. Seventh son of a seventh son, he learns from Merriman* Lyon on his eleventh birthday that he is an Old One, one of those immortals whose responsibility it is to save the world from the powers of the Dark. Among other deeds, he helps to save his village from the extreme cold sent by the Dark, assists Merriman in recovering the stolen Grail of King Arthur, wins a golden harp, awakens the Six Sleepers, and with Bran acquires the sword by which the silvery mistletoe is cut from the Midsummer Tree and the Dark is finally defeated (in *Silver on the Tree*, the last book in The Dark is Rising series). Will is not a memorable protagonist, serving more as a device or pivot than a flesh and blood heroic character, in spite the many, often dangerous adventures he goes through.

THE WINGED WATCHMAN (Van Stockum*†, Hilda, ill. author, Farrar, 1962), historical novel that follows a Dutch family from the summer of 1944 to May of 1945, the last year of the German occupation of Holland in World War II, and that deals primarily with their involvement in the war on the home front. The Verhagens are more fortunate than many Dutch families. Father runs the Winged Watchman, the windmill that drains some of the fields in Saterwoude, and the villagers pay him for his services in food, fuel, and goods as they can. Even so, the family must sometimes resort to the Black Market for things they need. When Joris, 10, from whose point of view most of the events are seen, his brother, Dirk Jan, 14, and their father go to Mr. Schenderhans, their neighbor, to buy Freya, a collie pup, they learn to their dismay, that Leendert, the eldest son, against his family's wishes has become a "landwatcher," one who enforces the rules of the Nazi occupation. Leendert's appointment is particularly threatening to the Verhagens. Trixie, 3, the youngest Verhagen, is really a Jewish child that the Verhagens have been raising as their own since her parents were arrested early in the Occupation. Having a Nazi official living so near makes efforts to help the Resistance more difficult, too. Joris discovers Charles King, a British airman, hiding in the Giant, an abandoned windmill. He and Dirk Jan help Uncle Cor, a Resistance worker, smuggle Charles out of the area, disguising him as a woman and actually tricking Leendert into giving him a lift on his motorbike, for one of the book's lighter episodes. Later Dirk Jan makes a perilous journey to Leyden, carrying a message for Uncle Cor to arrange for a weapons drop. From there, windmill operators send the message overland by setting the wings of their windmills in certain agreed-upon positions. During the winter, Mother responds generously to all who come to the Winged Watchman seeking help, and it becomes a haven for "underdivers," some temporary, some permanent. Among these are Betsy and Koba, the small daughters of a stationmaster who has gone into hiding, and Hildebrand, a student who is avoiding the German workforce. Christmas is happy, and St. Nicholas (really Uncle Cor) comes with small gifts and goodies for the little ones. After the holidays, cold and shortages intensify. When winter rains flood the fields, Father persuades the farmers to breach the dikes and to let him use the Winged Watchman to drain them, in the process demonstrating effectively his contention that wind power is more reliable than electricity. Spring brings the sad news of the execution of the legendary leader of the Resistance, Kip Kees, who the family now learns is their Uncle Cor. But Freya has puppies, to the children's great delight, and Holland is liberated at last. Those who have been hiding can now go home, and everyone looks forward to better days. The highly episodic plot moves unevenly, and the author makes little of its possibilities for suspense. She never works up, for example, the potential of Uncle Cor's double life, or the activities of Reina, the niece of the local doctor, who seems to wander in and out of the village and their lives on Resistance duties. The book does, however, give a low-keyed, unsentimental, unmelodramatic sense of what the Occupation must have been like from the child's point of view. Characters are flat, and some, like Leendert, are stock. Joris matures predictably through his experiences, and outspoken little Trixie, whose mother reclaims her at the end, is especially winsome. The themes include standing up for one's rights, keeping faith with God and neighbor, and generosity and neighborliness in adversity. Choice; Fanfare.

WINGS (Richard*, Adrienne, Little, 1974), episodic, realistic novel of family life. The almost plotless story covers a school year in the life of serious, strong-minded, little Pip (Ann Margaret) dePuyster, whose passion is airplanes. Pip and her older brother, bookish Parkman, return from spending the summer with their wealthy, proper father in Kansas City to stay with their beautiful and lively mother at her valley home somewhere in California in 1928. Pip resumes old friendships and makes new ones, particularly among her mother's Bohemian crowd, and starts a new school year. She suggests that her class raise chickens as a project and then chairs the committee to do it. She solves a distressing personal problem, how to get out of cleaning the coop, by promising to be friends with shy, quiet Harold* Hoffer, if he will do the detestable task for her. The moral aspects of the situation eventually compel her to fulfill her pledge. The end of May finds her and Parkman abruptly returning to the Midwest, when their father suspiciously reads sexual connotations into Pip's innocent relationship with Radyar*, her mother's motorcycle-riding, astrologist friend. Pip reluctantly agrees to go, wisely realizing that there are some things in life that one must accept. Characters are well realized, and it is through them that the reader gets to know and understand Pip. When Pip wheels out her wagon, whirls its imaginary propeller, pulls away its braking blocks, and goes for a spin through the village, she and the reader meet asthmatic Mr. Zick, who manages the local movie house, saves advertising posters for her, and plays flight features that thrill her to heights of ecstasy. Mrs. Huckaby, whose lima bean bread Pip's mother favors, ponders why tarantulas like her bathtub so much, sells health foods, and cures Pip's mother's headaches with strange, flat, electrical plates. There are also rich Aunt Andrea, whom Pip's naive comments send into peals of bubbling, silvery laughter; Yamaji*, the gentle Indian mystic; Pip's mother, Dorrit, who often does not understand Pip and at other times understands her all too well; Parkman, who usually shuns his mother's friends and who sometimes plays the airplane game with Pip, lifting her spirits to unspeakable heights; and Marjorie, her know-it-all classmate, against whom Pip uses her head as a battering ram to persuade to her way of thinking; and several others who walk in and out of Pip's life during the year. The fully rounded characters dominate the book. Although tinged with the eccentric, Pip and her friends are never made grotesque or ridiculous. The 1920s come alive with just enough details of dress, behavior, and current events to make the characters' lives real and give the book texture. The author demonstrates a literate and vigorous use of language, and her tone is consistently sympathetic and straightforward. National Book Finalist.

WINNIE FOSTER (*Tuck Everlasting**), overprotected ten-year-old who, in a spurt of independence, takes a walk in the woods by her house and is kidnapped by the wonderful Tuck family into a strange adventure. Being used to order in her life and her home, Winnie is amazed at the casual Tucks and their haphazard housekeeping, at first critical but soon adoring the family. She does her first really daring thing when she climbs into the jail window to take the place of Mae* Tuck, who is escaping after being held for murder. Jesse* Tuck has suggested that Winnie wait until she is seventeen, then drink some of the water from the spring that has kept the Tucks unchanged for eighty-seven years, and run off with him, but Mae and Angus* Tuck, many years later, find her tombstone that shows she led an ordinary life and died.

WINSTON LOCHMANN (*Ox Under Pressure**), owner of the house the Olmsteads rent on Long Island. An art collector, he has bet on a return to representational art and spent his fortune. He is described as both sinister and giggling, a thoroughly unpleasant man, whose idea of fun is to get his German butler, Hans*, to say, "My father was a dragoon," which in Hans's fractured English comes out "dragon," and then to laugh at him. Arabella's* father has encouraged him to think he will make a match with the girl when she becomes eighteen, although he is much older.

THE WISH GIVER: THREE TALES OF COVEN TREE (Brittain*, Bill, ill. Andrew Glass, Harper, 1983), fantasy set in a small New England town, apparently in the first third of the twentieth century, playing changes on the old three-wishes motif. The narrator, Stew Meat (Stewart Meade), owner of the Coven Tree General Store, is attending the annual church social when he notices a sign on one of the booths set up by outsiders at the far end of the lawn, "Thaddeus Blinn I can give you whatever you ask for only 50¢." The extravagant promise draws only four Coven Tree inhabitants, skeptical Stew Meat, eleven-year-old Polly Kemp, the most outspoken girl in town, Rowena Jervis, a giddy fifteen-year-old, and Adam Fiske, 16, who lives on a dry farm where in rain-poor seasons even drinking water must be hauled all the way from Spider Creek. To each of them, for fifty cents, Thaddeus Blinn gives a little white card with a red spot on it, telling them that they only have to press their thumbs against the red spot and utter a wish aloud and it will be granted—but only one. All four think they have been swindled, particularly when Blinn shuts up his tent and departs promptly. Polly, whose friends are Leland and Lenora Wickstaff, shy, half-wild twins who know all the secrets of nature, but who wants to make friends with Agatha Benthorn and Eunice Ingersoll, the richest, best-dressed girls in town, wishes to be the center of attention, making people smile, and to be invited to Agatha's house. The next day she finds that whenever she starts to say something, it comes out in a frog croak, "JUG-A-RUM!" It gets her the attention and the smiles, and though she begins to say other things, the JUG-A-RUM! comes out unpredictably. Lenora figures out that it is whenever Polly starts to say something hurtful or angry. Polly overhears Agatha and Eunice plotting to ask her to tea and get her riled so they can laugh at her frog sounds. She accepts their invitation but acts cool and polite as can be and realizes that the girls are mean and shallow and, above all, boring. Rowena has a crush on the traveling farm-implement salesman, Henry Piper, and ignores the hired boy, Sam Waxman. Infatuated, she wishes that Henry will put down roots in Coven Tree and never leave again. To her horror, this literally comes true. Henry begins to root in a grove of trees on her father's farm and each day becomes more tree-like. As Rowena and Sam try to help him, his bullying and crossness make her see him in quite another light, and Sam's evidence that all Henry's stories of traveling in exotic places are lies destroys the last of her illusions. Predictably, Adam Fiske, weary of hauling water in tubs with the team and wagon, wishes for water. His father has had the dowser, Uncle Poot, walk the whole farm with his forked applewood branch hunting for water to no avail. But after his wish Adam tries the forked branch and it wrestles and bucks in his hands. Shortly afterwards, water starts spouting like geysers from the holes he has dug for fence posts. At first, he and his parents are delighted, but the water keeps coming. Soon they are sitting in the middle of a lake and then start to raft their furniture to higher ground. Adam tries to tell his father, who is too busy to listen, about his wish, and when he finally does tell his story, as they camp by the lakeside, he is astonished at how understanding his father is. The problems are solved when the three young people converge on Stew Meat's store and beg him to use his wish to undo theirs. The lighthearted stories have enough humor to make the old pattern work again, and the colloquial style and small-town details give the solid foundation necessary for fantasy. Thaddeus Blinn is a strange and mesmerizing character, with eyes that seem to glow red, a description that sets the mood for unusual happenings, but the tone is always light and true belief is not expected. Fanfare.

WISLER, G(ARY) CLIFTON , teacher and writer of novels for young people and adults. His long and avid interest in the Civil War and in the battle of Shiloh resulted in *Thunder on the Tennessee** (Dutton, 1983), which received the Spur Award of Western Writers of America. This novel describes the involvement of a sixteen-year-old Texas youth in the regiment that saw service in the battles of Pittsburg Landing and Shiloh. It is the sequel to *Buffalo Moon* (Dutton, 1984), in which the same boy runs away from home to avoid being sent to school in New Orleans and lives for some months with Comanches. He has also written for young readers *Winter of the Wolf* (Dutton, 1981), about a youth who runs the family ranch in Texas during the Civil War and saves the life of a young Comanche, which was nominated for the Spur Award, and for adults *My Brother,* *the Wind* (Doubleday, 1979) and *A Cry of Angry Thunder* (Doubleday, 1980), both also involving Indians. He teaches school in Garland, Tex.

WITCHES (*A Wrinkle in Time**), Mrs. Who, Mrs. Whatsit, and Mrs. Which, three witchlike women who live in an old house across the woods from the Murry house. Mrs. Whatsit, the youngest of the three and the comforter among them, is plump and dresses like a tramp. Mrs. Who is a chubby, little, old lady who speaks in quotations from famous writers and thinkers of various periods. Mrs. Witch, the eldest of the three, stutters a lot. Although comic figures, they command respect. They have the ability to change their shapes, have more than human knowledge, and tesser (tesseract*) the children through space when they are trying to find Dr. Murry. They are dedicated to the cause of helping good triumph over evil. They show the children the great, dark shadow of evil that threatens to engulf the world.

THE WITCHES' BRIDGE (Carleton*, Barbee Oliver, Holt, 1967), mystery novel set near York, Mass., in the mid-twentieth century. An orphan, Dan Pride, 13, returns to the family home he has never seen and his uncle, dour Julian Pride, whom he does not know. Small for his age and insecure, he finds the house at Pride's Point isolated, his uncle morose and uncommunicative, and the people of York unfriendly. Part of the hostility goes back to Puritan times when Samuel Pride, builder of the house, was believed to call the devil up onto the salt marshes in the fog by his violin music and was pressed to death as a witch. By being silent rather than confessing, he saved the house from being confiscated, and it has come down in the family through Dan's grandfather, old Dan Pride, who died mysteriously one foggy night on the marsh and was believed to have been a victim of the Fiddler. His death gave new impetus to the feud between the Prides and the Bishops, the family who had brought the witchcraft charges against Samuel, because old Dan had left the Point that night with a briefcase full of cash to buy the local shipyards from the Bishops and the briefcase, which should have contained the receipts, was not found with his body. Dan is warned not to go out on the marshes at night, not to have anything to do with the Bishops, and to beware of his uncle's dog, huge, misshapen Caliban. His time is spent helping the handyman, Billy* Ben Corey, a young man who seems alternately friendly and threatening, and swimming and repairing a skiff with the help of the twins, Pip Cole and his sister, Gilly. It is only after their bonfire has started a grass fire which threatens the Point that Dan discovers they are the children of Ann Bishop, who was engaged to Uncle Julian before his father's death. About the same time, Dan realizes that Billy Ben hates him and is conducting a systematic search of the Point to find old Dan's briefcase. He also finds that Caliban is vicious only to Billy Ben, who crippled him with a beating. An old hermit, Lamie, who lives on an island nearby and is believed locally to be mad, helps him straighten out his true affection for the Cole twins and for Pride's Point. In an exciting denouement, Dan is accused of arson in York, hides in the marsh when he is chased by police, finds the "witches' chamber," a hiding place and escape route built by Samuel's son in case of further accusations, beneath the old chapel with an entrance under the Witches' Bridge to the marsh, is almost murdered by Billy Ben, and is saved by Caliban, who attacks the hired man. The briefcase, found in the witches' chamber, proves that not the Bishops but Billy Ben's father killed old Dan Pride. Full of Gothic props (ancient feuds, an isolated decaying mansion, fog, unexplained music, legends of witchcraft) the novel is not high on credibility or depth of characterization but keeps the reader on edge with a fast-paced, suspenseful plot skillfully handled. Poe Nominee.

THE WITCHES OF WORM (Snyder*, Zilpha Keatley, ill. Alton Raible, Atheneum, 1972), realistic novel set in an apartment house in a large city in California in the late 1900s. Plain, twelve-year-old Jessica Ann Porter feels neglected by her "beautiful-as-a-movie-star," divorced mother, Joy*, and deserted by her friends, Brandon Doyle, who lives in the same apartment building, and Diane, a school chum, both of whom have developed new interests and friends. A bookish, lonely child with an active imagination, Jessica becomes interested in witchcraft. In the cave in the hills where she and Brandon used to play pretend games, Jessica finds an ugly, newborn kitten which she names Worm and raises. When she vents her frustrations through spiteful and destructive acts against those around her, she rationalizes by telling herself that Worm has prompted her to do them. This leads her to believe that Worm is a demon sent by some witch to control her life. Her malicious phone call to Diane's mother gets her former friend in trouble, she preys upon the fears of Mrs.* Post, her sitter, by falsely asserting she saw a prowler in the back yard, and she spitefully ruins her mother's new, red dress to keep her from spending the weekend with her fiance's family. Each time, Jessica lies and dissembles her way out of punishment. The climax comes when she damages Brandon's trumpet by angrily shoving it from the window sill where he had left it. Mrs.* Fortune, the cat-keeping, elderly woman who owns the apartment complex, sees the deed and insists Jessica own up. Jessica first decides to get revenge, then goes to Mrs. Fortune with the cat-demon-witch story. Mrs. Fortune, an imaginative person herself, lends Jessica a book on exorcism. The ceremony completed, Worm races from the apartment and out the front door of the complex, with Jessica, and, later, Brandon in frantic pursuit. The two retrieve the animal, and Jessica confesses to Brandon, also telling him the cat-demon-witch story. Brandon assures her that the exorcism took and that he harbors no ill-will over the trumpet. Jessica apparently has a firmer grip on reality and is pleased to be friends with Brandon again. Events are seen from Jessica's point of view, and, though the picture is superficial, Jessica is quite convincing as a maladjusted personality, the victim of circumstances and her own too passionate nature. The action, which exploits a current fad, builds suspensefully to the climax, but the resolution is unsatisfying and illogical in view of previous events and Jessica's character as presented. The adults are not believable, and a few flashbacks illuminate the linear plot. This is an intriguing, if not wholly convincing, account of an angry, disturbed, early adolescent child's attempts to cope with painful realities in her life. National Book Finalist; Newbery Honor.

THE WITCH FAMILY (Estes*†, Eleanor, ill. Edward Ardizzone, Harcourt, 1960), episodic fantasy in which most of the action takes place in the unreal world and which begins and ends in, and occasionally reverts to, reality. Amy and Clarissa, both almost seven, live in Washington, D.C., in the mid–1900s. Best friends, they spend hours playing together mostly in Amy's house. Amy's mother often tells them stories about a wicked Old Witch. One day, Amy decides to banish the mean, crotchety, old creature to a barren, glass hill. She informs Old Witch that, if she's good, she can come back at Halloween. With Old Witch goes Malachi, a fuzzy, venerable bumble bee, which Amy regards as her "representatiff" on the glass hill. Malachi is a "spelling bee"; he speaks by spelling out his thoughts in words. He makes sure that things are orderly on the hill and stings anyone who misbehaves. Amy and Clarissa then imagine a family and adventures for Old Witch. They draw pictures about her activities, and the scenes come alive in the fantasy world. Hannah, a Little Witch Girl, joins Old Witch, goes to witches' school, and plays with Lurie, a mermaid, whom the girls also create and place by a waterfall inside the glass hill. The girls give the Little Witch Girl a baby sister, Beebee, and a birthday party, which all her witch classmates attend and to which Hannah "abracadabras" Amy and Clarissa against Old Witch's orders. In April, Old Witch relapses briefly into her wicked ways. She sets out to eat Easter eggs and rabbits (the dish she particularly enjoys), but Malachi warns the animals just in time, and she mistakenly consumes the stuffed rabbits and painted rocks they set out instead. On Halloween, Amy gives Old Witch leave to attend the annual revels. Hannah comes to earth, too, where she changes place with Amy and goes trick-or-treating, while, in a brief dream sequence, Amy has adventures on Little Witch's broomstick and even goes to witches' school. After that, Amy decides that she and Clarissa should relieve the barrenness of Old Witch's environment and flesh out their pictures with trees, flowers, and grass, additions to the scene that Hannah especially appreciates. The book ends inconclusively with Mother telling another story about wicked Old Witch. The plot ambles along as the girls think of adventures for their imaginary witch family. Most of the ideas are Amy's, but Clarissa helps to draw the pictures. Situations are strained, the book is overly long and seems dated, and sometimes the author intrudes and even occasionally lapses into a coy and patronizing tone. There is minimal character development, and the book lacks the charm and holding power of the author's realistic books about the Moffat family, *The Moffats†* and its successors. Fanfare.

WITCH OF THE GLENS (Watson*, Sally, ill. Barbara Werner, Viking, 1962), historical romance set in Scotland in 1644 when the English revolution is spreading into the Highlands. Young Kelpie*, about fifteen to seventeen, traveling with the gypsies, Black Bogle and Mina Faw, who stole her as an infant because she has the blue, triple-ringed eyes of second sight, begins to realize that she is being used by her companions, not only to pick pockets and steal from clothes lines, but also to look into the crystal and see the future. When the trio run into Ian Cameron and his foster brother, red-haired Alex MacDonald, both just returned from study at Oxford, she automatically throws herself in front of their horses, pretending to be hurt to get their sympathy and some money. To her surprise, she actually has hurt her shoulder, and Mina, for her own reasons, lets them take Kelpie to the Cameron home, Glenfern. There she meets the first kindness of her life, the love of Wee Mairi, the fascination of the twins, Donald and Ronald, who hope she is a witch as she claims to be, and the friendship of Ian and his sister, Eithne. Even cynical Alex, who twice catches her stealing, begins to banter with her good-humoredly, as she works as a servant in the informal household and begins to learn the rudiments of a decent life. Then, looking into a clear pool, she sees a vision of Alex with a sword upraised and Ian falling wounded. She turns bitterly on Alex and warns Ian, who fails to take alarm, but suddenly Mina and Bogle reappear, demand that she go with them, bribe her with a promise to teach her witchcraft, and threaten to curse the Glenfern family, particularly Wee Mairi, if she refuses. Again they use her, this time in collusion with a lowlander warlock, to become a servant of the witch-baiting head of the Campbell clan, head of the Covenant Army of the Lowlands, MacCailein Mor, the Marquis of Argyll, at Invary Castle. There the Puritan ways almost stifle her, but she finally succeeds in her mission to get some personal thing of MacCailein Mor, specifically a few hairs from his brush, with which the warlock will make a powerful curse. Kelpie is caught in Argyll's bedroom, however, and thrown into a dungeon to be burned later as a witch. Argyll's nephew, Ewen Cameron, who is really a hostage, helps her escape by a secret tunnel, and she makes her way alone, trying to go south and east to get out of Campbell territory. She runs into Ian and Alex, who are with Antrim's army loyal to the Stuart king, and joins the women and children who follow the army, which is soon inspirited by the arrival of the charismatic leader, Graham of Montrose. She is with the army through several victories against much larger forces, but when she runs into a crowd tormenting two witches and discovers they are Mina and Bogle, who turn the mob's anger to her, she sees Ian rushing to save her and Alex's sword upraised, just as in her vision. She gets away, assuming that Ian is dead, and wanders back to an old couple who had earlier given her shelter. Later she rejoins the army, learns that Ian is wounded, not dead, and that Alex is "away." Some time later, after leaving to try to get to Glenfern, she discovers the Campbell army and is able to send word to Montrose. Then she finds Alex with a sprained ankle, hiding in a cave. Both he and she are taken prisoner, and though she is able to get away, she hides and hears MacCailein Mor threaten to kill Alex if he cannot produce the one who sent word to Montrose. He knows her whereabouts but doesn't betray her so she, against all her training and better judgment, steps out to try to save him by confessing. Just then Montrose's army attacks; they are both wounded and are taken to Glenfern, where it is all straightened out. Alex is shown to have been saving, not harming, Ian. Alex confesses his love for Kelpie, and they plan to marry and head for the new world. Because Kelpie is an interesting character, tough and independent, yet touching, and the setting of the wild highlands and complex loyalties of the conflict are well presented, the story has power and interest as well as action. The final scene of explanation and Alex's declaration of love are too sudden and pat, and not worthy of the earlier unlikely but convincing story. Included are a historical note, a glossary of Gaelic terms, and notes on Gaelic pronunciation. Fanfare.

A WIZARD OF EARTHSEA (LeGuin*, Ursula K., ill. Ruth Robbins, Parnassus, 1968), first of a fantasy trilogy set in a pre-industrial world on an imaginary archipelago called Earthsea*. Duny, later known as Sparrowhawk, a boy of the island of Gont which is famous for wizards, has shown unusual abilities and so has been taught by his aunt, a village witch, some simple spells. He saves the village from invading Kargs by creating a fog, in which they are confused and led over a precipice. Ogion*, the wizard of Re Albi, gives him his secret name, Ged*, and takes him for an apprentice. Tempted by the daughter of the Lord of Re Albi, later known as Serret, he reads a spell from his master's lore-book and calls up a shadow but is saved by Ogion, who allows him to go to the great school for wizards on the island of Roke*. There Ged learns rapidly but forms a rivalry with a noble-born student, Jasper*, who goads him into a contest in which Ged in pride calls up the spirit of the long-dead Elfarran, woman from the hero tale, the Deed of Enlad, and accidentally with it a misshapen clot of black shadow that wounds him severely but is banished by the Archmage. After a long convalescence, Ged, humbled, takes a position at the poor fishing village of Low Torning, which has been threatened by the dragons of Pendor. Trying to save the life of his fisherman friend's son, Ged follows the boy's spirit even into the land of death and realizes that the Shadow still seeks him. Therefore, he travels to Pendor, kills the young dragons, and resists the temptation of the old dragon who suggests that he may tell Ged the Shadow's true name, thus giving him power over it. Instead, Ged binds the dragon by its true name never to fly east of Pendor and, having saved the archipelago, sets out to try to escape the Shadow, which is seeking him. His travels take him to the Court of Terrenon in Osskil, a castle in the medieval style, where Serret, now wife to the Lord Benderesk, tries to get him to use the Stone of Terrenon, which would have enslaved him. He turns into a falcon and flies to Ogion, who tells him he must stop fleeing and face the Shadow to overcome it. The rest of the book is a wild chase over the sea, including a wreck on an island where he finds two old people, a brother and sister who were abandoned there when they were royal children, a stop in West Hand where he obtains a new boat, *Lookfar**, and a stop at Iffish, where he is joined by his friend, Vetch*, from the school at Roke. Together they sail beyond the furthest island where Ged finally meets the Shadow and conquers it with its true name, Ged. The theme that one must face and know the evil in oneself to overcome it is just one of several strong themes in the novel, another being that one cannot change any small part of the universe without disturbing the balance and equilibrium. The tone is serious and dramatic, but since the fantasy elements are based on ideas from the oral tradition and the author also employs concrete detail in all the descriptions, it has both the quality of legend and the believability of fiction. One of the strongest American fantasies of recent years. Boston Globe Winner; Choice; Fanfare; Lewis Carroll.

WOJCIECHOWSKA (RODMAN), MAIA (1927–   ), born in Warsaw, Poland; author of a number of books, mostly for young adults. With her family she fled Poland during the Nazi invasion in World War II, to France, Portugal, England, and eventually the United States, an experience recounted in a book of memoirs, *Till the Break of Day* (Harcourt, 1972). She attended Immaculate Heart College in Hollywood, Calif., and worked at a variety of jobs, many of them in editing and publishing, then started to write for young people, publishing three of her books under the name of Maia Rodman during the period when she was married to the poet, Selden Rodman. Her Newbery winning novel, *Shadow of a Bull** (Atheneum, 1964), a story set in Spain, started as a short story for adults. Among her other books are *A Single Light* (Harper, 1968), a story of a mute girl, *Tuned Out* (Harper, 1968), a story of drug dependency, and *Winter Tales from Poland* (Doubleday, 1973), eight stories, some folktales, some original.

A WONDERFUL, TERRIBLE TIME (Stolz*†, Mary, ill. Louis S. Glanzman, Harper, 1967), realistic novel of family life set in an inner city apartment complex in New York City and in a girls' camp in the country in the mid twentieth century. Two black girls, Sue Ellen Forrest and Mady Guthrie, about ten, are best friends. Sue Ellen's mother, Lillian*, takes care of Mady while Mady's mother, Anna*, works. Now that school is out, the girls look forward to a summer of good times together, playing dolls, taking trips to the five and dime, and running through the hydrant. Sue Ellen's father, Dan*, a taxi driver, narrowly avoids hitting a pedestrian, Mr. Kusack, who, in gratitude, offers to send the girls to camp. Sue Ellen, always the leader, rejects the idea immediately, preferring to stay with her parents and friend on familiar territory, and assumes Mady will agree. To her surprise and disappointment, Mady, who loves animals and longs for a change of scenery, accepts with such elation that Sue Ellen reluctantly agrees to go, too. On the way up by train and for much of the two weeks they are in camp, Sue Ellen remains resentful, aloof, and disparaging. Swimming is the only activity that she enjoys, but mostly she longs for home. Mady, on the other hand, enters immediately and wholeheartedly into the swing of things, though never without concern for reluctant Sue Ellen. Mady makes friends with counselors and campers and participates eagerly in activities. In particular, she enjoys Maria, the warm, patient counselor who plans to become a vet and who helps her make a terrarium. When Sue Ellen overhears some girls remark that she is a natural for the part of gloomy Eeyore in the cabin skit, since she is such a Sour Sue, she takes the criticism positively and plays the part well. Her disposition even improves a little. She returns home joyfully; for her the two weeks have been terrible. Although she bubbles over with stories to tell her parents about camp, she declares she will never go again. Mady, on the other hand, wishes the two weeks had never ended. She comes home tearfully, sure that finances will prevent her from ever going again. She enters her empty apartment sadly, then sees the goldfish bowl her mother has prepared as a welcome home gift. She decides to make the best of things, greets her mother with a hug, gives her the terrarium, and sits down to have a quiet talk about this most wonderful summer of her life. The strength of this implausibly motivated story lies in its sympathetic portrayal of the way the two girls react to the same experience. Dialogue is extensive and accurate, and the parents, if a shade too perfect, are very likeable. Choice.

WOODS, GEORGE A(LLAN) (1926–   ), born in Lake Placid, N.Y.; review editor, author. He was graduated from Fordham University and served in India with the U.S. Army in World War II. Since 1963 he has been children's editor for the New York *Times Book Review* and has been lecturer at Fordham and at Marymount College. *To Catch a Killer** (Harper, 1972), a story of suspense, was an Edgar Allan Poe Award nominee.

WORCESTER, GURDON S(ALTONSTALL) (1897–   ), born in Philadelphia, Pa.; psychologist, writer, and inventor. He served with the U.S. Army in World War I, attended Harvard University, and worked as a consulting psychologist for many years. In the 1940s he collaborated with his wife, Natalie Shipman, in the writing of two novels, *Way of the Heart* (Greystone, 1941) and *Perchance to Dream* (Prentice, 1946). Since 1960 he has devoted his time to inventing and writing; among his books is the poetic *The Singing Flute** (Obolensky, 1963).

WORDS BY HEART (Sebestyen*, Ouida, Atlantic/Little, 1979), realistic novel set in Texas in 1910. When Lena Sills, 12, wins the school contest for knowing the most Bible verses by heart, she is confused by the worry of her step-mother, Claudie, who is tense and lonely being the only black woman in the area after having lived in Scattercreek, an all-black community before the family moved west. Claudie blames Lena's father, Ben*, who wants to give Lena a chance and to shield her from the ugly truth of racial prejudice. When they return that night they find a knife stabbed through a cloth-covered loaf of bread on their table and the next morning discover their dog dead. Lena is sure that Tater Haney, whose shiftless poor-white father has been replaced at the gin by Ben, is to blame. Lena has to miss school when Mrs.* Mary Tom Chism, the quarrelsome, eccentric employer, insists that she come to work. In cleaning up the attic, Lena finds books she covets, and when Mrs. Chism won't let her borrow them, she takes one without permission. It turns out to be an atlas, much admired by Winslow Starnes, the honor student she beat in the Bible contest. Later she sneaks it back and takes another, a poetry anthology, but that one is damaged when little Roy, 5, spills milk over it. Ben realizes that the book has not really been loaned by Mrs. Chism and takes Lena back to confess. The woman is furious but eventually makes a deal with Ben to give Lena permission to read the books if he will go mend fences at her property at Hawk Hill, a job he has been avoiding because it will keep him away from his family two or three nights. The job had originally been Mr. Haney's. While he is gone, someone lets their cow loose, and Claudie must hunt for it, leaving Lena with Roy, Armilla, 3, and the baby. Mr. Haney, drunk, comes belligerently yelling for Ben but is dragged away by Tater. When Ben does not return as expected, Lena sneaks out at night to go find him, walks to Hawk Hill, and finds the wagon with the horses still hitched up. She finally discovers Ben, shot by Tater, who has been thrown and dragged by the horse which was scared by the noise. Ben has been staying with him, keeping flies from his wounds. Ben, a religious man, tells Lena she must help Tater. With great difficulty she gets both of them into the wagon, but Ben dies. She delivers Tater to his house and takes the body of her father home. Winslow, the only student who has been nice to Lena, defies his father to come help with the younger children. Claudie, at first shocked into a stupor, pulls herself together and decides that they will stay rather than go back to Scattercreek, but that they will insist on their rights. The picture of prejudice in the community is rather heavy-handed, with even the teacher pointing out in school that the white race is superior, but probably true for the time and place. Lena is a believable child, but most of the others are stock characters. IRA.

WORMSER, RICHARD (EDWARD) (1908–   ), born in New York City; writer of science fiction, western novels, and film scripts. He attended Princeton University, worked as a newspaper reporter, in public relations, and in publishing. Since 1937, he has lived in the Southwest, where he has been editor of anthropological publications for the Museum of New Mexico and director of the Southwest Association on Indian Affairs. Besides many magazine stories, he has written a science fiction novel, *Pan Satyrus* (Avon, 1963), screen plays, including those for *The Last Days of Sodom and Gomorrah* and *Thief of Bagdad*, and a number of novels with a western setting. Among these are *Ride a Northbound Horse** (Morrow, 1964) and *The Black Mustanger** (Morrow, 1971), both of which not only give a good picture of the working cowboy in the late nineteenth century but also show an interesting relationship between a boy and a man for whom he works.

WOSMEK, FRANCES (1917–   ), born in Popple, Minn.; teacher, designer, writer. She attended Wadena Teachers Training College in Minnesota and Meinzinger's Art School, Detroit, Mich. Her varied career has included teaching school in rural Minnesota, designing greeting cards, working in layout and advertising art, writing juvenile novels, some self-illustrated, and illustrating books written by others. Among her novels is *Mystery of the Eagle's Claw** (Westminster, 1979), an Edgar Allan Poe Award nominee.

WRIGHT, BETTY REN , novelist and editor. She has worked in publishing, adapting a number of classics for Raintree Publishers of Milwaukee, including *Red Badge of Courage* by Stephen Crane, *The Time Machine* by H. G. Wells, and *Wuthering Heights* by Emily Bronte, and has had stories in *Redbook*, *Ladies' Home Journal*, *Young Miss*, and many other magazines. Among her novels for young people are *Getting Rid of Marjorie* (Holiday, 1981), a story of how an eleven-year-old schemes to get rid of a new stepgrandmother whom she fears will come between her and her grandfather, and *The Dollhouse Murders** (Holiday, 1983), a mystery most notable for its consideration of the problems of a child who must care for her retarded sister, which was a nominee for the Edgar Allan Poe Award. Among her other titles are *I Want to Read* (Golden Press, 1973), *The Day the TV Broke Down* (Raintree, 1980), and *The Secret Window* (Holiday, 1982). She lives with her husband in Kenosha, Wis.

A WRINKLE IN TIME (L'Engle*, Madeleine, Farrar, 1962), a fantasy novel that relies heavily on scientific innovation and conjecture set recently in the eastern part of the United States, probably New England, and on several planets in space, in particular, Camazotz*. The father in the closely knit Murry family, a gifted scientist, has disappeared while working on a classified government project, the tesseract*, or the ''wrinkle in time.'' Sensitive, warmhearted Meg*, about thirteen, her younger brother, prodigy Charles* Wallace, 5, and their neighbor, popular student and athlete, Calvin* O'Keefe, 14, are ''tessered'' away through time and space by three odd, witchlike, otherworld beings, Mrs. Whatsit, Mrs. Who, and Mrs. Which, to various planets. Among them is one in Orion's belt, where the Happy Medium, who lives in a cave and has a crystal ball, shows them the evil Dark Thing which threatens to engulf Earth. The witches* tesser them to Camazotz, a controlled society ruled by IT, a disembodied brain, where Charles Wallace is hypnotized by the man with the Red Eyes, IT's mouthpiece, and made to serve IT. Father has been captured by IT and imprisoned in a large, round, transparent column. Meg bravely enters the column and releases him, and the three are then tessered away by Dr. Murry to still another planet, Ixchel. Injured in the trip back through the Dark Shadow, Meg is nursed by Aunt Beast, a soft, furry, faceless, shapeless creature, who cuddles her and restores her to health with warmth and love. Because she is the closest in spirit to Charles Wallace, only Meg can save him. She is tessered back to Camazotz, and, through the power of her great love for her little brother, she breaks the hold IT has on him, and all return safely home to the Murrys' village and a happy reunion with Mother, also a gifted scientist in her own right, and twin brothers, Sandy and Dennys. This fast-moving story of the power of self-sacrificing love and the dangers of conformity and over-reliance on the intellect is inventive and suspenseful, if heavy on messages. It probes such concerns common to the genre as good and evil, free will, extra-sensory perception, and social responsibility. Human characters are convincingly drawn and likeable, but the otherworld beings are caricatures. Dialogue is extensive, and occasional humor relieves the tension. Others in series. Books Too Good; ChLA Touchstones; Choice; Fanfare; Lewis Carroll; Newbery Winner.

X

X15 (*Henry 3**), the most exclusive boy's club in Crestview. It consists of three boys who have built in the garage of one of them a car out of spare parts from fifteen different makes of cars. It is a smooth, sparkling, black, four-door sedan. Since all the boys are too young to drive, they go for pretend trips in the car every afternoon after school. Until Henry arrives, no other boy has ever been invited to join. Henry is chosen because he has the idea of taking a trip around the world.

Y

YAMAJI (*Wings**), Indian mystic who frequently visits at the dePuyster home, one of Pip's mother's circle of Bohemian friends. Although he has many followers, he feels quite doubtful about his ability to help others achieve the good life. He and Pip have conversations at her special places, the sycamore tree in the yard and the valley of the horses' bones, that help Pip put her relationship with Harold* Hoffer in its proper perspective. Pip sees Yamaji as a warm, kind man, who is searching for the right way to live.

YANUS (*Dragonsong**), Sea Holder at Half-Circle, a hidebound, tradition-loving leader, who is so afraid that anything unconventional will disgrace his hold that he tries to suppress his daughter's marvelous musical talent. Being more interested in fishing than anything else, he has never wanted to spare a man or boy to learn the music of the harper and so finds he has only his daughter to sing the deathsong for the old harper and to teach the children until the new harper comes, but he forbids her to play any music she has made up. When he catches Menolly playing a bit of a tune she has composed, he beats her and takes away her harp. To the new harper's inquiries he answers evasively, letting him think that the children have been taught their music by a lad who has left the Hold. Yanus, however, is a good sailor who leads his fishermen with great skill and efficiency and works as hard himself as he forces his followers to work.

THE YEAR OF THE RACCOON (Kingman*, Lee, Houghton, 1966), realistic novel of family life with problem story qualities, which takes place in a rural area in New England over several months in the mid–1900s. Everybody in the Larkin family is special in some way, except Joey, 15, a mediocre student who appears to be drifting aimlessly through life. His older brother, Jerry, is a talented pianist, and Jock, 9, is exceptional at math and science. Joey knows his brilliant, energetic father, an industrial consultant often away from home on problem-solving assignments, expects him to excel at something, too, and some day enter a profession. In early summer, Joey finds an injured baby raccoon which he insists on rearing, in spite of the warnings of old Reino, the Larkins' Finnish handyman. Caring for Bertie gives Joey the courage to demand some relief from such family chores as gardening, most of which have fallen to him because his presumably more talented brothers are pursuing more important interests. But the raccoon brings problems, too. Joey's preoccupation with Bertie separates him even more from his family and peers, and his grades suffer. Bertie destroys Jock's collection of exotic fish and is indirectly responsible for Jerry cutting himself on the lawnmower. Only Joey's quick thinking in recovering the tip of Jerry's severed finger makes it possible for Jerry to continue with his music. Christmas marks a turning point in their lives. Joey returns Bertie to the wilds after he ruins the Christmas tree, chews shingles on the house, and arouses Mr. Larkin's ire by his general intractability. Mr. Larkin threatens to send Joey to private school in Scotland if his marks do not improve. No one, however, except Joey, has noticed that Jerry is unhappy. Jerry confides to Joey that he knows he is not talented enough to continue at the conservatory but has been afraid to communicate his concerns to the family. When Jerry overdoses on sleeping pills, Joey resourcefully gets help in time to save his brother's life. Bertie returns from the wilds and soon dies of wounds he has received. Joey sees parallels between himself and Bertie but realizes that everyone must decide for himself what he will do with his life. He courageously points out to his father that he must work things out his own way. Mr. Larkin sees his children in a different perspective, and the family appreciates Joey for his own special qualities of quick thinking, cool head, and steady reliability. The slow-moving, awkwardly constructed plot ambles along too deliberately, showcasing such problems of upper middle-class family life as over-directive parents and the needs of middle children. Dialogue seems contrived and is often unlifelike, and most elements for predicting the outcome of things are on the surface. Characters are one dimensional types, and conversations, in particular at book's end, have a decidedly didactic flavor. Choice.

YELLOW HAIR SQUAW (*Cayuse Courage**), the Cayuse Indians' name for Narcissa Whitman, an actual historical figure and wife of the mid nineteenth century American missionary to Oregon Territory, Marcus Whitman*. In the novel the Indians dislike her very much, regarding her as loud, cold, and intimidating. The reader sees that she is hardworking, diligent, and generous in caring for her large family of foster children and in preparing for the white settlers and many visitors who pass through the mission. It is apparent also that she makes little effort to get to know the Indians who live nearby and regards them as inferiors. For example, she turns Samuel out with no thought about what effect the loss of his arm may have had on his position in the tribe. She simply has never bothered to learn about the Indians' ways, considering white ones naturally superior. She is killed in the uprising.

YELLOW WOLF (*The Horse Talker**), headstrong, deceitful Indian youth who pretends he wishes to steal the white colonel's horse as a bride price. He persuades Lan to help him, and then he abandons Lan to the white soldiers. Later, he joins the Inglés and Guero, the dishonest mustangers. He is a foil for Lan.

YEP, LAURENCE M(ICHAEL) (1948–   ), born in San Francisco, Calif.; author of novels for young people, mostly about the Chinese-American experience. He attended Marquette University and the University of Santa Cruz and earned his Ph.D. degree from the State University of New York at Buffalo. In 1970 he won a Book of the Month Club writing fellowship. A number of his science fiction stories have appeared in anthologies and he has published three science-fantasy novels for young people, *Sweetwater* (Harper, 1973), *Seademons* (Harper, 1977), and *Dragon of the Lost Sea* (Harper, 1982). He has also written a psychological novel of a boy and girl set in a Catholic prep school in San Francisco, *Kind Hearts and Gentle Monsters* (Harper, 1982) and *Liar, Liar* (Morrow, 1983), a novel of suspense, but his best-known writings are novels set in California's Chinese-American community, including *Dragonwings** (Harper, 1975), a Newbery honor book, and *Child of the Owl** (Harper, 1977), winner of both the Boston *Globe-Horn Book* Award and the Jane Addams Award. *The Serpent's Children* (Harper, 1984), set in China in the mid nineteenth century, has also received enthusiastic reviews.

Z

ZEELY (Hamilton*, Virginia, ill. Symeon Shimin, Macmillan, 1967), realistic novel set in a rural area of the United States in the mid–1900s. Elizabeth Perry, a black girl about twelve, and her younger brother, John, take the train to spend the summer with their Uncle Ross on his farm. An imaginative child, Elizabeth decides that she will be Geeder for the summer and that John will be Toeboy. By a combination of high-handed direction, threats, and occasional cajolery, she dominates her brother, whose only recourse when she gets too disagreeable is to start to write to his father. At the farm, where they have not been for three years, they rediscover the pump room, the pantry full of the food Uncle Ross has canned, the parlor, the pond, even the road, which Geeder renames "Leadback Road." They decide to sleep under the stars, and Geeder scares Toeboy by telling him about "night travelers" who resent having children see them. She herself is frightened when she sees a tall figure in white seeming to float down the road. Later she learns that this was Zeely Tayber, whose father, Nat, raises hogs on shares on Uncle Ross's land. Zeely is extremely tall, with a thin nose and high cheekbones. Both she and her father hold themselves aloof from the community. Geeder is tremendously impressed and begins to fantasize about Zeely. When she finds a picture of an African princess, a Watutsi, who looks very much like Zeely, she decides that Zeely is a queen. At a neighborhood bonfire, she announces this to the other children. Her hero worship is only increased when she sees Zeely helping Nat drive his prize hogs through town. Zeely appears unaware of Nat's brutal treatment of the animals but responds quickly when Geeder runs to her to prevent Nat's cruel prodding of a fallen sow. Without showing any emotion, Zeely forces Nat away and carefully helps the sow by feeding it from her hand, paying no attention to Geeder or the watching crowd. Later Zeely leaves word that she wants to talk to Geeder. They meet at the edge of the woods, walk into it, and sit and talk. Zeely, dressed in a Watutsi robe, tells Geeder an origin story of her people that her mother told her. She also tells Geeder that she gave up make-believe to become herself. Geeder understands, and when she returns to Uncle Ross's farm, she is Elizabeth again. The idea of an imaginative child building a fantasy world around a near stranger is genuine, but the action is not sufficient to carry the portentous significance with which it is endowed in the story. The only real characterization is Geeder's bossy and insensitive treatment of her brother. The story is slow moving and pretentiously written but has been highly acclaimed for treating the rural black girl with dignity. Choice.

Z FOR ZACHARIAH (O'Brien*, Robert C., Atheneum, 1974), fantasy set in the future in a secluded valley near Ithaca, N.Y. As far as she knows, Ann Burden, 16, is the only survivor of a nuclear war. For one year, she has been living on the family farm, her only companion Faro, the dog. Ann records in her journal the events of the three months following the arrival of John Loomis, chemist and apparently the last man alive, who comes on foot wearing a plastic safe-suit. Although she welcomes the prospect of human companionship, caution drives Ann into the hills from which she observes his movements. When Loomis gets radiation poisoning from bathing in a contaminated stream, Ann resumes living in the farmhouse and nurses him back to health. Remarks he makes while delirious disturb her, and bullet holes in the safe-suit confirm her suspicions that Loomis murdered a co-worker, Edward, over the safe-suit, the only one in existence. After he recovers, their relationship deteriorates rapidly. Her uneasiness about him changes to fear as Ann comes to see that Loomis is coldly determined to control the means of their existence and even Ann herself. When he attacks her one night while she is in her bedroom, she escapes to a hillside cave. He stalks her, shoots her in the ankle, and uses Faro to locate and destroy her camp. When she sees that Loomis will eventually track her down, she kills Faro by tricking him into the contaminated stream. Concluding that death in the outside world would be preferable to living as the slave of a psychopath, she steals the safe-suit, confronts Loomis with the reasons for her actions, and departs. She hopes to find another valley like her own which has escaped destruction and where perhaps there are people with whom she can make a good life. Ann's account of her struggle for survival is too detailed and well organized for suspense to be convincing as the journal it is purported to be, but her feelings and motivations are in character. The book is strong at arousing the emotions, and incidents are adroitly calculated for maximum tension without lapsing into sentimentality, melodrama, or sensation. The conclusion (written posthumously from O'Brien's notes) seems abrupt and implausible, since failing to protect the suit does not fit Loomis's character as revealed. Ann's romantic dreams, vacillation, and growing resolve seem appropriate, and Loomis is an intriguingly enigmatic and complex character. His actions at the end are particularly puzzling. Descriptive passages are rich with imagery and some symbolism. They provide texture, heighten the poignancy, and intensify the conflict. Addams; Fanfare; Poe Winner.

ZIA TROYANO (*The King's Fifth**), young Indian guide and interpreter whom Estéban* de Sandoval first takes for a boy when he meets her with Coronado's army. At thirteen she is a tomboy who wears a hat rimmed with bells of her Nayarit tribe and leaps around like a young animal, but she grows more womanly in the ensuing two years. High spirited and honest, Zia is interested in the maps which Estéban makes and loves the colt, which she names Blue Star, but she is immune from the gold fever that affects most of the other characters. When she comes to testify at Estéban's trial, she admits, obliquely, that love for him has brought her.

ZINDEL, PAUL (1936–   ), born on Staten Island, N.Y.; dramatist, author associated with the alienation of the 1960s. He attended Wagner College in New York and taught high school chemistry for nine years. In 1970 he won the New York Drama Critics Award and in 1971 the Pulitzer Prize in Drama. His novels for teenagers are mostly stories of rebellious young people betrayed or abandoned by adults, written in the slick, slangy language of the adolescent. Best known is *The Pigman** (Harper, 1968), a story of how the friendship of two high school sophomores with an elderly man leads to his death. Among other titles are *My Darling, My Hamburger* (Harper, 1969), *I Never Loved Your Mind* (Harper, 1970), *Pardon Me, You're Stepping on My Eyeball* (Harper, 1976), *Confessions of a Teenage Baboon* (Harper, 1977), *The Undertaker's Gone Bananas* (Harper, 1978), *The Pigman's Legacy* (Harper, 1980), and *Harry and Hortense at Hormone High* (Harper, 1984).

ZOOK, PETER (*Susy's Scoundrel**), Amish farmer who moves West to Oklahoma when his bishop expels him from the church because he has bought a tractor. He is a loving family man and is very close to his daughter, Susy, whose affection for wildlife he shares. He buys her two coyote pups to raise as pets and posts his land against hunting. He quietly and staunchly stands up for his conviction that coyotes are the farmer's friends.

INDEX

Names and titles in ALL CAPITAL LETTERS refer to the actual entries of the dictionary, and page numbers *in italics* refer to the location of the actual entries of the dictionary.

ARCHIE COSTELLO, *23*, 114–15
archipelagoes, Earthsea, 559, 666–67, 736
architects, 620, 687
architecture, 598
Archmage, 27, 207–8, 233, 736
Ardis, 579–80
Ardizzone, Edward, 10, 734
Aremis Slake, 602–4
ARE YOU IN THE HOUSE ALONE?, *23–24*,
    504
ARE YOU THERE GOD? IT'S ME,
    MARGARET., *24–25*, 63
Argess, 79, 159–60, 559
arguments: between brothers, 588; father-son,
    127; stormy, between husband and wife,
    437
Argyll, Marquis of, 353, 735
Arha, 652, 667
Arilla Adams, 25
ARILLA SUN DOWN, *25*, 269
Arizona: mid 16th century, 360–61, 703–4;
    mid 19th century, 15, 357–58; late 19th
    century, 599; mid 20th century, 21–22,
    497–98
Arkansas: mid 19th century, 294; early 20th
    century, 721–22; mid 20th century, 446–47,
    634; late 20th century, 513
Arkansas City, Kans., 368
Arkla, 65–66
Arkwright mill, 180, 243
Armamentarium, 101
Armijo, 173, 533, 726
ARMINTA HAYES, *25*, 125–26
Armistead family, 143–44
THE ARM OF THE STARFISH, *25–26*, 375,
    554
The Arm of Transvax (spaceship), 239–40
arms, broken, 415
ARMSTRONG, WILLIAM HOWARD, *26–*
    27, 617
Armstrong family, 119, 563, 658
army: brats, 333; decision to join, 668; life,
    318; sleeping, 623; Spanish, 750
Army of the Potomac, 591
Arnauld family, 546–47
ARNEATHA HAWKINS, *27*, 726
Arnie Cadle, 12–13
Arnie Nichols, 234
Arno, Enrico, 467
Arnold, General Benedict, 449
ARORA, SHIRLEY L(EASE), *27*, 710
ARREN, *27*, 207–8, 386

arrests: for disturbing peace, 186; for drug
    possession, 197–98; for speeding, 652; for
    theft, 653; of kids, 209; of printer, 244
arrogance, 674–75
arrowheads, 629
arson, accusations of, 732
art collectors, 730
art gallery owners, dishonest, 217–18
arthritis, 443–44, 489–90
Arthur, 336, 473
Arthur Bent, 385
Arthur Berryfield, 108
Arthur Dunn, 120
Arthur Elliot, 451–52, 515
Arthur, for the Very First Time, 393
Arthur Guttery, 293–94
Arthur Platt, 342
Arthur Sheldon, 230
article, newspaper: about treasure, 663;
    maligning peddlers, 658–59
artifacts; archeological, 460–61; golden goblet,
    246; Indian, 203, 314, 461, 548; iron, 338,
    668; of Pushcart War, 522; pre-Columbian,
    609
artisans, Indian, in N. Mex., 655
artists, 157, 307–8, 571, 583, 648; cartoonists,
    96–97; shoddy pop, 648; wood carvers,
    686. *See also* painters
arts, patrons of, 390, 501
Arts Festival, 111
Artro River, 662
art treasures, 609
Arva Williams, 401
Asa (*Belling the Tiger*), 47, 523, 661
Asa (*Village of the Vampire Cat*), 698
Asafa, 524
ASA HALE SHIPMAN, *28*
As a Speckled Bird, 336
Ash, 65–66
Ashe Norvell, 579
Ashkelon, 163
Ashlymine, 445–46
Ash Puck, 211
Asia: unspecified time, Japan, 176; 12th
    century, Japan, 406, 484–86; 16th century,
    Japan, 698–99; mid 19th century, India,
    322; early 20th century, China, 293–94; mid
    20th century, India, 710–11; Korea, 269–70;
    late 20th century, Vietnam, 63–64, 135–36,
    398–400
Ask Anybody, 256
aspirin, mouse finds for ill child, 436

576; changing character, 213–14; children assume for escape, 357; children assume for family support, 326, 494, 518; children assume for farm, 3–4, 175, 211, 332, 333; children assume for grandmother, 532–33; children assume for home, 40, 182–83, 217, 241–42, 272, 334, 548–49, 561; children assume for homeless, 217–18; children assume for sheep, 414; children assume for siblings, 156–57, 290; children assume for survival, 64; children overwhelmed by, 544; development of sense of, 371–72; girl assigned for retarded sister, 388; girl assumes debt, 655; girl assumes for another family, 593; girl assumes for autistic child, 659–60; girl assumes for baby, 285; girl assumes for boarding house, 379, 621, 646–47; girl assumes for brother, 450; girl assumes for family, 676–77; girl assumes for family on overland trail, 669; girl assumes general, 21; girl assumes for grandparents, 721; girl assumes for herb doctor, 721; girl assumes for household, 223–24, 224, 232, 556–57, 678, 681, 712–13, 739; girl assumes for invalid, 723–24; girl assumes for neighbor boy, 678; girl assumes for retarded brother, 634–35, 639–40; girl assumes for siblings, 473–74, 548–49, 561, 624, 640; ignored, 235; mysterious, 294; of children toward parents, 284; of government toward governed, 709–10; of learning, 710–11; personal, 159–60, 168–69, 316–17, 474–75, 515–16, 531–32, 687; slave exhibits strong sense of, 198; social, 740–41; strong sense of, 205–206, 229, 267–68, 589–60; suddenly exhibited, 6; to save world, 727; youth takes charge of war unit, 660–61

restaurants, 166, 343, 439
restaurateurs, 708
Resurrection Cemetery, 193
Ressurrection City, 401
retarded persons: girl developing potential, 388; youth developing potential, 377
retirements, from teaching, 427
RETTA ANDERSON, 336, 414, 473–74, *548–49*, 563, 592
returns: joyful, 738; tearful, 738; to accompany brother, 314. *See also* reunions
Return to Gone-Away, 197
Return to South Town, 148, 186, 250, 721
Reuben O'Neal, 483, 650

reunions: family with lost child, 311; happy, 740; joyful, 596, 680. *See also* returns
Revelator, 240
revenge, 329, 537, 583, 733; black girl on white, 561; for murder of husband, 517; killing of turkey, 260; on bus driver, 624; of slandered friends, 272; thwarted, 617
revenuers, 392
Revere Mansion, 572
REVEREND FARNLEE, *549*, 587
REVEREND JAMES WALLIS, 443, 443–44, 489–90, *549*
Reverend Prempey Moshombo, 720
Reverend Robb Fry, 642
Reverend Samuel Parris, 664–65
reversals, of names, 648
Revolution: American, 1, 5, 179–80, 187–88, 225, 225–26, 275, 333–34, 337–38, 379, 389, 449–50, 503, 508–509, 577–78, 587, 615, 637, 674–75; English, 734–35; Westmark, 354–55, 709–10
revolutionaries, 219, 404, 709
rewards, 109, 176; Bears' House, 427; carrying the flag, 157–58; courting rights, 630; denied, 164; dogs returned for, 300; expected, 190; for capturing bandit, 439; for saving life, 140; for swimming Ohio River, 411; gift of donkey, 246; money, 1; money for college, 392; $6,000 for apprehending thieves, 585; three horses for valor, 630; title of "story catcher," 630. *See also* prizes
Rhian Evans, 44, 630–31
RHODA COOPER, *549*, 572, 659
Rhode Island, 604; late 18th century, 146–47; early 20th century, 454–55; mid 20th century, 460–61
RHUN, 98, 286–87, *549–50*
Rhyme, 512
rhymes: containing clues, 584; girl speaks in, 469
Rhys, Megan, 726
RIBSY, 117, *550*
Ricardo, 391
Rich, 458
RICH, LOUISE DICKINSON, *550–51*, 659
RICHARD, ADRIENNE, 517, *551*, 729
Richard Crewe, 61–62
Richard Strang, 620
Richard Williams, 596
RICHIE GREATBEAR, *551*
Richmond, Va., 629

About the Authors

ALETHEA K. HELBIG is Professor of English Language and Literature at Eastern Michigan University. She has published articles in *Children's Literature, Children's Literature Association Quarterly, The Alan Review, American Women Writers,* and *Writers for Children* and compiled *Straight on Till Morning: Poems of the Imaginary World* and *Dusk to Dawn: Poems of Night* (with Agnes Perkins). She is Past-President of the Children's Literature Association (International).

AGNES REGAN PERKINS is Professor of English Language and Literature at Eastern Michigan University. Her articles have appeared in *A Tolkien Compass, Unicorn, Children's Literature, Children's Literature Association Quarterly,* and *Writers for Children.* In addition she is co-compiler of *New Coasts and Strange Harbors: Discovering Poems* (with Helen Hill).